5 EDITION

OUR Social WORLD

SAGE was founded in 1965 by Sara Miller McCune to support the dissemination of usable knowledge by publishing innovative and high-quality research and teaching content. Today, we publish more than 750 journals, including those of more than 300 learned societies, more than 800 new books per year, and a growing range of library products including archives, data, case studies, reports, conference highlights, and video. SAGE remains majority-owned by our founder, and after Sara's lifetime will become owned by a charitable trust that secures our continued independence.

Los Angeles | London | Washington DC | New Delhi | Singapore | Boston

5 EDITION

OUR Social WORLD

Introduction to Sociology

Jeanne H.
BALLANTINE
Wright State University

Keith A.
ROBERTS
Hanover College

Kathleen Odell
KORGEN
William Paterson University

SAGE

Los Angeles | London | New Delhi
Singapore | Washington DC | Boston

Los Angeles | London | New Delhi
Singapore | Washington DC | Boston

FOR INFORMATION:

SAGE Publications, Inc.
2455 Teller Road
Thousand Oaks, California 91320
E-mail: order@sagepub.com

SAGE Publications Ltd.
1 Oliver's Yard
55 City Road
London EC1Y 1SP
United Kingdom

SAGE Publications India Pvt. Ltd.
B 1/I 1 Mohan Cooperative Industrial Area
Mathura Road, New Delhi 110 044
India

SAGE Publications Asia-Pacific Pte. Ltd.
3 Church Street
#10-04 Samsung Hub
Singapore 049483

Printed in Canada

Cataloging-in-publication data is available for this title from the Library of Congress.

ISBN 978-1-4833-6860-3

Acquisitions Editor: Jeff Lasser
Development Editor: Nathan Davidson
Editorial Assistant: Alexandra Croell
Digital Content Editor: Gabrielle Piccininni
Production Editor: Laura Barrett
Copy Editor: Melinda Masson
Typesetter: C&M Digitals (P) Ltd.
Proofreader: Wendy Jo Dymond
Indexer: Robie Grant
Cover and Interior Designer: Scott Van Atta
Marketing Manager: Erica DeLuca

This book is printed on acid-free paper.

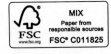

15 16 17 18 19 10 9 8 7 6 5 4 3 2 1

Brief Contents

Detailed Contents

Preface

TO OUR STUDENT READERS

This book will change how you view the world—and your place in it. You will gain a sociological perspective on the world that will change what you notice and how you make sense of your social world. Some of you will become sociology majors. All of you will find the subject matter of this course relevant to your personal and professional lives. You will learn how society works—and how you can influence it; develop interpersonal skills; and gain new information about social life in small groups and global social systems. As the broadest of the social sciences, sociology has a never-ending array of fascinating subjects to study.

Sociology and this book ask you to think outside the box. Why? The best way to become a more interesting person, to grow beyond the old familiar thoughts and behaviors, and to make life exciting is to explore new ways to view your social world. The world in which we live is intensely personal and individual in nature, with much of our social interaction occurring in intimate groups of friends and family. Our most intense emotions and most meaningful links to others are at this small-group "micro" level of social life.

However, these intimate micro-level links in our lives are influenced by larger social structures and global trends. The social world you face in the job markets of the 21st century is influenced by changes and forces that are easy to miss. Like the wind, which can do damage even if the air is unseen, social structures are themselves so taken for granted that it is easy to miss seeing them. However, their effects can be readily identified. Sociology's new perspectives will help you to better understand your family, friends, work life, leisure time, and place in a diverse and changing world.

The Social World Model

A well-constructed course, like an effective essay, needs to be organized around a central question, one that leads to other subsidiary questions and intrigues the participants. For you to understand sociology as an integrated whole rather than a set of separate chapters in a book, we have organized the chapters in this book around the *social world model*: a conceptual model that demonstrates the relationships between individuals (micro level); organizations, institutions, and subcultures (meso level); and national societies and global structures (macro level). At the beginning of each chapter, a visual diagram of the model will illustrate this idea as it relates to the topic of that chapter, including how issues related to the topic have implications at various levels of analysis in the social world, influencing and being affected by other parts of society. No aspect of society exists in a vacuum. On the other hand, this model does not assume that everyone always gets along or that relationships are always harmonious or supportive. Sometimes, different parts of the society are in competition for resources, and in conflict with one another.

This micro- to macro-level analysis is a central concept in the discipline of sociology. It will help you to develop a *sociological imagination*, an ability to see the complex links between various levels of the social system, from the micro level of close relationships to the macro level of globalization. Within a few months, you may not remember all the specific concepts or terms that have been introduced, but if the way you see the world has been transformed during this course, a key element of deep, lasting learning has been accomplished. Learning to see things from alternative perspectives is a precondition for critical thinking. This book will help you recognize connections between your personal experiences and problems and larger social forces of society. Thus, you will be learning to take a new perspective on the social world in which you live.

A key element of that social world is diversity. We live in societies in which there are people who differ in a host of ways: ethnicity, socioeconomic status, religious background, political persuasion, gender, sexual orientation, and so forth. Diversity is a blessing in many ways to a society because the most productive and creative organizations and societies are those that are highly diverse. This is the case because people with different backgrounds solve problems in very different ways. When people with such divergences come together, the outcome of their problem solving can create new solutions to vexing problems. However, diversity often creates challenges as well. Misunderstanding and "us" versus "them" thinking can divide people. These issues will be explored throughout this book. We now live in a global village, and in this book, you will learn something about how people on the other side of the village live and view the world.

We hope you enjoy the book and get as enthralled with sociology as we are. It genuinely is a fascinating field of study.

Jeanne H. Ballantine
Jeanne H. Ballantine
Wright State University

Keith A. Roberts
Keith A. Roberts
Hanover College

Kathleen Odell Korgen
Kathleen Odell Korgen
William Paterson University

Your authors—teaching "outside the box."

Instructors

HOW TO MAKE THIS BOOK WORK FOR YOU

Special features woven throughout each chapter support the theme of the book. These will help students comprehend and apply the material and make the material more understandable and interesting. These features are also designed to facilitate deep learning, to help students move beyond rote memorization, and to increase their ability to analyze and evaluate information.

For students to understand both the comparative global theme and sociology as an integrated whole rather than as a set of separate chapters in a book, we have organized the chapters in this book around the *social world model*: a conceptual model that demonstrates the relationships between individuals (micro level); organizations, institutions, and subcultures (meso level); and societies and global structures (macro levels of analysis). At the beginning of each chapter, a visual diagram of the model will illustrate this idea as it relates to the topic of that chapter, including how issues related to the topic have implications at various levels of analysis in the social world.

"THINK ABOUT IT"

So that students can become curious, active readers, we have posed questions at the outset of each chapter that we hope are relevant to everyday life, but that are also tied to the micro–meso–macro levels of analysis that serve as the theme of the book. The purpose is to transform students from passive readers who run their eyes across the words into curious active readers who read to answer a question and to be reflective. Active or deep reading is key to comprehension and retention of reading material (Roberts and Roberts 2008). Instructors can also use this feature to

encourage students to think critically about the implications of what they have read. Instructors might want to ask students to write a paragraph about one of these questions before coming to class each day. These questions might also provide the basis for in-class discussions.

Students should be encouraged to start each chapter by reading and thinking about these questions, looking at the topics in the chapter outlined just below the "Think About It" feature, and asking some questions of their own. This will mean that they are more likely to stay focused, remember the material long-term, and be able to apply it to their own lives.

"WHAT'S COMING IN THIS CHAPTER"

Each chapter begins with a simple listing of the key topic headings. Research on deep reading shows that if students begin to ask questions and become active as readers at the outset, they comprehend and retain more of the material. This new feature is added in response to requests by reviewers of the text.

A GLOBAL PERSPECTIVE AND THE SOCIAL WORLD MODEL

This book incorporates a global perspective throughout. This is done so that students can see not only how others live different but rewarding lives, but also the connections between others' lives and their own. Students will need to think and relate to the world globally in future roles as workers, travelers, and global citizens. Our analysis illustrates the interconnections of the world's societies and their political and economic systems, and demonstrates that what happens in one part of the world affects others.

We use this global approach to instill interest, understanding, and respect for different groups of people and their lifestyles. Race, class, and gender are an integral part of understanding the diverse social world, and these features of social life have global implications. The comparative global theme is carried throughout the book in headings and written text, in examples, and in boxes and selection of photos. As students read this book, they should continually think about how the experiences in their private world are influenced by and may influence events at other levels: the community, organizations and institutions, the nation, and the world.

OPENING VIGNETTES

Chapters typically open with an illustration relevant to the chapter content that will grab the attention of students. For instance, in Chapter 2, "Examining the Social World," the case of Hector, a Brazilian teenager living in poverty in a *favela*, is used to illustrate research methods and theory throughout the chapter. Chapter 3, "Society and Culture," begins with scenarios of mealtime scenes and foods from around the world to illustrate the variations in human cultures. In Chapter 4, "Socialization," the case of Phoebe Prince, a 15-year-old immigrant from Ireland, who was so harassed and bullied by peers that she hung herself, begins the discussion. Chapter 7 begins with a discussion of the royal wedding of Prince William and Kate Middleton. These vignettes are meant to interest students in the upcoming subject matter by helping them relate to a personalized story. In several cases, the vignettes serve as illustrations throughout the chapters.

"THINKING SOCIOLOGICALLY" QUESTIONS

Following major topics, students will find thought-provoking questions that ask them to think critically and apply the material just read to some aspect of their lives or the social world. The purpose of this feature is to encourage students to apply the ideas and concepts in the text to their lives, to develop critical thinking skills, and to use the material for better recall. These questions can be the basis for in-class discussions and can be assigned as questions to start interesting conversations with friends and families to

learn how the topics relate to their own lives. Note that some of these questions have a miniature icon—a small version of the chapter-opening model—signifying that these questions reinforce the theme of micro, meso, and macro levels of social influence.

"ENGAGING SOCIOLOGY"

Perhaps the most innovative feature in this book is called "Engaging Sociology"—and the double entendre is intentional. We want students to think of sociology as engaging and fun. These features—such as applying a population pyramid to the business world, taking a survey to understand why differences in social and cultural capital make first-generation students feel alienated on a college campus, and reading a map and learning to analyze the patterns—help students understand how interesting and useful sociology can be.

KEY CONCEPTS, EXAMPLES, AND WRITING STYLE

Key terms in **bold** are defined and illustrated within the running narrative and appear in the glossary. Other terms of less significance are italicized and defined. The text is rich in examples that bring sociological concepts to life for student readers. Each chapter has been student tested for readability. Both students and reviewers describe the writing style as reader friendly and accessible, but not watered down.

SPECIAL FEATURES

Featured inserts provide even more in-depth illustrations of the usefulness of the sociological perspective to understand world situations or events with direct relevance to a student's life. There are three kinds of special features. "Sociology in Our Social World" features focus on a sociological issue or story, often with policy implications. "Sociology Around the World" takes readers to another part of the globe to explore how things are different (or how they are the same) from what they might experience in their own lives. "Sociologists in Action" features appear in many chapters and examine profiles of public sociologists working in the field. This helps students grasp what they and professional sociologists can actually do with sociology.

TECHNOLOGY AND SOCIETY

Nearly every chapter examines the issues of technology as they are relevant to that chapter. We have especially sought out materials related to social media and other uses of the Internet.

SOCIAL POLICY AND BECOMING AN INVOLVED CITIZEN

Most chapters include discussion of some social policy issues and the relevance of sociological findings to current social debates. Furthermore, because students sometimes feel helpless and do not know what to do about social issues that concern them at macro and meso levels, we have concluded every chapter with a few ideas about how they might become involved as active citizens, even as undergraduate students. Some suggestions in the "Contributing to Our Social World: What Can We Do?" section may be assigned as extra credit, service learning, or term projects.

SUMMARY SECTIONS AND DISCUSSION QUESTIONS

Each chapter ends with review material: a "What Have We Learned?" feature that includes a "Key Points" bulleted summary of the chapter's core material. The summary is followed with probing discussion questions that ask students to go beyond memorization and apply the material in the chapter to their own lives. Research indicates that unless four discrete sections of the brain are stimulated, the learning will not be long term and deep but surface and short term (Zull 2002). These questions are carefully crafted to activate all four critical sections of the brain.

A LITTLE (TEACHING) HELP FROM OUR FRIENDS

Whether the instructor is new to teaching or an experienced professor, there are some valuable ideas in this text that can help invigorate and energize the classroom. As we have noted, substantial literature on teaching methodology tells us that student involvement is key to the learning process. In addition to the engaging questions and exercises in the text, there are a number of teaching suggestions in the supplements and teaching aids for active learning in large or small classes.

SAGE edge™

SAGE edge offers a robust online environment featuring an impressive array of tools and resources for review, study, and further exploration, keeping both instructors and students on the cutting edge of teaching and learning. SAGE edge content is open access and available on demand. Learning and teaching has never been easier!

SAGE edge for Instructors supports teaching by making it easy to integrate quality content and create a rich learning environment for students. SAGE edge instructor sites include tools and elements such as:

- Test banks that provide a diverse range of pre-written options as well as the opportunity to edit any question and/or insert personalized questions to effectively assess students' progress and understanding
- Sample course syllabi for semester and quarter courses provides suggested models for structuring one's course
- Editable, chapter-specific PowerPoint® slides that offer complete flexibility for creating a multimedia presentation for the course
- Chapter-specific discussion questions help launch classroom interaction by prompting students to engage with the material and by reinforcing important content.
- Lecture notes which summarize key concepts by chapter to ease preparation for lectures and class discussions
- A Course cartridge that provides easy LMS integration

SAGE edge for Students provides a personalized approach to help students accomplish their coursework goals in an easy-to-use learning environment.

- Mobile-friendly eFlashcards which strengthen understanding of key terms and concepts
- Mobile-friendly practice quizzes that allow for independent assessment by students of their mastery of course material
- An online action plan includes tips and feedback on progress through the course and materials, which allows students to individualize their learning experience
- Web exercises and meaningful web links facilitate student use of Internet resources, further exploration of topics, and responses to critical thinking questions
- Carefully selected chapter-by-chapter Video and Multimedia content which enhance classroom-based explorations of key topics.

- EXCLUSIVE! Access to full-text SAGE journal articles that have been carefully selected to support and expand on the concepts presented in each chapter

Visit http://edge.sagepub.com/ballantine5e to view the site.

WHAT IS NEW IN THE FIFTH EDITION?

In this major revision we have reorganized several chapters and updated all data, added many new studies, and included new topics in sociology. There are seven *new* boxed features in the fifth edition, replacing old ones; four of these are about "Sociologists in Action." Most chapters have *extensive* updates, with nearly 500 new references in the book and many old references dropped. The new edition also includes updated and new tables and maps. Considerable attention has also been given to clarifying and simplifying definitions throughout the book and determining what major concepts should be in the glossary. The core elements of the book—with the unifying theme and the social world model at the beginning of every chapter—have not changed. However, revised visual presentation of the model provides a clearer conceptual image.

Finally, although we had been told that the writing was extraordinarily readable, we have tried to simplify sentence structure in a number of places with the help of our new coauthor. In short, we have tried to respond to what we heard from all of you—both students and instructors (and yes, we *do* hear from students)—to keep this book engaging and accessible.

NEW TO THIS EDITION!

- A new coauthor who brings new ideas, a crisp writing style, and expertise in public sociology to the book: Kathleen Korgen.
- Redesign of our social world model at outset of each chapter for better clarity and eye appeal.
- Increased attention to public sociology, including description of the work of at least one public sociologist per chapter in a feature on "Sociologists in Action."
- Seven new featured essays, including four new "Sociologists in Action" features.
- Revised "Engaging Sociology" features, with more opportunity for data analysis by students.
- Clarified and often simplified definitions and updating the glossary.
- Scores of new examples.
- Nearly 100 new and updated tables, and more than 500 new references.
- Redesigned photo essays, with probing questions to facilitate analysis of visual material.
- Nearly 200 photos (well over half of them new to this book) and 15 new or updated maps.
- Revamping of the photography program with somewhat fewer photos, but strategically selected and enlarged.
- "Contributing to Our Social World" feature has additional ideas for volunteer work, internships, and careers.
- Reformulation of instructional strategies for the photo essays, which are now online.
- Considerable condensing of the material for more focused discussion of topics.

A Personal Note to the Instructor

What is truly distinctive about this book? This is a text that tries to break the mold of the typical textbook synthesis, the cross between an encyclopedia and a dictionary. *Our Social World* is a unique course text that is *a coherent essay on the sociological imagination—understood globally*. We attempt to radically change the feel of the introductory book by emphasizing coherence, an integrating theme, and current knowledge about learning and teaching, but we also present much traditional content. Instructors will not have to throw out the well-honed syllabus and begin from scratch, but they can refocus each unit so it stresses understanding of micro-level personal troubles within the macro-level public issues framework. Indeed, in this book, we make clear that the public issues must be understood as global in nature.

Here is a text that engages students. *They* say so! From class testing, we know that the writing style, the structure of chapters and sections, the "Thinking Sociologically" features, the wealth of examples, and other instructional aids help students stay focused, think about the material, and apply it to their lives. It neither bores them nor insults their intelligence. It focuses on deep learning rather than memorization. It develops sociological skills of analysis rather than emphasizing memorization of vocabulary. Key concepts and terms are introduced but only in the service of a larger focus on the sociological imagination. The text is both personal and global. It speaks to sociology as a science as well as addressing public or applied aspects of sociology. It has a theme that provides integration of topics as it introduces the discipline. This text is an analytical essay, not a disconnected encyclopedia.

As one of our reviewers noted,

Unlike most textbooks I have read, the breadth and depth of coverage in this one is very impressive. It challenges students with college-level reading. Too many textbooks seem to write on a high school level and give only passing treatment to most of the topics, writing in nugget-sized blocks. More than a single definition and a few sentences of support, the text forces students deep into the topics covered and challenges them to see interconnections.

Normally, the global-perspective angle within textbooks, which seemed to grow in popularity in the mid- to late 1990s, was implemented by using brief and exotic examples to show differences between societies—a purely comparative approach rather than a globalization treatment. They gave, and still give to a large extent, a token nod to diversity. This textbook, however, forces students to take a broader look at similarities and differences in social institutions around the world, and structures and processes operating in all cultures and societies.

So our focus in this book is on deep learning, especially expansion of students' ability to role-take or "perspective-take." Deep learning goes beyond the content of concepts and terms and cultivates the habits of thinking that allow one to think critically. Being able to see things from the perspective of others is essential to doing sociology, but it is also indispensible to seeing weaknesses in various theories or recognizing blind spots in a point of view. Using the sociological imagination is one dimension of role-taking because it requires a step back from the typical micro-level understanding of life's events and fosters a new comprehension of how meso- and macro-level forces—even global ones—can shape the individual's life. Enhancement of role-taking ability is at the core of this book because it is a *prerequisite* for deep learning in sociology, and it is the core competency needed to *do* sociology. One cannot do sociology unless one can see things from various positions on the social landscape.

This may sound daunting for some student audiences, but we have found that instructors at every kind of institution have had great success with the book because of the writing style and instructional tools used throughout. We have made some strategic decisions based on these principles of learning and teaching. We have focused much of the book on higher-order thinking skills rather than memorization and regurgitation. We want students to learn to think sociologically: to apply, analyze, synthesize, evaluate, and comprehend the interconnections of the world through a globally informed sociological imagination. However, we think it is also essential to do this with an understanding of how students learn.

Many introductory-level books offer several theories and then provide a critique of the theory. The idea is to teach critical thinking. We have purposefully refrained from extensive critique of theory (although some does occur) for several reasons. First, providing critique to beginning-level students does not really teach critical thinking. It trains them to memorize someone else's critique. Furthermore, it simply confuses many of them, leaving students with the feeling that sociology is really just contradictory ideas, and the discipline really does not have anything firm to offer. Teaching critical thinking needs to be done in stages, and it needs to take into account the building steps that occur before effective critique is possible. That is why we focus on the concept of deep learning. We are working toward building the foundations that are necessary for sophisticated critical thought at upper levels in the curriculum.

Therefore, in this beginning-level text, we have attempted to focus on a central higher-order or deep-learning skill—synthesis. Undergraduate students need to grasp this before they can fully engage in evaluation. Deep learning involves understanding of complexity, and some aspects of complexity need to be taught at advanced levels. While students at the introductory level are often capable of synthesis, complex evaluation requires some foundational skills. Thus, we offer contrasting theories in this text, and rather than telling what is wrong with each one,

we encourage students through "Thinking Sociologically" features to analyze the use of each and to focus on honing synthesis and comparison skills.

Finally, research tells us that learning becomes embedded in memory and becomes long lasting only if it is related to something that learners already know. If they memorize terms but have no unifying framework to which they can attach those ideas, the memory will not last until the end of the course, let alone until the next higher-level course. In this text, each chapter is tied to the social world model that is core to sociological thinking. At the end of a course using this book, we believe that students will be able to explain coherently what sociology is and construct an effective essay about what they have learned from the course as a whole. Learning to develop and defend a thesis, with supporting logic and evidence, is another component of deep learning. In short, this text provides instructors with the tools to teach sociology in a way that will make a long-term impact on students.

ORGANIZATION AND COVERAGE

Reminiscent of some packaged international tours, in which the travelers figure that "it is Day 7, so this must be Paris," many introductory courses seem to operate on the principle that it is Week 4 so this must be deviance week. Students do not sense any integration, and at the end of the course, they have trouble remembering specific topics. This book is different. A major goal of the book is to show the integration between topics in sociology and between parts of the social world. The idea is for students to grasp the concept of the interrelated world. A change in one part of the social world affects all others, sometimes in ways that are mutually supportive and sometimes in ways that create intense conflict.

Although the topics are familiar, the textbook is organized around levels of analysis, explained through the social world model. This perspective leads naturally to an integrated discussion in which all topics fit clearly into an overall view, a comparative approach, and discussions of diversity and inequality. It hangs together!

As seen in the Table of Contents, the book includes 16 chapters plus additional online materials, written to fit into a semester or quarter system. It allows instructors to use the chapters in order, or to alter the order, because each chapter is tied into others through the social world model. We strongly recommend that Chapter 1 be used early in the course because it introduces the integrating model and explains the theme. If any Part IV chapters are used, the four-page section opener on "Institutions" will be useful to include as well. Otherwise, the book has been designed for flexible use. Instructors may also want to supplement the core book with other materials, such as those suggested on the Instructor Teaching Site. Each chapter, for example, has an online exercise that helps students grasp the practical, public implications of sociology. While covering all the key topics in introductory sociology, the cost and size of a midsize book allows for this flexibility. Indeed, for a colorful introductory-level text, the cost of this book is remarkably low—roughly half the cost of some other very popular introductory texts.

A UNIQUE PROGRAM SUPPORTING TEACHING OF SOCIOLOGY

There is one more way in which *Our Social World* has been unique among introductory sociology textbooks. In 2007, the original authors (Ballantine and Roberts) teamed with SAGE to start a new program to benefit the entire discipline. Using royalties from *Our Social World,* we helped establish a new award program called the SAGE Teaching Innovations & Professional Development Award, designed to prepare a new generation of scholars within the teaching movement in sociology. People in their early-career stages (graduate students, assistant professors, newer PhDs) can be reimbursed $600 each for expenses entailed while attending the daylong American Sociological Association (ASA) Section on Teaching and Learning's preconference workshop. The workshop is the day before ASA meetings. In 2007, 13 young scholars—graduate students or untenured faculty members—received this award and benefited from an extraordinary workshop on learning and teaching. Since then, 23 other SAGE authors have supported this program from textbook royalties, and a total of 176 young scholars have been beneficiaries of more than $90,000 as of 2014. We are pleased to have had a hand in initiating and continuing to support this program.

We hope you find this book engaging. If you have questions or comments, please contact us.

Jeanne H. Ballantine
Wright State University
jeanne.ballantine@gmail.com

Keith A. Roberts
Hanover College
robertsk@hanover.edu

Kathleen Odell Koren
William Paterson University
korgenk@wpunj.edu

Acknowledgments

Knowledge is improved through careful, systematic, and constructive criticism. The same is true of all writing. This book is of much greater quality because we had such outstanding critics and reviewers. We, therefore, wish to honor and recognize the outstanding scholars who served in this capacity. These scholars are listed on this page and the next.

We also had people who served in a variety of other capacities. Authors of short sections within the book include Kevin Bales, Helen Berger, Jeremiah Castle, Mary Gatta, Susan Guarino-Ghezzi, Kirk Hadaway, Thomas Horejes, Melanie Hughes, Kichiro Iwamoto, David Kirk, Ruth Meizen-Dick, Wendy Ng, Amy Orr, Robert Pellerin, Elise Roberts, Susan St. John, Brent Staples, Jay Weinstein, Jackie Bergdahl, Nancy Diggs, Ellis Jones, Anna Misleh, Ossama Zyoud, Melissa Sheridan Embser-Herbert, Eric R. Wright, and five students from William Paterson University: Donna Yang, Christian Agurto, Michelle Benavides, Brianne Glogowski, Deziree Martinez, and Michele Van Hook. The religion chapter has some new approaches to denominationalism and to church polity, and David Yamane drafted early versions of much of that.

All three of us are experienced authors, and we have worked with some excellent people at other publishing houses. However, the team at SAGE Publications was truly exceptional in support, thoroughness, and commitment to this project. Our planning meetings have been fun, intelligent, and provocative. Jeff Lasser has provided wonderful support as the SAGE sociology editor, and Nathan Davidson, the development editor, has been a terrific photo researcher and supporter in other ways. Folks who have meant so much to the quality production of this book include Nick Pachelli, editorial assistant and excellent photo researcher, Sheri Gilbert, permissions editor, Erica DeLuca, senior marketing manager, and Melinda Masson, our wonderful copy editor extraordinaire who has also been more like a research assistant. We have become friends and colleagues with the staff at SAGE Publications. They are all greatly appreciated.

Thanks to the following reviewers:

Kristie Vise – Northern Kentucky University

Antonia Randloph – University of Delaware

Lisa Munson Weinberg – Florida State University

Matthew West – Bevill State Community College

Amy Donley – University of Central Florida

George Ansalone, PhD – Florida Gulf Coast University

Maureen Ellis-Davis – Bergen Community College

Charles Bittner – Texas Woman's University

Crystal V. Lupo – Auburn University

April Cubbage – Saddleback College

Jo Ry-Anne Feller – Palm Beach State College

Stacye Blount – Fayetteville State University

Nirmal Niroula – Walsh University, North Canton, OH

Skylar C. Gremillion – Louisiana State University

Robert B. Jenkot – Coastal Carolina University

Liza L. Kuecker – Western New Mexico University

David R. Dickens – University of Nevada, Las Vegas

Kevin Doran – Indiana University, Bloomington

Debra K. Taylor – Johnson County Community College

Dennis Veleber – Montana State University Northern

Hephzibah V. Strmic-Pawl – Coastal Carolina University

W. Trevor Brooks – Austin Peay State University

PART

I

Understanding Our Social World

The Scientific Study of Society

Can an individual make a difference? How does your family influence your chances of gaining a college degree and a high-paying job? If you were born into a poor family, what are your chances of becoming wealthy? How does your level of education impact your likelihood of marrying—and staying married? How can sociology help you understand and be an effective member of society? How does the wealth of your country affect your opportunities?

Those are some of the questions you will be able to answer as you develop a deeper understanding of our social world. Sociology is valuable because it gives us new perspectives on our personal and professional lives and because sociological insights and skills can help all of us make the world a better place. Sociology can change your life—and help you change the world.

By the time you finish reading the first two chapters, you should have an initial understanding of what sociology is, what you can gain from sociology, the roots of the sociological perspective, and how sociologists carry out research. We invite you to view our social world through a sociological lens and learn how you can use sociology to make a difference in your life, your community, and the world.

1 Sociology

A Unique Way to View the World

Sociology involves a transformation in the way one sees the world—learning to recognize the complex patterns that connect our everyday personal lives to local, regional, national, and global processes. It takes a sociological perspective to notice many social patterns, just like it takes a view from above to notice the patterns among these umbrellas.

MICRO

● **ME (MY FAMILY AND CLOSE FRIENDS)**

● **LOCAL ORGANIZATIONS AND COMMUNITY**
My school, place of worship, hangouts

MESO

● **NATIONAL ORGANIZATIONS, INSTITUTIONS, AND ETHNIC SUBCULTURES**
My political party, ethnic affiliation

MACRO

● **SOCIETY**
Type of national government and economic system

● **GLOBAL COMMUNITY**
United Nations, World Bank, Doctors Without Borders, multinational corporations

This model illustrates a core idea carried throughout the book—how your own life is shaped by your family, community, society, and world and how you influence them in return. Understanding this model can help you to better understand your social world and to make a positive impact on it.

THINK ABOUT IT

Micro: Small Groups and Local Community	How can sociology help me understand my own life and help me to be a more effective citizen in my community?
Meso: National Institutions, Complex Organizations, and Ethnic Groups	How do sociologists help us understand and even improve our lives in work organizations and health care organizations?
Macro: National and Global Systems	How might national and global events affect my life?

The womb is apparently the setting for some great bodywork. It may win the prize for the strangest place to get a back massage, but according to a recent scientific article, by the fourth month of gestation, twin fetuses begin reaching for their "womb-mates," and by 18 weeks, they spend more time touching their siblings than themselves or the walls of the uterus (Weaver 2010). Fetuses that have single-womb occupancy tend to touch the walls of the uterus a good deal to make contact with the mother. Nearly 30% of the movements of twins is directed toward their companions. Movements such as stroking the back or the head are more sustained and more precise than movements toward themselves—touching their own mouths or other facial features. As one team of scholars put it, we are "wired to be social" (Castiello et al. 2010). In short, humans are innately social creatures.

Shortly after birth, twins Jackson and Audrey were put in a warmer. Jackson cried until he found Audrey and then quickly intertwined his arms and legs with hers. Twins, like all humans, are hardwired to be social and in relationships with others.

The social world is not merely something that exists outside us. As the story of the twins illustrates, the social world is also something we carry inside. We are part of it, we reflect on it, and we are influenced by it, even when we are alone. The patterns of the social world engulf us in ways both subtle and obvious, with profound implications for how we create order and meaning in our lives. The point is that we need others—and that is where sociology enters.

Sometimes it takes a dramatic and shocking event for us to realize just how deeply embedded we are in our relationships in the social world that we take for granted. "It couldn't happen in the United States," read typical world newspaper accounts. "This is something you see in the Middle East, Central Africa, and other war-torn areas. . . . It's hard to imagine this happening in the economic center of the United States." Yet on September 11, 2001, shortly after 9 a.m., a commercial airliner crashed into New York City's World Trade Center, followed a short while later by another pummeling into the paired tower. This mighty symbol of financial wealth collapsed. After the dust settled and the rescue crews finished their gruesome work, nearly 3,000 people were dead and many others injured. The world as we knew it changed forever that day. This event taught U.S. citizens how integrally connected they are with the international community.

Such terrorist acts horrify people because they are unpredicted and unexpected in a normally predictable world. They violate the rules that support our connections to one another. They also bring attention to the discontent and disconnectedness that lie under the surface in many societies—discontent that can come to the surface and express itself in hateful violence. Such discontent and hostility are likely to continue until the root causes are addressed.

Terrorist acts represent a rejection of the modern civil society we know. The terrorists themselves see their acts as justifiable, as a way they can strike out against injustices

Social Rules and Disaster

and threats to their way of life. Few outside the terrorists' inner circle understand their thinking and behavior. When terrorist acts occur, we struggle to fit such events into our mental picture of a just, safe, comfortable, and predictable social world. The United States is a world power, yet its values challenge and threaten the views of many people around the world. For many U.S. citizens, a sense of loyalty to the nation was deeply stirred by the events of 9/11. Patriotism abounded. The nation's people became more connected as a reaction to an act against the United States.

A similar sense of patriotism and connectedness arose immediately after the bombing at the Boston Marathon in 2013. First responders and marathon runners pierced with shrapnel were held up as heroes and symbols of U.S. pride and perseverance in the face of terrorist attacks. As Émile Durkheim, one of the founders of sociology, first pointed out, acts that break normal rules of behavior, as terrorism does, can unite the rule-following members of society ([1895] 1982).

Most of the time, we live with social patterns that we take for granted as routine, ordinary, and expected. These social patterns are essential in social groups so we understand what is happening and know what to expect. Unlike our innate drives, social expectations come from those around us and guide (or constrain) our behaviors and

thoughts. Without shared expectations among humans about proper patterns of behavior, life would be chaotic. Our social interactions require some basic rules, and these rules create routine and normalcy in everyday interaction. It would be strange if someone broke the expected patterns. For the people in and around the World Trade Center on 9/11 and Boston on April 15, 2013, the social rules governing everyday life broke down.

This chapter examines the social ties that make up our social world, as well as sociology's focus on those connections. You will learn what sociology is, what sociologists do, how sociology can be used to improve your life and society, and how the social world model helps us understand how society works.

WHAT IS SOCIOLOGY?

Sociology *is the scientific study of social life, social change, and social causes and consequences of human behavior.* Sociologists examine how society both shapes and is shaped by individuals, small groups of people, organizations, national societies, and global social networks.

Unlike the discipline of psychology, which focuses on the attributes, motivations, and behaviors of individuals, sociology

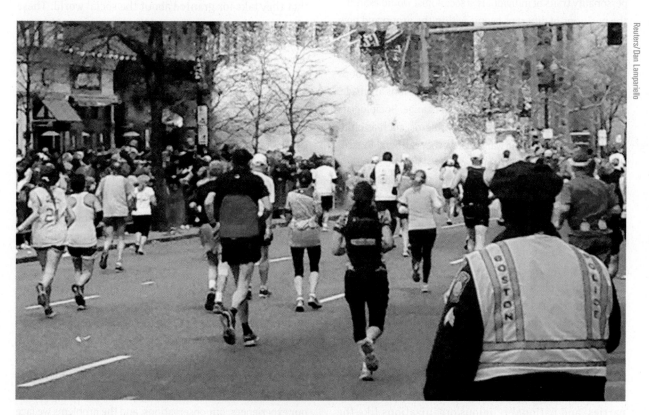

The terrorist bombing of the 2013 Boston Marathon inspired residents in the Boston area and marathon runners to come together in the face of terrorism. The 2014 Boston Marathon attracted even more participants and spectators.

Sociological Perspective

What values, skills, attitudes, and assumptions about life and social interaction do you think these young boys are learning?

can sometimes involve hundreds of millions of people. In the past several decades, social scientists have also pointed to globalization, the process by which the entire world is becoming a single interdependent entity. Of particular interest to sociologists is how these various groups are organized, how they function, why they can come into conflict, and how they influence one another.

 Thinking Sociologically

Identify several dyads, small groups, and large organizations to which you belong. Did you choose to belong, or were you born into membership in these groups? How does each group influence who you are and the decisions you make? How do you influence each of the groups?

focuses on group patterns. A group is *a unit involving two or more people who interact with each other because of shared common interests, goals, experiences, and needs.* Whereas a psychologist might try to explain behavior by examining the personality traits of individuals, a sociologist would examine the positions of different people within the group and how these positions influence what individuals do. Sociologists seek to analyze and explain why people interact with others and belong to groups, how groups work, why some groups have more power than other groups, how decisions are made, and how groups deal with conflict and change. Sociologists also examine the causes of social problems, such as child abuse, crime, poverty, and war and ways they can be addressed.

Two-person interactions—*dyads*—are the smallest units studied by sociologists. Examples of dyads include roommates discussing their classes, a professor and student going over an assignment, a husband and wife negotiating their budget, and two children playing. Next in size are small groups consisting of three or more interacting people who know each other—a family, a neighborhood or peer group, a classroom, a work group, or a street gang. Then come increasingly larger groups—organizations such as sports or scouting clubs, neighborhood associations, and local religious congregations. Among the largest groups contained within nations are ethnic groups and national organizations or institutions, such as the auto industry, the Republican and Democratic national political parties, and national religious organizations like the Southern Baptists. Nations themselves are still larger and

Ideas Underlying Sociology

The idea that one action can cause something else is a core idea in all science. Sociologists also share several ideas that they take for granted about the social world. These ideas about humans and social life are supported by considerable evidence, and they are no longer matters of debate or controversy. They are considered to be true. Understanding these core assumptions helps us see how sociologists approach the study of people in groups.

People are social by nature. This means that humans seek contact with other humans, interact with one another, and influence and are influenced by the behaviors of others. Furthermore, humans need groups to survive. Although a few individuals may become socially isolated as adults, they could not have reached adulthood without sustained interactions with others. We become who we are because other people and groups constantly influence us.

People live much of their lives belonging to social groups. It is in social groups that we interact with family, friends, and work groups; learn to share goals and to cooperate with others in our groups; develop identities that are influenced by our group affiliations; obtain power over others—or are relatively powerless; and have conflicts with others over resources we all want. Our individual beliefs and behaviors, our experiences, our observations, and the problems we face are derived from connections to our social groups.

Interaction between the individual and the group is a two-way process in which each influences the other. In our family or on a sports team, we can influence the shape and direction of our group, just as the group provides the rules and decides the expected behaviors for individuals.

Recurrent social patterns, ordered behavior, shared expectations, and common understandings among people characterize groups. Consider the earlier examples of the chaos created by 9/11 and the Boston Marathon bombing. These events were so troubling because they were unexpected and out of the normal range of expectations. Normally, a degree of continuity and recurrent behavior is present in human interactions, whether in small groups, large organizations, or society.

The processes of conflict and change are natural and inevitable features of groups and societies. No group can remain unchanged and hope to perpetuate itself. To survive, groups must adapt to changes in the social and physical environment, yet rapid change often comes at a price. It can lead to conflict within a society—between traditional and new ideas and between groups that have vested interests in particular ways of doing things. Rapid change can give rise to protest activities; changing in a controversial direction or failing to change fast enough can spark conflict, including revolution. The Arab Spring demonstrations illustrate the desire for rapid change from long-standing dictatorships, springing from citizens' discontent with corrupt or authoritarian rule. The problem is finding acceptable replacement governments to take over what has been overthrown.

As you read this book, keep in mind these basic ideas that form the foundation of sociological analysis: People are social; they live and carry out activities largely in groups; interaction influences both individual and group behavior; people share common behavior patterns and expectations; and processes such as change and conflict are always present. As you will see, in several important ways, sociological understandings provide new lenses for looking at our social world.

Sociological Findings and Commonsense Beliefs

Through research, sociologists have shown that many commonly held beliefs are not actually true, and some "commonsense" ideas have been discredited by sociological research. Here are some examples:

Belief: Most of the differences in the behaviors of women and men are based on "human nature"; men and women are plainly very different from each other. Research shows that biological factors certainly play a part in the behaviors of men and women, but the culture (beliefs, values, rules, and way of life) that people learn as they grow up determines who does what and how biological tendencies are played out. A unique example illustrates this: In the nomadic Wodaabe tribe in Africa, women do most of the heavy work, while men adorn themselves with makeup, sip tea, and gossip (Cultural Survival 2010; Loftsdottir 2004). Each year the group holds a festival where men show their white teeth and the whites of their eyes to attract a marriage partner. Such dramatic variations in the behavior of men and women around the world are so great that it is impossible to attribute behavior to biology or human nature alone.

Belief: Racial groupings are based on biological differences among people. Actually, racial categorizations are socially constructed (created by members of society) and vary among societies and over time within societies. A person can be seen as one race in Brazil and another in the United States. Even within the United States, racial categories have changed many times. All one has to do is look at old U.S. Census records and see how racial categories change over time—even within the same nation!

Belief: Given the high divorce rates in the United States and Canada, most marriages do not last. The highest divorce rates in the United States are found among those below the average in education and living in poverty. Those who are middle class or higher tend to have more stable marriages (Luscombe 2010; Pew Research Center 2010).

As these examples illustrate, the discipline of sociology provides a method to assess the accuracy of our commonsense assumptions about the social world. To improve the lives of individuals in our communities and in societies around the world, decision makers must have accurate information. Sociological research can be the basis for more rational and just social policies—policies that better meet the needs of all groups in the social world. The sociological imagination, discussed next, helps us gain an understanding of social problems.

The Sociological Imagination

Events in our social world affect our individual lives. If we are unemployed or lack funds for a college education, we may say this is a personal problem. Yet, broader social issues are often at the root of our situation. The sociological imagination holds that we can best understand our personal experiences and problems by examining their broader social context—by looking at the big picture.

Many individual problems (or private troubles) are rooted in social or public issues (what is happening in the social world outside one's personal control). Distinguished sociologist C. Wright Mills called the ability to understand this *complex interactive relationship between individual experiences and public issues* the sociological imagination. For Mills, many personal experiences can and should be interpreted in the context of large-scale forces in the wider society (Mills 1959).

Consider, for example, someone you know who has been laid off from a job. This personal trauma is a common situation during a recession. Unemployed persons often experiences feelings of inadequacy or lack of self-worth because of the job loss. Their unemployment, though, may be due to larger social forces such as unsound banking practices, corporate downsizing, or to a corporation taking operations to another country where labor costs are cheaper and where there are fewer environmental regulations on companies. People may blame themselves or each other for personal troubles such as unemployment or marital problems, believing that they did not try hard enough. Often, they do not see the connection between their private lives and larger economic and social forces beyond their control. They fail to recognize the public issues that create private troubles.

©Oliver Strewe/ Lonely Planet Images/ Getty Images

In the early 20th century, immigrants to the United States who were of Irish and Italian ancestry were not considered "white" in Virginia and several other states. In some cases where parochial schools were not options, Irish and Italian children were forced to go to racially segregated public schools with black students.

If you are having trouble paying for college, that may feel like a very personal trouble. High tuition rates, though, relate to a dramatic decline in governmental support for public higher education and financial aid for students. The rising cost of a college education is a serious public issue that our society needs to address. Individuals, alone, cannot reduce the high price of college.

As you learn about sociology, you will begin to notice how social forces shape individual lives, and how this knowledge helps us understand aspects of everyday life we take for granted. In this book, we investigate how group life influences our behaviors and interactions and why some individuals follow the rules of society and others do not. You will learn to view the social world and your place in it from a sociological perspective—the *sociological imagination*. Connecting events from the global and national levels to the personal and intimate level of our own lives is the core organizing theme of this book.

Thinking Sociologically

How has divorce, poverty, or war caused personal troubles for someone you know? Give examples of why is it inadequate to explain these personal troubles by examining only the personal characteristics of those affected.

Questions Sociologists Ask—and Don't Ask

Perhaps you have had late-night discussions with your friends about the meaning of life, the existence of God, the ethical implications of stem cell research, or the morality of abortion. These are philosophical issues that sociologists, like other scientists, cannot answer through scientific research. What sociologists *do* ask are questions about people in social groups and organizations—questions that can be studied scientifically. Sociologists may research how people feel about the above issues (the percentage of people who approve of umbilical cord stem cell research, for example), but sociologists do not say what are right and wrong answers to such value-driven opinions. They are more interested in how people's beliefs influence their behavior. They focus on issues that can be studied objectively and scientifically—looking for causes or consequences.

Sociologists might ask, *who gets an abortion, why do they do so, and how does the society as a whole view abortion?* These are matters of fact that a social scientist can explore. However, sociologists avoid making ethical judgments about whether abortion is sometimes acceptable or always wrong.

Likewise, sociologists might ask, *what are the circumstances around individuals becoming drunk and acting drunken?* This question is often tied more to the particular social environment than to the availability of alcohol. Note that a person might become very intoxicated at a fraternity party but not at a family member's wedding reception where alcohol is served. The expectations for behavior vary in each setting. The researcher does not make judgments about whether use of alcohol is good or bad or right or wrong and avoids—as much as possible—opinions regarding responsibility or irresponsibility. The sociologist does, however, observe variations in the use of alcohol in different social situations and the resulting behaviors. The focus of sociology is on facts and what causes behaviors and their results.

Thinking Sociologically

Consider the information you have just read. What are some questions sociologists might ask about cohabitation or same-sex unions? What are some questions sociologists would not ask about these topics, at least while in their roles as researchers?

The Social Sciences: A Comparison

Not so long ago, our views of people and social relationships were based on stereotypes, intuition, superstitions, supernatural explanations, and traditions passed on from one generation to the next. Natural scientists (e.g., chemists, astronomers, biologists, and oceanographers) first used the scientific method, a model later adopted by social scientists. Social scientists, including anthropologists, psychologists, economists, cultural geographers, historians, and political scientists, as well as sociologists, apply the scientific method to study social relationships, to correct misleading and harmful misconceptions about human behavior, and to guide policy decisions. Consider the following examples of specific studies various social scientists have conducted.

Some anthropological studies focus on garbage. They examine what people discard to understand what kind of lives they lead (Bond 2010). Anthropology is the study of humanity in its broadest context. It is closely related to sociology, and the two areas have common historical roots and sometimes overlapping methodologies and subject matter. However, anthropologists have four major subfields within anthropology: physical anthropology (which is related to biology), archaeology, linguistics, and cultural anthropology (sometimes called ethnology). This last field has the most in common with sociology. Cultural anthropologists study the culture, or way of life, of a society.

A psychologist may wire research subjects to a machine that measures their physiological reaction to a violent film clip, and then ask them questions about what they were feeling. Psychology is the study of individual behavior and mental processes (e.g., sensation, perception, memory, and thought processes). It differs from sociology in that it focuses on individuals rather than on groups, institutions, and societies. Although

Binge drinking, losing consciousness, vomiting, or engaging in sexual acts while drunk may be sources of storytelling at a college party but can be offensive at a wedding reception.

there are different branches of psychology, most psychologists are concerned with individual motivations, personality attributes, attitudes, perceptions, abnormal behavior, mental disorders, and the stages of normal human development.

A political scientist studies opinion poll results to predict who will win the next election, how various groups of people are likely to vote, or how elected officials will vote on proposed legislation. Political science is concerned with government systems and power—how they work, how they are organized, the forms of government, relations among governments, who holds power and how they obtain it, how power is used, and who is politically active. Political science overlaps with sociology, particularly in the study of political theory and the nature and uses of power.

Many economists study the banking system and market trends to try to predict trends and improve the global economy. Economists analyze economic conditions and explore how people organize, produce, and distribute material goods. They are interested in supply and demand, inflation and taxes, prices and manufacturing output, labor organization, employment levels, and comparisons between postindustrial, industrial, and nonindustrial nations.

In this psychological study, the researcher is using some equipment and a computer to measure how the eye and the brain work together to help create depth perception.

What these social sciences—sociology, anthropology, psychology, political science, and economics—have in common is that they study aspects of human behavior and social life. Social sciences share many common topics, methods, concepts, research findings, and theories, but each has a different focus or perspective on the social world. Each of these social sciences relates to topics studied by sociologists, but sociologists focus on human interaction, groups, and social structure, providing the broadest overview of the social world.

Thinking Sociologically

Consider the issue of unemployment in the United States. What is one question in each discipline that an anthropologist, a psychologist, a political scientist, an economist, and a sociologist might ask about this social issue?

WHY DOES SOCIOLOGY MATTER?

Sociology is important not only to understand our relationships with other people and because it can inform social policy decisions, but also because we can pursue a career in sociology or use skills developed through sociology in a wide range of career fields.

Why Study Sociology?

The sociological perspective helps us to be more effective as we carry out our roles as life partners, workers, friends, family members, and citizens. For example, an employee who has studied sociology may better understand how to work with groups and how the structure of the workplace affects individual behavior, how to approach problem solving, and how to collect and analyze data. Likewise, a schoolteacher trained in sociology may have a better understanding of classroom management, student motivation, the causes of poor student learning that have roots outside the school, and why students drop out. Consider the example in the next "Sociology in Our Social World" feature, which explores who drops out, why, the consequences of dropping out, and other variables that shape the professional life of teachers and the academic success of students.

A sociological perspective allows us to look beneath the surface of society and notice social patterns that others

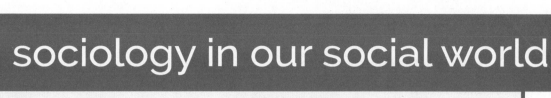

sociology in our social world

High School Dropouts: Causes, Consequences, and Cures

"Cesar entered Hacienda Middle School in the Los Angeles School District in the sixth grade. He lived with his mother and three younger siblings in a garage that was divided into sleeping quarters and a makeshift kitchen with no running water. His mother, who spoke only Spanish, supported the family by working long hours at a minimum-wage job" (Rumberger 2011:1). Because Cesar missed lots of school and did not complete assignments, he failed the first semester. However, a dropout prevention program helped him begin to pass courses. By eighth grade, peer pressure and gangs became part of his life. He was involved in a fight in school and was "transferred"— but stopped going to school. Cesar became a dropout (Rumberger 2011).

Sociologists studying education look for causes and results of students dropping out. The number of high school dropouts each year is approximately 3,030,000; that is 8,300 each day. In ninth grade, 36% of all dropouts occur, and only 59% of students in the 50 largest U.S. cities graduate from high school (Statistic Brain 2014). In 2010, there were almost 28 million dropouts ages 18 and over—and that is not counting students like Cesar who drop out before ninth grade (Rumberger 2011). Estimates are that 81% of students who entered a public high school in 2008 graduated four years later in 2012, but only 76% of Hispanic and 68% of African American students graduated compared to 93% of Asian and 85% of white students (National Center for Education Statistics 2014).

Sociologists, educators, parents, and policy makers, among others, are concerned about the high dropout rates because of economic factors—dropouts have difficulty finding jobs and cost the government money. If they do find a job, they earn much less than high school graduates do, on average about $260,000 less over their working life. Dropouts have poorer health, use more health services, and die younger. They also engage in criminal behavior and are in prison in much higher numbers. They are less likely to vote or be engaged in civic activities, pay less in taxes, and often receive public assistance. Dropouts from the class of 2010 alone will cost more than $337 billion in lost taxes and wages (National Education Association 2012).

Another concern is that those most likely to be dropouts are the fastest-growing groups in schools because of birthrates among these groups. In addition, schools are being held accountable for students achieving on grade level. Thus, schools are reluctant to promote students to the next grade level if they are not achieving on grade level, increasing the chances for retained students to drop out (Alliance for Excellent Education 2010; Rumberger 2011).

Why do students drop out? A few reasons stand out:

- High rates of absenteeism
- Low levels of school engagement
- Low parental education

(Continued)

(Continued)

- Work or family responsibilities
- Problematic/deviant behavior
- Moving to a new school in ninth grade
- Attending school with lower achievement scores (Child Trends 2013)

Sociologists and others propose many solutions for the dropout problem. Dropout counselors can identify students at risk and work with them, finding programs and curricula suited to their needs. Schools designed for at-risk students attempt to address issues in the students' lives such as living situations, poverty, poor health, lack of nutrition, gang membership, and

other barriers to success (Diggs 2014). Some dropouts return to school to obtain a GED or alternative certificate. Some research supports smaller schools and classrooms and more teacher engagement with individual students to reduce dropout rates.

Models of successful schools that have reduced dropout rates and increased the number of students going on to college provide examples of success in working with at-risk students. A key to success is addressing the whole child and some of the many problems students face.

tend to overlook. When you view our social world with a sociological perspective, you

1. become more self-aware by understanding your social surroundings, which can lead to opportunities to improve your life;
2. have a more complete understanding of social situations by looking beyond individual explanations to include group analyses of behavior;
3. understand and evaluate problems more clearly, viewing the world systematically and objectively rather than in strictly emotional or personal terms;
4. gain an understanding of the many diverse cultural perspectives and how cultural differences are related to behavioral patterns;
5. assess the impact of social policies;
6. understand the complexities of social life and how to study them scientifically;
7. gain useful skills in interpersonal relations, critical thinking, data collection and analysis, problem solving, and decision making; and
8. learn how to change your local environment and the larger society.

What Do Sociologists Do?

Graduates with a BA in sociology who seek employment immediately after college are most likely to find their first jobs in social services, administrative assistantships, or some sort of management position. The first jobs of

sociology majors are indicated in Figure 1.1. With graduate degrees—a master's or a doctoral degree—graduates usually become college teachers, researchers, clinicians, or consultants. Some work for governments, while others work for businesses or public service non-profit organizations.

FIGURE 1.1 Occupational Categories for Sociology Graduates' First Jobs

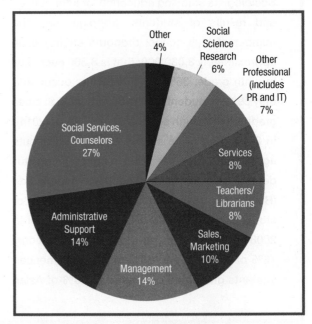

Source: Based on "21st Century Careers With an Undergraduate Degree in Sociology," American Sociological Association, 2009.

Sociology Career Data

Many sociologists work outside of academia, using their knowledge and research skills to address the needs of businesses, nonprofit organizations, and government. For example, they often work in human resources departments and as consultants for businesses. In government jobs, they provide data such as population projections for education and health care planning. In social service agencies they help provide services to those in need, and in health agencies they may be concerned with outreach to immigrant communities. Both sociologists who work in universities and those who work for business or government can use sociological tools to improve society. You will find examples of sociologists in the "Sociologists in Action" boxes throughout the book. In addition, at the end of some chapters you will find a discussion of policy related to that chapter topic.

Thinking Sociologically

From what you have read so far, how might sociological tools (e.g., social interaction skills and knowledge of how groups work) be useful to you in your anticipated major and career or current job?

What Employers Want

Ask employers what they want in a new hire, and the focus is likely to be on writing, speaking, and analytical skills—especially when the new employee will be faced with complex problems. Other desired skills in demand include the ability to cope with change, work effectively in diverse teams, and gather and interpret quantitative information. The left column in Table 1.1 indicates what employers want from college graduates; the right column indicates the skills and competencies that are part of most sociological training. Compare the two, noting the high levels of overlap.

We now have a general idea of what sociology is and what sociologists do. It should be apparent that sociology is a broad field of interest; sociologists study all aspects of human social behavior. The next section of this chapter shows how the parts of the social world that sociologists study relate to each other, and it outlines the model you will follow as you continue to learn about sociology.

Thinking Sociologically

Imagine that you are a mayor, legislator, police chief, or government official. You make decisions based on information gathered by social science research rather than on your own intuition or assumptions. What are some advantages to this decision-making method?

THE SOCIAL WORLD MODEL

Think about the different groups you depend on and interact with on a daily basis. You wake up to greet members of your family or your roommate. You go to a larger group—a class—that exists within an even larger organization—the college or university. Understanding sociology and the approach of this book requires a grasp of levels of analysis—that is, *social groups from the smallest to the largest*. It may be relatively easy to picture small groups, such as a family, a group of friends, a sports team, or a sorority or fraternity. It is more difficult to visualize large groups, such as corporations—Gap, Abercrombie & Fitch, Eddie Bauer, General Motors Company, or Starbucks—or organizations such as local or state governments. The largest groups include nations or international organizations, such as the sprawling networks of the United Nations or the World Trade Organization. Groups of various sizes shape our lives. Sociological analysis involves an understanding of these groups that exist at various levels of analysis and the connections among them.

The social world model helps us picture *the levels of analysis in our social surroundings as an interconnected series of small groups, organizations, institutions, and societies*. Sometimes these groups are connected by mutual support and cooperation, but sometimes there are conflicts and power struggles over access to resources. What we are asking you to do here and throughout this book is to develop a sociological imagination—the basic lens used by sociologists. Picture the social world as connected levels of increasingly larger circles. To understand the units or parts of the social world model, look at the model shown on page 15 (and at the beginning of each chapter).

We use this social world model throughout the book to illustrate how each topic fits into the big picture—our social world. The social world includes both *social structures* and *social processes*.

Social Structures

Picture the human body, held together by bones and muscles. The units that make up that body include the brain, heart, lungs, and kidneys. In a similar manner, social units are *interconnected parts of the social world ranging from small groups to societies*. These social units include dyads, small groups like the members of a family, community

Table 1.1 What Employers Want and What Sociology Majors Can Deliver

Employers Who Want Colleges to "Place More Emphasis" on Essential Learning Outcomes		Traits and Knowledge That Are Developed in Most Sociological Training
Knowledge of Human Culture	**% Seeking**	**Skills and Competencies**
1. Global issues	72	• Knowledge of global issues • Sensitivity to diversity and differences in cultural values and traditions
2. The role of the United States in the world	60	• Sociological perspective on the United States and the world
3. Cultural values and traditions— U.S. and global	53	• Understanding diversity • Working with others (ability to work toward a common goal)
Intellectual and Practical Skills	**% Seeking**	
4. Teamwork skills in diverse groups	76	• Effective leadership skills (ability to take charge and make decisions) • Interpersonal skills (working with diverse coworkers)
5. Critical thinking and analytic reasoning	73	• Analysis and research skills • Organizing thoughts and information • Planning effectively (ability to design, plan, organize, and implement projects and to be self-motivated)
6. Written and oral communication	73	• Communication skills (listening, verbal and written communication) • Working with peers • Effective interaction in group situations
7. Information literacy	70	• Knowledge of how to find information one needs— online or in a library
8. Creativity and innovation	70	• Flexibility, adaptability, and multitasking (ability to set priorities, manage multiple tasks, adapt to changing situations, and handle pressure) • Creative ways to deal with problems
9. Complex problem solving	64	• Ability to conceptualize and solve problems • Ability to be creative (working toward meeting the organization's goals)
10. Quantitative reasoning	60	• Computer and technical literacy (basic understanding of computer hardware and software programs) • Statistical analysis
Personal and Social Responsibility	**% Seeking**	
11. Intercultural competence (teamwork in diverse groups)	76	• Personal values (honesty, flexibility, work ethic, dependability, loyalty, positive attitude, professionalism, self-confidence, willingness to learn) • Working with others • Ability to work toward a common goal
12. Intercultural knowledge (global issues)	72	• Knowledge of global issues

Source: American Sociological Association 2009; Hansen and Hansen 2003; WorldWideLearn 2007. See also Association of American Colleges and Universities and Hart Research Associates 2013.

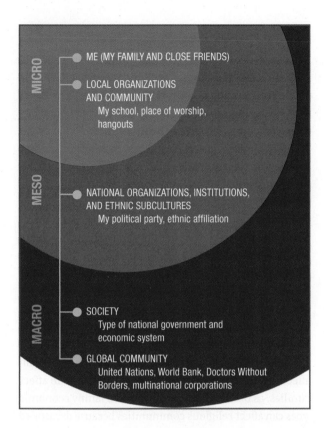

MICRO

ME (MY FAMILY AND CLOSE FRIENDS)

LOCAL ORGANIZATIONS
AND COMMUNITY
My school, place of worship,
hangouts

MESO

NATIONAL ORGANIZATIONS, INSTITUTIONS,
AND ETHNIC SUBCULTURES
My political party, ethnic affiliation

MACRO

SOCIETY
Type of national government and
economic system

GLOBAL COMMUNITY
United Nations, World Bank, Doctors Without
Borders, multinational corporations

organizations including schools and churches, large-scale organizations such as political parties or state and national governments, and global societies such as the United Nations.

All these social units connect to make up the social structure—*the stable patterns of interactions, statuses, roles, and organizations that provide stability for the society and bring order to individuals' lives.* Think about these parallels between the structure that holds together the human body and the structure that holds together societies and their units.

Sometimes, however, the units within the social structure are in conflict. For example, a religion that teaches that some forms of birth control are wrong may conflict with the health care system regarding how to provide care to women. This issue has been in the U.S. news as many religious organizations and religious business owners have fought against the requirements of the 2010 Affordable Care Act that employers provide birth control to those who wish to receive it.

Social institutions are *organized, patterned, and enduring sets of social structures that provide guidelines for behavior and help each society meet its basic survival needs.* Think about the fact that all societies have some form of family, education, religion, politics, and economics; in more complex societies there are also essential structures

that provide science, health care, and a military. These are the institutions that provide the rules, roles, and relationships to meet human needs and guide human behavior. They are the units through which organized social activities take place, and they provide the setting for activities essential to human and societal survival. For example, we cannot survive without an economic institution to provide guidelines and a structure for meeting our basic needs of food, shelter, and clothing. Likewise, society would not function without political institutions to govern and protect its members. Most social units fall under one of these institutions.

Like the human body, society and social groups have a structure. Our body's skeleton governs how our limbs are attached to the torso and how they move. Like the system of organs that make up our bodies—heart, lungs, kidneys, bladder—all social institutions are interrelated. Just as an illness in one organ affects other organs, a dysfunction in one institution affects the other institutions. A heart attack affects the flow of blood to all other parts of the body. Likewise, if many people are unable to afford medical treatment, the society is less healthy, and there are consequences for families, schools, workplaces, and society as a whole.

The national society, one of the largest social units in our model, includes *a population of people, usually living within a specified geographic area, connected by common ideas, and subject to a particular political authority.* It also

©WOLFGANG KUMM/DPA /Landov

All social institutions are interrelated, just as the parts of the body are interdependent: If the skeletal system of the body breaks down, the muscular system and nervous system are not going to be able to get the body to do what it needs to do.

This refugee mother and child from Mozambique represent the smallest social unit, a dyad. In this case, they are trying to survive with help from larger groups such as the United Nations.

features a social structure with groups and institutions. In addition to having relatively permanent geographic and political boundaries, a national society has one or more languages and a unique way of life. In most cases, national societies involve countries or large regions where the inhabitants share a common identity as members. In certain other instances, such as contemporary Great Britain, a single national society may include several groups of people who consider themselves distinct nationalities (Welsh, English, Scottish, and Northern Irish within the United Kingdom). Such multicultural societies may or may not have peaceful relations.

Thinking Sociologically

How might change in one national institution, such as health care, affect change in other national institutions, such as the family and the economy? Can you think of any human activities that do not fall into one of the institutions mentioned above?

Social Processes

If social structure is similar to the human body's skeletal structure, social processes are similar to what keeps the body alive—beating heart, lungs processing oxygen, stomach processing nutrients. Social processes *take place through actions of people in institutions and other social units.* The process of socialization teaches individuals how to behave in society. It takes place through actions in families, educational systems, religious organizations, and other social units. Socialization is essential for the continuation of any society because through this process members of society learn the thoughts and actions needed to survive in their society. Another process, conflict, occurs between individuals or groups over money, jobs, and other needed or desired resources. The process of change also occurs continuously in every social unit; change in one unit affects other units of the social world, often in a chain reaction. For instance, change in the quality of health care can affect the workforce. A workforce in poor health can affect the economy; instability in the economy can affect families, as breadwinners lose jobs; and family economic woes can affect religious communities because devastated families cannot afford to give money to churches, mosques, or temples.

Sociologists try to identify, understand, and explain the processes that take place within social units. Picture these processes as overlying and penetrating our whole social world, from small groups to societies. Social units would be lifeless without the action brought about by social processes, just as body parts would be lifeless without the processes of electrical impulses shooting from the brain to each organ or the oxygen transmitted by blood coursing through our arteries to sustain each organ.

The Environment of Our Social World

Surrounding each social unit, whether a small family group or a large corporation, is an environment—*the setting in which the social unit operates, including everything that influences the social unit, such as its physical and organizational surroundings and technological innovations.* Just as each individual has a unique environment, including family, friends, and other social units, each social unit has an environment to which it must adjust.

Some parts of the environment are more important to the individual or social unit than others. For example, your local church, synagogue, temple, or mosque is surrounded

A Social Theory of War ▶

by its unique environment. That religious organization may seem autonomous and independent, but it depends on its national organization for guidelines and support; the local police force to protect the building from vandalism; and the local economy to provide jobs to members so that the members, in turn, can support the organization. If the religious education program is going to train children to understand the scriptures, local schools are needed to teach the children to read. A religious group may also be affected by other religious bodies, competing with one another for potential members from the community. These religious groups may work cooperatively—organizing a summer program for children or jointly sponsoring a holy-day celebration—or they may define one another as evil, each trying to stigmatize the other. Moreover, one local religious group may be composed primarily of professional and business people and another group mostly of working-class people. The religious groups may experience conflict in part because they each serve a different socioeconomic constituency. The point is that to understand a social unit *or* the human body, we must consider the structure and processes within the unit as well as the interaction with the surrounding environment.

Perfect relationships or complete harmony among the social units is unusual. Social units, be they small groups or large organizations, are often motivated by self-interest and the need for self-preservation, with the result that they compete with other units for resources (time, money, skills, energy of members). Therefore, social units within a society are often in conflict. Whether groups are in conflict or they cooperate does not change their interrelatedness;

units are interdependent and can be studied using the scientific method.

Studying the Social World: Levels of Analysis

Picture for a moment your sociology class as a social unit in your social world. Students (individuals) make up the class, the class (small group) is offered by the sociology department, the sociology department (a large group, including faculty and students) is part of the college or university, and the university (an organization) is located in a community. It follows the practices approved by the social institution (education) of which it is a part, and education is an institution located within a nation. Practices the university follows are determined by a larger accrediting agency that provides guidelines and oversight for educational institutions. The national society, represented by the national government, is shaped by global events such as technological and economic competition between nations, natural disasters, global climate change, wars, and terrorist attacks. Such events influence national policies and goals, including policies for the educational system. Thus, global issues and conflicts may shape the content of the curriculum taught in the local classroom, from what is studied to the textbooks used.

Each of these social units is referred to as a level of analysis, as described earlier (see Table 1.2). These levels are illustrated in the social world model at the beginning of each chapter, and their relation to that chapter's content is shown through examples in the model.

Table 1.2 The Structure of Society and Levels of Analysis

	Level	Parts of Education
Micro-level analysis	Interpersonal	Sociology class; professor and student interacting; study group cramming for an exam
	Local organizations	University; sociology department
Meso-level analysis	Organizations and institutions	State boards of education; National Education Association
	Ethnic groups within a nation	Islamic madrassas or Jewish yeshiva school systems
Macro-level analysis	Nations	Policy and laws governing education
	Global community	World literacy programs

Micro-Level Analysis

A focus on *individual or small-group interaction in specific situations* is called micro-level analysis. The micro level is important because one-to-one and small-group interaction form the basic foundation of all social groups and organizations to which we belong from families to corporations to societies. We are members of many groups at the micro level.

To understand micro-level analysis, consider the problem of spousal abuse, most often involving women being abused. Why does a person remain in an abusive relationship, knowing that each year thousands of people are killed by their partners and millions more are severely and repeatedly battered? To answer this question, several possible micro-level explanations can be considered. One view is that the abusive partner has convinced the abused person that she is powerless in the relationship or that she "deserves" the abuse. Therefore, she gives up in despair of ever being able to alter the situation. The abuse is viewed as part of the interaction—of action and reaction—and some partners come to see abuse as what comprises "normal" interaction.

Another explanation for remaining in the abusive relationship is that battering is a familiar part of the person's everyday life. However unpleasant and unnatural this may seem to outsiders, it may be seen by the abused as a "normal" and acceptable part of intimate relationships, especially if she grew up in an abusive family.

Another possibility is that an abused woman may fear that her children would be harmed or that she would be harshly judged by her family or church if she "abandoned" her mate. She may have few resources to make leaving the abusive situation possible. To study each of these possible explanations involves analysis at the micro level because each focuses on interpersonal interaction factors rather than on large society-wide trends or forces. Meso-level analysis leads to quite different explanations for abuse.

Meso-Level Analysis

Meso-level analysis involves looking at *intermediate-sized units smaller than the nation but larger than the local community or even the region.* This level includes national institutions (such as the economy of a country, the national educational system, or the political system within a country), nationwide organizations (such as a political party, a soccer league, or a national women's rights organization), and ethnic groups that have an identity as a group (such as Jews, Mexican Americans, or Native

Americans in the United States). Organizations, institutions, and ethnic communities are smaller than the nation or global social units, but they are still beyond the everyday personal experience and control of individuals. They are intermediate in the sense of being too large to know everyone in the group, but they are not as large as nation-states. For example, state governments in the United States, provinces in Canada, prefectures in Japan, or cantons in Switzerland are at the meso level and usually more accessible and easier to change than the national bureaucracies of these countries.

In discussing micro-level analysis, we used the example of domestic violence. Recognizing that personal troubles can often be related to public issues—*the sociological imagination*—many social scientists look for broader explanations of spousal abuse, such as social conditions at the meso level of society (Straus, Gelles, and Steinmetz 2006). When a pattern of behavior in society occurs with increasing frequency, it cannot be understood solely from the point of view of individual cases or micro-level causes. For instance, sociological findings show that fluctuations in spousal or child abuse at the micro level are related to levels of unemployment in meso-level organizations and macro-level government economic policies. Frustration resulting in abuse erupts within families when poor economic conditions make it nearly impossible for people to find a stable and reliable means of supporting themselves and their families. The message here is that economic issues in the society must be addressed in order to decrease domestic violence.

Macro-Level Analysis

Studying the largest social units in the social world, called macro-level analysis, involves looking at *entire nations, global forces, and international social trends.* Macro-level analysis is essential to our understanding of how larger societal forces and global events shape our everyday lives. A natural disaster such as the recent droughts in North America and West Africa and massive hurricanes in Central America and the Caribbean may change the foods we can serve at our family dinner table, since much of what we consume comes from other parts of the world. (Figure 1.2 shows some of the most deadly natural disasters of the past few years.) Likewise, a political conflict on the other side of the planet can lead to war, which means that a member of your family may be called up on active duty and sent into harm's way more than 7,000 miles from your home. Each member of the family may experience individual stress, have trouble concentrating, and feel ill with worry. The entire globe has become an interdependent social unit. If we are to prosper and thrive in the world today, we need to understand connections that go beyond our local communities.

Even patterns such as domestic violence, considered as micro- and meso-level issues earlier, can be examined at the macro level. Violence against women (especially rape) occurs at very different rates in different societies, with some having a "culture of rape" (Kristof and WuDunn 2009). Consider the case in 2013 of the medical student in India who was gang raped on a bus and subsequently died. Her rape and that of a Swiss tourist and of girls as young as 2 shortly thereafter became headline news and shone a spotlight on the culture and lack of law enforcement in India that encourage violence against women. The most consistent predictor of violence against women is a macho conception of masculine roles and personality. Societies or subgroups within society that teach males that the finest expression of their masculinity is physical strength and domination tend to have more battered women (Lindow 2009).

India is far from the only nation with a culture that generates violence against women. South Africa has one of the highest levels of rape in the world, with one in four men (often under 20) having raped a woman, and 46% of those more than once. The men tend to show no remorse because the behavior is "accepted" by their segments of society; it is "macho" (Lindow 2009).

Understanding individual human behavior often requires investigation of the larger societal beliefs and values that support that behavior. Worldwide patterns may tell us something about a social problem and offer new lenses for understanding that problem.

Distinctions between each level of analysis are not always sharply delineated. The micro level shades into the meso level, and the lines between the meso level and the macro level are blurry on the continuum. Still, it is clear that in some micro-level social units, you know everyone, or at least every member of the social unit, is only two degrees of separation away. In other words, every person in the social unit knows someone whom you also know. Try the following "Engaging Sociology" on page 22 to test your understanding of levels of analysis and the sociological imagination.

FIGURE 1.2   Natural Catastrophes Worldwide, 2012

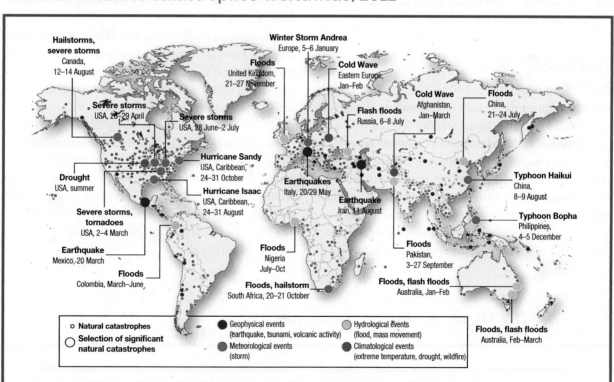

Source: Natural Catastrophes, 2012 World Map. © 2013 Münchener Rückversicherungs-Gesellschaft, Geo Risks Research, NatCatSERVICE.

Analyzing Outsourcing

We all participate in meso-level social units that are smaller than the nation but that can be huge. For example, thousands or even millions of individuals join organizations such as the Tea Party movement, Occupy Wall Street, MoveOn.org, or the environmental group 350.org. Those involved participate in dialogues online, and contribute money to political organizations. We share connections with the other members of these organizations, and our lives are interconnected, even if we never meet face-to-face.

The macro level is even more removed from the individual, but its impact can change our lives. For example, decisions by lawmakers in Washington, D.C., may determine whether or not your own family has health care coverage (and of what quality) and whether the United States will lead or stymie global efforts to address climate change. These government leaders will also determine whether or not interest rates on federal student loans for U.S. students go up.

The social world model presented in each chapter opening illustrates the interplay of micro-, meso-, and macro-level forces related to that chapter's content. Figure 1.3 shows how this micro-to-macro model should be seen as a continuum. In the "Sociology Around the World" below, we examine a village in Tunisia to see how macro-level forces influence a meso-level local community and individual micro-level lives.

The Social World Model and This Book

The social world engulfs each of us from the moment of our birth until we die. Throughout our lives, each of us is part of a set of social relationships that provides guidelines for how we interact with others and how we see ourselves. This does not mean that human behavior is strictly determined by our links to the social world. Humans are more than mere puppets whose behavior is programmed by social structure. It does mean, however, that the individual and the larger social world influence each other. We are influenced by, and we have influence on, our social environment. The social world is a human creation, and we can and do change that which we create. It acts on us, and we act on it. In this sense, social units are constantly emerging and changing in the course of human action and interaction.

The difficulty for most of us is that we are so caught up in our daily concerns that we fail to see and understand the social forces that are at work in our personal lives. What we need are conceptual and methodological tools to help us gain a more complete and accurate perspective on the social world. The ideas, theories, methods, and levels of analysis employed by sociologists are the very tools that will help give us that perspective. To use an analogy, each different lens of a camera gives the photographer a unique view of the world. Wide-angle lenses, close-up lenses, telephoto lenses, and special filters each serve a purpose in creating a distinctive picture or frame of the world. No one lens will provide the complete picture. Yet the combination of images produced by various lenses allows us to examine in detail aspects of the world we might ordinarily overlook. That is what the sociological perspective gives us: a unique set of lenses to see the social world around us with deeper understanding. In seeing the social world from a sociological perspective, we are better able to understand who we are as social beings.

Throughout this book, we use the social world model as the framework for understanding the social units, processes, and surrounding environment. We look at each social unit and process. We take the unit out, examine it, and then return it to its place in the interconnected social world model so that you can comprehend the whole social world and its parts, like putting a puzzle together. Look for the model at the beginning of every chapter. We will also explain the micro-, meso-, and macro-level dimensions of issues throughout the text. Test your understanding of these concepts by identifying the levels of analysis in the following "Engaging Sociology" on page 24.

FIGURE 1.3   The Micro-to-Macro Continuum

Micro social units   Meso social units   Macro social units

Movement Popularity on Different Levels

Sociology Around the World

Tunisian Village Meets the Modern World

This is a story of change as macro-level innovations enter a small micro-level traditional village. As you read, try to identify the units, the levels of analysis being discussed, and the impact of globalization on a community that does not know what these changes will bring.

The workday began at dawn as usual in the small fishing village on the coast of Tunisia, North Africa. Men prepared their nets and boats for the day, while women prepared breakfast and dressed the young children for school. About 10 a.m., it began—the event that would change this picturesque village forever. Bulldozers arrived first, followed by trench diggers and cement mixers, to begin their overhaul of the village.

Villagers had suspected something was afoot when important-looking officials arrived two months earlier with foreign businessmen, followed by two teams of surveyors. Without their approval, the government had sold the land that the village had held communally for generations to the foreigners so that they could build a multimillion-dollar hotel and casino. When concerned citizens asked what was happening in their village, they were assured that their way of life would not change. The contractor from the capital city of Tunis said that they would still have access to the beach and ocean for fishing. He also promised them many benefits from the hotel project—jobs, help from the government to improve roads and housing, and a higher standard of living.

The contractor had set up camp in a trailer on the beach, and word soon got around that he would be hiring some men for higher hourly wages than they could make in a day or even month of fishing. Rivalries soon developed between friends over who should apply for the limited number of jobs.

As the bulldozers moved in, residents had mixed opinions about the changes taking place in their village and their lives. Some saw the changes as exciting opportunities for new jobs and recognition of their beautiful village. Others viewed the changes as destroying a lifestyle that was all they and generations before them had known.

Today, the village is dwarfed by the huge hotel, and the locals are looked on as quaint curiosities by the European tourists. Fishing has become a secondary source of employment to working in the hotel and casino or selling local crafts and trinkets to souvenir-seeking visitors. Many women are now employed outside the home by the hotel, creating new family structures as grandparents, unemployed men, and other relations take over child-rearing responsibilities.

To understand the changes in this one small village and other communities facing similar change, a sociologist uses the sociological imagination. This involves understanding the global political and economic trends affecting this village and its inhabitants (macro-level analysis). It requires comprehension of the transformation of social institutions within the nation (meso-level analysis). Finally, sociological investigation explores how change affects the individual Tunisian villagers (micro-level analysis).

To sociologically analyze the process of change, it is important to understand what is going on in this

(Continued)

(Continued)

situation. The government officials and the international business representatives negotiated a lucrative deal to benefit both Tunisia and the business corporation. The community and its residents presented few obstacles to the project from the point of view of the government, and in fact, government officials reasoned that the villagers could benefit from new jobs. However, the economic and family roles of

the villagers—how they earned a living and how they raised their children—changed dramatically with the disruption of their traditional ways. The process of change began with the demand of people far from Tunisia for vacation spots in the sun. Ultimately, this process reached the village's local environment, profoundly affecting the village and everyone in it. For this Tunisian village, the old ways are gone forever.

ENGAGING SOCIOLOGY

Micro-Meso-Macro

The distinctions between levels of analysis are gray rather than precise. Levels of analysis should be viewed as a continuum—from micro to macro social units. Clear criteria help identify groups at each level. One criterion is size (number of people) of the group. A second is the geographic range of influence:

- intimate or very close personal relationships (micro),
- social units in the local community (micro),
- social units that cover a large geographic region (like a state or commonwealth) and even nationwide groups that—despite size—are still a small portion of the entire nation (meso), and
- the nation itself (macro) and units with global reach (macro).

A third criterion is degree of separation. If you know someone personally, that is one degree of separation. If you do not know the mayor of your town, but you know someone who knows the mayor, that is two degrees of separation. If you have a friend or a relative who knows someone who is a friend or relative of the governor in your state or province, that is three degrees of separation. Some research

indicates that every person on the planet is within seven degrees of separation from every other human being. Let us see what this means for various levels of analysis in our social world.

Micro-level groups are small, local community social units such as families and school classrooms within which everyone knows everyone else or knows someone who knows a group member. So the degree of separation is usually not more than two degrees.

Meso-level groups are social units of intermediate size such as state governments (with limited geographic range), ethnic groups, and religious denominations (with large geographic range but population size that makes them a minority of the entire nation). Typically the group is large enough that members have never heard the names of many other members. Many members may have little access to the leaders, yet the group is not so large as to make the leaders seem distant or unapproachable. Almost anyone within the social unit is only three or four degrees of separation apart. Everyone in the unit is likely to know someone who is an acquaintance of someone who knows a particular member.

(Continued)

(Continued)

Macro-level groups are large social units, usually quite bureaucratic, that operate at a national or a global level, such as national governments or international organizations. Most members are unlikely to know or have communicated with the leaders personally or know someone who knows the leaders. The "business" of these groups is of international importance and implication. A macro-level system is one in which most of the members are at least five degrees of separation from one another—that is, they know someone who knows someone who knows someone who knows someone who knows the person in question.

----

1. Micro social units

----

2. Meso social units

----

3. Macro social units

Look at the list of social units below. Identify which level each group is most likely to belong to—(1) micro, (2) meso, or (3) macro. Why did you answer as you did? The preceding definitions should help you make your decisions. Again, some are "on the line" because this is a continuum from micro to macro, and some units could legitimately be placed in more than one group. Which ones are especially "on the line"?

_____ Your nuclear family

_____ The United Nations

_____ A local chapter of the Lions Club or the Rotary Club

_____ Your high school baseball team

_____ India

_____ NATO (North Atlantic Treaty Organization)

_____ The First Baptist Church in Muncie, Indiana

_____ The World Bank

_____ A family reunion

_____ Google, Inc. (international)

_____ The Department of Education for the Commonwealth of Kentucky

_____ The show choir in your local high school

_____ African Canadians

_____ The Dineh (Navajo) people

_____ Canada

_____ The Republican Party in the United States

_____ The World Court

_____ A fraternity at your college

_____ The International Monetary Fund (IMF)

_____ The Ministry of Education for Spain

_____ The Roman Catholic Church (with its headquarters at the Vatican in Rome)

_____ Australia

_____ The Chi Omega national sorority

_____ Boy Scout Troop 3 in Marion, Ohio

_____ Al-Qaeda (an international alliance of terrorist organizations)

_____ The provincial government for the Canadian providence of Ontario

_____ The United States of America

See how your authors rate these at edge.sagepub .com/ballantine5e.

ENGAGING SOCIOLOGY

Micro-Meso-Macro: An Application Exercise

Imagine that there has been a major economic downturn (recession) in your local community. Identify three possible events at each level (micro, meso, and macro) that might contribute to the economic troubles in your town.

The micro (local community) level:

1.

2.

3.

The meso (intermediate—state, organizational, or ethnic subculture) level:

1.

2.

3.

The macro (national/global) level:

1.

2.

3.

When we say we know something about society, how is it that we know? What is considered evidence in sociology, and what lens (theory) do we use to interpret the data? In the next chapter, we turn to how we gather data to help us test theories to understand and influence the social world.

WHAT HAVE WE LEARNED?

How can sociology help you see new aspects of your life and change society? Throughout this book you will find ideas and examples that will help answer this question. You will learn how to view the social world through a sociological lens and use the *sociological imagination*. Understanding how the social world works from the micro through the meso to the macro level helps us interact more effectively in it. Using the sociological imagination enables us to see how individual troubles can be rooted in social issues, and best addressed with an understanding of the meso or macro level. This knowledge enables us to be better family members, workers, citizens, and members of the global community.

We live in a complex social world with many layers of interaction. If we really want to understand our own lives, we need to comprehend the levels of analysis that affect our lives and the connections between those levels. To do so wisely, we need both objective lenses for viewing this complex social world and accurate, valid information (facts) about the society. As the science of society, sociology can provide both tested empirical data and a broad, analytical perspective, as you will learn in the next chapter. Here is a summary of points from Chapter 1.

KEY POINTS

- Humans are, at our very core, social animals—more akin to pack or herd animals than to individualistic cats. (See pp. 4–5.)

- Sociology is based on scientific findings, making it more predictable and reliable than opinions or commonsense beliefs in a particular culture. (See pp. 5–6.)

- A core idea in sociology is the sociological imagination. It requires that we see how our individual lives and personal troubles are shaped by historical and structural events outside our everyday lives. It also prods us to see how we can influence our society. (See pp. 8.)

- Sociology is a social science and, therefore, uses the tools of the sciences to establish credible evidence to understand our social world. As a science,

sociology is scientific and objective rather than value laden. (See pp. 9–10.)

- Sociology has pragmatic applications, including those that are essential for the job market. (See pp. 10–13.)

- Sociology focuses on social units or groups, social structures such as institutions, social processes that give a social unit its dynamic character, and social environments. (See pp. 13–15.)

- The social world model is the organizing theme of this book. Using the sociological imagination, we can understand our social world best by clarifying the interconnections between micro, meso, and macro levels of the social world. Each chapter of this book will examine society at these three levels of analysis. (See pp. 17–20.)

DISCUSSION QUESTIONS

1. Think of a problem that impacts you personally (e.g., the high cost of tuition, unemployment, or divorce) and explain how you would make sense of it differently if you viewed it as (a) only a personal problem or (b) influenced by a public issue. How do possible solutions to the problem differ depending on how you view it?

2. How can sociology help you become a more informed citizen and better able to understand how government policies impact society?

3. What are three ways the sociological perspective can help you succeed in college and the workforce?

4. Think of some of the ways the social institutions of government and education are connected. Why is it in the interest of the government to support higher education? How has government support (or lack of support) impacted your college experience?

5. Imagine you would like to look at reasons behind the high college dropout rate in the United States. How might your explanations differ based on whether your analysis was on the micro, meso, or macro level? Why? Which level or levels would you focus on for your study? Why?

CONTRIBUTING TO OUR SOCIAL WORLD: WHAT CAN WE DO?

At the end of this and all subsequent chapters, you will find suggestions for work, service learning, internships, and volunteering that encourage you to apply the ideas discussed in the chapter. Suggestions for Chapter 1 focus on student organizations for sociology majors and nonmajors.

At the Local (Micro) Level

- *Student organizations and clubs* enable students to meet other students interested in sociology, carry out group activities, get to know faculty members, and attend presentations by guest speakers. These clubs are usually not limited to sociology majors. If no such organization exists, consider forming one with the help of a faculty member. Sociologists also have an undergraduate honors society, Alpha Kappa Delta (AKD). Visit the AKD website at http://alphakappadelta.org/ to learn more about the society and what it takes to form a chapter.

At the Regional (Meso) Level

- *State, regional, and specialization (education, criminology, social problems) sociological associations* are especially student friendly and feature publications and sessions at their annual meetings specifically for undergraduates. The American Sociological Association lists regional and specialty organizations and their websites, with direct links to their home pages, at www.asanet.org/about/Aligned_Associations.cfm.

At the National and Global (Macro) Levels

- The *American Sociological Association (ASA)* is the leading professional organization of sociologists in the United States. Visit the ASA website at www.asanet.org, and take a look around it. You will find many programs and initiatives of special interest to students. If you are interested in becoming a sociologist, be sure to look at the links under the heading "News on the Profession." ASA also sponsors an honors program at the annual meeting that introduces students to the profession and gives them a heads-up on being successful in sociology. For more information, go to www.asanet.org/students/honors.cfm.

- The *International Sociological Association (ISA)* serves sociologists from around the world. Every four years, the organization sponsors a large meeting (Toronto, Canada, in July 2018). Specialty groups within ISA hold smaller conferences throughout the world during the other years. Check out www.isa-sociology.org.

2 Examining the Social World

How Do We Know?

Science is about knowing—through careful systematic investigation. Of course, there are other ways of seeking knowledge, such as finding a good library on a beach!

MICRO

ME (MY FAMILY AND CLOSEST FRIENDS)

LOCAL ORGANIZATIONS AND COMMUNITY

I am active in local church, school, clubs, and sports teams.

MESO

NATIONAL ORGANIZATIONS, INSTITUTIONS, AND ETHNIC SUBCULTURES

I am active in a religious denomination, part of an educational system, and perhaps an ethnic group.

MACRO

SOCIETY

I am a citizen of the United States, Canada, or another country.

GLOBAL COMMUNITY

I am influenced by actions of the United Nations, the World Health Organization, or Doctors without Borders.

IN THIS CHAPTER

- The Development of Sociology

- Sociology's Major Theoretical Perspectives

- Ideas Underlying Science

- How Sociologists Study the Social World

THINK ABOUT IT

Micro: Local Community	When you are trying to convince neighbors or people in your community to accept your opinion, why are facts and evidence important?
Meso: National Institutions, Complex Organizations, and Ethnic Groups	How do sociologists gather accurate data about families, educational institutions, or ethnic groups?
Macro: National and Global Systems	How can theories about national and global issues help us understand our own lives at the micro level?

Let us travel to the Southern Hemisphere to meet a teenage boy, Hector. He is a 16-year-old living in a *favela* (slum) on the outskirts of São Paulo, Brazil. He is a polite, bright boy, but his chances of getting an education and a steady job in his world are limited. Like millions of other children around the world, he comes from a poor rural family that migrated to an urban area in search of a better life. However, his family ended up in a crowded slum with only a shared spigot for water and one string of electric lights along the dirt road going up the hill on which they live. The sanitary conditions in his community are appalling—open sewers, no garbage collection—which makes the people susceptible to various diseases. His family is relatively fortunate, for they have cement walls and wood flooring, but no bathroom, running water, or electricity. Many adjacent dwellings are little more than cardboard walls with corrugated metal roofs and dirt floors.

Hector wanted to stay in school but was forced to drop out to help support his family. Since leaving school, he has picked up odd jobs—deliveries, trash pickup, janitorial work, gardening—to help pay for the family's dwelling and to buy food to support his parents and six siblings. Even when he was in school, Hector's experience was discouraging. He was not a bad student, and some teachers encouraged him to continue, but other students from the city teased the *favela* kids and made them feel unwelcome. Most of his friends dropped out before he did. Hector often missed school because of other obligations—looking for part-time work, visiting a sick relative, or taking care of a younger sibling. The immediate need to put food on the table outweighed the long-term value of staying in school.

What is the bottom line for Hector and millions like him? Because of his limited education and work skills, obligations to his family, and limited opportunities, he most likely will continue to live in poverty.

Sociologists are interested in the factors that influence the social world of children like Hector: family, friends, school, community, and the place of one's nation in the global political and economic structural systems. Sociologists use social theories and scientific methods to examine poverty and many other social issues. In this chapter you will learn about some of the different data collection methods sociologists use to collect information and the theories they utilize to make sense of their data.

Sociological research helps us to understand how and why society operates and how we might change it. It can also help you make sense of why people in your family, neighborhood,

Slum dwellers of São Paulo, Brazil. Hector lives in a neighborhood with shelters made of available materials such as boxes, no electricity or running water, and poor sanitation.

© Christopher Pillitz/In Pictures/Corbis

The Kindness of Strangers

college campus, and workplace act the way they do. You will, no doubt, find yourself in a situation where conducting a research study will help your organization or community.

This chapter will introduce you to the basic tools used to plan studies and gather dependable information on topics of interest. It will also help you understand how sociology approaches research questions. To this end, we begin this chapter by discussing the development of sociology as a discipline and the core principles of sociology's major theoretical perspectives. We then explore sociology as a science—core ideas that underlie any science, how to collect data, ethical issues involving research, and practical applications and uses of sociological knowledge. We start with the beginnings and emergence of sociology as a field of study.

THE DEVELOPMENT OF SOCIOLOGY

Throughout recorded history, humans have been curious about how and why society operates as it does. Religion had a major influence on the way individuals thought about the world and their social relationships. Christianity dominated European thought systems during the Middle Ages, from the end of the Roman Empire to the 1500s, while Islamic beliefs took hold in much of the Middle East and parts of Africa. The North African Islamic scholar Ibn Khaldun (1332–1406) was the first person on record to suggest a systematic approach to explain the social world. Khaldun was particularly interested in understanding the feelings of solidarity that held tribal groups together during his day, a time of great conflict and wars (Alatas 2006; Hozien n.d.).

Social philosophers provided another approach to understanding society, one that invariably had a strong moral tone. For example, Plato's *Republic*, written around 400 BCE, outlines plans for an ideal state—complete with government, family, economic systems, class structure, and education—designed to achieve social justice. These philosophers' opinions were derived from abstract reflection about how the social world should work but were not tested scientifically.

The Rise of Modern Sociology

Several conditions from the 1600s to the 1800s gave rise to sociology. First, European nations were imperial powers extending their influence and control by establishing colonies in other cultures. This exposure to other cultures

encouraged at least some Europeans to learn more about the people in and around their new colonies. Second, they sought to understand the rapid changes in their own societies brought about by the Industrial Revolution (which began around the middle of the 1700s) and the French Revolution (1789–1799). Finally, advances in the natural sciences demonstrated the value of the scientific method, and some wished to apply this scientific method to understand the social world.

In the early and mid-1800s, no one had clear, systematic explanations for why the old social structure, which had lasted since the early Middle Ages, was collapsing or why cities were exploding with migrants from rural areas. French society was in turmoil, members of the nobility were being executed, and new rules of justice were taking hold. Churches were made subordinate to the state, equal rights under the law were established for citizens, and democratic rule emerged. These dramatic changes marked the end of the traditional monarchy and the beginning of a new social order.

It was in this setting that the scientific study of society emerged. Two social thinkers, Henri Saint-Simon (1760–1825) and Auguste Comte (1798–1857), decried the lack of systematic data collection or objective analysis in social thought. These Frenchmen argued that a science of society could help people understand and perhaps control the rapid changes and unsettling revolutions taking place.

Comte officially coined the term *sociology* in 1838. His basic premise was that religious or philosophical speculation about society did not provide an adequate understanding of how to solve society's problems. Just as the scientists compiled basic facts about the *physical* world, so, too, was there a need to gather scientific knowledge about the *social* world. Only then could leaders systematically apply this scientific knowledge to improve social conditions.

Comte asked two basic questions: What holds society together and gives rise to a stable order in lieu of anarchy? Further, why and how do societies change? Comte conceptualized society as divided into two parts: (1) *Social statics* referred to aspects of society that give rise to order, stability, and harmony. (2) *Social dynamics* referred to change and evolution in society over time. Comte was concerned with what contemporary sociologists and the social world model in this book refer to as *structure* (social statics) and *process* (social dynamics). By understanding these aspects of the social world, Comte felt that leaders could strengthen the society and respond appropriately to change. His optimistic belief was that sociology would be the "queen of sciences," guiding leaders to construct a better social order (Comte [1855] 2003).

Scientific Method

The Bastille, a state prison in Paris, France, and a symbol of oppression, was seized by the common people during the French Revolution, a social upheaval that forced social analysts to think differently about society and social stability. Today, rallying points for social movements and revolutions such as Tahrir Square in Cairo, Egypt, illustrate that uprisings of the common people are still changing societies.

Sociology continued developing as scholars contemplated further changes brought about by the Industrial Revolution. Massive social and economic changes in the 18th and 19th centuries brought about restructuring and sometimes the demise of political monarchies, aristocracies, and feudal lords. Scenes of urban squalor were common in Great Britain and other industrializing European nations. Machines replaced both agricultural workers and cottage (home) industries because they produced an abundance of goods faster, better, and cheaper. Peasants were pushed off the land by new technologies and migrated to urban areas to find work; at the same time a powerful new social class of capitalists was emerging. Industrialization brought the need for a new skilled class of laborers, putting new demands on an education system that had served only the elite. Families now depended on work and wages in the industrial sector to stay alive.

These changes stimulated other social scientists to study society and its problems. The writings of Émile Durkheim, Karl Marx, Harriet Martineau, Max Weber, W. E. B. Du Bois, and many other early sociologists set the stage for the development of sociological theories. Accompanying the development of sociological theory was the utilization of the scientific method—the systematic gathering and recording of reliable and accurate data to test ideas. First, we turn to sociology's major theoretical perspectives.

SOCIOLOGY'S MAJOR THEORETICAL PERSPECTIVES

A theoretical perspective is a basic view of society that guides sociologists' research and analysis. Theoretical perspectives are *the broadest theories in sociology, providing overall approaches to understanding the social world and social problems.* Sociologists draw on major theoretical perspectives at each level of analysis to guide their research and to help them understand social interactions and social organizations.

A good theory *or statement or explanation regarding how and why two or more facts* are related to each other and the connections between these facts also allows social scientists to make predictions about the social world.

Recall the description of the social world model presented in Chapter 1. It stresses the levels of analysis—smaller units existing within larger social systems. Some theories are especially useful when trying to understand micro-level interactions, while others tend to be used to make sense of macro-level structures. Either type of theory—those most useful at the micro or macro levels—can be used at the meso level, depending on the research question being asked. To illustrate four of the major theoretical perspectives on the social world, we delve into our examination of Hector's circumstances, described at the beginning of this chapter.

Micro- to Meso-Level Theories

If we want to study Hector's interactions with his friends and their influence on him or his school performance, we would turn to micro- and meso-level theories to guide our research. Two theories most often used at the micro and meso levels of analysis are symbolic interaction and rational choice theory.

Symbolic Interaction. Symbolic interaction theory (also called social constructionism or interpretative theory) *sees humans as active people who create shared meanings of symbols and events, and then interact on the basis of those meanings.* Through these interactions, we learn to share common ideas, understand what to expect from others, and gain the capability to shape society. As we interact, we make use of symbols, *actions or objects that represent something else and therefore have meaning beyond their own existence*—such as flags, wedding rings, words, and nonverbal gestures. Symbolic communication (e.g., language) helps people construct a meaningful world. Humans continually create and re-create society through their construction and interpretation of the social world. More than any other theory in the social sciences, symbolic interaction theory stresses human agency—the active role of individuals in creating their social environment.

George Herbert Mead (1863–1931), one of the founders of the symbolic interaction perspective, explored the mental processes associated with how humans define or make sense of situations (Mead [1934] 1962). He placed special emphasis on human interpretations of gestures and symbols (including language) and the meanings we attach to our actions. He also examined how we learn our social roles in society that include *expected behaviors, rights, obligations, responsibilities, and privileges assigned to a social status* (such as mother, child, teacher, and friend) and how we learn to carry out these roles. Indeed, as we will see in Chapter 4, he insisted that our notion of who we are—our *self*—emerges from social experience and interaction with others. Language is critical to this process, for it allows us to step outside of our own experience and reflect back on how others see us. Indeed, human language is a unique and powerful human trait, as is illustrated in the next "Sociology in Our Social World."

These ideas of how we construct our individual social worlds and have some control over them represent one approach of symbolic interactionism (known as the Chicago School). Another symbolic interaction approach (the Iowa School) makes a clear link between a person's individual identity and position within organizations. This connects the micro and the meso level of the social system (Kuhn 1964). If we hold several positions—honors student, club president, daughter, sister, student, athlete, thespian, middle-class person—those positions form our *self*. We will interpret new situations in light of our social positions, some of which are very important and anchor how we see the social *world*. Once a core *self* is established, it guides and shapes the way we interact with people in many situations—even new social settings (Kuhn 1964). Thus, if you are president of an organization and have the responsibility for overseeing the organization, part of your self-esteem, your view of responsible citizenship, and your attitude toward life will be shaped by that position. Thus, the Iowa School of symbolic interaction places less emphasis on individual choice, but more on recognizing the link between the micro, meso, and macro levels of society (Carrothers and Benson 2003; Stryker 1980).

To summarize, the modern symbolic interaction theory emphasizes the following:

- People continually create and re-create society through interacting with one another.
- People interact by communicating with one another through the use of shared symbols.
- We learn who we are (our sense of self) and our place in society through interacting with others.

Critique of the Symbolic Interaction Theory. Each theory has its critics. Although symbolic interaction theory is widely used by sociologists today, it is often criticized for neglecting the macro-level structures of society that affect human behavior. By focusing on interpersonal interactions, large-scale social forces such as an economic depression or a political revolution that shape human destinies are given less consideration. With the focus on the ability of each individual to create his or her meaning in social situations (called *agency*), symbolic interaction has

1250s Family Dinner

sociology in our social world

Human Language and the Marvel of a College Classroom

A college classroom is a magical place, and this is true mostly because of human language. Human language is distinctive. All other species communicate with a fairly limited number of sounds they can make. Other animals, except perhaps for dolphins, whales, and chimpanzees, communicate only about something that is happening in the present time and location (Phillips 2013).

Each human language identifies about 50 sounds that come to be designated as meaningful language sounds. In English, this includes such sounds as *sss, mmm, nnn, ttt, kkk, bbb,* and *ooo.* We take this designated collection of sounds and combine them in various ways to make words: *cat, dog, college, student.* This ability to combine sounds into words and words into sentences is called a *distinctive feature system*. A distinctive feature system allows you to say something to your instructor that he or she has never heard any other human say before. The sounds are familiar, as are the words themselves, but you may combine them in a novel way that causes a new idea to occur to your listener. This is actually the root of much humor. For example, you can say a sentence or tell a story that has such a surprising ending that it causes the listener to laugh.

Your animal companions at home clearly have memory. They can recognize you when you get home. Your dog may well remember the other pups in his litter. However, they cannot remember together. They cannot gather to recall and share stories about "good old Dad" the way you can recall the quirky traits of your professors with friends. Your dogs and cats cannot plan for the future—planning a litter reunion for next summer, for example.

The fact that our communication is a *distinctive feature system* allows something unique: temporal and spatial sharing. We can remember together our experiences of the past, and we can pass ideas from one person to another. We can discuss the ideas of people who have died and have perhaps been gone for more than a century. A mare cannot transmit to her colt the racing ideas of Man o' War, the great racehorse of the 1920s, let alone the experiences of horses involved in the Trojan War, or even the more recent derby winner, Secretariat. However, whether in a classroom or a pub, humans can discuss the ideas of Plato, or Muhammad, or Karl Marx. Further, humans, because of words, can take other perspectives—to vicariously visit the other side of the planet or to go back in history to experience a time when an entirely different set of ideas about life was common.

When we come into a classroom, something mysterious, something amazing, happens. Language allows us to see things from a new point of view. What a remarkable gift that we can share ideas and see things through the eyes of someone different from ourselves, and it is largely because of the human *distinctive feature system* of communication. What an interesting species to study! What a marvel that we can do so in a classroom.

often been less attuned to important macro-level issues of social class position, social power, historical circumstances, or international conflict between societies (Meltzer, Petras, and Reynolds 1975). For example, if we focused only on how Hector interacts with his family and friends in trying to determine why he dropped out of school, we would overlook macro forces (e.g., how the lack of government supports for poor families impacted his decision to drop out of school). Another critique is that it is difficult to study abstract ideas like "the development of the self," key to symbolic interaction theory.

Despite these limitations, theorists from the symbolic interaction perspective have made significant contributions to understanding the development of social identities and interactions that underlie groups, organizations, and societies. Many of these studies are discussed in chapters throughout the book.

Rational Choice (Exchange) Theory. According to rational choice theory, *humans are fundamentally concerned with self-interests, making rational decisions based on weighing costs and rewards of the projected outcome of an action.* Someone from this perspective would say Hector would picture the situation as if it were a mental balance sheet: For example, on the plus side, staying in school may lead to future opportunities not available to the uneducated. On the minus side, school is a negative experience, and the family needs help to feed its members now, so going to school is a "waste of time." Which side will win depends on Hector's balance sheet and on family and friends' influence over the rewards versus costs.

Rational choice, also called *exchange theory*, has its roots in several disciplines—economics, behavioral psychology, anthropology, and philosophy (Cook, O'Brien, and Kollock 1990). Social behavior is seen as an exchange activity—a transaction in which resources are given and received (Blau 1964; Homans 1974). Every interaction involves an exchange of something valued—money, time, material goods, attention, sex, allegiance, and so on. People stay in relationships because they get something from the exchange, and they leave relationships that have more costs than benefits for them. They constantly evaluate whether there is reciprocity or balance in a relationship, so that they are receiving as much as they give. Simply stated, people are more likely to act if they see some reward or success coming from their behavior. The implication is that self-interest for the individual is the guiding element in human interaction.

The idea of rational choice theory is that people avoid cost or pain and seek benefits. Thus, people in authority try to control others—like this small child—by imposing cost for behaviors that are unwanted. The cost for this girl of "time-out" in school is both boredom and humiliation, and the authority figure—a teacher—hopes it will lead to more desired behaviors.

In summary, rational choice theory involves the following key ideas:

- Human beings are mostly self-centered and are driven in their behavior by self-interest.
- Humans calculate costs and benefits (rewards) in making decisions.
- Humans are rational in that they weigh choices in order to maximize their own benefits and minimize costs.
- Every interaction involves exchanges entailing rewards and penalties or expenditures.
- A key element in exchanges is reciprocity—a balance in the exchange of benefits.
- People keep a mental ledger in their heads about whether they owe someone else or that person owes them.

Critique of the Rational Choice Theory. Rational choice theorists give little attention to micro-level internal mental processes, such as self-reflection. They see human conduct as self-centered, with rational behavior implying that people seek to maximize rewards and minimize costs. Charitable, unselfish, or altruistic behavior is not easily explained by this view. Why would a soldier sacrifice his or her life to save a comrade? Why would a starving person in a Nazi concentration camp share a crust of bread with another? Proponents of rational choice counter the criticism by arguing that if a person feels good about helping another, that in itself is a reward that compensates for the cost.

Thinking Sociologically

How can symbolic interaction and rational choice perspectives help explain dating behavior? For example, how might a "hookup" mean something different to females as opposed to males? How would each of the micro theories above answer this question a bit differently?

Meso- and Macro-Level Theories

Meso- and macro-level theories consider large units in the social world: organizations (e.g., General Motors or the Episcopal Church), institutions (such as education, religion, health care, politics, or economics), societies (Canada or Mexico), or global systems (the World Trade

The Tanzanian village elders in this photo continue to have authority to make local (micro-level) decisions about the traditional irrigation canals being improved in their village, but their expanded water supply is possible in part because of international financial support (meso- and macro-level decisions).

Organization or World Bank). For example, Hector's government at the national and international levels affects his life in a variety of ways. As Brazil industrializes, the nature of jobs and the modes of communication change. Local village cultures adjust as the entire nation gains more uniformity of values, beliefs, and norms. Similarly, resources such as access to clean water may be allotted at the local level, but local communities need national and sometimes international support, as illustrated in the photo of tribal elders from Tanzania. We can begin to understand how the process of modernization influences Hector, this village in Tanzania, and other people around the globe by looking at two major macro-level perspectives: the structural-functional and conflict theories.

Structural-Functional Theory. The **structural-functional theory**, also called **functional theory**, *assumes that all parts of the social structure (including groups, organizations, and institutions), the culture (values and beliefs), and social processes (e.g., social change or child rearing) work together to make the whole society run smoothly and harmoniously*. To understand the social world from this perspective, we must look at how the parts of society (structure) fit together and how each part contributes to the maintenance of society. For instance, two functions (purposes) of the family include having children and teaching them to be members of society. These and other functions help perpetuate society, for without reproducing and teaching new members to fit in, societies would collapse.

Émile Durkheim (1858–1917) was the founder of the functionalist perspective. He theorized that society is made up of necessary parts that fit together into a working whole. Durkheim believed that individuals conform to the rules of societies because of a *collective conscience*—the shared beliefs in the values of a group (Durkheim 1947). People grow up sharing the same values, beliefs, and rules of behavior as those around them. Gradually, individuals internalize these shared beliefs and rules. A person's behavior is, in a sense, governed from within because it feels right and proper to behave in accordance with what is expected. As such, the functionalist perspective of Durkheim and subsequent theorists places emphasis on social consensus, which gives rise to stable and predictable patterns of order in society. Because people need groups for survival, they adhere to the group's rules so that they do not stand apart from it. This means that most societies run in an orderly manner, with most individuals fitting into their positions in society.

Functions (consequences of an action or behavior) can be manifest or latent. **Manifest functions** are *the planned* *outcomes of interactions, social organizations, or institutions.* Some of the planned consequences of the microwave oven, for instance, have been to allow people to prepare meals quickly and easily, facilitating life in overworked and stressed modern families. **Latent functions** are *unplanned or unintended consequences of actions or of social structures* (Merton 1938, [1942] 1973). Some of the unplanned consequences of microwave ovens were the creation of a host of new jobs and stimulation of the economy, as people wrote new cookbooks and as businesses were formed to produce microwavable cookware and prepared foods ready for the microwave.

Latent functions can be functional or dysfunctional. Functional actions contribute to the stability or equilibrium of society while **dysfunctions** are *those actions that undermine the stability or equilibrium of society* (Merton 1938). For example, by allowing people to prepare meals without using a stove or an oven, the microwave oven has contributed to some young people having no idea how to cook, thus making them highly dependent on expensive technology and processed foods, and in some cases adding to problems of obesity.

From a functionalist theory perspective, it is important to examine the possible functional and dysfunctional aspects of life in society in order to maintain harmony and balance.

To summarize, the structural-functional perspective

- examines the macro-level organizations and patterns in society.
- focuses on what holds societies together and enhances social continuity.
- considers the consequences or "functions" of each major part in society.
- focuses on the way the structure (groups, organizations, institutions), the culture, and social processes work together to make society function smoothly.
- considers manifest functions (which are planned), latent functions (which are unplanned or secondary), and dysfunctions (which undermine stability).

Critique of the Structural-Functional Perspective. Some ideas put forth by functional theorists are so abstract that they are difficult to test with data. Moreover, functionalism does not explain social changes in society, such as conflict and revolution. As we try to understand the many societal upheavals in the world, from suicide bombings in the Middle East to the economic privatization movements in China, it is clear that dramatic social

Although the microwave oven and fast-food restaurants have had many benefits for a society in a hurry, one dysfunction is the deterioration of health—especially due to obesity.

change is possible. The functionalist assumption is that if a system is running smoothly, it must be working well because it is free from conflict. It assumes that conflict is harmful, even though we know that stability may come about because of ruthless dictators suppressing the population. In short, stability is not always good.

Thinking Sociologically

Describe a manifest and a latent function of the system of higher education in the United States today. Is the latent function dysfunctional? Why or why not?

Conflict Theory. In many ways, **conflict theory**, *which focuses on societal groups competing for scarce resources,* turns the structural-functionalist theory on its head. Conflict theorists contend that conflict is inevitable in any group or society. They claim that inequality and injustice are the source of the conflicts that permeate society. Resources and power are distributed unequally in society, so some members have more money, goods, and **prestige**—or *esteem, recognition, and respect based on wealth, position, or accomplishment*—than others. The rich protect their positions by using the power they have accumulated to keep others in their places. From the perspective of poor people such as Hector, it seems the rich get all the breaks. Most of

Obesity and Health   Perspectives Applied to Fear and Germs us want more of the resources in society (money, good jobs, nice houses, and cars), causing the possibility of conflict between the haves and the have-nots. These conflicts sometimes bring about a change in society.

Modern conflict theory has its origins in the works of Karl Marx (1818–1883), a German social philosopher who lived in England during the height of 19th-century industrial expansion. Capitalism had emerged as the dominant economic system in Europe. *Capitalism* is an economic system in which individuals and corporations, rather than the state, own and control the means of production (e.g., factories). As they compete for profits, some win while others lose.

Marx recognized the plight of workers toiling in factories in the new industrial states of Europe and viewed the ruling elites and the wealthy industrial owners as exploiters of the working class. Marx wrote about the new working class crowded in urban slums, working long hours under appalling conditions, without earning enough money for decent housing and food. Few of the protections enjoyed by many (but not all) workers today—such as retirement benefits, health coverage, sick leave, the 40-hour workweek, and restrictions against child labor—existed in Marx's time.

Marx believed that two classes, the capitalists (also referred to as the bourgeoisie or "haves"), who owned the **means of production** (*property, machinery, and cash owned by capitalists*), and the workers (also referred to as the proletariat or "have-nots"), would continue to live in conflict until the workers shared more equally in the profits of their labor. The more workers came to understand their plight, the more aware they would become of the injustice of the situation. Eventually, Marx believed that workers would rise up and overthrow capitalism, forming a new, classless society. Collective ownership—shared ownership of the *means of production*—would be the new economic order (Marx and Engels [1848] 1969).

The idea of the *bourgeoisie* (the capitalist exploiters who own the factories) and the *proletariat* (the exploited workers who sell their labor) has carried over into analysis of modern-day conflicts among groups in society. For example, from a conflict perspective, Hector in Brazil and millions like him in other countries are part of the reserve labor force—a cheap labor pool that can be called on when labor is needed and disregarded when demand is low, thus meeting the changing labor needs of industry and capitalism. This pattern results in permanent economic insecurity and poverty for Hector and those like him.

Many branches of the conflict perspective have grown from the original ideas of Marx. Here, we mention three contributions to conflict theory, those of the American sociologists Harriet Martineau ([1837] 1962), W. E. B. Du Bois ([1899] 1967), and Ralf Dahrendorf (1959). As you can see, social conflict has been a major focus of sociological investigation.

Harriet Martineau (1802–1876), generally considered the first female sociologist, wrote several books that contribute to our understanding of modern sociological research methods and provided a critique, at the time, of the failure of the United States to live up to its democratic principles, especially as they related to women. She argued that social laws influence social behavior and that societies can be measured on their social progress (including how much freedom they give to individuals, and how well they treat the most oppressed members of society). Her work represents the foundation of current feminist and conflict theories (Martineau 1838).

Another early American conflict theorist was W. E. B. Du Bois, the first African American to receive a doctorate from Harvard University. Du Bois, like other early sociological theorists, believed that, although research should be scientifically rigorous and fair-minded, the ultimate goal of sociological work was social improvement—not just human insight. Throughout his life, Du Bois documented and lambasted the status of black Americans, noting that African Americans were an integral part of U.S. society but not fully accepted into it.

Du Bois helped establish the National Association for the Advancement of Colored People (NAACP). He stressed the need for minority groups to become advocates for their rights—to object loudly when those in power act to disadvantage minorities—and to make society more just (Du Bois [1899] 1967). He was—and continues to be—an inspiration for many sociologists who believe that their findings should have real applications and be used to create a more humane social world (Mills 1956).

A half-century later, in 1959, Ralf Dahrendorf argued that society is always in the process of change and affected by forces that bring about change. Dahrendorf refined Marx's ideas in several ways. He pointed out that capitalism had survived, despite Marx's prediction of a labor revolt, because of improved conditions for workers (e.g., unions, the establishment of labor laws and workplace regulations). Dahrendorf also maintained that, instead of divisions based on ownership, conflict had become based on authority.

Dahrendorf noted that those with lower-status positions, such as Hector, could form interest groups and engage in conflict with those in higher positions of authority. *Interest groups*, such as the members of Hector's *favela*, share a common situation or interests. In Hector and his neighbors' case, these interests include a desire for

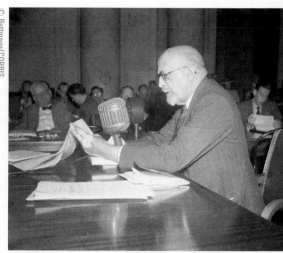

Harriet Martineau (left) published a critique of the United States' failure to live up to its democratic principles 11 years before Karl Marx's most famous work, but she was not taken seriously as a scholar for more than a century because she was female—the first feminist theorist. Karl Marx (center) is known as the founder of conflict theory. W. E. B. Du Bois (right) continued the development of conflict theory and was among the first to apply that theory to U.S. society, especially to issues of race.

sanitation, running water, electricity, jobs, and a higher standard of living. From within such interest groups, *conflict groups* arise to fight for changes. There is always potential for conflict when those without power realize their common position and form interest groups. How much change or violence is brought about depends on how organized those groups become.

Dahrendorf's major contribution is the recognition that conflict over resources results in a conflict not just between the proletariat and the bourgeoisie but among a multitude of interest groups including old people versus young people, rich versus poor, one region of the country versus another, Christians versus non-Christians, and so forth. This acknowledges multiple rifts in the society based on interest groups.

Whereas Marx emphasized the divisive nature of conflict, other theorists have offered a modified theory of conflict in society. American theorist Lewis Coser took a very different approach to conflict from that of Marx, arguing that it can strengthen societies and the organizations within them. According to Coser, problems in a society or group lead to complaints or conflicts—a warning message to the group that all is not well. Resolution of the conflicts shows that the group is adaptable in meeting the needs of its members, thereby creating greater loyalty to the group. Thus, conflict provides the message of what is not working to meet people's needs, and the system adapts to the needs for change because of the conflict (Coser 1956; Simmel 1955).

In summary, conflict theorists advance the following key ideas:

- Conflict and the potential for conflict underlie all social relations.
- Groups of people look out for their self-interest and try to obtain resources and make sure they are distributed primarily to members of their own group.
- Social change is desirable, particularly changes that bring about a greater degree of social equality.
- The existing social order reflects powerful people imposing their values and beliefs upon the weak.

Critique of the Conflict Theory. First, many conflict theorists focus on macro-level analysis and lose sight of the individuals involved in conflict situations, such as Hector and his family. Second, empirical research to test conflict theory is limited. The conflict perspective often paints a picture with rather broad brushstrokes. Research to test the picture involves interpretations of broad spans of history and is more difficult to claim as scientific. Third, conflict theorists tend to focus on social stress, power dynamics, and disharmony. Conflict theory is not very effective in explaining social cohesion and cooperation. Fourth, many critics of conflict theory argue that altruism and cooperation are common human behaviors but are not recognized by conflict theory.

Multi-Level Analysis. Many of the more contemporary theorists try to bridge the gap between micro and macro levels of analysis, offering insights relevant at each level. We examine two of these below.

▶ Private War Contractors

Thinking Sociologically

Imagine you are a legislator. You have to decide whether to cut funding for a senior citizens' program or slash a scholarship program for college students. You want to be reelected, and you know that approximately 90% of senior citizens are registered to vote and most actually do vote. You also know that less than half of college-age people are likely to vote. These constituencies are about the same size. What would you do, and how would you justify your decision? How does this example illustrate conflict theory?

Max Weber's Contributions. Max Weber (1864–1920), a German-born social scientist, has had a lasting effect on sociology and other social sciences. Weber (pronounced VAY-ber) cannot be pigeonholed easily into one of the theoretical categories or one level of analysis, for his contributions include both micro- and macro-level analyses. His emphasis on *Verstehen* (meaning deep empathetic understanding in humans) gives him a place in micro-level theory, and his discussions of power and bureaucracies give him a place in meso- and macro-level theory (Weber 1946).

Verstehen stems from the interpretations or meanings individuals at the micro level give to their social experiences. Weber argued that to understand people's behaviors, you must step into their shoes and see the world as they do. Following in Weber's footsteps, sociologists try to understand both human behavior and the meanings that people attach to their experiences. In this work, Weber is a micro theorist who set the stage for symbolic interaction theorists.

However, the goal-oriented, efficient new organizational form called bureaucracy was the focus of much of Weber's writing at the meso level. This organizational form was based on rationality (*the attempt to reach maximum efficiency with rules that are rationally designed to accomplish goals*) rather than relying on long-standing tradition for how things should be done. As we describe in Chapter 5, Weber's ideas about society at the meso level have laid the groundwork for a theoretical understanding of modern organizations.

Weber also attempted to understand macro-level processes. For instance, in his famous book *The Protestant Ethic and the Spirit of Capitalism* (Weber [1904–1905] 1958), he asked how capitalists (those who have money and control production) understood the world around them. His work was influenced by Marx's writings, but where Marx focused on economic conditions as the key factor shaping history and power relations, Weber argued that Marx's focus was too narrow. Weber felt that politics, economics, religion, psychology, and people's ideas are interdependent—affecting each other. In short, Weber thought that society was more complex than Karl Marx's theory that focused only on two groups—the haves and the have-nots—in conflict over economic resources.

Feminist Theory. Much of feminist theory has foundations in the conflict perspective. **Feminist theory** *critiques the hierarchical power structures that disadvantage women and other minorities* (Cancian 1992; Collins 2008). They note that men form an interest group intent on preserving their privileges. Feminists also argue that sociology has been dominated by a male perspective that does not give a complete view of the social world.

Some branches of feminist theory come from interaction perspectives, emphasizing the way gender socialization, cues, and symbols shape the nature of much human interaction. Thus, feminist theory moves from meso- and macro-level analysis (e.g., looking at national and global situations that give privileges to men) to micro-level analysis (e.g., looking at inequality between husbands and wives in marriage). In particular, feminist theory points to the importance of gender as a variable influencing social patterns (Brettell and Sargent 2008; Burn 2011; Kramer 2010; Lorber 2009).

Many people face inequality due to multiple factors, and it is the interplay of these factors that interests Patricia Hill Collins. An important contemporary scholar, Collins examines the discrimination and oppression people face because of their race, class, gender, sexuality, or nationality, all of which are interconnected. Collins used the term *intersectionality,* meaning individuals have multiple identities (e.g., race, class, and gender) that intersect and impact their life chances (2005, 2008).

Thinking Sociologically

To what extent are human beings free agents who can create their own social world and come up with their own ideas about how to live their lives? To what extent are our lives determined or influenced by the social systems around us and by our positions in the economic and political system?

Using Different Theoretical Perspectives

Each of the theoretical perspectives described in this chapter begins from a set of assumptions about humans. Each makes

Patricia Hill Collins, an innovative feminist scholar, has challenged sociologists to look at the ways experiences of race, social class, gender, and sexuality can intersect and reinforce one another.

a contribution to our understanding, but each has limitations or blind spots, such as not taking into account other levels of analysis (Ritzer 2011). Figure 2.1 provides a summary of cooperative versus competitive perspectives to illustrate how the theories differ.

The strength of a theory depends on its ability to explain and predict behavior accurately. Each theoretical perspective focuses on a different aspect of society and level of analysis and gives us a different lens through which to view our social world. The social world model helps us picture the whole system and determine which theory or theories best suits our needs in analyzing a specific social process or structure.

Thinking Sociologically

Consider the issue of homelessness in cities around the world. How could each of the theories discussed in this chapter be used to help us understand the problem of homelessness?

Scientists, including sociologists, often use theories to predict changes in society and under what conditions they are likely to occur. Theory tells the researcher what to look for and what concepts or variables need to be measured. However, explanations about the relationships between social variables need to be tested. This is where research methods—the procedures one uses to gather data—are relevant. Data must be carefully gathered and then used to assess the accuracy of theory. If a theory is not supported by the data, it must be reformulated or discarded. Theory and research are used together and are mutually dependent.

To study Hector's life in Brazil, researchers might focus on the micro-level interactions between Hector and his family members, peers, teachers, and employers as factors that contribute to his situation. For example,

FIGURE 2.1 Cooperative Versus Competitive Perspectives

	Macro analysis	Micro analysis
Humans viewed as cooperative (people interact with others on the basis of shared meanings and common symbols)	*Structural-Functional Theory*	*Symbolic Interactionism Theory*
Humans viewed as competitive (behavior governed by self-interest)	*Conflict Theory* (group interests)	*Rational Choice Theory* (individual interests)

one theory could be that Hector's family has socialized him to believe that certain activities (for example, working) are more realistic or immediately rewarding than others (such as attending school). A meso-level focus might examine the influence of the organizations and institutions—such as the business world, the schools, and the religious communities in Brazil—to see how they shape the forces that affect Hector's life. Alternatively, the focus might be on macro-level analysis—the class structure (rich to poor) of the society and the global forces, such as trade relations between Brazil and other countries, that influence opportunities for Brazilians who live in poverty. Whatever the level of analysis, as social *scientists*, sociologists utilize scientific methods of gathering evidence to disprove or to support theories about society.

IDEAS UNDERLYING SCIENCE

Throughout most of human history, people came to "know" the world by the traditions passed down from one generation to the next. Things were so because authoritative people in the culture said they were so. Often, there was reliance on magical, philosophical, or religious explanations of the forces in nature, and these explanations became part of tradition. For example, just 260 years ago, the conventional wisdom was that lightning storms were a sign of an angry god, not electricity caused by meteorological forces. As ways of knowing about the world shifted, tradition and magic as the primary means to understand the world were challenged. With advances in the natural sciences, observations of cause-and-effect processes became more systematic and controlled.

The scientific approach is based on several core ideas: First, there are real physical and social worlds that can be studied scientifically. Second, there is a certain order to the world, with identifiable patterns that result from a series of causes and effects. The world is not merely a collection of unrelated random events; rather, events occur in a systematic sequence and in patterns—that is, they are *causally* related. Third, the way to gain knowledge of the world is to subject it to empirical testing. **Empirical knowledge** *is founded on information gained from evidence (facts), rather than on intuition.* **Evidence** refers to *facts and observations that can be objectively observed and carefully measured using the five senses (sometimes enhanced by scientific instruments).*

For knowledge to be scientific, it must come from phenomena that can be observed and measured. Phenomena that cannot be subject to measurement are not within the realm of scientific inquiry. For example, the existence of God, the devil, heaven, hell, and the soul cannot be observed and measured and therefore cannot be examined scientifically. Religion, however, can be studied scientifically by looking at the role it plays in society and our lives, its impact on our values and behavior (the sociology of religion), the historical development of specific religious traditions (the history of religion), or the emotional comfort and stability it brings to people (the psychology of religion). Finally, science is rooted in **objectivity**; that is, *one must take steps to ensure that one's personal opinions or values do not bias or contaminate data collection and analysis.* Scientists are obliged to not distort their research findings so as to promote a particular point of view. Scientific research is judged first on whether it relies on careful efforts to be objective. Social scientists, like all scientists, must explain what the data reveal, not what they wish it would reveal! Researchers must be open to finding results that support *or* disprove their **hypothesis** (*an educated guess or prediction*).

Failure to meet these standards—empirical knowledge, objectivity, and scientific evidence—means that a study is not scientific. Someone's ideas can seem plausible and logical but may still not be supported by the facts. This is why evidence is so important. Sociology is concerned with using accurate evidence, and it is important to know what is or is not considered accurate. Perhaps you have seen an episode of the *CSI: Crime Scene Investigation* or *Bones* series on television. The shows in these series depict the importance of careful collection of data and commitment to objective analysis. Sociologists deal with different issues, but the same sort of concern for accuracy in gathering data guides their work. When sociologists establish theories as to why society works as it does, they must test those theories using scientific methods.

HOW SOCIOLOGISTS STUDY THE SOCIAL WORLD

Suppose you have a research question you want to answer, such as "Why do boys like Hector drop out of school?" In order for your research to be scientific, you must follow the basic steps of the scientific research process.

A. PLANNING A RESEARCH STUDY
- *Step 1:* Define a topic or problem that can be studied scientifically.

- *Step 2:* Review existing relevant research studies and theory to refine the topic and define **variables**, *concepts (ideas) that can vary in frequency of occurrence from one time, place, or person to another* (such as age, ethnicity, religion, level of education).
- *Step 3:* Formulate hypotheses or research questions and determine how to define and measure the variables.

B. DESIGNING THE RESEARCH PLAN AND METHOD FOR COLLECTING THE DATA

- *Step 4:* Design the research plan that specifies how the data will be gathered.
- *Step 5:* Select a **sample**, *a group of systematically chosen people who represent a much larger group,* to study.
- *Step 6:* Collect the data using appropriate research methods.

C. MAKING SENSE OF THE DATA

- *Step 7:* Analyze the data and relate it to previous findings on the topic, concluding exactly what the study says about the research question(s) from Step 3.
- *Step 8:* Draw conclusions and present the final report, including suggestions for future research. Recommendations for actions may be part of the report.

Planning a Research Study

To study Hector's situation, the researcher uses Step 1 to define a topic or problem, including the variables to be studied. Step 2 requires the researcher to review past studies on related topics to see what has been done and how variables were defined in other studies. This review provides the basis for Step 3.

In Step 3, researchers must link concepts, such as poverty or dropping out of school, to specific measurements. For example, the researcher could hypothesize that poverty is a major cause of *favela* teenagers dropping out of school because they need to earn money for their families. Who is a dropout might be determined by school records indicating whether that child has attended school during the past six months. Poverty could be defined as having a low annual income—say less than half of the average income for that size of family in the country—or by assessing ownership of property such as cattle, automobiles, and indoor plumbing. It is important for

National Census Data

researchers to be clear, precise, and consistent in how they measure the variables in their hypothesis or research question.

In order to conduct research to test a theory, researchers formulate a hypothesis, a statement they can test to determine if it is true. This is called *deductive research*. It starts with a theory that you then test. *Inductive research* starts with observations that then lead to hypothesis development and, potentially, theory formation. Researchers make an observation and then begin to collect more data to determine if what they witnessed initially was a social pattern. Once they start to notice social patterns, they can begin to analyze those patterns using appropriate existing theories, or they can create a new theory if existing ones do not provide needed explanations.

Thinking Sociologically

Think of a research question based on a theoretical perspective. For example, you might ask how Hector's peers affect his decisions, using a micro-level theory. Then write a hypothesis and identify your variables in the hypothesis.

Whether you use inductive or deductive research, you must always carefully define your variables and determine how they interact with and relate to one another. The relationship between variables is central to understanding *causality*. Causal reasoning is discussed in the next "Sociology in Our Social World."

Designing the Research Method and Collecting the Data

Researchers must always make clear how they collect their data. Every research study should be replicable—capable of being repeated—by other researchers. So, enough information must be given to ensure that another researcher could repeat the study and compare results.

The appropriate data collection method depends on the level(s) of analysis of the research question (micro, meso, or macro) the researcher is asking. For example, if you want to answer a macro-level research question, such as the effect of poverty on students dropping out of school in Brazil, you should focus on large-scale social and economic data sources such as the Brazilian census. To learn about micro-level issues such as the influence of peers on an individual's decision to drop out of school, you will need to examine small-group interactions at the micro level. Figure 2.2 illustrates the different levels of analysis.

sociology in our social world

Being Clear About Causality

Sociology as a science tries to be very careful about language—more precise than we usually are in our everyday conversations. What do we really mean when we say that something causes something else? At the heart of the research process is the effort to find causal relationships (i.e., one variable causes another one to change). The following key terms are important in understanding how two variables (concepts that vary in frequency and can be measured) are related:

CORRELATION

Correlation *refers to a relationship between variables (such as poverty and low levels of education), with change in one variable associated with change in another.* The hypothesis above predicts that poverty and teenagers dropping out of school are related and vary together. That is, when the poverty level is high, dropping out of school is also high. If we claim that there is a correlation, however, that is only the first step. We have not yet established that change in one variable causes a change in the other.

CAUSE-AND-EFFECT VARIABLES

Cause-and-effect relationships *occur when there is a relationship between variables so that one variable stimulates a change in another.* Once we have determined that there is probably a relationship, or correlation (the fact that the two variables, such as poverty and dropping out of school, both occur in the same situation), we need to take the next step: analyzing which comes first and seeing if one variable causes

change in another. The **independent variable** *is the variable in a cause-and-effect relationship that comes first in a time sequence and causes a change in another variable*—the **dependent variable**. If we hypothesize that poverty causes Hector and others to drop out of school, *poverty* is the independent variable in this hypothesis, and *dropping out of school* is the dependent variable, dependent on the poverty. In determining cause and effect, the independent variable must always precede the dependent variable in time sequence if we want to try to determine whether the independent variable causes a change in the dependent variable.

SPURIOUS RELATIONSHIPS

Spurious relationships *occur when there is no causal relationship between the independent and dependent variables, but they vary together, often due to a third variable affecting both of them.* For example, if the quantity of ice cream consumed is highest during those weeks of the year when most drownings occur, these two events are correlated. However, eating ice cream did not cause the increase in deaths. Indeed, hot weather may have caused more people both to purchase ice cream and to go swimming, with the larger number of swimmers resulting in more drowning incidents. The connection between ice cream and drownings is a *spurious relationship*.

CONTROLS

Controls *are steps used by researchers to eliminate all variables except those related*

to the hypothesis—especially those variables that might be spurious. Using controls helps ensure that the relationship is not spurious. Using the ice cream example, we might have studied beaches where lots of ice cream is sold and beaches where none is available in order to compare water death incidents. If there is no difference in death rates, the drownings cannot be caused by the ice cream.

FIGURE 2.2 **The Social World Model and Levels of Analysis**

Micro Level

Individual	Hector
Small group	Hector's family and close friends
Local community	The *favela*; Hector's local school, church, neighborhood organizations

Meso Level

Organizations	Brazilian corpora tions, Catholic Church, and local school system in Brazil
Institutions	Family; education; political, economic, and health systems in the region or nation of Brazil
Ethnic subcultures	Native peoples, African-Brazilians

Macro Level

| National society | Social policies, trends, and programs in Brazil |
| Globlal community of nations | Status of Brazil in global economy; trade relations with other countries; programs of international organizations or corporations |

Designing a Method for Collecting Data. The primary methods used to collect data for research studies include questionnaires, interviews, observational studies, secondary data analysis, content analysis, and experiments. Some methods produce *quantitative* (numerical) data while others supply *qualitative* (nonnumerical data such as individuals' open-ended responses). Questionnaires and secondary data analysis tend to be quantitative and used when conducting macro- and meso-level studies. Interviews, observational studies, and content analysis usually produce qualitative data or a blend of quantitative and qualitative data, and are primarily used for micro-level research. Some studies include both quantitative and qualitative data.

Interviews are conducted by talking directly with people and asking questions in person or by telephone. Both unstructured and semistructured interviews, which allow respondents to answer questions in a more open-ended manner, evolve in response to what the researcher learns as the research progresses.

Questionnaires contain questions and other types of items designed to solicit information from individual respondents appropriate to analysis of research questions (Babbie 2014). They are convenient for collecting large amounts of data because they can be distributed by mail or sent by e-mail to respondents.

Observational studies (also called field research) involve *systematic, planned observation and recording of interactions or human behavior in their natural settings (where the activity normally takes place rather than in a laboratory).* They can take different forms: (1) observations in which the researcher actually participates in the activities of the group being studied or (2) observations in which the researcher is not involved in group activities but observes or videotapes the activity. It is important for observers to avoid influencing or altering group functioning and interaction by their presence.

 Thinking Sociologically

If you were trying to compare how effectively two professors teach a research methods course offered in your department, what variables might you use, and what variable might you need to control? How would you set up your study? What methods would you use?

© Jeanne H. Ballantine

Census questionnaires are taken in the United States and many other countries every 10 years. Sometimes it is difficult to gather accurate data on the entire population, as in the situation with this census worker, who is counting homeless people in Penn Station in New York City.

Secondary analysis *uses existing data, information that has already been collected.* Often, large data-collecting organizations, such as the United Nations or a country's census bureau, the national education department, or a private research organization, will make data available for use by researchers. Consider the question of the dropout rate in Brazil. Researchers can learn a great deal about the behavior of school dropouts as a group from analysis of information gathered by ministries or departments of education. Likewise, if we want to compare modern dropout rates with those of an earlier time, we may find data from previous decades to be invaluable. Secondary analysis can be an excellent way to do meso- or macro-level studies that reveal large-scale patterns in the social world.

Content analysis *involves systematic categorizing and recording of information from written or recorded sources.* With content analysis (a common method in historical research and study of organizations), sociologists can gather the data they need from printed materials— books, magazines, newspapers, laws, letters, comments on websites, e-mails, videos, archived radio broadcasts, or even artwork. They develop a coding system to classify the source content. A researcher trying to understand shifts in Brazilian attitudes toward youth poverty in *favelas* could do a content analysis of popular magazines to see how many pages or stories were devoted to child poverty in the Brazilian media each decade from the 1960s to the present. Content analysis has the advantage of being relatively inexpensive and easy to do. It is also *unobtrusive*, meaning that the researcher does not influence the participants being investigated by having direct contact with them. Furthermore, examining materials in historical sequence can be effective in recognizing patterns over time.

An example of historical research using existing materials to examine social patterns is illustrated in the next "Sociology in Our Social World." In this case the researcher, Virginia Kemp Fish, studied records and writings of early women sociologists in Chicago to discover their contributions to sociology and to the betterment of society.

In **experiments**, *all variables except the one being studied are controlled so researchers can study the effects of the variable under study.* An experiment usually requires an **experimental group**, *in which subjects in the group are exposed to the variable being studied to test the effects of that variable on human behavior,* and a **control group**, *in which the subjects are not exposed to the variable the researcher wants to test.* The control group provides a baseline to which the experimental group can be compared.

Experiments are powerful because they are the most accurate test of cause and effect. They make it possible to control most variables (eliminating irrelevant spurious variables) and determine the sequence in which variables affect each other. By separating the sample into experimental and control groups, the researcher can see if the study's independent variable makes a difference in the behavior of people who are exposed to that variable compared to those who are not. Psychologists use lab experiments, but few sociologists use this method because many sociological questions cannot be studied in controlled settings. For example, Hector's environment in the *favela* cannot be studied in a laboratory setting.

Control and experimental research projects outside of a lab setting are more common among sociologists. For example, researchers may want to determine whether a new teaching method using technology might help children from Hector's *favela*. We can do so by comparing a control group, exposed to the usual teaching, and an experimental group, provided with the new method or experimental technology. We must ensure that the control and experimental groups of children are at the same academic level and that the teachers are equally motivated and prepared when teaching both classes. With this carefully designed research project, we can conclude that the new approach increases learning if the children in the experimental group score significantly higher on the final exam than those in the control group.

Triangulation refers to the *utilization of two or more methods of data collection to enhance the amount and type of data for analysis and the accuracy of the findings.*

sociology in our social world

The Hull House Circle: Historical Content Analysis in Sociology

Wikipedia

Jane Addams, social researcher, critic, and reformer.

Hull House was a settlement house in Chicago, one of several such residences established in urban immigrant neighborhoods. Settlement houses created a sense of community for residents and offered a multitude of services to help residents and neighbors negotiate poverty. In addition to offering services, Hull House was the location for a group of women social researchers, reformers, and activists. The well-known social activist Jane Addams (1860–1935), who received a Nobel Peace Prize, was one of them. These women had obtained college degrees in some of the few fields then open to women (political science, law, economics), and they used their education and skills to help others and to do research on social conditions, contributing to the development of the science of sociology.

Until recently, women sociologists, such as the members of the Hull House Circle, have not received much attention for their contributions to the science of sociology. Yet some of the earliest social survey research was conducted by the women connected with Hull House, sometimes employing the Hull House residents to collect data. For example, these women led the first systematic attempt to describe an immigrant community in an American city, a study found in *Hull House Maps and Papers* (Residents of Hull House [ca. 1895] 1970).

Historical research can be an important source of data for sociological analysis, for historical circumstances help us understand why things evolved to the present state of affairs. Virginia Kemp Fish, who originated the designation Hull House Circle, researched historical literature to learn more about the lives and contributions of these women and their place in the sociological literature. She examined records, letters, biographies, and other historical sources to piece together their stories (Fish 1986). By studying their writings and their activist work, Fish showed how they supported each other's work and scholarship and provided emotional encouragement and intellectual stimulation. Fish also considered these women's professional styles as compared with the styles of men. While men often received their training and support from a mentor (an older, established, and respected man in the field), the women of Hull House operated within a network of egalitarian relationships and interactions.

According to Fish's research, the data and documents collected by their leader, Jane Addams, and other Hull House women provide baseline information that has been used as a starting point or comparison for later studies—for social researchers in the fields of immigration, ethnic relations, poverty, health care, housing, unemployment, work and occupations, delinquency and crime, war, and social movements.

Reuter/Ray Stubblebine

Social scientists aren't the only professionals who use triangulation. Journalists also consult a variety of sources—including, at times, social scientists—to put together news broadcasts.

To study Hector's situation, a research study could use macro-level quantitative data on poverty and on educational statistics in Brazil and micro-level interviews with Hector and his peers to determine their goals and their attitudes toward education. If all findings point to the same conclusion, the researcher can feel much more confident about the study results.

Selecting a Sample. It would be impossible to interview or send a questionnaire to every school dropout in Brazil to determine why the teenage dropout rate is so high. A part of the research design is determining how to make sure the study includes people who are typical of the total group (or population) you want to learn about. This involves careful selection of a sample.

Researchers use many types of samples. A common one, the representative sample, attempts to accurately reflect the group being studied so that the sample results can be generalized or applied to the larger group or population. In the case of studying why so many boys from Hector's *favela* drop out of school, a representative sample for a study could be drawn from all 13- to 16-year-olds in his region or city in Brazil.

The most common form of representative sample is the *random sample*. People from every walk of life and every group within the population have an equal chance of being selected for the study. By observing or talking with this smaller group selected from the total

population under study, the researcher can get an accurate picture of the total population and have confidence that the findings apply to the larger group. Developing an effective sampling technique is often a complex process. In the case of Brazil, people constantly move in and out of the *favela*. Those who have just arrived may not have the same characteristics as those who have been living there a long time, but it is important to have a sample that represents the whole group being studied. Samples also must be large enough to accurately represent a population and to use statistical programs to analyze the data. If you take a methods course, you will delve further into these details of sampling and data analysis discussed next.

Making Sense of the Data: Analyzing Data and Drawing Conclusions

Once you have collected your data from your sample, you have to analyze it. Imagine that you have 100 interviews from residents of Hector's *favela*, plus a notebook full of field observation notes from "hanging out" with the youth there. What do you do with the data? Social researchers use multiple techniques to analyze data, but whatever techniques they use, they look for patterns in the data and then use theories and findings from past research on the topic to make sense of those patterns.

Presenting Your Findings. The final step in the research process is a report that presents a discussion of the results, draws conclusions as to whether or not the hypotheses were supported or answers were found for the research question, interprets the results, and makes recommendations on how to use the findings, if appropriate. As part of the presentation and discussion of results, the report may contain tables or figures presenting summaries of data to help the reader easily understand the patterns found in the data. The next "Engaging Sociology" on page 50 provides useful tips on reading research tables found in journal articles and news magazines.

Ethical Issues in Social Research

What happens if a scientist conducts research that has negative impacts on the participants? It is due to this concern that most universities and other research organizations, especially those receiving public money, have

Breast Cancer Research Table

human subjects review boards. The boards review the proposed research plans and methods to be used to be sure they will *not* hurt the subjects. Of special concern are research projects in medical sciences, but social scientists must also have their research reviewed.

Sociologists and other scientists are bound by the ethical codes of conduct governing research. The American Sociological Association (ASA) code of ethics outlines standards that researchers are expected to observe when doing research, teaching, and publishing. They include

- explaining the uses and consequences of the research, and gaining informed consent from respondents;
- taking steps to ensure the privacy of respondents;
- being objective, reporting findings and sources fully;
- making no promises to respondents that cannot be honored;
- accepting no support that requires violation of these principles;
- completing contracted work; and
- delineating responsibilities in works with multiple authors.

Examples of unethical research include studying people without their knowledge or consent, only including data that support the results you would like to see, and violating the confidentiality of your subjects by revealing their identity. The bottom line is that researchers must do everything they can to protect their subjects from harm.

Thinking Sociologically

What might be some ethical problems in a research project you would like to conduct? What, for example, might be the ethical issues of studying a setting or a situation but not informing the people involved that you are studying them?

Putting Sociology to Work: Public Sociology

Most early sociologists—including Lester Ward, the first president of the American Sociological Association—promoted sociology as means for improving society (Calhoun 2007). As the discipline of sociology grew from its early days and became an acknowledged social science, some sociologists advocated for "pure" research disconnected from the public sphere. Throughout the history of the discipline, sociologists have debated their proper role in society.

However, like physicists, chemists, and geologists, many sociologists believe that there are both important practical applications of the discipline and many policy issues that need to be informed by good science. Today, there is a movement to recall the roots of sociology and make sociology more "public" and of use to society. **Public sociologists** *use sociological tools to understand and inform citizens about how society operates, and to improve society*. Some help create and advocate for social policies that their research indicates will make a positive impact on society. Public sociologists—whether professors or those in a variety of professions outside academia—share a common goal: to better understand how society operates *and* to make practical use of their sociological findings (Pickard and Poole 2007).

Some public sociologists work outside of academia and use sociological knowledge and research skills to address organizational needs or problems in government, education, health care settings, social service agencies, and business organizations. They work for clients or organizations who often determine the research questions they address. Depending on their positions, they may be known as sociological practitioners, applied sociologists, clinical sociologists, policy analysts, program planners, or evaluation researchers, among other titles. They focus on pragmatic ways to improve organizations or society, sometimes recommending major changes and sometimes proposing modest policy proposals.

So far, we have focused on what sociology is and how sociologists know what they know. The rest of the book examines our social world as informed by methods and theories discussed in this chapter. The next chapter explores how you can understand your culture and society at the various levels of analysis in our social world.

Public Sociologists

ENGAGING SOCIOLOGY

How to Read a Research Table

A statistical table is a researcher's labor-saving device. Quantitative data presented in tabular form are clearer and more concise than the same information presented in several written paragraphs. A good table has clear signposts to help the reader avoid confusion. For instance, Table 2.1 shows many of the main features of a table, and the list that follows explains how to read each feature.

HEADNOTE (or Subtitle): Many tables will have a headnote or subtitle under the title, giving information relevant to understanding the table or units in the table.

For this table, the reader is informed that it includes all persons over the age of 25 and the units will be reported in thousands.

Table 2.1 **Educational Attainment by Age: 2010, for Persons 25 Years Old and Over, Reported in Thousands**

TITLE: The title provides information on the major topic and variables in the table.

"Educational Attainment by Age: 2010"

HEADINGS AND STUBS: Tables generally have one or two levels of headings under the title and headnotes. These instruct the reader about what is in the columns below.

In this table, the headings indicate the level of education achieved so that the reader can identify the percentage with a specified level of education.

The table also has a stub: the far-left column under "Characteristic." This lists the items that are being compared according to the categories found in the headings. In this case, the stub indicates age.

Characteristic	Population (1,000)	Percent of Population—Highest Level					
		Not a High School Graduate	High School Graduate	Some College, but No Degree	Associate's Degree[1]	Bachelor's Degree	Advanced Degree
Total persons	199,928	12.9	31.2	16.8	9.1	19.4	10.5
Age							
25–34 yrs old	41,085	11.6	27.2	18.9	9.5	24.0	8.9
35–44 yrs old	40,447	11.7	28.6	16.3	10.3	21.9	11.2
45–54 yrs old	44,387	10.4	32.8	16.7	10.6	19.0	10.4
55–64 yrs old	35,359	10.4	31.3	17.3	9.2	18.6	13.1

MARGINAL TABS: In examining the numbers in the table, try working from the outside in. The marginals, the figures at the margins of the table, often provide summary information.

In this table, the first column of numbers is headed "Population (1,000)," indicating (by thousands) the total number of people in each category who were part of the database. The columns to the right indicate—by percentages—the level of educational attainment for each category.

CELLS: To make more detailed comparisons, examine specific cells in the body of the table. These are the boxes that hold the numbers or percentages.

In this table, the cells contain data on age in education.

Table 2.1   Educational Attainment by Age: 2010, for Persons 25 Years Old and Over, Reported in Thousands   (Continued)

UNITS: Units refer to how the data are reported. They could be in percentages, in number per 100 or 1,000, or in other units.

In this table, the data are reported first in raw number in thousands and then in percentages.

FACTS FROM THE TABLE: After reviewing all the above information, the reader is ready to make some interpretations about what the data mean.

In this table, the reader might note that young adults are more likely to have a college education than older citizens.

Likewise, people in the Northeast and West have the highest levels of education. What other interesting patterns do you see?

Characteristic		Percent of Population—Highest Level					
	Population (1,000)	Not a High School Graduate	High School Graduate	Some College, but No Degree	Associate's Degree[1]	Bachelor's Degree	Advanced Degree
65–74 yrs old	20,956	17.0	35.4	15.7	6.6	14.1	11.1
75 yrs or older	17,657	24.6	37.6	14.0	4.6	11.9	7.3
Region							
Northeast	36,834	11.4	33.7	13.0	8.4	20.6	12.9
Midwest	43,380	10.1	34.6	17.6	10.0	18.2	9.5
South	73,682	14.5	31.9	16.9	8.7	18.1	9.8
West	46,032	14.0	25.0	19.0	9.5	21.6	10.8

Source: U.S. Census Bureau (2012a).

[1] Includes vocational degrees.

Features of the table adapted from Broom and Selznick (1963).

SOURCE: The source note, found under the table, points out the origin of the data. It is usually identified by the label "Source."

Under this table, the source note says "U.S. Census Bureau (2012a)."

FOOTNOTES: Some tables have footnotes, usually indicating something unusual about the data or where to find more complete data.

In this table, a footnote is provided so that the reader does not make mistakes in interpretation.

WHAT HAVE WE LEARNED?

The core features of **scientific** research are (1) a commitment to empirically validated evidence, facts, and information that are confirmed through systematic processes of testing using the five senses; (2) allowing us to be convinced by the evidence rather than by our preconceived ideas; (3) absolute integrity and objectivity in how we conduct and report on our research; and (4) continual openness to having our findings reexamined and new interpretations proposed. We must always consider the possibility that we have overlooked alternative explanations of the data and alternative ways to view the problem.

Science—including social science—does not consist of just facts to be memorized. Science is a process that is made possible by a social exchange of ideas, a clash of opinions, and a continual search for truth. Knowledge in the sciences is created by vigorous debate. We hope you will engage in the creation of knowledge by entering into these debates.

Theories serve as lenses to help us make sense of the data that we gather using various research strategies. The data themselves can be used to test the theories, so there is an ongoing reciprocal relationship between theory (the lens for making sense of the data) and research (the evidence used to test the theories). The most important ideas in this chapter are what sociology considers data or evidence and how sociology uses methods to be a science. These ideas form the framework for the content of sociology.

KEY POINTS

- Attempts to understand society have existed for at least two-and-a-half millennia, but gathering of scientific evidence to test hypotheses and validate claims is a modern idea. (See pp. 31–32.)

- Theories are especially important to science because they raise questions for research, and they explain the relationships among facts. Sociology has four primary, overriding, theoretical perspectives or paradigms: symbolic interaction theory, rational choice theory, structural-functional theory, and conflict theory. Other perspectives, such as feminist theory, serve as correctives to the main paradigms. Most of these theories are more applicable either at the micro to meso level or at the meso to macro level. (See pp. 32–42.)

- Sociology is a science used to study society, and therefore, it is essential to understand what is—and what is not—considered data or evidence. For a scientist, this means that ideas must be tested empirically—that is, scientifically. (See pp. 42.)

- As social scientists, sociologists use eight systematic steps to gather data and test theories about the social world. (See pp. 42–43.)

- The *independent variable* is the variable in a cause-and-effect relationship that comes first in a time sequence and causes a change in another variable—the *dependent variable.* (See pp. 44–45.)

- Major methods for gathering data in sociology include questionnaires, interviews, observational studies, secondary data analysis, content analysis, and experiments. (See pp. 45–46.)

- Quantitative data come in the form of numbers (e.g., derived from questionnaires, some secondary sources such as the Census), and qualitative data come in nonnumerical form (e.g., derived from semistructured and unstructured interviews, observation studies). (See pp. 45.)

- Use of multiple methods—triangulation—increases confidence in the findings. (See pp. 47.)

- Scientific confidence in results requires representative samples, usually drawn randomly. (See pp. 48.)

- Responsible research requires sensitivity to the ethics of research—ensuring that gathering scientific data does no one harm. (See pp. 48–49.)

- Public sociologists use sociological tools to understand and inform citizens about how society operates, and to improve society. (See pp. 51.)

DISCUSSION QUESTIONS

1. Why do research questions have to be asked in a precise way? Give an example of a precise research question. How do precise questions make it possible for you to test and measure your topic?

2. As stated in this chapter, "sociologists must be continually open to having their findings reexamined and new interpretations proposed." Describe a time when you changed your mind due to new information. Was it difficult for you to change your mind? Why or why not?

3. Why is the ability to be open to new ideas and interpretations so vital to the scientific perspective? Do you think you could carry this aspect of the scientific process out successfully—no matter how you feel about a topic? Why or why not?

4. If you were to examine the relationship between the government and the economy in the United States today, which of the four major theoretical perspectives outlined in the chapter would be most helpful? Why?

5. Imagine you would like to conduct a sociological study of the students with whom you attended the fourth grade, to determine what key factors influenced their academic achievements. Which of the four major theoretical perspectives would you employ in your study? Why?

6. If you were to conduct a study to measure student satisfaction with a particular academic department on campus, what research method(s) would you use? Why? How would the method(s) you select vary according to (a) the size of the department and (b) the type of information you sought?

CONTRIBUTING TO OUR SOCIAL WORLD: *WHAT CAN WE DO?*

At the Local Level

- *Local service organizations* are found in every community and work to provide for the unmet needs of community members: housing, legal aid, medical care, elder care, and so on. United Way works with most local service organizations and may be able to let you know which ones need help in your area. Going to idealist.org is also a great way to find volunteer opportunities in your area. Volunteer to work with

an organization in its applied needs assessment research, and practice the sociological principles and research methods described in this chapter. If your college or university has a service-learning office, it will offer connections to many service opportunities, sometimes linked to specific fields of study. Many colleges and universities also offer Academic Service Learning (ASL) credit in which course assignments include such community work under the supervision of the instructor.

At the State/Meso Level

- *State agencies* often have ongoing projects to gather data for more accurate information about the state and the needs of its citizens. Go to www .nationalservice.gov/about/contact-us/state-ser vice-commissions to find volunteer opportunities through your state government.

At the National and Global Levels

- *The U.S. Bureau of the Census* is best known for its decennial (every 10 years) enumeration of the population, but its work continues each year as it prepares special reports, population estimates, and regular publications (including *Current Population Reports*). Visit the Bureau's website at www.census .gov, and explore the valuable and extensive quanti-tative data and other information available. Visit your local Census Bureau office or click on www .census.gov/hrd/www/jobs/student.html to find vol-unteer and other opportunities for students at the Census.

PART II

Social Structure, Processes, and Control

Picture a house. First there is the foundation, then the wood frame, then the walls and roof. This provides the framework or structure. Within that structure, activities called *processes* take place—electricity to turn on lights and appliances, water to wash in and drink, and people to carry out these processes. If something goes wrong in the house, we take steps to control the damage and repair it.

Whether we are building a house or a society, the process of constructing our social world is parallel. Social structure is the framework of society with its groups and organizations; social processes are the dynamic activities of society. This section begins with a discussion of the structure of society, followed by the processes of culture and socialization through which individuals are taught cultural rules—how to function and live effectively within their society's structure. Although socialization of individuals takes place primarily at the micro level, we will explore its implications at the meso and macro levels as well.

If we break the social structure into parts, such as the wood frame, walls, and roof of a house, it is the groups and organizations (including bureaucracies) that are parts of the social structure. To work smoothly, these organizations depend on people's loyalty so that these participants do what society and its groups need to survive. However, these components do not always join together well. Things break down. Those in control of societies try to control disruptions and deviant individuals in order to maintain control and smooth functioning.

As we explore the next few chapters, we will continue to examine social life at the micro, meso, and macro levels, for each of us as individuals is profoundly shaped by social processes and structures at larger and more abstract levels, all the way to the global level.

3 Society and Culture

Hardware and Software of Our Social World

Depending on what resources are available where we live and what is considered usable and edible, we humans eat a wide range of plants and animals. This international market is bustling with activity as people shop for the kinds of foods that are considered nutritious and tasty in their culture.

MICRO

- ME (AND MY FAMILY)

- LOCAL ORGANIZATIONS
  AND COMMUNITY
  Local soccer teams and scout
  troupe have a microculture.

MESO

- NATIONAL ORGANIZATIONS,
  INSTITUTIONS, AND ETHNIC
  SUBCULTURES
  Ethnic groups have a subculture.

MACRO

- SOCIETY
  A nation has a national culture.

- GLOBAL COMMUNITY
  Multinational organizations like the World
  Health Organization have a global culture.

IN THIS CHAPTER

- Society: The Hardware

- Culture: The Software

- Society, Culture, and
  Our Social World

- Theories of Culture

- The Fit Between
  Hardware and Software

⬤ THINK ABOUT IT

Micro: Local Community	How do microcultures (e.g., your fraternity, study group, or team) influence you?
Meso: National Institutions, Complex Organizations, and Ethnic Groups	How do subcultures (such as your ethnic group) and countercultures (such as youth gangs) shape the character of your nation and influence your own life?
Macro: National and Global System	How do your nation's social structures and culture influence who you are and how you dress, eat, work, and live your life?

What do people around the world eat? Mrs. Ukita, the mom in the Ukita family, rises early to prepare a breakfast of miso soup and a raw egg on rice. The father and two daughters eat quickly and rush out to catch their early morning trains to work and school in Kodaira City, Japan. The mother cares for the house, does the shopping, and prepares a typical evening meal of fish, vegetables, and rice for the family.

The Ahmed family lives in a large apartment building in Cairo, Egypt. The 12 members of the extended family include the women who shop for and cook the food—vegetables, including peppers, greens, potatoes, squash, tomatoes, garlic, spices, and rice, along with pita bread and often fish or meat. The adult men work in shops in one of the many bazaars, while the school-age children attend school, then help with the chores.

In the Breidjing refugee camp in Chad, many Sudanese refugees eat what relief agencies can get to them—and that food source is not always reliable. Typical for the Aboubakar family, a mother and five children, is rice or some other grain, oil for cooking, dried legumes, occasionally some root plants or squash that keep longer than fresh fruits and vegetables, and a few spices. The girls and women go into the desert to fetch firewood for cooking and to get water from whatever source has water at the time. This is a dangerous trip as they may be attacked and raped or even killed outside the camps.

The Walker family from Norfolk, Virginia, grabs dinner at a fast-food restaurant on their way to basketball practice and an evening meeting. Because of their busy schedules and individual activities, they cannot always find time to cook and eat together—a behavior that would be unthinkable in most societies around the world.

Although most diets include some form of grain and starch, locally available fruits and vegetables, and perhaps meat or fish, broad variations in food consumption exist even within one society. Yet all of these differences have something in common: Each represents a society with a unique culture that includes what people eat. Food is one aspect of our way of life and what is necessary for survival. Ask yourself why you sleep on a bed, brush your teeth, or listen to music with friends. Our way of life is called culture.

Culture *refers to the way of life shared by a group of people—the knowledge, beliefs, values, rules or laws, language, customs, symbols, and material products (such as food, houses, and transportation) within a society that help meet human needs.* Culture provides guidelines for living. Learning our culture puts our social world in an understandable framework, providing a toolkit we can use to help construct the meaning of our world and behaviors in it (Bruner 1996; Nagel 1994). We compare culture to *software* because it is the human ideas and input that make the society work. Otherwise, society would just be structures, like the framework of a house.

A **society** is an *organized and interdependent group of individuals who live together in a specific geographic area, who interact more with each other than they do with outsiders, who cooperate for the attainment of common goals, and who share a common culture over time.* Most often societies are the same as the countries that make up the world. Each society includes key parts called institutions, such as family, education, religion, politics, economics, and health care or medicine, that meet basic human needs. This structure that makes up society is what we refer to here as the hardware, like the structure of a computer. Culture, the software, is learned, transmitted, shared, and reshaped from generation to generation. All activities in the society, whether educating young members, preparing and eating dinner, selecting leaders for the group, finding a mate, or negotiating with other societies, are guided by cultural rules and expectations. In each society, culture provides the social rules for how individuals carry out necessary tasks.

Society—organized groups of people—and *culture*—their way of life—are interdependent. The two are not the same thing, but they cannot exist without each other, just

Culture and Food 📄

as computer hardware and software are each useless without the other.

This chapter explores the ideas of society and culture and their relation to each other, what society is and how it is organized, how it influences and is influenced by culture, what culture is, how and why culture develops, the components of culture, cultural theories, and policy issues. After reading this chapter, you will have a better idea of how you learn and make use of your society's culture.

SOCIETY: THE HARDWARE

The structures that make up society include micro-level positions (parents, students, workers), the groups to which we belong (family, work groups, and clubs), and the larger groups, organizations, or institutions in which we participate (education, political, and economic organizations). This "hardware" (structure) of our social world provides the framework for "software" (culture) to function.

Societies differ because they exist in different places with unique resources—mountains, coastal areas, jungles. Societies change over time with new technology and leadership. Although human societies have become more complex, especially in recent human history, people have been hunters and gatherers for 99% of human existence. Only a few groups remain hunters and gatherers today. As Table 3.1 illustrates, if all human history were to be compressed into the lifetime of an 80-year-old person, humans would have started cultivating crops and herding animals for their food supply only a few months ago. Note the incredible rate of change that has occurred just in the past two centuries.

Thinking Sociologically

What major changes took place in your grandparents' lifetimes that affect the way you and your family live today? Take a look at the timeline inside the cover of this book. It will provide some ideas.

Societies are organized in particular patterns shaped by factors including the way people procure food, the availability of resources, contact with other societies, and cultural beliefs. For example, people can change from herding to farming only if they have the knowledge, skills, and desire to do so and only in environments that will support agriculture. As societies develop, changes take place in the social structures and relationships between people. For example, in industrialized societies, relationships between people typically become more formal

Members of the Aboubakar family of Sudan gather here in front of their tent with a week's worth of food.

because people must interact with strangers and not just their relatives. It is important to note that not all societies go through all stages. Some are jolted into the future by political events or changes in the global system, and some resist pressures to become modernized and continue to live in simpler social systems.

Evolution of Societies

The Saharan desert life for the Tuareg tribe is pretty much as it has been for centuries. In simple traditional societies, individuals are assigned to comparatively few social positions or statuses. Today, however, few societies are isolated from global impact. Even the Tuareg are called on to escort adventurous tourists through the desert for a currency new to them and unneeded until recently. In 2012, Al Qaeda in the Islamic (or Arabian) Maghreb challenged the Tuareg's control over their desert homeland in a war in northern Mali, Africa. The Tuareg, a nomadic tribe living in northern Mali, staged a rebellion from January to April 2012 to gain greater autonomy in their region, called Azawad. Islamic groups joined in the battle, helped the Tuareg gain control, and then imposed strict Sharia law on the region, including the Tuareg. A force including French military and African troops pushed out the Islamists, and a peace deal was signed between Mali and the Tuareg. However, that has not held as the Tuareg's demands were not met. As of May 19, 2014, the rebellion continues ("Mali 'at War'" 2014).

In such traditional societies, men teach their sons everything they need to know, for all men do much the same jobs, depending on where they live—hunting, fishing, or farming and protecting the community from danger.

Table 3.1   One Million Years of Human History Compressed Into One 80-Year Lifetime

Approximate Year	Age	Event	
2.5 million years ago	Birth	*Homo habilis* is born—the first ancestor to make/use tools and have culture; evidence of sharing food, congregating, and probably sharing housing	Photographed by Lillyundfreya
2 million years ago	2 years old	*Homo erectus* shows early evidence of family structures; findings of longer life spans and three generations alive simultaneously	
15,000 years ago	79 years old	Six months ago: North America settled by early humans, hunters and gatherers	
11,000 years ago	79 years old	Five months ago: in the Middle East, the first agricultural communities emerge, indicating food cultivation	
10,000 years ago	79 years old	Twenty weeks ago: the last ice age is over; humans spread more widely over the planet	http://www.belovedegypt.com/29_-_Sphinx_and_Pyramid.jpg
5,000 years ago	79 years old	Ten weeks ago: humans begin to cast and use metals and built the pyramids	
2,000 years ago	79 years old	Seven weeks ago: beginning of the Common Era (under the Holy Roman Empire)	Library of Congress
220 years ago	79 years old	Two and a half weeks ago: the United States begins a new experiment with democracy	
100 years ago	79 years old	Yesterday morning: the airplane is invented	
30 years ago	79 years old	Yesterday afternoon: humans first set foot on the moon; after dinner, we break the DNA (genetic) code	Wikimedia http://starchild.gsfc.nasa.gov/Images/StarChild/space_level2/aldrin_big.gif

Likewise, girls learn their jobs from their mothers—such as child care, fetching water, food preparation, farming, weaving, and perhaps house building. In contrast, in more complex societies, such as industrial or "modern" societies, thousands of interdependent job statuses are based on complex divisions of labor with designated tasks.

Émile Durkheim, an early French sociologist, pictured a continuum between simple and complex societies ([1893] 1947). He described simple premodern societies as held together by mechanical solidarity—*social cohesion and integration based on the similarity of individuals in the group, including shared beliefs, values, and emotional ties between members of the group*. Furthermore, the division of labor is based largely on male/female distinctions and age groupings; everyone fulfills his or her expected social positions. This provides the glue that holds the society together. The entire society may involve only a few hundred people, with no meso-level institutions, organizations, or subcultures. Prior to the emergence of nation-states, there was no macro level either—only tribal groupings.

According to Durkheim, as societies transformed, they became more complex through increasingly multifaceted divisions of labor and changes in the ways people carried out necessary tasks for survival ([1893] 1947). Organic solidarity refers to *social cohesion (glue) based on division of labor, with each member playing a highly specialized role in the society and each person being dependent on others due to interdependent, interrelated tasks*. The society has cohesion regardless of whether people have common values and shared outlooks. Prior to the factory system, for example, individual cobblers made shoes to order. With the Industrial Revolution, factories took over the process, with many individuals carrying out interdependent tasks. The division of labor is critical because it leads to new forms of social cohesion based on interdependence, not on emotional ties. Gradual changes from mechanical (traditional) to organic (modern) society also involve harnessing new forms of energy and finding more efficient ways to use them (Nolan and Lenski 2008). For example, the use of steam engines and coal for fuel triggered the Industrial Revolution, leading to the development of industrial societies (see Figure 3.1).

As societies changed toward organic solidarity, they added large organizations and institutions that reached individuals and families as never before. The meso level—institutions and large bureaucratic organizations—became more influential. Still, as recently as 200 years ago, even large societies had little global interdependence, and life for the typical citizen was influenced mostly by

events at the micro and meso levels. As communication and transportation around the world developed and expanded, the global level grew.

As you read about each of the following types of societies, from the simplest to the most complex, notice the presence of these variables: (a) division of labor, (b) interdependence of people's positions, (c) increasingly advanced technologies, and (d) new forms and uses of energy. Although none of these variables alone is *sufficient* to trigger evolution to a new type of society, they may all be *necessary* for a transition to occur.

According to Durkheim, then, in traditional societies with mechanical solidarity, interpersonal interaction and community life at the micro level were the most important aspects of social life. Meso- and macro-level societies developed as a result of changes toward more organic solidarity. As societies become more complex, meso- and macro-level institutions become more important and have more profound impacts on the lives of individuals.

Hunter-Gatherer Societies. In the Kalahari Desert of southwestern Africa live hunter-gatherers known as the !Kung. (The ! is pronounced with a click of the tongue.) The !Kung live a nomadic life, moving from one place to

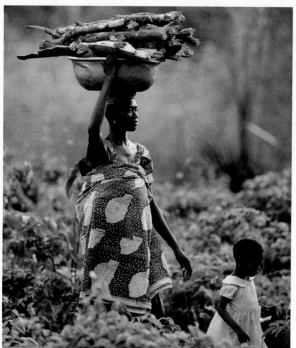

A mother in Côte d'Ivoire (West Africa), carrying her load on her head, returns to the village with her daughter after gathering wood. Carrying wood and water is typically women's work in this hunter-gatherer society.

FIGURE 3.1 Timeline of the Industrial Revolution, 1712–1903

another as food supplies become available or are used up. As a result, they carry very few personal possessions and live in temporary huts, settling around water holes for a few months at a time. Settlements are small, rarely more than 20 to 50 people, for food supplies are not plentiful enough to support large, permanent populations (Lee 1984). !Kung women gather edible plants and nuts, while !Kung men hunt. Beyond division of labor by gender and age, however, there are few differences in roles or status.

In **hunter-gatherer societies,** *people rely on the vegetation and animals occurring naturally in their habitat to sustain life.* Generally, life is organized around kinship ties and reciprocity—that is, mutual assistance—for the well-being of the whole community. When a large animal is killed, people gather from a wide area to share in the bounty, and great care is taken to ensure that the meat is distributed fairly. Resources are shared among the people, but sharing is regulated by a complex system of mutual obligations. A visitor who eats food at another's hearth is expected to repay that hospitality in the future.

The !Kung are a typical hunter-gatherer society. People make their clothing, shelter, and tools from available materials or obtain goods through trade with other nearby groups. People migrate seasonally to new food sources. Population size remains small as the numbers of births and deaths in the society are balanced.

From the beginning of human experience until recently, hunting and gathering (or foraging) were the sole means of sustaining life. Other types of societies emerged only recently. Today, only a handful of societies still rely on hunting and gathering (Nolan and Lenski 2008). The hunter-gatherer lifestyle is becoming extinct.

Herding and Horticultural Societies. A seminomadic herding society, the Masai of Kenya and Tanzania move camp to find grazing land for their animals and set up semipermanent shelters for the few months they will remain in one area. Settlements consist of huts constructed in a circle with a perimeter fence surrounding the compound. At the more permanent settlements, the Masai grow short-term crops to supplement their diet.

Herding societies *have food-producing strategies based on domestication of animals whose care is the central focus of their activities.* Domesticating animals has replaced hunting them. In addition to providing food

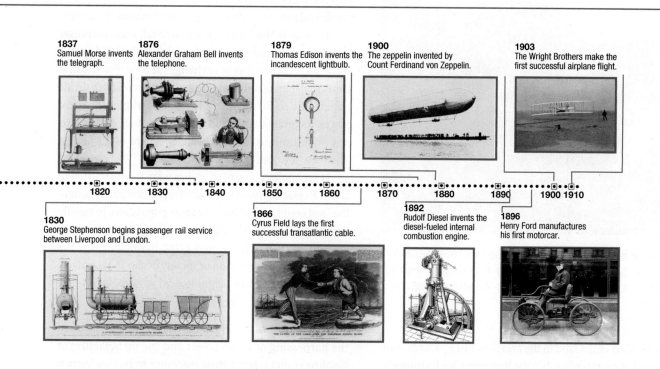

Timeline of Industrial Revolution, 1700-1900 is adapted from Industrial Revolution: Timeline, Facts, and Resources. Research by B. Sobey, TheFreeResource.com.

1837
Samuel Morse invents the telegraph.

1876
Alexander Graham Bell invents the telephone.

1879
Thomas Edison invents the incandescent lightbulb.

1900
The zeppelin invented by Count Ferdinand von Zeppelin.

1903
The Wright Brothers make the first successful airplane flight.

1820 1830 1840 1850 1860 1870 1880 1890 1900 1910

1830
George Stephenson begins passenger rail service between Liverpool and London.

1866
Cyrus Field lays the first successful transatlantic cable.

1892
Rudolf Diesel invents the diesel-fueled internal combustion engine.

1896
Henry Ford manufactures his first motorcar.

and other products, cattle, sheep, goats, pigs, horses, and camels represent forms of wealth that result in more social prestige for members of the group with large herds.

Horticultural societies are *those in which the food-producing strategy is based on domestication of plants, using digging sticks and wooden hoes to cultivate small gardens*. They may also keep domesticated animals, but they focus on simple agriculture or gardening. They cultivate tree crops, such as date palms or bananas, and plant garden plots, such as yams, beans, taro, squash, or corn. This is more efficient than gathering wild vegetables and fruits. Both herding and horticultural societies differ from hunter-gatherer societies in that they make their living by cultivating food and have some control over its production (Ward and Edelstein 2009).

The ability to control food sources was a major turning point in human history. Societies became more settled and stored surpluses of food, which led to increases in population size. A community could contain as many as 3,000 individuals. More people, surplus food, and greater accumulation of possessions encouraged the development of private property and created new status differences between individuals and families. Forms of social inequality started to become pronounced.

The technological breakthrough that moved many societies from the horticultural to the agricultural stage was the plow, introduced more than 6,000 years ago. It marked the beginning of the agricultural revolution in Europe, the Middle East, and other parts of the world, and it brought about massive changes in social structures in many societies. The end of the horticultural stage also saw advances in irrigation systems, the fertilization of land, crop rotation, more permanent settlements, land ownership, human modification of the natural environment, higher population density (cities), and power hierarchies.

Agricultural Societies. Pedro and Lydia Ramirez, their four young children, and Lydia's parents live as an extended family in a small farming village in Nicaragua. They rise early, and while Pedro heads for the fields to do some work before breakfast, Lydia prepares his breakfast and lunch and sees that their eldest son is up and ready to go to school, while Lydia's mother looks after the younger children. After school, the oldest boy also helps in the

©istockphoto.com/Britta Kasholm-Tengve

Plows, essential for agricultural societies to develop, were pushed by people and then pulled by animals and finally machines. Harnessing energy ever more effectively is a prerequisite to a society becoming more complex.

fields. Most of the land in the area is owned by a large company that grows coffee, but the Ramirezes are fortunate to have a small garden plot where they grow some vegetables for themselves. At harvest time, all hands help, including young children. The family receives cash for the coffee they have grown, minus the rent for the land. They plow the land with the help of strong animals such as horses and oxen, and use fertilizers and water the garden when needed.

The Ramirezes' way of life is typical of life in an agricultural society. Agricultural societies *rely primarily on raising crops for food, but make use of technological advances such as the plow, irrigation, animals, and fertilization to continuously cultivate the same land.* The continuous cultivation of the same land results in permanent settlements and greater food surpluses. Agricultural societies utilize energy more efficiently than foraging societies. For example, the plow circulates nutrients better than a digging stick, and when an animal pulls the plow, the farmer can marshal strength beyond that of a person. As increasingly sophisticated agricultural technology resulted in surplus food, the size of population centers increased to as much as a million or more.

As surpluses accumulated, land in some societies became concentrated in the hands of a few individuals. Wealthy landowners built armies and expanded their empires. During these periods, fighting for land took precedence over technological advance. War was prevalent, and societies were divided increasingly into rich and poor

classes. Those who held the land and wealth could control the labor sources and acquire serfs or slaves. Thus, the feudal system was born. Serfs (the peasant class) were forced to work the land for their survival. Food surpluses also allowed some individuals to leave the land and to trade goods or services in exchange for food. For the first time, social inequality became extensive enough to divide society into social classes. At this point, religion, political power, a standing army, and other meso-level institutions and organizations came to be independent of the family. The meso level became well established.

As technology advanced, goods were manufactured in cities. Peasants moved from farming communities, where the land could not support the large population, to rapidly growing urban areas, where the demand for labor was great. It was not until the mid-1700s in England that the next major transformation of society began to take place, resulting largely from technological advances and additional harnessing of energy.

Industrial Societies. The Industrial Revolution involved the harnessing of steam power and the manufacture of gasoline engines, permitting machines to replace human and animal power. A tractor can plow far more land in a week than a horse, and an electric pump can irrigate more acres than an ox-driven pump. As a result of such new technologies, raw mineral products such as ores, raw plant products such as rubber, and raw animal products such as hides could be transformed into mass-produced consumer goods. The Industrial Revolution brought about enormous changes in occupations, division of labor, specialization, products produced, and social structures.

Industrial societies *rely primarily on mechanized production, resulting in greater division of labor based on expertise.* Economic resources were distributed more widely among individuals in industrial societies, but inequities between owners and laborers persisted. Wage earning gradually replaced slavery and serfdom, and highly skilled workers earned higher wages, leading to the rise of a middle class. Farmworkers moved from rural areas to cities to find work in factories, which produced consumer goods. Cities grew, and many became populated by millions of people.

Family and kinship patterns at the micro level also changed. Agricultural societies need large, land-based, extended family units to do the work of farming (recall how the Ramirez parents, grandparents, and children in Nicaragua all help out at harvest time), but industrial societies need individuals with specific skills, ability to move to where the jobs are, and smaller families to support. Family roles change. Children are an asset in agricultural societies and begin work at an early age. However, from a purely economic perspective, children become a liability in an industrial society because they contribute less to the finances of the family.

Meso- and macro-level dimensions of social life expand in industrializing societies and become more influential in the lives of individuals. National institutions and multinational organizations develop. Today, for example, global organizations such as the World Bank, the World Court, the United Nations, and the World Health Organization address social problems and sometimes even make decisions that change national boundaries or national policies. Corporations such as Nike and Gap are multinational organizations (located in many countries). Some voluntary associations—such as Doctors without Borders, which serves medical needs, and Amnesty International, which lobbies for human rights— do their work across the globe.

Perhaps the most notable characteristic of the industrial age is the rapid rate of change compared with other stages of societal development. The beginning of industrialization in Europe was gradual, based on years of population movement, urbanization, technological development, and other factors of modernization. Today, however, societal change occurs so rapidly that societies at all levels of development are being drawn together into a new age— the postindustrial era.

Postindustrial or Information Societies.

Postindustrial societies are *those that have moved from human labor and manufacturing to automated production and service jobs, largely processing information.* For example, postindustrial societies require workers with high levels of technical and professional education. Those without technical education are less likely to find rewarding employment in the technological revolution. This results in new class lines being drawn, based in part on skills and education in new technologies.

The shift to an information-based society has also enhanced cross-border workplaces. As your authors finished chapters for this book, they were sent to India for typesetting in the evening, and returned by morning. Technology, the efficiency of overnight delivery, and the lower cost of production have led many publishing companies to turn to businesses halfway around the world for much of the book production process. As India and other developing countries increase their trained, skilled labor force, they are being called on by national and multinational companies to carry out global manufacturing processes. India has some of the world's best technical training institutes and modern technology—*the practical application of tools, skills, and knowledge to meet human needs and extend human abilities.* Although many people in India live in poverty, a relatively new middle class is rapidly emerging in major business centers around the country.

After World War II, starting in the 1950s, the transition from industrial to postindustrial society began in the United States, Western Europe (especially Germany), and Japan. This shift was characterized by movement from human labor to automated production and from a predominance of manufacturing jobs to a growth in service jobs, such as computer operators, bankers, scientists, teachers, public relations workers, stockbrokers, and salespeople. More than two thirds of all jobs in the United States now reside in organizations that produce and transmit information, thus the reference to an "Information Age." Daniel Bell (1973) describes this transformation of work, information, and communication as "the third technological revolution" after industrialization based on steam (the first technological revolution) and the invention of electricity (the second technological revolution). According to Bell, the third technological revolution was the development of the computer, which has led to this postindustrial era or Information Age. To examine this transformation, see Table 3.2 in the next "Engaging Sociology" on page 66.

Postindustrial societies rely on new sources of power, such as atomic, wind, thermal, and solar energy, and new uses of computer automation. Computer-controlled

This Buddhist monk uses modern technology, including a laptop that can connect him with colleagues on the other side of the globe.

ENGAGING SOCIOLOGY

Demographics of Internet Users

Below is the percentage of each group of U.S. adults who use the Internet, according to a January 2014 survey of the Pew Internet and American Life Project. For instance, 86% of women use the Internet.

Table 3.2   Internet Users in 2014

Among adults, the % who use the Internet, e-mail, or access the Internet via a mobile device

Category	Percent who Use the Internet
All Adults	87
Sex	
a. Men	87
b. Women	86
Race/ethnicity	
a. White	85
b. African American	81
c. Hispanic	83
Age group	
a. 18–29	97
b. 30–49	93
c. 50–64	88
d. 65+	57
Education level	
a. High school grad or less	76
b. Some college	91
c. College+	97
Household income	
a. Less Than $30,000/yr	77
b. $30,000–$49,999	85
c. $50,000–$74,999	93
d. $75,000+	99
Community type	
a. Urban	88
b. Suburban	87
c. Rural	83

Source: Table on p. 5. "Demographics of Internet Users in 2000 and 2011." *Digital Differences,* by Kathryn Zickuhr and Aaron Smith. April 13, 2012. Pew Internet and the American Life Project.

Engaging With Sociology

Interview 10 people you know to find out about their Internet use, keeping records on the gender, age, ethnicity, educational attainment, and income bracket of each. Then compare your figures with those in Table 3.2. Are they similar? If not, what possible geographic, social class, or other social factors might cause your figures to be different from those in this national survey?

robots have taken over many jobs once carried out by humans. The control of information and the ability to develop technologies or provide services have become key sources of money and power.

Twenty-first-century postindustrial societies favor scientific and creative approaches to problem solving, research, and development, along with attitudes that support the globalization of world economies. Satellites, cell phones, fiber optics, and especially the Internet continue to transform postindustrial societies of the Information Age, linking people from societies around the world.

In a study of postmodern communities, sociologist Richard Florida links creativity to the local cultural climate and to economic prosperity. His research has important applied dimensions and is useful to policy makers in local communities. As his research, described in the next "Sociologists in Action" on page 68 makes clear, the organization of society and the means of providing the necessities of life have a profound impact on values, beliefs, lifestyle, and other aspects of culture.

Thinking Sociologically

Why do some communities attract creative people? What are some characteristics of these communities? What might be advantages—or disadvantages—to living in a creative community? Would you like to live in such a community? Why or why not? How do you think growing up in such a community would impact your choice of a career?

What will the future bring? Futurologists predict new trends based on current activities and predictions of new advances and technologies on the horizon. Among the many ideas for the future, technological advances dominate the field. Predictions include the increasing use of cell phones connecting the poorest corners of the globe with the rest of the world. One billion mobile phone users are predicted for China by 2020, with 80% of the population having cell phones. With discovery and efficient use of energy being central to sociocultural evolution, alternative energy sources from wind to solar power will become essential to meet demand. Plug-in hybrids, natural gas, and electric batteries may replace gasoline motors. One million hydrogen-fueled cars are predicted for the United States by the year 2035, and far more for Europe and Japan. Gas may be on the way out. Rechargeable batteries that run for 40 hours without interruption will run most home appliances by 2030. Brain computer interfaces will give paralyzed people the ability to control their environments (News of Future 2012). These are just a few of the

many predictions of what will affect societies and alter some human interactions.

In much of this book we focus on complex, multilevel societies, for this is the type of social environment in which most of us reading this book now live. Much of this book also focuses on social interaction and social structures, including interpersonal networking, the growth of bureaucratic structures, social inequality within the structure, and the core institutions necessary to meet the needs of individuals and society. In short, *hardware*—society—is the focus of many subsequent chapters. The remainder of this chapter focuses primarily on the social *software*—culture.

CULTURE: THE SOFTWARE

Cultures—the ideas and "things" passed on from one generation to the next in a society, including knowledge, beliefs, values, rules and laws, language, customs, symbols, and material products—vary greatly as we travel across the globe. Each social unit of cooperating and interdependent people, whether at the micro, meso, or macro level, develops a unique way of life with guidelines for the actions and interaction of individuals and groups within society.

As you can see, the sociological definition of culture refers to far more than "high or elite culture" shared by a select few—such as fine art, classical music, opera, literature, ballet, and theater—and also far more than "popular culture"—such as reality TV, professional wrestling, YouTube, and other mass entertainment. *Popular culture* is mass produced and consumed, and becomes part of everyday traditions through its practices, beliefs, and material objects. It influences public opinion and values. One type of pop culture is music in its many forms; for example, rap music often focuses on urban culture's politics, economics, and inequality and provides an outlet for frustrations through musical commentary. Much of pop culture has been shaped by technology, as we see in texting and social media. The very rapid change in this aspect of popular culture is illustrated in the next "Engaging Sociology" on pages 70–71.

Characteristics of Culture

Cultures have certain characteristics in common. These characteristics help define culture and illustrate the purposes it serves for our societies.

SOCIOLOGISTS IN ACTION: RICHARD FLORIDA

Creativity, Community, and Applied Sociology

Like the transformations of societies from the hunter-gatherer to the horticultural stage or from the agricultural to the industrial stage, our own current transformation seems to have created a good deal of "cultural wobble" within society. How does one identify the elements or the defining features of a new age while the transformation is still in progress? This was one of the questions that intrigued sociologist Richard Florida, who studied U.S. communities.

Professor Florida combined several methods of data collection (2002, 2012). First, he traveled around the country to communities that were especially prosperous and seemed to be on the cutting edge of change in U.S. society. In these communities, he did both individual interviews and focus-group interviews. *Focus-group interviews* are semistructured group interviews with seven or eight people where ideas can be generated from the group by asking open-ended questions. Professor Florida recorded the discussion and analyzed the transcript of the discussion. The collected data helped Professor Florida identify the factors that caused people to choose the place where they decided to live. His informants discussed quality of life and the way they make decisions. As certain themes and patterns emerged, he tested the ideas by comparing statistical data for regions that were vibrant, had growing economies, and seemed to be integrated into the emerging information economy. He used another method to compare communities and regions of the country—analyzing already existing (secondary) archival data collected by various U.S. government agencies, especially the U.S. Bureau of Labor Statistics and the U.S. Census Bureau.

Florida argues that the economy of the 21st century is largely driven by creativity, and creative people often decide where to live based on certain features of the society. Currently, more than one third of the jobs in the United States—and almost all the extremely well-paid professional positions—require creative thinking. These include not just the creative arts but scientific research, computer and mathematical occupations, education and library science positions, and many media, legal, and managerial careers. People in this "creative class" have an enormous amount of autonomy in their work; their employers give them problems to solve and the freedom to figure out how to do so. Florida found that modern businesses flourish when they hire highly creative people. Thus, growing businesses tend to seek out places where creative people locate.

Through his research, Florida identified regions and urban areas especially attractive to the creative class. Florida's research led him to collaborate with Gary Gates, a scholar who was doing research on communities hospitable to gays and lesbians. Gates and Florida were amazed to find that their lists were nearly identical. Florida found that creative people thrive on diversity—ethnic, gender, religious, and

Creative, highly productive people tend to be attracted to communities that embrace diversity and have locally owned stores like this Village Lights bookstore in Madison, Indiana.

otherwise—for when creative people are around others who think differently, it tends to spawn new avenues of thinking and problem solving. Tolerance of difference and even the enjoyment of individual idiosyncrasies are hallmarks of thriving communities.

Florida is now very much in demand as a consultant to mayors and urban-planning teams, and his books have become required reading for city council members. Some elected officials have decided that fostering an environment that attracts creative people leads to prosperity because business will follow. Key elements of creative communities include local music and art festivals, organic food grocery stores, legislation that encourages interesting mom-and-pop stores (and keeps out large "box stores" that crush such small and unique endeavors), quaint and locally owned bookstores and distinctive coffee shops, provisions for bike and walking paths throughout the town, and ordinances that establish an environment of tolerance for people who are "different."

• •

Richard Florida heads the Martin Prosperity Institute at the Rotman School of Management at the University of Toronto. He also runs a private creative class institute. He earned his bachelor's degree from Rutgers University and his doctorate in urban planning from Columbia University.

All people share a culture with others in their society. Culture provides the rules, routines, patterns, and expectations for carrying out daily rituals and interactions. Within a society, the process of learning how to act is called socialization (discussed in Chapter 4). From birth, we learn the patterns of behavior approved in our society.

Culture evolves over time and is adaptive. What is normal, proper, and good behavior in hunter-gatherer societies, where cooperation and communal loyalty are critical to the hunt, differs from appropriate behavior in the Information Age, where individualism and competition are encouraged and enhance one's position and well-being.

The creation of culture is ongoing and cumulative. Individuals and societies continually build on existing culture to adapt to new challenges and opportunities. Your culture shapes the behaviors, values, and institutions that seem natural to you. Culture is so much a part of life that you may not even notice behaviors that outsiders find unusual or even abhorrent. You may not think about it when handing food to someone with your left hand, but in some other cultures, such an act may be defined as disgusting and rude.

The transmission of culture is the feature that most separates humans from other animals. Some societies of higher primates have shared cultures but do not systematically enculturate (teach a way of life to) the next generation. Primate cultures focus on behaviors relating to obtaining food, use of territory, protection, and social status. Human cultures have significantly more content and are mediated by language. Humans are the only mammals with cultures that enable them to adapt to and even modify their environments so that they can survive on the equator, in the Arctic, or even beyond the planet.

Thinking Sociologically

Imagine playing a game of cards with four people in which each player thinks a different suit is trump (a trump is a rule whereby any card from the trump suit wins over any card from a different suit). In this game, one person believes hearts is trump, another assumes spades is trump, and so forth. What would happen? How would the result be similar to a society with no common culture?

Ethnocentrism and Cultural Relativity

As scientists, sociologists must rely on scientific research to understand behavior. The scientific method calls for *objectivity*—the practice of considering observed behavior independently of one's own beliefs and values. The study of social behavior thus requires both sensitivity to a wide variety of human social patterns and a perspective that reduces bias. This is more difficult than it sounds because sociologists themselves are products of society and culture. All of us are raised in a particular culture that we view as normal or natural. Yet not every culture views the same things as "normal."

▶ Power of Technology

ENGAGING SOCIOLOGY

Pop Culture and Technology Timeline

©Getty/Bernhard Lang

How surprising to think that digital telephones, high-speed lines for computers, digitized print media, and the World Wide Web were all invented within about the past half-century, many within the last 20 years. Vinyl records, dial telephones, and VHS tapes have been surpassed by CDs, cell phones, DVDs, and streamlined and downloaded movies and music. Slim laptops, iPads, and handheld computers have replaced bulky desktop computers. The following timeline shows the rapid advances of the Internet and World Wide Web in recent years; the point of this timeline is to illustrate the rapid advance of technology and the place it holds in our lives. Technology is now a primary conveyor of culture, especially pop culture.

An Internet and World Wide Web Timeline

1946:   Electronic Numerical Integrator and Computer (ENIAC), the first general-purpose computer, is developed for military purposes.

1951:   UNIVersal Automatic Computer (UNIVAC) becomes the first civilian computer.

1965:   A highly usable computer language, Beginner's All-Purpose Symbolic Instruction Code (BASIC), is developed.

1971:   Microprocessors are developed, making possible personal computer (PC) technology.

1977:   The first fiber-optic network is created.

1978:   Cellular phone service begins.

1982:   The National Science Foundation sponsors a high-speed communications network, leading to the Internet.

1984:   Apple Macintosh introduces the first PC with graphics.

1991:   The Internet opens to commercial uses, HyperText Markup Language (HTML) is developed, and the World Wide Web is launched.

1993:   The first point-and-click web browser, Mosaic, is introduced.

1996:   Google makes its debut.

2001:   Instant messaging services expand to allow exchanges between different service providers.

2002:   Broadband technology is developed in South Korea.

2004:   Mark Zuckerberg begins Facebook while a student at Harvard University.

2005:   YouTube is created by PayPal employees Chad Hurley, Steve Chen, and Jawed Karim.

2005 to present: Cloud computing enables users to run programs on many connected computers at the same time; video glasses have a head-mounted display screen and video capability; smart (computerized) watches connect to the Internet and smartphones.

The continuing rapid advances in technology have paralleled the development of shared pop culture in the United States and around the world, culture that is accessible to everyone, not just the elite. Music groups from other continents have gained audiences in the United States, with musical groups becoming instant success stories through YouTube. Webcasting allows access to audio and video presentations on demand, and streaming allows people around the world to listen to broadcasts on the Internet. The spread of pop culture—music, mass art, fashion, books, you name it—has been made possible by advances in technology. "There is no turning back the clock once an innovation is introduced that makes communication more rapid, cheap, and broadly accessible" (Danesi 2008:21).

Engaging With Sociology

1. Identify four of the historic innovations that you feel are particularly significant. What are some ways in which they have impacted your life?

2. Identify three positive and three negative ways these rapid advances in technology might impact less developed parts of the world.

3. How can the spread of pop culture across the globe (a) bring different societies closer together and (b) cause tensions within and between societies?

Views of premarital sex and pregnancy vary among societies (Library of Congress 2010). For example, in one 1970 study of 154 societies, about 42% of the societies encouraged premarital sex, while 29% forbade such behavior and punished those who disobeyed this rule (Ford 1970). The remainder fell in between those two extremes. As you can see, social values, beliefs, and behaviors can vary dramatically from one society to the next. These differences can be threatening and even offensive to people who judge others according to their own perspectives, experiences, and values.

The tendency to view one's own group and its cultural expectations as right, proper, and superior to others is called ethnocentrism—"ethno" for ethnic group and "centrism" for centered on. If you were brought up in a society that forbids premarital or extramarital sex, for instance, you might judge many Americans to be immoral. In a few Muslim societies, people who have premarital sex may be severely punished or even executed, because such behavior is seen as an offense against the faith and the family and as a weakening of social bonds. It threatens the lineage and inheritance systems of family groups. In turn, some Americans would find such strict rules of abstinence to be strange and even wrong.

Societies instill some degree of ethnocentrism in their members because ethnocentric beliefs hold groups together and help members feel that they belong to the group. Ethnocentrism promotes loyalty, unity, high morale, and conformity to the rules of society. Fighting for one's country, for instance, requires some degree of belief in the rightness of one's own society and its causes. Ethnocentric attitudes also help protect societies from rapid, disintegrating change. If most people in a society did not believe in the rules and values of their own culture, the result could be widespread dissent, deviance, or crime.

Unfortunately, ethnocentrism can lead to misunderstandings between people of different cultures. The same ethnocentric attitudes that strengthen ties between some people may encourage hostility, racism, war, and genocide against others—even others within the society—who are different. Virtually all societies tend to "demonize" their adversary—in movies, the news, and political speeches—especially when a conflict is most intense. Dehumanizing another group with labels makes it easier to torture or kill its members or to perform acts of discrimination and brutality against them. We see this in the current conflict in Syria in which both sides in the conflict feel hatred for each other. However, as we become a part of a global social world, it becomes increasingly important to accept those who are "different." Bigotry and attitudes of superiority do not enhance cross-national cooperation and trade—which is what the increasing movement toward a global village and globalization entail. The map in Figure 3.2 challenges our ethnocentric view of the world. Note how you react.

U.S. foreign relations illustrate how ethnocentrism can produce hostility. Many U.S. citizens are surprised to learn that the United States—a great democracy, world power, and disseminator of food, medicine, and technological assistance to developing nations—is despised in many countries. Anti-U.S. demonstrations in South America, the Middle

FIGURE 3.2   "Southside Up" Global Map

Source: Map by Anna Versluis.

Note: This map illustrates geographic ethnocentrism. U.S. citizens tend to assume it is natural that the north should always be "on top." The fact that this map of the world is upside-down, where south is "up," seems incorrect or disturbing to some people. Most people think of their countries or regions as occupying a central and larger part of the world.

East, and Asia have brought this reality to life through television. The 10 countries with the most negative feelings according to polls are Pakistan, the Palestinian territories, Algeria, Lebanon, Egypt, Iran, Iraq, Yemen, Greece, and Serbia (Sauter, Weigley, and Hess 2013). One cause is the political dominance of the United States and the threat it poses to other people's way of life. In many places of the world, people believe U.S. citizens think only about their own welfare as their country exploits weaker nations. U.S. tourists are sometimes seen as loudmouthed ignoramuses whose ethnocentric attitudes prevent them from seeing value in other cultures or from learning other languages.

Note that even referring to citizens of the United States as "Americans"—as though people from Canada, Mexico, and South America do not really count as Americans—is seen as ethnocentric by many people from these other countries. *America* and the *United States* are not the same thing, but many people in the United States, including some presidents, fail to make the distinction, much to the dismay of other North and South Americans. If you visit Mexico, people might ask you where you are from. Say "America," and they, too, will say they are from America. Say North America, and Mexicans will say, "From Canada or the United States?"

Not all ethnocentrism is hostile; some of it is just a reaction to the strange ways of other cultures. An example is making judgments about what is proper food to eat and what is just not edible. While people everywhere eat, we can see widespread cultural differences in what people eat, as noted in the first part of this chapter. Some of the New Guinea tribes savor grasshoppers, Europeans and Russians relish raw fish eggs (caviar), Inuit children may find seal eyeballs a treat, some Indonesians eat dog, and some Nigerians prize termites. Whether it is from another time or another society, variations in food can be shocking to us.

In contrast to ethnocentrism, cultural relativism *requires setting aside cultural and personal beliefs and prejudices to understand another group or society through the eyes of its members and using its own community standards.* Instead of judging cultural practices and social behavior as good or bad according to one's own cultural practices, the goal is to be impartial in learning the purposes and consequences of practices and behaviors of the group under study. Cultural relativism does not require that social scientists accept or agree with all the beliefs and behaviors of the societies or groups they study. Yet it allows them to try to understand those practices in the social and cultural contexts in which they occur.

Applying Cultural Relativity   Cultural Diversity

Being tolerant and understanding is not always easy. Some behaviors or ideas in other cultures can be difficult for even the most objective observer to understand. The notion of being "on time," for example, which is so much a part of the cultures of the United States, Canada, Japan, and parts of Europe, is a rather bizarre concept in some societies. Among many Native American people, such as the Dineh (Apache and Navajo), it is ludicrous for people to let a piece of machinery such as a cell phone govern the way one constructs and lives life. The Dineh orientation to time—that one should do things according to the natural rhythm of the body and not according to an artificial electronic mechanism—is difficult for many people outside that culture to grasp. Misunderstandings occur when some North Americans think that "Indians are always late" and jump to the erroneous conclusion that "Indians" are undependable. Native Americans, on the other hand, think Whites are neurotic about letting some instrument control them (Basso 1979; Farrer 2011; Hall 1959, 1983).

 Thinking Sociologically

Small, tightly knit societies with no meso or macro level often stress cooperation, conformity, and personal sacrifice for the sake of the community. Complex societies with established meso- and macro-level linkages tend to be individualistic, stressing personal uniqueness, individual creativity, and critical thinking. Why do you think this is the case?

THE COMPONENTS OF CULTURE: THINGS AND THOUGHTS

Things (material) and thoughts (nonmaterial) make up much of our culture. Together they provide the guidelines for our lives.

Material Culture: The Artifacts of Life

Material culture *includes all the human-made objects we can see or touch, all the artifacts of a group of people—* their grindstones for grinding cassava root, microwave ovens for cooking, bricks of mud or clay for building shelters, hides or woven cloth for making clothing, books or computers for conveying information, tools for reshaping their environments, vessels for carrying and sharing food, and weapons for dominating and subduing others.

Some material culture is from the local community; it is of micro-level origin. The kinds of materials with which homes are constructed and the materials used for clothing often reflect the geography and resources of the local area. Houses are an especially good example of material culture, since they result from local ideas of what a "home" looks like and shape the interactions and attitudes of people in the society. Likewise, types of jewelry, pottery, musical instruments, or clothing reflect tastes that emerge at the micro and meso levels of family, community, and subculture. At a more macro level, national and international corporations interested in making profits work hard to establish trends in fashion and style that may cross continents and oceans.

Material culture helps drive the globalization process. Workers in Asia and Central American countries now make many of our clothes. Our shoes may come from the Philippines. The last banana each of us ate probably grew in Costa Rica, Guatemala, Honduras, or Panama. That romantic diamond engagement ring—a symbol that represents the most intimate tie—may well be imported from a South African mine using low-paid or even slave labor. Our cars consist of parts produced on nearly every continent.

Thinking Sociologically

Think of examples of material culture that you use daily: stove, automobile, cell phone, computer, refrigerator, clock, money, and so forth. How do these material objects influence your way of life and the way you interact with others? How would your behavior be different if these material objects, say, iPhones or money, did not exist?

Nonmaterial Culture: Beliefs, Values, Rules, and Language

Saluting the flag, saying a blessing before meals, flashing someone an obscene gesture, and a football coach signaling what defensive formation to run for the next play are all symbolic acts. In the case of the salute and the prayer, the acts undergird a belief about the nation or about a higher spiritual presence. In each case something is communicated, yet each of these acts refers to something more abstract than any material object.

Nonmaterial culture refers to *the thoughts, language, feelings, beliefs, values, and attitudes that make up much of our culture.* They are the invisible and intangible parts of culture that involve society's rules of behavior, ideas, and beliefs that shape how people

Material Culture

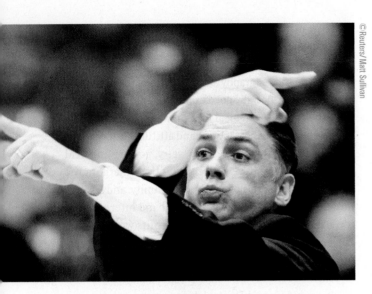

Coaches and players use hand signals to cue each other into an upcoming play or to convey what defense or offense to set up—an example of nonverbal communication.

interact with others and with their environment. Although we cannot touch the nonmaterial components of our culture, they pervade our life and influence how we think, feel, and behave. Nonmaterial culture is complex, comprising four main elements: values, beliefs, norms or rules, and language.

Values are *shared judgments about what is desirable or undesirable, right or wrong, good or bad. They express the basic ideals of any group of people.* In industrial and postindustrial societies, for instance, a good education is highly valued. That you are in college shows you have certain values toward learning and education. Gunnar Myrdal (1964), a Swedish sociologist and observer of U.S. culture, referred to the U.S. value system as the "American creed," so much a part of the way of life that it acquires the power of religious doctrine. We tend to take our core values for granted, including freedom, equality, individualism, democracy, free enterprise, efficiency, progress, achievement, and material comfort (Macionis 2012; Williams 1970).

At the macro level, conflicts may arise between groups in society because of differing value systems. For example, there are major differences between the values of various Native American groups and the dominant culture—whether that dominant culture is in North, Central, or South America (Lake 1990; Sharp 1991). Consider the story in the next "Sociology Around the World" about Rigoberta Menchú Tum and the experiences of Native American populations living in Guatemala.

The conflict in values between First Nations and the national cultures of Canada, the United States, and many Latin American countries has had serious consequences. Cooperation is a cultural value that has been passed on through generations of Native Americans in both North and South America. Their survival has always depended on group cooperation in the hunt, in war, and in daily life. The value of cooperation can place Native children at a disadvantage in North American schools that emphasize competition. Native American and Canadian First Nation children experience more success in classrooms that stress cooperation and sociability over competition and individuality (Lake 1990; Mehan 1992).

Beliefs are *ideas we hold about life, about the way society works, and about where we fit into the world.* They are expressed as specific statements that we hold to be true. Many Hindus, for example, believe that fulfilling behavioral expectations of one's own social caste will lead to rewards in one's next birth, or incarnation. In the next life, good people will be born into a higher social status. In contrast, some Christians believe that one's fate in the afterlife depends on whether one believes in certain ideas—for instance, that Jesus Christ is one's personal savior. Beliefs come from traditions established over time, sacred scriptures, experiences people have had, and lessons given by parents and teachers or other individuals in authority. Beliefs, based on values, influence the choices we make. For example, one value might be that the environment is worth preserving. A belief based on that value would be that humans should make efforts to curb global warming.

Values and beliefs, as elements of nonmaterial culture, are expressed in two forms: an ideal culture and a real culture. **Ideal culture** consists of *practices, beliefs, and values regarded as most desirable in society and consciously taught to children.* Not everyone, however, follows the approved cultural patterns, even though they may say they do. Sometimes our values contradict one another. **Real culture** refers to *the way things in society are actually done.* For example, family time and money are both highly valued in U.S. society. However, in order to make money, we often have to sacrifice time with our families.

Thinking Sociologically

The experiences of Rigoberta Menchú Tum provide some examples of clashes between dominant and less powerful groups within a single nation. What are some examples of cultural conflict among groups in your society? Which (if any) do you think should prevail? Why? How do these conflicts impact the stability of the overall society? Why?

Language and Labels

Sociology Around the World

Social Justice in a Guatemalan Village

Rigoberta Menchú Tum

In her five decades of life, Rigoberta Menchú Tum has experienced the closeness of family and cooperation in village life. These values are very important in Chimel, the Guatemalan hamlet where she grew up. She also experienced great pain and suffering with the loss of her family and community. A Quiché Indian, Menchú became famous throughout the world in 1992, when she received the Nobel Peace Prize for her work to improve conditions for Indian peoples.

Guatemalans of Spanish origin hold the most power in Guatemala and have used Indians almost as slaves. Some of the natives were cut off from food, water, and other necessities, but people in Menchú's hamlet helped support each other and taught children survival techniques. Most people had no schooling. Menchú's work life in the sugarcane fields began at age 5. At 14, she traveled to the city to work as a domestic servant. While there, she learned Spanish, which helped her be more effective in defending the rights of the indigenous population in Guatemala. Her political coming of age occurred at age 16, when she witnessed her

brother's assassination by a group trying to expel her people from their native lands.

Menchú's father started a group to fight the repression of the indigenous and poor, and at 20, Menchú joined the movement Comité de Unidad Campesina (CUC, meaning "Peasant Unity Committee"), which the government claimed was communist inspired. Her father was murdered during a military assault, and her mother was tortured and killed. Menchú moved to Mexico with many other exiles to continue their nonviolent fight for rights and democracy.

The values of the native population represented by Menchú and the values of the dominant culture in Guatemala conflict with one another. The culture of the indigenous population focuses on respect for and a profound spiritual relationship with the environment, equality of all people, freedom from economic oppression, and the benefits of cooperation over competition. Those with the most power in Guatemala tend to stress the freedom of people to pursue their individual self-interests (even if inequality resulted), competition, and the right to own property and to do whatever one desired to exploit that property for economic gain. They think individual property rights are more important than the preservation of indigenous cultures. Among this cultural group, economic growth and profits are held in higher regard than religious connectedness to the earth.

Rigoberta Menchú Tum continues to fight for the rights of her people and for the values they hold dear. She won the Nobel Peace Prize for her work advocating for the rights of indigenous people and is a UN ambassador for indigenous people around the world.

Norms are *rules of behavior shared by members of a society and rooted in the value system.* Examples include our rather routine behaviors, from saying "Hi" to people we meet to obeying traffic signs. Norms range from religious warnings such as "Thou shalt not kill" to the expectation in many societies that young people will complete their high school education. Sometimes the origins of particular norms are quite clear. Few people wonder, for instance, why there is a norm to stop and look both ways at a stop sign. Other norms, such as the rule in many societies that women should wear skirts but men should not, have been passed on through the generations and have become unconsciously accepted patterns and a part of tradition. Sometimes we may not know how norms originated or even be aware of norms until they are violated.

Norms generally fall into two categories—folkways and mores—based largely on their importance and people's response to the breach of those norms. *Folkways* are customs or desirable behaviors, but they are not strictly enforced: Examples of folkways include responding appropriately and politely when introduced to someone, speaking quietly in a library, not scratching your genitals in public, using proper table manners, and covering your mouth when you cough. Violation of these norms causes people to think you are weird or even uncouth but not necessarily immoral or criminal.

Mores are norms that most members observe because they have great moral significance in a society. Conforming to mores is a matter of right and wrong, and violations

of many mores are treated very seriously. The person who deviates from mores is considered immoral or criminal. Being honest, not cheating on exams, and being faithful in a marriage are all mores. Table 3.3 provides examples of violations of folkways and mores.

Taboos are the strongest form of mores. They concern actions considered unthinkable or unspeakable in the culture. For example, most societies have taboos that forbid incest (sexual relations with a close relative) and prohibit defacing or eating a human corpse. Taboos are most common and numerous in societies without centralized governments to establish formal laws and to maintain jails.

Taboos and other moral codes are of the utmost importance to a group because they provide guidelines for what is right and wrong. Yet behaviors that are taboo in one situation may be acceptable at another time and place. The incest taboo is an example found in all cultures, yet the application of the incest taboo varies greatly across cultures (Brown 1991). In medieval Europe, if a man and a woman were within seven degrees of relatedness and wanted to marry, the marriage could be denied by the priest as incestuous. (Your first cousin is a third degree of relatedness from you.) Of course, in Europe, exceptions were made for the royal families, where cousins often married. By contrast, the Balinese permit twins to marry because it is believed they have already been intimately bonded together in the womb (Leslie and Korman 1989). In some African and Native American societies, one cannot marry a sibling but might be expected to marry a first cousin. As Table 3.4 illustrates, the definition of what is and what is not incest varies even from state to state in the United States.

Laws are *norms formally encoded by those holding political power in society with formal punishment attached,* such as laws against stealing property or killing another person. The violator of a law is likely to be perceived not just as a weird or immoral person but also as a criminal who deserves formal punishment. Many mores are passed into law, and some folkways are also made into laws with formal punishments imposed for their violation. Behaviors may be folkways in one situation and mores or laws in another, with gradually more serious consequences. For example, nudity or various stages of near nudity may be only mildly questionable in some social settings (the beach or certain fraternity parties) but would be quite offensive in others (a four-star restaurant or a house of worship) and against the law in still other situations, incurring a penalty, or sanction.

Table 3.3 Violations of Norms

Folkways: Conventional Polite Behaviors Violations Viewed as "Weird"
Swearing in a house of worship
Wearing blue jeans to the prom
Using poor table manners
Picking one's nose in public
Mores: Morally Significant Behaviors Violations Viewed as "Immoral"
Lying or being unfaithful to a spouse
Buying cigarettes or liquor for young teens
Having sex with a professor as a way to increase one's grade
Parking in handicap spaces when one is in good physical condition

Taboo: Assisted Suicide   Folkways

Table 3.4   Incest Taboos in the United States: States That Allow First-Cousin Marriage

Alabama	Connecticut	Hawaii	New Mexico	South Carolina
Alaska	District of Columbia	Maryland	New York	Tennessee
California	Florida	Massachusetts	North Carolina	Vermont
Colorado	Georgia	New Jersey	Rhode Island	Virginia

Source: National Conference of State Legislatures 2013.

Sanctions *reinforce norms through rewards and penalties.* Sanctions vary with the importance of the norm and can range from a parent frowning at a child who fails to use proper table manners to a prison term or a death sentence. Formal sanctions *are rewards or punishments conferred by recognized officials to enforce the most important norms.* Fines for parking illegally, failing grades for plagiarism, or expulsion for bringing drugs or weapons to school are formal negative sanctions your school might impose. Positive sanctions include honors and awards. Informal sanctions *are unofficial rewards or punishments such as smiles, frowns, or ignoring unacceptable behaviors.* A private word of praise by your professor after class about how well you did on your exam would be an informal positive sanction; gossip or ostracism by other students because of the clothes you wear would be an informal negative sanction. Most often, adherence to norms is ingrained so deeply that our reward is simply "fitting in."

Language is *the foundation of every culture. It conveys verbal, written, and nonverbal messages among members of society.* The mini-drama between infant and adult is played out every day around the world as millions of infants learn the language of the adults who care for them. In the process, they acquire an important part of culture, which is learned. Although many animals can communicate with a limited repertoire of sounds, the ability to speak a language is unique to humans (Phillips 2013). Transport a baby from France to the Arapesh tribe in New Guinea and another baby from New Guinea to France, and each will learn to speak the language and adhere to the culture in which it is brought up. Language conveys verbal, written, and nonverbal messages among members of society. Simply put, without language there would be little, if any, culture. Through the use of language, members of a culture can pass on essential knowledge to children and can share ideas with other members of their society. Work can be organized, and the society can build on its experiences and plan its future. Through language, members express their ideas, values, beliefs, and knowledge, a key ingredient in the ability of humans to sustain social life.

Language takes three primary forms: spoken, written, and nonverbal. There are an estimated 5,000 languages spoken in the world. The most common first languages are Chinese (with 1.9 billion speakers), Spanish (406 million), English (335 million), Hindi (260 million), and Arabic (223 million) (Infoplease 2012). English, on the other hand, is the top Internet language around the world with 536.9 million users (Internet World Stats 2014).

Written language enables humans to store ideas for future generations, accelerating the accumulation of ideas on which to build. It also makes possible communication over distances. Members of a society learn to read these shared symbols, some of which are displayed in Figure 3.3.

Nonverbal language consists of gestures, facial expressions, and body postures. This mode of communication may carry as much as 90% of the meaning of a message (Samovar and Porter 2003). Every culture uses nonverbal language to communicate, and just like verbal language, those cues may differ widely among cultures.

The power to communicate nonverbally is illustrated in American Sign Language, designed for the hearing challenged and the mute. Complex ideas can be transmitted without vocalizing a word. Indeed, one can argue that the deaf have a distinctive culture of their own rooted in large part in the unique sign language that serves them (discussed further later). In addition, technology has aided communication among the hearing impaired through text messaging.

FIGURE 3.3 Societies Use Various Symbols to Communicate Their Written Language

福
Поздравляю!
Θεος
לחם שׁר בא
-십 시 요
العربية
राम

Thinking Sociologically

Think about a time when you were trying to understand what someone was saying when you could not hear his or her words (at a concert, a bar, a loud party, etc.). How did you rely on the other person's nonverbal communication to interpret what he or she was trying to convey? How successful were you? How did you know whether or not you were successful?

Language also plays a critical role in our perceptions and in thought organization. The *linguistic relativity theory* posits that the people who speak a specific language make interpretations of their reality—they notice certain things and may fail to notice certain other things (Sapir 1929, 1949; Whorf 1956). "A person's 'picture of the universe' or 'view of the world' differs as a function of the particular language or languages that person knows" (Kodish 2003:384). While language does not totally determine thinking, most scientists agree that it does influence thinking (Casasanto 2008; Gumperz and Levinson 1996; Levinson 2000). For example, in some Native Alaskan cultures where life is dependent on the elements, there are a number of words for snow, each giving members of the

group a description that could mean life or death—wet snow, dry snow, heavy snow, melting snow. Children in each different culture will learn about the world within the framework provided by their language.

In the English language people tend to associate certain colors with certain qualities in a way that may add to the problem of racist attitudes (Levinson 2000). The definition of the word *black* includes "dismal," "boding ill," "hostile," "harmful," "inexcusable," "without goodness," "evil," "wicked," "disgrace," and "without moral light." The word *white*, on the other hand, is defined as "honest," "dependable," "morally pure," "innocent," and "without malice" (Merriam-Webster 2014; *Webster's Unabridged English Dictionary* 1989). If the linguistic relativity thesis is correct, it is more than a coincidence that bad things are associated with the *black sheep* of the family, the *blacklist*, or *Black Tuesday* (when the U.S. stock market dropped dramatically and crashed in 1929).

This association of blackness with negative images and meanings is not true of all languages. The societies that have negative images for *black* and positive images for *white* are the same societies that associate negative qualities with people of darker skin. Blackness associated with something evil is not true of many African languages (Jordan 2012). The use of *white* as a synonym for good or innocent—as in reference to a "white noise machine" or a

White and black as colors have symbolic meaning—with phrases like "blackballed from the club" or "black sheep of the family" indicating negative judgment associated with blackness. Athletic teams wearing black are called for more fouls than are teams wearing white.

"white lie"—may contribute to a cultural climate that devalues people of color. In essence, the language may influence our perception of color in a manner that contributes to racism. Interestingly, there is empirical evidence supporting this claim of color symbolism. Athletic teams that wear black uniforms have more penalties called on them than teams with lighter-colored uniforms (Frank and Gilovich 1988).

When grouped together, material and nonmaterial components form cultural patterns. People's lives are organized around these patterns. For example, family life includes patterns of courtship, marriage, child rearing, and care of the elderly. For additional visual support for understanding material and nonmaterial cultural patterns, see Table 3.5.

We have seen that material artifacts and nonmaterial beliefs, values, norms, and language comprise the basic components of culture. Next, we explore the theoretical explanations for culture.

SOCIETY, CULTURE, AND OUR SOCIAL WORLD

Whether their people are eating termite eggs, fish eggs, or chicken eggs, societies always have a culture, and culture is always linked to a society. Culture provides guidelines for behaviors and actions at each level of society, from the global system to the individual family. The social world model at the beginning of the chapter, with its concentric circles, represents the micro to macro levels of society. Smaller social units such as a school operate within a larger community, which is also part of a region of the country. The culture determines what takes place in each of these units. There is a social unit—a structural "hardware"—and a culture—or "software"—at each level.

Microcultures: Micro-Level Analysis

Micro-level analysis focuses on social interactions in small groups. Groups of people, if those people meet with regularity and have some common interests or purpose, will develop insider language, jokes, symbols, and ways of interacting that may differ from other groups in which those same people participate. The social unit at this level of analysis only affects a small portion of one's daily life (a business office, a book group, or a poker club) or shapes a limited time of one's life (a Boy Scout troop or a gremlin soccer team for 8-year-old girls) (Gordon 1970). The social unit at the meso or macro level affects larger groups or societies and has more long-term impacts. So a microculture is *the culture that develops at the micro level in groups or organizations and affects only a segment of one's life or influences a limited period of one's life*. Other classic examples from sociology include a street gang, a college sorority, and a business office.

Hospitals are communities of people who share a microculture. People in different-colored uniforms scurry around carrying out their designated tasks, part of the division of labor in the organization, each having

Table 3.5   Material and Nonmaterial Cultural Patterns in Sport

Material objects	Balls: football, soccer ball, tennis ball, volleyball.
Nonmaterial cultural components	Competition and fair play.
Beliefs	Sports are healthy, create community around the sport. They express core American ideals of competition, work ethic, and the meritorious prevailing.
Values	One should support one's sports team—it is the best—and one should admire athletes.
Rules	Referees uphold the rules. Fans, players, and coaches sometimes challenge the refs' decisions, but are expected to engage in fair play.
Language or symbols	Each team has certain plays that it communicates by language or symbols. Supporters of teams use mascots, colors, and chants to cheer the team on.

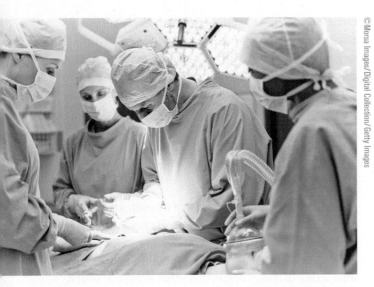

Hospitals provide one example of a microculture. Hospital employees share terminology, rules of interaction, and values regarding objectifying human body parts so that the patient is not sexualized.

symbolic significance indicating positions at the hospital. Hospital workers interact among themselves to attain goals of patient care. They have a common in-group vocabulary, a shared set of values, a hierarchy of positions with roles and behaviors for each position, and a guiding system of regulations for the organization—all of which shape interactions during the hours when each member works in the hospital. Yet the hospital microculture may have little relevance to the rest of the employees' everyday lives. Microcultures may survive over time, with individuals coming in and leaving as workers and patients, but in a complex society, no one lives his or her entire life within a microculture. The values, rules, and specialized language used by the hospital staff continue as one shift ends and other medical personnel enter and sustain that microculture.

Every organization, club, and association is a social group and therefore must have a culture (a microculture) with its own set of rules and expectations. Schools develop their own unique cultures and traditions; as students graduate and move out of that microculture, others move into it. Many microcultures exist for a limited time or for a special purpose. A summer camp microculture may develop but exists only for that summer. The following summer, a very different culture may evolve because of new counselors and campers. A girls' softball team may develop its own cheers, jokes, insider slang, and values regarding competition or what it means to be a good sport, but next year, the girls may be realigned into different teams, and the transitory culture of the previous year

changes. In contrast to microcultures, subcultures continue across a person's life span.

Subcultures and Countercultures: Meso-Level Analysis

A subculture *is the culture of a meso-level subcommunity that distinguishes itself from the dominant culture of the larger society.* A subculture is smaller than a nation but, unlike a microculture, is large enough to support people throughout the life span—such as an ethnic group. A subculture is in some ways unique to the smaller group yet at the same time shares the culture of the dominant society (Arnold 1970; Gordon 1970). Many ethnic groups within the larger society have their own subculture with their own sets of conventions and expectations. For example, picture a person who is African Canadian, Chinese Canadian, or Hispanic Canadian, living within an ethnic community that provides food, worship, and many other resources. Despite unique cultural traits, that person is still a Canadian citizen, living within the national laws, norms, and way of life. It is just that the person's life has guidelines from the subculture in addition to the dominant culture of the society.

Because the social unit, such as the ethnic groups mentioned above, plays a more long-term and pervasive role in the life span of group members than a summer camp or a sorority (microcultures), we analyze subcultures at the meso level. (Table 3.6 illustrates the connection between the social unit at each level and the type of culture at that level.)

Note that many of the categories into which we group people are not subcultures. For example, redheads, left-handed people, tall people, individuals who read *Wired* magazine, people who are single, visitors to Chicago, and DVD watchers do not make up subcultures because they do not interact as social units or share a common way of life. A motorcycle gang, a college fraternity, and a summer camp are also not subcultures because they affect only a segment of one's life (Gordon 1970; Yablonski 1959). A subculture, by contrast, is likely to influence a person throughout life. You may participate in many different groups with microcultures in a single day (the choir, a Greek organization, an athletic team, a classroom), but you are likely to live your entire life within the same subculture.

In the United States, subcultures include ethnic groups, such as Mexican American and Korean American; restricted religious groups, such as the Orthodox Jews in New York City; and social class groups, including the elite

Subculture: 1967 Hippie Temptation

Table 3.6   Level of Social Units and of Culture

Social Unit (People who interact and feel they belong)	Culture (The way of life of that social unit)
Dyads; small groups; local community	Microculture
Ethnic community or social class community	Subculture
National society	Culture of a nation
Global system	Global culture

upper class on the East and West Coasts of the United States. The superwealthy have networks, exclusive clubs, and the Social Register, which lists the names and phone numbers of the elite, so they can maintain contact with one another. They have a culture of opulence that differs from middle-class culture, and this culture is part of their experience throughout their lives.

Many societies have subcultures based on ethnicity or religion or other historical characteristics, but broad-based subcultures with extensive social networks can emerge in other ways as well. Perhaps the most fascinating is the deaf subculture in the United States, which is explained in the next "Sociology in Our Social World" on page 82.

A give-and-take exists between subcultures and the dominant culture, with each contributing to and influencing the other. Sometimes the differences between the two lead to tension and conflict. When conflict with the larger culture becomes serious and important norms of the dominant society are violated, a different type of culture emerges.

A **counterculture** is *a group with expectations and values that contrast sharply with the dominant values of a particular society* (Yinger 1960). An example of a counterculture is the Old Order Amish of Pennsylvania and Ohio. The Amish drive horse-drawn buggies and seldom use electricity or modern machines. They reject many mainstream notions of success and replace them with their own work values and goals. The Old Order Amish prefer to educate their children in their own communities, insisting that their children not go beyond an eighth-grade education in the public school curriculum. They also do not use automobiles or conventional tractors. The Amish are pacifists and will not serve as soldiers in the national military.

Other types of countercultures seek to withdraw from society, to operate outside its economic and legal systems, or even to bring about the downfall of the larger society. Examples include survivalist groups such as racist militia and skinheads, who reject the principles of

democratic pluralism. In the United States, the number of antigovernment "Patriot" groups who believe "that the

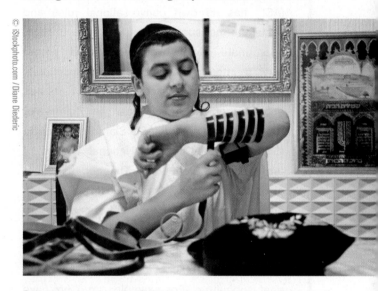

Subcultures, such as the Orthodox Jewish faith community, impact their members throughout life—from infancy to death. Here, an Orthodox Jewish boy prepares to pray according to Jewish law by wrapping the leather strap of his tefillin around his arm and a tallit (prayer shawl) around his shoulders.

The Amish, a counterculture, rejects important aspects of the mainstream or dominant culture—technology and consumerism—replacing it with biblical principles calling for a simple lifestyle.

Counterculture and the Mainstream   ▶ Amish Culture

sociology in our social world

Deaf Subculture in the United States

By Thomas P. Horejes

The deaf subculture possesses its own language, norms, and social networks that are unique to the deaf. American Sign Language (ASL) has its own conversational rules and social norms such as mandatory eye gaze, appropriate facial expressions, and proper ways to interject ideas. Like other subcultures, the deaf subculture celebrates its own arts and entertainment, including Deaf View/Image Art (De'VIA), deaf poetry (ASL Slam), deaf music (Signmark), deaf theater (National Theatre of the Deaf and Deaf West Theatre), and deaf cinema (WORLDEAF Cinema Festival). The arts and entertainment of the deaf subculture are often expressed visually through perspectives, experiences, and/or metaphors only understood by those who are fluent in ASL and a part of the deaf subculture. For example, *"true biz have VP? GA to SK no more? PAH!"* would probably get a chuckle from someone who is immersed in the deaf subculture. Additionally, there are social gatherings and events by associations within the deaf subculture that host annual conferences and tournaments ranging from the Deaf World Softball Championships, to the National Black Deaf Advocates, to the Rainbow Alliance of the Deaf (an LGBTQ organization). As with other subcultures, there is a deaf history and heritage that is passed on from generation to generation.

Many of the 5% to 10% of deaf children born to deaf parents are immediately enculturated into their own deaf subculture. In contrast, a large majority (90%–95%) of deaf children (including myself, born to hearing parents) start with an identity from the larger world (hearing society). As we progress throughout life, however, our identities become negotiated as we become more aware of a subculture—a deaf subculture that each of us has embraced quite differently. Some reject the deaf subculture in favor of total immersion into hearing society while others navigate in the deaf subculture, but in different ways. In addition to those born deaf, there are many individuals who become deaf later in life whether it is due to age, illness, or even prolonged exposure to loud sounds.

Regardless of how one becomes deaf, some individuals rely on technology (hearing aids or cochlear implants), communicate with hearing individuals via spoken/written English or through an ASL interpreter, and express willingness to work in the workplace dominated by members of the hearing society. Other deaf individuals become fully immersed into the deaf subculture or what they call the deaf "world." They may attempt to depart from the hearing culture by rejecting values and beliefs possessed by the hearing society, such as assistive-listening devices and speech therapy, and by not placing their deaf child in hearing schools. These people typically attend only deaf plays, read about deaf history, take on jobs where communication is through sign language, and forbid any voiced English in favor of equal "access" in all aspects their daily activities. There are also numerous people who become situated on the margins and/or the borderlands between the hearing world and the deaf subculture. They do not seem fully welcome in either social space.

It is possible to navigate through the deaf social landscapes in different phases of one's life. For example, some deaf people may immerse themselves into the counterculture at one time in their lives after being isolated from the dominant culture. Others come from a strong deaf culture and deaf "world" (those whose entire family is deaf) and are later immersed into the hearing world with peers from a different culture. Still others grow up being the only deaf person in a family, not having learned

any sign language. One common denominator in shaping deaf identity and deaf subculture is language: the incorporation or lack of sign language in the deaf individual's life.

Thomas P. Horejes received his PhD at Arizona State University in justice studies and teaches sociology at Gallaudet University, the world's only university with programs and services specifically designed to accommodate students who are deaf or hard of hearing. He is the author of Social Constructions of Deafness: Examining Deaf Languacultures in Education.

federal government is conspiring to take Americans' guns and destroy their liberties as it paves the way for a global 'one-world government'" has increased dramatically over the past decade (Potok 2013b).

Some countercultures such as the Amish continue over time and can sustain members throughout their life cycle. Like subcultures, they operate at the meso level but reject mainstream culture. However, many countercultural groups, such as punk rock groups or violent and deviant teenage gangs, are short-lived or are relevant to people only at a certain age—operating only at the micro level.

Countercultures are not necessarily bad for society. According to conflict theory, which was introduced in Chapter 2, the existence of counterculture groups is clear evidence that there are contradictions or tensions within a society that need to be addressed. Countercultures often challenge the unfair treatment of groups in society that do not hold power and sometimes develop into social organizations or protest groups. Extremist religious and political groups, whether Christian, Islamic, Hindu, or any other, may best be understood as countercultures against Western or global influences that they perceive as threatening to their way of life. Figure 3.4 illustrates the types of cultures in the social world and the relationship between countercultures and their national culture. Countercultures, as depicted, view themselves and are viewed by others as "fringe" groups—partial outsiders within a nation.

Thinking Sociologically

Describe a counterculture group whose goals are at odds with those of the dominant culture. Do you see any evidence to show that the group is influencing behavioral expectations and values in the larger society? What effect, if any, do countercultures have on your life?

National and Global Culture: Macro-Level Analysis

Canada is a national society, geographically bounded by the mainland United States to the south, the Pacific Ocean

FIGURE 3.4 Cultures at Various Levels in the Social World

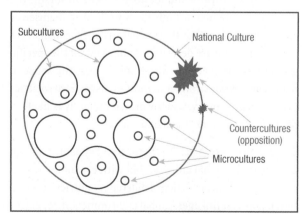

and Alaska to the west, the Atlantic Ocean to the east, and the Arctic to the north. The government in Ottawa passes laws that regulate activities in all provinces (which are similar to states or prefectures), and each province passes its own laws on regional matters. These geographic boundaries and political structures make up the national society of Canada.

National Society and Culture. The national society, introduced in Chapter 1, is a population of people, usually living within a specified geographic area, who are connected by common ideas, cooperate for the attainment of common goals, and are subject to a particular political authority. Within the nation, there may be smaller groups, such as ethnic, regional, or tribal subcultures, made up of people who identify closely with each other. Most nations have a national culture of *common values and beliefs that tie citizens of a nation together.* The national culture affects the everyday lives of most citizens. For example, within some countries of Africa and the Middle East, local ethnic or religious loyalties are much stronger than any sense of national culture, in part because the nation-state boundaries were originally imposed by foreign colonial powers. However, subcultural differences divide many nations. Consider the loyalties of Shiites, Sunnis, and Kurds in Iraq to their subcultures, where the national culture struggles for influence over its citizens through laws, traditions, and military force.

In colonial America, people thought of themselves as Virginians or Rhode Islanders rather than as U.S. citizens. Even during the "War Between the States" of the 1860s, the battalions were organized by states and often carried their state banners into battle. The fact that some Southern states still call it the War Between the States rather than the Civil War communicates the struggle over whether to recognize the nation or states as the primary social unit of loyalty and identity. People in the United States today are increasingly likely to think of themselves as U.S. citizens (rather than as Iowans or Floridians), yet the national culture determines only a few of the specific guidelines for everyday life. Nonetheless, the sense of nation has grown stronger in most industrialized societies over the past century, and the primary identity is likely to be "United States" or "Canadian" citizen.

Global Society and Culture. Several centuries ago there was no "global culture," but with expanding travel, economic interdependence of different countries, international political linkages, global environmental concerns, and technology allowing for communication throughout the world, people now interact across continents in seconds. Globalization refers to *the process by which the entire world is becoming a single sociocultural entity— more uniform, more integrated, and more interdependent* (Pieterse 2004; Robertson 1997; Robertson and Scholte 2007). Globalization is a process of increased connectedness, uniformity, and interdependency across the planet (Eitzen and Zinn 2012).

Western political and economic structures dominate in the development of this global society, largely as a result of the domination of Western (European and U.S.) worldviews and Western control over resources. For example, the very idea of governing a geographic region with a bureaucratic structure known as a nation-state is a fairly new notion. Formerly, many small bands and tribal groupings dominated areas of the globe. However, with globalization, nation-states now exist in every region of the world.

Global culture includes *behavioral standards, symbols, values, and material objects that have become common across the globe* (International Beliefs and Values Institute 2012). We need to understand global culture to engage in human rights issues, global education, conflict resolution, sustainability, and religious and cultural understanding. For example, beliefs that monogamy is normal; that marriage should be based on romantic love; that people have a right to life, liberty, and the pursuit of happiness; that people should be free to choose their leaders; that women should have rights such as voting; that wildlife and fragile environments should be protected; and that everyone should have a cell phone and television set are spreading across the globe (Newman 2009).

During the 20th century, the idea of the primacy of individual rights, civil liberties, and human rights spread around the world, creating conflicts within nations that traditionally lack democratic institutions and processes. Backlashes against these and other Western ideas also can be seen in the acts of groups that have embraced terrorism (Eitzen and Zinn 2012; Kurtz 2007; Turner 1991a, 1991b). This has resulted in Western societies scapegoating, or blaming, certain groups for economic and social crises, when those groups see themselves as trying to preserve their culture (Morey and Yaqin 2011; Peek 2011).

Still, these trends are aspects of the emerging global culture. Even 100 years ago, notions of global cooperation and competition would have seemed quite bizarre (Lechner and Boli 2005). However, in nations all over the globe, people who travel by plane know they must stand in line, negotiate airport security, squeeze their bodies into confined spaces, and stay seated in the airplane until they are told they can get up (Lechner and Boli 2005). Regardless of nationality, we know how to behave in any airport in the world.

As the world community becomes more interdependent and addresses issues that can only be dealt with at the global level (such as global warming, pirates from Somalia and other countries, massive human rights violations as in the Syrian revolution or Sudanese war, international terrorism, global food shortages, and global financial crises), the idea of a common "software" of beliefs, social rules, and common interests takes on importance. Common ideas for making decisions allow for shared solutions to conflicts. Global culture at the macro level affects our individual lives, and its influence will only increase.

However, global culture is not the only pattern that is new. Today, we see a counterculture at the global level. Stateless terrorist networks such as al-Shabaab, al-Qaeda, and the Taliban reject the values of international organizations such as the World Court, the Geneva Convention, and other international systems designed to resolve disputes. Terrorists do not recognize the sovereignty of nations and do not acknowledge many values of respect for life or for civil discourse. This counterculture at the global level is a more serious threat than those at the micro and meso levels, in part because they do not fit into the global system of nations and its norms. (See the discussion of terrorism in Chapter 13.)

Thinking Sociologically

Make a list of social units of which you are a part. Place these groups into categories of microculture, subculture, national culture, and global culture. Consider which of them affects only a portion of your day or week (such as your place of work) or only a very limited time in your entire life span. Consider which groups are smaller than the nation but will likely influence you over much of your life. To what cross-national (global) groups do you belong? Do you belong to fewer groups at the national culture and global culture levels? If so, why do you suppose that is the case?

THEORIES OF CULTURE

Cultural Theory at the Micro Level

To understand our interactions with family and friends, we turn to the micro level of analysis. Although external forces at the national and global (macro) levels shape us in

Many simple norms or beliefs about how to behave in public—like waiting in line for a train—have become accepted in cultures throughout the world.

many ways, that is not the whole story as we see when we examine the symbolic interaction approach to culture.

Symbolic Interaction Theory. How amazing it is that babies learn to share the ideas and meanings of complex cultures with others in those cultures. Symbolic interaction theory considers how we learn to share the meanings of symbols, whether material or nonmaterial. Culture is about symbols, such as rings, flags, and words that stand for or represent something. A ring means love and commitment. A flag represents national identity and is intended to evoke patriotism and love for one's country. A phrase such as *middle class* conjures up images and expectations of what the phrase means, a meaning shared with others in our group. Together in our groups and societies, we define what is real, normal, and good.

Symbolic interaction theory maintains that our humanness comes from the impact we have on each other through these shared understandings of symbols that humans have created. When people create symbols, such as a new greeting (e.g., a fist bump instead of a handshake) or a symbolic shield for a fraternity or sorority, symbols come to have an existence and importance for the group.

Symbolic interaction theory pictures humans as consciously and deliberately creating their personal and collective histories. The theory emphasizes the part that verbal and nonverbal language and gestures play in the shared symbols of individuals and the smooth operation of society. More than any other theory in the social sciences, symbolic interaction stresses the active decision-making

 Symbolic Interaction

role of individuals—the ability of individuals to do more than conform to the larger forces of the society.

Many of our definitions of what is "normal" are shaped by what others around us define as "normal" or "good." The **social construction of reality** *is the process by which individuals and groups shape reality through social interaction.* Our construction of reality, influenced by our social relations, has a profound effect on our daily lives, our life chances, and what we believe is possible in our lives. One illustration of this is the notion of what is beautiful or ugly. In the late 18th and early 19th centuries, in Europe and the United States, beaches were considered eyesores since there was nothing there but crushed stone and dangerous water. A beach was not viewed as a place to relax in a beautiful environment. Likewise, when early travelers to the West encountered the Rocky Mountains, with soaring granite rising to snowcapped peaks, the idea was that these were incredibly ugly wounds in the earth's surface. The summits were anything but appealing. Still, over time, some individuals began to redefine these crests as breathtakingly beautiful. We now see both as beautiful, but the social construction of scenery has not always been so (Lofgren 1999, 2010). So even what we experience as relaxing and peaceful in nature is shaped by how our society constructs those experiences.

This notion that individuals shape culture and that culture influences individuals is at the core of the symbolic interaction theory. Other social theories tend to focus at the meso and macro levels.

In the late 1700s and early 1800s, this mountain view would have been considered an eyesore—too ugly to enjoy. The social construction of reality—the definition of what is beautiful in our culture—has changed dramatically over the past two centuries.

Design Pics Inc/National Geographic Creative

 Thinking Sociologically

Think about how you communicate with one or more of your close friends. What are some of the symbols you use to communicate with one another? How do these forms of communication indicate that you are close friends and help you feel connected to them?

Cultural Theories at the Meso and Macro Levels

How can we explain such diverse world practices as eating termites and worshipping cows? Why have some societies allowed men to have four wives, whereas others—such as the Shakers—prohibited sex between men and women entirely? Why do some groups worship their ancestors, while others have many gods, and yet others believe in a single divine being? How can societies adapt to extremes of climate and geographical terrain—hot, cold, dry, wet, mountainous, and flat? Humankind has evolved practices so diverse that it would be hard to find a practice that has not been adopted in some society at some time in history.

To explain these cultural differences, we will use two already familiar perspectives that have made important contributions to understanding culture at the meso and macro levels: structural-functional and conflict theories.

Structural-Functional Theory. Structural-functional theorists ask why members of an ethnic subculture or a society engage in certain practices. To answer, structural-functionalists look at how those practices contribute to the survival or social solidarity of the group or society as a whole. An example is the reverence for cattle in India. The "sacred cow" is protected, treated with respect, and not slaughtered for food. The reasons relate to India's ancient development into an agricultural society that required sacrifices (Harris 1989). Cattle were needed to pull plows and to provide a source of milk and dried dung for fuel. Cows gained religious significance because of their importance for the survival of early agricultural communities. They must, therefore, be protected from hungry people for the long-term survival of the group. Protecting cows was functional; that is, the practice served a purpose for society.

Functionalists view societies as composed of interdependent parts, each fulfilling certain necessary functions or purposes for the total society (Radcliffe-Brown 1935). Shared norms, values, and beliefs, for instance, serve the function of holding a social group together. At a global macro level, functionalists see the world moving in the direction of having a common culture, potentially reducing "we" versus "they" thinking and promoting unity across boundaries. Synthesis of cultures and even the loss of some cultures are viewed as a natural result of globalization.

Although most cultural practices serve positive functions for the maintenance and stability of society, some practices, such as slavery, may be functional for those in power (those using child labor) but dysfunctional for minority groups or individual members of society. The fact that some societies are weak or have died out suggests that their way of life may not have been functional in the long run. Consider the case of Haiti, a country weakened in part because all the forests have been cut down to provide firewood. The resulting erosion made much of the land unusable for growing crops and led to a scarcity of food (Diamond 2005). Add to the existing poverty and hunger the devastation brought about by the January 12, 2010, earthquake that damaged or destroyed most buildings. The country and its people must rely on external support and donations from other countries to survive as it tries to rebuild.

The functionalist perspective has been criticized because it fails to consider how much dysfunction a society has, how much conflict a society can tolerate, and how much unity is necessary for a society to survive. Some critics argue that functional theory overemphasizes the need for consensus and integration among different parts of society, thus ignoring conflicts that may point to problems such as inequality in societies (Dahrendorf 1959).

Conflict Theory. Whereas functionalists assume consensus exists because all people in society have learned the same cultural values, rules, and expectations, conflict theorists do not view culture as having this uniting effect. Conflict theorists describe societies as composed of meso-level groups—class, ethnic, religious, and political groups—vying for power. Each group protects its own self-interests and struggles to make its own cultural ways dominant in the society. Instead of consensus, the dominant groups may impose their cultural beliefs on minorities and other subcultural groups, thus laying the groundwork for conflict. Conflict theorists identify tension between meso and macro levels, whereas functionalists tend to focus on harmony and smooth integration between those levels.

Actually, conflict may contribute to a smoother-running society in the long run. German sociologist Georg Simmel believed that some conflict could serve a positive purpose by alerting societal leaders to problem areas that need attention (1955).

Conflict theorists believe that society is composed of groups, each acting to meet its own self-interests. One example is the conflict in Egypt in 2012 over who won a presidential election and where the country is headed in the future.

Conflict theorists argue that the people with privilege and power in society manipulate institutions such as religion and education. In this way, average people learn the values, beliefs, and norms of the privileged group and accept the dominant group's beliefs, self-interests, power, and advantage. The needs of the privileged are likely to be met, and their status will be secured. For instance, schools that serve lower-class children usually teach obedience to authority, punctuality, and respect for superiors—behaviors that make for good laborers and compliant workers. The children of the affluent, meanwhile, are more likely to attend schools stressing divergent thinking, creativity, and leadership, attributes that prepare them to occupy the most professional, prestigious, and highly rewarded positions in the society. Conflict theorists point to this control of the education process by those with privilege as part of the overall pattern by which the society benefits the rich.

Conflict theory can also help us understand global dynamics. Many poor nations feel that the global system protects the self-interests of the richest nations and that those rich nations impose their own culture, including their ideas about economics, politics, and religion, on the poorer nations of the global South. Some scholars believe there is great richness in local customs that is lost when homogenized by cultural domination of the powerful nations (Ritzer 2007; Eitzen and Zinn 2012).

Conflict theory is useful for analyzing the relationships between societies (at a macro level) and between subcultures (at a meso level) within complex societies. It also helps illuminate tensions in a society when local

Conflict in America: Immigrant Rights

(micro-level) cultural values clash with national (macro-level) trends. Conflict theory is not as successful, however, in explaining simple, well-integrated societies in which change is slow to come about and cooperation is an organizing principle.

THE FIT BETWEEN HARDWARE AND SOFTWARE

Computer software cannot work with incompatible machines. Some documents cannot be easily transferred to a different piece of hardware, although sometimes a transfer can be accomplished with significant modification in the formatting of the document. The same is true with the hardware of society and the software of culture. For instance, consider the size of families: the value (software) of having a large extended family, typical in agricultural societies, does not work well in the structure (hardware) of industrial and postindustrial societies that are mostly urban and crowded. Children in urban settings are generally a liability compared to those who work on the farm in agricultural societies. In short, there are limits to what can be transferred from one type of society to another, and the change or "formatting" may mean the new beliefs transferred to a different social setting are barely recognizable.

Attempts to transport U.S.-style "software" (culture)—individualism, capitalism, freedom of religion, and democracy—to other parts of the world illustrate that these ideas are not always successful in other settings. The hardware of other societies may be able to handle more than one type of software or set of beliefs, but there are limits to the adaptability. Thus, we should not be surprised when our ideas are transformed into something quite different when they are imported to another social system. If we are to understand the world in which we live and if we want to improve it, we must first fully understand other societies and cultures.

 Thinking Sociologically

Some anthropologists argue that *team sports*, groups playing each other in coordinated competition, were first developed by Native American groups. Yet team sports are now a core component of U.S. society. How does participating in team sports help prepare people to successfully navigate life in the United States? For example, what lessons learned through playing on an organized team might be relevant to life in the business world?

Because there is such variation among societies and cultures in what they see as *normal*, how do we learn our particular society's expectations? The answer is addressed in the next chapter. Each society relies on the process of **socialization** to teach the culture to its members. Humans go through a lifelong process of socialization to learn social and cultural expectations. The next chapter discusses the ways in which we learn our culture and become members of society.

WHAT HAVE WE LEARNED?

Individuals and small groups cannot live without the support of a larger society, the hardware of the social world. Without the software—culture—there could be no society, for there would be no norms to guide our interactions with others in society. Humans are inherently social and learn their culture from others. Furthermore, as society has evolved into more complex and multileveled social systems, humans have learned to live in and negotiate conflicts among multiple cultures, including those at micro (microcultures), meso (subcultures), and macro (societal and global cultures) levels. Life in an Information Age society demands adaptability to different sociocultural contexts and tolerance of different cultures and subcultures. This is a challenge to a species that has always had tendencies toward ethnocentrism.

KEY POINTS

- *Society* refers to an organized and interdependent group of individuals who live together in a specific geographic area, interact with each other more than with outsiders, cooperate to attain goals, and share a common culture over time. Each society has a culture, the way of life shared by a group of people, including ideas and "things" passed on from one generation to the next; the culture has both material and nonmaterial components. (See pp. 58–59.)

- Societies evolve from very simple societies to more complex ones, from the simple hunter-gatherer society to the information societies of the post-industrial world. (See pp. 59–67.)

- The study of culture requires that we try to avoid ethnocentrism (judging other cultures by the standards of our culture). Instead, we should use the view of cultural relativism, so that we can understand culture from the standpoint of those inside it. (See pp. 71–73.)

- Just as social units exist at various levels of our social world, from small groups to global systems, cultures exist within different levels of the social system—microcultures, subcultures, national cultures, and global cultures. Some social units at the micro or meso level stand in opposition to the dominant national culture, and they are called counter-cultures. (See pp. 79–85.)

- Various theories offer different lenses for understanding culture. While symbolic interaction illuminates the way humans bring meaning to events (thus generating culture), the functionalist and conflict paradigms examine cultural harmony and conflict between cultures, respectively. (See pp. 85–88.)

- The metaphor of hardware (society's structure) and software (culture) describes the interdependent relationship of society and culture, and, as with computers, there must be some compatibility between the structure of a society and the culture. If there is none, either the cultural elements that are transported into another society will be rejected, or the culture will be "reformatted" to fit the society. (See pp. 88.)

DISCUSSION QUESTIONS

1. Think about the evolution of societies described in this chapter. In which type of society (hunter-gatherer, herding, horticultural, agricultural, industrial, or postindustrial) would you prefer to live? Why? In which would you most likely be (a) economically successful and (b) content? Why?

2. This chapter points out that today material culture "drives the globalization process." Look around at what your classmates are wearing and carrying and come up with some examples that support that point.

3. Think of a subculture to which you belong. What are the norms, values, and material artifacts that distinguish members of your subculture from those who do not belong to it?

4. Every classroom has norms of behavior. Some are mores, and some are folkways. Describe two of each in a typical classroom at your school. How are both enforced? How do you help enforce these norms?

5. Are you part of a counterculture? Why or why not? In what ways might a counterculture benefit a society?

VISUAL SOCIOLOGY: *HOME AS MATERIAL CULTURE*

© Keith Roberts

Homes are good examples of material culture. Their construction is influenced not only by local materials but also by ideas of what a home is. Homes shape the context in which family members interact, so they can influence the nonmaterial culture—including beliefs, values and symbols. Houses, like clothes, act as symbols that communicate levels of prestige. Visit **edge .sagepub.com/ballantine5e** for an interactive photo essay about homes as material culture.

CONTRIBUTING TO OUR SOCIAL WORLD: *WHAT CAN WE DO?*

At the Local and National Levels

- *Ethnic group* organizations and clubs focus on the interests of specific ethnic groups: Arab Americans, Chinese Americans, Italian Americans, Polish Americans, and so on. You may have one or more on your own campus. Contact one of these groups (of your own background or of a background that differs from your own). Arrange to attend one of the group's meetings, and learn about the subculture and activities in which its members are involved. To find an ethnic association on campus, call your campus activities office. To find one in your local area, try Googling the name of the ethnic group, "club," and the name of your town or city.

- *Immigrant aid groups* are ethnically oriented organizations that assist recent immigrants in dealing with adjustment to life in a new country. Contact one of these groups, and explore the possibility of volunteering or serving as an intern. You should be able to determine if one is in your area by Googling the

name of your town or city, the name of the ethnic group, and "immigrant aid group."

At the Global Level

- *The United Nations Permanent Forum on Indigenous Issues* assists indigenous people around the world who face threats to their cultures, languages, and basic rights as the process of globalization accelerates. We have experienced this in North America in relation to Native American and Inuit populations, but it is occurring throughout the world. Visit the forum's website at http://undesadspd.org/ IndigenousPeoples.aspx, and contact the forum about the possibility of volunteering.

- *Cultural Survival* is an example of a leading nongovernmental organization (NGO) engaged in action-oriented programs. It partners with indigenous people to "defend their lands, languages, and cultures." Look at its website (www.cs.org) for internship and volunteer opportunities.

© REUTERS/ Lucy Nicholson

4 Socialization

Becoming Human and Humane

Whether at the micro, meso, or macro level, our families, friends, associates, and various organizations teach us how to be human and humane in our society. Skills are taught, as well as values such as loyalty and compassion, by watching others.

MICRO

ME (MY FAMILY AND CLOSEST FRIENDS)

LOCAL ORGANIZATIONS AND COMMUNITY

Families and friends serve as agents of socialization.

MESO

NATIONAL ORGANIZATIONS, INSTITUTIONS, AND ETHNIC SUBCULTURES

Citizens are socialized for national loyalty and patriotism.

MACRO

SOCIETY

Political parties and religious denominations transmit values.

GLOBAL COMMUNITY

People are socialized for tolerance and respect across borders.

IN THIS CHAPTER

- Nature *Versus* Nurture—or *Both* Working Together?

- The Importance of Socialization

- Socialization and the Social World

- Development of the Self: Micro-Level Analysis

- Agents of Socialization: The Micro–Meso Connection

- Socialization and Macro-Level Issues

- Policy and Practice

THINK ABOUT IT

Micro: Local Community	What does it mean to have a "self"? How have your family, local religious congregation, and schools shaped who you are?
Meso: National Institutions, Complex Organizations, Ethnic Groups	How do various subcultures or organizations of which you are a member (your ethnic group, political party, or religious affiliation) influence your position in the social world?
Macro: National and Global Systems	What would you be like if you were raised in a different country? How might globalization or other macro-level events—such as a terrorist attack on your country—impact you and your sense of self?

Phoebe Prince was a 15-year-old immigrant from Ireland. She and her family had recently settled in South Hadley, Massachusetts, and she enrolled in the high school. Unfortunately, she made a mistake! She dated a popular senior on the football team. This was not acceptable to a clique of girls who had it out for Phoebe. These "mean girls" sent her threatening text messages, threw things at her, called her "Irish slut" and "whore" on social networking sites such as Facebook and Twitter, and engaged in other bullying behaviors. Other students and even faculty who were aware of the bullying did nothing. After months of such treatment, one day the "mean girls" threw a can at Phoebe—and she went home and hung herself (Crime Library 2012).

Phoebe's story and stories of hundreds of other bullied and abused children point to a problem in the process of socialization, both in what the victim is experiencing and in what the perpetrators are doing. In this chapter we examine the process of socialization, how it involves development of our "self," and what can happen when socialization goes wrong.

Socialization is *the lifelong process of learning to become a member of the social world, beginning at birth and continuing until death*. It is a major part of what the family, education, religion, and other institutions do to prepare individuals to be members of their social world. In Phoebe's case, she had a negative socialization experience from peers, resulting in a damaged self-concept.

From the day they are born, infants are interactive, ready to be socialized into membership in the social world. As they cry, coo, or smile, they gradually learn that their behaviors elicit responses from other humans. This interaction is *the exchange of verbal and nonverbal messages that form the basic building block of socialization through which a child learns its culture and becomes a member of society*. This process of interaction shapes the infant into a human being with a social self—the perception we have of who we are.

Three main elements provide the framework for socialization: human biological potential, culture, and individual experiences. Babies enter this world unsocialized, totally dependent on others to meet their needs, and completely lacking in social awareness and an understanding of the rules of their society. Despite this complete vulnerability, they have the potential to learn the language, norms, values, and skills needed in their society. Socialization is necessary not only for the survival of the individual but also for the survival of society and its

Socialization starts at the beginning of life as babies interact intensively with their parents, observing and learning what kinds of sounds or actions elicit response from the adults.

© Michelle Garrett/CORBIS

Socialization in Schools 📄

groups. The process continues in various forms throughout our lives as we enter and exit various positions—from school to work to retirement to death.

In this chapter, we explore the nature and importance of socialization and how individuals become socialized. We also look at development of the self, who or what socializes us, macro-level issues in the socialization process, and a policy example illustrating socialization. First, we briefly examine an ongoing debate: Which is more influential in determining who we are—our genes (nature) or our socialization into the social world (nurture)?

NATURE *VERSUS* NURTURE—OR *BOTH* WORKING TOGETHER?

What is it that makes us who we are? Is it our biological makeup or the family and community in which we grow up? One side of the contemporary debate regarding nature versus nurture seeks to explain the development of the self and human social behaviors—violence, crime, academic performance, mate selection, economic success, gender roles, and other behaviors—by examining biological or genetic factors (Harris 2009; Winkler 1991). Sociologists call this sociobiology, and psychologists refer to it as evolutionary psychology. Researchers in these fields claim that our human genetic makeup wires us for social behaviors (Wilson et al. 1978).

The idea is that we perpetuate our own biological family and the human species through our social behaviors. Human groups develop power structures, are territorial, and protect their kin. Examples of behaviors that sociobiologists see as rooted in the genetic makeup of the species include a mother ignoring her own safety to help a child, soldiers dying in battle for their comrades and countries, communities feeling hostility toward outsiders or foreigners, and people defending property lines against intrusion by neighbors. Sociobiologists say that these behaviors continue because they result in an increased chance of survival of the family and species as a whole (Lerner 1992; Lumsden and Wilson 1981; Wilson 1980, 1987).

Most sociologists believe that sociobiology and evolutionary psychology explanations have flaws. Sociobiology is a *reductionist* theory; that is, it often reduces complex social behaviors to single inherited traits such as an altruism gene, an aggression gene, or any other behavioral gene. However, evidence for such inherited traits is weak,

at best. Sociologists point to the fact that there are great variations in the way members of different societies and groups behave. People born in one culture and raised in another adopt social behaviors common to the culture in which they grow up, not based on inherited traits (Gould 1997). If a specific social behavior is genetic, then it should be present regardless of the culture in which humans are raised. What sets humans apart from other animals is not so much our biological heritage but our ability to learn the ways of our culture through socialization.

Most sociologists recognize that individuals are influenced by biology, which limits the range of human responses and creates certain needs and drives, but they believe that nurture is far more important. Some sociologists propose theories that consider both nature and nurture. Alice Rossi, former president of the American Sociological Association, has argued that we need to build both biological and social theories—or biosocial theories—into explanations of social processes such as parenting (Rossi 1984). One group of sociologists has developed an approach called evolutionary sociology, which takes seriously the way our genetic makeup—including a remarkable capacity for language—shapes our range of behaviors. However, biological research also shows that living organisms are often modified by their environments and the behaviors of others around them—with even biological or genetic structure changing due to social interaction and experiences (Dobbs 2013; Lopreato 2001; Machalek and Martin 2010).

In short, biology influences human behavior, but human action and interaction can also modify biological traits. For example, the nutritional history of grandparents can affect the metabolism of their grandchildren, and what grandparents ate was largely shaped by cultural ideas about food (BBC's Science and Nature 2009; Freese, Powell, and Steelman 1999). Our cultural values shape what we eat today and whether we share food with the less privileged in our society. The bottom line is that *socialization* is key in the process of "becoming human and becoming humane."

THE IMPORTANCE OF SOCIALIZATION

If you have lived on a farm, watched animals in the wild, or seen television nature shows, you probably have noticed that many animal young become independent shortly after birth. Horses are on their feet in a matter of hours, and by

▶ Music and Development

the time turtles hatch from eggs, their parents are long gone. Many species in the animal kingdom do not require contact with adults to survive because their behaviors are inborn and instinctual. Generally speaking, the more intelligent the species, the longer the period of gestation and of nutritional and social dependence on the mother and family. Humans clearly take the longest time to socialize their young. Even among primates, human infants have the longest gestation and dependency period, generally 6 to 8 years. Chimpanzees, very similar to humans in their DNA, take only 12 to 28 months.

Table 4.1 compares human infants and other primate babies. This extended dependency period for humans— what some have referred to as the *long childhood*—allows each human being time to learn the complexities of culture. This suggests that biology and social processes work together.

Normal human development involves learning to sit, crawl, stand, walk, think, talk, and participate in social interactions. Ideally, the long period of dependence allows children the opportunity to learn necessary skills, knowledge, and social roles through affectionate and tolerant interaction with people who care about them. Yet what happens if children are deprived of adequate care or even human contact? The following section illustrates the importance of socialization by showing the effect of deprivation and isolation on normal socialization.

Isolated and Abused Children

What would children be like if they grew up without human contact? Among the most striking examples are the few cases we know of severely abused and neglected children whose parents kept them isolated in cellars or attics for years without providing even minimal attention and nurturing. When these isolated children were discovered, typically they suffered from profound developmental disorders that endured throughout their lives (Curtiss 1977; Davis 1947). Most experienced great difficulty in adjusting to their social world's complex rules of interaction, which people normally start to learn from infancy onward.

In case studies comparing two girls, Anna and Isabelle, who experienced extreme isolation in early childhood, Kingsley Davis found that even minimal human contact made some difference in their socialization (Davis 1947). Both "illegitimate" girls were kept locked up by relatives who wanted to keep their existence a secret. Both were discovered at about age 6 and moved to institutions where they received intensive training. Yet the cases were different in one significant respect: Prior to her discovery by those outside her immediate family, Anna experienced virtually no human contact. She saw other individuals only when they left food for her. Isabelle, on the other hand, lived in a darkened room with her deaf-mute mother, who provided some human contact. Anna could not sit, walk, or talk and learned little in the special school in which she was placed. When she died from jaundice at age 11, she had learned the language and skills of a 2- or 3-year-old. Isabelle, on the other hand, did progress. She learned to talk and played with her peers. After 2 years, she reached an intellectual level approaching normal for her age but remained about 2 years behind her classmates in skill and competency levels. By age 14, she was attending regular school and participating in social activities (Davis 1940, 1947).

Contemporary cases of children neglected or abused in their family settings or forced into slavery, prostitution, or fighting wars reinforce the importance of early social

Table 4.1   Dependence on Adults Among the Primates

Primate Form	Pregnancy Period	Period of Absolute Nutritional Dependency on Mother or Mother-Surrogate	Nursing Period	Social Independence
Human	266 days	1 year or more	1–2 years	6–8 years
Ape: chimpanzee	235 days	3–6 months	2–3 months	12–28 months
Monkey: rhesus	166 days	1–3 weeks	2–4 weeks	2–4 months
Lemur	111–145 days	1–3 days	2–14 days	2–3 weeks

Note: Lemurs and monkeys, among the less complex members of the primate order, depend on adults for food for a much shorter time than do apes and humans. The period of dependence affords human infants time to absorb the extensive knowledge important to the survival of the species.

This African family shares a playful moment together as they interact with one another. Even in such carefree moments, parents act as socializing agents for their children.

interaction. Although not totally isolated, these children also experience problems and disruptions in the socialization process. They have to deal with socially toxic abusive, violent, and dead-end environments with harmful developmental consequences for children (War Child 2014). Consider the case of child soldiers. A recent video, *Invisible Children*, went viral on YouTube, showing the plight of these children kidnapped by Joseph Kony's Lord's Resistance Army into a world of drugs, sex, and violence (Terra Networks 2013). Most will have a difficult time integrating back into society—if they have the chance to do so—although there are organizations trying to help them.

These cases illustrate the devastating effects on socialization of isolation, neglect, and abuse early in life. Humans need more from their environments than food and shelter. They need positive contact, a sense of belonging, affection, safety, and someone to teach them knowledge and skills. This is children's socialization into the world, through which they develop a self. Before we examine the development of the self in depth, however, we consider the complexity of socialization in the multileveled (micro, meso, and macro) social world.

SOCIALIZATION AND THE SOCIAL WORLD

Ram, a first grader from India, had been in school in Iowa for only a couple of weeks. The teacher was giving the first test. Ram did not know much about what a test meant, but he rather liked school, and the red-haired girl next to him, Elyse, had become a friend. He was catching on to reading a bit faster than she was but she was better at the number exercises. They often helped each other learn while the teacher was busy with a small group in the front of the class. The teacher gave each child the test, and Ram saw that it had to do with numbers. He began to do what the teacher had instructed the children to do with the worksheet, but after a while, he became confused. He leaned over to look at the page Elyse was working on. She hid her sheet from him, an unexpected response. The teacher looked up and asked what was going on. Elyse said that Ram was "cheating." Ram was not quite sure what that meant, but it did not sound good. The teacher's scolding of Ram left him baffled, confused, and entirely humiliated.

This incident was Ram's first lesson in the individualism and competitiveness that govern Western-style schools. He was being socialized into a new set of values. In his parents' culture, competitiveness was discouraged, and individualism was equated with selfishness and rejection of community. Athletic events were designed to end in a tie so that no one would feel rejected. Indeed, a well-socialized person would rather lose in a competition than cause others to feel bad because they lost. Like Ram, each of us learns the values and beliefs of our culture. In Ram's case, he moved from one cultural group to another and had to adjust to more than one culture within his social world. At the micro level, most parents teach children proper behaviors to be successful in life, and peers influence children to "fit in" and have fun. In fact, the process of socialization in groups allows the self to develop as individuals learn to interact with others in their culture. Interaction theory, focusing on the micro level, forms the basis of this chapter, as you will see.

At the meso level, religious denominations and political groups teach their versions of the truth, and educational systems teach the knowledge and skills considered by leaders as necessary for functioning in society. At the nationwide macro level, television ads encourage viewers to be more masculine or feminine, buy products that will make them better and happier people, and join the military. From interactions with our significant others to dealing with government bureaucracy, most activities are part of the socialization experience that teaches us how to function in our society.

Keep in mind that socialization is a lifelong process. Even your grandparents are learning how to live at their stage of life. The process of socialization takes place at each level of analysis, linking the parts. Groups at each level have a stake in how we are socialized because they all need trained and loyal group members to survive. Organizations need citizens who have been socialized to devote the time, energy, and resources that these groups need to survive and meet their goals. For example, volunteer and charitable organizations cannot thrive unless people are willing to volunteer their energy, time, skills, and money. Lack of adequate socialization means social organizations will not receive the support they need to thrive or even, possibly, to survive.

Most perspectives on socialization focus on the micro level because socialization takes place in each individual. However, meso- and macro-level theories add to our understanding of how socialization prepares individuals for their roles in the larger social world. *Structural-functionalist perspectives* of socialization tend to see organizations at different levels supporting each other. For example, families often organize holidays around patriotic themes, such as a national independence day, or around religious celebrations. These activities can strengthen family members' commitment to the nation and buttress the moral values emphasized in churches, temples, and mosques. All these values, in turn, help prepare individuals to support national political and economic systems.

At the meso level, the purposes and values of organizations or institutions sometimes directly contrast with one another or conflict with other parts of the social system. From the *conflict perspective*, the linkages between various parts of the social world are based on competition with or even direct opposition to another part. Socialization into a nation's military forces, for example, stresses patriotism and ethnocentrism, sometimes generating conflict and hostility toward other groups and countries. Demands from various organizations for people's time, money, and energy may leave little to give to our religious communities or even our families. Each organization and unit competes to gain our loyalty in order to claim some of our resources.

Conflict can occur in the global community as well. For example, religious groups often socialize their members to identify with humanity as a whole ("the family of God"). However, in some cases, nations do not want

their citizens socialized to identify with those beyond their borders. Leaders of nations may seek to persuade Christians to kill other Christians, Jews, or Muslims whom they define as "the enemy." If religion teaches that all people are "brothers and sisters" and if religious people object to killing, the nation may have trouble mobilizing its people to arms when the leaders call for war.

Conflict theorists believe that those who have power and privilege use socialization to manipulate individuals to support the power structure and the self-interests of the elite. Those in power have significant influence on the socialization of others through schools and political institutions. Although individuals may not realize it, most have little control over their futures. For example, parents decide how they would like to raise their children and what values they want to instill in them, but as soon as their children enter school, parents must share the socialization process with school personnel. One reason why some parents choose to homeschool their children is to control external influences on the socialization process.

Whether we stress harmony in the socialization process or conflict rooted in power differences, the development of a sense of self through the process of socialization is an ongoing, lifelong process. Let us now focus on the micro level: How does the *self* develop?

 Thinking Sociologically

Although the socialization process occurs primarily at the micro level, it is influenced by events at each level in the social system. Give examples of family, community, subcultural, national, or global events that influenced how you were socialized or how you might socialize your child.

DEVELOPMENT OF THE SELF: MICRO-LEVEL ANALYSIS

A baby is born with the potential to develop a *self*, but that self can evolve in many directions. Think of a baby you have observed; what influences that baby from birth? Can you see how those influences contribute to the developing self? The main product of the socialization process is *the self*. Fundamentally, self refers to *the perceptions we have of who we are*. Throughout the socialization process, our self develops largely from the way others respond to us—praising us, disciplining us, ignoring us. The development of the self allows individuals to interact with other people and to learn to function at each level of the social world.

Humans are not born with a sense of self. It develops gradually, beginning in infancy and continuing throughout adulthood. Selfhood emerges through interaction with others. Individual biology, culture, and social experiences all play a part in shaping the self. The hereditary blueprint each person brings into the world provides broad biological outlines, including particular physical attributes, temperament, and a maturational schedule. Each person is also born into a family that lives within a particular culture, illustrating that nature is shaped by nurture. This hereditary blueprint, in interaction with family and culture, helps create each unique person, different from any other person yet sharing the types of interactions by which the self is formed.

Most sociologists, although not all (Irvine 2004), believe that we humans are distinct from other animals in our ability to develop a self and to be aware of ourselves as individuals or objects. Consider how we refer to ourselves in the first person—*I* am hungry, *I* feel foolish, *I* am having fun, and *I* am good at basketball. We have a conception of who we are, how we relate to others, and how we differ from and are separate from others in our abilities and limitations. We have an awareness of the characteristics, values, feelings, and attitudes that give us our unique sense of self (James [1890] 1934; Mead [1934] 1962).

Thinking Sociologically

Who are some of the people who have been most significant in shaping your *self*? How have their actions and responses helped shape your self-concept as musically talented, athletic, intelligent, kind, assertive, clumsy, or any of the other hundreds of traits that might make up your self?

The Looking-Glass Self and Role-Taking

Ty: "Hi! What's up?" (Ty has had his eye on this girl in his class, so approaches her before class)

Valerie: "Nothin' much."

Ty: "So what do you think of our sociology class?"

Valerie: "It's OK." (She turns around, spots a friend, and walks away) "Hey Julie, did you get your soc assignment done?"

Ty is left to reflect on how to interpret Valerie's response. Take this common interaction and apply it to interactions you have had. First you approach someone and open a conversation (or someone approaches you); second, the person takes you up on the conversation—or not; third, you evaluate the individual's response and modify your behavior based on your interpretation. These steps make up the *looking-glass self,* and they are repeated many times each day. We now explore these seemingly simple interactions that are key in developing our *self* and our socialization process.

The looking-glass self idea is part of *symbolic interaction theory,* and offers important insights into how individuals develop the self. Two of the major scholars in this approach were Charles H. Cooley ([1909] 1983) and George Herbert Mead ([1934] 1962). Cooley believed that the self is a social product, shaped by interactions with others from the time of birth. He likened interaction processes to looking in a mirror wherein each person reflects an image of the other.

Each to each a looking-glass

Reflects the other that doth pass. (Cooley [1909] 1983:184)

For Cooley, the **looking-glass self** is a *reflective process that develops the self based on our interpretations and on our internalization of the reactions of others* ([1909] 1983). In this process, Cooley believed that there are three principal elements, shown in Figure 4.1: (1) We imagine how we appear to others, (2) others judge our

FIGURE 4.1   The Looking-Glass Self Process of Self-Development

1. We imagine how we want to appear to others.
2. Others make judgments and respond.
3. We experience feelings and react based on our interpretations.

Recovering Reputations

appearance and respond to us, and (3) we react to that feedback. We experience feelings such as pride or shame based on this imagined judgment and respond based on our interpretation. Moreover, throughout this process, we actively try to manipulate other people's view of us to serve our needs and interests. This is one of the many ways we learn to be boys or girls—the image we see reflected back to us lets us know whether we have behaved in ways socially acceptable according to gender expectations. The issue of gender socialization in particular will be discussed in Chapter 9. Of course, this does not mean our interpretation of the other person's response is correct, but our interpretation does determine how we respond.

Our self is influenced by the many "others" with whom we interact, and each of our interpretations of their reactions feeds into our self-concept. Recall that the isolated children failed to develop this sense of self precisely because they lacked interaction with others.

Taking the looking-glass self idea a step further, Mead explained *that individuals take others into account by imagining themselves in the position of that other*, a process called **role-taking**. When children play mommy and daddy, doctor and patient, or firefighter, they are imagining themselves in another's shoes. Role-taking allows humans to view themselves from the standpoint of others. This requires mentally stepping out of our own experience to imagine how others experience and view the social world. Through role-taking, we begin to see who we are from the standpoint of others. In short, role-taking allows humans to view themselves as objects, as though they were looking at themselves through the eyes of another person. For Mead, role-taking is a prerequisite for the development of our sense of self. The next "Sociology in Our Social World" illustrates the looking-glass self process for African American males. This situation experienced by Brent Staples vividly illustrates the impact of others on us.

Mead also argued that role-taking is possible because humans have a unique ability to use and respond to symbols ([1934] 1962). *Symbols*, first described in Chapter 2, are actions or objects that represent something else and therefore have meaning beyond their own existence. Language and gestures are examples, for they carry specific meaning for members of a culture. Symbols such as language allow us to give names to objects in the environment and to infuse those objects with meanings. Once the person learns to symbolically recognize objects in the environment, the self can be seen as one of those objects. This starts with possessing a name that allows us to see our self as separate from other objects. If we said the name LeBron James, most listeners would immediately think of the same person: an extraordinary athlete who largely turned around the fortunes of the Miami Heat professional basketball team to win back-to-back NBA championships.

In the process of symbolic interaction, we take the actions of others and ourselves into account. We may blame, encourage, praise, punish, or reward ourselves. An example would be a basketball player missing the basket because the shot was poorly executed and thinking, "What did I do to miss that shot? I'm better than that!" Reflexive behavior, being able to look at oneself and one's behaviors as though from the outside looking in, includes the simple act of taking mental notes or mentally talking to one's self.

Parts of the Self

According to the symbolic interaction perspective, the self is composed of two distinct but related parts—dynamic parts in interplay with one another (Mead [1934] 1962). The most basic element of the self is what George Herbert Mead refers to as the **I**, *the spontaneous, unpredictable, impulsive, and largely unorganized aspect of the self*. The *I* initiates behavior without considering the possible social consequences. We can see this at work in the "I want it now" behavior of a newborn baby or even a toddler. Cookie Monster on the children's television program *Sesame Street* illustrates the *I* in every child, gobbling cookies at every chance and insisting on more *now*.

The *I* continues as part of the self throughout life, tempered by the social expectations that surround individuals. In stages, humans become increasingly influenced by interactions with others who instill society's rules. Children develop the ability to see their *self* as others see them (role-taking), allowing them to critique the behavior that was initiated by the *I*. Mead called this reflective capacity of the self the *Me*. The **Me** is *the part of the self that has learned the rules of society through interaction and role-taking, and it controls the I and its desires*. Just as the *I* initiates the act, the *Me* gives direction to the act. In a sense, the *Me* channels the impulsive *I* in an acceptable manner according to societal rules and restraints, yet meets the needs of the *I* as best it can. When we stop ourselves just before saying something and think to ourselves, "I'd better not say that," it is our *Me* monitoring and controlling the *I*. Notice that the *Me*

Imposters 🎙

sociology in our social world

Black Men and Public Space

By Brent Staples

Many stereotypes—rigid images of members of a particular group—surround the young African American male in the United States. How these images influence the young men and their social world is the subject of this feature. Think about the human cost of stereotypes and their effect on the socialization process as you read the following essay. If your sense of self is profoundly influenced by the ways others respond to you, how might the identity of a young African American boy be affected by public images of black males?

* * * * * * *

My first victim was a woman—white, well dressed, probably in her early-twenties. I came upon her late one evening on a deserted street in Hyde Park, a relatively affluent neighborhood in an otherwise mean, impoverished section of Chicago. As I swung onto the avenue behind her, she cast back a worried glance. To her, the youngish black man—broad, six-feet two-inches tall, with a beard and billowing hair, both hands shoved into the pockets of a bulky military jacket—seemed menacingly close. After a few more quick glimpses, she picked up her pace and was running in earnest. Within seconds, she disappeared into a cross street.

That was more than a decade ago. I was 22 years old, a graduate student newly arrived at the University of Chicago. It was in the echo of that terrified woman's footfalls that I first began to know the unwieldy inheritance I'd come into. . . . It was clear that she thought herself the quarry of a mugger, a rapist, or worse. Suffering a bout of insomnia, however, I was stalking sleep, not defenseless wayfarers. . . . I was surprised, embarrassed, and dismayed all at once. Her flight . . . made it clear that I was indistinguishable from the muggers who occasionally seeped into the area from the surrounding ghetto. That first encounter, and those that followed, signified that a vast, unnerving gulf lay between night-time pedestrians—particularly women—and me. And I soon gathered that being perceived as dangerous is a hazard in itself. I only needed to turn a corner into a dicey situation, or crowd some frightened, armed person in a foyer somewhere, or make an errant move after being pulled over by a policeman. Where fear and weapons meet—and they often do in urban America—there is always the possibility of death.

In that first year, my first away from my hometown, I was to become thoroughly familiar with the language of fear. At dark, shadowy intersections, I could cross in front of a car stopped at a traffic light and elicit the thunk, thunk, thunk, thunk of the driver—black, white, male, or female—hammering down the door locks. On less-traveled streets after dark, I grew accustomed to but never comfortable with people crossing to the other side of the street rather than pass me. Then there was

(Continued)

(Continued)

the standard unpleasantness with policemen, doormen, bouncers, cabdrivers, and those whose business it is to screen out troublesome individuals before there is any nastiness.

After dark, on the warren-like streets of Brooklyn where I live, I often see women who fear the worst from me. They seem to have set their faces on neutral, and with their purse straps strung across their chests bandolier style, they forge ahead as though bracing themselves against being tackled. I understand, of course, that . . . women are particularly vulnerable to street violence, and young black males are drastically overrepresented among the perpetrators of that violence. Yet these truths are no solace against the kind of alienation that comes of being ever the suspect. . . .

Over the years, I learned to smother the rage I felt at so often being taken for a criminal. Not to do so would surely have led to madness. I now take precautions to make myself less threatening.

I move about with care, particularly late in the evening. I give a wide berth to nervous people on the subway platforms during the wee hours. . . . I have been calm and extremely congenial on those rare occasions when I've been pulled over by the police.

On late-evening constitutionals, I employ what have proved to be excellent tension-reducing measures: I whistle melodies from Beethoven and Vivaldi and the more popular classical composers. Even steely New Yorkers hunching toward nighttime destinations seem to relax, and occasionally they even join in the tune. Virtually everybody seems to sense that a mugger wouldn't be warbling bright, sunny selections from Vivaldi's Four Seasons. It is my equivalent of the cowbell that hikers wear when they know they are in bear country.

• •

Source: Staples (2001).

Thinking Sociologically

Brent Staples goes out of his way to reassure others that he is harmless. What might be some other responses to this experience of having others assume one is dangerous and untrustworthy? How might one's sense of self be influenced by these responses of others? How are the looking-glass self and role-taking at work in this scenario?

requires the ability to take the role of the other, to anticipate the other's reaction.

Stages in the Development of the Self

The process of developing a social self occurs gradually and in stages. Mead identified three critical stages—(1) the imitation stage, (2) the play stage, and (3) the game stage—each of which requires the unique human ability to engage in role-taking (Mead [1934] 1962). In the imitation stage, *children under 3 years old are preparing for role-taking by observing others and imitating their behaviors, sounds, and gestures*. The play stage involves *a child, usually from 3 to 5, having the ability to see things (role-take) from the perspective of one person at a time: simple role-taking or playacting*. Listen to children who are 3 to 5 years old play together. You will notice that they spend most of their time telling each other what to do. One of them will say something like, "You be the mommy, and José can be the daddy, and Julie, you be the dog. Now you say 'Good morning, Dear,' and I'll say, 'How did you sleep?' and Julie, you scratch at the door like you want to go out." They will talk about their little skit for 15 minutes and then enact it, with the actual enactment

Childhood Development

taking perhaps 1 minute. Small children mimic or imitate role-taking based on what they have seen as they learn and practice future roles (Handel, Cahill, and Elkin 2007).

Society and its rules are initially represented by **significant others**—*parents, guardians, relatives, siblings, or important individuals whose primary and sustained interactions are especially influential.* That is why much of the play stage involves role-taking based on these significant people in the child's life. The child does not yet understand the complex relations and multiple role players in the social world outside the immediate family. Children may have a sense of how their mommy or daddy sees them, but children are not yet able to comprehend how they are seen by the larger social world. Lack of role-taking ability is apparent when children say inappropriate things such as "Why are you so fat?"

The third stage in the process of developing a social self, the **game stage**, begins *when a child develops the ability to take the role of multiple others concurrently and conform to societal expectations.* The child goes beyond the significant other such as the parent to value the opinion of all peers or expectations of the community.

Have you ever watched a team of young children play T-ball (a pre–Little League baseball game in which the children hit the ball from an upright rubber device that holds the ball), or have you observed a soccer league made up of 6-year-olds? If so, you have seen Mead's point illustrated vividly. In soccer (or football), 5- or 6-year-old children will not play their positions despite constant urging and cajoling by coaches. They all run after the ball, with little sense of their interdependent positions. Likewise, a child in a game of T-ball may pick up a ball that has been hit, turn to the coach, and say, "Now what do I do with it?" Most still do not quite grasp throwing it to first base, and the first-base player may actually have left the base to run for the ball. It can be hilarious for everyone except the coach, as a hit that goes 7 feet turns into a home run because everyone is scrambling for the ball.

Prior to the game stage, the vision of the whole process is not possible. When children enter the game stage at about age 7 or 8, they are developmentally able to play the roles of various positions and enjoy a complex game. Each child learns what is expected and the interdependence of roles because she or he is able, at this stage, to respond to the expectations of several people simultaneously (Hewitt and Schulman 2011; Meltzer 1978). This allows the individual to coordinate his or her activity with others.

Courtesy of Wendy Shermano

This child is learning both adult roles and empathy with others through play.

In moving from the play stage to the game stage, children's worlds expand from family and day care to neighborhood playmates, school, and other organizations. *This process gradually builds up a composite of societal expectations that the child learns from family, peers, and other organizations*, what Mead refers to as the **generalized other**. The child learns to internalize the expectations of society—the generalized other—over and above the expectations of any "significant others." Behavior comes to be governed by abstract rules ("no running outside of the baseline" or "no touching the soccer ball with your hands unless you are the goalie") rather than guidance from and emotional ties to a "significant other." Children become capable of moving into new social situations such as school, organized sports, and (eventually) the workplace to function with others in both routine and novel interactions.

©Ana Abejon/E+/Getty Images

Very young children who play soccer do not understand the role requirements of games. They all—including the goalie—want to chase after the ball. Learning to play positions is a critical step in socialization.

The common human experience of feeling embarrassed illustrates how the generalized other becomes internalized into one's conception of self. Making an inappropriate remark at a party or having another call undue attention to one's appearance can cause embarrassment. Feeling embarrassed may occur when one violates a social norm and then thinks about how others view that behavior. According to this role-taking view, we see ourselves as objects from the standpoint of others, and we judge ourselves accordingly. Very young children, however, do not feel embarrassment when they do things such as soiling their pants or making inappropriate comments because they have not incorporated the generalized other. They have not yet learned the perspective of others. The capacity to feel embarrassed is not only an indicator of having internalized the generalized other but also a uniquely human outcome of our role-taking ability (Hewitt and Schulman 2011; Koschate-Reis 2009).

As we grow, we identify with new in-groups such as a neighborhood, a college sorority, or the military. We learn new ideas and expand our understanding. Some individuals ultimately come to think of themselves as part of the global human community. Thus, for many individuals, the social world expands through socialization. However, some individuals never develop this expanded worldview, remaining narrowly confined and drawing lines between themselves and others who are different. Such narrow boundaries often result in prejudice against others.

Thinking Sociologically

Who are you? Write down 15 or 20 roles or attributes that describe who you are. How many of these items are characteristics associated with the *Me*—nouns such as *son, mother, student,* and *employee*? Which of the items are traits or attributes—adjectives such as *shy, sensitive, lonely, selfish,* and *vulnerable*? How do you think each of these was learned or incorporated into your conception of your *self*?

The Self and Connections to the Meso Level

In the preceding "Thinking Sociologically" exercise, we asked you to think about how you see yourself and what words you might use to portray yourself. If you were describing yourself for a group of people you did not know, we suspect that you would use mostly nouns describing a status or a social position within the society: *student, employee, athlete, violinist, daughter, sister, Canadian, Lutheran,* and so forth. To a large extent, our sense of who we are is rooted in social positions that are part of organizations and institutions in the society (Kuhn 1964; Stryker 1980). This is a key point made by what is referred to as the Iowa School of symbolic interaction: The *self* is relatively stable because we develop a core self—a stable inner sense of who we are regardless of the immediate setting in which we find ourselves. This core often centers on the most important social positions we hold in the larger structure of society. Your sense of core self may shape your sexual behavior, the honesty with which you conduct business with others, and whether you are willing to cheat on an exam—even though you may not be around other people of your moral or political persuasion at the time (Kuhn 1964; Stryker 1980, 2000; Stryker and Stratham 1985; Turner 2003).

The Chicago School of symbolic interactionism emphasizes the role of the *I* and focuses on individuals' involvement in their own development and their agency in creating their world. The Iowa School places somewhat more emphasis on the *Me*—on the role of others and the external social environment in shaping us (Carrothers and Benson 2003).

Socialization Throughout the Life Cycle

The naming ceremony begins with an introduction of the 6-week-old baby, followed by the rituals surrounding the naming and welcoming of the newcomer into his tribe in

Socialization in Sports

Nigeria, Africa. By 6 weeks, the baby is considered likely to survive and thus given a name and incorporated into the group. Markers such as the naming ceremony point to movement from one stage to the next in the socialization process: birth, naming ceremonies or christenings, starting school at age 5 or 6, officially joining a church or temple at early puberty, obtaining a driver's license at about age 16, becoming eligible for military draft, being able to vote at age 18 and drink alcohol at age 21, getting married, having children, developing a career, and retiring from the workforce. Most social scientists emphasize the importance of *rites of passage*—celebrations or public recognitions when individuals shift from one status to another. The importance of this shift resides in how others come to perceive the individual differently, the different expectations that others hold for the person, and changes in how the person sees himself or herself.

Socialization is a lifelong process with many small and large passages. Infants begin the socialization process at birth. In childhood, one rite of passage is a child's first day at school—entrance into the meso-level institution of education. This turning point marks a child's entry into the larger world. The standards of performance are now defined by the child's teachers, peers, friends, and others outside the home. Adolescence is an important stage in Western industrial and postindustrial societies, but this stage is far from universal. Indeed, it is largely an invention of complex societies over the past two centuries, characterized by extensive periods of formal education and dependency on parents (Papalia and Feldman 2011). Adolescence is, in a sense, a structurally produced mass identity crisis because Western societies lack clear rites of passage for adolescents. Teens come to view themselves as a separate and distinct group with their own culture, slang vocabulary, clothing styles, and opinions about appropriate sexual behavior and forms of recreation.

Most of our adult years are spent in work and home life, including marriage and parenting roles. It is not surprising, then, that graduation from one's final alma mater (whether it be high school, college, or graduate school), marriage, and acceptance of one's first full-time job serve as rites of passage into adulthood in modern societies.

 Thinking Sociologically

Find someone who has grown up in a different culture and ask her or him about rites of passage from adolescence to adulthood where she or he was raised. How are the patterns similar to or different from your own?

Even the retired and elderly members of society are constantly undergoing socialization and resocialization in the process of developing their sense of self. The type of society influences the socialization experience of the elderly and how they carry out their roles, as well as their status in society. Consider the changes that have taken place in the lifetimes of those born before 1945, as described by one group of elders.

If you were born before 1945:

We were born before television, before polio shots, frozen foods, Xerox, plastic contact lenses, Frisbees, and the Pill. We were born before credit cards, split atoms, laser beams and ballpoint pens; before pantyhose, dishwashers, clothes dryers, electric blankets, air conditioners in our homes, drip-dry clothes and before man walked on the moon. . . . We were before house husbands, gay rights, computer dating, dual careers, and commuter marriages. We were before day care centers, group therapy, and nursing homes. We never heard of FM radio, tape decks, electric typewriters, artificial hearts, word processors, yogurt, and guys wearing earrings. For us time sharing means togetherness—not computers and condominiums. A chip meant a piece of wood, hardware meant hardware and software wasn't even a word. . . . smoking was fashionable, grass was mowed, coke was a cold drink and pot was something you cooked in. And we were the last generation that was so dumb as to think that you needed a husband to have a baby.

Oh my, how the world has changed! (Grandpa Junior 2006)

The elderly are vitally important to the ongoing group in more settled agricultural societies. They are the founts of wisdom and carry group knowledge, experiences, and traditions valued in societies where little change takes place. In industrial and postindustrial countries, the number of the elderly is growing rapidly as medical science keeps people alive longer, diets improve, and diseases are brought under control. As of 2013, the average life expectancy in the United States was 76 for men and 81 for women ("U.S. Life Expectancy" 2013). Yet, in modern societies, social participation by the elderly often drops after retirement.

Retirement is a rite of passage to a new status, like that of marriage or parenthood, for which there is little preparation. As a result, retired people sometimes feel a sense of

📄 Aging Population   ▶ Aging in America

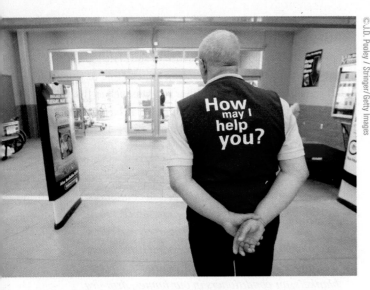

Some retirees, rather than taking up hobbies, decide on a part-time job, like this man who enjoys people and is now a "greeter" at a Walmart. Others take on a postretirement job because they need the income.

uselessness when they abruptly lose their occupational status. Retirees in Western societies generally have many years of life yet to live. The most socially satisfied retirees tend to develop hobbies, enjoy sports, or have new jobs they can pursue after they retire.

Dying is the final stage of life (Kübler-Ross 1997). Death holds different meanings in different cultures: passing into another life, a time of judgment, a waiting for rebirth, or a void and nothingness. In some religious groups, people work hard or do good deeds because they believe that they will be rewarded in an afterlife or with rebirth to a better status in the next life on earth. Thus, beliefs about the meaning of death can affect how people live their lives and how they cope with dying and death.

Each stage of the life cycle involves socialization into new roles in the social world. Many social scientists have studied these developmental stages and contributed insights into what happens at each stage (Clausen 1986; Erikson 1950; Freud [1923] 1960; Gilligan 1982; Handel et al. 2007; Kohlberg 1971; Papalia and Feldman 2011; Piaget 1989). For example, some sociologists focus their research on the study of old age (gerontology), and death and dying.

Death ends the lifelong process of socialization, a process of learning social rules and roles and adjusting to them. When the individual is gone, society continues. New members are born, are socialized into the social world, pass through roles once held by others, and eventually give up those roles to younger members. Cultures provide guidelines for each new generation to follow. The social world perpetuates itself and outlives the individuals who populate it.

Thinking Sociologically

How were you socialized to view death and dying? What have you learned in your family about how to cope with death? Is death a taboo topic for your family?

The Process of Resocialization

If you have experienced life in the military, a boarding school, a convent, a mental facility, or a prison, or had a major transition in your life such as divorce or the death of a spouse or child, you have experienced resocialization. **Resocialization** is *the process of shedding one or more social positions and taking on others, which involves learning new norms, behaviors, and values suitable to the newly acquired status* (Goffman 1961). Resocialization may take place in a **total institution**—*a place that cuts people off from the rest of society and totally controls their lives in the process of resocialization*. These include prisons, mental hospitals, monasteries, concentration camps, boarding schools, and military barracks. Bureaucratic regimentation and the manipulation of residents for the convenience of the staff is part of the routine (Goffman 1961).

We often associate resocialization with major developmental stages in adult life—leaving home to go to college, marriage, having a baby, divorce, retirement, and widowhood. Changes in status present opportunities to move in new and often exciting directions, such as going to college. Resocialization can also mean adjusting to living alone, raising children alone, loneliness, and possible financial problems. One divorcée of three years told the authors, "There are many things to commend the single life, but I still have not adjusted to eating alone and cooking for myself. Worse than that are Sunday afternoons. That is the loneliest time."

Sometimes, resocialization occurs when individuals are forced to correct or reform behaviors defined as undesirable or deviant. Prison rehabilitation programs provide one example. However, research suggests that the difficulty in resocializing prisoners is rooted in the nature of the prison environment itself. Prisons are often coercive and violent environments, which may not provide the social supports necessary for bringing about positive change in a person's attitudes and behaviors.

Resocialization of Mentally Ill Offenders ▶

Although resocialization is the goal of self-help groups such as Alcoholics Anonymous, Gamblers Anonymous, Parents Anonymous, drug rehabilitation groups, and weight loss groups, relapse is a common problem among participants. Some public sociologists work on trying to understand why there are such high rates of reversion to previous patterns of behavior. Former prison inmates are at especially high risk of repeating a crime, so public sociologists want to know what might make the resocialization "stick." In the next "Sociologists in Action" feature on page 108, David Kirk shows how he used lessons from the aftermath of Katrina to solve a puzzle and make policy recommendations.

There are multiple individuals, groups, and institutions involved in the socialization process. These socialization forces are referred to as agents of socialization.

AGENTS OF SOCIALIZATION: THE MICRO–MESO CONNECTION

Agents of socialization are *the transmitters of culture—the people, organizations, and institutions that help us define our identity and teach us how to thrive in our social world*. Agents are the mechanism by which the self learns the values, beliefs, and behaviors of the culture. Agents of socialization help new members find their place, just as they prepare older members for new responsibilities in society. At the micro level, one's family, one's peer group, and local groups and organizations help people know how they should behave and what they should believe. At the meso level, formal sources of learning (e.g., education and religion) and other informal sources of learning, such as the media and books, are all agents that contribute to socialization. They transmit information to children and to adults throughout people's lives.

In early childhood, the family acts as the primary agent of socialization, passing on messages about respect for property and authority, and the value of love and loyalty (Handel et al. 2007). **Peer groups**—*people who are roughly equal in some status within the society, such as the same age or the same occupation*—are also important, especially during the teenage years. Some researchers even argue that the peer group is most important in the socialization process of children and

As children become teenagers, peers become increasingly important socializing agents, shaping their norms, values, and attitudes.

 Thinking Sociologically

As you read this section, make a list of socializing agents. Indicate two or three central messages each agent of socialization tries to instill in people. Are there different kinds of messages at the micro, meso, and macro levels? Do these messages conflict, and if so, why?

teens (Aseltine 1995; Harris 2009). Each agent has its own functions and is important at different stages of the life cycle, but meso-level institutions play a more active role as one matures. For example, schools and religious bodies become more involved in socialization as children become 6 years old and older, compared with when they were preschool age.

The next "Sociology in Our Social World" on page 110 discusses socialization in schools by exploring an important and widely cited research project. Note what kinds of data are viewed as evidence for understanding gender socialization.

Lessons from one agent of socialization generally complement those from other agents. Parents work at home to support what school and religion teach. However, at times, agents provide conflicting lessons. For example, family and faith communities often give teens messages that conflict with those of peer groups regarding sexual activity and drug use. This is an example of mixed messages given by formal and informal agents.

Formal agents of socialization are *official or legal agents (e.g., families, schools, teachers, religious*

SOCIOLOGISTS IN ACTION:
DAVID S. KIRK

Using Evidence-Based Research to Inform Public Policy: Resocialization Lessons From Hurricane Katrina

I have spent much of my professional career using the tools of sociology to examine the myriad consequences of criminal justice policies in the United States. Part of my focus has been on the influence of communities on the *resocialization* of ex-prisoners. Research reveals that on leaving prison ex-prisoners tend to be geographically concentrated in a relatively small number of neighborhoods within metropolitan areas; they often return to the very same neighborhoods and they find themselves surrounded by the socializing agents that helped lead them to criminal behavior in the first place. Thus, it is not surprising that large proportions of ex-prisoners end up back in prison within just three years.

If criminal behavior is influenced by the types of neighborhoods we live in, then it seems counterproductive to prisoner reintegration for ex-offenders to return to the same locales where they got into trouble. The hope for ex-prisoners is that they will become *resocialized*, shedding their criminal identity as they learn the norms, behaviors, and values of law-abiding citizens.

These well-known facts about crime and justice in the United States serve as the backdrop of my research on prisoner reentry, the process of leaving prison and returning to the community. The tragedy of Hurricane Katrina, which devastated the gulf coasts of Louisiana and Mississippi in August 2005, afforded me a unique opportunity to examine what would happen if ex-prisoners did not return home to their old neighborhoods upon exiting prison. Katrina provided a natural experiment for investigating the importance of residential change because it forced some people to move who otherwise would not have. Residential change may serve as a catalyst for sustained behavioral change by providing an opportunity for individuals to separate from the former contexts and associates that facilitated their prior criminal behavior. A fresh location enhanced resocialization efforts.

As I had hypothesized, prisoners exiting incarceration following Hurricane Katrina were much less likely to reside in the New Orleans neighborhoods where they resided prior to incarceration. Among those who did return to the same parish (a parish is the equivalent of a county) where they resided prior to incarceration, 26% were reincarcerated within one year of release from prison. By comparison, only 11% of offenders who moved to a new parish faced reincarceration one year after leaving prison. Based on these results, I concluded that separating individuals from their former residential environment reduces their likelihood of recidivism. Moving allows an individual to separate from the peers and routine activities that contributed to his or her criminal behavior in the past.

One critical component of disseminating information about scientific discoveries is to communicate the implications of the research. For instance, in most states, prisoners released on parole are legally required to return to their county of last residence, contributing to a return to old neighborhoods. So, parole policies, while designed to enhance public safety, may in fact undermine it. One implication of my research that I have discussed with key policy makers is that removing the institutional barriers to residential change may enhance public safety by lessening repetition

(Continued)

(Continued)

of crime. Additionally, providing incentives for individuals to move to new neighborhoods, such as public housing vouchers, may benefit public safety. Thus, in my experience, redesigning public policies is part of a methodical process that involves good science, communication of results, and further testing in a real-world environment.

David S. Kirk, PhD, is an associate professor in the Department of Sociology and a faculty research associate of the Population Research Center at the University of Texas at Austin. This excerpt is adapted from Sociologists in Action: Sociology, Social Change, and Social Justice *(Sage 2013).*

organizations) whose purpose it is to socialize the individual into the values, beliefs, and behaviors of the culture. For example, a primary goal of families is to teach children to speak and to learn proper behavior. In addition, schoolteachers educate by giving formal instruction, and religious organizations provide moral instruction. (These formal agents of socialization are discussed in Chapters 10–12.)

Informal agents of socialization are *unofficial forces that shape values, beliefs, and behaviors in which socialization is not the express purpose.* Examples include the media, books, advertising, and the Internet. They bring us continuous messages even though their primary purpose is not socialization but entertainment or selling products. Children watch countless advertisements on television, many with messages about what is good and fun to eat and how to be more attractive, more appealing, smarter, and a better person through the consumption of products. This bombardment is a particularly influential part of socialization for children and teenagers.

Thinking Sociologically

What confusion might be created for children when the formal and informal agents of socialization provide different messages about values or acceptable behaviors? Is this contradiction something that parents should be concerned about? Why or why not?

Micro-Level Socialization

Perhaps the most important micro-level formal agent of socialization is our own family—parents, siblings, and other family members. One way in which families teach children what is right and wrong is through rewards and

punishments, called *sanctions.* Children who lie to their parents may receive a verbal reprimand or a slap on the hand, be sent to their rooms, have "time out," or receive a spanking, depending on differences in child-rearing practices among families. These are examples of negative sanctions. Conversely, children may be rewarded for good behavior with a positive sanction, such as a smile, praise, a cookie, or a special event. The number and types of sanctions dispensed in the family shape the socialization process, including development of the self and the

© Tibor Bognar/Corbis

A Japanese mother helps her son at Heian Shinto Shrine during Shichi-go-san Matsuri, also called the Seven-Five-Three Festival, a celebration with prayers of long life for children aged 3 to 7.

sociology in our social world

Gender Socialization in U.S. Public Schools

Pause for a moment as you pass a school yard, and observe the children at play. Children's behavior on the school playground translates into a powerful agent of gender socialization in a very complex world. Consider the evidence reported in the ethnographic study of Barrie Thorne, recounted in her award-winning book, *Gender Play* (1993).

Many people assume that gender differences are natural and that we are "born that way." In contrast, Thorne provides evidence that gender differences are social constructions, influenced by the setting, the players involved in the situation, and the control people have over the situation. She suggests that we need to look at well-known everyday patterns from a fresh point of view. As an astute observer and researcher, Thorne suspected that girls and boys have complex relations that play out in the classroom and school yard. She chose the playground as the focus of her observation of the separate worlds of girls and boys (Thorne 1993). Through systematic participant observation, she found that children and adults play an active role in defining and shaping gender expectations through the collective practices of forming lines, choosing seats, teasing, gossiping, and participating in selected activities.

Thorne used two schools for her research—one in a small California city and another in a Midwest suburb. She entered the world of the children, sometimes sitting apart on the playground taking notes, sometimes participating in their activities such as eating and talking in the lunchroom. In each setting, she recorded her observations and experiences. For example, she noted what children call themselves and how they think of themselves. She was intrigued by the reference to the "opposite sex"—a term that stresses difference and opposition rather than similarity and the sense of "we." Thorne was struck by the active meaning construction involved as the children gained a notion of "normal" gender behavior. The real focus of her work is in taking seriously how children themselves make sense of sex differences.

Previous studies concluded that boys tend to interact in larger, more age-heterogeneous groups and in more rough-and-tumble play and physical fighting. Thorne also found that boys' play involves a much larger portion of the playground, and their play space was generally farther from the building, making them less subject to monitoring and sanctioning. Boys not only used roughly 90% of the playground, they would also often run "sneak invasions" into the girls' space to take things belonging to the girls. Many boys felt that they had a right to the geographical space that was occupied by girls. Girls played close to the buildings in much smaller areas and rarely ventured into the boys' area.

Girls' play tended to be characterized by cooperation and taking turns. They had more intense and exclusive friendships,

(Continued)

(Continued)

which took shape around keeping and telling secrets, shifting alliances, and indirect ways of expressing disagreement. Instead of direct commands, girls more often used words such as *let's* or *we gotta*. However, Thorne found that these notions of "separate girls' and boys' worlds" used in most previous studies miss the subtleties of race, class, and other factors.

In follow-up research, Valerie Ann Moore examined children at a summer day camp (2001). Like Thorne, she watched children play and interact with one another, and found that the children also use play to construct the meaning of gender, race, and age. The boys in the camp showed their independence by defying the adults' rules, which unified them across racial and age boundaries. The girls at the camp,

on the other hand, were much more likely to separate by age and by race when interacting with other campers. Narratives of romance were likely to break the physical boundaries among older campers (Moore 2001). These romances, however, emphasize gender differences. The camp counselors reinforced this difference by constantly creating and maintaining gender boundaries to prohibit romances from forming between the teens.

The major contribution of these two studies is to alert us to the complexity of the gender socialization process, helping us see the extent to which children are active agents creating their own definitions of social relations, not just short automatons who enact adult notions of what gender means.

perceptions we have of who we are and even whether we are good and clever or bad and stupid. Note that family influence varies from one culture to another.

In Japan, the mother is a key agent in the process of turning a newborn into a member of the group, passing on the strong group standards and expectations of family, neighbors, community, and society through the use of language and emotion. The child learns the importance of depending on the group and therefore fears being cast out. The need to belong creates pressure to conform to expectations, and the use of threats and the fear of shame help socialize children into Japanese ways (Hendry 1987; Holloway 2001).

Nonconformity is a source of shame in Japan. The resulting ridicule is a powerful means of social control. In some cases, the outcast is physically punished by peers. Thus, to bring shame on oneself or the family is behavior to be avoided. In the most extreme cases, young people have committed suicide because they did not conform to group expectations and felt profoundly ashamed as a result.

The interaction of family and formal education in Japan is explored in more detail in the next "Sociology Around the World" on page 112.

Thinking Sociologically

Recall your own playground days or watch a sibling, a relative, or another child on the playground. What do your observations tell you about the role of play in gender socialization?

In contrast to the values of conformity and fitting into the group espoused in many Asian countries, in the United States, most parents teach their children to value friendliness, cooperation, orientation toward achievement, social competence, responsibility, and independence. However, subcultural values and socialization practices may differ within the diverse groups in the U.S. population. Conceptions of what makes a "good person" or a "good citizen" and varied goals of socialization bring about differences in the process of socialization around the world.

Meso-Level Socialization

Meso-level agents also work to socialize people into specific cultural values and roles they must learn to fulfill. Education and religion are two obvious influences—both being institutions with primary responsibility for

Sociology Around the World

Socialization in Japan: The Family and Early Schooling

By Wendy Ng

Each of our families prepares us through the socialization process for the culture we are entering. How families carry out this process differs around the world, just as the cultures for which they are preparing their children differ. Here we consider meso-level family and early schooling in Japanese socialization.

The family is one of the most important socializing influences in Japan. The basis of the family unit in Japan is called the *ie* (pronounced ee-ay). Traditionally, it is made up of blood relatives who reside in the same household, as well as their ancestors and the descendents not yet born. Thus, family in Japan goes beyond those who belong to the immediate nuclear grouping and includes a broader array of individuals. Compared with the past, the modern *ie* in Japan relies more on the nuclear and living extended family and serves as the major reference group that socializes individuals within the family. Thus, family members within the *ie* are responsible for teaching individuals their family roles, values, and norms within the culture.

A unique feature of interdependence found within the family structure is *amae* (ah-may), which roughly translated means passive love but is often referred to as an emotional bond usually held between mother and child. Through this relationship, children are socialized to understand that they are an important part of the family, and they also learn that parents are to be respected and obeyed as the adults within the family. Although this appears hierarchical, the emotional bond of *amae* sets up a relationship of interdependency between child and parent for their lifetime. As children grow into adulthood, they will take care of their parents in the way that they were taken care of as children. This bond of loyalty between parent and child within the family structure carries over into other social structures outside the family. For example, in a business organization, there is a similar expectation of group loyalty.

In terms of early childhood socialization, Japanese children learn the distinction between two related yet distinct concepts: *uchi* (inside) and *soto* (outside). These concepts apply to material distinctions of clean and unclean spaces. In behavior, this means taking one's shoes off outside the house because the inside is clean and the outside is unclean. In Japanese households, the bathroom has similar clean and unclean designations. The bath is "clean" and the toilet, used to dispose of bodily wastes, is "unclean." Thus, one would never wear the same shoes or slippers in the toilet room and the room for bathing because that would be mixing unclean and clean elements.

Within the family, immediate members are "insiders" and other people are "outsiders." Children learn that the family is a safe and secure environment where the emphasis is on harmony among the various family members. Interactions between individuals stress cooperation, and interpersonal disputes are avoided. If a disagreement happens, children are taught to apologize to one another. Reciprocity is yet another behavior emphasized within the family. Children are taught to put themselves in the role of the other person and to think of the consequences of their behavior before acting out. This type of role behavior suggests that harmony between and among family members is important and sets the foundation for the child's educational socialization.

Whereas the family serves as the central socializing force when children are very young, as they grow the educational system continues to socialize children through group interaction and learning. When children enter kindergarten they become familiar with participating in a social group with peers. The Japanese kindergarten system emphasizes group equality among children and thus socializes children to be loyal to their classmates and group. Other children now form their new *uchi* or "inside" associations and friendships. The emphasis on group over individual identities is accomplished through wearing identical uniforms or smocks, having similar educational tools for all students, and having children take turns in different duties in the classroom. For example, the responsibility of passing out paper in the classroom, or food at lunchtime, is rotated among all the children in the classroom. Thus, cooperation and group participation becomes an important defining feature of kindergarten socialization.

At first glance, the emphasis on equality among individuals in the kindergarten classroom setting might seem to conflict with the emphasis on hierarchical authority present in much of Japanese society. In fact, the emphasis on group socializing helps to encourage a sense of belonging and group identity that works well within hierarchical authority structures. By learning these behaviors at a young age, the children learn that they are individuals within a larger group and that their actions reflect not only on themselves but also on their family, school, or whatever social group they belong to as adults.

• •

Wendy Ng, PhD, is chair of the Department of Sociology at San Jose State University. She has written about Asian cultures, among other things.

 ### Thinking Sociologically

How did agents of socialization influence who you are today, and how did your experience differ from that of Japanese children described in the essay above?

socialization. We discuss those in more detail in Chapters 11 and 12; here we illustrate meso-level socialization influences with a focus on social class and the media.

Social Class. Our education level, our occupation, the house we live in, what we choose to do in our leisure time, the foods we eat, and our religious and political beliefs are just a few aspects of our lives affected by socialization. Applying what we know from sociological research, the evidence strongly suggests that socialization varies by social class, or *the wealth, power, and prestige rankings that individuals hold in society* (Paxton and Pearce 2009). Meso-level patterns of distribution of resources, based in part on the economic opportunities created by state and national policies, affect who we become, as we see below.

Upper-middle-class and middle-class parents in the United States usually have above-average education and managerial or professional jobs. They tend to pass on to their children the skills and values necessary to succeed in the subculture of their social class. Subcultures, you will recall, operate at the meso level of the social system. Subcultural values such as autonomy, creativity, self-direction (the ability to make decisions and take initiative), responsibility, curiosity, and consideration of others are especially important for middle-class success and are part of middle class subculture (Kohn 1989). If the child misbehaves, for example, middle-class parents typically analyze the child's reasons for misbehaving, and punishment is related to these reasons. Sanctions often involve instilling guilt and denying privileges.

Working-class parents tend to pass on to children their cultural values of respect for authority and conformity to rules, lessons that will be useful if the children also have blue-collar jobs (Kohn 1989). Immediate punishment with no questions asked if a rule is violated functions to prepare children for positions in which obedience to rules is important to success. They are expected to be neat, clean, well-mannered, honest, and obedient students and workers (MacLeod 2008). Socialization experiences for boys and girls are also often different, following traditional gender-role expectations of the working class subculture.

©Digital Vision/Jeff Randall/ Thinkstock

This parent passes on a love for the piano to his young son. Because of the social class of this father, his son is likely to receive many messages about creativity, curiosity, and self-direction.

Members of each class, as you can see, socialize their children to be successful in their social class and to meet expectations for adults of that class. Schools, like families, participate in this process and socialize children to adapt to the settings in which they grow up and are likely to live. Children's social class position on entering school, in turn, has an effect on the socialization experiences they have in school (Ballantine and Hammack 2012).

Social class, however, is only one of many influencing agents of socialization. As we saw in *Black Men and Public Space* (p. 000), race and ethnicity are very important factors in socialization, as is gender. We discuss gender socialization in more detail in Chapter 9, but note here

that race, class, and gender act as structural constraints on some members of the population, as they receive different messages about who they are and how they should behave. Therefore, it is important to recognize the interplay of these variables in people's lives.

Electronic Media. Television and computers are important informal agents of socialization at the meso level. They are intermediate-sized social units—larger than a local community, but smaller than a nation. They impact both nation-states and global agencies at the macro level by shaping public attitudes, and they affect family notions of what is normal or not normal at the micro level. In developed countries, there is scarcely a home without a television set, and over 78% of homes have computers and Internet access (New Media Trend Watch 2013).

Researchers have collected nearly five decades of information on how television has become a way of life in homes. By the time an average child in the United States reaches age 18, he or she will have spent more time watching television than doing any other single activity besides sleeping. On average, children between ages 8 and 18 spend 3 hours a day watching television, 1 hour 11 minutes watching videos or DVDs, 1 hour 44 minutes with audio media, 1 hour using computers, and 49 minutes playing video games, with a total media exposure in a typical day of 8 hours and 33 minutes. Ninety-five percent of teens are online (Madden et al. 2013). More than 75% of teens own cell phones, and text an average of 60 times a day (Ahuja 2013; Pew Research Center Internet & American Life Project 2012). There is a marked increase in Internet use by children under the age of 9, with 40% of parents owning a tablet (Rideout 2013; Shapiro 2013). The next "Engaging Sociology" feature shows the total media exposure of children by several variables. Examine this issue in more depth by answering the questions following Tables 4.2 and 4.3.

The moguls of the mass media—a meso-level social system—are able to influence socialization within the most intimate of environments. "Children [in the United States] use computers at very young ages. Over 80% of children under age 5 use the Internet weekly" (Kessler 2011).

Parents who play an active role in helping children understand the content of television and computer games can have a powerful effect on mitigating media's negative impacts and enhancing the positive aspects of media. The media usage habits of parents can also influence how their children respond to media (Jordan et al. 2006; National Consumers League 2013).

An alarming concern with Internet socialization is its role in radicalizing some young people and involving them in terrorism. The Tsarnaev brothers—Tamerlan and

ENGAGING SOCIOLOGY

Media Exposure and Socialization

Examine Tables 4.2 and 4.3 and respond to the questions below.

Table 4.2 Total Media Exposure

		average hours per day
Age	8 to 10 years old	7:51
	11 to 14 years old	11:53
	15 to 18 years old	11:23
Gender	Boys	11:12
	Girls	10:17
Race	White	8:36
	Black	12:59
	Hispanic	13:00
Parent education	High school or less	11:26
	Some college	11:30
	College graduate	10:00

Source: Based on Rideout, Foehr, and Roberts 2010; Kaiser Family Foundation 2010.

Table 4.3 Average Amount of Time per Day Spent with Each Medium (8- to 18-year-olds)

Medium	1999	2009
Television	3:47	4:29
Music/audio	1:48	2:31
Computer	:27	1:29
Video games	:26	1:13
Print	:43	:38
Movies	:18	:25
Total media exposure	7:29	10:45
Multitasking proportion	16%	29%

Source: Based on Rideout, Foehr, and Roberts 2010; Kaiser Family Foundation 2010.

Sociological Data Analysis

1. Considering the data in Tables 4.2 and 4.3, how would you describe television-watching and other media-engaged patterns among different groups?

2. Are the trends in media exposure over the first decade of the 21st century a matter of concern? Why or why not?

3. How might media time affect other aspects of socialization of children?

4. What might be the social consequences of ethnic minorities (blacks and Hispanics) and those children whose parents do not have a college education having so much higher media exposure each day, compared to whites and those with more education?

5. Do your conclusions indicate any cause for concern about the use of media in your society? Why or why not?

Source: Kaiser Family Foundation (2010); Rideout, Foehr, and Roberts (2010.

Dzhokhar—were apparently well-adjusted teens while in high school, but they were deeply influenced by Internet exchanges and by political websites. Eventually they teamed together to plot the Boston Marathon bombings on April 15, 2013. Three people were killed, and roughly 280 people were injured, many losing limbs. The actions of these young men were spawned when they adopted ideologies deeply antagonistic to the United States through Internet socialization. In a country that values free speech, controlling such antisocial influences is a real dilemma (Crary and Lavoie 2013).

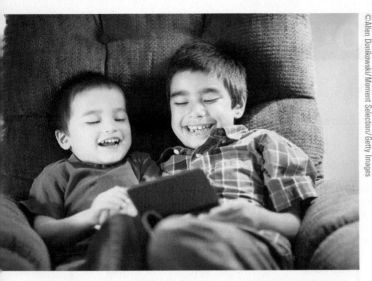

The children above illustrate how such computer games and other electronic devices influence the socialization process of even young children.

Perhaps the most important aspect of television and computers is something that we do not fully understand but that has frightening potential. For the first time in human history, we have powerful agents of socialization in the home from a child's birth onward. Time spent watching television or playing computer games means less time spent engaging in interaction with caregivers and peers. Intimate family bonds formed of affection and meaningful interaction are being altered by the dominant presence of electronic media in the home. In addition, those who control the flood of mass media messages received by children may have very different interests and concerns than parents.

Without a doubt, a significant part of the informal socialization process occurs with the assistance of electronic equipment that shares the home with parents and siblings and that commands a significant portion of a child's time and attention. We also know that macro forces, such as globalization, have influenced school curricula and media content. We move next to a discussion of some of the national and global processes that influence socialization.

SOCIALIZATION AND MACRO-LEVEL ISSUES

Sense of Self in New Global Context

Immigration patterns and ethnic conflicts around the world have resulted in a fairly new phenomenon: transnationalism. Transnationalism is *the process by which immigrants have multinational social relations that link*

together their original societies with their new locations. This means that an individual or a family has national loyalty to more than one country (Levitt 2001, 2007; Levitt and Waters 2006). Often, it occurs after the migration of war refugees, whose roots lie in their country of origin and whose close family members may continue to live there.

Consider transnational children raised in war-torn countries. In the Palestinian territories, especially Gaza, and in Israeli settlements along the border, children grow up with fear and hatred that result in major influences on their socialization. Some war refugees spend childhoods in refugee camps and may never return to their native countries. For people experiencing transnationalism, there are conflicting messages about culturally appropriate behaviors and the obligations of loyalty to family and nation. Events of a national or global nature directly impact how an individual is socialized—with some of the socializing influences being from outside one's country of residence.

However, one need not migrate to another country to experience global pressures. The Internet and cell phones have increasingly created a sense of connectedness to other parts of the world and an awareness of global interdependencies (Brier 2004; Roach 2004). Some commentators have even suggested that the Internet is a threat to the nation-state as it allows individuals to develop friendships, loyalties, and norms that are not in the interests of the state (Drori 2006). Ideas of social justice or progress may be shaped not just by the government that rules the country but by international human rights organizations and ideas obtained from media that cross borders, such as the Internet. In recent uprisings in some Middle Eastern and North African countries, social networking kept movement participants in touch with others in the uprisings and with outside media and supporters. So socialization can include agents beyond the local community and even beyond national boundaries.

As more people have access to the Internet, they also have access to international information and friendships across borders and boundaries. Figure 4.2 on Internet use around the world illustrates not only variability of access but also how widespread this access has become. One interesting question is how access or lack of access will influence the strength of "we" versus "they" feelings between citizens of different countries, insofar as sense of self is connected to belonging to a group—to a sense of "we."

At a time when people lived in isolated rural communities and did not interact with those unlike themselves, there was little price to pay for being bigoted or chauvinistic

Children and Technology

FIGURE 4.2   Internet Users per 100 People

Source: World Bank (2013).

toward those who were different. However, we now live in a global village where we or our businesses will likely interact with very different people in a competitive environment. If we hold people in low regard because they are unlike us or because we think they are destined for hell, there may be a high cost for this animosity. Among other problems, terrorism is fostered when people feel alienated. Therefore, training in cultural sensitivity toward those "others" has become an economic and a political issue.

The reality is that children today live in a globalized world. Increasing numbers of children around the world learn multiple languages to enhance their ability to communicate with others. Some college campuses require experiences abroad as part of the standard curriculum because faculty members and administrators feel that a global perspective is essential in our world today and part of a college education. Global sensitivity and tolerance of those once considered "alien" has become a core element of our day (Robertson 1992; Schaeffer 2003; Snarr and Snarr 2008).

Sometimes, global events can cause a different turn—away from tolerance and toward defensive isolation. When 19 young men from Saudi Arabia and other Middle Eastern countries crashed planes into the World Trade Center in New York City and into the Pentagon in Washington, D.C., the United States was shocked and became mobilized to

defend itself and its borders. The messages within schools and from the government suddenly took a more patriotic turn. So this event and other terrorist acts, clearly tragedies rooted in global political conflicts, can intensify the boundaries between people and loyalty to the nation-state. Global forces are themselves complex and do not always result in more tolerance.

Indeed, the only thing that we can predict with considerable certainty is that in this age of sharing a small planet, the socialization of our citizens will be influenced by events at the macro level, whether national or global.

POLICY AND PRACTICE

Should preschoolers living in poverty be socialized in day care settings? Should adolescents work while going to school? Should we place emphasis in high school and college on in-group loyalty and patriotism or on developing a sense of global citizenship? Should new parents be required to take child-rearing classes? How should job-training programs be structured? How can communities use the talents and knowledge of retirees? Can the death process be made easier for the dying person and the family? These are all policy questions—issues of how to establish governing principles that will enhance our common life.

These policy questions rely on an understanding of socialization—how we learn our beliefs and our positions on issues facing society. For example, making decisions about how to provide positive early-childhood education experiences at a time when young children first learn the ways of their culture depends on understanding the socialization they receive at home and at school. The quality of child care we provide for young children will affect not only how effective our future workforce is but also whether the children turn out to be productive citizens or a drain on society. These are all questions public sociologists can help to answer.

Now that we have some understanding of the process of socialization, we look at the next level in the process of interaction and how individuals become members of small groups, networks, and large complex organizations.

WHAT HAVE WE LEARNED?

Human socialization is pervasive, extensive, and life-long. We cannot understand what it means to be human without comprehending the impact of a specific culture on us, the influence of our close associates, and the complex interplay of pressures at the micro, meso, and macro levels. Indeed, without social interaction, there would not even be a self. We humans are, in our most essential natures, social beings. The purpose of this chapter has been to open our eyes to the ways in which we become the individuals we are. We move now to a discussion of how we use our socialization in interactions with groups and organizations to be a part of society.

KEY POINTS

- Human beings come with their own biological makeup, but most of what makes us uniquely human we learn from our culture and society—through socialization. Humans who live in isolation from others do not receive the socialization necessary to be part of culture and are sometimes barely human. (See pp. 95–97.)

- The self consists of the interaction of the *I*—the basic impulsive human with drives, needs, and feelings—and the *Me*. We develop a reflective self through role-taking to see how others might view us. (See pp. 99–102.)

- The self is profoundly shaped by others, but it also has agency—that is, it can be an initiator of action and a maker of meaning. (See pp. 102–104.)

- The self develops through stages, from mimicking others (the play stage) to more intellectually sophisticated abilities to role-take and to see how various roles complement each other (the game stage). (See pp. 102–104.)

- The self is modified as it moves through life stages, and some of those stages require major resocialization—shedding old roles and taking on new ones as one enters new statuses in life. (See pp. 107–108.)

- A number of agents of socialization are at work in each of our lives, communicating messages relevant at the micro, meso, or macro level of social life. At the meso level, for example, we may receive different messages about what it means to be a "good" person depending on our ethnic, religious, or social-class subculture. (See pp. 107–116.)

- Some of these messages may be in conflict with each other, as when global messages about

tolerance for those who are different conflict with a nation's desire to have absolute loyalty and a sense of superiority. (See pp. 116–117.)

DISCUSSION QUESTIONS

1. Cooley's idea of the "looking-glass self" helps us understand that how we think other people view us influences our view of ourselves. How has your sense of your ability to succeed in college been influenced by the feedback you have processed from those around you (particularly teachers, peers, and family members)?

2. Socialization occurs throughout the life cycle. Into what role have you been socialized most recently? Who were the primary agents in this socialization process? Did you find the process relatively easy or difficult? Why?

3. Sociological studies have shown that middle-class and working-class parents tend to socialize

their children differently. Explain the differences and describe how they relate to how you were socialized by your family of origin.

4. How has your socialization been influenced by television and video games? Do you think the extent to which these informal agents of socialization influence children these days has a positive or a negative impact on our society? Why?

5. If you were asked to create a government policy to promote positive socialization experiences that would strengthen our society, what might you propose? Why?

VISUAL SOCIOLOGY: *DEATH RITUALS*

When people die, their bodies are handled according to the religious and cultural practices of the groups they belong to. This celestial burial master feeds the body of a dead Tibetan to the vultures in northwest China's Qinghai province. In Tibetan regions, where people believe in rebirth and thus no need to preserve the body, they speak of this practice as "giving alms to the birds." Visit **edge.sagepub.com/ ballantine5e** for an interactive photo essay about death rituals.

CONTRIBUTING TO OUR SOCIAL WORLD: WHAT CAN WE DO?

At the Local Levels

- In every community, numerous opportunities exist for volunteer work helping children from economically and otherwise disadvantaged backgrounds to succeed in school. *Opportunities to help disadvantaged children succeed in school include tutoring or mentoring in the local schools.*

- *Head Start centers for poor preschool children* often have opportunities to do something concrete to help children. An education faculty member at your college can give you contact information, or go to the association's website at www.nhsa.org.

- *Helping in a local Boys and Girls Club* that provides socialization experiences for children through their teens. You can find a club near you by going to www.bgca.org/whoweare/Pages/FindaClub.aspx.

- *Taking service learning course credits.* Locate the service learning office at your college or university to learn about service learning programs on your campus that help disadvantaged children.

At the National and Global Levels

- *Literacy* is a vital component of socialization, yet remains an unmet need in many parts of the world, especially in the less-developed countries of Africa and Asia.

- *World Education* provides training and technical assistance in nonformal education in economically disadvantaged communities worldwide. Go to the organization's website at www.worlded.org to learn about its wide variety of projects and volunteer/work opportunities.

- *Care International* (www.care-international.org) and *Save the Children* (www.savethechildren.org) provide funding for families to send children to school and to receive specialized training.

- *Free The Children* (www.freethechildren.com), an organization that empowers young people to help other young people, has built more than 650 schools and schoolrooms for children in various parts of the world. Go to the organization's website to learn how you can work with others to help create more educational opportunities for children.

- *UNESCO (the United Nations Educational, Scientific, and Cultural Organization)* promotes literacy around the world in many ways. Learn more about its efforts at www.unesco.org/new/en/education.

Opportunities exist for fund-raising, internships, and eventually jobs with these organizations.

5 Interaction, Groups, and Organizations

Connections That Work

Human interactions result in connections—networks—that make life more fulfilling and our economic efforts more productive. These connections link everything from small micro groups to large bureaucratic organizations.

MICRO

● ME (MY FAMILY AND CLOSEST FRIENDS)

● LOCAL ORGANIZATIONS AND COMMUNITY

Networks form in local organizations like civic and alumni groups.

MESO

● NATIONAL ORGANIZATIONS, INSTITUTIONS, AND ETHNIC SUBCULTURES

Ethnic organizations, political parties, and religious denominations are important to many people.

MACRO

● SOCIETY

Citizen of a nation develop connections and common identity.

● GLOBAL COMMUNITY

The United Nations, international courts, and transnational corporations influence our lives.

THINK ABOUT IT

Micro: Local Community	How does interaction with family and friends affect who you are and what you believe?
Meso: National Institutions, Complex Organizations, and Ethnic Groups	Is bureaucratic red tape necessary and inevitable?
Macro: National and Global Systems	What are some ways national trends, such as the decline in the percentage of U.S. citizens who smoke, influence your quality of life? What are some ways networks across the globe affect your daily life, your education, and your chosen profession?

As we wrote these words, Kathleen, one of the authors of this book, turned to CNN.com on her smartphone and saw that the relatives of a U.S. woman just killed in Syria were able, while at their home in Michigan, to identify her body via a picture posted online (Watkins 2013). Likewise, people online all over the world were able to follow the recent protests and uprisings in nations such as Iran, Tunisia, Yemen, Egypt, and Bahrain. Peaceful demonstrators and violent fighters used their cell phones, blogs, Twitter, and Facebook to send pictures and video footage documenting these events. Some have referred to this as "the Twitter Revolution." Cyberspace links people around the world in seconds in ways that few governments can stop (Stone and Cohen 2009). The information superhighway is opening new communication routes and allowing individuals with common interests to network instantly.

By contrast, Jeanne, another of the authors of this book, took a leave of absence in the mid-1980s to conduct some research in Japan. A benefit of that leave was that she escaped the distractions of ringing phones and she could concentrate. Fax was almost unknown, and e-mail hardly existed for the civilian population. In 2007, she taught on Semester at Sea. Even in the middle of the ocean, she was in instant contact with her office, her publisher, and her family over the international Internet superhighway. She could insert earphones into her laptop computer and have a Skype conversation by voice or pick up a mobile phone and call her family or coauthor. What a change in 25 years! Technology is creating a smaller world, connected through global networks.

This chapter lays the groundwork for understanding how we fit into the structure of our social world—exploring the link between the individual and the social structure. The process starts when we are born and continues with group activities as we join playgroups, preschool, and kindergarten classes. It broadens as we become members of larger organizations and bureaucracies within universities, workplaces, national political parties, and national and international religious organizations. First, we consider how networks and connections link individuals and groups to different levels of analysis. Then, we focus on micro-level interactions, meso-level groups, and meso- and macro-level organizations and bureaucracies. Finally, we consider macro-level national and global networks.

© REUTERS/Eric Gaillard

No longer are paper and pencil the sole tools of learning. From as early as kindergarten on, students use electronic devices and the Internet at school.

NETWORKS AND CONNECTIONS IN OUR SOCIAL WORLD

Try imagining yourself at the center of a web, such as a spider's web. Attach the threads that spread from the center first to family members and close friends, on out in the web to peers, then to friends of friends. Some thread connections are close and direct. Others are more distant but connect more and more people in an ever-expanding web.

Have you ever used the Six Degrees of Kevin Bacon search tool? Perhaps you have heard that just about any actor can be connected to Kevin Bacon in six or fewer steps. It is also true that the typical person in the United States is now fewer than six steps (or degrees removed) from any other person in the country. Stanley Milgram and his associates studied social networks by selecting several target people in different cities (Korte and Milgram 1970; Milgram 1967; Travers and Milgram 1969). Then, they identified "starting persons" in cities more than 1,000 miles away. Each starting person was given a folder with instructions and the target person's name, address, and occupation, as well as a few other facts. The starting person was instructed to mail the folder to someone he or she knew on a first-name basis who lived closer to or might have more direct networks with the target person than the starting person had. The number of links in the chain to complete delivery ranged from 2 to 10, with most having 5 to 7 intermediaries. This is the source of the reference to "six degrees of separation" and the original inspiration for the Kevin Bacon game.

More recently, research by scientists at Facebook and the University of Milan showed that the average number of acquaintances separating any two people in the world is now 4.74. Within the United States the separation was only 4.37 people (Markoff and Sengupta 2011). Clearly, networks are powerful linkages and create a truly small world.

Our social networks, then, *refer to individuals linked together by one or more social relationships, connecting us to the larger society*. We use our social network to get jobs or favors, often from people not very far removed from us in the web. Networks begin with micro-level contacts and exchanges between individuals in private interactions and expand to small groups, then to large (even global) organizations (Granovetter 2007; Tolbert and Hall 2008). The stronger people's networks, the more influential they can be in a person's life (see Figure 5.1).

Networks at the Micro, Meso, and Macro Levels

As noted above, networks span the micro, meso, and macro levels of analysis. For example, at the *micro level*, you develop close friends in college—bonds that may

This woman takes a "selfie" with a mobile phone in front of activists during a rally near the Ukrainian Elections Commission. Within seconds her friends throughout the world could see her at this rally through her Facebook page.

continue for the rest of your life. You introduce your friends from the student government to your roommate's friends from the soccer team, and the network expands. These acquaintances may have useful information about which professors to take, what campus organizations to join, and how to get a job in your field. You most likely carry out all of these interactions both in-person and online.

FIGURE 5.1   Networks: A Web of Connections

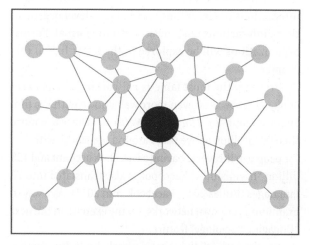

The blue circle represents an individual—perhaps you—and the yellow circles represent your friends and acquaintances. Your network looks a bit like a web but is less complete in terms of every point connected to the adjacent point, since some of your friends do not know each other.

▶ Social Media Fame

When you graduate from your university, you will be part of the university's alumni association, and this may become important to you for social contacts, business connections, or help with settling in a new location. When people refer to the Old Boy network, they are talking about contacts made through general association with people such as alumni. Men have used networks quite successfully in the past, and networks of working women—New Girl networks—are expanding rapidly. One of the reasons for the persistent inequality in our society is that members of certain groups may not have access to these privilege-enhancing networks.

Thinking Sociologically

Map your social network web (as far as you can). What advantages do you get from your network? How might this network help you to advance in your chosen career?

Network links create new types of organizational forms at the *meso level*. These networks often cross societal, racial, ethnic, religious, and other lines that divide people. Networks also link groups at different levels of analysis. In fact, you are linked through networks to (1) micro-level college, athletic, and faith communities; (2) meso-level formal, complex organizations such as a political party or national fraternity and ethnic or social class subcultures; (3) the macro-level nation of which you are a citizen; and (4) global entities such as the United Nations. These networks may open opportunities, but they also may create obligations that limit your freedom to make your own choices. As we move from micro-level interactions to larger meso- and macro-level organizations, interactions tend to become more formal. Formal organizations will be explored in the latter half of this chapter.

Probably the most famous networking site is Facebook, and it became even more well known with the film about its founder, *The Social Network*. There are more than 901 million active users around the world, with 1 in 7.7 people in the world having a Facebook account and 125 billion "friendships." Facebook is also translated into 70 languages (Bullas 2012; Facebook.com 2011). As a way of examining your own networks, try the exercise in the next "Engaging Sociology" feature.

We can network through Facebook, LinkedIn, Twitter, Instagram, Vine, and other sites, and we can keep in touch constantly through text messaging. However, this means that people spend more time interacting with a piece of technology and may feel less comfortable interacting face-to-face with someone. Likewise, online courses are in one sense less intimate—the instructor and the student may never meet face-to-face. Yet, through the Internet, more people can take college-level courses than ever before. We are only beginning to understand the implications of this technology on human interaction and on interpersonal skills.

Thinking Sociologically

How does online technology shape your interactions with friends?

THE PROCESS OF INTERACTION: CONNECTIONS AT THE MICRO LEVEL

Each morning as you rouse yourself, you consider what the day might bring. You evaluate what is in store for you, what roles you will play during the day, and with whom you are likely to interact.

Should you wear the ragged but comfy jeans and T-shirt? Perhaps that will not work today, since there is that class trip to the courthouse. Something a bit less casual is in order. Then, you are meeting with your English professor to discuss the last essay you wrote. What approach should you take? You could act insulted that she failed to think of you as a future J. K. Rowling, Veronica Roth, or Suzanne Collins. Maybe a meek, mild "Please tell me what I did wrong, I tried so hard" approach would work. She seems a nice, sympathetic sort. After class, there is a group of students who chat in the hall. It would be nice to meet them. What strategy should you use? Tell a joke? Make small talk? Talk to the students individually so you can get to know each before engaging the whole group? Each of these responses is a strategy for interaction, and each might elicit different reactions.

The Elements of Social Interaction

"Let's have a drink!" Such a simple comment might have many different meanings. We could imagine two thirsty children playing together, men going to a bar after work, a couple of friends getting together to celebrate an event,

ENGAGING SOCIOLOGY

Networking via Facebook

If you are on Facebook, go to your Facebook account and note the number of friends you have listed. Then, look at them carefully to see if you can answer the following questions:

1. What is the age range of the friends on your list?

2. What is the gender composition of your list?

3. How many members of each of the following racial or ethnic groups are on your list?

    ___ African Americans

    ___ Whites

    ___ Hispanics

    ___ Asians

    ___ Other racial and ethnic group (or some combination)

    ___ International contacts

4. What is the socioeconomic status of your friends?

    ___ Blue collar (families in which the primary wage earner works for an hourly wage)

___ Middle class (families in which the primary wage earner earns a salary of less than $100,000 per year)

___ Professional (families in which the primary wage earner earns a salary of $100,000 to $500,000 per year)

___ Highly affluent corporate executive (families in which the primary wage earner earns a salary of $500,000 to $10 million)

___ Upper class (families in which much of the wealth is inherited and annual income is in the multimillions)

* * * * * * *

Engaging With Sociological Data

- Now look at the data you have collected. What have you learned about your own networks?

- How much socioeconomic, age, and ethnic diversity do the data reveal about your networks?

---

fraternity brothers at a party, or a couple on a date. In all these cases, social interaction consists of *two or more individuals purposefully relating to each other*.

"Having a drink," like all *interaction*, involves action on the part of two or more individuals, is directed toward a goal that people hope to achieve, and takes place in a social context that includes cultural norms and rules governing the situation, the setting, and other factors shaping the way people perceive the circumstances. The action, goal, and social context help us interpret the meaning of statements such as "Let's have a drink."

The norms governing the particular social context tell us how to behave. Recall from Chapter 3 that norms are

rules that guide human interactions. People assume that others will share their interpretation of a situation. These shared assumptions about proper behavior provide the cues for your own behavior that become a part of your social self. You look for cues to proper behavior and rehearse in your mind your actions and reactions. In the "Let's have a drink" scenario, the dress, mannerisms, speech, and actions you consider appropriate depend on expectations from your socialization and past experience in similar situations. You will, no doubt, have learned to dress and act differently depending on whether you are having the drink with an old friend or a potential romantic partner. In turn, you will expect that the person with whom you are drinking will be making the same sort of

▶ Facebook Networking

In North America, friends interact at a close distance, 1.5 to 4 feet, as in the top photo. A more formal setting calls for a distance of 4 to 12 feet and can feel cold and intimidating, as in the interview at the right.

decisions on what to wear and how to behave when you get together.

Although most people assume that talking, or *verbal communication*, is the primary means of communication between individuals, words themselves are actually only a part of the message. In most contexts, they make up less than 7% of the communication, with body language 55% and tone of voice 38% (Debenham 2014). We communicate primarily through nonverbal communication—*interactions without words using facial expressions, the head, eye contact, body posture, gestures, touch, walk, status symbols, and personal space* (Cherry 2012; Givens 2012). We learn these important

elements of communication through socialization as we grow up.

People who travel to a country other than their own often use gestures as they try to be understood. Like spoken language, however, nonverbal gestures vary from culture to culture. Communicating with others in one's own language can be difficult enough. Add to this the complication of individuals with different language, cultural expectations, and personalities using different nonverbal messages, and misunderstandings are likely. Although one may master another written and verbal language, nonverbal messages are the hardest part of another language to master because they are specific to a culture and learned through socialization.

Consider the following example: You are about to wrap up a major business deal. You are pleased with the results of your negotiations, so you give your hosts the thumb-and-finger A-OK sign. In Brazil, you have just grossly insulted your hosts—it is the equivalent of giving them "the finger." In Japan, you have asked for a small bribe. In the south of France, you have indicated the deal is worthless. Intercultural communication takes more than knowing the language of a different culture.

Another example of nonverbal communication involves personal space. Most people have experienced social situations, such as parties, where someone gets too close. One person backs away, the other moves in again, and the first backs away again—into a corner or a table with nowhere else to go. Perhaps the person approaching was aggressive or rude, but it is also possible that the person held different cultural norms or expectations in relation to personal space.

The amount of personal space an individual needs to be comfortable or proper varies with the cultural setting, gender, status, and social context of the interaction. Individuals from Arab countries are often comfortable at very close range. However, people from Scandinavia generally need a great deal of personal space. Consider the following four categories of social distance and social space based on a study of middle-class people in the United States (though there may be some variation within the middle class depending on ethnicity). Each category applies to particular types of activity (Hall and Hall 1992):

1. *Intimate distance:* from zero distance (touching, embracing, kissing) to 18 inches. Children may play together in such close proximity, and adults and children may maintain this distance, but

Social Groups

between adults, this intimate contact is reserved for private and affectionate relationships.

2. *Personal distance:* from 18 inches to 4 feet. This is the public distance for most friends and for informal interactions with acquaintances.

3. *Social distance:* from 4 feet to 12 feet. This is the distance for impersonal business relations, such as a job interview or class discussions between students and a professor. This distance implies a more formal interaction or a significant difference in the status of the two people.

4. *Public distance:* 12 feet and beyond. This is the distance most public figures use for addressing others, especially in formal settings and in situations in which the speaker has a very high status.

Personal space also communicates one's position in relation to others. The higher the position, the greater the control of space. In social situations, individuals with higher positions spread out, prop their feet up, put their arms out, and use more sweeping gestures.

Thinking Sociologically

Describe a time when you experienced miscommunication. Who was involved? What happened? How can what you read in this chapter help you to explain why the miscommunication occurred?

Theoretical Perspectives on the Interaction Process

Sociologists study interactions, including verbal and nonverbal communication, to better understand why people behave the way they do. Symbolic interactionists and rational choice theorists examine how and why people communicate with one another. As you will see, their different perspectives lead them to focus on different aspects of interactions and come up with distinctive conclusions as to why they occur.

Symbolic Interaction Theory. With whom do you interact? What determines whether the interaction will continue or stop? How do you know how to behave and what to say around each other? What other processes are taking place as you "talk" to each other? Why do you act differently with different people?

Symbolic interactionism is based on the idea that humans create society through interacting with one another. We act toward people and objects on the basis of

When the pope speaks, it is not only the Vatican Security that keeps people at a formal distance; it is a sense of awed respect for the office: 12 feet or more is the standard distance kept between public figures and other people.

the meanings those things have for us. The meanings are derived by individuals as they interact with others. Together, through our interactions with one another, we agree that objects, gestures, and phrases, like "Let's have a drink," symbolize certain things. Likewise, the word *hello* can signify the beginning of a conversation and *good-bye* the end of one because we agree on the meanings of those words and agree to act accordingly. Symbols are the key to understanding human life, and we go about the task of fitting our actions together through our shared perceptions and meanings of those symbols. Through our mental manipulation of symbols and interpretation of meaning, we *define situations* and determine how we should act in a given situation or how we should make sense of it (Charon 2010; Hewitt and Shulman 2011). More than any other theory in the social sciences, symbolic interactionism stresses the agency—the active decision-making role—of humans within their societies (Charon 2010; Hewitt and Schulman 2011).

Have you ever laughed at a joke you did not hear or understand because those around you laughed? In ambiguous situations, humans look to others to see how they have made sense of the situation or interaction taking place—do people around us look frightened, annoyed, bored, or amused? When in doubt, we tend to follow the cues of those around us. Once one person defines the situation and acts, especially if that person is highly regarded or very self-confident, others will often accept that response as "normal." This is how social interaction is involved in the **social construction of reality**—*the process by which individuals and groups shape reality through social interaction.* This imposed notion of reality then takes on a life of its own, often constraining and even coercing people to conform (Berger and Luckmann 1966; Hewitt and Shulman 2011; O'Brien 2011; Ritzer 2013b). For example, our career goals tend to be influenced by those with whom we interact. If you had been a woman in the United States in the 1910s, you would be unlikely to think you could pursue a career in the "male" field of engineering.

However, socially constructed constraints can be challenged by individuals and lead to different realities, which, in turn, begin to influence people's perceptions of what is true and what is possible. For example, until recently, it seemed impossible for gay artists to gain acceptance in the hip-hop community. If you were gay, the choice seemed to be to choose a different genre or keep your sexual orientation hidden. This began to change when Frank Ocean publicly proclaimed that his first love was a man and his announcement drew support, rather than condemnation, from many other prominent hip-hop artists. The public embrace and acceptance of renowned hip-hop DJ Mister Cee by Ebro Darden, the program director for Hot 97, has also helped lead to the "the gradual easing of hip-hop's internalized homophobia" and the possibility to be both openly gay and a hip-hop artist (Caramanica 2013; McKinley 2012).

A different approach to interaction analysis—called *dramaturgy*—analyzes life as a play or drama on a stage, with scripts and props and scenes to be played. The play we put on creates an impression for our audience. In everyday life, individuals learn new lines to add to their scripts through the socialization process, including influence from family, friends, films, and television. They perform these scripts for social audiences to maintain certain images, much like the actors in a play.

Consider the following familiar example: Every day in high schools around the world, teenagers go on stage—in the classroom or the hallway with friends and peers and with adult authorities who may later be giving grades or writing letters of reference. The props these students use include their style of clothing, a backpack, a phone, and a smile or a "cool" look. The set is the classroom, the cafeteria, and perhaps the athletic field. The script is shaped by the actors: Teachers and coaches may establish an authoritarian relationship with students; classmates engage in competition for grades; peers seek social status

among companions. The actors include hundreds of teens struggling with issues of identity, changing bodies, and attempting to be accepted and avoid humiliation. Each individual works to assert and maintain an image through behavior, clothing, language, and friends.

Each part or character an individual plays and each audience requires a different script. For example, interacting with peers at a bar differs from meeting a professor in her office. As we perform according to society's script for the situation, we take into consideration how our actions will influence others. By carefully managing the image we project—a process called *impression management*—we try to create an impression that works to our advantage. Most of the time, we engage in front-stage behavior. This is the largely scripted behavior we use with strangers or casual acquaintances. A poor or unacceptable performance, such as wearing out-of-style clothes or spilling our lunch, is embarrassing both for us and for our audience. We learn to develop strategies to cover up weaknesses or failures, such as laughing at a joke even though we do not understand it.

Sometimes we avoid situations that will require us to play a role with which we are unfamiliar or uncomfortable. Have you ever avoided interacting with a certain group of people because you were unsure of how to act when around them or decided against trying out for a team or a theater production or running for office because you were afraid you might not make it or it was not an "in" thing to do? We learn to avoid those performance activities that are likely to result in humiliation or failure or that contradict the image we have worked to create.

At home or with close friends with whom we are more intimate, we engage in "backstage behavior," letting our feelings show and behaving in ways that might be unacceptable for other audiences (Goffman 1967, [1959] 2001). We feel that with them we can relax and be our "true" selves, without possible negative repercussions. So, as you can see, dramaturgical analysis, and its front- and backstage concepts, can help us to better understand our interactions and how our behavior changes with the setting.

Thinking Sociologically

Describe some ways in which your life feels like a dramatic production. Identify front-stage and backstage behaviors you carry out on a daily basis.

Rational Choice Theory. Rational choice or exchange theorists look at a different aspect of interaction—why relationships continue, considering the rewards and costs of interaction for the individual. They argue that the choices we make are guided by reason ("rational choices"). If the benefits of the interaction are high and if the costs are low, the interaction will be valued and sustained. Every interaction involves calculations of self-interest, expectations of reciprocity (a mutual exchange of favors), and decisions to act in ways that have current or eventual pay-off for the individual (Smelser 1992).

Reciprocity is a key concept for rational choice theorists. The idea is that if a relationship is imbalanced over a period of time, it will become unsatisfying. As theorists from this perspective see human interaction, each person tends to keep a mental ledger of who "owes" whom. If I have done you a favor, you owe me one. If you have helped me in some way, I have an obligation to you. If I then fail to comply or even do something that hurts you, you will likely view it as a breach in the relationship and have negative feelings toward me. Moreover, if one person has more power in the relationship, there is an imbalance in what each brings to the relationship.

In the study of families, scholars use the "principle of least interest," which states that the person with the least interest in the relationship has the most power. The person with the least interest is the person who brings more resources (financial, physical, social, personal) to the relationship and receives less. That person could easily leave. The person who offers less to the relationship or who has fewer assets is more dependent on the relationship. This person is likely to give in when there is a disagreement, so the person with less interest gets her or his way.

Sometimes a person may engage in a behavior where there is little likelihood of reciprocity from the other person—as in cases where the behavior is altruistic or self-giving. Rational choice theorists would argue that there is still a benefit. It might be enhanced feelings of self-worth, positive recognition from others, hope for a place in heaven, or just the expectation of indirect reciprocity. This latter notion is akin to the idea of "paying it forward": The person you help might not help you, but if you are in a similar situation, you could hope for and expect someone to come to your assistance (Gouldner 1960; Turner 2003).

Social Status: Individuals' Link to Groups

As you will recall from Chapter 4, a **social status** is *a social position in society*. We interact with others, and they react to us, based in part on the statuses we hold. We interact differently when in the daughter status with our parents,

in a student status with our professor, or in friend status with our peers. Each individual holds many statuses, and this combination held by any individual is called a *status set:* for instance, daughter, sister, worker, teammate, and student.

Statuses affect the type of interactions individuals have. In some interactions (as with classmates), people are equals. In other situations, individuals have interchanges with people who hold superior or inferior statuses. If you are promoted to supervisor, your interaction with former peers and subordinates will change. Consider the possible interactions shown in Figure 5.2, in which the first relationship is between equals and the others are between those with unequal statuses.

With a friend, these status relationships are constantly being negotiated and bargained: "I'll do what you want tonight, but tomorrow I choose." By contrast, when individuals are in dominant or subordinate positions, power or deference affects their interactions. Gender, power, and hierarchical relationships are important in determining interaction patterns. The more powerful person, such as one who has more wealth or privilege, can interrupt in a conversation with his or her partner and show less deference in the interaction (Kim et al. 2007; Reid and Ng 2006; Wood 2008).

People have no control over certain statuses they hold. These **ascribed statuses** are *often assigned at birth and do not change during an individual's lifetime.* For example, while a few people undergo sex change operations, for most people sex is an ascribed characteristic. Ascribed statuses are assigned to a person without regard for personal desires, talents, or choices. In some societies, the caste or social position into which one is born (e.g., "Untouchables" or "Dalits" in India) is an ascribed status because it is usually impossible to change.

FIGURE 5.2 Types of Status Relationships Experienced by You

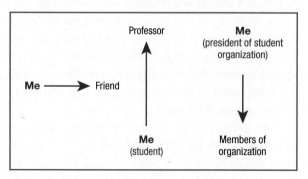

Achieved status, on the other hand, *is chosen or earned by the decisions one makes and sometimes by personal ability*. Attaining a higher education, for example, improves an individual's occupational opportunities and thus his or her achieved status. Being a guitarist in a band is an achieved status and so is being a criminal, for both are earned positions based on the person's own decisions and actions.

At a particular time in life or under certain circumstances, one of an individual's statuses may become most important and take precedence over others; this is called a **master status**. Whether it is an occupation, parental status, or something else, it dominates and shapes much of an individual's life, activities, self-concept, and position in the community for a period of time. For a person who is very ill, for instance, that illness may occupy a master status, needing constant attention from doctors, influencing social relationships, and determining what that person can do in family, work, or community activities.

Thinking Sociologically

What are your statuses? Which ones are ascribed, and which are achieved statuses? Do you have a master status? How do these statuses affect the way you interact with others in your network of relationships?

The Relationship Between Status and Role

Every status (position) in your network includes certain behaviors and obligations as you carry out the **roles**, *the expected behaviors, rights, obligations, responsibilities, and privileges assigned to a social status*. Roles are the dynamic, action part of statuses in a society. They define how each individual in an interaction is expected to act (Linton 1937). The role of a person holding the status of "college student" includes behaviors and obligations such as attending classes, studying, taking tests, writing papers, and interacting with professors and other students. We enter most statuses with some knowledge of how to carry out the roles dictated by our culture. Through the process of socialization, we learn roles by observing others, watching television and films, reading, and being taught by family members, teachers, and others how to carry out the status.

Both statuses (positions) and roles (behavioral expectations of people holding the status) form links with other people in the social world because they must be carried out in relationships with others. For example,

a father has certain obligations (or roles) toward his children and their mother. The position of father exists not on its own but in relationship to significant others who have reciprocal ties.

Your status of student requires certain behaviors and expectations, depending on whether you are interacting with a dean, a professor, an advisor, a classmate, or a prospective employer. This is because the role expectations of the status of student vary as one interacts with specific people in other statuses. In Figure 5.3, the student is the subject, and the others are those with whom the student interacts in the status of student.

Within a group, individuals may hold both formal and informal statuses. One illustration is the formal status of high school students, each of whom plays a number of informal roles in cliques that are not part of the formal school structure. A student may be known, for example, as one of the popular crowd, a jock, a nerd, a loner, a goth, a clown, a prep, or an outcast. Each of these roles takes place in a status relationship with others: teacher-student, peer-peer, coach-athlete. The connections between statuses, roles, and environment are illustrated in Table 5.1.

Social networks may be based on ascribed characteristics, such as age and sex, or on achieved status, such as education, occupation, or common interests. These links, in turn, form the basis for social interactions and group structures (Hall 2002). However, at times, individuals cannot carry out their roles as others expect them to, creating role strain or conflict.

FIGURE 5.3 Types of Interactions Students Have With Reciprocal Status Holders

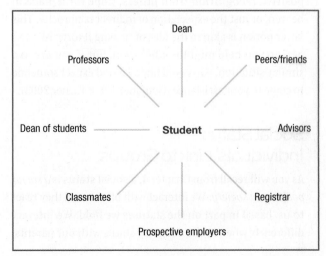

Table 5.1   The Relationship Between Statuses and Roles

Status (position in structure)	Role (behavior, rights, obligations)
Student	*Formal*
	Study, attend class, turn in assignments
	Informal
	Be a jock, clown, partier, nerd
Parent	*Formal*
	Provide financial support, child care
	Informal
	Be a playmate, lead family activities
Employee	*Formal*
	Carry out work responsibilities, be on time
	Informal
	Befriend coworkers, join lunch group, represent company in bowling league

Role Strain and Role Conflict

Most people have faced times in their lives when they simply could not carry out all the obligations of a status, such as student—write two papers, study adequately for two exams, complete the portfolio for the studio art class, finish the reading assignments for five classes, and memorize lines for the oral interpretation class, all in the same week. Every status carries role expectations, the way the status is supposed to be carried out according to generally accepted societal or group norms. Yet in these cases, individuals face role strain, the *tension among roles within a status.* Role strain causes the individual to be pulled in many directions by various obligations of the single status, as in the example regarding the status of "student." Another such strain is often experienced by first-time fathers as they attempt to reconcile their role expectations of fathering with ideas held by their wives.

To resolve role strain, individuals can cope in several possible ways, such as passing the problem off lightly (and thus not doing well in classes), considering the dilemma humorous, becoming highly focused and pulling a couple of all-nighters to get everything done, or becoming stressed, tense, fretful, and immobilized because of the strain. Most often, individuals set priorities based on their values and make decisions accordingly: "I'll work hard in the class for my major and let another one slide."

Role conflict refers to *conflict between the roles of two or more social statuses.* It differs from role strain in that conflict is *between* the roles of two or more statuses, rather than tension between roles within one of the statuses. For example, college athletes face role conflicts from competing demands on their time (Adler and Adler 1991, 2004). They must complete their studies on time, attend practices and be prepared for games, perhaps attend meetings of a Greek house to which they belong, and get home for a little brother's birthday. Similarly, a student may be going to school, holding down a part-time job to help make ends meet, and raising a family. If the student's child gets sick, the status of parent comes into conflict with that of student and worker. In the case of role conflict, the person may choose—or be informed by others—which status is the master status. Figure 5.4 illustrates the difference between role conflict and role strain.

Most statuses and accompanying roles come and go. For example, you will not always be a student. You may or may not be married at different points in your life. You will retire from your job. As people grow older, they disengage from some statuses and engage in new and different statuses and roles.

Our statuses connect us to and make us integral parts of meso- and macro-level organizations. Our place within the social world, then, is guaranteed, even obligatory, because of

Role Strain of Student Athletes

FIGURE 5.4   Role Strain and Role Conflict

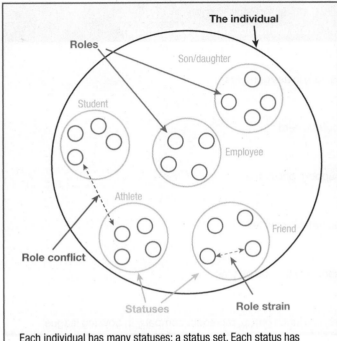

Each individual has many statuses: a status set. Each status has many roles: a role set. A conflict between two roles of the same status is a *role strain*. A conflict between the roles of two different statuses is a *role conflict*.

Thinking Sociologically

Using Figure 5.4 as a model, fill in the statuses you hold in your social world and the roles you perform in these statuses. Then, list three examples of role conflicts and three examples of role strains that you experience.

statuses we hold—within small groups (family and peers), in larger groups and organizations (school and work organizations), in institutions (political parties or religious denominations), and ultimately as citizens of the society and the world (citizens, and workers in global corporations). Each of these statuses connects us to a group setting.

GROUPS IN OUR SOCIAL WORLD: THE MICRO–MESO CONNECTION

Groups refer to *units involving two or more people who interact with each other because of shared common interests, goals, experiences, and needs* (Drafke 2008). As we have seen, humans are social beings. We become members of society and gain a sense of self through social interaction. Groups meet our social needs for belonging and acceptance, support us throughout our lives, and place restrictions on us. We also need groups for protection, to obtain food, to manufacture goods, and to get jobs done. Groups can be small, intimate environments—micro-level interactions with family or friends—or they can become quite large meso-level organizations. In any case, it is through our group memberships that the micro and meso levels are connected.

Not all collections of individuals are groups. For instance, your family is a group, but people shopping at a mall or waiting for a bus are not a group because they do not regularly interact or acknowledge shared common interests.

Groups form through a series of succeeding steps. Consider people forming a soccer team in a new league: The first step is initial interaction. If the interactions with the other members are rewarding and meet individuals' needs, the individuals will attempt to maintain the benefits the group provides and form a team (Mills 1984). In the second step, a collective goal emerges. For example, team members may work together to plan practice and game schedules, buy uniforms, and advertise the games. In the third and final step, the group attempts to expand its collective goals by building on the former steps and by pursuing new goals. For example, the team may reach out to new players, to coaches, and to supporters for funding.

As noted earlier, groups impact both society and individuals. Neither would function properly without groups. The importance of groups becomes especially clear when we consider two social problems: anomie and suicide.

Group Solidarity, Anomie, and Suicide

Who commits suicide? Did you know that the answer to this is closely related to an individual's group affiliations? Early sociologist Émile Durkheim took a unique approach to making sense of suicide trends. In his volume, *Suicide* ([1897] 1964), he discussed the social factors contributing to suicide. Using existing statistical data to determine suicide rates in European populations, Durkheim looked at variables such as sex, age, religion, nationality, and the season in which the suicide was committed. His findings demonstrate that individual problems cannot be understood without also understanding the group context in which they occur.

Durkheim found that Protestants committed suicide more often than Catholics, urban folks more often than people living in small communities, people in highly developed and complex societies more frequently than those in simple societies, and people who lived alone more than those situated in families. The key variable linking these findings was the degree to which an individual was integrated into a group, that is, the degree of social bond with others. Those who belonged to more tightly knit groups were least likely to commit suicide, while those whose lives were less tied to those of others were most likely to kill themselves. Durkheim described this type of suicide, when the individual feels little social bond to the group or society and lacks ties, such as family or friends, that might prevent suicide, as *egoistic suicide*.

A second type, *anomic suicide*, occurs when a society or one of its parts is in disorder, turmoil, or rapid change and lacks clear norms and guidelines for social behavior. With the rapid changes and continued breakdown of institutional structures in many modern and modernizing societies, religious and political groups may vie for power and offer contrasting definitions of reality. Social controls (police and military forces) may be strained, and leaders struggle to cope with the turmoil and lack of consensus. The result of the collapse of norms is anomie, *the state of normlessness that occurs when the rules for behavior in society break down under extreme stress from rapid social change or conflict* (Merton 1938). This anomie tends to lead to higher rates of suicide.

Durkheim's third type of suicide, *altruistic suicide*, differs from the others in that it involves such a strong bond and group obligation that the individual is willing to die for the group. Self-survival becomes less important than group survival (Durkheim [1897] 1964). Examples of altruistic suicide include the young suicide bombers in Iraq, Afghanistan, and Pakistan carrying out suicide missions against their country's police forces and sometimes against NATO or American military forces, which they have defined as invading forces. U.S. military Medal of Honor recipients who sacrificed their own lives to save those of the men in their units are another example. These suicides usually occur in social groups that have very clear norms and high levels of consensus about values arising from their religious or political commitments.

Durkheim's work revealed that suicide rates are strongly influenced by social and psychological factors that can operate at the meso or macro level. His findings

Jorge Parra was one of a group of disabled workers in a General Motors plant in Colombia who were disabled while working and then fired for their inability to do the work. He and more than a dozen other injured workers went on a hunger strike, sewing their mouths closed so they could ingest only liquids. Jorge decided he would fast until death, if necessary. He had gone more than 70 days without food by January 2013, when the United Auto Workers intervened and agreed to help negotiate a solution, provided that Parra end his death fast. Jorge was willing to commit *altruistic suicide*—to die voluntarily for the good of his group.

and those of others show that groups impact our lives and even our desire to continue living (Hall 2002; Nolan, Triplett, and McDonough 2010; Pescosolido and Georgianna 1989). No individual is an island. The importance of groups and social influence from various levels in the system is an underlying theme of this text. To more fully understand the influence of groups over us, though, we must become familiar with the different types of groups in which we interact.

Types of Groups

Each of us belongs to several types of groups. Some groups provide intimacy and close relationships, whereas others do not. Some are required affiliations, and others are voluntary. Some provide personal satisfaction, and others are obligatory or necessary for survival.

Primary groups are at the most micro level and *characterized by cooperation among close, intimate, long-term relationships*. Your family members and best friends, school classmates, and close work associates are all of primary importance in your everyday life. Primary groups provide a sense of belonging and shared identity. Group members care about you, and you care about the other group members, creating a sense of loyalty. Approval and disapproval from the primary group influence the activities you choose to pursue. Belonging to the group is the main reason for membership. The group is of intrinsic value—enjoyed for its own sake—rather than for some utilitarian value such as making money.

For individuals, primary groups provide an anchor point in society. You were born into a primary group—your family. You hold many statuses and play a variety of roles in primary relationships—those of child, sibling, partner, parent, relative, close friend, and so on. You meet with other members face-to-face or keep in touch on a regular basis and know a great deal about their lives. What makes them happy or angry? What are sensitive issues? In primary groups you share values, say what you think, let down your hair, dress as you like, and share your concerns and emotions, your successes and failures (Goffman 1967, [1959] 2001). Charles H. Cooley ([1909] 1983), who first discussed the term *primary group*, saw these relationships as the source of close human feelings and emotions—love, cooperation, and concern.

Secondary groups are *those with formal, impersonal, and businesslike relationships, often temporary, and based on a specific limited purpose or goal*. Secondary groups are usually large and task-oriented because they have a specific purpose to achieve and focus on accomplishing a goal. In the modern world, people cannot always live under the protective wing of primary group relationships. As children grow, they move from the security and acceptance of primary groups—the home and neighborhood peer group—to a secondary group—the large school classroom, where each child is one of many students vying for the teacher's (and others') approval and competing for rewards. Similarly, the job world requires formal relations and procedures: applications, interviews, contracts. Employment is based on specific skills, training, and job knowledge—competence to carry out the role expectations in the position.

Because each individual in a secondary group carries out a specialized task, communication between members is often specialized as well. Contacts with doctors, store clerks, and even professors are generally formal and impersonal parts of organizational life. Sometimes associations with secondary groups are long lasting, sometimes of short duration—as in the courses you are taking this term. Secondary groups operate at the meso and macro levels of our social world, but they affect individuals at the micro level.

As societies modernize, they evolve from small towns and close, primary relationships to predominantly urban areas with more formal, secondary relationships. In the postindustrial world, with family members scattered across countries and around the world, secondary relationships have come to play ever greater roles in people's lives. Large work organizations may provide day care, health clinics, financial planning, courses to upgrade skills, and sports leagues.

Small micro-level and large macro-level groups often occur together. Behind most successful secondary groups are primary groups. Consider the small work group within a large organization that eats together or goes out for a beer on Friday afternoons. These relationships help individuals feel a part of the larger organization, just as residents of large urban areas have small groups of neighborhood friends. Table 5.2 summarizes some of the dimensions of primary and secondary groups.

Problems in primary groups can affect performance in secondary groups. Consider the problems of a student who has an argument with a partner or roommate, or experiences a failure of his or her family support system due to divorce or other problems. Self-concepts and social skills diminish during times of family stress and affect group relationships in other parts of one's life (Drafke 2008).

Thinking Sociologically

In the past, raising children was considered a family task, done by the primary family group. Today, many children are in child care settings, often run by secondary groups. What differences do you see between the experiences a child receives in a family and in child care? What might be the advantages and disadvantages of each? Can a secondary group provide care comparable with that provided by a family? Can the secondary group provide better care than families? Why or why not?

Reference groups are *composed of members who act as role models and establish standards against which members measure their conduct*. Individuals look to reference groups to set guidelines for behavior and decision making. Successful businesses can serve as reference groups for other businesses. Ethnic groups can also be reference groups. Ethnic groups can provide adolescent members with strong reference group standards by which to judge themselves. The stronger the ethnic pride and identification, the more some teens may separate themselves from contact with members of other ethnic groups (Schaefer and Kunz 2007). This can be functional or

Office Politics

Table 5.2   **Primary and Secondary Group Characteristics**

	Primary Group	Secondary Group
Quality of relationships	Personal orientation	Goal orientation
Duration of relationships	Usually long term	Variable, often short term
Breadth of activities	Broad, usually involving many activities	Narrow, usually involving a few largely goal-directed activities
Subjective perception of relationships	As an end in itself (friendship, belonging)	As a means to an end (to accomplish a task, earn money)
Typical examples	Families, close friendships	Coworkers, political organizations

dysfunctional for the teens, as shown in the next section on in-groups and out-groups.

An in-group is *one to which an individual feels a sense of loyalty and belonging.* It also may serve as a reference group (any group may fit into more than one category of group). An out-group is *one to which an individual does not belong, but more than that, it is a group that competes with or acts in opposition to an in-group.*

Membership in an in-group may be based on sex, race, ethnicity, social class, religion, political affiliation, the school one attends, an interest group such as the fraternity or sorority one joins, or the area where one lives. People tend to judge others according to their own in-group identity. Members of the in-group—for example, supporters of a high school team—often feel hostility toward or reject out-group members—boosters of the rival team. The perceived outside threat or hostility is often exaggerated, but it does help create the in-group members' feelings of solidarity. Another example might be the "preps" in a high school who control many resources because they control the school's student council and many of the leadership positions in the school. They are an in-group, but the goths, punks, or burnouts (the out-group) reject the preps and seek alternatives to the activities planned by the preps. Unfortunately, these feelings of hostility can result in prejudice and ethnocentrism, overlooking the individual differences of in-group members.

Thinking Sociologically

What are some examples of your own group affiliations: Primary groups? Secondary groups? Peer groups? Reference groups? In-groups and out-groups?

ORGANIZATIONS AND BUREAUCRACIES: THE MESO–MACRO CONNECTION

Our days are filled with activities that involve us with complex organizations: from the doctor's appointment to college classes; from the political rally for the issue we support to worship in a church, temple, or mosque; from paying state sales tax for our toothpaste to buying a sandwich at a fast-food franchise. Figure 5.5 shows the institutions of society, each made up of thousands of

© REUTERS/Soe Zeya Tun

Even Buddhist nuns, who spend much of their lives devoted to private meditation, need the support and solidarity of a group.

FIGURE 5.5 Our Social World: Institutions, Organizations, and Individual Status

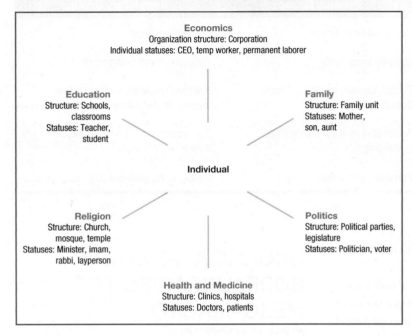

Economics
Organization structure: Corporation
Individual statuses: CEO, temp worker, permanent laborer

Education
Structure: Schools, classrooms
Statuses: Teacher, student

Family
Structure: Family unit
Statuses: Mother, son, aunt

Individual

Religion
Structure: Church, mosque, temple
Statuses: Minister, imam, rabbi, layperson

Politics
Structure: Political parties, legislature
Statuses: Politician, voter

Health and Medicine
Structure: Clinics, hospitals
Statuses: Doctors, patients

organizations (medical organizations, educational organizations, religious groups, economic corporations, political movements, the government itself), and each following the cultural norms of the society. We have statuses and roles in each group, and these link us to networks and the larger social world. We now look at how the modern forms of these organizations developed.

Modern Organizations and Their Evolution

Recall from Chapter 3 the discussion of types of societies, from hunter-gatherer to postindustrial. Each type of society entails different organizational structures (Blau 1956; Nolan and Lenski 2010). The development of modern organizations and bureaucracies began with the industrial revolution in the 1700s and 1800s. Increasingly complex organizations required and helped create what Max Weber called the rationalization of social life—*the attempt to maximize efficiency by creating rules and procedures focused solely on accomplishing goals* (Weber 1947). No longer were decisions made by tradition, custom, or the whim of a despot. Instead, trained leaders planned policies to achieve organizational efficiency. Tasks became more specialized, and some manual jobs were taken over by machines. People were expected to behave in purposeful, coordinated ways to advance organizational efficiency.

Formal organizations (also called *modern "rational" organizations*), *composed of complex secondary groups deliberately formed to pursue and achieve certain goals*, were created to standardize production and increase productivity, precision, and speed. They are called "formal organizations" because of the written charters, constitutions, bylaws, and procedures that govern them. Google, General Electric (GE), the Red Cross, the National Basketball Association (NBA), the Republican Party, and your university are all formal organizations.

Bureaucracies are *specific types of very large formal organizations that have the purpose of maximizing efficiency. They are characterized by set relations between participants, clearly laid-out procedures and rules, and pursuit of stated goals.* Bureaucratization evolved as the most efficient way of producing products economically for mass markets (Ritzer 2013b).

An example of a bureaucratic organization can be found in the fast-food empires and chain "box" stores spreading all around the world. The next "Sociology Around the World" feature describes the trend toward the "McDonaldization of society"—sociologist George Ritzer's pop culture term for rationalization in organizations.

Formal Organizations and Modern Life

Think about the many organizations that regularly affect your life: the legal system that passes laws, your college, your workplace, and voluntary organizations to which you belong. Human interactions take place in formal organizations, and formal organizations require human interaction to meet their organizational needs. Some organizations, such as the local chapter of the Rotary Club or a troop of the Girl Scouts, function at the micro level. Everyone is in a face-to-face relationship with every other member of the organization. However, those local groups are part of a nationwide meso-level organization. At the macro level, the federal government is a complex formal organization that influences the lives of every citizen and organization in the United States. Meanwhile

McDonaldization 📖

Sociology Around the World

The McDonaldization of Society

The process of rationalization described by Max Weber—the attempt to reach maximum bureaucratic efficiency—comes in a new modern version, expanded and streamlined, exemplified by the fast-food restaurant business that began to spread in the 1950s and chain "box" stores now found around the world. Efficient, rational, predictable sameness is sweeping the world—from diet centers such as Weight Watchers to Nutrisystem to 7-Eleven and from Walmart to Gap clothing stores with their lookalike layouts. Most major world cities feature McDonald's or KFC in the traditional main plazas of train stations for flustered foreigners and curious native consumers.

The McDonaldization of society, as George Ritzer (2013b) calls it, refers to several trends: First, *efficiency* is maximized by sameness—same store plans, same mass-produced items, same procedures. Second is *predictability*, the knowledge that each hamburger or piece of chicken will appear and taste the same, leaving nothing to chance. Third, everything is *calculated* so that the organization can ensure that everything fits a standard—every burger is cooked the same number of seconds on each side. Fourth, there is *increased control* over employees and customers so there are fewer variables to consider—including substitution of technology for human labor as a way to ensure predictability and efficiency.

What is the result of this efficient, predictable, planned, automated new world? According to Ritzer, the world is becoming more dehumanized, and efficiency is replacing individual creativity and human interactions. The mom-and-pop grocery, bed and breakfasts, and local craft or clothing shops are rapidly becoming a thing of the past. This process of the McDonaldization of society, meaning principles of efficiency and rationalization exemplified by fast-food chains, is coming to dominate more and more sectors of our social world (Ritzer 2013b). While there are aspects of this predictability that we all like, it also entails a loss of the uniqueness and local flavor that individual entrepreneurs bring to a community.

Some large corporations have started a movement toward "Starbuckization" to impress consumers tired of McDonaldization. For examples, Starbucks, with its own music mixes, comfortable seats, and Wi-Fi, makes customers feel like they are purchasing a cultural product along with their coffee. This culture, however, is as controlled as any other McDonaldized endeavor, making Starbucks a McClone at its core.

McDonaldization is so widespread and influential that many modern universities are now McDonaldized. A large lecture hall is a very efficient way of teaching sociology or biology to many students at once. Similarly, massive online classes, PowerPoint presentations, multiple-choice exams, and a limited choice of textbooks for professors increase the predictability of content in course offerings. Finally, grade point averages and credit hours completed are very calculated—and efficient—ways to judge student accomplishments.

Thinking Sociologically

To what extent do you think your college is McDonaldized? Why? What can you and your fellow students do to address the problem of the McDonaldization of higher education?

The Mall of America near Minneapolis is the largest mall in North America, with 4.3 miles of storefront footage, 520-plus stores on five stories, 4.2 million total square feet, and 25 amusement park rides. Yet many of the stores look like clones of one another, and this cathedral to consumerism can feel like an experience in the McDonaldization of society.

Characteristics of Bureaucracy

If you have been to a Caribbean, African, Asian, or Middle Eastern market, you know that the bartering system is used to settle on a mutually agreeable price for goods. This system is more personal and involves intense interaction between the seller and the buyer, but it also takes more time and is less efficient than the buying process to which shoppers from North America are accustomed. Bartering can be frustrating to the uninitiated visitor used to the relative efficiency and predictability of bureaucracy: going to a store, selecting a product, and paying a set price. As societies become more complex, they tend to adopt bureaucratic forms of organization.

At the beginning of the 20th century, Max Weber (1864–1920) looked for the reasons behind the transition from traditional society to bureaucratic, capitalist society. He wanted to understand why bureaucracy came to dominate the forms of organization in some countries more rapidly than in others. He found that bureaucracies arise first in more democratic nations with capitalist, industrial economic systems. As these countries established systems of government and economics whereby positions were granted based on merit, rather than tradition, their economies could grow much faster. This growth, in turn, required more efficient and rational means of organization—bureaucratization (Weber 1947).

Weber's concept of the *ideal-type bureaucracy* refers to the dominant and essential characteristics of organizations designed for reliability and efficiency (Weber 1947). The term simply describes an organization with a particular set of traits, not a necessarily good or perfect organization. Any particular bureaucracy is unlikely to have all the characteristics of the ideal type, but the degree of bureaucratization is measured by how closely an organization resembles the core characteristics of the ideal type. The following shows Weber's ideal-type bureaucracy with examples related to schools today:

1. *Division of labor based on technical competence:* Administrators lead but do not teach, and instructors teach only in areas of their certification; staff are assigned positions for which their credentials make them most qualified, and recruitment and promotion are governed by formal policies.
2. *Administrative hierarchy:* There is a specified chain of command and designated channels of communication, from school board to superintendent to principal to teacher.

multinational corporations and entities like the United Nations are global in their reach.

Some organizations provide us with work necessary for survival. Others are forced on us—prisons, psychiatric hospitals, military draft systems, and even education—up until a certain age. Still others are organizations we believe in and voluntarily join—scouts, environmental groups, sports leagues, and religious organizations. Residents of the United States tend to volunteer for organizations at higher rates than people in many other countries do (Charities Aid Foundation 2012).

3. *Formal rules and regulations:* Written procedures and rules—perhaps published in an administrative manual—spell out system-wide requirements, including discipline practices, testing procedures, curricula, sick days for teachers, penalties for student tardiness, field trip policies, and other matters.

4. *Impersonal relationships:* Formal relationships tend to prevail between teachers and students and between teachers and administrative staff (superintendents, principals, counselors); written records and formal communication provide a paper trail for all decisions.

5. *Emphasis on rationality and efficiency to reach goals:* Established processes are used, based on the best interests of the school. Efficiency is defined in terms of the lowest overall cost to the organization in reaching a goal, not in terms of personal consequences.

Although the list of characteristics makes bureaucracies sound formal and rigid, informal structures allow organizational members to deviate from rules both to meet the goals of the organization more efficiently and to humanize an otherwise uncaring and sterile workplace. The *informal structure* includes the unwritten norms and the interpersonal networks that people use within an organization to carry out roles. Likewise, although bylaws, constitutions, or contracts spell out the way things are supposed to be done, people often develop unwritten shortcuts to accomplish goals. For example, the U.S. Postal Service has rules specifying that letter carriers are not supposed to walk across people's lawns, yet if they did not find shortcuts, it would take much longer for mail to be delivered.

Informal norms are not always compatible with those of the formal organization. For example, what if the norm at your organization is to do the least amount of work possible? Have you ever been pressured to *not* work hard by your coworkers? Consider the following example from a famous classical study. In the Western Electric plant near Chicago, the study found that new workers were quickly socialized to do "a fair day's work" and those who did more or less than the established norm—what the work group thought was fair—were considered "rate busters" or "chiselers" and experienced pressure from the group to conform. These informal norms help give workers a degree of power but make the formal goals of the organization harder to achieve (Roethlisberger and Dickson 1939).

They also indicate a lack of clear communication or enforcement of the rules of the bureaucratic system.

Thinking Sociologically

How closely does each of Weber's characteristics of ideal-type bureaucracy describe your college or your work setting? Is your college highly bureaucratized, with many rules and regulations? Are decisions based on efficiency and cost-effectiveness, educational quality, or both? To what extent is your work setting characterized by hierarchy, and formal rules governing your work time? To what extent is it shaped by informal relationships?

Issues in Bureaucracies

Despite the fact that some informal norms and red tape can hamper bureaucratic efficiency, bureaucracies are likely here to stay. They are the most efficient form of modern organization yet devised. Nonetheless, several individual and organizational problems created by bureaucratic structures are important to understand. These deficiencies arise from our roles in organizations or our interactions with organizations. Some examples of problems that can arise in bureaucracies are decreased levels of professionalism in bureaucracies, alienation, oligarchy, and goal displacement.

Bureaucracy, some argue, can be the number one enemy of *professionalism*, for it reduces individuals' autonomy. First, bureaucrats insist that authority rests in the person who holds an organizational status or title in the hierarchy rather than the person with the most expertise. Second, bureaucrats tend to reward people with external rewards such as bonuses rather than internal motivations, such as greater freedom in how they do their work. Third, bureaucrats focus on the needs of the organization as primary rather than on the needs of the client or professional. For example, a scientist hired by a tobacco company faced a dilemma when his research findings did not support the company position that nicotine is not addictive. They wanted him to falsify his research, which would be a violation of professional ethics. The potential clash between professionals and bureaucracy raises key concerns as universities, hospitals, and other large organizations are governed increasingly by bureaucratic principles (Roberts and Donahue 2000).

Alienation, *feeling uninvolved, uncommitted, unappreciated, and unconnected to the group or the society,* occurs when workers are assigned routine, boring tasks or dead-end jobs with no possibility of advancement. Marx believed that alienation is a structural feature of capitalism, with serious consequences: Workers lose their sense of purpose and become dehumanized and objectified in their work, creating a product that they often do not see completed and for which they do not get the profits (Marx [1844] 1964). Workers who see possibilities for advancement put more energy into the organization, but those stuck in their positions are less involved and put more energy into activities outside the workplace (Kanter 1977).

● Thinking Sociologically

How might giving workers increased autonomy, more participation in decision making, and stockholder shares in the company enhance commitment and productivity in your place of work? What might be some risks or downsides to such worker input and freedom?

©REUTERS/Desmond Boylan

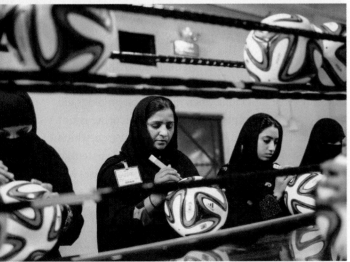

©Reuters/Sara Farid

Women in many countries tend to have low-paid, dead-end jobs that result in alienation. Most, however, need the work to support themselves and their families, such as the women in these photos.

Oligarchy, *the concentration of power in the hands of a small group,* is a common occurrence in bureaucratic organizations. In the early 1900s, Robert Michels, a French sociologist, wrote about the *iron law of oligarchy,* the idea that power becomes concentrated in the hands of a small group of leaders in political, business, voluntary, or other organizations. Initially, organizational needs, more than the motivation for power, cause these few stable leaders to emerge. As organizations grow, however, a division of labor emerges so that only a few leaders have access to information, resources, and the overall picture. This, in turn, causes leaders who enjoy their elite positions of power to become entrenched (Michels [1911] 1967).

Goal displacement occurs *when the original motives or goals of the organization are displaced by new, secondary goals.* Organizations are formed to meet specific goals. For example, religious organizations are established to worship a deity and serve humanity on behalf of that deity, schools are founded to educate children, and social work agencies are organized to serve needy citizens. Yet, over time, the original goals may be met or become less important as other motivations and interests emerge. These organizations can sometimes become focused on the benefits they can bring to patrons or employees, rather than on fulfilling the goals for which they were established (Merton 1938; Whyte 1956). For example, in 2012, Pedro Espada Jr., a former New York State senator, pleaded guilty to charges of stealing money from health care clinics he ran in the Bronx. The clinics were created to care for poor people in the area, but Espada used them to enrich himself, family, and friends (Federal Bureau of Investigation 2012b).

Thinking Sociologically

In what areas of your college or workplace do you see goal displacement? In other words, where do you see decisions being driven by goals other than the original purpose of the organization?

Diversity and Equity in Organizations. In a global and diverse society, it makes sense to have a diverse workforce. The interaction of people who see things differently because of religious beliefs, ethnic backgrounds, and gender experiences increases productivity and creativity in many organizations. Having a wide range of perspectives can lead to better problem solving (Florida 2004; Molotch 2003). Successful business owners know they need to have a diverse group of employees in order to thrive. That is also one reason why colleges promote diversity on college campuses. The U.S. Supreme Court held hearings in 2013 on affirmative action programs in higher education, programs that promote diversity on campuses and prepare a diverse workforce by actively seeking qualified underrepresented minority students for positions. Fifty large corporations, including Walmart, Pfizer, Halliburton, and American Express, joined together to write a brief in support of affirmative action programs in higher education. While these corporations gave most of their political donations to Republicans, they supported the Obama administration's arguments in favor of affirmative action, because they know a diverse workforce is good for business (Wilson 2012).

Despite efforts to diversify the workplace, women and other minorities in bureaucracies are underrepresented in upper management positions. They often find themselves with little authority and less pay than others with similar skills and credentials (Arulampalam, Booth, and Bryan 2007). It is also often much harder for minorities to even make it onto the lowest rung of bureaucratic organizations. For example, in New York City, among *equally qualified* whites, blacks, and Latinos applying for low-wage jobs, Latinos were less likely than, and blacks were *half* as likely as, white applicants to receive a job or callback. Even whites with criminal records were just as likely as, if not more likely than, black and Latino applicants *without* a criminal record to get a callback or job offer (Pager, Western, and Bonikowski 2009). These discriminatory actions are irrational and dysfunctional to organizations (Florida 2004, 2012a; Molotch 2003).

NATIONAL AND GLOBAL NETWORKS: THE MACRO LEVEL

Understanding people unlike us, networking with people from different cultures, and being open to new ideas have become core competencies in our globalizing social world. Increasingly, colleges have study-abroad programs and corporations seek multilingual employees with cultural competence in diverse settings. One young college graduate with a sociology degree found that she could use her sociology skills in leading groups of college-age students in international travel experiences. She explains this use of sociology in the next "Sociologists in Action."

With modern communication and transportation systems and the ability to transfer ideas and money with a touch of the keyboard, global networks are superseding national boundaries. Some businesses are global and can easily move their physical headquarters from one nation

Global organizations like United Nations Women and microfinance groups like the Grameen Bank and FINCA provide loans and other supports for women to begin their own business enterprises. Such assistance for women often helps whole communities.

SOCIOLOGISTS IN ACTION:
ELISE ROBERTS

Using Sociology in International Travel and Intercultural Education

By Elise Roberts

After graduating from college with a bachelor's degree in sociology, I left the country to backpack through Mexico and Central America. My studies helped me to be more objective and aware as I experienced other societies. My international travel helped me examine my own societal assumptions and further understand how society creates so much of one's experience and view of the world. Eventually, I found a job leading groups of teenagers on alternative-education trips abroad. I was excited to get the job, but I was soon to learn that leading groups of teenagers in other countries is actually very hard work.

What struck me on meeting my first group was that I had very few students who initially understood this sociological perspective that I took for granted and that was so helpful in dealing with others. At times, my students would make fun of the way things were done in other countries, calling them "weird" or "stupid." They would mock the local traditions, until we discussed comparable traditions in U.S. culture. These students were not mean or unintelligent. In fact, they loved the places we were seeing and the people we were meeting. They just thought everything was factually, officially weird. They had been socialized to understand their own society's ways as "right" and "normal." They were fully absorbed in the U.S. society, and they had never questioned it before.

It was rewarding to apply concepts from my textbooks in the real world. My coleaders and I learned to have fun while encouraging our students to become more socially conscious and analytical about their travel experience. We sent the groups out on scavenger hunts, and they would inevitably

come back proudly announcing what they had paid for a rickshaw ride—only to learn that they had paid 10 times the local price. We would use this experience to talk about the role of foreigners, the assumptions that the local population made due to our skin color, and the culture of bartering. They had to learn to understand "odd" gestures, like pointing with the lips or side-to-side nodding. We would use these experiences to discuss nonverbal communication and gestures that we take for granted in U.S. culture.

We would encourage our novice travelers to interact with the people around them, which helped them understand the struggles facing immigrants and non-English speakers in the United States. We would force them to have conversations while standing toe-to-toe with each other, and they would finish with backaches from leaning away from one another. We would not allow them to explain their behavior with "because it's creepy to stand so close together," even though this was the consensus. "Why do you feel uncomfortable?" we would ask. "Why is this weird?" The answer has to do with social constructions of what is "normal" in any society.

Of course, while traveling internationally, one is surrounded by various other sociological issues, such as different racial or ethnic conflicts, gender roles, or class hierarchies, and learning about these issues was a part of our program as well. Without realizing it, many group conversations and meetings began to remind me of some of my favorite undergraduate sociology classes. "Study sociology!" I would say, plugging my major to the most interested students.

I have always thought that travel was an incredibly useful means not only to learn about the society and culture one is visiting but also to learn much about oneself and one's home society. For teenagers who otherwise might never step back to think about the role of being a foreigner or the traditions and social patterns they take for granted, it is even more important. Traveling abroad on my own and leading programs overseas were such extremely rich and rewarding experiences not only due to the cross-cultural exchanges and the intense personal examination that I saw in my students but also because it was fascinating and rewarding to

be able to use my sociology degree every day on my job.

• •

Elise Roberts graduated from Macalester College with a major in sociology. Her postcollege travels took her through Central America, the South Pacific, and many parts of Asia. She recently graduated from Columbia University with a master's degree in international social work and is a regional organizer for Witness for Peace.

to another (Ritzer 2007). This has helped many companies avoid paying millions of dollars in taxes. Apple, one of the multinational companies best at avoiding taxes, has managed to reduce its taxes by billions of dollars through "routing profits through Irish subsidiaries and the Netherlands and then to the Caribbean." This practice is now common as many corporations can move freely from nation to nation, in search of the largest profit possible (Duhigg and Kocieniewski 2013).

Profit, efficiency, and calculability are highly prized in multinational corporations. However, as these Western notions of public life are exported to other countries, a severe backlash has occurred in some nations. In many Middle Eastern Islamic countries, for example, these values clash with Muslim loyalties and priorities. The result has been high levels of anger at the United States and Western Europe. Many scholars believe that Middle Eastern anger at the United States is based not just on opposition to freedom and democracy but also on what some Middle Easterners see as the crass greed and impersonal organizational structures we try to import into their micro-, meso-, and macro-level worlds. They feel that their very culture is threatened (Ritzer 2007).

Radical fundamentalist movements—groups fueled by religious beliefs and socioeconomic stressors and view the world in absolutes—are mostly antimodernization movements turned militant (Antoun 2008; Marty and Appleby 2004). They have emerged in Christian, Jewish, Islamic, Sikh, and other groups, largely as a response to perceived threats to their ways of life (Armstrong 2000). Some aspects of global terrorism and international conflict are a response to the way the Western world organizes its social life and exports it to other parts of the world. These conflicts, in turn, have resulted in the mobilization of the

armed forces in the United States. A consequence is that members of your own family might be serving abroad even as you read these pages.

 Thinking Sociologically

How has global interaction been transformed during your lifetime through Internet technology? Give an example of how you can learn about what is happening in, say, Syria right now by using the Internet. Does this make you feel more connected to people there? Why or why not?

POLICY ISSUES: WOMEN AND GLOBALIZATION

Women in many parts of the world are viewed as second-class citizens, the most economically, politically, and socially marginalized people on the planet, caught in expectations of religion, patriarchy, and roles needed to sustain life (Schneider and Silverman 2006). They run households, and are often the main support for children in poor countries. Women produce 80% to 90% of the food crops in sub-Saharan Africa, and almost 50% in the world (Food and Agriculture Organization of the United Nations 2010–2011). Yet, they account for 70% of the world's population living in absolute poverty (Global Fund for Women 2012). To help their children survive, most women do whatever their situation allows to make money: street selling, low-paying factory assembly line work, piecework (i.e., sewing clothing in their homes), prostitution and sex work, and domestic service. Throughout this book, we discuss causes of and policies to address the many problems facing women at each level of analysis.

Tax Shelter   Corporate Social Responsibility

One macro-level organization with policies to help raise the status of women through development is the United Nations. The UN and other organizations concerned with women's status advocate for women to have more ownership or control of land and an even larger role in agriculture, estimating that this could boost food production 20% to 30%, while improving the lives of women (Boulding and Dye 2002; Global Fund for Women 2012).

A world development report outlines four priorities for improving the conditions for women: "1. Reducing excess female mortality (especially maternal mortality during birth) and closing education gaps; 2. Improving access to economic opportunities for women; 3. Increasing women's voice and agency in the household and society; and 4. Limiting the reproduction of gender inequality across generations" (World Development Report 2012). Many projects have emerged, including microlending organizations (Grameen Bank, SEWA, FINCA, CARE), allowing individuals and groups of women to borrow money to start cooperatives and other small-business ventures. These organizations can have very beneficial effects if used wisely by policy makers who care about the people involved and the participants are given proper support and technical assistance. In the next few chapters, we will learn about some of the factors that cause some individuals and countries to be poorer than others.

Our networks play a major role in setting norms and controlling our behaviors, usually resulting in our conformity to the social expectations of those in our network. This, of course, contributes to the stability of the entire social system because deviation can threaten the existence of "normal" patterns, as we see in the next chapter.

WHAT HAVE WE LEARNED?

Each of us has a network of people and groups that surround us. The scope of our networks has broadened with the increased complexity of societies and includes the global social world. Indeed, it is sometimes hard to recognize how far our networks reach. Although some of our social experiences are informal (unstructured), we are also profoundly affected by another phenomenon of the past three centuries—highly structured bureaucracies. As a result of both, our experiences and personal lives are far more extensively linked to meso- and macro-level events and to people and places on the other side of the globe than were those of our parents. If we hope to understand our lives, we must understand this broad context. Although it may have been possible to live without global connections and bureaucratic systems several centuries ago, these networks are intricately woven into our lifestyles and our economic systems today. The question is whether we will control these networks or they will control us.

KEY POINTS

- People in the modern world are connected through one acquaintance to another in a chain of links, referred to as networks, that can now span the globe. (See pp. 125–126.)

- We interpret interpersonal interactions at the micro level through unspoken assumptions based on the social context, nonverbal communication, and the physical space between people. (See pp. 127–128.)

- Many of our behaviors are shaped by the statuses (social positions) we hold and the roles (expectations associated with a status) we play. However, our multiple-status occupancy can create role conflicts (between the roles of two statuses) and role strains (between the role expectations of a single status). (See pp. 131–134.)

- When the norms of behavior are unclear, we may experience anomie (normlessness), and when anomie spreads in a society, suicide rates rise. (See pp. 134–135.)

- Various types of groups affect our behavior—from primary and secondary groups to peer groups and reference groups. (See pp. 135–136.)

- At the meso and macro levels, we find that formal organizations in the contemporary modern world have become bureaucratized. Bureaucratic organizations are ruled by rational calculation of the organization's goals rather than by tradition or emotional ties, tend to expand, are governed by impersonal formal rules, and stress efficiency and rational decision making. (See pp. 137–138.)

- Bureaucracies often create particular issues that may make them inefficient or destructive, such as alienation, oligarchies, and goal displacement. (See pp. 138–141.)

- In a global and diverse society, it makes sense to have a diverse workforce. Discrimination against minorities in promotion and hiring is irrational and dysfunctional for organizations. (See pp. 142–143.)

- Some scholars think that the impersonal mode of organizing social life—so common in the West for several centuries now—is a critical factor in anti-American and anti-Western resistance movements. (See pp. 143–145.)

DISCUSSION QUESTIONS

1. Think about your social network. How useful might it be in helping you get a job (or a better job) once you graduate from college? Why?

2. During a typical day, when do you engage in front- and backstage behavior? Why? With whom do you engage in each? Why?

3. Have you ever experienced role strain because of your status as a student? Explain why or why not. If so, how did/do you cope with it?

4. Most college students, particularly those with family, work, and/or sports team obligations, deal with role conflict. Describe a time when you dealt with a conflict between the roles you carry out and what you did about it. How might colleges and universities diminish role conflict among students?

5. To what primary and secondary groups do you belong? How does your involvement (or lack thereof) in primary groups on your campus impact your feelings of attachment to your school?

6. Would you rather live in a bureaucratic society or in a society without bureaucratic forms of organizations? Why? How does the informal structure at your college or university impact how the school functions? Does it do more to help or hurt students? Why?

VISUAL SOCIOLOGY: *MONEY AS A SOCIAL CONSTRUCTION*

© Keith A. Roberts

Depicted here are Japanese *yen*. Your local department store or restaurant will not accept *yen* in exchange for the piece of furniture or the meal you just consumed, any more than they would accept monopoly money. We exchange goods and services based on some pieces of paper because we have a general agreement that this is "good currency"—a *social construction of reality*. Visit **edge.sagepub.com/ballantine5e** for an interactive photo essay about money.

CONTRIBUTING TO OUR SOCIAL WORLD: *WHAT CAN WE DO?*

At the Local Level

- *Tutoring and mentoring* programs help students struggling with their studies. Contact the Student Affairs or Tutoring Office and arrange to observe and/or volunteer in a program. Helping students build *social capital*, which includes their knowledge of ways to obtain the help they need, can increase their chances of success.

- Workers' Centers for employed people not represented by unions have developed in many metropolitan areas, often with the aid of local clergy. Workers' Centers help these workers to organize and develop the social capital to obtain better wages, benefits, and workplace dignity. For a list of Workers' Centers, go to www.iwj.org/worker-center-network/locations.

At the Organizational or Institutional Level

- The social capital theory can also be applied to meso-level community organizations: *Community organizations* that work to build power and implement social change, such as *IAF (the Industrial Areas Foundation* at www.industrialareasfoundation.org), *Gamaliel* (www.gamaliel.org), and *PICO National Network* (www.piconetwork.org), provide their members with social capital. Find a group affiliated with one of these organizations near you.

- *Unions* also develop social capital for their members. Although far fewer U.S. citizens are unionized today than in past decades, membership in a union can improve the economic prospects of workers. For some workers, this can make the difference between living in poverty and obtaining a living wage. At 2.1 million members, the *Service Employees International Union (SEIU)* is the fastest-growing union in North America. Internships with unions like SEIU are a great way to learn about organizing and social capital. You can find information about internships on the SEIU website (www.seiu.org).

- *The Anti-Defamation League* (www.adl.org), the *American-Arab Anti-Discrimination Committee* (www.adc.org), and the *National Association for the Advancement of Colored People* (www.naacp.org) are examples of organizations that defend the rights of minority groups. These organizations often use volunteers or interns and can provide you with the opportunity to learn about the extent to which social contacts and networks play a role in managing social conflict.

At the National or Global Level

- Well-run *microfinance organizations* can help poor people, particularly women, gain social capital and economic independence. Three well-known and respected groups are CRS (Catholic Relief Services at http://crs.org/microfinance), FINCA (www.finca.org), and Kiva (www.kiva.org). Check out their websites to learn how you can support their efforts.

6 Deviance and Social Control

Sickos, Weirdos, Freaks, and Folks Like Us

We often think of deviants as bad people who do not care about rules or other members of society; we contrast them to people like us. Sometimes, though, people need to commit deviants acts to change unjust social structures and to topple tyrants. Further, enforcement of conformity is often experienced as authoritarian.

ME (MY FAMILY AND CLOSEST FRIENDS)

LOCAL ORGANIZATIONS AND COMMUNITY
People violate local ordinances and commit thefts.

NATIONAL ORGANIZATIONS, INSTITUTIONS, AND ETHNIC SUBCULTURES
People violate state laws, and they commit crimes using corporations.

SOCIETY
People commit federal crimes; the national government itself may commit crimes such as torture.

GLOBAL COMMUNITY
Crimes may result in global environmental destruction or violations of human rights across national boundaries.

IN THIS CHAPTER

- What Is Deviance?

- What Causes Deviant Behavior? Theoretical Perspectives

- Crime and Individuals: Micro-Level Analysis

- Crime and Organizations: Meso-Level Analysis

- National and Global Crime: Macro-Level Analysis

- Controlling Crime: Social Policy Considerations

THINK ABOUT IT

Micro: Local Community	Are you deviant? Who says so? Why do some people in your community become deviant while others do not?
Meso: National Institutions, Complex Organizations, and Ethnic Groups	What are the consequences of organized crime or occupational crime for large bureaucratic organizations?
Macro: National and Global Systems	What are the costs—and the benefits—of deviance for a nation? How can a global perspective on crime enhance our understanding of international and national criminal activities?

Wafa did not stand out from the girls around her as she grew up, but she was destined to make world headlines—as the first female suicide bomber in the Palestinian-Israeli conflict. She was the age of most university students reading this book, but she never had an opportunity to attend college. Her task was to smuggle explosives across the Israeli border for the intended bomber, her brother. Instead, on January 27, 2002, she blew up herself and an Israeli soldier. She was declared a martyr, a *sahida*, by the al-Aqsa Martyrs Brigade, and the organization took credit for the attack. The group's political leadership indicated their approval of her act, opening the way for other women to follow. Why did this happen? What motivated her to commit suicide and take another life in the process? Was she driven by ideology to participate in the Palestinian–Israeli struggle? Were there social and structural factors that affected her decision? Most important, was she deviant in carrying out this act, and according to whom?

Wafa Idris grew up in Palestine. She was married at a young age but did not produce children. As a result, her husband divorced her and remarried. She had no future, for who would want a barren, divorced woman in a society that values women for their purity and their childbearing ability? She was a burden to her family. Her way out of an impossible and desperate situation was to commit suicide, bringing honor and wealth to her family and redeeming herself in the process. Other women who followed Wafa have similar stories: Most shared an inability to control their own lives in the patriarchal (male-controlled) society (Gonzalez-Perez 2011; Handwerk 2004; Victor 2003).

Our question is this: Are such women deviant criminal terrorists, hapless victims of terrorist groups, mentally ill "crazies," invisible victims in a patriarchal society, or martyrs who should be honored for their acts? And who says so? Each of these views is held by someone interested in

this situation. From this opening example, we can begin to see several complications that arise when defining deviance and deviants. In this chapter, we consider who is deviant, under what circumstances, and in whose eyes.

First, we discuss deviance—*the violation of social norms*—and the social control mechanisms that keep most people from becoming deviant. Occasionally, most of us violate a norm, and depending on its importance and on the severity of the violation, we may or may not be seen as deviant. Wearing strange clothes may be seen as amusing and nonconformist once in a while, but you will be labeled deviant if you do so regularly. If enough people start wearing similar clothes, however, this once deviant act will no longer be deviant. Getting a tattoo or wearing skintight jeans to school are good examples of once deviant acts now considered normal behavior in many communities. We also examine crime in this chapter, *deviant actions for which there are formal penalties imposed by the government, such as fines, jail, or prison sentences.*

You may be surprised to learn that we are all deviant at some times and in some places and almost all of us have committed crimes. The self-test in the next "Engaging Sociology" illustrates this point.

WHAT IS DEVIANCE?

While some acts, such as murder, assault, robbery, and rape, are considered deviant in almost every time and place, some deviant acts may be overlooked or even viewed as understandable under certain circumstances, such as when a family steals water and diapers from a destroyed supermarket after a natural disaster. Some acts of deviance are considered serious offenses in one society but tolerated in another. Examples include prostitution, premarital or extramarital sex, gambling, corruption, and bribery. Even

ENGAGING SOCIOLOGY

Who Is Deviant?

Please jot down your answers to the following self-test questions. There is no need to share your responses with others.

Have you ever engaged in any of the following acts?

1. stolen anything, even if its value was under $10
2. used an illegal drug
3. misused a prescription drug
4. run away from home prior to age 18
5. used tobacco prior to age 18
6. drunk alcohol prior to age 21
7. engaged in a fistfight
8. carried a knife or gun
9. used a car without the owner's permission
10. driven a car after drinking alcohol
11. forced someone to have sexual relations against her or his will
12. offered sex for money
13. damaged property worth more than $10
14. been truant from school
15. arrived home after your curfew
16. been disrespectful to someone in authority
17. accepted or transported property that you had reason to believe might be stolen
18. taken a towel from a hotel room after renting the room for a night

All of the preceding are delinquent acts (violations of legal standards), and most young people are guilty of at least one infraction. However, few teenagers are given the label of *delinquent*. If you answered yes to any of the preceding questions, you committed a crime in many states. Your penalty or sanction for the infraction could range from a stiff fine to several years in prison—*if* you got caught!

Engaging in Sociological Analysis

1. Do you think of yourself as a deviant? Why or why not?
2. Are deviants only those who get caught? For instance, if someone steals your car but avoids being caught, is he or she deviant?
3. Who is considered deviant—and by whom?

---

within a single society, different groups may define deviance and conformity quite differently. The state government may officially define alcohol consumption by 19-year-olds as deviant, but on a Saturday night at a fraternity party, the 19-year-old "brother" who does *not* drink may be viewed as deviant by his peers. What do these cases tell us about deviance?

Deviance is socially constructed and dependent on the time and social context. Members of groups in societies define (construct) what is deviant. As we noted earlier, these socially constructed definitions of deviance can change over *time* and depend on the social situation or *context* in which the behavior occurs.

Thinking Sociologically

Have you ever dressed or styled your hair in a deviant way? Why? Did you have any role models to guide you on how to do so? If so, does this mean you really were *not* being deviant? Why or why not? Who determines whether or not your clothes or hairstyle are deviant?

If we take the same behavior and place it in a different social context, perceptions of whether the behavior is deviant may well change. For example, in Greece, Spain, and other Mediterranean countries, the clothing norms on beaches are very different from those in most of North America. Topless sunbathing by women is not at all

▶ Standing Out

Miley Cyrus was purposefully deviant when she crossed the lines of appropriate behavior on television and "twerked"—a sexually provocative dance move—throughout her performance at the 2013 Video Music Awards. Perhaps chastened by the outcry that ensued, she stated in an interview at the 2014 VMAs that she had "retired" from twerking.

uncommon, even on beaches designated as family beaches. The norms vary, however, even within a few feet of the beach. Women will sunbathe topless, lying only 10 feet from the boardwalk where concessionaires sell beverages, snacks, and tourist items. If these women become thirsty, they cover up, walk the 10 feet to purchase a cola, and return to their beach blankets, where they again remove their tops. To walk onto the boardwalk topless would be considered highly deviant.

An individual's status or group may be defined as deviant. Some individuals have a higher likelihood of being labeled deviant because of the group into which they were born, such as a particular ethnic group, or because of a distinguishing mark or characteristic, such as a deformity. Others may escape being considered deviant because of their dominant status in society. The higher one's status, the less likely that one will be suspected of violating norms and the less likely that any violations will be characterized as "criminal." Who would suspect that a respectable, white-collar husband and father is embezzling funds from his company?

The looting that happened following Hurricane Katrina was addressed differently depending on whether it was done by whites or African Americans (Huddy and Feldman 2006; Thompson 2009). The media showed photos of black "looters" who "stole food," but the same media described whites who "broke into grocery stores" in search of food as "resourceful." Likewise, gays and lesbians are often said to be deviant and accused of flaunting their sexuality. Heterosexuals are rarely accused of "flaunting" their sexuality, regardless of how overtly flirtatious or underdressed they may be. So one's group membership or ascribed traits may make a difference in whether or not one is defined as deviant.

Deviance can be functional for society. As structural functionalists point out, deviance serves vital functions by setting examples of unacceptable behavior, providing guidelines for behavior necessary to maintain social order, and bonding people together through their common rejection of the deviant behavior. Deviance is also functional because it provides jobs for those who deal with deviants—police, judges, social workers, and so forth (Gans 2007). Furthermore, deviance can signal problems in society that need to be addressed and can therefore stimulate positive change. Sometimes deviant individuals break the model of conventional thinking, thereby opening society to new and creative paths of thinking. Scientists, inventors, activists, and artists have often been rejected in their time but have been honored later for accomplishments that positively affected society. Famous artist Vincent van Gogh, for example, lived in poverty and suffered from schizophrenia. During his life, his artistic gifts were overlooked, but he became recognized as a renowned painter after his death. His paintings now sell for millions of dollars. Likewise, Nelson Mandela, Martin Luther King Jr., and Mahatma Gandhi were once considered deviant and dangerous, but today they are regarded as social justice heroes.

Thinking Sociologically

Think of examples in your life that illustrate the *relative nature of deviance*. For instance, are some of your behaviors deviant in one setting but not in another, or were they deviant when you were younger but not deviant now?

Crime: Deviance That Violates the Law

Governments create laws and impose formal sanctions—punishments—for some acts of deviance, and the social disapproval associated with being convicted of these violations results in the perpetrator being identified as "criminal." *When members of society are in general agreement about the seriousness of certain crimes*, these acts are referred to as **consensus crimes** (Brym and Lie 2007; Goodman and Brenner 2002). **Predatory crimes** (*crimes—usually violent—against humans, such as premeditated murder, forcible rape, and kidnapping for ransom*) are consensus crimes in most nations.

Just as what is considered deviant varies over time and place, so does what is regarded as criminal behavior. For example, at the end of the 1920s, 42 of the 48 U.S. states had laws forbidding interracial marriage (Coontz 2005; see Figure 6.1). Legislatures in half of these states removed those restrictions by the 1960s, but 16 states still had antimiscegenation laws on the books until 1967, when the U.S. Supreme Court ruling in *Loving v. Virginia* made these laws unconstitutional. Today, this legal ban on interracial marriage has been eliminated completely, illustrating that most laws change to reflect the times and sentiments of the majority of people. Likewise, the move to legalize same-sex marriage, with 19 states and the District of Columbia legally recognizing same-sex marriages as of September 2014, reflects changing views toward homosexuality.

We now look at theoretical perspectives that help explain deviance, how some deviant acts become crimes, and what policies might control or reduce crime.

WHAT CAUSES DEVIANT BEHAVIOR? THEORETICAL PERSPECTIVES

Helena is a delinquent. Her father deserted the family when Helena was 10, and before that, he had abused Helena and her mother. Her mother has all she can cope with; she is just trying to survive financially and keep her

Some sociologists point out that crime can be "functional" because it creates jobs for people such as those above and it unifies society against the nonconformists.

three children in line. Helena gets little attention and little support or encouragement in her school activities. Her grades have fallen steadily. As a young teen, she sought attention from boys, and in the process, she became pregnant. Now, the only kids who have anything to do with her are others who have been in trouble; her friends are other young people who have also been labeled delinquent. Helena's schoolmates, teachers, and mother see her as a delinquent troublemaker, and it would be hard for Helena to change their views and her status.

Until recently, this same-sex couple would have been considered deviant throughout the United States. Today, the federal government recognizes same-sex marriages, as do many states.

🎙 Crime Scenes

FIGURE 6.1   **Historical Restrictions on Interracial Marriage in the United States**

Date When Restriction Against Interracial Marrage Was Lifted

| ■ 1780 – 1855 | ■ 1856 – 1890 | 1891 – 1966 | 1967 | Never had restrictions |

Source: Wallenstein (2002:253–254). Map by Anna Versluis.

How did this happen? Helena's situation is, of course, only one unique case. Sociologists cannot generalize from Helena to other cases, but they do know from their studies that there are thousands of teens with problems like Helena's. In the following we consider some theories of deviance that help us recognize and explain patterns among delinquent teens like Helena.

Throughout history, people have proposed explanations for why some members of society "turn bad"—from biological explanations of imbalances in hormones and claims of innate personality defects to social conditions within individual families or in the larger social structure. Biological and psychological approaches focus on personality disorders or abnormalities in the body or psyche of individuals, but they generally do not consider the social context in which deviance occurs.

Sociologists place emphasis on understanding the interactions, social structure, and social processes that lead to deviant behavior, rather than on individual characteristics. They consider the socialization process and interpersonal relationships, group and social class differences, cultural and subcultural norms, and power structures that influence individuals to conform to or deviate from societal expectations. Theoretical explanations about why people are deviant influence social policy decisions and strategies to curb deviant behavior and deal with deviants.

Some theories explain particular types of crime better than others (say, theft as opposed to sexual assault), just

Why deviance?

as some illuminate micro-, meso-, or macro-level processes better than others. Taken together, these theories help us understand a wide range of deviant and criminal behaviors.

Micro-Level Explanations of Deviance

No one is born deviant. Individuals learn to be law-abiding citizens or to be deviant through the process of socialization. Why do some people learn to become deviant and others learn to follow the norms of society? Symbolic interaction and rational choice theories focus primarily on micro-level answers to this question.

Rational Choice Approaches to Deviance. Rational choice theory, as noted in previous chapters, suggests that when individuals make decisions, they calculate the costs and benefits to themselves. They consider the balance between pleasure and pain. Turning to crime is therefore a conscious, rational, and calculated decision made after weighing the costs and benefits of alternatives.

Rational choice theorists believe that punishment—imposing high "costs" for criminal behavior, such as fines, imprisonment, or even the death penalty—is the best way to dissuade criminals from choosing the path of crime. When the cost outweighs the potential benefit and opportunities are restricted, it deters people from thinking that crime is a "rational" choice (Earls and Reiss 1994; Winslow and Zhang 2008).

Positive sanctions reward those behaviors approved by society. This is the reason why schools have honor ceremonies, companies reward their top salespeople, and communities recognize civic leadership with "Citizen of the Year" awards. All these actions enhance the rewards for conventional behavior. Negative sanctions (or punishments) increase the cost to those who deviate from the norm. They range from fines for traffic violations to prison sentences for serious crimes and even death, in many states, for acts considered most dangerous to society.

Social Control Theory. One of sociology's central concepts is social control—why people obey norms (Hagan 2011). A specific rational choice application, control theory focuses on why most people conform most of the time and do not commit deviant acts. If human beings were truly free to do whatever they wanted, they would likely commit more deviant acts. Yet to live near others and with others requires individuals to control their

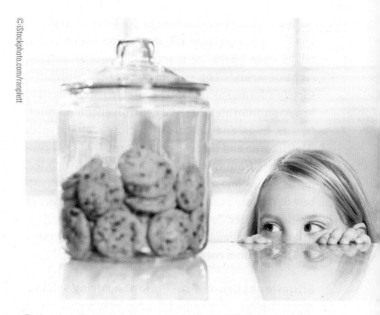

Rational choice theorists would note that this little girl is weighing the costs and benefits of taking cookies, and the benefits are looking pretty sweet!

behaviors based on social norms and sanctions—in short, social control.

A perpetual question in sociology is the following: How is social order possible in the context of rapidly changing society? A very general answer is that social control results from social norms that promote order and predictability in the social world. When people fail to adhere to these norms, or when the norms are unclear, the stability and continuance of the entire social system may be threatened.

Control theory contends that people are bonded to others by four powerful factors:

1. *Attachment* to other people who respect the values and rules of the society. Individuals do not want to be rejected by those to whom they are close or whom they admire.
2. *Commitment* to conventional activities (such as school and jobs) that they do not want to jeopardize.
3. *Involvement* in activities that keep them so busy with conventional roles and expectations that they do not have time for mischief.
4. *Belief* in the social rules of their culture, which they accept because of their childhood socialization and indoctrination into those conventional beliefs.

These factors can decrease the likelihood that that a person would commit deviant acts (Hirschi [1969] 2002).

Two primary forces shape our tendency to conform. The first is internal controls, those voices within us that tell us when a behavior is acceptable or unacceptable, right or wrong. The second is external controls—society's formal or informal controls against deviant behavior. Informal external controls include smiles, frowns, hugs, and ridicule from close acquaintances (Gottfredson and Hirschi 1990). Formal external controls come from the legal system through the police, judges, juries, and social workers. In both cases, the cost-benefit ratio shifts, making either conformity or deviance a rational choice. Social control comes from shifting the balance toward more pain and fewer benefits for those who deviate from norms.

Situational Crime Prevention.

Applying rational choice theory to crime prevention has led to measures that focus on making it harder and less rewarding to commit crimes. For example, improved lighting (making it harder to commit a crime unnoticed), marking goods that may be stolen (for easy tracking and recovery), and creating positive alternatives to crime (such as summer jobs for teens) make crime both harder and less appealing (Clarke 1997).

Thinking Sociologically

Think of a time when you committed a deviant act or avoided doing so despite a tempting opportunity. What factors influenced whether you conformed to societal norms or committed a deviant act?

According to differential association theory, people who abuse drugs, like this young man, tend to learn this behavior through close associations with other illicit drug users. They come to see the drugged state as enjoyable *and* learn the techniques for using them.

Symbolic Interaction Approaches to Deviance.

Symbolic interactionists focus on how our interactions with others influence whether or not we will commit deviant acts. Because symbolic interaction theorists stress variables other than pure self-interest, they are less inclined to think that increasing the penalties or changing the costs will change behavior and reduce deviance. One interactionist approach, differential association theory, describes how people learn to commit delinquent acts through their social relationships with peers and family members.

Differential Association Theory.

Differential association theory focuses on the process of learning deviant behavior from those with whom we interact (e.g., family, peers, fellow employees) (Hagan 2011; Sutherland, Cressey, and Luckenbil 1992). Helena, for example, came to be surrounded by people who made dropping out of school and other delinquent acts seem normal. If her close friends and siblings were also sexually active as teens, her teen pregnancy might not be remarkable and might even be a source of some prestige within her group of peers.

According to differential association theory, the possibility of becoming deviant depends on four factors related to associating with a deviant group: the *duration* of time spent with the group, the *intensity* of interaction, the *frequency* of interaction, and the *priority* of the group in one's friendship network (Sutherland et al. 1992). If people have regular and frequent exposure to deviance among their longtime, close friends they are likely to learn to behave in deviant ways.

Some theorists contend that life in poverty often involves immersion in a distinctive subculture in which poor people learn delinquent behavior patterns through socialization. The values, beliefs, norms, and practices that have evolved in poor communities over time can often encourage violation of laws. Just as upper-class youth learn norms that help them to succeed in middle- and upper-class areas of society, lower-class youth may learn other behaviors that help them to survive in their poor neighborhoods but that those with privilege have defined as delinquent and criminal (Bettie 2003; Chambliss 1973).

Elijah Anderson's book, *Code of the Street* (2000), describes two types of groups that coexist in poor neighborhoods: "decent people" and "street people." "Street-oriented people" learn a code of the street that involves hanging out on the street with peers; seeking immediate gratification through sex, violence, and drugs; and adopting a certain look with their clothes and jewelry—an image expected by the group. Peers become more important than society's social control agents. "Decent families" accept mainstream values and often find support systems in church communities or other organizations. In order to survive in such neighborhoods and avoid violent sanctions from street-oriented peers, however, those from decent families must dress and carry themselves in a way that conforms with the street-oriented image. The result is that other members of society, including the police, view both the street-oriented and those from decent families as deviant (Anderson 2000).

Today, we know that members of all social classes commit crimes, and no socioeconomic class has a monopoly on violence, corruption, or dishonesty. However, *labeling* theory, another explanation of deviance based on the symbolic interactionist perspective, explains why some individuals and groups are more likely to be caught and punished for deviance.

Labeling Theory. Labeling theory *explains how people can be labeled deviant after committing a deviant act, which can then lead them to carry out further acts that reflect that label.* Labels (such as "juvenile delinquent") are symbols that have meanings affecting an individual's self-concept and the way others see the individual.

Labeling theorists define two stages in the process of becoming a deviant. **Primary deviance** is *a violation of a norm that may be an isolated act or an initial act of rule breaking,* such as a young teenager shoplifting something on a dare by friends. Most people commit acts of primary deviance. However, many of us avoid being labeled "deviant" when we commit one of these primary acts. Remember how you marked the deviant behavior test that you took at the beginning of this chapter? If you have engaged in deviant acts, you were probably not labeled deviant for the offense. If you had been so labeled, you might not be in college or taking this class.

If an individual continues to violate a norm and begins to take on a deviant identity because of being labeled as deviant, this is referred to as **secondary deviance.** Secondary deviance becomes publicly recognized, and the individual is identified as deviant, beginning a deviant career. If a teenager like Helena is caught, her act becomes known, perhaps publicized in the newspaper. She may spend time in a juvenile detention center, and parents of other teens may not want their children associating with her. Employers and store managers may refuse to hire her. Soon, there are few opportunities open to her because others expect her to be delinquent. The teen may continue performing the deviant acts and associating with delinquent acquaintances, in part because few other options are

Shoplifting, when done by young people without a criminal record, provides an example of primary deviance.

available. Society's reaction, then, is what defines a deviant person and may limit options for that person to change the label (Lemert 1951, 1972).

The process of labeling individuals and behaviors takes place at each level of analysis, from individual to society. If community or societal norms define a behavior as deviant, individuals are likely to believe it is deviant. Sanctions against juvenile delinquents can have the effect of reinforcing the deviant behavior by (a) increasing alienation from the social world, (b) forcing increased interaction with deviant peers, and (c) motivating juvenile delinquents to positively value and identify with the deviant status (Kaplan and Johnson 1991).

A **self-fulfilling prophecy** *occurs when a belief or a prediction becomes a reality, in part because of the prediction.* A false perception of a person, perhaps based on a stereotype, can become true if it provokes behavior that fulfills that false perception or stereotype. For example, James is 8 years old and already sees himself as a "bad" kid who will end up in prison, just like his father, whom he has never met. His mother tells him he was born "bad" because he resembles his father, and his teachers and peers tell him he is "bad" because he struggles in school. In keeping with the idea of self-fulfilling prophecy, James accepts the label and acts accordingly, refusing to do his homework and stealing other kids' lunch money. Unless someone—such as an insightful teacher—steps in to give him another image of himself, James is likely to end up in prison—not because he was born "bad" but because he was treated by others as if he were (Merton 1948).

Those fighting crime also need to keep in mind the power of the self-fulfilling prophecy. For example, law enforcement trainers can have a huge influence on whether or not their students (police officers, FBI agents, etc.) succeed. If the trainers treat their trainees as though they are not capable of learning the crime prevention skills needed to do the job, the trainees' chances of failing are much higher. Realizing this, the FBI has made efforts to inform trainers of the self-fulfilling prophecy and ways to avoid imposing its negative effects on their students (Fitch 2010).

Thinking Sociologically

What labels do you carry? How do you know you carry these labels? How do they affect your self-concept and behavior?

A major explanation of why certain individuals and groups are labeled deviant has to do with their status and power in society—a concern of conflict theory. Those on the fringes, away from power—the poor, minorities, members of new religious movements, or others who in some way do not fit into the dominant system—are more likely to be labeled deviants. On the other hand, because the powerful have the influence to define what is acceptable, they tend to avoid the deviant label. Their behavior, even when it has a negative impact on society, is less likely to be labeled deviant or criminal.

A study by Chambliss (1973) illustrates the process of labeling in communities and groups. Perhaps during your high school years you witnessed situations similar to that described in his study. Chambliss looked at the behavior of two small peer groups of boys and at the reactions of community members to their behavior. The Saints, boys from "good" families, were some of the most delinquent boys at Hannibal High School. Although the Saints were constantly occupied with truancy, drinking, wild driving, petty theft, and vandalism, none was officially arrested for any misdeed during the two-year study. The Roughnecks, who were from less affluent families, were constantly in trouble with the police and community residents, even though their rate of delinquency was about equal to that of the Saints.

What was the cause of the disparity in the labeling of these two groups? Community members, the police, and teachers alike labeled the boys based on their perceptions of the boys' family backgrounds and social class. The Saints came from stable, white, upper-middle-class families; were active in school affairs; and were precollege students who everyone expected would become professionals. In fact, the Saints almost all did become professionals, living up to their images in the community. On the other hand, the general community feeling was that the Roughnecks would amount to nothing. They carried around a negative label that was hard to change. Two Roughnecks ended up in prison, two became coaches, and little is known of the others. For a number of these boys, the prophecy became self-fulfilling (Chambliss 1973).

Labels are powerful and can stigmatize an individual—stigma refers to branding the person with a negative mark that *discredits a person's claim to a "normal" identity*. This process can be extended to a number of issues, including obesity, as the next "Sociology in Our Social World" illustrates.

While labeling theory is mostly based on symbolic interaction (a micro-level theory), labeling theorists also point to the role of macro-level social forces—social inequality or lack of access to power—in determining whether people are labeled or whether they can avoid being labeled as deviant. Thus, labeling theory is also sometimes used by conflict theorists. When members of the dominant group in society see certain behaviors as potentially threatening or disruptive to the society or to their privileged statuses, they label those who carry them out as deviant. For example, writing less-than-positive things on the Internet about a government can lead to being treated as a criminal in some countries. Recent news stories have relayed that, after their online writings displeased powerful government officials, a blogger in Turkey was imprisoned, bloggers in Iran were sentenced to death, and a blogger in China was sent to a labor camp for a year (AFP 2013; Louk 2012; Watson and Tuysuz 2013).

Thinking Sociologically

Imagine you have a friend who is using drugs illegally. From what you know about the above theories, how might you explain her behavior? What insights can you gain, if any, on what might lead your friend to stop using these drugs?

Meso- and Macro-Level Explanations of Deviance

While micro-level interactions can lead a person to become and to be labeled as deviant, meso- and macro-level analysis can help us gain a greater understanding of the societal factors leading to deviance. As we have noted, meso-level analysis focuses on ethnic subcultures, organizations, and institutions. Macro-level analysis focuses on national and global social systems.

The Obesity Stigma

sociology in our social world

Stigmatizing Fatness

By Leslie Elrod

©TIM SLOAN / Staff/Getty Images

Obesity in America

The United States is now the fattest country in the world. "American society has become 'obesogenic,' characterized by environments that promote increased food intake, unhealthy food, and physical inactivity . . . One in seven low-income preschool children is obese" (Centers for Disease Control and Prevention [CDC] 2009). The CDC has found that more than 60% of U.S. adults are classified as overweight or obese, and 25% of children are classified as obese.

The obsession with thinness and body image in U.S. culture can make being overweight particularly painful for many. When a physical attribute is assigned social significance, violators of this norm are likely to endure negative labeling because of perceived physical imperfections.

According to Cooley's theory of *the looking-glass self*, we generally define ourselves based on how we think others perceive us (see Chapter 4). Obese people tend to suffer lower self-esteem and have negative self-images, thus creating heightened levels of psychological distress (Cooley (1902; [1909] 1983). The obese, labeled as self-indulgent, gluttonous, lazy, sloppy, and selfish, experience social condemnation. Some research shows that even doctors tend not to be as nice to their overweight patients, treating their thin ones with more warmth and empathy (Parker-Pope 2013).

Socialized by the media to believe that their physical appearance should be a valuable commodity, obese women tend to experience greater stigmatization than do obese men. Such messages come from images in print ads, magazines, television programming, and movies as well as merchandizing directed toward females of all ages. These messages portray unrealistic images of women. In fact, as real women grew heavier, models and "beautiful" women were portrayed as increasingly thinner. "In 1965, the average model weighed just 8 percent less than the average American woman . . . the average fashion model today is . . . thinner than 98% of women" (National Eating Disorders Association 2009). Failing to meet this standard of beauty not only jeopardizes a woman's happiness but also challenges her femininity.

While much of the research on women's obsession with weight assumes that all women and girls are affected by the culture of thinness, there is evidence to suggest that not all women are affected equally. Obesity rates

(Continued)

(Continued)

are highest among minorities, the poor, and the disenfranchised. Yet "few black women seem to have eating disorders . . . and less emphasis (is placed) on eating and weight in general among black college students compared to while students" (Powell and Kahn 1995:190). When compared to black females, white women feel under significantly greater social pressure to be thin. Some research, however, has found that eating disorders, an outcome of dissatisfaction with one's body, are no longer confined to upper-class white females, indicating that the

effects of body mass on self-esteem may be changing (Hesse-Biber 2007). This is not a good sign—and a clear indication that more attention must be paid to the dangers of unrealistic body images in the media and the stigmatization of fatness.

• •

Leslie Elrod is associate professor of sociology at University of Cincinnati, Blue Ash College. Two of her specialties are sociology of the body and deviance.

 Thinking Sociologically

On your campus, what physical characteristics can affect people's self-perception or cause them to be labeled as different or even deviant by others?

Structural-Functional Approaches to Deviance. Structural-functional theories of deviance include (1) *anomie*, the breakdown of norms guiding behavior, which leads to *social disorganization*, and (2) *strain theory*, which shows that the difference between definitions of success (goals) in a society and the means available to achieve those goals can lead to deviant behavior.

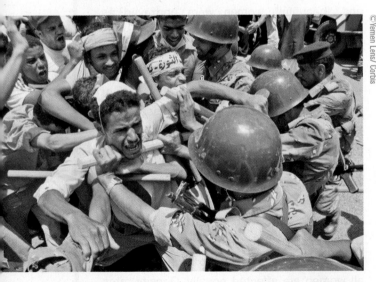

©Yemen Lens/ Corbis

The autocratic Yemeni president, Ali Abdullah Saleh, claimed that the recent protests against him were leading to anomie and general social chaos. In the picture above, Yemeni army soldiers try to stop anti-government protesters.

Anomie and Social Disorganization. Sociologists use the term *anomie*, or the state of normlessness that occurs when rules for behavior in society break down under extreme stress from rapid social change or conflict (Merton 1968). Émile Durkheim (1858–1917) first described this normlessness as a condition of weak, conflicting, or absent norms and the changes in values that arise when societies are disorganized. As discussed in Chapter 5, this situation is typical in rapidly urbanizing, industrializing societies; at times of sudden prosperity or depression; during rapid technological change; during a war; or when a government is overthrown.

Imagine you were raised in a small village where your family and all those around you have been farmers for as far back as anyone can remember. You were raised to become one yourself and thought you would raise your children to become farmers as well. Over the past few years, though, due to climate change, the rains have not come, and the fields no longer support crops. You have no choice but to leave everyone and everything you have ever known to try to find work in the nearest city. This may thrust you into a situation where norms of interaction—including mutual support and friendliness—are very different and you feel like you are in a different country.

Millions of people are now living out similar stories. Villagers in industrializing countries in Africa, Asia, and Latin America find themselves pushed off marginally productive rural lands and pulled into rapidly expanding cities to seek better lives and means for survival. They hope to find good jobs in these urban areas, but when they arrive, they often face disappointment. Poor, unskilled, and homeless, they move into crowded apartments or shantytowns of temporary shacks and try to adjust to the new style of life, which often includes unemployment. Old village norms that have provided the guidelines for proper behavior crumble, sometimes without clear expectations emerging to take their places. The lack of clear norms in the rapidly changing urban environment leads to high levels of social disorganization and deviant behavior.

This general idea of anomie led a group of Chicago sociologists to study the social conditions of that city that correlate with deviance. The Chicago School, as the research team is known, linked life in transitional slum areas to the high incidence of crime. Certain neighborhoods or zones in the Chicago area—generally inner-city transitional zones with recent settlers—have always had high delinquency rates, regardless of the group that occupied the area. Low economic status, ethnic heterogeneity, residential mobility, family disruption, and competing value systems (because of the constant transitions) led to community disorganization. Although new immigrant groups have replaced the older groups over time, the delinquency rate has remained high because each generation of newcomers experiences anomie (Shaw and McKay 1929). The high in-migration and out-migration in these communities in itself explains the lack of stability in families. Peer group norms become influential, and models of nondeviant behavior are scarce for many teenagers and adults (Anderson 2000).

Strain Theory. What happens when you know what your goal is but you cannot find a socially acceptable path to reach it? How do you proceed? *Strain theory* focuses on the contradictions and tensions between the shared values and goals of a society, on one hand, and the opportunity structures in the society, on the other—and your chance of reaching your goals.

Strain theory suggests that the gap between an individual's or a society's *goals* and the legitimate ways of attaining those goals—*the means*—can lead to strain in the society (Merton 1968). Individuals may agree with the society's *goals* for success (say, financial affluence) but may not be able to achieve them using the socially acceptable means of achieving that success. The strain created can lead to deviance. Merton uses U.S. society as an example because it places a heavy emphasis on success as measured by wealth and social standing. He outlines five ways by which individuals adapt to the strain (Merton 1968). Figure 6.2 shows these five types and their relationship to goals and means.

FIGURE 6.2 Merton's Strain Theory

To further illustrate strain theory, we trace the choices of a lower-class student who realizes the value of an education and knows it is necessary to get ahead but who has problems finding time to study because she has to work many hours a week to help support her family.

1. *Conformity* means embracing the society's definition of success and adhering to the established and approved means of achieving success. The student works hard despite the obstacles, pulling all-nighters and trying to do well in school to achieve success and a good job placement. She uses legitimate, approved means—education and hard work—to reach goals that the society views as worthy.

2. *Innovation* refers to the use of illicit means to reach approved goals. Our student uses illegitimate means to achieve her education goals. She may cheat on exams or get papers from Internet sources. Success in school is all that matters. How she attains that success does not matter.

3. *Ritualism* involves strict adherence to the culturally prescribed rules, even though individuals give up on the goals they hoped to achieve. The student may give up the idea of getting good grades and going to college but, as a matter of pride and self-image, continues to try hard and to attend school. She conforms to expectations, but with no sense of purpose. She just does what she is told.

4. *Retreatism* refers to giving up on both the goals and the means. The student either bides her time, not doing well, or drops out, giving up on future job goals. She abandons or retreats from the goals of a professional position in society and the means to get there. She may even turn to a different lifestyle—for example, becoming a user of drugs and alcohol—as part of the retreat.

5. *Rebellion* entails rejecting socially approved ideas of success and the means of attaining that success. It replaces those with alternative definitions of success and alternative strategies for attaining new goals. Rebelling against the dominant cultural goals and means, a student may leave her family, abandon thoughts of college and a profession, and join a radical political or religious group or become a terrorist, seeking to destabilize the government and establish a new type of society.

Deviant behavior results from retreatism, rebellion, and innovation. According to Merton, the reasons why individuals resort to these behaviors lie in the social conditions that prevent access to success, not in their individual biological or psychological makeup (Merton 1968).

The structural-functional approaches to deviance focus on what occurs if deviance disrupts the ongoing social order. They explore what causes deviance, how to prevent disruptions, how to keep change slow and nondisruptive, and how deviance can be useful to the ongoing society. However, anomie and strain theories fail to account for class conflicts, inequities, and poverty, which conflict theorists argue cause deviance.

Conflict Theory of Deviance. As you will recall from previous chapters, conflict theorists assume that conflict among groups is inevitable. Conflict theory focuses on a meso- and macro-level analysis of deviance, looking at deviance as the result of social inequality or of the struggle among groups for power.

Wealthy and powerful elites want to maintain their control and their high positions (Domhoff 2009). They have the power to pass laws and define what is deviant, sometimes by effectively eliminating the opposition groups. The greater the cultural difference between the dominant group and other groups in society, the greater the possibility of conflict. This is because minority groups and subcultures challenge the norms of the dominant groups and threaten the consensus in society (Huizinga, Loeber, and Thornberry 1994).

Some conflict theorists blame capitalist systems for the unjust administration of law and unequal distribution of resources, arguing that the ruling class uses the legal system to further the capitalist enterprise (Quinney 2002). The dominant or ruling class defines deviance, applies laws to protect its interests, represses efforts to make laws more just, and, in effect, may force those in subordinate classes to carry out actions that the dominant class has defined as deviant. These deviant actions become necessary for survival when the affluent restrict legitimate avenues to resources. In most cases, the dominant class consists of one racial or ethnic group that distinguishes itself from the racial or ethnic groups found in the subordinate classes. So, conflict and definitions of deviance often have racial and ethnic implications as well as social class dimensions. When people believe that those in power treat them unfairly, they have less loyalty to the society and to its rules.

To reduce deviance and crime, conflict theorists believe that we must change the structure of society. For instance, legal systems in many countries claim to support equal and fair treatment for all, but when one looks at the law in action, another picture emerges. Recall the example of the Saints and Roughnecks; the students from powerful families and higher social classes received favored treatment. Unequal treatment of groups that differ from the dominant group—the poor, laboring class and racial or ethnic minorities in particular—is rooted in the legal, political, and occupational structures of societies. Today, we can see evidence of this disparity in treatment by comparing the treatment of black and white Americans who use marijuana (see Figures 6.3a and 6.3b). Similar percentages of white and black Americans use marijuana but blacks are almost *four times* as likely as whites to be arrested for marijuana possession (American Civil Liberties Union [ACLU] 2013).

 Thinking Sociologically

Meso- and macro-level social forces can be even more powerful than micro-level forces in explaining deviance. What might be the factors at the meso and macro levels that contribute to deviance such as prostitution or shoplifting? Pick a recent example of deviance now in the news. Which sociological theories help explain this deviant behavior?

A Multilevel Analysis of Deviance: Feminist Theories. As we have indicated in previous chapters, feminist theories sometimes take a macro approach very akin to conflict theory, and sometimes they are more micro in approach. In any case, feminist theorists consistently argue that traditional theories do not give an adequate picture or understanding of women's situations. These theorists look for explanations of violence against women and the secondary status of most women in gender relations and social structures. Although there are several branches of feminist theory, most see the macro-level causes of abuses suffered by women as rooted in the capitalist patriarchal system.

FIGURE 6.3a   Marijuana Use by Race, 2001–2010

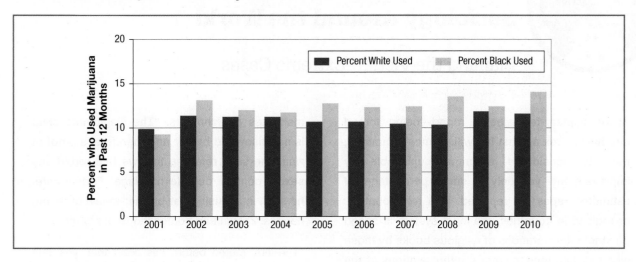

Source: Substance Abuse and Mental Health Services Administration.

FIGURE 6.3b   Arrest Rates for Marijuana Possession by Race, 2001–2010

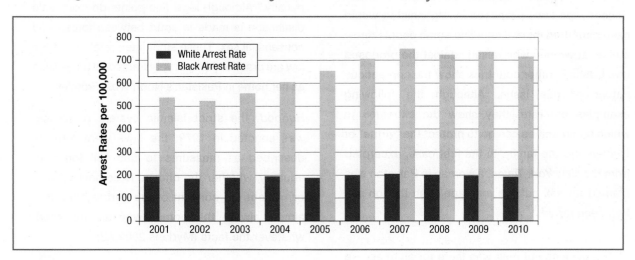

Source: FBI/Uniform Crime Reporting Program Data and U.S. Census Data.

One result of women's secondary status is that they are often victims of sexual crime, and those who commit such crimes against women do not face severe, or in some cases *any*, punishment. Criminal acts against women, including honor killings, sex trafficking, and rape, take place around the world (Bales 2004; Bales and Trodd 2008). Globally, 7 out of 10 women report being sexually assaulted at some point during their lives (United Nations 2013). Often, women are blamed for "letting it happen" (Boy and Kulczycki 2008). The next "Sociology Around the World" on page 166 feature illustrates this pattern.

According to feminist theory, women's work in the private sphere—including housework, child care, and sexual

satisfaction of their husbands—is undervalued, as are the women who carry out these roles. In some societies, women are the property of their husbands, with men's strength and physical force the ultimate means of control over women. Some branches of feminist theory argue that men exploit women's labor power and sexuality to continue their dominance. The system is reproduced through new generations socialized to maintain the patriarchy and to view inequality between the sexes as "normal" and "natural." Women who deviate from the cultural expectations of "normal" behavior are condemned.

No one theory of why deviance occurs can explain all the forms of deviance. Depending on the level of analysis of

Sociology Around the World

Blaming the Victim: Extreme Cases

Every woman fears being raped—being forced into having sex against her will. In most countries, rape is considered a crime punishable by imprisonment—yet only a small percentage of estimated rapes are reported. In a few countries or regions in countries, the legal system is based on strict interpretations of religious books by those who practice fundamentalist interpretations of the religion, in an attempt to guard against loss of a woman's virtue, shame, and illegitimate children. These laws also maintain patriarchal control. Recent rape laws proposed in Afghanistan would have permitted marital rape and some people threw stones at women who rallied against the proposed law. Cases in other countries show the contentious nature of this issue. Although the following examples are rare, they show the extremes to which communities can go to protect the "virtue" of women and the family. In the first case, excerpted from the *New York Times*, a woman in Pakistan was blamed for sex outside marriage even though she had been raped.

The evidence of guilt was there for all to see—a newborn baby in the arms of its mother, a village woman named Zafran Bibi. Her crime: She had been raped. Her sentence: death by stoning. Now, Ms. Zafran, who is about 26, is in solitary confinement in a death row cell in Kohat, a nearby town. The only visitor she is allowed is her baby daughter, now a 1-year-old being cared for by a prison nurse.

Thumping a fat, red statute book, the white-bearded judge who convicted her—Anwar Ali Khan—said he had simply followed the letter of the Koran-based law, known as *hudood*, that mandates punishments. "The illegitimate child is not disowned by her and therefore is proof of *zina*," he said, referring to laws that forbid any sexual contact outside marriage. Furthermore, he said, in accusing her brother-in-law of raping her, Ms. Zafran had confessed to her crime.

"The lady stated before this court that, yes, she had committed sexual intercourse, but with the brother of her husband," Judge Khan said. "This left no option to the court but to impose the highest penalty." Although legal fine points do exist, little distinction is made in court between forced and consensual sex. These strict interpretations of the law are practiced only in very traditional areas such as her home in Pakistan's North West Frontier.

Hudood, the strict Islamic system of justice, was enacted in 1979; the laws were formally described as measures to ban "all forms of adultery, whether the offense is committed with or without the consent of the parties," but it is almost always the women who are punished, whatever the facts (Mydans 2002:A3).

Zafran Bibi appealed the adultery decision. Women's rights groups and the international community protested the charge; this may have helped the court to find her "not guilty," and she was released from prison under the Federal Sharia Act in Pakistan. Although the Women's Protection Bill was passed in 2006, she still fears that she will be the victim of violence. Because she became a public figure through the publicity her case received and because the individuals who opposed her acquittal know where she lives and what she looks like, she is subject to possible retaliation.

In another case, covered extensively by American and European news, a young Pakistani woman, Mukhtar Mai, was ordered to be raped as punishment for the acts of her brother who was seen with a woman from another, more powerful tribe. In 2004, Pakistani governments (mostly those of small towns and villages) ordered about 400 rapes as punishment for both sexual and nonsexual offenses. Higher policing groups do occasionally arrest the rapists in these cases for sexual violation, but this is not uniform. For Mai, 6 of her 14 rapists have been charged with rape, and Mai has asked that the men not be acquitted (*Mukhtar Mai* 2005). However, on April 21, 2011, five of the six alleged rapists were freed by the courts, and Mai says she fears for her life (Shackle 2012; Taseer 2011).

In Saudi Arabia, a 19-year-old woman was abducted at knifepoint, gang-raped for being seen with a man who had blackmailed her and her family and then beaten by her brother for disgracing the family. A Saudi court sentenced the woman to 90 lashes and several months in prison for being seen with the man who was blackmailing them and who may have lured her into the trap. After the court ruling, there was an international outcry. In response, King Abdullah of Saudi Arabia pardoned the woman ("Gang-Rape Victim Faces Lashes" 2007; Shihri 2007).

Although these are extreme cases illustrasting *blaming the victim*, the practice takes place in many settings and is sometimes justified by the law.

Thinking Sociologically

How might a feminist theorist explain why some women face punishment for being raped? Do you agree with this perspective? Why? What is the counterargument to your position?

the questions sociologists wish to study (micro, meso, or macro), they select the theory that best fits the data they find. In the following sections, we explore in more detail the micro–meso–macro connections as they apply to one manifestation of deviance—crime. This illustrates how the sociological imagination can be applied to deviance at each level in the social system.

CRIME AND INDIVIDUALS: MICRO-LEVEL ANALYSIS

In the United States, more than 2,800 acts are listed as federal crimes. These acts fall into several types of crime, some of which we discuss below. First, we consider how crime rates are measured.

How Much Crime Is There?

How do sociologists and law enforcement officials know how much crime occurs? Not all crime is reported to the police, and when crime is reported, the methods of

© Reuters/Andrew Biraj

Feminist scholars point out that domestic abuse, such as that inflicted on this woman and child, disproportionately impacts women. Asma and her 11-month-old daughter Afsana were attacked with acid because she was helping her sister with a divorce.

collecting data may differ. Each country has its own methods of keeping crime records. For instance, the official record of crime in the United States is found in the Federal Bureau of Investigation's *Uniform Crime Reports* (UCR). The FBI relies on information submitted voluntarily by law enforcement agencies and divides crimes into two categories: Type I and Type II offenses. Type I offenses, also known as *FBI index crimes*, include murder, forcible rape, robbery, aggravated assault, burglary, larceny theft, motor vehicle theft, and arson. Type II offenses include fraud, simple assault, vandalism, driving under the influence of alcohol or drugs, and running away from home. In fact, there are hundreds of Type II crimes. Table 6.1, the Crime Clock, summarizes UCR records on Type I offenses.).

Table 6.1   2013 Crime Clock

A Violent Crime occurred every	27.1 seconds
One Murder every	37.0 minutes
One Forcible Rape every	6.6 minutes
One Robbery every	1.5 minutes
One Aggravated Assault every	43.5 seconds
A Property Crime occurred every	3.7 seconds
One Burglary every	16.4 seconds
One Larceny-theft every	5.3 seconds
One Motor Vehicle Theft every	45.1 seconds

Source: U.S. Department of Justice (2014).

Although the UCR data provide a picture of how much crime gets *reported* to the police and leads to arrest, the FBI does not provide complete information on how much crime there is in the United States. The UCR does not show most corporate crimes or white-collar crimes, and *many* street crimes are not reported for a host of reasons. Further, sometimes a crime reported to the police does not lead to an arrest, or an arrest is made but the case is never prosecuted in court, or a prosecutor will initiate prosecution but the case never comes to trial. A majority of cases end in plea bargains—a suspect agrees to plead guilty in exchange for being given a lesser charge, perhaps because the suspect expresses feelings of guilt, does not have the resources to fight the charges with a good attorney, or is willing to exchange information for a lighter sentence. The reduction in the number of cases at each level of the criminal justice system contributes to the difficulty of determining accurate crime rates.

Self-reporting surveys—asking individuals what criminal acts they have committed—provide another way to measure crime rates. Criminal participation surveys typically focus on adolescents and their involvement in delinquency. *Victimization surveys* ask people how much crime they have experienced. The Bureau of Justice Statistics carries out the National Crime Victimization Survey each year. These NCVS indicates that the tendency to report crime to the police varies by the type of crime, with violent victimizations having the highest reporting rate.

Thinking Sociologically

Imagine that you work for the Bureau of Justice Statistics. Congress asks you to predict how many FBI agents will be needed to deal with different types of crime. How would you go about determining this, and what data sources might you use?

Although differences in crime reports are often difficult to reconcile, each measurement instrument provides a different portion of the total picture of crime. By using several data-gathering techniques (triangulation), a more accurate picture of crime begins to emerge. All data-gathering techniques indicate that the rate of violent and nonviolent crime in the United States has dropped since the mid-1990s, so we can be confident that the crime rate has really fallen. In 1990, there were 732 violent crimes per 100,000 residents, but in 2012, that number was 386 (see Figure 6.4).

The violent crime rate decreased further from June 2012 to June 2013 by the following percentage points: murders 6.9%, forcible rapes 10.6%, aggravated assaults 6.6%, and robbery offenses 1.8% (FBI 2014a). Researchers have yet to come to a consensus as to why crime has declined. Some ideas now under review include the following:

- Changing demographics—a decline in the number of young people (those most likely to commit crimes)
- Rising rates of incarceration (though those rates have declined over the past few years)
- New policing strategies, including computer-assisted planning and closer focus on gun use by youth
- Greater access to abortion after the 1973 *Roe v. Wade* Supreme Court decision, which led to fewer unwanted children (relatively more likely to commit crimes due to their negative treatment)
- The phasing out of lead in gasoline in the 1970s (lead can cause brain damage related to violent behavior) (Cohn et al. 2013)

Though crime is down, it is still the common subject of news headlines. Crime reporting is relatively inexpensive, as reporters can rely on information about index crimes that officials regularly make public. So, the crimes that grab the attention of average citizens of countries around the world tend to be violent crimes committed by individuals or small groups.

Types of Crime

Predatory Crimes. Citizens of the United States tend to be most afraid of violent predatory crime—crimes with a

FIGURE 6.4   U.S. Violent Crime Rate Since 1990 (per 100,000 residents)

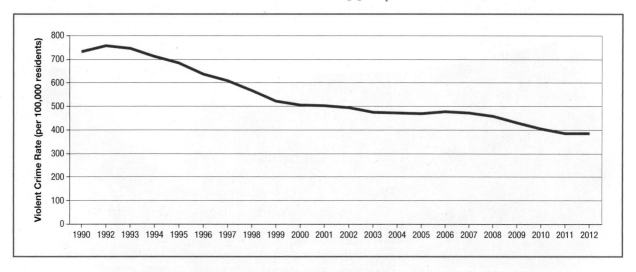

Source: FBI (2014b).

human victim. Many citizens feel they cannot trust others. Some keep guns to protect themselves from this perceived danger. Some neighborhoods *are* dangerous; however, as noted earlier, the total violent crime victimization rate has declined over the past several decades. In the following, we discuss more crimes committed by individuals—but stay tuned because most criminologists feel there are more serious crimes, to be discussed under meso- and macro-level deviance.

Crimes Without Victims. *Acts committed by or between individual consenting adults* are known as victimless or public order crimes. These can include prostitution, gambling, drug use, and public drunkenness. While these crimes do not result in specific victims, they are deemed harmful to society (and, thus, criminal) because they violate the dominant values and norms. While illegal, they may be tolerated (the police may look the other way) as long as they do not become highly visible. For example, it would be rare for police in the United States to crack down on a low-stakes monthly poker game friends play behind closed doors.

Victimless crimes involving drugs result in a variety of policies, from execution in Iran and hanging in Malaysia to legalization in Holland. As noted earlier, U.S. drug policies have led to huge numbers of people being imprisoned. Half of all drug arrests in 2010 were related to marijuana usage (ACLU 2013). However, proposals to legalize drugs in the United States have recently gained traction. As we write these words, 23 states and Washington, D.C., allow for the medical use of marijuana, and 2 states (Colorado and Washington) have legalized recreational use of the drug (see Figure 6.5). A 2013 Gallup poll indicated that 58% of Americans favor decriminalization of marijuana (Nagourney and Lyman 2013).

California has the longest experience with legalization of medical marijuana—nearly two decades. Fears among some that legalization would lead to civic disorder, increased lawlessness, and drastic increases in other drug usage have all been unfounded. Due to careful monitoring of the age of buyers, teen use of marijuana in California has not increased since legalization in 1996 (Nagourney and Lyman 2013). Further, some scholars think more teen use of marijuana would not be a bad trend. When teens

This photo shows how what we consider deviant can change over time.

The Sociology of Drug Use

FIGURE 6.5 Medical Marijuana Laws 2013

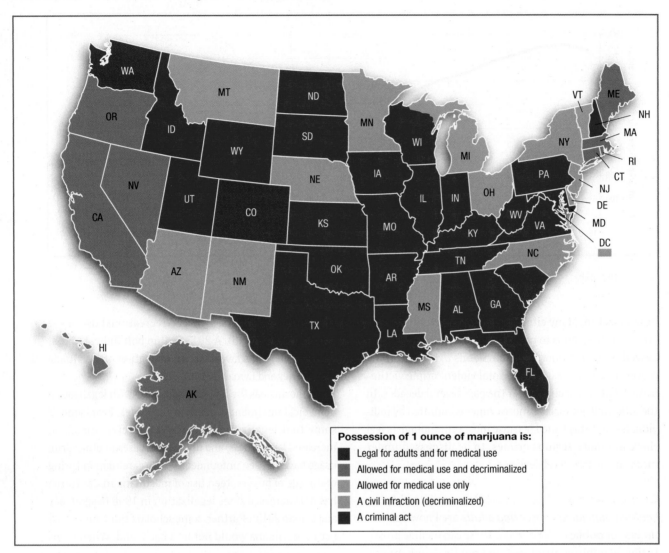

Possession of 1 ounce of marijuana is:

- ■ Legal for adults and for medical use
- ■ Allowed for medical use and decriminalized
- ■ Allowed for medical use only
- ■ A civil infraction (decriminalized)
- ■ A criminal act

switch to marijuana, they tend to reduce alcohol usage, and alcohol is more likely to result in death from overuse or from drunk driving (Anderson and Rees 2013).

Thinking Sociologically

Can a person be victimized by drugs even if he willingly uses them? Many prostitutes only consent to sex acts because poverty or drug addiction leaves them with few other options and because, like many women without resources, they are vulnerable to domination by men. Are they victims, or are these crimes without victims? Why?

Hate Crimes. A hate crime is a *"criminal offense against a person or property motivated in whole or in part by an offender's bias against a race, religion, disability, ethnic*

origin or sexual orientation" (FBI 2014c). The FBI reported 5,790 hate crimes in 2012, with the breakdown by bias indicated in Figure 6.6. Hate crimes are underreported, with many victims not believing the police can help them. From the data that are available, though, it is clear that hate crimes based on religion and sexual orientation have increased over the past few years (FBI 2013; Langton Planty, and Sandholtz 2013; Potok 2013a).

Those who commit hate crimes feel rage against the victim as a representative of a group they despise. In the case of some white supremacy movements, philosophical, political, and even religious principles guide their group beliefs (Blee 2008). As minority groups gain notoriety *or* acceptance in society, they can face more hate crimes. For example, hate crime incidents against Muslim Americans increased after September 11, 2001, and the Boston

Drug Legalization 💻

FIGURE 6.6   Breakdown of the 5,790 Single-Bias Hate Crime Incidents Reported in 2012

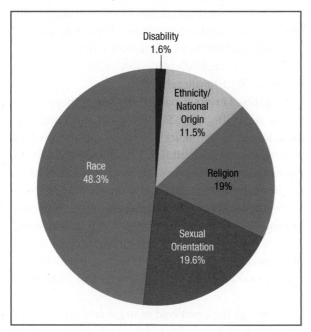

Source: http://www.fbi.gov/news/stories/2013/november/annual-hate-crime-statistics-show-slight-decease

Marathon bombing in 2013. The numbers of white supremacist groups increased dramatically after Barack Obama, the first U.S. president of color, was elected; and antigay hate crimes have become more common with the growing success of the same-sex marriage movement (Peek 2011).

The examples above represent only three of the many types of micro-level crimes, characterized by individual or small-group actions. We now turn to crime in organizations and institutions at the meso level. Organizations usually commit the crimes most harmful to society.

CRIME AND ORGANIZATIONS: MESO-LEVEL ANALYSIS

Crime and organized crime control efforts are part of the social structure of modern societies. First, as societies modernize, there is an almost universal tendency for crime rates to increase dramatically due to the anomie that new migrants and the poor experience in urban areas where old norms are no longer relevant (Merton 1938).

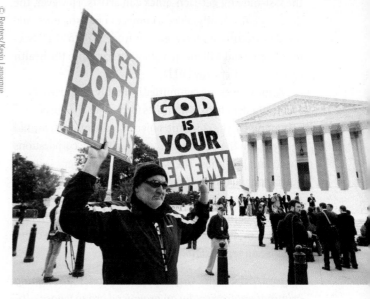

These photos reveal how various subcultures can have sharply different views on what they consider deviant. They also help illustrate why hate crimes tend to increase as minority groups gain more power in society and their definitions of reality come to be normalized.

Second, as societies become modernized and urban, they become more reliant on meso-level formal or bureaucratic mechanisms of control rather than small community pressures and conformity. They develop a criminal justice system.

Crimes Involving Organizations and Institutions

Jeanne, one of the authors of this book, recently got a call from a fraud office at an online retailer saying that her credit card had been compromised. Someone had ordered online items from Atlanta-based Bloomingdale's, Coach, and DSW (Designer Shoe Warehouse) using her credit card—and it was not Jeanne! How did the retailer catch it? "Unusual behavior on the account." Credit card fraud and identity theft are two types of organized crime prevalent today.

High rates of fraud can also be seen in the medical system. Approximately 20% of every Medicare dollar in 2011 went to fraud (Konrad 2012). For example, in South Florida, criminals open storefronts claiming to sell medical equipment. Often these businesses are located in dying strip malls. Once the criminals have sent in false claims for Medicare payments, sometimes amounting to millions of dollars, they close the storefronts and move on so that they cannot be traced. The federal government has had a small number of investigators in the past—hardly a match for the fast-moving get-rich-quick con artists. However, the government recently added a number of investigators, and fraud prosecutions increased 85% from 2010 to 2011. Savings from fraud will mean money put back into the health care system (Kennedy 2011).

Some crimes are committed by highly organized, hierarchically structured syndicates formed for the purpose of achieving their economic objectives through criminal behavior. On the other hand, some legitimate corporations also commit crimes. Their crimes are often very serious, but the public image of such organizations is not criminal so they are not always suspected or caught. We will look first at organized criminal organizations and then at crimes committed by people within their legitimate occupations and organizations.

Organized Crime. Organized crime refers to *ongoing criminal enterprises by an organized group whose ultimate purpose is economic gain through illegitimate means* (Siegel 2009). Our image of this type of crime is sometimes glamorized in films such as *No Country for Old Men, The Godfather, Goodfellas,* and *Gangs of New York*. On television, *The Sopranos* is the ultimate media "mob" depiction. Despite the alluring view of these idealized stories, organized crime is a serious problem in many countries. It is essentially a counterculture with a hierarchical structure, from the boss down to the underlings. The organization relies on power, control, fear, violence, and corruption. This type of deviance is a particular problem when societies experience anomie and social controls break down.

Marginalized ethnic groups that face discrimination may become involved in a quest to get ahead through organized crime. Early in U.S. history, Italians were especially prominent in organized crime, but today, many

groups are involved. Organized crime around the world has gained strong footholds in countries in transition (European Commission 2014). For example, in Russia, the transition from a socialist economy to a market economy has provided many opportunities for criminal activity. The *Mafiya* is estimated to include over 100,000 people, and some estimate that the members control 70% to 80% of all private business and 40% of Russia's wealth (Lindberg and Markovic n.d.; Schmalleger 2012).

Organized crime usually takes one of three forms: (1) the sale of illegal goods and services, including gambling, loan sharking, trafficking in drugs and people, selling stolen goods, and prostitution; (2) infiltrating legitimate businesses and unions through threat and intimidation and using bankruptcy and fraud to exploit and devastate a legitimate company; and (3) racketeering—the extortion of funds in exchange for protection (i.e., not being hurt). Activities such as a casino or trash collection service often appear to be legitimate endeavors on the surface but may be cover operations for highly organized illegal crime rings.

Although the exact cost of organized crime in the United States is impossible to determine, estimates of the annual gross income of organized crime activity range from $50 billion to $90 billion per year (CNBC 2010; Siegel 2011). Internationally, criminal proceeds for all transnational organized crime is estimated at $870 billion a year (United Nations Office on Drugs and Crime 2014a); recorded criminal activities $2.1 trillion (Bjelopera and Finklea 2012; Fedotov 2012).

Transnational organized crime takes place across national boundaries, using sophisticated electronic communications and transportation technologies. The major crime clans in the world include (a) Hong Kong–based organized crime organizations, (b) South American cocaine cartels, (c) Italian mafia, (d) Japanese yakuza, (e) Russian Mafiya, and (f) West African crime groups. Each operates across borders. Organized crime is responsible for thousands of deaths every year through drug trafficking and murders, and contributes to the climate of violence in many cities (Siegel 2009).

The value of the global illicit drug market is estimated at more than $320 billion at the retail level (based on retail prices). Add other types of crimes (transporting migrants, selling human organs, trafficking in women and children for the sex industry, drug sales, and sales of weapons and nuclear material), and the estimates of profits for international crime cartels are as high as $1.5 trillion a year ("Transnational Crime in the Developing World" 2011).

Mafia in the United States

Occupational Crime. Bernard (Bernie) Madoff, a well-respected investor and former chair of the NASDAQ stock exchange, developed a Ponzi scheme that was probably the largest investment fraud Wall Street has ever seen. The scheme defrauded and wrecked thousands of investors, public pension funds, charitable foundations, and universities of billions of dollars, with more than $65 billion missing from investor accounts when the scam became public in 2008. Named after Charles Ponzi, the first to be caught (in 1919), Ponzi schemes involve promises of large returns on investments, paying old investors with money from new investors. Money is simply shifted among investors to make it appear as though the investments earn money ("The Madoff Case" 2009). Meanwhile, those running the scam pocket enormous sums of the money invested.

Ponzi schemes are one example of white-collar or occupational crime, *a violation of the law committed by an individual or a group in the course of a legitimate, respected occupation or financial activity* (Coleman 2006; Hagan 2011). Occupational crime can be committed by individuals from virtually any social class, and it can occur at any organizational level. However, most often this refers to white-collar crimes.

These crimes receive less attention than violent crimes because they are less visible, do not always cause obvious physical injury to identifiable people, and are frequently committed by people in positions of substantial authority and prestige. Reports of violent crimes that appear on the television news each night attract more attention. Yet occupational crime is far more costly in money, health, and lives. Victims of financial scams who have lost their life savings or workers who have lost their good health because of unsafe and illegal work conditions are well aware of this.

Sociologists divide occupational crimes into four major categories: (1) against the company, (2) against employees, (3) against customers, and (4) against the general public or other organizations (Hagan 2011).

Crimes against the company include pilfering (using company resources such as the photocopy machine for personal business) and employee theft (taking company supplies for your own use, stealing from the till, and embezzlement). Those who commit occupational crimes say they do so for several reasons. First, they feel little or no loyalty to the organization, especially if it is large and impersonal. It is like stealing from nobody, they say. Second, workers feel exploited and resentful toward the company. Stealing is getting back at the company. Third, the theft is seen as a "fringe benefit" or "informal compensation" that they deserve. Such workers may spend time on a side business while at work or take paper and ink cartridges for their printer at home. Fourth, workers may steal because of the challenge. It makes the job more interesting if they can get away with it. It is important to note that these people do not see themselves as criminals, especially compared with "street" criminals (Altheide et al. 1978).

The other three types of corporate crime benefit the company at the expense of employees or members of the larger society. *Crimes against employees* refer to corporate neglect of worker safety. In 1970, the U.S. government established the Occupational Safety and Health Administration (OSHA) to help enforce regulations to protect workers, but there are still many problems. Government agencies estimate that the death rate each year from job-related illness and injuries is *five times* the number of deaths from street crimes. For example, one out of every five cancer cases has been traced to pollutants in workplaces, and many of these cases were preventable (Simon 2006; U.S. Bureau of Labor Statistics 2011). *Wage theft*, underpaying or not paying workers, is another widespread corporate crime that harms millions of workers. Many employers do not pay workers their due wages by requiring them to work "off the clock," not paying them minimum wage, stealing their tips, not paying them overtime, refusing to give them their last check, or simply not paying them at all. A 2009 study revealed that almost half (43.6%) of low-wage, urban U.S. workers surveyed had experienced wage theft during the previous year (Bernhardt et al. 2009).

Neglect of worker safety is a particularly serious problem in many developing or peripheral countries trying to attract multinational corporations with low taxes, cheap labor, and few regulations. The decisions of many corporations and factory owners illustrate *rational choice theory*. Too often they decide the benefits (profit) that come from exploiting labor outweigh the costs (harm to workers). The collapse of a shoddily constructed factory building in Bangladesh that killed over 1,127 workers in 2013 is a powerful example of what can result from this type of thinking.

As *strain theorists* point out, almost all corporations have the goal of making the greatest short-term profit possible, and one (deviant) method to do that is to cut expenses at the expense of worker safety. Government regulatory agencies responsible for reducing environmental hazards and workplace dangers do not have sufficient staff to police companies for adherence to laws. Internationally, there is little oversight. Multinational corporations generally look for the cheapest labor costs and fewest

Employees in the Rana Plaza building in Bangladesh made clothing for many multinational apparel companies who failed, along with the building owner, to ensure that they had a safe place to work. This is an example of corporate crime against employees.

environmental regulations, and governments of poor countries try to attract foreign corporations to keep the poor populace employed regardless of the personal illnesses and environmental or workplace consequences.

Since the building collapse in Bangladesh, momentum is (for the moment, at least) on the side of workers' rights organizations. After the government had done nothing following several factory fires that killed hundreds of workers, the building collapse was the last straw for many workers in Bangladesh and for millions of people seeing the carnage in the media. Protesters took to the streets in Bangladesh and across the world. This organized outrage has led to promises from the Bangladesh government to raise the minimum wage for workers and ease antiunion laws. Many multinational corporations, fearing further negative exposure, have pledged to ensure better working conditions for Bangladeshi workers who make their products.

Consumers, as well as workers, can be victims of corporate crime. *Crimes against customers* involve acts victimizing patrons, such as selling dangerous foods or unsafe products, consumer fraud, deceptive advertising, and price-fixing (i.e., setting prices in collusion with another producer). The purpose of advertising is to convince customers to buy the product—appealing to their vanity, sexual interests, or desire to keep up with their neighbors. Sometimes these techniques cross the line between honesty and deception, and customers purchase defective and even dangerous products—all with the full knowledge of company officials.

Crimes against the public include acts by companies that negatively affect large groups of people. One example is hospitals or medical offices that overbill Medicare (discussed above), or insurance companies pressuring hospitals to discharge patients too early to save on costs. Surreptitiously dumping pollutants into landfills, streams, or the air is another crime against the public. Proper disposal of contaminants can be costly and time-consuming for a company, but shortcuts can cause long-term effects for the public (Coleman 2006). Pollutants from industrial wastes have caused high rates of miscarriages, birth defects, and diseases among residents.

These examples help illustrate that white-collar crime committed by company executives is by far our most serious crime problem. The economic cost of white-collar crime is vastly greater than the economic cost of street crime. White-collar criminals kill considerably more people than all violent street criminals put together (Coleman 2006).

 Thinking Sociologically

Why are meso-level crimes (occupational/white-collar crimes) more dangerous and more costly to the public than micro-level crimes? Why do they get so much less attention?

NATIONAL AND GLOBAL CRIME: MACRO-LEVEL ANALYSIS

As we have seen, national boundaries continue to blur as people migrate around the globe and many corporations move headquarters across national lines in search of lower costs and higher profits. Crime syndicates, too, are multinational, as they move money, goods, and people surreptitiously across borders. Likewise, terrorist organizations have no boundaries. We now turn to the macro-level crime of terrorism.

Terrorism is the *planned use of random, unlawful (or illegal) violence or threat of violence against civilians to create (or raise) fear and intimidate citizens in order to advance the terrorist group's political or ideological goals* (U.S. Department of Defense 2011). Terrorist groups can be anarchist, state sponsored, right wing or left wing, nationalist, or religious (Rice 2013; Schmalleger 2006). Table 6.2 shows the major types of terrorist groups.

Governments can commit *state-organized crime.* Often overlooked by the public and by social scientists, this form of

Table 6.2 Types of Terrorist Groups

Anarchist	Some contemporary antiglobalization groups
State sponsored	Hezbollah (Iran), Abu Nidal Organization (Syria)
Right wing	Neo-Nazis, skinheads, white supremacists; paramilitary groups in Colombia
Left wing	Revolutionary Armed Forces of Colombia (FARC); Revolutionary People's Liberation Party–Front (Turkey)
Nationalist	Irish Republican Army, Basque Fatherland and Liberty
Religious	Al-Qaeda, Hamas, ISIS (Syria and Iraq), Aum Shinrikyo (Japan)

Sources: Rice (2013); Schmalleger (2006).

crime includes acts defined by law as criminal but committed by state or government officials. For example, a government might be complicit in smuggling, assassination, or torture, which is then justified in terms of "national defense." Government offices may also violate laws that restrict or limit government activities such as eavesdropping. In some countries, political prisoners such as the Guantánamo Bay detainees held in Cuba by the United States are imprisoned for long periods without charges, without access to lawyers, and without trials, and some have been tortured, violating both national and international laws (Center for Constitutional Rights 2013). The U.S. Supreme Court has ruled (2006 and 2008), that the U.S. administration violated the rights of these people (Global Security 2009). The Obama administration planned to shut down the Guantánamo Bay facility in 2010, but that closure has not yet occurred, and, as we write these words, 149 detainees remain at "Gitmo" (Haberkorn 2014). Although countries may violate their own laws, it is difficult to prosecute when the guilty party is the government.

Bribery and corruption are the way of life in many governments, businesses, and police forces. The percentage of citizens who said that they had paid a bribe to obtain services is as high as 79% in Nigeria, 72% in Cambodia, and 71% in Albania. The institutions perceived to be most affected by corruption globally include political parties, the police, the judiciary, legislatures, and business (Transparency International 2012). Figure 6.7 shows an index of the perception of corruption (from 1 to 10) in various countries around the world.

Thinking Sociologically

Sometimes government officials and even heads of state are the perpetrators of crimes. When, if ever, is it justified for a government official to violate the law of the nation?

The forms of global corruption are too extensive to catalog here, so we will settle for an illustration of one of the newest manifestations of global crime against people and property: cyber-crime. Internet deviance or cyberspace crime is growing faster than a cybergeek can move a mouse. This new world of crime ranges from online identity theft and gambling to cybersex and pornography, to hate sites and stalking, to hacking into government and military files, and to terrorist recruiting sites. Global law enforcement gridlock due to national and international jurisdictional confusion impedes efforts to prevent such crime. For example, as many as five different federal U.S. agencies can be involved in preventing financial

© Ron Sachs/CNP/Corbis

Detainees sit in a holding area at the naval base in Guantánamo Bay, Cuba, in the "temporary" detention center. It violates U.S. law, but the facility continues to hold prisoners and to operate.

FIGURE 6.7   Corruption Perceptions Index 2013

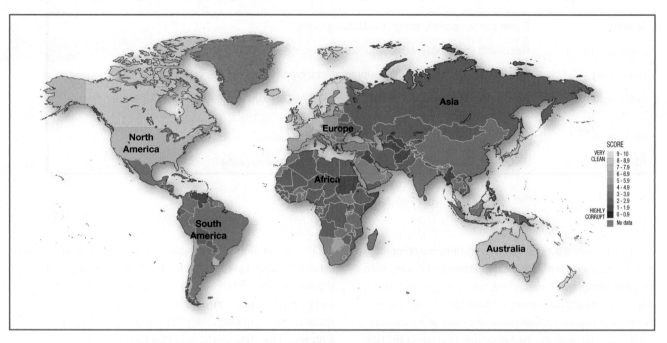

Note: Transparency International's Corruption Perceptions Index measures the perceived level of public sector corruption in countries and territories around the world.

Source: Data taken from Transparency International CPI 2013. Copyright © Transparency International. All Rights Reserved. For more information, visit http://www.transparency.org

fraud on the Internet, not to mention the state and local agencies that might play a role. If the fraud involves international cybercrime, the customs services and other branches of government also may enter the investigation. The resulting confusion and lack of clear authority can play into the hands of lawbreakers. For example, most big corporations have been the victim of hacking and cybertheft from China and other nations. The federal government, however, does not yet have an effective way to make companies do all they can to safeguard their customers' information or to coordinate effective defenses against such illegal cyber intrusions from other nations ("Cybercrime: Smoking Gun" 2013; Perlroth and Sanger 2013).

Cross-National Comparison of Crimes

The vending machine was on the corner near the Ballantines' house in Japan. The usual cola, candy, and sundries were displayed, along with cigarettes, beer, whiskey, sake, and pornographic magazines. Out of curiosity, Jeanne and her family watched to see who purchased what from the machines, and not once did they see teenagers

sneaking the beer, cigarettes, or porn. It turns out that the Ballantines were not the only ones watching! The neighbors also kept an eye on who did what. Because of the stigma attached to deviant behavior in Japan, the teens tend to avoid violating norms, and vigilant neighbors help keep the overall amount of deviance low. The many eyes in the neighborhood remind people that deviant behavior is unacceptable and provide informal social control over those who might be tempted to commit crimes.

Japan and the United States are both modern, urban, industrial countries, but their crime rates and the way they deal with deviant behavior and crimes differ. The overall crime rate in the United States is 3 times that of Japan, and the U.S. murder rate is *10 times* higher. Japan has 0.5 murders for every 100,000 people, whereas the United States has 5.0 per 100,000 residents (Cowen and Williams 2012; Spacey 2012).

How can these extreme differences in crime rates be explained? Researchers look at cultural differences: Japan's low violent crime rate is due in part to Japan's culturally homogeneous society and loyalty to a historic tradition of cooperation that provides a sense of moral order, a network of group relations, strong commitment to social norms, and respect for law and order. The example of vending machines in Japan illustrates this idea. In addition, guns are outlawed and much harder to come by in Japan.

Japan does not attain its lower crime rate through heavy investment in its criminal justice system. In fact, the Japanese government actually spends far less of its gross national product on the police, courts, and prisons than does the United States. For many crimes in Japan, the offender may simply be asked to write a letter of apology. This is frequently a sufficient sanction to deter the person from further violation of the law. The humiliation of writing an apology and the fear of shame and embarrassing one's family are strong enough to curb deviant behavior (Lazare 2004). Table 6.3 provides information on crimes in selected countries; it allows you to see differences in crime rates per 100,000 individuals in the population. Differences are due in part to the much higher disparity in income between rich and poor and the heterogeneity of populations. Two sources of international data are Interpol (the International Criminal Police Organization) and the United Nations.

Thinking Sociologically

Study Table 6.3. Which countries have especially striking crime rates—either high or low? Why? Why might the rankings of countries for violent crimes (the first two columns) and economic crimes (the third column) be different?

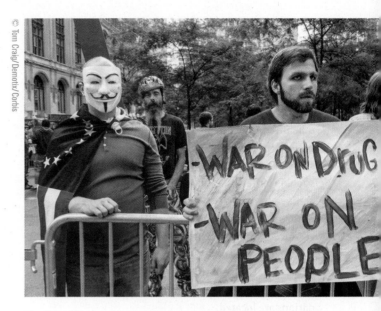

The U.S. "War on Drugs" has meant that the United States has pressured Mexico and other global South nations to crack down on drug producers and traffickers. This has made drugs more scarce and mob-run drug trafficking a major source of crime and violence, negatively impacting innocent people in many nations.

Global Crimes

Increasingly, crimes are global in nature. Some scholars use the *world systems theory* to understand global crime, arguing that the cause of global crime lies in the

Table 6.3 Crime Rates per 100,000 People in Selected Countries

Country	Murders	Rapes	Robberies
Mexico	18.1	13.3	607
United States	5.0	28.6	133
Israel	2.1	17.5	40
Canada	1.8	1.4	96
New Zealand	1.5	30.6	52
Australia	1.2	91.9	18
England and Wales	1.1	27.7	137
Denmark	0.9	6.4	73
Germany	0.8	8.9	60
Japan	0.5	1.1	4

Source: Cowen and Williams (2012).

global economy, the inequalities between countries, and the competition between countries for resources and wealth. As a result of the capitalist mode of production, an unequal relationship has arisen between core nations (the developed, wealthy nations in the Global North) and periphery nations (the Global South). Core nations often take unfair advantage of peripheral nations. Peripheral nations, in turn, must find ways to survive in this global system, and they sometime turn to illegal methods—such as violating global environmental standards—to achieve their goals (Chase-Dunn and Anderson 2006). Some nations, though not wealthy, have many natural resources and are semiperipheral nations. Benefiting from extensive trade, they are less vulnerable than the poorest nations. Map Figure 6.8 helps you see where some of these core, peripheral, and semi-peripheral nations are located.

As you look at this figure, note that the developed or affluent countries are almost all located in the Northern Hemisphere. Although some poor countries are north of the equator, the pattern is obvious. To avoid some misleading implications of the words *developed* and *developing*, many scholars now prefer the term *Global South* to refer to less affluent nations. If you see or hear the phrase *Global South*, this figure should help you see why it refers to developing or poor countries.

CONTROLLING CRIME: SOCIAL POLICY CONSIDERATIONS

What is the best way to control crime? While all modern societies have criminal justice systems, their crime prevention strategies vary. We now look at the mechanisms used by societies to curb deviant behavior and punish deviants.

Dealing With Crime: The Criminal Justice Process

Structural-functionalists see the justice system as a crucial means of ensuring order and social control in society. Conflict theorists, on the other hand, argue that the criminal justice system works in the interest of those in power, at the expense of the other members of society. It is in the interests of those in power to maintain the image that crime is primarily the work of outsiders and the poor. This deflects citizen discontent and hostility from the powerful, and helps them retain their positions of power (Reiman and Leighton 2010a, 2010b). Conflict theorists point out that there will always be crime in society because the powerful will make sure that some things and some people are labeled deviant.

FIGURE 6.8   Global Status of the Death Penalty, 2012

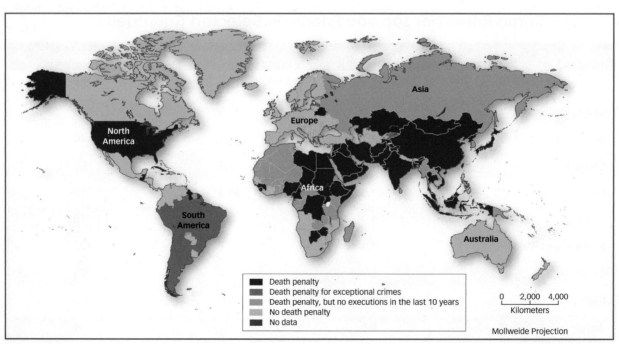

Source: Data from Amnesty International. Map by Anna Versluis.

Depending on whether one uses a structural-functional or conflict theoretical perspective, criminal justice policy generally focuses on either how to deter deviant acts or the injustices of the criminal justice system. In the United States today, prisons provide one of the primary means of controlling individual criminal behavior. Think about which theoretical perspective, structural functionalism or conflict theory, you would use to better understand the function of prisons in U.S. society as you read the following section.

Prisons. Prisons are a form of *total institution* that completely controls the prisoners and regulates all their activities. Inmates' lives are drastically changed through the processes of *degradation*, which marks the individual as deviant, and *mortification*, which breaks down the individual's original self as the inmate experiences resocialization (Goffman 1961; Irwin 1985; Irwin and Owen 2007). The inmate cannot have any personal property. Guards allow prisoners only limited communication and often verbally abuse inmates. Uniforms and standard buzz cuts (for men) are required, and inmates' have strictly controlled schedules.

In a famous study that simulated a prison situation, researchers illustrated the social organization that develops and the roles that individuals play within the prison system. College students were assigned roles as prisoners or prison guards. Within a short time, the individuals in the study were acting out their roles, and behaving in ways very different from their normal behavior, outside of the prison situation. The students playing the role of "guard" became cruel and sadistic, causing the researcher, Philip Zimbardo, to end the experiment early. Participants had taken their roles so seriously that the abuse was beginning to have alarming consequences (Zimbardo et al. 1973).

The recent abuse of prisoners in Iraq and at the Guantánamo Bay prison in Cuba parallels the findings from Zimbardo's earlier study of the roles that develop in these social situations (Zimbardo 2004).

Conflict theorists believe that social class and demographic makeup of prisons reveal that prisons are mostly about controlling or "managing" minorities and poor people, not about public safety. African American males, for example, are more than 5 times more likely to be incarcerated than are white men, and African American women are 2.5 times more likely than are white women to be in imprisoned (Fathi 2009; Sentencing Project 2014). While whites made up 63% of the overall population of the United States in 2011, just 35% of prisoners in the United States were white (Sentencing Project 2014). The makeup of U.S. prisons is presented in Table 6.4.

The recent decrease in incarceration rates in the United States stems from more people being released from prison due to overcrowding and fewer lockups for minor offenses. Still, the "War on Drugs" and "Zero Tolerance Policies" (that prevent judges from adjusting punishments to fit particular circumstances) keep the prison population high compared with that in any other global North country, and account for the highest number of causes for imprisonment (Alexander 2011; Guerino et al. 2011). In fact, the 2013 U.S. incarceration rate of 716 per 100,000 people is the highest in the world (Wing 2013). While the United States contains only 5% of the world's population, it has 25% of the world's prisoners (Kirchhoff 2010). Nearly half (48%) of prisoners in federal prisons were sentenced for drug offenses (Carson and Sabol 2012). Table 6.5 compares incarceration rates among countries with the highest percentages of people in prison and among other industrialized nations.

Table 6.4 Characteristics of People in Prison

	Makeup of U.S. Prison Population	Makeup of U.S. Population*	Ratio of the Population 30–34 Years Old in Prison	Chance of Spending Time in Prison During Lifetime
Black	38%	12.6%	1:13	32%
Hispanic	21%	16.3%	1:36	17%
White	35%	63.7%	1:90	6%

Source: Sentencing Project (2014).

*According to the 2010 U.S. Census (www.census.gov/prod/cen2010/briefs/c2010br-02.pdf).

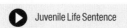 Juvenile Life Sentence

Table 6.5   World Comparative Rates of Incarceration (per 100,000 People), 2013

Top 10 Countries (a)	Incarceration Rate	Other Industrialized Countries (b)	Incarceration Rate
United States	716	England and Wales	148
St. Kitts and Nevis	649	Australia	133
Seychelles	490	Canada	118
Virgin Islands	539	France	103
Rwanda	527	Italy	100
Cuba	510	Switzerland	87
Russia	490	The Netherlands	82
Anguila	487	Germany	78
Georgia	473	Sweden	60

Source: (a) Wing (2013); (b) International Center for Prison Studies (2014).

Thinking Sociologically

Why do you think the United States has 5% of the world's population but 25% of the world's prisoners? How has this impacted your life? Why? How do you think your age, gender, social class, and race influenced your answer?

The Purposes of Prisons. What purpose do you believe prisons serve? From the structural-functional perspective, prisons serve several purposes for society: (1) fulfilling the desire for revenge or retribution, (2) removing dangerous people from society, (3) deterring would-be deviants, and (4) rehabilitating deviants through counseling, education, and work training programs inside prisons (Johnson 2002). However, in prison, inmates are exposed to more criminal and antisocial behavior, so rehabilitation and deterrence goals are often undermined by the nature of prisons. According to a recent Bureau of Justice Statistics report, roughly 5% of prison inmates are sexually assaulted by other prisoners or prison guards, and 12% of youth in juvenile detention facilities are victims, often in gang rapes ("New Federal Report" 2010). This ongoing problem of assault, rape, and threat of violence in prison so brutalizes inmates that it becomes difficult for them to reenter society as well-adjusted citizens ready to conform to societal norms (Fathi 2009; Hensley, Koscheski, and Tewksbury 2005; Liptak 2008).

Prisons and Profits. There is money to be made by locking up prisoners. All prisons can be a source of jobs for the communities in which they are located. Traditionally run by local, state, or federal governments, for-profit companies operate increasing numbers of prisons. While privatization of prisons started in the 1980s, it has taken off in the last two decades. The number of people in private prisons has grown by 1,664% in the past 19 years, and today approximately 130,000 people are in for-profit institutions (Wade 2013). Seven states put more than one of every four of their prisoners in private prisons (Carson and Sabol 2012; Lee 2012).

Prison privatization advocates claim that private businesses driven by a profit motive and competition will operate prisons more efficiently. Private prisons can save on labor costs by not paying the high benefits that states must pay to employees. Those against privatization argue that incarcerating (imprisoning) people for profit is a bad idea, morally and financially. They point out that costs per prisoner often rise after the initial contract with the state (Smith 2012). Some states must incarcerate a certain number of people due to contracts with private prisons, thereby manipulating the criminal justice system (Kirkham 2012). When profit motive is the bottom line, these critics argue, quality of food, training of guards, health care, educational opportunities, and other treatment of inmates can deteriorate.

Profits are also found through inmate labor. As of 2013, 37 states had legalized the contracting of prison labor to private corporations. While prisoners in some state prisons receive minimum wage, many receive less. Some make as little as 17 cents an hour. These low wages lead to high profit margins for those invested in these companies, and business for such contracts is booming (Pelaez 2013).

As one step in an effort to revamp the U.S. federal criminal justice system, the Obama administration has proposed releasing low-level, nonviolent drug offenders who have not committed serious crimes. Thousands of federal offenders could be eligible for early release, easing overcrowding in the prison population (Johnson 2014). The hope is that state criminal justice systems will follow the federal lead.

The Death Penalty. Crimes of murder, assault, robbery, and rape usually receive severe penalties because citizens consider them the most dangerous crimes. The most controversial (and irreversible) method of control is for the state to put the deviant to death. The most common argument for using the death penalty, more formally known as capital punishment, is to deter people from crime. The idea is that not only will the person who has committed the crime be punished but also that others will be deterred from committing such a crime because they know that the death penalty is a possibility for them too.

However, the death penalty does not deter murder (Alarcon and Mitchell 2011; Radelet and Lacock 2009). In addition, it costs far more to use the death penalty than prison as a punishment. For example, a study in California showed that over $4 billion has been spent on 13 executions there since 1978, a cost of $308 million per execution. Because of the costs of a capital trial, various appeals processes (many of which are mandated by law to avoid mistakes), and special death row incarceration requirements, the cost is much greater than for life imprisonment (Alarcon and Mitchell 2011).

Moreover, more murders occur in states with the death penalty than in those without it. The average murder rate in death penalty status was 4.7 per 100,000 persons, while the average murder rate of states without the death penalty was 3.7 (not weighted by population) (Death Penalty Information Center 2013). Despite this, 32 states still have the death penalty (Death Penalty Information Center 2014).

Few Global North countries use the death penalty, and in 2007 the United Nations passed a resolution calling on all nations to abolish it as "cruel and unusual punishment" (Amnesty International 2012; UN News Center 2010). As you can see from Figure 6.9, the United States is one of the

FIGURE 6.9   Global Status of the Death Penalty, 2012

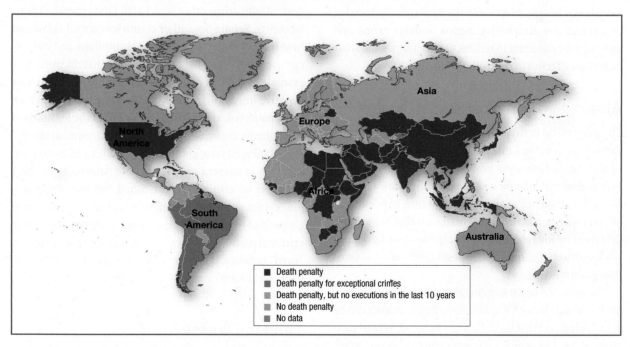

Legend:
- ■ Death penalty
- ■ Death penalty for exceptional crimes
- ■ Death penalty, but no executions in the last 10 years
- ■ No death penalty
- ■ No data

Source: Amnesty International. Map by Anna Versluis.

Criminal Rehabilitation

few countries that utilizes the death penalty out of 198 where records are available. A total of 22 countries carried out executions in 2013, with Iran and Iraq having high numbers of executions, China's true numbers are unknown but suspected to be in the thousands every year, Saudi Arabia with 79, and the United States with 39 (Amnesty International 2014). Only China and Yemen officially recorded more executions in 2010 than the United States (World Coalition 2012).

Thinking Sociologically

How can you explain the higher murder rates in U.S. states that have the death penalty? Why do you think the U.S. death penalty rate is high compared to the rate in most other countries in the world?

Race and class status relate to who receives the death penalty. In most U.S. states with capital punishment, a disproportionate number of minority and lower-class individuals are put to death. Of those executed since 1976, 56% have been white and 34% black. Yet the percentage of blacks in the total population is less than 13%. In 2013, Maryland became the 18th state to abolish the death penalty. In describing why, the governor said, "Maryland has effectively eliminated a policy that is proven not to work. Evidence shows that the death penalty is not a deterrent, it cannot be administered without racial bias, and it costs three times as much as life in prison without parole" (Sutton 2013). These problems with the death penalty have led to a search for alternative means to deter crime and spurred policy analysts to rethink assumptions about what factors are effective in controlling human behavior.

Alternative Forms of Social Control

The disturbing reality is that, despite the high rates of incarceration in the United States, recidivism rates—*the likelihood that someone who is arrested, convicted, and imprisoned will later be a repeat offender*—are also very high. More than half of all men who do time in prison will be confined again for a crime. This means that as a specific deterrent or for rehabilitation, imprisonment does not work very well (Quinney 2002; Siegel 2009). What options does government have?

Based on the understanding that most criminal behavior is learned through socialization, that criminals can be resocialized, and that tax dollars can be saved, several sociological theories of crime suggest early community intervention to reduce crime rates. Some of these ideas include high-quality schools, preventing young people from

entering the criminal justice system in the first place, and methods of treatment other than brutalizing incarceration for those who do find themselves in trouble with the law. Each of these approaches increases the social capital of criminals and those at risk of becoming criminals.

Social capital, as mentioned in the "Contributing to Our Social World" section in Chapter 5, *refers to social networks within and among groups and access to important resources* (Flavin 2004). Social capital encompasses one's relationships, support systems, and access to community resources (Jarrett, Sullivan, and Watkins 2005). Increasing an individual's social capital by increasing educational attainment, job skills, and the ability to take advantage of available resources can reduce the chances of that person going to prison in the first place and of recidivism. Creating positive, rather than negative, relationships between youth and police is one means of social capital production that can help keep young people out of prison. One public sociologist, Susan Guarino-Ghezzi, found that hostile relations between young delinquents and police officers had developed into a cycle that simply made for more crime. She explains in the next "Sociologists in Action" how efforts to improve youth-police relations can lead to positive bonds and behavior.

It is difficult to determine how best to deter crime. Not many people think that the apology technique used in Japan would work as a deterrent to crimes in other countries. On the other hand, there is a wide range of options available for dealing with crime other than harsh (and expensive) punishments. Seeing how other countries control crime can help us take a new look at our assumptions and help us come up with creative new solutions that do work. For example, is the War on Drugs having more of a positive or negative impact on crime? What can we learn from how other nations deal with drugs? How might the legalization of marijuana in some U.S. states affect incarceration rates?

Sociologists use comparative studies and evaluation research of current policies to help determine the best strategies for crime and recidivism deterrence. For example, evidence shows that prison education, substance abuse, and job training programs can be used to reduce criminal justice expenses by allowing some prisoners to "earn" reduced sentences. These programs also lead to lower recidivism rates (Lawrence 2009).

Thinking Sociologically

How has what you read in this chapter affected your ideas about deviance, crime, and the criminal justice system?

SOCIOLOGISTS IN ACTION:
SUSAN GUARINO-GHEZZI

Police and Delinquent Youth: Changing Stereotypes and Making Peace

In the 1990s, I conducted research in Boston on two groups of people—police and gang-involved male juvenile offenders held at the Massachusetts Department of Youth Services (DYS). I was interested in how each group defined encounters with one another. Police and juveniles were each frustrated by the relentless violence and record homicide rate, and they blamed one another for the situation. Within both groups were subcultures that reinforced fallacies and stereotypes. These misunderstandings were perceived as "real" and locked each group into routine, ritualized behaviors, guaranteeing that they would clash.

My goal was to uncover these patterns, expose misleading stereotypes, and use these new understandings to change behaviors on both sides. Previous research I had conducted revealed that the youths who were the most alienated from police had the most frequent encounters with them (Guarino-Ghezzi and Carr 1996; Guarino-Ghezzi and Kimball 1996). Negative encounters with police were at the center of their lives, and I came to realize that while the offenders claimed to hate police, they actually looked forward to negative confrontations as opportunities to reinforce peer bonds.

At the same time, I learned that police painted all ex–juvenile offenders with the same brush. If a juvenile offender returned to the community after a long program of rehabilitation, regardless of his or her willingness to reform, the individual was still a juvenile offender as far as the police were concerned. If a juvenile offender became a victim of crime, the police showed less sympathy than if the juvenile were a law-abiding victim.

I contacted the deputy superintendent of the experimental neighborhood policing district in Boston and shared my concerns. Together, with some other police officers, we established a program called "Make Peace With Police" (MPWP), which arranged communications sessions, role-plays, and other nonconfrontational encounters between police and gang-involved juveniles. As executive director, I oversaw 41 group meetings run by MPWP facilitators on a weekly basis. These sessions helped us to understand the sources of hostility on both sides, but more importantly, they helped to create useful dialogue between juveniles and police.

A key finding of the MPWP project was that without sincere efforts to establish relationships, juveniles lacking positive social bonds learn to define police negatively from their social environments. While some of the most defiant and hostile-seeming youths were biased against police based on their peer subcultures, our sessions became turning points for developing positive relationships.

Police told us that they were surprised to learn that young gang members were really "just kids." An officer who arrived at a session feeling tough and somewhat angry at the youths quickly attached to a youth during the session who was visibly upset when mentioning a death in his family. The officer offered to help the youth find a job when he was released from the DYS facility. When asked what made him change, the officer explained that he had no idea how young and vulnerable the youths were because he'd never looked beyond the "street tough" exteriors that were so common among groups of youths in high-crime communities.

Another officer received a surprise one weekend when a youth he had met in the detention facility

(Continued)

(Continued)

recognized him in his cruiser and went out of his way to initiate a pleasant conversation. It was especially fulfilling because the boy was one of a small number who refused to even speak to police in his first MPWP session. The communication sessions provided a necessary "bridge" for redefining social norms.

This excerpt is adapted from Korgen, White, and White's Sociologists in Action: Sociology, Social Change, and Social Justice. *Susan Guarino-Ghezzi is a professor of sociology and criminology at Stonehill College. She is the former director of research of the Massachusetts Department of Youth Services, and is a frequent consultant on juvenile crime.*

One of the dominant characteristics of modern society is social inequality, and as we have seen, inequality is often an issue in criminal activity. Indeed, many of our social problems are rooted in issues of inequality. Extreme inequality may even be a threat to the deeper values and dreams of a society, especially one that stresses individualism and achievement. In the following three chapters, we look at three types of inequality: socioeconomic, ethnic or racial, and gender-based inequity.

WHAT HAVE WE LEARNED?

Deviance is socially constructed and varies across time and societies. What is considered deviant now may not be considered deviant in another place or 100, or even 10, years from now. All societies must fashion responses to deviant behaviors, which can threaten their stability and safety. The criminal justice system tends to be a conservative force in society because of its focus on ensuring social conformity.

To make our society run more smoothly, we must understand why deviance and crime happen. Good policy must be based on accurate information and careful analysis of the information. We must also understand that deviance and conformity operate at various levels in the social world: micro, meso, and macro. In addition, it is important to understand that there may be positive aspects of deviance for any society, from uniting society against deviants to providing creative new ways to solve problems.

KEY POINTS

- Deviance—the violation of social norms, including those that are formal laws—has both positive and negative consequences for individuals and for society. (See pp. 152–155.)

- We can use many different sociological theories to explain deviance—rational choice (including social control), symbolic interaction's anomie and labeling theories at the micro level, structural functional theory's differential association and strain theory, and conflict and feminist theory at the meso and macro level. (See pp. 155–167.)

- Many of the formal organizations concerned with crime (such as the FBI and the media) focus on crimes involving individuals—predatory crimes,

crimes without victims, and hate crimes—but the focus on these crimes may blind us to occupational crimes that actually are more harmful and more costly to society. (See pp. 167–171.)

- At the meso level, organized and occupational crimes may cost billions of dollars and pose a great risk to thousands of lives. Occupational crime may be against the company, employees, customers, or the public. (See pp. 171–174.)

- At the macro level, national governments some-times commit state-organized crimes, sometimes in violation of their own laws or in violation of interna-tional laws. These crimes may be directed against their own citizens (usually the minorities) or people from other countries. (See pp. 174–178.)

- Controlling crime has generated many policy debates, from the use of prisons to the death pen-alty and even to alternative approaches to the con-trol of deviance. (See pp. 178–182.)

DISCUSSION QUESTIONS

1. List five acts that were once considered deviant but are now considered acceptable or even cou-rageous. Have you ever committed a deviant act because you believed it was the moral thing to do? If yes, please explain why. If not, in what sort of situation might you consider carrying out a deviant act?

2. Have you ever been labeled deviant? Why or why not? How does your social class, level of educa-tion, gender, race or ethnicity, and nation of origin impact the chances you will be considered devi-ant in your country?

3. Which of the following theories of deviance described in the chapter—rational choice, differ-ential association, labeling theory, anomie and social disorganization, strain theory, and conflict theory—best explain the recent increase in cheat-ing among college students? Why?

4. Why is occupational crime not given as much attention as violent crime? What are some exam-ples of occupational crimes that hurt millions of Americans every day? Have you ever been the victim of one of these crimes? What would you suggest policy makers do to curb these crimes?

5. How do conflict theorists explain the makeup of prisoners in the U.S. prison system? Do you agree with their explanation? Why or why not?

6. How can social capital help keep people out of prison and help former prisoners avoid returning to prison? How will your social capital help you conform (or not?) to the norms of society?

VISUAL SOCIOLOGY: DEVIANCE AS A SOCIAL CONSTRUCTION

© Jose Fuste Raga/Corbis

Is this man deviant by virtue of his appearance? Why or why not? Visit **edge.sagepub.com/ballantine5e** for an interactive photo essay about deviance.

CONTRIBUTING TO OUR SOCIAL WORLD: WHAT CAN WE DO?

At the Local Level

- *LGBT groups* support lesbian, gay, bisexual, and/or transgender students. The Consortium of Higher Education LGBT Resource Professionals, a national organization of college and university groups, maintains a website at www.lgbtcampus.org. Regardless of your own sexual identity/orientation, consider contacting your campus LGBT group, attending meetings, and participating in its support and public education activities.

- *Boys and Girls Clubs* provide local programs and services to promote healthy development by instilling a sense of competence, usefulness, belonging, and influence in young people. Organizations for youth like Boys and Girls Clubs need interns and volunteers to provide role models for youth. Consider volunteering to help children with homework or activities. You can find a club near you by going to www.bgca.org/whoweare/Pages/FindaClub.aspx.

At the Organizational or Institutional Level

- The extensive and rapidly growing *criminal justice system* in the United States focuses on crime prevention, law enforcement, corrections, and rehabilitation. Identify the aspect of the system that interests you most and, using faculty and community contacts, select an appropriate organization for volunteer work, an internship, or a job.

- *Criminal courts* play a central role in the administration of criminal justice, and trials are often open to the public. Attending a trial and/or contacting a judge or magistrate could provide a good introduction to the court system and some of the people who work within it.

- *Crime prevention programs* are designed to reduce crime. You can find information about such programs at the National Crime Prevention Council at www.ncpc.org/programs. In order to obtain a better understanding as to what types of crime prevention programs are most effective, go to the Center for the Study and Prevention of Violence's (CSPV) Blueprints for Healthy Youth Development website at www.colorado.edu/cspv/blueprints.

At the National and Global Levels

- *The Polaris Project* works to reduce global trafficking of women and children (www.polarisproject.org). Volunteers participate in letter-writing campaigns, support antitrafficking legislation, and conduct research on the problem.

PART III

Inequality

Why are you rich, while others in your sociology class or community are poor—or vice versa? Why do some people rise to the top of society with wealth, power, and prestige at their fingertips, and others languish near the bottom? Does ethnicity, race, or gender affect your position in society? What are your chances of moving out of your current social position? These are the underlying questions in the following three chapters. They focus on stratification, how individuals and groups are layered or ranked in society according to how many valued resources they possess (e.g., wealth, power, and prestige) or to which they have access. Inequality results from the *process of stratification through which some people "make it" and others do not*. At the very bottom of the human hierarchy are those starving and diseased world citizens who have no hope of survival for either themselves or their families. This compares with corporate executives and some world politicians or royalty who have billions of dollars at their disposal. The implications of social stratification extend from the individual all the way to global social networks.

Sometimes the basis for social stratification and inequality is one's socioeconomic status, but other characteristics such as race, ethnicity, gender, sexual orientation, nationality, religion, or age can also help determine where you fall in the social stratification system. These differences often result in strong feelings like "us " versus "them" thinking.

In this section, we focus on issues of social inequality related to social class, race, ethnicity, and gender. Chapter 7 focuses on local and global socioeconomic stratification resulting in inequality; subsequent chapters examine ethnic and gender stratification.

7 Stratification

Rich and Famous—or Rags and Famine?

Will you live under the bridge or above it—rags or riches? While hard work can often make a difference, your future success also depends on your society's system of stratification and amount of inequality.

ME (AND MY RAGS OR RICHES)

LOCAL ORGANIZATIONS AND COMMUNITY
How I am regarded by my peers.

NATIONAL ORGANIZATIONS, INSTITUTIONS, AND ETHNIC SUBCULTURES
Institutions support the privileged; ethnic subcultures are often disadvantaged.

SOCIETY
The privileged control resources, health care, economic markets, and tax rates.

GLOBAL COMMUNITY
Rich countries have more access to resources than poor ones.

IN THIS CHAPTER

- The Importance of Social Stratification

- Theoretical Explanations of Stratification

- Individuals' Social Status: The Micro Level

- Social Mobility: The Micro–Meso Connection

- Major Stratification Systems: Macro-Level Analysis

- Poverty and Social Policy

- National and Global Digital Divide: Macro-Level Stratification

⬤ THINK ABOUT IT

Micro: Local Community	Why are some people in your community wealthier than others?
Meso: National Institutions, Complex Organizations, and Ethnic Groups	How do institutions—such as the family, education, religion, health, politics, and the economy—help keep people in the class they were born into?
Macro: National and Global Systems	Why are some nations affluent and others impoverished? How does the fact that we live in a global society affect you and your social position?

Pomp and circumstance surrounded the April 29, 2011, royal wedding of Prince of Wales William (heir to the British throne) and Catherine (Kate) Middleton. All eyes in Britain and many eyes around the world were glued to their TVs and computer monitors. Thousands waited for hours to see the happy couple in person, as they lined the royal route to the palace. The wedding for this young couple included flower arrangements for $800,000, a wedding dress that cost about $400,000, and a cake for just under $80,000. The bill for the entire wedding (security included) came in at $70 million (Mawani 2011).

Members of royal families such as Prince William and Prince Harry of Britain grow up in a privileged world, with wealth, prestige, and access to power. Their lifestyles include formal receptions, horse races, polo games, royal hunts, state visits, and other social and state functions. The family has several elegant residences at its disposal. However, like most royalty, Wil-

liam, Harry, and now Kate Middleton also live within the confines of their elite status, with its strict expectations and limitations. They cannot show up for a beer at the local pub or associate freely with commoners. Their family problems or casual antics are subject matter for front pages of tabloids, as seen in the behavior of Prince Harry during a trip to Las Vegas that thrilled the paparazzi and dismayed the royal household. Thanks to a cell phone camera, what he did in Vegas did not stay in Vegas. While there is no official royalty in the United States, wealthy entrepreneurs, stockbrokers and bankers, and entertainment and sports figures hold positions that allow for a life of comfort similar to that of royalty.

On the other hand, rags and famine pervade the planet. Hidden from the public eye in Britain and the United States are people with no known names and no swank addresses; some have no address at all. Around the globe, wars, natural disasters, famines, economic crises, slavery, and human trafficking point to the presence of inequality. **Inequality** is *a social condition in which privileges, opportunities, and substantial rewards are given to people in some positions in society but denied to others.* Examples of media portrayals of suffering include refugees from the wars in Syria and South Sudan; impoverished victims of natural disasters such as Typhoon Haiyan, a record-setting strong storm on November 8, 2013, that devastated the Philippines; and famines occurring in Ethiopia, Somalia, and other poor countries. The earthquake and tsunami in Japan in March 2011 affected people of all socioeconomic levels, but poor and working-class people were most likely to live in areas vulnerable to flooding. That quake triggered 35-foot waves that left 16,447 people dead and 4,666 missing. Most victims were people who lived in the lower socioeconomic range and in poverty (Diep 2011; Vervaeck and Daniell 2011). The point is that inequality leaves many people vulnerable.

As noted in Chapter 6, climate change and economic hard times have pushed many low-income people from

©Reuters/Dylan Martinez

Prince William and Kate Middleton, now the Duchess of Cambridge, were married in 2011 in Westminster Abbey with all the trappings of British royalty. He is second in line to inherit the throne of England.

their rural homes to cities in hopes of finding jobs. However, with few jobs for unskilled and semiskilled workers in today's postindustrial service economies, many of the poor are left homeless. They live in abandoned buildings or sleep in unlocked autos, on park benches, under bridges, on beaches, or anywhere they can stretch out and hope not to be attacked or harassed. In the United States, cities such as Houston, Los Angeles, New York and Washington, D.C., try to cope with the homeless by setting up sanitary facilities and temporary shelters, especially in bad weather. Cities also rely on religious and civic organizations to run soup kitchens and shelters.

Of the 1.9 billion children in the world, 2.2 million die every year (6,000 a day, mostly from Global South countries) from malnutrition, diseases related to unsafe water, poor sanitation, and inadequate health care. According to a recent report on the world's urban children, 1 in 3 city dwellers lives in a slum, but that ratio is as high as 6 in 10 in Africa (UN News Center 2012). These urban children grow up in poverty, with lack of electricity, clean water, education, sanitation, health care, or adequate food. They die of preventable diseases.

In some areas of the world, such as India and sub-Saharan Africa, the situation is even more desperate, and many families are starving. At daybreak, a cart traverses the city of Kolkata (Calcutta), India, picking up bodies of diseased and starved homeless people who have died on the streets during the night. Mother Teresa, who won the Nobel Peace Prize for her work with those in dire poverty, established a home in India where these people could die with dignity. She also founded an orphanage for children who would otherwise wander the streets begging or lie on the sidewalk dying. The micro and meso efforts of Mother Teresa and her fellow Missionaries of Charity are noble but only a small Band-Aid on a massive macro-level social problem.

What group of people is lower on the social hierarchy than those living in the street? That would be *slaves*. It may surprise you to know that slavery—*when an individual or a family is bound in servitude as the property of a person or household, bought and sold, and forced to work*—is alive and flourishing around the world (Free the Slaves 2014). An estimated 30 million people, mostly women and children from poor families in poor countries, are slaves, auctioned off or lured into slavery each year by gangs, pimps, and cross-border syndicates to work in forced labor or prostitution, as child soldiers or brides in forced marriages, or as children working on plantations or in factories (Walk Free Foundation 2013). Slavery caught the world's attention in April 2014 when the terrorist organization Boko Haram kidnapped close

The United States does not have royalty with inherited thrones and titles. However, it does have enormous gaps in wealth with some people living in splendor and luxury beyond the imagination of the average citizen.

New York, like most cities, has a large homeless population. This person seeks shelter and some sleep in a New York subway station.

to 300 Nigerian schoolgirls to sell them into slavery and to give to men as wives. The group argues that women are the property of men and instruments of reproduction; girls, according to their ideas, should not receive education, especially not Western education.

A global phenomenon, slavery exists in all of the 162 countries studied by Walk Free Foundation (2013).

Mauritania has the most slaves (1 in every 25 members of the population). Next is Haiti with many children in slavery, followed by India and Pakistan. Sex trafficking is most common in South Asia and Eastern Europe (especially Ukraine), Myanmar (Burma), Laos, Nepal, and the Philippines. It is so profitable that businesspeople invest in involuntary brothels much as they would in a mining operation (Bales 2007, 2012; Bales and Trodd 2008). Today, approximately 60,000 people (1 in every 5.000 members of the population) are enslaved in the United States (Walk Free Foundation 2013). Figure 7.1 provides a visual image of where most slaves are located, and the next "Sociology Around the World" examines the issue of slavery in chocolate and coffee production.

As we write these words, at least 2.5 million people are suffering the abuse of *human trafficking*. A form of slavery, human trafficking consists of "the recruitment, transport, transfer, harbouring or receipt of a person by such means as threat or use of force or other forms of coercion, of abduction, of fraud or deception for the purpose of exploitation" (United Nations Office on Drugs and Crime [UNODC] 2014b). Most, but not all, of the victims of trafficking are women. The vast majority of trafficking (79%) results in the sexual exploitation of the victims. Most of the other victims (18%) find themselves forced to work as slaves (UNODC 2014b).

Around the stadiums of international events such as the recent Russian and Brazilian Olympics, major soccer matches, and the Super Bowl, traffickers use cheap hotels and brothels to buy and sell child prostitutes (Elam 2011). Young foreign girls are brought in from other countries to be sex slaves. Sometimes, poor families sell their daughters for the promise of high wages and money sent home.

Because slavery exists in many forms, it is difficult to eradicate. For example, debt bondage, another form of modern-day slavery, involves extremely poor families—often people with differences in appearance or culture from those with power—working in exchange for housing and meager food. Severe debt, passing from generation to generation, often results when farmers borrow money because they face drought or need cash to keep their families from starving. The only collateral they have on the loan is themselves—put up for bondage until they can pay off the loan. Often, no one but the wealthy landowner keeps accounting records, which results in there being no accountability—and no paying off of loans, resulting in slavery.

In the slavery of the 19th century, slaves were expensive, and there was at least some economic incentive to care about their health and survival so that they could be productive workers. In the new slavery, humans are

FIGURE 7.1 Where in the World Slaves Live

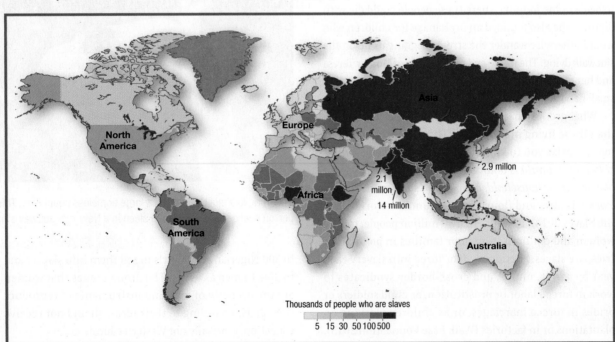

Source: Fisher (2013a). "How 35 Countries Compare on Child Poverty." April 15. *The Washington Post.*

Sociology Around the World

Chocolate and Coffee: A Moral Dilemma?

Yum! Chocolate and coffee are addictive, and most of us depend on one or both. The average U.S. citizen eats over 11 pounds of chocolate (that's 120 bars) a year, and 83% drink coffee (Perez 2013). However, the ugly side of these tasty, stimulating treats is that over 70% of the production is from West Africa (Ivory Coast and Ghana), and most involves child labor or child slaves. Let's look at this more closely.

"Boys and girls, usually between the ages of 12 and 16 but some as young as 5 years, are smuggled from neighboring countries such as Mali and Burkina Faso, and sold to cocoa bean plantation owners . . . The children are forced to engage in grueling manual labor, carrying extremely heavy bags, working with machetes and pesticides. They often work long hours, as many as 80 a week, but they are rarely, if ever, paid" (Food Empowerment Project 2014; Nall 2012). Large chocolate companies such as Hershey's, Mars, Cadbury, and Nestlé use these cocoa beans. However, Hershey's has stated that by 2020 it will only use Fair Trade Certified chocolate, made without forced child labor (children whose parents send them to work or who are orphaned or abandoned and have no choice but to work but are paid little or not at all) or slavery (children who have been bought or kidnapped and are owned by others and not paid). Other companies are considering similar actions (International Labor Rights Forum 2012).

U.S. adults are the world's biggest coffee consumers, with 63% drinking at least one cup of coffee every day (Perez 2013). Workers on coffee plantations in Ivory Coast, Colombia, and Guatemala are often forced child laborers and child slaves. Coffee

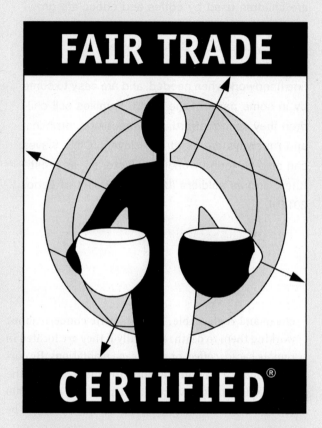

The Fair Trade Certified symbol signifies that products such as coffee, tea, and chocolate (made from cacao) meet sustainable development goals, help support family farmers at fair prices, and are not produced by slave labor.

growers receive less than 1% of our consumer cost when we buy our coffee and cappuccino. Most of the profits go to companies that sell the coffee products to consumers. Plantation workers who do get paid receive between $2 and $3 a day. Folgers, Maxwell House, Nescafé, and other major coffee companies import coffee from many plantations that use forced child labor and child slaves. Therefore, they pay very little for the coffee beans, allowing them to maintain high profit levels (Wilhoit 2014).

(Continued)

(Continued)

As of 2014, the International Labour Organization (ILO) estimated that there are 168 million child laborers throughout the world (Esim 2014). Why are children used by coffee and chocolate growers? To put it simply, they are cheap or free labor and easy to exploit. Child slaves eat little, can be abused without consequence to the owner, can do fine handwork when needed, and are easy to come by in some parts of the world. Families sell children they cannot afford, and street kids, orphans, and runaways are lured into slavery. Child slaves can also be found working in factories, as prostitutes, and as soldiers (U.S. Department of Labor 2011b).

What can we do to get our coffee and chocolate fix and help solve the problem? A number of organizations including Free the Slaves, Mercy Project, Slavery Footprint, and Ark of Hope for Children work to stop and prevent child slavery. Makers of "Fair Trade Certified" products such as "Equal Exchange" use fair labor practices and practice sustainable farming. By studying labels and buying Fair Trade goods, we can help fight child slavery. Supporting organizations that fight for children's rights or that reduce the poverty at the root of child slavery can go a long way toward making our chocolate and coffee guilt free. The logo below is a common one for indicating that a product is Fair Trade Certified.

cheap and replaceable. There is little concern about working them to death, especially if they are located in remote cacao, coffee, or sugar cane plantations. By current dollars, a slave in the southern United States in the mid-1800s would have cost the equivalent of $40,000 today, but contemporary slaves are cheap. They can be procured from poor countries for an average of $90 (Bales 2012).

As noted with the recent positive developments in the production of chocolate, there are ongoing efforts by public sociologists among others to do away with modern-day slavery. A sociologist most at the forefront of the current movement to eradicate slavery is featured in the next "Sociologists in Action."

Child laborers fill up empty cigarettes manually with locally grown tobacco in a small *bidi* (cigarette) factory at Haragach in Rangpur district, Bangladesh, in 2013.

©REUTERS/Andrew Biraj

Thinking Sociologically

Poor people around the world often lose control over their lives. What situations can lead to this condition, and what are some consequences for these people? What solutions would you propose?

As we can see from the examples above, our social world is stratified in ways that result in high levels of inequality. The rest of this chapter discusses (a) why stratification is important, (b) different systems of stratification, (c) the consequences of social rankings for individuals, (d) whether one can change social class positions (social mobility), (e) characteristics of major stratification systems, (f) poverty and social policies to address problems, and (g) the global digital divide.

SOCIOLOGISTS IN ACTION:
KEVIN BALES

Stopping Slavery in the 21st Century

In the following excerpt from "Confronting Slavery With the Tools of Sociology," Kevin Bales describes how he has used his sociological training to draw attention to and work to combat modern slavery, living the life of a public sociologist.

* * * * * * *

Becoming an abolitionist sociologist crept up on me. The first tiny prodding was a leaflet I picked up at an outdoor event in London. The front of the leaflet read "There are Millions of Slaves in the World Today." I was a university professor, and I confess to an unpleasant mixture of pride and hubris in my reaction to the bold title of the leaflet. Having been involved in human rights for many years, I thought, "How could this be true if I don't know about it already?"

Something began to itch in my mind . . . what if? What if there were millions of people in slavery? What if almost all of us, governments, human rights groups, the media, the public, were simply unaware? Millions of hidden slaves seemed unlikely, but my nagging thought was that if there were millions of people in slavery, then finding them was the job of a social researcher. If there were not millions of slaves, this type of literature needed debunking.

I pulled in students to help dig and sift through information, and paid one researcher to look further afield. As a faint picture of global slavery began to emerge, I came to understand why this issue was invisible. Slavery was hidden under a thick blanket of ignorance, concealed by the common assumption that it was extinct. With slavery illegal in every country, criminal slaveholders kept their activities hidden.

As I built up a picture of slavery, every new set of facts generated new questions. I began to realize that a large-scale research project was needed and I went in search of modern slavery, traveling to India, Pakistan, Thailand, Mauritania, and Brazil—often going undercover as I studied slave-based businesses in each country. The result was the book, *Disposable People: New Slavery in the Global Economy* (1999, 2004, 2012).

Some years later, I was able to build a database of slave prices over time that showed that slaves had been high-ticket capital purchase items in the past (even though occasional gluts caused prices to dip) and are normally low-cost disposable inputs today.

In 2000, I, with three others, helped found Free the Slaves, the American sister-organization of Anti-Slavery International, the world's oldest (1787) and original human rights group. Free the Slaves works with local partners to liberate slaves around the world and change the systems that allow slavery to exist. In addition to addressing the crime of enslavement, this work often involves confronting gender inequality, racism, ethnic and religious discrimination, and the negative outcomes of global economic growth. We have learned that freedom and empowerment are viral, and that freed slaves will stop at nothing to stay free and help others to liberty.

Not every part of liberation and reintegration requires sociological training, but it would be very hard to be successful without it. Without carefully constructed longitudinal surveys of villages in slavery we could never have demonstrated the "freedom dividend," the powerful and positive economic change that comes to whole communities when slavery is abolished.

(Continued)

Slavery Today

(Continued)

Without training in the empathetic understanding of a social researcher we could never have developed the "slavery lens," a way of seeing this hidden crime, that the U.S. government now requires of all its foreign aid program workers. Without learning about the complex interplay of culture, society, economics, politics, and social vulnerability, we would never be able to build the unique methodologies of liberation tailored to specific and culturally rooted forms of slavery. And there is nothing like the ugly reality of a crime like slavery to push young sociologists to do their best work—using solid social science to change the world.

• •

Kevin Bales is a sociologist and professor of contemporary slavery at the Wilberforce Institute for the Study of Slavery and Emancipation (WISE) at the University of Hull, England, and co-founder of Free the Slaves in Washington, D.C. This excerpt is taken from Korgen, White, and White's Sociologists in Action: Race, Class, Gender, and Intersections *(SAGE, 2013).*

THE IMPORTANCE OF SOCIAL STRATIFICATION

Consider your own social ranking in society. You were born into a family that holds a position in society—upper, middle, or lower class. The position of your family influences the neighborhood in which you live and where you shop, go to school, play sports, engage in the arts or other activities, and attend religious services. Most likely, you and your family carry out the tasks of daily living in your community with people who share your social class status.

Your position in the stratification system affects the opportunities available to you and the choices you make in life. Note the social world model at the beginning of the chapter. It provides a visual image of the social world and socioeconomic stratification. The stratification process affects everything from individuals' social rankings at the micro level of analysis to positions of countries in the global system at the macro level.

Social stratification refers to *how individuals and groups are layered and ranked in society according to their access to and possession of valued resources.* The society's culture (rules, values, beliefs, and artifacts) determines and legitimizes the society's system of sorting its members.

Each society also determines what it considers to be valued resources. For example, in an agricultural society, members are ranked according to how much land or how many animals they own. In an industrial society, ownership of the *means of production* (property, machinery, and cash owed by capitalists) and occupational skills determine class status. In postindustrial information societies, education, access to technology, and information dissemination (in addition to ownership of the means of production) become key determinants in the ranking process.

What members of each society value and the criteria they use to rank other members depends on events in the society's history, its geographic location, its level of development in the world, the society's political philosophy, and the decisions of those in power. The more powerful individuals tend to get the best positions, the most desirable mates, and the greatest opportunities. They may have power because of birth status, personality characteristics, age, physical attractiveness, education, intelligence, wealth, race, family background, occupation, religion, or ethnic group—whatever the basis for power is in that particular society. Those with relatively high amounts power have advantages that perpetuate their power, and they try to hold onto those advantages through laws, customs, power, ideologies, and sometimes force. Note that each level of analysis—micro, meso, and macro—adds to our understanding of the stratification process as shown below.

Micro-Level Prestige and Influence

Remember how some of your peers on the playground were given more respect than others? Their high regard may have come from belonging to a prestigious family, having a dynamic or domineering personality, being good at games, or owning symbols that distinguished them—"cool" clothing or shoes, a desirable bicycle, or expensive toys. This is stratification at work.

Property, power, and prestige are accorded to those who have **cultural capital** (*knowledge, skills, language mastery, style of dress, and values that provide a person with access to a particular status in society*) and **social capital** (*networks with others who have influence*). Individual qualities such as leadership skills, an engaging personality, self-confidence, quick-wittedness, and physical attractiveness, or ascribed characteristics such as the most powerful gender or ethnic group, influence cultural and social capital. Interactions with meso-level organizations help shape the influence of these individual traits.

Meso-Level Access to Resources

Many of the resources we use come from institutions at the meso level: family, education, religion, economic and political institutions, and health care. We first learn our social status and the roles associated with it through our interactions with family members. The socialization we undergo in our families influences how we see ourselves, how others perceive us, and our access to resources such as education and jobs. For example, we learn grammar and manners from our families; that in turn affects how our teachers and peers view and judge us. Educational organizations treat children differently according to their social status, and social status is revealed through such symbols as language (e.g., speaking standard English) and manners (e.g., not interrupting, saying "please" and "thank you" when appropriate, addressing adults by their proper titles). Our education can result in differential access to prestigious jobs and affect our social status in society—and, therefore, our position in the social stratification hierarchy.

Macro-Level Factors Influencing Stratification

The global economic position of a nation affects the opportunities available to individuals in that nation, illustrating that macro-level factors also influence placement in the stratification system (see Figure 7.2). Haiti provides a powerful illustration of this fact. Located on the island of Hispaniola in the Caribbean, Haiti is the poorest country in the Western Hemisphere and one of the poorest countries in the world, with little technology, few resources, ineffective government, a very weak educational system, and an occupational structure based largely on subsistence farming. Even its forest resources are essentially gone, as desperately poor people cut down the last trees for firewood and shelters, leaving the land to erode (Diamond 2005).

Even the sports one plays—such as polo or stickball—are greatly influenced by social class and convey different kinds of social and cultural capital. Polo clearly requires a good deal of economic capital in order to play, whereas stickball requires only a ball and a straight stick.

The economy is in a downward cycle, pushing many already poor people still lower in the world's stratification system. The 2010 earthquake and floods added to

FIGURE 7.2 Gross National Income (in Dollars) per Capita in 2013

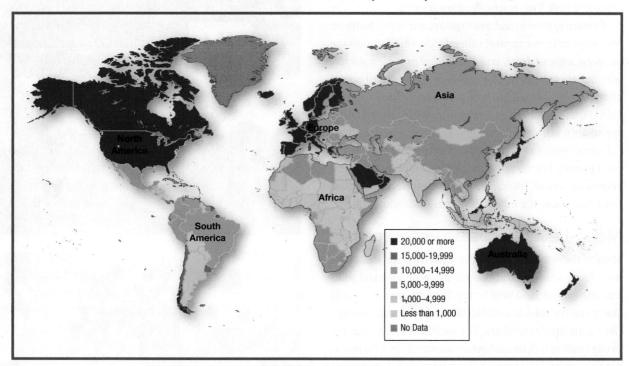

20,000 or more
15,000–19,999
10,000–14,999
5,000–9,999
1,000–4,999
Less than 1,000
No Data

Source: World Bank.

Haitians' economic woes and misery. Residents were driven from what meager shelters they had, and then faced a cholera epidemic from contaminated water. Haitians now have very few opportunities to get ahead and be successful. This is but one example of macro-level factors (failing economy, eroded land, lack of infrastructure such as schools and health facilities, lack of opportunity to participate in the global economy) affecting the opportunities available to people in the country.

Almost all societies stratify members, and societies themselves are stratified in the world system, so that each individual and nation experiences the world in unique ways related to its position. Stratification is one of the most powerful forces that we experience, but we are seldom conscious of how it works or how pervasive it is in our lives. This is the driving question sociologists ask when developing theories of stratification: How does it work?

 Thinking Sociologically

Place yourself in the center of the social world model. Working from micro-level interactions toward the meso-level institutions and the macro-level global stratification system, indicate what has influenced where you fall in the stratification system.

THEORETICAL EXPLANATIONS OF STRATIFICATION

As we traverse the world, we see continuous examples of rich and poor—those who have more resources than they need and those who do not have enough to survive. Why is the distribution of resources so uneven? Is the unequal distribution inevitable, healthy, or harmful for society?

Sociologists have developed different theories to explain social stratification, based on the lens through which they view society. These explanations range from individual micro-level to national and global macro-level theories (e.g., symbolic interaction, rational choice, structural-functional, and conflict theories).

Micro-Level Theory

Our now familiar theories that relate to the micro level help us again, this time to understand differences among individuals in the stratification hierarchy.

Symbolic Interaction Theory. Have you ever been to a party where almost everyone came from a social class that had either much more or much less money than you? Even if you have not, you can probably imagine what it might be like. Awkward! Each social group has norms that members learn through the socialization process. These norms are recognized within that group and can make clueless outsiders feel like space aliens. People learn what is expected in their groups—family, peer group, social class—through interaction with others. For instance, children are rewarded or punished for behaviors appropriate or inappropriate to their social position.

The socialization process transmits and perpetuates our positions in the social stratification system. Learning our position means learning values, speech patterns, consumption habits, appropriate group memberships (including political, economic, and religious affiliations), and even our self-concept. This knowledge provides us with the cultural capital necessary to interact effectively with people who share our social position.

Cultural capital (knowledge, skills, language, and values) is learned by children at home; they then bring that with them to school. Some home environments teach children to obey rules and authority, and to develop skills repairing houses and cars. Other families teach children by expanding vocabularies; developing good grammar; experiencing concerts, art, and theater; visiting historical sites; providing reading materials; and modeling engagement with reading. The higher-class parents tend to stress thinking and questioning skills as opposed to primarily obeying authority figures. The result of this learning at home is that all children attain cultural capital that helps them interact with others at their social class level. The class difference in the types of cultural capital, though, means that children from the middle and upper classes or higher castes are more likely to get the best education, setting them up to be future leaders with better life chances. Schools place children into courses and academic groups, influenced in part by the labels children receive due to their cultural capital. In this way, children's home experiences and education help reproduce the social class systems and perpetuate the family's social class position in society (Ballantine and Hammack 2012).

Like language, other symbols can also represent social positions. Clothing, for example, sets up some people as special and privileged. In the 1960s, wearing blue jeans was a radical act by college students to reject status differences—showing solidarity with and support for the working class. Today, many young people wear expensive designer jeans that low-income people cannot afford. Drinking wine that most people do not have the means to buy, driving a Jaguar rather than a less expensive car, and

living in a home that has six or eight bedrooms and is 5,000-plus square feet is an expression of *conspicuous consumption*—displaying goods in a way that others will notice and that will presumably earn the owner respect (Veblen 1902). Thus, purchased products become symbols intended to define the person as someone of high status in the stratification hierarchy.

Privacy can also symbolize affluence. For example, in most of the Global North, one symbol of middle-class "decency" is the right to bathe and do one's grooming in private. Indeed, many young people in the United States have their own bedrooms and expect no interruptions when sprucing up for the day. Homeless people in the United States do not have this luxury, and in India, bathing on the streets is not uncommon. Privacy requires money.

A core idea in symbolic interaction theory is that reality is constructed, that as we figure out what our circumstances mean, we construct the reality we live. This idea is explored in further depth in the next "Sociology in Our Social World" on page 201.

Rational Choice Theory. As you now know, rational choice theorists focus on individuals and the way they make decisions regarding their own self-interest. From this view, people make decisions influenced by their perception of costs and benefits. Some people evaluate potential benefits with a view to the long-term. They are willing to endure short-term expense or "pain" if the long-term gains are substantial. In order to take

©iStockphoto.com/tomazi

Look at all those forks and knives. Some people know what to do with each of them! Knowing which fork or knife to use for each course of a meal is a sign of cultural capital that can influence your chances of acceptance into elite society or success on a job interview.

In India, many people must bathe every day in public in whatever water supply they can find. Even many people with homes do not have their own water supply. Privacy for one's grooming is a symbol of privilege for the affluent.

this view, one needs a sense of *delayed gratification*—delaying rewards or benefits until a later time. People who are willing or in a position to do this—living austerely now in order to experience prosperity later—may be more likely to have upward mobility and to experience greater affluence at a later time. While your friend from high school may have a job and drive a nicer car than you can afford, you may be building debts and living in a drab dormitory in hopes of a better future. Thus, rational choice theorists would focus on how personal choices influence one's place in the social system. The idea is that one's socioeconomic position is shaped largely by individual decisions. What, though, influences those individual decisions?

In high school, many college prep students make "rational" decisions to become involved in athletic programs, student council, the Spanish Club, leadership roles in the National Honor Society, or community service because they want to list those involvements on college applications. They commit effort now—sometimes in activities that they care little about—in hopes of having a payoff in admission or scholarships to the college of their choice. Those same students become discouraged with classmates who will not help with student council activities or with building the junior class float. However, for young people whose parents did not go to college and whose past experiences do not lead them to believe that they, themselves, could ever attain a college

degree, spending time decorating a float makes no sense. It is not seen as a "rational" choice. Thus, past experiences and social position can influence the way one evaluates costs and benefits.

These micro-level theories help us to understand how our daily interactions and decisions can impact our social positions (and vice versa) within society's stratification hierarchy. We now look at theories that examine the larger social structures, processes, and forces that affect stratification and inequality: structural-functional theory and various forms of conflict theory.

Meso- and Macro-Level Theories

Structural-Functional Theory. Structural-functionalists view stratification within societies as an inevitable, and generally necessary, part of the social world. The stratification system provides individuals a place or position in the social world and motivates them to carry out their roles. Societies survive by having an organized system into which each individual is born and raised, and contributes to the maintenance of the society.

The basic elements of the structural-functional theory of stratification were explained by Kingsley Davis and Wilbert Moore (1945), and their work still provides the main ideas of the theory today. Focusing on stratification by considering the rewards given to people in various occupations, Davis and Moore argue the following:

1. *Value of positions*: Some positions are more important to society than others. For example, society needs physicians and CEOs, both of which require specialized training. Societies must motivate talented individuals to prepare for and occupy the most important and difficult positions.

2. *Preparation requires talent, time, and money*: To motivate talented individuals to make the sacrifices necessary to prepare for difficult positions such as physician or CEO, differential rewards of income, prestige, power, or other valued goods must be offered. Thus, doctors and CEOs receive high income, prestige, and power as incentives.

3. *Unequal distribution of rewards*: The differences in rewards, such as pay for most valued positions, in turn, lead to the unequal distribution of resources—or inequality—for occupations in society. The result is that stratification is inevitable.

Look at the example of poverty. Some sociologists argue that poverty serves certain *functions* for society, thus making it difficult to eliminate (Gans 1971, 1995).

sociology in our social world

Understanding Urban Homeless People

Homeless people may find themselves sleeping under bridges or in parks, vacant lots, cars, or unused subway tunnels. Although many people look down on the homeless, most have held respectable jobs and had housing in the past. Bad economic times, untreated mental illnesses, or other problems have left these citizens without jobs and with few opportunities. On any given night, there are an estimated 610,042 homeless people in the United States (National Alliance to End Homelessness 2014). Housing and Urban Development (HUD) officials in the United States measure overall homelessness via funding applications for housing services and state that even this number is a large underestimation of the total number of people who experience homelessness (HUD 2008).

In trying to make sense of homelessness, researchers identified key variables that distinguished different types of homelessness, and uncovered a wide range of causes, circumstances, and coping methods. Snow and Anderson have studied the micro culture of street people, how they lend each other support and help each other make sense of their circumstances. They point to many forces at work on the homeless, from global economic trends to the way their families relate to them (Snow and Anderson 1993).

One question is how homeless people affirm a positive sense of self in this humiliating situation. After all, to be a person of worth in American society is to (1) own some property, (2) have someone who cares about you enough to take you in if you are really desperate, and (3) occupy a significant status in society by earning some money and having a career or

position deserving of respect. The homeless not only lack all these, but their master status—"homeless person"—is one that elicits disrespect. "Dignity and worth are not primarily individual characteristics, but instead flow from the roles we play," write the authors (Snow and Anderson 1993:9). To be homeless, then, is far more than to be without a residence or shelter. It is to be without a place to restore one's dignity. So how do the homeless cope?

This research showed a number of coping strategies. Sometimes, the homeless people explained away their circumstances as temporary "bad luck" or part of a normal cycle in which they just happened to be on the down end for a short period of time. Others would distance themselves from the role of homelessness, pointing out that they were "different" from other homeless people, "did not really belong," and did not really deserve to be seen as homeless at all. Some people coped by fictive storytelling, pointing to pronounced achievements in the past (often fictionalized or embellished) or creating stories of their phenomenal accomplishments when they finally do get on their feet. By affirming another identity in the past or the future, their self-esteem was salvaged. However, perhaps the most surprising strategy to preserve self-worth was to embrace the role of being homeless with pride—to boast about how one was the best at being a survivor, the best at being a friend to the homeless, or the best at rejecting shallow values of materialism in our commercial society. They could thus affirm themselves for coping skills, for caring qualities, or for deep spirituality. They had defined reality in a way that allowed them to see themselves in a positive light. They had changed the social construction of reality, at least among themselves (Snow and Anderson 1993).

Some people may actually benefit from having poor people kept poor. Consider the following points:

1. *Poverty provides us with a convenient scapegoat*— someone to blame for individual and societal problems. We can put the blame for poverty on the poor individuals themselves. That way we can ignore the meso- and macro-level causes of poverty—like economic and political systems—that would be expensive to resolve.
2. *Having poor people creates many jobs for those who are not poor*, especially in the "helping" professions such as social workers and law enforcement jobs such as police, judges, and prison workers.
3. *The poor provide an easily available group of surplus laborers* to do undesirable jobs when needed.
4. *The poor reinforce and legitimate our own lives and institutions*. Their existence allows the rest of us to feel superior to someone, enhancing our self-esteem.
5. *Their violation of mainstream values helps reaffirm the values among the affluent* (Gans 1971, 1995).

In the mid-20th century, structural-functional theory was the dominant theory used to explain stratification. However, it has been criticized for its inability to explain why some people in society who do not provide vital services for society (e.g., professional basketball players, hedge fund managers) receive great rewards. It also does not explain why CEOs now make so much more money compared to the typical worker than they once did. For example, in 1965, CEOs made, on average, 18 times the average worker's salary. In 2011, CEOs made 209 times the pay of the average worker (Mishel and Sabadish 2012). Functionalist explanations of stratification have also been critiqued for an inability to fully explain the conflict societies experience. This is the primary focus of conflict theory.

Conflict Theory. Conflict theorists see stratification as the outcome of struggles for dominance and scarce resources, with some individuals in society taking advantage of others. Individuals and groups act in their own self-interest by trying to exploit others, leading inevitably to a struggle between those who have advantages and want to keep them and those who want a larger share of the pie.

Conflict theorist Karl Marx (1818–1883) described four possible ways to distribute wealth, according to (1) what each person needs, (2) what each person wants, (3) what each person earns, or (4) what each person can take. It was this fourth way, Marx believed, that was dominant in

competitive capitalist societies (Cuzzort and King 2002; Marx and Engels 1955).

Marx viewed the stratification structure as composed of two major economically based social classes: the *haves* and the *have-nots*. The *haves* consist of the owners (capitalist bourgeoisie), whereas the *have-nots* are the working-class (proletariat). Individuals in the same social class have similar lifestyles, share ideologies, and hold common outlooks on social life. The struggle over resources between haves and have-nots is the cause of conflict (Hurst 2013).

The *haves* control what Marx called the *means of production*—property, machinery and cash owned by capitalists—the valued resources in society (Marx [1844] 1964). The haves dominate because the lower-class have-nots cannot accumulate enough money and power to change their positions. The norms and values of the haves dominate the society because of their power and ability to make the distribution of resources seem "fair" and justified. Laws, religious beliefs, and educational systems spread ideas that support the domination of the haves. This keeps the *have-nots* from understanding their own self-interests and is why working-class people often support politicians whose policies really favor the wealthiest 1%. The haves' control of political structures, policies, and police or military forces ensures their continued dominance in society.

The unorganized lower-class have-nots cannot overcome their exploitation until they develop a *class consciousness*—a shared awareness that they, as a class, have interests that differ from those of the haves. They need to understand that what is good for the haves is bad for the have-nots. Marx contended that, with the help of enlightened intellectuals (like him), the working class would develop a class consciousness, rise up, and overthrow the haves, culminating in a classless society in which wealth would be more equally shared (Marx and Engels 1955).

 Thinking Sociologically

How would conflict theorists explain the fact that CEOs make over 209 times the pay of the average worker? Does their argument make sense? Why or why not?

Unlike the structural-functionalists, then, conflict theorists maintain that money and other rewards are not necessarily given to those in the most important positions in the society. Can we argue that a rock star or baseball player is more necessary for the survival of society than a teacher or a police officer? Yet the pay differential is tremendous. It takes most teachers (even those with a master's degree, an entire career to earn as much as many celebrities earn in a matter of months.

As you know, not all of Karl Marx's predictions have come true. While many nations have labor laws that require owners to pay workers a minimum wage, provide safe working conditions, and prevent them from discriminating on the basis of race, gender, or religion, inequality still exists throughout the world. Even societies that claim to be classless, such as China, have privileged classes and poor peasants. In recent years, the Chinese government has allowed more private ownership of shops, businesses, and other entrepreneurial efforts, motivating many Chinese citizens to work long hours at their private businesses to "get ahead." The only classless societies are a few small hunter-gatherer groups that have no extra resources that would allow some members to accumulate wealth.

Some theorists criticize Marx for his focus on only the economic system, pointing out that noneconomic factors enter into the stratification struggle as well. Max Weber (1864–1920), another influential theorist, agreed with Marx that group conflict is inevitable, that economics is one of the key factors in stratification systems, and that those in power try to perpetuate their positions. However, he added two other influential factors that he argued determine stratification in modern industrial societies: power and prestige. Sometimes these are identified as the "three *P*s"—property, power, and prestige.

Recent theorists suggest that using the three *P*s, we can identify five classes—capitalists, managers, small business owners or the petty bourgeoisie, workers, and the underclass—rather than just the *haves* and *have-nots*. *Capitalists* own the means of production, and they purchase and control the labor of others. *Managers* sell their labor to capitalists and manage the labor of others for the capitalists. The *petty bourgeoisie*, such as small shop or business owners, own some means of production but control little of the labor of others; nevertheless, they have modest prestige, power,

Who do you think makes more money, Selena Gomez or this teacher? What does this imply about the structural-functionalist argument that societies motivate (through higher salaries) talented individuals to prepare for and occupy the most important and difficult positions?

and property (Sernau 2010). *Workers* sell their labor to capitalists and are low in all three *P*s. Finally, the *underclass* has virtually no property, power, or prestige.

In the modern world, conflict theorists argue that workers are still exploited but in different ways. As noted earlier, owners and CEOs get more income than many analysts feel is warranted by their responsibilities and education. For example, in 2013, *Forbes* magazine reported that the CEO of Kinder Morgan (an energy company), Richard Kinder, received $1.1 billion in income for the year, the highest income for billionaires that year. The money came from income on stocks and other assets. The second highest income for the year among billionaires, $288.6 million, went to Daniel Och of Och-Ziff Capital Management Group. Howard Schultz, CEO of Starbucks, received $118 million (Smith 2013).

Income is money received from work or investments while **wealth** is *your income, property, and total assets* or how much you are worth when you subtract the value of what you own from what you owe. The distribution of wealth and income in the United States has not been as uneven as today since before the Great Depression hit in 1929. Today, the richest 1% of U.S. households own more wealth than *all* of the bottom 90% combined (Saez 2012), and 40% of the nation's total wealth (Archer 2013). In the world, the richest 1% own 46% of the world's wealth, and the richest 10% own 86% (Reuters 2013).

The Evolutionary Theory of Stratification: A Synthesis

Evolutionary theory, developed by Gerhard Lenski, borrows assumptions from both structural-functional and conflict theories in an attempt to determine how scarce resources are distributed and how that distribution results in stratification (Lenski 1966; Nolan and Lenski 2008). The basic ideas are as follows: (a) To survive, people must cooperate; (b) despite this, conflicts of interest occur over important decisions that benefit one individual or group over another; (c) valued items such as money and status are always in demand and in short supply; (d) there is likely to be a struggle over these scarce goods; and (e) customs or traditions in a society often prevail over rational criteria in determining distribution of scarce resources. After the minimum survival needs of both individuals and the society are met, power determines who gets the surplus: prestige, luxury living, the best health care, and so forth. Lenski believes that privileges (including wealth) flow from having power, and prestige usually

results from having access to both power and privilege (Hurst 2006).

Lenski tested his theory by studying societies at different levels of technological development, ranging from simple to complex. He found that the degree of inequality increases with technology until it reaches the advanced industrial stage. For instance, in subsistence-level hunter-gatherer societies, little surplus is available, and everyone's needs are met to the extent possible. As surplus accumulates in agrarian societies, those who acquire power also control surpluses, and they use this to benefit their friends and relations. However, they must share at least some of the wealth or fear being overthrown.

When societies finally reach the advanced industrial stage, there should be less inequality. Industrialization brings surplus wealth, a division of labor, advanced technology, and interdependence among members of a society. No longer can one individual control all the important knowledge, skills, or capital resources. The surplus can be spread to more people without diminishing that received by those who have the most. Therefore, this should eliminate the extreme gaps between haves and have-nots because resources would normally be more evenly distributed. Also, at this point in history, societies tend to have constitutions and recognize the rights of citizens, making it harder to exploit them.

Evolutionary theory takes into consideration an idea shared by the structural-functionalists and rational choice theorists—that talented individuals need to be motivated to make sacrifices. This produces motivated, competent, and well-educated people in the most important social statuses. The theory also recognizes exploitation leading to inequality, a factor that conflict theorists find in systems of stratification.

The reality is that while some inequality may be useful in highly complex societies, as functionalists have argued, extraordinary amounts of inequality may undermine motivation and productivity. The most talented people will not even try to attain the most demanding and important jobs if upward mobility seems impossible. Therefore, high levels of inequality do not make sense for a healthy industrial or postindustrial society (Nolan and Lenski 2008).

Each of the theories discussed earlier—symbolic interaction, rational choice, structural-functional, conflict, and evolutionary—provides different explanations for understanding stratification in modern societies. These theories provide the basis for micro- to macro-level discussions of stratification. Our next topic looks at some factors that influence an individual's position in a stratification system and the ability to change that position.

Thinking Sociologically

Why is the income gap between the rich and the poor currently increasing in the United States? Which theory seems most helpful in explaining this pattern? What are some possible ramifications of this widening income gap?

INDIVIDUALS' SOCIAL STATUS: THE MICRO LEVEL

You are among the world's elite. Less than 7% of the world's population has a college degree (Erickson and Vonk 2012). Being able to afford the time and money for college is a luxury beyond the financial or personal resources of almost 93% of people in the world. However, the global number of college students is expanding rapidly as countries such as China provide more higher education opportunities to support their growing economies.

In fact, enrollment of Chinese students in higher education surpassed the percentage enrolled in the United States in 2011 (People's Daily Online 2011). Because the demand for a college education far exceeds the opportunity in China, many Chinese college students are studying abroad, adding to their opportunities and enhancing China's knowledge of the world. Chinese students make up the largest number of international students studying in the United States—236,000 in 2013—accounting for more than a quarter of all international students (Paulson 2013).

In the United States, access to higher education is greater than in many other countries because there are more levels of entry—including technical colleges, community colleges, large state universities, and private four-year colleges. However, with limited government help, most students must have enough financial resources to cover tuition and the cost of living.

The prestige of the college that students choose can also make a difference in their future opportunities. Students born into wealth can afford private preparatory schools and tutors to increase SAT and ACT test scores that increase their chances of gaining acceptance to prestigious colleges. Such colleges offer social networking and other opportunities not available to those attending the typical state university or nonelite college (Jaschik 2013; Persell 2005). For men, attending an elite college makes a significant difference in future earnings, but for women

These college graduates share the privilege of a college education with just 7% of the world's population.

entering a field that pays well makes more of an impact on future earnings than the college they attended (Ma and Savas 2014).

Ascribed characteristics, such as gender, can also affect one's chances for success in life. Embedded gender stratification systems may make it difficult for women to rise in the occupational hierarchy. Many Japanese women, for example, earn college degrees but leave employment after getting married and having children, in part because of gender discrimination in the workforce (Globe Women 2013). We examine gender stratification in more depth in Chapter 9, but note that it intersects with socioeconomic status and must be viewed as part of a larger pattern resulting in inequality in the social world.

Individual Life Chances

Life chances refer to one's opportunities, depending on both achieved and ascribed statuses in society. That you are in college, probably have health insurance and access to health care, and are likely to live into your late 70s or 80s are factors directly related to your life chances. Let us consider several examples of how placement in organizations at the meso level affects individual experiences and has global ramifications.

Education. Although education is valued by most individuals, the cost of books, clothing, shoes, transportation, child care, and time taken from income-producing work may be insurmountable barriers to school attendance for many people. One's level of education affects

Average Wealth

many aspects of life, including political, religious, and family attitudes and behavior. Generally speaking, the higher the education level, the more active individuals are in political life, the more mainstream or conventional their religious affiliation, and the more likely they are to marry and remain married and have good health.

Health, Social Conditions, and Life Expectancy. If you have a sore throat for an extended period of time, you will probably go see a doctor. Yet many people in the world will never see a doctor. Access to health care requires doctors and medical facilities, money for transportation and treatment, access to child care, and released time from other tasks. The poor sometimes do not have these luxuries. In contrast, the affluent eat better food, are less exposed to polluted water and unhygienic conditions, and are able to pay for health insurance, medical care, and drugs when they do have ailing health. As a result, they tend to live much longer than poorer people.

Examining causes of death among different classes illustrates some of the deadly results of the differences in access to health care among people at different places in the stratification hierarchy. For example, in the poor Global South, shorter life expectancies *or the average number of years a person in particular society can expect to live*—and deaths, especially among children, are due to controllable infectious diseases such as cholera, malaria, AIDS, typhoid, tuberculosis, and other respiratory ailments. In contrast, in affluent countries, heart disease, stroke, and lung cancer are the most common causes of death, and most deaths are of people above the age of 65. With improvements in immunizations, mosquito nets to prevent malaria, better sanitation and water quality, access to medicines, better nutrition, and female literacy, life expectancy rises. The chance to live a long and healthy life is a privilege available to those living in wealthy countries. By studying Table 7.1 in the next "Engaging Sociology" feature, you can compare life expectancy with two other measures of life quality for the poorest and richest countries: the gross national product (GNP) per capita income—the average amount of money each person has per year—and the infant mortality rates (death rates for babies). Note that life expectancy in poor countries is as low as 49 years in Chad, South Africa, and Guinea-Bissau in Africa (many of the people in these countries are subsistence farmers), and as high as 89.6 years in the wealthy country of Monaco, and 84 in Macau, Japan, and Singapore. In the United States, life expectancy is 79.6 (World Factbook 2014c). Average annual income is as low as $600 in Zimbabwe and $400 in the Democratic Republic of Congo, and as high as $102,100 in Qatar and $89,400 in

Liechtenstein. The average U.S. income is $52,800 a year (World Factbook 2014a). Infant mortality is as high as 117.2 deaths per 1,000 births in Afghanistan (over 1 in 10), and as low as 1.8 in Monaco and 2.2 in Japan. In the United States, the estimated 2014 rate is 6.2 per 1,000 births (World Factbook 2014b).

One does not have to look beyond the borders of the United States, though, to see the relationship between health and wealth. The United States has much larger gaps between rich and poor people than most other wealthy nations, and that has led to a corresponding gap in health and life expectancy among social classes much wider than those in other highly developed nations. As the video *In Sickness and In Wealth: Health in America* (2008) reveals, there is "a health-wealth gradient" in the United States, in "which every descending rung of the socioeconomic ladder corresponds to worse health." The result is that 41 other nations have higher life expectancy rates than the United States (Meyer 2012; World Factbook 2014c).

Individual life chances are determined in part by the per capita income of individuals. If a country is poor, many individuals have little disposable income. This means a life of poverty, with less access to education, health, and other social conditions that determine life chances and lifestyle.

 Thinking Sociologically

Explain how some specific factors at the micro, meso, and macro levels affect your life expectancy and that of your family members.

Individual Lifestyles

Your individual lifestyle includes *your attitudes, values, beliefs, behavior patterns, and other aspects of your place in the world, as shaped by socialization*. As individuals grow up, the behaviors and attitudes consistent with their culture and their family's status in society become internalized through the process of socialization. Lifestyle is not a simple matter of having money. Acquiring money—say, by winning a lottery—cannot buy a completely new lifestyle (Bourdieu and Passeron 1977). This is because values and behaviors are ingrained in our self-concept from childhood. A person may gain material possessions, but that does not mean he or she has the lifestyle of the upper-class rich and famous. Remember the awkward party when you were around people of a different social class? Even if you suddenly made the same amount of money as those at an elegant party, you would not

ENGAGING SOCIOLOGY

Life Expectancy, Per Capita Income, and Infant Mortality

Analyzing the meaning of data can provide an understanding of the health and well-being of citizens around the world. A country's basic statistics including life expectancy, per capita gross national product, and infant mortality tell researchers a great deal about its economic health and vitality.

1. What questions do the data in Table 7.1 raise regarding differences in mortality and life expectancy rates around the world?

2. Considering what you know from this and previous chapters and from Table 7.1, what do you think are some differences in the lives of citizens in the richest and poorest countries?

Table 7.1   Life Expectancy, per Capita Income, and Infant Mortality for Selected Poor and Rich Countries

Poor Countries	Life Expectancy (in years)	Infant Mortality (deaths per 1,000 births)	Per Capita GDP ($)	Rich Countries	Life Expectancy (in years)	Infant Mortality (deaths per 1,000 births)	Per Capita GDP ($)
Chad	49.4	90.3	2,500	Monaco	89.6	1.8	65,500
South Africa	49.6	41.6	11,500	Japan	84.5	2.1	37,100
Afghanistan	50.5	117.2	1,100	Singapore	84.4	2.5	62,400
Somalia	51.6	100.1	600	Hong Kong	82.8	2.7	52,700
Zambia	51.8	66.6	1,800	Switzerland	82.4	3.7	54,800
Mozambique	52.6	72.4	1,200	Sweden	81.9	2.6	40,900
Nigeria	52.6	74.1	2,800	Australia	82.1	4.4	43,000
Uganda	54.5	60.8	1,500	Canada*	81.7*	4.7*	43,100
Niger	54.7	86.3	800	France	81.7	3.3	35,700
Zimbabwe	55.7	26.6	600	United States**	79.6**	6.2**	52,800

Source: World Factbook (2014b) (2014c) for infant mortality and life expectancy; World Factbook (2014a) for per capita income.

Note: Infant mortality is per 1,000 live births.

*Canada is 14th in life expectancy and 43rd in infant mortality rate.

**United States is 42nd in life expectancy and 56th in infant mortality rate.

know the norms associated with that social class. Some examples of factors related to your individual lifestyle that tend to differ among social classes include attitudes toward achievement, family life and child-rearing patterns, religious membership, and political involvement.

Increasing Life Expectancy

Attitudes Toward Achievement. Attitudes toward achievement differ by social status and are generally closely correlated with life chances. As noted previously, motivation to get ahead and beliefs about what we can achieve are in part products of our upbringing and the opportunities we see as available to us. These attitudes differ greatly depending on the opportunity structure around us, including what our families and friends see as possible and desirable. For example, the primary concern of poor families in poor nations may be to put food on the family's table. They may view education as a luxury not appropriate for people of their social class. In Global North countries, opportunity is available for most children to attend school at least through high school and often beyond. However, some students do not learn to value achievement in school due to lack of support from their primary socializing agents: family, peers, and teachers (Ballantine and Hammack 2012).

Family Life and Child-Rearing Patterns. Attitudes toward achievement are not the only things that differ among socioeconomic groups. Child-rearing patterns also vary and serve to reinforce one's attitude toward achievement and social position in society. When you were growing up, were your after-school hours, weekends, and summers filled with adult-organized activities (e.g., formal lessons, youth sports, camps), or were you pretty much free to play on your own, watch TV, or hang out with friends or extended family?

A family's social class location shapes the daily rhythms of family life (Lareau 2003). Upper- and middle-class parents engage in the "concerted cultivation" of their kids. They schedule their kids in multiple activities, engage in more elaborate verbal communication with them, and intervene on their behalf with teachers and other authority figures. Working-class parents, other than providing daily essentials, tend to be more hands-off, an approach that researcher Annette Lareau labeled the "accomplishment of natural growth" (2003: 238). Their kids engage in more casual, unstructured play, have fewer opportunities to hear and use extended vocabularies, and are left to fend for themselves in dealings with adults. Their parents tell them what to do with orders, rather than reasoning with them, as many middle- and upper-class parents do with their children. Their parents also tend to use more physical punishment than middle-class parents, who utilize guilt, reasoning, time-outs, and other nonphysical sanctions to control children's behavior. These differences help shape their assumptions about how authority is exercised and whether it is acceptable to challenge authority figures.

Differences in parenting behavior also lead to the "transmission of differential advantages to children" (Lareau 2003:5). Through their socialization by their parents, middle-class children are better able to navigate the educational and, later, occupational worlds than working-class children. This, in turn, influences the social class destinies of each group (Lashbrook 2009).

Religious Membership. Religious affiliation also correlates with the social status variables of education, occupation, and income. For instance, in the United States, upper-class citizens are found disproportionately in Episcopalian, Unitarian, and Jewish religious groups, whereas lower-class citizens tend to be attracted to Nazarene, Southern Baptist, Jehovah's Witness, and other holiness and fundamentalist sects. Although there are exceptions such as Catholicism, most religious groups attract members predominantly from one social class, as Chapter 12 illustrates (Roberts and Yamane 2012).

Political Involvement. Political party identification and general ideological beliefs affect voting, and they are, in turn, affected by social factors such as race, religion, region of the country, social class, gender, marital status, and age (Interuniversity Consortium for Political and Social Research 2011). Throughout the world, the lower the social class, the more likely people are to vote for parties that support greater distribution of wealth, and the higher the social status, the more likely people are to be conservative on economic issues—consistent with protecting their wealth (Domhoff 2005; Kerbo 2008). However, those with lower levels of education and income tend to vote conservatively on many social issues relating to minorities and civil liberties (e.g., rights for homosexuals, same-sex marriage, and abortion) (Gilbert 2011; Kerbo 2008). In the 2012 election in the United States, many voters had to make choices about economic policies they liked and whether those policies were more important than their preferences on some social issues. President Obama was reelected due to support from young people, racial and ethnic minorities, women, those who made less than $50,000 a year, and both low-educated voters (those with just a high school or less than a high school education) and the highly educated (those with postgraduate degrees).

In 2012, 61.8% of the voting population voted, with increases since 2008 of 117 million black votes, 1.4 million Hispanic votes, and 550,000 Asian votes. The white vote decreased by about 2 million. Approximately 60% of the votes cast came from those who made *over* $50,000 (Current Population Survey 2013).

Money also influences who can run successful campaigns. For example, during the 2012 congressional elections, the average candidate running for a position in the House of Representatives or the Senate spent, respectively, $526,818 and $2,318,358. During the presidential campaign of 2012, President Obama and Mitt Romney (along with their allies) raised approximately a billion dollars each. This contributes to the fact that those with more money, who can help support such campaigns, also have more influence in elections (King 2012; OpenSecrets.org 2012a, 2012b).

Status Inconsistency. Some people experience high status on one trait, especially a trait achieved through education and hard work, but may experience low standing in another area. For example, a professor may have high prestige but low income. Max Weber called this unevenness in one's social standing *status inconsistency*. In societies with high levels of racism and sexism, racial minorities and women in high-status positions experience status inconsistency. If their lowest ascribed status is treated as most important, they are likely to experience discontent with the current system and become more liberal in political views (Weber 1946).

Life experiences such as hunger, unnecessary early death of family members, or pain of seeing one's child denied opportunities are all experienced at the micro level, but their causes are usually rooted in events and actions at other levels of the social world. This brings us to our next question: Can an individual move up or down in a stratification system?

Thinking Sociologically

Describe your own lifestyle and life chances. How do these relate to your socialization experience and your family's position in the stratification system? What difference do they make in your life today and for what you think you will accomplish in the future? What can you do to improve your life chances?

SOCIAL MOBILITY: THE MICRO–MESO CONNECTION

The LeBron Jameses and Peyton Mannings of the world make millions of dollars—at least for the duration of their playing careers. For professionals in the world of sport, each hoop, goal, or touchdown throw is worth thousands of dollars. These riches give hope to those in rags that if they "play hard," they too may be on the field or court making millions. The problem is that the chances of making it big are so small

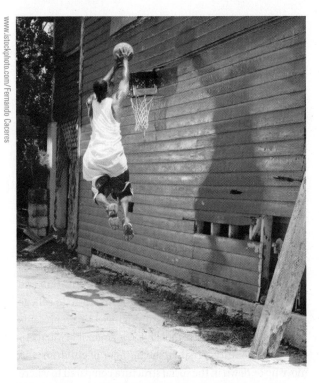

This young street basketball player has dreams of glory on the courts. Despite many grand hoop dreams, few experience dramatic social mobility through sports.

that such hopes are some of the cruelest hoaxes perpetrated on poor young African Americans and others in the lower or working class today. It is a false promise to think of sports as the road to wealth when chances of success are extremely limited (Dufur and Feinberg 2007; Edwards 2000).

Those few minority athletes who do "make it big" and become models for young people tend to experience "stacking," holding certain limited positions in a sport. Moreover, those young players who make it into the major leagues may have done so by going in right after high school or leaving college after a single year. This thwarts their postathletic career opportunities. When retired from playing, few black athletes rise in the administrative hierarchy in the sports of football and baseball (basketball has a better record of hiring black coaches and managers). If young people put all their hopes and energies into developing their muscles and physical skills, they may lose the possibility of moving up in the social class system, which requires developing their minds and technical skills.

Social mobility refers to *the extent of individual movement up or down in the class system, changing one's social position in society—especially relative to one's parents* (Gilbert 2011). What is the likelihood that your status will be different from that of your parents over your lifetime? Will you start a successful business?

Social Mobility

Marry into wealth? Win the lottery? Experience downward mobility due to loss of a job, illness, or inability to complete your education? What factors at different levels of analysis might influence your chances of mobility? These are some of the questions addressed in this section and the next.

The four issues that dominate the analysis of mobility are (1) types of social mobility, (2) methods of measuring social mobility, (3) factors that affect social mobility, and (4) whether there is a "land of opportunity" for those wishing to improve their lot in life.

Types of Social Mobility

Mobility can be up, down, or sideways. *Intergenerational mobility* refers to change in social class status compared with one's parents, usually resulting from education and occupational attainment. If you are the first to go to college in your family and you become an engineer, this represents intergenerational upward mobility. The amount of intergenerational mobility—that is, the number of children who move up or down in the social structure compared to where their parents are—measures the degree to which a society has an *open class system*. The more movement there is between classes, the more open the class system.

You can change positions at the same level in the stratification system. For example, you could move from your job as a postal worker and become a firefighter. This type of mobility is called *horizontal mobility*. You have changed your position, but your social prestige remains the same.

Intragenerational mobility (not to be confused with *inter*generational mobility) refers to a change in position within a single individual's life. For instance, if you begin your career as a teacher's aide and end it as a school superintendent, that is upward intragenerational mobility. However, mobility is not always up. *Vertical mobility* refers to movement up *or* down in the hierarchy and sometimes involves changing social classes. You may start your career as a waitress, go to college part-time, get a degree in computer science, and get a more prestigious and higher-paying job, resulting in upward mobility. Alternatively, you could lose a job and take one at a lower status and pay. In today's slow growth economy, people at all levels of the occupational structure have experienced downward intragenerational mobility after being laid off from one job and having difficulty finding another at the same level and pay grade.

How Much Mobility Is There? Measures of Social Mobility

One traditional method of measuring mobility is to compare fathers with sons, and in more recent research with daughters. Determining the mobility of women is more difficult because they often have lower-level positions, and their mothers may not have worked full-time, but a conclusion that can be drawn is that both women's and men's occupational attainment is powerfully influenced by class origins. As Figure 7.3 indicates, the level of social mobility in the United States is lower than in most other Global North nations (Gould 2012). This figure shows correlations, and a lower number in this case means a higher likelihood that sons will end up in the same social class as their fathers.

While the dramatic growth of the U.S. economy in the decades following World War II led to rising prosperity and upward mobility for most (particularly white, male Americans), mobility has decreased since the early 1970s. There is quite a bit of movement in the middle of the class system (between the lower-middle and upper-middle classes), but not much movement at the upper and lower ends. People born poor or wealthy tend to remain poor or wealthy when they are adults (Haskins, Isaacs, and Sawhill 2008; Pew Charitable Trusts 2012).

Factors Affecting an Individual's Mobility

Why are some people successful at moving up the ladder, while others lag behind? Mobility is driven by many factors, from your family's background to global economic variables. One's chances to move up depend on micro-level factors (e.g., cultural capital, socialization, personal characteristics, and education)—and meso- and macro-level factors (e.g., the occupational structure and economic status of countries; population changes in the number of births, deaths, or people migrating; the numbers of people vying for similar positions; discrimination based on gender, race, or ethnicity; and the global economic situation).

Studying mobility can be a complicated process because these key variables are interrelated. Macro-level forces (such as the occupational structure and economic status in a country) are related to meso-level factors (such as access to education and type of economy) and micro-level factors (such as socialization, family background, and education level) (Blau and Duncan 1967). An individual's family background accounts for nearly half of the factors affecting what job one gets (Jencks 1979). Consider a few of the variables that can make a difference in your chances for mobility.

Family Background, Socialization, Marriage, and Education. Whether you marry and whom you marry can move you up or down the social class ladder. As

FIGURE 7.3   Social Mobility: Correlations Between Earnings of Fathers and Sons

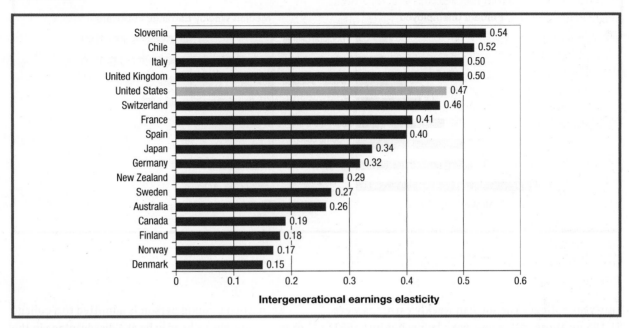

Source: Gould (2012).

Note: The higher the number, the lower the intergenerational social mobility.

men's wages have fallen over the past few decades and more women have joined the workforce, household incomes (rather than just male incomes) play more of a role in people's social class positions. As people increasingly tend to marry those of similar income levels, marriage makes even more of an impact on family income. Two high-income earners make much more than two low-income earners (and *much* more than one low-income or even middle-income worker) (Haskins et al. 2008; Pew Charitable Trusts 2012).

As we have noted throughout this chapter, our family background has a major influence on our chances for upward mobility on the social class ladder. For example, recent research discusses the continuing social class "word gap" between children from different classes. Disparities in vocabulary are noticeable as early as 18 months (National Public Radio [NPR] 2013). Children from higher social classes learn nuances in language whereas lower-class children learn primarily commands and short directive sentences. Professional parents use three times as many different words at home as parents in low-income families. By the time the children of professional families are 3 years old, they have a vocabulary of about 1,100 words and typically use 297 different words per hour. Children in working-class families have a 700-word vocabulary and use 217 words per hour, while children from low-income families have 500 words and

use 149 per hour. These numbers represent a gap in the range of words they hear at home and illustrate the difference family background and socialization can make in education and future opportunities. A University of Chicago study recommends a "3-Ts" approach—tune in, talk more, take turns—to increase vocabulary (Hart and Risley 2003; NPR 2013). Because language usage at home impacts school success, that in turn plays a role in a child's chances of getting into college and climbing the stratification ladder.

Thinking Sociologically

How might your vocabulary affect your success in school? How might an expanded vocabulary affect your opportunities in life (e.g., impress a potential employer)? What can you do to increase your vocabulary?

A college degree helps those at the bottom of the stratification system move up and helps those in the middle and upper classes to remain in those higher positions. This positive impact on social class position relates to the fact that, as Figure 7.4 reveals, employment rates and earnings tend to go up dramatically with a college degree. For example, in 2012, the unemployment rate for those with just a high school degree was 7.5%, but just 4.0% for those with a degree from a

FIGURE 7.4   **Earnings and Unemployment Rates by Educational Attainment**

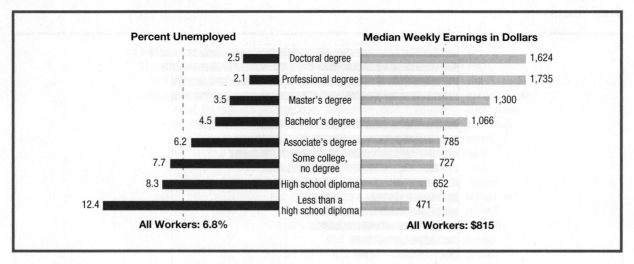

Source: U. S. Bureau of Labor Statistics, Current Population Survey.

four-year college. The median weekly earnings were $1,108 for those with a four-year degree but just $651 for those with only a high school diploma (Pew Charitable Trusts 2012; U. S. Bureau of Labor Statistics 2013b).

As Table 7.2 indicates, most people who go to college are already in the middle and upper classes. When we look at actual college degrees, however, the pattern is more extreme; 50% of college diplomas go to students in the top-status groups, compared with only 10% to graduates coming from the bottom half of income levels. If U.S. society were truly a **meritocracy,** *positions would be allocated in a social group or organization according to individuals' abilities and credentials.* One would expect cognitive ability to be the most important variable (Gilbert 2011).

Table 7.2   College Attendance by Social Class and Cognitive Ability (percent in college)

Cognitive Ability Quartile	Family Socioeconomic Status Quartile			
	Top	Third	Second	Lowest
Top	83	74	63	51
Second	69	51	42	33
Third	57	40	24	23
Lowest	35	20	13	13

Source: Gilbert (2011:149).

Even when a young person is admitted to a college or university, she or he may be at a disadvantage in the classroom and alienated from past social ties. The culture of four-year colleges is typically the culture of the well-educated upper-middle class and may be different and uncomfortable for those from other class backgrounds (Dews and Law 1995). The alienation many poor and working-class students experience at four-year colleges is explored in more detail in the next "Engaging Sociology."

Population Trends and Economic Vitality Within a Country. The economic vitality of a country affects the chances for individual mobility, since there will be fewer positions at the top if the economy is stagnant. As agricultural work decreases and technology jobs increase in most areas of the world, these changes in the composition and structure of jobs affect individual opportunity (Hurst 2013). Thus, macro-level factors such as a country's economy and its place in the global system shape the employment chances of individuals.

The U.S. nationwide baby boom following World War II resulted in a flood of job applicants and downward intergenerational mobility for the many who could not find work comparable with their social class at birth. In contrast, the smaller group following the baby boomer generation had fewer competitors for entry-level jobs. Baby boomers hold many of the executive and leadership positions today, so promotion has been hard for the next cohort. As baby boomers retire, opportunities will open up, and mobility should

ENGAGING SOCIOLOGY

First-Generation College Students: Issues of Cultural and Social Capital

Socioeconomic classes develop subcultures that can be quite different from one another, and when one changes subcultures, it can be confusing and alienating. College campuses provide an example. Generally they are dominated by middle-class cultures. First-generation college students often find themselves in a world as alien to them as visiting another country. Students whose parents went to college are more likely to have cultural and social capital that helps them adjust to and understand their professors who are generally part of the middle-class culture. Answer the following survey questions. How might your own cultural and social capital cause you to feel at home or alienated, privileged or disprivileged, hopeful or despairing in a four-year college environment?

A. Which of the following *experiences* were part of your childhood?

☐ Had a library of books (at least 50 adult books) in your childhood home

☐ Had parents who subscribed to a newspaper

☐ Had parents who subscribed to news magazines (*Time, The Economist*)

☐ Listened to music as a family, including classical or instrumental music such as harp or flute

☐ Traveled to at least 20 other states or to at least 5 other countries

☐ Took regular trips to the library

☐ Took regular trips to museums

☐ Attended movies

☐ Attended plays (theater productions)

☐ Attended concerts

☐ Played a musical instrument

☐ Took dance lessons

☐ Listened to National Public Radio (NPR)

☐ Watched PBS (Public Broadcasting Station) on television

B. Which of the following *relationships* were part of your childhood?

☐ My parents knew at least two influential people in my community on a first-name basis— such as the mayor, members of the city council, the superintendent of schools, members of the school board, the local county sheriff, the chief of police, the prosecuting attorney, the governor, or the district's representative to Congress.

☐ The regional leader of my religious group— church, temple, or mosque—knew and respected my family.

☐ My parents knew, on a first-name basis, at least three CEOs of corporations.

☐ When I entered new situations in high school, it was likely that my parents were known by the coaches, music directors, summer camp counselors/directors, or other authority figures who were "running the show."

☐ When I came to college, one or more professors and administrators at the college knew my parents, a sibling, or another family member.

☐ I have often interacted directly and effectively (in a nonadversarial way) with authority figures.

Engaging in Sociological Analysis

1. If you experienced many of the items under *A* at home, you had fairly high cultural capital. If you

(Continued)

marked most of the items under *B*, you had a lot of social capital. If you did not mark many of the items above you may find the culture of a college campus to be alien and even confusing. How well does your background match up with the cultural capital of a college?

2. Which of the following aspects of a college campus do you think might make a first-generation

college student feel most alienated at your college: *economic* capital (money), *social* capital (networks with those who have resources), or *cultural* capital (knowledge of important aspects of the culture)? Why?

Source: Survey constructed in part using ideas from Morris and Grimes (1997).

increase. The *fertility rates*, or number of children born at a given time, influence the number of people who will be looking for jobs.

Gender, Race, Ethnicity, and Earnings. Many women and ethnic minority groups, locked in a cycle of poverty, dependence, and debt, have little chance of changing their status. For example, African Americans tend to remain poor or fall from the middle-class more often than people in other racial groups (Pew Charitable Trusts 2012). Likewise, while women have made some gains, women in the U.S. workforce are more likely than men to be in dead-end

clerical and service positions with no opportunity for advancement. Overall, women also still make less money than men (U.S. Department of Labor 2011a). Table 7.3 shows the earnings for population groups including gender and race/ethnicity.

Women, on average, earn less money than men, but they now have more degrees than men do. Women are much more likely than men (32% compared to 24%) to earn a bachelor's degree by the time they are 27. While women are still woefully underrepresented in upper-level management positions (only 4.2% of *Fortune* 500 CEOs are women), their increasing edge in education should,

Most four-year colleges have middle-class cultures—or even upper-class cultures. The environment can be quite alienating—"chilly" in more ways than one—to first-generation students who do not have social and cultural capital that fits their new environment.

Table 7.3 Median Annual Earnings by Race/Ethnicity and Sex

Race/Gender	Earnings	Wage Ratio
White men	$46,176	100.0%
White women	37,596	81.4
Black men	34,632	75.0
Black women	31,044	67.0
Hispanic men	30,863	66.8
Hispanic women	27,612	59.8
All men	$45,084	
All women	$36,608	
Gender wage gap for all ethnic groups		81.2%

Source: Adapted from U.S. Department of Labor (2013).

eventually, lead to more women in high-level positions in the workforce (U. S. Bureau of Labor Statistics 2013a; Catalyst 2013; DeBoskey 2012).

The Interdependent Global Market. All members of an economy are vulnerable to international events and the swings in the global marketplace. If the Chinese or Japanese stock markets hiccup, it sends ripples through world markets. If high-tech industries in Japan or Europe falter, North American companies in Silicon Valley, California, may go out of business, costing many professionals their lucrative positions. In ways such as these, the interdependent global economies affect national and local economies, and that in turn affects individual families.

Whether individuals move from "rags to riches" is not determined solely by their personal ambition and work ethic. As the information in this chapter indicates, mobility for the individual, a micro-level event, is linked to a variety of events at other levels of the social world. What we see and hear in the media, though, may have us believe otherwise.

Thinking Sociologically

Think of family members or friends who have recently lost or acquired jobs. Using your sociological imagination, how can you connect those individual experiences to the national and global economy? How do you think the national and global economies will impact your experience in the marketplace after you earn your college degree?

Is There a "Land of Opportunity"? Cross-Cultural Mobility

Television shows bombard us with images of rich bachelors and the desirability of marrying a millionaire to improve our status in life. By playing a game of trivia or being challenged on an island on a TV show, we too might "strike it rich." Another possibility is that we might win the lottery by buying a ticket at our local convenience store. In reality, these quick fixes and easy get-rich-fast plans are seldom realized, and the chances of us profiting are slim indeed.

The question for this section concerns your realistic chances for mobility and whether you have a better chance to improve your status by moving to some other country. The answer is not simple. Countless immigrants have sought better opportunities in new locations. Their economic future depended on the historical period, the economic conditions, attitudes toward immigrants, their job skills, and their ability to blend into the new society.

During economic growth periods, many immigrants have found great opportunities for mobility in the United

States and Europe. However, opportunities for upward mobility have changed significantly with globalization. Multinational corporations look for the cheapest sources of labor in the Global South with low taxes, few labor unions and workplace safety regulations, and many workers needing jobs. This has drained away low-skilled, manufacturing jobs from Global North countries, making it even more essential to have advanced educational credentials (such as a bachelor's or master's degree).

Most jobs in the United States today focus on providing services. These service-sector jobs tend to require either a great deal of education (e.g., lawyers, computer engineers, or doctors) or minimal training (e.g., retail sales, nurse's aides, fast-food workers, or security guards). The low-skill jobs do not pay well, and labor unions, with declining memberships and political clout, have increasingly limited influence on the wages and working conditions of workers.

Although the new factories for multinational industries springing up in Global South countries such as Malaysia, Mexico, and the Philippines, provide opportunities for mobility to those of modest origins, much of the upward mobility in the world is taking place among those who come from small, highly educated families with individualistic achievement-oriented values (Featherman and Hauser 1978; Rothman 2005). They are positioned to take advantage of the changing occupational structure and high-tech jobs. As the gap between rich and poor individuals widens, education becomes more important.

Thinking Sociologically

What social factors in your society limit or enhance the likelihood of upward social mobility for you and other members of your generation? Explain.

MAJOR STRATIFICATION SYSTEMS: MACRO-LEVEL ANALYSIS

Mansa works on a plantation in Mozambique. He tries in vain to pay off the debts left by his father. However hard he and his wife and children work, they will always be in debt because they cannot pay the total amount due for their hut or food from the owner's store. Basically, they are slaves—they do not have control over their own labor. They were born into this status, and there they will stay.

Imagine being born into a society in which you have no choices or options in life because of your family background, age, sex, and ethnic group. You

 Extreme Wealth

cannot select an occupation that interests you, cannot choose your mate, and cannot live in the part of town you prefer. You see wealthy aristocrats parading their advantages and realize that this will never be possible for you. You can never own land or receive the education of your choice.

This situation is reality for millions of people in the world—they are born this way and will spend their lives this way. In ascribed stratification systems, *characteristics beyond the control of individuals—such as family background, age, sex, and race—determine their position in society.* In contrast, achieved stratification systems *allow individuals to earn positions through their ability, efforts, and choices.* In an open-class system, it is possible to achieve a higher ranking by working hard, obtaining education, and choosing an occupation that pays well.

Ascribed Status: Caste and Estate Systems

Caste systems are the *most rigid ascribed stratification systems. Individuals are born into a status, which they retain throughout life.* That status is deeply embedded in religious, political, and economic norms and institutions. Individuals born into caste systems have predetermined occupational positions, marriage partners, residences, social associations, and prestige levels. A person's caste is easily recognized through clothing, speech patterns, family name and identity, skin color, or other distinguishing characteristics. From their earliest years, individuals learn their place in society through the process of socialization. To behave counter to caste prescriptions would be to go against religion and social custom and to risk not fitting into society. That can be a death sentence in some societies.

In caste-based societies, the institution of religion works together with the family, education, economic, and political institutions to shape both expectations and aspirations and to keep people in their prescribed places in caste systems. For example, Hindu ideas dictate that violating the caste prescriptions can put one's next *reincarnation* or rebirth (in the Hindu tradition) in jeopardy. Stability in Hindu societies is maintained in part by the belief that people can be reborn into a higher status in the next life if they fulfill expectations in their ascribed position in this life.

The clearest example of a caste system is found in India, a predominantly Hindu society. The Hindu religion holds that individuals are born into one of four *varnas,*

broad caste positions, or into a fifth group below the caste system, the *outcaste* group. The first and highest *varna,* called *Brahmans,* originally was made up of priests and scholars but now includes many leaders in society. The second *varna, Kshatriyas* or *Rajputs,* includes the original prince and warrior *varna* and now embraces much of the army and civil service. The *Vaishyas,* or merchants, are the third *varna.* The fourth *varna,* the *Sudras,* includes peasants, farmers, artisans, and laborers. The final layer, below the caste system, encompasses profoundly oppressed and broken people—"a people put aside"— referred to as untouchables, outcastes, *Chandalas* (a Hindu term), and *Dalits* (the name preferred by many "untouchables" themselves). Although the Indian Constitution of 1950 granted full social status to these citizens, and a law passed in 1955 made discrimination against them punishable, deeply rooted traditions can be difficult to change. Caste distinctions are still very prevalent in India, especially in rural areas, as seen in the next "Sociology Around the World."

Estate systems are characterized by *the concentration of economic and political power in the hands of a small minority of political-military elite, with the peasantry tied to the land* (Rothman 2005). They existed in ancient Egypt, the Incan and Mayan civilizations, Europe, China, and Japan. In estate systems, an individual's rank and legal rights are clearly spelled out, and arranged marriages and religion bolster the system. In Europe, during the Middle Ages, knights defended the realms and the religion of the nobles. Behind every knight in shining armor were peasants, sweating in the fields and paying for the knights' food, armor, and campaigns. For farming the land owned by the nobility, peasants received protection against invading armies and enough of the produce to survive. Their lives were often miserable. If the yield of crops was poor, they ate little. In a good year, they might save enough to buy a small parcel of land. A very few were able to become independent in this fashion. Today, similar systems exist in some Central and South American, Asian, and African countries on large banana, coffee, cacao, and sugar plantations.

Thinking Sociologically

What might be some advantages, for both the society and the individuals living in it, of a society where status is ascribed rather than achieved? Do you think you would enjoy living in such a society? Why or why not?

Sociology Around the World

The Outcastes of India

The *Dalits*—sometimes called "untouchables"—are the most impoverished people in India and some of the poorest in the world. These are *Dalit* children, attending a school so destitute that they do not have books, pencils, chairs, or desks.

The village, south of Chennai (Madras) in the state of Tamil Nadu, lies on an isolated dirt road, 1 kilometer from the nearest town. It consists of a group of mud and stick huts with banana leaf–thatched roofs. As our group of students arrived, the *Dalit* villagers lined the streets to greet us—and stare. Many had never seen Westerners. They played drums and danced for us and threw flower petals at our feet in traditional welcome.

Through our translator, we learned something of their way of life. The adults work in the fields long hours each day, plowing and planting with primitive implements, earning about 8 cents from the landowner, often not enough to pay for their daily bowl of rice. Occasionally, they catch a frog or bird to supplement their meal. In the morning, they drink rice gruel, and in the evening, they eat a bowl of rice with some spices. Women and children walk more than a kilometer to the water well—but the water is polluted during the dry season. There are no privies but the fields. As a result of poor sanitation, inadequate diet, and lack of health care, many people become ill and die from health problems easily cured in Western societies. For instance, lack of vitamin A, found in many fruits and vegetables to which they have little access, causes blindness in many village residents. Although the children have the right to go to the school in the closest village, many cannot do so because they have no transportation, shoes, or money for paper, pencils, and books. Also, the families, in order to survive, need the children to work in the fields alongside their parents or to help care for younger siblings.

Many taboos rooted in tradition separate the *Dalits* from other groups in India. For instance, they are forbidden to draw water from the village well, enter the village temple, or eat from dishes that might be used later by people of higher castes. The latter prohibition eliminates most dining at public establishments. About 95% are landless and earn a living below subsistence level.

Dalits who question their status have been attacked. The Human Rights Education Movement of India states that every hour, two *Dalits* are assaulted, three *Dalit* women are raped, two *Dalits* are murdered, and two *Dalit* houses are burned (Dalit Liberation Education Trust 1995; Thiagaraj 2006); Wilson 1993). Violence is used to control *Dalits* who try to uplift themselves and thus create threats to the social status and dominance of higher caste groups (Karthikeyan 2011). This group on the bottom rung of the stratification system has a long fight ahead to gain the rights that many of us take for granted.

(Continued)

(Continued)

A few *Dalits* have migrated to cities, where they blend in, and some of them have become educated and now lead the fight for the rights and respect guaranteed by law. Recently, unions and interest groups have started representing the *Dalits*, and some members turn to religious and political groups more sympathetic to their plight, such as Buddhists, Christians, or Communists.

One educated *Dalit* social activist, Henry Thiagaraj, has committed his life to improving conditions for the *Dalits*. Thiagaraj works on the micro, meso, and macro levels. On the micro level, he encourages educated *Dalits* with some power in government or business to organize the people who live in *Dalit* slums. At the meso level, Thiagaraj and other *Dalit* activists work to initiate microlending to the *Dalits* and to improve their education and labor training. On the macro level, Thiagaraj works with nongovernmental organizations to increase support for *Dalit* interests. He also works to improve media coverage of the *Dalits* to raise awareness of their experiences. Thiagaraj's (2006) book *Human Rights From the Dalit Perspective* provides an outstanding retrospective of how India has addressed caste discrimination since the 1980s.

Achieved Status: Social Class in the United States

In contrast to ascribed status systems, *achieved stratification systems* maintain that everyone is born with common legal status and equality before the law. In principle, all individuals can own property and choose their own occupations. However, in practice, most achieved status systems, like the class system found in the United States, pass privilege or poverty from one generation to the next. Individual upward or downward mobility is more difficult than the ideology invites people to believe.

Social class refers to *the wealth, power, and prestige rankings that individuals hold in society*. Members of the same social class have similar income, wealth and economic position, lifestyles, levels of education, cultural beliefs, and patterns of social interaction. Our families, rich or poor and educated or unskilled, provide us with an initial social ranking and socialization experience. We tend to feel a kinship and sense of belonging with those in the same social class and tend to live, attend school, and work with people from our social class. We think alike, share interests, and probably look up to the same people as a reference group.

Our social class position is based on the three main factors in the stratification system: (1) property, (2) prestige, and (3) power. This is the trio—the three *P*s—that, according to Max Weber, determines where individuals rank in relation to each other (Weber 1946, 1947). By *property* (wealth), Weber refers to owning or controlling the means of production. *Power*, the ability to control others, includes not only the means of production but also the position one holds. *Prestige* involves the esteem and recognition one receives, based on wealth, position, or accomplishments. Chances of being granted high prestige improve if one's patterns of behavior, occupation, and lifestyle match those valued in the society (e.g., in U.S. society today that would include scientists, physicians, military officers, lawyers, and college professors). However, recent news events—such as the Boston Marathon bombings—may increase the rankings of occupations in which people such as first responders (police and firefighters) have been portrayed as "heroes."

Although these three dimensions of stratification are often found together, this is not always so. Recall the idea of *status inconsistency*: an individual can have a great deal of prestige yet not command much wealth (Weber 1946). Consider winners of the prestigious Nobel Peace Prize such as Wangari Maathai, a Kenyan environmentalist who won the prize for starting a movement to plant trees and for her political activism, or Betty Williams and Mairead Corrigan of Northern Ireland, founders of the Community of Peace People who won for their efforts to find a peaceful end to their country's problems. None of them was rich, but each made contributions to the world that gained them universal prestige. Likewise, some people gain enormous wealth through crime or gambling, but this wealth may not be accompanied by respect or prestige.

Money and Behavior 🎙 Social Class ▶

Still, some theorists see power as the key element in systems of stratification. Conflict theorists maintain that those who hold power control the economic capital and the means of production in society (Ashley and Orenstein 2009). Consistent with Marx, many recent conflict theorists argue that a **power elite** comprised of *top leaders in corporations, politics, and the military* rules society. These interlocking groups of elites (Domhoff 2005, 2014; Mills 1956). grow up together, attending the same private schools and belonging to the same private clubs. There is an unspoken agreement to protect each other's positions and ensure that their power is not threatened. Those not in this interlocking elite group do not hold real power and have little chance of breaking into the inner circles (Dye 2002).

Pluralist power theorists, on the other hand, argue that *power is not held exclusively by an elite group but shared among many power centers, each of which has its own self-interests to protect* (Ritzer and Goodman 2004). Well-financed special interest groups (e.g., the insurance industry, dairy and cattle farmers, or truckers' trade unions) and professional associations (e.g., the American Medical Association or the American Bar Association) have considerable power through collective action. From the pluralist perspective, officials who hold political power are vulnerable to pressure from influential interest groups, and each interest group competes for power with others. Creating and maintaining this power through networks and pressure on legislators is the job of lobbyists. For example, in the intense U.S. debate over health care legislation, interest groups from the medical community, insurance lobbies, and citizens' groups wielded their power to influence the outcome, but because these major interests conflict and no one group has the most power, no one group attained all it wanted. Some groups wanted to nationalize health care, and others wanted to completely privatize it; the Affordable Care Act did neither. The core idea of pluralist theorists, then, is that many centers of power create at least some checks and balances on those in elite positions.

Examples of Social Classes in the United States

Imagine that you are a politician. The public is clamoring for more help for the middle class. Flash back to the most recent U.S. presidential campaign. All the candidates were talking about the middle class. Did you ever hear the politicians define what they meant? You probably did not, because the broader and more inclusive the definition, the more useful it is to politicians who are trying to appeal to a range of voters.

When given a choice among lower, middle, and upper class, almost all Americans will say they are middle class. When given a choice that includes working class, however, 45% say middle class, and another 45% define themselves as working class (Gilbert 2011). You can see sociologist Dennis Gilbert's social class model in Figure 7.5. Most social scientists measure social class by looking at the income, education, and profession of respondents. Middle class generally requires extensive education and training and a salary rather than an hourly wage—teachers, nurses, accountants, managers, and other mid-level jobs—falling at around 50% of the income distribution (Gilbert 2011).

Sometimes, social scientists break down members of the middle class into two groups: the white-collar middle class and the working class. Most white-collar workers have a college education, have professions with salaries (rather than jobs where they are paid by the hour), work in an office setting, and earn within a specified range around the median income. Members of the working class work for hourly wages, do manual labor, and do not usually have a college degree.

FIGURE 7.5 Gilbert Model of Social Class

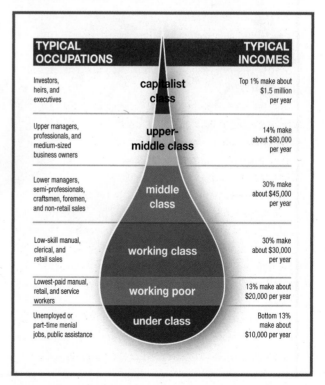

Source: Gilbert (2011:14).

Middle Class

Thinking Sociologically

How does today's popular culture on TV and in films, magazines, and popular music reflect interests of different social classes? How are rich and poor people depicted? Who appears responsible for their wealth or poverty—the individuals, the society, or some other combination? Do any of these depictions question the U.S. class system?

POVERTY AND SOCIAL POLICY

Nothing describes poverty more vividly than hunger. Stories about hunger and famine in Global South countries fill the newspapers. Around the world, nearly 870 million people, or roughly 1 in every 8 people on Earth, go to bed hungry every night. Yet chronic hunger has declined by 130 million people since 1990 (World Food Programme 2013; World Hunger Education Service 2013). Figure 7.6 shows where hunger is most severe.

One hardly expects to see hunger in rich countries, yet in the United States over 50 million people, or 1 in 6 in the U.S. population and 1 in 5 children, are hungry some of the time (Feeding America 2013; Sauter and Hess 2013). States most severely affected by food insecurity (lack of consistent access to food) include Mississippi, Arkansas, Texas, Alabama, North Carolina, Georgia, Missouri, Nevada, Tennessee, and Ohio. These states also have among the highest obesity rates due to poor diets (Sauter and Hess 2013). Households led by single women are more likely to be food insecure (36.8%). Race also influences the likelihood of food insecurity. One out of four black (25.1%) and Hispanic (26.2%) households are food insecure (Coleman-Jensen et al. 2012).

Most people living in poverty have no property-based income and no permanent or stable work, only casual or intermittent earnings in the labor market. They often depend on help from government agencies or private organizations to survive. In short, they have personal troubles in large part because they have been unable to establish linkages and networks in the meso- and macro-level organizations of our social world. They have little collective power and therefore little representation of their interests and needs in the political system.

 Thinking Sociologically

Explain how your family's ability to provide food for its members at the micro level is largely dependent upon its connectedness to the meso and macro levels of society.

FIGURE 7.6   Global Hunger Index

■ >30.0 (Extremely alarming)
■ 20.0–29.9 (Alarming)
■ 10.0–19.9 (Serious)
■ 5.0–9.9 (Moderate)
■ <4.9 (Low)
■ No data
■ Industrialized country

Source: International Food Policy Research Institute (2013).

Sociologists recognize two basic types of poverty: (1) absolute poverty and (2) relative poverty. **Absolute poverty,** *not having resources to meet basic needs,* means no prestige, very little access to power, no accumulated wealth, and insufficient means to survive. Whereas absolute poverty in the United States is quite limited, the *Dalits* of India (described earlier in "Sociology Around the World: The Outcastes of India") provide an example of absolute poverty. Some die of easily cured diseases because the bodies of those in absolute poverty are weakened by chronic and persistent hunger and almost total lack of medical attention.

Relative poverty occurs when *one's income falls below the poverty line, resulting in an inadequate standard of living relative to others in the individual's country.* In the United States, relative poverty means shortened life expectancy, higher infant mortality, and poorer health. While few people starve on the street and suffer from the easily cured diseases more common among the poor in global South nations, food insecurity and the stress and hardships of relative poverty lead to more health problems and earlier deaths for the poor in the United States and other global North nations with high levels of inequality.

The *feminization of poverty* refers to the trend in which single females with children make up a growing proportion of those in poverty. In 2012, 13.6% of males and 16.3% of females in the United States lived in poverty. For women aged 18 to 64, the rate was 15.4%, and for men in this age group 11.9% (DeNavas-Walt, Proctor, and Smith 2013). If you were raised by a single mother, chances are good that you experienced poverty. More than half (57.2%) of children under age 6 living with just a female head of household in the United States (with no husband present) were in poverty in 2011 (DeNavas-Walt et al., 2012). Some of those in poverty find themselves without a home. As of January 2013, there were 610,042 homeless people in the United States (U.S. Department of Housing and Urban Development 2013). Among them, 65% were in transitional or emergency shelters, and 35% were unsheltered. Almost one out of four of the homeless (23%) were children under the age of 18. Families now make up over one third (36%) of the homeless population.

The Obama administration has made a concerted effort to combat homelessness and has used social scientific research to do so. Studies have shown that "mainstream housing, health, education, and human service programs must be fully engaged and coordinated to prevent and end homelessness" (Sullivan 2013). Research

This little boy sits at the feet of an aid worker. His family has little power to improve their situation or his life chances. Compare his circumstances to those of the little girl riding in a limousine while talking on her cell phone.

also reveals that providing a wide range of services for the homeless actually saves taxpayers money in the long run "by interrupting a costly cycle of emergency room visits, detoxes, and even jail terms" (Sullivan 2013). Thanks to strategies based on these findings, the number of both the homeless, in general, and homeless families has declined by, respectively, 6% and 8% since 2010, despite growing levels of inequality in our society.

How can we effectively address inequality? First, we must become aware of the problem. As this chapter has described, almost every society has some system of stratification. We do not all have the same chances of "making it." Most of us, though, do not fully realize the extent of the inequality in some societies including the society we call home.

For example, in a recent study, a nationally representative sample of U.S. citizens were shown three charts that display different distributions of wealth ranging from somewhat equal to very unequal. When asked which of the three charts illustrate how wealth was distributed in the United States, most respondents chose the chart that actually described wealth distribution in Sweden, the nation with the *lowest level* of economic inequality in the world. The chart most often picked by respondents as an "ideal" distribution of wealth illustrated an even *more equitable* distribution of wealth than that found in Sweden (Norton and Ariely 2011). Figure 7.7 shows the actual U.S. wealth distribution plotted against the estimated and ideal distributions across all respondents.

Thinking Sociologically

What distribution of wealth and income would you favor for your nation, and why? What changes would you make to approach your favored distribution?

After reading this chapter, you understand that the United States has higher levels of inequality and poverty and less class mobility than most other wealthy nations have. Once we understand the extent of inequality and poverty, we can start to develop ways to address these issues. We can also critique poverty reduction programs now under way in different nations and help to create more effective ones, if needed.

Solutions to Poverty: Some Policy Considerations

Government programs exist in the United States and many other countries to help individuals through difficult times, especially during economic downturns. The

FIGURE 7.7 Wealth Inequality in the United States: Actual, Estimated, and Perceived Ideal Percent Wealth Owned

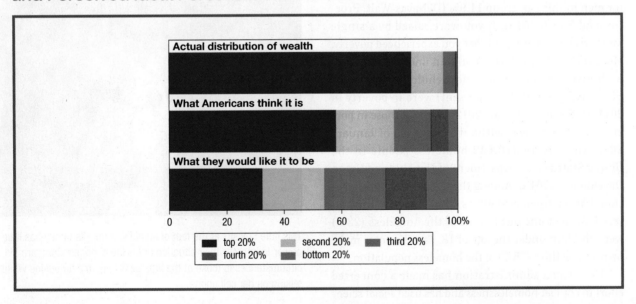

Source: Norton and Ariely (2011).

Note: The actual U.S. wealth distribution plotted against the estimated and ideal distributions across all respondents. Because of their small percentage share of total wealth, both the "4th 20%" value (0.2%) and the "Bottom 20%" value (0.1%) are not visible in the "Actual" distribution.

The bar labeled "What Americans think it is", represents the actual distribution of wealth in Sweden not the U.S.

stated goal of most public and private poverty reduction and welfare programs is to change factors that perpetuate poverty, but this requires money, jobs, and remodeling our social institutions. Sociologists and other social scientists work to understand social problems. They also devise programs to mitigate them, and evaluate programs in existence to help ensure that only effective programs continue to receive funds. Some policy makers suggest attacking the problem of poverty institution by institution, offering incentives for family stability, for students to finish high school, and for job training.

Welfare, Workfare, and Other Aid Programs. Most Global North countries provide assistance to citizens who need help when they are unemployed, sick, or elderly. The United States established the Great Society programs of the 1960s and 1970s, as part of the "War on Poverty" of that era. Some of these programs still exist, including the Special Supplemental Nutrition Program for Women, Infants, and Children (WIC), which provides nutritional help, and Head Start, which provides early childhood education. Both programs have received high grades for effectiveness. Yet child poverty rates are still high compared with those of 35 other Global North countries, with the United States ranked 34th (meaning only one other nation in the group has higher rates of child poverty) (Fisher 2013b).

In addition to micro-level incentives such as child care and work training, success in helping people out of poverty depends on meso-level economic conditions: Are there jobs available at living wages? Are taxpayers, many of whom are attracted to politicians who cut taxes, willing to provide money for social programs to help the "invisible" poor out of poverty as well as provide subsidies for other groups, including farmers, homeowners, college students, and corporations? Ironically, government institutions such as prisons and the criminal justice system absorb public funds that could go to poverty reduction. Yet, as we discussed in Chapter 6, crime itself is often a result of people in poverty feeling that they have no other options for survival.

Since the 2007–2009 Great Recession and the slow recovery that has followed, jobs have become harder to find, and the success story of workfare has been challenged. Social workers and others working with people living in poverty have seen increases in the number of people needing food stamps, food pantries and food kitchens, temporary shelter, and other stopgaps for the destitute. Caseloads of welfare workers have increased over 10% since 2007, by more than 4.6 million

households (Johnson 2012). As you can see, there are multiple, often intersecting reasons one can fall into or remain mired in poverty. Policy analysts look at how poverty reduction may require addressing different issues at once. This is one way sociologists can help form public policy efforts aimed at reducing poverty. In the next "Sociologists in Action" on page 224, Dr. Mary Gatta provides an example of a sociologist making just such a contribution. She uses her sociological training to create policy and programs that help working-poor mothers gain education and skills training.

© Elise Roberts

©Arthur Dries/Stone/Getty Images

In Laos, where many people live in grass houses such as this one (top), families do not have access to electronic devices or the Internet. Their homes and their life chances stand in stark contrast to those of the children seen here working on computers—seen as necessary equipment.

The Great Recession   America in Recession

SOCIOLOGISTS IN ACTION:
MARY GATTA

Poor Women, Work, and School—Help to Accomplish It All!

Gender, race, class, age, and educational levels, among other variables, impact the effectiveness of public policies. Yet public officials and policy makers are not often trained to understand the effects of such variables. Working-poor women face a dual challenge: How will they survive economically in the present, and, then, how will they attain the skills that will enable them to be more marketable in the future? Women, and in particular single, poor working mothers, face a system of structural barriers—child care, elder care, irregular work hours, and transportation inequities—that make it hard for them to gain education in traditional classroom settings.

Using a sociological framework, Dr. Mary Gatta examines why so many policies have not succeeded in helping poor working women. With data gathered from posing as a client at workforce development centers, Gatta concludes that working-poor women are caught in a system in which they are not only unable to support themselves, but are also unable to acquire human capital resources to attain self-sufficiency via the traditional mechanisms of education and skills training.

Gatta helps create social policy and programs that take into account the effects of variables such as race and gender on marginalized groups. Specifically, Gatta has helped to create and implement workforce development programs that provide access to education and skills training for single, working-poor mothers in ways that attend to their work and family needs. She has crafted programs that are flexible so that women can receive their education without compromising their family or work responsibilities.

To address education and work issues, Gatta has overseen a new and rapidly expanding system of training single working mothers via the Internet, and she conducts research on workplace flexibility for low-wage workers in a variety of professions. Her work enables single mothers to obtain better jobs and become more active participants in U.S. society by providing them with flexible educational alternatives. The Internet is available around the clock, so women can fit education into their lives, as opposed to fitting their lives into educational structures. In addition, these programs provide computers for the women and their children, helping bridge the digital divide.

Gatta's background in sociology helps her educate policy makers on the gender effects of policy. Her book, *Not Just Getting By: The New Era of Flexible Workforce Development* (2005), coauthored with Kevin McCabe, is an excellent example of her ability to use sociology for the public good. Gatta's use of sociological training in her work helps policy makers to do their jobs more effectively and ensures that gender is taken into account at the policy table.

• •

Mary Gatta is Senior Scholar at Wider Opportunities for Women, a national organization based in Washington, D.C. This excerpt is adapted from Korgen and White's Engaged Sociologist: Connecting the Classroom to the Community *(Sage, 2013).*

Thinking Sociologically

Recalling what you have learned about poverty, how would you develop a plan to attack the problem of poverty within your community or nation, taking into account micro, meso, and macro levels of analysis? Consider job training, changing family values, providing child care for working parents, raising the minimum wage, and other possible strategies. First, describe the root causes of poverty and then suggest solutions.

NATIONAL AND GLOBAL DIGITAL DIVIDE: MACRO-LEVEL STRATIFICATION

Mamadou from Niger and Eric from Ghana answer their iPhones to the sound of chimes from London's Big Ben clock tower and a Bob Marley song. One speaks in Kanuri and French and the other in Twi to friends thousands of miles away. They are the future generation of elites from the Global South, fluent in the languages of several countries, adept in computer software, and at the forefront of their countries in digital technology. Many of their fellow citizens in Niger and Ghana in Africa are not so fortunate. In their Global South subsistence lives and with insufficient education to participate in the changing economy and new technologies, they have little contact with the digital world swirling overhead through satellite connections.

Global economic and political institutions increasingly produce and transmit information through digital technology. Few tools are more important than computers, smartphones, and the Internet. In nearly every salaried and professional position, computer knowledge and ability to navigate the Internet are critical employment skills. The *digital divide* refers to the gap between those with knowledge and access to information technology and those without it. The lines of the divide are drawn by the position of the country in the world, socioeconomic status of citizens, minority group membership, and urban versus rural residence (Mehra, Merkel, and Bishop 2004).

Many individuals in Global South countries have insufficient technology and education to participate in this new economy (Drori 2006; Nakamura 2004). Still, the number of Internet users in the world is increasing rapidly. In 2000 just 250 million people could access the Internet, but by December 2013 nearly 40% of the world's population had used the Internet (Renick 2011; Internet World Stats 2014). As Table 7.4 makes clear, this varies greatly by region of the world. *Internet penetration* refers to the percentage of Internet users in each country.

Researchers have laid out three tiers in the digital divide, based on the following: (1) personal computers per 100 in the population, (2) Internet users per 100 in the population, and (3) Internet bandwidth per person. Using these standards, all developed countries plus some additional countries in the Caribbean, Eastern Europe, and the Middle East are Tier 1—the places with most access. The second tier includes Brazil, Russia, China, and some smaller countries in South America. African nations account for the majority of members in the lowest tier, reflecting the disadvantage of the continent in terms of lack of computers, computer use, and bandwidth ("The International Digital Divide" 2011). However, undersea fiber-optic cables are being laid around Africa to provide faster and more reliable Internet access (African Undersea Cables 2013).

As Internet technology expands, it brings the world to remote villages, opening new horizons and options and changing lifestyles. Some poor countries are transitioning

Table 7.4 World Internet Usage by Region: December 2013

World Regions	Internet Penetration (% population)	% of Total Global Internet Users
Africa	21.3	8.6
Asia	31.7	45.1
Europe	68.6	20.2
Middle East	44.9	3.7
North America	84.9	10.7
Latin America/Caribbean	49.3	10.8
Oceania/Australia	67.5	0.9
WORLD TOTAL	34.3	100.0

Source: Internet World Stats (2014).

World Internet Usage

into the electronic age and making policies that facilitate rapid modernization. They are passing over developmental stages that rich global North countries went through. As an illustration, consider the telephone. Most telephones in the world are cell phones, many using satellite connections. Some countries never did get completely wired for landlines and have chosen to skip that step in development. With the satellite technology now in place, some computer and Internet options are available to them without landlines (Drori 2006). Use of cell phones in poor countries has boomed, giving people access to health care and other services. By 2014, the number of mobile phones in the world was over 7 billion (enough for 96% of the world's population), with 77% of growth from smartphones (Cisco 2014). Africa had the lowest number of subscribers at 63% (Pramis 2013; Whitney 2012).

The growing use of cell phones has helped shrink the digital divide more than anything else. For example, around the world people can buy and sell goods, and send money through their cell phones. The influence is felt from the micro to the macro level, as it improves the lives of individuals, increases business in the area in which they live, and helps connect them to the global economy by allowing individuals to save and invest money in the local and global economies (Langfitt 2011).

Haiti, one of the poorest nations in the world, also provides a great example of the potential positive power of Internet technology. While only 10% of Haitians have bank accounts, 80% have cell phones. They can now use these phones to do banking and as debit cards to make purchases. Aid agencies, after the earthquake of 2010, have also been able to make use of this technology, distributing aid to far-flung refugees via their cell phones (Beaubien 2011; Partners in Prepaid 2012).

Using the Internet to promote savings and investment is one powerful means, just now being tapped, of addressing global poverty and inequality. The potential is enormous, and sociologists in action like Dr. Mary Gatta (described earlier) can help us determine how to make the most effective use of the new technologies. Digital technology is an example of one important force changing the micro- to macro-level global stratification system—a spectrum of people and countries from the rich and elite to the poor and desperate.

We leave this discussion of stratification systems, including class systems, with a partial answer to the question posed at the beginning of this chapter: Why are some people rich and others poor? In the next two chapters, we expand the discussion to include other variables in stratification systems—race, ethnicity, and gender. By the end of these chapters, the answer to the opening question—why some have riches and some have only rags—should be even clearer. Socioeconomic status is important as a measure in any society, but it is not the sole basis for stratification. In the next chapter, we look at the role of race and ethnicity in social inequality.

WHAT HAVE WE LEARNED?

The issue of social stratification calls into question the widely held belief in the fairness of our economic system. By studying this issue, we better understand why some individuals are able to experience prestige (respect) and to control power and wealth at the micro, meso, and macro levels of the social system, while others have little access to those resources. Few social forces affect your personal life at the micro level as much as stratification. That includes the decisions you make about what you wish to do with your life or whom you might marry. Indeed, stratification played a role in why you are reading this book.

KEY POINTS

- *Stratification*—the layering or ranking of people within society—is one of the most important factors shaping the life chances of individuals. This ranking is influenced by micro, meso, and macro forces and resources. (See pp. 196–198.)

- Depending on the theoretical perspective, stratification can be viewed as either functional or destructive for society and its members. (See pp. 198–204.)

- The United States has less social mobility and higher levels of inequality and poverty than most other Global North nations. (See pp. 209–210.)

- For individuals, where they stand in the system of stratification is highly personal, but it is influenced by the way the social system works at the meso and macro levels—due to access to education; the problems created by gender, racial, and ethnic discrimination; and the vitality of the global economy. (See pp. 210.)

- People without much social capital have fewer connections to the meso and macro levels and are less likely to attain power, wealth, and prestige. (See pp. 210–215.)

- Some macro systems stress ascribed status (assigned to one, often at birth, without consideration of one's individual choices, talents, or intelligence). Other systems purport to be open and based on achieved status (depending on one's contributions to the society and one's personal abilities and decisions). (See pp. 215–219.)

- Poverty is a difficult social problem, one that can be costly to a society as a whole. Various solutions at the micro, meso, and macro levels have had mixed results, partially because it is in the interests of those with privilege to have an underclass to do the unpleasant jobs. (See pp. 220–225.)

- Technology is both a contributor to and a possible remedy for inequality, as the digital divide creates problems for the poor, but electronic innovations may create new opportunities in the social structure for networking and connections to the meso and macro levels—even for those in the Global South, the poorer regions of the world. (See pp. 225–226.)

DISCUSSION QUESTIONS

1. Were you surprised to learn that among rich nations, life expectancy in the United States is among the lowest? Explain. What sociological theory best explains this fact? Support your answer.

2. How has the social class of your parents and your upbringing influenced your success in school and your professional aspirations?

3. What is the social status of most of the people with whom you hang out? Why do you think you tend to associate with people from this social status?

4. Describe factors at the (a) micro, (b) meso, and (c) macro levels that impact your ability to move up the social class ladder.

5. How do the forces that have led to the shrinking of the middle class impact your chance of becoming (or remaining) a member of the (a) middle, (b) upper-middle, or (c) upper class after you graduate from college?

6. How can bridging the global digital divide lead to a decrease in inequality across the world? How does your ready access (or lack of access) to a computer and the Internet impact *your* life chances?

CONTRIBUTING TO OUR SOCIAL WORLD: WHAT CAN WE DO?

At the Local Level

- *Volunteer to serve a meal* at an area soup kitchen. Your campus activities office should be able to help you find one in your area and even connect you with a group on campus that regularly volunteers at one.

- *Tip service people in cash.* Housekeepers in hotels and motels, maids, meal servers at restaurants, and food delivery employees may depend on tips to survive. In order to make it more likely that they receive the tips intended for them, be sure to tip in cash, rather than using a credit card.

At the Organizational or Institutional Level

- *Habitat for Humanity* pairs volunteers with current and prospective homeowners in repairing or constructing housing for little or no cost. Habitat projects are under way or planned for many communities in the United States and around the world. See the organization's website at www.habitat.org for more details and to see if you can volunteer for a project in your area.

- Founded in the early 1990s, *AmeriCorps* includes a variety of programs from intensive residential programs to part-time volunteer opportunities in communities across the United States. For more information, go to the organization's website at www.americorps.gov.

At the National and Global Levels

- *The Peace Corps* involves a serious, long-term (two-year) commitment, but most who have done it agree that it is well worth the time and energy. The Peace Corps is an independent agency of the U.S. government, founded in 1961. Volunteers work in foreign countries throughout the world, helping local people improve their economic conditions, health, and education. The Peace Corps website (www.peacecorps.gov) provides information on the history of the organization, volunteer opportunities, and reports of former and present volunteers.

- *Grameen Bank* (www.grameen-info.org or www.grameenfoundation.org), a microcredit organization, was started in Bangladesh by Professor Muhammad Yunus, winner of the 2006 Nobel Peace Prize. It makes small business loans to people who live in impoverished regions of the world and who have no collateral for a loan. Consider doing a local fundraiser with friends for the Grameen Bank or other microcredit organizations, such as FINCA (www.finca.org), Kiva (www.kiva.org), and CARE International (www.care-international.org).

- *Free The Children* is a youth-focused organization whose international programs help free people across the globe from the cycle of poverty by providing clean water, schools, health care, and sanitation. You can learn more about this organization and how you can join its efforts at www.freethechildren.com.

©REUTERS/Danish Ismail

8 Race and Ethnic Group Stratification

Beyond "Us" and "Them"

As human beings, we are all part of "us," but there is a tendency to define those who look or behave differently as "them." Those labeled as "them" are often separated, even dehumanized and mistreated, from "us" and from each other.

MICRO

- **ME (AND MY MINORITY FRIENDS)**

- **LOCAL ORGANIZATIONS AND COMMUNITY**
  Locally, members of ethnic groups may experience exclusion and prejudice.

MESO

- **NATIONAL ORGANIZATIONS, INSTITUTIONS, AND ETHNIC SUBCULTURES**
  Policies in large organizations may discriminate—intentionally or unintentionally.

MACRO

- **SOCIETY**
  National laws or court rulings often set policies that relate to discrimination.

- **GLOBAL COMMUNITY**
  Racial and ethnic hostilities around the world may result in wars, genocide, and "ethnic cleansing."

IN THIS CHAPTER

- What Characterizes Racial and Ethnic Groups?

- Prejudice: Micro-Level Analysis

- Discrimination: Meso-Level Analysis

- Dominant and Minority Group Contact: Macro-Level Analysis

- Policies Governing Minority and Dominant Group Relations

THINK ABOUT IT

Micro: Local Community	Why do people in the local community categorize "others" into racial or ethnic groups?
Meso: National Institutions, Complex Organizations, and Ethnic Groups	How might your education, religion, politics, economics, and health experiences differ depending on your ethnicity?
Macro: National and Global Systems	Why are minority group members in most countries economically poorer than dominant group members? In what ways might ethnicity or race shape international negotiations and global problem solving?

DeBrun was a well-liked African American college student, actively involved in extracurricular activities. Like many college students, he enjoyed both alcohol consumption on weekends and the outrageous things that happened when people were inebriated. However, DeBrun's anger, normally kept in check, tended to surface when he was drunk. One weekend, some racial slurs were thrown around at a party, and when one of the perpetrators pushed DeBrun too far—including a sucker punch—DeBrun exploded in a fury of violence. No one died, but there were some serious injuries—the worst inflicted by the muscular DeBrun—and at one point a weapon was pulled. DeBrun was expelled from the university, and felony charges were leveled against him. Because there had been a weapon—one that did not belong to DeBrun but at one point ended up in his hand—the university president would not consider readmission. The local white prosecutor, who saw a powerfully built young black man with tattoos and dreadlocks, assumed that this campus leader was a "thug" and insisted on the most severe felony charges and penalties.

DeBrun, who had no previous encounters with law enforcement, ended up with a felony record and two years in prison. Because of both state and federal laws, the felony charges meant that he no longer qualified for any federal financial aid. As his family had very few resources, his hopes for a college degree were crushed. As a convicted felon, he would not be able to vote in many states for the rest of his life, his future employment prospects were greatly diminished, and his family's hopes that he would be their first college graduate were crushed. The president of the college was not a bigot, but the professors who knew DeBrun well were convinced that neither his expulsion, nor his arrest, nor his conviction as a serious felon would have occurred had he been white.

This recent incident represents a way that African American males can experience a different United States of America than middle-class white males. The cause is not necessarily personal bigotry by people in power. Differential treatment and harmful actions against minorities can sometimes occur at individual and small-group levels, but is particularly problematic at the meso or institutional level. In any case, life in the United States can be very different for people whose skin tone is dark.

In a recent study, sociologists interviewed black and white schoolchildren whose ages ranged from 11 to 14, and asked them "what would happen if an alien entered their room at night and turned them into black [or white] children." The majority (65%) of the white children and an overwhelming majority (93%) of the black children thought their lives would be different if their race changed (Risman and Banerjee 2013).

What do you think? Would your life change if your race changed? Imagine that you were given the opportunity to choose your own racial and ethnic background. What would you do? Why? How do you think your life would be different if you chose a different racial and ethnic background? In this chapter, we explore racial and ethnic stratification. In doing so, we look at related issues, such as the social construction of race, prejudice, racism, and discrimination. Some are micro-level issues, while others are best addressed at the meso and macro levels.

WHAT CHARACTERIZES RACIAL AND ETHNIC GROUPS?

In this section, we consider the characteristics of racial and ethnic groups and their positions within the stratification system. **Minority groups** *differ from other groups in some characteristics and are subject to less power, fewer privileges, and discrimination.* Like all minority groups, racial and ethnic minority groups have less power than the dominant group in society.

Minority Groups

Several factors characterize minority groups and their relations with dominant groups in society (Dworkin and Dworkin 1999). Minority groups

1. can be distinguished from the group that holds power by physical appearance, dress, language, or religion;

2. are excluded from or denied full participation at the meso level of society in economic, political, educational, religious, health, and recreational institutions;

3. have less access to power and resources within the nation and are evaluated less favorably, based on their characteristics as minority group members;

4. are stereotyped, ridiculed, condemned, or otherwise defamed, allowing dominant group members to justify and not feel guilty about unequal and poor treatment; and

5. develop collective identities to insulate themselves from the un-accepting world; this in turn perpetuates their group identity by creating ethnic or racial enclaves, intragroup marriages, and segregated group institutions such as religious congregations.

● Thinking Sociologically

Based on the preceding list of minority group characteristics, explain how membership in dominant or minority groups influences people's interactions at the micro family level, the meso institutional level, and the macro levels of society.

Minority and majority status can change over time and among societies. For example, throughout England's history, wars and assassinations changed the ruling group from Catholic to Protestant and back several times. Today, in Iraq, Shiite Muslims are dominant, but they were a minority group, and Sunni Muslims were the dominant group, when Saddam Hussein ruled Iraq.

As in the case of Iraq under Saddam Hussein, dominant groups are not always the numerical majority. In the case of South Africa, possession of advanced European

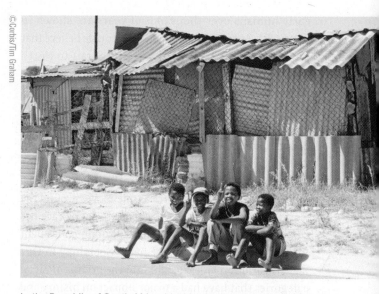

In the Republic of South Africa, blacks are almost three quarters of the population, but they are still considered a minority group because they face racial discrimination and have far less access to economic power and privilege than the "majority" of white South Africans, who comprise 9% of the population.

weapons placed the native African Bantu population under the rule of a relatively small number of White British and Dutch descendants in what became a complex system of planned discrimination called *apartheid*. From 1948 to 1994, each major racial group in South Africa—White, Asian, Colored, and Black—had its own living area, and members carried identification cards showing the "race" to which they belonged. Racial classification and privilege were defined by the laws of the dominant group.

The Concept of Race

Race is a *socially created concept that identifies a group as "different" based on certain biologically inherited physical characteristics.* This allows them to be singled out for dissimilar treatment. Most attempts at racial classifications have been based on combinations of appearance, such as skin color and shade, stature, facial features, hair color and texture, head form, nose shape, eye color and shape, height, and blood or gene type. As you will see, though, racial categories are social constructions that vary over time and place.

The Social Construction of Race. From our earliest origins in Ethiopia and around the Olduvai Gorge in East Africa, about 200,000 years ago, *Homo sapiens* slowly spread around the globe, south through Africa, north to Europe, and across Asia. Original migration patterns of

 Race Relations

early humans over thousands of years are shown in Figure 8.1. As the map shows, most theorists believe that humans crossed Asia and the Bering Strait to North America around 20,000 BCE and continued to populate North and South America (Diamond 1999, 2005). However, continuing archaeological research indicates that indigenous human populations may have reached South America well before the figure indicates (Mann 2005). The point is that the mixing of peoples over the centuries has left few if any genetically isolated people, only gradations in appearance as one moves around the world. Thus, the way societies choose to define race has come about largely through what is culturally convenient for the dominant group. The next "Sociology in Our Social World" provides insight into the origins of racial categories that have had a major impact on history and form the basis for many conflicts today.

In 1978, the United Nations, concerned about racial conflicts and discrimination based on scientifically inaccurate beliefs, issued a "Declaration on Race and Racial Prejudice" (UNESCO 1969, 1978) prepared by a group of eminent scientists from around the world. This and similar statements by scientific groups point out the harmful effects of racist arguments, doctrines, and policies. The conclusion of their document upheld that (a) all people are born free and equal both in dignity and in rights, (b) racial prejudice impedes personal development, (c) conflicts (based on race) cost nations money and resources, and (d) racism foments international conflict. Racist doctrines lack any scientific basis, as all people belong to the same species and have descended from the same origin. In summary, problems arising from race relations are social, not biological, in origin. Differential treatments of groups based on "race" falsely claim a scientific basis for classifying humans.

Thinking Sociologically

How would you describe the other people in your sociology class? Do you use racial terms for everyone? Why or why not? How does your own racial background influence how much you notice the racial characteristics of others? Why?

Symbolic Interactionist Analysis of the Social Construction of Race. Why are sociologists concerned about a concept that has little scientific accuracy and is ill defined? The answer is its *social significance*. The social reality is that people's group membership can influence how they are treated by others and how they view themselves. Remember the *looking-glass self* concept—we see ourselves based on how we think others perceive us. Our self-concept can be greatly affected by whether or not we see ourselves as members of a dominant or minority racial group.

FIGURE 8.1 The Spread of Humans Around the World

This map shows the historical spread of humans around the globe and the approximate time periods of the movements.

sociology in our social world

Historical Attempts to Define Race

Throughout history, political and religious leaders, philosophers, and even scientists have struggled with the meaning and significance of race. The first systematic classification of all living phenomena was published in 1735 by Carl von Linné (Linnaeus). His hierarchy of species was actually quite complex, including monkeys, elephants, and angels. His work was based on the study of fossil remains of various species, implying evolution of the species over time. Then, in 1758, he published *Systema Naturae*, in which he suggested four human types: Americanus (Native Americans), Asiaticus, Africanus, and Europeanus (Cashmore and Troyna 1990). Other scientists proposed other divisions. Johann Blumenbach was the first to use the word *race* in his 1775 classification system: Caucasian, Mongolian, Ethiopian, American, and Malay.

By the 19th century, race began to take on a biological meaning, and many began to use it to theorize about inherent inequalities among races and to justify slavery and colonialism. For example, John Calhoun, a U.S. Senator from South Carolina, declared in 1840 that Africans were incapable of self-care and would become mentally ill under the "burden of freedom." Therefore, "it is a mercy to him to give him the guardianship and protection" of slavery (Deutsch 1944; Feagin 2012:71). During this same period, Joseph Arthur—also known as Comte de Gobineau (1816–1882)—questioned why once great societies had declined and fallen. He argued that each race has specific characteristics, and he attributed the demise of societies to the mixing of the white race with other (inferior) races. His book *Essay on Inequality of the Human Races*, published in 1853–1855, earned him the title "father of modern racism."

A major event in theories of race was the publication of Charles Darwin's *On the Origin of Species* ([1859] 1909). Among his many ideas was that human races *might* represent the stages or branches of a tree of evolution. This idea implied that those groups of humans who were biologically best suited to the environment would survive. He argued that "natural selection," or "survival of the fittest," was true of all races in the human species, not of individuals within a species. From Darwin's ideas emerged the concepts of *survival of the fittest* and *ever-improving races*.

These two late-19th-century concepts were taken out of context and became the foundation for a number of theories of superior races. For instance, in 1899, the Brit-turned-German Houston Stewart Chamberlain ([1899] 1911) published an aristocratic, anti-Semitic work in which he argued that northern and western European populations, Teutonic in particular, were superior. He argued for racial purity, a theme the Nazis of the 1930s and 1940s adopted. Gustaf Kossinna introduced the idea of *Volk* in his writings, claiming a commonality of traits among Germans that, he felt, qualified the German people to become the "ruling elite" (Cashmore and Troyna 1990).

In the United States, a book by lawyer and eugenicist Madison Grant—*The Passing of the*

(Continued)

Slavery

(Continued)

Great Race—was published in 1916 claiming the superiority of the "Nordic race." Grant proposed a eugenics or breeding program to "save" this "endangered" racial strain. The argument was later discredited by the horrific Nazi program of supposed racial purity.

Mein Kampf (1939) was Adolf Hitler's contribution to the concept of a superior race. In it, he conceptualized two races, the Aryans and Others. He focused attention on several groups, in particular the Jews, which he claimed caused the economic and social problems of Germany. What followed in the name of German purity was the extermination of millions of Jews, Poles, Roma, Catholics, gay men, and other groups and individuals who were deemed "less human" or who opposed the Nazis. The extent to which Hitler succeeded exemplifies what can happen when one group needs to feel superior to others, blames other groups for its shortcomings, and has the power to act against those minorities.

Looking through history, one can see many more examples of how racial categorizations have been misused across time and societies. For example, in the United States, Irish and Italians were once seen as distinct races that were clearly inferior to the white race. These examples help reveal that racial categories are social, rather than biological, constructions.

Strangely, we might be seen as part of a dominant group in one society and a minority group in another. For example, imagine it is 1970 and you have white parents, three white grandparents, and one black grandparent. Imagine, too, that no one would guess by your appearance that you had an ancestor who was not white. In South Africa, you would be treated as "Colored" (between black and white). On the other hand, in many U.S. states, you would be defined as black. If you were in Brazil, you would be perceived as white (Kottack 2010). In 1977, the U.S. Office of Management and Budget issued a directive to ensure consistent ethnic and racial categories for both statistical and administrative goals. Federal programs directed toward specific racial and ethnic groups use these categories. Many very different groups have been combined under the five government racial and ethnic categories (American Indian or Alaska Native, Asian or Pacific Islander, black, Hispanic, and white. Hispanic/Latino Americans are an ethnic group and can be of any race). For example, in North America, those racially classified as Native American or Alaska Native use 600 independent tribal nation names to define themselves, including the Ojibwa (Chippewa), the Dineh (the Navajo), the Lakota (the Sioux), and many others. Most consider themselves very different from other "Native American" groups. Some even fought against one another in past wars. Likewise, in the U.S. Census, Koreans, Filipinos, Chinese, Japanese, and Malaysians are all identified as *Asian Americans,* but they come from very different cultures (including some that were mortal enemies). Likewise, people from Brazil, Mexico, and Cuba and many other nations are grouped together in an ethnic category called *Hispanics* or *Latinos.*

Before civil rights laws were passed in the United States in the 1960s, a number of states had laws that spelled out differential treatment for racial groups. These were commonly referred to as Jim Crow laws. States in the South passed laws defining who was African American or Native American. In many cases, it was difficult to determine to which category an individual belonged. For instance, African Americans in Georgia were defined as people with any ascertainable trace of "Negro" blood in their veins. In Missouri, 1/8 or more "Negro" blood was the standard, whereas in Louisiana, 1/32 Negro blood defined one as black. Differential treatment was spelled out in other states as well. In Texas, for example, the father's race determined the race of the child. Federal law now prohibits discrimination on the basis of "racial" classifications, and most state laws that are explicitly racial have been challenged and dropped, but race remains a *social concept*!

The Continuing Significance of Race. The civil rights legislation of the 1960s that prohibited racial discrimination in voting, housing, and employment has helped diminish discrimination. Unfortunately, though, racial discrimination still exists, and the combination of the impact of past and present discrimination has led to disparities in wealth and income among black, Hispanic, and white Americans. As Tables 8.1 and 8.2 make clear, income levels for African Americans, Hispanics, and whites, even when controlling for education level, are still far apart. A clear racial economic hierarchy exists with white Americans on the top and other racial groups below. Differences in *wealth* (one's income, property, and total assets) by race are even more stark. For every $1 of wealth a white person has, Hispanic and black persons have just 7 and 6 cents, respectively. So whites have roughly 20 times the wealth of blacks and Hispanics (Tippett et al. 2014).

As we described in Chapter 7, education is one of the key means of social mobility (despite the fact that even well-educated racial minorities make less than whites). While 52.4% of Asian Americans and 30.3% of white Americans 25 and older have a college education, only 19.8% of black and 13.9% of Hispanic Americans have college degrees (U.S. Census Bureau 2012c). This is clearly an area that must be addressed if we want to reduce racial economic inequality. Although explicit racial bias has decreased at the micro (interpersonal) level, it is still a significant determinant in the lives of African Americans, especially those in the lower class.

 Thinking Sociologically

Were you aware of the race-based disparities in income and wealth? Why do you think income among races differs, even when controlling for education?

Table 8.1   Race/Ethnicity and Family Income

	White	Black	Hispanic	Median in United States
Median family annual income	$62,545	$38,409	$39,730	$60.088
Percentage under $15,000	6.6	23.9	17.0	8.7
Percentage above $100,000	20.4	8.2	8.27	19.1

Source: U.S. Census Bureau (2012b).

Table 8.2   Income by Educational Level and Race/Ethnicity

Education	White	Black	Hispanic
Not a high school graduate	$20,457	$18,936	$19,816
High school graduate	31,429	26,970	25,998
Some college, no degree	33,119	29,129	29,836
College graduate	57,762	47,799	49,017
Master's degree	73,771	60,067	71,322
Professional degree	127,942	102,328	79,228

Source: U.S. Census Bureau (2012d).

Ethnic Groups

Ethnic groups *are based on cultural factors: language, religion, dress, foods, customs, beliefs, values, norms, a shared group identity or feeling, and sometimes loyalty to a homeland, monarch, or religious leader.* Members are grouped together because they share a common cultural heritage, often connected with a national or geographical identity. There can be many ethnic groups under one racial category (e.g., black Americans include African immigrants, West Indian immigrants, African Americans, and so on, and Asians include Japanese, Chinese, Indians, and others). Visits to ethnic enclaves in large cities in the United States give a picture of ethnicity. Indian, Chinese, and Dominican neighborhoods may have non-English street signs and newspapers, ethnic restaurants, culture-specific houses of worship, and clothing styles that reflect the ethnic subculture.

How is ethnicity constructed or defined? As noted earlier, the U.S. government has combined many different ethnic and racial groups into singular racial and ethnic categories. When government aid is tied to such categories, people must identify as such in order to receive funds. When federal funds for social services were made available to Asian Americans or American Indians, these diverse people began to think of themselves as part of a larger grouping for political purposes (Esperitu 1992). The federal government essentially created an ethnic group by

Ethnic enclaves can foster a strong sense of local community, hosting festivals from the old country and helping members develop networks in the new country. This photo depicts a street in San Francisco's Chinatown.

naming and providing funding to that group. If people wanted services (health care, legal rights, and so forth), they had to become a part of a particular group—such as "Asian Americans." This process of merging many ethnic groups into one broader category—called *panethnicity*—emphasizes that ethnic and racial identity are socially shaped and created.

Census 2010 data show the ethnic ancestry of millions of Americans and their distribution across the United States. Germans make up the largest group at almost 50 million, followed by African Americans at 41 million, Irish at 36 million, Mexican at 32 million, and English at

30 million. Twenty million claim "American" as their ancestry. American Indian or Alaska Natives, the original Americans, make up about 5 million people (O'Connor, Lubin, and Spector 2013).

Figure 8.2 shows where each ethnic group, by county, has the largest concentration, though this does not necessarily mean the group makes up more than 50% of the population of that county.

Biracial and Multiracial Populations: Immigration, Intermarriage, and Personal Identification

The patterns shown in Figure 8.1 illustrate that "push" factors drive people from some countries and "pull" factors draw them to other countries. The most common push-pull factors today are job opportunities, the desire for security, individual liberties, and availability of medical and educational opportunities. The target countries of migrants are most often in North America, Australia, or Western Europe, and the highest emigration rates are from Africa, Eastern Europe, Central Asia, and South and Central America.

The United States was once considered to have a two-tiered racial hierarchy, black and white (which disregarded the Native American population). However, immigration into the United States from every continent has led to a more diverse population, with 13% of the current U.S. population born elsewhere (Grieco et al. 2012). With new immigration, increasing rates of intermarriage, and many more individuals claiming multiracial identification, the picture is much more complex today, and the color lines have been redrawn (DaCosta 2007; Lee and Bean 2004, 2007). In 2012, almost 1 in 5 Americans under 18 were identified with two or more racial groups (Alpert 2013). Figure 8.3 illustrates the current ethnic group distribution and projections for the future for the United States.

Some scholars such as Eduardo Bonilla-Silva say that the United States is moving from a black-white racial hierarchy to a three-tiered racial hierarchy with "*Whites at the top* ('traditional' whites, new 'white' immigrants; and, in the near future, assimilated Latinos, some multiracials [light-skinned ones], and individual members of other groups [some Asian Americans, etc.])" (Bonilla-Silva and Embrick 2005:33).

Next will come a middle group consisting of "*honorary Whites* (most light-skinned Latino Americans, Japanese Americans, Korean Americans, Asian Indian [Americans], Chinese Americans, the bulk of multiracials . . . and most Middle Eastern Americans" (Bonilla-Silva and

FIGURE 8.2 Ancestry With Largest Population in Each County, 2010

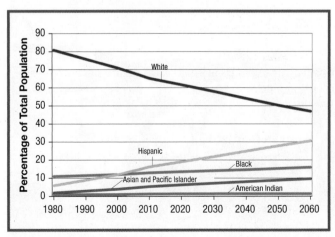

Source: U.S. Census Bureau.

Embrick 2005:33). The bottom group, the *"collective Black,"* will contain black Americans, dark-skinned Latino Americans, Vietnamese Americans, Cambodian Americans, Laotian Americans, and maybe Filipino Americans. The lines are shifting, but the racial hierarchy remains (Bonilla-Silva 2009; Bonilla-Silva and Embrick 2005).

 Thinking Sociologically

Identify one dominant and one minority group in your community or on campus. Where does each group fit into the stratification system in the United States? How are the life chances of individuals in these groups influenced by factors beyond their control?

PREJUDICE: MICRO-LEVEL ANALYSIS

Have you ever found yourself in a situation in which you were viewed as different, strange, or undesirable? Perhaps you have felt the sting of rejection, not based on judgment of you as a person but solely because of the ethnic or racial

FIGURE 8.3 Percent of the Population, by Race and Hispanic Origin: 1980–2060

Source: U.S. Census Bureau (2014).

group into which you were born. Then again, you may have been insulated from this type of rejection if you grew up in a homogeneous community or in a privileged group.

Where and when we are born can determine how we are treated, our life chances, and many of our experiences and attitudes.

Prejudice influences dominant-minority group relations. **Prejudice** refers to *attitudes of prejudgment about a group, usually negative and not based on facts.* Prejudiced individuals lump together people with certain characteristics without considering individual differences. Although prejudice can refer to positive attitudes and exaggerations (e.g., all Asians are good at math), in this chapter, we concentrate on the negative aspects of prejudice. We also focus on the negative uses of the concept of *stereotyping*, when prejudiced individuals use distorted, oversimplified, or exaggerated ideas to categorize a group of people and attribute personal qualities to them. While prejudice and stereotypes can be stimulated by events such as conflicts at the institutional level and war at the societal level, attitudes are held by individuals and can be best understood as a micro-level phenomenon.

Prejudice refers to attitudes rather than actions. **Discrimination**, on the other hand, is *differential treatment and harmful actions against minorities.* These actions at the micro level might include refusal to sell someone a house because of the religion, race, or ethnicity of the buyer or not hiring someone because of her or his minority status (Feagin and Feagin 2010). Discrimination in

the legal system, such as laws that deny opportunities or resources to members of a particular group, operates largely at the meso or macro level, discussed later in this chapter.

The Nature of Prejudice

Prejudice is an understandable response of humans to their social environment. To survive, every social group or unit—a sorority, a sports team, a civic club, or a nation—needs to mobilize the loyalty of its members. Each organization needs to convince people to voluntarily commit energy, skills, time, and resources so the organization can meet its needs. As people commit themselves to a group, they invest a portion of themselves and feel loyalty to the group. This loyalty leads to a preference for the group and attempts to distinguish it from others. It is important to recognize prejudice, though, and how it can foster discriminatory actions.

In wartime, the enemy may be depicted in films or other media as villains. During World War II, American films often showed negative stereotypes of Japanese and German people. These negative images helped lead to the decision to intern more than 110,000 Japanese Americans, the majority of whom were U.S. citizens, in detention camps following the bombing of Pearl Harbor.

Similar issues and stereotypes have arisen for Muslim Americans in recent years. For example, hate crimes against Muslims spiked after the attacks on the New York World Trade Center on September 11, 2001, and the Boston Marathon bombing on April 15, 2013 (Potok 2013c). Sociologist Saher Selod examines some of the results of anti-Muslim sentiment after 9/11 in the next "Sociology in Our Social World."

Explaining Racial Discrimination at the Micro Level. Why do individuals commit acts of racial discrimination? Why would people be so angry at racial minorities that they would act to harm them? The following is one theory that has attempted to explain acts of racial discrimination.

Frustration-aggression theory. In Greensboro, North Carolina, in 1978, a group of civil rights activists and African American adults and children listened as a guitarist sang freedom songs. A nine-car cavalcade of white Ku Klux Klan (KKK) and American Nazi Party members arrived. The intruders unloaded weapons from the backs of their cars, approached the rally, and opened fire for 88 seconds. They left as calmly as they had arrived. Four White men and a Black woman were dead (Greensboro Justice Fund 2005).

After Japan bombed Pearl Harbor on December 7, 1941, more than 110,000 Japanese Americans, including those pictured here, were forcibly removed from many western states and sent to relocation camps.

sociology in our social world

Anti-Muslim Sentiments in the United States

By Saher Selod

On September 11, 2001, the United States experienced the largest terrorist attack on U.S. soil. Four airplanes were hijacked by terrorists. Two of the airplanes were flown into the World Trade Center, causing the two buildings to collapse. Another airplane crashed into the Pentagon, and the fourth plane crashed due to a revolt by the passengers on board. The attacks claimed the lives of close to 3,000 Americans. The terrorists were Muslims from Saudi Arabia, United Arab Emirates, and Egypt. These horrific events changed the lives of all Americans, including Muslim Americans and immigrants.

A few sociologists studied the impact 9/11 had on Muslims living in the United States (Bakalian and Bozorgmehr 2009; Cainkar 2009; Peek 2011). Some of the findings revealed that Muslims have become targets for antiterrorist laws and policies that were a part of a government-led campaign known as the "War on Terror" (Cainkar 2009). For example, a little over a month after the attacks, the USA PATRIOT (Uniting and Strengthening America by Providing Appropriate Tools Required to Intercept and Obstruct Terrorism) Act was signed into law. This 300-page document restricted the civil liberties of Muslims and any other American who could be connected to terrorism. The document loosely defined terrorism, justifying the surveillance of Muslims due to an inaccurate association of Islam with terrorism. As a result, mass deportations of

Muslim immigrants for minor infractions of their visas were hidden from the public through the application of the Patriot Act. There was also an increase in visitations of Muslims by the Federal Bureau of Investigation (FBI) following 9/11.

Another policy passed after 9/11 was the National Security Entry-Exit Registration System, initiated in September 2002 by the Immigration and Naturalization Service. This law required noncitizen men over the age of 16 from 25 countries (of which 24 were Muslim countries) to register with the government. Muslim men were forced to submit fingerprints and had their photos taken as if they were potential criminals. One of the consequences of these laws and policies is they created an environment where innocent people were treated as if they were guilty due to their shared religious identity with the perpetrators of the terrorist attacks. Since 9/11, over a thousand Muslims (mostly noncitizens) have been detained even though no connection to terrorism was determined. Furthermore, these policies have encouraged the distrust of Muslims.

Muslims living in the United States have reported a rise in prejudice and discrimination. Lori Peek's study, *Behind the Backlash: Muslim Americans After 9/11,* highlights the backlash Muslims living in New York City and Colorado experienced in the few weeks after 9/11. Although it has been over 10 years since the terrorist attacks, anti-Muslim sentiments remain strong today. According to a Gallup report, 43% of Americans admitted to feeling some prejudice toward Muslims, and 31%

(Continued)

Muslim Americans

(Continued)

of Americans view Islam unfavorably (Gallup 2009). These rising anti-Muslim sentiments have had a direct impact on the everyday life of the Muslim population. Statistics compiled by the FBI reveal hate crimes against Muslims increased by almost 50% from 2009 to 2010. In August 2012, a mosque in Joplin, Missouri, was burned to the ground by an arsonist. As a consequence of government policies targeting Muslims and the perpetuation of stereotypes and myths that Muslims are a threat to national security and American cultural values, Muslims are living with a new racialized identity.

Organizations such as the Council on American-Islamic Relations (CAIR) strive to counter stereotypes about Muslims and "enhance the understanding of Islam, encourage dialogue, protect civil liberties, empower American Muslims, and build coalitions that promote justice and mutual understanding" (CAIR 2014). Working with other organizations, like the American Civil Liberties Union, they fight bigotry and discrimination against Muslims living in the United States.

• •

Saher Selod is an assistant professor of sociology at Simmons College. Her areas of research are race and ethnicity and sociology of religion—especially the Muslim experience in the United States.

According to *frustration-aggression theory*, many of the perpetrators of this and other heinous acts felt angry and frustrated because they could not achieve their work or other goals. Frustration-aggression theory focuses largely on poorly adjusted people who express their frustration through aggressive attacks on others.

When they cannot take out their aggression on its source and turn it on innocent victims, they are *scapegoating*. The word *scapegoat* comes from the Bible, Leviticus 16:5–22. Once a year, a goat (which was obviously innocent) was laden with parchments on which people had written their sins. The goat was then sent out to the desert to die. This was part of a ritual of purification, and the creature took the blame for the sins committed by the people. Scapegoating occurs when a minority group is blamed for the failures of others. It is often difficult to look at oneself to seek reasons for failure but easy to transfer the blame for one's failure to others. Individuals who feel they are failures in their jobs or other aspects of their lives may turn the blame toward minority groups. From within such a prejudiced mind-set, violence toward the out-group may seem acceptable. The key point is that hate groups evolve from like-minded individuals, often because of prejudice and frustration (see Figure 8.4).

Forms of Racial Prejudice

A bigot is someone who blindly insists that certain other people are so different that they are inferior—even, perhaps, less than human. Hate groups in the United States, Europe, and many other countries justify themselves on the basis of such bigoted thinking. They loudly proclaim that those outside their racial or ethnic group deserve to face discrimination.

Many other people are not bigoted but are simply oblivious to racial inequality and the hidden privileges that whites experience in U.S. society. They do not want to hear about the realities of racial inequality. In fact, they maintain that race no longer matters. A racial ideology that grew out of opposition to affirmative action programs in the 1980s, the *color-blind ideology*, is now the dominant racial ideology in the United States (Bonilla-Silva 2009; Brunsma 2006; Korgen and Brunsma 2012). Promoters of the color-blind ideology maintain that we should all act as though we are "color-blind" when it comes to race and avoid the topic in personal interactions.

Those who have a color-blind perspective on race do not notice the "invisible privileges" of whites in U.S. society (Rothenberg 2011). Consider the following privileges that most people who are part of the dominant group take for granted (McIntosh 2002:97–101):

- I can avoid spending time with people who mistrust people of my color.
- I can protect my children most of the time from people who might not like them.

FIGURE 8.4 **Active Hate Groups in 2013**

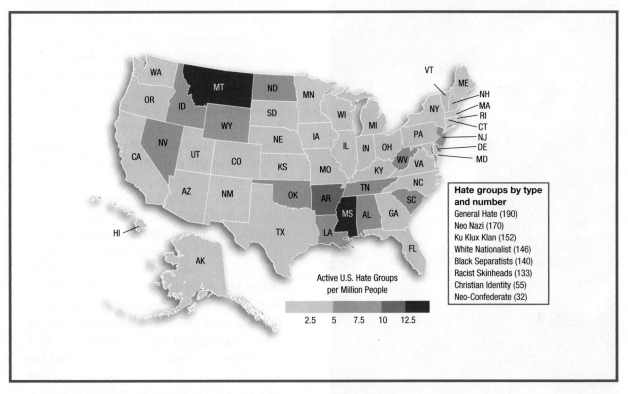

Hate groups by type and number
General Hate (190)
Neo Nazi (170)
Ku Klux Klan (152)
White Nationalist (146)
Black Separatists (140)
Racist Skinheads (133)
Christian Identity (55)
Neo-Confederate (32)

Active U.S. Hate Groups
per Million People

2.5   5   7.5   10   12.5

Source: Active Hate Groups in the U.S., 2012 is reprinted with permission and originally appeared in *The Atlantic – The Geography of Hate* by Richard Florida, May 2011. Map by Zara Matheson, Martin Prosperity Institute. Data source: http://www.splcenter.org/get-information/hate-map.

- I can criticize our government and talk about how I fear its policies and behavior without being seen as a cultural "outsider" or not patriotic.
- I can easily buy posters, postcards, picture books, greeting cards, dolls, toys, and children's magazines featuring people of my race.
- I can arrange my activities so that I will never have to experience feelings of rejection owing to my race.

 Thinking Sociologically

What is your reaction to this list? How does your own racial and ethnic background influence your reaction?

In an award-winning book, white sociologist Joe Feagin (2012) has analyzed how the "white frame"—the lens through which whites view history and understand everyday life—shapes what white people see. He documents the many ways that frame or lens is so much a part of the socialization process that it is like water to fish—it is the unnoticed, unconscious environment in which we live. Unfortunately this frame involves assumptions that reinforce images, ideologies, interpretations, narratives, and emotional triggers that sustain white privilege. It in fact blinds white people to subtle realities so that it is entirely impossible for them to actually be color-blind (Feagin 2012). Furthermore, for many people, their blackness or brownness is so integral to their identity that to say one is "color-blind" is to fail to see the whole person. They feel they are being made invisible and forced to be part of the mainstream culture—to be assimilated (Dalton 2012; Dyer 2012; Feagin 2012).

The color-blind perspective on race allows discrimination hidden within the society's institutions to remain in place. Advocates of the color-blind racial ideology reject blatant bigotry as crude and ignorant, but fail to recognize that their own actions may perpetuate inequalities at the institutional or meso level, discussed below. Racism is *any meso-level institutional arrangement that favors one racial group over another; this favoritism may result in intentional or unintentional consequences for minority groups.* Note that many people without social science training see racism as just a micro-level issue—one involving individual actions or attitudes—whereas social scientists recognize racial discrimination in meso-level organizations and macro-level policies or laws as the very core of the problem of racism (Bonilla-Silva 2003).

A neo-Nazi protester makes a white power salute at the opening ceremony for the Illinois Holocaust Museum and Education Center in Skokie, Illinois, in 2009. The group of protesters chanted epithets expressing their hatred of Jews and other minority groups.

Although frustration-aggression theory can shed light on the most extreme cases of individual or small-group prejudice and racism, there is much this theory does not explain. It says little about the everyday hostility and reinforcement of prejudice that most of us experience or engage in, and fails to deal with discrimination embedded in institutions.

DISCRIMINATION: MESO-LEVEL ANALYSIS

Dear Teacher,

I would like to introduce you to my son, Wind-Wolf. He is probably what you would consider a typical Indian kid. He was born and raised on the reservation. He has black hair, dark brown eyes,

and an olive complexion, and, like so many Indian children his age, he is shy and quiet in the classroom. He is 5 years old, in kindergarten, and I can't understand why you have already labeled him a "slow learner." He has already been through quite an education compared with his peers in Western society. He was bonded to his mother and to the Mother Earth in a traditional native childbirth ceremony. And he has been continuously cared for by his mother, father, sisters, cousins, aunts, uncles, grandparents, and extended tribal family since this ceremony. . . .

Wind-Wolf was strapped (in his baby basket like a turtle shell) snugly with a deliberate restriction on his arms and legs. Although Western society may argue this hinders motor-skill development and abstract reasoning, we believe it forces the child to first develop his intuitive faculties, rational intellect, symbolic thinking, and five senses. Wind-Wolf was with his mother constantly, closely bonded physically, as she carried him on her back or held him while breast-feeding. She carried him everywhere she went, and every night he slept with both parents. Because of this, Wind-Wolf's educational setting was not only a "secure" environment, but it was also very colorful, complicated, sensitive, and diverse.

As he grew older, Wind-Wolf began to crawl out of the baby basket, develop his motor skills, and explore the world around him. When frightened or sleepy, he could always return to the basket, as a turtle withdraws into its shell. Such an inward journey allows one to reflect in privacy on what he has learned and to carry the new knowledge deeply into the unconscious and the soul. Shapes, sizes, colors, texture, sound, smell, feeling, taste, and the learning process are therefore functionally integrated—the physical and spiritual, matter and energy, and conscious and unconscious, individual and social.

It takes a long time to absorb and reflect on these kinds of experiences, so maybe that is why you think my Indian child is a slow learner. His aunts and grandmothers taught him to count and to know his numbers while they sorted materials for making abstract designs in native baskets. And he was taught to learn mathematics by counting the sticks we use in our traditional native hand game. So he may be slow in grasping the methods and tools you use in your classroom, ones quite familiar to his white peers, but I hope you will be patient with him. It takes time to adjust to a new cultural system and learn new things. He is not culturally "disadvantaged," but he is culturally different. (Lake 1990:48–53)

This letter expresses the frustration of a father who sees his son being labeled and discriminated against by the school system without being given a chance. *Discrimination,* introduced earlier in this chapter, refers to differential treatment and harmful actions taken against members of a minority group. It can occur at individual and small-group levels but is particularly problematic at the organizational and institutional levels—the meso level of analysis.

 Thinking Sociologically

How might schools unintentionally misunderstand Wind-Wolf and other minority children in ways that have negative consequences for children's success?

Institutional racial discrimination is *any meso-level institutional arrangement that favors one racial group over another; this favoritism may result in intentional or unintentional consequences for minority group*s (Farley 2011). This form of discrimination results from the normal or routine part of the way an organization operates that systemically disadvantages members of one group. It can include intentional actions, such as laws restricting minorities, as well as unintentional actions, that have consequences restricting minorities. Jim Crow laws, passed in the late 1800s in the United States, and laws that barred Jews in Germany from living, working, or investing in certain places are examples of intentional discrimination embedded in organizations.

Often, though, institutional racial discrimination is done quite unintentionally. For example, in some states, local funding of schools leads to schools with racial minorities receiving fewer funds than most predominantly white schools. This type of funding policy can be supported by nonracists who simply want local control over schools. Whether intended or not, though, such a policy benefits a particular race at the expense of others. As you can see, racial discrimination does not have to be the result of a nasty or mean-spirited person bullying others; it often operates independently of prejudice (Bonilla-Silva 2003; Rothenberg 2011).

Side-effect discrimination and past-in-present discrimination are two other types of unintentional institutional discrimination (Feagin and Feagin 1986; Rydgren 2004). **Side-effect** discrimination *refers to practices in one institutional area that have a negative impact because they are linked to practices in another institutional area; because institutions are interdependent, discrimination in one results in unintentional discrimination in others.* Figure 8.5 illustrates this idea. Each institution uses information from the other institutions to make decisions. So, discrimination in one can lead to discrimination in others.

Side-effect discrimination occurs when discrimination in the criminal justice system leads to discrimination in the employment sector. For example, in an interview conducted by one of the authors, a probation officer in a moderate-sized city in Ohio said that he had never seen an African American in his county get a not-guilty verdict and that he was not sure it was possible. He had known of cases in which minorities had pled guilty to a lesser charge even though they were innocent because they did not think they could receive a fair verdict in that city. When people apply for jobs, however, they are required to report the conviction on the application form. Employers discriminate against applicants with a criminal record, whether or not the applicant was guilty of the crime. The side-effect discrimination is *unintentional discrimination*; the criminal

FIGURE 8.5 Side-Effect Discrimination

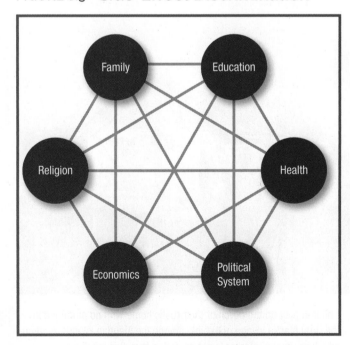

Racism in Schools

justice system has reached an unjust verdict, and the potential employer is swayed unfairly.

A second example of side-effect discrimination shows that the Internet also plays a role in institutionalized discrimination and privilege. For example, in Alaska, 15.2% of the population is Native, but Natives hold only 5% of state jobs, and 27.3% of Native men and 16% of Native women are unemployed (AAANativeArts 2011; U.S. Census Bureau 2011). Consider that the State of Alaska uses the Internet as its primary means of advertising and accepting applications for state jobs (State of Alaska 2006). In the early 2000s, Internet access was unavailable in the 164 predominantly Native villages in Alaska—a state so large and spread out that it is 2.2 times the size of Texas and has only 1.2 people per square mile (Denali Commission 2001; Hudson 2011). Although efforts have been made in recent years to expand Internet access, Alaska remains far behind other states in communications access, with less than half of Alaskan villages having Internet facility in 2012 (Hudson 2011, 2012). Other options for application for state jobs include requesting applications by mail, but a person must first know about the opening. The usefulness of this process is limited, however, by the reliability and speed of mail service to remote villages and the often short application periods for state jobs. State officials may not intentionally try to prevent Aleuts, Inupiats, Athabaskans, or other Alaska Natives from gaining access to state jobs, but the effect can be institutionalized discrimination. Here, Internet access plays a role in the participation of minorities in the social world (Nakamura 2004).

Children play on the porch of their rustic home with no plumbing in the rural Alaska village of Akhiok, among the Aleutian Islands. Finding jobs through the Internet is not an option from this location.

The point is that whites, especially affluent whites, benefit from privileges not available to low-income minorities. The privileged members may not purposely disadvantage others and may not be prejudiced, but the playing field is not level. The discrimination may be completely unintentional (Rothenberg 2011).

 Thinking Sociologically

Imagine you run a business that is hiring people. You routinely do a criminal background check on applicants. You have just read this chapter and realize that some of that information may be a source of unintended side-effect discrimination for a minority group member. What will you do now? Why?

Past-in-present discrimination *refers to practices from the past that may no longer be allowed but that continue to have consequences for people in the present* (Feagin and Feagin 1986; Verbeek and Penninx 2009). Examples of this abound if you dig deep enough. For example, in Mississippi, during the 1950s, state expenditures to educate a white child averaged $147 per pupil, whereas the average was $34 per black pupil in segregated schools (Luhman and Gilman 1980). Such blatant segregation and inequality in use of tax dollars is no longer legal. This may seem like ancient history, yet some African Americans who were in school in the 1950s and 1960s are receiving low Social Security checks because their earning power was diminished due to their poor schooling. Today, they cannot help pay for their grandchildren to go to college. To those who received a substandard education and did not have an opportunity for college, this is not ancient history; it affects their opportunities today.

Another example can be seen in the economic inequality between whites and blacks. The great disparity in wealth between white and black Americans relates to the legal discrimination many generations of black Americans experienced that stymied efforts to amass and pass down wealth to future generations. Events from the past continue to echo into our current times, creating barriers for some citizens and clear paths for others. The next "Engaging Sociology" feature explores how discrimination can occur at different levels and in intentional or unintentional ways.

In the United States, we have a president who had both a black and a white parent. It is also true, though, as Table 8.3 indicates, that no senators are black and only two are Hispanic (out of 100) in 2014.

We have also seen in Table 8.2 that college-educated African Americans earn $10,000 per year less than white

ENGAGING SOCIOLOGY

Using and Relating Key Concepts

Figure 8.6 indicates the levels at which discrimination can operate and how such acts can be intended or unintended.

FIGURE 8.6 Understanding Key Concepts

	Micro Level	Meso and Macro Level
Conscious and Intended	*Prejudice and individual* acts of direct discrimination	*Direct Institutional Discrimination*
Unconscious and Unintended	*Color-Blind* perspective	*Indirect Institutional Discrimination* Side-effect discrimination Past-in-present discrimination

Engaging With Sociology

1. Define and give an example of the term or concept in each box above.

2. Identify ways that each of these elements of intergroup conflict might foster the others.

3. Describe how you might take steps to counter each of the various types of discrimination.

Table 8.3 Representation in the U.S. Congress, 2013–2014

	Native American	Asian	Black	Hispanic
Senate	0	2 **(2%)**	0 **(0%)**	2 **(2%)**
House	1 **(0.2%)**	7 **(1.6%)**	44 **(10%)**	25 **(5.7%)**
% of Population	**0.9%**	**4.8%**	**12.6%**	**16.3%**

Source: ThisNation.com (2014).

college graduates. Whites with a professional degree earn, on average, $128,000 per year ($25,000 per year more than blacks with the same degree), while Hispanics with the same degree earn, on average, $79,000 (U.S. Census Bureau 2012a). This means that over a 40-year career, whites could earn $1 million more than blacks and nearly $2 million more than Hispanics with the same credentials. African Americans and other minorities also continue to have higher unemployment than whites do.

As long as these and other examples of discrimination exist, we must acknowledge and take steps to address racial inequality.

Thinking Sociologically

How do the different types of discrimination, as discussed earlier, help us understand world conflicts, such as the intense hostility between Palestinians and Jews in Israel?

DOMINANT AND MINORITY GROUP CONTACT: MACRO-LEVEL ANALYSIS

Meso-level analysis is essential to understanding the primary issues of racism in contemporary global North countries, but ultimately the tone for interracial relationships is set at the macro level. The first question is how those in power decide to structure relationships between racial and ethnic groups.

Majority Group Policies to Manage Racial and Ethnic Relations

Dominant-minority relations depend on the time, place, and circumstances. However, majority groups tend to structure or manage the majority and minority relationships with one of five policies, indicated in Figure 8.7.

Genocide is *the systematic effort of one group, usually the dominant group, to destroy a minority group.* Examples of race- and ethnicity-based genocide exist throughout history. In the 13th century, Mongols under Temüjin Genghis Khan destroyed entire nations in their path. Germany's Adolf Hitler sent Jews and other non-Aryan groups into concentration camps to be gassed in the 1930s and 1940s. In Rwanda, in the mid-1990s, members of the Hutu tribe committed mass murders of people from the Tutsi tribe. More recently, the terrorist group ISIS tried to wipe out the Yazidis, a religious minority group, in Iraq. Genocide has existed at many points in history, and it still exists today (see Figure 8.8). These examples illustrate the lethal consequences of racism, one group at the meso level systematically killing off another, often a minority, to gain control and power.

Subjugation refers to *the subordination of one group to another that holds power and authority.* Haiti and the Dominican Republic share the island of Hispaniola in the Caribbean. Many Haitians cross the border into the Dominican Republic, lured by promises of jobs in the sugarcane fields of that wealthier nation. However, once there, many are forced to work long hours for little pay and not allowed to leave until they have paid for housing and food, which may be impossible to do on their low wages.

Slavery is one form of subjugation that has existed throughout history. When the Roman Empire defeated other lands, the captives became slaves. This included ancient Greeks, who also kept slaves at various times in their history. African tribes enslaved members of neighboring tribes, sometimes selling them to slave traders, and slavery has existed in Middle Eastern countries such as Saudi Arabia. As mentioned in Chapter 7, slavery still flourishes in many parts of the world today (Bales 2000, 2007, 2012). *Segregation*, a specific form of subjugation, separates minorities from the dominant group and deprives them of access to the dominant institutions, such as occurred in the United States under the Jim Crow laws discussed earlier (Alexander 2010; Feagin and Feagin 2010).

Population transfer refers to *the removal, often forced, of a minority group from a region or country.* Generally, the dominant group wants land, or resources. For example, Native Americans in the United States were removed to reservations. The Cherokee people were forced to walk from Georgia and North Carolina to new lands west of the Mississippi—a "Trail of Tears" along which 40% of the people perished, so that whites in these states could have access to Cherokee land. As noted previously, during World War II, Japanese Americans were forcibly moved to "relocation centers" and had their land and property confiscated. In 1972, Idi Amin, dictator of Uganda, gave Asian Ugandans 36 hours to pack their bags and leave—even though it had been the homeland for many of them from birth—because they had great economic resources that he argued should belong to native Ugandans.

FIGURE 8.7   Types of Dominant-Minority Group Relations

Most Hostile to "Others" ⟶				Most Accepting of "Others"
Genocide	**Subjugation**	**Population Transfer**	**Assimilation**	**Pluralism**
Extermination of minorities	Oppression, slavery	Removal to new location	Cultural blending of groups	Groups share in legitimacy and power

FIGURE 8.8   **Select Genocides Around the World, 1914–Present**

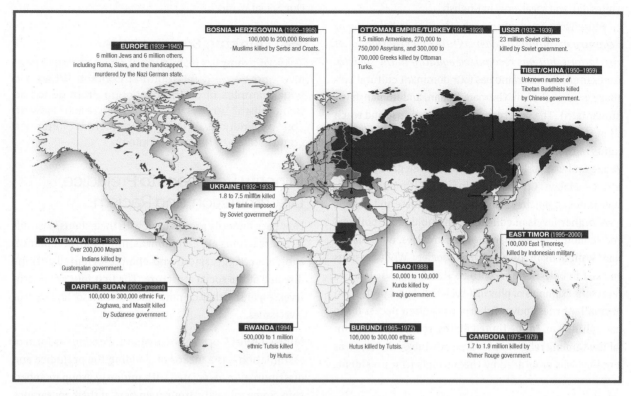

BOSNIA-HERZEGOVINA (1992–1995)
100,000 to 200,000 Bosnian
Muslims killed by Serbs and Croats.

EUROPE (1939–1945)
6 million Jews and 6 million others,
including Roma, Slavs, and the handicapped,
murdered by the Nazi German state.

OTTOMAN EMPIRE/TURKEY (1914–1923)
1.5 million Armenians, 270,000 to
750,000 Assyrians, and 300,000 to
700,000 Greeks killed by Ottoman
Turks.

USSR (1932–1939)
23 million Soviet citizens
killed by Soviet government.

TIBET/CHINA (1950–1959)
Unknown number of
Tibetan Buddhists killed
by Chinese government.

UKRAINE (1932–1933)
1.8 to 7.5 million killed
by famine imposed
by Soviet government.

GUATEMALA (1981–1983)
Over 200,000 Mayan
Indians killed by
Guatemalan government.

DARFUR, SUDAN (2003–present)
100,000 to 300,000 ethnic Fur,
Zaghawa, and Masalit killed
by Sudanese government.

IRAQ (1988)
50,000 to 100,000
Kurds killed by
Iraqi government.

EAST TIMOR (1995–2000)
100,000 East Timorese
killed by Indonesian military.

RWANDA (1994)
500,000 to 1 million
ethnic Tutsis killed
by Hutus.

BURUNDI (1965–1972)
100,000 to 300,000 ethnic
Hutus killed by Tutsis.

CAMBODIA (1975–1979)
1.7 to 1.9 million killed by
Khmer Rouge government.

Source: Adapted from Online Resources from The Choices Program, Brown University.

Assimilation *refers to the social and cultural merging of minority and majority groups.* It is often a voluntary process during which members of minority groups choose to adopt the values, norms, and institutions of the dominant group. Assimilation is more likely to occur when the minority group is culturally similar to the dominant group. For instance, in the United States, the closer a group is to being white and English speaking, the faster its members will be assimilated into the dominant group, adopting the culture and blending in biologically through intermarriage. While some assimilation happens naturally when different groups interact in housing, schooling, employment, political circles, family groups, friendships, and social relationships, some assimilation policies in certain times and places have forced ethnic minorities to change their cultural attributes (language, religion, style of eating, etc.) in order to avoid ridicule or even death (Marger 2012).

Forced assimilation occurs when members of a minority group are compelled to suppress their cultural identity. For example, in the late 1800s and early 1900s, Native American children were forced to leave their families and go to white-run boarding schools. There, they had to cut

National Archives and Records Administration

One of the most horrific results of discriminatory racial or ethnic policies was the Holocaust, the murder of 11 million people, including 6 million Jews, by the Nazi government in Germany under Adolf Hitler. This photo is difficult to view, but this is the consequence of bigotry that leads to genocide.

their hair, attend Christian religious services, dress as whites did, and speak only in English.

Pluralism *occurs when each ethnic or racial group in a country maintains its own culture and separate set of institutions, but has recognized equality in the society.* For example, Switzerland has four dominant cultural language groups: French, German, Italian, and Romansh (or Rumantsch). The government and schools use and teach all of these official languages. Each group respects the rights of the other groups to maintain a distinctive language and way of life. In Malaysia, three groups share power—Malays, Chinese, and Indians. Although the balance is not completely stable because Chinese and Indians have higher levels of education and hold more political and economic power than the native Malays, most Malaysians want to maintain a pluralistic society. While tensions do exist in both nations, both Switzerland and Malaysia represent examples of pluralist societies. Legal protection of smaller or less powerful groups is often necessary to have pluralism. In the United States, religious pluralism (at least among religions practiced by white Americans), as a policy, was embraced by the nation's first president,

George Washington, as explained in the next "Sociology in Our Social World."

 Thinking Sociologically

Think of examples from current news stories of positive and harmful intercultural contact. Where do your examples fit on the continuum from genocide to pluralism? What is your reaction to each? How do your experiences of intercultural contact influence your reaction to these examples?

Minority Reactions to Prejudice, Discrimination, and Racism

How have minority groups dealt with their status? Five different reactions are common: assimilation, acceptance, avoidance, aggression, and change-oriented actions directed at the social structure. The first four are micro-level responses; they do not address the meso- and macro-level issues.

Micro-Level Coping Strategies. *Passing*—a form of assimilation—is a means of avoiding the prejudice and discrimination associated with minority group membership. Some minority group members, if their appearance allows them to do so, attempt to *pass* as members of the dominant group. This strategy usually involves abandoning their own culture and turning their back on family roots and community ties, a costly strategy in terms of self-esteem and sense of identity. People who select this coping strategy must deny their minority background and live with the fear that it will be exposed. They often live in constant anxiety, feeling as though they must hide something about themselves.

Acceptance is another reaction to minority status. Some members of minority groups have learned to live with their minority status and do not challenge the system. They may or may not hold deep-seated hostility, but they ultimately conclude that change in the society is not very likely, and acceptance may be the rational means to survive within the existing system.

There are many possible explanations for this seeming indifference. For example, religious beliefs allow poor Hindus in India to believe that if they accept their lot in life, they will be reincarnated in a higher life-form. If they rebel, they can expect to be reincarnated into a lower life-form. Their religion is a form of social control. In other cases, members of minority groups believe that they are, in fact, inferior and, therefore, should be treated that way. Socialized in a society that treats them as second-class citizens, they begin to accept this image of themselves.

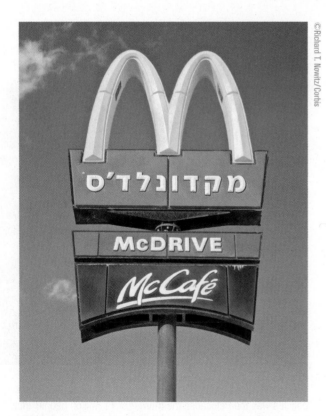

©Richard T. Nowitz/Corbis

This picture of a McDonald's in the United States helps illustrate that the country is a pluralistic society. The "McDonald's" on this sign is in the Hmong language.

sociology in our social world

Pluralism: A Long-Standing History in the United States

© Keith A. Roberts

This Jewish synagogue, the oldest in the United States, proudly displays a letter from George Washington enshrining pluralism in the new nation's policies.

It is no surprise that the oldest Jewish synagogue in the United States is in Rhode Island, for separation of church and state and tolerance of other religious traditions was a founding principle of the colony of Rhode Island. After George Washington was elected president of the new nation, he received a letter from that early Jewish congregation in Newport, Rhode Island, asking about his policies of pluralism or multiculturalism (though those words had not been coined yet). In response in 1790, Touro Synagogue received a handwritten letter signed by President Washington (and now proudly on display at the synagogue) embracing an open and "liberal" policy to all U.S. citizens, regardless of origins or religious affiliation. In this letter, George

Washington affirmed a policy of pluralism from the very beginning of the country's existence as a nation. Passages from that letter follow.

* * * * * * *

The Citizens of the United States of America have a right to applaud themselves for having given to mankind examples of an enlarged and liberal policy: a policy worthy of imitation. . . . It is now no more that toleration is spoken of, as if it was by the indulgence of one class of people, that another enjoyed the exercise of their inherent natural rights. For happily the Government of the United States, which gives to bigotry no sanction, to persecution no assistance, requires only that they who live under its protection should demean themselves as good citizens.

. . . May the children of the Stock of Abraham, who dwell in this land, continue to merit and enjoy the good will of the other Inhabitants; while everyone shall sit in safety under his own vine and fig tree, and there shall be none to make him afraid. May the father of all mercies scatter light and not darkness in our paths, and make us all in our several vocations useful here, and in his own due time and way everlastingly happy.

—G. Washington

Others may simply fear the negative consequences of refusing to accept their minority status.

Avoidance entails coping with minority group status through shunning all contact with the dominant group. This can involve an active and organized attempt to leave the culture or live separately as some political exiles have done. For example, in the United States, Marcus Garvey

organized a Back-to-Africa movement in the 1920s, encouraging blacks to give up on any hope of justice in U.S. society and to return to Africa. Today, some Native Americans on reservations avoid contact with other Americans and do all they can to live as their ancestors once did—before the intrusion of white people onto their land. For example, among some groups of isolated

Apaches in New Mexico and Arizona, nearly half of the older population speaks no English and has no need or desire to learn it. They live according to traditional cultural ways in rather isolated desert climates. They have simply withdrawn from contact with the larger society (Farrer 2011).

Aggression resulting from anger and resentment over minority status and from subjugation may lead to retaliation or violence. Direct confrontation can be very costly to those lacking political or economic power. So, aggression often takes one of two forms, indirect aggression or displaced aggression. Indirect aggression includes biting assertiveness in the arts—literature, art, racial and ethnic humor, and music—and in job-related actions such as inefficiency and slowdowns by workers. Displaced aggression, on the other hand, involves hostilities directed toward individuals or groups other than the dominant group, such as happens when youth gangs attack other ethnic or racial gangs in nearby neighborhoods. They substitute aggression against the dominant group by acting out against other minority groups. The arts can represent indirect aggression or efforts toward social change, as shown in the following photo.

The four responses discussed thus far address the angst and humiliation that individual minorities feel. Each strategy allows an individual person to try to cope, but none addresses the structural causes of discrimination. The final strategy is *change-oriented action*.

The Penumbra theatre in St. Paul, Minnesota, uses the performing arts to promote social change. It fosters laughter at socially absurd norms and ideas, often a form of biting commentary. As the theater company tells the story of African American in the United States, they carry out their mission to use theater to "teach, criticize, comment, and model."

Meso- and Macro-Level Efforts to Bring Change: Resistance. Passing, acceptance, and avoidance are forms of adaptation to the existing structures. Aggression, if not used strategically, can also work to support the status quo by creating opposition to changes that would help the minority group. Yet rather than accepting the current system and adapting to it, minority groups may choose strategic resistance. Resistance to the white framing of what life is like in the United States can take place through offering positive definitions of one's racial or ethnic group and preserving pride in one's culture (Feagin 2012). This is what was at work in the "black is beautiful" theme that emerged early in the civil rights movement. That movement led to more books and films that relate the stories of courage, stamina, and contribution by minority groups. These media images provide a challenge and an alternative to those developed through the white perceptions of minority groups and U.S history.

Efforts to change cultural attitudes towards minority groups have been complemented by work within the legal system to challenge unjust laws. The National Association for the Advancement of Colored People (NAACP) sought to bring about legal changes through lawsuits that created new legal precedents supporting racial equality. Often, these lawsuits addressed side-effect discrimination—a meso-level problem. Many other associations for minorities—including the Anti-Defamation League (founded by Jews) and La Raza Unida (a Mexican American organization)—also seek to address problems both within organizations and institutions (meso level) and in the nation as a whole (macro level).

One of the most important efforts to bring change in the United States has been nonviolent resistance. The model for nonviolent resistance by minority groups comes from Mahatma Gandhi who, from 1915 to 1947, led the struggle for India's independence from Britain. Although Britain clearly had superior weapons and armies, Indian boycotts, sit-ins, and other forms of resistance eventually led to British withdrawal as the ruling colonial power. This strategy has been used by workers and students to bring about change in many parts of the world.

In the United States, Martin Luther King Jr. followed in the nonviolent resistance tradition of Gandhi, who sought to change India's laws so that minorities could have equal opportunities within the society. King's strategy involved nonviolent popular protests, economic boycotts, and other challenges to racially discriminatory norms of the society. His nonviolent disruptive efforts brought attention to the plight of black people in the United States and created the political pressure needed to pass the civil rights legislation of the 1960s.

Integration

Mahatma Gandhi, leader of the Indian civil disobedience revolt, led nonviolent protests against unjust laws such as a march to collect salt, an illegal act.

W. E. B. Du Bois, Martin Luther King Jr. (who had an undergraduate degree in sociology), and many other public sociologists have used their training to address issues of discrimination through empowerment and change. Their efforts to strategically counter the power of the dominant group have helped create a more equitable society for all residents of the United States.

 Thinking Sociologically

The preceding discussion presents five types of responses by minorities to the experience of discrimination and rejection. Four of these are at the micro level, and one is at the meso and macro levels. Why do you think most of the coping strategies of minorities are at the micro level?

Theoretical Explanations of Dominant-Minority Group Relations

Dominant-minority group relations take place on the micro, meso, and macro levels. Therefore, we must utilize a wide variety of theoretical perspectives in order to fully understand these types of group interactions. For example, psychological and social-psychological theories are most relevant when examining prejudice in individuals and small groups. To understand discrimination embedded in institutions, studying meso-level organizations is helpful, and to understand the pervasive nature of prejudice and stereotypes over time in various societies, cultural explanations are useful. Finally, we must turn to macro-level theories to understand national and global group relations.

Structural-Functional Theory. Some functionalists point out that prejudice, discrimination, and institutional racism are dysfunctional for society, resulting in loss of human resources, costs to societies due to poverty and crime, hostilities between groups, and disrespect for those in power. For example, Durkheim divided social inequalities into *internal* (based on people's natural abilities) and *external* (those forced upon people). He argued that the existence of *external inequality* in an industrial society indicates that its institutions are not functioning properly. Because an industrial society needs all its members doing what they do best in order for it to function most effectively, external inequality—like racial discrimination—that prevents some people from fulfilling their innate talents damages all of society. Prejudice, discrimination, and institutional racism, then, are dysfunctional for society, resulting in loss of human resources, costs to societies due to poverty and crime, hostilities between groups, and disrespect for those in power (Schaefer 2012).

However, other functionalists note that maintaining a cheap pool of laborers (e.g., members of a minority group) who are in and out of work serves several purposes for society. Not only does this minority group function to provide a ready labor force for dirty work or menial unskilled jobs, but these laborers also serve other functions for society. Having minority groups makes possible occupations that service the poor, such as social work, public health, criminology, and the justice and legal systems. The oppressed buy goods others do not want—day-old bread, old fruits and vegetables, and secondhand clothes (Gans 1971, 1994). In short, having a supply of people in desperate need at the bottom of the social structure, according to some analysts, has some useful functional aspects, and this makes change more difficult.

Conflict Theory. Conflict theorists argue that creating a less powerful group protects the dominant group's advantages. Because privileges and resources are usually limited, those who have them want to keep them. One strategy used by privileged people, according to conflict theory, is to perpetrate prejudice and discrimination against minority group members. For example, in the 1840s, as the United States set out to build a transcontinental railroad, large numbers of laborers emigrated from China to do the hard manual work. When the railroad was completed and competition for jobs became stiff, the once-welcomed Chinese became targets of bitter prejudice, discrimination, and sometimes violence. Members of these minority groups banded together in towns or cities for protection, founding the Chinatowns we know today (Kitano, Aqbayani, and de Anda 2005). Non-Chinese Asian groups suffered discrimination as well, because the bigoted generalizations were applied to all Asians (Winders 2004).

Karl Marx argued that exploitation of the lower classes is built into capitalism because it benefits the ruling class. Unemployment creates a ready pool of labor to fill the marginal jobs, with the pool often made up of identifiable minority groups. This pool allows people to remain in their higher-level positions and prevents others from moving up in the stratification system and threatening their jobs. Three critical factors contribute to animosity between groups, according to one conflict theorist (Noel 1968): First, if two groups of people can each be identified by their appearance, clothing, or language, then "us" versus "them" thinking and ethnocentrism may develop. However, this by itself does not mean there will be long-term hostility between the groups. Second, if the two groups conflict over scarce resources that both want, hostilities are very likely to arise. The resources might be the best land or cattle, the highest-paying jobs, access to the best schools for one's children, energy resources such as oil, or positions of prestige and power. If the third element is added to the mix—one group having much more power than the other—then intense dislike between the two groups and misrepresentation of each group by the other is fairly certain to occur.

The group with more power uses that power to ensure that its members (and their offspring) get the most valued resources. However, because they do not want to see themselves as unfair and brutish people, they develop stereotypes and derogatory characterizations of "those other people" so that it seems reasonable and justified not to give "them" access to the valued resources. Discrimination (often at the macro level) comes first, and bigoted ideology comes later to justify the discrimination (Noel 1968). Thus, macro- and meso-level conflicts can lead to micro-level attitudes.

Split labor market theory, a branch of conflict theory, characterizes the labor market as having two main types of jobs. The primary market involves clean jobs, largely in supervisory roles, and provides high salaries and good advancement possibilities, whereas the secondary market involves undesirable, hard, and dirty work, compensated with low hourly wages and few benefits or career opportunities. Competition for lesser jobs pits minorities against each other and low-income whites against minorities. By encouraging division and focusing antagonism between worker groups, employers reduce threats to their dominance and get cheaper labor in the process. Workers do not organize against employers who use this dual system because they are distracted by the antagonisms that build up among themselves—hence, the *split labor market* (Bonacich 1972, 1976). This theory maintains that competition, prejudice, and ethnic animosity serve the interests of the powerful owners of capital because that atmosphere keeps the laboring classes from uniting.

Conflict theory has also been used to illuminate issues of ethnic hostility on other continents, for this theory has wide application. Kichiro Iwamoto, who does sociological work on race relations issues in Africa and elsewhere, discusses such conflicts in Africa in the next "Sociology Around the World."

Conflict theory has taught us a great deal about racial and ethnic stratification. However, conflict theorists often focus on people with power quite intentionally oppressing others to protect their own self-interests. They often depict the dominant group as made up of nasty, power-hungry people. As we have seen in the meso-level discussion of side-effect and past-in-present discrimination, racial discrimination is often subtle and unconscious and can continue even without conscious ill will among those in the dominant group.

Thinking Sociologically

Do you think the split labor market perspective is useful when examining the racial and ethnic hierarchy in the United States? Why or why not? Can you see any evidence on your campus or in your local community to support the split labor theorists' view of racial and ethnic stratification?

POLICIES GOVERNING MINORITY AND DOMINANT GROUP RELATIONS

The dominant ethnic group in northern Sudan is Arabs—led by President Omar al-Bashir and his armies. In South

Sociology Around the World

Violence in Kenya

By Kichiro Iwamoto

In January 2008, violence gripped Kenya as rival political leaders representing different ethnic groups fought for control of the country in a contested election. Former Secretary General of the United Nations Kofi Annan said, while visiting western Kenya during the unrest, "What we saw was heart-wrenching. We saw houses burning, grandmothers and children being pushed out of their homes, and people suffering everywhere." He told the rival political leaders to resolve the political conflict as the violence was out of control in the country (UPI 2008).

At a small Assembly of God church in Kiambaa, Kenya, armed men trapped Kikuyu women, children, and elderly people inside; barricaded all the doors; and burned the building down, killing an estimated 50 people. The attackers were reported to be members of a rival tribe, the Kalenjin (Gettleman 2008). Viewing the violence through a sociological lens can help us to understand why it occurred.

Political conflicts over power can incite age-old rivalries and erupt into genocide, systematic killing of "others." Tribalism leads to discrimination against other tribes that are viewed as economic and power rivals, "different," and often inferior, and then resentments result in reprisals. In Kenya, tribalism led to the Kalenjin and Kikuyu attacking each other. Violence escalated in a vicious cycle of "us" versus "them" animosity.

In Kenya, the mob violence and social chaos may have been advantageous for those in high political positions as the "reign of terror" kept many frightened people from protesting the controversial national election of December 2007. The tribal violence kept the population fragmented, weakening opposition to those in power.

• •

Kichiro Iwamoto has taught for many years in the sociology/anthropology department at Santa Clara University in California.

Sudan, a newly formed country, the citizens are dark-skinned Africans who have a very different culture. Until a tenuous peace was brokered by the United Nations, the southern Sudanese people were tortured and killed and their villages burned by the more powerful northern Sudanese. Two issues at stake are (1) cultural and ethnic differences and (2) oil reserves. Conflict over oil, primarily located near the border between the two countries, has made the peace plan tenuous. While the hope was that the new border would separate warring factions, skirmishes continue to threaten the peace. In this case, macro-level policies from the United Nations and world powers intervened to stop the atrocities, but this has not eliminated the meso-level causes of conflict—cultural differences and resources such as land and oil. Remember that conflict over resources is usually the cause of animosity between groups.

War, famine, and economic dislocation force families to seek new locations where they can survive and perhaps improve their circumstances. Refugees may end up in a new country, perhaps on a new continent. The degree of acceptance children and their families find in their newly adopted countries varies depending on the government's policies, the group's background, economic conditions in the host country, and whether the refugee group poses a threat to residents (Rumbaut and Portes 2001). Some formerly refugee-friendly countries are closing their doors to immigration because of the strain on their economy and threats of terrorism. In this section, we consider the policies that emerge when dominant and minority groups come into contact and interact.

Policies to Reduce Prejudice, Racism, and Discrimination

In the preceding pages, we considered some of the costs to individuals, groups, societies, and the global community inflicted by discriminatory behavior and policies. Discrimination's influence is widespread, from slavery and subjugation to unequal opportunities in education, work and political arenas, and every other part of the social world. If one accepts the premise that discrimination is destructive to both individuals and societies, then ways must be found to address the root problems effectively.

The photo above shows a section of the wall built to keep undocumented immigrants from crossing the Mexican–American border and entering the United States. Some believe that walls of this sort foster "us" versus "them" thinking.

From our social world perspective, we know that no problem can be solved by working at only one level of analysis. A successful strategy must bring about change at every level of the social world—individual attitudes, organizational discrimination, cultural stereotypes, societal stratification systems, and national and international structures. However, most current strategies focus on only one level of analysis. Figure 8.9 shows some of the programs enacted to combat prejudice, racism, and discrimination at the individual, group, societal, and global levels.

Thinking Sociologically

What purpose do walls between different groups serve? Do walls such the one pictured create more positive or negative repercussions? Why and for whom?

Individual or Small-Group Solutions. Programs to address prejudice and stereotypes through human relations workshops, and group encounters, can achieve goals at the micro level. Two groups with strong multicultural education programs are the Anti-Defamation League and the Southern Poverty Law Center's Teaching Tolerance program. Both groups provide schools and community organizations with literature, videos, and other materials aimed at combating intolerance and discrimination toward others. Schools can also create interracial friendship opportunities with racially integrated classrooms where students of different racial and ethnic backgrounds interact regularly (Cheng and Xie 2013; Ellison and Powers 1994).

Group Contact. Some social scientists advocate organized group contact between dominant and minority group members to improve relations and break down stereotypes and fears. Although not all contact reduces prejudice, many studies have shown the benefits of structured

FIGURE 8.9   Problems and Solutions

Types of Problems at Each Level	Types of Solutions or Programs at Each Level
Individual level: stereotypes and prejudice	Therapy, tolerance-education programs
Group level: negative group interaction	Positive contact, awareness by majority of their many privileges
Societal level: institutionalized discrimination	Education, media, legal-system revisions
Global level: deprivation of human rights	Human rights movements, international political pressures

Race and Ethnicity

contact. Some essential conditions for success are equal status of the participants, noncompetitive and nonthreatening contact, and projects or goals on which to cooperate (Farley 2011).

In a classic study of group contact, social psychologists Muzafer Sherif and Carolyn Sherif and their colleagues ran summer camps for 11- and 12-year-old boys and studied how they interacted with one another under different circumstances. On arrival, the boys were divided into two groups that competed periodically. The more fierce the competition, the more hostile the two cabins of boys became toward each other. The experimenters tried several methods to resolve the conflicts and tensions:

1. *Appealing to higher values (be nice to your neighbors)*: This proved of limited value.
2. *Talking with the natural leaders of the groups* (compromises between group leaders): The group leaders agreed, but their followers did not go along.
3. *Bringing the groups together in a pleasant situation* (a mutually rewarding situation): This did not reduce competition; if anything, it increased it.
4. *Introducing a superordinate goal* that could be achieved only if everyone cooperated: This technique worked. The boys were presented with a dilemma: The water system had broken, or a fire needed to be put out, and all were needed to solve the problem. The groups not only worked together, but their established stereotypes eventually began to fade away. Such a situation in a community might arise from efforts to get a candidate elected, a bill passed, or a neighborhood improved. At the global macro level, representatives from hostile countries could sit together to solve issues that threatened all nations. (Sherif and Sherif 1953)

Students can be actively engaged in this level of change, even while undergraduates, by confronting and challenging bigotry and stereotypes, as illustrated in the next "Sociologists in Action" on page 258.

Positive group contact experiences can be effective in improving relations in groups at a micro level by breaking down stereotypes, but to solidify the positive gains, we must also address institutionalized inequalities.

Institutional and Societal Strategies to Improve Group Relations. Sociologists contend that institutional and societal approaches to reduce discrimination get closer to the core of the problems and affect larger numbers of people than do micro-level strategies. Changes at the macro level that can impact racial and ethnic stratification include legislation and government programs that enforce laws mandating racial and ethnic equality. For example, laws requiring equal treatment of minorities, such as the Civil Rights Act of 1964 that prohibited discrimination on the basis of race, religion, sex, or nation of origin, have resulted in increased tolerance and opened doors once closed to minorities. The U.S. Civil Rights Commission and the Equal Employment Opportunity Commission are government organizations that protect rights and work toward equality for all citizens.

In the United States, executive action to end discrimination has been taken by a number of presidents. In 1948, Harry Truman moved to successfully end military segregation, and subsequent presidents have urged the passage of civil rights legislation and equal employment opportunity legislation. Affirmative action laws, first implemented during Lyndon Johnson's administration, have been used to fight pervasive institutional racism (Crosby 2004; Farley 2011).

Affirmative Action. One of the most contentious policies in the United States has been affirmative action. The following discussion addresses the goals and forms of policies under the umbrella of "affirmative action."

As a societal policy for change, affirmative action actually involves three different policies.

Strict affirmative action, its simplest and original form, involves taking affirmative or positive steps to make sure that unintentional discrimination does not occur. It requires, for example, that an employer who receives federal monies must advertise a position widely and not just through internal or friendship networks. If the job requires an employee with a college education, then by federal law, employers must recruit through minority and women's colleges as well as state and private colleges in the region. If employers are hiring in the suburbs, they are obliged to contact unemployment agencies in poor and minority communities as well as those in their affluent neighborhoods.

After taking these required extra steps, employers are expected to hire the most qualified candidate who applies, regardless of race, ethnicity, sex, religion, or other external characteristics.

The focus is on providing opportunities for the best-qualified people. For many people, this is the meaning of affirmative action, and it is inconceivable that this could be characterized as "reverse discrimination," for members of the dominant group will be hired if they are in fact

▶ Affirmative Action

SOCIOLOGISTS IN ACTION:
ANNA MISLEH

Challenging Bigotry Toward the Roma

In the spring of 2013, a group of students from St. John's University in Queens, New York, were involved in a study-abroad program in Rome, Italy, and performed weekly service work in a Roma (Gypsy) population to better understand an ethnic group that experienced discrimination. In the process we, as college students, learned we could raise awareness of the discrimination of the Roma and its impact. We worked one-on-one with Roma children living in Monachina, a settlement camp of Roma that is not officially recognized, but is tolerated, by the Italian government. Through our work at the camp, interviewing Italians knowledgeable about the Roma and interacting closely with one of the families at Monachina, my peers and I were able to better understand the Roma lifestyle and the discrimination they face in Rome.

To deepen our understanding of the Roma population in Rome, we interviewed two Italian women involved in a *doposcuola* (after-school) program at Monachina. These women had been visiting Monachina for several years and understood the culture at the camp and the views of Italians toward the Roma. We also read and researched all we could about the Roma to supplement the information given to us by the women involved in the *doposcuola* program. The Roma who reside in Rome, and other European cities, have come from dozens of different countries. Most have fled political unrest in their home countries. The Roma at the Monachina camp, for example, migrated to Rome in the early 1990s when the country of Yugoslavia dissolved and ethnic wars broke out across the area.

Italians were not pleased by the arrival of the Roma. Generally, Italians stereotype them as an inferior ethnic group that is lazy, dirty, uncooperative, and unwilling to assimilate into Italian culture. This has led to a self-fulfilling prophecy. The discrimination the Roma face prevents them from obtaining reputable jobs, owning property, receiving a good education, and generally integrating into Italian society.

Our response to this discrimination of the Roma, which we saw evidenced in the Monachina community, was to raise awareness. We invited students from several U.S. universities to visit Monachina with us and meet the Roma. Through this experience, they gained a deeper understanding of the Roma and how they are an oppressed minority group in Italian society. They were able to see that the stereotype of all Roma being lazy pickpockets was far from the truth. We also took time to discuss with them how this discrimination negatively impacts Italian society, as well as all other European countries that host these Roma populations and see them through the eyes of negative stereotypes. Being seen only as a societal nuisance hurts both the life chances of the Roma and their ability to fully contribute to the societies in which they live.

After experiencing the plight of the Roma population firsthand, my peers and I were able to use our sociological imagination to relate what we saw to the social issue of racial and ethnic discrimination. Sociology has taught me that a well-functioning society has institutions that support and respect the rights and dignity of all its members. Seeing the discrimination against the Roma at the Monachina camp in Rome has brought this truth home to me in a very real way and made me more committed than ever to teach others that racial and ethnic discrimination hurts everyone in a society—not just those who are its direct victims.

• •

Anna Misleh is a student at St. John's University in Queens, New York, studying sociology with minors in social justice, Spanish, and theology. She is a leader in the Ozanam Scholars social justice scholarship program at St. John's.

the most qualified. These policies do not overcome the problem that qualified people who have been marginalized may be competent but do not have the traditional paper credentials that document their qualifications (Gallagher 2004).

A *quota system*, the second policy, is a requirement that employers *must* hire a certain percentage of minorities. For the most part, quotas are now unconstitutional. They apply only in cases where a court has found a company to have a substantial and sustained history of discrimination against minorities and where the employment position does not have many requirements (if the job entails sweeping floors and cleaning toilets, there would not be an expectation of a specific academic degree or a particular grade point average).

Preference policies are the third form, the one that has created the most controversy among opponents of corrective action. Preference policies are based on the concept of equity, the belief that sometimes people must be treated differently in order to be treated fairly. This policy was enacted to level the playing field, which was not rewarding highly competent people because of institutional racism. To overcome these inequalities and achieve certain objectives (e.g., a diverse workforce to serve a diverse population), employers and educational institutions take account of race or sex by making special efforts to hire and retain workers or accept students from groups that have been underrepresented. In many cases, these individuals bring qualifications others do not possess. Consider the following examples.

A goal of the medical community is to provide access to medical care for underserved populations. There is an extreme shortage of physicians on the Navajo reservation. Thus, a Navajo applicant for medical school might be accepted, even if her scores are slightly lower than those of another candidate's, because she speaks Navajo and understands the culture. One could argue that she is more qualified to be a physician on the reservation than someone who knows nothing about Navajo society but has a slightly higher grade point average or test score. Some argue that tests should not be the only measure to determine the merit of applicants.

Likewise, an African American police officer may have more credibility in an African American neighborhood and may be able to defuse a delicate conflict more effectively than a white officer who scored slightly higher on a paper-and-pencil placement test. Thus, being a member of a particular ethnic group can actually make one more qualified for a position.

Many colleges and universities admit students because they need an outstanding point guard on the basketball team, an extraordinary soprano for the college choir, or a student from a distant state for geographic diversity. These students are shown preference by being admitted with lower test scores than some other applicants because they are "differently qualified." Many colleges also give preference to children of former graduates. In order to achieve gender balance, male students tend to be given preference, even if more qualified females apply. The controversy about whether minority students should be given preference follows this same reasoning. Consider the following example.

A landmark case filed in a Detroit district court in 1997 alleged that the University of Michigan gave unlawful preference to minorities in undergraduate admissions and in law school admissions. In this controversial case, the court ruled that these undergraduate admissions were discriminatory because numbers rather than individualized judgments were used to make the admission determination (University of Michigan Documents Center 2003). Consider the next "Engaging Sociology" feature on page 260 and decide whether you think the policy was fair and whether only race and ethnicity should have been deleted from the automatic preferences allowed.

In 2013, the Supreme Court in the case of *Fisher v. University of Texas*, No. 11-345, upheld the 1997 ruling, saying that affirmative action was permissible in order to achieve the goal of a diverse student body. In the deciding decision, however, Justice Kennedy wrote that universities must "verify that it is necessary for a university to use race to achieve the educational benefits of diversity . . . and that the university could [not] achieve sufficient diversity without using racial classifications" (Liptak 2013). In April 2014, the Supreme Court went further, upholding a ban on affirmative action for racial or ethnic groups that was approved by 58% of Michigan voters, arguing that a lower court did not have the authority to overturn the referendum. Thus, publicly funded colleges in Michigan cannot grant preferential treatment on the basis of race, sex, color, ethnicity, or national origin (Mears 2014). So now all such policies are illegal in Michigan.

The question remains: Should preferences be given to accomplish diversity? Some people feel that programs involving any sort of preference for minorities are unfair and should not be allowed. Others believe that such programs do much more good than harm. They have encouraged employers, educational institutions, and government to look carefully at hiring policies and minority candidates, and many more competent minority group members are working in the public sector as a result of these policies. What is the truly equitable thing to do?

ENGAGING SOCIOLOGY

Preference Policies at the University of Michigan

To enhance diversity on the campus—a practice that many argue makes a university a better learning environment and enhances the academic reputation of the school—many colleges have preference policies in admissions. However, the University of Michigan was sued by applicants who felt they were not admitted because others replaced them on the roster due to their racial or ethnic background.

The University of Michigan is a huge university where a numbering system is needed to handle the volume (tens of thousands) of applicants; the admissions staff cannot make a decision based on personal knowledge of each candidate. Thus, they give points for each quality they deem desirable in the student body. A maximum of 150 points is possible, and a score of a 100 would pretty much ensure admission. The university feels that any combination of points accumulated according to the following formula will result in a highly qualified and diverse student body.

For academics, up to 110 points are possible:

- 80 points for grades (a particular grade point average in high school results in a set number of points; a 4.0 results in 80 points; a 2.8 results in 56 points)

- 12 points for standardized test scores (ACT or SAT)

- 10 points for the academic rigor of high school (so all students who go to tougher high schools earn points)

- 8 points for the difficulty of the curriculum (e.g., points for honors curriculum vs. keyboarding courses)

For especially desired qualities, including diversity, up to 40 points are possible for any combination of the following

- Geographical distribution (10 for Michigan resident; an additional 6 for underrepresented Michigan county)

- Legacy—a direct relative has attended Michigan (4 points for a parent; 1 point for a grandparent or sibling)

- Quality of submitted essay (3 points)

- Personal achievement—a special accomplishment that was noteworthy (up to 5 points)

- Leadership and service (5 points each)

- Miscellaneous (only one of these can be used):

  ___ Socioeconomic disadvantage (20 points)

  ___ Underrepresented racial or ethnic minority (black, Hispanic, or Native American) (20 points; disallowed by the court ruling)

  ___ Men in nursing (5 points)

  ___ Scholarship athlete (20 points)

  ___ Provost's discretion (20 points; usually the son or daughter of a large financial donor or of a politician)

In addition to race or ethnicity, athleticism, musical talent, having a relative who is an alum, or being the child of someone who is noteworthy to the university are also considered. Some schools also give points for being a military veteran. The legal challenge to this admissions system was based only on the points given for race or ethnic background, not on the other reasons for which some students are given preference.

* * * * * * *

Engaging With Sociology

1. Does this process seem reasonable as a way to get a diverse and highly talented incoming class of students? Why or why not?

2. Does it significantly advantage or disadvantage some students? Explain.

3. Should there be preferences for predominantly white students—such as "legacy" students, whose family members attended the university? Why or why not?

4. How would you design a fair system of admissions, and what other factors would you consider?

Global Movements for Human Rights

The rights granted to citizens of any nation used to be considered the business of each sovereign nation, but after the Nazi Holocaust, German officers were tried at the Nuremberg Trials, and the United Nations passed the Universal Declaration of Human Rights. Since that time, many international organizations have been established, often under the auspices of the United Nations, to deal with health issues, world poverty and debt, trade, security, and many other issues affecting world citizens—the World Health Organization, the World Bank, the World Trade Organization, and numerous regional trade and security organizations.

The United Nations and privately funded advocacy groups speak up for international human rights as a principle that transcends national boundaries. The most widely recognized private group is Amnesty International, a watchdog group that lobbies on behalf of human rights and supports political prisoners. When Amnesty International was awarded the Nobel Peace Prize in 1997, the group's visibility dramatically increased. Some activist sociologists have formed groups such as Sociologists Without Borders, or SSF (*Sociólogos Sin Fronteras*; www.sociologistswithoutborders.org), a transnational organization committed to the idea that "all people have equal rights to political and legal protections, to socioeconomic security, to self-determination, and to their personality."

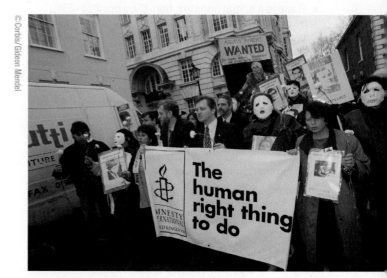

Some human rights movements focus on international justice issues in countries around the world. Amnesty International is one such movement that has strong support on many college campuses.

Everyone can make a positive difference in the world, and one place to start is in our own communities (see "Contributing to Our Social World"). We can counter prejudice, discrimination, and socially embedded racism in our own groups by teaching children to see beyond "us" and "them" and by speaking out for fairness and against stereotypes and discrimination.

Socioeconomic inequality and racial and ethnic stratification create many problems for a society. However, a full understanding of inequality also requires insights into discrimination based on gender. We turn to issues of gender inequality in Chapter 9.

WHAT HAVE WE LEARNED?

If there is competition over resources in a society, groups tend to form. Groups with the most power become dominant, and those with less power become minority groups. Those with the most power stratify their society in a way that ensures that their group has more access to power, money, and status. Racial and ethnic prejudice and discrimination at the micro, meso, and macro levels work to uphold dominant-minority group relations.

KEY POINTS

- Race is a social construction. (See pp. 233–236.)

- Racial and ethnic stratification are common throughout the world. Racial and ethnic minority groups have less power and less access to resources than majority groups. (See pp. 236–239.)

- Prejudice operates at the micro level of society while discrimination can occur at the micro, meso, and macro levels. (See pp. 239–242.)

- The racial ideology of color-blindness does not acknowledge the reality of racial discrimination. (See pp. 242–244.)

- At the meso level, institutionalized discrimination operates through two processes: side-effect and past-in-present. These forms of discrimination are unintended and unconscious—operating quite separately from any prejudice of individuals in the society. (See pp. 244–247.)

- The policies of the dominant group may include genocide, subjugation, population transfer, assimilation, or pluralism. (See pp. 248–250.)

- The costs to society from racial discrimination are high, including loss of human talent and resources. (See pp. 253.)

- The coping devices used by minorities include five main strategies: assimilation, acceptance, avoidance, aggression, and organizing for societal change. Only the last of these addresses the meso- and macro-level causes. (See pp. 250–253.)

- Policies to address problems of prejudice and discrimination range from individual and small-group efforts at the micro level to institutional, societal, and even global social movements. (See pp. 256–253.)

- Affirmative action includes three different sets of policies that are quite distinct and have different outcomes. (See pp. 257–259.)

DISCUSSION QUESTIONS

1. Have you ever experienced being stereotyped because of your race or ethnicity? Why or why not? How can racial stereotypes harm societies, as well as groups and individuals?

2. What is the difference between the color-blind perspective on race and blatant bigotry? Why is it often so difficult to recognize and address racial discrimination in the United States today?

3. Give two examples, respectively, of both side-effect discrimination and past-in-present discrimination. How have they impacted you and your life chances? Why?

4. We know that efforts to reduce prejudice, racism, and discrimination must take place at all levels (micro, meso, and macro). Most organizations, though, must choose one level on which to focus

their particular efforts. If you were going to start an organization to decrease racial or ethnic prejudice, would you focus on the micro, meso, or macro level? Why? Explain what your organization would do.

5. Do you agree with preferences for college applicants at the University of Michigan who were scholarship athletes or the sons or daughters of a large donor or a politician, but not for racial or ethnic minorities? Why or why not? Was the Supreme Court correct in ruling that a referendum passed by voters in Michigan should trump concerns about diversity? Why?

CONTRIBUTING TO OUR SOCIAL WORLD: WHAT CAN WE DO?

At the Local Level

- *African American, Arab American, and Native American student associations* are examples of student organizations dedicated to fighting bigotry and promoting understanding and the rights of racial minorities. Identify one of these groups on your campus and arrange to attend a meeting. If appropriate, volunteer to help with its work.

At the Organizational or Institutional Level

- The *Leadership Conference on Civil and Human Rights* is a national coalition dedicated to combating racism and its effects. It maintains a website that includes a directory of its membership of more than 200 organizations (www.civilrights.org). On its website you can find a "take action" link that will help you to explore ways in which you can participate in its efforts.

- *Teaching Tolerance* (www.splcenter.org/center/tt/teach.jsp), a program of the Southern Poverty Law Center, has curriculum materials for teaching about diversity and a program for enhancing cross-ethnic cooperation and dialogue in schools. Check into internship opportunities in local primary and secondary schools, and explore ways in which the Teaching Tolerance approach can be incorporated into the curricula in your school district with local teachers and administrators.

At the National and Global Levels

- The *Anti-Defamation League* (www.adl.org) acts to "stop the defamation of the Jewish people and to secure justice and fair treatment to all." Members of this organization develop and implement educational programs on interfaith/intergroup understanding, scrutinize and call attention to hate groups, monitor hate speech on the Internet, and mobilize communities to stand up to bigotry throughout the United States and abroad. Job listings, summer internships, and opportunities in Israel and other locations are listed on the ADL website.

- *National Relief Charities* strives "to help Native American people improve the quality of their lives by providing opportunities for them to bring about positive changes in their communities." To do so, it partners with tribal and other groups on the ground in the tribal regions of the Plains and Midwest. You can find out how to support the work of this group and its partner organizations by going to www.nrcprograms.org/site/PageNavigator/index.

- *Cultural Survival and the UN Permanent Forum on Indigenous Issues* (www.cs.org and www.un.org/esa/socdev/unpfii) provide opportunities for combating racism globally.

- Consider purchasing only Fair Trade Certified (packages are clearly marked as such) coffee, and especially chocolate, and encouraging your school to sell Fair Trade products. You can learn more about Fair Trade products and issues by reading this article—www.nytimes.com/2012/09/28/business/media/green-mountain-coffee-begins-fair-trade-campaign-advertising.html—and looking at educational materials provided by the Fair Trade Resource Network at www.fairtraderesource.org.

- *Amnesty International* campaigns against abuses of human rights. It relies heavily on volunteers organized into chapters, many of them campus based. You can join the organization and learn how to participate in its action through its website at www.amnesty.org. Consider joining or starting one on your campus.

©REUTERS/Pierre Marsaut

9 Gender Stratification

She/He—Who Goes First?

Social inequality is pervasive in gender relations, and although in some societies women are treated with deference, they are rarely given first access to positions of significant power or financial reward. The men often "go first."

MICRO

- **ME (AND MY GENDER GROUPS)**

- **LOCAL ORGANIZATIONS AND COMMUNITY**
  Peers, neighbors, teachers, and religious congregations socialize us into gendered expectations.

MESO

- **NATIONAL ORGANIZATIONS, INSTITUTIONS, AND ETHNIC SUBCULTURES**
  Organizations and institutions limit access to many positions based on gender.

MACRO

- **SOCIETY**
  National policies provide sex-based privileges.

- **GLOBAL COMMUNITY**
  Gender status is determined by laws and power structures; The United Nations champions equal rights for women.

THINK ABOUT IT

Micro: Local Community	How does being female or male affect your thoughts, behaviors, and opportunities? Why do some people face violence in their homes and communities because of their sexuality?
Meso: National Institutions, Complex Organizations, and Ethnic Groups	Can anything be done in our organizations and institutions to make men and women more equal?
Macro: National and Global Systems	Why do women have second-class status in many societies?

As women around the world wake up to International Women's Day, each woman, no matter where she lives, holds the same basic goals: a trusting and happy relationship; the option of having healthy, educated children with a fair chance in life; enough food on the table; self-respect; access to health care; and whatever individual desires are relevant in her society. Consider the following example from a Global North country that illustrates the problems some women face in meeting basic goals.

Jocelyn, who lives in the United States, is now retired and having trouble making ends meet. After training in nursing, including a master's degree, she married and dropped her career to raise her family. The marriage did not work out, and 15 years after college she found herself with no credit, two children, little job experience, and mounting expenses. She was a conscientious and hard worker, but with two children and meager child support from their father, she could not put much away for retirement. Nursing does not pay well in her town in the Midwest, but there had been few other career options for females in the early 1960s when she was getting her education.

Moreover, two decades does not build a very large retirement annuity, and she had never been able to buy an adequate home on her income. If she had been a typical male with a master's degree, her lifetime earnings would have been over $1 million more in cumulative income (Catalyst 2014c; Julian and Kominski 2011). Her life chances were clearly affected by the fact that she was a female.

Due to changes in gender roles and opportunities over the past 50 years, Jocelyn's granddaughter, Emma, will have a range of opportunities that were beyond consideration for her grandma. Ideas about sex, gender, and appropriate roles for women and men not only transform over time, but they also vary a great deal from one society to the next. Some practices of your own society may seem very strange to women and men in another society. Gender identities and roles are not stagnant; they change over time, reflecting the economic, political, and social realities of the society. For instance, women in today's India, with the exception of some rural areas, seldom commit *sati* (suicide) on their husband's funeral pyre (Greenan 2013; Ziel 2013); however, before the practice of *sati* was outlawed, it was a common way to deal with widows who no longer had a social role or means of support (Ahmad 2009).

In this chapter, we explore the concepts of sex, gender, and sexuality. We combine these issues with race and class for further understanding of the stratification system, or why people hold the positions they do in society. Although gender refers to a range of social behaviors, more emphasis will be on women's status and roles than men's as this is generally more relevant to our concern about stratification and minorities. At the micro level, we consider gender socialization or how girls and boys learn to be men and women in their respective societies. At the meso and macro levels we consider gender stratification, or placement of women and men in the society's stratification system. A discussion of costs and consequences of gender stratification plus policy implications will end this chapter.

SEX, GENDER, AND THE STRATIFICATION SYSTEM

You name it, and some society has probably done it! Gender relations are no exception. Variations around the world show that most roles and identities are not biological but rather socially constructed. In Chapter 7, we discussed factors that stratify individuals into social groups (castes and classes), and in Chapter 8, we discussed the roles that race and ethnicity play in stratification. Add the concepts of sex and gender, and we have a more complex and complete picture of how class, race and ethnicity, and gender together influence the experiences that make us who we are and our positions in society. Consider the following examples from societies that illustrate some unusual human social constructions based on sex and gender. These examples show that gender roles are created by humans to meet the needs of their societies. We then move to more familiar societies.

The Wodaabe, a subgroup of the Fulani ethnic group, are herders and traders in the Sahel region of Africa (especially Niger and Nigeria). The men would be defined as effeminate by most Western standards because of their behavior patterns. They are like birds, showing their colorful feathers to attract females. They take great care in doing their hair, applying makeup, and dressing to attract women. They also gossip with each other while sipping their tea. What are the women doing? They are cooking meals, caring for the children, cleaning, tending to the animals, planting small gardens, and preparing for the next move of this nomadic group (Beckwith 1993; Human Planet 2012; Saharan Vibe 2007). These patterns have developed over time and carry on as traditions. The point is that groups have developed cultural norms over time that cause gender behaviors to differ widely.

Women of the Tchambuli tribe, now known as the Chambri, in New Guinea seem unacceptably aggressive, assertive, businesslike, and competitive to people of the Arapesh tribe in New Guinea, where gentleness and non-aggression are the rule for both women and men. Men of the Tchambuli, on the other hand, exhibit expressive, nurturing, and gossipy behavior. The Mbuti and !Kung peoples of Africa value gender equality in their division of labor and treatment of women and men, and among the Agta of the Philippines, women do the hunting. In West African societies such as the Ashanti and Yoruba kingdoms, women control much of the market system (Dahlberg 1981; Mead [1935] 1963; Turnbull 1962). Each tradition has evolved over time to meet the basic human needs and to provide order to society. Each person, in all these diverse societies, knows how to behave appropriately.

Under the Taliban rule in Afghanistan at the turn of this century—and still in some areas today—women could not be seen in public without total body covering that meets strict requirements. Anyone not obeying could be stoned to death. Women could not hold public positions or work outside their homes. If they became ill,

Wodaabe men in Niger go to great pains with makeup, hair, and jewelry to ensure that they are highly attractive, a pattern thought by many people in other parts of the world to be associated with females.

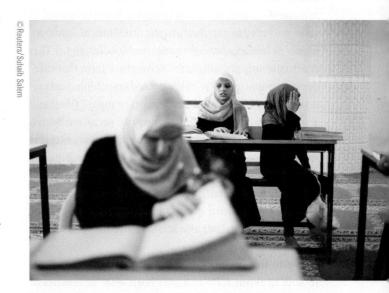

Muslim girls in some parts of the world cover their faces when in public. The display of skin, even in a classroom, would be immoral to many Muslims. However, in other Muslim countries such coverings would be unusual.

women could not be examined by a physician because all doctors were male. Instead, they had to describe their symptoms to a doctor through a screen (Makhmalbaf 2003; Trust in Education 2013).

Certain tasks must be carried out by individuals and organizations in each society for members to survive. Responsibilities include raising children, providing people with the basic necessities (such as food, clothing, and shelter), leading, defending the society, and resolving conflicts. One's sex and age are often used to determine who holds what positions and who carries out what tasks. Each society develops its own way to meet its expectations, and interpretations of right and wrong gender role behaviors. This results in gender role variations from one society to the next. If the genders are identified as fundamentally different, distinguishing symbols such as dress, head coverings, and hairstyle become important for each gender's identity.

Thinking Sociologically

Why did societies in different corners of the globe develop such radically different ways of organizing their gender roles?

Sex and Sexuality

At birth, when doctors say, "It's a . . . !" they are referring to the distinguishing primary characteristics that determine sex—that is, the penis or vagina. **Sex** is *a biological term referring to ascribed genetic, anatomical, and hormonal differences between males and females*, right? This is actually only partially true. *Sex* is also a term that categorizes people using *"socially agreed upon* biological criteria for classifying persons as females or males" (West and Zimmerman 1987:127). In other words, occasionally this binary male–female categorization by biological criteria is not clear. Occasionally, babies are born with ambiguous genitalia, not fitting the typical definitions of male or female (the *intersexed*). Germany has recently recognized "intersex" as a third group, an indeterminate gender option; Australian laws also acknowledge the intersex status (Agius 2013).

Up to five variations in sexes have been identified, including about 1.7% of babies born with "anomalies of sex chromosomes, internal procreative organs, and external genitalia in a variety of combinations" (Fausto-Sterling 2000:50–54). In Global North countries, these babies often undergo surgeries to clarify their gender, with hormonal treatments and possible further surgery at adolescence (Chase 2000). However, governments in some Global North countries are discouraging surgeries in favor of more acceptance of intersexed individuals. A new law in Germany, for example, allows the category of "indeterminate gender" on birth certificates, arguing that surgery is unnecessary and cosmetic. Whether this will result in more acceptance is unclear (Agius 2013).

Where medical interventions are not possible, people with sex anomalies may have special status, such as the transgendered Hijras (or Aravanis) in India. These unique people are called on for special religious observances and other ceremonial occasions (Gannon 2009). Whether male, female, or intersexed, anatomical differences at birth and chromosomal typing before birth result in attempts by people in various cultures to clearly categorize people based on their sex. The word *sex* when applied to a person refers largely to elements of one's anatomy. The struggles that some individuals have with their sexual identity are especially compelling in studies of *transgender*—when intersexed individuals do not fit clearly into female or male sex classifications (Kinsey Institute for Research in Sex, Gender, and Reproduction 2012; Leeder 2004). *Transgender* refers to "identification as someone who is challenging, questioning, or changing gender from that assigned at birth to a chosen gender—male-to-female, female-to-male, transitioning between genders, or gender 'queer' (challenging gender norms)" (Lorber and Moore 2007:6). Transgendered individuals interest sociologists because of their ambiguous life—living on the boundaries. Due to the pressure to fit in, most transgendered people change themselves, sometimes through surgery, to fit into their chosen gender.

The reason many societies go to great lengths to assign a sex to an infant is that sex constitutes a major organizing principle in most societies. Surgeries to clarify the sex of an infant are done mainly because of stigma and psychological reasons for those who do not fit socially approved categories. Despite emphasis on "achieved status" in modern societies, society's expectations guiding roles and statuses are largely ascribed—determined by a person's sex. Our attraction to others is expressed by our sexuality and our sexual identity. Most people fall into the category of heterosexual (other sex), homosexual (same sex), bisexual (both sexes), or "varied" (such as transgendered). In most societies our sexual identities follow the prevailing belief that a "normal" girl or boy will be sexually attracted to and eventually have sex with someone of the other sex (Lorber and Moore 2007). However, as we have seen, sex is not always a straightforward distinction and is as social as it is biological.

Sexuality refers to *culturally shaped meanings both of sexual acts and of how we experience our own bodies—especially in relation to the bodies of others*. Strange as it may seem, sexuality is socially constructed. A sex act is a "social enterprise," with cultural norms defining what is normal and acceptable in each society, how we should feel, and hidden assumptions about what the act means (Steele 2005). Even what we find attractive is culturally defined. For a period, in China, men found tiny feet a sexual turn-on—hence, the bound feet of women. In some cultures, legs are the attraction, and in others, men are fascinated by breasts. Likewise, the ideal male body as depicted in popular magazines in contemporary Western cultures, is "over 6 feet tall, 180 to 200 pounds, muscular, agile, with straight white teeth, a washboard stomach, six-pack abs, long legs, a full head of hair, a large penis (discreetly shown by a bulge), broad shoulders and chest, strong muscular back, clean shaven, healthy, and slightly tanned if White, or a lightish brown if Black or Hispanic" (Lorber and Moore 2011:89–90). We grow up learning what is appealing.

As individuals mature, they are expected to adopt the behaviors appropriate to their anatomical features as defined by their society. In addition to the physical sex differences between males and females, a few other physical conditions are commonly believed to be sex linked, such as a prevalence of color blindness, baldness, learning disabilities, autism, and hemophilia in males. Yet some traits that members of society commonly link to sex are actually learned through socialization. There is little evidence, for instance, that emotions, personality traits, or ability to fulfill most social statuses are determined by inborn physical sex differences. However, the social messages urging people to conform to expectations for their sex category are strong. What is defined as normal behavior for a male, a female, or an intersexed person in one society could get one killed in another.

Gender

Gender refers to a *society's notions of masculinity and femininity—socially constructed meanings associated with being male or female—and how individuals construct their identity in terms of gender within these constraints*. Gender identity, then, is how individuals form their identity using the categories of sex and gender, and negotiate the constraints they entail. The examples at the beginning of this section illustrate some differences in how cultures are structured around gender.

Statuses are positions within the structures of society, and roles are expected behaviors within those statuses (Rothenberg 2010). **Gender roles**, then, are *those commonly assigned tasks or expected behaviors linked to an individual's sex-determined statuses* (Lips 2010, 2013). Members of each society learn the structural guidelines and positions expected of males and females (West and Zimmerman 1987). Our positions, which affect access to power and resources, are embedded in institutions at the meso level with culture defining what is right and wrong. There is not some global absolute truth governing gender

or gender roles. While both vary across cultures, gender is a learned cultural idea, and gender roles are part of the structural system of roles and statuses in a society.

In summary, although the terms *sex*, *sexuality*, and *gender* are often used interchangeably, they do have distinct meanings. The distinctions between these terms are not always as clear-cut as the definitions would imply. One can be a masculine heterosexual female, a masculine homosexual male, or any of a number of possible combinations. Individuals who negotiate the meanings attached to gender and sexuality are *doing gender*, a process discussed later in this chapter ("Doing Gender" 2011; West and Zimmerman 1987).

Sex, Gender, and Sexuality: The Micro Level

"It's a boy!" brings varying cultural responses. In many Western countries, that exclamation results in blue blankets, toys associated with males (footballs, soccer balls, and trucks), roughhousing, and gender socialization messages. In some Asian societies, boys are sources for great rejoicing, whereas girls may be seen as a burden. Abortion rates in some countries are much higher when ultrasound tests show that the fetus is female ("Gendercide" 2010). In China and India, *female infanticide* (killing of newborn girl babies) is sometimes practiced in rural areas, in part because of the cost to poor families of raising a girl and the diminished value of girls. In China, the male preference

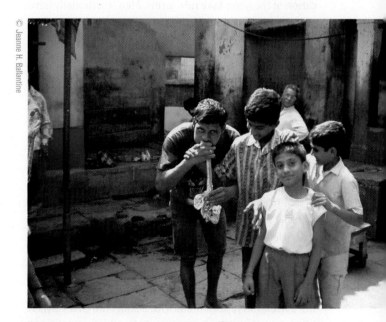

This extended family helps illustrate the growing sex imbalance in some parts of the world, such as China and India.

🔊 Gendercide

system has been exacerbated by the government's edict that most couples may have only one child, although this has changed for some couples in some areas of China. As a result of government policy and female infanticide and abortion, a sex imbalance is growing and causing other consequences such as a shortage of brides.

At the micro level we can trace stages in an individual's life as a female or male: early childhood socialization, school and community activities and experiences, adult statuses and roles of females and males, and so on through the life cycle. At each stage, there are messages that reinforce appropriate gender behavior. Cultural traditions learned from birth guide individuals into proper gender roles. These gender expectations are inculcated into children by parents, siblings, grandparents, neighbors, peers, and even day care providers. If we fail to respond to the expectations of these significant people in our lives, we may experience negative sanctions: teasing, isolation and exclusion, harsh words, and stigma. Therefore, children usually learn to conform, at least in their public behavior.

The lifelong process of gender socialization continues once we reach *school age* and we become more involved in activities separate from our parents. Other people in the community—teachers, religious leaders, coaches, and peers—influence us. We are grouped by sex in many of these social settings: boys versus girls, us versus them. Even if our parents are not highly traditional in their gender expectations, we still experience many expectations to conform from peers, school, and other sources.

With adulthood, the differential treatment and stratification of the sexes take new forms. Men traditionally have more networks and statuses, as well as greater access to resources outside the home. This has resulted in many women around the world having less power, because they depend more on husbands or fathers for resources. The subtitle of this chapter asks, "Who goes first?" When it comes to the question of who walks through a door first, the answer is that in many Western societies, *she* does—or at least, formal etiquette would suggest this is proper. The strong man steps back and defers to the weaker female, graciously holding the door for her, and women are served first at restaurants. This seems little compensation for the fact that doors are often closed to women at the meso and macro levels of society.

Language can be powerful in shaping the behavior and perceptions of people, as discussed in Chapter 3 on culture. Women often end sentences with tag questions, ending a declarative statement with a short tag that turns it into a question: "That was a good idea, don't you think?" This pattern may cause male business colleagues to think

women are insecure or uncertain about themselves, preventing a woman from getting the job or the promotion. The women themselves may view it as an invitation to collaboration and dialogue. On the flip side, when women stop using these "softening" devices, they may be perceived as strident, harsh, or "bitchy" (Sandberg 2013; Wood and Reich 2006). Women also tend to use more words related to psychological and social processes, while men prefer more discussion of objects and impersonal topics (Newman et al. 2008). The same adverb or adjective, when preceded by a male or female pronoun, can take on very different meanings. When one says, "He's easy" or "He's loose," it does not generally mean the same thing as when someone says, "She's easy" or "She's loose." The word *spinster* is supposed to be the female synonym for *bachelor*, yet it has very different connotations. Even the more newly coined *bachelorette* is not usually used to describe a highly appealing, perhaps lifelong role. What might be the implications of these differences?

Those who invoke the biological argument that women's options to participate in public affairs and politics are limited by pregnancy, childbirth, or breast-feeding ignore the fact that in most societies, these biological roles are time limited and that women play a variety of social roles in addition to keeping the home and hearth. They also ignore those societies in which males are deeply involved in nonaggressive and nurturing activities such as child rearing.

Thinking Sociologically

Until recently, words like *mankind* and phrases like "all men are created equal" were commonly used. Today, some people always write *he* first when writing "he and she." Others sometimes put *she* first. How do these examples—and others you can think of—reveal how language relates to gender roles?

Sex, Gender, and Sexuality: The Meso Level

By whatever age is defined as being an "adult" in a society, members are expected to assume leadership roles and responsibilities in the institutions of family, education, religion, government, economics, health care, and the military. Our roles in these institutions often differ depending on our sex, which determines our placements and many of our experiences in the social world (Brettell and Sargent 2012). This makes it difficult—but not impossible—for women to attain the most powerful positions in a society.

In most societies, sex and age stipulate when and how we experience *rites of passage*—rituals and ceremonies in institutions that mark a change of status in the family and community—the meso levels of society. These rites include any ceremonies or recognitions that admit one to adult duties and privileges. Rites of passage are institutionalized in various ways: religious rituals such as the Jewish male bar mitzvah or the female bat mitzvah ceremonies; education celebrations such as graduation ceremonies, which often involve caps and gowns of gender-specific colors or place females on one side of the room and males on the other; and different ages at which men and women are permitted to marry. Other institutions also segregate us by sex. For example, in traditional Greek Orthodox Christian churches and Orthodox Jewish synagogues, men sit on one side of the sanctuary and women on the other.

Empowerment of Women. Thirty village women gather regularly to discuss issues of health, crops, their herds, the predicted rains, goals for their children, and how to make ends meet. They are from a subsistence farming village in southern Niger on the edge of the Sahara desert. Recently, a microcredit organization was established with a small grant of $1,500 from abroad. With training from CARE International, an international nongovernmental organization (NGO), the women selected a board of directors to oversee the loans. Groups of five or six women joined together to explain their projects to the board and request small loans. Each woman is responsible for paying back a small amount on the loan each week once the project is established and bringing in money. Typical microcredit participants are women with several children, living at or below poverty, and sharing shelter with other families. With loans, women can make and sell items, and build businesses to feed, clothe, and educate children (Foundation for Women 2012). A loan of between $20 and $50 from the microcredit organization is a tremendous sum considering that for many of these women it is equivalent to 6 months' earnings. Strong social norms are instituted to encourage repayment. Participation in the program encourages women and grants them economic and social capital otherwise unavailable to them.

With the new possibilities for their lives, these women have big plans: For instance, one group plans to buy a press to make peanut oil, a staple for cooking in the region. Currently, people pay a great deal for oil imported from Nigeria. Another group will buy baby lambs, fatten them, and sell them for future festivals at a great profit. Yet another group plans to set up a small bakery. Women are also discussing the possibility of making local craft products to sell to foreign fair-trade organizations such as Ten

Thousand Villages (a Fair Trade organization that markets products made by villagers and returns the profits back to the villagers).

Some economists and social policy makers claim that grassroots organizations such as microcredits may be the way out of poverty for millions of poor families, and that women are motivated to be small-business entrepreneurs to help support their families and buy education and health care for their children. Muhammad Yunus, the founder of Grameen Bank—a microcredit lender for the very poor—received the Nobel Prize for Peace in 2006.

Microcredit organizations often build significant economic and social capital for their participants. Critics, though, suggest such organizations work on a micro level to address macro-level national and international problems of inequality (Mayoux 2008). For better or worse, microloans also may shift relations between husbands and wives, leaving men in a less powerful position within marriages, and changing gender dynamics. While this has led to more respect for women in some areas, this shift of power has also left some women vulnerable to criticisms, harassment, and isolation (Business Insider 2012). Most economists agree that microlending works best alongside macro-level initiatives seeking to address national economic problems.

Microcredit banks have provided a variety of opportunities for public sociologists to make a positive impact. For example, the next "Sociologists in Action" feature on page 274 describes how one class of sociology undergraduate students raised awareness of how meso-level organizations—banks—can impact people at the micro level.

Catarina lives in Guatemala. She started a weaving business—and turned her life around—with the help of a microfinance loan from FINCA.

SOCIOLOGISTS IN ACTION:
DONNA YANG, CHRISTIAN AGURTO, MICHELLE BENAVIDES, BRIANNE GLOGOWSKI, DEZIREE MARTINEZ, AND MICHELE VAN HOOK

Sociology Students Engage With Microfinance

Students at William Paterson University describe their participation in a microcredit organization and how they used the sociological tools they gained in their Principles of Sociology course. They educated their classmates about Kiva, a microfinance project designed to aid women and diminish poverty globally, and raised money for the organization's efforts.

Kiva is an international microfinance organization dedicated to helping ordinary people across the globe become lenders to beginning entrepreneurs. Using various sociological concepts, we sought not only to raise money for Kiva loans but also to generate awareness about microfinance's ability to empower women and help fight poverty. The website, www.kiva.org, is designed to facilitate partnerships between people willing to donate and low-income entrepreneurs seeking financial services. Kiva loans typically range from $25 to $3,000, and are temporarily financed by Kiva users who have browsed the profiles of potential entrepreneurs uploaded on the website.

Although *gender inequality* was central to our Kiva project, we used two other key sociological ideas: using a sociological eye and promoting social activism. We recognized patterns of inequality intersecting along both class and gender lines. Social stratification has created hierarchies through which women are marginalized economically, politically, and socially. Microfinance programs such as Kiva seek to mitigate this unequal access to wealth by creating greater accessibility for low-income individuals, mostly women, to financial services. As a group, we felt passionate about Kiva because of its commitment to improve society by providing more equal lending opportunities.

We raised more than $150 toward a group loan for the communal bank "Mujeres Progresistas" (Progressive Women) in Cuenca, Ecuador. This bank is composed of 11 women, and our specific loan was distributed to 2 women—both mothers of four seeking loans to help finance their personal businesses in order to help support their families. Maria Huerta invested the money in chickens and chicken feed to begin running a chicken farm. Maria Suqui used her loan to help establish a snack shop through which she hopes to earn enough money to eventually own a home.

In order to promote awareness about our project and Kiva's initiatives, we created informational pamphlets and distributed them to students on our college campus. The pamphlets explained microfinance, how Kiva utilizes this process of lending to help low-income individuals around the globe, and how students can get involved. This project helped us to realize the importance of sociology, its applicability within everyday life, and our obligation to act as socially conscious individuals in order to help promote greater social justice.

• •

This excerpt is adapted from Korgen and White's The Engaged Sociologist: Connecting the Classroom to the Community *(SAGE, 2013).*

Thinking Sociologically

How might the lack of women in positions of authority in organizations and institutions—the meso level of society—influence females' roles at the micro level? How might it influence their involvement at the macro level?

Sex, Sexuality, and Gender: The Macro Level

People around the world go to school, drive a car, and work, but in some parts of the world, school, driving, and work are forbidden for women. Fourteen-year-old Malala Yousafzai, a girl from northwest Pakistan, was shot and severely wounded by a Taliban gunman for both going to school and speaking out for other girls to have educational opportunities (Mehsud 2012). The Taliban, a regional organization that extends beyond the local boundaries, is opposed to girls going to school. Malala gained worldwide fame and since her recovery has spoken out about the right for education for all children.

When we turn to the national and global level, we witness inequality between the sexes quite separate from any form of personal prejudice or animosity toward women. Patterns of social action embedded in the entire social system may influence women and men, providing unrecognized privileges or disadvantages. This is called *institutionalized privilege* or *disprivilege*.

Over the past decade, the number of women in governing roles has increased in many parts of the globe. Although women are still denied the right to vote in Saudi Arabia, in most elections in the United Arab Emirates, and in the Vatican, voting is a universal right for most. In the United States, women have voted in federal elections for more than 90 years, following the passage of the Nineteenth Amendment in 1920 prohibiting voter discrimination on the basis of sex. Yet in the entire history of the United States, only 45 women have served in the U.S. Senate, and 297 have been elected to the House of Representatives. The first woman was elected in 1917. As of 2014, however, just 20 of 100 senators and 79 of 435 representatives in the House were women—and that was an all-time high. Still, though, women comprise just 18.5% of all national representatives (Center for American Women and Politics 2014).

The nation with the highest percentage of women in the national parliament or congress is Rwanda (sub-Saharan Africa) with 63.8% women—one of only two

In 2013, 19 women served as the head of their nations, including Angela Merkel (top), the chancellor of Germany, and Ellen Johnson Sirleaf (bottom), the president of Liberia and the first elected female head of state in Africa. Sirleaf is coordinating Liberian efforts to fight the Ebola virus.

countries to reach or surpass 50%. Canada is 61st among nations, and the United States, tied with Sao Tome and Principe, ranks 101st—well below Global North countries like Sweden (#4), Spain (#11), Denmark (#16), and

Workplace Equality

Germany (#22) and trailing Global South countries like Afghanistan (#45), Iraq (#57), and Saudi Arabia (#90) (Inter-Parliamentary Union 2014). Nations like Rwanda, with political systems that stress proportional representation and have adopted gender quotas for government positions, have more women in political offices (Yoon 2011a, 2011b). Without such systems and quotas, democratization of governmental systems is sometimes linked to a *decrease* in representation by women, a sad reality for those committed to establishing democracy around the world (Yoon 2005). Globally, women's access to power and prestige is highly variable, with African and northern European countries having a position of leadership when it comes to gender equity in government (see Table 9.1). As you study Table 9.1, note that researchers find that the needs and interests of women are not fully represented unless a critical mass of female representatives is reached, and that critical mass is usually about 35% (Yoon 2011b).

Table 9.1   Percentage of Women in National Governments (Selected Countries), 2014

	Country	Lower Chamber (e.g., House of Representatives) or Single Chamber	Upper Chamber (Senate)
1	Rwanda	63.8	38.5
2	Andorra	50.0	—
3	Cuba	48.9	—
4	Sweden	45.0	—
5	Seychelles	43.8	—
6	Senegal	43.3	—
7	Finland	42.5	—
8	Nicaragua	42.4	—
9	Ecuador	41.6	—
10	South Africa	40.8	35.2
11	Iceland	39.7	—
11	Spain	39.7	—
13	Norway	39.6	—
14	Belgium	39.3	50
15	Mozambique	39.2	—
22	Germany	36.5	27.5
27	New Zealand	33.9	—
45	Afghanistan	27.7	27.5
53	Australia	26.0	38.2
57	Iraq	25.2	—
61	Canada	25.1	39.6
74	United Kingdom	22.6	23.4
90	Saudi Arabia	19.9	—
101	United States	18.2	20.0

Source: Taken from Inter-Parliamentary Union (IPU) (2014). www.ipu.org. Reprinted with permission of the Inter-Parliamentary Union.

Note: To examine the involvement of women in other countries or to see even more recent figures, go to http://www.ipu.org/wmn-e/classif.htm.

Thinking Sociologically

What factors might explain why the United States and Canada rank so poorly in representation of women in their governments?

Cross-cultural analyses confirm that gender roles that have evolved over centuries can be transformed by sweeping government reforms, economic upheaval, or wars. In many societies, though, gender roles are passed down from one generation to the next. The fact that women in China generally work outside the home whereas women in some Muslim societies hardly venture from their homes is due to differences in cultural norms about gender roles dictated by traditions, religious beliefs, and governments, and learned through the socialization process.

GENDER SOCIALIZATION: MICRO- AND MESO-LEVEL ANALYSES

"Sugar and spice and everything nice—that's what little girls are made of. Snips and snails and puppy dog tails—that's what little boys are made of." As the verse implies, different views of little girls and little boys start at birth, based on gender and stereotypes about what is biologically natural. Behavioral expectations stem from cultural beliefs about the nature of men and women, and these expectations guide socialization from the earliest ages and in intimate primary group settings.

Gender role socialization is the process by which people learn the cultural norms, attitudes, and behaviors appropriate to their gender. That is, they learn how to think and act as boys or girls, women or men. Socialization reinforces the "proper" gender behaviors and punishes the improper behaviors. This process, in turn, reinforces gender stereotypes.

In many societies, traits of gentleness, passivity, and dependence are associated with femininity, whereas boldness, aggression, strength, and independence are identified with masculinity. For instance, in most Western societies, aggression in women is considered unfeminine, if not inappropriate or disturbing (Sandberg 2013). Likewise, the gentle, unassertive male is often looked on with scorn or pity, stigmatized as a "wimp." Gender stereotypes in the United States are less rigid than in the past, but they are still a big part of popular culture and provide guidelines for parents, and especially

for boys' behavior. Girls' norms of femininity have expanded more than norms of masculinity, and more girls have aspirations for law and medical school than boys have for nursing. Girls have more flexibility in sports they choose and in toys they can play with ("Gender Stereotypes" 2011).

Stages in Gender Socialization

Bounce that rough-and-tumble baby boy and cuddle that precious, delicate little girl. Thus begins gender socialization, starting at birth and taking place through a series of life stages, discussed in Chapter 4 on socialization. Examples from infancy and childhood show how socialization into gender roles takes place.

Infancy. Learning how to carry out gender roles begins at birth. Parents in the United States describe their newborn daughters as soft, delicate, fine featured, little, pretty, cute, awkward, and resembling their mothers. They depict their sons as strong, firm, alert, and well coordinated (Lindsey 2011). Although gender stereotypes have declined in recent years, they continue to affect the way we handle and treat male and female infants.

Clothing, room decor, and toys also reflect notions of gender. An interesting fact is that only a century ago pink was considered the "manly" color and self-respecting men were steered away from the very soft feminine color—blue ("Finery for Infants" 1893). A trade publication, *Earnshaw's Infants' Department*, published an article in June 1918 that advises parents that "[t]he generally accepted rule is pink for the boys, and blue for the girls. The reason is that pink, being a more decided and stronger color, is more suitable for the boy, while blue, which is more delicate and dainty, is prettier for the girl." In 1927, *Time* magazine printed a chart showing sex-appropriate colors for children: pink is for boys—blue for girls (Maglaty 2011). Moreover, prior to the 20th century, both boys and girls in the United States were dressed mostly in frilly dresses until they were about 6 (Maglaty 2011).

Childhood. Once they are out of infancy, research shows that boys receive more encouragement than girls to be independent and exploratory. More pressure is put on boys to behave in "gender-appropriate" ways, with an emphasis on achievement, autonomy, and aggression (Kramer and Beutel 2014). Boys are socialized into this "boy code" that provides rigid guidelines for their behavior as described in the next "Sociology in Our Social World."

Being a Girl   ▶ Tough "Guise"

sociology in our social world

The Boy Code

The Old Boy network in U.S. society favors adult men over women through a system of networks. This system actually starts with "the boy code," the rules about boys' proper behavior. Young boys learn "the code" from parents, siblings, peers, teachers, and society in general. They are praised for adhering to the code and punished for violating its dictates. William Pollack (1999) writes that boys learn several stereotyped behavior models exemplifying the boy code:

1. "The sturdy oak": Men should be stoic, stable, and independent; a man never shows weakness.

2. "Give 'em hell": From athletic coaches and movie heroes, the consistent theme is extreme daring, bravado, and attraction to violence.

3. "The 'big wheel'": Men and boys should achieve status, dominance, and power; they should avoid shame, wear the mask of coolness, and act as though everything is under control.

4. "No sissy stuff": Boys are discouraged from expressing feelings or urges perceived as feminine—dependence, warmth, empathy.

The boy code is ingrained in society; by 5 or 6 years of age, boys are less likely than girls to express hurt or distress. They have learned to be ashamed of showing feelings and of being weak. This gender straitjacket, according to

Pollack, causes boys to conceal feelings in order to fit in and be accepted and loved. As a result, some boys, especially in adolescence, become silent, covering any vulnerability and masking their true feelings. This affects boys' relationships, performance in school, and ability to connect with others. It also causes young males to put on what Jackson Katz calls the "tough guise," when young men and boys emphasize aggression and violence to display masculinity (Katz 2006). Moreover, if fathers emphasize competition and toughness, their sons are much more likely to become bullies and are likely to have few deep friendships, especially in the later teen years (Kindlon and Thompson 2000; Way 2011).

Although boys are innately as capable of expressing emotion as girls, they learn to suppress emotions—except for anger, which is seen as a legitimate masculine emotion (Kindlon and Thompson 2000). This inability to share feelings has serious repercussions for inner well-being and for healthy relationships.

Today, many boys are a part of a resistance movement against the boy code (Way 2011). They have quite intimate relationships with male friends—sharing emotions, vulnerabilities, and secrets—especially during childhood and early adolescence. Sadly, research shows that while most boys deeply value intimate same-sex friendships, those ties, under pressure from the boy code, can weaken considerably by late adolescence and many boys struggle privately with the loss. However, some men are forming more supportive and less competitive

Male Socialization

relationships with other men, and there are likely to be continued changes in and broadened definitions of "appropriate" behavior for men (Kimmel and Messner 2009; Way 2011).

Pollack suggests that we can help boys resist norms that are destructive to them by

1. giving some undivided attention each day just listening to boys;

2. encouraging a range of emotions;

3. avoiding language that taunts, teases, or shames;

4. looking behind the veneer of "coolness" for signs of problems;

5. expressing love and empathy;

6. dispelling the "sturdy oak" image; and

7. advocating a broad, inclusive model of masculinity (Pollack 1999).

Thinking Sociologically

What evidence do you see of the boy code when you observe your friends and relatives? What is the impact of the boy code? Is there a similar code for girls?

On the other hand, girls are trained to express aggression in more subtle ways: through gossip, rumors, name-calling, backbiting, and excluding other girls from social activities (Beran 2012). Friendship and needing to belong are the weapons—rather than the "sticks and stones" used by boys. This form of bullying is subtle and hard to detect, but it can have long-lasting effects on girls (Beran 2012; Girls Health 2009; Simmons 2002).

Names for children also reflect stereotypes about gender. Boys are more often given strong, hard names that end in consonants. The top 10 boys' names include Jackson, Aiden, Liam, Lucas, Noah, Mason, Jayden, Ethan, Jacob, and Jack. Girls are more likely to be given soft pretty names with vowel endings such as most of the top 10: Sophia, Emma, Olivia, Isabella, Mia, Ava, Lily, Zoe, Emily, and Chloe (BabyCenter 2013).

Alternatively, girls may be given feminized versions of boys' names—Roberta, Jessica, Josephine, Nicole, Michelle, Donna, Charlotte, Georgia, or Antonia. Sometimes traditional boys' names are given to girls without first feminizing them. Names such as Lynn, Stacey, Tracey, Faye, Dana, Jody, Lindsay, Robin, Carmen, Kelly, Kim, Beverly, Ashley, Dana, Carol, Shannon, and Leslie used to be names exclusively for men, but within a decade or two after they were applied to girls, parents stopped using them for boys (Kean 2007). So a common name for males may for a time be given to either sex, but then, it is given

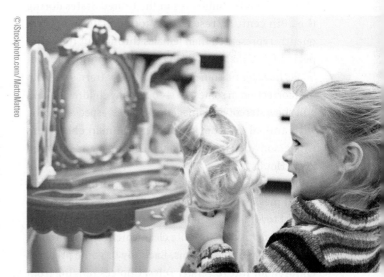

©iStockphoto.com/MattoMatteo

Boys and girls, like the one in this picture, begin to conform to gender expectations once they are old enough to understand that their sex is permanent.

primarily to girls. The pattern rarely goes in the other direction. Once feminized, the names seem to have become tainted and unacceptable for boys (Lieberson, Dumais, and Bauman 2000).

As children are rewarded for performing proper gender roles, these roles are reinforced, setting the stage for gender-related interactions, behaviors, and choices in later life. We now turn to meso-level agents of gender socialization.

Meso-Level Agents of Gender Socialization

Clues to proper gender roles surround children in materials produced by corporations (books, toys, games), in technology and mass media images, in educational settings, and in religious organizations and beliefs. In Chapter 4, we learned about agents of socialization. Those agents play a major role in teaching children proper gender roles. The following examples demonstrate how organizations and institutions in our society teach and reinforce gender assumptions and roles.

Corporations. Corporations create many materials that help socialize children into conduct socially approved for their gender. Publishers, for example, produce books that present images of expected gender behavior. The language and pictures in preschool picture books, elementary children's books, stories for teenagers, and school textbooks are steeped in gender role messages, reflecting society's expectations and stereotypes. In a recent study of children's books published in the United States during the 20th century, researchers found males more frequently represented than females throughout the entire period (McCabe et al. 2011). Studies on more recent books have found some change in this pattern—even an overcorrection in some cases—but many children's books still show stereotyped images of females, especially those with animal or other types of nonhuman characters (Anderson and Hamilton 2005; Diekman and Murmen 2004; Houlis 2011).

Producers of toys and games also contribute to traditional messages about gender. Wall posters and store-bought toys fill rooms in homes of children in the Western world, and it is usually quite clear which are boys' rooms and which are girls' rooms. Each toy or game prepares children for future gender roles. Choices ranging from college major to occupational choice appear to be affected by these early choices and childhood learning experiences (Deerwester 2013).

Boys' rooms are filled with sports equipment, army toys, building and technical toys, and cars and trucks. Girls' rooms have fewer toys, and most are related to dolls and domestic roles. Boys have more experience manipulating blocks, Tinkertoys, LEGO bricks, and Erector Sets—toys paralleling masculinized activities outside the home in the public domain, from constructing and building trades to military roles and sports. Girls prepare for domestic roles with toys related to domestic activities and play with Barbie dolls that stress physical appearance, consumerism, and glamour. Toy stores are generally divided into distinct boys' and girls' sections, shaping parents' and children's choices, and girls' and boys' future skills and interests (Abadi 2013; Williams 2006). Each toy or game

prepares children through anticipatory socialization for future gender roles. The bottom line is that gender portrayals are unequal and the females presented in books, video games, and toys tend to be in stereotypical roles—supporting, needing rescue, or sexually alluring.

Mass Media. Mass media comes in many forms—magazines, ads, films, music videos, Internet sites—and is a major agent of socialization into gender roles. We can see its influence all around us, even during a typical weekend evening for many boys. It is Friday night and a group of adolescent males gather to play games. Their two favorites are the card game *Magic: The Gathering* (MTG or Magic) and the online game *World of Warcraft* (WoW). WoW is played with many online players, and the individual players can sit in front of their computers alone, interacting only online. Popular video games that primarily attract boys include *Grand Theft Auto: Vice City* (adventure), *Halo 2* (action), *Gran Turismo 3: A-Spec* (driving), and *Madden NFL* (sports). One study found that over 80% of characters in video games are male (Williams et al. 2009). Research shows that adolescents identify with characters in video games, and often view them as role models (Mou and Peng 2009). Girls are generally missing or peripheral to the play. Notice the next time you are around people playing video games that the fighting characters are typically male and often in armor. When fighting women do appear, they are usually clad in skin-revealing bikini-style attire—odd clothing in which to do battle! (Martins et al. 2009).

Thinking Sociologically

Why are video and role-playing games primarily a boy thing? Where are the girls? What effect might girls' and boys' different activities have on their futures?

Some recent action films include adventurous and competent girls and women, helping to counter images of sexy and helpless females. *The Hunger Games* heroine, Katniss Everdeen, has become a brave idol for teenage girls; Mattel has even made a Barbie version of the heroine. *The Girl With the Dragon Tattoo* and other films in that series present an extremely clever and unique heroine in Lisbeth. Despite these new examples of young women in strong leadership roles, highly competent females are still seen less frequently than men are in the media.

Young men and women, desiring to fit in, can be influenced in harmful ways by messages from the media. For instance, the epidemic of steroid use or hormones among boys to stimulate muscle growth results from desire to be successful in sports and have an appealing body image. Professional athletes set an example, and the dark side of steroids is often overlooked: acne, mood swings, depression, elevated suicide attempts, aggressive behavior, high blood pressure, heightened sex characteristics, and liver damage (Global Sports Development 2013). Adolescent girls are more prone to dieting, binging, and purging (Stephen et al. 2014). Dieting among girls, driven in part by ads, is a health concern in the United States and some other countries (Taub and McLorg 2010). Studies show that between 40% and 60% of children age 6 to 12 are worried about their weight. Eighty percent of 10-year-olds have dieted. Over half (53%) of 13-year-old and more than three out of four (78%) 17-year-old girls have issues with their bodies (Hepworth 2010; Roberts 2012).

Television is another part of the media that works as a powerful socializing agent. Children born after 2005 in the United States spend—on average—35 hours watching TV per week, a 12% increase over the previous 9 years. Television presents a simple, stereotyped view of life, from advertisements to situation comedies to soap operas. Women in soap operas and ads, especially those working outside the home, are often depicted as having problems in carrying out their role responsibilities (Boston Women's Health Book Collective 2006). Even the extraordinary powers of superheroes on Saturday morning television depict the female characters as having gender-stereotyped skills such as superintuition.

Films and television series in the United States seldom feature average-size or older women (although a greater variety of ages and body types is seen in British Broadcasting Corporation and other British productions such as the recent films *The Best Exotic Marigold Hotel* and *Philomena* featuring older stars). Most U.S. films feature stars who are attractive and thin, presenting an often unattainable model for young women, making many feel inadequate and feeding the diet frenzy (Taub and McLorg 2010). In U.S. media, overweight women are almost entirely depicted as comic figures on television.

In addition to watching television, the average child in the United States also spends approximately 10 hours a week using other electronic devices. In part, because of this sedentary lifestyle, children today are much more likely to be overweight, even obese (Joint Center for Political and Economic Studies 2013; Mercola 2013). Ironically, this makes it harder for them to live up to the stereotypical buff male and slender female body images they see in the media.

Mattel's Barbie dolls have been criticized for their extremely traditional and highly sexualized images of young women. The boy looks at toys marketed for boys, and the message he receives is very different.

 Thinking Sociologically

Think of recent images of popular men and women you have seen in the media. What type of body images do they portray? How might these meso-level depictions affect young men and women individually at the micro level?

Educational Systems. Girls and boys often have very different experiences in school. As noted in the following examples, education systems socialize children through

Like most U.S. glamour stars, Paris Hilton (left—arriving at the MTV Video Movie Awards with Nicky Hilton) must conform to the image of very thin, shapely femininity. By contrast, an older not-particularly-thin actor, Stephanie Cole (right) plays the leading role in the BBC series *Waiting for God*—a comedy about people in an assisted living nursing home.

classroom academics, lunchroom, and playground activities; students' popularity and recognition; sports and Title IX programs; and teachers' attitudes and expectations. In academics, girls are achieving at a higher level than boys overall. According to a recent study, overall girls have better social and behavioral skills than boys and are more likely to study, whereas boys have lower engagement in school and weaker preparation (DiPrete and Buchmann 2013). However, in subjects that lead to high-paying jobs, there is a lag for some girls, such as high-level physics and math courses. Recent research indicates, however, that girls are equally represented with boys in physics courses in communities where women are employed in STEM (science, technology, engineering, and math) fields and girls have a model for pursuing STEM courses. Thus, girls may excel in physics and other STEM courses in communities where traditional gendered status is not the norm (Riegle-Crumb and Moore 2013).

A study of gender and math also showed that girls perform as well as boys, but differently. For example, boys in the United States tend to do either very well or very poorly on tests, whereas girls are more often in the middle range. Pursuing a STEM career does not necessarily require stellar math scores, but some girls are socialized to believe they are not good in math and therefore do not take higher-level courses or expect to do well on tests (Wade 2013b).

In sports, boys are encouraged to join competitive team sports and girls to support them. Some argue that this simulates hierarchical adult roles of boss/secretary and physician/nurse. Girls and boys' separate experiences in grade school and middle school reinforce boundaries of "us" and "them" in classroom seating and activities, in the lunchroom, and in playground activities, as girls and boys are seated, lined up, and given assignments by sex (Sadker and Sadker 2005). Those who go outside the boundaries, especially boys, are ridiculed by peers and sometimes teachers, reinforcing stereotypes and separate gender role socialization (Sadker and Sadker 2005; Thorne 1993).

Part of the issue of male–female inequality in schools is tied to the issue of *popularity*, which seems to have less to do with being liked than with being known and visible. If everyone knows a person's name, she or he is popular. At the middle school level, there are more ways by which boys than girls can become known. In sports, even when there are both boys' and girls' basketball teams, many spectators come to the boys' contests and very few to the girls' games. Thus, few people know the female athletes by name. In fact, a far more visible position is cheerleader—standing on the sidelines cheering for the boys teams, and sometimes for girls teams—because those girls are at least seen. One effort is to redefine cheerleading as a legitimate sport in its own right (Eder, Evans, and Parker 1995; Hu 2007; Milner 2006). The bottom line is that there are far more visible positions for the boys than for girls in middle and high school, allowing them to be recognized and become leaders.

Title IX of the U.S. Education Amendments of 1972 was a major legislative attempt to level the educational and sports playing field. Passed in order to bar gender discrimination in schools receiving federal funds, this legislation mandates equal opportunity for participation in school-sponsored programs (Lindsey 2011). The law has reduced or eliminated blatant discrimination in areas ranging from admissions and health care to counseling and housing, sex-segregated programs, financial aid, dress codes, and other areas of concern. However, the biggest impact of Title IX legislation has been in athletics.

Women's athletic programs and scholarship opportunities have grown since 1972, but still lag behind those for men. By 2011, the number of girls competing in high school sports had climbed to almost 3.2 million, yet that is still 1.3 million more boys than girls participating in high school sports. In collegiate sports, the number of female athletes has grown from fewer than 30,000 to about 200,000. Men's sports, though, both bring in and receive more money and have more airtime on TV (Dusenbery and Lee 2012). Participation in athletics, especially team sports, is important because sports can foster skills in teamwork, strategic thinking, and anticipating counteractions by a competitor, useful skills in business and government.

Religious Organizations. Religious organizations serve as agents of gender socialization by defining, reinforcing, and perpetuating gender roles and cultural beliefs. Religious teachings provide explanations of proper male and female roles. Although the specific teachings vary, the three major monotheistic religions that affirm that there is only one God—Christianity, Islam, and Judaism—are traditionally patriarchal, stressing separate female and male spheres (Kramer and Beutel 2014).

Some interpretations of the Adam and Eve creation story in the Hebrew Bible (the Old Testament in the Christian Bible) state that man was created first and that men are, therefore, superior. Because Eve, created from the rib of man, was a sinner, her sins keep women forever in an inferior, second-class position. For these and other reasons, in some branches of these religions, women are restricted in their roles within the family and religious organizations. They cannot be priests in Catholic churches

High school and college athletics are much less reliable paths for women to become known since so few people come to the games. Even at this professional Lynx game with a team that twice won the national title, there is a sparse attendance (left). By contrast, women in very sexy outfits can become celebrities when they perform as cheerleaders in front of 80,000 fans at men's sporting events (right).

and cannot vote on business matters in some religious organizations. However, recent work by feminist scholars challenges the notion of patriarchy in Judaic and Christian history, pointing out that women may have played a much broader role in religious development than currently recognized (Hunter College Women's Studies Collective 2005). Even *Yahweh*—the name for God in the Hebrew Bible—had both male and female connotations, and when God was referred to as a source of wisdom in the wisdom literature (Psalms, Proverbs, and so forth), feminine pronouns and references were used (Borg 2001). Increasingly, denominations are granting women greater roles in the religious hierarchies, ministries, and priesthood.

Women in Judaism lived for 4,000 years in a patriarchal system where men read, taught, and legislated while women followed (Lindsey 2011). Today, three of the five main branches of Judaism allow women equal participation, illustrating that religious practices do change over time. However, Hasidic and Orthodox Jews have a division of labor between men and women following old laws, with designated gender roles for the home and religious life.

Some Christian teachings have treated women as second-class citizens, even in the eyes of God. For this reason, some Christian denominations have excluded women from a variety of leadership roles and told them they must be subservient to their husbands. Other Christians point to the admonition by Saint Paul that theologically speaking, the distinction between men and women is not relevant and that women and men are not spiritually different.

Traditional Hindu religion painted women as seductresses, strongly erotic, and a threat to male spirituality and asceticism. To protect men from this threat, women were kept totally covered in thick garments and veils and seen only by men in their immediate families. Today, Hinduism comes in many forms, most of which honor the woman's domestic sphere of life—as mothers, wives, and homemakers—while accepting women in public roles (Lindsey 2011).

Traditional Islamic beliefs also portrayed female sexuality as dangerous to men, although many women in Islamic societies today are full participants in the public and private sphere. The Quran (also spelled Qur'an or Koran), the Muslim sacred scripture, has a few passages that seem to favor men, but most of the text actually supports women's rights (Aslan 2011). Still, aspects of the traditional Sharia law, strict Islamic law, have carried over in several countries and among some groups. It has been used to punish women accused of violating rules about gender behavior (Proudman 2012; Mydans 2002).

Women in strict literalist Muslim societies such as Algeria, Iran, Syria, and Saudi Arabia are separated from men (except for fathers and brothers) in work and worship. They generally remain covered. *Purdah*, which means curtain, refers to practices of seclusion and separate worlds for women and men in Islamic cultures. Screens in households and veils in public enforce female modesty and prevent men from seeing women where this is dictated (Ward and Edelstein 2014). In the days of Muhammad, only his wives wore such veils for privacy, and there were no commandments in the Quran instructing women to be covered, so these patterns are more cultural and national than Islamic. In any case, today some women argue that the veil they wear is for modesty, for cosmetic purposes, or to protect them from the stares of men.

Meso-level religious systems influence how different societies interpret proper gender roles and how sometimes these belief systems change with new interpretations of scriptures. (Further discussion of the complex relationship between religion and gender appears in Chapter 12.) From family and education to media and religion, meso-level agents of socialization reinforce "appropriate" gender roles in each society.

 Thinking Sociologically

What are some of the books, toys, games, television shows, school experiences, religious teachings, and peer interactions that have influenced your gender role socialization? In what ways did they do so?

GENDER STRATIFICATION: MESO- AND MACRO-LEVEL PROCESSES

The phrase *glass ceiling* generally applies to processes that limit the progress of women and other minorities to the highest job or status positions because of invisible barriers that bar promotion within an organization. Although they may have superior skills or experience, they are passed over (Berrey 2013). "The *glass ceiling* keeps women from reaching the highest levels of corporate and public responsibility, and the 'sticky floor' keeps the vast majority of the world's women stuck in low-paid jobs" (Hunter College Women's Studies Collective 2005:393). This discrimination results in a loss of talent, and lower salaries for women, who make up almost half of the workforce and are the main or equal breadwinners in 4 out of 10 families.

Although there are high-profile women serving as CEOs and in government leadership positions in the United States, they occupy only 4.6% of both the Fortune 500 and the Fortune 1000 CEO positions (Catalyst 2014b). Women now represent 52.2% of the U.S. PhDs (Council of Graduate Schools 2014) and 67% of college graduates, but they earn only about 80 cents for every dollar earned by men, a 23% wage gap. This holds across occupations (DeBoskey 2012; Hegewisch et al. 2014; Matson 2013; U.S. Bureau of Labor Statistics 2014).

Men, on the other hand, often face the "glass escalator," especially in traditionally female occupations. Even if they do not seek to climb in the organizational hierarchy, occupational social forces push them up the job ladder to the higher echelons (Williams 2013). The next "Engaging Sociology" on page 286 provides an exercise to think about how our ideas may subtly maintain the glass ceiling and the glass escalator.

Women and Men at Work: Gendered Organizations

"How can I do it all—marriage, children, education, career, social life?" This is a question that many college students ask. They already anticipate a delicate balancing act. Work has been central to the definition of masculinity in U.S. society, and for the past half-century women have been joining the workforce in greater numbers (Kramer and Beutel 2014). In 2012, women made up 46.9% of the labor force; 57.7% of all women 16 and over were in the labor force, compared to 70.2% of all men (Catalyst 2014a). Figure 9.1 shows the average pay for women in an

FIGURE 9.1   **Ratio of Women's to Men's Earnings for Selected Occupations, 2010**

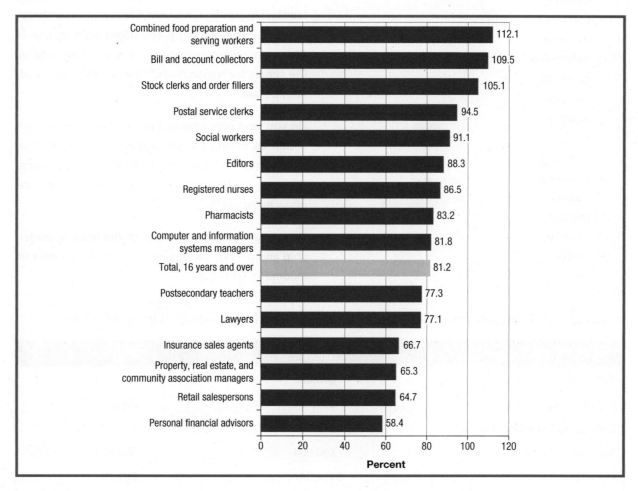

Source: US Bureau of Labor Statistics.

Note: The yellow line is the average income ratio for women compared to men—that is, on average, women earn 81% of what men earn.

occupation as a ratio of what men earn. For example, women who are personal financial advisors earn 58.7% of what men in that occupation earn. The pattern of unequal pay is true in a number of global North countries (20-First 2010).

Among countries of the global North, Sweden has the highest percentage of working women at more than 8 out of 10 women participating in the labor force. Yet even in Sweden, with its parental leave and other family-friendly

ENGAGING SOCIOLOGY

Masculinity and Femininity in Our Social World

Mark each characteristic with an *M* or an *F* depending on whether you think it is generally defined by society as a masculine or feminine characteristic.

__ achiever

__ aggressive

__ analytical

__ caring

__ confident

__ dynamic

__ deferential (defers to others; yields with courtesy)

__ devious

__ intuitive

__ loving

__ manipulative

__ nurturing

__ organized

__ passive

__ a planner

__ powerful

__ sensitive

__ strong

__ relationship oriented (makes decisions based on how others will *feel*)

__ rule oriented (makes decisions based on *abstract procedural rules rather people's feelings*)

Next, mark an *X* just to the right of 10 characteristics that you think are the essential qualities for a leadership position in a complex organization (business, government, etc.). You might want to ask 20 of your acquaintances to do this and then add up the scores for "masculinity," "femininity," and "leadership trait."

Do you (and your acquaintances) tend to view leadership as having the same traits as those marked "masculine" or "feminine"? What are the implications of your findings for the "glass ceiling" or "the glass escalator"?

How might correlations between the traits of leadership and gender notions help to explain the data on income in Table 9.2?

Table 9.2   U.S. Income by Educational Level and Sex—Full-Time Workers

Education	Men	Women
Not a high school graduate	$23,036	$15,514
High school graduate	$35,468	$24,304
College graduate (bachelor's)	$69,479	$43,589
Master's degree	$90,964	$58,534
Doctorate	$114,347	$83,708
Professional degree	$150,310	$89,897

Source: U.S. Census Bureau, *Statistical Abstract of the United States* (2012).

policies, women and men feel pressures of work and family responsibilities (Eshleman and Bulcroft 2010). Dual-career marriages raise questions about child rearing, power relations, and other factors in juggling work and family.

Every workplace has gendered relationships: ratios of female to male workers; gender reflected in subordinate-supervisor positions; and distribution of positions between men and women. This, in turn, affects our experiences in the workplace. Consider the example of mothers breast-feeding their babies. Must they quit their jobs or alter their family schedules if the workplace does not provide a space for breast-feeding? Some workplaces accommodate family needs, but many do not.

Using data from Organisation for Economic Co-operation and Development, *The Economist* constructed a "glass-ceiling index" using the five indicators: the number of men and women respectively with college educations;

female labor-force participation; the gender wage gap; the proportion of women in senior positions in corporations and professions; and net child-care costs compared to incomes. Cross-national comparisons indicate that New Zealand, Norway, Sweden, and Canada have the best conditions for working women. Nations that scored least women-friendly in employ were Japan and South Korea where few women can reach top jobs. Among the 26 nations that were studied, the United States rated 12th for women's employment conditions (Khazan 2013). The results of the ranking appear in Figure 9.2.

 Thinking Sociologically

If corporate structures were reversed so that women organized the workplace, how might the workplace environment change? How might these changes impact women, men, and their families?

FIGURE 9.2   **Glass-Ceiling Index**

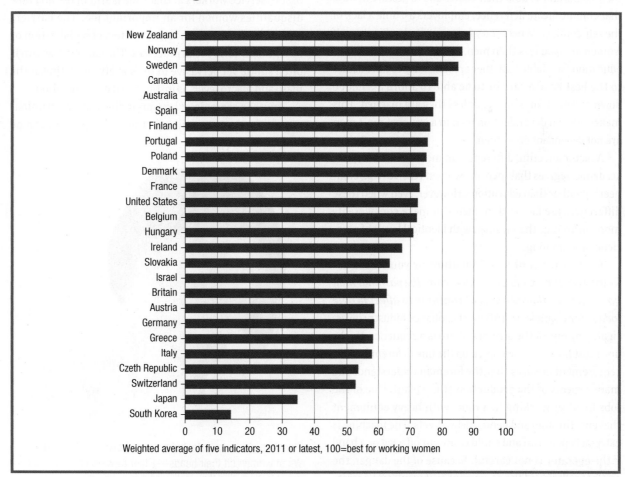

Weighted average of five indicators, 2011 or latest, 100=best for working women

Source: "The Glass Ceiling Index," *The Economist,* March 7, 2013.

Institutionalized Gender Discrimination

Gender stratification at the meso level—like race and ethnic stratification—can occur quite independently of any overt prejudice or ill will by others. It becomes part of the social system, and we are not even conscious of it. *Discrimination* is often built into organizations and cultural expectations and includes both intentional actions and unintentional actions or structures that have consequences harmful to minorities. It is embedded in institutions.

Recall from the previous chapter that side-effect discrimination involves *practices in one institutional area that have negative impact because they are linked to practices in another institutional area.* Institutions are interdependent, so discrimination in one can result in unintentional discrimination in others. For example, when roles of women in family life are determined by rigid gender expectations, women find it more difficult to devote themselves to gaining job promotions. In addition, as long as little girls learn through socialization to use their voices and to hold their bodies and to gesture in ways that communicate deference, employers assume a lack of the self-confidence necessary for major leadership roles. If women are paid less than men, despite the same levels of education (see Table 9.2), they are less likely to have access to the best health care or to be able to afford a $40,000 down payment for a house, unless they are married. This makes women dependent on men in a way that most men are not dependent on women.

A factor affecting differences in incomes is the type of academic degrees that men and women receive (e.g., engineering rather than education). However, even when these differences are factored in, men still make considerably more on average than women with identical levels of experience and training.

Past-in-present discrimination, as you will recall from Chapter 8, refers to *practices from the past that may no longer be allowed but that continue to affect people today.* For example, in a Midwest appliance industry investigated by one of the authors, there is a sequence of jobs one must hold to be promoted up the line to foreman. This requirement ensures that the foreman understands the many aspects of the production at the plant. One of the jobs involves working in a room with heavy equipment that cuts through and bends metal sheets. The machine is extremely powerful and could easily cut off a leg or a hand if the operator is not careful. Because of the danger, the engineers designed the equipment so it would not operate unless three levers were activated at the same time. One

lever was triggered by stepping on a pedal on the floor. The other two required reaching out with one's hands so that one's body was extended. When one was spread-eagled to activate all three levers, there was no way one could possibly have a part of one's body near the blades.

It was brilliant engineering, but there was one unanticipated problem: The hand-activated levers were 5 feet, 10 inches off the ground and 5 feet apart. Few women had the height and arm span to run this machine, and therefore, no women had yet made it through the sequence of positions to the higher-paying position of foreman. The equipment cost millions of dollars, so it was not likely to be replaced. Neither the engineers who designed the machine nor the upper-level managers who established the sequence of jobs to become foreman had deliberately tried to exclude women. Indeed, they were perplexed when they looked at their employee figures and saw so few women moving up through the ranks. The cause of women's disadvantage was not mean-spirited men but features of the system that had unintended consequences resulting in past-in-present discrimination. A machine built in the past to service workers at that time is still in use and now disqualifies women for an important job. The barriers women face, then, are not just matters of socialization or other micro-level social processes. The nature of sexism is often subtle yet pervasive in the society, operating at the meso and macro levels as institutional discrimination.

Another example of how prejudices and discrimination in the past can still affect us in the present can be

© iStockphoto.com/ Pathathai Chungyam

This little girl looks cute, but not very powerful or confident. When women tilt their heads—either forward or to one side—they also look like they lack confidence, and this hurts their chances of promotion in the corporate world.

seen in children's books. Earlier in this chapter we discussed inequalities and stereotypes in children's books. Although more recent books show expansion in the roles of males and females, the tens of thousands of older, classic books in public and school libraries mean that a parent or a child picking a book off of the shelf is still likely to select a book that has old stereotypical views of boys and girls.

Men often get defensive and angry when people talk about sexism in society because they feel they are being attacked or asked to correct past injustices. However, the empirical reality is that the playing field is not level for men and women. Most men do not do anything to intentionally harm women, and they may not feel prejudiced toward women, but sexism operates so that men are given privileges they never asked for and may not even recognize.

Gender Differences in Internet Use

Internet-related gender stratification exhibits itself not just in terms of *whether* a person uses the Internet but also in terms of *how* a person uses the Internet. In the United States, women tend to use social networking sites 12% more than men (women 74%, men 62%) (Pew Research Center Internet & American Life Project 2014), with the intent of keeping up with family and friends. Women's use focuses on personal growth, maintaining a social group, and getting information about products and brands. Globally, women account for 47.9% of visitors to social networking sites, and spend 30% more time on social networking sites than men (ComScore 2010; Morrison 2010).

Men tend to use the Internet to gather information and to exchange ideas, gain job skills, and form and maintain professional networks. Thus, women use social media more than men for their private lives, and men are more likely to use the Internet for engaging in the public sphere. The difference also reflects dissimilarities in the professional positions men and women tend to hold. Men's greater use of the Internet to enhance their careers relates to the preponderance of men in upper-level management positions. In the United States, where women have recently caught up with or outpaced their male peers in education, the direction of U.S. usage parallels that of other Global North countries and may predict the future for other countries (Madden and Zickuhr 2011).

In some countries, there is a huge gender digital divide, and research shows that women and men tend to use computers in different ways. These women in Afghanistan are learning computer skills.

Thinking Sociologically

Ask several people from different generations and different genders how they use computer technology and the Internet and how they learned these skills. What do you conclude from their responses about the impact of gender on Internet use? How do your findings compare to those discussed in the book? Why?

GENDER STRATIFICATION: MICRO- TO MACRO-LEVEL THEORIES

Recent research by some biologists and psychologists has considered whether there are innate differences in the makeup of women and men. For instance, males produce more testosterone, a hormone found to be correlated with aggression. Research shows that in many situations, males tend to be more aggressive and concerned with dominance, whether the behavior is biologically programmed or learned or both. Other traits, such as nurturance, empathy, and altruism, show no clear gender difference (Fausto-Sterling 1992; Sapolsky 2011).

Although biological and psychological factors are part of the difference between females and males, our focus here is on the major contribution that *social factors* make in the social statuses of males and females in human society (DiPrete and Buchmann 2013). This section explores social theories that explain gender differences.

Symbolic Interaction Theory: Micro-Level Analysis

Traditional notions of gender are hard to change. Confusion over proper masculine and feminine roles creates anxiety and even anomie in a society. People want guidelines. Thus, many believe it is best to adhere to traditional notions of gender that are reinforced by religious or political dogmas, making those ideas appear sacred, absolute, and beyond human interference. Others believe the male prerogatives and privileges of the past were established by men to protect their rights and should be challenged. Change in concepts of gender can be hard to bring about precisely because they are rooted in the meaning system and status and power structures present in the social world.

Symbolic interactionists look at gender as socially constructed. Sex is the biological reality of different "plumbing" in our bodies, and interactionists are interested in how those physical differences come to be symbols, resulting in different social rights and rewards. The meaning assigned to one's sex is connected to notions of masculinity and femininity. The symbolic interaction perspective has been forceful in insisting that notions of proper gender behavior are not intrinsically related to a person's sex. Rather, gender is a socially created or constructed idea.

More than any other theory, symbolic interaction stresses the idea of *human agency*—the notion that humans not only are influenced by the society in which they live but also actively help create it (Charon 2010; Hewitt and Shulman 2011). In a study of elementary children in classrooms and on playgrounds, Barrie Thorne (1993) found that while teachers influenced the children, the children themselves were active participants in creating the student culture that guided their play. As children played with one another, Thorne noticed the ways in which they created words, nicknames, distinctions between one another, and new forms of interaction. This is a very important point: Humans do not just passively adopt cultural notions about gender; they *do gender*. They create it as they behave and interact with others in ways that define "normal" male or female conduct (West and Zimmerman 1987). *Doing gender* is an everyday, recurring, and routine occurrence. It is a constant ongoing process that defines each situation, and takes place in organizations and between individuals. Understanding the process of *doing gender* helps us understand why we think and act as we do.

When children are in an ambiguous situation, they may spontaneously define their sex as the most relevant trait about themselves or others. Indeed, even when children act as if gender matters, they are helping make it a reality for those around them. As the next child adopts the "definition of reality" from the first, acting as if sex is more important than hair color or eye color, it makes gender the most prominent characteristic in the mind of the next child. Yet each child, in a sense, could choose to ignore gender and decide that something else is more important. This is part of *human agency*—the freedom to define reality differently from others. The same principle applies to adults. When a person "chooses" to recognize gender as a critical distinction between two individuals or two groups, that person is "doing gender." We *do gender* all the time, every day. In fact, we cannot avoid it! It is present in our interactions, and we are conscious that we will be judged by others on how well we follow our gender roles. That judgment could be harsh if we go outside accepted boundaries of gender behavior (Hewitt and Shulman 2011; O'Brien 2011; Schoepflin 2011).

Through interaction, people do gender, and although this process begins at a micro level, it has implications all the way to the global level. The next section explores meso- and macro-level forces that shape gender and stratification based on sex. One example of *doing gender* is illustrated in eating—as discussed in the next "Sociology in Our Social World." This shows how gender socialization affects our attitudes toward everyday events that we take for granted.

 Thinking Sociologically

How do you do gender*? How did you learn these patterns of behavior? How do you think people would react if you did not follow the behavior patterns assigned to your gender? How comfortable would you feel when violating those gender norms? Why?*

Structural-Functional and Conflict Theories: Meso- and Macro-Level Analyses

Structural-Functional Theory. From the structural-functional perspective, each sex has a role to play in the interdependent groups and institutions of society. Some early theorists argued that men and women carry out different roles and are, of necessity, unequal because of the needs of societies and practices that have developed since early human history. Social relationships and practices that have proved successful in the survival of a group are likely to continue and to be reinforced by society's norms, laws, and religious beliefs.

sociology in our social world

Gender and Food
By Jacqueline Bergdahl

Behavior is generally considered *gendered* when it has symbolic meaning that differs for men versus women. Food is gendered—embedded with symbolic meanings. In food preparation, women are more likely than men to be the primary food preparer in households, while there are more male professional chefs than female ones. Women are more likely to bake than are men, and men are more likely to grill than are women. Food practices are shaped by gender, even though we prefer to think that what and how we eat are due to personal preferences, rather than larger social forces.

Some food items are considered to have a gender. Meat, potatoes, and coffee are foods that many people consider to be masculine, while yogurt and fruit are feminine, and chicken and oranges are gender neutral (Rappoport 2003). When researchers asked subjects to sort the pictures of food items into men's foods and women's foods, salad, fish, couscous, and stir-fry were generally considered women's foods while pizza, hot dogs, macaroni and cheese, pot roast, and bacon cheeseburgers were considered men's foods (McPhail, Beagan, and Chapman 2012).

Many food preferences were also seen by respondents as gendered. Salads were considered food for women, and red meat for men. Women were said to eat daintily and men heartily. Some argue that part of these differences could be biological, as men generally require more calories to maintain their greater muscle mass than women do, but generally these expectations about who eats what have more to do with cultural gender constructions than the physicality of bodies (McPhail et al. 2012).

Food was considered women's food when it was colorful, delicate, in smaller portions, lighter, or healthier. Part of the attribution of foods to women had to do with weight control. Women were perceived as needing to be more concerned with maintaining or losing weight. Men were thought to prefer both heartier fare and larger portions—with little worry about controlling their food intake or weight (McPhail et al. 2012).

Women were more adventurous than men when it came to food choices, while ease of preparation and consumption were the primary considerations for men. Men were also found to be less concerned about their health, more reluctant to eat vegetables, and more likely to prefer spicy foods. Most participants in the study considered meat, and particularly red meat, to be men's food.

Some foods were less gendered. Fish was generally considered women's food as it was healthy and light, but some respondents considered fish to be men's food because more men than women like to catch and eat their own fish. Sushi was seen by some as women's food because of its appearance, but as men's food by others because it contained raw fish. Despite all these clearly gendered ideas about food, all of the subjects involved in the study denied that their eating was gendered. All

(Continued)

The Truth About Men, Women, and Food

(Continued)

identified their food preferences as a matter of individual choice, not the result of social patterns or forces (McPhail et al. 2012).

Why is it important to understand that food is gendered—that it has symbolic as well as nutritional substance? It allows us to see that our behavior is under the influence of larger structural forces. We may recognize the influence generally (in this case by being willing to sort food photographs into piles according to gender), but we prefer to view our own behavior

as simply a matter of choice. Until we acknowledge the effects of gender in all spheres, it will be difficult to eradicate gender inequality. Thinking about how food is gendered is a way of seeing the effects of gender in our lives and would make interesting dinner conversation.

• •

Jacqueline Bergdahl is associate professor of sociology at Wright State University. She studies food, gender, and obesity, among other topics.

Thus, relationships between women and men believed to support survival are maintained. In traditional hunter-gatherer, horticultural, and pastoral societies, for instance, the division of labor and social roles are based on sex and age. The females often take on the primary tasks of child care, gardening, food preparation, and other duties near the home. Men do tasks that require movements farther from home, such as hunting, fishing, and herding.

As societies industrialize, roles and relationships change due to structural changes in society. Émile Durkheim described a gradual move from traditional societies held together by *mechanical solidarity* (the glue based on shared beliefs, values, and traditions) to modern societies united through *organic solidarity* (social coherence based on division of labor, with each member playing a highly specialized role) (Durkheim [1893] 1947). According to early functionalists, gender-based division of labor exists in modern societies because it is efficient and useful to have different but complementary male and female roles. They believed this helps members of society to accomplish essential tasks and maintains societal stability (Lindsey 2011).

In the structural-functionalist view of the traditional family, the father works, the mother stays at home, and they have two children. The female plays the expressive role through childbearing, nursing, and caring for family members in the home. The male carries out the instrumental role by working outside the home to support the family (Dilon 2009; Parsons and Bales 1953). Although this pattern was relevant for white, middle-class, and wealthier families during the Industrial Revolution and for some

decades before and after World War II, when men returned to take jobs women had held during the war, it characterizes relatively few families in the United States now.

Today, more children are being raised by single moms than married couples, and the turnover in partners has created complex families not seen before (Aulette 2010; Coontz 2011b). Fewer people are marrying, and those who do tend to be older than in previous decades. Increasing numbers of women do not have children (about 20% now, compared to just 10% in the 1970s) (Angier 2013). In addition, many families today thrive with two adult partners of the same sex.

Conflict Theory. Conflict theorists view gender relations through the lens of power. Men are the *haves*—controlling the majority of power positions and most wealth—and women are the *have-nots*. By keeping women in subordinate roles, males control the means of production and protect their privileged status.

A classical conflict explanation of gender stratification is found in the writings of Karl Marx's colleague, Friedrich Engels ([1884] 1942). In traditional societies, where size and strength were essential for survival, men were often dominant, but women's roles were respected as important and necessary to the survival of the group. Men hunted, engaged in warfare, and protected women. Over time, male physical control was transformed into control by ideology, by the dominant belief system itself. Capitalism strengthened male dominance by making more wealth available to men and their sons. Women became dependent on men, and their roles were transformed into "taking care of the home" (Engels [1884] 1942).

Ideologies based on traditional beliefs and values have continued to be used to justify the social structure of male domination and subjugation of women. It is in the interest of the dominant group, in this case men, to maintain a position of privilege. Conflict theorists believe it unlikely that those in power by virtue of sex, race, class, or political or religious ideology will voluntarily give up their positions as long as they are benefiting from them. By keeping women in traditional gender roles, men maintain control over institutions and resources (Collins 1971).

Feminist Theory. Feminist theorists agree with Marx and Engels that gender stratification is based on power struggles, not biology. On the other hand, some feminist theorists argue that Marx and Engels failed to consider fully a key variable in women's oppression: patriarchy. Patriarchy involves a few men dominating and holding authority over all others, including women, children, and the less powerful men (Arrighi 2000; Lindsey 2011). According to feminist theory, no matter what the economic or political system, women will continue to be oppressed by men until patriarchy is eliminated. There is a range of feminist theories. However, all feminist theories argue for bringing about a new and equal ordering of gender relationships to eliminate the patriarchy and sexism of current gender-stratification systems (Kramer and Beutel 2014).

Feminist theorists try to understand the causes of women's lower status and seek ways to change the systems to provide more opportunities, to improve the standard of living, and to give women control over their bodies and reproduction. Feminist theorists also feel that little change will occur until group consciousness is raised so that women understand the system that limits their options and do not blame themselves for their situations (Sapiro 2003).

As societies become technologically advanced and need an educated workforce, women of all social classes and ethnic groups around the world are likely to gain more equal roles. Women are entering institutions of higher education in record numbers, and evidence indicates they are needed in the world economic system and the changing labor force of most countries. Countries in which women are not integrated into the economic system generally lag behind other countries. Feminist theorists examine these global and national patterns, but they also note the role of patriarchy in micro-level interpersonal situations—such as domestic violence.

Violence against women perpetuates gender stratification, as is evident in the intimate environment of many homes. Because men have more power in the larger society, they often have more resources within the household as

Men—like these Jordanians—are much more likely than women to play cards, games, or sports together and to develop networks that enhance their power and their ability to "close deals." When women are not part of the same networks, they are denied the same insider privileges.

well (an example of side-effect discrimination). Women are often dependent on the man of the house for his resources, meaning they must yield on many decisions. Power differences in the meso- and macro-level social systems also contribute to power differentials and vulnerability of women in micro-level settings. In addition, women have fewer options when considering whether to leave an abusive relationship. Although there are risks of staying in an abusive relationship, many factors enter into a woman's decision to stay or leave; rational choice theory has been used by some researchers to evaluate the gains and losses from staying versus leaving (Copp et al. 2013; Estrellado and Loh 2013). The following "Sociology Around the World" on page 294 discusses one form of violence around the world that is perpetuated predominantly against women: rape.

In summary, feminist analysis finds gender patterns embedded in social institutions of family, education, religion, government, economics, and health care. If the societal system is patriarchal, ruled by men, the interdependent institutions are likely to reflect and support this system. Feminist theory helps us understand how patriarchy at the meso and macro level can influence patriarchy at the micro level and vice versa.

Thinking Sociologically

Imagine you were asked to decrease the occurrence of domestic abuse in your society. How would you address it differently if you were to look at it as a social issue, rather than just as a problem for the individuals directly affected by it?

Gender Equality

Sociology Around the World

Rape and the Victims of Rape

For many women around the world, rape is the most feared act of violence and the ultimate humiliation. Rape is a sexual act but closely tied to macho behavior. Often it is a power play to intimidate, hurt, and dominate women. As a weapon of war, rape humiliates the enemies who cannot protect their women (Audette 2014; Larsen 2013). Some societies are largely free from rape whereas others are prone toward rape. Why the difference?

When a society is relatively tolerant of interpersonal violence, holds beliefs in male dominance, and strongly incorporates ways to separate women and men, rape is more common ("Male Dominance Causes Rape" 2008; Pazzanese 2013; Sanday and Goodenough 1990). Rape is also more common when gender roles and identities are changing and norms about interaction between women and men are unclear.

An alarming problem is rape on college campuses in the United States. What does this say about the United States, where 1 in 4 to 5 college women will be raped or survive a rape attempt during her college years (R. Gray 2012)? That is 1 every 21 hours. Ninety percent of rapes occur with one or both parties under the influence of alcohol (R. Gray 2012). Eighteen percent of women in the whole United States have survived a complete or an attempted rape—22 million women. In the United States, someone is sexually assaulted or raped every two minutes, averaging more than 2,000 rapes daily (R. Gray 2012). These figures are most likely low given that the U.S. Justice Department estimates that only 26% of rapes and attempted rapes are reported (Anti-Violence Resource Guide 2012; National Center for Injury Prevention and Control 2011).

The fallout from rape and attempted rape is that victims "often experience anxiety, guilt, nervousness, phobias, substance abuse, sleep disturbances, depression, alienation, sexual dysfunction, aggression, and distrust of others." Physical disorders are also common, including sexually transmitted diseases (Anti-Violence Resource Guide 2012). All of this indicates that rape and sexual assault intimidate a significant portion of the population, making the targeted group feel vulnerable and less confident—in short, less powerful.

Men who hold more traditional gender roles view rape very differently than both women and less traditional men do. The former tend to attribute more responsibility to the female victim of a rape, believe sex rather than power is the motivation for rape, and look less favorably on women who have been raped. Moreover, many males who are sexually aggressive toward women do not define their behavior as rape. This points to the stereotypes and misunderstandings that can occur because of gendered beliefs and attitudes. Rape causes deep and lasting problems for women victims as well as for men accused of rape because of "misreading" women's signals. Some college men define gang rape as a form of male bonding. To them, it is no big deal. The woman is just the object and instrument. Her identity is immaterial (Barry and Choksi 2013).

Many citizens and politicians see rape as an individualized, personal act, whereas social scientists tend to see it as a structural problem that stems from negative stereotypes of women, subservient positions of women in society, and patriarchal systems of power. Many sociologists and anthropologists believe that rape will not be substantially reduced unless our macho definitions of masculinity are changed (McEvoy and Brookings 2008).

Rape Victim-Blaming

The Interaction of Class, Race, and Gender. Zouina is Algerian in her background and ethnicity, but she was born in France to her immigrant parents. She lived with them in a poor immigrant suburb of Paris until she was forced to return to Algeria for an arranged marriage to a man who already had one wife. That marriage ended, and she returned to her "home" in France. Since she returned to France, Zouina has been employed wherever she can find work. The high unemployment rate and social and ethnic discrimination, especially against foreign women, makes life difficult.

The situation is complex. Muslim women from Tunisia, Morocco, and Algeria living in crowded slum communities outside Paris face discrimination in the workplace and their communities (Lazaridis 2011). Expected to be both good Muslim women and good family co-providers—which necessitates working in French society—they face ridicule when they wear their *hijabs* (coverings) to school or to work (Lentze 2013). However, they encounter derision in their community if they do not wear them. They are caught between two cultures and may be the scapegoats for frustrated young men who cannot find work.

Because of high unemployment in the immigrant communities, many youth roam the streets. Gang rapes by North African youth against young women have been on the rise in France and elsewhere abroad. The victims of these rapes face rejection and disdain in France in their immigrant community, and in their original African communities (Killian 2006).

Some feminist theorists look at the ways in which discrimination related to class, race, and gender intersects in society (Anderson and Collins 2010). In the process, some groups of people face multiple forms of oppression that reinforce one another. For example, "many women of color . . . are burdened by poverty, child care responsibilities, and the lack of job skills. These burdens, largely the consequence of gender and class oppression, are then compounded by the racially discriminatory employment and housing practices women of color often face, as well as by the disproportionately high unemployment among people of color" (Crenshaw 1991). Table 9.3 shows the median earnings of workers in the United States by race and sex and helps illustrate how racism and sexism can reinforce one another and lead to the "double marginalization" of women of color.

These examples illustrate that race, class, and gender have crosscutting lines that may affect one's status in the society. Sexual orientation, age, nationality, and other factors also have the effect of either diminishing or

Table 9.3   Median Usual Weekly Earnings of Workers by Race, Sex, and Percent of Men's Earnings by Women, Second Quarter 2014

Race and Ethnicity	Male	Female	Women's % of Men's Earnings
Asian American	$1,139	$855	75.1
White	884	725	82.0
African American	667	631	94.6
Hispanic or Latino	609	532	87.4

Source: U.S. Department of Labor (2014).

increasing minority status of specific women, and theorists are paying increasing attention to these intersections (Rothenberg 2010). Chapter 8 discussed the fact that race and class lines may be either crosscutting or parallel. However, gender always affects one's prestige and privilege within class or ethnic groups. Thus, to get a full picture, these three variables—race, class, and gender—need to be considered simultaneously.

Thinking Sociologically

How have race, class, and gender intersected in your life and impacted your life chances? Do you think your experience is common among other members of your local community? Why or why not?

Women of color can face the triple status determinants of being poor (class), women (gender), and of color (race or ethnicity). LGBTQ women face yet another form of oppression that intersects with the other three. As members of a minority group, females may face threats especially if they are from poor families (see the next "Sociology Around the World" on page 296).

Gender, Homosexuality, and Minority Status

We have already learned that sex, gender, and sexuality are complex concepts. *Heterosexism* is an assumption that

Sociology Around the World

Dowry and Death: Some Dangers of Marriage

Dowry is a long-standing tradition in India, Bangladesh, Pakistan, Sri Lanka, and other countries. It involves "payment from the bride's family to the groom and groom's family at the time of marriage" and includes the money, goods, and estate or property that a woman brings her husband in marriage (Srinivasan and Lee 2004:1108). When a son is married, the son's family receives a dowry. Though once a practice of the wealthy, it is now most common in poorer families where sons are often more "valuable" than daughters because they will receive a dowry, and a dowry can amount to the equivalent of a year's salary. The bride receives her inheritance at the time of the wedding rather than at the time of death of her parents.

Although dowry payments were officially prohibited in India by the Dowry Prohibition Act in 1961, this traditional practice is still widespread ("Dowry Deaths" 2013). These marriages are typically arranged between families and generally do not involve consent or love. It is a business deal. Misunderstandings surrounding dowry agreements and payments can result in a form of dowry death, also called bride burning. When the business deal fails or results in disagreement, the bride may be found soaked in kerosene or other flammable liquid and burned to death, usually in the kitchen. Authorities often rule these bride burnings as suicides. The husband can then seek another bride and another dowry (Ward and Edelstein 2014). In 2012, 8,233 dowry death cases were reported across India; that is, one bride burned to death every hour ("Dowry Deaths" 2013). In addition, hundreds of cases are estimated to go unreported. Although police receive many calls, there are very few convictions for the crime.

Women's groups in South Asia have formed to protest against both dowries and the problems they bring, especially to poor young women who have no power or options. Some women's shelters and burn wards in hospitals have been established. The Dowry Project, established in 1995, does research on the practice, especially the link between attitudes toward violence and death, or bride burning. However, traditions are strong and poverty great; bride burnings are likely to continue until the penalties make it unprofitable and the guilty are punished.

every person is heterosexual, legitimizing heterosexuality as the only normal lifestyle and marginalizing persons who do not identify as heterosexual (Gender Equity Resource Center 2013). Heterosexism operates at all levels of society. For example, it can be seen at the micro level in the United States, where it is strongest in small towns and rural areas where LGBTQs (lesbian, gay, bisexual, transgender, and queer) experience housing discrimination, property damage, and employment discrimination (Swank, Fahs, and Frost 2013).

Despite this, homosexuality and transgendered people have always existed. They have been accepted and even required for certain positions at some times and places, and rejected or outlawed in others. In some cases, homosexuals and transgendered individuals have been placed in a separate sexual category with special roles. For example, the *Hijras* in India and some other areas in South Asia are usually physiological males who have feminine gender identity. Many live in *Hijra* communities and have designated roles in Indian festivals and celebrations.

Some societies ignore the existence of LGBTQ members of the community. Some consider them to have psychological illnesses or forms of depraved immorality. Some societies even consider these forms of sexuality a crime (as in 38 out of 54 African nations today and in most states in the United States during much of the 20th century). To be accused of homosexuality can result in the death penalty in Sudan, Somalia, Mauritania, and the northern part of Nigeria (Nossiter 2014). In each case around the world, the government or dominant religious group determines the status of homosexuals. The reality is that deviation from a society's gender norms, such as attraction to a member of the same sex, may cause one to experience minority status. (See Figure 9.3.)

Homophobia—intense fear and hatred of homosexuality and homosexuals, whether male or female—is highly correlated with and perhaps a cause of people holding traditional notions of gender and gender roles (Shaw and Lee 2005). This concept, which operates on the micro level, was coined by a psychologist who noted that intense hatred of LGBTQs is due to a personality disorder or illness (Weinberg 1972).

Some homosexuals deviate from traditional notions of masculinity and femininity and therefore from significant norms of many societies. This may result in hostile reactions and stigma from the dominant group. Indeed, homosexual epitaphs are often used to reinforce gender conformity, particularly among men, and to intimidate anyone who would dare to be different from the norm.

A transsexual (*Hijra*) dances at a gathering in Bangladesh, where a group met in the capital to demand government action to provide legal protection from persecution. They are treated as social outcasts and typically earn their livings by singing, dancing, and other performances.

Because in many societies women are economically dependent on men, their status in society is typically based on their relationship with men. Therefore, lesbians—women who are attracted to other women—are in some

FIGURE 9.3 Lesbian and Gay Laws Around the World, 2014

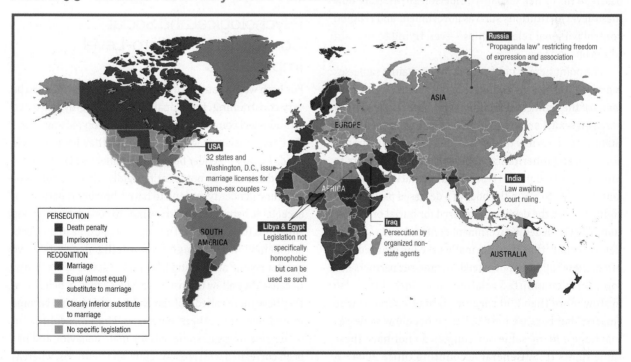

Source: Lesbian and Gay Rights Around the World, 2012 is from "ILGA launches 2013 ILGA State-Sponsored Homophobia Report," 2013. Reprinted by permission of the International Lesbian, Gay, Bisexual, Trans and Intersex Association.

▶ Homophobia

instances perceived as a threat to men's power (Burn 2011; Ward and Edelstein 2014).

The mass media have begun to include LGBTQ characters in films such as *Behind the Candelabra* (2013), *Dallas Buyers Club* (2013), *In Bloom* (2013), *Beginners* (2011), *A Single Man* (2009), *Milk* (2008), *Shelter* (2007), and *Brokeback Mountain* (2005). Television shows with positive images of lesbians and gays—such as *Ellen, Will and Grace, Pretty Little Liars, Glee, Modern Family, Grey's Anatomy, Chicago Fire,* and *The Good Wife*—have also become popular. In addition, there are many well-known lesbian and gay news commentators and show hosts, reflecting an increased level of acceptance of LGBTQ people in many nations.

Gallup polls reveal that U.S. public acceptance of lesbians and gays is up 19 points in the past 12 years to 59% today (Newport and Himelfarb 2013). Over half (52%) of all Americans and 69% of 18- to 34-year-olds say they would vote in favor of laws legalizing same-sex marriage (Saad 2013). As of October 2014, 32 states and Washington, DC, permit same-sex marriage (Freedom to Marry 2014b; Wolf 2014). In 2013, Walmart initiated partner benefits for same-sex couples. It is among the 62% of Fortune 500 companies that now offer health insurance and other "marriage" benefits to same-sex couples ("Same-Sex Couples" 2013).

Despite these indications of greater openness in attitudes, in 2014 it was still legal in 29 states to fire someone based on his or her sexuality (Eidelson 2014). Note how meso-level institutions such as government and religion control personal relationships—even trying to restrain whom one can love.

The point here is not to argue for or against same-sex marriage but to note that gays and lesbians do not have many of the rights that heterosexuals have, a discrepancy based on sexual preferences. Heterosexuals in the United States have a variety of rights—ranging from insurance coverage and inheritance rights for lifelong partners to jointly acquired property, hospital visitation rights as family, rights to claim the body of a deceased partner, and rights to have the deceased prepared for burial or cremation. The U.S. federal government confers 1,138 rights on heterosexuals that they normally take for granted, but often, these rights do not extend to same-sex partners in a long-term committed relationship. Most states also bestow more than 200 specific rights to persons who "marry," but because most states do not allow same-sex marriages, many same-sex couples do not have these same rights (U.S. General Accounting Office 2004). A number of other countries, including Canada and many European countries, have legalized same-sex marriage,

reducing the number of inequities in rights. In short, cultural notions about gender and sexuality are influencing the structure of society at the meso level, including institutions such as family, politics, and religion. Gender is very personal and private but also a public issue with macro-level implications.

Thinking Sociologically

What are some societal changes that have influenced the dramatic changes over the past decade in attitudes in the United States toward same-sex marriage? Have they impacted your perspective on this issue? Why or why not?

COSTS AND CONSEQUENCES OF GENDER STRATIFICATION

The consequences of gender stratification affect every level of society. They impact life chances for individuals and how institutions, nations, and the global society function. As illustrated in the following examples, sex- and gender-based stratification limits individual development and causes problems in education, health, work, and other parts of the social world.

Psychological and Social Consequences: Micro-Level Implications

For both women and men, rigid gender stereotypes can be very constraining. Individuals who hold highly sex-typed attitudes feel compelled to behave in stereotypic ways, ways that are consistent with the pictures they have in their heads of proper gender behavior (Kramer 2011). However, individuals who do not identify rigidly with masculine or feminine gender types tend to have a broader repertoire of acceptable behaviors and know how to cope with changing situations (Cheng 2005). They are more flexible in thoughts and behavior, score higher on intelligence tests, have greater spatial ability, and have higher levels of creativity. Because they allow themselves a wider range of behaviors, they have more varied abilities and experiences and become more tolerant of others' behaviors. High masculinity in males sets up rigid standards for male behavior and has been correlated with anxiety, guilt, and neuroses, whereas less rigid masculine expectations are associated with emotional stability, sensitivity, warmth, and enthusiasm. Rigid stereotypes and resulting sexism can limit our activities, behaviors, and perspectives.

Results of Gender Role Expectations. Women in many societies are expected to be beautiful, youthful, and sexually interesting and interested, while at the same time prepare the food, care for the children, keep a clean and orderly home, bring in money to help support the family, and be competent and successful in their careers. Multiple, sometimes contradictory, expectations for women can cause stress and even serious psychological problems. The resulting strain contributes to depression and certain health problems such as headaches, nervousness, and insomnia (Slaughter 2012; Wood 2008).

Gender expectations also affect women's self-concepts and body images. As noted earlier, beautiful images jump out at us from billboards, magazine covers, and TV and movie screens. Some of these images are unattainable for most women because they have been created through surgeries, eating disorders, and the use of airbrushing on photographs. Disorders, including anorexia and bulimia nervosa, relate to societal expectations of the ideal woman's appearance (Taub and McLorg 2010). In the United States, close to 24 million people suffer from eating disorders. Women are more likely to have eating disorders, but men are less likely to seek help when they do have a problem, resulting in serious health problems including death (James 2013).

Thinking Sociologically

How much time, energy, and money do you spend on your physical appearance? Why? From what socializing agents did you learn how to judge your physical appearance? Overall, how have those socializing agents impacted how you view yourself?

Men die earlier than women, in part due to environmental, psychological, and social factors. Problems in Global North countries such as heart disease, stroke, cirrhosis, cancers, accidents, and suicides are linked in part to the role expectations that males should appear tough, objective, ambitious, unsentimental, and unemotional—traits that require men to assume great responsibility and suppress their feelings (Leit, Gray, and Pope 2002; Tull 2012). So gender expectations can have a substantial cost for men as well as for women.

Societal Costs: Meso- and Macro-Level Implications

Gender stratification creates costs for societies around the world in a number of ways. *Poor educational achievement*

of female children leads to the loss of human talents and resources, a serious loss for societies. *Social divisiveness*—"us" versus "them" thinking based on sex—can create alienation, if not hostility, and this can result in physical or emotional aggression, discrimination, and violence against women.

Human capital—the resources of the human population—is central to social prosperity in societal systems. Yet resistance to expanding women's public sphere and professional roles is often strong. For example, Japanese women make up close to 50% of the workforce, but only 10.1% hold managerial positions, and many leave the workplace when they marry (Fackler 2007a). In Japan and Korea, women make only 61% of what men do, the largest wage gap among Global North countries (Catalyst 2014c). Although Japanese women score higher in science than boys and are almost half of university graduates, few can break through the glass ceiling they face in the job market (Hewlett 2013).

CHANGING GENDER STRATIFICATION AND SOCIAL POLICY

Is it better for a woman in the Global South to have a poor-paying job and poor working conditions, or no job? On the one hand, few wage-paying jobs are available in some countries, and most of these positions in manufacturing and assembly positions that do become available are held by women. Yet women in factories around the globe face dangerous conditions and low pay. Sweatshops exist because poor women and sometimes men have few other job options to support their families and because people in rich countries want to buy the cheap products that perpetuate the multinational corporate system. For example, over one million Mexicans work in *maquiladoras* (foreign-owned manufacturing and assembly plants) in Mexican border towns for very low wages.

The maquiladoras are owned by U.S., European, and Japanese conglomerates, and hire primarily unskilled young women. Wages are 18% of what U.S. workers receive (Stevenson 2013). The employees produce electronic equipment, clothing, plastics, furniture, appliances, and auto parts, most of which are shipped to the United States (Rosenberg 2012). The hours worked per week range from 50 to 75, although some governments are trying to pass a law limiting working hours per week to 48. Some maquiladoras pay $40 to $50 for a 60-hour

▶ Gender in Advertising

week. Women and children often make less than men ("Misery of the Maquiladoras" 2011). The maquiladoras are but one example of multinational corporations based in the Global North using workers in the Global South to make their products for very little money and in harsh working conditions.

One result of companies offering low wages and poor working conditions is exploitation of women workers in other parts of the world. Another is loss of income for workers in the United States, including men. Manufacturers within the United States are starting to hire after the economic recession, but the wages they are offering are $10 to $15 an hour less than before the recession (Kelber 2012). So the "race to the bottom" by multinationals (seeking the lowest price for labor) is affecting earnings of men and women in the United States. We really live in an interconnected world.

What can be done about the abusive treatment of women workers around the world? This is a tough issue: Governments have passed legislation to protect workers, but governments also want the jobs that multinational corporations bring and therefore do little to enforce regulations. International labor standards are also difficult to enforce because multinational corporations are so large and located in many different parts of the world. Trade unions have had little success attracting workers to join because companies squash their recruiting efforts immediately.

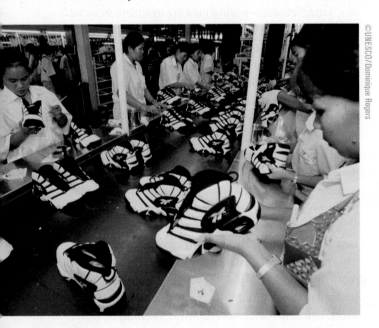

Women in Thailand produce shoes for extremely low pay. These jobs are better than no employment at all, but before pressures from Global North societies changed their cultures, most people were able to feed their families on farms in small villages.

One way activist groups protest for fair wages and conditions for workers is to adopt practices that have worked for other groups facing discrimination in the past. Consider the following strategies used by groups to combat unfair labor practices: holding nonviolent protests—sit-down strikes and walkouts—encouraging companies to help the communities in which their factories are located; using the Internet to carry the message to others; carrying out boycotts against companies that mistreat employees; employing the arts, storytellers, and teachers to mobilize resistance; and building on traditions of student, community, and religious activism (Collins 2008; Maquila Solidarity Network 2014). Most of these strategies require organized movements, but such efforts may antagonize the companies so much that they move to other countries. It is a delicate balance. To be successful, the fair labor effort must be as globalized as the corporations whose practices they wish to impact.

Thinking Sociologically

Take a look at the clothing in your closet and your drawers. Figure out where it was made either by reading the labels or by looking up the companies' factories on the Internet. Would you be willing to pay more for that clothing so that other people could have better conditions? Why or why not? What about your friends? How can the plight of workers across the globe impact you and other workers in your nation?

Some sociologists have dedicated their professional careers to using sociological skills to help women gain more power and more access to resources. This is challenging but highly rewarding work. One example of a sociologist who has tried to improve the lives of women in Rwanda is described in the next "Sociologists in Action" feature.

At women's conferences around the world, policy makers debate the means to create solutions to women's problems. Most United Nations member countries have at least fledgling women's movements fighting for the improved status of women and their families. The movements attempt to change laws and other social practices that negatively impact women. One example is the Better Factories movement in Cambodia (Kampuchea), sponsored by the International Labour Organization, that works to address worker problems, especially garment workers (International Labour Organization 2014). Such efforts are but one example of how organized people can impact society and work together to address gender discrimination.

Factory Worker Exploitation

SOCIOLOGISTS IN ACTION:
MELISSA SHERIDAN EMBSER-HERBERT

Using Sociology to Promote Gender Equity and Peace in Postgenocide Rwanda

During the summer of 2011, I had the opportunity to make my first visit to Rwanda, explore the culture, plan a course bringing students to Rwanda, and learn, more directly than books allow, about the 1994 genocide. Yes, I saw the mountain gorillas—up close and personal—and I bought too many hand-woven baskets, but I also saw—and smelled—stacks of bones and piles of bloodied clothing at genocide memorials. In 2012, with a colleague and 12 students, I returned to study restorative justice and reconciliation in postgenocide Rwanda.

It's one thing to watch a video or read a book about genocide. It's another to visit the country where it happened and see the mass graves, the number of people missing limbs, and—as my colleague experienced—talk with someone who says, "I killed seven people. I've made peace with six families. I hope to with family seven." While our central aim was to learn about restorative justice and reconciliation, we also considered other issues that impact postgenocide Rwandan society. One key issue is the role of women in Rwanda.

While we were there, we visited the market in Musanze. In Rwanda, most women are employed in agriculture with "off-farm" opportunities being quite limited. Women are far less likely to have access to financial services, including the microcredit often required for starting their own businesses. If the independent participation of women in the nonagricultural labor market is to increase, more support must be found for women who have the skills and initiative to become entrepreneurs. Via our interpreter, one student, Angela, started talking with one of the women at the market who sewed, wanting to know about her life. From our class blog: "Mama Joyce went on to tell me that she makes 30,000 RWF [Rwandan francs], or about 50 USD [U.S. dollars] per month, and from that she pays 20,000 RWF or 33 USD in rent for her sewing machine. . . . Her income supports the majority of her family's basic needs and definitely doesn't allow for anything extra. They [each] net only 17 USD a month. I was astounded to learn that the cost to purchase her own machine would be about 70,000 RWF or 115 USD. Cripes. I spend approximately that much on my cell phone bill each month."

Angela decided to make a personal donation so that Mama Joyce could purchase a sewing machine. But, she had also received $100 from her department in case she had the opportunity to conduct interviews while in Rwanda. Angela was told that should that not be possible, she could donate the money as she wished. She decided to give Mama Joyce that money for the purchase of a second sewing machine. The idea was that the women who sewed together might start a cooperative, a business that they would run together, sharing in its profits. But, she didn't stop there. Upon her return to the United States, Angela started exploring how to establish her own nonprofit to help other women in Musanze, Rwanda. *Begin* was begun.

Still a fledgling nonprofit, *Begin* aims to raise funds to allow more women in Musanze to purchase their own sewing machines. Referring to the money that would no longer be spent renting machines, Angela writes, "This is money that she [Mama Joyce] could be using to buy food and clothes for her children . . . or money

(Continued)

(Continued)

she could be using to reinvest in her community . . . By building a park, for example. Or maybe a kindergarten." Mama Joyce is the primary wage earner for her family. Her husband, having left military service, has been unable to find permanent, full-time work. This shift in responsibility is not unique to Mama Joyce, or to Rwanda. Women across the globe share these experiences. Angela recognized this need and then took steps to address it.

My students and I used our sociological imaginations to recognize patterns of systemic inequality in the institutions of Rwanda, including the economy. Our commitment to using that knowledge to make a positive impact on society led some to take action. While these steps are relatively small, we know that there are many other sociologists in action—some reading this piece right now—taking steps of their own. Together, we can change the world for the better.

Inequality based on class, race, ethnicity, and gender takes place at all levels of analysis and is often entrenched at the meso level within the institutions found in every society—family, education, religion, government, economics, and health care. Complex societies incorporate other institutions as well, including science and technology, sports, and the military. We turn now to a discussion of institutions in our social world.

WHAT HAVE WE LEARNED?

At the beginning of this chapter, we asked how being born female or male affects our lives. Because sex is a primary variable on which societies are structured and stratified, our sex affects our public and private sphere activities, our health, our ability to practice religion or participate in political life, our opportunities for education, and just about everything we do.

KEY POINTS

- Whereas sex is biological, notions of gender identity and gender roles are socially constructed and learned, and vary across cultures. (See pp. 268–271.)

- While "she" may go first in micro-level social encounters (served first in a restaurant or the first to enter a doorway), "he" goes first in meso and macro settings—with the doors open wider for men to enter leadership positions in organizations and institutions. (See pp. 272–287.)

- Greater access to resources at the meso level makes it easier to have entry to macro-level positions, but it also influences the respect one receives in micro settings. (See pp. 271–275.)

- Notions of gender are first taught in micro settings—in the intimacy of the home—but reinforced at the meso and macro levels. (See pp. 277–284.)

- Much of the gender stratification today is unconscious and unintended—not caused by angry or bigoted men who purposefully oppress women.

Gender inequality is rooted in institutionalized privilege and disprivilege. (See pp. 284–289.)

- Various social theories shed different light on the issues of inequality in gender roles assigned to various sexes. (See pp. 289–298.)

- For modern postindustrial societies, there is a high cost for treating women like a minority group—individually for the people who experience it and for the society, which loses many potential contributions from women. (See pp. 298–299.)

DISCUSSION QUESTIONS

1. Describe some of the ways socializing agents (e.g., family, peers, the media, religion, schools) encouraged you to conform to traditional gender norms. Do you think you will encourage (or have you encouraged) your own children to conform to traditional gender norms? Why or why not?

2. Give two examples of side-effect gender discrimination that lead to economic inequality between men and women.

3. How does gender socialization influence who runs for office and for whom we vote? How are female politicians treated by the media, compared to male politicians? How has that impacted your own perception of female politicians?

4. How does gender discrimination harm society? What could be done on your campus to improve the status of women or men? How might you join these efforts?

5. What are your career goals? Do they follow traditional gender roles? Why or why not? How has your gender socialization impacted your career plans?

6. More women than men are now in college. How do you think this fact will impact gender roles on campus and in the larger society?

CONTRIBUTING TO OUR SOCIAL WORLD: *WHAT CAN WE DO?*

At the Local Level

- *To learn about gender discrimination on your campus,* schedule an interview with the director or other staff members of the human resources or affirmative action offices on your campus to learn about your school's policies regarding gender discrimination. What procedures exist for hiring? Do women and men receive the same salaries, wages, and benefits for equal work? Explore the possibility of working as a volunteer or an intern in the office, specifically in the area of gender equity.

At the Organizational and National Levels

- *The National Organization for Women (NOW)* is the world's leading advocate for gender equity. It deals with issues such as reproductive rights, legislative outreach, economic justice, ending sex discrimination, and promoting diversity. Several internship programs are listed on the organization's website, www.now.org, along with contact information, state and regional affiliates, and "NOW on Campus" links.

- *Sociologists for Women in Society (SWS)*, an organization that "works to improve women's lives through advancing and supporting feminist sociological research, activism and scholars," provides many resources for students. SWS provides students with scholarships, opportunities to be mentored, and an award to recognize students who improve the lives of women through activism.

- The *New Leadership Institute at the Center for American Women and Politics* is an annual 6-day residential summer program that "educates college women about the important role that politics plays in their lives and encourages them to become effective leaders in the political arena." To learn more about New Leadership and to find out how to apply to the program, go to www.cawp.rutgers .edu/education_training/NEWLeadership/newlead ership_about.php.

At the Global Level

- *MADRE*, an international women's rights organization, works primarily in less-developed countries. You can find numerous opportunities for working on

issues of justice, human rights, education, and health on its website at www.madre.org.

- *Equality Now*, an international nongovernmental organization, provides many venues for those interested in promoting equality for women and curbing gender violence and discrimination. You can find more about this organization at www.equalitynow.org.

- The *United Nations Inter-Agency Network on Women and Gender Equality* works on global issues, including violence against women and women's working conditions. Its WomenWatch Website at www.un.org/womenwatch contains news, information, and ideas for contributing to the worldwide campaign for women's rights.

PART IV

Institutions

Picture a house, a *structure* in which you live. Within that house there are the actions and activities that bring the house alive—the *processes*. Flip a switch, and the lights go on because the house is well wired. Adjust the thermostat, and the room becomes more comfortable as the structural features of furnace or air-conditioning systems operate. If the structural components of the plumbing and water heating systems work, you can take a hot shower when you turn the knob. These actions taken within the structure make the house livable. If something breaks down, you need to get it fixed so that everything works smoothly.

Institutions, too, provide a *structure* for society, a framework that promotes stability. *Processes* are the action dimension within institutions—the activities that take place. They include the interactions between people, decision making, socialization, and other actions in society. These processes are often dynamic and can lead to significant change within the structure—like a decision about whether new homeowners should remodel their kitchen. Institutions are meso-level structures because they are larger in scope than the face-to-face social interactions of the micro level, and yet they are smaller than the nation or the global system.

Institutions such as family, education, religion, politics, economics, and health care include certain patterns and expectations that differ in each society. They are interdependent and mutually supportive, just as the plumbing, heating system, and electricity in a house work together to make a home functional. However, a breakdown in one institution or conflict over limited resources between institutions affects the whole society, just as a malfunction in the electrical system may shut the furnace off and cool down the water heater.

THE IMPORTANCE OF INSTITUTIONS

Institutions are not anything concrete that you can see, hear, touch, or smell. The concept of *institutions* is a way of describing and understanding how society works. For example, the institution of family meets certain needs found in almost all societies. Family as an institution refers to the behavior of thousands of people, which—taken as a whole—forms a social structure. Think of your own family. It has unique ways of interacting and raising children, but it is part of a community with many families. Those many families, in turn, are part of a national set of patterned behaviors we call "the family." This pattern meets the basic needs of the society for producing and socializing new members and providing an emotionally supportive environment.

Institutions do not dictate exactly how you will carry out the roles within your family. However, they do specify certain needs families will meet and statuses (spouse/partner, parent, child) that will relate to each other in certain mutually caring ways and filling certain seminegotiable roles. An institution provides a blueprint (much like a local builder needs a blueprint to build a house), and in your local version of the institution you may make a few modifications to the plans to meet your individual micro-level needs. Still, through this society-encompassing structure and interlocking set of statuses, the basic needs for individuals at the micro level and for society at the macro level are met. Table IV.1 illustrates the impact of social institutions in society at each level of analysis.

Thinking Sociologically

Using Table IV.1, try placing other institutions (mass media, science, sports, the military) in the framework. Where do organizations you belong to fit into the institutional structure?

Institutions, then, *are organized, patterned, and enduring sets of social structures that provide guidelines for behavior and help each society meet its basic survival needs. While institutions operate mostly at the meso level, they also act to integrate micro and macro levels of society.* Let us look more deeply at this definition.

1. *Organized, patterned, and enduring sets of social structures* means that institutions are not bricks and mortar of buildings but refer to a complex set of groups or organizations, statuses within those groups, and norms of conduct that guide people's behavior. These structures ensure socialization of children, education of the young, sense of meaning in life, companionship, and production and distribution of needed goods (food, clothing, automobiles, cell phones, computers) for the members of the society. If this patterned behavior were missing, these needs might not be addressed. At the local level, we may go to a neighborhood school, or we may attend worship at a congregation we favor. These are local organizations—local franchises, if you will—of a much more encompassing structure (education and religion) that provides guidelines for education or addresses issues of meaning of life for an enormous number of people. The Catholic Church in your town, for example, is a local "franchise" of an organization transnational in scope and global in its concerns.

2. *Guidelines for behavior* help people know how to conduct themselves and obtain basic needs in their society. Individuals and local organizations actually carry out the institutional guidelines in each culture; the exact ways they do so vary by locality. In local "franchises" of the political system, people know how to govern and how to solve problems at the local level because of larger norms and patterns provided by the political institution. Individual men and women operate a local hospital or clinic (a local "franchise" of the medical institution) that follows a national blueprint of how to provide health care. The specific activities of a local school, likewise, abide by the guidelines and purposes of the larger goals of "formal education" in a given nation.

3. *Meeting basic survival needs* is a core component of institutions because societies must meet needs of their members; otherwise the members die, or the society collapses. Institutions, then, are the structures that support social life in a large bureaucratized society. Common to all industrialized societies are family, education, religion, economics, politics, and health. We discuss the institutions in the following chapters.

4. *Integrating micro and macro levels of society* is also critical because one of the collective needs of society is coherence and stability—including some integration between the various levels of society. Institutions help provide that integration for the entire social system. They do this by meeting needs at the local franchise level (food at the grocery, education at the local school, health care at the local clinic) at the same time they coordinate national and global organizations and patterns.

Table IV.1 The Impact of Institutions at Each Level of Analysis

	Family	Education	Economic Systems	Political Systems	Religion	Medicine
Macro (National and global social systems and trends)	Kinship and marriage structures, such as monogamy versus polygamy; global trends in family, such as choice of partners rather than arranged marriages	National education system; United Nations Girls' Education Initiative	Spread of capitalism around the world; World Bank; International Monetary Fund; World Trade Organization	National government; United Nations; World Court; G7 (most powerful seven nations in the world)	Global faith-based movements and structures: National Council of Churches; World Council of Churches; World Islamic Council; World Jewish Congress	National health care system; World Health Organization; transnational pandemics
Meso (Institutions, complex organizations, ethnic subcultures, state/provincial systems)	The middle-class family; the Hispanic family; the Jewish family	State/provincial Department of Education; American Federation of Teachers*	State/provincial offices of economic development; United Auto Workers*	State/provincial governments; national political parties; each state or province's supreme court	National denominations/ movements (e.g., United Methodist Church or American Reform Judaism)	HMOs; Minnesota Nurses Association; American Medical Association
Micro (Local "franchises" of institutions)	Your family; local parenting group; local Parents Without Partners; county family counseling clinic	Your teacher; local neighborhood school; local school board	Local businesses; local Chamber of Commerce; local labor union chapter	Neighborhood crime watch program; local city or county council	Your local religious study group or congregation	Your doctor and nurse; local clinic; local hospital

*These organizations are national in scope and membership, but they are considered meso level here because they are complex organizations *within* the nation.

Again, if all this sounds terribly abstract, that is because institutions *are* abstractions. You cannot touch institutions, yet they are as real as air, love, or happiness. In fact, in the modern world institutions are as necessary to life as is air, and they help provide love and happiness that make life worth living.

THE DEVELOPMENT OF MODERN INSTITUTIONS

If we go all the way back to early hunting and gathering societies, there were no meso or macro levels to their social experience. People lived their lives in one or two villages, and while a spouse might come from another village or one might move to a spouse's clan, there was no national or state governance, and certainly no awareness of a global social system. In those simple times, family and community provided whatever education was needed, produced and distributed goods, paid homage to a god or gods, and solved conflicts and disputes through a system of familial (often patriarchal) power distribution. One social unit such as the family served multiple functions.

As societies became more complex and differentiated, multiple levels of the social system and various new institutions emerged. Sociology textbooks in the 1950s identified only "five basic institutions": family, economic systems, political systems, religion, and education (formal public education only having been created in the mid-19th century). These five institutions were believed to be the core structures that met the essential needs of individuals and societies in an orderly way.

Soon thereafter, *medicine* moved from the family and small-town doctors to become another institution. Medicine has become bureaucratized in hospitals, medical labs, professional organizations, and other complex structures that provide health care. *Science* is also now something more than flying kites in thunderstorms in one's backyard. It is a complex system that provides training, funding, research institutes, peer review, and professional associations to support empirical research. New information is the lifeblood of an information-based or postindustrial

society. Science, discussed in Chapter 16, is now an essential institution. Although it is arguable whether sports are an essential component for social viability, sports have clearly become highly structured in the past 50 years, and many sociologists consider sports an institution. The mass media and military also fall into the category of institutions in more advanced countries. There are gray areas as to whether something is considered an institution, but the questions to ask are (a) whether the structure meets basic needs of the society for survival, (b) whether it has become a complex organization providing routinized structures and guidelines for society, and (c) whether it is national or even global in its scope, while also having pervasive local (micro) impact.

CONNECTIONS AMONG INSTITUTIONS

The Great Recession of 2007–2009 illustrates how institutions can impact one another. Many individuals in the United States became unemployed as credit for companies dried up and companies reduced their payrolls. Their families then also faced various stresses that come with an unemployed breadwinner. In turn, the government faced pressure, as citizens expected political leaders to intervene and find ways to bring the nation out of an economic recession. At the same time, religious congregations experienced increased demands at their food banks and soup kitchens *and* declining contributions from religious congregants who lost their jobs. Funding for schools also suffered during the Great Recession, as tax revenues fell. Connections among meso-level institutions are a common refrain in this book. As you read these chapters, notice that change in one institution affects others. Sociologists studying the legal system, mass media, medicine, science, sports, or the military as institutions would raise similar questions and would want to know how these institutions influence the micro, meso, and macro levels of a society. We begin with the family—an institution that is such an intimate part of our lives and that is often called the "most basic" institution of society.

10 Family

Partner Taking, People Making, and Contract Breaking

Through the institution of the family, we take partners and "make people"—both biologically and socially speaking. While families can experience conflict, violence, and contract breaking, they can also give us a sense of belonging, love, and great joy.

ME (AND MY FAMILY)

**LOCAL ORGANIZATIONS
AND COMMUNITY**

Family is the basic unit
of action within a community.

**NATIONAL ORGANIZATIONS,
INSTITUTIONS, AND ETHNIC
SUBCULTURES**

Families socialize children into social roles so they
can function in society.

SOCIETY

Governments develop family policies.

GLOBAL COMMUNITY

International organizations support
families, and children.

IN THIS CHAPTER

- What Is a Family?

- Theoretical Perspectives
  on Family

- Family Dynamics: Micro-
  Level Processes

- The Family as an Institution:
  Meso-Level Analysis

- National and Global Family
  Issues: Macro-Level Analysis

- Marriage, Divorce, and
  Social Policies

THINK ABOUT IT

Micro: Local Community	How do people find life partners?
Meso: National Institutions, Complex Organizations, and Ethnic Groups	Why is family seen as the core or basic institution of society?
Macro: National and Global Systems	What, if anything, should be done by government to strengthen families? What are some common and different traits among families around the world?

A Guatemalan family in a rural village prepares for the day's chores. Maria Hernandez prepares the breakfast as Miguel cares for the animals. The children fix their lunches of tortillas, beans, rice, and banana to take to school. When they return home, they will help with the farm chores. They live together with their extended family, several generations of blood relatives living side by side.

It is morning in Sweden. Anders and Karin Karlsson are rushing to get to their offices on time. They hurry their children, a 12-year-old son and an 8-year-old daughter, out the door to school. All will return in the evening after a full day of activities and join together for the evening meal. In this dual-career family, common in many postindustrial societies, both parents are working professionals.

The gossip at the village water well this day in Niger, Africa, is about the rich local merchant, Abdul, who has just taken his fourth and last wife. She is a young, beautiful girl of 15 from a neighboring village. She is expected to help with household chores and bear children for his already extensive family unit. Several of the women at the well live in affluent households where the husband has more than one wife.

Tom and Henry in Minneapolis, Minnesota, recently adopted Ty into their family. The couple share custody of the 5-year-old boy. Ty's two fathers attend his school events and teach him what all parents are expected to teach their children. Adoption by same-sex couples is legal in only 16 U.S. states and the District of Columbia ("Gay Adoption Nationwide" 2011). However, both political candidates in the 2012 U.S. presidential campaign supported a policy allowing gay couples to adopt children (Cronkite 2012).

Dora, a single mom with two children, lives next door to Tom, Henry, and Ty. She bundles the children off to school before heading to her job. After school, she has an arrangement with other neighbors to care for the children until she gets home.

What do these very different scenes have in common? Each describes a family, yet not everyone agrees on what constitutes a family. Groupings officially recognized as families by governments tend to receive hundreds of privileges and rights, such as health insurance and inheritance rights (Degenova, Stinnett, and Stinnett 2011). In this chapter, we discuss characteristics of families, theoretical perspectives on the family, family dynamics, the family as an institution, family issues, and policies regarding marriage and family dissolution.

Families come in many shapes, sizes, and color combinations. We begin our exploration of this institution with a discussion of what *is* family.

In recent decades, the definition of family has broadened in many areas of the world to include families with parents of the same sex, like these two families.

© STRINGER/SPAIN/ Reuters/ Corbis42-48574498

WHAT IS A FAMILY?

Who defines what constitutes a family: individuals, the government, or religious groups? Is a family just Ma, Pa, and the kids? Let us consider several definitions. The U.S.

Census Bureau says "a group of two people or more (one of whom is the householder) related by birth, marriage, or adoption and residing together; all such people (including related subfamily members) are considered as members of one family" (U.S. Census Bureau 2013a). Thus, a family in the United States might be composed of siblings, cousins, a grandparent and grandchild, or other groupings. Some sociologists define family more broadly, such as "two or more individuals who maintain an intimate relationship that they expect will last indefinitely—or in the case of parent and child, until the child reaches adulthood—and who usually live under the same roof and pool their incomes and household labor" (Cherlin 2010:14). This definition would include same-sex couples and many cohabiting heterosexuals as families. Some religious groups define family as a mother, a father, and their children, whereas others include several spouses, multiple generations, or several siblings living under the same roof.

The definition and the typical composition of family are changing as societies and social norms change (Angier 2013). The traditional family of married parents with a mother who tends to the household, a father who brings in the income, and biological children living in an intact family comprises only 15% of all families and 7% of all households in the United States (Population Reference Bureau 2013c). Indeed, Table 10.1 indicates family makeup today.

Thinking Sociologically

Look at the information in Table 10.1. If you could choose among the different types of families described in the table, in which would you prefer to be raised? Why? Do you think your answer would change if you were raised a generation earlier or later? Why?

As noted earlier, the family is often referred to as the most basic institution of any society. First, it is the place where we learn many of the norms for functioning in the larger society. Second, most of us spend our lives in the security of a family. People are born and raised in families, and many will die in a family setting. Through good and bad, sickness and health, most families provide for our needs, both physical and psychological. Therefore, families meet our primary, our most basic, needs. Third, major life events—marriages, births, graduations, promotions, anniversaries, religious ceremonies, holidays, funerals—take place within the family context and are celebrated with family members. In short, family is where we invest the most emotional energy and spend much of our leisure time. Fourth, the family is capable of satisfying a range of social needs—belonging to a group, economic support, education or training, raising children, religious socialization, resolution of conflicts, and so forth. One cannot conceive of the economic system providing emotional support for each individual or the political system providing

Table 10.1 Family Diversity: Families With Children Under Age 18

Nuclear Families With Two Parents	50%
Single-Parent Families	27%
Blended Families With Children From Previous Marriages	20%
Adoptive/Foster Families	nearly 1%

Same-Sex Parent Families—roughly 2 million children have parents who are gay, lesbian, or bisexual.

Cross-Generational Families 670,000 families with children under age 18 include a family member age 65 or older.

2.5 million children under age 18 live with one or both parents in their grandparents' home.

Never-Married Families—1.5 million unmarried couples have at least one child living with them.

Grandparents as Parents—approximately 1.3 million children live with grandparents.

Source: American Academy of Pediatrics (2013).

Living in the mountains of Nepal, the Chepang family lives a simple life, but the children learn many survival skills, and the most basic needs of the children, physical and psychological, are met.

socialization and personalized care for each child. Family carries out these functions (Benokraitis 2012).

We *make people*—not just biologically but also socially, in families. In the family, we take an organism that has the potential to be fully human, and we mold this tiny bit of humanity into a caring, compassionate, productive person—at least that is the ideal plan.

In global North societies, most individuals are born and raised in the **family of orientation**, *the family into which we are born*. This family consists of parent(s) and possibly sibling(s); individuals are born and raised in this family, receive early socialization, and learn the language, norms, core values, attitudes, and behaviors of the community and society. A **family of procreation** *is the family we create ourselves*. We find a life mate and/or have children. The transmission of values, beliefs, and attitudes from our family of orientation to our family of procreation generally preserves and stabilizes the family system. Because family involves emotional investment, we have strong feelings about what form it should take.

Whether we consider families at micro, meso, or macro levels, sociological theories can help us understand the role of families in the social world.

THEORETICAL PERSPECTIVES ON FAMILY

Things on the family front are not always a fairytale. Consider the case of Felice, a young mother locked into a marriage that provides her with little satisfaction. For the first year of marriage, Felice tried to please her husband, Tad, but gradually he seemed to drift farther away. He began to spend evenings out. Sometimes, he came home drunk and yelled at or hit her. Felice became pregnant shortly after their marriage and had to quit her job. This increased the financial pressure on Tad, and they fell behind in paying the bills.

Then came the baby. They were both ecstatic at first, but Tad soon reverted to his old patterns. Felice felt trapped. She was afraid and embarrassed to go to her parents. They had warned her against marrying so young without finishing school, but she was in love and had gone against their wishes. She and Tad had moved away from their hometown, so she was out of touch with her old support network and had few friends in her new neighborhood. Her religious beliefs told her she should try to stick it out, suggesting that the trouble was partly her fault for not being a "good enough wife." Lacking a job or skills to get a job that paid more than minimum wage, she could not live on her own with a baby. She thought of marriage counseling, but Tad refused to consider this and did not seem interested in trying to work out the problems. He had his reasons for behaving the way he did, including feeling overburdened with the pressure of caring for two dependents. The web of this relationship seems difficult to untangle, but sociological theories provide us with some tools to analyze such family dynamics.

Micro-Level Theories of Family and the Meso-Level Connection

To understand our own families it is useful to think about how our familiar micro-level theories—symbolic interaction and rational choice—help give us new understanding and perspectives.

Symbolic Interaction Theory. Symbolic interaction theory can help us understand Felice's situation by explaining how individuals learn their particular behavior patterns and ways of thinking. We create relationship roles through socialization and interaction with others. Felice, for example, developed certain expectations and patterns of behavior by modeling her experiences on her family of orientation (the family into which she was born), observing others, and developing expectations based on her initial interactions with Tad. Tad developed a different set of expectations for his role of husband, modeled after his father's behavior. His father had visited bars after work,

Role of Fathers

had affairs with other women, and expected "his woman" to be at home and to accept this without question.

Two related concepts in symbolic interaction theory (introduced in Chapters 2 and 3) are the *social construction of reality* and the *definition of a situation*. What significant others around us accept as ordinary or acceptable shapes our definition of normal family relations. Children who grow up in homes where adults argue or hit one another or shout at one another with sarcastic put-downs may come to think of this behavior as typical or a normal part of family life. They simply have known no other type of interaction. Thus, without seeing other options than what they have learned, they may create a similar pattern of family interaction in their own families of procreation (the families they create). Concepts such as *family*, *partner*, and *parenting* may mean something very different to the person sitting beside you in class or to a potential mate.

Thinking Sociologically

Think about how the family in which you were raised influenced your attitudes toward family life and your perceptions of how family members should interact with one another. How do you think you would react if you were suddenly thrust into a very different type of family? Why?

One of the great challenges of newlyweds is meshing their ideas about division of labor, family holidays, discipline of children, spousal relations, and economic necessities, along with their assumptions about being in a committed relationship. A new couple socially constructs a new relationship, blending the models of life partnership from their own childhood homes or creating an entirely new model as they jointly define their relationship. Furthermore, the meaning of one's identity and one's obligations to others change dramatically when one becomes a parent. The mother and father have to work out what this means for each of them, for their interactions with each other, and for their interactions with the child. This brings us back to a central premise of symbolic interaction: Humans are active agents who create their social structure through interaction. We not only learn family patterns, but we *do family* just as we *do gender* in the sense that we create roles and relationships and pass them on to others as "normal."

Institutional arrangements at the meso level shape our individual identities and family patterns. For example, corporations, religious bodies, legal systems, and other government entities define the roles of "wife" and "husband." Each U.S. state actually spells out in its legal codes the duties of husbands and wives. Those who do not fulfill these duties may be in "neglect of duty." These family roles are embedded at the macro level in ways that many people do not realize.

Rational Choice Theory. Rational choice theory can also shed light on Felice's situation, helping us understand why people seek close relationships and why they stay in abusive relationships. As discussed in Chapter 2, rational choice theory asserts that individuals evaluate the costs and rewards of engaging in interaction. We look for satisfaction of our needs—emotional, sexual, and economic—through interaction. Patterns in the family are reinforced to the extent that exchanges benefit members. When the costs outweigh the rewards, the relationship is unlikely to continue. Women in abusive relationships weigh the costs of suffering abuse against the rewards of having social legitimacy, income, social and religious acceptance, a home, and companionship. Many factors enter into the complex balance of the exchange. Indeed, costs and benefits of various choices are often established by meso-level organizations and institutions: insurance programs, health care options, and legal regulations that make partnering decisions easy or difficult.

This cost–benefit consideration also includes whether there is *reciprocity*—"if you scratch my back, I will scratch yours." Rational choice theorists maintain that humans will not extend assistance to others unless they think there will be a payback and some balance in the relationship. If people feel like they give more than they receive, the relationship turns sour. This pattern is no less true of family relationships than any other human interactions. Humans are ultimately seen in this perspective as focused on self-interest.

According to rational choice theorists, an exchange calculation shapes even the mate selection process. People estimate their own assets—physical, intellectual, social, and economic—and try to find the "best deal" they can make, someone with at least the level of resources they possess, even if those assets are in different areas. Marrying someone with more assets gives the other person more power and forces one to put up with things that equal partners would not tolerate. As noted in Chapter 5, this is called the "principle of least interest"—the person with least interest had more power because the person with most interest (most invested in the relationship) is likely to give in when there is conflict rather than jeopardize the relationship. Cost/benefit, according to this view, affects the forming of the relationship and the power and influence in the relationship.

Thinking Sociologically

How can the rational choice perspective help you understand why some couples you know (a) got together and (b) stayed together or broke up? Does it help you to better understand some of your own experiences? Why or why not?

Meso- and Macro-Level Theories of the Family

Structural-Functional Theory. Why do all societies have families? One answer is that families fulfill certain purposes, or functions, for societies that enhance survival of individuals and societies. Traditionally, there have been at least six ways the family has contributed to the stability of the society, according to structural-functional theory.

Sexual Regulation. Physically speaking, any adult human could engage in sex with any other human. However, in practice, no society allows total sexual freedom. Every society attempts to regulate the sexual behavior of its members in accordance with its own particular values. This is most often accomplished through marriage. Regulation ensures that this strong biological drive is satisfied in an orderly way that does not create ongoing disruption, conflict, or jealousy. Certain people are "taken" and "off limits" (Ward and Edelstein 2014).

Reproduction and Replacement. Societies need children to replace members who die, leave, or are incapacitated. Reproduction is controlled to keep family lineage

This woman in New Guinea became more attractive to men as a potential wife after she had proved her fertility by having a child.

and inheritance clear. Parent and caretaker roles are clearly defined and reinforced in many societies by ceremonies: baby showers, birth announcements, christenings, and naming ceremonies that welcome the child as a member of the family. In some places, such as New Guinea, procreation is so important that a young girl who has had children before marriage is more desirable because she has established her fertility. This practice is possible in matriarchal societies where the child is absorbed into the female side of the family.

Socialization. The family is the main training ground for children. In our families, we begin to learn values and norms, proper behavior, roles, and language. In most societies, schools, religious organizations, and other institutions carry out later socialization, but the family remains the most important initial socializing agent to prepare us for roles in society. Parents do most of the socializing in the family, but siblings, grandparents, and other relatives are important socializing agents as well.

Emotional Support and Protection. Families are the main source of love and belonging in many societies, giving us a sense of identity, security, protection, and safety from harm. The family is one place where people may experience unqualified acceptance and feelings of being cherished. Problems of children in youth shelters and incidents of family violence and neglect are reminders that this function is not always successfully provided in families. Still, the family is usually the environment most capable of meeting this need.

Status Assignment. Our family of orientation is the most important determinant of our social status, life chances, and lifestyles. It strongly affects our educational opportunities, access to health care, religious and political affiliations, and values. In fact, in societies with caste systems, the ascribed position at birth is generally the position at death. Although in class societies individuals may achieve new social statuses, our birth positions and the early years of socialization have a strong impact throughout life on who and what we are.

Economic Support. Historically, the family was a unit of production—running a farm, a bakery, or a cobbler shop. Although this function is still predominant in many societies, the economic function carried out in individual families has pretty much disappeared in most Global North families. However, the family remains an economic unit of consumption. Who paid for your clothing, food, and other needs as you were growing up? Who helps many of you pay your college tuition and expenses? Taxing agencies, advertising and commercial enterprises, workplaces, and other social organizations also treat the family as the primary economic unit.

Functional theorists ask about the consequences of what takes place in the family for other parts of the society. They note that the micro-level processes of the family meet structural needs of society at the meso and macro levels (e.g., in the United States, the need for motivated workers who thrive on competition). Each part of the system, according to functionalists, works with other parts to create a functioning society.

Changing Family Functions. As societies change, so do family systems. The sociohistorical perspective of family tells us that changes in intimate relationships—sexuality, marriage, and family patterns—have occurred over the centuries. Major transitions from agricultural to industrial to postindustrial societal systems change all the institutions within those societies. The institution of family in agricultural societies is often large and self-sufficient, with families producing their own food and providing their own shelter; this is not the case in contemporary urban societies. Industrialization and urbanization typical in 18th- and 19th-century Europe and the United States created a distinct change in roles. The wife and child became dependent on the husband who "brought home the bread." The family members became consumers rather than independent and self-supporting coworkers on a farm.

In addition to evolving roles, other changes in society have brought shifts to the family. Improved technology, for example, brought medical advances, new knowledge and skills to be passed on in schools, recreation outside the family unit organized according to age groups, and improved transportation. Socialization is increasingly done in schools, and in some cases teachers have become substitute parents. They do a great deal of the preparation of the child for the larger world. However, family remains a critical institution in society. Most families still function to provide stable structures to carry out early childhood socialization and to sustain love, trust, affection, acceptance, and an escape from the impersonal world.

Thinking Sociologically

How does your family interact with educational and economic institutions? For example, how did the family in which you were raised influence your success in school and your chances of attaining a good job?

 Family Conflict

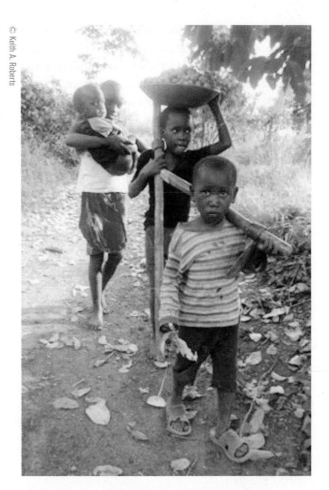

In Kimukunda, a village in southern Uganda, orphaned siblings between the ages of 4 and 8 return from working as day laborers on a nearby farm. Their parents died of AIDS, and their 60-year-old grandmother now takes care of them. Together they struggle to fulfill the functions of a family.

Conflict Theory. Conflict theorists study both individual family situations and broad societal family patterns. They argue that conflict in families is natural and inevitable. It results from the struggle for power and control in the family unit and in the society at large. As long as there is an unequal allocation of resources, conflict will arise.

Family conflicts take many forms. For instance, conflicts occur over allocation of resources, a struggle that may be rooted in conflict between men and women in the society: Who makes decisions, who gets money for clothes or a car, who does the dishes? On the macro level, family systems are a source of inequality in the general society, sustaining class inequalities by passing on wealth, income, and education opportunities for their own members or perpetuating disadvantages such as poverty and lack of cultural capital.

Yet some conflict theorists argue that conflict within the family can be positive because it forces constant negotiation among individual family members and may bring about change that can strengthen the unit as a whole. Believing that conflict is both natural and inevitable, these theorists focus on root causes of conflict and how to deal with the discord. For conflict theorists, there is no assumption of a harmonious family. The social world is characterized more by tension and power plays than by social accord.

An Alternative Theory for Analysis of the Family

One approach to analysis of family and the place of family within the society can be either a micro- or a macro-level theory and offers a different lens for understanding interaction within family structures: feminist theory.

Feminist Theory. Because women often occupy very different places in society than men, feminist theorists argue the need for a feminist perspective to understand family dynamics. Feminist scholars begin by placing women at the center, not to suggest their superiority but to spotlight them as subjects of inquiry and as active agents in the working of society. In doing so, they uncover and examine biases rooted in patriarchal assumptions (Eshleman and Bulcroft 2010).

A micro-level branch of feminist theory, the interpretive approach, considers women within their social contexts—the interpersonal relations and everyday reality facing women as they interact with other family members. It does not ignore economic, political, social, and historical factors but focuses on the ways women construct their reality, their opportunities, and their place in the family and community. According to feminist theorists, this results in a more realistic view of family and women's lives than many other theories provide.

Applying this feminist approach to understand Felice's situation, for example, the theorists would consider the way she views her social context and the way she assesses her support systems. This approach is similar to Max Weber's concept of *Verstehen*—understanding people and social units from *within* the experience—and has much in common with symbolic interaction theory, since it focuses on what interaction means to the women themselves. Felice's religious background, her reference group of close women friends, and her parents and siblings can have a profound effect on how she understands marriage, her rights and responsibilities within family roles, and her view of herself as mistreated or not.

Many branches of feminist theory have roots in conflict theory, and are therefore more macro in focus. These theorists argue that patterns of patriarchy and dominance lead to inequalities for women. One of the earliest conflict theorists, Friedrich Engels (Karl Marx's close associate), argued that the family was the chief source of female oppression and that until basic resources were reallocated within the family, women would continue to be oppressed. However, he said that as women become aware of their collective interests and oppression, they will insist on a redistribution of power, money, and jobs (Engels [1884] 1942).

One vivid example of how women and men can be viewed as groups with competing interests is through a feminist analysis of domestic violence. In the United States, one in four (25%) women experiences domestic violence in her lifetime. With an estimated 1 million to 3 million women assaulted by an intimate partner each year, there is an incident of domestic violence every 25 seconds in the United States. Approximately 85% of the victims of domestic violence are women (Domestic Violence Resource Center 2012; Safe Horizon 2014). Boys who witness domestic violence are more than twice as likely to abuse their own wives later in life. Thirty-five percent of female murder victims are murdered by a spouse or boyfriend, with three women and one man killed each day by a spouse or intimate partner (Domestic Violence Resource Center 2012).

Recent United Nations data indicate that one in three women in the world has experienced physical or sexual abuse, and some men openly admit having raped or abused women with no consequences. Although women's situation has improved in many areas, especially in education, there is a long way to go to eliminate brutality (Sengupta 2014; United Nations Population Fund 2014).

Women are most severely exploited in societies that treat them as property and in which the family is a key political unit for power and status. Consider the practice of *sati* found in some patriarchal Asian societies, in which a widow is expected (or forced) to throw herself on her husband's funeral pyre because there is no structural place for her in the family after her husband's death. Although outlawed in India for almost two centuries now, the practice lingers in some rural areas of the nation.

Feminist theorists point out that changes in the patriarchal family structure, education and employment opportunities for women, and child care availability can lead to greater freedom of choice, equality, and autonomy for women.

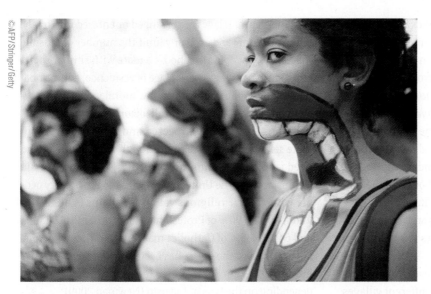

Women with their upper bodies painted pose as they take part in a protest against domestic violence against women on International Women's Day.

FAMILY DYNAMICS: MICRO-LEVEL PROCESSES

The Agabi family belongs to the Hausa tribe of West Africa. They share a family compound composed of huts or houses for each family unit of one wife and her young children, plus one building for greeting guests, one for cooking, one for the older children, and one for washing. The compound is surrounded by an enclosure. Each member of the family carries out certain tasks: food preparation, washing, child care, farming, herding—whatever is needed for the well-being of the group. Wives live with their husbands' families. Should there be a divorce, the children generally belong to the husband's household because in this tribe the family lineage is patrilineal through the father's side.

The eldest male of the Hausa tribe is the leader and makes decisions for the group. When a child is born, he presides over a ceremony to name and welcome the child into the group. When the child reaches marrying age, the eldest male then plays a major role in choosing a suitable mate. On his death, the power he has held passes to his eldest son, and he and his other sons inherit his property.

However, the eldest Agabi son has moved away from the extended family to the city, where he works in a factory to support himself. He lives in a small room with several other migrants. He has met a girl from another tribe and may marry her, but he will have to do so without his family's blessing. He will probably have a small family because

of money and space constraints in the city. His lifestyle and even values have already altered considerably. These micro-level changes are connected to a global trend of urbanization and industrialization altering cultures around the world and changing family life.

Families can be studied at each level of analysis: as interdependent micro-level social units with family members in the immediate household; as meso-level institutions that can be seen as economic units; and as part of the macro-level social system. Many individual family issues that seem very intimate and personal are actually affected by cultural norms and forces at other levels (such as migration, urbanization, and economic conditions). Likewise, decisions of individuals at the micro level affect meso- and macro-level social structures (such as size of families). Individual families are, in essence, local franchises of a larger social phenomenon.

Thinking Sociologically

What kinds of changes in families would you anticipate as societies change from agricultural to industrial to information technology economies and as individuals move from rural to urban areas? What changes has your family undergone over several generations?

Mate Selection: How Do New Families Start?

At the most micro level, two people get together to begin a new family unit. In 2011 the world population passed 7 billion people, but your partner was or will not be randomly selected from the entire global population. Even in Global North societies, where we think individuals have free choice of marriage partners, mate selection is not an entirely individual choice. Indeed, mate selection is highly limited by geographical proximity, ethnicity, age, social class, and a host of other variables. As we shall see, micro- and macro-level forces influence each other even in a process as personal as mate selection.

Norms Governing Choice of Marriage Partners: Societal Rules and Intimate Choices. A number of cultural rules—meso- and macro-level expectations—govern the choice of a mate in any society. Most are unwritten societal norms. They vary from culture to culture, but in every society we learn them from an early age. One of the cultural rules is exogamy, *norms governing the choice of a mate that requires individuals to marry outside of their own immediate group.* The most universal form of exogamy is the *incest taboo,* including restrictions against father–daughter, mother–son, and brother–sister marriages. Some countries, including about half the U.S. states, forbid first cousins to marry (see Table 3.3 on page 77). Others, such as some African groups and many Syrian villages, encourage first-cousin marriages to solidify family ties and property holdings.

Some societies require village exogamy (marriage outside one's own village) because it bonds different villages together and reduces the likelihood of armed conflict between neighboring groups. Exogamy also alleviates sexual jealousy within groups. For example, if father and son became jealous about who was sleeping with the wife/mother/sister, relationships would be destroyed and parental authority sabotaged. Likewise, if the father was always going to the daughter for sexual satisfaction, the mother and daughter bond would be severely threatened (Williams, Sawyer, and Wahlstrom 2013). No society can allow this to happen to its family system. Any society that has failed to have an incest taboo self-destructed long ago.

On the other hand, norms of endogamy *require individuals to marry inside certain human boundaries, whatever the societal members see as protecting the homogeneity of the group.* The purpose is to encourage group bonding and solidarity, and to help minority groups survive in societies with different cultures. Endogamous norms may require individuals to select mates of the same race, religion, social class, ethnic background, or clan (Williams et al. 2013). Examples of strictly endogamous religious groups include the Armenian Iranians, Orthodox Jews, Old Order Amish, Jehovah's Witnesses, and the Parsis of India. Such a practice results in less biologically diversified groups, but protects the minority identity (Belding 2004).

Each group may have different definitions of where the exogamy boundary is. For Orthodox Hasidic Jews, marriage to a Reform Jew is exogamy—strictly forbidden. For the Amish, the marriage of a Hostetler Amish woman to a Beachy Amish man is beyond consideration. Marriage of a Hopi to a Navajo has also been frowned on as marriage to an "Other"—even though many Anglos would think of this as an endogamous marriage of two Native Americans.

Whether marriages are arranged or entered into freely, both endogamy and exogamy limit the number of possible mates. Most people also choose a mate with similar social characteristics—age, race, place of residence, educational background, political philosophy, moral values, and psychological traits—a practice called *homogamy.*

Going outside the expected and accepted group in mate selection can make things tough for newlyweds who need family and community support. Few take this risk. For instance, in the United States, close to 90% marry people with similar religious values (Williams et al. 2013). About 80% to 90% of Protestants marry other Protestants, and 64% to 85% of Catholics marry within their religious faith. For Jews, the figure has been as high as 90% but has dropped in recent decades to as low as 50% for some Jews, depending on the type of Judaism (Newman 2009).

So cultural norms of societies limit individual decisions about micro-level matters such as choice of a spouse, and they do so in a way that most individuals do not consciously recognize. Exogamy and endogamy norms and expectations generally restrict the range of potential marriage partners. Some of these norms are weakening, however, as the rapidly rising number of interracial marriages in the United States reveals. Still, the question remains: How do we settle on a life partner?

Finding a Mate. In most societies, mate selection takes place through arranged marriages, free-choice unions, or some combination of the two. In either case, selection is shaped by cultural rules of the society.

Kako and Hiroshi of Japan met for the first time for tea after a matchmaker had worked with each one's family to find a suitable mate. If they get along and do not object to the match, the wedding will be planned. Abdul's father has arranged a marriage for him with a girl from a nearby village. This marriage will solidify bonds between the families and the villages, reducing the chance of future conflict. Love has nothing to do with such arranged marriages, but political and economic factors matter big time! Some marriages are based on individual choice and love, and some are based on what is good for the family and community group. Arranged marriages involve *a pattern of mate selection in which someone other than the couple—elder males, parents, a matchmaker—selects the marital partners.* This method of mate selection is most common in traditional, often patriarchal, societies. For many girls in traditional Muslim societies, marriage is a matter of necessity, for their support comes from the family system. Marriages create and strengthen economic

Arranged Marriages ▶

arrangements and political alliances between family groups. Daughters serve as valuable commodities in negotiations to secure these ties between families (Burn 2011). Beauty, youth, talent, and pleasant disposition bring a high bride price and a good match. Should the young people like each other, it is icing on the cake. Daughters must trust that their families will make the best possible matches for them. Most often, the men hold the power in this vital decision.

Seated front and center with the bride and groom at many Japanese weddings is the matchmaker, the person responsible for bringing the relationship into being. After both families agree to the arrangement, the couple meets over tea several times to decide whether the match suits them. Today, about 30% of marriages in Japan are still arranged this way, the rest being called "love marriages" ("Getting Married in Japan" 2014).

Where arranged marriages are the norm, love has a special meaning. The man and woman may never have set eyes on each other before the wedding day, but respect and affection generally grow over time as the husband and wife live together. People from societies with arranged marriages are assured a mate and have difficulty comprehending marriage systems based on love, romance, and courtship—factors believed to be insufficient grounds for a lifelong relationship. They wonder why anyone would want to place themselves in a marriage market, with all the uncertainty and rejection. Such whimsical and unsystematic methods would not work in many societies, where the structure of life is built around family systems.

While most arranged marriages involve adults, in some parts of the world, arranged marriages of children also occur. Girls as young as 6 have been married to much older men who can afford to take them in or so the girl's family can pay off a debt. In some cases, they become slaves of the man's household, working long hours and bearing children at a young age (Ghosh 2014; Murray 2012).

Free-choice marriage is *a pattern of mate selection in which the partners select each other based primarily on romance and love.* The idea that each person has the right to choose a partner with minimal interference from others has become increasingly prevalent as societies around the world become more Westernized, women gain more rights and freedoms, and families exert less control over their children's choice of mates (Eshleman and Bulcroft 2010). Sonnets, symphonies, rock songs, poems, and plays have been written to honor romantic love and the psychological and physiological pain and pleasure that the mating game

Child marriage is especially common in parts of West Africa, South Asia, and East and Central Africa. In some countries, as many as 1 out of every 10 girls is married by the time she is 15 years old, and nearly half are married by age 18.

brings. However impractical romance may seem, in industrial and postindustrial societies people generally value love and individualism and tend to have high marriage rates, low fertility rates, and high divorce rates.

Many people in arranged marriage systems are bewildered about how people can meet possible mates in free-choice systems. The Internet facilitates romance and mate selection in many modern societies, helping people of all ages enter into relationships and find compatible mates. Internet mate shoppers spend more than $900 million a year on online dating.

Many of the e-dating services claim that their profiles and processes are based on social science research. The burgeoning business in e-romance introduces people with common interests, backgrounds, ages, and other variables. Several popular sites are Match.com, Zoosk, eHarmony, OurTime, and HowAboutWe. For example, according to eHarmony, each day approximately 15,000 individuals fill out its extensive 258-question questionnaire to create a personality profile that the company claims is a "scientifically proven" compatibility-matching system. More than 33 million users from 150 countries hope for one or more matches from the system. If the reported average of 236 members who marry every day is an indication, many would-be mates are finding their partners (eHarmony 2014). Many specialized niche dating services have sprung up based on race, religion, sexual orientation, occupations, and other interests (Hu 2014).

Thinking Sociologically

Recent studies reveal a lower divorce rate among those who met online than those who met in more traditional ways. How might a rational choice theorist explain those findings?

Starting with the assumption that eligible people are most likely to meet and be attracted to others who have similar values and backgrounds, sociologists have developed various mate selection theories, several of which view dating as a three-stage process—a series of sequential decisions (see Figure 10.1).

1. *Stimulus:* We meet someone to whom we are attracted by appearance, voice, dress, similar ethnic background, sense of humor, or other factors. Something serves as a stimulus that makes us take notice. Of course, sometimes the stimulus is simply knowing the other person is interested in us.

2. *Value comparison:* We are more likely to find someone compatible if he or she affirms our own beliefs and values toward life, politics, religion, and roles of men and women in society and marriage. If our values are not compatible, the person does not pass through our filter. We look elsewhere.

3. *Roles and needs stage:* Another filter comes when the couple explores roles of companion, parent, housekeeper, and lover. This might involve looking for common needs, interests, and favored activities. If the roles and needs are not complementary, desire for a permanent relationship wanes.

Thinking Sociologically

Conduct a small survey of dating and married couples you know. Ask them about how they became involved in their relationship and their process of deciding to get together or marry. How do their comments mesh with the three-stage process described above?

FIGURE 10.1 Mate Selection "Filtering"

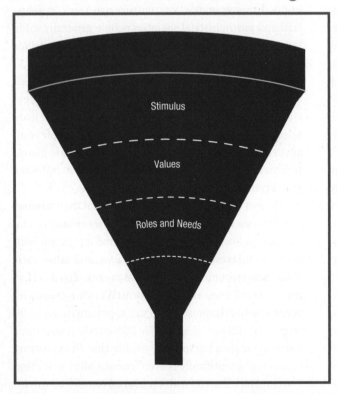

Stimulus

Values

Roles and Needs

The notion of mate selection described above is sometime referred to as a filter theory. It is as though you were filtering specs of gold, and the first filter holds out the large stones, the second filter holds back pebbles, the third filter stops sand, but the flakes of gold come through. Each stage in the mate selection process involves filtering some people out of the process. For you there may be other filter factors as well—such as religious similarities or common ethnicity.

Who Holds the Power? Authority in Marriage

Power relations, another micro-level issue shaped by cultural norms at the macro level, affect the interactions and decision making in individual families. Two areas that have received particular sociological attention are decision making in marriage and work roles.

Decision Making in Marriage. Cultural traditions establish the power base in society and family: patriarchy, matriarchy, or egalitarianism. The most typical authority pattern in the world is patriarchy, or male authority. Matriarchy, female authority, is rare. Even where the lineage is traced through the mother's line, males usually dominate decision making.

Egalitarian family patterns—in which power, authority, and decision making are shared between the spouses and perhaps with the children—are emerging, but they are not yet a reality in most households. For example, research indicates that in many U.S. families, decisions concerning vacation plans, car purchases, and housing are reached democratically. Still, most U.S. families are not fully egalitarian. Males generally have a disproportionate say in major decisions such as whether to move to a new city or buy a new home (Lindsey 2011). However, social scientists find no evidence that there are any inherent intellectual or personality foundations for male authority as opposed to female authority (Kramer 2010; Ward and Edelstein 2014).

Resource theory attempts to explain power relations by arguing that the spouse with the greater resources—education, occupational prestige, income—has the greater power. In many societies, income is the most important factor because it represents identity and power. If only one spouse brings home a paycheck, the other is usually less powerful. In families where the wife is a professional, other factors in addition to income such as persuasion and egalitarian values may enter into the power dynamic (Jory & Yodanis 2014; Lindsey 2011). Regardless of who has greater resources, men in two-earner couples tend to have more say in financial matters and less responsibility for children and household tasks.

Who Does the Housework?. The *second shift*, a term coined by Hochschild (1989), refers to the housework and child care that employed women do after their "first-shift" jobs. The gap in household work for men and women has closed dramatically in recent decades; studies indicate that women spend 2.6 hours and men 2.1 hours per day doing household chores (U.S. Bureau of Labor Statistics 2014a). Still, on an average day, 83% of women compared to 65% of men spend some time doing household activities (U.S. Bureau of Labor Statistics 2014a). Furthermore, men spend just 16% of their time doing child care activities while women spend 25% of their day caring for children (U.S. Bureau of Labor Statistics 2014a). The next "Engaging Sociology" on page 324 shows the breakdown in hours spent by men and women at various household activities.

Employment schedules also affect the amount of time each spouse contributes to household tasks. Husbands who are at home during hours when their wives are working tend to take on more tasks. Employment, education, and earnings give women more respect and independence and a power base for a more equitable division of labor across tasks (Cherlin 2012; Kramer 2010). Recent research also clearly shows a narrowing of the gap in time spent by men and women on household tasks, though such factors as the ages of children, how many years the mother has worked outside the home, and socioeconomic status of the family influence how involved men are and how much real "free time" each experiences. When women do have free time, it is much more likely to be interrupted than men's free time (Kan, Sullivan, and Gershuny 2011; Mattingly and Sayer 2006; Saxbe, Repetti, and Graesch 2011).

A positive relationship exists between equity in households and successful marriages. Husbands who do an equitable share of the household chores actually report higher levels of satisfaction with the marriage, and such couples are less likely to divorce (Dockterman 2014; Lorillard 2011). The success or failure of a marriage depends in large part on patterns that develop early in the marriage for dealing with the everyday situations including power relationships and division of labor.

While women in the world are more often economically dependent on men, men are more often dependent on women emotionally, for they are less likely to have same-sex friends with whom they share feelings and vulnerabilities. Men bond with one another, but they seldom develop truly intimate ties that provide support in hard times. So women are not entirely without power even where they are economically dependent. It is just that their power frequently takes a different form and results in fewer privileges (Newman 2009).

THE FAMILY AS AN INSTITUTION: MESO-LEVEL ANALYSIS

We experience family life at a very personal level, but the sum total of hundreds of thousands of families interacting in recognizable patterns results in *family as an institution* at the meso level. In this section, we look at the structure and parts of family as an institution, and the family and its relationship to other institutions. Some of the changes in the family have resulted from—or caused—changes in other institutions.

The Structure and Parts of the Family Institution

The family institution varies among societies in some interesting ways. For example, in some societies men marry more than one woman. Institutions lay out the general framework for families in any society and include types of marriages, extended and nuclear families, and other structural models of families. Individual families are local expressions of a larger system of families that make up the institution of family in a society.

Types of Marriages. Monogamy and polygamy are the main forms of marriage found around the world. **Monogamy** refers to *marriage of two individuals* and is the most familiar form of marriage in industrial and postindustrial societies. Polygamy, *marriage of one person to more than one partner at the same time*, is most often found in agricultural societies where multiple spouses and children mean more help with the farmwork. There are two main forms of polygamy—*polygyny* and *polyandry*. Anthropologist George Murdock found that

 Polygamy   Why get married?

ENGAGING SOCIOLOGY

Household Tasks by Gender

In many families, household talks are highly gendered. As recently as the 1980s, wives and daughters spent two or three times as much time as fathers and sons in household tasks such as cleaning and laundry and yard work. However, the tides have been shifting, and while they are not entirely equal, they are more balanced.

Sociological Data Analysis

1. What is the division of labor (by gender) for household maintenance in your family?

2. How did it evolve?

3. Is it considered fair by all participants?

4. How does it compare to the data in Figure 10.2?

FIGURE 10.2   Percentage of Men and Women Who Engage in Some Type of Household Task Each Day

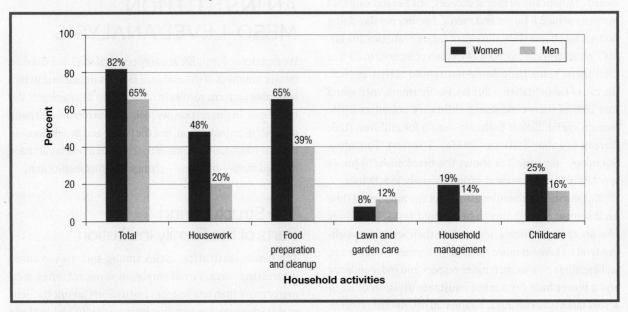

Source: U.S. Bureau of Labor Statistics (2014a).

polygyny, a marital system in which a husband can have more than one wife, was allowed (although not always practiced) in 709 of the 849 tribal groups and societies he cataloged in his classic *Ethnographic Atlas* (1967). Only 16% (136 societies) were exclusively monogamous (Barash 2002). Polygyny is limited due to the expense of maintaining a large family, the high cost of brides in some societies, and religious and political pressures plus a global movement toward monogamy. Also, there are seldom enough extra women to go around. Polygyny tends to increase during or immediately after wars when war casualties result in reduced numbers of men.

Polyandry, a marital system in which a wife has more than one husband, is practiced in less than 1% of the world's societies. Murdock found only four societies in the world that practice polyandrous marriage. In one such society, the Todas of Southern India, brothers can share a wife (O'Connel 1993). The Marquesan Islanders also allow wives to have more than one husband. A Tibetan practice originating in the country's system of land ownership and inheritance permits a woman to marry several men, usually brothers (O'Connel 1993). This often happens when the men are poor and must share a single plot of land to eke out a meager livelihood, so they decide to remain a single household with one wife.

Members of global North societies often find the practice of polygamy hard to understand, just as those from polygamous societies find monogamy strange. Some societies insist on strict monogamy: Marriage to one other person is lifelong, and deviation from that standard is prohibited. Yet most global North societies practice what could be called a variation of polygamy—*serial monogamy*. With high divorce and remarriage rates, Western societies have developed a system of marrying several spouses, but one at a time. One has spouses in a series rather than simultaneously.

Extended and Nuclear Families. The Ma-Pa-and-kids monogamous model familiar in many industrialized parts of the world is not as typical as it appears to those from such societies. From a worldwide perspective, it is only one of several structural models of family.

Extended families *include two or more adult generations that share tasks and living quarters. This may include brothers, sisters, aunts, uncles, cousins, and grandparents*. In most extended family systems, the eldest male is the authority figure. This is a common pattern around the world, especially in agricultural societies. Some ethnic groups in the United States, such as Mexican Americans and some Asian Americans, live in extended monogamous families with several generations under one roof. This is financially practical and helps group members maintain their traditions and identity.

As societies become more industrialized and fewer individuals and families engage in agriculture, the nuclear family, *consisting of two parents and their children—or any two of the three*—becomes more common. A worldwide movement toward more nuclear families is under way because of urbanization, fewer arranged marriages, and growing equality between men and women (Burn 2011; Goode 1970).

No matter what form the family takes in a society, the family, like all of the other major institutions, is interdependent at the meso level with each of the other institutions. For example, if the health care institution is unaffordable or not functioning well, families may not get the care they need to prevent serious illness. If the economy goes into a recession and jobs are not available, families experience stress, abuse rates increase, and marriages are more likely to become unstable. In worst-case scenarios, families who lose their incomes may become homeless.

This polyandrous family poses for a photo in front of their tent in northwest China (which does not officially permit such marriages). The children—no matter who is their biological father—call the oldest brother father and all the other brothers uncle.

Thinking Sociologically

Under what social and economic circumstances would an extended family be helpful? Under what circumstances would it be a burden? Would you rather live in an extended or a nuclear family unit? Why?

The Economic Institution and the Family

The family is the primary economic unit of consumption, so what happens when economic times are rough? In the

In many societies, the family is still the primary unit of economic production. This family of farmers selling mangoes waits for customers at the side of a road on the outskirts of Havana, Cuba.

Economics and the Family   Nuclear Family

past several years much of the world economy has been troubled, resulting in employment instability and uncertainty, economic strain, and even poverty causing strained family relations. Low-income families, especially single-parent families headed by women, are particularly hard-hit and often have to struggle for survival. In some cases, families are so financially devastated that they become homeless—an especially difficult situation for children.

Poverty and Families in the United States. The poverty threshold for a family of four was $23,850 in 2014, and for a single person $11,670 (U.S. Department of Health and Human Services 2014b). In 2012, 15% of those living in the United States (46.5 million people) lived below the poverty line. This was 2.5% higher than the poverty rate in 2007, reflecting the recession's effect on families. For children under 18, the poverty rate was 21.8% (U.S. Census Bureau 2013b). Table 10.2 shows the percentage of individuals and families in poverty.

The *feminization of poverty*, discussed in earlier chapters, is a global problem. It occurs where single motherhood is widespread and where there are few policies to reduce poverty, especially for this group (Williams et al. 2013). Single mothers, whether in capitalist or socialist countries, have some common experiences, including dual roles as workers and mothers, lower earnings than men, irregular paternal support payments, and underrepresentation in policy-making bodies. What differ around the world are governmental policies that help mothers with child support, child care, health care, maternity leave, and family allowances. Single mothers are as prevalent in Sweden as in the United States, but U.S. single mothers are many times more likely to be poor because of fewer support systems from the state (Winkler 2002). For single teens, early motherhood, lack of education, and insufficient income lead to a multiproblem family pattern.

One cause of single-parent families has been divorce. However, the change in birthrates in which more children are born to single women is also a factor. Table 10.3 shows

Table 10.2   Poverty Status of U.S. Families by Family Type in 2011

Poverty Status and Family Type	Total Percentage Below Poverty Level
Total (all) families	11.8% (9.5 million)
Married-couple families	6.3% (3.7 million)
Single female householder	30.9% (4.8 million))
Single male householder	16.4% (1.0 million)

Source: U.S. Census Bureau (2013b).

Table 10.3   Percentage of Births to Unmarried and Married Women: United States

Year	Births to Unmarried Women (%)	Births to Married Women (%)
2012	40.7	59.3
2000	33.2	66.8
1995	32.2	67.8
1990	28.0	72.0
1985	22.0	78.0
1980	18.4	81.6

Source: DeParle and Tavernise (2012); CDC (2014); ChildStats.gov (2013).

the shift in 30 years from 18.4% to 40.7% of babies born outside of marriage (Centers for Disease Control and Prevention [CDC] 2014b).

Due to high mortality and incarceration rates of African American males, relatively few African American women marry. More than 70% of African American women between 25 and 29 are not married (Stanley 2011). Although African Americans value family, many cannot fulfill the economic role of husband and father because of racial discrimination, discrimination against those with criminal records, and the declining number of jobs available to less-educated men (MacLeod 2008; Madyun and Lee 2010; Wilson 1987).

Some argue that a culture of poverty, a set of attitudes and values including a sense of hopelessness and passivity, low aspirations, feelings of powerlessness and inferiority, and present-time orientation (concern only for the present and not planning for the future) is passed from one generation to the next (Lewis 1961, 1986). However, many sociological researchers support the argument that poverty itself causes the values and attitudes that develop as survival mechanisms in poor communities. The poverty is largely a result of macro-level factors such as government policies, not the values and attitudes of the poor (MacLeod 2008).

Dual-Worker Families. A different kind of economic influence can be seen in dual-career marriages. Two incomes may relieve economic strain on a household, but family life in dual-worker families may be quite complicated. Browse through the checkout-line magazine racks next time you are in a grocery store. Note the number of articles offering advice on how to cope with stress and overload or how to budget time, cook meals in minutes, rise to the top, and "make it" together. Stress, role conflict, and work overload are common, but most couples are aware of these strains and have chosen or feel financially compelled to combine marriage, sometimes children, and dual careers.

A recent debate emerged after publications by several influential women. Anne-Marie Slaughter, the U.S. State Department's director of policy planning under Hillary Clinton, left her position to spend more time with her family. Slaughter argued in a 2012 article explaining her departure that smart, productive career women often find they have to give up ambitions because institutional social mores make it difficult to have successful family lives and high-powered careers. This raised the question, *Can* women "have it all"—family and satisfying professional lives?

The debate about women's roles escalated, especially among women academics and students, when Sheryl Sandberg, Facebook's chief operating officer, wrote a book

This young woman sits at the wheel of her car with all of her possessions inside and her children in the backseat. These are not conditions that make for effective parenting.

arguing that women can and should pursue professional success and leadership positions (Sandberg 2013). The debate is not whether there are ambitious and talented women, but whether the structure and norms of the workplace and society are allowing women to exercise their full potential in the current system.

In many global North societies, government and industry support dual-career families with various family-friendly policies: readily available child care facilities, parental leaves for childbirth and illness, and flexible work hours or telecommuting (working from one's home). These policies allow families to combine work and family lives and even have some time for leisure. The United States, however, has been slower than other global North countries to adopt family-friendly policies. The U.S. government passed the Family and Medical Leave Act in 1993, allowing for 12 weeks of unpaid leave for the birth of a baby or care of a newborn, foster care or adoption, serious health issues in the immediate family, or serious medical conditions of the employee (U.S. Department of Labor 2013a). However, few employers can afford to take unpaid time off. Many corporations in the United States have also been slow to respond to dual-career family needs. Company-sponsored day care and parental leave for fathers are still rare. A few businesses are experimenting with family-friendly policies such as flextime (allowing individuals to schedule their own work hours within certain time frames) and job sharing (allowing individuals to split a job, with one family member working in the morning and the other in the afternoon).

In comparison to other countries, however, the government in the United States does little to ensure that women can take time off to have a baby and not lose their jobs. Figure 10.3 indicates the legal requirements of maternal leave in several countries.

As we have seen, family is a diverse and complex social institution. It interacts with other institutions and in some ways reinforces them. Families prepare the next generation. They talk—and many pray—together about what happens after death. They provide care of disabled, infirm, or sick members. As a basic institution, the family plays a role in the vitality of the entire nation. So it should not be surprising that at the macro level, many national and global policy decisions concern how to strengthen the family institution.

Thinking Sociologically

What are the challenges facing dual-career families? What social policies might relieve some of the stress on families with two working parents?

NATIONAL AND GLOBAL FAMILY ISSUES: MACRO-LEVEL ANALYSIS

An effective way to explore macro-level issues pertaining to families is through policy matters that impact families. After exploring issues of national concern—cohabitation,

same-sex families, and divorce—we look at some global trends in marriage and family life.

Cohabitation

Cohabitation—living together in a sexual relationship without marriage—is a significant micro-level trend in many countries that has implications for national family laws, tax laws, work benefits, and other macro-level issues. In European and North American countries, cohabitation has become the norm for many groups. In the United States, by the age of 30 three out of four women have lived with a partner without marriage. Forty percent of cohabitants marry within 3 years, according to a recent CDC report (Lopatto 2013). This has become a common step toward marriage for some, and an alternative to marriage for others. The overall trend in the number of "unmarried households" has risen for several decades. Two thirds of couples married in the past decade cohabited before marriage (Jay 2012).

Some argue that a newly emerging pattern for young adults between 25 and 34 is serial cohabitation (Lichter, Turner, and Sassler 2010). As Figure 10.4 shows, the increases in cohabiting households (same-sex and different-sex couples) in the United States over 30 years are dramatic. Still, at any given point in time, only about 9% of the population in the United States is cohabiting (Benokraitis 2012).

FIGURE 10.3   Total Duration of Paid Leave After Childbirth: Selected Countries

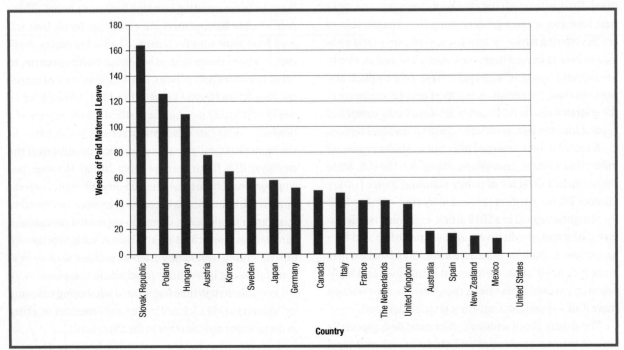

Source: Organisation for Economic Co-operation and Development (2014).

Divorce 📖

FIGURE 10.4   Cohabiting Households in the United States, 1960–2012

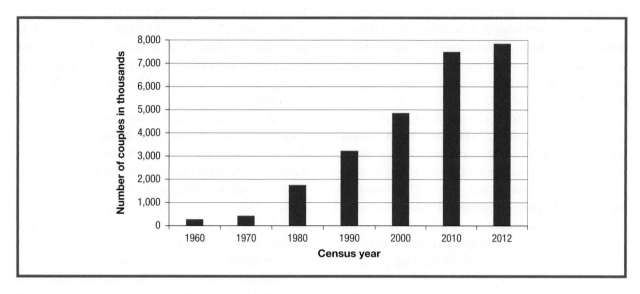

Sources: Fitch, Goeken, and Ruggles (2005); Kreider (2010b); Vespa, Lewis, and Kreider (2013).

Countries in Europe with the highest percentage of cohabiting couples between the ages of 20 and 34 include Denmark (28.6%), Estonia (23.5%), Finland (28.3%), France (21.3%), the Netherlands (21.9%), Norway (22.7%), and the United Kingdom (22.2%) (OECD Family Database 2010). Latin American and Caribbean surveys indicate that more than one in four women between the ages of 15 and 49 are in relationships they call consensual unions, living together without official sanction. Such women typically have far less legal protection than European women do during or after such unions.

Rates and reasons for marriage versus cohabitation vary significantly by ethnicity. For whites in the United States, cohabitation is often a precursor to marriage. For African Americans, it is more of an alternative to marriage. As noted earlier in the chapter, financial problems encourage cohabitation in African American families. Many African American men avoid marriage if they do not think they can support a family and fulfill the breadwinner role. Although childbearing increases the chance of marriage, it is a much stronger impetus for white than for black cohabitants.

We might assume that cohabiting would allow couples to make more realistic decisions about entering permanent relationships if they do get married. However, some studies have shown that this is not always the case. When couples have different objectives for cohabiting, or have not discussed the future of the relationship before moving in together, problems may arise, and dissolution of

the relationship can result. Some studies have linked cohabitation prior to marriage to higher rates of divorce (Sassler and Miller 2011). However, that correlation has changed in the past decade. Recent research indicates that the fairly large gap in divorce rates between cohabitants and those who did not live together prior to marriage has nearly evaporated (Cohen and Manning 2010).

 Thinking Sociologically

For about four decades, cohabitation by a couple was linked to greater likelihood of divorce. In very recent years this pattern has changed. What hypotheses on the micro, meso, and macro levels can you generate to explain the shift in outcomes for cohabitation? For which hypothesis do you think you would find the most evidence? Why?

Same-Sex Marriage and Civil Unions

A hotly debated macro-level policy matter concerning the family is the official status of same-sex couples. Policy decisions affect rights and benefits for partners, but there is intense disagreement over whether this issue is about human rights or about divinely determined rights and wrongs.

In the United States, the 1996 Defense of Marriage Act declared that states were not compelled to recognize same-sex marriages performed in other states and that the federal government would not grant rights guaranteed to opposite-sex married couples. In essence, this act ensured that same-sex couples would not receive 1,138 federal rights given to heterosexual married partners (U.S. General Accounting Office 2004). In 2013, however, the U.S. Supreme Court ruled that the section of the Defense of Marriage Act dealing with federal recognition of same-sex marriages was unconstitutional and that these rights cannot be limited to heterosexual citizens ("Supreme Court DOMA Decision" 2013).

As same-sex relationships become more widely acknowledged and accepted in the global North, increasing numbers of gay and lesbian couples live together openly as families. Denmark was the first country to recognize same-sex unions in 1989, granting legal rights to such couples. In 2001, the Netherlands was the first country to allow same-sex marriages. As of June 2014, 17 countries allow same-sex marriages: Argentina, Belgium, Brazil, Canada, Denmark, England/Wales, France, Iceland, the Netherlands, New Zealand, Norway, Portugal, Scotland, South Africa, Spain, Sweden, and Uruguay (Freedom to Marry 2014a). Some countries, however, punish openly gay individuals. Uganda almost passed a bill authorizing the death penalty for homosexuals, but it was deterred by international condemnation. Nigeria has passed a bill outlawing homosexuality, and mobs have attacked homosexuals (Goodstein 2012).

In the United States, a court ruling in 2014 suddenly increased the number of states that allow same sex marriage from 19 (plus the District of Columbia) to 32, so a majority of states now allow it, and that will soon increase the numbers (Moen 2014; Pew Research Center Religion & Public Life Project 2014). The U.S. Census reports over 600,000 same-sex couples in the United States, or about 1% of all couple households (U.S. Census Bureau 2013c). Most scholars acknowledge that this is probably an underreporting because of the stigma of reporting that one is gay or lesbian. One out of every nine unmarried cohabiting couples are gay or lesbian, and one quarter of these couples are raising children (Benokraitis 2012; James 2011).

One reason many people in the *lesbigay* community are so intent on the legalization of same-sex marriage is that same-sex partnerships or civil unions are "insufficiently institutionalized," making them somewhat less stable and creating ambiguity about their roles and rights (Cherlin 1978; Stewart 2007). They argue that if we actually believe that stable relationships and families make for a healthier and more stable society, then families with same-sex adults need public recognition.

Those who favor gay and lesbian marriages claim that supportive lifelong relationships are good for individuals and good for society. They see the growing support for the legalization of same-sex marriage as an encouraging sign about how important the family is to society (see Figure 10.5). Moreover, because many societies offer tax benefits, insurance coverage, and other privileges to married couples, the denial of marriage on the basis of one's gender attraction is discriminatory and costly to partners denied rights, and to societies that must care for the needs of the uninsured or unemployed.

Those opposed to the legalization of same-sex marriage argue that marriage has been a function of the church, temple, and mosque for centuries. Marriage was historically governed in Europe by the church or temple until Martin Luther insisted that the government play a role. Gradually after that time, marriage came to be monitored and recorded by governments. Still, that did not happen in England until as recently as 1837, so religious groups have defined marriage for most of Western history (England Church Records 2014). None of the religious traditions have historically recognized same-sex relationships as legitimate (although a few are doing so now). Some opponents appeal to biology with the assertion that marriage is a legitimate way to propagate the species. Because same-sex unions do not serve this purpose, they do not serve the society, according to these opponents of same-sex marriage. However, many same-sex couples are providing loving, supportive homes for children, their own or adopted.

The whole issue of same-sex marriage has been a policy issue for which some legislators have turned to public

©REUTERS/Philippe Laurenson

This couple celebrates after hearing that their marriage and those of other same-sex couples will be legally recognized in their state.

FIGURE 10.5   Changing Attitudes of U.S. Adults Toward Same-Sex Marriage, 2001–2012

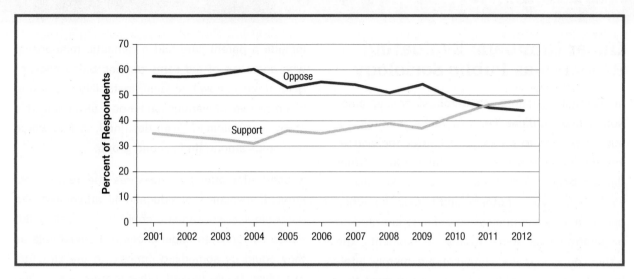

Source: Adapted from Newport, F. (2012, May 8). *Half of Americans Support Legal Gay Marriage.* Gallup Politics.

sociologists for accurate information. One of these is Tey Meadow, whose work is featured in the next "Sociologists in Action" on page 332.

Divorce: Contract Breaking

Is the family breaking down? Is it relevant in today's world? Although most cultures extol the virtues of family life, the reality is that not all partnerships work. Support is not forthcoming for the partner, trust is violated, abuse is present, and relationships deteriorate. So we cannot discuss family life without also recognizing the often painful side of family life that results in contract breaking.

Some commentators view divorce rates and declining marriage rates as evidence that the family is losing importance. They see enormous problems created by divorce. There are costs to adults who suffer guilt and failure, to children from divided homes, and to the society that does not have the stabilizing force of intact lifelong partnerships. Many children around the world grow up in homes without both natural parents present. For example, 24% of children in the United States live in mother-only families, and 6% live with grandparents (Child Trends 2013b). Nearly half of all U.S. children today live at least part of their lives in single-parent families (Kreider and Ellis 2011). In 2012, 51% of African American, 28% of Hispanic, 10.6% of Asian, and 19% of white children lived in mother-only households (Child Trends 2012).

Others argue that marriage is not so much breaking down as adapting to a different kind of social system. Indeed, more people today express satisfaction with marriage than at any previous time period, and 6% of currently married couples reach their 50th wedding anniversary, 35% their 25th, and 50% their 15th anniversary (U.S. Department of Commerce 2011). As recently as the late 19th century, the average length of a marriage was only 13 years—mostly because life expectancy was relatively short. "'Til death do us part" was not such a long time then as it is today, when average life expectancy in Global North countries reaches into the 80s (Coontz 2005). There are many misconceptions about divorce in the 21st century as well, and the next "Sociology in Our Social World" on page 334 addresses some of those.

 Thinking Sociologically

Micro-level issues of divorce are often rooted in the personalities and relationships of the individuals involved. Talk with friends and family members who have divorced about micro-level factors that contributed to the dissolution of their marriages. Now, based on information from this chapter, make a list of meso-level factors (e.g., religious, economic, legal, educational) that contribute to or reduce divorce rates. What connections do you see between the micro and meso factors?

SOCIOLOGISTS IN ACTION:
TEY MEADOW

Queer Numbers: Evaluating Research as Public Sociology

Intellectual questions have robust social, emotional, and political lives. At times, our role as sociologists is to create new knowledge and to introduce new stories into the public realm. Other times, it becomes important to use our expertise to evaluate the work of others, and to help the public understand the impact of how things are studied on controversial social issues. At moments, the issues on which we comment are merely intellectual; other times, they touch on the most fundamental and intimate aspects of our selves and relationships.

In July 2012, University of Texas at Austin professor Mark Regnerus published a study purported to show that children raised by same-sex couples fared worse psychologically than peers raised by heterosexuals (Regnerus 2012). As a queer person, a parent, and a sociologist of gender and sexual diversity, I found that this finding contradicted everything I knew to be true about gay families. I decided to look more closely and to determine its validity for myself.

First, I discovered that the research subjects he considered children of gay and lesbian parents never actually identified their parents as gay at all. Instead, they simply replied in the affirmative to a question about whether either of their parents ever had a romantic relationship with someone of the same gender. Parents of his subjects did not necessarily identify as gay and, it seems, probably never cohabitated with a same-sex partner (Sherkat 2012). Instead, he likely captured individuals who separated, divorced, or had affairs. This is an apples-to-oranges comparison: On one side we have always-married, heterosexual co-parents, and on the other we have a group of families that include a parent who had a romantic relationship with someone of the same gender. Since sociologists already know that family instability of any kind is predictive of various childhood struggles, this study was destined, even designed, to find worse outcomes among that second group.

Second, the outcome measures the researchers studied, measures of educational attainment and psychological adjustment, could be as easily influenced by repeated experiences of homophobia as they could by something intrinsic to the structure of a given family. Indeed, other researchers do find that it is more often experiences of homophobia that affect emotional well-being than any particular family structure.

Finally, Regnerus's study was both funded by an antigay political group and rushed through a biased peer review process and into print (Sherkat 2012). Not coincidentally, the study was entered into evidence in several court cases, including, only one day after its publication, the Supreme Court case challenging the constitutionality of the Defense of Marriage Act and California's controversial Proposition 8 (banning same-sex marriage in the state). Regnerus himself appeared frequently in conservative news media, continuing to describe his results as if they were incontrovertible findings. Thus, what I, as a sociologist, understand to be total junk science was portrayed as a value-free truth about social life. The consequences for legal recognition for LGBTQ families and more general social and political conversations about family diversity are huge. That's why I was among more than 200 social scientists who signed a letter protesting the review and publication of Regnerus's article and why I write and speak publicly about the limitations of the study's methodology and the political motivations behind it. As a result of the collective responses of sociologists like me, the

American Sociological Association filed a response brief with the court, outlining the study's limitations and declaring its findings invalid; the court, in turn, rejected the study and ruled in favor of legally recognizing LGBTQ families.

Tey Meadow is an assistant professor of sociology and women's, gender, and sexuality studies at Harvard University. She studies the ways individuals understand, make use of, and resist social categories related to gender and sexuality.

Macro-level social issues also contribute to divorce. These in turn result in micro-level individual family problems. The reason for the dramatic increases in the U.S. divorce rate after the early 1970s was a policy change: no-fault divorce laws. For centuries in the United States, in order to get a divorce one had to prove that the other party was in breach of the marriage contract. When U.S. divorce laws became more lenient in the 1970s, there was a boomlet of divorces, stimulated by the increasing number of women who entered the labor force and changed family dynamics.

All this makes divorce in the United States much easier to obtain than in previous years. However, some ask if divorces are being sought for the slightest offense. Some critics believe this easing has led to a *divorce culture*—a society in which people assume that marriages are fragile rather than assuming that marriages are for life (a *marriage culture*) (Emery 2013).

Despite this perception, divorce rates for most groups in the United States have been dropping since the early 1980s (Cherlin 2010; Clarkson 2011). The divorce rate has fallen from 5.9 per 1,000 citizens in 1979 to 3.6 per 1,000 people in 2011 (CDC 2013). See Figure 10.6 for the trend line which shows that divorce rates today are as low as they were in 1970. There is also variation by region of the country. Figure 10.7, indicates where in the United States the divorce rates are the highest. You may be surprised by which states have especially high or low divorce rates. Why do you think there would be so much variation by state?

Thinking Sociologically

In your social group, do most people have parents who have remained married to one another? Why? What social and economic factors played a role in your answer?

FIGURE 10.6   Divorce Rate in the United States From 1950 to 2011

Source: CDC (2013).

sociology in our social world

Debunking Misconceptions About Divorce

By David Popenoe

Divorce Fallacy 1: Because people learn from their bad experiences, second marriages tend to be more successful than first marriages.

Fact: Although many people who divorce have successful subsequent marriages, the divorce rate of remarriages is in fact higher than that of first marriages.

Divorce Fallacy 2: Having a child together will help a couple improve their marital satisfaction and prevent a divorce.

Fact: Many studies have shown that the most stressful time in a marriage is after the first child is born. Couples who have a child together have a slightly decreased risk of divorce compared to couples without children, but the decreased risk is far less than it used to be.

Divorce Fallacy 3: When parents don't get along, children are better off if their parents divorce than if they stay together.

Fact: A recent large-scale, long-term study suggests that while parents' marital unhappiness and discord have a broad negative impact on virtually every dimension of their children's well-being, so does going through a divorce. It was only the children in very high-conflict homes who benefited from a divorce. In lower-conflict marriages that end in divorce—as many as two thirds of divorces—the situation of the children was made much worse following a divorce. Therefore, except in high-conflict marriages, it is better for the children if their parents stay together and work out their problems than if they divorce.

Divorce Fallacy 4: Being very unhappy at certain points in a marriage is a good sign that the marriage will eventually end in divorce.

Fact: All marriages have their ups and downs. Recent research using a large national sample found that 86% of people who were unhappy in their marriages but stayed with the marriage indicated five years later that they were happy. Indeed, three fifths of the formerly unhappily married couples rated their marriages as either "very happy" or "quite happy."

Divorce Fallacy 5: It is usually men who initiate divorce proceedings.

Fact: Two thirds of all divorces are initiated by women.

Divorce and Its Social Consequences. Many find the emotional aspects of divorce are most difficult. Divorce is often seen as a failure, rejection, or even punishment. Moreover, a divorce often involves splitting with more than just a spouse. It often entails separating from some family and friends, a religious community, and other social contexts in which your identity is tied to your marriage (Amato 2000). No wonder divorce is so wrenching. Unlike simple societies, most modern ones have no ready mechanism for absorbing people back into stable social units such as clans.

Adjustment to divorced status varies by gender: Men typically have a harder time emotionally adjusting to singlehood or divorce than women do. Divorced men must

Divorce Myths

FIGURE 10.7   U.S. States With the Highest and Lowest Divorce Rates

Divorce rate per 1,000 people, age 15 and older

6.05–7.65	7.66–9.31	9.32–10.97	10.98–12.63	12.64–14.35

Source: Reich (2013).

often leave not only their wives but also their children, and whereas many women have support networks, fewer men have developed or sustained friendships outside marriage. Finances, on the other hand, are a bigger problem for divorced women and their children than for men. Women are more likely to be living in poverty than men across all racial and ethnic groups in the United States (Reason 2011). Single mothers are twice as likely to be in poverty as single fathers, and over 35% experience food insecurity (not enough food) (E. Gray 2012). Support from the non-custodial parent can help relieve the poverty, yet 29% of custodial parents receive no help at all, 30% receive some of what is owed, and 41% receive full child support (Child Trends 2013a).

Divorce also entails other costs for children whose lives are often turned upside down. Many children move to new houses and locations, leave one parent and friends, and must make adjustments to new schools and to reduced resources. Adjustment depends on the age of the children and the manner in which the parents handle the divorce. As noted earlier, children in families with high levels of marital conflict may be better off long-term if their parents divorce (Booth and Amato 2001; Sobolewski and Amato 2007).

Overall, children have an easier time with divorce if they can remain in their home and in their familiar school, keep both parents in their lives, and maintain their friendship networks. Grandparents, too, can provide stability during these traumatic times.

MARRIAGE, DIVORCE, AND SOCIAL POLICIES

Family systems around the world are changing in similar ways, pushed by industrialization and urbanization, migration to new countries or refugee status, changing kinship and occupational structures, and many other influences from outside the family. The most striking changes include greater choice of spouse, more equal status for women, equal rights in divorce, neolocal residency (when partners in a married couple live separate from either set of parents), and bilateral kinship systems (tracing lineage through both parents) (McKie and Callan 2012). However, countermovements in some parts of the world call for strengthening of marriage through modesty of women, separation of the sexes (in both public and private spheres), and rejection of some Global North trends such as high divorce rates and other Western practices.

National Family Patterns and Policies in the United States

As we discussed previously, obtaining a divorce in the United States is relatively easy compared with the process in many other countries. All 50 U.S. states now have no-fault provisions based on "irreconcilable differences" or "irreconcilable breakdown of the marriage" (Benokraitis 2012). Conservative U.S. organizations, such as the Family Research Council, maintain that the family is being challenged by many forces that weaken the family structure and impede it from carrying out its purpose (Family Research Council 2014). They argue that the United States should go back to fault divorce to make it less easy to end a marriage in what they consider this "divorce culture." They argue that many couples enter marriages assuming that the marriage will probably not last. An assumption of impermanence is no way to begin a marriage, they believe, insisting that pro-family policies promote stability and are a precursor to

One aspect of covenant marriage is that couples must choose which kind of contract they want—which critics think makes marriage a consumer choice, rather like choosing toothpaste.

healthy relationships. Other scholars think that making the divorce process more restrictive would leave many women in highly vulnerable positions in relationships with abusive men, and while such a strategy may create more marriages that stay together, it would not necessarily create healthy ones. Healthy marriages are what help the society, not unhappy ones, say the defenders of no-fault divorce.

The covenant marriage law implemented in Louisiana (1997), Arizona (1998), and Arkansas (2002) created a contract to make it harder to end a marriage. In these states, couples can choose whether they want a standard marriage or an "upgraded" covenant marriage. If they opt for a covenant marriage, they make a lifelong commitment to marriage and agree to forego the option for a no-fault divorce. They must undergo premarital counseling before the wedding and, if they seek a divorce, a year of counseling before a fault divorce is permitted (HG.org 2014; Leon 2009; Nock, Sanchez, and Wright 2008). Covenant marriage is just one example of efforts to create policy that will strengthen marriages and families, but like all policies they may or may not work, and they may have unexpected consequences.

Global Family Patterns and Policies

As we have seen, family life, which seems so personal and intimate, is actually linked to global patterns. For example, global aid is activated when drought, famine, refugee status, or other disasters affect communities and a country cannot provide for families. In such cases, international organizations such as the United Nations, Doctors Without Borders, Oxfam, and the Red Cross mobilize to support families in crises. Support varies from feeding starving children to opposing the slavery that occurs when parents are reduced to selling their children to survive. International crises can lead to war, perhaps removing the main breadwinner from the family or taking the life of a son or daughter drafted to fight. Homes and cultivated fields may be destroyed and the families forced into refugee status.

National policies can limit families' access to birth control and knowledge about family planning. Consider cases of governments that prohibit birth control in attempts to increase declining populations. These policies in turn affect the economic circumstances of people with large families to raise and support. Such policies also lead to more single-parent families created by

Family Planning in Thailand ▶

Sociology Around the World

Cross-Cultural Differences in Family Dissolution

Family conflict and disorganization occur when members of the family unit do not or cannot carry out roles expected of them by spouses, other family members, the community, or the society. This may be due to voluntary departure (divorce, separation, desertion), involuntary problems (illness or other catastrophe), a crisis caused by external events (war or deteriorating economic conditions), or failure to communicate role expectations and needs. Many of these role failures are a direct consequence of societal changes due to globalization. Once again, the social world model helps us understand macro-level trends and patterns that affect us in micro-level contexts.

Divorce is still very limited in some parts of the world, and it may be an option for only one gender. In some Arab countries, for example, only the husband has had the right to declare "I divorce thee" in front of a witness on three separate occasions, after which the divorce is complete. The

wife returns, sometimes in disgrace, to her family of orientation, while the husband generally keeps the children in the patriarchal family and is free to take another wife (Khazaleh 2009). Despite a seemingly easy process for men to divorce, the rate remains rather low in many global South countries because family ties and allegiances are severely strained when divorces take place. Thus, informal pressures and cultural attitudes restrain tendencies to divorce.

Still, when family turmoil and conflict are too great to resolve or when the will to save the family disappears, the legal, civil, and religious ties of marriage may be broken. The methods for dissolving marriage ties vary, but most countries have some form of divorce. Table 10.4 (see page 338) compares marriage and divorce rates in selected industrial countries. Notice that while the divorce rate in countries such as the United States is quite high, the marriage rate is also high.

out-of-wedlock births. In addition, as individuals and couples around the world make decisions such as choosing a spouse based on love, rejecting multiple wives, or establishing a more egalitarian family, the collective impact may rock the foundations of the larger society. Because governments make policies that influence families, the interaction between policy makers and social scientists can lead to laws based on better information and more comprehensive analysis of possible consequences. This is part of the contribution of public sociology—providing accurate information and analysis for wise public policy decisions.

Do marriage and divorce rates indicate that the family is in crisis? To answer this question, we need information on current patterns and historical trend lines in various parts of the world. The above "Sociology Around the World" provides cross-cultural data on marriage and divorce ratios.

The Chinese government recently relaxed its one-child policy to allow families to have two children, if one of the parents was an only child. This picture shows one such happy family holding a birth permit for their second child.

 China's Child Policy   Covenant Marriage Law

Table 10.4   Marriage and Divorce Rates in Selected Countries, 1980–2010

Country	Marriages per 1,000 Persons in Population				Divorces per 1,000 Persons in Population			
	1980	1990	2000	2010	1980	1990	2000	2010
USA	10.2	9.8	8.3	10.6	5.2	4.7	4.1	3.6
Canada	7.8	6.8	5.1	4.4	2.5	2.8	2.3	2.1
Denmark	5.2	6.1	7.2	5.6	2.7	2.7	2.7	2.6
France	7.2	5.1	5.0	3.9	1.5	1.9	1.9	2.1
Germany	6.3	6.5	5.1	4.7	1.8	1.9	2.4	2.3
Ireland	6.4	5.1	5.5	4.6	na	na	0.7	0.7
Italy	5.7	5.6	5.0	3.6	0.8	0.5	0.7	0.9
Netherlands	6.4	6.5	5.5	4.5	1.8	1.9	2.2	2.0
Spain	5.9	5.7	5.4	3.6	na	0.6	0.9	2.2
Sweden	4.7	4.5	4.7	5.1	2.4	2.3	2.4	2.5
United Kingdom	6.6	7.4	5.2	4.5	2.6	2.7	2.6	2.1

Source: Employment and Social Development Canada (2014); European Commission (2012); Statistics Canada (2013); U.S. Census Bureau (2012g).

Note: na = not available

Thinking Sociologically

Would it strengthen marriages to remove all no-fault divorce laws and return to a fault divorce where one member of the couple must prove that the other person was in breach of contract? Why or why not? If you were making divorce policies, what would you do? What are the positive and negative aspects of your policy?

The family is a powerful socializing agent and the first social experience of most human beings. As children grow up and branch out from the embrace of the family, the social environments they experience first are usually the local school and a religious organization. These provide lifelong training for participation in society. It is to the institution of education that we turn next.

WHAT HAVE WE LEARNED?

Despite those who lament the weakening of the family, the institution of family is here to stay. Its form may alter as it responds and adapts to societal and global changes, and other institutions will continue to take on functions formerly reserved for the family. Still, the family is an institution crucial to societal survival, and whatever the future holds, the family will adapt in response to changes in other parts of the social world. It is a resilient institution that shapes the way we partner and "make people" in any society.

Our happiest and saddest experiences are integrally intertwined with family. Family provides the foundation through which individuals' needs are met. Societies depend on families as the unit through which to funnel services. It is the political, economic, health, educational, religious, and sexual base for most people and essential for societies.

KEY POINTS

• Families are diverse entities at the micro level, having a wide range of configurations, but families also collectively serve as a core structure of society—an institution—at the meso and macro levels. (See pp. 312.)

• The family is sometimes called the most basic unit of society, for it is a core unit of social pairing into groups (partner taking), a primary unit of procreation and socialization (people making), and so important that when it comes unglued (contract breaking), the whole social system may be threatened. (See pp. 312–314.)

• Various theories—rational choice, symbolic interactionism, functionalism, conflict theory, and feminist theory—illuminate different aspects of family and help us understand conflicts, stressors, and functions of families. (See pp. 314–318.)

• At the micro level, people come together in partner-taking pairs, but the rules of partner taking (exogamy/endogamy, free choice/arranged marriage, polygamy/monogamy) are meso and macro level. (See pp. 319–322.)

• Power within a partnership—including distribution of tasks and authority—is assigned through intimate processes largely controlled by rules imposed from another level in the social system. (See pp. 322–323.)

- At the macro level, nations and even global organizations try to establish policies that strengthen families. Issues of concern to some analysts include cohabitation patterns, same-sex households (including same-sex marriage), and contract breaking (divorce). (See pp. 328–339.)

DISCUSSION QUESTIONS

1. What do you believe is the ideal makeup of a family? Why? How does your description relate to the functions the family performs in society?

2. Which of the main theoretical perspectives discussed in this chapter (functionalist, conflict, rational choice, and feminist) is most useful when examining the families with which you are familiar? Why?

3. A majority of Americans and a strong majority of young Americans (those younger than 30) now support same-sex marriages. What are some cultural and structural changes that have led to this increase in support for marriage equality over the past decade?

4. Does (or did) your family expect you to marry someone of a particular (a) race or ethnicity, (b) social class, (c) educational background, or (d) religion? Why or why not? How do you think endogamous norms impact (a) individual marriages and (b) society?

5. How does your family's income influence the (a) amount and (b) quality of the time family members spend together? How might more or less money influence your family members' relationships with one another? Why?

6. Do you think the establishment of no-fault divorce laws have been good or bad for (a) the institution of the family in the United States, (b) married couples, and (c) children? Explain your answers.

VISUAL SOCIOLOGY: *WHAT IS A FAMILY?*

© Kate Ballantine

Families vary a great deal from one culture to another. This polygynous family from Tibet illustrates one variation. Sociologists look for certain patterns within the great diversity of family life: mutual support, a sense of identity, and feelings of belonging and caring. Visit **edge.sagepub.com/ballantine5e** for an interactive photo essay about the meaning of family.

CONTRIBUTING TO OUR SOCIAL WORLD: *WHAT CAN WE DO?*

At the Local Level

- *Support groups for married or partnered students* respond to the needs of an ever-increasing number of undergraduate students living on or near campus with spouses, partners, and children. If your campus has a support group, arrange to attend a meeting and work with members to help them meet the challenges associated with their family situation. If such a group does not exist, consider forming one.

- Is there *day care available on your campus*? Day care on campus can be invaluable for parents. If there is, look at the cost and availability of care for the children of faculty, staff, and students. If there is not a day care, look at the possibilities of creating, funding, and staffing one. How might it benefit the college or university, as well as the families it will serve?

At the Organizational or Institutional Level

- *Support groups for multigeneration households* provide an important opportunity to support this growing population. Approximately one in five households contains more than one generation of adults.

- *House builders* have begun to change how they design some houses in order to meet the needs of multigeneration households. Contact your local *Habitat for Humanity* chapter (www.habitat.org) and ask if you can help the organization create more homes suitable for such households. You can find some ideas for such homes at http://articles .chicagotribune.com/2012-09-10/special/chi-primetime-multigen-091412_1_bedroom-floor-plan-designs.

At the National and Global Levels

- *Influencing marriage policies* is another way for sociology students to make a difference in our social world. Select a family-related issue about which you feel strongly—pro or con (for example, covenant marriage, no-fault divorce options, or same-sex marriage policies). Find out about the laws of the United States or your state regarding the issue. Next, identify your members in the U.S. House of Representatives (www.house.gov), the Senate (www.senate.gov), and/or your state legislature (www.ncsl.org/about-us/ncslservice/state-legislative-websites-directory.aspx). Contact those people via letter or e-mail, stating your views.

- *Voices* is a multi-issue advocacy group for children with member organizations across the nation. The organization strives to improve the lives of children and their families, particularly those most at risk. You can learn about the issues on which this group is working and join its efforts, if you would like to do so, by going to its website at www.voices.org.

- *Hofstra University* maintains a resource site on international family law at http://people.hofstra .edu/lisa_a_spar/intlfam/intlfam.htm where you can learn more about the field.

©REUTERS/Samsul Said

11 Education

What Are We Learning?

In schools, students learn much more than the three *Rs*. The communities in which learning occurs play a major role in what and how students learn and the place of education within societies.

MICRO

- **ME (AND MY TEACHERS AND CLASSMATES)**

- **LOCAL ORGANIZATIONS AND COMMUNITY**
  Neighborhood schools and classrooms within those schools affect our everyday lives.

MESO

- **NATIONAL ORGANIZATIONS, INSTITUTIONS, AND ETHNIC SUBCULTURES**
  State or provincial funding, regulations, and learning standards affect local schools.

MACRO

- **SOCIETY**
  National policies are also developed to improve schools.

- **GLOBAL COMMUNITY**
  United Nations programs try to improve education in poor countries.

THINK ABOUT IT

Micro: Local Community	What did you learn—both formally and informally—in your local school?
Meso: National Institutions, Complex Organizations, and Ethnic Groups	How do families help or hurt children's school achievement? Explain.
Macro: National and Global Systems	How is education changing in your nation? Why is education a major concern around the world?

Tomás is a failure. At 9 years of age, he cannot read, write, or get along with his peers, and out of frustration, he sometimes misbehaves. His parents have told Tomás over and over that he will not amount to anything if he does not shape up. His teachers have noticed that he is slow to learn and has few friends. So two strikes against him are the judgments of his parents and his teachers. The third strike is Tomás's own acceptance of the label "failure." He has little evidence to contradict their judgment. Tomás is an at-risk child, identified as having characteristics inclining him toward failure in school and society. He will likely drop out of school, and may even get in trouble with the law unless caring people intervene, encouraging him to realize his potential.

Tomás goes to school in Toronto (Ontario), Canada, but he could live in any country. Although successful children develop a positive self-concept that helps them deal with disappointments and failures, children like Tomás internalize failures. Successful children negotiate the rules and regulations of school, and school provides them with necessary skills for future occupations. Tomás carries a label of "failure" with him that impedes his chances for academic success and a good job. What factors could change the educational outcomes for students such as Tomás?

At least Tomás is (for now) in the education system. *Schooling*—learning skills such as reading and math via systematic instruction, by a trained professional—is a luxury some children will never know. On the other hand, in most urban areas around the world and in all areas of affluent countries, formal education has become a necessity. Education of the masses in a school setting is a modern concept that developed when literacy and math skills became essential for many jobs (even if just to read instructions for operating machinery). Literacy is also necessary for the smooth functioning of societies with democratic forms of government. Citizens must be able to read information about elected officials and proposed policies in order to effectively participate in a democracy.

In this chapter, we explore the state of the world's education, micro-level interactions in educational organizations, what happens in schools after the school bell rings, education at the macro level, whether education is the road to opportunity, and educational social policy issues.

STATE OF THE WORLD'S EDUCATION: AN OVERVIEW

Every society educates its children. Most societies create national education systems for this task. **Formal education**—*schooling that takes place in a formal setting with the goal of teaching a predetermined curriculum*—has expanded dramatically in the past several decades as higher percentages of students in many countries attend school and learn to read and write. (See Figure 11.1.)

Global macro-level organizations concerned with education contribute to efforts to educate the world population. For example, UNESCO (the United Nations Educational, Scientific, and Cultural Organization) provides teacher training, curricular guidance, and textbook sources. It also gathers and disseminates international statistics on educational achievement. Many countries have adopted UNESCO standards, including the organizational model of 6 years of primary school, typically for students from 6 to 12; 2 to 3 years of middle school or junior high school; and 4 years of high school (UNESCO Institute for Statistics 2012). A nation's level of development, cultural values, and political ideology also influence the

FIGURE 11.1 Adult Literacy Rates by Country

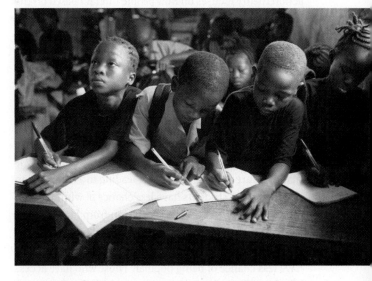

Global literacy rate
- No data
- <35
- 35–50
- 50–60
- 60–70
- 70–80%
- 80–90%
- 90–97%
- >97%

Source: UNESCO Institute for Statistics (2013). "Adult and Youth Literacy," UIS Fact Sheet, September 2013, No. 26.

development of *curriculum*, the courses taught in schools and the overall goals of their educational systems. What is considered essential knowledge to be taught in schools is based largely on a country's level of development, its cultural values and political ideology, and guidelines from international standards.

Leaders believe that a literate population is necessary for economic development and expansion, a thriving political system, and the well-being of the citizenry. In the world today, an estimated 793 million adults (two thirds of whom are women) cannot read or write, and have no experience with technology. In some poor Global South countries in Southeast Asia and sub-Saharan Africa, fewer than 50% of adults are literate (have basic reading skills) (UNESCO Institute for Statistics 2012). These adults cannot participate in the global economy and suffer from far higher rates of unemployment and poverty. If a woman stays in school just one additional year, her earnings can increase by 10% to 20% over a lifetime, and her children are more likely to survive (Bokova and Bush 2012). The next section provides a summary of how various theories

Overcrowding in classrooms is not uncommon in Global South countries, such as Sierra Leone, where these schoolchildren work to gain the skills they will need to "make" it in our global economy.

look at issues in education and explain how the institution of education functions in society.

THE INS AND OUTS OF LOCAL SCHOOLS: MICRO-LEVEL INTERACTIONS IN EDUCATIONAL ORGANIZATIONS

The process of education takes place at the micro level in the classrooms and corridors and on the playgrounds of local schools, with players who enact the everyday drama of teaching and learning. At the micro level, much sociological analysis has focused on interpersonal exchanges within the classroom and on the school as a social setting within a community. At this level, sociologists look at roles and statuses in educational settings and the informal norms and interaction patterns that evolve in those settings. We will begin by reviewing two micro-level theories, and how they make sense of some common in-school interactions.

Micro-Level Theories: Individuals Within Schools

Symbolic Interaction Perspective and the Classroom. As discussed previously, the symbolic interaction theory focuses on how people interact based on the meaning they have assigned to various traits, behaviors, or symbols (such as clothing). Children actively create distinctions among individuals and groups, becoming agents in determining the social reality in which they live. Popularity, a major issue for many children, especially in middle and high school years, is mostly a function of being well known. Students may increase their popularity by being attractive, representing the school in an athletic contest, or being in a leadership position. The difficulty is that there are few such positions, leading to a competition in which some students have less chance of winning than others. In the United States, children from families that cannot afford to purchase trendy clothing or other status symbols or send their children to sports training or camps have less chance of being popular. Those who have access to material and symbolic resources that give them high visibility have a step up in the competition for popularity. They often gain special privileges in the school (e.g., if elected to a student office or captain of a sports team) and are more likely to develop leadership skills and to feel good about themselves—forms of social and cultural capital (Vijayakumar 2012).

Classrooms are small societies of peers that reflect the interaction patterns and challenges of the larger world (Durkheim 1956). These challenges include students learning to interact with their peers and teachers in ways that earn positive, rather than negative, sanctions. Research findings indicate that girls around the world have more struggles with self-esteem and gender inequality than do boys, especially in middle schools (American Association of University Women Educational Foundation 2001; Vijayakumar 2012).

The micro interactions of the school help form our sense of self. The extensive time we spend in school from 6 to 18 years of age has an enormous impact on how we see ourselves. How we think our peers view us can begin to mold our sense of competence, intelligence, and likability.

The larger school organization creates a structure that influences how individuals make sense of their reality and interact with others. Some symbolic interaction theorists, including those representing the Iowa School, emphasize the link between the self and meso-level positions or statuses (Stryker 2000). Official school positions—such as president of the student council, senior class president, or varsity athletic team member—become important elements of one's *self*.

Thinking Sociologically

Describe how (a) your teachers and (b) your classmates in high school influenced how you view yourself. Why did they have this influence on you? Has your view of yourself changed since? Why or why not?

Rational Choice Theory and Education Settings. Rational choice theory, as you will recall, focuses on the cost-benefit analysis that individuals undertake in virtually everything they do. What are the costs—in terms of money, relationships, self-esteem, or other factors—and what are the benefits?

How might weighing costs and benefits influence decisions about education? Students who consider dropping out of school go through some analysis of costs to themselves—for example, a decision may be shaped by battered self-esteem in school. Similarly, teachers make rational choices about staying in the teaching profession. Approximately 10% of teachers leave the teaching profession after one year (Kaiser and Cross 2011). Rational choice theorists explain teacher attrition by looking at perceived costs, such as poor salary given one's educational attainment; lack of respect from parents, students, and administrators; 12- to 14-hour days for 9 months of the year; and lack of professionalism in treatment of teachers. Teachers compare these costs with the benefits of teaching—the feeling of making a contribution to society and helping children; getting time off in the summer; and enjoying many aspects of teaching and working with children.

Over the past several years, teacher satisfaction has declined dramatically, with 62% indicating they were very satisfied in 2008, compared to just 39% in 2012. In a survey conducted in 2012, approximately half (51%) of teachers said they were under great stress several days a week (up from 36% in 1985). Less-satisfied teachers tend to work in schools that have experienced declining budgets, reduced professional growth opportunities, and less time for collaboration with other teachers over the past year. Adding to their dissatisfaction, very few teachers (17%) believe that the new Common Core curriculum, which almost all states have agreed to put into place, will improve the academic achievement of students (MetLife 2013).

Thinking Sociologically

Think of the teachers you had before coming to college. What seem to be the costs and benefits of the various roles teachers fulfill? Do you think that most teachers base their actions on this kind of rational choice calculation?

Schools are important organizations in local communities, a source of pride and a unifying symbol of identity. Local communities rally around their school. Moreover, in many communities, the school system is a large employer with real importance to the economic vitality of the area. At the micro level, much of the sociological analysis has focused on the school as a social setting within a community. At the meso level, sociologists look at schools as organizations with roles and statuses, informal norms, and interaction patterns that evolve in educational settings.

Statuses and Roles in the Education System

Students, teachers, staff, and administrators hold statuses, or positions, in educational systems. These statuses are part of the larger school organization at the meso level, and individuals hold them only during their tenure in the organization. The roles associated with each status in educational organizations bring both

obligations and challenges. When those in each status agree on expected behaviors (role expectations), schools function smoothly. When they do not agree, conflicts can arise. In the United States, girl students seem more capable of fulfilling their roles in schools than do boy students (Wire Side Chat 2014).

Students and the Peer Culture of Schools. In a private Rwandan secondary school, students crowd onto benches. They are quiet, respectful, and very hardworking. They know that they are in a privileged position, and many students are lined up to take their place on the bench should they not carry out their roles, work hard, and succeed. Although they have no written texts, students write down the lectures in their notebooks and memorize the material. In some countries such as Rwanda, going to high school is a privilege. In others such as the United States, it is a necessary part of life that many students resist.

Schools exist to serve students and to expand their skills and knowledge. Still, there are many dynamics within a school that may undermine that primary objective. The role expectations of anyone in the status of student can be complicated by variables such as ethnicity, gender, sexual orientation, and socioeconomic standing. Thus, the experience of being a student can be quite different for different students. Consider a child whose family has recently immigrated to the United States and does not yet understand English. She may feel that her entire culture is being denigrated because her language and ethnic history is ignored or even scorned. This would not

© Keith A. Roberts

In Rwandan secondary schools, as many as 45 students may be in a classroom with little more than wooden benches and tables. They value school and are diligent students.

be an environment in which she would feel safe or respected, both of which are needed for learning to occur.

Experiences of harassment provide another example of a factor that affects some children's student status. In 2010–2011, 48% of students in Grades 7 through 12 dealt with some form of sexual harassment and reported negative effects. Abuse was verbal, physical, and electronic, with over 30% experiencing harassment through electronic media such as Twitter and Facebook—cyberbullying (Alvarez 2013). Girls reported more harassment than boys (52% compared to 35%), and electronic harassment, in particular (36% compared to 24%). A major problem is that few students report harassment to parents or school personnel (Hill and Kearl 2011; Munsey 2012). Compared with boys, girls experience "hostile hallways" in more physically and psychologically harmful ways, and students who identify themselves as gay, lesbian, bisexual, or transgendered

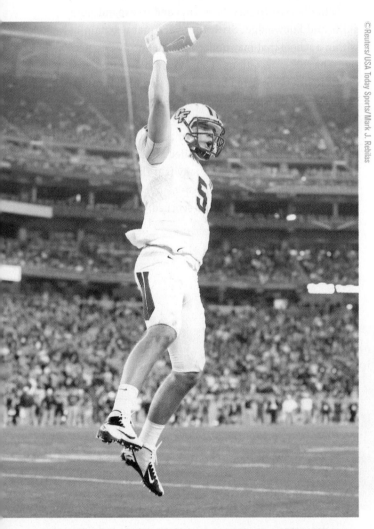

Males have many ways of becoming known and respected. Male athletic competitions draw bigger crowds than do female athletic competitions, and one can become a local celebrity based on skills on the field or court.

experience very high levels of bullying and assaults. In 2010, 31% of gay youth were threatened or injured at school (Mental Health America 2011).

Gender is a complex issue for students. Research for several decades had shown that boys were given many privileges, were favored by teachers, and scored higher in many academic areas than girls. However, researchers point out the incredible gains in recent years made by females, who tend to study and be more compliant in school than boys. One indicator of girls' success in education in the United States is the "feminization" of higher education. Since 1980, more women in the United States have gone to and graduated from college than men. In 2012, 71% of women entered college right after high school versus 61% of men. This gender pattern held true for all U.S. racial groups: whites (72% vs. 62%), blacks (69% vs. 57%), Hispanics (76% vs. 62%), and Asian (86% vs. 83%) (Lopez and Gonzalez-Barrera 2014).

An estimated 18% of youth between the ages of 16 and 24—mostly ethnic minorities—are without postsecondary education and are disconnected—neither in school nor employed. In particular, many black teenaged boys have not witnessed education as a path to better jobs for their peers or themselves. According to 2013 data, the unemployment rate for African American youth aged 16 to 19 was 43.1%, for Hispanics 25.1%, and for whites 22.5% (Center for American Progress 2013; U.S. Bureau of Labor Statistics 2013).

This lack of confidence in education as an avenue to success has resulted in high dropout rates, and a phenomenon that the Children's Defense Fund calls the "cradle to prison pipeline," with one of every three African American boys expected to eventually be imprisoned (Children's Defense Fund 2013). This is a failure of institutions in our society that has long-term consequences. The experience of being a student is clearly not the same for all, with gender, ethnicity, race, sexual orientation, and socioeconomic factors shaping the experience and affecting learning. Research such as that presented in the next "Sociology in Our Social World" discusses the concerns that have been raised about gender differences, especially in U.S. schools.

Teachers: The Front Line. Teachers in the classroom occupy the front line in implementing the goals of the school, the community, and the society. Teachers serve as gatekeepers, controlling the flow of students, activities, resources, and privileges. One scholar estimated that teachers have more than a thousand verbal exchanges a day in their roles as classroom managers (Jackson 1968). As primary socializers and role models for students,

How to Talk to Kids   School Dropouts

sociology in our social world

Where the Boys Are—and Where the Men Are Not?

The Fragile Girl, The War Against Boys, Failing at Fairness, How America's Schools Cheat Girls, and *At Colleges, Women Are Leaving Men in the Dust*—these are just a few titles of articles on research in a debate about whether girls or boys have the biggest advantage or disadvantage in schools. For many years, concern focused on the factors that inhibited minorities' and girls' educational attainment in school. Recently, some authors are turning the tables and focusing their concern on boys.

Statistics indicate that educational achievement varies greatly by sex, age, race or ethnicity, and socioeconomic status. Among the many reasons for the differences, researchers point out the incredible gains made by girls and women and the fact that they tend to study more and take school more seriously as a necessity for success. In the United States, African American, Hispanic, and low-income males lag behind all other groups, including females from their own ethnic or socioeconomic group. Asians and Pacific Islanders have a higher high school completion rate (96.6%) than whites (96.2%), blacks (90.1%), Hispanics (82.3%), and Native Americans (86.4%). The high school gap has been narrowing in recent years, but the gap in higher education is widening as seen in Table 11.1 but Figure 11.2 shows that the high school graduation gap is narrowing (Stillwell, Sable, and Plotts 2011).

"More than 60% of the people in prison are now racial and ethnic minorities. For Black males in

Table 11.1   College Attendance Rates and Graduation Rates

Race	College Attendance Rate
Asian	92.2%
White, non-Hispanic	72%
Hispanic	64%
Black	56%
Males	66%
Females	72%

Source: National Center for Education Statistics (2012c); U.S. Department of Education (2012).

their 30s, 1 in every 10 is in prison or jail on any given day," further reducing their chances for education, good jobs, and a stable family life (Sentencing Project 2012b). The reasons are many, but the bottom line is that these young men feel disconnected from a society that they feel helps women with children but ignores the vulnerabilities of men, and they do not see education as a path to success (Mincy 2006). Unemployment for African Americans typically runs at twice the rate for whites in the United States (Allegretto et al. 2011).

One result of disillusion with education and lower high school graduation rates among males is that higher education is experiencing "feminization." While 77% of 18-year-old women attend college, just 66% of 18-year-old men are college students. While upper-class men prove an exception, attending college at

Students Today

FIGURE 11.2   High School Completion Rate by Race/Ethnicity: 1964–2012

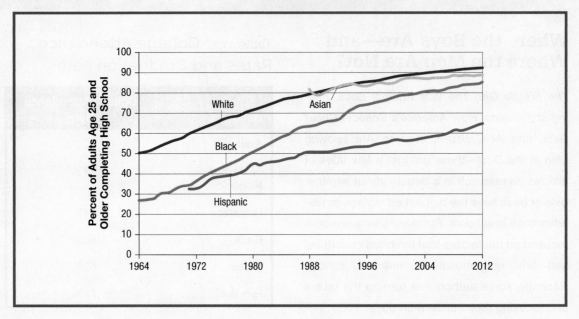

Source: Plumer (2013).

a slightly higher rate than women in that social class, men from low-income families—disproportionately African American and Hispanic in composition—are the most underrepresented in higher education (Lewin 2006).

By 2020 colleges are expected to be 58.6% women and 41.4% men (Hennigan 2012). To combat this trend, some colleges have even added activities such as football to attract more male students ("Colleges' Gender Gap" 2010). Not only do women receive more of the undergraduate diplomas; women have surpassed men in the number of doctoral degrees received in the United States (Jaschik 2010). So we do know where men are not—and this is in college and higher education. This is cause for concern.

teachers are expected to support and encourage students and, at the same time, judge their performance—giving grades and recommendations. This creates role strain, which can interfere with the task of teaching and contribute to teacher burnout. U.S. teachers are held accountable for students' progress as measured on standardized tests. While teachers play a role in how students do on these tests, other factors, such as the influence of students' families and peers, also influence test scores. This can cause stress for teachers and an overemphasis on teaching what will help students earn high scores on the standardized tests (Dworkin and Tobe 2012).

In some other nations of the world, like Japan, teachers are treated with great respect and honor. They receive salaries and respect commensurate with those in industry and professions such as law and medicine (Ballantine and Hammack 2012). In Europe, many high schools are organized like universities. Teachers think of themselves as akin to professors. In contrast, studies in Australia and the United States show teachers feel they are unappreciated and not treated with much respect (Saha and Dworkin 2006). In the United States, secondary school teachers think of themselves as more like middle school teachers than like university professors (Legters 2001).

Raising the respect for teaching requires better recruiting, training, and upgrading the status and pay of teachers (Ingersoll and Merrill 2012). For example, we may learn something from Finland, which tops other OECD nations in test scores. Finland has very competitive teaching programs, and all teachers, even in primary schools, must have a master's degree. Teachers have higher-than-average salaries, freedom to create their own curriculum, and high status in their society ("How Finnish Schools Shine" 2012).

 Thinking Sociologically

Who should create curricula for public schools? Who should enforce high teacher standards—the federal, state, or local government? Teachers unions? Explain your answers and describe how to carry out what you envision.

Administrators: The Managers of the School System. Key administrators—superintendents, assistant superintendents, principals and assistant principals, and headmasters and headmistresses—hold the top positions in the educational hierarchy of local schools. They are responsible for a long list of tasks: issuing budget reports; engaging in staff negotiations; hiring, firing, and training staff members; meeting with parents; carrying out routine approval of projects; managing public relations; preparing reports for boards of directors, local education councils, legislative bodies, and national agencies; keeping up with new regulations; and many other tasks.

The Informal System: What Really Happens Inside a School?

It is the first day of high school, and the teacher asks a question. Should you respond or let someone else answer? If you respond, the teacher might be impressed, but the other students might think you are showing off or "brown-nosing." What if you answer incorrectly and sound foolish? Does that scenario sound familiar to you?

The informal system of schooling includes the unspoken, unwritten, and implicit norms of behavior that we learn, whether in kindergarten or later in college. These norms may be created or enforced by teachers or by the student peer culture. The informal system does not appear in written goal statements or course syllabi but nevertheless influences our experience in school in important ways. Dimensions of the informal system include the hidden curriculum, the educational climate, the value

climate, power dynamics, and coping strategies in the classroom.

The *hidden curriculum* refers to the implicit "rules of the game" that students learn in school (Snyder 1971). It includes everything not explicitly taught, such as unstated social and academic norms. Students have to learn and respond to these rules to be socially accepted and succeed in the education system (Snyder 1971).

In many societies, children attend preschool and kindergarten, which provide the basis for schooling in the society (Neuman 2005). During these early school years, teachers teach children to follow rules, to cooperate with each other, and to accept the teacher as the boss who gives orders and controls how time is spent (Gracey 1967). Sometimes students learn that being tardy has a bigger impact on grades than whether one has actually learned the material. Teachers instill such lessons in students even though they are not part of the formal curriculum of reading, writing, and arithmetic. These less formal messages form an alternative set of "three *R*s"—rules, routines, and regulations.

According to functional theorists, it is through the hidden curriculum that students learn the expectations, behaviors, and values necessary to succeed in school and society. For conflict theorists, the hidden curriculum is a social and economic agenda that maintains class differences. Many working-class schools stress order and discipline, teaching students to obey rules and accept their lot as responsible, punctual workers (Willis 1979). More is expected of elites, and in higher-income schools students have greater responsibility and opportunities for problem solving that result in higher achievement (Brookover and Erickson 1975).

Thinking Sociologically

What are some examples of the hidden curriculum you learned in your K–12 education? How has this training impacted how you act now in college?

The Educational Climate of Schools. Schools can be comfortable and stimulating or stifling and unfriendly places. Some have an atmosphere of excitement about learning, with artwork and posters on the walls and enthusiastic noises coming from classrooms. In other schools, students tend to speak as little as possible, for fear of punishment. These are aspects of *school climate*, a general social environment that characterizes a group, organization, or community such as a school (Brookover, Erickson, and McEvoy 1996).

School architecture, classroom layouts, teacher expectations, and student groupings by age and ability—all

Four-year-old preschoolers recite the Pledge of Allegiance. Developing patriotism is part of the implicit and informal curriculum of schools—and sometimes part of the formal curriculum.

affect the educational and cultural climate of the school. Schools also have ceremonies and rituals that contribute to the climate—logos, symbols, athletic events, pep rallies, and awards ceremonies. Teachers' use of discipline and encouragement, the organization of tasks and opportunities for student interaction, and the grouping and seating arrangements also influence classroom climates. These aspects of the school experience can create an atmosphere that celebrates or stifles student achievement (Ballantine and Hammack 2012).

Teachers' responses to class, ethnicity or race, and gender differences also create climates that have subtle but profound impacts on students' experiences and learning. For example, studies indicate that teachers give boys more attention. They call on them and encourage them to speak up more often and accomplish tasks independently (Raina 2012; Sadker and Sadker 2005; Spade 2004). Another study found that teachers unconsciously tend to groom white girls for academic attainment while encouraging African American girls to emphasize social relationships over academic work. Teachers tend to groom white boys for high attainment and high-status social roles, while focusing on carefully monitoring and controlling black boys in the classroom. This disparate treatment leads to inequality in the way teachers and administrators discipline students. Black students are 3.5 times, and Hispanic students 1.5 times, as likely to be suspended as white students. Students of color also tend to receive harsher punishments than white students for similar infractions (Grant 2004; U.S. Department of Education for Civil Rights 2012).

Immigrant students who do not speak English well and students of color also tend to end up in lower-ability groups, guaranteeing their lower levels of achievement (Oakes 2005; Rubin 2008). The result is that students' and teachers' perceptions of themselves and the learning environment help shape the school climate and influence achievement. Table 11.2 illustrates teacher expectations. Note that all of these are social variables that impact learning in the classroom.

Students in poor and minority neighborhoods are also less likely to have access to advanced classes. For example, in school districts with a high percentage of minority students, just two thirds of high schools offer Algebra II courses, 40% offer Physics, and less than one third offer Calculus. These schools also tend to have inadequate equipment and outdated textbooks. Some, also, do not provide adequate guidance and support for their students of color. For example, in one school district in the United States, "African American students were encouraged to enroll in an ethnic literature course rather than an AP course based on the belief that the students would 'connect better' and 'be more comfortable' in the ethnic literature class" (U.S. Department of Education for Civil Rights 2012:6).

Value Climate of Schools. Many black, Latino, and Native American students do not engage in their schools and schoolwork because they do not feel as though they fit into the school culture. So an issue is that ethnic minorities feel like the dominant culture is being rammed down their throats and their own culture is ignored or belittled. Educators must make efforts so that *all* students feel welcome and supported in their school environments (Carter 2007; George 2011).

The *value climate* of a school also includes students' motivations and aspirations. Sociologists know that families influence students' educational motivation. Recall the opening case of Tomás, who received only negative comments and little encouragement at home and school. As you will recall from Chapter 7, parents' backgrounds and current social class location provide the basis for child rearing and transmission of class values. These influence the child's motivation and academic achievement (Roksa and Potter 2011).

Schools that value diversity and practice integration within classrooms can help more students succeed. Racially and ethnically integrated classrooms frequently raise the level of motivation and achievement for all students (Lucas and Berends 2002). High expectations of students by teachers can also make a difference and lead to higher college enrollments. Students expected to do very well generally

Table 11.2   **Teacher Expectations**

Teachers are influenced by the same stereotypes as others, and those perceptions can lead to lower expectations for some children. The following factors can create lower expectations for certain groups of students.	
Sex	Boys and girls are sometimes the recipients of low academic expectations because of beliefs about boys' maturation and gender assumptions about girls' mathematics skills.
Socioeconomic status	Low expectations are typically held for children from families with low income and education levels, low-status jobs, and an undesirable neighborhood residence.
Race and ethnic identifiers	Teachers are less likely to expect African American, Hispanic, and Native American students to succeed. They are also less likely to expect them to attend college. In contrast, school personnel often have high expectations for Asian American students.
The location of the school	Rural and inner-city schools often have lower expectations than suburban schools. This sometimes evolves into a negative "can't do anything" climate.
Appearance and neatness	Lower expectations are associated with clothes and grooming that are out of style, made of cheaper material, not branded, or purchased at thrift or discount stores. Poor handwriting and other sloppiness in presentation can also create assumptions about the intellectual abilities of students.
Oral language patterns	Nonstandard English grammar and vocabulary is a basis for holding lower expectations for students.
The halo effect	There is a tendency to label a student's current achievement based on past performance evaluations of the child. Therefore, blind grading—evaluation of student work without knowledge of who wrote the material until after it is graded—is important.
The seating position	Lower expectations are typically transmitted to students who sit on the sides and in the back of a classroom.
Student behavior	Teachers tend to have lower academic expectations of students with nonacademic behaviors deemed inappropriate by middle-class standards.
Tracking or grouping	Students in lower academic tracks are presumed to have been placed there for a good reason (i.e., they have limited capacities and cannot be expected to learn at a high level), yet in some cases, placements may have been arbitrary or incorrect.

Source: Adapted from *Creating Effective Schools: An In-Service Program for Enhancing School Learning Climate and Achievement* by Wilbur B. Brookover, Fritz J. Erickson and Alan W. McEvoy. Copyright 1997, 1982, Wilbur B. Brookover, Fritz J. Erickson and Alan W. McEvoy Published by Learning Publications, Inc.

rise to meet these expectations (Downey and Pribesh 2004; Morris 2005). Whether throughout the school or in a particular classroom, the atmosphere that pervades the learning environment has an impact on students' educational achievement and, ultimately, their life chances.

Thinking Sociologically

How might teachers and school administrators unintentionally misunderstand minority children in ways that have negative consequences for the children's success?

Power Dynamics and Coping Strategies in the Classroom. For teachers, getting students to cooperate or take responsibility can be challenging. Some students wish to wrest control from teachers and gain some freedom from the rules of the classroom or the school. Both students and teachers develop strategies to cope with pressures and difficult situations. Student coping strategies range from complete compliance to outright rebellion. Do the following five strategies sound familiar? They are adapted from Merton's (1938) strain theory of deviance (see Chapter 6) and represent strategies students use to cope with school pressures:

- *Conformity:* acceptance of goals and means—doing the schoolwork expected
- *Innovation:* finding alternative or unapproved methods to achieve conventional goals—cheating or plagiarizing to pass a course or to win an academic contest
- *Retreatism:* rejection of goals and means—rebelling against school establishment by not conforming or cooperating
- *Ritualism:* indifference toward goals—"getting by" through following rules but not learning anything
- *Rejection with replacement:* rejection of goals and means in favor of another strategy—being a discipline problem or dropping out of school to pursue other activities (Hammersley and Turner 1980; Merton 1968)

Teachers try to elicit cooperation and participation from students by creating a cost-benefits ratio that favors compliance. Manipulating the classroom can be an effective means of control: putting students at specific tables or in a circle, breaking up groups of chattering friends, or leading a discussion while standing beside the most disruptive child.

AFTER THE SCHOOL BELL RINGS: MESO-LEVEL ANALYSIS OF EDUCATIONAL ORGANIZATIONS

Schools can be like mazes, with passages to negotiate, hallways lined with lockers, and classrooms that set the scene for the education process. Schools are mazes in a much larger sense as well. They involve complex interwoven social systems at the meso level—the state agencies above the local community that affect a school's operations. At this level, we encounter the formal organization of the school system in a more bureaucratized form.

Formal Education Systems

Formal education came into being in the Western world in 16th-century Europe. Schools were seen as a way for Catholics to indoctrinate people into religious faith and for Lutherans to teach people to read so that they could interpret the Bible for themselves. The first compulsory education was provided by a Lutheran monastery in Germany in 1619. By the 19th century, schooling was seen as necessary to teach the European lower classes better agricultural methods, skills for the rapidly growing number of factory jobs, national loyalty, and obedience to authorities (Gatto 2003).

After 1900, national state school systems were common in Europe and its colonial outposts and former colonial empires. These systems shared many common organizational structures, curricula, and methods, as nations borrowed ideas from other countries. The Prussian model, with strict discipline and ties to the military, became popular in Europe in the 1800s, for example.

Thus, formal education systems came into being when other social institutions required new roles, skills, and knowledge that parents could not teach. Knowledge needed by the young became too complex to be taught informally in families through example, moral lessons, and stories. Industrializing societies required workers with reading and math skills, and eventually, they would need electronic technology skills. Schooling that formerly served only the elite gradually became available to the masses, and some societies began to require schooling for basic literacy (usually third-grade level). Schools emerged as major formal organizations and eventually developed extensive bureaucracies. The post–World War II period from 1950 to 1970 brought about a rapid rise in education worldwide, with worldwide enrollment in primary schooling jumping from 36% to 84% and secondary enrollments going from 13% to 36% (Boli 2002). Figure 11.3 shows trends since 1970, with worldwide primary schooling up to 90% by 2009 and secondary schooling reaching 68% (UNESCO 2012).

Sometimes, differing goals for education systems lead to conflict. What need, for example, does a subsistence farmer in Nigeria or Kenya have for Latin? Yet Latin was often imposed as part of the standard curriculum in colonialized nations by those who wished them to follow the standards of the colonizing nation. Since the colonial era, many Global South countries have revised curricula based on the goals and needs of their own economies.

The Bureaucratic School Structure

Organizational requirements of education systems at a meso level can influence the personal student–teacher relationship at the micro level. The meso-level formal

FIGURE 11.3 Number of Students (in millions) Worldwide Enrolled in School, From Primary to Tertiary Education, 1970, 2000, and 2009

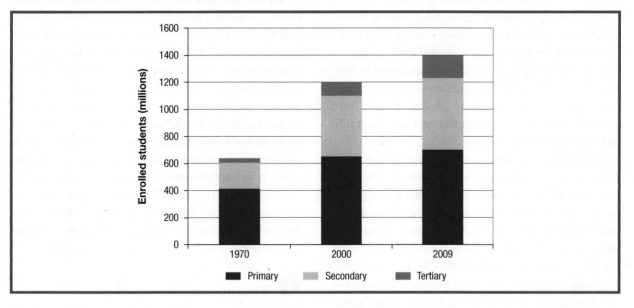

Source: UNESCO (2012).

bureaucratic atmosphere that permeates many schools arose because it was cost-effective, efficient, and productive. Bureaucracy provided a way to document and process masses of students coming from different backgrounds. Recall Weber's bureaucratic model of groups and organizations, discussed in Chapter 5:

1. Schools have a division of labor among administrators, teachers, students, and support personnel. The roles associated with the statuses are part of the school structure. Individual teachers or students hold these roles for a limited time and are replaced by others coming into the system.
2. The administrative hierarchy incorporates a chain of command and channels of communication.
3. Specific rules and procedures in a school cover everything from course content to discipline in the classroom and use of the schoolyard.
4. Personal relationships are downplayed in favor of formalized relations among members of the system, such as placement on the basis of tests and grades.
5. Rationality governs the operations of the organization; people are hired and fired on the basis of their qualifications and how well they do their jobs (unless or until they attain tenure) (Weber 1947).

One result of bureaucracy is that some children's special needs—such as personal problems or learning difficulties—are not met (Kozol 2006; Sizer 1984; Waters

2012). Impersonal rules can lock people into rigid behavior patterns, leading to apathy and alienation. In schools, these feelings cause passivity or acting out among students, which in turn frustrates teachers. Children like Tomás in the opening example do not fit into neat cubbyholes that bureaucratic structures invariably create. These children view school not as a privilege but as a requirement imposed by an adult world. Caught between the demands of an impersonal bureaucracy and individual goals for their students, teachers cannot always give every child the personal help she or he needs. Thus, we see how organizational requirements of education systems at a meso level can influence the personal student-teacher relationship at the micro level. This is another example of how the social world model helps us understand human behavior in organizations.

Education and the Social Institution of Family

We discuss interactions among meso-level institutions throughout this book. The social institutions of family and education impact each other in many ways, some of which we have already mentioned. When children enter kindergarten or primary school, they bring their prior experience, including socialization experiences and cultural capital from a parent or parents, brothers, sisters, and other relatives (Jaeger 2011). Family background, according to many sociologists, is the single most important

🎙 Bureaucracy in Schools

influence on children's school achievement. Children succeed in large part because of what their parent(s) do to support them in their educations (Jaeger 2011).

Most families stress the importance of education, but they do so in different ways. Middle-class parents in the Global North tend to manage their children's education, visiting schools and teachers, having educational materials in the home, and holding high expectations for their children's achievement. In these families, children learn the values of hard work, good grades, and deferred gratification for reaching future goals.

Often, teachers' perceptions of their students and behavior toward them are influenced by their interactions with parents. Middle- and upper-class parents are more likely to ask about their children's progress, consult with teachers on strategies to help them learn better at home and in the classroom, and make it clear that they want teachers to focus on their children. Teachers interested in pleasing (or appeasing) these parents will be sure to pay attention to their children. Parents from lower-socioeconomic-status families tend to be less involved in their children's schooling, with less time to help with homework and fewer interactions with teachers. Language barriers (for new immigrants), lack of time (for single parents and those working many hours per week), and views toward teachers (as authority figures who should be left alone to do their job) are some of the reasons many lower-income parents do not play an active role in their children's schooling (Cheung and Pomerantz 2012). Children who must make educational decisions on

their own have a greater likelihood of doing poorly or dropping out of school (Jaeger 2011).

Wealthier students also tend to be healthier students—another advantage in the educational institution. Healthier children do better academically. Children from low-income families tend to have less access to nutritious food and safe areas to play. Providing a variety of healthy food choices at school and devising ways to make exercise fun and available for all students can impact the health gap between poor and wealthier students, as well as educational inequality. Recognizing the connection between health and educational achievement, as well as the obesity epidemic, the Obama administration, in 2012, established higher nutritional standards for school lunches so that low-income students who rely on free or reduced-price lunches can have healthy meals to eat.

 Thinking Sociologically

Provide some examples of links between academic success in schools and at least two other social institutions.

Educational Decision Making at the Meso Level

Who should have the power to make decisions about what children learn? In relatively homogeneous countries such as Japan and Sweden, centralized goal setting and school decisions are possible. Educational decision making typically causes little controversy. In contrast, heterogeneous societies such as Canada, Israel, and the United States include many different racial, ethnic, regional, and religious subcultures, each with its own needs and interests. In many such nations, without a strong central government that controls the educational system, teachers, administrators, school boards, parents, and interest groups all claim the right to influence the curriculum. Consider the following examples of influences from micro and macro levels on the educational institution, a meso-level organization.

Local-Level Influences. At the U.S. local community level, curricular conflicts occur routinely over the selection of reading material and sex education courses, as well as over any content thought to contain obscenity, sex, nudity, political or economic bias, profanity, slang or nonstandard English, racism or racial hatred, and antireligious or presumed anti-American sentiment. For example, Tucson, Arizona, suspended its Mexican American

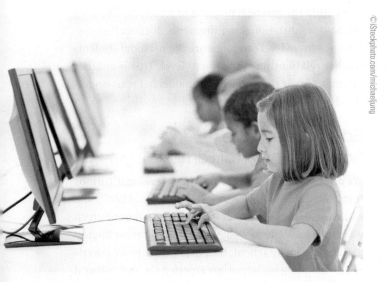

Computer skills are increasingly essential in societies and schools, yet some children come from families without access to computers. Children who have computers at home have a significant advantage.

©iStockphoto.com/michaeljung

studies program and banned a number of books related to the program because they were thought by some parents to "promote resentment toward a race or class of people" (Delfattore 2004; Goodman and Gonzalez 2012). Another example comes from Family Friendly Libraries, an online grassroots interest group that started in Virginia and argues that the popular *Harry Potter* books should be banned from school libraries. The members of this group believe the series promotes the religion of witchcraft (DeMitchell and Carney 2005). Banned books in the past have included *The Wonderful Wizard of Oz, Rumpelstiltskin, Anne Frank: The Diary of a Young Girl, Madame Bovary, The Grapes of Wrath, The Adventures of Huckleberry Finn,* Shakespeare's *Hamlet,* Chaucer's *Miller's Tale,* and Aristophanes's *Lysistrata* (Ballantine and Hammack 2012). Table 11.3 shows the most frequently challenged books in 2013. Off the top 10 list this year, but on in previous years, are *ttyl, ttfn,* and *l8r, g8r* (a series by Lauren Myracle); *The Color of Earth; My Mom's Having a Baby; Alice* (series); *Brave New World; What My Mother Doesn't Know; Gossip Girl* (series); and *To Kill a Mockingbird* (American Library Association 2014).

A growing number of large city school districts, concerned with teen pregnancy and sexually transmitted diseases, including AIDS, now provide teens with sex education, information about contraception, counseling, and sometimes condoms. Decisions about sex education curricula are often fraught with controversy. Many oppose sex education in schools, believing it should be left to families and religious institutions. Some argue that these programs encourage premarital sex rather than abstinence and teach teens how to have sex. However, the numbers of sexually active teens have remained steady since 1991, and even dropped in recent years. In 2014, the number of sexually active teens was 16% at age 15, 33% at age 16, 48% at age 17, and 71% at age 18 (Guttmacher Institute 2014). The rate of teen pregnancies and births among teens has dropped to half of what it was two decades ago, due to more access to birth control and better sex education. Counties with sex education programs typically have much lower teen pregnancy rates (Kulkarni 2012; Memmott 2013).

National-Level Influences. Whether or not the national government should control education is a question in all

Table 11.3   The 10 Most Challenged Children's Books of 2013

	Title	Reason for Banning
1	*Captain Underpants* by Dav Pikey	Offensive language; unsuited to age group, violence
2	*The Bluest Eye* by Toni Morrison	Offensive language, sexually explicit, unsuited to age group, violence
3	*The Absolutely True Diary of a Part-Time Indian* by Sherman Alexie	Drugs/alcohol/smoking, offensive language, racism, sexually explicit, unsuited to age group
4	*Fifty Shades of Grey* by E. L. James	Nudity, offensive language, religious viewpoint, sexually explicit, unsuited to age group
5	*The Hunger Games* by Suzanne Collins	Religious viewpoint, unsuited to age group
6	*A Bad Boy Can Be Good for a Girl* by Tanya Lee Stone	Drugs/alcohol/smoking, nudity, offensive language, sexually explicit
7	*Looking for Alaska* by John Green	Drugs/alcohol/smoking, sexually explicit, unsuited to age group
8	*The Perks of Being a Wallflower* by Stephen Chbosky	Drugs/alcohol/smoking, homosexuality, sexually explicit, unsuited to age group
9	*Bless Me, Ultima* by Rudolfo Anaya	Occult/Satanism, offensive language, religious viewpoint, sexually explicit
10	*Bone* (series) by Jeff Smith	Political viewpoint, racism, violence

Source: American Library Association (2014).

societies. Because the U.S. Constitution leaves education in the hands of each state, the involvement of the federal government has been more limited than in most countries. Education is centralized in almost all other countries around the world, and the U.S. system is more fragmented and uneven than most. Even in the United States, though, the federal government wields enormous influence through its power to make federal funds available for special programs, such as mathematics and science, reading, and special education. The government may withhold funds from schools not in compliance with federal laws and the U.S. Constitution. For example, the federal government, courts, and public opinion forced all-male military academies to become coeducational, despite the schools' resistance to such change. School changes as a result of the Civil Rights Act and the Americans with Disabilities Act are other examples of federal government influence on local schools through the enforcement of federal laws. Schools now accommodate people with various disabilities—people who in the past would have been left out of the system. With their classroom experiences and working with other teachers and children, many differently abled children can participate fully in society. However, as the following "Sociology in Our Social World" shows, this process is not always smooth.

Since the establishment of the U.S. Department of Education in 1980, each president has put his mark on the U.S. education system. President George W. Bush's controversial No Child Left Behind (NCLB) initiative was a prime example. It tied federal funds to school performance and required annual competency testing of students. Under this program, schools were required to administer achievement tests for accountability—tests that focus on math and reading. Schools failing to meet guidelines were penalized. The result was that 70% of schools reduced instructional time in other subject areas (Center for Education Policy 2006; Ginicola and Saccoccio 2008). Some states such as Wisconsin have reported improvement in math and reading (New America Foundation 2014a). So, even in the decentralized United States, where only 12% of education dollars come from the federal government, macro-level policies have an impact on what happens in the intimate environment of classrooms (New America Foundation 2014b).

Critics argued that NCLB ignored much of what educators and social scientists know from research about teaching and learning. It overemphasized testing, penalized schools with many low-income students, demoralized and deprofessionalized teachers, and failed to provide adequate funding for the mandates (Bracey 2005; Hallett and Meanwell 2012; Karen 2005).

President Obama and his education secretary, Arne Duncan, changed the NCLB plan by funding parts of the law that were left unfunded, allowing states to opt out of certain parts of the program, and establishing funding for new initiatives as part of the "Race to the Top" agenda to improve schools. This approach included adding new assessment measures of student learning, providing some alternatives to the high-stakes testing, stressing rewards for high-performing teachers, and nationalizing some of the standards previously in the hands of states. Still, critics charge that the Obama administration maintained many of the NCLB policies that caused problems in the previous administration, especially the use of high-stakes testing and centralized control ("Plan for Lifetime Success Through Education" 2008).

The Obama administration placed new emphasis on "zero to five" education by expanding Head Start funding for preschoolers. Early-childhood education has been touted as providing the start that many low-income

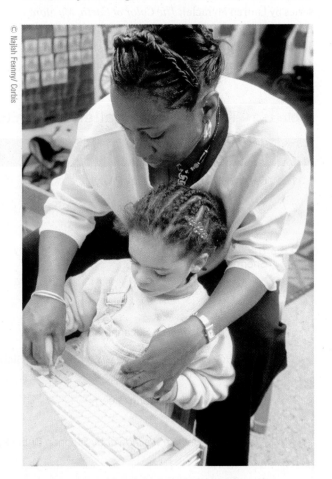

No Child Left Behind and other federal education policies put in place in recent years attempt to close education gaps between social classes and races and provide the resources needed for all children to learn and contribute to society. The girl in this picture is learning how to use a computer thanks to a government-supported program.

Special Education   Government Programs

sociology in our social world

Disability and Inequality
By Robert M. Pellerin

Living with a visual disability for over 40 years has provided me with lived experience. I have also been doing research on experiences of others with disabilities as part of my PhD research. My results show that having a disability puts people at a disadvantage in education, employment, media images, and personal relationships. Technologies for those with disabilities have advanced, legislation has been introduced and sometimes passed, and advocacy for rights abound, but I still have to remind others, including professionals, that due to visual impairments some methods of communication, such as print media, do not work. Additionally, most of the technology from which those with visual impairment could benefit is unaffordable, and most mainstream companies do not include features that would make products disability-friendly. The bottom line is that many of us are ready, willing, and able to advance in education and be productive citizens, but we are often precluded from positions because of our disabilities and difficulty obtaining accommodation.

Disability in the United States has undergone a significant transition since the late 1800s. Most of those who have helped bring disability to the forefront have been U.S. veterans who were wounded in war and notable figures like Helen Keller who influenced societal perceptions of disability. They have helped define disabilities as being a relative disadvantage instead of a tragedy. Historically, disability has been synonymous with an inability to engage in education or employment. During the 1800s and early 1900s, people deemed unfit were often warehoused in asylums or institutions and placed in residential schools where they were provided with less-than-adequate instruction. For several decades in the early 20th century, some countries—including the United States—sterilized people with disabilities. However, advocates campaigned during the late 1960s to change such laws and to close asylums for the disabled.

The most well-known legislation seeking to end exclusion and increase participation in areas of education and employment is the Rehabilitation Act of 1973 and the Americans with Disabilities Act (ADA) of 1990. The 1973 and 1990 regulations apply to the states and public accessibility (that is, access to jobs, public services, and telecommunications). Despite this legislation, approximately 70% of people with disabilities do not participate in the workforce. As a result, unfortunately, people with disabilities are at higher risk for engaging in drug and alcohol use, sexual promiscuity, higher levels of abuse, and suicidal ideation than other groups.

Prior to the 1970s, people with disabilities were excluded from public education. Due to advocacy and legislation, today approximately 75% of school-age students with disabilities attend public school. Legislation regarding full inclusion has not proven as useful as planned, although exposure to students with disabilities has increased comfort levels of teachers and nondisabled peers. Recent deficiencies in providing equal education include lack of adequate technology and skills needed in college or in vocational or social settings.

(Continued)

(Continued)

Regarding employment, historically people with disabilities have gone from being evaluated on the same standards as nondisabled individuals to being assessed according to how well they know themselves, their accommodation needs, and their job qualifications. Despite legislation, courts have generally ruled in favor of employers in discrimination suits. Some social scientists advocate for improving the social and human capital of those with disabilities as a way to increase the level of educational and workforce participation. Many employers believe the candidate is responsible for ensuring employment is attained, while some potential employers continue to believe people with disabilities are too difficult to hire and accommodate despite their academic achievement. Employees with disabilities, including myself, concur with recommendations such as improving social and human capital, educating employers about the benefits of hiring people with disabilities, and dispelling misconceptions and negative stereotypes.

The tragedy is that people with disabilities, despite their efforts, continue to meet with virtual hoops posed by court decisions, changes in education, and negative labeling. I believe that until society views people as having abilities and strengths as opposed to disabilities, stigma will predominate and society will be deprived of talents and qualities from which all can benefit.

• •

Robert M. Pellerin earned an interdisciplinary sociology and psychology PhD in family studies from Union Institute and University. His research has been on employment barriers for people with visual disabilities, and he is currently a clinician doing marriage and family therapy in California.

children need to be successful in school, as we will discuss in more detail later. Evaluations of the Head Start program in the United States, designed for 3- to 5-year-olds from disadvantaged backgrounds, show that program participation tends to increase cognitive development, social skills, and school progress. Yet, fewer than half of the eligible children take part in the program due to lack of adequate funding (Barnett 2013; Camilli et al. 2010).

The Obama administration is also trying to ensure that all U.S. students have the same basic academic preparation by putting into place the Common Core State Standards. Note that recent presidents from both major political parties have supported an expansion of national rather than local control of school curriculum.

 Thinking Sociologically

The discussion above shows that educational issues at the micro (individual), meso (institutional or ethnic group), and macro (national) levels can be very different. Identify an issue and indicate who would be involved in the discussion of that issue at each level and what they might support or push for.

EDUCATION, SOCIETY, AND THE ROAD TO OPPORTUNITY: THE MACRO LEVEL

In Dalton, Georgia, Mexican students make up over half the school-age population. In the school that researcher Hector Tobar visited there, 80% of the students were first- or second-generation Mexican Americans. The town has been unable to recruit bilingual teachers to this rural community, so the community recruited teachers from Mexico for three-year terms and sent some of its own teachers to Mexico to learn about the cultures and educational systems there. Since that time, some of the teachers from Mexico have decided to stay in Dalton. The teachers do instruction in both English and Spanish. The state support for education covers less than half of the cost, which means that the town's carpet factories and local taxpayers (many of them low income) cover most of the expenses. The cofounder of the Georgia

Project, which assisted new immigrants in their adjustment to Dalton, believes that carpet factories made a self-interested decision when they decided to support the local schools. "The factories need the workers, and the workers come with families . . . Without good schools for the workers' children, the county would leave itself wide open to a whole host of social problems down the road. Giving Dalton's Mexican kids a decent education was the sensible thing to do, 'pure self-interest'" (Diggs 2011:59–60).

Other states have not been so accommodating—or pragmatic—with Mexican immigrants. In 2000, voters in Arizona approved the most restrictive English-only education law in the country, and since that time non-English-speakers in Arizona public schools have been part of an English-only program, with no Spanish spoken in school. Mexican students start behind and stay behind according to teachers (Diggs 2011).

Educational decisions made by states and national governments affect individual families and their kids, communities, states, and national economic and education systems. This next section focuses on the role of education in the stratification system. As you will see, education is deeply interwoven into the macro-level inequalities of a society.

Why Societies Have Education Systems: Macro-Level Theories

The average number of years of schooling of adults in India is 5.1 years. This average should increase soon, though, as enrollment in primary school has increased dramatically. Almost 94% of children in India are enrolled in primary school (NationMaster 2014a; UNESCO 2014. However, in some rural areas of India and other Global South countries, little more than basic literacy is considered necessary or possible, especially for girls. In addition, transportation to get to schools can be a problem. For example, youngsters in India must deal with overloaded school buses, and some children in Myanmar have to crowd onto a gondola to get to school.

In our global society, education plays a major role in providing children with skills for their adult lives—but how education takes place varies across societies. Village children in many Global South countries around the world go to the community school, tablets in hand, but when the family needs help in the fields or with child care, older children often stay at home. Even though attending several years of school is mandated by law in

© Elise Roberts

These children, who live near Inle Lake in Myanmar (Burma), take the only available mode of transportation to get to school, a gondola school bus.

most countries, not all people become literate. Learning survival skills—how to grow crops, care for the home, treat diseases, and make clothing—takes up the available time and energy of many people in the Global South.

Functionalist Perspective on Education. Functional theorists argue that formal and informal education serve certain crucial purposes in society, especially as societies modernize. The functions of education as a social institution are outlined in Figure 11.4. Note that some functions are planned and formalized (manifest functions), whereas others are unintended and unorganized—the informal results of the educational process (latent functions). Latent functions of schooling are often just as important to the society as manifest functions. For example, imagine what would happen to productivity if schools did not give parents release time from child care responsibilities so that they could perform other roles.

In the functionalist view, the structure and processes within the educational institution remain stable when they help society function smoothly and achieve its goals. Government proposals for education reforms can stem from complaints from business owners about inadequately prepared workers and other indications of poor educational outcomes, such as the nation's students falling behind in international test comparisons or achievement gaps among races and ethnicities, sexes, or socioeconomic classes. We look at each of these functions of education in more detail in the following.

Curricular Innovation and School Reform

FIGURE 11.4 Key Functions of Education

Manifest Functions (intended; formalized)

- Teach students the skills necessary to become educated, effective participants of society.

- Socialize children to be productive members of society.

- Select individuals for key positions in society.

- Promote social participation, change, and innovation.

- Enhance personal independence and social development.

Latent Functions (unintended; informal)

- Confine and supervise underage citizens.

- Weaken parental controls over youths.

- Provide opportunities for peer cultures to develop.

- Provide contexts for the development of friendships and mate selection.

Teach Students the Skills Necessary to Become Educated, Effective Participants of Society. This function is the most obvious one. Schools help students cultivate the skills needed for jobs. It also teaches students to read, think clearly, and understand the history of their country in order to be active and effective members of a democratic society.

Socialize Children to Be Productive Members of Society. Societies use education to pass on essential information of a culture—especially the values, skills, and knowledge necessary for survival. Sometimes this process occurs in formal classrooms and other times in informal places. For example, in West African villages, children may have several years of formal education in a village school, but they learn what is right and wrong, values, and future roles informally by observing their elders and by "playing" at the tasks they will soon undertake for survival. The girls help pound cassava root for the evening meal, while the boys build model boats and practice negotiating the waves and casting nets.

In postindustrial Global North societies, elders and family members cannot teach all the skills necessary for survival. Formal schooling emerged as a meso-level institution to meet the needs of macro-level industrial and postindustrial societies, furnishing the specialized training required by rapidly growing and changing technology. Schools also teach students culture beyond what some families in heterogeneous societies can provide. Diverse groups must learn common rules that maintain the social order, for example. These rules come from the dominant culture of the society, and schools teach them through both their regular and hidden curriculum (Brint, Contreras, and Matthews 2001).

Select Individuals for Positions in Society. Students take standardized tests, receive grades at the end of the term or the year, and ask teachers to write recommendation letters. These activities are part of the selection process prevalent in competitive societies with formal education systems. Individuals accumulate credentials—grade point averages, standardized test scores, and degrees—that determine the colleges or job opportunities available to them, the fields of study or occupations they can pursue, and ultimately their positions in society. In some societies, education systems enact this social function through tracking, ability grouping, grade promotion and retention, high-stakes and minimum-competency testing, and pullout programs that contribute to job training, such as vocational education and service learning.

Thus, from a functionalist perspective, education outfits people for making a living in their society, contributing to the economy, and maintaining the stability of society. Income levels and standards of living for individuals, families, communities, states, and nations relate positively to education levels. Consider Figure 11.5 in the next "Engaging Sociology," showing the distribution of college degrees in the United States.

Promote Social Participation, Change, and Innovation. In our high-tech age, critical thinking and analytical skills, and familiarity with information systems—computers, Internet resources, electronic library searches, and so forth—lead to increased employment opportunities and greater prosperity for society. For example, India has developed technology institutes, and many graduates find employment in multinational companies with offices in India. These jobs have helped create a growing middle class in India. Well-trained, efficient engineers and computer experts working in India for lower wages than workers in many highly developed countries have become an essential part of the global economy (Friedman 2005).

ENGAGING SOCIOLOGY

Consequences of High or Low Numbers of Bachelor's Degrees

FIGURE 11.5   Percentage of the U.S. Population Holding a Bachelor's Degree or Higher by State

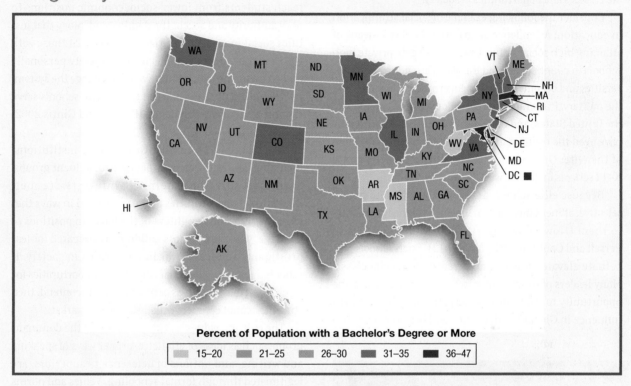

Percent of Population with a Bachelor's Degree or More

| 15–20 | 21–25 | 26–30 | 31–35 | 36–47 |

Source: StateMaster.com (2013).

Engaging With Sociological Data

1. How does your state rank?

2. How might the economy of a state be affected when an especially low percentage of the population has a college degree?

3. What kinds of businesses, industries, or professionals are more likely to locate in a state with a very high percentage of college-educated citizens?

4. Do you think some businesses might be attracted to states where relatively few people have a college education? Why or why not?

5. How might educational levels in a state influence its political, health, and science institutions?

6. Look at the states that have especially high or especially low levels of the population with college degrees. What might be some causes for these high or low rates of college graduation?

7. Come up with at least two questions this map raises.

Enhance Personal Independence and Social Development. In school, children are taught educational and social skills and ethical conduct that will enable them to function in society. For example, in addition to the three *R*s, they learn to get along with others, resolve disputes, stay in line, follow directions, obey the rules, take turns, be kind to others, be neat, tell the truth, listen, plan ahead, work hard, meet deadlines, and so on.

Conflict Perspectives on Stratification and Education.

A small percentage of students around the world receive elite educations, but many others do not. Conflict theorists emphasize the role of education in social stratification and competition between groups. They focus on the impact education or lack thereof has on children's life chances and opportunities in society.

Consider the following example of social stratification in education: Attendance at an elite school is a means of attaining high social status. Graduates of elite private high schools in countries around the world attend the best universities and become leaders of government, business, and the military. Preparatory (prep) schools in England, Japan, the United States, and many other countries traditionally have been the training ground for the sons and daughters of the elite. Only 8% of U.S. students attended private K–12 schools in 2011 (Ewert 2013).

Because elite schools are very expensive and highly selective, affluent members of society have the most access to them (Howard and Gaztambide-Fernandez 2010; Persell and Cookson 1985; Wade 2012). Such schools perpetuate elevated prestige and "reproduce social class." Many leaders of former colonized countries have had the opportunity to study abroad, perpetuating Global North influence in Global South countries. Those not born into

positions of advantage have very limited chances to participate in elite education and leadership positions.

According to conflict theory, when elites of society protect their educational advantages, the result is **reproduction of class**—*the socioeconomic positions of one generation passing on to the next.* This process takes place in part through the socialization of young people into adult work roles and compliance with the modern economic and political institutions and their needs. Schools teach students from lower-socioeconomic positions to obey authority and accept the dominant ideology that justifies social inequality. If citizens believe that those with the best educations and jobs in their society personally earned them, they are not motivated to change the system. By promoting the legitimacy of the system, schools serve the interests of the privileged (Bowles and Gintis 2002; Collins 2004).

At a macro level, conflict theorists see institutions, including education, as tools of powerful affluent groups, used to ensure that their self-interests are met. Educational opportunities are manipulated in ways that keep the sons and daughters of the haves in positions of privilege, while lower-class children are prepared for less prestigious and less rewarding positions in society. If schools do not provide equal educational opportunities for all children in a society, as conflict theorists contend, then students cannot compete equally in the job market.

The cultural values and social norms of the dominant group, such as ideas of etiquette, proper ways of speaking and writing, and notions of deference to superiors, are legitimated through formal schooling. Values and norms that are important in ethnic or socioeconomic subcultures are marginalized (Kozol 2005, 2012). According to conflict theorists, this process enhances power and confirms the privileges of the dominant group. The education system is not equally beneficial to all citizens in society. In addition, private schools sometimes become sanctuaries for those who do not want race- and class-integrated schools, perpetuating religious, economic, and racial segregation.

Critics of the increasing efforts to promote school choice and more charter schools (publicly funded independent schools) fear that public schools might be left with the least capable students and teachers, further stratifying an already troubled system. Students often gain entrance into charter schools through a lottery for which some, but not all, parents register. This can result in a "creaming process" that leaves students with parents not involved in their educational process, in traditional public

© Karen Kasmauski/ Corbis

Schoolgirls in Kenya wait for classes to begin. Children like this, whose parents can afford to send them to school, will have more life chances than those who cannot attain an education. Conflict theorists point out that inequality is deeply embedded in the institution of education.

schools (Chubb and Moe 1990). This issue was at the root of the Chicago teachers' union strike in September 2012 that closed down the schools for over a week (Tareen and Keyser 2012).

Having explored some lenses through which sociologists analyze education systems, we now focus on the classrooms, corridors, local schools, and key players where the everyday drama of teaching and learning plays out.

 Thinking Sociologically

Consider the community in which you went to high school. Do you think the education there enhances upward social mobility and serves all students and the community, or serves the affluent, reproducing social class and training people to fulfill positions at the same level as their parents, or some combination? Explain.

Can Schools Bring About Equality in Societies?

Equal opportunity exists when all people have an equal chance of achieving high socioeconomic status in society regardless of their class, ethnicity, race, or gender (Riordan 2004). James Coleman describes the meaning and goals of equal educational opportunity:

- To provide a common curriculum for all children regardless of background
- To allow children from diverse backgrounds to attend the same school
- To provide equality within a given locality (Coleman 1968, 1975, 1990)

Equal opportunity means that children are provided with equal facilities, financing, and access to school programs. Schools in poor neighborhoods or in rural villages in the United States and around the world, however, often lack the basics—safe buildings, school supplies and books, and funds to operate. Lower-class minority students who live in these areas fall disproportionately to the bottom of the educational hierarchy. Many children face what seem to be insurmountable barriers to educational success, such as poverty, lack of health care, homelessness, hunger, and pressure to drop out to help the family (Kozol 2012; Noguera 2011). These conditions at home and in neighborhoods affect children's achievement in school and on standardized tests (Boger and Orfield 2009; Coleman 1990).

Who Gets Ahead and Why? The Role of Education in Stratification

Any school or educational institution is supposed to be a **meritocracy,** *a social group or organization in which people are allocated to positions according to their abilities and credentials, as in level of education attained.* This, of course, is consistent with the principles of a meritocratic social system where the most qualified person is promoted and decisions are impersonal and based on "credentials" (Charles, Roscigno, and Torres 2007). Still, in societies around the world, we see evidence that middle-class and elite children receive more and better education than equally qualified poor children. Children do not attend school on an equal footing, and in many cases, meritocracy does not exist at all.

Three practices that tend to lead to inequality in schools—testing, tracking, and funding—illustrate how schools reproduce and perpetuate social class and social stratification systems. They also give clues as to what might be done to mitigate inequality in education.

Assessing Student Achievement: Testing. Testing is one means of placing students in schools according to their achievement and merit and of determining academic progress. Yet many scholars, including sociologists of education, argue that standardized test questions, the vocabulary employed, and testing situations disadvantage lower-class, minority, and immigrant students. These disadvantages often result in lower scores among these groups, relegating these students to lower tracks in the education system (Gardner 1987, 1999; Smith 2008).

Moreover, higher-income parents have the means to seek educational opportunities outside of school that give their children a further edge over other students on standardized tests. Families with more economic resources can provide more chances to learn through travel, going to museums, and mixing with members of the elite. They can also provide *shadow education* opportunities outside of school, such as tutoring, test prep, and summer programs that help prepare students for tests such as the SAT and ACT. Shadow education gives those students an advantage in the college selection process that relies, in part, on standardized test scores (Buchmann, Condron, and Roscigno 2010). Relatively few African American and Hispanic students participate in shadow education, and students from these racial and ethnic groups tend to score lower on standardized tests (Corbett, Hill, and Rose 2008; Strauss 2011). Table 11.4 in the next "Engaging Sociology" shows differences in ACT and SAT scores depending on sex, race,

··· ENGAGING SOCIOLOGY ···

Test Score Variations by Gender and Ethnicity

Evaluate your testing experiences and compare them to those of other groups:

Table 11.4 ACT and SAT Scores by Sex and Race/Ethnicity

ACT Scores: 2013	Average	SAT Scores: 2013	Average
Composite, total scores	20.9	SAT Writing, all students	488
Male*	21.2	Male	482
Female*	20.9	Female	493
White	22.2	White	515
African American	16.9	Black/African American	417
American Indian/Alaska Native	18	American Indian/Alaska Native	462
Hispanic	18.8	Hispanic	442
Asian American	23.5	Asian/Pacific Islanders	528
SAT Scores: 2013	**Average**	**SAT Scores: 2013**	**Average**
SAT Critical Reading, all students	496	SAT Math, all students	514
Male	496	Male	531
Female	494	Female	499
White	528	White	535
Black/African American	428	Black/African American	428
Hispanic	450	Hispanic	461
Asian/Pacific Islanders	518	Asian/Pacific Islander	595
American Indian/Alaska Native	482	American Indian/Alaska Native	489

Source: ACT (2013); College Board (2013).

* No male/female scores listed for 2013 ACT; scores reflect 2011 data.

Sociological Data Analysis

1. Do you think your scores were an accurate measure of your ability or achievement? Why or why not?
2. Do you think your race or ethnicity, social class, or gender affected your scores? Why or why not?
3. Have your scores affected your life chances? Are there ways in which you have been privileged or disprivileged in the testing process?
4. What might be some causes of the variation in test scores between groups or categories of students?

and ethnic group. Answer the questions posed as you engage with the sociological data.

Student Tracking. Judgments by school administrators, counselors, and teachers affect children for a lifetime. There are several forms of separating students by ability in schools. *Ability grouping* places students into different level groups within classes. *Tracking* separates students into different-level classes within a school. *Streaming,* practiced in Europe and Asia but not in the United States, separates students into different secondary schools. All of these groups have the goal of allowing educators to more effectively address the needs of students of different abilities.

Many sociologists of education have argued against tracking, pointing out that it contributes to the stratification process that perpetuates inequality. Research finds that levels at which students are tracked correlate with factors such as the child's background and ethnic group, language skills, appearance, and other socioeconomic variables (Rosenbaum 1999; Wells and Oakes 1996). Students from lower social classes and minority groups tend to be clustered in the lower tracks and complete fewer years of school (Lucas and Berends 2002; Oakes et al. 1997). In other words, track placement is not always a measure of a student's ability. It can be arbitrary, based on teachers' impressions or questionable test results. Even language differences between teachers and students can affect placement.

On the other hand, tracking provides many benefits for teachers and students. In tracked classes, teachers do not have to slow down to help some students catch up, while trying to make sure that their more advanced students are not bored. Students tend to make more progress when working in groups with similar academic aptitudes. For example, in comparing Massachusetts middle schools that track students with those that have "detracked" students, researchers found that schools that track in math courses have more advanced math students than those that do not. High-achieving students learn more when they are around other high achievers (Loveless 2009).

While tracking decreased in the 1990s, amid much criticism, the practice has rebounded somewhat in recent years, with most schools placing students into different-level math classes. Ability grouping has become much more common over the past several years, with the majority of fourth-grade teachers separating students into such groups when they teach reading (71%) and math (54%) (Loveless 2009, 2013). Sociologists now know enough about the possible negative repercussions of tracking to emphasize that, if a school district does place students into different ability groups or tracks, it should find ways to eliminate possible race, class, and gender bias, and students should be tracked in each subject independently, not in a single track for all subjects. Students should also have the opportunity to move among tracks, as their progress indicates they should.

Thinking Sociologically

Were you tracked in any subjects? What effect, if any, did this have on you? What effect did tracking have on friends of yours? How might tracking shape friendship networks?

School Funding. The amount of money available to fund schools affects the types of programs they can offer, an important issue for nations that must compete in the global social and economic system. Money for education, in some societies, comes from central governments and, in others, from a combination of federal, state, and local government and private sources, such as tuition, religious denominations, and philanthropies. In Uganda, for example, the government runs the schools, but most of the funding comes from tuition paid by each student or by the student's family. Whatever the source, schools sometimes face budget crises and must trim staff and programs.

In the United States, public school spending comes from local property taxes as well as state and federal funds. On average, local governments provide 44% of education funding for elementary and secondary school budgets from income taxes, corporate taxes, sales taxes, and fees. States provide about 43%, mostly from property taxes; however, this percentage is dropping with tight state budgets. About 12% of education funding comes from the federal government (New America Foundation 2014b). Spending is closely related to the racial and class composition of schools and to student achievement levels. Schools in low-income communities are disadvantaged by smaller tax bases and fewer local resources (Condron and Roscigno 2003; Kozol 1991, 2005; "School Finance" 2011). Controversies over equitable school funding in the United States have reached the courtroom in a number of states.

The Elementary and Secondary Education Act, first passed by Congress in 1965, requires equitable state and local funding for high-poverty and low-income schools. Some states have chosen (or have been mandated in court) to target state funds to poorer school districts in their states. However, despite these efforts, over 40% of

School Funding

low-income schools across the United States receive less state and local funding than other, wealthier, schools in their districts (Heuer and Stullich 2011). The states with the most equitable funding were Connecticut, Iowa, Massachusetts, New Jersey, and Vermont, whereas Wyoming, Illinois, Louisiana, Missouri, and North Carolina provided the least equitable school funding in the United States in 2010 (Baker, Sciarra, and Farrie 2010).

Economically disadvantaged schools tend to pay teachers less and have lower-achieving students. Many of their teachers leave for jobs elsewhere after a few years. The result is that these schools tend to have more inexperienced teachers than those in wealthier districts (Haycock and Hanushek 2010).

While not all experienced teachers are effective, experienced teachers tend to be more effective than new ones, who have not yet honed their skills (Haycock and Hanushek 2010). This leaves students at low-income schools at a further disadvantage in relation to their peers at higher-income schools.

Policies related to funding, tracking, and testing, therefore, seriously impact the educational experiences of students. We now take a closer look at issues impacting education policies today.

EDUCATIONAL AND SOCIAL POLICY ISSUES

In the 21st century, school systems around the world face dramatic changes. The need for technological training of citizenry, increased demand for access to high school and higher education, changes in the student composition of the classroom, and increased accountability and testing of students and teachers are but a few of the many issues facing schools. Because education reflects societal politics and problems, policies change, depending on who is in power and their agenda.

Recently in the United States, the issues of accountability, standardized testing, and teaching basic skills have been at the forefront of educational policy, but

Students pictured in this computer class attend a British school where many students come from challenging situations: having refugee status, living in temporary shelters, or coming from non-English-speaking homes. Positively transformed by new management and increased governmental funding, this school has become a "government beacon school" (model school) in Britain.

movements toward individualization of education and developing the whole child are reappearing (ASCD 2013; The Whole Child 2012). Although the past century brought some improvement in equality in education, much remains to be done to level the playing field. The greatest barrier to equal education in the 21st century, both within and between countries, may prove to be socioeconomic, with many racial and ethnic minorities represented in lower classes. Sociologists of education contribute to the policy discussions in their roles as researchers, consultants, policy analysts, and public sociologists.

Educational Policies in the United States

What path should nations take to improve their education systems? In the United States, there is constant debate about fair and equitable funding policies, the best methods for teaching children, and accountability. At the core of these issues lies the question of who should make decisions about education. Should the centralized leadership of the federal government be dominant so that there is some coherence and consistency in educational policy across states? Should states that provide the majority of funding for schools determine educational policies? Should local districts have the most power since they may best know the local situation and needs?

Today, despite numerous U.S. government policies and reports, the data on school success show that most students do not graduate from high school ready for college or a career. In 2012, only 25% of high school graduates who took the ACT met the college readiness benchmark in all four subjects (English, reading, math, and science) (ACT 2012). There are 32 million U.S. adults who cannot read, or 14% of the population, and 21% of adults in the United States read below the fifth-grade level ("The U.S. Illiteracy Rate" 2013). Although the high school graduation rate increased over the past three decades to reach 78.2%, as of 2013, there were still 1,434 high schools in the United States in which 60% or more of students did not graduate on time (Balfanz and Gomperts 2013; Brenchley 2013; Layton 2012).

Occasionally, private policy makers initiate school programs that provide models for other schools. One example is public sociologist Geoffrey Canada who has had success with implementing programs for poor children in Harlem, from preschool to high school, as discussed in the next "Sociologists in Action" feature on page 370.

Global Policy Issues in Education

Approaches to learning tend to reflect a society's social and economic values. Countries with capitalist economic systems are more likely to have an education system that stresses individualism and competition, pitting students against one another for the best grades and the best opportunities. Socialist economic systems often encourage cooperation and collaboration among students, with the collective needs of society viewed as more important than those of individuals (Rankin and Aytaç 2006).

Political and economic trends outside a country can also have an impact on the education system within the country. For example, as China has become a more powerful economic nation and trading partner with the United States, many U.S. schools have added Mandarin classes to their curriculum. Also, since 9/11, many colleges and universities have developed courses covering issues of terrorism.

An important factor in access to education is where one lives. In Niger, for instance, only 12% of the girls in rural areas are in primary school compared with 83% in the capital city, Niamey. In refugee camps in Africa, only 6% of children receive any secondary education due to hardships from lack of teachers, the impact of AIDS, and orphaned status. Even when children do receive some primary education, the quality is such that many children leave school without basic skills (UNESCO 2005). For example, in just two refugee camps in Djibouti, Africa, 29,000 children do not go to school because there are no classrooms or teachers, and no toilets or exercise books (AlertNet 2012). Even when schools do exist in a region, an ongoing issue is proximity to those schools and transportation.

One of the notable global patterns has to do with gender. Throughout the world, enrollment among girls rose from 32% of school enrollees in 1950 to almost 50% in 2010 (World Bank 2013c). In Global North countries, women attend university at levels equal to or exceeding men. In some countries however, a gender gap favoring boys and men remains. For example, for every 100 boys, there are 66 girls in primary and secondary school in Afghanistan, 69 in Central African Republic, and 68 in Chad (World Bank 2013c). Studies show, though, that schooling has a very positive influence on the life chances of women, their children, and the whole society.

Education and Gender

SOCIOLOGISTS IN ACTION:
GEOFFREY CANADA

Harlem Children's Zone

Geoffrey Canada has an ambitious agenda—to have all young people in Harlem graduate from college. Sometimes policy agendas are forwarded by citizens who have knowledge, organizational skills, and a saleable idea to raise funds. Canada's life experience prepared him to work as a social activist and educator. He grew up in the South Bronx, was raised by a single mom and then had a lucky break. He moved to the suburbs with his grandparents and went on to earn a college degree from Bowdoin College and a master's degree from the Harvard Graduate School of Education.

Having been given the opportunity to earn an elite education, Canada is now using his expertise in education to help achieve academic success. As president and CEO of the Harlem Children's Zone (HCZ) in New York, he works with students to increase high school and college graduation rates. HCZ started out as a 24-block area of Harlem but has grown to 97 blocks due to its success. In the 97-block neighborhood, his center follows the academic careers of youth, providing social, medical, and educational services for free to the 10,000 children who live in the Zone. He has built his own charter school, the Promise Academy, with 1,200 students. Tuition to the school is free, and admission is done by lottery. For those in the Zone who do not win the school's admissions lottery, Harlem Children's Zone still provides services, including parenting classes, preschool language classes, school preparation classes, and SAT tutoring. HCZ supports the idea that strong communities produce strong schools and well-educated children.

The Promise Academy has long days and a short summer vacation, a dress code, and strict discipline. The schools also provide students with meals and after-school and Saturday tutoring and enrichment programs. The student–teacher ratio is 6 to 1. For students who work hard and achieve, there are rewards. Canada rewards students for their achievements. Some get free trips to Disneyland for good grades, and others get paid for good high school grades.

The Zone is not cheap to run at $16,000 per student (not including after-school programs, administrative and building costs, student rewards, and so on) compared to the $14,452 spent on each public school student in New York City, but Canada points out that the costs of a child ending up in the criminal justice system are much greater (Otterman 2010). HCZ, like other charter schools, receives, per student, 73% of the funds allocated for each public school student. Much of the rest of the funding comes from the business community and Wall Street.

To test the effectiveness of the school and program, a Harvard economics professor studied the data from tests of achievement and other academic indicators. He found that the Promise Academy elementary school had closed the gap in math and reading between its students and students in white or mixed schools, and outperformed many of the comparison schools. Those middle school students who started at the Promise Academy were behind, but they caught up with students in comparison schools. Another study found that students who attended the HCZ Promise Academy performed impressively better than those from the same background who attended a typical public school in New York City. According to the evaluator, the results were "stunning" (Croft and Whitehurst 2010). President Obama has taken notice of the success of HCZ and advocates replicating the program in other cities.

• •

Geoffrey Canada received his undergraduate degree from Bowdoin College and his master's in education from Harvard. He has written several books and articles, including Reaching Up for Manhood: Transforming the Lives of Boys in America *(Beacon Press, 1998).*

Some of the benefits of educating girls include "higher wages, greater agricultural productivity, and faster economic growth, but also health benefits" (Sperling 2006). More educated girls and women

- have lower fertility rates,
- are less likely to die in childbirth,
- are less likely to have their infants die,
- are less likely to contract HIV/AIDS,
- have increased labor force participation and earnings,
- provide better health care and education to their children,
- lift households out of poverty, and
- pass these benefits on to the next generation (World Bank 2014).

The influence of different cultural values and beliefs on the social construction of gender roles becomes obvious when looking at attitudes toward education for girls and women in different societies. For example, in a survey of respondents in 22 nations, majorities in 18 of the 22 countries disagreed that "a university education is more important for a boy than for a girl." However, almost two thirds of those in India (63%) and about half in Pakistan (51%), Egypt (50%), and China (48%) believe that a college education is more important for a boy than for a girl, and strong minorities in several countries agree. The case of Malala Yousafzai, who was shot by the Taliban in Pakistan in 2012 for her support of the education of girls, and the kidnapping of 300 school girls by the terrorist organization Boko Haram (which means "no Western education") in Nigeria in 2014 are vivid reminders of the continuing hostility toward education for girls.

A gender gap in views toward the importance of higher education for boys and girls can be found in many nations (including a slight one in the United States), but tends to be most evident in Muslim nations. For example, "while majorities of men in Egypt and Jordan say it is more important for a boy to receive a university education (60% and 56%, respectively); 60% of women in Egypt and 67% in Jordan disagree. In Pakistan, where more than twice as many men agree (64%) as disagree (30%) that a university education is more important for boys than it is for girls, about half (48%) of women disagree and 36% agree" (Pew Research Center 2010b:11).

The availability of clean drinking water is a major issue in the global South. Because women and girls must spend as much as six hours a day carrying water home (26% of a woman's day in Africa), the daughters are needed to care for children. Indeed, research by WaterAid estimates that in the Global South, 443 million school days are lost each year due

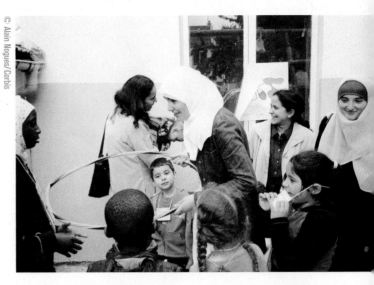

The French government does not permit public displays of religion and forbids Islamic girls and women from wearing the traditional head covering (hijab) to school. Government officials believe they contribute to the "us" versus "them" polarization between Muslims and non-Muslims.

The women above are carrying water. Their daughters are often needed to either fetch the water or stay home with young children while the mothers tote the filled water jugs, making school attendance for girls difficult.

to water-related issues and diseases. When wells were built and usable water became more accessible, the school attendance of girls immediately increased by 11% because of better sanitation and local access to water (WaterAid 2013).

Thinking Sociologically

How might education be important to children in a rural agricultural area? How might education in a local community or refugee camp be affected by global events, such as a war or a worldwide economic recession?

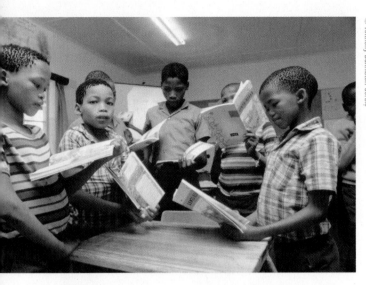

In Namibia, as elsewhere around the globalized world, education is increasingly necessary as skills in literacy and numeracy become critical to survival and hopes of prosperity.

The Future of Education in the Global System

The search for the best model of education is never ending. School systems around the world are under pressure to meet the diverse needs of their societies and their individual citizens. A major concern in Global North countries in the Information Age is this: What will become of those students who do not complete enough education to attain the skills needed today and in the near future? In these countries, high school used to prepare most young people for a job. By the 1990s in the Global North, high school had become preparation for college, which was itself necessary to find a decent job in the globalizing world. Forty-seven European countries have joined forces to reform higher education, create comparable and compatible systems of higher education throughout Europe, promote student mobility to fill job needs, and train young people for jobs of the future. The Bologna Declaration was fully implemented in 2010, and is influencing the market for college graduates (European Higher Education Area 2014). However, those students who do not attend college can take another route in Germany where businesses sees a trained workforce as key to maintaining their advanced industrial capacity. This idea meets needs of both the companies that are training students in skilled labor through apprenticeships, and need for younger workers to get a decent-paying job (Schwartz 2013).

Although college has become much more expensive, those with college degrees tend to earn much higher salaries and lifelong earnings (McArdle 2012). The role of technology in the future of education is expanding. The technological cyber gap may be closing in some parts of the world, but Global South countries need to invest further in Internet bandwidth and other technologies to allow more of their citizens to access the Internet easily ("The International Digital Divide" 2011). Electronic textbooks and materials have the potential to give students in both the affluent Global North and the poor Global South immediate access to new knowledge and ideas that can continually be updated.

Corporations, the government, and the military use video games to educate, sell products, and recruit. Advocates argue that "[t]hey let players . . . *inhabit* roles that are otherwise inaccessible to them" (Shaffer et al. 2005:105). Researchers are now creating video games for use in schools (Plass et al. 2012). Much learning will take place without walls, clocks, or age segregation, as students study via distance learning and through digital technology on their own time.

As governments develop educational policies, we again see the interconnections of our social world. Curricula respond to global events, international markets, and technological advances. They are also shaped by micro-level effectiveness or ineffectiveness of teachers and students in individual classrooms. The macro-level concerns and the micro-level processes come together in education, with the ultimate objective of preparing individuals in each classroom to meet the needs of the community, the state, the nation, and the world.

After the family, education is one of the first institutions that a child encounters, and like the family, it is primarily concerned with the process of socialization of the populace. Another institution deeply concerned with socialization and the inculcation of values into young people is religion. Both religion and education tend to address issues of "what" and "why," but whereas education tends to focus on answers that have to do with knowledge—causality and the relationship between facts—religion tends to address questions of ultimate meaning in life. We turn in the next chapter to a sociological perspective on religion.

Liberal Arts Education ▶

WHAT HAVE WE LEARNED?

Education systems are typically viewed as the means to reduce inequality, the source of upward mobility, the way to improve the economy, and the path for reduction of prejudice in societies. However, institutions such as education also have a vested interest in stability. Schools foster patriotism and loyalty toward the political system, families support schools and education, and education is expected to support the economic vitality of the nation. Institutions and organizations are driven by interest in their own survival, and risk-taking behaviors on behalf of change are not necessarily those that foster survival. Taking risks may threaten those who have power, privilege, and influence. It should not be surprising, therefore, that education does more to enhance stability than to create change. Still, those who seek to improve the society see tremendous potential in education as an agent of change, if its influence can be harnessed. It works largely with young minds in the socialization process—carrying out what powerful policy makers feel is important.

KEY POINTS

- Education is one of the primary institutions of society, focusing on the socialization of children and adults into their cultures so that they become contributing members. (See pp. 344–345.)

- At the micro level, various statuses and roles interact within a school, and classrooms develop their own cultures that may or may not enhance learning. (See pp. 346–351.)

- At the micro level, social theory is attentive to interaction in classrooms and local schools, using concepts of symbolic interaction or cost–benefit analysis to understand the climate of learning. (See pp. 346–347.)

- What we learn in schools goes far beyond the formal curriculum. We also learn a "hidden curriculum" in school that helps socialize us into our roles in society. (See pp. 348–351.)

- At the meso level, education can be understood as a formal organization that works toward certain goals (bureaucracy) but that has many of the dysfunctions of other bureaucracies. (See pp. 354–360.)

- At the macro level, national governments often try to see that their national needs are met by shaping educational policy, and their actions often create tension with those administrators and teachers at the meso and micro levels who do the actual work of teaching. (See pp. 360–361.)

- Macro-level theories focus on how education supports the social system (functionalism) or on how education serves the interests of the "haves" and reproduces social inequality (conflict theory). (See pp. 361–365.)

- Education is also a global concern, with curriculum influenced by global, as well as national, events. (See pp. 369–372.)

DISCUSSION QUESTIONS

1. Why is a good system of education important for a democracy? How can gaining a sociological perspective help people become more effective participants in a democratic society?

2. Who were the most popular kids in your high school? What made them popular? How did the reasons for their popularity vary based on their gender?

3. How do functionalist and conflict theorists describe the "hidden curriculum" in schools? What description best matches your own school experience? Why?

4. Do you think there should be tracking in schools? Why or why not? How has tracking (or an absence of tracking) in your schools impacted your

education and sense of yourself as a student? How does tracking in schools impact society?

5. This chapter describes several ways social class influences educational success. How has the social class of the family in which you were raised influenced your educational achievement? How did it influence your selection of a college to attend?

6. How do schools reproduce and perpetuate social stratification? If you had the power and desire to use the school system to reduce inequality, what policies would you implement? What do you think the chances are of your policies actually being put into place? Why?

VISUAL SOCIOLOGY: *GETTING TO SCHOOL*

Thierry Tronnel/Corbis

For many children around the world, just getting to school can be a challenge. These children and their families have taken refuge in Jordan to escape the violence of the civil war in Syria. The boys and girls in this picture attend a school run by UNICEF and the Jordanian government, and are returning to their temporary homes at the end of a school day. What are some of the structural forces that make it difficult for children to get an education? Visit **edge.sage pub.com/ballantine5e** for an interactive photo essay about transportation to school.

CONTRIBUTING TO OUR SOCIAL WORLD: *WHAT CAN WE DO?*

At the Local Level

- Some colleges and universities have established programs called *FIGs (First-Year Interest Groups)* to assist first-year students as they adjust to college and help them form a community with other students. Learn more about FIGs at schools such as the University of Wisconsin (http://figs.wisc.edu/), the University of Washington (http://fyp.washington.edu/figs/), and the University of Missouri (http://reslife.missouri.edu/fig/). If your school does not have a FIG program, try to initiate one.

- Every college and university provides opportunities for students to *tutor and mentor other students*. Ask the chair of your department or an office that coordinates mentoring how you can help!

At the Organizational or Institutional Level

- Most primary schools welcome *reading and math tutors,* volunteers, and service learning students who can read to young students and tutor them in reading and math. Contact a faculty member on your campus who specializes in early-childhood education and investigate the opportunities for such volunteer work.

- *Volunteers of America* (www.voa.org) chapters organize to provide low-income and homeless children with school supplies and backpacks every year through "Operation Backpack." You can learn more about the program and how to locate your local VOA chapter at the VOA website or by Googling "VOA" and "Operation Backpack" and the name of your state.

At the National and Global Levels

- *Teach for America* (www.teachforamerica.org), a national organization modeled along the lines of AmeriCorps and Peace Corps, places recent college graduates in short-term (approximately two-year) assignments teaching in economically disadvantaged neighborhood schools. "Teach for America is the national corps of outstanding recent college graduates and professionals of all academic majors and career interests who commit 2 years to teach in urban and rural public schools and become leaders in the effort to expand educational opportunity. . . . [Its] mission is to build the movement to eliminate educational inequity by enlisting our nation's most promising future leaders in the effort."

- *Teaching abroad* provides an opportunity to make a difference in the lives of children. Consider teaching English abroad through one of many organizations that sponsor teachers. Visit www.globaltesol.com, www.teachabroad.com, www.jetprogramme.org, and related websites.

©REUTERS/ Bazuki Muhammad

12 Religion

The Social Meaning of Sacred Meaning

Religion takes many forms and is expressed in many ways, but it is always about
a sense of meaning and purpose in life. That meaning and actions associated with
the meaning affect many aspects of daily life.

MICRO

ME (AND MY FAITH COMMUNITY)

LOCAL ORGANIZATIONS AND COMMUNITY

People find meaning and support in a local church, temple, or mosque.

MESO

NATIONAL ORGANIZATIONS, INSTITUTIONS, AND ETHNIC SUBCULTURES

Religious groups and denominations influence family life, government, education, and the economy.

MACRO

SOCIETY

Religious groups foster national social movements and influence the national culture.

GLOBAL COMMUNITY

Transnational religious organizations cross national borders and religious outreach programs span the globe.

IN THIS CHAPTER

- What Does Religion Do for Us?

- Becoming Part of a Faith Community: Micro-Level Analysis

- Religion and Modern Life: Meso-Level Analysis

- Religion in Society: Macro-Level Analysis

- Religion in the Modern World

- Social Policy: Same-Sex Marriage and Gay/Lesbian Clergy

THINK ABOUT IT

Micro: Local Community	How do various local religious congregations interact with the local community in your town?
Meso: National Institutions, Complex Organizations, and Ethnic Groups	How does the institutionalization of a religion help it survive? Why do ethnic groups often have specific religions or branches of religions?
Macro: National and Global Systems	How do religions foster solidarity and conflict within your country? How do religions help solve world problems (war, poverty, hunger, disease, bigotry) or help create them?

Abu Salmaan, a Muslim father and shopkeeper in Syria, prays frequently in keeping with the commands of the Quran, the holy book of his faith. Like his neighbors, when he hears the call to prayer, he goes to the village square, faces Mecca, and prostrates himself, with his head to the ground, to honor God and to pray for peace. Doing this five times a day is a constant reminder of his ultimate loyalty to God, whom he calls Allah. As part of the larger Abrahamic religious tradition (which includes Judaism, Christianity, and Islam), he believes in one God and accepts the Hebrew Bible and the authority of Jeremiah, Isaiah, Amos, and Jesus as prophets. He believes that God also revealed Truth through another voice—that of Muhammad. He is devoted, worshipping as commanded by the Quran, cherishing his family as directed by his scriptures, giving generously to charities, and making business decisions based on the moral standards of a God-loving Muslim.

Trevor Weaver is a Presbyterian living in Louisville, Kentucky. He attends church services most Sundays and prays to God in church and during emergencies, when he feels helpless. Trevor once took theological studies at a church-related college, and he has a strong knowledge of the scriptures. When he makes daily decisions, he thinks about the ethical implications of his behavior as "a member of the larger family of God." He opposes prayer in schools because he thinks this would make some children feel ostracized. He values diversity and acceptance of other traditions, and he believes people need to "work out their own theology."

Tuneq, knowledgeable Netsilik Eskimo hunter that he is, apologizes to the soul of the seal he has just killed. He shares the meat and blubber with his fellow hunters, and he makes sure that every part of the seal is used or consumed—skin, bones, eyes, tendons, brain, and muscles. His Inuit religion provides rules that help enforce an essential

ecological ethic among these arctic hunters to preserve the delicate natural balance. His faith has taught Tuneq that, if he fails to honor the seal by using every morsel or if he violates a rule of hunting etiquette, an invisible vapor will come from his body and sink through the ice, snow, and water. This vapor will collect in the hair of Nuliajuk, goddess of the sea. In revenge, she will call the sea mammals to her so the people living on the ice above will starve.

Before going to bed, Nandi Nwankwo from Nigeria sets out a bowl of milk and some food for the ancestors who, he believes, are present outside the family's dwelling at night. Respected ancestors protect family members, but they are also a powerful and even frightening force in guiding social behavior. Children learn that they must behave or the ancestors will punish them.

These are but a few examples from the world's many and varied religious systems. What they have in common is that each system provides directions for appropriate and expected behaviors and serves as a form of social control for individuals within that society. Religious sanctions that encourage conformity are strong. Indeed, they are made *sacred*, a realm of existence different from mundane everyday life. Religion, according to Andrew M. Greeley, the well-known Catholic priest and sociologist, pervades the lives of people of faith (Greeley 1989). It cannot be separated from the rest of the social world. Members of societies believe so strongly in their religions that conquests and wars throughout history have been based on spreading or defending the faith.

Sociologists are interested in these relationships—in the way social relationships and structures affect religion and in the consequences of religion for individuals and for society. In this chapter, we explore religion as a complex social phenomenon that interrelates with other processes and institutions of society. We investigate what religion does for individuals, how individuals become religious, how religion and modern societies interact, and what religious policies have to say about teen sexuality, gay rights, and other social issues.

WHAT DOES RELIGION DO FOR US?

What do people have to gain from religious practices, beliefs, and organizations? Religion helps explain the meaning of life, death, suffering, injustice, and events beyond our control. As sociologist Émile Durkheim pointed out, humans generally view such questions as belonging to a realm of existence different from the mundane or profane world of our everyday experience (Durkheim [1915] 2002). He called this separate dimension the *sacred realm*. This sacred realm elicits feelings of awe, reverence, and even fear. It is viewed as being above normal inquiry and doubt. Religious guidelines, beliefs, and values dictate "rights and wrongs," provide answers to the big questions of life, and instill moral codes and ideas about the world in members of each society or subculture. For these reasons, religions can have enormous control over people's attitudes and behavior (Ammerman 2009; Durkheim [1915] 2002).

Religion is more than a set of beliefs about the supernatural. It often *sacralizes* (makes sacred and unquestionable) the culture in which we live, the class or caste position to which we belong, the attitudes we hold toward other people, and the morals to which we adhere. Religion impacts our lifestyles, gender roles, and social status. Around the world, billions of people believe that they have found the Truth—the ultimate answers—in their religions. Many are willing to die for their faith.

Note the various wars between Hindus and Muslims in India and Pakistan, between Catholics and Protestants in Northern Ireland, or between the two Muslim sects of Sunni and Shi'ite in several Muslim countries. Although the root causes of these wars are political and economic, religious differences help polarize "us" versus "them" sentiments. Religion can convince the members of each group that God is on their side.

Thinking Sociologically

Consider your own religious tradition. Which of the purposes or functions of religion mentioned earlier does your religious faith address? If you are not part of a faith community or do not hold religious beliefs of a particular group, are there other beliefs or groups that fulfill these functions for you?

Components of Religion

Religion normally involves at least three components: (1) a faith or worldview that provides a sense of meaning and purpose in life (which we will call the *meaning system*), (2) a set of interpersonal relationships and friendship networks (which we will call the *belonging system*), and (3) a stable pattern of roles, statuses, and organizational practices (which we will call the *structural system*) (Roberts and Yamane 2012).

The meaning system operates mostly at the micro level; the belonging system is also critical at the micro level but part of various meso-level organizations as well; and the structural system tends to have its major impact at the meso and macro levels. These components of religion may reinforce one another and work in harmony toward common goals, or there may be conflict among them.

Meaning System. The *meaning system* of a religion includes the ideas and symbols it uses to provide a sense of

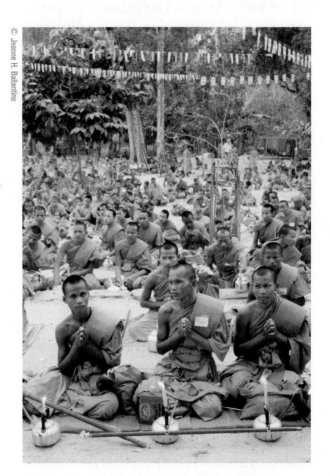

© Jeanne H. Ballantine

Buddhist monks pray at Bayon Temple in Angkor Thom, Cambodia. Their religious system not only gives them a sense of meaning and purpose in life but also provides social ties.

Stories of Faith

The Bat Mitzvah, shown here, is an initiation ceremony into the faith for Jewish girls.

purpose in life and to help explain why suffering, injustice, and evil exist. It provides a big picture to account for events that would otherwise seem chaotic and irrational. For example, although the loss of a family member through death may be painful, many people find comfort and hope in their religion's teachings on the meaning of life and death.

Meaning systems of religion reflect the needs of the societies in which the religion is practiced. Because each culture has different problems to solve, the precise needs reflected in each society's meaning system vary. In agricultural societies, the problems revolve around growing crops and securing the elements necessary for crops—water, sunlight, and good soil. Among the Zuni of New Mexico and the Hopi of Arizona, for example, water for crops is a critical concern. These Native American people typically grow corn in a climate that averages roughly 10 inches of rain per year, so it is not surprising that the central focus of their religious dances and of their supernatural beings—*kachinas*—is to bring rain. In other societies, the death rate is so high that high fertility has been necessary to perpetuate the group. Thus, fertility goddesses take on great significance. In some other societies, strong armies and brave soldiers have been essential to preserve the group from invading forces; hence, gods or rituals of war have been popular.

Belonging System. *Belonging systems* are profoundly important in most religious groups. A belonging system refers to the interpersonal networks and emotional ties that develop among adherents of a particular faith. Many people remain members of religious groups not so much

because they accept the meaning system of the group but because that is where they find their belonging system— their friendship and kinship network. A prayer group may be the one area in their lives in which people can be truly open about their personal pain and feel safe to expose their vulnerabilities. This builds bonds and belonging. For many religious people, their religious group is a type of extended family that tends to become more important as their own families age. The religious groups that have grown the fastest in recent years are those that have devised ways to strengthen the sense of belonging and to foster friendship networks within the group.

Structural System. A religion involves a group of people who share a common meaning system. However, if each person interprets the group's beliefs in his or her own way and if each attaches his or her own meanings to the symbols, the meaning system becomes so individualized that *sacralization* of common values can no longer occur. Therefore, almost all religions (the Unitarian Universalist religion is an exception) have developed a system of control and screening of new revelations. Religious leaders in designated statuses have the authority to interpret theology and define the essentials of the faith.

Religious groups also need methods of designating leaders, raising funds to support their organizations, and ensuring continuation of the group. To teach the next generation the meaning system, members need to develop a formal structure to determine the content and form of their educational materials, and then they must produce and distribute them. If the religion is to survive past the death of a charismatic leader, it must undergo institutionalization. In other words, it must establish a *structural system* of established statuses, norms, ways to access resources, and routine procedures for addressing problems.

Because religion is one institution in the larger society, it is interdependent and interrelated with the political, economic, family, education, health, and information systems. Changes in any one of these areas can bring change to religion, and changes in religion can bring changes to other institutions of society. Consider the furor in parts of the United States over the decision of some school districts to teach "intelligent design," creationism alongside evolution, as part of the science curriculum in public schools. The conflict reverberates in congregations, schools, legislative chambers, courts, and scientific communities.

Although some people dislike the idea of organized religion, one insight of sociology is that a group cannot

Benefits of Religion

survive in the modern world unless it undergoes *routinization of charisma*. That is, religious organizations must develop established roles, statuses, groups, and routine procedures for making decisions and obtaining resources in order to survive more than a generation (Weber 1947).

At the local level, a formal religious structure develops, with committees doing specific tasks, such as overseeing worship, maintaining the building, recruiting religious educators, and raising funds. These committees report to an administrative board that works closely with the clergy (the ordained ministers) and has much of the final responsibility for the life and continued existence of the people who regularly gather for religious services, referred to as the *congregation*. The roles, statuses, and committees make up the structural system. The structure is every bit as important as the meaning system if the group is to thrive.

Like any other formal organization in society, meso-level religious structures consist of individuals and committees doing specialized tasks. Contemporary branches of Christianity in the United States, for example, may have national commissions on global outreach, evangelism, worship, world peace, social justice, and so forth. In addition, bishops, presbyters, or other leaders provide guidelines for pastors who lead their own congregations. Most religious organizations are, among other things, bureaucracies. The formal organization may be caught up in some of the dysfunctions that can plague any organization: goal displacement, the iron law of oligarchy, alienation, and other problems discussed in Chapter 5.

Just as any organization needs data on its effectiveness, religious organizations collect information to help inform policy. "Sociologists in Action" on page 382 describes the work of a sociologist who does research within such a denominational structure.

The three components of religion—meaning, belonging, and structure—are interconnected and interdependent. One member of a faith community may be committed to the meaning system, another to the belonging system through strong friendship networks, and a third to the structural system, making large financial donations to a congregation even though he or she rarely attends services. In most cases, however, commitment to one of these systems will reinforce commitment to the others. They usually go together. (See Figure 12.1.)

FIGURE 12.1   Three Components of Religion

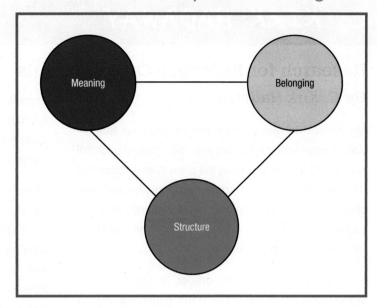

Thinking Sociologically

Think about the meaning, belonging, and structural systems of a religion with which you are familiar. How do these elements influence—and how are they influenced by—the larger social world, from individual to national and global systems?

BECOMING PART OF A FAITH COMMUNITY: MICRO-LEVEL ANALYSIS

We are not born religious, although we may be born into a religious group. We learn our religious beliefs through socialization, just as we learn our language, customs, norms, and values. Our family usually determines the religious environment in which we grow up, whether it is an all-encompassing message or closer to a one-day-a-week commitment. We start imitating religious practices, such as praying before bed or saying grace before dinner, before we understand these practices intellectually. Then, as we encounter the unexplainable events of life, religion is there to provide meaning. Gradually, religion becomes an ingrained part of many people's lives.

It is unlikely that we will adopt a faith not practiced in our society. For instance, if we were born in most parts of India, we would be raised in and around the Hindu, Muslim, or Sikh faiths. In most Arab countries, we would become Muslim; in South American countries, we would

SOCIOLOGISTS IN ACTION:
C. KIRK HADAWAY

Research for Religious Organizations

By C. Kirk Hadaway

My interest in research on and for religious institutions began when I worked with my graduate school mentor on a grant studying the growth and decline of denominations. I explored demographic change and church growth, denominational switching, and the impact of new church development on the growth of established denominations.

I am a church research officer, a position that entails everything from mundane gathering of statistics to serious social research. Our office of six persons collects membership, attendance, and giving data from all United Church of Christ (UCC) churches and analyzes those data. We do surveys among our churches, pastors, staff, and lay leaders on a wide variety of topics (issues related to congregational health, leadership, use of denominational resources, beliefs and attitudes, and so forth). I also conduct research on the state of religion/churches in modern society and on social trends that might impact our churches. We communicate the results of this research in reports and books that give advice to our churches and pastors.

I speak to clergy groups regularly on related topics. My clients get an interpretation of data based on a broad, sociologically grounded understanding of religious trends.

I have studied church trends (patterns of growth and decline) using data from local congregations and studies of religious participation and religious marginality. Also, I have conducted large-scale surveys with pastors from several denominations as key informants. It is particularly gratifying to see theories confirmed with real data on real churches. I find helping church leaders see their situation from a different, sociological, perspective, and using that perspective to make a positive difference in their work, the most rewarding aspect of my job.

• •

Dr. C. Kirk Hadaway received his PhD in sociology from the University of Massachusetts, Amherst. He has worked for various boards and agencies of the Southern Baptist Convention, has been director of research at the United Church of Christ, and is currently director of research for the Episcopal Church.

likely become Catholic or evangelical Christian; and in many Southeast Asian countries, Buddhist. Although our religious affiliation may seem normal and typical to us, no religion has a majority of the people in the world as its adherents, and we may in fact be part of a rather small minority religious group when we think in terms of the global population. Table 12.1 shows this explicitly.

Learning the meaning system of a religious group is both a formal and an informal process. In some cultures, religious faith pervades everyday life. For the Amish, farming without machines or the use of electricity is part of their Christian teachings, which affect their total lifestyle.

Formal teaching in most religions takes place primarily in the temple, church, or mosque. The formal teaching may take the form of Bar or Bat Mitzvah classes, Sunday school, or parochial school. Informal religious teaching occurs when we observe others "practicing what they preach."

Again, the meaning (believing) and belonging systems are linked in important ways. Most people do not belong to a religious group because they accept its belief system, at least initially. Rather, they come to believe because they want to belong and are socialized to feel they are an integral part of the group (Greeley 1972; Roberts and Yamane 2012). Research on people who switch religious affiliations or join new religious movements (NRMs) indicates that loyalty to a friendship network usually comes first, followed by commitment to the meaning and structural systems. In many cases, accepting a new meaning system is the final stage rather than the initial stage of change (Roberts and Yamane 2012).

There is more fluidity in religious membership now than at any other time in history. Historically, most people remained part of the same religious group for a lifetime. Current studies show that 28% of U.S. citizens have either left the religious group in which they were raised for another religion or no longer have any religious affiliation (Pew Forum on Religion and Public Life 2012b). Increase in interreligious marriages plays a role in changing religions, as 37% of current marriages involve spouses with different religious affiliations. Most often, the change is to a different branch of the same umbrella religion (e.g., from one form of Christianity to another) (Pew Forum on Religion and Public Life 2012b).

Because changing religious groups occurs most often through change of friendship networks or marriage, religious groups frequently try to control the boundaries and protect their members from outside influences. The Amish in the United States have done this by living in their own communities and attempting to limit schooling of their children by outside authorities. To help perpetuate religious beliefs and practices, most religious groups encourage *endogamy*, marrying within the group. For example, Orthodox Jews have food taboos and food preparation requirements that limit the likelihood that they will share a meal with "outsiders." In order to have a wedding in the Catholic Church, Catholics who want to marry a non-Catholic must receive permission from their local bishop to marry "despite the disparity of cult" between them.

Religious groups also try to socialize members to make sacrifices of time, energy, and financial resources on behalf of their faith. If one has sacrificed and devoted one's resources and energy for a cause, one is likely to feel a commitment to the organization—the structural system (Kanter 2005; Sherkat and Ellison 1999). Single young people in their late teens and early twenties who are members of the Church of Jesus Christ of Latter-Day Saints (Mormons) are strongly encouraged to devote two years of their lives to missionary work. They must save money in advance to support themselves. This sacrifice of other opportunities and investment of time, energy, and resources in the church creates an intense commitment to the organization. Few of them later feel that they wasted those years or that the investment was unwise. So, commitment to the structural

Table 12.1 Religious Membership Around the Globe

Religion	Membership (in millions)	Percentage of World Population
Christian (Total)	2,319.8	33.1
Roman Catholic	1,200.9	17.0
Protestant	430.6	6.0
Independent	356.7	5.0
Orthodox	277.6	3.8
Unaffiliated	110.1	1.6
Muslim	1,609.2	22.9
Hindu	967.2	13.8
Nonreligious	679.0	9.7
Buddhist	504.8	7.2
Chinese Folk Religions	437.1	6.2
Other Ethnoreligions	247.5	3.5
Atheist	136.3	1.9
Sikh	24.8	0.4
Jewish	15.0	0.2
Spiritist	13.7	0.2
Taoist	8.5	0.1
Confucianist	8.2	0.1
Baha'i	7.5	0.1
Jain	5.5	0.1
Shintoist	2.8	a
Zoroastrian	0.2	a

Source: World Almanac (2014). "World Adherents of Religions by Continental Area 2012." New York: World Almanac Books: 701.

Note: Numbers add up to more than the total world population because some people identify themselves with more than one religious tradition. Thus, the percentages will also add up to more than 100%. Percentages are rounded.

a = Less than 0.05%.

An Amish family enjoys a trip to the beach. Amish faith influences every aspect of their lives, including their beach attire.

system is connected to strong commitment to the meaning and belonging systems.

The survival of a religious group depends in part on how committed its members are and whether they share freely of their financial and time resources. Most religious groups try, therefore, to socialize their members into commitment to the meaning system, the belonging system, and the structural system of their religion.

Thinking Sociologically

How did you or individuals you know become committed to a faith tradition? Did you (or they) think about the process as it occurred, or were you (or they) born into it? If you left a religious organization, why did you leave?

Symbols and the Creation of Meaning: A Symbolic Interactionist Perspective

Dina is appalled as she walks passed the Laundromat. The *gaje* (the term Roma use to refer to non-Roma) just do not seem to understand cleanliness. These middle-class North American neighbors of hers are very concerned about whether their clothes are *melalo*—dirty with dirt. In contrast, they pay no attention to whether they are *marime*—defiled or polluted in a spiritual sense. She watches in disgust as a woman not only places the clothing of men, women, and children in a single washing machine but also includes clothing from the upper and lower halves of the body together. No respectable Roma (sometimes called Gypsies by outsiders) would allow such mixing, and if it did occur, the cloth could be used only as rags. The laws of spiritual purity make clear that the lower half of the body is defiled. Anything that comes in contact with the body below the waist or that touches the floor becomes *marime* and can never again be considered *wuzho*—truly "clean." Food that touches the floor becomes filthy and inedible.

Ideally, a Roma woman would have separate washtubs for men's upper-body clothing, men's lower-body clothing, women's upper-body clothing, women's lower-body clothing, and children's clothing. Roma know too well that the spirit of Mamioro brings illness to homes that are *marime*. The lack of spiritual cleanliness of non-Roma causes Roma to minimize their contact with these *gaje*, to avoid sitting on a chair used by a *gaje*, and generally to recoil at the thought of assimilation into the larger culture (Sutherland 1986, 2001; Sway 1988).

How we make sense of the world takes place through meaning systems, as illustrated in the preceding example. Roma interpret objects and actions in ways that differ from members of the larger society, and the different meanings result in different behaviors and sometimes distancing from "outsiders."

Symbolic interaction theory focuses on how we make sense of and construct our worlds. When we see religious symbols, we react to them based on our experiences with and understanding of the religion they symbolize. Think about how you feel attracted to, or perhaps put off by, someone who wears a cross or another religious symbol, such as a yarmulke, worn by Orthodox Jewish men to cover the crown of the head, or a head scarf worn by Muslim women. Symbols affect micro-level interaction—the way we feel about people and whether we are inclined to form a relationship.

It is the meaning system that most interests symbolic interactionists—the worldview or conceptual framework by which people make sense of life and cope with suffering and injustice. Religious meaning systems are made up of three elements: myths, rituals, and symbols.

Myths are *stories that transmit values and embody ideas about life and the world*. When sociologists of religion use the word *myth*, they are not implying that the story is untrue. A myth may relate historical incidents that actually occurred, fictional events, or abstract ideas, such as reincarnation. Regardless of the literal truth or fiction of these stories, myths transmit values and a particular outlook on life. If a story, such as the Exodus from Egypt of ancient Hebrew people, elicits some sense of sacredness, communicates certain attitudes and values, and helps make sense of life, then it is a myth. The Netsilik Eskimo myth of the sea goddess Nuliajuk (explained in the third story that opened this chapter) reinforces and makes sacred the value of conservation in an environment of scarce resources. It provides messages for appropriate behavior in that group. Thus, whether a myth is factual or not is irrelevant. Myths are always "true" in some deeper metaphorical sense. Indeed, stories that do not carry truth or deep meaning are simply not "myths."

Rituals are *ceremonies or repetitive practices, often used to invoke a sense of awe of the divine and to make certain ideas sacred.* Ceremonies may include music, dancing, kneeling, praying, chanting, storytelling, and other symbolic acts. A number of religions, such as Islam, emphasize devotion to orthopraxy (conformity of behavior) more than to orthodoxy (conformity to beliefs or doctrine) (Preston 1988; Tipton 1990). Praying five times a day while facing Mecca, mandated for the Islamic faithful, is an example of orthopraxy.

Often, rituals involve acting out myths. In almost all Christian churches, the cleansing of the soul is enacted by immersing people in water or pouring water on the head during baptism. Likewise, Christians frequently reenact the last supper of Jesus (Communion or Eucharist) as they accept their role as modern disciples. Among the Navajo, rituals enacted by a medicine man may last as long as five days. An appropriate myth is told, and sand paintings, music, and dramatics lend power and unique reality to the myths.

The group environment of the ritual is important. Ethereal music, communal chants, and group actions such as kneeling or taking off one's shoes when entering the shrine or mosque create an aura of separation from the everyday world and a mood of awe so that the beliefs seem eternal and beyond question. They become sacralized. Rituals also make ample use of symbols.

As you will recall from earlier chapters, a **symbol** is an *object or an action that represents something else and therefore has meaning beyond its own existence* (e.g., flags and wedding rings). Because religion deals with the transcendent—a realm that cannot be experienced or proven with the five senses—sacred symbols are a central part of religion. They have a powerful emotional impact on the faithful and reinforce the sacredness of myths.

Sacred symbols store an enormous amount of information and can deliver that information with powerful

A Romanian Roma woman uses different tubs to wash upper- and lower-body clothing and men's and women's apparel separately so that they will not become spiritually defiled.

Removal of shoes before entering a mosque is a ritual expression of respect for the sacred among Muslims. Hundreds of Iraqi Shi'ite Muslim pilgrims have arrived to pray at this mosque in northern Baghdad.

▶ Religious Rituals

immediacy. Seeing a cross, for example, can flood a Christian's consciousness with a whole series of images, events, and powerful emotions concerning Jesus and his disciples. Tasting the bitter herbs during a Jewish Seder service is meant to elicit memories of the story of slavery in Egypt, recall the escape under the leadership of Moses, and send a moral message to the celebrant to work for freedom and justice in the world today. The mezuzah, a plaque consecrating a house, fixed to the doorpost of a Jewish home, is a symbol reminding the occupants of their commitment to obey God's commandments and reaffirming God's commitment to them as a people. Because symbols are often heavily laden with emotion and can elicit strong feelings, they are used extensively in rituals to represent myths.

Myths, rituals, and symbols are usually interrelated and interdependent (see Figure 12.2). Together, they form the meaning system—a set of ideas about life or about the cosmos that seem uniquely realistic and compelling. They reinforce rules of appropriate behavior and even political and economic systems by making them sacred. They can also control social relationships among different groups.

The Roma revulsion at the filthy *marime* practices of middle-class Americans, like the Kosher rules for food preparation among the Jews, creates boundaries between "us" and "them" that nearly eliminate prospects of marriage or even of close friendships outside the religious community. Some scholars think that these rituals and symbolic meanings are the key reason why Roma and Jews have survived for millennia as distinct groups without being assimilated or absorbed into dominant cultures. The symbols and meanings have created barriers that prevent the obliteration of their cultures.

When symbolic interactionists study religion, they tend to focus on how symbols influence people's perception of reality. Symbolic interactionists stress that humans create, shape, and interpret the meaning of events. Clearly, no other institution focuses as explicitly on shaping and interpreting the meaning of life and its events as religion.

 Thinking Sociologically

In a religious tradition with which you are familiar, how do symbols and sacred stories reinforce a particular view of the world or a particular set of values and social norms?

FIGURE 12.2 The Meaning System of Religion Is Composed of Three Interrelated Elements

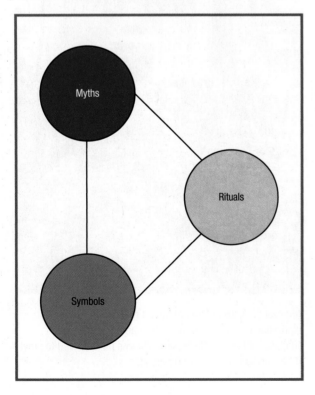

Seeking Eternal Benefits: A Rational Choice Perspective

Rational choice theorists maintain that people decide whether or not they should join or leave a religious group by asking, "What are the benefits, and what are the costs? Do the benefits outweigh the costs?" The benefits, of course, are nonmaterial when it comes to religious choices—feeling that life has meaning, belonging to a community, gaining a sense of communion with God, confidence in an afterlife, and so forth (Finke and Stark 2005; Warner 1993).

The rational choice approach views churchgoers as consumers out to meet their needs or obtain a "product." It depicts churches as entrepreneurial establishments, or "franchises," in a competitive market, with "entrepreneurs" (clergy) as leaders. Competition for members leads churches, for example, to "market" their religion to consumers. Converts, and religious people generally, are regarded as active and rational agents pursuing self-interests. In order to grow, churches must meet "consumer demand" (Finke and Stark 2005; Jelen 2002). Religious groups produce religious "commodities" (rituals, meaning systems, a sense of belonging, symbols, and so forth) to meet the "demands" of consumers (Christiano, Swatos, and Kivisto 2008).

Rational choice theorists believe that aggressive religious entrepreneurs who seek to produce religious products appealing to a target audience will reap the benefits of a large congregation. Competitive enterprises, churches, temples, and mosques must make investments of effort, time, and resources to attract and keep potential buyers. There are many religious entrepreneurs seeking to increase the number of people in their congregations. The challenge for the various groups is to beat the competition by meeting the demand of the current marketplace (Finke and Stark 2005). For instance, because the U.S. Constitution separates church from state, organized religions had to offer their product on an open market, in competition with other religions. This prompted most religions in the United States to put much energy into recruiting more followers. Rational choice theorists note that where religion is an ascribed identity (adopted based on one's family of birth or the country's official religion), it is likely to be much less vigorous than in places where there is a competitive religious marketplace and religion is an achieved identity chosen freely from many options (Finke and Stark 2005; Iannaccone and Bainbridge 2010). Competition for the hearts and minds of members stimulates concern about spiritual matters and commitment to religion. Religious pluralism and spiritual diversity increase the rates of religious activity as each group seeks to increase its market share and meet the needs of individuals in the society (Finke and Stark 2005; Iannaccone and Bainbridge 2010).

Not everyone agrees that religion is a competitive enterprise. This strictly utilitarian economic analysis of religion seems counter to the way most religious people understand their own behavior. As one religious scholar put it,

> *It is one thing to describe a person's decision to join a church as if the person were trying to maximize his or her benefits; it is something different to claim that the person's actual thought in joining measured his or her potential gains against potential losses. (McGuire 2002:298–99)*

While costs and benefits may exist, people may not consciously measure them when determining whether to join a religious organization.

Thinking Sociologically

Does the rational choice explanation for religious behavior seem correct to you? Why? Is religious behavior similar to self-interested economic behavior? Why or why not?

RELIGION AND MODERN LIFE: MESO-LEVEL ANALYSIS

Cassandra is a chaplain at a hospital in Minneapolis. She works closely with doctors and other professionals in health care who value her work. Many of the physicians at her hospital are convinced that when people have emotional support, feel a sense of love and connection, and have hope for the future, they are more likely to improve their health. Cassandra prays for the people she counsels, but she also is convinced that God often works through science and modern medicine. The clergy and medical professionals collaborate as a team to help people either recover from ill health or face death with dignity.

We begin this meso-level discussion by exploring various types of religious organizations and then examining how religion as an institution interacts with other institutions. As you will see, different religions structure themselves in various ways. All, though, interact with the other social institutions in society.

Types of Religious Organizations

The unique history of religious organizations in the United States led Andrew Greeley to describe the country as a "denominational society" (1972). In doing so, though, he stressed the heterogeneity among religious denominations in the American colonies and then the United States.

© O'Rourke, Skip/ZUMA Press/Corbis

Chaplains, members of the religious institution, often work closely with professionals in another institution—health care. Here we see a hospital chaplain at work.

The country is religiously diverse in two senses: multiple religious groups living side by side with no single faith tradition being dominant, and church and state given their own autonomous realms by the U.S. Constitution (Stark and Finke 2000).

Denominations and Denominationalism.

In the United States and most other Western countries, local congregations tend to be part of larger centralized organizations. These *centralized coordinating bodies or associations that link local congregations with a similar history and theology* are called **denominations**.

In the long history of human society, denominationalism is a unique and rather recent way of organizing religion (Ammerman 2006). For most of human history, religion was diffused through all of life. Under these conditions, religion and the rest of life have been seamless and undifferentiated (Bellah 1970). Over time, religion gradually became distinct from other social institutions in most Western societies, particularly in the political or governmental structures. The result is that specifically religious organizations arose.

Initially, a single religious organization dominated a particular geographic area. For several centuries, the Roman Catholic Church was the dominant religious group in Europe. Eventually, however, the religious sphere itself came to be diverse, as various groups within the Catholic Church developed distinct missions (the Dominicans, the Jesuits, and so forth). It became more distinct when the Reformation Era (1517–1648) launched Protestantism and brought about the emergence of different, oppositional, Christian groups with different beliefs and organizational structures. Most of them were splinter groups that broke away from Catholicism, such as the Lutherans (Gorski 2000).

Each religious group attempted to become the official and government-approved church in its territory. Conflict rather than peaceful coexistence came to characterize Europe, and many people were forced to flee the lands in which they were raised because of their faith.

Some of those driven out of Europe for religious reasons were followers of the Calvinist Puritan movement seeking to reform the Church of England, a church that split from the Catholic Church in 1534 largely because King Henry VIII wanted to legitimize a divorce. The Puritans ended up playing a major role in the founding of the New England colonies and, in so doing, created religious establishments of their own. Four of the colonies (Rhode Island, Delaware, New Jersey, and Pennsylvania) were quite religiously diverse and had no state-sponsored church. As a result, no single religious group established dominance or control in North America. This development led to necessary peaceful coexistence: religious pluralism and official separation of church and state.

Freedom of religion and prohibition of a state-endorsed church are key conditions for denominationalism. When scholars refer to the United States as a "denominational society," they mean a society characterized by religious congregations united into denominations presumed equal under the law and that generally treat other religious bodies with an attitude of mutual respect (Greeley 1972). As a consequence of this organizational pattern of religious pluralism, there are hundreds of denominations in the United States (Mead, Hill, and Atwood 2005). Indeed, the *Handbook of Denominations in the United States* lists 31 different Baptist denominations alone (Mead et al. 2005). Denominationalism has become a global phenomenon. The *World Christian Encyclopedia* reports 33,830 denominations within Christianity worldwide (Barrett, Kurian, and Johnson 2001; Roberts and Yamane 2012).

Although diversity within Protestantism was a key force for denominationalism, it has become fully incorporated by all major religious groups in the United States. Some scholars have even identified Jewish "denominationalism" in reference to the four branches of Judaism—Orthodox, Conservative, Reform, and Reconstructionist (Lazerwitz et al. 1998). The Nation of Islam and American Society of Muslims are distinctively American Islamic denominations (though the former is often viewed negatively by traditional Muslims). There are also denominations of Islam that are more global (Sunni and Shi'ite are the largest). Buddhism and Hinduism also have different branches or schools, though; like Islam, they were brought to America in large numbers only recently, so it remains to be seen whether there will be an evolution of those branches into recognizable denominations.

Denominational Structures and the Micro-Meso Connection.

The organizational structures of denominations vary. Most, however, are congregational, episcopal, or presbyterian (Ammerman 2006; Roberts and Yamane 2012). Note that these are *not* the same as churches by those names, but rather the organizational structure (or "polity") of a number of churches.

In a *congregational* polity or structure, the authority of the local congregation is supreme. For example, the thousands of Baptist and United Church of Christ congregations in the United States hire and fire their own ministers, control their own finances, own their own property, decide whether to ordain women, and make other decisions about the congregation themselves (Ammerman 1990, 2009).

The *episcopal*—also called "hierarchical"—pattern of governance places ultimate authority over local churches in the centralized hands of bishops (the word *episcopal* means "governed by bishops"). Each of the Roman Catholic Church's nearly 20,000 U.S. congregations (or "parishes") is geographically defined. They are clustered into a "diocese" under the authority of the local bishop and, ultimately, the Bishop of Rome—the pope. In an episcopal structure, a bishop, in consultation with his or her executive staff, decides who will be the priest or minister of the local church. A committee of the local congregation may be consulted, but the bishop has the final say. Christian churches that have some form of episcopal organization include Anglican, Episcopalian, Eastern Orthodox, Methodist, African Methodist Episcopal (AME), AME Zion, and some Lutherans. So, the local United Methodist church building in your community is actually owned by the larger denomination and

only maintained by the local congregation, and a bishop decides who will be the minister for the community.

Presbyterian polity, quite simply, is a middle ground between episcopal (with a bishop having tremendous power) and congregational (where the congregation has total authority). In presbyterian polity, authority is shared so that neither a single local congregation nor the hierarchy can trump the other. The Presbyterian Church is the best example of this compromise position. Presbyterian structure usually involves a local board in a congregation that can make decisions—called Sessions. There are also organizations composed of groups of congregations at regional and national levels that, in order of regional to national, are typically called Presbyteries, Synods, and then the National Assembly. Almost all Reformed churches use this approach: Dutch Reformed, Swiss Reformed, and the Presbyterian Church, which is an offshoot of the Scottish Reformed tradition. Table 12.2 provides some examples of which churches tend to follow which polity.

Table 12.2 Polity or Organizational Structures of Selected Churches

Episcopal Polity	Presbyterian Polity	Congregational Polity
Roman Catholic Church	Reformed Churches	United Church of Christ (Congregationalists)
Episcopal Church	Dutch Reformed	National Baptist
Anglican Church	Swiss Reformed	Southern Baptist
United Methodist	French Reformed	Christian Church (Disciples of Christ)
African Methodist Episcopal	Church of Scotland	Churches of Christ
Evangelical Lutheran	Presbyterian Church USA	Unitarian Universalists

One cannot tell by looking at these buildings, but the organizational structure to which each belongs is quite different. The Methodist church on the left is episcopal in structure; the Presbyterian church in the center has a presbyterian organization; and the Congregational church on the right is congregational in structure.

sociology in our social world

Islam, Mosques, and Organizational Structure

Most mosques in the United States are relatively new, with almost all founded after 1970. Since, 2000, the number of mosques has increased 74%. At the turn of the century, there were 1,209 mosques in the United States, and by 2010 there were 2,106 (Grossman 2012a).

According to the Islamic scholar Ihsan Bagby, "most of the world's mosques are simply a place to pray. . . . A Muslim cannot be a member of a particular mosque" because mosques belong to God, not to the people (Bagby 2003:115). In some countries, mosques are government supported. The role of the imam—the leader of a mosque—is simply to lead prayers five times a day and to run the services on the Sabbath, including delivery of a sermon. Unlike many Christian and Jewish leaders in the United States, an imam does not run an organization and does not need formal training at a seminary. Mosques in the United States cannot depend on government funding and need to adapt to the congregational model: recruiting members who will support it. Many have constructed buildings with multiple meeting spaces, which became community centers rather than simply a place to pray. They have also begun to put more emphasis on religious education (which had

been managed largely by extended families). Religious holidays are celebrated at the mosque rather than with families, and life cycle celebrations (births and marriages) are events for the congregation. This is a major change in the role of the mosque and the imam for many Muslims.

Mosques in the United States tend to be attended primarily by immigrants or African Americans. African American mosques represent only 27% of the total number of mosques, and these are in some important ways different in organizational structure from those attended by immigrants. Most important, 93% of African American mosques are led by an imam, compared with only 38% of immigrant-attended mosques.

Just 33% of all mosques in the United States have a paid, full-time imam, and only 13% of imams have a master's degree in theology, which is the standard expected for most mainstream Christian and Jewish clergy. So despite having exceptionally high levels of well-educated members in professional and managerial positions, Islamic mosques are less bureaucratized, with less emphasis on professional credentials, membership roles, or denominational connections. Mosques have already made some adjustments to U.S. society, however, and will likely assimilate further to the religious organizational patterns of the larger society.

While denominational structure or polity strongly affects the structure of a local congregation and how it works, the social environment can also cause a certain amount of adaptation. The tendency to assimilate to the organizational patterns in the social environment impacts religious groups as much as it does individuals, as shown "Sociology in Our Social World."

New Religious Movements (NRMs) or Cults. New religious movements, or NRMs, *arise to meet specific needs* *not met through traditional religious organizations. If NRMs survive for several generations, become established, and gain some legitimacy, they become new religions rather than a new denomination of an existing faith. Cult* was once the common term for this kind of movement, but the media and the public have so completely misused the word that its meaning has become unclear and often negative. The term *cult*, as sociologists have historically used it, is simply descriptive, not judging the group as good, bad, or kooky. Most sociologists of religion now prefer to use the term *NRM* to describe these religious forms (Christiano et al. 2008).

NRMs are either imported into a country as immigrants enter from other lands or founded on a new revelation (or insight, often directly from God) by a charismatic leader. They are usually out of the mainstream religious system, at least in their early days. Christianity, Buddhism, and Islam all began as NRMs or cults. The estimated number of NRMs in North America at the turn of the century was between 1,500 and 2,000 (Melton et al. 2009; Nichols, Mather, and Schmidt 2006). There are an estimated 10,000 more NRMs in Africa and perhaps tens of thousands worldwide (Religious Worlds 2007). An NRM usually originates with a charismatic leader, someone who claims to have received a new insight, usually straight from God. For example, Reverend Sun Myung Moon founded an NRM called the Unification Church, the members of which are often referred to as *Moonies*. While claiming to be a part of Christianity, the Unification Church has its own additional scripture to complement the Bible, and Reverend Moon has a standing in the Unification Church equal to Jesus—an idea offensive to most Christian groups.

Some sensational NRMs have ended in tragedy: In 1978, Reverend Jim Jones led his devoted followers to a retreat in Guyana, South America, and ultimately directed them to commit mass suicide, in the belief that heaven was awaiting them (Lacayo 1993; Wright 1995). In 1997, the members of the Heaven's Gate NRM also committed group suicide. They believed supernatural beings were coming to take them away in a flying saucer and that they had to kill themselves so that their souls could board the spaceship (Wessinger 2000).

Most new religious groups, however, are not dangerous to members. Furthermore, most religious groups now accepted and established were stigmatized as strange or evil when they started. Early Christians, for example, were characterized by Romans as dangerous cannibals. In the 19th century and early decades of the 20th century in the United States, Roman Catholics were depicted in the media as dangerous, immoral, and anti-American (Bromley and Shupe 1981). When we encounter media reports about NRMs, we should remember that not all cults are like the sensational ones.

NRMs tend to be hard to study because the members feel they might be persecuted for their faith and beliefs. Witchcraft (or Wicca) is one example of a religion forced to remain secretive; the next "Sociology in Our Social World" on page 392 explores the strategies of one sociologist to examine this religious community.

 Thinking Sociologically

What factors might lead to the birth of an NRM? Imagine the leaders of an NRM have asked you for advice on how they might succeed. What advice would you give them?

Religion and Other Social Institutions

The dominant religion(s) in any society generally supports the dominant political system and ideology of the society. It also closely relates to the economic and education systems and legitimates the family system through sacred rites of passage for marriage, birth, and death. Religion interacts with the health system, as well. Some religions establish rules related to health care. Also, those who regularly attend religious services are healthier (and happier) than those who do not (Newport 2012f).

Religion not only supports other institutions but may also experience support or pressure from these other institutions. The Catholic Church, for example, has faced increasing criticism from international organizations, political movements, governments, religious groups, and educational institutions for its ban on artificial birth control. Due to AIDS and rapid population growth, especially in poor Catholic nations, many interested parties have encouraged the Catholic Church to ease its strict ban on artificial birth control. In 2010, faced with mounting pressures and high death rates in Africa, Pope Benedict XVI indicated some openness to accepting the use of condoms among married couples to prevent the spread of AIDS (*Pope Condones Condom Use* 2010). If the church does not change and adapt with the times, it must expend considerable effort to defend its position in order to keep from losing credibility in the eyes of members and nonmembers alike. We now consider the relationship between religion and three other social institutions: family, politics, and economics.

Religion and Family. Our parents provide our first contact with religion. They may say prayers, attend worship services, and talk about proper behavior as defined by their religious group. Many religions recognize Mother's Day,

sociology in our social world

Witchcraft in the United States

Wiccans participate in a lunar ritual in Illinois.

In *A Community of Witches: Contemporary Neo-Paganism and Witchcraft in the United States*, Helen Berger applies sociological analysis to conduct a fascinating study of contemporary Wicca (Berger 1999; Religious Tolerance 2012). She carried out participant observation in a newly formed coven in New England. A coven is a small congregation of witches, usually with no more than 10 or 12 members. It took considerable effort to establish trust with the members, but this method of gathering data allowed her to experience firsthand the close-knit support group and the actual behaviors and interactions within the group. A national organization provided her with a wealth of printed material produced by Neo-Pagans and allowed her entry to several national Neo-Pagan festivals, where she observed the rituals. She also did in-depth, open-ended interviews with 40 members from a number of covens. By using a variety of methods, Berger was able to gain in-depth information and get an idea of whether her qualitative data accurately described most covens.

Wicca was established in the first half of the 20th century from various pieces of occult lore. Every member is clergy, all priests and priestesses; worship is of two deities, a god and a goddess; and the rites and rituals are learned at initiation. It comes from a feminist perspective, believing in a goddess and emphasizing gender equality, though some branches of Wicca include men. It also celebrates the spiritual unity of humans with nature and has a strong ecology ethic. The religion encourages self-awareness, self-transformation, and an intuitive approach to decision making (rather than using logic). As a nature-based religion, it also celebrates the senses and embraces sexuality, fertility, and being at one with the universe.

Father's Day, and Grandparents' Day, thereby honoring and connecting parenting and family ties to the religion. Many of the sacred ceremonies in religion are family affairs: births, christenings or naming of new members, marriages, and funerals. Jews, Muslims, and Latter-Day Saints (Mormons) are especially known for their many ceremonies and gatherings designed specifically for family units, and their moral codes place a high value on family loyalty and responsibility.

Religiosity, a person's degree of religious involvement, is positively associated with moral beliefs and behavior in youth and influences interaction with children and support of spouses in marriages. Various faiths spread distinct messages on how marriage partners should relate to one another and raise a family. For example, some fundamentalist Christian groups (those that believe in a literal interpretation of the Bible) produced parenting manuals and manifestos to guide families that promote their perspective on family life. Some of these have created controversy because of their emphasis on hierarchical and authority-centered parenting models (Carlson and Mero 2005; Grille 2005). The conservative Christian organization Focus on

Witchcraft

the Family has a syndicated newspaper column, radio programs, books, DVDs, and a monthly magazine that it uses to spread its perspective on family life.

Sometimes, tensions can arise between family and religion over social control. Among the Amish, for example, if the bishop orders a member of the church "shunned," the family must comply and refuse to speak to or associate with that person. If the family does not comply, it will be ostracized by the other members of the community (Clarke 2007; Hostetler 1993).

Religion and Politics: Theocracies and Civil Religion. Jan, a Swede, belongs to a state religion: Lutheranism. He was raised a Lutheran and does not really think about the possibility of other religious beliefs, although there is a growing Pentecostal movement in Sweden. The Nwankwo family, mentioned in the chapter opening, practices an ancient tribal religion, also with no thought that another religious belief might have something better to offer. Most of us are raised in a particular belief system from childhood and adhere to that religion because it is part of the custom and tradition most familiar to us. We seldom question our "choice" until we interact with members of different religions.

In a pure **theocracy**, or rule by God, *religious leaders, like those in Iran, rule society in accordance with God's presumed wishes.* In other nations, political rather than religious leaders govern, but an official state religion receives support from tax money. Sweden, Britain, and Italy are examples of societies with state religions. In China, citizens have some limited freedom to practice certain religions, but the Chinese government gives itself the right to select religious leaders (like the Dalai Lama and Catholic bishops serving in China). Some countries, such as the former Soviet Union, have outlawed religion altogether so that nothing competed with loyalty to the nation. The continuum in Figure 12.3 shows the possible relationships between church and state.

Although religion often reinforces the power of the state, it may also be a source of conflict and tension on issues regarding morality, justice, and legitimate authority. Even in the United States, which professes separation between church and state matters, religious groups seek to influence policies such as prayer in school, selection of textbooks and reading matter, and abortion laws. In some countries, religious groups strongly oppose the government and seek to undermine the authority and power of political leaders. In Nazi Germany, for example, some church leaders formulated the Barmen Declaration in opposition to Hitler. Many Christian groups in South Africa opposed apartheid. In some parts of Latin America, church leaders work for human rights and more equitable distribution of land and resources. Indeed, depending on the organizational structures, religion can provide a source of authority that offers a real challenge to the power of the state when that government has become oppressive, as shown in the next "Sociology Around the World" on page 394.

In simple homogeneous societies, religion serves as a kind of glue, making sacred the existing social system by offering it supernatural legitimacy. In complex and heterogeneous societies, on the other hand, no single religion can provide the core values of the culture. In such circumstances, an alternative form of religion called civil religion frequently evolves. **Civil religion** *is the set of beliefs, rites, and symbols that sacralize the values of the society and*

FIGURE 12.3 Links Between Religion and the State

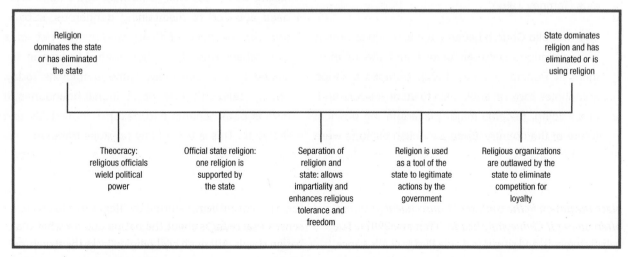

Religion dominates the state or has eliminated the state

State dominates religion and has eliminated or is using religion

Theocracy: religious officials wield political power

Official state religion: one religion is supported by the state

Separation of religion and state: allows impartiality and enhances religious tolerance and freedom

Religion is used as a tool of the state to legitimate actions by the government

Religious organizations are outlawed by the state to eliminate competition for loyalty

Civil Religion   ▶ Abortion

Sociology Around the World

Transnational Religion: The Catholic Church and Political Systems

The Roman Catholic Church was one of the first truly transnational organizations, external to any one nation and including representation from many countries. It must be sympathetic to the circumstances of people in many nations, for its membership and its organizational reach span the globe. It cannot align itself with the economic and political interests of one nation or set of nations without risking the alienation of tens of millions of members in another part of the world (Roberts and Yamane 2012).

Sometimes, however, multinational religious organizations such as the Catholic Church can have a real impact on the social and economic policies within a nation, protecting the welfare of the people against a tyrannical state. In Poland during the 1970s and 1980s, the citizenry often felt colonized by a foreign power—the Soviet Union. The communist government in Poland was extremely unpopular, but the people had no real way to make the government more responsive to their needs. In 1983, only 3% of Poles surveyed felt that the government-dominant political hierarchy represented the interests of the Polish people. In contrast, 60% identified the Catholic Church and the pope as protecting Polish interests (Tamney 1992).

The Catholic Church became a major power broker in negotiations between unions and the government in Poland (Tamney 1992). Catholic bishops sometimes took on a role akin to union leaders and, in so doing, became major players in the political future of the country. Because Polish bishops were ultimately responsible to the pope and had a source of support external to the nation, they experienced a good deal of independence from the communist party in power. Clergy supported by a church financed with tax dollars would not have had the same freedom to challenge the government. The global nature of the Catholic Church influenced the role bishops could play in the Polish situation.

In many single-nation religious denominations, the primary function of churches is to support the political power of the state or affirm an ethnic or national identity (Turner 1991b). Poland is an especially intriguing case in that a single religion tended to be identified with national pride and culture but that religion was global in its nature. That combination provided an exceptionally strong platform for challenging governmental policies not in the interests of the citizens (Tamney 1992).

A religion that crosses national boundaries can also foster suspicion among members of society who do not belong to it. For example, until a few decades ago, many people in the United States suspected the national loyalty of Roman Catholics, derisively calling them "papists." Likewise, Jews have often been accused of maintaining dangerous, subversive ties because of their international networks with others who share their faith. Muslims in the United States face these same suspicions today. When a religion transcends national boundaries, it carries both benefits and risks for individuals and the state. This is true of any religious tradition.

place the nation in the context of *transcendent meaning, often giving it divine significance* (Yamane 2007). The beliefs, symbols, and rituals (e.g., the Pledge of Allegiance, the national anthem, saluting the flag) serve to create a sense of sacredness about the nation and for what that nation stands. Although civil religion lacks the structural system of organized religion, it is often supported by various types of patriotic groups. These small voluntary associations develop intense belonging systems, and civil religion tends to strengthen the sense of belonging citizens feel as members of that society (Bellah 1992; Roberts and Yamane 2012).

American civil religion is not explicitly Christian, for it must appeal to those who are non-Christian as well, but it involves reference to God in many areas of civilian life and a legitimation of the U.S. political system. It attempts to give the nation and the government supernatural blessing and authority (Bellah 1970). It also calls the nation to a higher standard of justice and may be used by change agents, such as Dr. Martin Luther King Jr., to make social change more acceptable and compelling.

Although civil religion is supposed to unite a country, in some nations, civil religion can itself be a point of intense conflict (McGuire 2002; Yamane 2007). In Northern Ireland, part of the conflict between Protestants and Catholics is over civil religion. Protestants and Catholics not only come from different economic strata and different ethnic backgrounds but also have different visions for the future of the country and different ideas about what gives the country its special place in history. These disparate outlooks and backgrounds make a unified civil religion very difficult to achieve.

Thinking Sociologically

How does civil religion manifest itself in your country? Give specific examples.

Religion and the Economy: The Protestant Ethic and Capitalism. Why do most of us study hard, work hard, and strive to get ahead? Why are you sacrificing time and money now—taking this and other college courses—when you might spend that money on an impressive new car? Our answers probably have something to do with our moral attitudes about work, about people who lack ambition, and about the proper way to live. Max Weber provided an answer to this question with his research on the relationship between the Protestant work ethic and capitalism. He gathered information by studying many documents, including the diaries of Calvinists (a branch of Protestantism), sermons and religious teachings, and other historical papers (Weber [1904–1905] 1958).

Weber noted that the areas of Europe where the Calvinists had the strongest followings were the same areas where capitalism had grown the fastest. Weber argued that four elements in the Calvinist Protestant faith created the morals and value system necessary for the

Civil religion blends reverence for the nation with more traditional symbols of faith. The above picture, for example, shows a chapel at Punchbowl, the Pacific cemetery for U.S. military personnel, located in Hawaii. Note the relative prominence of the flags in the altar.

growth of capitalism: predestination, a calling, self-denial, and individualism.

1. *Predestination* meant that one's destiny—whether one would eventually go to heaven or hell—was predetermined. Nothing anyone could do would change what was to happen. Because God was presumed to be perfect, he was not influenced by human deeds or prayer. Those people who were chosen by God were referred to as the *elect* and were assumed to be a small group. Therefore, people looked for signs of their status—salvation or damnation. High social status was sometimes viewed as a sign of being among the elect. This view motivated people to succeed in *this* life, so that they would appear to be headed toward salvation in the next.

2. The *calling* referred to the concept of doing God's work. Each person was put on Earth to serve God, and each had a task to do in God's service. One could be called by God to any occupation, so the key was to work very hard and with the right attitude. Because work was a way to serve God, laziness or lack of ambition came to be viewed as a sin. These ideas helped create a society in which people's self-worth and their evaluation of others were tied to a work ethic. The Calvinists, therefore, worked hard.

3. *Self-denial* involved living a simple life. If one had a good deal of money, one did not spend it on a lavish home, expensive clothing, or various forms of entertainment. Such consumption would be offensive to God. Therefore, people worked hard and began to accumulate resources, saving or investing in a business. This self-denial was tied to an idea that we now call *delayed gratification*, postponing the satisfaction of one's present wants and desires in exchange for a future reward. The reward they sought was in the afterlife. Because Calvinists believed in predestination, they did not expect to *earn* salvation through this way of life, but they believed that they could demonstrate to themselves and others that they were among the elect.

4. *Individualism* meant that each individual faced his or her destiny alone before God. Previous Christian theology had emphasized group salvation, the idea that an entire community would be saved or damned together. The stark individualism of Calvinistic theology stressed that each individual was on his or her own before God. Likewise, in the emerging capitalist economic system, individuals were on their own. The person who thrived was an individualist who planned wisely and charted his or her own course. Religious individualism and economic individualism reinforced one another (Weber [1904–1905] 1958).

The Protestant ethic that resulted from these elements stressed hard work, simple living, and rational decision making by individualists. Businesspeople and laborers spent long hours working at their calling, and reinvested profits into new equipment or expansion of the company. The rise of individualism allowed people to focus on their own efforts to accumulate and reinvest wealth—and not feel guilty for doing so. The growth of the Calvinist Protestant church led to major changes in cultural values, which, in turn, helped transform the economy into a capitalistic system (Weber [1904–1905] 1958).

Gradually, the capitalistic system, stimulated by the Protestant ethic, spread to other countries and to other religious groups. Many of the attitudes about work and delayed gratification no longer have a supernatural focus, but they are part of the larger cultural value system nonetheless. They influence our feelings about people who are not industrious and our ideas about why some people are poor. In fact, some religious groups see individuals as responsible for their own fate, believing that the poor and jobless should solve their own problems rather than depend on government aid (Davidson 2008). This view was expressed by Mitt Romney in the 2012 presidential election and a large number of Americans share it (Brooks 2012; Rubin 2012).

Weber recognized that other factors also had to be present for capitalism to develop, but he believed that the particular set of moral values and attitudes that Calvinism instilled in the people was critical. Whereas Marx argued that religion encouraged workers to stay in their places and allowed the capitalists to exploit the system and maintain their elite positions, Weber focused on the change brought about in the economic system as a result of religious beliefs and values.

Religion interacts with the economy in other ways as well. First, religion is a major part of the economy. In the United States, more than 322,485 religious congregations received donations in June 2013. Of the total estimated charitable contributions ($101.54 billion) in the United States in 2012, 32% went to religious organizations (Center on Philanthropy 2013). In most countries, religions (a) employ clergy and other people who serve the church, (b) own land and property, and (c) generate millions through collections and fundraising. Some of this money goes to salaries and the upkeep of buildings, some to charitable and advocacy activities, and some to investments. Religious ventures continue to expand into many areas, from shopping centers to homes and apartment buildings for the elderly. In the United States, televangelism and megachurches (congregations with upward of 10,000 members) are multimillion-dollar industries with sophisticated marketing strategies. The televangelism industry, for example, involves the sale of books, CDs, and DVDs and donations of hundreds of millions of dollars by listeners. These megachurches become corporations and use information from the corporate world (e.g., how to structure their organization and market their product) to increase their chances of success. Indeed, many televangelists and megachurches preach a version of the "gospel of prosperity"—that God wants people to be prosperous and even wealthy. They argue that worshipping God in their style and giving to their church will contribute to wealth. This embracing of the search for wealth fits with the interests of capitalists and capitalism.

There are other ways in which religion and economic institutions are linked. When large religious organizations take a moral stand on poverty, for example, they may influence government investment into the economy. Moreover, troubled economic times tend to lead to the creation of certain kinds of religious movements. For example, millenarian religious movements, which anticipate the end of the world, almost always gain adherents when economic prospects are bleak (Roberts and Yamane 2012).

Religion interacts with and impacts the other major social institutions in society, but the interaction between religion and society is a two-way street. While religions can influence other social institutions, religions also find themselves influenced by the society in which they exist.

Megachurches, such as this one in Illinois, which sometimes draw 20,000 to 30,000 worshippers on a weekend, offer high-entertainment worship and a range of other services. These churches are run—and marketed—like a business.

 Thinking Sociologically

In postindustrial societies, the media influence religion and individuals' views toward religion. What messages from the media (movies, TV, music) about religion are prevalent in your society? How have these messages influenced your views toward religion? Why?

RELIGION IN SOCIETY: MACRO-LEVEL ANALYSIS

As an integral part of society, religion meets the needs of individuals and of the social structure. In this section, we explore functionalist and conflict theories as we consider some functions of religion in society, the role of religion in supporting stratification systems, and various conflicts within societies and in the global system.

The Contribution of Religion to Society: A Functionalist Perspective

Regardless of their personal belief or disbelief in the supernatural, sociologists of religion acknowledge that religion has important social consequences. Functionalists contend that religion has some positive consequences—helping people answer questions about the meaning of life and providing part of the glue that helps hold a society together. Let us look at some of the social functions of religion, keeping in mind that the way religion affects society varies depending on the structure of the society and the time period.

Social Cohesion. Religion helps individuals feel a sense of belonging and unity with others, a common sense of purpose with those who share the same beliefs. It serves to hold social units together and gives the members a sense of camaraderie. You will recall that Durkheim's widely cited study of suicide stresses the importance of belonging to a group, such as a congregation (Durkheim ([1897] 1964). Research shows that communities with religious homogeneity and a high rate of congregational membership have lower rates of suicide. This lower suicide rate among the highly religious appears to hold in Muslim as well as U.S. societies (Ellison, Burr, and McCall 1997; Lotfi, Ayar, and Shams 2012). In societies with competing religions, or religions inconsistent with other values of society, however, religions may reduce cohesion and even be a source of conflict and hatred (Bainbridge and Stark 1981). As mentioned earlier, societies with competing religions often develop a civil religion—a theology of the

Religion and Academic Achievement

nation—that serves to bless the nation and to enhance conformity and loyalty.

Legitimating Social Values and Norms.

Functionalists note that religion often sacralizes social norms—grounds them in a supernatural reality or a divine command that makes them larger than life. Whether those norms have to do with care for the vulnerable, the demand to work for peace and justice, the immorality of extramarital sex, the sacredness of a monogamous heterosexual marriage, or proper roles for men and women, the foundations of morality from scripture create feelings of absoluteness. This lends stability to society: Agreement on social control of deviant behavior is easier, and society needs to rely less on coercion and force to get citizens to follow social norms. Of course, the absoluteness of the norms also makes it more difficult to change them as the society evolves. This inflexibility is precisely what pleases religious conservatives and distresses theological liberals, with the latter often seeking new ways to interpret the norms.

Social Change.

Depending on the time and place, religion can work for or against social change. Some religions fight to maintain the status quo or return to norms from an earlier era. This is true of many fundamentalist religions—whether they are branches of Christian, Jewish, Hindu, or Islamic faiths—that seek to simplify life in the increasingly complex industrial world. Other religious traditions support or encourage change. For example, Japan made tremendous strides in industrialization in a short time following World War II, in part, because the Shinto, Confucian, and Buddhist religions provided no obstacles and, in fact, supported the changes needed to move their economy forward. In the United States, African American religious leaders led the civil rights movement in the 1950s and 1960s, utilizing the established networks and communication channels created by African American religious organizations (Farley 2011; Lincoln and Mamiya 1990; McAdam 1999, 2003).

 Thinking Sociologically

Which religious groups in your community have a stabilizing influence, and which ones have a disruptive influence? Which faith communities make the existing system seem sacred and beyond question? Which push for more social equality and less ethnocentrism toward others? Are there mosques, temples, or churches that oppose the government's policies, or do they foster unquestioning loyalty?

The Link Between Religion and Stratification: A Conflict Perspective

At times, religions reinforce socially defined differences between people, giving sacred legitimacy to racial prejudice, gender bias, and inequality. Conflict theory considers the ways in which religion relates to stratification and the status of minority groups. Our religious ideas and values and the way we worship are shaped not only by the society into which we are born but also by our family's position in the stratification system. Religion serves different primary purposes for individuals, depending on their positions in the society. People of various social statuses differ in the type and degree of their involvement in religious groups.

The Class Base of Religion. Conflict theorist Karl Marx states clearly his view of the relationship between religion and class—religion perpetuates the prevailing power structure (Marx [1844] 1963). For the proletariat or working class, religion is a sedative, he asserts, a narcotic that dulls people's sensitivity to and understanding of their desperate situation. He labels religion the "opiate of the people." Faith provides workers an escape from reality—from the tedium and suffering in everyday life. At the same time, it helps those in power discourage workers from rebelling, as it promises life in the hereafter if they work hard and contentedly. Some religions justify the positions of those who are better off by saying they have earned it.

Because the needs and interests of socioeconomic groups differ, most societies have class-based religions. With some exceptions (e.g., Catholics and Muslims) in the United States, religious affiliation tends to correlate with social class measures such as education, occupation, and income (Pyle 2006; Smith and Faris 2005). Table 12.3 indicates the specific links between denominational affiliation and socioeconomic measures in the United States today. Some religious traditions tend to attract lower- and working-class worshippers because they focus on the problems and life situations faced by people in the lower social classes. People with higher social status attend worship more regularly and know more about the historical and social context of scriptures than do people with less education and income, but people with lower socioeconomic status are more likely to pray and read scripture daily (Roberts and Yamane 2012).

Max Weber referred to this pattern of people belonging to religious groups that espouse values and characteristics compatible with their social status as *elective affinity* (Weber 1946). For example, people in laboring jobs usually find obeying the rules of the workplace and adhering to the

Table 12.3 Socioeconomic Profiles of American Religious Groups

Religious Group	Education Level (in percentage)		Annual Household Income (in dollars)
	% With at Least a College Degree	% With No High School Degree	% Over 100,000
Hindu	74	4	43
Jewish	59	3	46
Episcopal Church in USA	57	1	35
Unitarian	51	3	26
Buddhist	48	3	22
Presbyterian in USA	47	7	28
Orthodox	46	6	28
United Church of Christ	42	4	18
Atheist	42	8	28
United Methodist	35	8	22
Disciples of Christ	35	10	20
Evangelical Lutheran in USA	30	6	17
Nondenominational	29	6	18
Latter-Day Saint (Mormon)	28	8	15
Catholic	26	17	19
Muslim	24	21	16
Southern Baptist	21	15	15
Seventh-Day Adventist	21	24	11
Religious but Unaffiliated	17	21	12
American Baptist	14	23	8
Assemblies of God	12	24	8
Other Pentecostal	11	26	7
Jehovah's Witness	9	19	9
Black Baptist	8	19	8

Source: Pew Forum on Religion and Public Life (2008):78–80, 84–86. Published by the Pew Forum on Religion and Public Life, www.pewforum.org.

instructions of the employer or supervisor essential for success on the job (Bowles and Gintis 1976; McLeod 2009).

Likewise, the faith communities of the poor and the working class tend to stress obedience, submission to "superiors," and the absoluteness of religious standards. The values of the workplace are reenacted and legitimated in churches to help socialize children to adapt to noncreative laboring jobs.

Many people in affluent congregations are paid to be problem solvers and break the mold of conventional thinking. They will not do well professionally if they merely obey rules. Instead, they must help create rules while trying to solve organizational or management problems (Bowles and Gintis 1976). It is not surprising, then, that the denominations of the affluent (Unitarian Universalists, Jews, Episcopalians, Presbyterians, and United Church of Christ) are more likely to value tolerance of other perspectives, religions, or values and to view factors that limit individual opportunity (e.g., institutional racism and sexism) as evil. They tend to embrace tolerance of differences and condemn rigidity, absolutism, and conventionalism. Their religious communities are likely to encourage each member to work out his or her own theology, within limits, and value divergent thinking and a streak of independence (Roberts and Yamane 2012; Roof 1999).

Whatever the particular belief, one's religion and one's social status affect everything from life expectancy, the likelihood of divorce, and mental health to attitudes regarding sexual behavior, abortion, and fetal stem cell research.

Thinking Sociologically

How do the social class and religious affiliation of people you know relate to this discussion? How do denominations in your community whose members have higher-than-average levels of education (Unitarians, Jews, Episcopalians, Presbyterians, and members of the United Church of Christ) differ from those with less-educated members?

Racial Bias, Gender Prejudice, and Religion. Most religious groups profess to welcome all comers. Many, however, have practiced discrimination against some group at some time, often related to political and economic factors in the society. In fact, some studies show positive relationships among religion, prejudice, and discrimination. However, it is important to recognize that religion has multiple and even contradictory effects on societies. For example, most Christian denominations have formal statements that reject racial prejudice as un-Christian. The meaning system teaches tolerance. However, informal group norms in a local congregation— the belonging system—may be tolerant of ethnic jokes and may foster distrust of certain races. Among whites in

the United States, for instance, active church members have historically displayed more prejudice than inactive church members or the unchurched (Chalfant and Peck 1983; Roberts and Yamane 2012).

The structural system of religion can also play a role in supporting prejudice and discrimination. Promotions to larger churches are usually awarded to well-liked ministers, who have growing, harmonious congregations and financially sound organizations. Such ministers are sometimes reluctant to speak out forcefully on issues such as racial or gender equality, for fear of offending their parishioners. Bishops may not promote a minister or priest to a larger church if his or her current congregation is racked with dissention and donations have declined. Even though the denomination's meaning system may oppose prejudice, the structural system may reward clergy who do not defend that meaning system and who allow bigotry to remain unchecked (Campbell and Pettigrew 1959; Roberts and Yamane 2012).

Women have often been the most active members of Christian congregations and appear to be more spiritual than men, as discussed in the next "Engaging Sociology." In some denominations, they hold leadership positions (Chaves 2004). Many Christian and Jewish denominations, for example, have female ministers and rabbis (Chaves 2004; Religious Tolerance 2012). Several Christian denominations allow women to become bishops.

More conservative denominations and conservative members within more moderate denominations oppose moves to grant women leadership positions. The Anglican Church of England's internal division among progressives who support, and social conservatives who oppose, allowing women to be bishops has made headlines in recent years, with both groups vociferously arguing for their side (Jourdan 2013). Similar divisions exist within the Catholic Church, but because of the organizational structure of the Church, there is less open debate. In 2012, 59% of Catholics in the United States supported the ordination of women priests (Levitt 2012). However, the Pope and Bishops of the Roman Catholic Church have taken a strong position in opposition, threatening excommunication and categorizing any attempt by woman to be ordained as a grave crime against the church—in the same category as crimes committed by priests who sexually abuse children (Donadio 2010).

Men and women sit separately in some houses of worship today. These include some Christian, Islamic, and Jewish worship services. Religious rules regarding attire also help reinforce the differentiation of the sexes in some houses of worship.

ENGAGING SOCIOLOGY

Women and Spirituality

FIGURE 12.4   The Spirituality Gap

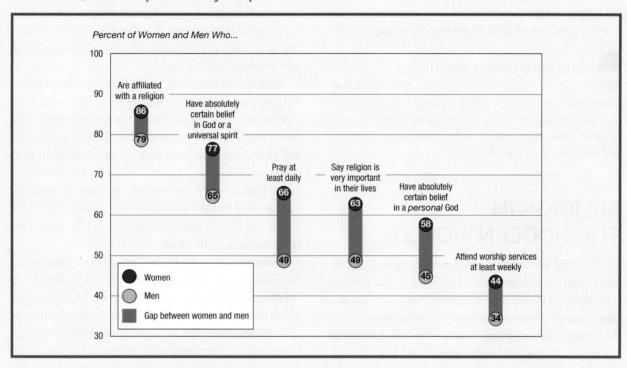

Source: Pew Forum on Religion and Public Life (2008). http://religions.pewforum.org/

Sociological Data Analysis

1. Are you convinced by this evidence that women are more spiritual than men? Why or why not?

2. If so, why do you think this is the case? If not, why do the data seem to suggest less involvement of men?

3. Is the message of religious communities and faith traditions (altruism, self-sacrifice, trusting others) less in tune with the everyday experiences of men than of women?

While most mainline Christian denominations now have official statements on the equality of women and formal policies against discrimination in ordaining or hiring women pastors, the official meaning system does not tell the whole story. Again, religious structures play a role. Local congregational search committees who screen and hire new ministers usually care deeply about the survival and health of the local church. Studies show that, often, members of these committees are themselves not personally opposed to women in the pulpit but believe that others in their church would be offended if they hired a woman and would stop coming and giving money to the church. Thus, the local belonging and structural systems of the religion may perpetuate unequal treatment of

Women and Religion

clergywomen, even if the meaning system says they are equal (Chaves 2004; Lehman 1985).

As noted earlier, some religions may reinforce and legitimize social prejudices, while others may be powerful forces for change and for greater equality in a society. Religion elicits strong emotions and influences people's definition of reality. Religion has promoted social strife, but it has also been the motivation for altruism and service to others, and a major contributor to social solidarity.

 Thinking Sociologically

From what you know about the status of racial and ethnic minority groups, LGBTQ people, and women in your society, how are the problems they face in religion and other institutions (education, politics, economics, health care) similar?

RELIGION IN THE MODERN WORLD

Name almost any religion, and a group representing that belief system can probably be found in the United Kingdom, the United States, Canada, Kenya, and several other countries where religious diversity is the norm. In the United States, religious pluralism has been a founding principle since Roger Williams founded the state of Rhode Island in 1636 and advocated religious toleration and separation of church and state. This makes for a complex religious pattern. In this section we look at the vitality of major religions in North America, with empirical data that track religious trends over time (Pew Forum on Religion and Public Life 2012b; Stark 2000).

In order to make sense of religious trends, we must first define the variables we want to measure. If we want to know whether being highly religious is correlated with other social factors or with specific behaviors, how do we measure religiosity? This question is discussed in the next "Engaging Sociology."

Is Religion Dying or Reviving in North America?

Depending on the survey, 16% to 20% of Americans report no religious affiliation, with many more younger than older people reporting a lack of affiliation (Grossman 2012b; Pew Forum on Religion and Public Life 2012a). On the other hand, 65% of people in the United States say that religion is "very important" to them, and the number is especially high—80%—for Muslim Americans (Gallup 2009). Indeed, even among those not affiliated with a religious community, roughly half say that spirituality is important to their lives—calling themselves spiritual but not religious (Pew Forum on Religion and Public Life 2012a). Spirituality is a more individual experience of feeling there is something sacred in life beyond the realm of the everyday empirical world, while religion is a communal or social expression of that outlook. In any case, it is safe to say that religion and spirituality still have a significant influence in U.S. society.

Religion has somewhat less influence in Canadian life. Well over half of Canadians regularly engage in some form of religious activity over the course of a year, though, and a third claim to attend worship services monthly. Close to half (44%) say religion is very important in their lives (Clark and Schellenberg 2008). While the Canadian indicators have dropped a bit over the last several years, the indicators of religious commitment in both the United States and Canada are higher than those in most other religiously pluralistic nations.

Religious affiliation in the United States today is also high in comparison to earlier periods in U.S. history. In the days of colonial America, only about 17% of the population belonged to a church. Religious membership rose fairly steadily from the 1770s until the 1960s. Although there has been a modest decline in the past 30 years, self-reports of membership in a faith community have fluctuated between 64% and 70% for the past two decades (Newport 2010). Another measure of religious strength is belief in God. Gallup poll results for the past three decades indicated that 92% of the U.S. population believes in God or a universal spirit or higher power (Newport 2012e). Tables 12.4a and 12.4b in "Engaging Sociology" show the results from Gallup polls regarding indicators of the importance of religion in people's lives.

Attendance at worship in a church, temple, or mosque is also an indicator of religious involvement. While attendance rates vary by faith community, Gallup polls indicate self-reports of attendance have been fairly steady in the United States for more than 70 years at 37% to 49% of the population, hovering close to 40% in 2013 (Newport 2014). (See Figure 12.5.) Figure 12.6, however, shows that there are significant geographical variations in affiliation with a religious group.

Religion in the United States has adjusted to changes in society and taken on new forms. For example, the number of Protestants in the United States has declined from two thirds of the population to less than half (48%) in the past 30 years, as the country has become more religiously diverse.

ENGAGING SOCIOLOGY

Determining What It Means to Be "Religious"

- Study the list of items in Table 12.4a. Do measures such as belief in God, church membership, and frequency of attendance seem like good measures of one's religiosity? Why might the answer to this question indicate something other than the depth of one's religious faith?

- Attendance at Sabbath worship varies greatly, with Mormons and members of the conservative Church of Christ reporting weekly attendance at about 67% to 68%; Muslims at 56%; mainline Methodists, Presbyterians, Lutherans, and Roman Catholics at 43% to 45%; and Jews at 15%. Given the fact that attendance varies so much by religious group, does this mean that members of some groups are less religious, or does it mean attendance is not a very good measure of religiosity for some groups?

- Is asking whether religion is very important in one's life, whether one believes religion answers problems in life, or how much confidence one has in religious organizations a good indicator of a person's religiosity? (See Table 12.4b for indications of how stable "importance in life" has been over time.) What might be some misleading dimensions of using one or more of these measures to indicate "religiosity"?

- Some scholars have argued that how religious beliefs affect one's behavior is a good indicator of religiosity. So in studying Islam, Judaism, or some forms of Christianity, one measure of religiosity has been how much one gives to charitable causes—both to one's faith community and to people living in poverty. Is this measure an accurate way to understand levels of religious influence in the society? Why or why not?

- Imagine you have been asked to conduct a study to determine the religiosity of various demographic groups in the United States. How would you define religiosity?

Table 12.4a Leading Religious Indicators (in Percent)

Belief in God	92[a]
Member of a church, temple, or mosque	63[b]
Say they attend worship services regularly	43[c]
Religion *very important* in life	55[a]
Pray daily	58[d]
High confidence in organized religion	44[e]

Sources:

a. Newport (2012e).

b. Newport (2009).

c. Newport (2010).

d. Pew Forum on Religion and Public Life (2009).

e. Saad (2012).

Table 12.4b How Important Is Religion in Your Life (in Percent)?

	Very[a]	Fairly	Not Very
2012	58	23	19
2000	59	29	12
1992	58	29	12

Source: Gallup (2013).

These figures vary by religious affiliation. Note, for example, that Muslims rated among the highest—at 80% *very important*—in a 2009 Gallup survey.

Religious Knowledge

FIGURE 12.5 Weekly Attendance at Church, Synagogue, or Mosque in the United States: Annual Averages

Source: Newport (2013).

FIGURE 12.6 Percentage of U.S. Population Affiliated With a Church, Mosque, or Temple

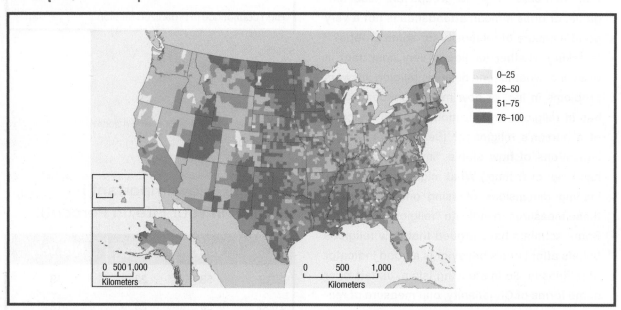

Source: Religious Congregations and Membership Study (2010).

Note: This map is based on data reported by local congregations and includes both members and other regular attendees; it does not represent weekly attendance. The numbers indicate overreporting (people report attendance at higher rates than they actually attend), but that does not change the overall geographical pattern of religious affiliation.

This decline stems in part from decreasing numbers of white Protestant families (due to the changing ethnic composition of the country) and an increase in the number that no longer affiliate with any faith community (Pew Forum on Religion and Public Life 2012a, 2012b). The latter half of the 20th century also saw a wide range of religious groups forming and growing in North America, from the occult and astrology to New Age spirituality and Zen Buddhism. Today, approximately 46% of U.S. adults hold a creationist view of human origin, indicating the strong influence of fundamentalist Christianity in the United States. Creationists reject the theory of evolution and believe the creation story of Earth found in the Bible is scientifically factual (Newport 2012c).

Religious identity influences how people view the world and their political choices. The religiosity of candidates has been raised in political campaigns throughout the history of the United States, including the most recent presidential elections. In June 2012, just as the 2012 presidential primaries ended, 18% of the population said that they would not vote for a Mormon. Despite this, the "highly religious" tended to support Romney over Obama—except for "highly religious" Hispanic Catholics who leaned toward Obama (Newport 2012a, 2012b, 2012d).

Demographic changes in the makeup of the United States and Canada have influenced the religious landscape. Although two out of every three native-born U.S. citizens are Protestant, two out of every three Christian immigrants are Catholic. This influx of Catholic immigrants has helped the Catholic Church maintain the membership of a steady percentage of U.S. citizens. Some other religious faiths are represented among those new residents of the United States as well (Pew Forum on Religion and Public Life 2012b).

Religion and Secularization: Micro-, Meso-, and Macro-Level Discord

Secularization refers to *the diminishing influence and role of religion in everyday life*. At the meso and macro level, religion becomes one of many institutions in the society—no longer having authority in governing, health, and other realms. Secularization at the micro level involves a movement away from supernatural and sacred interpretations of the world and toward decisions based on empirical evidence and logic. Before the advent of modern science and technology, religion helped explain our social and physical world. However, the scientific method, its emphasis on logical reasoning, and the fact that there are many different religions rather than one have challenged religious and spiritual approaches to the world. As part of micro-level secularism, we might expect to see most individuals working out their own faith systems rather than adhering to the faith affirmations of their denomination or religious leaders. If secularization were uniform, it might look like the pattern indicated in Table 12.5.

Table 12.5 Secularization in the Social World

	Institutional Differentiation (separation of religion so it does not dominate other institutions)	Decision Making
Macro Level	In the larger society, government, education, and the economic institutions are independent and autonomous from religious organizations.	Decision making about social policies uses logic, empirical data, and cost/benefit analysis rather than scripture, theological arguments, or proclamations of religious authorities.
Meso Level	**Organizations** look to other social associations for accepted practices of how to operate, not to religious organizations and authorities.	Decision making about an organization's policies is based on analyses of possible consequences, rather than on scripture, theological arguments, or proclamations of religious authorities.
Micro Level	Individuals emphasize being "spiritual rather than religious," formulate their own meaning system or theology, and may believe that spirituality has little to do with other aspects of their lives.	Decision making about life decisions is based on individual self-interest without concern for the teachings of the religious group or the clergy.

Source: From *Religion in Sociological Perspective,* 4th edition by ROBERTS. Copyright 2004 Wadsworth, a part of Cengage Learning, Inc.

Religion in Schools

However, we have seen that most indicators of traditional religiosity—belief in God, attendance, affirmation that religion affects all of life, and confidence in religious organizations—are high. Religion is still a strong force in the lives of many individuals. However, it does not have the extensive control over other institutions of education, health, politics, or family that it once did. In most Global North countries, it is just one institution among others, rather than the dominant one. Whereas in 1957, 69% of the population thought religion was increasingly important in U.S. society, in 2012, 77% felt it was declining in importance (Newport 2014).

Some scholars have argued that secularization is an inevitable and unstoppable force in the modern postindustrial world (Dobbelaere 2000; Gorski and Altinordu

2008). Others argue that secularization is far from inevitable and that it has almost reached its limit (Gardom 2011; Stark 2000). Our social world model helps us understand that, like religion, secularization is a complex phenomenon that occurs at several levels and affects each society differently (Chaves and Gorski 2001; Yamane 1997).

Secularization may be occurring at the societal level, but the evidence noted earlier suggests that this is not so pervasive at the individual level in North America (Chaves and Gorski 2001). When religious faith guides people's everyday lives—their conduct on the job, their political choices, their sexual behavior, or their attitudes toward race relations—then secularization at the micro level is weak and religious influence is strong. Faith still matters to many people.

Secularization is more obvious at the meso and macro levels. For example, religiously affiliated organizations (e.g., Catholic nursing homes, Presbyterian colleges, Jewish social service foundations), make most, though not all, of their decisions about how to deliver services or whom to hire or fire based on systematic policies designed for organizational efficiency, not religious dogma. Likewise, policies in the society at large are usually made with little discussion of the theological implications (health care policies are one notable exception, as we will discuss in Chapter 14). In morally ambiguous cases, policy makers defend positions with human rights arguments, rather than ideas on what is sinful—again suggesting that society has become secular at the macro level (Chaves 1993; Roberts and Yamane 2012; Yamane 1997). On the other hand, debates about prayer in schools, abortion, same-sex marriage, and economic inequality; the involvement of religious leaders in political issues; and the influence of religion in presidential politics indicate a continuing impact of religion on the meso and macro levels in U.S. society. *Secularization* even at the macro level is not complete.

In short, most sociologists of religion believe that religion continues to be a particularly powerful force at the individual level while secularization is more pervasive in the larger culture (at the meso and macro levels) (Roberts and Yamane 2012; Sommerville 2002). At the global level, no particular theological authority has the power to define reality or determine policies, and secularization is well established. Perhaps this is one reason why conservatives of nearly every religious faith are leery of global processes and global organizations, such as the United Nations. Our global political organizations are governed by rational-legal (secular) authority, not religious doctrines.

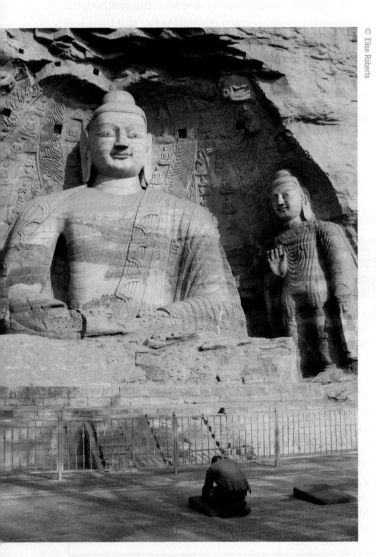

© Elise Roberts

Despite the process of secularization in some parts of the world, the sense of awe before the holy remains strong for many people. This enormous Buddha at the Yungang Buddhist Caves at Wuzhou Mountain in China has been a source of veneration for generations.

Thinking Sociologically

What might be the results if a society is secularized at the meso and macro levels but much less so at the micro level? Is this a problem? Does it create problems for decision making and social coherence? Is separation of church and state, with government policies based on secular calculations of the interests of the nation, a good idea or a bad idea? Why or why not?

Religion: Fostering War or Peace?

Can religion bring peace to the world? Most religious systems advocate living in harmony with other humans and with nature, yet peace has not been the reality. Although Christianity, Judaism, and Islam embrace a world of peace and justice, Christian denominations often foster nationalistic loyalty—with displays of the flag and even pledges of allegiance to the flag during worship. This endorsement of national pride can foster "us" versus "them" thinking and undermine peace.

Congregations that take peace activities seriously may decline in membership and financial stability if seen as "anti-American," whereas those that foster in-group or nationalistic sentiments can attract large numbers. So, the structural system may actually undermine the message of the meaning system because growth and financial vitality are major concerns for many local church leaders. Despite the rhetoric, fiscal concerns can actually trump claims to worship the "Prince of Peace." The linking of nationalistic loyalty to religion can also lead to the conflation of nation and God and, in some cases, the perception that leaders are divinely chosen.

Liberal theologies suggest that God may speak to people through a variety of channels, including the revelations of other religious traditions. While religious leaders may feel that their theology provides the fullest and most complete expression of God's Truth, some hold that other faiths also provide paths to salvation. This pluralism has resulted in more tolerance, but it may also be an indication of secularization of theology itself.

Members of fundamentalist groups—whether they are Jewish, Muslim, or Christian—generally believe in a literal interpretation of their holy books. They usually believe that they have the only Truth, which they must defend and

spread. This generates ethnocentrism and sometimes hatred, causing people to fight and die to defend their belief systems and way of life. Fundamentalist religious groups attempt to preserve their distinctive identities (Marty and Appleby 1991, 2004). They seldom believe in pluralism or tolerance of other beliefs but rather believe that they have the only true religion. Consequently, they resist and defend themselves against threats to their beliefs and way of life (Ebaugh 2005; Stern 2003; Wessinger 2000).

Conflict between religious groups is especially intense if there are also ethnic, economic, and religious differences between the groups. On the other hand, cross-cutting social categories reduces social hostilities, as Figure 12.7 illustrates. When you are in a group that includes adherents of different religions, different ethnicities, and different socioeconomic classes, it becomes much less likely that you will vilify people from those other groups. They no longer—as a category—can be seen as uniformly evil or as the enemy. This is what is meant by crosscutting divisions.

Religion has the greatest potential for reducing hatred between groups when the groups share some type of common identification. If the conflict is over ethnicity and economics, a common religious heritage can lessen the likelihood of violent confrontation. Likewise, some religious groups (including Christian, Jewish, and Muslim) have joined together in peaceful enterprises such as attempts to ban nuclear weapons or to address global poverty or climate change. These common purposes provide for cooperation and collaboration, thus lessening animosity and "us" versus "them" thinking.

Many countries today make clear separations between religion and the state because of their histories of religious

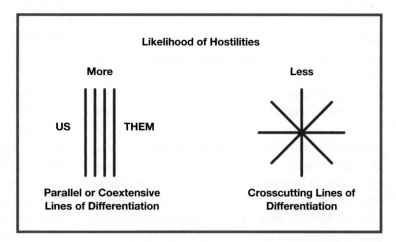

FIGURE 12.7 Lines of Differentiation Between "Us" and "Them"

hostilities. The conflicts in Europe between Protestant and Catholic religious groups were very brutal. Intense religious in-group loyalties led to a willingness to kill those following other religions or other denominations of the same faith. The horrific religious conflicts in European societies—known as the Hundred Years' War—did not reach closure until the beginning of the Enlightenment period in the mid-1600s. Acceptance of other religious traditions and separation of religion from the state were needed to restore civility (Dobbelaere 1981, 2000; Lambert 2000).

The global rise of *religious nativism*—absolutist religious groups that insist only their own view of life and the divine is Truth—appears to be a local reaction against global modernization (Fernandez 2011; Salzman 2008). Rapid global change has resulted in *anomie* as people confront

- threats to traditional cultures and religious perspectives,
- the increasing secularization of society,
- the threat to the material self-interests of religious organizations, and
- increased interdependence among nations.

All these threats have strengthened religious nativism (Fernandez 2011).

Thinking Sociologically

What specific religious beliefs or behaviors might influence the way in which religions and countries relate to one another? How might religious organizations influence international relations? For example, how might anti-Muslim prejudice by Christians influence U.S. relations with predominantly Islamic countries? How might the growing persecutions of Christians around the world, particularly in Global South nations, impact U.S. international relations?

Religion, Technology, and the World Wide Web

Technology and the Internet affect not only nations but also religions. From television broadcasts of megachurch services to Muslim chat rooms using technology to communicate, religious messages travel in new ways.

Prior to the wide distribution of religious texts to people who were not ordained priests, the hierarchies of Christendom controlled what was disseminated as Truth. The common (and typically illiterate) member of the local church did not have any basis for challenging the Pope or other church leaders. Those leaders were the authority. However, Martin Luther, founder of the Lutheran church, used the printed word in many powerful ways. He and other

reformers claimed that the Bible alone was the ultimate source of Truth and religious authority. The church leaders were to be believed only insofar as they were faithful to the scriptures. Luther himself used the printed word to spread his version of Christian Truth, and he did so with a vengeance. He not only wrote more than the other dissenters; he out-published the entire legion of Vatican defenders.

The invention of the printing press in 1450 allowed Luther to widely distribute his "95 Theses," written in 1517, containing his objections against Catholic Church practices. With his publications in the common languages of the people, rather than in Latin, Luther launched the Protestant Reformation and changed the course of religious history. It is doubtful whether this could have happened without the printing press. The printing press had similar revolutionary effects within Judaism (Brasher 2004).

Today, television and multimedia worship have enhanced the marketing of religion, including the modification of aspects of the faith to meet "consumer" demand (Ebaugh 2005; Roberts and Yamane 2012; Sargeant 2000). Tens of millions of religious websites relay information about an extraordinarily wide range of religious beliefs and practices (ReligiousTolerance.org 2013). Even conservative Christians such as the late Jerry Falwell, who once dubbed the Internet an evil Tower of Babel, have used it to spread their message.

It is too early to tell for sure what impacts these most recent technologies might have on religions around the world, but one outcome is clear: The Internet allows instant access to information about religions that otherwise might be obscure or nonexistent for many people. Note the immediacy of access to the derogatory YouTube *Innocence of Muslims* video that led to riots in many Islamic countries in 2012. This would not happen without the instant communication technology.

SOCIAL POLICY: SAME-SEX MARRIAGE AND GAY/ LESBIAN CLERGY

Ordination of gay ministers and same-sex marriage in churches make for heated debate over church policy and threaten to split some denominations. Most established religious groups assume the normality of heterosexuality, but as noted in Chapter 10, public opinion is shifting. More Americans favor same-sex marriage than oppose it. Americans under 30 are those most likely to favor same-sex marriage and do so by a more than two-to-one ratio (65% in favor with only 30% opposing) (Pew Research Center for the People and the Press 2012). So the public, especially the younger generation, is increasingly willing to grant gay and lesbian households a status as legitimate families.

Marriage is sanctified by religious ceremony in all major religious groups, and some religious bodies have recently officially sanctioned weddings for same-sex couples. Most of the largest denominations (e.g., Roman Catholic Church, Southern Baptist Church, United Methodist Church, Church of Jesus Christ of Latter-Day Saints [Mormons]) define marriage as between a man and a woman and prohibit same-sex marriage. However, a growing number of smaller denominations have begun to allow them. The Unitarian Universalist Association of Congregations sanctioned them in 1996, and the United Church of Christ began to perform same-sex marriages in 2005. Fifty-four percent of Catholics and 55% of white mainline Protestants now support same-sex marriage (Pew Forum on Religion and Public Life 2013). Conservatives see liberal notions about same-sex marriage and gender roles as a threat to society, family, and the moral social order. Liberals typically see no moral issue and no threat to society when sexuality is expressed within a committed relationship. The real moral issue for them is bigotry—lack of tolerance for other lifestyles. Thus, conservatives and liberals have socially constructed the meaning of morality differently.

Some mainstream denominations have developed policies supportive of lesbian, gay, and bisexual persons in local churches: More Light (Presbyterian), Open and Affirming (United Church of Christ and Christian Church), Reconciled in Christ (Lutheran), and Reconciling Congregations (Methodist). These designations apply to about 300 congregations that wish to be known as "gay and lesbian friendly" (Phoenix Declaration 2012). A new denomination, Universal Fellowship of Metropolitan Community Churches (UFMCC), affirms homosexuality as a legitimate lifestyle for Christians (Rodriguez and Ouellette 2000). It also has more than 172 local churches in 17 countries (Metropolitan Community Churches 2012).

Many denominations face internal divisions on the issue of same-sex marriage. The Methodists provide one example. The governing document for the United Methodist Church states that "homosexuality is incompatible with Christian teaching." This statement has been used to prevent same-sex marriages and ordination of gay and lesbian clergy. After the church's national legislative body voted to keep that line in church policy, the West Coast regional organization issued a statement of "Gospel Obedience" that, in keeping with Christian faith, the West Coast Methodist church would act as though that policy "does not exist." Thus, same-sex marriage is affirmed by Methodists in at least one region of the country (Western Jurisdictional Conference 2012). Methodists in southern states, in particular, are outraged by this stand.

One of the most controversial issues in several mainline denominations is over ordination of gays and lesbians as ministers. A divide between the global North and global South countries has arisen on this issue within some denominations. For example, in 2003, when the Episcopal Church in the United States elected gay clergyman Gene Robinson as bishop, nearly 1,000 Episcopal congregations in the United States and Canada broke away and formed the Anglican Church in North America. Likewise, African Anglican leaders made clear their "outrage" over the Church of England's decision to allow gay clergy to become bishops, declaring their communion with the mother Church "broken" (Anglican Church in North America 2013; Zaimov 2013).

In our social world, religious organizations influence society, and the larger society influences religious groups. Today, catalysts for change in religious organizations include (1) the emphasis on the equality of all people before God in Christian theology and (2) secularization in society—especially in the global North—that involves emphasis on placing people in leadership roles based on competence and commitment rather than on traits beyond their control (skin color, gender, or sexual orientation).

Thinking Sociologically

How has religion impacted your views about same-sex marriage? What other institutions have impacted your attitudes toward same-sex marriage? Which have influenced you more? Why?

Religion deals with issues of meaning and, like education, serves as a core socialization agent in the society. It provides socialization of members of society on important values, which sometimes makes cooperation more possible within a society. However, conflict cannot always be overcome by appeals to values, and sometimes the issues between individuals and groups come down to matters of power and access to resources. In the next chapter, we examine the influence of power and privilege in society and in our own lives. We turn now to the institutions of politics and economics.

🎙 Sin as Subjective

WHAT HAVE WE LEARNED?

Religion is a powerful force in the lives of people around the world. It typically elicits passions and deep loyalties, and in so doing, it can stimulate great acts of self-sacrificing charity or horrible atrocities and intergroup bigotries. People's religious affiliation strongly relates to their nationality, ethnic and racial group, and lifestyle. Religion is the one institution in most societies that consistently professes a desire for peace and goodwill, yet there may be inconsistencies between what people say and what they do. Religion can provide us with the hope that the world's problems may be dealt with in humanitarian ways.

Religion can provide a sense of purpose to our lives, and religious symbols come to have sacred meaning. Systems of meaning, belonging, and structure are interdependent components of religion.

Humans in the modern world tend to be spiritual. They may also live in states with massive governmental bureaucracies that hold power, and they participate in economic systems that produce and distribute the goods and services needed for survival. The next institutions we will examine are politics and economics—how power relations are negotiated at each level in the social world.

KEY POINTS

- Religion makes our most important values sacred, operating through three interconnected systems: (1) a meaning system, (2) a belonging system, and (3) a structural system. (See pp. 379–381.)

- We become committed through these three systems, by our attachment to a reference group that becomes a belonging system, by making investments in the organization (the structural system), and by holding as real the system of ideas (the meaning system). (See pp. 381–384.)

- At the micro level, symbolic interaction theory illuminates how the meaning system works, with an interaction of myths, rituals, and symbols coming to define reality and making the values and the meaning system sacred. Rational choice theory focuses on the costs and benefits that influence the decisions individuals make about religious commitments. It also examines how religious organizations go about seeking a "market share" in the competition for members. (See pp. 384–387.)

- Denominationalism organizes religious life when there are a plurality of religious groups and when religious authority is separated from governmental authority. New religious movements (NRMs) also arise in pluralistic social contexts. (See pp. 387–397.)

- At the macro level of analysis, functionalists maintain that religions can serve as a kind of glue to help solidify the country and meet the basic needs of the populace. In contrast, conflict theorists focus on the ways in which religion reinforces conflicts and inequalities in society, whether socioeconomic, racial, or gender. (See pp. 397–402.)

- In the United States and Canada, secularization is dominant at the meso and macro levels but does not seem to be as strong at the micro level. This is a source of tension in societies. (See pp. 402–406.)

- At the global level, religion can be involved in issues of war and peace (sometimes unwittingly undermining peace), and its influence in this area has expanded through television and the Internet. (See pp. 407–408.)

• Same-sex marriage and the ordination of gay or lesbian clergy are examples of religious policy issues causing considerable controversy among religions and their denominations. (See pp. 408–409.)

DISCUSSION QUESTIONS

1. What are some ways that religion and government are interdependent and interrelated in the United States?

2. If you are a person of faith and affiliated with a religious community, how did you become so? If you are not, explain why you are not. How did your family members and peers influence your views toward religion?

3. What motivates you to work hard and try to succeed professionally? Think about how Weber perceived the relationship between the development of the capitalist economic system and thoughts about sacrifice and work. Does it relate to your answer to the first part of this question? Why or why not?

4. Do you think religion is more of a unifying or divisive force in (a) the United States and (b) the world today? Why? Do you have many friends from different religious groups? Why or why not?

5. What do you think might happen to society if religions did not exist? Why? How would an absence of religion impact you personally?

VISUAL SOCIOLOGY: *RELIGIOUS AND SECULAR LIFE IN THE U.S.*

©Bloomberg/Getty Images

Although religious faith is very strong at the micro level in the U.S., public policy and the operation of organizations and government are secularized—based on principles of pluralism and rational deliberation. This town council prays as it opens its monthly meeting, after the Supreme Court ruled that prayers are allowed in this setting if there is a long tradition of having prayer. Was that a wise decision? Visit **edge.sagepub.com/ballantine5e** for an interactive photo essay about the balance between religious and secular practices.

CONTRIBUTING TO OUR SOCIAL WORLD: *WHAT CAN WE DO?*

At the Local Level

• *Campus religious foundations or ministries.* Most colleges and universities, including many of those not affiliated with a religion, have religious groups on campus. If you are not already a member and would like to join such an organization on your campus, contact a student representative or faculty sponsor, attend a meeting, and become involved. Most of these organizations participate in various types of outreach work, including volunteering for soup kitchens, food pantries, or thrift stores for the poor. If you attend a religiously affiliated college or university, you will find many and varied options.

At the Organizational or Institutional Level

- *College-based religious organizations.* Many religious campus organizations such as the Newman Foundation (Roman Catholic; http://new manfnd.org), InterVarsity (Christian; www.intervar sity.org), Muslim Students Association (MSA; http://msana tional.org), and Hillel Foundation (Jewish; www.hil lel.org) are branches of larger organizations. You can find out more about them and how to start or join a chapter by going to their websites.

- *American Atheists* (www.atheists.org) provides similar services to atheists. According to the group's website, "Now in its fourth decade, American Atheists is dedicated to working for the civil rights of Atheists, promoting separation of state and church, and providing information about Atheism." Volunteers assist in this work through contributions, research, and legal support.

At the National and Global Levels

Several religious groups are committed to working for justice and peace at the national and global levels.

- *Tikkun Community* (www.tikkun.org) is an interreligious organization, started by progressive members of the Jewish community, to "mend, repair, and transform the world." It is an "international community of people of many faiths calling for social justice and political freedom."

- *The American Friends Service Committee* (www .afsc.org), a Quaker organization, "includes people of various faiths who are committed to social justice, peace, and humanitarian service."

- *Catholic Relief Services* (www.crs.org) "carries out the commitment of the Catholic bishops of the United States to assist the poor and vulnerable" in over 100 countries.

- *Lutheran World Relief* (www.lwr.org) "extends the hand of Christian love to people overcoming poverty and injustice in 50 countries."

These and similar faith-based organizations sponsor many relief, peace, and justice projects around the world. You can find out more by going to their websites.

©REUTERS/ Kevin Lamarque

13 Politics and Economics

Probing Power, Dissecting Distribution

Power probes every aspect of our lives with intimidating force, even as economic distribution cuts across the social fabric. Sociology helps us probe and dissect the sources and consequences of each.

MICRO

● ME (AND MY FAMILY)

● LOCAL ORGANIZATIONS
AND COMMUNITY
Power struggles and finances
influence how well a local
fraternity or a women's
civic club functions.

MESO

● NATIONAL ORGANIZATIONS,
INSTITUTIONS, AND ETHNIC
SUBCULTURES
State or provincial governments,
political parties, and corporations
within the state affect quality of life.

MACRO

● SOCIETY
National governments and court systems
set rules that resolve conflicts and establish
standards for conducting business.

● GLOBAL COMMUNITY
Cross-national organizations such as the
United Nations and the World Court and
global human rights movements like Amnesty
International set standards for nations.

IN THIS CHAPTER

- What Is Power?

- Power and Privilege in
Our Social World

- Theoretical Perspectives
on Power and Privilege

- Micro-Level Analysis:
Individuals, Power,
and Participation

- Meso-Level Analysis:
Distributions of Power and
Privilege Within a Nation

- Macro-Level Analysis:
National and Global Systems
of Governance and Power

THINK ABOUT IT

Micro: Local Community	How do people in my local community use power in constructive or destructive ways?
Meso: National Institutions, Complex Organizations, and Ethnic Groups	How does the political institution interact with the economic institution? How are different ethnic groups affected by power and privilege?
Macro: National and Global Systems	How does economic instability threaten a national government? Why do struggles over power and privilege often evolve into war and terrorism?

Imagine that a nuclear disaster has occurred. The mortality rate is stunning. The survivors gather together for human support and collectively attempt to meet their basic survival needs. They come from varying backgrounds and have diverse skills. Before the disaster, some—the stockbroker and the business executive, for instance—earned more money and held higher social status than the others, but that is in the past. Faced with the new and unfamiliar situation, different skills are more immediately important for survival.

Where should this group begin? Think about the options. Some sort of organization seems essential, a structure that will help the group meet its needs. Food, shelter, and medical care are paramount. Those with experience in agriculture, building trades, and health care are likely to take leadership roles to provide these initial necessities. As time goes on, the need for clear norms and rules emerges.

These survivors decide that all members must work—must contribute their share of effort to the collective survival. At first, these norms are unwritten, but gradually some norms and rules are declared more important than others and are recorded, with sanctions (penalties) attached for noncompliance. Survivors form committees to deal with group concerns, and a semblance of a judicial system emerges. One person is appointed to coordinate work shifts and others to oversee emerging aspects of this small society's life. This scenario could play out in many ways.

What is happening? A social structure is evolving. Not everyone in the group will agree with the structure, and some people will propose alternatives. Whose ideas will be adopted? Leadership roles may fall to the physically strongest, or perhaps the most persuasive, or those with the most skills and knowledge for survival. Those most competent at organizing may become the leaders, but that outcome is by no means assured.

In our world of power and privilege, a war, an invading power, or a revolutionary overthrow of an unstable government can change the form of a political system overnight, necessitating rapid reorganization. The daily news brings stories of governments overthrown by military leaders in coups, with new governments emerging to fill the gap, as has been happening in various parts of the Middle East and Africa. The opening scenario and the political activity in our modern society share a common element—power. The concept of power is critical to understanding many aspects of our social world.

In this chapter, we focus primarily on the political and economic dimensions of society, since both political and economic systems enforce the distribution of power and resources in a society. Political systems involve the power relationships between individuals and larger social institutions. Economic systems produce and distribute goods and services. Not everyone gets an equal share, thus giving some citizens privileges that others do not have.

©Reuters/Jeff Haynes

U.S. vice president Joe Biden (left) makes a point during the vice presidential debate in 2012. This debate helped determine what political party—Democrats or Republicans—would control the power of the executive branch of the U.S. government.

In this chapter, we consider the nature of power, politics, and economics at each level in our social world: individuals and power; political systems and the distribution of power and privilege through political and economic institutions; and national and global systems of governance, including international conflicts, war, and terrorism. Because the topic of economics has been explored in many chapters of this book, we put more emphasis on political systems and their relation to economic systems.

Thinking Sociologically

Imagine that global climate change has caused massive flooding on your island nation. Only a few people have survived. How would you construct a new social system? What are the issues you would need to resolve in order to build a new society?

WHAT IS POWER?

Power is an age-old theme in many great scholarly discussions. Social philosophers since Plato, Aristotle, and Socrates have addressed the issue of political systems and power. Machiavelli, an early 16th-century Italian political philosopher, is perhaps best known for his observation that "the ends justify the means." His understanding of how power was exercised in the 15th, 16th, and 17th centuries significantly influenced how monarchs used the powers of the state (the means) to obtain wealth, new territories, and trade dominance (the ends) (Machiavelli [1532] 2010).

The most common definition of power used in social sciences today comes from Max Weber, who saw **power** as *the ability of a person or group to realize its own will in group action, even against resistance of others who disagree* (Weber 1947). Building on Weber's idea of power, we can identify various power arenas. Two key arenas of power are the nation state and the economic system. The leaders of a national government attempt to control the behavior of individuals through (a) *physical force and the threat of violence* (through a police force), (b) *symbolic control*, such as the manipulation of people (control of the media), and (c) *rules of conduct* that channel behavior toward desired patterns (laws). For example, the dictator and military in Syria have used torture, rape, and death to intimidate dissidents and their families and media to present the opposition as terrorists. The opposition has also used force and social media, but does not have the same degree of power.

Control of the economy is another important source of power. Conflict theorists argue that those with power over the economy can control government officials (who are dependent on campaign contributions from the wealthy)

and can convince the public that what is good for the wealthy is good for everyone. The members of the middle and working classes become convinced via the media that further tax breaks and advantages to the wealthy are—in the long run—in their own self-interest. In the United States, the media is largely controlled by wealthy owners of large corporations. Six companies (Comcast, News Corp, Disney, Viacom, Time Warner, and CBS), each operated by wealthy owners, control 90% of television, radio, and newspaper outlets (Lutz 2012).

 ### Thinking Sociologically

Weber's definition of power involves control over group action from the micro to macro levels. At what level do you have the most power? Why? Be sure to give examples.

POWER AND PRIVILEGE IN OUR SOCIAL WORLD

Power can be found at even micro levels of interaction, from individuals to family groups. In family life, relations often involve negotiation and sometimes conflict over how to run a household and spend money. Interactions between parents and children also involve power issues, as parents socialize their children. Indeed, the controversy over whether spanking is an effective discipline or an abusive imposition of pain is a question of how parents use their power to teach their children and control their behavior.

At the meso level, power operates in cities, counties, and states/provinces. Governments make decisions about which corporations receive tax breaks to locate their plants within the region. They pass laws that regulate everything from how long one's grass can grow before a fine is imposed, to how public schools will be funded. Therefore, people have an interest in influencing governments by contributing to political campaigns and helping elect the people who support their views. Interest groups such as environmental advocacy, flat tax, and gay rights organizations also wield power and try to influence the political process at the meso level.

Power processes pervade the micro, meso, and macro levels. Locally organized groups can force change that influences politics at the local, state/provincial, national, or global levels. Provincial or state laws shape what can and cannot be done at the local level. These laws may either limit or enhance the ability of citizens to protest or express their views by determining where and when protests can occur.

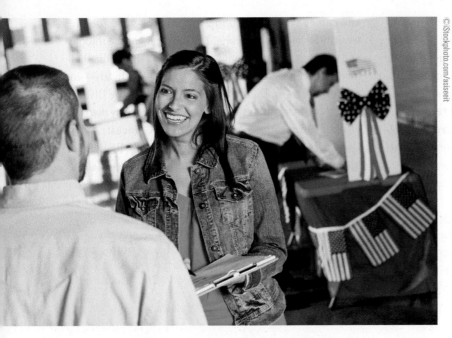

©iStockphoto.com/asiseeit

Individual campaign workers in local communities try to influence voters at the micro level to determine who will wield power in meso and the macro systems.

Laws at the national and global levels influence state, provincial, and county politics and policies. Global treaties, for example, affect national autonomy. Reluctance to yield national autonomy is the main reason the United States and a few other countries have refused to ratify seemingly very benign global treaties, such as the Convention on the Rights of the Child (UNICEF 2005).

Power can also be understood in terms of the allocation of economic resources in a society and what factors influence patterns of resource distribution. Both economic and political systems are important in the sociologist's consideration of power distribution in any society. Let us first consider the theoretical lenses that help us understand power and politics.

THEORETICAL PERSPECTIVES ON POWER AND PRIVILEGE

Do you and I have any real decision-making power? Can our voices or votes make a difference, or do leaders hold all the power? Many sociologists and political scientists have studied these questions and found several answers to who holds power and the relationship between the rulers and the ruled.

Among the common theoretical perspectives on power are our familiar ones: symbolic interaction, rational choice, structural-functional, and conflict theories.

Symbolic interaction theorists focus on symbols and constructions of reality that help some people assume power. A core concern is the legitimacy of power, or whether those who are ruled accept the right of their leaders to have power over them. *Rational choice* theorists emphasize that people calculate their own self-interests and make choices—including political choices—based on perceived benefits and costs to themselves. Much analysis of voting behavior has to do with how people vote to advance themselves, but also how they sometimes fail to understand which policies would truly be economically advantageous to them.

Focusing on the macro level, *structural-functionalists* believe that citizens legitimize political systems by supporting them through their votes or traditions. They do this because political systems serve important functions, or purposes, in society. They establish and coordinate societal goals—for example, promoting stability, providing law and order, engaging in relations with other countries, providing protection, and meeting social needs. *Conflict theorists* believe that the state protects the privileged position of a few, allowing them to consolidate power and wealth, and perpetuate inequalities that keep them in power. This power elite theory stems from conflict theory's contention that power is concentrated in the hands of an elite few and the masses have little power.

Micro- and Meso-Level Perspectives: Legitimacy of Power

Symbolic interactionists look at how loyalty to the power of the state is created—a loyalty so strong that citizens are willing to die for the state in a war. In the early years of the United States, citizens' loyalty tended to be mostly to individual states. Even as late as the Civil War, Northern battalions fought under the flag of their own state rather than that of the United States.

Most people in the United States now tend to think of themselves as U.S. citizens more than Virginians, Pennsylvanians, or Oregonians, and they are willing to defend the whole country. National symbols such as anthems and flags help create loyalty to nations. The treatment of flags illustrates the social construction of meaning around national symbols. The next "Sociology in Our Social World" explores this issue.

sociology in our social world

The Flag, Symbolism, and Patriotism

Flags have become pervasive symbols of nations, helping to create a national identity (Billig 1995). In some countries, loyalty to the nation is taught with daily pledges to the flag at work or school. National loyalty becomes sacred, and that sacredness is imbedded in the flag as a symbol of patriotism. Émile Durkheim maintained that one's national group elicits loyalty and, thereby, becomes sacred. He believed that sacredness is a form of respect for that which transcends the individual (such as the nation) (Durkheim 1947).

In the United States, the design of the flag and the respect of the public for it illustrate key ideas in symbolic interaction theory. The stars and stripes each have specific meaning related to states and the nation. Flag etiquette instructions also highlight the respect it holds as a symbol. Government instructions on how to care for the flag (the "Flag Code") make it clear that flying a faded, soiled, or dirty flag is an offense to the flag. We should either burn or bury a damaged flag as a way to honor and respect it (U.S. Flag Code 2008).

Some citizens and legislators have proposed a constitutional amendment prohibiting burning of the U.S. flag to prevent protesters from using the flag as a protest statement against certain U.S. policies. Because such protests show disrespect for the flag, some patriots have a visceral reaction of outrage. As recently as June 2006, the Senate came within one vote of sending the flag-burning amendment to the individual states for ratification ("Flag-Burning Amendment" 2006). Supporters want flag burners punished and disrespect for the flag outlawed.

© Can Stock Photo Inc. / jackyric

This man no doubt feels he is expressing his patriotism, yet technically he is violating the U.S. Flag Code and "desecrating" the American flag. During the Vietnam War, when more people were aware of the Flag Code, protesters risked attacks for dressing this way and "disrespecting" the flag and country.

Those who oppose this amendment feel that only tyrannical countries limit freedom of speech. They feel that the principle of free speech, central to democracy, must be allowed even if a sacred symbol is at stake. Indeed, opponents of the amendment think passing such a law would be a desecration of what that flag stands for. Supporters and opponents of the amendment have each attached different meanings to what is considered desecration of the national symbol. In the meantime, if you have a tattered or fading flag, burning it is the way you honor that flag—so long as you do so in private!

(Continued)

(Continued)

Other aspects of the U.S. Flag Code are interesting precisely because many people violate this code unknowingly when they think they are displaying their patriotism (U.S. Flag Code 2008):

1. The flag should never be used for advertising in any manner whatsoever. It should not be embroidered on cushions, handkerchiefs, or scarves, or reproduced on paper napkins, carry-out bags, wrappers, or anything else that will soon be thrown away.

2. No part of the flag—depictions of stars and stripes that are in any form other than that approved for the flag design itself—should ever be used as a costume, a clothing item, or an athletic uniform.

3. Displaying a flag after dark should not be done unless it is illuminated, and it should not be left out when it is raining.

4. The flag should never be represented flat or horizontally (as many marching bands do). It should always be aloft and free.

5. The flag should under no circumstances be used as a ceiling covering. (U.S. Flag Code 2008)

According to the standards established by U.S. military representatives and congressional action, any of these forms of display may be considered a desecration of the flag, yet the meaning that most citizens give to these acts may be quite different. Symbolic interactionists are interested in the meaning people give to actions and how symbols themselves inform behavior.

Thinking Sociologically

Do you think wearing a shirt or sweater with the U.S. stars and stripes in some sort of artistic design is an act of desecration of the flag or a statement of patriotism? Why or why not? How does this issue illustrate that respect is, in the words of a symbolic interactionist, "socially constructed"?

Socialization of individuals at the micro level generally instills a strong sense of the legitimacy and authority of the reigning government in a particular society. This includes loyalty to a flag or another symbol that represents the nation, as illustrated above. Individuals learn their political and economic attitudes, values, and behaviors—their political socialization—from family, schools, the media, and their nation. For example, national leaders provide much of the information for newspapers and other media and can spin that information to suit their needs and manage the perceptions of the public. Governments also play a role in what is taught in schools, which shapes attitudes of the citizenry regarding democracy, capitalism, socialism, and other political and economic systems (Glasberg and Shannon 2011).

Social Constructions of Politics: Legitimacy, Authority, and Power. Max Weber distinguished

between legitimate and illegitimate power. *Power that people consider legitimate* is authority, and *is recognized as rightful by those subject to it* (Weber 1947). Governments are given legitimate power when citizens acknowledge that the government has the right to exercise power over them. They adhere to a judge's rulings because they recognize that court decrees are legitimate. In contrast, illegitimate power, or coercion, includes living under force of a military regime or being kidnapped or imprisoned without charge (see Figure 13.1). These distinctions between legitimate and illegitimate power are important to our understanding of how leaders or political institutions establish the right to lead. To Weber, illegitimate power is sustained by brute force or coercion. Authority, on the other hand, is granted by the people subject to the power. They believe in the legitimacy of the authority so they willingly obey (Weber 1946).

How Do Leaders Gain Legitimate Power? Generally, leaders with legitimate power gained their positions in one of three ways:

1. *Traditional authority* is passed on through the generations, usually within a family line, so that positions are inherited. Tribal leaders in African societies pass their

FIGURE 13.1 Weber's Formula Regarding Power

Force + Consent = Power

Force < Consent = Legitimate Power (authority)

Force > Consent = Illegitimate Power (e.g., dictatorship)

titles and power to their sons. Japanese and many European royal lines pass from generation to generation. Usually called a monarchy, this has been the most common form of leadership throughout history. Authority is seen as "normal" for a family or a person because of tradition. It has always been done that way, so no one challenges it. When authority is granted based on tradition, authority rests with the position rather than the person. The authority is easily transferred to another heir of that status.

2. *Charismatic authority* is power based on a claim of extraordinary, even divine, personal characteristics. Charismatic leaders often emerge at times of change when strong, new leadership is needed. For charismatic leaders, unlike traditional authority leaders, the right to lead rests with the person, not the position. Followers believe power is rooted in the personality of a dynamic individual. This is an inherently change-oriented and unstable form of leadership because authority resides in a single person. The most common pattern is that, as stability reemerges, power will become institutionalized—rooted in stable routine patterns of the organization. Charismatic leaders are effective during transitional periods but often replaced by rational-legal leaders once affairs of state become stable.

Some examples of charismatic religious leaders include Jesus, Muhammad, Joan of Arc, and the founder of the Mormon Church, Joseph Smith. Charismatic political leaders include Mao Zedong in China and Mahatma Gandhi in India. Both men led their countries to independence and had respect from citizens that bordered on "awe." One charismatic leader today is Aung San Suu Kyi, pro-democracy activist and Nobel Prize winner who was imprisoned for many years by the military leadership in Myanmar (formerly known as Burma).

3. *Rational-legal authority* is the most typical type of legitimate power in modern nation-states. Authority is given not to a particular person, but to the position the person holds. Such authority is often found in political and economic bureaucracies in the modern states. For example, the president of the United States has authority due to the office he holds, just as the CEO of a corporation does. Individuals are granted authority because they have proper training or have proven their merit.

Japan's Emperor Akihito (right) and Empress Michiko leave after praying at the altar of the late Prince Tomohito. Japan has the only monarch in the world with the title *Emperor*, a position that is inherited through the family line. This is an example of traditional authority.

Each of these three types of authority is a "legitimate" exercise of power because the people being governed give their consent, at least implicitly, to the leaders (Weber 1947, [1904–1905] 1958). However, on occasion, leaders overstep their legitimate bounds and rule by force. Some of these rulers, such as Muammar Gaddafi in Libya and Hosni Mubarak of Egypt, are challenged and overthrown.

Self-Interest as a Path to Legitimacy. In contemporary democratic politics, politicians and political commentators often explicitly refer to the self-interests of voters. This reflects the *rational choice perspective* that humans tend to vote for their own benefit, regardless of whether the actions of government would be fair to all citizens.

Both U.S. Republican and Democratic parties try to convince the public and donors that their policies will

Aung San Suu Kyi, Nobel Prize winner and opposition leader in Myanmar (Burma), spent 15 years under house arrest after an authoritarian military junta took over the government. Released from house arrest to participate in the changing political situation in Burma, she and her party recently won 40 of 45 elected seats in the government. She has charismatic authority.

serve their self-interests. Democrats tend to argue that their government policies benefit citizens directly, with government programs for the middle and working classes, such as government support for preschool and higher education. Republicans, on the other hand, often stress that less government and lower taxes create a greater stimulus to the economy than anything the government can do. Again, the appeal is to self-interests. Members of both political parties promise to help those who support and vote for them, once they are put in positions of power.

Many voters do not understand the issues at play in elections and vote for people who support policies that would actually harm them. To make it even more complex, some people vote based on values—right to life,

support for the needy, or protection of the environment, for example—because they think it is the right thing to do. The policy may not be in the person's economic self-interests—unless the person is considering the interest of his or her children and grandchildren or long-term non-economic interests, such as a desire to build a society pleasing to God.

Macro-Level Perspectives: Who Rules?

Pluralist Model of Power. As noted in previous chapters, the pluralist model holds that power is distributed among various groups so that no one group has complete power. According to pluralists, it is primarily through interest groups that you and I influence decision-making processes. Groups such as unions or environmental organizations represent our interests and act to keep power from being concentrated in the hands of an elite few (Dahl 1961; Dye and Zeigler 1983). One current example of an interest group in the United States is the Tea Party, which is discussed in the next "Sociology in Our Social World."

Politics involves negotiation and compromise among competing groups. Interest groups can influence laws and policies by mobilizing large numbers of voters or political donors. Examples include efforts to influence health care reform in the United States, combat global climate change, and reform government, business, and banking industry practices. Greenpeace, Common Cause, Earth First!, Bread for the World, Focus on the Family, the Family Research Council, the Service Employees International Union, and other consumer, environmental, religious, and political action groups have had impacts on policy decisions. According to pluralists, shared power is found in each person's ability to join groups and influence policy decisions and outcomes.

National or international nongovernmental organizations (NGOs) can have a major impact on global issues and policy making, as exemplified by the Grameen Bank, BRAC, and other microcredit organizations that work in the field of international development (The Global Journal 2013; Yunus and Jolis 1999). NGOs exert influence on power holders because of the numbers they represent, the money they control, the issues they address, and the effectiveness of their spokespeople or lobbyists. Sometimes they form coalitions around issues of concern such as the environment, human rights, health care, or women's and children's issues. The efforts of religious, business,

sociology in our social world

Interest Groups in Politics: The Tea Party

According to pluralist theorists, interest groups influence the decision-making process, though ideally no one group has complete power. The Tea Party movement in the United States began as a small group of disaffected individuals opposed to government expansion and higher taxes. With big wins in the 2010 congressional election, it has become a major determinant of Republican Party politics. Its accomplishments include electing a number of new members to the U.S. Congress, resulting in the House of Representatives being controlled by the fiscally conservative wing of the Republican Party (Skocpol and Williamson 2012). Tea Party members have also won approximately 700 seats in state legislatures around the country. Their impact moved the Republican platform to the right, and focused debates in Congress on the national debt and reducing the size of the federal government (Martin and Meckler 2012; Tanenhaus 2012).

Though sometimes short on specific proposals, the Tea Party relies on ideas from conservative think tanks like the Heritage Foundation and the Cato Institute. In addition to electing fiscal conservatives, their goals include encouraging disaffection with the Washington establishment and reducing support for big government programs including health care and social programs (Mann and Ornstein 2012; Ryan, Cantor, and McCarthy 2010). Citizens join such a movement because of a common core of concerns—a central one being the staggeringly large national debt (U.S. Debt Clock 2013; U.S. Government Accountability Office 2014).

The second driving concern of the movement is lower taxes, with the idea that lower taxes will allow those who have more resources to spend them on new businesses and expand the economy.

Rational choice theorists contend that people support programs serving their own interests. The citizens who join the movement, therefore, might fit into *at least* one of four categories: those who (1) see government programs as expensive to themselves and as benefitting those who contribute least to society, (2) are quite affluent and would benefit most from tax cuts, (3) have aspirations and expectations of attaining such wealth in the future, and (4) believe that the current system has not addressed their own needs.

Symbolic interactionists tend to focus on another social reality—the way people socially construct what a good and fair society looks like. Tea Party advocates are less likely to see a good society as one that stresses collective well-being and community enhancement, and more likely to want society to maximize individualism and personal autonomy (Tanenhaus 2012).

and labor unions for immigration reform provide an example of such a coalition. Each of these groups, with their own set of constituents, believes that immigration reform is in its best interest.

According to pluralists, multiple power centers offer the best chance to maintain democratic forms of government because no one group dominates and many citizens are involved. Although an interest group may dominate decision making on a specific issue, no one group dictates all policy. On the other hand, some theorists maintain that only a small group of elite people really have much power.

Elite Model. The power elite model asserts it is inevitable that a small group of elite will rule societies. As we discussed in earlier chapters, they argue that this is the nature of individuals and society and that pluralists are imagining a world that does not exist. Individuals have limited power through interest groups, but real power is held by the power elite (Domhoff 2005, 2008; Dye 2002; Mills 1956). They wield power through their institutional roles and make decisions about war, peace, the economy, wages, taxes, justice, education, welfare, and health issues—all of which have serious impact on citizens. These powerful elites attempt to maintain, perpetuate, and even strengthen their rule. Robert Michels, a well-known political philosopher, believed that elite rule is inevitable. He described this pattern of domination as the *iron law of oligarchy*. In democratic and totalitarian societies alike, leaders have influence over who is elected to succeed them and to whom they give political favors. This influence eventually leads those in elite positions to abuse their power (Michels [1911] 1967).

The social philosopher Vilfredo Pareto expanded on this idea of abuse of power, pointing out that abuse would cause a countergroup to challenge the elite for power. Eventually, as the latter group gained power, its members would become corrupt as well, and the cycle—a *circulation of elites*—would continue. Corruption in many countries illustrates this pattern (Pareto [1911] 1955), as can be seen in current headlines from such various nations as Greece, Guatemala, Zimbabwe, and Bangladesh.

C. Wright Mills also argued that there is an invisible but interlocking power elite in U.S. society, consisting of leaders in military, business, and political spheres, wielding their power from behind the scenes. They make the key political, economic, and social decisions for the nation and manipulate what the public hears (Mills 1956).

According to the power elite model of G. William Domhoff, a wealthy few citizens of the United States form a cohesive economic-political power structure that represents their interests. Through interactions from a very young age in private clubs and schools, the elite socialize with one another and prepare to become "rulers." One can see today that many of those who hold top positions on corporate boards or in the foreign policy-making agencies of national government attended the same private preparatory schools and Ivy League colleges—Brown, Columbia, Cornell, Harvard, University of Pennsylvania, Dartmouth, Princeton, and Yale (Domhoff 2005, 2008; Howard 2007; Persell and Cookson 1985).

Domhoff analyzed leaders of large corporations and financial institutions and showed that their common characteristics promote a network of connections, or "higher circles," and constitute a pool of potential appointees to top government positions. Key government officials come from positions in industry, finance, law, and universities. They are linked with an international elite that helps shape the world economy. According to the power elite model, Congress ultimately has minimal power. The elected representatives accede to the power elite. Elite theorists believe that government seldom regulates business. Instead, business co-opts politicians to support its interests by providing the financial support needed to run political election campaigns (Domhoff 2008).

Pluralists, however, disagree, believing that a powerful government serves as a balance to the enormous power of the corporate world. Big business and big government are safety checks against tyranny—and each is convinced that the other is too big.

Thinking Sociologically

Do you think your national society is controlled by pluralist interest groups or a power elite? Can an individual outside of the power elite help influence policies in your nation? What makes you think so?

MICRO-LEVEL ANALYSIS: INDIVIDUALS, POWER, AND PARTICIPATION

Whether you have health insurance or are subject to a military draft depends in part on the political and economic decisions made by the government in power. Political systems influence our personal lives in myriad ways, some of which are readily apparent: health and safety regulations, taxation, a military draft, regulations on food and the drugs we buy, and even whether the gallon of gas pumped into our car is really a full gallon—or is really gasoline. In this section, we explore the impact individuals have on the government and the variables that influence participation in political and economic policy-making processes. At the micro level, individuals decide to vote or otherwise participate in the political system. This private decision is, in turn, affected by where those individuals fall in the stratification system of society, not just by personal choices.

Participation in Democratic Processes

Citizens in democratic countries have the right to free and fair elections. Many social scientists, including sociologists, have tried to understand what influences citizens' decisions on whether and how to vote. Political sociologists want to know how participation affects (and is affected by) an individual's perception of his or her power in relationship to the state. The next "Sociologists in Action" on page 426 focuses on a political sociologist who examines the voting patterns of U.S. citizens in red, blue, and purple states.

Ideology and Attitudes About Politics and Economics. What kind of government do you think is best? If you believe that individuals are not naturally social people and, instead, are motivated only by selfish considerations and desire for power, you may feel as the 17th-century English philosopher Thomas Hobbes did—that order must be imposed by an all-powerful sovereign. In that scenario, individuals do not have rights, and rulers of states may control them in any way necessary. Control over people is more important than individual freedom and liberty because people cannot exist without the state.

On the other hand, you may believe, as did John Locke, another 17th-century political philosopher, that humans are naturally social and free and that governments have a right to exist only if they preserve that freedom. Humans, Locke argued, should have their needs and interests met by the state, and among these needs are liberty, ability to sustain life, and ownership of property. Unlike Hobbes, Locke believed that governments must have the consent of the people.

What kind of economic system do you favor? Do you believe in equal distribution of resources—wealth, property, and income—or do you think that those who are most able or have inherited high status should receive more of the wealth? Some social scientists, politicians, and voters think that individuals have different abilities and are therefore entitled to different rewards. Some people are successful, and some are not. (Recall the structural-functional theory discussion in Chapter 7 on stratification about the inevitability of inequality.) Others think

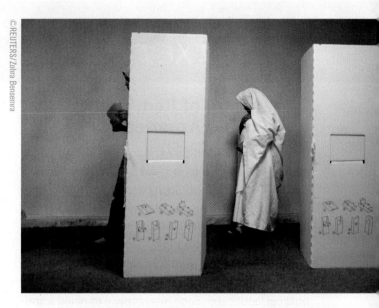

A woman in Libya commits an act of courage as she casts her ballot during the 2012 national Congress elections. The elections were considered a crucial step for Libya, but they occurred amid fears of violence.

government should facilitate a more equal distribution of resources, so that all have similar life chances. Conflict theorists tend to support this view.

 Thinking Sociologically

How might your decision about how to vote (a micro-level decision) be affected by your ideology and attitudes about politics and economics? How might those decisions on how to vote make a difference in how state/provincial, national, or global systems work?

Levels of Participation in Politics. As mentioned in previous chapters, wealthier people are more likely to vote for various reasons. For example, they tend to

- have been socialized to believe they can make an impact on the political process;
- benefit from an educational background that allows them to understand the issues at hand and how their own self-interests are at stake;
- have the time to follow the news and political issues; and
- experience a more flexible schedule that allows them the time to vote.

Those with little money, on the other hand, tend to feel that politics has little relevance for them (apathy) or

SOCIOLOGISTS IN ACTION:
RUY TEIXEIRA

The Future of Red, Blue, and Purple America

Presidential elections are exciting times in the political arena. Prominent among those studying elections is Dr. Ruy Teixeira, a sociologist and specialist in political demography and geography. Teixeira conducts research on U.S. politics with its red (Republican) and blue (Democratic) states and, particularly, "purple" or swing states. He convened a group of researchers to consider social changes that have affected the U.S. political landscape. Each researcher examined a specific aspect of the political scene. Teixeira focused particularly on the purple or swing states.

Teixeira and his colleagues note that five major trends influenced the 2012 presidential election:

1. Minority voters increased their share of the voting population from 26% in 2008 to 28% in 2012.

2. Minority voters maintained their overwhelming support for Obama.

3. The gender gap got even bigger; Obama carried women, 55% to 44%, but lost men, 45% to 52%.

4. Professionals continued their strong support for Democrats.

5. Young voters (the Millennials) turned out again in droves for the Democrats, comprising 19% of the electorate, up from 18% in 2008 (Teixeira 2012b).

(See Figure 13.2 for the political breakdown of states in the 2012 presidential election.)

The political strength and orientations of various groups has shifted over the past several decades, resulting in deadlock on each side of the political spectrum. However, Teixeira and other researchers believe that this deadlock is likely to ease by the 2016 elections. Growth in Hispanic and Asian groups, shifts of the population to different regions of the country and from rural to urban areas, changing family structures and shifting women's roles, aging of baby boomers, and the high levels of political engagement by Millennials who generally value diversity all combine to suggest major changes by the 2016 election (Teixeira and Halpin 2012).

Teixeira predicts that "culture wars"—the polarization and clashes between segments of society over differences in values—will not be as important in the future. Issues such as how to help nontraditional families, improve education, and provide health care will be shared concerns that unite people. Therefore, he predicts that the polarization that has divided some communities will not last.

Teixeira has found that sociology provides exceptionally useful theory and methods to help understand our political world.

• •

Note: Ruy Teixeira is a senior fellow at the Century Foundation and the Center for American Progress, and a fellow at the Brookings Institution. Being a fellow means employment as a scholar to carry out research that meets the goals of the organization or think tank.

FIGURE 13.2   States That Voted Republican (Romney/Ryan) or Democratic (Obama/Biden) in the U.S. Presidential Election of 2012

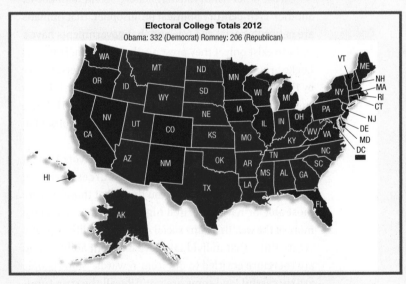

Source: "Latest Presidential Election 2012 Map: Obama Beats Romney 303 to 206 Electoral Votes, But Florida Still Too Close to Call." *Latinos Post,* November 7, 2012. www.latinospost.com/articles/6570/20121107/latest-presidential-election-2012-map-obama-beats.htm

Swing Voters

that they cannot affect the process and are disaffected by the scandals or corruption in politics (alienation from a system that does not value them). Participation in elections in the United States is the second lowest of the Global North democracies, as indicated in Table 13.1.

Structural factors also influence voting. The 2012 debates over U.S. voter registration are a case in point, with some states combing their voter lists for ineligible

voters or making registration and voting difficult for some citizens, usually the elderly, minorities, and people in poverty who may have problems obtaining acceptable ID. By contrast, in 22 countries voting is compulsory, a legal obligation of citizenship, and voter turnout is above 90%. For example, 10 countries that enforce voting are Argentina, Australia, Brazil, Democratic Republic of Congo, Ecuador, Luxembourg, Nauru, Peru, Singapore, and Uruguay; it is a violation of the law not to vote (Frankal 2011; World Factbook 2011). Fines, community service, and even jail time are penalties for not voting. Elections are held over many days to ensure that people can get to the polls. Some other countries also make sure that ethnic minorities and women have a voice by structuring elections to ensure broad representation. Even inmates in prison are expected to vote in some countries. The next "Sociology Around the World" on page 429 examines the reasons that an African country—the war-torn nation of Rwanda—emerged early in the 21st century with the highest percentage of women in government of any nation in the world.

In the 2012 presidential election, a higher percentage than normal, 58.7%, of eligible voters turned out (Nonprofit Vote 2012; U.S. Elections Project 2012), and the numbers have generally been higher in the 21st century than in the three decades from 1970 to 2000 (Lederman 2012). A higher African American and Latino participation was a major reason why voter participation was relatively high during the last few presidential elections (Sherwood 2012; Short 2009). Another key factor was a resurgence of interest in politics among those under 30 years old during the 2008 and 2012 presidential campaigns as discussed in the next "Sociology in Our Social World" feature on page 431.

Table 13.1 Average Voter Participation Over 60 Years (all elections)*

Country	Voter Participation % (all elections for 60 years)	Most Recent Parliamentary Election
Italy	92.5	75.2% (2013)
Iceland	89.5	81.4% (2013)
New Zealand	86.2	74.2% (2011)
South Africa	85.5	77.3% (2009)
Austria	85.1	81.7% (2008)
The Netherlands	84.8	74.6% (2012)
Australia	84.4	93.2% (2010)
Denmark	83.6	87.7% (2011)
Sweden	83.3	84.6% (2010
Germany	80.6	70.8% (2009)
United Kingdom	74.9	65.8% (2010)
Argentina	70.6	79.4% (2011)
Japan	69.0	59.3% (2012)
Canada	68.4	61.4% (2011)
France	67.3	55.4% (2012)
Bolivia	61.4	94.6% (2009)
USA	48.3	58.7% (2012)
Mexico	48.1	62.5% (2012)

Source: International Institute for Democracy and Electoral Assistance (2012).

*The figures are averages of voter participation for all elections since 1945. Note that enfranchisement of women and various ethnic minorities changed in some countries during that time, so these should be viewed as very crude overall indicators of voting patterns.

Note: To see the voting participation figures for 172 countries in the world, go to www.idea.int/vt/.

Thinking Sociologically

How did you, your parents, and your grandparents vote (or whom did you favor, if you did not actually vote) in the last presidential election? Why? Do you think your respective ages played a role in whom you supported? Why or why not?

In off-year elections—when many senators, congressional representatives, and state governors are elected—the turnout hovers in the low 40s or even below. This means that if 40% of the eligible population votes and it is a very close election, only slightly more than 20% of the citizenry may have elected the new officeholder. So voter turnout is an important issue for a society that purports to be a democracy. Figure 13.3 indicates voter turnout since 1990.

FIGURE 13.3 Voter Turnout in the United States: 1990–2012 (by percentage of eligible voters)

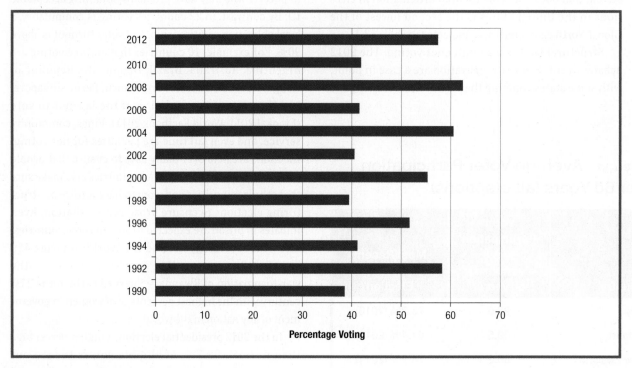

Source: U.S. Elections Project (2012).

MESO-LEVEL ANALYSIS: DISTRIBUTIONS OF POWER AND PRIVILEGE WITHIN A NATION

In southern Africa, Bantu tribal groups provide for heirs to take on leadership when a leader dies. When there is no male heir to the position, a female from the same lineage is appointed. This woman must assume the legal and social roles of a male husband, father, and chief by acting as a male and taking a "wife." The wife is assigned male sexual partners, who become the biological fathers of her children. This provides heirs for the lineage, but the female chief is their social father because she has socially become a male. This pattern has been common practice in many southern Bantu societies and among many other populations in four separate geographic areas of Africa. Anthropologists interpret this as a means of maintaining public positions of dominance and power in the hands of males in a particular family and community (O'Brien 1977). Ruling groups in society, in this case a meso-level tribal society under the jurisdiction of a nation-state, have mechanisms for ensuring a smooth transition of power to keep the controlling structure functioning.

Meso-level political institutions include state or provincial governments, national political parties, and large formal organizations within the nation. Those political institutions also influence and are influenced by other meso-level institutions: family, education, religion, health care, and economics.

What Purposes Do Political and Economic Institutions Serve?

We have learned in earlier chapters that each institution has purposes or functions it serves for society. Just as family, education, health care, and religion meet certain

Sociology Around the World

Women and Political Change in Post-Genocide Rwanda

By Melanie Hughes

In 2003, Rwanda became the new global leader in women's political representation. In 2011, women were elected to 56% of the seats in Rwanda's Chamber of Deputies, plus the speaker's chair and cabinet positions, making it the most gender balanced of any national legislature in the history of the world (McCrummen 2008; Paxton and Hughes 2007; see also Table 9.1). For the first time since 1988, a country outside of Scandinavia garnered the top spot in women's political representation, and for the first time in history, the position was held by an African country. From just 10 years earlier, the number of women serving in Rwanda's parliament almost tripled.

Many were particularly surprised about Rwandan women's involvement, given the country's recent history of economic upheaval and civil war. The instability culminated in 1994, when during a span of 100 days an estimated 800,000 ethnic Tutsis and moderate Hutus died at the hands of their countrymen and -women in a horrific ethnic genocide. So, how did Rwanda bounce back within a decade to lead the world in women's political representation?

At the micro level, research suggests that the behavior of individual women during and after the Rwandan genocide generated support for their empowerment (Hughes 2004). During the civil war, women served on the front lines with men, led military actions, and worked as mediators to help end the insurgency. After conflict subsided, women played key roles in the reconstruction effort

(UNIFEM 2002). Interviews with Rwandans suggest that the burdens taken on by women during this period generated both the political will and the public support necessary to advance women in politics (Mutamba 2005).

Important changes also occurred at the meso level. Immediately after the killing subsided, women's associations, both new and old, began to step into the void (Longman 2005). Women's organizations took action early on to shape the new state. For example, in 1994, an organization of women's

The Rwanda government has a higher percentage of women in its legislature than any government in the world.

associations drafted a document addressing Rwanda's postconflict problems and suggesting how women could foster reconciliation (Powley 2003). Building up to the adoption of the new constitution in 2003, women's organizations served as a bridge, taking suggestions from women at the grassroots level into meetings with the transitional government.

(Continued)

(Continued)

Women at all levels were supported by international organizations and foreign aid. Rwanda's economic troubles meant that dependence on international funding was unavoidable, and women were well situated to take advantage of foreign monies. The empowerment of women, especially in the Global South, was on the agenda of the United Nations and other global bodies. Therefore, many international organizations helped advance the idea that women's incorporation into political decision-making positions was essential for sustainable peace (Hughes 2004).

Action by individual women, native women's associations, and international organizations all helped encourage the government to adopt female-friendly political institutions. Women's councils and women-only elections were established to guarantee female representation down to the grassroots level. In addition, the new constitution mandated that women fill 30% of all policy-making posts in Rwanda.

Rwanda today has a democratically elected government, but with a fairly authoritarian leader. However, since the election in 2003, women have still been able to revise inheritance laws, pass a law banning discrimination against women, and strengthen rape laws (Longman 2005). Rwanda has come a long way toward giving women a political voice.

• •

Melanie M. Hughes is an associate professor of sociology at the University of Pittsburgh. She is coauthor of Women, Politics, and Power: A Global Perspective *(SAGE 2014), now in its second edition.*

societal needs, so do the political and economic systems. The following six activities are typical societal purposes (functions) of meso-level political and economic institutions. They set the stage for power and privilege carried out at the macro level in national and international arenas.

1. *To maintain social control:* We expect to live in safety, to live according to certain "rules," to be employed in meaningful work, and to participate in other activities prescribed or protected by law. Ideally, governments help clarify expectations and customs and implement laws that express societal values.

2. *To serve as an arbiter in disputes:* When disputes arise over property or the actions of another individual or group, a judicial branch of government can intervene. In some systems, such as the tribal groups mentioned earlier, a council of elders or powerful individuals performs judicial functions. In other cases, elected or appointed judges have the right to hear disputes, make judgments, and carry out punishment for infractions.

3. *To protect citizens:* Governments are responsible for protecting citizens from takeover by external powers or disruption from internal sources.

4. *To represent the group in relations with other groups or societies:* Individuals cannot negotiate agreements with foreign neighbors. Official representatives deal with other officials to negotiate arms and trade agreements, protect the world's airways, determine fishing rights, and establish military bases in foreign lands, among other agreements.

The four functions listed thus far are rather clearly political in nature; the two that follow are areas of contention between political and economic realms.

5. *To make plans for the future of the group:* As individuals, we have little direct impact on the direction our society takes, but the official governmental body—be it elected, appointed, or imposed through force—shares responsibility with economic institutions for planning in the society. In some (but not all) socialist societies, this planning determines how many engineers, teachers, or

sociology in our social world

The 2012 Presidential Election and the Youth Vote
By Jeremiah Castle

The 2012 U.S. presidential election was a competitive race between incumbent Barack Obama and challenger Mitt Romney. The election saw the creation or evolution of several trends that impact younger voters. Recognizing that the 18–29 age group was a key part of Obama's coalition in 2008, both campaigns attempted to reach out to this constituency in debates and advertisements. Social media again played an important role, as the campaigns used platforms like Facebook and Twitter to keep followers updated on news and appearances. These trends suggest that both parties are increasingly realizing the impact of younger voters.

Throughout the campaign, both candidates stressed how their policies would improve life for recent graduates. For example, during the debate where undecided voters asked the candidates questions, a 20-year-old college student asked the candidates what they could do to make sure college students would have jobs after graduation. Romney assured the young voter that he would maintain the Pell Grant and student loan programs and promised to improve the economy, thereby creating more jobs for recent graduates. Obama emphasized how creating new manufacturing jobs, increasing jobs in green energy, and reducing the deficit would create employment opportunities for younger voters

("Full Transcript of the Second Presidential Debate" 2012). Their responses suggest that both candidates were keenly aware of the impact of economic conditions on the plight of younger voters.

In an effort to appeal to younger voters, both parties explored new ways to use social media in 2012. Obama kicked off his reelection campaign with a video posted on YouTube (Cillizza 2011; "It Begins With Us" 2012). Throughout the campaign, both Obama (@BarackObama) and Romney (@MittRomney) used Twitter accounts to spread news, advocate policies, and keep supporters energized over the course of the campaign. While both campaigns used social media, data suggest that the Obama campaign was able to reach a wider audience. For example, as of November 6, 2012, Obama's Facebook page had 32 million likes, while Romney's page had just 12 million. Obama's advantage appeared to be even greater on Twitter: As of November 6, 2012, Obama had over 22 million followers, while Romney had just 1.7 million followers.

Obama also had the advantage among youth voters at the polls. Early exit polls confirmed that, while Obama's advantage among younger voters was not as large as it was in 2008, it remained substantial. In 2012, 60% of voters ages 18 to 29 supported Obama (down from 66% of younger voters in 2008), while 36% supported Romney. Exit polls also showed that younger voters represented about 19% of the total electorate, up roughly a point from

(Continued)

(Continued)

2008 (Kingkade 2012). One study showed that if the votes of those under 30 were not counted, Romney would have won the crucial battleground states of Ohio, Florida, Virginia, and Pennsylvania, thereby giving him the presidency ("At Least 80 Electoral Votes Depended on Youth" 2012). This finding leaves little doubt that younger voters had a significant impact on the outcome of the election.

The pattern of increasing turnout from younger voters led experts, including Rock the Vote president Heather Smith, to speculate that higher youth turnout is due to differing norms among the Millennial generation (the current youth generation, born between the 1980s and 2000s) and Generation X (those born between the 1960s and 1980s) (Robillard 2012). However, it remains to be seen whether this trend will continue in the future, and candidates will need to show they can appeal to younger voters. While nothing is certain, current evidence suggests that younger voters will continue to play an important role in national politics in the coming years.

• •

Jeremiah Castle minored in sociology in college and is now a PhD candidate in political science at the University of Notre Dame.

nurses are needed. The appropriate numbers of people are then trained according to these projections. In other societies, power is much less direct. In capitalist systems, for instance, supply and demand are assumed to regulate the economic system, and there is less governmental planning in economic matters than in socialist societies. The question of who plans for the future is often a source of stress between the political and economic institutions: Are the planners elected politicians/public servants or private entrepreneurs?

6. *To provide for the needs of their citizens:* Governments differ greatly in the degree to which they attempt to meet the material needs of citizens. Some provide for most of the health and welfare needs of citizens, whereas others tend to leave this largely to individuals, families, local community agencies, and other institutions, such as faith communities. Not everyone agrees that providing for needs is an inherent responsibility of the state. Some people believe that the economy will produce jobs, goods, and services for the population if the government gets out of the way and lets individuals make decisions based on their self-interests. The debates over health care and welfare systems in the United States point to conflicts over who should be responsible—the state or private individuals. Should such services be coordinated by the government or left to "the invisible hand" of market forces?

The ways in which governments and economic institutions carry out these six functions are largely determined by society's dominant philosophies of power and political structures. Political and economic institutions, like family and religious institutions, come in many forms. In essence, these variations in political institutions reflect variations in human ideas of power.

Thinking Sociologically

In an era of terrorist threats, how do you think the "protecting the safety of the citizens" function has affected the ability of governments to perform other functions?

Meso- and Macro-Level Systems of Power and Privilege

While *politics* refers to the social institution that determines and exercises power relations in society, *economics* is the social institution that deals with the production and distribution of goods and services. Both politics and economics focus on questions related directly to the concept of power and power relationships among and between individuals, organizations, nation-states, and societies. Economic and political systems overlap in part because those who have power also have access to resources. How goods are distributed to the members of society—a major function of economics—is often determined by who has political power.

Successful political campaigns, except at the most local level, require significant financial resources, so attaining political positions involves cultivating relationships with leaders in the economic system. Thus, there is a reciprocal relationship between economics and politics. In many countries, the government is the largest employer, purchaser of goods, controller of exports and imports, and regulator of industry and of interest rates. In the United States, many government regulatory agencies, such as the Food and Drug Administration, Department of Agriculture, and Justice Department, attempt to watch over the economic sector to protect consumers.

Government officials have a vested interest in the well-being of the economy, for should the economy fail, the state is likely to fail as well. Recessions, depressions, and high rates of inflation put severe strains on governments that need stable economies to run properly. When problems occur, government officials are inclined to increase their roles in the economic sector. Witness the volatile money markets from 2008 to 2012 and measures, such as bailouts, taken by many governments to stabilize their economies.

On September 29, 2008, the Dow Jones index dropped an unprecedented 777 points and fell another 782 points a week later. President Bush and Congress immediately began to look for "stimulus packages" to keep the economy from going into a deep recession. When Obama became president in 2009, turning the economy around became one of the key challenges of his presidency.

A dramatic drop in financial markets indicates a loss of the population's confidence in the economy and a mass reluctance to invest in it. Lending institutions cannot loan money easily, business stagnates, unemployment rates skyrocket, and the entire government may be held responsible for a lack of economic vitality. When a country goes into a recession, the party in power is often held responsible and will not likely be reelected if the recovery takes too long. Economic recessions can destroy the careers of politicians but can also create such dissatisfaction that the entire government may be at risk

One function of governments is to provide protection from external threats—the role of the military establishment. These soldiers are in training for that role.

of a citizen uprising. Indeed, in 2009, Dennis Blair, the U.S. director of national intelligence, declared the global economic crisis the most serious national security issue facing the nation, calling it a "bigger threat than Al Qaeda terrorists" (Haniffa 2009).

Types of Governments

The major systems of government in the world range from fascist totalitarianism to democracy. However, each culture puts its own imprint on the system it uses, making for tremendous variation in actual practice.

Authoritarian Governments. In authoritarian governments, *one absolute monarch or dictator, or a small group of unelected people, holds all of the political power.* They often have the backing of the military to keep them in power. Authoritarian regimes are common forms of government. Some are helpful to citizens—benevolent dictators—but almost all exert tremendous power and discourage dissent. The Castro brothers—Fidel and more recently Raúl—have maintained absolute political control of Cuba since 1959 (and exercised control, to various extents, over other institutions as well). While they are despised by many Cuban immigrants in the United States and subject to U.S. government embargos, they are admired by many Cubans as ruling in the best interests of the people, even if autocratically.

A stable economic system is essential to political stability, and extreme fluctuations in the economy threaten those in power. On September 29, 2008, the Dow Jones index dropped dramatically and the New York Stock Exchange, usually bustling with activity, emptied out. Recession in one country influences other countries around the world because of global trade and international markets.

Totalitarian Governments. A totalitarian government *is any form of government that almost totally controls people's lives.* They differ from authoritarian governments in that the political leaders also control the social and economic institutions. Totalitarian states are often based on a specific political ideology and run by a single ruling group or party, referred to as an *oligarchy.* Russia under Joseph Stalin, Germany under Adolf Hitler, Libya under Muammar Gaddafi, and North Korea under Kim Jong-un are examples. The state typically controls the workplace, education, the media, and other aspects of life. All actions revolve around state-established objectives. Dissent and opposition are discouraged or forcefully eliminated as we had when Gaddafi was in power, with violent crackdowns on demonstrators. Interrogation by secret police, imprisonment, and torture are used to quiet dissenters. Terror is used as a tactic to deal with both internal and external dissent, but when it is used by the state to control the citizenry or to terrorize those of another nation, it is called *state terrorism.*

Throughout history, most people have lived under authoritarian or totalitarian systems. Under certain conditions, totalitarian regimes can turn into democratic ones, and of course, democratically elected leaders can change or ignore laws to retain their positions of power, as was the case of a number of elected leaders who changed the constitutions to allow for them to run again (Venezuela, Zimbabwe, and Russia are examples). The next "Sociology Around the World" provides an example of one totalitarian regime.

Democratic Systems of Government. In contrast to totalitarian regimes, democratic governments are *characterized by accountability of the government to citizens and a large degree of control by individuals over their own lives.* Democracies always have at least two political parties that compete in elections for power and that generally accept the outcome of elections. Mechanisms for the smooth transfer of power are laid out in a constitution or another legal document. Ideal-type

Sociology Around the World

The Khmer Rouge Revolution: A Totalitarian Regime

These skulls are the remains of people massacred by the Khmer Rouge government in the Killing Fields in Cambodia (also called Kampuchea).

When the Khmer Rouge faction took over the government of Cambodia in 1978, it abolished private property, relocated urban dwellers to rural areas, seized personal property, classified some people as peasants, workers, or soldiers—and killed the rest. The group's most impressive feat was the total evacuation of the capital city, Phnom Penh, ordered to remove urban civilization and isolate Cambodia from other economic and political influences, such as free markets and democracy, which the Khmer Rouge opposed.

This complete social and economic revolution under the leadership of Pol Pot was planned in Paris by a small group of intellectual revolutionaries. They believed that it would allow Kampuchea (their name for Cambodia), to rebuild from scratch, eliminating all capitalism, private property, and Western influence.

After urban dwellers were resettled in rural camps, the totalitarian regime tried to break down the family system by prohibiting contact between members, including sexual relations between husbands and wives. Approximately 1.7 million people (21% of the population), including defeated soldiers, bureaucrats, royalty, businesspeople, intellectuals with opposing views, Muslims, and Buddhist monks, were slaughtered for minor offenses. Hence, the term *The Killing Fields* is used to describe the execution sites (Cambodian Genocide Program 2013).

Famine followed the killings, causing many Cambodians to flee their land, traveling by night and hiding by day to reach refugee camps across the border in Thailand. Pol Pot was finally overthrown in 1979, when Vietnam defeated Cambodia militarily and established a new government with Khmer Rouge defectors. Today, with increases in global demand for manufacturing, the economy in Cambodia is growing, especially in the areas of garment work and tourism. Violence still exists in Cambodia, however. The Human Rights Center reports chaos, corruption, poverty, and a reign of terror, as the military kills and extorts money from citizens. Killings, violence, and intimidation have surrounded elections, though the parliamentary elections of 2012 had somewhat fewer problems than in the past (Loy 2012).

Khmer Rouge Revolution

democracies share the following characteristics, although few democracies fit this description exactly:

1. *Citizens participate in selecting the government:* There are free elections with anonymous ballots cast, widespread suffrage (voting rights), and competition between members of different parties running for offices. Those who govern do so by the consent of the majority, but political minorities have rights, representation, and responsibilities.

2. *Civil liberties are guaranteed:* These usually include freedom of association, freedom of the press, freedom of speech, and freedom of religion. Such individual rights ensure dissent, and dissent creates more ideas about how to solve problems. These freedoms are therefore essential for a democracy to thrive.

3. *Government powers are limited by a constitution:* The government can intrude only into certain areas of individuals' lives. Criminal procedures and police power are clearly defined, thus prohibiting harassment or terrorism by police. The judicial system helps maintain a balance of power.

4. *Governmental structure and process are spelled out:* Generally, some officials are elected whereas others are appointed, but all are accountable to citizens. Representatives are given authority to pass laws, approve budgets, and hold the executive officer accountable for activities. The two main forms of democratic constitutional government are the parliamentary and presidential systems. In typical parliamentary governments, the head of government is a prime minister, chancellor, or premier, and there is also a president or a monarch, with less power. Countries with this model include Belgium, Canada, Denmark, the United Kingdom, Japan, Sweden, Ireland, India, Israel, Pakistan, and Turkey. Examples of presidential governments include France, Italy, the United States, Germany, Argentina, Brazil, Kenya, and the Philippines.

Proportional representation means that each party is given a number of seats corresponding to the percentage of votes it received in the election. In "winner-takes-all" systems, the individual with more than 50% of the votes gets the seat. In the United States, the winner-takes-all presidential electoral system has come under attack because the winner of the nationwide presidential popular vote can lose the election. This actually happened in two presidential elections in the United States: once in 1876 and the other time in 2000. Al Gore received the most votes for president in 2000, but because of the system for electing the Electoral College, George W. Bush became the next president, as elected by the Electoral College. Defenders of this system of choosing the president argue that this protects the voice of each state, even if each individual voice is not given the same weight.

Constitutional governments may include representatives from two to a dozen or more parties, as has been the case in Switzerland. Most have four or five viable ones. In European countries, typical parties include Social Democrats, Christian Democrats, Communists, Liberals, and other parties tied to specific local or state issues, such as Green parties.

Modern electronic technology can also have a complex relationship to democracy, enhancing it in some ways and undermining it in others. The next "Sociology in Our Social World" examines some of the impacts of electronic media on democracy.

Types of Economic Systems. As societies become industrialized, one of two basic economic systems evolves: a planned system or a market system. Planned or centralized systems involve state-based planning and control of

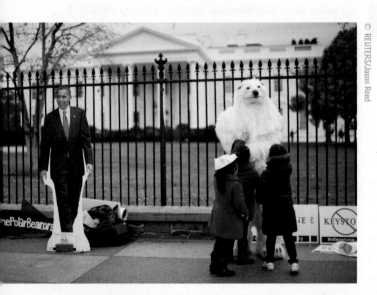

© REUTERS/Jason Reed

Children interact with a person dressed as a polar bear advocating against the proposed Keystone XL oil pipeline project, near a cutout of U.S. President Barack Obama outside the White House in 2013. Protests are one way citizens try to keep a government accountable and influence policy.

sociology in our social world

Technology and Democracy

In the modern world, there are new challenges and issues that face democracies. Electronic technology—the Internet and other tele-communications technologies—can be a boon to democracy, an opportunity for people around the world to gain information necessary to be an informed electorate, or a burden that hinders thoughtful debate and civic engagement in ideas, these being essential ingredients of a functioning democracy (Barber 2006). For example, the 2012 election for U.S. president had unlimited political contributions that funded negative campaign ads. These ads were often deceptive and required good analytical skills to avoid being manipulated by them.

The Internet, cell phones, and other tele-communications devices have been major instruments for indigenous people, linking them to the outside world and helping them to combat oppressive governments. On the other hand, blogs, talk shows, web pages, and Internet discussions are often known more for sound bites and polemical attacks on opponents than for reasoned debates in which opposing sides express views. Technology can be used by elected officials and those running for elected positions in myriad ways. In representative democracies, such as the United States, one key contribution that these technologies bring is speed—helping citizens stay in touch with their elected representatives. This allows them to follow and try to influence policy making as it unfolds.

However, speed is not always good for democracy. Legislation requires the ability to debate and compromise, but digital media has the tendency to reduce political discourse to simplistic sound bites of opposites, as though only two choices are possible (Barber 2006).

Technology can also invade citizens' privacy, even in democracies. For example, the leaking of classified information in 2013 revealed that the U.S. government keeps track of its citizens' communications by having direct access to the servers of Google, Apple, Facebook, and other Internet companies (Greenwald and MacAskill 2013). These intrusions are done in the name of protecting the public from terrorists, but some citizens believe that it violates their right to privacy.

Thinking Sociologically

How can the above issues of technology be problems for representative democracy? Which are benefits? What effect do they have on direct participatory democracy?

property, whereas market systems stress individual planning and private ownership of property, with much less governmental coordination or oversight. These basic types vary, depending on the peculiarities of the country and its economy. For instance, China has a highly central-ized planned economy with government control, yet some private property and incentive plans exist, and these are expanding. The United States is a market system, yet the government puts many limitations on business enterprises and regulates the flow and value of money. Distinctions between the two major types rest on the degree of centralized planning and the ownership of

▶ Economic Systems   🖥 Obama's Blackberry

property. In each type of system, decisions must be made concerning which goods to produce (and in what quantity), what to do in the event of shortages or surpluses, and how to distribute goods. Who has the power to make these decisions helps determine what type of system it is.

Market/Capitalist Economic Systems. Market or capitalist economic systems *are driven by the balance of supply and demand, allowing free competition to reward the efficient and the innovative with profits. They stress individual planning and private ownership of property.* As noted earlier, the goal of capitalism is profit, made through free competition between competitors for the available markets. Proponents of pure capitalism assume that the laws of supply and demand will allow some to profit, while others fail. Needed goods will be made, and the best product for the price will win out over the others. No planning by an oversight group is necessary, because the invisible hand of the market will ensure sufficient quality control, production, and distribution of goods. This system also rewards innovative entrepreneurs who take risks and solve problems in new ways, resulting in potential growth and prosperity.

Capitalist manufacturers try to bring in more money than they pay out to produce goods and services. As Marx described, because workers are a production cost, getting the maximum labor output for the minimum wage benefits capitalists. Therefore, multinational corporations look throughout the world for the cheapest sources of labor with the fewest restrictions on employment and operations. This potential and practice of labor exploitation leads most governments to exercise some control over manufacturing and the market, although the degree of control varies widely.

Capitalism was closest to its pure form during the Industrial Revolution, when some entrepreneurs gained control of large amounts of capital and resources, and legislation to control owners and protect workers did not yet exist. Using available labor and mechanical innovations, these entrepreneurs built industries and, soon, monopolies (exclusive control over supplying certain goods). Craftspeople such as cobblers could not compete with the efficiency of the new machine-run shops, and many were forced to become laborers in new industries to survive.

As we noted in earlier chapters, Marx predicted that capitalism would cause citizens to split into two main classes: the *bourgeoisie*, capitalists who own the means of production (the "haves"), and the *proletariat*, those who sell their labor to capitalists (the "have-nots"). He argued that institutions such as education, politics, laws, and religion work to preserve the privileges of the elite.

Religious ideology often stresses hard work and deference to authority, allowing entrepreneurs to increase profits that benefit the owners. Furthermore, members of the economic and political elite usually encourage patriotism to distract the less privileged from their conflicts with the elite. According to Marx, the elite want the masses to draw the line between "us" and "them" based on national loyalty, not based on lines of economic self-interests (Gellner and Breuilly 2009). So, in Marxist thought, even patriotism is a tool of the elite to control the workers. However, Marx believed that ultimately the workers would realize their plight, develop a class consciousness, and rebel against their conditions. They would overthrow the "haves" and bring about a new and more egalitarian society

The revolutions that Marx predicted have not occurred in most countries. Labor unions have protected workers from the severe exploitation that Marx witnessed in the early stages of industrialization in England, and capitalist governments have created and expanded a wide array of measures to protect citizens, including antimonopoly legislation, social security systems, unemployment compensation, disability programs, welfare systems, and health care systems. Therefore, most workers have not been discontent to the point of trying to overthrow their governments. Marx's vision of a small group of owners controlling the economy has borne out, however. For example, today, among all transnational companies, just 1% controls 40% of all of the world's collective wealth (Coghlan and MacKenzie 2011). Fewer than 740 multinational corporations control 80% of corporate wealth. These figures are out of 37 million companies and investors and 43,060 transnational corporations in the world, each with interlocking networks (Upbin 2011).

One of the major criticisms of pure capitalism is that profit is the only value that drives the system. Human dignity and well-being, environmental protection, rights of ethnic groups, and other social issues are important only as they affect profits. This leaves some people deeply dissatisfied with capitalism.

Planned Economic Systems. In planned (or centralized) economic systems, *the government or another centralized group oversees production and distribution.* They deemphasize private control of property and economic autonomy and have the government do economic planning. Matters of production and labor are, in theory,

governed with the "communal" good in mind. There is deep suspicion of the exploitation that can occur when individuals all pursue their own self-interests. Those who hold this philosophy believe that the market system results in oligarchy—a system run by the financial elite in the pursuit of their own self-interests. Therefore, they believe the state needs to oversee the total economy. China, Cuba, and about 24 nations in Africa, Asia, and Latin America have planned economies with industry controlled by the state (Freedom House 2002).

In reality, however, no system is a perfect planned state with the complete elimination of private property or differences in privilege. China, based on a planned, government-controlled system, made rapid progress in tackling hunger, illiteracy, drug addiction, and other problems by using its strong central government to establish five-year economic development plans. Today, however, charges of corruption among those who control state-run companies and a desire for increased economic growth has led it to experiment with new economic plans, including limited private entrepreneurship, more imported goods, and trade and development agreements with other countries. China is now the largest trading nation, and expected to be the world's largest economy by 2016 (Organisation for Economic Co-operation and Development 2012).

One key criticism of planned systems is that placing both economic and political power in the hands of the same people can lead to control by a few leaders, resulting in tyranny. Multiple power centers in government, the business world, and the military can balance each other and help protect against dictatorships and tyranny (Heilbroner and Milberg 2007).

Mixed Economies. Some systems are mixed economies, sometimes called "democratic socialism" because they try to balance societal needs and individual freedoms. Democratic socialism, for example, refers to *collective or group planning of the development of the society, but within a democratic political system*. Private profit is less important than in capitalism, and the good of the whole is paramount. Planning may include goals of protecting the environment, wealth redistribution through progressive taxation, universal health care, or supporting families through government-subsidized health care and family leave legislation, but individuals' rights to pursue their own self-interests are also allowed within certain parameters. Mixed economies seek checks and balances so that both political and economic decision makers are accountable to the public. Several countries, including

Sweden, the United Kingdom, Norway, Austria, Canada, France, and Australia, have incorporated some democratic socialist ideas into their governmental policies, especially in public services. Many Western European democracies redistribute income through progressive tax plans that tax according to people's ability to pay. The government uses these revenues to nationalize education, health plans and medical care, pensions, maternity leaves, and sometimes housing for its citizens. Although much of the industry is privately run, the government regulates business and assesses high taxes to pay for government programs. Typically, public service industries such as transportation, communications, and power companies are government controlled.

When U.S. President Obama was first elected, he was faced with a major economic crisis caused by the deregulation of banks and the system of loans for home mortgages and businesses. He—as his Republican predecessor, George W. Bush, did before him—pushed a massive ($787 billion) stimulus plan through Congress (Espo 2009). The problem was lack of regulation of the economy, and the solution was massive support for corporations and businesses, actions that some called socialistic. Other programs and policies in the United States that follow the structure of democratic socialism include Social Security, Medicaid, Medicare, farm subsidies, federal unemployment insurance, the national parks system, public schools, environmental policies, and thousands of other programs that support and protect U.S. citizens. So despite hostility to the term *socialism*, any government program that "bails out" the economy (such as rescuing a failing bank) or that "protects consumers" is part of a mixed economy that includes some socialist policies. Note that both Republican and Democratic administrations have supported such policies, and the policies have been very popular. Marx believed that the worst of all governments was *state capitalism*—a system in which the state controlled the economy. His early writings, in particular, put much more emphasis on decentralization and even a withering away of the government (Marx [1844] 1963). So, it is ironic that the states perceived as "communist" today (China and Cuba) have such governments in authoritarian forms. They are far from what Marx would advocate.

Just two centuries ago, it was widely believed that democracy could not work. The notion of self-governance by the citizenry was discredited as a pipe dream. Yet this experiment in self-governance is continuing, despite some flaws and problems. In a speech to the British

House of Commons in 1947, then prime minister Winston Churchill said that "democracy is the worst form of government, except for all those other forms that have been tried" (Churchill 2009). Some economists and social philosophers have argued that if the people can plan for self-governance, they certainly should be able to plan for economic development in a way that does not put economic power solely in the hands of a political elite.

The institutions of politics and economics cannot be separated. In the 21st century, new political and economic relationships will emerge as each institution influences the other. Both institutions ultimately have close connections to power and privilege.

MACRO-LEVEL ANALYSIS: NATIONAL AND GLOBAL SYSTEMS OF GOVERNANCE AND POWER

Each nation-state develops its own systems of power and privilege in unique ways, depending on its history, leaders, needs, and relations with other nations. A macro-level analysis of national and global systems of governance and power includes both individual nation-states and international organizations, including terrorist groups that cross borders.

Power and the Nation-State

A *nation-state* is a political, geographical, and cultural unit with recognizable boundaries and a system of government. These boundaries change as disputes over territory are resolved by force or negotiation. For example, the boundaries of Israel have changed multiple times since the establishment of the nation in 1948.

There are officially 195 nation-states in the world today that are recognized by each other's governments in the United Nations, and 6 more with partial recognition, making 201 nation-states (Political Geography Now 2014). Only the Vatican, Taiwan, and Kosovo do not have UN representation. The number of nations increases as new independent nation-states continue to develop in Europe, Asia, Africa, and other parts of the world. One of the newest countries is South Sudan, which broke away from Sudan in 2011.

Within each nation-state, systems of power govern people through leaders, laws, courts, the tax structure, the military, and the economic system. Different forms of power dominate at different times in history and in different geographical settings.

The notions of the nation-state and of nationalism are so accepted that we rarely stop to think of them as social constructions of reality, created by people to meet group needs. In historical terms, though, nationalism is a rather recent or modern concept, emerging only after the nation-state (Gellner 1983, 1993; Gellner and Breuilly 2009). Medieval Europe, for example, knew no nation-states. One scholar writes that

throughout the Middle Ages, the mass of inhabitants living in what is now known as France or England did not think of themselves as "French" or "English." They had little conception of a territorial nation (a "country") to which they owed an allegiance stronger than life itself. (Billig 1995:21)

Some argue that the nation-state has "no precedent in history" prior to the 16th century and did not become widely acknowledged until nation-states formed throughout Europe in the 19th century (Giddens 1987:166). This raises an interesting question: Why did nation-states emerge in Europe and then spread throughout the rest of the world? The answer to this puzzle of modern history has to do with the change to rational organizational structures (Billig 1995). It is noteworthy that today every square foot of the Earth's land space is thought to be under the ownership of a nation-state. Yet, even today, a sense of nationalism or patriotism linking one's personal identity to the welfare of a nation is a foreign idea in many areas of the world. For example, people in Kenya, Pakistan, and Afghanistan have loyalty to their region, their ethnic or tribal group, their religious group, or their local community, but a sense of being Pakistani, Kenyan, or Afghani is weak at best. Yet, in places such as the United States, having a passionate sense of national loyalty for which one would die is so taken for granted that anyone lacking this loyalty is suspect or deviant. Note the earlier discussion of the role of the flag. The nation is largely an imagined reality, something that exists because we choose to believe that it exists, but it can exert tremendous influence over us (Anderson 2006; McCrone 1998). Indeed, for some people, belonging to the nation has become a substitute for religious faith or belonging to local ethnic groups (Theroux 2012).

Revolutions and Rebellions

From the 1980s to the present, significant social and political changes have taken place throughout the world. The

Berlin Wall was dismantled, leading to the reunification of East and West Germany. The government of South Africa that supported apartheid fell. The Baltic states of Estonia, Latvia, and Lithuania became independent. In Eastern Europe, political and social orders established since World War II underwent radical change. When the Soviet Union and Yugoslavia broke apart, national boundaries were redrawn. Internal strife resulted from ethnic divisions formerly kept under check by the strong centralized governments in these areas. In addition, the "Arab Spring" of 2011 to 2012 led a number of dictators in the Middle East to fall from power.

Were these changes around the world revolutions? **Revolution** refers to *social and political transformations of a nation that result when states fail to fulfill their expected responsibilities* (Skocpol 1979). Revolutions can be violent, and generally result in altered distributions of power. Revolutions typically occur when the government does not respond to citizens' needs and when leadership emerges to challenge the existing regime. News reports from around the world frequently announce that nation-states have been challenged by opposition groups attempting to overthrow the regimes. This is the case in Syria and some other Middle Eastern nations today. These days, revolutions are enhanced by new technologies, as is discussed in the next "Sociology Around the World" on page 442.

The Meso-Macro Political Connection

State or provincial governments and national political parties are meso-level organizations that operate beyond the local community, but with less widespread influence than national or federal governments or global systems. Still, decisions at the state or provincial government level can have a major impact on political processes at the national level. For example, in 2012 some state governors refused federal funds for expanding Medicaid to cover more poor residents, which may impact national health care policies and costs. Here we look at another issue: the recent controversies about how to nominate and elect a president within the United States. Although the focus is on the U.S. political system, this discussion should be seen as illustrative of the tensions and peculiarities of the meso-macro link in any complex political system.

In some U.S. states, only members of the respective political parties (e.g., Democrat and Republican) can vote in their selection of candidates for office. In other states, citizens registered as Independents can help select either party's candidate in a primary election. In other states,

One revolution is the Zapatista movement in southern Mexico (Chiapas). Here we see Zapatista commanders holding a Mexican flag as they attend a mass rally in Mexico City's main square. They have fought for indigenous rights, including clean water, and schooling through sixth grade for their children. The Zapatistas wear masks to avoid identification and persecution by the government, but they have become a symbol of the antiglobalization movement.

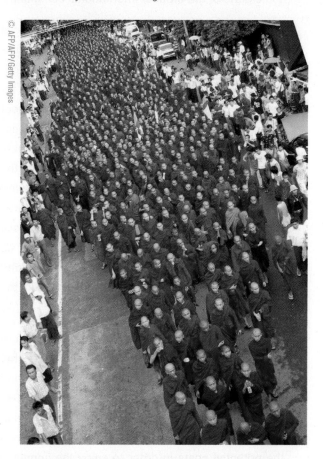

Revolutions can involve a violent attack on governments or nonviolent events such as this protest march by Burmese monks that the government in Myanmar (Burma) brutally suppressed.

Revolutionary Movements

Sociology Around the World

Social Media and Political Protests

By Jeremiah Castle

Recent events confirm that social media is playing a significant role in modern political protests. For example, social media has helped maintain news coverage of events going on inside Syria since the civil war began there in 2011. After the Syrian government attempted to restrict non-state reporters following the outbreak of protests, members of the rebel groups and bystanders tweeted and uploaded YouTube videos of government-led violence going on there (Mackey 2011). These videos helped bolster support for the rebels both inside Syria and in some parts of the broader international community.

There are a number of potential benefits to social media, the most obvious of which is a nearly limitless audience. Social media websites like Facebook, Twitter, and YouTube make it possible for networks of people with similar opinions to connect across great distances. Social media and text messaging can help large groups of people coordinate actions quickly, and the greater anonymity of the Internet can facilitate communication of political ideologies that might otherwise go unshared (Woods 2011). However, critics point out that social media–based networks are often not as "deep" as more traditional networks like those that provided a foundation for the civil rights movement in the United States (Gladwell 2010).

Crackdowns on protesters in Iran and other countries have provided support for growing fears that governments will use social media to identify and silence dissidents (Howard 2011; Morozov 2009). However, the events in Syria are part of a growing pattern that suggests protesters are willing to face the potential costs in order to enjoy the immense organizational benefits of social media. In 2009, protesters in Moldova used Twitter, Facebook, and text messages to mobilize opposition to the Communist Party's election wins (Barry 2009). A few months later, citizens and reporters in Iran used social media to keep more traditional media outlets informed of events following the disputed 2009 elections (Landler and Stelter 2009). Protesters used YouTube to distribute videos of police beating crowds, raiding Tehran University, and shooting women in the streets, causing concerns among traditional media outlets due to the graphic nature of the videos and the difficultly in verifying their authenticity (Stelter 2009).

In 2011, Twitter, Facebook, and YouTube all played a role in the protests that ended Egyptian president Hosni Mubarak's tenure in office. A Facebook group titled "We are all Khaled Said," dedicated to the memory of an Alexandrian man beaten to death by police, had over 1.8 million subscribers (Preston 2011). In the fall of 2012, citizens of the Philippines protested a new law that might allow social media users to be prosecuted for libel by replacing their Facebook profile pictures with black silhouettes and making blank posts (Whaley 2012). Widening Internet access, faster connection speeds, and improvements in strategy provide reasons to believe that social media will play an increasing role in the future of political protest.

New evidence suggests that social media can also cause protests in a more direct fashion. Social media has dramatically expanded the marketplace of ideas, and now anyone with a keyboard, phone, or camera can distribute his or her thoughts to a worldwide audience. In one recent case, an American filmmaker who published an anti-Islamic film on YouTube helped spark a series of protests in numerous Muslim countries, including Egypt, Syria, Pakistan, and Sudan (Mackey and Stack 2012). These incidents serve as a reminder that, with the democratization of ideas brought by social media, one person's actions have the potential to affect the lives of others around the world.

• •

Jeremiah Castle minored in sociology in college and is now a PhD candidate in political science at the University of Notre Dame.

 ## Thinking Sociologically

Some states never get any say in the nomination of presidential candidates because the process is completed before they vote. One state has written into its constitution that it must have the first primary election. Should these decisions be made at the state or national level? Who has the authority to tell a state it cannot put into its constitution a regulation that it must have the first presidential primary?

Democrats and Republicans can cross over and vote in the primary for the other party. What are the implications of having different rules in different states about crossover party voting?

In some U.S. states, each political party runs its own caucuses (face-to-face meetings of voters in homes, schools, and other buildings) to discuss policy and to carry out public votes. In caucus states, the political party funds and operates the process of selecting delegates who will nominate the presidential candidate—so the political party rather than the state sets the rules. In contrast, other states have primary elections run by the state government. (See Table 13.2 for caucus and primary states.) However, even states that use a primary are not all the same. In most states, delegates to the convention are selected based on the proportion of the vote won by a candidate in that state. If a candidate wins 40% of the vote, she wins 40% of the delegates. However, in some states on the Republican side, the delegate selection process is a winner-takes-all system. In such elections, even if one candidate wins by a hundred votes, he or she wins all the delegates for that state. Still others have a formula by which some delegates are elected in the primary based on proportion of the statewide vote, while others are chosen based on who wins each congressional district. In short, there is not uniformity. In addition, one state, New Hampshire, has in its state constitution a clause that the state *must* have the first presidential primary, and this means the state has more influence on winnowing down the presidential candidates than other states. (To see the processes for various states—whether winner-takes-all or proportional—go to www .sagepub.com/ballantine5e/.)

Only some state governments decide when primaries will be held, while elsewhere the political parties control the process of selecting nominees. The contentious 2008 U.S. election raised several controversial questions. Can a political party tell a state when to have its elections and then punish that state if it does not obey by refusing to seat or taking away the votes of its delegates at the party convention? This is what happened in Michigan and Florida. Can a state legislature—a meso-level political entity—tell a major national political party—another meso-level political entity—how to run its nomination process? The answers to these questions are not clear, yet they can have profound effects on who becomes the president of the most powerful nation on Earth.

In two states—Montana and Nebraska—the Republican primary is a "beauty contest" with no binding outcome. The results are purely advisory, and the delegates from that state are free to ignore the outcome of the election. The delegates are selected by party leaders in that state, not by the voters. The Democratic Party has only recently passed a national policy banning this kind of primary. On the other hand, the Democratic Party has 915 "superdelegates"—party leaders who have not been elected by the populace and who may commit their votes to anyone they please. So both parties allow delegates not representing any constituency to help choose the presidential nominee. What are the implications for a democracy when there are such irregularities?

Even selection of the Electoral College, which truly decides who will be president after the general election, is not uniform in policy across the states. Two states—Nebraska and Maine—have proportional distribution of

Table 13.2 Meso-Level Presidential Nomination Variations in the United States

"Open" Allowing citizens to cross over to vote in the other party's election	Semiclosed Allowing Independents to vote in the other party's election	States With Caucuses Rather Than Primaries Controlled by the political parties rather than the state
AL MN TN	AK IL NH	AK ME NV
AR MS VT	CA IA OH	CO MN ND
ID MO VA	GA MA RI	IA ME WA
IN ND WA		KS NE WY
MI SC WI		
Open in the Democratic but closed in the Republican processes: MT UT WV	Semiclosed in the Democratic but closed in the Republican processes: KS	Texas has both a primary and a caucus

Sources: Bowen (2008); Center for Voting and Democracy (2008), Green Papers (2008, 2008b); National Archives and Records Administration (2008); "Primary Calendar" (2008); Project Vote Smart (2008); State of Delaware (2008); U.S. Elections Map (2008); Voting and Democracy Research Center (2008).

Note: States that are not listed in the first two columns have closed voting systems—one can only vote if registered in that party.

electors, and all the others have winner-takes-all system. Should there be consistency between the states in the way the Electoral College is selected? Should state elections all be a proportional or a winner-takes-all system?

Because the Constitution grants considerable autonomy to states to make these decisions, how does the nation ever get consistency? At the state (meso) level, legislatures are very protective of their right to make their own decisions. Yet governance of the nation and the nation's relationships with the global community may be at stake. As you can see, meso-level political power can shape power at the macro level, which then influences policies relevant to individual lives. The three levels are intimately linked. The next "Engaging Sociology" raises questions about where authority for decisions resides at each level in the social system.

Global Interdependencies: Cooperation and Conflicts

The most affluent countries in the Global North are democracies, but a democratic system of government may not be functional in poor countries with different cultural values and systems (Etounga-Manguelle 2000). Despite the movement toward political liberalization, democracy, and market-oriented reforms in countries such as Chile, Mexico, Nigeria, Poland, Senegal, Thailand, and Turkey, not all of these societies are ready, willing, or able to adopt democratic forms of governance (Diamond 1992, 2009).

Foreign powers can do little to alter the social structure and cultural traditions of other societies, and as indicated, these structures are key to the successful development of democracy. If the imposed system is premature or incompatible with the society's level of development and other institutional structures, authoritarian dictatorship rather than democracy may emerge as the traditional authority structure breaks down. We can see signs of this in Afghanistan and Iraq, two nations in which the United States tried to establish democratic forms of government. Certain preconditions tend to be necessary for the successful emergence of democracy:

- High levels of economic well-being
- The absence of extreme inequalities in wealth and income
- Social pluralism, including a particularly strong and autonomous middle class

ENGAGING SOCIOLOGY

Political Decisions: Social Processes at the Micro, Meso, and Macro Levels

Imagine that your state legislature is considering a change in the presidential election process. Your state's representatives in the Electoral College would be selected according to the percentage of the popular vote in your state going to each candidate (Republican, Democratic, Libertarian, and Green Party). (*Note:* Currently, almost all states distribute their electors on a winner-takes-all basis.)

1. Identify two possible micro-level consequences of this policy change. (For example, how might it affect an individual's decision to vote or how the local board of elections does its job?)

2. Identify three consequences at the macro level. (For example, how might the change affect how presidential candidates spend their resources and time, how might Congress respond to such an initiative, and so forth?)

3. How does this illustrate the influence of meso-level organizations on micro and macro levels of the social system? For example, is it a problem for a *national* democracy when the delegate selection system is so variable at the meso level, or does this make elections even more democratic because states can make their own autonomous decisions? Explain your answer.

4. Which system—winner-takes-all or percentage of the popular vote—would produce the fairest outcome? Why?

- A market-oriented economy
- Influence in the world system of democratic states
- A culture relatively tolerant of diversity that can accommodate compromise
- A functioning and impartial media that will hold the government accountable
- A literate population (80% or more) informed about issues
- A written constitution with guarantees of free speech and freedom of assembly (Bottomore 1979; Inglehart 1997)

Thinking Sociologically

Why might some analysts believe that Iraq or Afghanistan—where the United States has attempted to set up democracies—may not be ready for a successful democratic government? Can you describe societies with which you are familiar that are—or are not—ready for democratic government? If you are not able to answer these questions, discuss why it is important for you, as a citizen of your own society, to be knowledgeable about other nations (and what you will do to become better informed).

An outside power like the United States can help establish the structures necessary to support democracy, but can seldom successfully impose those structures. If countries in the Global North want more democracies around the world, a more successful strategy would focus on supporting economic development in less affluent countries. Again, politics and economics are intertwined.

Some Global South countries see discussions of democracy as a ploy—a cover-up used by dominant affluent nations for advancing their wealth. For example, the Global North nations have combined to form a coalition of nations calling itself the Group of Seven (or the G7—the United States, Japan, Germany, Canada, France, Great Britain, and Italy). Russia was in what was called the G8, but was asked to leave because of political disputes over the country of Ukraine. The G7 uses its collective power to regulate global economic policies to ensure stability (and thereby ensure that its members' interests are secure). The G7 has the power to control world markets through the World Trade Organization, the World Bank, and the International Monetary Fund

(Brecher, Costello, and Smith 2012; Kaiser Family Foundation 2010). Global South nations have responded to the G7 with an organization of poor countries that they called the G77 to create collective unity and gain enough power to determine their own destinies (Brecher et al. 2012; Eitzen and Zinn 2012; Hearn 2012). Figure 13.4 shows the location of G7 and G77 nations.

Political systems can face threats from internal sources such as disaffected citizens, the military, and interest groups vying for power, or they can be challenged by external sources such as other nations wanting land or resources or by coalitions of nations demanding change. This is the situation for North Korea and Iran, as coalitions of nations demand that they drop their nuclear enrichment programs. Sometimes these power struggles erupt into violence. The following section discusses how war, terrorism, and rebellion challenge existing systems.

Violence on the Global Level. Although some wars in the past were brutal and entire populations were slaughtered (Genghis Khan's ruthless campaigns providing one example), it is also true that in the Middle Ages gallant knights in shining armor went forth to battle with good luck tokens from their ladies and the cause of their religion or their monarch to spur them on. They seldom died in these battles, and the daily life of the society went on as usual. Likewise, battles between First Nations in North America often resulted in four or five deaths. In contrast, since the invention of modern weaponry and chemical and nuclear weapons, no one has been safe from death and destruction in war. Weapons can destroy whole civilizations. A malfunctioning computer, a miscalculation, a deranged person, a misunderstanding between hostile factions, or a terrorist attack could kill millions of people.

War is *armed conflict occurring within, between, or among societies or groups*. It is sometimes called "organized mass violence" (Nolan 2002:1803). War is a frequent but not inevitable condition of human existence. Many countries are now engaged in wars detrimental to their economies and morale. Some of these wars (between India and Pakistan, between the Palestinian Territories and Israel, and between rival factions in the Congo) have lasted for years. Others have been short and decisive, such as the "Desert Storm" war with Iraq under the first President Bush. Table 13.3 lists ongoing world conflicts as of 2013.

FIGURE 13.4 Countries of the Group of 7, Major Emerging Economies, and Countries of the Group of 77

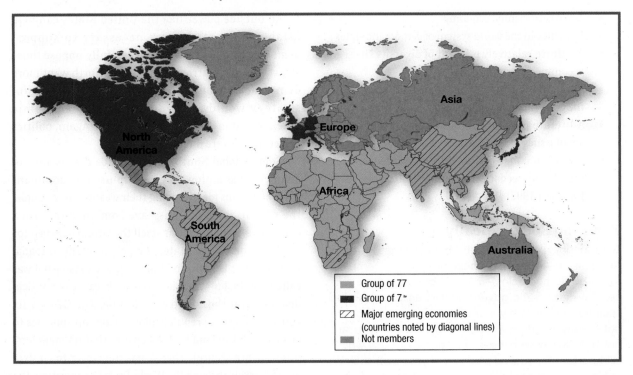

Source: www.g77.org, retrieved April 2008. Map by Anna Versluis.

Note: Russia was a member until 2014.

The U.S. and Iran ▶

Table 13.3 Significant Ongoing Armed Conflicts, 2013

Main Warring Parties	Year Conflict Began*
Middle East	
Syria vs. Free Syrian Army and other militants	2011–present
Iraq vs. Islamic State of Iraq and Syria (ISIS)	2003–present
Israel vs. Palestine	1948–present
Yemen: government forces vs. the rebel group Shabab al-Moumineen and other militants	2004–present
Turkey: government forces vs. the Kurdistan Workers' Party (PKK) and Kurdistan Freedom Falcons (TAK)	2003–present
Libya: fighting between militia groups	2012–present
Asia	
Afghanistan: U.S., U.K., and coalition forces vs. al-Qaeda and Taliban	1978–present
Burma (Myanmar) vs. Kachin Independence Army (Kachin and Rakhine states)	1988–present
India vs. Kashmir Harkat-ul-Ansar, Northeast United People's Democratic Front, Maoist insurgents (and other splinter groups)	1947–present
Philippines vs. the Mindanaoan separatists (MILF/ASG), the Bransamoro Islamic Freedom Fighters (BIFF), the New Democratic Front (NDFP), and New People's Army (NPA)	1969–present
Thailand vs. antigovernment insurgents	2004–present
Africa	
Algeria vs. Al Qaeda in the Islamic Maghreb	1992–present
Chad vs. Chadian Popular Front for Recovery (FPR)	1965–present
Democratic Republic of Congo vs. March 23 Movement (M23)	1990–present
Ethiopia vs. Ogaden National Liberation Front (ONLF)	2007–present
Kenya vs. Somali Islamists	1991–present
Nigeria vs. Boko Haram	1990–present
South Sudan vs. Sudan People's Liberation Army (SPLA) and Darfur	1983–present
Europe	
Russia vs. Chechen separatists in Chechnya	1999–present
Latin America	
Colombia vs. Revolutionary Armed Forces of Colombia (FARC)	1964–present

Sources: Project Ploughshares (2013).

Note: As of 2013.

*Where multiple parties and long-standing but sporadic conflict are concerned, date of first combat deaths is given.

Why Do Nations Go to War? Leaders use moral, religious, or political ideology to legitimize war, although the cause may be conflicts over economic resources or ethnic tensions. Wars have been waged to support religions through crusades and jihads; to liberate a country from domination by a foreign power; to protect borders, resources, and cultural customs; and to capture resources, including slaves, land, and oil. War can also distract citizens from other problems in their country, and may therefore be used by politicians intent on staying in power. The United States has been at war 193 out of the 237 years since the colonies declared independence. Indeed, during the entire 20th century, there were only 6 years when the United States was not engaged in some sort of military action around the world (Brandon 2005; Noguera and Cohen 2006). On the other hand, in some cultures, war is virtually unknown. These groups, often isolated, live in peace and cooperation, with little competition for land and resources. War is not inevitable but a product of societies and their leaders, created by societies and learned in societies.

Two familiar sociological theories attempt to explain the social factors that can lead to war. Functionalist theorists think underlying social problems cause disruptions to the system, including war, terrorism, and revolution. If all parts of the system were working effectively, they contend, these problems would not occur.

Agents of social control and a smooth-running system would prevent disruptions. However, some functionalists also argue that war brings a population together behind a cause, resulting in social solidarity.

Conflict theorists see war, terrorism, and revolution as the outcome of oppression by the ruling elite and powerful countries, and an attempt to eliminate that oppression. Other conflict theorists note, however, that many businesses profit from wars because their manufacturing power is put to full use. In fact, more money is spent on war than on prevention of disease, illiteracy, and hunger.

Those with power have the most control over decisions to go to war, but citizens from the lower classes and racial minorities join the military, fight, and die in disproportionate numbers. They are more likely to join the military as an avenue to employment and job training. They join as enlistees who serve on the front lines and are more at risk.

All sociological theorists agree that war is not a natural or biological necessity but a social construction (Stoessinger 1993). Likewise, societies create ways to resolve and avoid war.

How Might Nations Avoid War? What can nations do to avoid war? Here we discuss two methods used primarily by powerful nations: deterrence and negotiation. *Deterrence* is a theory of conflict management and a strategy aimed at preventing undesirable behavior by another group or country. Any parties contemplating action against others are deterred because the costs to them, should they strike, exceed any possible gains (Lebow 1981:83). This rational cost-benefit calculus is similar to rational choice theory with which you are familiar. This approach was paramount during the Cold War between the United States and the Soviet Union, and many argue it worked since no nuclear war ensued. Today those who advocate building defense capability as a deterrent against nuclear attacks or war align themselves with this theory.

However, a major problem today is that of terrorism, and some argue that this deterrent will not work against an "irrational" group that is difficult to locate and willing to incur loss of lives to achieve goals. Since some current threats do not lead to the possibility of conventional warfare, deterrence has more limited

The Vietnam Veterans Memorial Wall in Washington, D.C.—like many European war memorials do—expresses and elicits a sense of the anguish and suffering of war. This man mourns the loss of a close friend and comrade.

©Ursilla Catherine/ Getty

The Iraq War

effectiveness (Kroenig and Pavel 2012; U.S. Department of Defense 2012). Moreover, continual buildup of weapons increases mistrust and raises the potential for misunderstandings, mistakes, or disaster. Furthermore, military personnel often have a vested interest in war. The military trains for war and proves it is necessary through success in war. Business interests and economies may also profit from supporting successful wars.

The world spent $1.75 trillion on defense in 2013, with only 15 countries accounting for 79% of global defense spending. In 2013, the United States accounted for over 37% of world military spending, an estimated $640 billion. China was second, accounting for 11% of global defense spending with a budget of $188 billion. Russia was third, spending $88 billion (Keck 2014). Military spending usually comes at the expense of social programs such as education and health care, simply because there is not usually enough money to fund all these programs when the military consumes so much money (Hinton 2010). Still, many people feel that protection of the citizenry is the government's most essential responsibility, and deterrence is the way to achieve security.

Negotiation is the second approach to avoiding war and involves resolving conflicts by discussions to reach agreement. For example, diplomacy and treaties have set limits on nuclear weapons and their use. President Obama has pointed out that, as well as increasing the threat of nuclear war, maintaining Cold War weapons systems is expensive and can drain weakened economies. He negotiated a treaty with Russia in 2010 that led to a reduction in deployed, long-range nuclear warheads by 30% (Sheridan and Branigin 2010; Zeleny 2009).

Some citizens, not satisfied to leave peacekeeping efforts to their government leaders, form and participate in nongovernmental peace organizations. Strong grassroots peace movements in Europe, the Middle East, the United States, South Africa, and other countries attempt to decrease tensions and address conflicts around the world. The widespread demonstrations in many European and U.S. cities by people opposed to the wars in Iraq and Afghanistan were examples of such efforts.

Many peace groups sponsor educational programs and museum displays. The horrors depicted in the Hiroshima Peace Memorial Museum in Japan; the Killing Fields Museum in Cambodia; the Holocaust Memorial Museum in Washington, D.C.; the Anne Frank Museum in Amsterdam, Netherlands; the Rwanda Genocide Memorial; and the Korean War and Vietnam Veterans Memorials in Washington, D.C., all help sensitize the public and politicians to the effects of war. Interestingly,

most war memorials in the United States glorify the wars and lionize the heroes who fought in them. In Europe, many memorials stress the pathos and agony of war. The Vietnam Veterans Memorial Wall in Washington, D.C., also sends a message about the sorrows of war. Peace advocates and veterans of the war have stood and wept together in front of that memorial.

Scholars draw several conclusions from studies of war in the past century: (a) No nation that began a major war in the 20th century emerged a clear winner; (b) in the nuclear age, war between nuclear powers could be suicidal; and (c) a victor's peace plan seldom lasts. Peace settlements negotiated on the basis of equality tend to be much more permanent and durable. Economic issues such as an inequitable distribution of resources can incite a war. Therefore, a lasting peace requires attention to at least semi-equitable distribution of resources.

As long as discrimination, hunger, and poverty exist, the roots of violence are present. The world is a complex interdependent system. When the linkages between peoples are based on ideologies that stress "us" versus "them" polarities and power differentials that alienate people, then war, terrorism, and violence will not disappear from the globe.

Terrorism. "Geronimo! Bin Laden, mastermind of 9/11, is dead!" was the headline on May 2, 2011. For the 10 years since September 11, 2001, the search had been on. That was when three commercial airplanes became the missiles of terrorists, two crashing into the Twin Towers of the World Trade Center in New York City and one into the Pentagon in Washington, D.C. Another crashed into the fields of Pennsylvania after the passengers heroically attacked the terrorists piloting the plane. Together more than 3,025 people from 68 nations died, and countless others were injured. This was an act of terrorism. Why did Bin Laden and his followers do it?

Terrorism refers to *the planned use of random, unlawful (or illegal) violence or threat of violence against civilians to create (or raise) fear and intimidate citizens in order to advance the terrorist group's political or ideological goals* (U.S. Department of Defense 2012). Terrorism usually refers to acts of violence by private nonstate groups to advance revolutionary political goals, but *state terrorism*—government use of terror to control people—also proliferates. Terrorists are found at all points on the political continuum: anarchists, nationalists, religious fundamentalists, and members of ethnic advocacy groups. Worldwide, terrorist attacks rose by 43% from 2012 to 2013, killing 17,891 globally and wounding 32,577. There were almost 3,000 kidnapping and hostage-taking victims in just 2013. Most of these terrorist activities took place outside the United States (Ackerman 2014).

What makes terrorism effective? Terrorists strike randomly and change tactics so that governments have no clear or effective way of dealing with them. This unpredictability causes public confidence in the ability of government to protect citizens and deal with crises to waver. Private terrorist groups tend to be most successful when attacking democratic governments. They seldom attack targets in oligarchic or dictatorial societies because these countries ignore their demands despite the risk to innocent civilians and hostages' lives (Frey 2004).

Why do terrorists commit hostile acts? In our anger against terrorists, we sometimes fail to look at why they commit these atrocities. Who are the terrorists, and what have they to gain? Without understanding the underlying causes of terrorism, we can do little to prevent it.

Few terrorists act completely alone. They tend to be members or connected in some way (even if only through the Internet) to groups highly committed to an ideology or a cause—religious, political, or both. Class, ethnic, racial, or religious alienation often lies at the roots of terrorism. The ideology of terrorist groups stresses "us" versus "them" perceptions of the world, viewing "them" as evil. Those committing terrorist acts often feel victimized by

more powerful forces, and sometimes, they see their lives as the only weapon they have to fight back. Many believe they have nothing to lose by committing terrorist acts, even suicidal terrorist acts. One person's terrorist may be someone else's freedom fighter—it is in *the eye of the beholder.*

Ahmad is a 20-year-old terrorist. All his life, his family has been on the move, forced to work for others for barely a living wage, and controlled by rules made up by other people—ones that he feels are hostile to his group. When he was very young, his family's home was taken away, and the residents of his town scattered to other locations. He began to resent those who he thought had dislocated his family, put neighbors in jail, and separated him from friends and relatives. Ahmad sees little future for himself or his people, little hope for education or a career of his choosing. He feels that he has nothing to lose by joining a resistance organization to fight for what he sees as justice. Its members keep their identities secret. They are not powerful enough to mount an army to fight, so they rely on terrorist tactics against those they see as oppressors.

Ahmad puts the "greater good" of his religious and political beliefs and his group above his individual well-being. When he agrees to commit a terrorist act, he truly believes it is right and is the only way he can retaliate and bring attention to the suffering of his people. If killed, he knows he will be praised and become a martyr within his group. His family may even receive compensation for his death.

Religious and political beliefs are usually at the root of what leads terrorists to commit violent acts. Timothy McVeigh and Terry Nichols, convicted of bombing the Alfred P. Murrah Federal Building in Oklahoma City, Oklahoma, in 1995, had connections to paramilitary, antigovernment militia groups, many of which opposed government intervention in the private lives of U.S. citizens. These groups are white supremacist and antigovernment (despite their fanatic pro-Americanism). Most such paramilitary groups consider themselves to be devoutly Christian, and they believe that their religion and "good intentions" justify their acts. Figure 8.4 on page 243 shows how such groups are scattered throughout the United States.

Structural explanations help predict when conditions are ripe for terrorism. Again, terrorism and war tend to be sparked by conflict and strife within and between societal systems. Ahmad learned his attitudes, hatreds, and stereotypes from his family, his friends, charismatic leaders, and media such as the Internet. These beliefs were

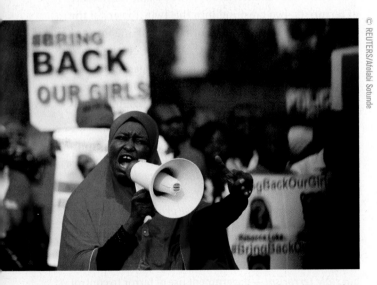

© REUTERS/Afolabi Sotunde

A protester addresses the "Bring Back Our Girls" protest group as they march to the presidential villa to deliver a protest letter to Nigeria's President Goodluck Jonathan in Abuja. The letter calls for the release of the Nigerian schoolgirls kidnapped by the Islamist militant group Boko Haram on May 22, 2014.

reinforced by his leaders, religious beliefs, and schools. However, their origin was anger and economic despair.

Conflict theory explanations of terrorism lie in the unequal distribution of world resources and the oppression of minority groups. Countries such as Germany, China, and the United States and multinational corporations control immense resources and capital and have considerable economic and cultural influence and power over peripheral nations. This inequity results in feelings of alienation and hostility—and sometimes terrorism.

Terrorism, then, is a means by which those with less power can gain attention to their cause and some power in the global system, even if it involves hijackings, bombings, suicides, kidnappings, and political assassinations. Terrorists feel justified in their actions. The victims of these acts are understandably outraged.

Democracy comes in many forms and structures. If you want to live in a society where you have a voice, get involved in the political system and stay well informed about the policies your government is considering or has recently enacted. Political systems need diverse voices and critics—regardless of what party is currently in power—to create vibrant societies that represent the citizens. They also need healthy citizens. The following chapter focuses on the institution of health care and explores its interaction with other institutions—such as the economy and the political system.

WHAT HAVE WE LEARNED?

Political and economic systems are both sources of power and are highly interlinked. Those who have high status in one institution tend to also have high status in the other. However, some political and economic systems do a better job of producing and distributing resources, ensuring accountability of power so it is less probing, and providing checks on abuses of power.

KEY POINTS

- Power involves the ability to realize one's will, despite resistance. (See p. 417.)

- Power and economics impact our intimate (micro-level) lives, our (meso-level) organizations and institutions, and our (macro-level) national and global structures and policies. (See pp. 417–418.)

- Leadership facilitates getting things done in any social group. It can be accomplished through raw power (coercion) or through authority (granted by the populace). Different types of leadership invest authority in the person, the position, or both. (See pp. 418–421.)

- Various theories illuminate different aspects of political power and view the United States' policy-making processes very differently—as dominated by the power elite or as distributed among various groups so that no one group has complete power (pluralism). (See pp. 421–424.)

- At the micro level of a political institution, individuals decide whether or not to vote or participate in politics. These decisions are not just individual choices but are shaped by culture and structures of the society. (See pp. 424–428.)

- At the meso level, the political institution (when it functions well) works to resolve conflicts and to address social needs within the political system. This may be done with authoritarian or democratic structures. Within nations, meso-level policies can also have major implications for national power distribution. (See pp. 428–436.)

- The economic system ensures production and distribution of goods in the society, and the type of economy in a society determines who has the power to plan for the future and who has access to resources. (See pp. 436–440.)

- At the macro level, nation-states have emerged only in the past few centuries as part of modernity. (See pp. 440.)

- At the global level, issues of power, access to resources, alienation, and ideology shape economic policies, war, terrorism, and the prospects for lives of peace and prosperity for citizens around the planet. (See pp. 444–451.)

DISCUSSION QUESTIONS

1. As you were growing up, did your parents encourage you to try to influence your local community or society? Why or why not? Was their perspective on power more like the pluralist or elite theoretical perspective? Explain. How have their views about power influenced your own?

2. Is your family of origin part of what G. William Domhoff refers to as the "power elite"? What makes you think so? Are you a member of the power elite? Why or why not? If you are not, what do you think your chances are of becoming a member of the power elite? Why?

3. Do you think that large corporations have undue influence over the U.S. government? Why or why not?

4. If you had the choice, would you rather live in a society with a planned/centralized economic system or market/capitalist economic system? Why?

5. How do conflict theorists explain terrorism? Do you agree? Why or why not? How would you suggest the U.S. government try to stem terrorism? What theoretical perspective do you think is most helpful in terms of understanding and dealing with terrorism? Why?

CONTRIBUTING TO OUR SOCIAL WORLD: WHAT CAN WE DO?

At the Local Level

- Consider getting involved in the *student government* on your campus. Most students do not know the power they have on their own campus. Organized students can have a major impact. If you would like to see something changed on your campus, establish relationships with key administrators and organize other students. Consider running for a leadership position in a student club or the student government association. Doing so will help you learn how to gain and use power and to better understand the basic principles of the democratic process.

- *Model Legislature or Model UN programs* may be found on most campuses, and are usually administered through the department of political science. Consider joining yours and gain valuable knowledge and skills in debating and governing.

- *Arrange a campus visit by a local political candidate or officeholder.* If this can be done through a sociology club, it would be especially appropriate to have the visitor discuss the political system as a social institution.

At the Organizational or Institutional Level

- *Government internships.* Consider doing an internship in your state/provincial legislature (www.ncsl .org/legislative-staff.aspx?tabs=856,33,816), in Congress (www.senate.gov/reference/Index/

Employment.htm and www.house.gov/content/educate/internships.php), in the governor's office (Google "governor's office," "internship," and the name of your state), or with a court judge (Google "court judge," with the name of your district, and "internship").

- *Special interest parties.* Become involved in a special interest political group such as the Green Party (www.gp.org), the Libertarians (www.lp.org), the Socialist Party (www.sp-usa.org), the Tea Party (www.teaparty.org), Occupy Together (www.occupytogether.org), Bread for the World (www.bread.org), PETA (People for the Ethical Treatment of Animals at www.peta.org), or any number of others.

At the National and Global Levels

- *Internships at the White House or one of the executive offices, such as the Departments of State, Agriculture, or Commerce,* can be a great learning experience. You can learn about the White House internship program and how to apply for one at www.whitehouse.gov/about/internships. Google the name of a cabinet office to obtain contact information for the other executive offices.

- Several agencies of the *United Nations* hire interns. The general contact for relevant information is www.un.org/Depts/OHRM/sds/internsh/.

14 Health Care

An Anatomy of Health and Illness

Health and illness are social matters, influenced by social interactions, affected by complex organizations intended to provide health care, and shaped by social policies at national and global levels. A sociological analysis looks deeply into these processes.

MICRO

ME (AND MY MEDICAL PROVIDERS)

LOCAL ORGANIZATIONS AND COMMUNITY
Local community health clinics and hospitals are the local franchises of the health care institution.

MESO

NATIONAL ORGANIZATIONS, INSTITUTIONS, AND ETHNIC SUBCULTURES
State governments regulate health care and deal with public health issues.

MACRO

SOCIETY
National governments regulate drug companies for safety standards and fund research.

GLOBAL COMMUNITY
International organizations establish health programs and control pandemics.

THINK ABOUT IT

Micro: Local Community	What does it mean for you to be sick or healthy? Why is being sick a social status and not just an individual concern? How does the health or illness of family and community members affect the functioning of you and your local community?
Meso: National Institutions, Complex Organizations, and Ethnic Groups	What type of health care system keeps people healthiest? Why?
Macro: National and Global System	What are costs to the nation of having a national health care system, and what are the costs of not having one? How do health care systems vary around the world?

Two tragic cases, both brain-dead pregnant women on life support. One is carrying a nonviable fetus, meaning the baby will die. The other is carrying a viable baby that is growing inside her even though she, herself, is brain dead. The ethical decisions and political pressures in these two cases show the dilemmas faced by family, medical practitioners, and even politicians. Health care is not just an individual matter.

In the case of brain-dead Marlise Muñoz from Texas, her husband and family wanted her taken off life support, but Texas state law prohibited that because of the fetus, even though the fetus was not viable and she would not recover. She finally was taken off life support by order of

Piergiorgio Welby, an Italian poet and artist, suffered from advanced muscular dystrophy and was confined to a bed, attached to a respirator. He was lucid and spoke via a computer that interpreted his eye movements. He petitioned the Italian government to let him commit medically assisted suicide and "find peace for my tortured and shattered body." The government finally granted his wish, but the church denied him a Catholic burial.

©Claudio Peri/ Corbis

the district court in Tarrant County, Texas, on January 26, 2014 ("Experts Weigh In" 2014). The husband and doctors of Robyn Benson from Victoria, British Columbia (Canada), decided to keep her alive with feeding tubes and ventilators until the baby was delivered by C-section even though she had been declared dead from a brain hemorrhage 16 days earlier (Payne 2014). Who has the right to decide what to do in situations like this, when a patient cannot communicate?

Another end-of-life situation involved Debbie, a 20-year-old woman in Portland, Oregon, lying in pain and dying from ovarian cancer. She had not eaten or slept for two days and was struggling for air. She said to the young medical resident (doctor, in training) on duty, "Let's get this over with." The resident then gave her an injection of morphine, causing her to die four minutes later (Standler 2012). These cases and others like them raise great controversy in medical, legal, and religious communities. End-of-life legislation that determines if patients have the legal right to decide when to die has led to vociferous debates and varies among nations throughout the world and the U.S. states.

Today, anyone can sign a "Living Will" or "Right to Die" or "Do Not Resuscitate" form, requesting that no extraordinary efforts be made to help keep him or her alive when death would naturally occur (passive euthanasia). However, just three U.S. states (Oregon, Washington, and Vermont) give competent, terminally ill adults the legal right to commit suicide (Death with Dignity National Center 2012; Hyde n.d.). Similar legislation has been proposed, and is now being debated, in many other states. Belgium, the Netherlands, and Switzerland have permitted physician-assisted suicide since 1942, even for nonterminal patients ("Assisted Suicide" 2012).

Under "Death with Dignity" laws in the United States, patients themselves, not doctors, administer the drugs. Patients and doctors who carry out these laws must go through many steps to ensure that patients making this decision are terminally ill and sure that they want to end their lives. Those who wish to obtain a prescription under the Oregon, Washington, or Vermont law must

- prove residency in one of the three states;
- be 18 years or older;
- be able to make and communicate health care decisions for themselves;
- be diagnosed with a terminal illness, expected to lead to death within the next six months;
- have two physicians determine they have met the criteria above; and
- make two written requests for the prescription from the physician, witnessed by two people who are not family members or primary caregivers.

The physician filling out the prescription must share with the patient all other possible options (e.g., hospice, pain management) and attest that the patient is mentally competent (Death with Dignity National Center 2012). A scenario like the one with Debbie and the medical resident would be considered illegal under the Death with Dignity laws.

Those who favor euthanasia argue that (a) physicians should be able to create comfortable environments for death to occur, (b) terminally ill individuals have a right—without interference by the state—to determine how they die and to make the decision to die, (c) legal safeguards are available to prevent abuse of physician-assisted suicide, (d) high rates of self-induced suicide already exist among terminally ill patients, (e) a majority of the public favors legalization of physician-assisted suicides, and (f) extending life with no hope of recovery is costly to families as well as to the medical care system.

Those opposed to euthanasia argue that (a) physicians are obligated to sustain life; (b) medical measures are available to relieve pain, so few have to suffer; (c) religious beliefs affirm the sanctity of life, which means supporting life at every turn; (d) terminally ill individuals who request to die often act out of depression, or they may feel pressured to accept a facilitated death to save the family's resources; and (e) a terminally ill patient's acceptance of active euthanasia may make suicide a more acceptable option for those people who are depressed, disabled, elderly, or mentally disabled (Weiss and Lonnquist 2012).

Relatively few people have chosen to use the Death with Dignity laws to arrange their own deaths. Assisted suicides account for approximately 0.2% of deaths in Oregon (77 in 2012, 71 in 2011, 65 in 2010, and 59 in 2009), and similarly low numbers of assisted suicide deaths occur in the European nations that allow them ("Assisted Suicide" 2012). Almost all those who died through the act in Oregon were whites (97.4%) with college degrees (43%), and more than half were in hospice care (Death with Dignity National Center 2012; Oregon Public Health Division 2012; Schadenberg 2013).

The cost of dying differs tremendously, from nothing in many poor Global South countries with no health care for the dying, to many thousands per person in the United States. Medicare, the government insurance for those 65 and older, spent $554 billion in total costs in 2011. More than $1 out of every $4 (28%, or approximately $170 billion) was spent on patients' final six months of life (Pasternak 2013). As the U.S. population ages, the Medicare system faces great pressure to cover expenses. At this rate, the Medicare system will deplete its funds by 2026 (Social Security and Medicare Boards of Trustees 2013).

Policy analysts point out that costs for elder care could be reduced and quality of care improved by providing more in-home services to allow people to die at home or in a hospice setting, rather than in an intensive care unit of a hospital. Efforts to encourage this have yielded some positive results. The percentage of people dying at home or in hospice increased, respectively, from 23% to 27% and 21.6% to 42.2% between 2000 and 2009 (Centers for Disease Control and Prevention [CDC] 2013a; "Drop in Hospital Death Rates" 2013; Jaslow 2013).

How we die, where we die, who is with us when we die, and whether we have a choice about when to die are decisions bound in cultural values, beliefs, and laws. Death and its various issues are but one aspect of the interrelationship between our physical condition and our social system. In this chapter, we consider why health is a social issue and examine theoretical perspectives on health and illness, the status and roles of sick people, modern health care systems, and health care policy issues at the national and global levels.

WHY IS HEALTH A SOCIAL ISSUE?

Starting in 2003, vaccination campaigns were suspended in parts of Nigeria. Muslim religious and political leaders in the northern part of the African country refused to allow international medical teams to immunize children against polio, a disease that had almost been eradicated elsewhere. The leaders had little trust in the motives of

Western medical teams, as rumors circulated that immunization efforts were a plot to sterilize Muslims. They recalled the results of a decision by Pfizer, a U.S. drug company, to use an experimental drug to immunize Nigerian children against meningitis in 1996. Eleven children died, and many more were disabled (Otieno 2013).

The refusal to accept the polio vaccine led to the spread of the disease and much suffering. Two-year-old Abubarkar Al Hassan is just one of the children who can no longer run around with his friends. Stricken with polio, he must now be carried everywhere. The government now mandates such vaccines, and thanks to a nationwide vaccination program carried out with UNICEF, cases in Nigeria have declined. Still, health care workers distributing the vaccine in the northern part of the nation confront much distrust and have faced attacks (Cooke 2012; Otieno 2013). This illustration points out how drug companies, national policy decisions, and religious conflict can have an effect on the health of a society, and shows the importance of international medical organizations and efforts to control world pandemics such as polio.

Outbreaks of illness and death also occur within countries due to food poisoning, environmental problems such as leaks of toxic chemicals, or contamination of medicines. In the fall of 2012, cases of a rare type of meningitis cropped up in many U.S. states. The common factor was a batch of contaminated drugs used to treat a form of back pain. About 14,000 people received the

©REUTERS/Jim Young

Sandy Wright looks over her bag of medications at her home in Peoria, Illinois. Wright has neuromyelitis optica and has a certified nursing assistant who both helps her cope with the illness and monitors budding health problems before they require a costly emergency room trip or an extended hospital stay.

steroid shots with a fungal contamination. They made 751 people very ill and led to the deaths of 64 people in 20 states (CDC 2013b; Lavoie 2013).

Let us explore some of the other factors that affect health, illness, and death in the world. **Health** is *a state of physical, mental, and social well-being or the absence of disease*. **Illness**, or *lack of health*, affects the way we perform our individual responsibilities in the social world. Like any social institution, *health care*—our efforts to foster health and treat illness—affects how individuals and groups carry out their lives at the micro, meso, and macro levels.

Health at the Micro Level

Sociologists examine how our state of health affects our individual ability to carry out social responsibilities. Our everyday lives are shaped by our own state of health or illness and those of our loved ones and close associates. If a roommate, significant other, or child is ill, it affects our lives in a number of ways. It alters our schedules, causes us to worry, and costs us time and (usually) money. If a parent is dying of cancer or a child has epilepsy, our lives are influenced in profound and disruptive ways.

Health at the Meso Level

The health of individual citizens can impact how a society functions. The institution of health care provides for the physical, mental, and social well-being of citizens. For example, one sick child can lead to a serious outbreak of influenza in the public schools, a meso-level institution. This could cause repercussions in workplaces throughout the community as parents struggle to deal with child care issues and visits to the doctor. No doubt the outbreak would quickly lead to citizens demanding that their government act to stem the outbreak. Thus, health status affects other institutions in the society, such as the government, the family, the educational system, and the workplace.

To illustrate how health care connects to the major social institutions in society, consider the following examples:

- Economy: Economically successful nations have more money to devote to health care.
- Education: Well-educated citizens are more likely to develop health-enhancing lifestyles.
- Family: Families often have responsibility to care for the sick.

A Patient's Experience

- Political systems: Governments often determine standards for health care and regulate medical drugs.
- Religion: Religious organizations establish support systems and health services, sometimes offer faith-healing alternatives to supplement the established medical system, and offer solace in times of illness and death.

These examples help reveal the interconnections between health and other institutions at the meso level.

Health at the Macro Level

Each society has a vested interest in the health of its citizenry because the general state of health affects the quality of life of the people and the state of the economy. Imagine a society in which citizens had "permission" to be sick frequently. How would that society continue to function? Cultural beliefs about illness and how to treat the sick vary by society.

Consider the case of the former, now-dissolved Soviet Union. After the Soviet victory over Czarist Russia in 1917, the new revolutionary government was faced with an underdeveloped nation that still produced its food with human-powered plows and simple hoes. The task of leading the country out of the 16th century and into the 20th was formidable. It called for a total effort from the nation's workforce. The new government determined that absenteeism at work, regardless of excuse, had to be kept very low. Accordingly, the government instituted rules that required workers who were ill to obtain a certificate allowing them to be absent from work because of illness (Weiss and Lonnquist 2012). These certificates could be obtained only from government clinics, and each clinic could issue only a limited number of permits. In some cases, the government encouraged physicians to compete with one another to see how few certificates they could issue. Thus, absence due to illness was controlled, and the human resources needed for rebuilding the nation were augmented. The macro-level needs were met at the expense of individuals.

Global health focuses on several issues, including possible pandemics of highly contagious diseases, which have become worldwide threats as global travel increases. A *pandemic* is a disease prevalent throughout an entire country that may infect a continent or reach around the world. Figure 14.1 illustrates the global nature of the AIDS pandemic.

FIGURE 14.1   Estimated Percentage of Adults Living With HIV in 2012

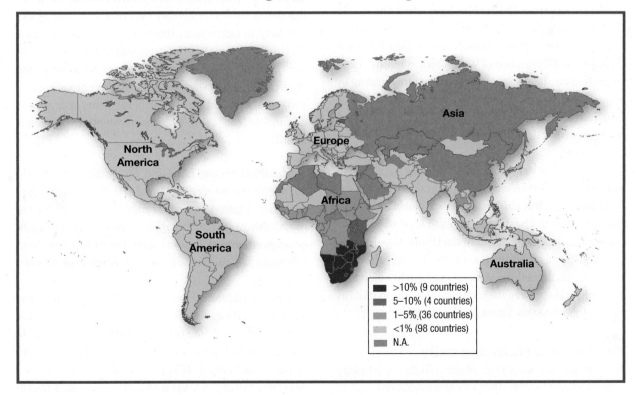

Legend:
- >10% (9 countries)
- 5–10% (4 countries)
- 1–5% (36 countries)
- <1% (98 countries)
- N.A.

Source: Kaiser Family Foundation (2013).

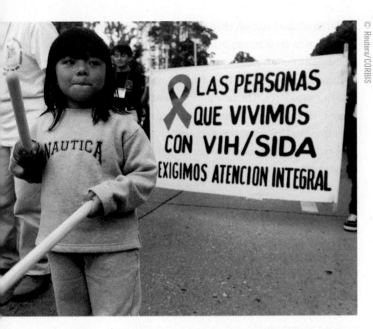

© Reuters/CORBIS

A Guatemalan child infected with HIV marches outside the site of an AIDS conference in Guatemala City. Hundreds of people from different countries marched to bring attention to the lack of government aid and medical assistance for those infected with the virus that causes AIDS.

Controlling such diseases requires cooperation across national boundaries by organizations such as the United Nations. Smallpox, for example, remained a serious global threat from the Middle Ages until the World Health Organization of the United Nations eliminated the disease completely in the 1960s. Likewise, river blindness once afflicted thousands of West Africans but has been eradicated due to international cooperation. Funding by organizations such as the Bill and Melinda Gates Foundation supports research, treatment, and eradication of killer diseases such as malaria, AIDS, and tuberculosis.

When you are sick, illness may seem like an individual problem, but as shown in the above examples, it is far more than that. It is also a national and global issue. This chapter examines health care at each level of analysis, from individual behaviors and decisions, to religious, political, and economic aspects, to the effect of stratification and ethnic status on the quality of health care one receives. Keep the social world model in mind as you read about health, illness, and health care.

 Thinking Sociologically

Why might diseases that affect a local community require international attention and solutions?

THEORETICAL PERSPECTIVES ON HEALTH AND ILLNESS

In the analysis of institutions, each major paradigm or perspective in sociology offers a lens for understanding different aspects of the institution. Let us consider how the major theoretical perspectives help us understand health and illness.

Micro-Level Theoretical Perspectives

Whereas once unruly schoolchildren faced punishments for being "bad," many now receive medications. New understandings of medical disorders have led to the diagnosis of millions of children with medical labels such as attention deficit and other disorders. Advances in medical science have also led to diagnosis and treatment of learning disabilities such as dyslexia, which make it harder for some children to achieve academic success. The changes in the labeling of such conditions result in changes in social stigma and different policies to deal with disorders.

The Symbolic Interaction Perspective and Labeling Theory. Symbolic interactionists point out that definitions of illness vary over time and from society to society. In recent years, the definition of illness in many Global North societies has expanded to encompass substance abuse and some forms of deviant behavior, giving physicians more power and authority over broad areas of social life. As noted earlier, many behaviors once seen as criminal or "bad" are now viewed as symptoms of medical disorders.

Medicalization and Labeling. Medicalization refers to *handling some forms of deviance as well as some normal human functions (such as pregnancy and childbirth) in the health care system rather than the family, legal, or religious arenas*. In some cases, the shift is away from individual self-control and toward medical diagnosis and treatment.

Consider addictive behaviors such as alcoholism and drug abuse. How we define alcoholism influences our understanding of the problem, whether or not we hold the patient to blame, and the course of treatment we pursue (Cockerham 2012). If we see alcoholism as a personal failing, we view the alcoholic as a moral degenerate who needs to start abiding by the norms of society. On the other hand, if we define alcoholism as a disease, we see the alcoholic as a sick person in need of medical care (Conrad, Mackie, and Mehrotra 2010). The next "Sociology in Our Social World" on page 462 explores social policy toward alcoholism.

As societal norms change, so do perceptions of behavior once considered signs of mental or physical disorders. For example, up until 1986, homosexuality appeared in the American Psychiatric Association's (APA) *Diagnostic and Statistical Manual of Mental Disorders*. Since that time, it has lost the label of a mental disorder. The increasing acceptance of gay people in the United States has led, in this case, to demedicalization. We turn now to how forces at the meso and macro levels in our social world shape the experience of illness or health at the micro level.

Meso- and Macro-Level Theoretical Perspectives

Different cultures have different perspectives on illness. Consider the conflicting ideas of illness between the Hmong culture in the United States, made up of immigrants from regions of Laos, Thailand, Vietnam, and China, and the U.S. medical community. In *The Spirit Catches You and You Fall Down* (1997), Anne Fadiman describes the contrasts between how an immigrant Hmong family views an epileptic child and how the hospital in the family's U.S. community sees the situation. The Hmong family attributes the seizures to spirits, but the medical staff treats the epileptic seizures with Western medical methods that utilize drugs, surgery, and other science-based techniques.

Some Hispanic cultures practice a unique, ancient, and complex system of healing known as *curanderismo*. The origins can be found in traditional herbal medicine, precolonial religious belief systems, witchcraft, and Spanish Catholicism. Members of these subcultures view good health and a strong body as God's blessing for the faithful. Illness comes either when one has sinned or as a message from God to help the person learn to be good. The relationship between the *curandero*, or healer, and the patient is close, relying on psychological and spiritual as well as physical treatments. Many Hispanics combine Western medicine and *curanderismo*. For "non-Hispanic illnesses," the physician is the healer of choice. However, for culture-specific conditions such as *susto* (characterized by extreme fright), the *curandero* may be

consulted because many believe that such conditions are impervious to even the highest technology of the scientific physician (Weiss and Lonnquist 2012). The role of the *curandero* combines elements of a psychologist and a healer.

Definitions of mental illness and treatment of the mentally ill can also vary greatly across societies. Consider the case of Manuel, a schizophrenic who "goes crazy" when the moon is full (from which the concept of lunacy derives) and is put in a Nicaraguan mental hospital during that time. Otherwise, he lives a relatively normal life with his parents. In another culture, he might be put in long-term hospital care or given drugs to control the condition. His mental instability might even be given a different definition (Fernando 2002).

How people perceive, experience, and react to pain also varies by culture (Addictionblog.org 2011; Galanti 2008). For example, Asian patients rarely ask for pain medication, but patients from Mediterranean cultures readily ask for help to relieve the slightest pain. Why is there a difference? In a classic U.S. hospital-based study of reactions to pain, researchers observed that patients' responses fell into two main categories: stoic and emotive. Patients with Jewish and Italian cultural backgrounds tended to respond to pain emotionally, while patients of English background were usually stoic and tried to bravely endure pain. Those of Irish descent often denied pain altogether. Although the Jewish American and Italian American patients exhibited similar reactions to pain, their reasons for these reactions were different. The Jewish American patients took a long-term view toward pain. They were concerned about its meaning for their future, and their reactions did not subside when pain-relieving drugs were administered. The Italian American patients, on the other hand, were mainly concerned with the pain itself, and drugs relieved both the pain and their complaints (Lasch 2002; Thomas and Rose 1991; Zborowski 1952). Other studies of culturally learned differences have linked expressive, emotive responses to Hispanic, Middle Eastern, and Mediterranean patients, while stoic patients were more often from Northern European and Asian backgrounds (D'Arcy 2009; Galanti 2008; In the Face of Pain 2013). Even young children show cultural differences in reacting to pain (Azize et al. 2013). Sociological theories and cross-cultural knowledge help us to understand these and other cultural differences in approaches to health care.

The Functionalist Perspective. Functional theorists focus primarily on the macro level of the health care

Mental Illness

sociology in our social world

Alcoholism, Medicalization, and Policy

Perhaps you know someone who struggles with an alcohol problem. The American Medical Association (AMA) officially designated alcoholism as an illness in 1956 (Jellinek 1960). Alcoholism is a dependency on alcohol (alcohol addiction), a chronic disease that includes strong craving, continued use of alcohol despite physical and social problems, and inability to limit drinking (CDC 2013c). The disease is often progressive and fatal.

Some health care professionals, however, argue that the disease concept is the wrong approach—that what is really at stake is "heavy drinking" as a way of life. Rather than treating a "disease," they feel that professionals should be concerned with approaches that will change the way in which individuals organize their behaviors. These researchers and practitioners argue that heavy drinkers can become nondrinkers or moderate drinkers who can control their drinking.

Some sociological theorists see medicalization as one more form of social control by the government and medical establishment. By labeling alcoholism as a disease, the medical profession gains more power and influence as an agent of social control (Conrad 2007). While the Alcoholics Anonymous approach to alcoholism treatment involves laypeople in groups, helping each other stay away from

© istockphoto.com/ Suzanne Toro

The label *alcoholic* has a number of implications, including the fact that the stigma associated with the term may prevent some people from seeking help. Many alcohol treatment centers have recast alcoholism as a disease, hoping that the redefinition will remove stigma.

alcohol in a spiritually oriented manner, the "medicalization of alcoholism" calls for treatment by professionals—psychiatrists, psychologists, hospitals, and clinics. Some people see these approaches as complementary, but others think they are incompatible and conflict with one another (Conrad 2007; Roisen 2012).

A third possibility exists—that there is truth in both models based on individual differences. Treatment programs can be found based on both of these models, and the debate about the best approach continues. Recent approaches to alcoholism often combine medical and social-behavioral treatments, some of which have been illustrated in the TV show *Intervention* (A&E 2012; Roisen 2012). All approaches concur on the need to help alcoholics recognize that they require help.

 Thinking Sociologically

After reading the "Sociology in Our Social World" piece, answer the following questions: Many of us have a friend or relative who struggles with alcohol problems. What labels do others place on that person? Do you think the problem comes from a lack of self-discipline or a physical illness requiring medical treatment? What might you do to help the person?

system. Studies of suicide, carried out by the French sociologist Émile Durkheim (discussed in Chapter 5), illustrate that social conditions and events in the larger society and people's group affiliations affect inclinations to commit suicide. Other studies have linked illnesses such as heart disease, kidney failure, stroke, mental illness, and infant mortality to macro-level processes and trends in societies. For example, economic recessions cause social stress and disruption in lifestyles, which, in turn, can result in health problems.

According to functionalists, the purpose of the health care system in society is to maintain the social structure and a harmonious balance between individuals and institutions in society. Illness is potentially disruptive to the balanced social world because it "robs" the society of normal role functioning. As we saw in the Soviet example, if too many people claim the sick role at the same time, the tasks necessary to maintain the society cannot be performed. The primary task, or function, of the medical profession is to control illness and ensure that individuals can perform their social roles. Sociologists can help organizations within the health care system work well together, as seen in the next "Sociologists in Action" feature on page 464.

Functionalists like Talcott Parsons (1971) see positive value in the hierarchical structure of the medical profession and in the power of the physician over the patient. Parsons believed that having "experts" in charge led to better care for patients. That view, however, is not shared by all, as we will see. We now turn to conflict theory for a different perspective on the health care system.

The Conflict Perspective. Poverty, unemployment, low wages, malnutrition, and a host of other economic conditions affect people's access and ability to compete for health care and medicine in many countries. Differential access is a key theme in conflict theorists' approach to health issues. Consider the case of Nkosi, a 4-year-old boy in a rural Ghanaian village. He came down with an infection due to polluted water, causing diarrhea and vomiting. Nkosi was already weakened by malnutrition and parasites, and by the time his family got medical help, he was so dehydrated that he died. Why was health care for this treatable condition not available in time?

Nkosi had less access to medical treatment, immunizations, antibiotics, vitamins, and a balanced diet than children in the Global North countries or even in urban areas of the Global South. Many children in poor countries around the world suffer from malnutrition and

Malnutrition

Gerardo Queupukura, a renowned shaman of the Mapuche tribe in Chile, attends to a line of patients and looks at the urine samples to determine the patients' health status.

chronic disease before succumbing to pneumonia or other infections, diseases for which treatment is normally available. Relatively new "emerging infectious diseases" such as AIDS, Brazilian purpuric fever, new strains of Ebola, various insect- and bird-transported diseases such as SARS and bird flu, and swine flu (H1N1) add to the problems faced by health care workers in the Global South. Efforts by medical activists such as Dr. Paul Farmer, a U.S. infectious disease specialist and anthropologist, help poor countries. He set up an organization, Partners in Health, with the goal of conquering diseases among the world's poor, especially in Haiti, Russia, and Peru where tuberculosis kills many (Kidder 2004). With life expectancy (average length of life) as low as 46 years in some drought-ridden and war-torn countries, the challenge is formidable.

Conflict theorists point out that individuals suffer different illnesses depending on the level of development of their society and their position in it. Many low-income residents in Global North nations live in *food deserts,* areas that lack grocery stores and other means of access to affordable, healthy food. The residents in these food deserts tend to eat highly processed foods full of artificially cheap, corn-based ingredients, sugar-laden soft drinks, and other addictive foods that spark cravings for more such food. The movie *Super Size Me* illustrates this well.

Meanwhile, poor people in Global South countries die from ailments that are curable in rich countries. Swaziland, in sub-Saharan Africa, provides an example. Many people in Swaziland die of treatable diseases;

SOCIOLOGISTS IN ACTION:
ERIC R. WRIGHT

Improving State-Level Substance Abuse Prevention Policy

The State of Indiana launched a comprehensive initiative to improve the state's alcohol and drug abuse prevention policies and programs. As part of those 2006 efforts, the Office of the Governor and staff from the Indiana Division of Mental Health and Addiction (IDMHA) approached me to develop and lead Indiana's State Epidemiology and Outcomes Workgroup (SEOW). Former governor Mitch Daniels was an early political champion of "data-driven decision-making," and his administration was keen to reform Indiana's behavioral health system to target scarce resources where needed.

The SEOW was established to serve as an inter-agency workgroup with representatives from the many state agencies in setting policy and funding programs related to the prevention of drug and alcohol abuse. As the SEOW chair, I was tasked with facilitating the regular meetings, improving communication among the agencies, and using epidemiological data (data to help understand the nature and extent of substance use, abuse, dependence, risks, and protective factors) to improve the coordination of efforts to prevent alcohol and drug abuse across Indiana (Substance Abuse and Mental Health Services Administration n.d.).

Initially, this was a formidable task. The state agencies I worked with existed in an isolated "policy silo"; each agency had its own preferred way of understanding substance abuse prevention using evidence to support its priorities. I had to draw extensively on my knowledge of the sociology of organizations and research methods to find ways to facilitate new dialogues, challenge long-standing beliefs, repair damaged communication channels,

and build new collaborative working relationships. The early SEOW meetings revolved around intense debates regarding the strengths and limitations of different types of data, building trust, and, ultimately, reaching an agreement on a plan to analyze the available data in a careful and coordinated way.

The result was the publication of a comprehensive public report, titled *The Consumption and Consequences of Alcohol, Tobacco, and Drugs in Indiana: A State Epidemiological Profile*, which summarized the existing data for policy makers and the people of Indiana. We tried hard to write the report in an objective way and to draw only conclusions that all members of the SEOW agreed were clearly evident in the statistical analyses presented. The SEOW then used the key findings from the report to prepare a list of strategic priorities to guide policy making and the allocation of funding across all state agencies involved in the prevention of alcohol and other types of substance abuse.

The data from that initial report, and our subsequent annual updates of the report and strategic priorities, continue to impact policy making and public awareness about the negative impact of drug and alcohol abuse on communities. While it has taken several years and much work remains to be done to reduce the burden of substance abuse in the Hoosier state, our efforts clearly have begun to pay off.

I have learned a great deal from my experience as SEOW chair. I regularly give public lectures, participate in media interviews, and consult with people involved in community and governmental prevention programs. Our research has been informed by collaboration with communities and individuals actively working on important social problems.

This project also thrust me into the public eye and transformed me into a "public sociologist"—that is, someone who not only studies society but also is actively involved in shaping social change. Most important, my work in this area has taught me that sociological research can be a powerful force in the public and political conversations, but sociologists must be prepared to be active participants in those

discussions and take responsibility for helping communities understand what research can and cannot tell us about a social problem.

• •

Eric R. Wright is a professor of sociology and public health at Georgia State University in Atlanta. As a medical sociologist, he works with local and state government as well as treatment organizations and community nonprofit agencies to improve the effectiveness of health programs and policy.

however, the dominant killer is AIDS. No other nation has a higher percentage of its population infected by HIV/AIDS, approximately one out of every four people (Doctors without Borders 2012). Among pregnant women, the number of HIV infections reaches about 41% (UNAIDS 2012b). Thanks in large part to PEPFAR (the U.S. President's Emergency Plan for AIDS Relief), the number of treated adults has now surpassed the number of new infections, but great efforts must still be made to provide health care and preventative treatment for those with HIV/AIDS in this economically struggling nation (PEPFAR 2013).

Many governments officially proclaim that health care is a basic right of all citizens, but they do not have the funds or infrastructure to meet the health needs of citizens. One country that has revolutionized its health care system is Venezuela. With oil revenues and tax dollars, the government has built clinics called *Mission Barrio Adentro* to serve those living in urban and rural poverty. Before the socialist government came to power in Venezuela in 1999, many poor people had no access to care. Today, clinics provide free medical services for communities. As a result, the infant mortality rate has been cut in half and life expectancy has risen (Sedghi 2013). However, many poor countries do not have oil or other natural resources to help pay for health care. Cuba, for example, now struggles to support its universal health care system, as explained in the next "Sociology Around the World" on page 466.

At the global level, many multinational companies that build factories in the poor Global South provide examples of the profit motive's influence on health conditions.

Businesses seeking large profit margins and cost-cutting opportunities may move operations to countries with lower health and safety standards than those in the Global North, which has more stringent health regulations. For example, many factories in Bangladesh spew untreated waste without regard to the health of their workers or those living in the area. These textile and garment factories, through making clothes for companies such as Walmart, J. C. Penney, and H&M, in the cheapest way

Abdur Rahman holds a family photo of his wife Cahyna Akhter, a garment worker who died when the Rana Plaza building collapsed, killing more than 1,000 people. Bangladeshi factory workers face risks from both unsafe working conditions and pollution created by the factories. Conflict theorists argue that self-interest of the affluent to increase profits results in unsafe conditions.

Sociology Around the World

Health Care: Cuba's Pride

One thing all Cubans were promised under the Communist regime of Fidel Castro was access to good health care, which he viewed as a basic right of all people. When Cuba had trading partners and support from the former Soviet Union and allied nations in Europe's eastern bloc, its system was considered a model, especially for a Global South country. Now, the country has lost external support due to the collapse of the Soviet system and must still deal with the long-standing U.S.-imposed embargo on goods going to Cuba. Shortages of drugs, diagnostic equipment, and medical supplies have forced Cuba's well-trained doctors to be creative. They use herbal remedies, hypnosis, and acupuncture in place of needed supplies and equipment.

Cuba's health care system has the best doctor-patient ratio in the world—1 doctor to every 155 inhabitants compared to 1 to 396 in the United States. Cuba spends $503 per capita compared to the U.S. expenses of over $7,500 per person (Souers 2012). Hospitals and clinics are spread throughout the country. Infant mortality in 2013 at 4.2 (deaths per 1,000 live births in the first year), and life expectancy rates (78 in 2013) compare well with those of most Global North developed countries (Global Post 2014; Index Mundi 2013a). However, because of economic hardships and lack of medicine and equipment that could easily control some illnesses and diseases, some experts fear these numbers will begin to slip.

Diary entries of a recent visitor to Cuba tell of the impact that economic sanctions have on the health of ordinary citizens:

I visited Dr. Barbara, a young family doctor, in her neighborhood *consultorio* in Havana, Cuba. Her waiting room was full of young mothers holding plump and healthy babies, sitting against a wall covered with a hand-painted wall mural. A portrait of Fidel Castro (Cuba's former head of government) hung next to a painted caricature of Mickey Mouse on the wall behind her desk. Her eyes bright, her long hair bouncing against her shoulders, she said she was very proud to be a Cuban physician and to care for a patient community of 200 families.

However, she added with a pause, sometimes she felt helpless to provide the care that her patients needed. She explained that diagnostic tests were often missed or delayed because of shortages of X-ray film or replacement parts for equipment. Blood work was limited by lack of reagents needed in the labs. Her prescription choices were restricted to the medicines available at the time, a situation that she found very frustrating when her patient had multiple medical problems that dictated the use of one medicine rather than another. Prozac and other state-of-the-art antidepressants were unheard of, and only a few drugs for treating depressive and anxiety disorders were available. Many anticancer medicines were difficult or impossible to get. She said that people were dying sooner than necessary because of these scarcities (Lemkau 2006).

The problems described in this diary entry and the preceding description of Cuba illustrate the connections among health, economic resources, and countries' relations with other nations.

possible, have helped create a pollution crisis. The pollution from their factories damages or destroys the food, water, and air sources people rely upon to eat, drink, and breathe.

The unsafe conditions in many factories in Bangladesh, and the death of at least 1,127 workers in the Rana Plaza building alone, also illustrates a problem in Global South countries. Pressures from buyers in Global North multinational companies for manufacturers to produce cheap goods, and corrupt government officials who fail to enforce regulations designed to provide safe buildings and control the treatment and dispersal of factory waste, result in unsafe practices (Yardley 2013).

Conflict theorists also point out that most physicians work in affluent, urban areas and go into specialties that pay more than primary (general, family care) doctors receive. The most lucrative positions with the most prestige are generally located in major global urban areas and at well-known clinics, where people can pay for private care. As a result, a severe shortage of primary care doctors exists in rural areas of the world, including the rural United States (Snyderman and Sottile 2013). This pattern also leads some conflict theorists to describe the doctor-patient relationship as an association in which the doctor exercises control, and loyalty of the doctor to the patient depends in part on the social status of the patient (White 2002).

Conflict theorists emphasize that poverty and inequality—whether in the Global North or the Global South—have a major impact on quality of life and health care. The next "Engaging Sociology" on page 468 illustrates the impact a lack of health care can have on individuals in the United States.

Feminist Theory. Feminist theorists examine the impact of gender on health, illness, and health care, among other topics. They argue that the patriarchal control of women carries over to health care systems and reinforces the dependence and submission of women.

In the Global North, women tend to spend more money on health care than do men. Some of the procedures practiced on women, although recommended by doctors, are unnecessary, according to feminists in medical professions. For example, many doctors recommend that women deliver their babies via cesarean section surgery rather than vaginally. The percentage of cesarean births has risen dramatically from 5% in 1970 to approximately 30% today. Some of them are necessary, but

others may be for convenience or to avoid lawsuits (Lake 2012; Weiss 2010). According to feminist theorists, controlling women's reproductive health and defining women's normal biological experiences as medical problems reflect and support a patriarchal (male-dominated) society.

To regain control of women's health, some feminists have formed health organizations concerned with reproductive health. Such organizations may provide midwifery and natural childbirth services, and help women deal with issues related to menopause. With increasing numbers of women physicians, attitudes toward women's health and communication practices between women and physicians have also started to change. Thanks to these changes, more doctors recognize the importance of listening to and working *with* patients on their health issues.

Gender also plays a role in doctors' specialty positions. Women now account for almost half of all those in medical school but, more than men, tend to opt for medical specialty areas with less prestige and less money but with more family-friendly emphases and hours. Women, for example, comprise 30% of all physicians in the United States but make up over half of all pediatricians and primary care doctors (American Medical Association 2012; Dotinga 2011).

Feminist theorists also point out that the social status of girls and women can be detrimental to their health. For example, many girls in Global South countries face pressure to marry at a young age, which can lead to major health problems. The risk of dying during childbirth increases the lower the age of the mother, yet 7.3 million girls under 18 in the Global South give birth each year, 2 million of them 14 and under (Vinograd 2013). One of the most socially difficult problems for young girls who give birth at a young age is *obstetric fistula*, a childbirth injury in which tissue is torn between the vaginal wall and the bladder or rectum. This causes ulcerations, incontinence, and infections (Burn 2011). More than 2 million young women suffer from this injury, and many are ostracized and abandoned. Several international organizations, including USAID, carry out the simple operation to repair the damaged area and return these young girls to their lives, but there is a backlog of those needing the surgery. Moreover, the girls must have access to such care and in many cases need permission from their husband to receive it (USAID 2014).

As you can see, each theory illuminates a different set of issues in health, illness, and health care at the meso and

···· ENGAGING SOCIOLOGY ·····················

Decisions About Health Care When Living in Poverty

Look at the following list of basic needs. Most of us provide these for our families through our jobs. Now imagine that you and your family are faced with a major financial crisis, and you simply cannot meet all your needs.

- Health care and health insurance
- A car or other reliable transportation
- Food for the family
- Clothing—appropriate for the weather and your occupation
- Housing in a safe neighborhood
- Access to good schools for your children
- Other essentials . . .

    1. Which of the items listed above would you give up? If that was still not sufficient to make ends meet, what decisions would you make to balance the budget?

2. Many people choose to postpone or sacrifice health care insurance or doctors' visits. How might poor health care affect your income *and* at least three of the items listed previously?

    1. _____

    2. _____

    3. _____

3. Now consider items you chose to eliminate in Question 1. How might those decisions have a long-term impact on other aspects of your quality of life—*including* the health of family members?

    1. _____

    2. _____

    3. _____

macro levels. We now examine health and illness at a micro level. In doing so, we focus on the status and roles of the sick person.

THE STATUS AND ROLES OF THE SICK PERSON: MICRO-LEVEL ANALYSIS

How do you know if you are sick? How you answer this question depends on your culture, as well as your physical symptoms (Weiss and Lonnquist 2012). A poor Central American woman, asked if she has been sick, illustrates this point by commenting that she wished she knew what it meant to be sick. Sometimes she felt so bad she thought she could curl up and die, but she kept going because the kids needed her, and she lacked money to spend on a doctor. She did not have time to be sick. She asks, "How does one know when someone is sick?" Some of us can go to bed almost any time with any illness, but many of the world's

people cannot be sick, not even when they need to be (Koos 1954).

To the poor, Central American woman, being sick was not just a physical condition or how she felt or any physical symptoms she displayed. From a cultural perspective, she had responsibilities that could not be ignored, little access to health care, and no money to buy medicine or care. So who defines the poor woman described earlier as sick? She herself? Her friends and family? Her employer? A health care professional? The answer is ambiguous. Illness, then, is in part socially constructed. Health care providers, schools, and workplaces acknowledge illness only if certain society-defined conditions are present.

Surveys of health in populations around the world indicate that most people have some physical disorder. Yet the presence of such disorders does not mean that individuals will seek treatment or that the illness will be recognized and treated. Both individual (micro) and structural (meso or macro) factors influence health care decisions and treatment. The political and economic environment, access to medical services, and the predisposition by an individual to seek medical care all enter into health care decisions.

Thinking Sociologically

How do you determine whether you are sick? How do your obligations influence your perceptions of your health? Was it easier for you to be sick as a child than it is now? Why or why not?

The Sick Role

Think of all the social relationships, engagements, and responsibilities affected when you are sick. You miss class and work, and have to avoid your friends so that you do not infect them with your germs. Most people are sympathetic for a few days, but then they expect you to get back to your usual routines and responsibilities. Unless those around you perceive you as *very* ill, you probably cannot play the "sick role" for a long period of time without facing negative sanctions.

Ill people occupy a special status in society that requires them to perform a certain role. The sick role is *a special position in society in which one is temporarily relieved of responsibilities and accepts a position of dependence.* This role allows one to deviate from usual role expectations, and other people must pick up those responsibilities. Unlike other acts of deviance, however, the sick role is not punished—as long as the sick individual cooperates and acts to overcome illness, returning as soon as possible to fulfill his or her usual social roles. That can be difficult for people facing chronic illness, as seen in the model below (Varul 2010).

In an early contribution to the sociology of health, Parsons (1951a) presented a functional theoretical model of the "sick role," outlining four interrelated behavioral expectations—two rights and two obligations:

Right 1: The sick person has the right to be excused from normal social responsibility as needed to be restored to normal functioning in the society. For example, sick students expect to receive permission to miss class or to make up a missed exam.

Right 2: The sickness is not the individual's fault. The sick person did not mean to deviate from normal social expectations and cannot become well by self-decision or by willing it so.

Obligation 1: The sick person should define being sick as undesirable. To avoid the accusation of laziness or malingering, the sick person must not prolong illness unnecessarily to avoid social obligations.

Obligation 2: Those in the sick status should seek technically competent help and cooperate in getting well. In Western countries, the help most often comes from a medical doctor.

Parsons describes the physicians' roles as complementing the "sick role"—to restore routine behavior and "orderliness" in patients. The model presented by Parsons clearly relates to functionalist thought. Functionalists focus on integrating all aspects of medical care into a working social system (Parsons 1951a).

Some individuals, however, might like being excused from tasks and allowed to deviate from social responsibility (such as taking tests or doing an arduous task). Certainly, being sick requires a less demanding lifestyle than going to work or school or taking care of a family. The sick role can also legitimize failure by providing a ready excuse for poor performance at some task. People who believe they are permanently unable to fulfill their normal social roles may be motivated to define themselves as sick. Yet an excess of sick people could be disruptive to the social fabric, so it is necessary to develop means to control who enters the sick status and to guard against misuse of illness as an excuse for avoiding social responsibility. In most societies today, possible negative sanctions, ranging from colleagues' raised eyebrows to being fired, discourage many people from pretending to be sick to get out of work.

Thinking Sociologically

What duties and responsibilities do you relinquish when you occupy a sick role? Which ones do you continue during your illness?

Individuals can also earn negative sanctions for engaging in unhealthy behavior. For example, if you smoke, there is a very good chance that someone has chastised you for doing so. Your decisions about what you eat and drink, your use of alcohol and other drugs, and your sexual behavior affect your health. Any of these taken to extremes can result in illness.

Attitudes toward health, illness, and death vary from society to society. In countries with high infant mortality rates and low life expectancy, illness and death are all too familiar. As we describe in more detail in Chapter 15, many people in Global South nations have many children because they expect some to die before reaching adulthood.

Social Factors and Attitudes Toward Health, Illness, and Death. A U.S. Peace Corps volunteer in a South American village could not understand the passive attitude of the mother, Mónica, as she held her dying baby. He offered to help Mónica get the baby to the clinic 15 miles away, but she seemed resigned to its death. The expectations that shaped Mónica's behavior were learned in her cultural setting. Three of her seven children had died already. In this rural Global South setting, as many as half of the babies born will die in infancy because of curable illness, poor sanitation, lack of clean water, and lack of health care and medicine. People come to accept infant deaths, often easily preventable, as part of life. Many parents do not even name their children until they have displayed indications of good health for several weeks after birth.

Social Predictors in Individual Health and Illness. Individual micro-level variables such as age, gender, ethnicity, economic factors, social status, and urban or rural residence help determine patterns of health and illness. For example, *age* affects health in several ways. People 65 years or older tend to need more medical intervention than younger people (Cherry, Lucas, and Decker 2010). Medicare covers this group and accounts for 20% of the national health expenditures. Of the 41.4 million citizens 65 years and older (or 1 in 8 citizens), 24.7% were in fair or poor health and required more doctors' visits than younger groups (U.S. Department of Health and Human Services 2012).

Gender patterns are clear, too: As noted earlier, in Global North cultures, women are more inclined to go to the doctor than men, and receive more preventive and reproductive care. In contrast, men tend to go to the doctor less and receive less preventative care. As a result, they tend to use emergency services more than women (Weiss and Lonnquist 2012).

Ethnic groups socialize individuals into lifestyles that help or harm their health. Ethnicity also influences people's perceptions of health, the medical interventions they seek, and their response to medical treatment. Recall the cases of Hispanic *curanderismo*, the Hmong concepts of illness, and the different experiences of pain discussed earlier. Socialization into possible health care options ranges from modern medical practitioners to alternative medical practitioners (from traditional folk healers to modern chiropractors), nonmedical professions (e.g., social workers and clergy), lay advisers, and self-care (Pescosolido 1992).

As we saw in Chapter 8, *racial privilege and disprivilege* can result from how institutions—including health care institutions—treat people. In the United States, for example, African Americans, Hispanics, and Native Americans are less likely to have regular health care providers and more likely to use hospital emergency rooms and health clinics than white Americans. Racial and ethnic minority residents tend to live in poor and rural areas, where there is less available health care. On average, most women of color receive less prenatal care than white women, and the infant mortality gap (i.e., the number of live-born infants who die in their first year per 1,000 births) reflects this disparity, as shown in Table 14.1 (MacDorman and Mathews 2011). The relatively high infant-mortality rate in the United States compared to rates in other affluent countries stems largely from the lack of adequate health care available to low-income U.S. citizens and racial and ethnic minorities (DeSantis 2013). Infant mortality also varies widely within the United States as health care varies; Figure 14.2 illustrates this well.

Wealthier individuals tend to seek professional help earlier for physical or psychological distress because they can better afford the cost and time for such treatment. Despite this fact, people in the lowest income group have more contact with physicians (7.6 doctor visits per year compared with an average of 6 for the entire population) (Weiss and Lonnquist 2012). This is one powerful indicator that lower-income people are less healthy.

Lower-income citizens' perceptions of necessary health consultation often involve responses to crises. The

Table 14.1 Infant Deaths per 1,000 Live Births by Race of Mother (in the United States)

Race or Ethnic Origin	Number per 1,000
All racial/ethnic groups	6.2
Black	11.5
American Indian/Alaska Native	8.3
Hispanic	5.3
White	5.2
Asian American	4.3

Source: CDC (2013d).

Health Care Costs 🎙

FIGURE 14.2 Infant Mortality Rates by State in the United States

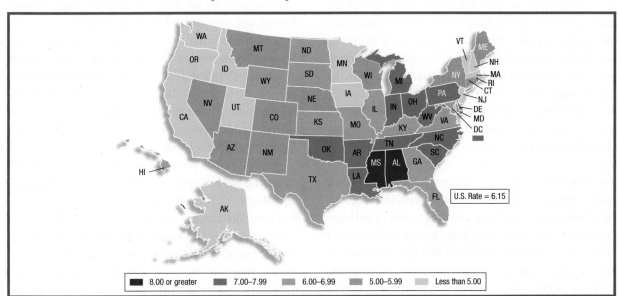

| 8.00 or greater | 7.00–7.99 | 6.00–6.99 | 5.00–5.99 | Less than 5.00 |

U.S. Rate = 6.15

Source: Center for Disease Control. Retrieved from http://www.cdc.gov/nchs/data/databriefs/db120.pdf

"working poor" who do not qualify for Medicaid but cannot afford private insurance or medical care tend to delay care (Weiss and Lonnquist 2012). Roughly one in four adults in the United States lacked health care in 2010, and one in five did not receive the needed health-related services because they could not afford to visit a doctor (CDC 2012; Schiller et al. 2012.). The number of U.S. citizens without health insurance has dropped from about 25% to 16% as of February 2014 as more citizens sign up for the Affordable Care Act insurance (Levy 2014). Without universal access to health care, income affects health status.

Differences in access to health care also relate to meso and macro levels of the social system, as discussed in the next sections.

MODERN HEALTH CARE SYSTEMS: MESO-LEVEL ANALYSIS

At one time, health care was largely an issue addressed in homes by families. Today, in wealthy countries, health care has become institutionalized. Much of the treatment of diseases depends on research funded by governments or foundations, and bureaucratized corporations deliver care. This section explores the institution of medicine: organization of health care systems, hospitals as complex organizations, and changes of professional status for physicians.

The Organization of Health Care Systems

Citizens' access to health care depends on several factors: the cultural values concerning the government's role in providing health care—whether health care is seen as a human right for all citizens or a privilege for those who can pay for

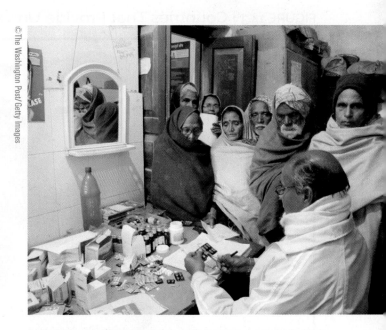

Availability of health resources is an important structural factor in health. This primary health care center in rural India does not have a pharmacist; a filing clerk makes decisions about who gets what drugs.

it, and the type of health care available. Societies around the world struggle with issues of cost, quality, and access to care and medical technology. In the Global North, these struggles result from aging populations with more health needs and smaller numbers of citizens in the taxpaying working population to support health care programs. Nations in the Global South struggle with problems that result in high death rates from curable diseases and epidemics. Nations develop health care philosophies and systems based on population needs and their ability to address them.

Types of National Health Care Systems. The two most common national models for providing health care—socialized medicine and decentralized national health care programs—are based on the philosophy of health care as a human right. The United States has moved closer to that philosophy with the passage of the Affordable Care Act, or Obamacare, signed into law in 2010. Figure 14.3 shows the countries of the world that have universal health care as of 2012.

Socialized medicine *provides a government-supported consumer service that ensures equal access to health care for all citizens of a country* (Cockerham 2012). The political system controls the organization and financing of health services and owns most facilities, pays providers directly, and allows private care for an extra fee. Global North

countries that have different forms of socialized medicine systems include Canada, Great Britain, Israel, Norway, Sweden, and several other European countries.

Countries with decentralized national health programs have many of the same characteristics, but the government's role is different. The government has less direct control over health care and acts to regulate the system, but not operate it (Cockerham 2012). Countries with decentralized systems include France, Germany, Japan, and the Netherlands.

The United States, unique among Global North countries, has had a mix of socialized (Medicaid for poor and Medicare for elderly) and private health care programs. Both tend to rely on *fee-for-service health care*, in which doctors and hospitals are paid for each service they perform, and decide the prices charged for every service. They typically can order as many tests as they feel necessary, and decide the price for each. The fee-for-service aspect has led to doctors and hospitals charging enormous (and varying) fees for every conceivable thing used (e.g., ibuprofen, sponges) and exceedingly high health care costs (Brill 2013). Under the current plan, called the Affordable Care Act, individuals who do not have a group plan or are low income (but do not qualify for Medicaid) can acquire health insurance through exchanges—organizations that facilitate the purchase of

FIGURE 14.3   Countries That Provide Universal Health Care

Source: Fisher (2012).

health insurance in each state at rates subsidized by the federal government. Those without insurance and not on Medicare or Medicaid after a certain deadline must pay a fine and pay out-of-pocket for medical services (Centers for Medicare and Medicaid Services [CMS] 2013).

Thinking Sociologically

What kind of access do you have to health care? Are you able to see a physician without worrying about the cost? Why or why not?

Most governments in Europe decided to support health care as a human right for all citizens and put their universal health care systems into place beginning in the late 1800s (in Germany) through the mid-1900s. Their motivations were to develop healthier populations, strengthen their military forces and economic systems, and reduce the possibility of revolution. The next "Sociology Around the World" on page 474 describes the philosophy of the health care system in Canada, developed right after World War II.

Global health organizations serve many poor countries, primarily with immunizations and humanitarian aid during wars or epidemics. The Red Cross, Doctors without Borders, and other international aid organizations work to address the emergency needs of dislocated populations and of those in war-torn nations. The World Health Organization, among other international organizations, helps provide immunizations and treatment for epidemics, but does not provide services for ongoing health needs.

Hospitals as Complex Organizations. *Hospitals* are organizations that provide care and treatment for the sick and injured, providing centralized medical knowledge and technology for treatment of illnesses and accidents. Rational, systematic approaches to health care replaced individual folk remedies in the late colonial period in North America. The first colonial hospital opened in 1752, and the first medical school began accepting students in 1765. The focus of these early hospitals was on segregating the destitute and terminally ill, who might be contagious and were likely to die. At this time, most hospitals were still small, but improvements in medical knowledge and competency began to change both these institutions and the entire medical profession. In the late 1800s, the number of hospitals, many of which were sponsored by religious organizations, grew very rapidly.

The status of the hospital shifted dramatically in the early 1900s, due to advances in medical science. Trained staff, sterile conditions, and more advanced techniques and technology changed hospitals from being the last resort of the urban poor and the dying to places of healing for all classes. Small community hospitals became an essential element of town life.

The post–World War II period produced huge growth in health care facilities and numbers of employees in the U.S. health care system. Medicines and vaccines controlled many infectious diseases that had formerly killed and disabled individuals. This period also saw the growth of medical schools and large medical facilities that provided not only patient care but also education and research. Thus began the dominance of the hospital in providing medical care. Today, many hospitals are centers of medical knowledge and technology, housing not only patients and surgical units but also laboratories and diagnostic centers, specialty clinics, and rehabilitation centers.

High-tech medical equipment (top) is expensive, but in places such as Ethiopia (bottom), hospitals have few resources, and physicians must use whatever limited technology is available.

Sociology Around the World

Comparing Health Care Systems: The Canadian Model

Two principles underlie Canada's health care system: All Canadians should have the right to health care, and financial barriers to care should be eliminated. After World War II, the Canadian government established a group of health insurance plans ("socialized insurance") that provided universal health insurance to improve the health of all Canadians. Most of the costs are paid for by public funding through general taxation, 70% in 2012. Financing by private households represents 15% of total health expenditures, mostly for dental care, long-term care, prescription drugs, and vision care. Much of the rest is for copayments. The government, in consultation with medical professionals, sets prices for services (Commonwealth Fund 2013).

Infant mortality and life expectancy rates, two key measures of a country's health status, reveal that Canada has lower infant mortality than the United States (4.71 deaths per 1,000 live births in Canada vs. 6.17 in the United States) (World Factbook 2014f). Canada also has higher life expectancy—81.0 years (12th in the world) compared to 78.7 years (53rd in the world) in the United States (Organisation for Economic Co-operation and Development [OECD] 2014). Taxes in Canada are 10% to 15% higher than those in the United States, but total cost per capita (per person) is 33% less for health care. In other words, the overall cost to consumers means higher taxes but lower costs overall. In 2011, Canada spent 11.3% of its gross domestic product (GDP) on health expenditures, while the United States spent 17.4% of its GDP on health care ("10 Countries Spending the Most" 2012).

Comparing Canada and the United States with 16 developed countries shows that the United States spent the most per capita ($7,960) in 2011. Norway is second in cost per citizen at $5,352, and Canada is only about half as expensive at $4,478 (see Table 14.2.) In addition, controls by insurance companies result in hospital stays in the United States that are 20% to 40% shorter than in most other countries for similar procedures.

No system, including the Canadian one, is perfect. For example, in Canada, waiting periods for nonessential procedures are longer, and there are shortages of health care providers in some areas. As in the United States, if they have the funds, individual Canadians can sometimes pay for private, more rapid treatment. This fact indicates that even the Canadian universal health care system does not treat all patients equally.

Table 14.2 Health Expenditures in the Most Expensive Countries and Life Expectancy Outcomes

	Cost per Citizen	% of Gross Domestic Product	Average Life Expectancy
Denmark	$4,438	11.5%	79.0 years
Canada	$4,478	11.3%	81.5 years
Netherlands	$4,914	12.0%	80.6 years
Switzerland	$5,344	11.6%	82.3 years
Norway	$5,352	9.6%	81.0 years
United States	$7,960	17.4%	78.5 years

Note: Switzerland has the health care system most similar to the newly passed U.S. Affordable Care Act.

Source: "10 Countries Spending the Most" (2012).

Canadian Health Care

Thinking Sociologically

Based on the "Sociology Around the World" feature on health care in Canada compared to the United States, what do you conclude about the pros and cons of these two approaches to health care?

Although medical health systems differ across societies, hospitals generally exhibit many characteristics similar to other large, bureaucratic organizations: hierarchical structures, rules and regulations, statuses (doctors, nurses) based on competency and training, hiring and promotion based on merit, and contracts for work performed. Primary-care physicians and other gatekeepers control client access to hospitals. Historically, U.S. hospitals were designed for the convenience of physicians. However, today two rather independent bureaucracies function within modern large-scale hospital organizations. Physicians dominate the medical operations, while lay administrators control the other areas of the hospital (e.g., finance, human resources, support services).

Health care systems act as major employers in most affluent nations. In the United States, for instance, more than 14 million people work in 5,723 hospitals (American Hospital Association 2012, 2014). They hold jobs as nurses, hospital administrators, pharmacists, physical therapists, physician's assistants, and imaging specialists (those who work with X-rays, MRIs, and the like), and the number of employees continues to grow. Nurses comprise the largest group of health care workers, with licensed registered nurses (2,711,500) and licensed practical and vocational nurses (738,400) accounting for nearly six nurses per physician (U.S. Bureau of Labor Statistics 2014). In the hospital, the nurse manages the patient care team under the authority of the physician, who is the prime decision maker. Under the nurse's authority in this hierarchical structure come increasing numbers of ancillary personnel.

As more for-profit corporations own and operate hospitals and other medical facilities in the United States, the power of the professional or medical line is giving way to corporate management—the lay or administrative line. Physicians have become the customers of the hospital, buying space and time to carry out their functions. Sometimes, the cost-saving goals of administrators and medical decisions of physicians come into conflict.

Changing Professional Status of Employees in the Health Care System

Special features distinguish the hospital from other large-scale organizations or bureaucracies. The division of labor in the hospital is extensive and more highly specialized than other formal organizations. The hospital has a hierarchical structure based on prestige and power, and hospitals depend on the cooperation of highly skilled people who must coordinate their work. Hospital employees rigidly follow patterns of authority and wear clothing and symbols indicating particular positions in the hospital hierarchy. At the top of the stratification ladder, the physicians exercise the most power and receive the highest financial and prestige rewards. Signs of their superior status include wearing long white coats or not wearing special uniforms at all.

Physicians rank among the most respected professionals in most societies. The widespread acceptance of physician authority is relatively recent, however. The status of physicians began to climb after medical discoveries in the 1800s led to greater success rates in treatment and more specialized training for physicians (Pescosolido and Boyer 2010). The transformation of physicians to a position of professional recognition gained great traction in the United States when some 250 physicians meeting in Philadelphia in May 1847 established the American Medical Association (AMA). This umbrella organization became the means to gain legitimacy and power over health care practice (Cockerham 2012). The powerful new AMA delegitimized predominantly female health care areas such as midwifery and other holistic approaches such as osteopathy, chiropractic medicine, and homeopathy. Only one approach was granted credibility: *allopathy*, medical treatment supported by the AMA and most Western medical organizations, involving remedies based on directly countering a patient's symptoms with drugs or surgery.

 Thinking Sociologically

Who controls the medical facilities in your community? What structure do they have, and what roles predominate? Do you see evidence of hospitals focusing on efficiency and profit over medical care? How are the hospitals in your community regarded by the community? Why?

Hospital Ratings Fatigue

Included in the professionalization of doctors was the relationship with patients. Parsons presented a model of the doctor role that had rights and obligations, just as patients had. Among the expectations were that doctors would have a high degree of skill and knowledge, act for the patient and community welfare, be objective and emotionally detached, and be professional. These expectations are still valid in today's changing system (Parsons 1951a).

Deprofessionalization is the *process through which a professional occupation loses autonomy, respect, and service orientation because the professionals come to be controlled by nonprofessionals and outside forces such as financial concerns, government regulations, technological changes, and administrators or management.* While their position entails a very high status in society, physicians have lost some control over health care to insurance companies and hospital administrators. Many physicians now work for managed care systems, by whose established guidelines for medical care they must abide, reducing their autonomy (Pescosolido and Boyer 2010). Nurses also face work situations that can cause burnout as discussed in the following "Sociologists in Action."

We have explored issues of health care at the micro level (the role of sick people) and at the meso level (organization of health care and hospitals as complex organizations). We now move on to macro-level policy issues at national and global levels.

 Thinking Sociologically

What meso- and macro-level forces lead to some people in the world having more access to health care than others? At the micro level, what does this mean for the health and productivity of individuals, and their ability to support their families? What might it mean for societies as a whole?

HEALTH CARE ISSUES AT NATIONAL AND GLOBAL LEVELS: MACRO-LEVEL ANALYSIS

The Health Care System in the United States

The United States has the best—and the worst—health care system among Global North countries in terms of quality medical care, trained practitioners, facilities, and advanced medical technology. People from around the world seek training and care in the United States. It is also the worst system, with the highest cost per capita in the world, unequal access, inefficiencies, and competing interests. The Affordable Care Act (Obamacare), as it is phased in, will address some of these issues.

People like Eloise have suffered from some of the weaknesses of the U.S. health care system. She knew something was seriously wrong when she lost her appetite, vomited when she ate more than a few bites, and did not have her usual, abundant energy. Without health insurance and fearing she would lose her job if she missed work to see a doctor, she tried home remedies and hoped the symptoms would go away. When she finally did go to the hospital, she was in serious condition. Eloise spent a few days in intensive care and is now on a treatment plan, but without income from her job, she cannot pay the bills for herself and her child.

Similar medical emergencies occur across the United States for more than 50.7 million people who lack medical insurance (U.S. Census Bureau 2010). Because of cases like Eloise's, some critics claim that the U.S. health care system is, itself, a social problem. It developed without specific direction and responded to demands piecemeal, allowing practitioners, medical facilities, and insurance and drug companies to establish themselves and then protect their self-interests, sometimes at the expense of patients.

Health Care Advances. Medical research into gene therapy, understanding of the human genome, and research into new drug and technological therapies make research one of the most rapidly advancing medical fields. New therapies will help people live longer, more comfortable and productive lives—*if* they can afford the care. As science moves rapidly, ethical questions about the use of fetal tissue in experiments and treatments, cloning, prolonging life, and other issues challenge ethicists and lawmakers.

In addition to advances in medical science, there have been other positive steps taken to increase the health of the population. *Public health* refers to efforts to fight disease, promote health, and raise life expectancy rates. Recent public health accomplishments include improved motor vehicle safety, safer workplaces, control of more infectious diseases, greater access to family planning and prenatal care, and education of citizens about the dangers of tobacco and other unhealthy substances.

Problems in the U.S. Health Care System. The U.S. health care system is one of extremes. As we have seen, it

 Tissue Engineering

SOCIOLOGISTS IN ACTION:
JAMES ANDERSON AND KATHY ABRAHAMSON

The Case of Nurse Burnout

With a shortage of trained nurses in the health care industry and a growing elderly population living in long-term care facilities, the United States cannot afford to lose nurses to burnout. This problem of nurse burnout in retirement communities is what Dr. James G. Anderson and his former doctoral student, Dr. Kathleen Abrahamson, set out to study.

Burnout occurs when workers feel unappreciated and disrespected, have low status, lack the autonomy needed to do their job properly, and feel unsupported by the establishments for which they work. To learn about the experiences of nurses in long-term care facilities, the researchers analyzed interview data from the Partners in Caregiving study, funded by the National Institute on Aging. Using computer simulations, Anderson and Abrahamson were able to look at the impact of conflict between nurses and the families of patients on burnout among nurses (Abrahamson et al. 2009). Nursing home employers expect nurses to deliver care efficiently and uniformly, while the families of patients often expect individualized, special care for their loved ones. This can result in conflicts between family members and nurses, as nurses face competing expectations from employers and families of their patients. The researchers found that burnout was highest early in the nurse's career cycle, and then leveled off but did not go away.

Anderson and Abrahamson's findings that burnout among nurses in nursing homes tends to peak during the first year of their careers led them to suggest strategies to avoid burnout that should be initiated as soon as a patient enters a long-term care facility. They point out that training for both nurses and families of patients that culminate in written agreements on the caregiving roles of family members and nurses reduces the likelihood of unmet expectations and tension between nurses and family members. Such training also improves positive communication between the two and leads to better and more complete care for the patient. In short, Anderson and Abrahamson's findings can help those who manage long-term care facilities and improve the lives of both the nurses and residents at those facilities.

• •

Dr. James G. Anderson received engineering degrees and a PhD in sociology and education at Johns Hopkins University in Baltimore. He is a professor of medical sociology and health communication. Dr. Kathleen Abrahamson, an RN with her PhD from Purdue, is currently an assistant professor in the Purdue University School of Nursing.

provides the best and worst results among the Global North countries. Although the United States is the country of choice for many types of surgeries and the health care is exceptional for those with plenty of money, issues like life expectancy are alarming, as Figure 14.4 indicates. The yellow bar labeled OECD is the average for countries in the Organisation for Economic Co-operation and Development, not all of which are Global North countries. The United States is below the average. It loses three times as many years of life to infectious diseases and two times as many to metabolic diseases than the average for an OECD nation (Kliff 2014). Much of this is because health care is so unevenly distributed in the United States.

FIGURE 14.4   Life Expectancy at Birth

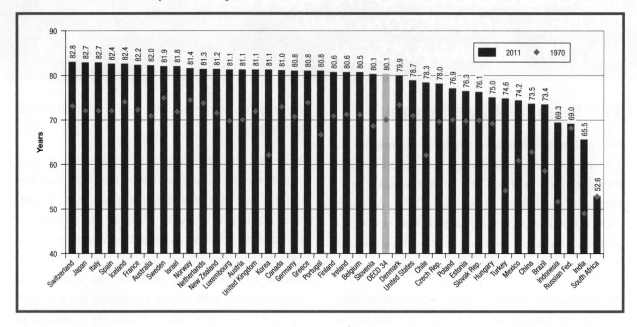

Source: OECD (2013).

Maldistribution of Health Care. In addition to a lack of doctors in rural and poor areas, inequality in U.S. health care also relates to the unequal distribution of doctors by state. Some states have higher ratios of physicians per residents than other states. Massachusetts has the most "active patient care doctors" per 100,000 residents with 314; Mississippi has the fewest with 159. Look at Figure 14.5 to see the variation. Given the discussion above, how might where you live affect your health care?

Health Care Cost and Funding. One of the most serious problems for health care systems and consumers in the United States, however, is the cost of health care. Since 1947, and up until the past several years, expenditures for health care in the United States (now at 17.2% of the gross national product) increased more rapidly than expenditures for other areas of the economy, and the United States spends twice as much per year on health care as many other Global North countries (CMS 2014b). The cost of drugs is also higher than in most other countries, and some U.S. citizens are mail-ordering drugs from foreign pharmacies, a practice that critics say lacks quality controls and could be dangerous (Rosenthal 2013). About 30% of health care costs in the United States go to administration, an unusually high figure compared to other Global North countries (Reinhardt 2008). Table 14.3 shows the increases in costs of health care over time in the United States.

Table 14.3   National Health Expenditures: United States

Year	In Billion Dollars	Percentage of Gross Domestic Product
1960	126.9	5.1
1970	173.2	7.1
1980	1,247.2	8.9
1990	1,699.5	12.2
2000	1,309.4	13.3
2012	2,800.0	17.2

Source: CMS (2014a).

Over the past several years, however, the rise of health care costs has slowed dramatically for several reasons (Lowrey 2013).

- Millions of Americans became unemployed in the Great Recession, leading to a loss of health insurance and reluctance to see a doctor.
- As corporations and governments cut spending during the Great Recession, they required many

FIGURE 14.5 Active *Patient Care* Physicians per 100,000 Population by State, 2012

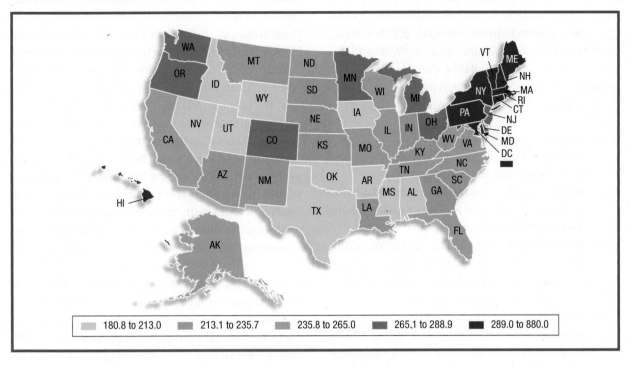

180.8 to 213.0	213.1 to 235.7	235.8 to 265.0	265.1 to 288.9	289.0 to 880.0

Source: American Association of Medical Colleges (2013). Copyright 2013 Association of American Medical Colleges. Reprinted with permission.

employees to pay higher copayments when seeking medical care, leading to a decline in doctor visits.

- As noted earlier, the Affordable Care Act encourages health providers to move away from the fee-for-service model. Increasing numbers of providers now take "bundled payments" for a course of treatment, and payments based on the quality, rather than the quantity, of care they deliver. These steps have reduced the cost of health care.

This slowdown in the rise of health care costs has given the federal government of the United States a little more breathing room to fix the serious Medicare funding problems and help reduce the national deficit.

Health Care Security and the Affordable Care Act. The greatest criticism of the U.S. system has been the lack of health insurance for millions, making health security unattainable. For people who do not have access to health insurance through their employer, lose a job that did provide it, or have a preexisting condition, health care has been unattainable. More than one out of four U.S. citizens, or between 48 and 50 million people below 65 years of age,

were uninsured at some point in 2011, in part due to loss of jobs (Morgan 2012). The estimated uninsured population in March 2014 was 15.9% and dropping as more people signed up for the Affordable Care Act (Levy 2014). As of April 2014, 8 million people had signed up for health insurance through the Affordable Care Act's Health Insurance Marketplace (U.S. Department of Health and Human Services 2014a).

The United States, however, still remains the only Global North nation without a national health insurance program providing health care coverage for all legal residents. The Affordable Care Act will lead to more, but not all, U.S. citizens having coverage. The Supreme Court upheld most of the Affordable Care Act. It also ruled, however, that states cannot be forced to expand Medicaid programs (government insurance for low-income residents primarily funded by the federal and state governments), and many have refused to do so, even though the federal government will pay for almost all of the extended coverage. The expansion of Medicaid was a key part of the law, and the Supreme Court ruling (and the decision of some states) means that many poor citizens will remain without health insurance and that access to health care will become even more disparate among states. In Massachusetts, which has a state-mandated health care plan on which the Affordable Care Act was based, only 4.9% of state residents did not have health insurance in 2013. This compares to an uninsured rate of 27% in Texas, the state with the fewest insured residents (Witters 2014). Provisions of the Affordable Care Act declared constitutional by the Supreme Court include the following (National Conference of State Legislatures 2011):

- Requiring employers to provide health coverage for their workers, or pay penalties, with exceptions for employers with under 50 employees.
- Requiring individuals to have insurance (with some exceptions, and with tax credits to help lower-income people pay for it)
- Requiring insurance plans to cover young adults up until age 26 on parents' health insurance plan.
- Prohibiting lifetime caps, and limiting the use of annual caps, on insurance coverage.
- Prohibiting the exclusion of people with preexisting conditions from private (as well as public) insurance plans (individual health insurance plans—bought by individuals, not through an employer—are grandfathered and can refuse to cover someone because of a preexisting condition).
- Establishing a limit on the percentage of insurance payments used for nonmedical payments (e.g., salaries and other administrative costs).

Health Care Around the Globe

During a yearlong sabbatical in England, the Ballantine family signed up with a local surgeon, as the British call family physicians. Their sore throats, upset tummies, and

bruised feet were taken to the doctor at no direct cost. The school referred their daughter to the hospital eye clinic for glasses at no cost. Their son was diagnosed and treated for "glandular fever" (mononucleosis), again at no cost. In Great Britain, all citizens have access to treatment by family physicians and dentists, to the dispensing of prescribed drugs, to eye care, and to community nursing and health visitor services. Taxes fund universal health care coverage at an expense much less than the U.S. cost for health care.

The demographic makeup, value systems, and financial status of each country have an effect on how health care is delivered. Global North societies, with a high proportion of elderly and a low proportion of young people, have very different needs from those of Global South societies with many dependent children. In societies with many elders, special care for chronic illness is more necessary, whereas societies with many children must deal with more childhood illnesses.

The maldistribution of physicians is a global, as well as a U.S., issue. As illustrated in Figure 14.6 in the next "Engaging Sociology," the countries with the most doctors—the highest number of physicians per 1,000 people—are Greece (6.2), Belarus (5.2), Austria (4.9), Georgia (4.8), Norway (4.2), and Switzerland (4.1). The United States has 2.4 doctors per 1,000 people, and Canada has 2.0. The lowest numbers can be found in Global South countries such as Colombia, Ghana, and Mauritania with 0.1 physicians per 1,000 people, and Afghanistan and Cambodia with 0.2 physicians per 1,000 people (World Bank 2012). Most of these physicians are found in urban areas. The World Health Organization recommends at least 1 physician for every 600 citizens. In some Global South countries, local rural residents are trained both in emergency medicine and to recognize illnesses. In Rwanda, Africa, health care workers make house calls to inquire about diseases and provide the required treatment, referring those with serious illnesses to regional hospitals.

Each society organizes its health care system in ways congruous with its culture. All nations search for ways to contain costs; provide accessible, high-quality, and effective care; manage care for disabilities and chronic illnesses; and find treatments for infectious diseases (Pescosolido and Boyer 2010). Western scientific medicine has spread throughout the world, but some of the ideas from other parts of the world now influence Western approaches to health and illness, as the following example from China illustrates.

The People's Republic of China: Medicine in a Communist State. Little was known outside China about

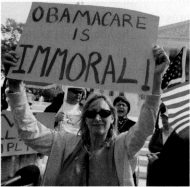

© REUTERS/Joshua Roberts

Supporters (left) and opponents (right) of the Affordable Care Act rally on the sidewalk at the Supreme Court in Washington, D.C., illustrating the controversy over national health care policy.

ENGAGING SOCIOLOGY

Access to Health Care for Rich and Poor

FIGURE 14.6 Number of Physicians per 1,000 People

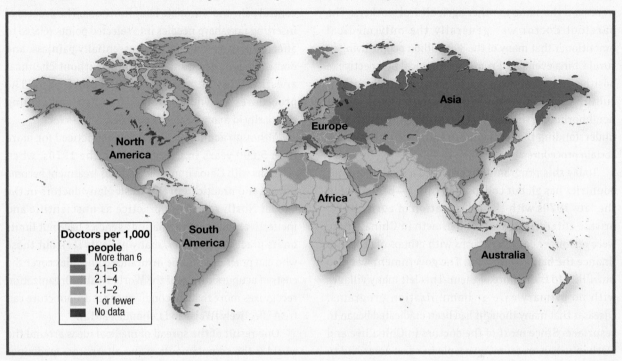

Source: NationMaster.com (2014b).

Engaging With Sociology

Study the map on physicians per 1,000 people. Then, answer the following questions:

1. How do you think the scarcity of physicians in the Global South and rural areas affects the health care of individuals and the functioning of communities and society?

2. How might a surplus of physicians influence health care?

3. How could a nation increase the number of qualified medical workers and people who have access to health care?

4. How might health care differ depending on where one lives in the United States?

China's health care system until the 1970s, when visitors, including health observers, were welcomed by the once-reclusive government. When the "bamboo curtain" that isolated China was raised in 1971, the outside world learned that, despite a background of poverty, the government had established an effective network of health services.

Jeanne, one of the coauthors of this text, met Xi (pronounced "She") on a train in China. He was returning to his village after completing a medical training course

that covered first-aid treatment, immunizations, and recognition of serious symptoms. He was one of more than a million "barefoot" doctors or *countryside doctors*—paramedics trained in basic medicine to provide health care for rural residents in China's villages. The program, begun in 1951, was very successful in curbing infectious diseases. In fact, the program has provided a model for reaching out into the countryside for several Global South countries, including Kenya and Rwanda.

Barefoot doctors were generally local peasants selected by fellow members of their agricultural communes. Many continued to work on the farm but, after some training, took responsibility for preventive medicine and some aspects of primary care in the local neighborhood. If they passed an exam, they could become a village doctor, licensed to carry out additional medical procedures. They were paid the same as other agricultural workers. The barefoot doctor was generally the only medical practitioner that many of the 800 million people living in rural China ever saw. From a sociological perspective, a positive feature of these practitioners was their within-culture socialization. Given the homogeneity of peasant neighborhoods, the barefoot doctor had little difficulty understanding the local culture and their resistance to certain procedures.

Today this program that provided a model for poor countries has all but collapsed in China—beginning in the late 1970s with the privatization of agriculture, private enterprises, and rapid growth in China. There were no longer collective farms with groups of people to finance the barefoot doctors. The government was also unwilling to train more of them. This left many villages with no primary care or immunization programs. Diseases that many thought had been eradicated began to resurface. Since most of the doctors in China live and work in urban areas, many people in rural areas had to depend on home remedies (Casella 2009). A remaining element of the rural medicine program is the Lifeline Express train in Xinjiang Province; it travels the countryside providing cataract eye surgery for residents across China. Today, the remaining village clinics provide basic services to poor and elderly, though they are poorly funded; doctors and health care workers often support themselves with money from medical drugs they sell (Babiarz, Yi, and Luo 2013; Hays 2011).

Recently, the central government allocated funds to increase basic coverage and improve hospitals in regional areas. The doctor-to-patient ratio is now 1,000 doctors per 1.05 patients, but few physicians work in rural areas. Further, many of those trained as physicians in China choose to practice in African nations where the wages and social standing are higher (Hays 2011).

Once introduced, Western-style medicine expanded rapidly in China, and Chinese practices expanded in Global North countries. After China opened itself up to the rest of the world in the 1970s, the number of medical personnel with training in Western medicine increased significantly. Many health care workers now blend Western medicine practices with traditional Chinese approaches.

Increasingly, doctors are trained in both. The opening up of China also led to the spread of traditional Chinese medical practices to the West. Consider the example of acupuncture, an ancient Chinese method for treating certain physical problems and relieving pain.

Acupuncture, along with related treatments, is based on the idea that the body has 700 points that ease and control pain and stimulate body functions. The process of inserting fine sharp needles into selected points related to affected organs in the body is essentially painless, and doctors have even done operations without chemical anesthesia using acupuncture to block pain. The procedures are widely practiced in Asia and gaining popularity in many Western countries.

Although acupuncture has been practiced for more than 5,000 years in China, only in the 1970s, when relations with China improved, did this treatment become known and practiced in the West. Many doctors in the Global North reject the practice as unscientific and ineffective, and some regulating agencies have put limits on its practice. However, many patients seek out those who can practice it. Some insurance companies cover the costs of acupuncture, and the World Health Organization recognizes more than 40 conditions that acupuncture can treat effectively (Weiss and Lonnquist 2012).

One result of the spread of medical ideas around the world is the complementary and alternative medicines (CAM) movement in the United States and other Global North countries. CAM includes health care systems, practices, and products used to complement conventional medicine or as alternative medicine used in place of conventional medicine. CAM therapies include acupuncture and chiropractic, natural products, special diets, and megavitamin therapy, and nearly 40% of U.S. citizens use one or more of these approaches (GoodTherapy.org 2012; National Center for Complementary and Alternative Medicine 2013).

The Chinese health care system faces a variety of problems. In urban areas, air pollution and other urban environmental issues are causing increasing numbers of health problems. In rural areas, many people practice only traditional folk medicine, and diseases, poor sanitation, and particularly high smoking rates result in lowered life expectancy (Watts 2012). China accounts for about 30% of the world's tobacco consumption, with more than 300 million smokers—about 31% of the population—and 740 million people exposed to secondhand smoke. China produces and consumes more tobacco than any other nation—with over 1.31 trillion cigarettes consumed per year. Smoking-related illnesses result in 1 million deaths

The Costs of Smoking   Maggot Medicine

yearly (ChinaDaily.com 2012). Government efforts to control smoking have been uneven because the government receives money from foreign tobacco sales.

Health care systems around the world illustrate the impact of national and global political and economic factors on the health care available to citizens. The political systems of countries and their economic status influence the philosophy toward health care and the money each country puts into it. International events such as wars and refugees influence availability of health care within countries. International organizations, such as the World Health Organization, play a key role in addressing epidemics and pandemics throughout the world.

Thinking Sociologically

What can countries learn by studying other health care systems? Give examples.

Globalization of Medical Problems. The international sale of body parts reveals how health care relates to social stratification and crosses national borders. In some countries, people at the bottom of the stratification system are so desperately poor that they sell parts of their body to help their families survive. For example, mothers and fathers in some poor slums of Mumbai and other cities in India and Pakistan sell their kidneys to those willing to resell them to patients (primarily in Global North nations) in need of a new kidney and with the money to buy one. The individuals who sell their body parts tend to do so for money to pay for housing, food, education for their children, and dowries for their daughters to marry. In the process, their health can suffer due to complications during

Many people around the world engage in tobacco use, a serious health hazard that lowers productivity and increases health care costs. Palestinian tunnel workers beneath the Gaza–Egypt border smoke cigarettes as they take a rest inside a tunnel where they work.

or after the surgery to remove their organ, and when the money is gone, life is even more difficult. Although laws were passed in India in 1994 banning the sale of human organs, few violators face capture and punishment ("Body Parts for Sale" 2008). At last report, the only nation where the sale of body organs was legal was Iran, which permits the sale of blood, breast milk, hair, eggs, sperm, and even the womb ("Body Parts for Sale" 2008; Kasperkevic 2014).

Body parts can also be harvested by corrupt medical personnel who treat persons for an ailment that may or may not exist and take organs in the process. Most commonly trafficked are kidneys, livers, and any other

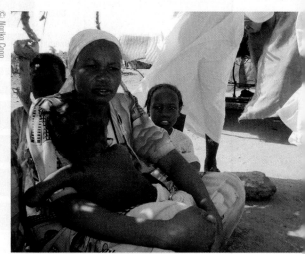

These two women are of similar age, both in their 30s. Health facilities make an enormous difference in one's life chances, one's health, and how one ages. The woman on the left lives in North America; the woman on the right raises a family in Senegal, West Africa.

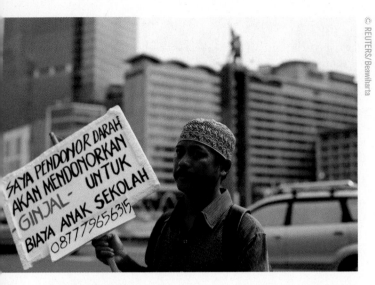

An unemployed man, Dwi Waryono, holds a placard advertising his kidney for sale in Jakarta in 2013. The placard reads "I was a blood donor. I will donate my kidney to pay for the cost of my children's schooling." For people in severe poverty, selling a body organ is a way to care for their family, for it can raise several thousand dollars.

organs that can be removed (UN.GIFT 2014). Recently, sales of skin, bones, tissue, and dental implants from fresh corpses have grown, with a center of such activity in Ukraine. The United States is the biggest market, with 2 million such products bought by U.S. citizens each year. These body parts allow those who buy them to see with cornea transplants, walk with recycled tendons, and replace a dying kidney with a healthy one (Wilson et al. 2012).

Body parts tend to go for high prices that only the relatively wealthy can afford. The transplant trade, for example, attracts medical tourists from Europe who visit impoverished countries in Latin America and Asia for transplants and other "cheap" treatments. This example of stratification within the world health care system reveals how health care for the rich can come at the expense (of the health) of the poor.

The global stratification of health care can also be seen in the different causes of death in affluent/Global North versus poor/Global South countries for the 55 million people who die worldwide every year (World Health Organization 2014b). Relatively few people in the Global North die of infectious diseases. Yet infectious diseases still cause the majority of deaths in the Global South, reducing life expectancy in some poor countries to 50 years or less. Figures 14.7 and 14.8 show the leading causes of death in low- and high-income nations.

FIGURE 14.7 Top 10 Causes of Death in Low-income Countries, 2012

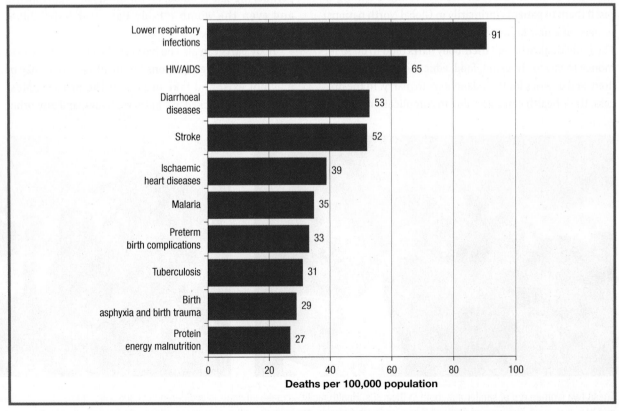

Source: World Health Organization (2014b).

FIGURE 14.8   **Top 10 Causes of Death in High-income Countries, 2012**

Ischaemic heart disease — 158
Stroke — 95
Trachea bronchus, lung cancers — 49
Alzheimer's disease and other dementias — 42
COPD — 31
Lower respiratory infections — 31
Colon rectum cancers — 27
Diabetes mellitus — 20
Hypertensive heart disease — 20
Breast cancer — 16

Deaths per 100,000 population

(x-axis: 0, 32, 64, 96, 128, 160)

Source: World Health Organization (2014b).

Thinking Sociologically

What are some factors that account for the differences in causes of death between high- and low-income countries? What might be done to tackle these disparities?

Globalization and the Mobility of Disease.

Traveling humans throughout history have provided passage to pathogens on their bodies and in their luggage—great plagues, smallpox, syphilis, and others. Today influenza, SARS, polio, and other diseases thought to be under control many years ago are resurfacing (Ostroff 2013). Consider measles in the United States, which has reemerged in several areas. Measles, a vaccine-preventable disease, has ranged from 37 U.S. cases in 2004 to 220 in 2011, 187 in 2013, and a growing number of cases in 2014. Why? One source of the disease is travelers returning from trips to foreign countries where the disease still exists. For example, U.S. residents who visited the Philippines in 2014 brought back the disease and infected others (CDC 2014a; Iannelli 2014).

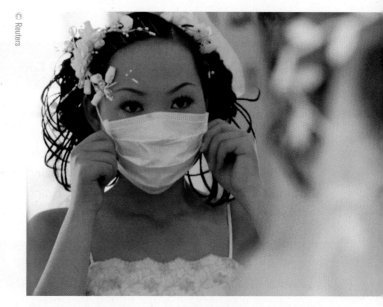

© Reuters

Even young brides on their wedding day wore masks to protect themselves from SARS, severe acute respiratory syndrome, in 2003. People traveling around the world have spread this dangerous disease.

The density and urbanization of the world's population (discussed in Chapter 15) also affects human health. For example, use of land and space determines the number of rodents and insects, the water supplies, and the direct contact people have with one another. Currently, about half of the world's people live in urban areas, many in slums surrounding major cities. Problems such as open sewers, inadequate sanitation, lack of electricity, and polluted water pervade these slums. Overcrowding combined with these problems causes infectious diseases to spread more rapidly. Even climate change and antimicrobial resistance affect the spread of diseases (World Health Organization 2013a).

Growing numbers of locations with shared circulated air (airplanes, domed stadiums, air-conditioned office buildings and hotels), also spread disease. A World Health Organization study indicates that of the infections leading to death, 65% stem from person-to-person contact; 22% come from food, water, or soil contamination; 13% from insects; and 0.3% directly from animals (bird flu, rabies, etc.). Because far more people travel around the globe today than in the past, diseases can spread more widely and quickly than in the past.

The growing threat of pandemics is one cause for global concern, but the global disparity in the handling of treatable diseases remains an even more pressing issue. The uneven distribution of health care, doctors, and medicines around the world and the resistance of some religious groups to inoculating their children have led to many preventable and curable diseases going untreated. In spite of increasingly sophisticated medical technology, as long as there is inequality in countries of our social world, adequate health care will not reach all people and all countries equally.

 Thinking Sociologically

We live in a global world, yet our most immediate experiences are local. How might you and your family benefit if international agencies resolve health problems in Africa, Asia, and South America?

Our social institutions—from family, education, and religion to politics, economics, and health—maintain stability in societies. However, the world in which we live is a dynamic one. In the final two chapters, we turn to an examination of how change occurs. First, we examine two forces that have changed exponentially in the past two centuries—population patterns and urbanization. We close with an examination of the many manifestations of social change.

WHAT HAVE WE LEARNED?

Sickness and the roles of sick people are social constructions that vary across societies. Although health is a private, personal concern, it is also a public concern, delivered through organizations dispensing health care and government practices determining access and funding of health care. Distant from your daily life but important to your well-being are the global health organizations that concern themselves with global epidemics. In addition, whether you can afford or have access to medical care depends in part on the economic conditions in society and the global marketplace of health care delivery.

KEY POINTS

- Sociology examines the social implications of health and illness—from the micro level of individuals coping with illness to the meso level of institutional interactions and complex organizations that manage health and illness, to the global issues of controlling the spread of diseases around the world. (See pp. 457–459.)

- Whether looking at the medicalization of social problems through labeling or examining functions and socioeconomic conflicts regarding health care in society, various social theories offer alternative lenses through which to view health care systems. (See pp. 460–468.)

- At the micro level, we can look at issues such as the "sick role," how social and cultural factors affect our responses to pain and ill health, and how our age, gender, and other personal aspects of identity relate to our responses to health and illness. (See pp. 468–471.)

- Hospitals and other elements of organizational complexity, the issues of professionalism and of deprofessionalization of medical personnel, and the linkages between institutions such as the economy, politics, education, and family are all aspects of health care at the meso level. (See pp. 471–476.)

- Health care is a national issue that relates to the nation's resources, issues of security of citizens, and types of health care delivery. (See pp. 476–480.)

- Globally, diseases spread around the planet much faster in our age of rapid travel and migrations. Different forms of health care have also spread throughout the world and influence the approaches we each choose in our own local communities. (See pp. 480–485.)

- The disparity in health care within and among nations remains the most pressing health care issue facing societies today. (See pp. 486.)

DISCUSSION QUESTIONS

1. Imagine that your state has a law on the ballot that would legalize assisted suicide, following the model of Oregon's, Vermont's, or Washington's law. Would you vote for or against the ballot question? Why? Would the conditions necessary for the legality of assisted suicide described in Oregon's law influence your vote? Why or why not? Why do you think most of those who participated in the Death with Dignity program in Oregon were whites with college degrees?

2. Think of the last time you or someone close to you was seriously ill. What were the repercussions of the illness on the micro level? How did these repercussions relate to health care issues on the meso and macro levels?

3. What are three ways social class impacts health? Describe how social class has impacted your health and the health of your family members.

4. Do you think health care is a human right? Why or why not? How can inequality in health care negatively impact a society?

5. If you were a policy maker, how might you try to curb binge drinking or smoking among college students?

VISUAL SOCIOLOGY: *HOSPITAL CLOTHING*

© iStockphoto.com/Sean Locke

The clothing worn by health care workers is significant. It communicates status, authority, and rights to certain prerogatives within the hospital or clinic. What sort of attire do nurses, technicians, and aids wear in your local hospital? Visit **edge.sagepub.com/ballantine5e** for an interactive photo essay about hospital clothing.

CONTRIBUTING TO OUR SOCIAL WORLD: *WHAT CAN WE DO?*

At the Local Level

- *Obesity in America* (www.obesityinamerica.org) provides information on a wide range of resources related to studies on eating behavior, many of which are directly applicable to problems faced by students. Plan a support group for those facing weight issues.

- Can you find *healthy food on campus*? If your school does not offer enough healthy options, start a petition and present it to your campus administrators asking them to address this issue. An article that describes some schools' attempts to go healthy can be found at www.hercampus.com/health/10-healthi est-college-dining-halls-america?page=2.

At the Organizational or Institutional Level

- *Free or low-cost clinics.* Most communities provide health screening and other services to uninsured individuals and families. The U.S. Department of Health and Human Services has a locator website at findahealthcenter.hrsa.gov/Search_HCC.aspx that searches for free clinics by state and city. Most have volunteer and internship opportunities that afford interesting and valuable experiences, especially if you are considering a career in a health care field.

At the National and Global Levels

- *The Joint United Nations Program on HIV/AIDS* works throughout the world to fight the pandemic. If you are interested in learning more about and possibly raising funds for this effort, go to www.unaids .org/en/.

- *World Vision* (www.worldvision.org) helps children, their families, and their communities in an effort to combat malnutrition, AIDS, and other health- and poverty-related problems across the world. The organization's Hope Child program lists several suggestions for getting involved, including sponsorship of a child.

- *AVERT*, an international AIDS charity, provides material to educate yourself and your classmates about AIDS on the organization's website at www.avert.org/.

PART V

Social Dynamics

Social structures such as institutions tend to resist change. Nonetheless, this entire book demonstrates that societies are dynamic and changing. Institutions and organizations come alive with processes that are fluid and vibrant. Globalization, a major theme in this book, is a process bringing transformation to our social world, as shown by the very different world inhabited by our grandparents. The macro- and meso-level dimensions of society have become increasingly powerful, which is exactly why we need a sociological imagination to understand how the events in our own micro worlds are influenced by the larger society.

This section looks at some of those dynamic, fluid, and vibrant processes: population changes, urbanization, expansion of technology, social movements, and more. In periods of rapid change, understanding how and why that change occurs can help us to influence the direction those changes take in our society. From global climate change to terrorism and from new digital technologies to immigrants in our communities, we need to understand causes and consequences in order to respond constructively. To do so, we must grasp the micro-, meso- and macro-level dimensions of change in our lives and the linkages between parts of our social world. We turn first to population dynamics and urbanization.

© REUTERS/ Dinuka Liyanawatte

15 Population and Urbanization

Living on Planet Earth

Humans are confined to this one moderate-sized planet on which we depend for survival. The challenges of controlling population size, migration patterns, the spread of disease, and climate change add to the need for global cooperation.

MICRO

● ME (AND MY NEIGHBORS)

● LOCAL ORGANIZATIONS
AND COMMUNITY
Local schools and community
organizations serve the local
population.

MESO

● NATIONAL ORGANIZATIONS,
INSTITUTIONS, AND ETHNIC
SUBCULTURES
Population trends influence institutions such as
politics, economics, and education.

MACRO

● SOCIETY
National governments set policies that influence
birth incentives, birth control, and immigration.

● GLOBAL COMMUNITY
Cross-national migration patterns can spread
epidemics or meet pressing needs for labor.

THINK ABOUT IT

Micro: Local Community	What is the population profile of your hometown: economic status of residents, ethnic and racial composition, recent immigrant groups? Where do you fit into that population profile?
Meso: National Institutions, Complex Organizations, and Ethnic Groups	Why do people move from rural areas to urban areas? What problems might this pattern of movement create?
Macro: National and Global Systems	How do global issues relating to demographic changes, urbanization, and the environment affect your family and your local community?

When Sally Ride, the first U.S. woman in space, looked down at the Earth, she, like other astronauts who have the opportunity to see the planet from far above, experienced the "overview effect." This occurs when the Earth is viewed from a new angle, from the perspective of space. Ride described the impact it had on her.

> Mountain ranges, volcanoes, and river deltas appeared in salt-and-flour relief, all leading me to assume the role of a novice geologist. In such moments, it was easy to imagine the dynamic upheavals that created jutting mountain ranges and the internal wrenching that created rifts and seas. I also became an instant believer in plate tectonics; India really is crashing into Asia, and Saudi Arabia and Egypt really are pulling apart, making the Red Sea wider. Even though their respective motion is really no more than mere inches a year, the view from overhead makes theory come alive. (Quoted in Beaver 2012)

Ride's perspective changed, and thus, her ability to recognize and understand the world also changed. Ride saw and noticed things she had not seen or noticed before, because of this new view of the world. In this chapter, you will learn to observe changes in the world's population from a sociological perspective and, in the process, see and notice patterns you may not have paid attention to before.

Since the emergence of *Homo sapiens* in East Africa almost 200,000 years ago, human populations have grown in uneven surges and declines due to births, deaths, and migrations. The World Population Clock (see Table 15.1) illustrates the current state of the human population. As you can see, there are now more than 7 billion people on Earth, and the number is increasing rapidly.

The world's human population grew sporadically over the millennia, but the explosion of human beings on the planet in the past two-and-a-half centuries is stunning. If we collapsed all human history into one 24-hour day, the time period since 1750 would consume 1 minute. Yet 25% of all humans have lived during this 1-minute time period. In the 200 years between 1750 and 1950, the world's population mushroomed from 800 million to 2.5 billion. On October 12, 1999, the global population reached 6 billion. It has now expanded to over 7.2 billion with almost all of the latest growth in the Global South (Population Reference Bureau 2012c; Worldometers 2014).

Let us start by focusing on one area of our world, Kenya in East Africa. We begin here partly because East Africa, where Kenya and Tanzania are located, is believed to be home to Earth's earliest human inhabitants. Scientists believe that bones found in the dry Olduvai Gorge area are the oldest remains of *Homo sapiens* ever recovered. We also focus here because today Kenya is making human history for another reason. With a population of 45 million people, and a growth rate of 2.11% annually, Kenya has one of the most rapidly growing populations on Earth (World Factbook 2014g). Kenya is made up of many tribal groups. With different religions and value systems, the tribes have clashed in power struggles in recent years. Still, there are several themes that pervade most Kenyan subcultures, as illustrated by the following example.

Wengari, like Kenyan girls of most tribal affiliations, married in her teens. She has been socialized to believe that her main purpose in life is to bear children, to help with the farming, and to care for parents in their old age. Children are seen as an asset in Kenya. Religious beliefs and cultural value systems encourage large families. However, due to high birthrates and high death rates caused by AIDS, the working-age population has declined

Table 15.1 **Population Clock, 2013 (in thousands)**

	World	Global South	Global North
Population	7,136,796	5,890,885	1,245,911
Births per day	390,696	352,521	38,175
Births per year	142,634	128,670	13,934
Deaths per day	153	120	34
Deaths per year	55,973	43,668	12,305
Infant deaths per day	15,789	15,597	193
Natural annual increase	86,661	85,002	1,629

Source: Haub, Carl and Toshiko Kaneda, 2013 *World Population Data Sheet* Washington, DC: Population Reference Bureau 2013.

and cannot continue to feed the growing population. Almost half (44.8%) of the Kenyan population consists of *dependents*: people under 15 or over 65 years of age, who rely on working-age citizens to support them (World Factbook 2014g). Almost all of the dependent population in Kenya consists of children under 15, rather than adults over 65 (42.1% compared to 2.7% of the population). Adding to Kenya's problems are severe droughts that kill animal herds and destroy crops. These facts, however, have little impact on the behavior of young women like Wengari, who, socialized to conform to the female role within their society, plan on having many children.

By contrast, far to the north in many of the industrialized, urbanized countries of Europe, birthrates are below population replacement levels, meaning population size has begun to drop. The population growth rate in Germany is 0.19%, in France 0.47%, and in the United Kingdom 0.55%. Russia, Hungary, Latvia, the Czech Republic, and many other countries in Eastern Europe are also losing population (IndexMundi 2013d). Germany, the most prosperous nation in Europe, does not have enough working-age people to support the pensions of older Germans. Much of Europe faces this problem (Daley and Kulish 2013).

While Asia's share of world population may continue to hover around 60% through the next century, Europe's portion has declined sharply and will likely drop even more during the rest of the 21st century. Africa and Latin America each will gain part of Europe's portion. By 2100, Africa is expected to capture the greatest share. Countries outside of Europe growing by less than 1% annually include Japan, Australia, New Zealand, and Russia (Population Reference Bureau 2013a).

USAID

Changes in the environment and in the global economy compel these Kenyan children to join the worldwide urbanization trend and move to the nearest city in search of work. Much of the socialization they receive in villages will not be relevant to their adult urban lives.

As societies develop, birthrates tend to go down. For example, typical European young people often wait until their late 20s or even 30s to start a family, postponing children until their education is complete and a job is in hand. Moreover, they have access to effective birth control options, widely used throughout their societies. Unlike many children in the Global South, most children born in Europe will survive to old age. Parents do not feel as though they must have many children in order to see some grow to maturity. **Life expectancy,** the *number of years a person in a particular society can expect to live,* is 63.5 years in Kenya (World Factbook 2014g). In Japan and some European countries, it is more than 82 years.

China, the country with the largest population in the world (1.35 billion people), had the greatest drop in population growth in the late 20th century, due to strict governmental family planning practices (World Factbook 2014b). India, the second-largest country, has a current population growth rate (increase in a country's population during a specified period of time) of 1.25% a year, just over replacement level (World Factbook 2014e).

Although some countries have birthrates below population replacement levels, the world's population continues to grow because of the skyrocketing growth rate in other countries and because of *population momentum* caused by the large number of individuals of childbearing age having children. After a baby boom, even though birthrates per couple may drop, the number of women of childbearing age becomes very high, resulting in continued growth in population size. Most of the countries with the highest growth rates are in the Global South, where societies value large families, and have less access to birth control and fewer resources to support the additional population.

 Thinking Sociologically

Do you have a choice in how many children you have or will have? Explain. If you do, what factors go into your decision? How might your decision differ if you lived in a different country? Should global patterns—which include food shortages and climate change—be a consideration in the size of your family and your neighbors' families? Why or why not?

We know the information above thanks to research gained through **demography**, the *study of human populations*. When demographers speak of **populations**, they mean *all permanent societies, states, communities, adherents of a common religious faith, racial or ethnic groups, kinship or clan groups, professions, and other identifiable categories of people*. Demographers examine various aspects of a population, including the size, location, movement, concentration in certain geographical areas, and changing characteristics. For example, the next "Engaging Sociology" asks you to imagine that the entire world population was only 100 people and look at how it would be composed given the current distribution of certain characteristics.

With few jobs to support populations in rural areas (areas outside of cities and their surrounding suburbs), many people move to cities in hopes of finding employment. This *pattern of movement from rural areas to cities* is called **urbanization**. The second half of this chapter will consider the evolution, growth, and development of populated areas, including movements from rural areas to cities, the organization of micro-level urban life, the relationship between individuals and the city, and some problems facing cities. The previous chapters have moved from micro- to macro-level analysis, but in this chapter, because of the nature of the material and the need to explain certain issues before the micro issues make sense, we discuss macro-level patterns in world population growth first. We then describe meso-level institutional influences on population, and micro-level factors affecting population patterns.

MACRO-LEVEL PATTERNS IN WORLD POPULATION GROWTH

Earlier, we noted that Global North societies tend to see reduced population growth as they continue to develop. What happens before this, though? Why did the world's population grow so slowly and then recently, so rapidly? Sociologists look for patterns in population growth over time to answer these demographic questions.

Patterns of Population Growth Over Time

Members of the small band of early *Homo sapiens* who inhabited the Olduvai Gorge moved gradually, haltingly, from this habitat into what are now other parts of Africa, Asia, and Europe. The process took thousands of years. At times, births outnumbered deaths and populations grew, but at other times, plagues, famines, droughts, and wars decimated populations. From the beginning of human existence, estimated as perhaps one million years ago, until modern times, the number of births and deaths

The overcrowding in some cities means that governments have a difficult time providing the infrastructure and services needed for the growing urban population. Rio de Janeiro, Brazil, is one example.

© Getty/Mario Tama

ENGAGING SOCIOLOGY

If the World Were 100 People

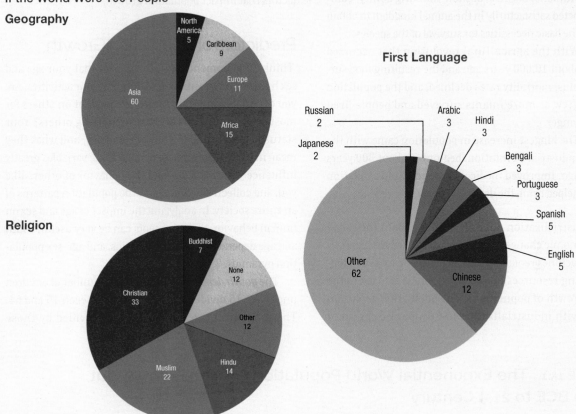

Geography

North America 5
Caribbean 9
Europe 11
Asia 60
Africa 15

First Language

Russian 2
Japanese 2
Arabic 3
Hindi 3
Bengali 3
Portuguese 3
Spanish 5
English 5
Other 62
Chinese 12

Religion

Buddhist 7
None 12
Christian 33
Other 12
Muslim 22
Hindu 14

Literacy	83 would be able to read and write
	12% of males would not be able to read and write
	21% of females would not be able to read and write
Education	7 would have a college degree
Urban/Rural	51 would be urban dwellers; 49 would be rural dwellers
Water	87 would have access to safe drinking water; 13 would not
Food	15 would be undernourished and 1 starving; 21 would be overweight
Poverty	48 would live on *less than* 2 U.S. dollars per day
	Half of the children would live in poverty
Electricity	78 would have electricity; 22 would not
Technology	30 would be active Internet users; 75 would be cell phone users

Engaging With Sociological Facts

1. Did any of these facts surprise you? If so, which ones? Why? If not, where did you learn these facts before?

2. In which ways are you highly privileged compared to most others in the world?

3. Which of the factors in this list cause the most suffering?

4. If you were a public sociologist and could improve two of these factors, which ones would you focus on? Why?

balanced each other over the centuries (Diamond 2005). The large population we see today resulted from three phases of population evolution:

1. Humans, because of their thinking ability, competed satisfactorily in the animal kingdom to obtain the basic necessities for survival of the species.
2. With the agricultural revolution that occurred about 10,000 years ago and the resulting food surplus, mortality rates declined, and the population grew as more infants survived and people lived longer.
3. The biggest increase in population came with the Industrial Revolution, beginning about 300 years ago. Improved medical knowledge and sanitation helped bring the death rate down.

Industrialization not only brought about the social and economic changes in societies discussed in Chapter 3 (e.g., machines replacing human labor and mass production using resources in new ways), but it also led to the rapid growth of populations. The population explosion began with industrialization in Europe and spread to widely scattered areas of the globe. Figures 15.1 and 15.2 show population growth throughout history. The worldwide *rate* of population growth reached its peak in the 1960s (Worldometers 2014). We now take a closer look at factors that impact population growth.

Predictors of Population Growth

Think for a moment about the impact that your age and sex have on your position in society and your activities. Are you of childbearing age? Are you dependent on others for most of your needs, or are you supporting others? Your status is largely due to your age and sex, and what they mean in your society. These demographic variables greatly influence your behavior and the behavior of others like you, and collectively they shape the population patterns of an entire society. In analyzing the impact of age and sex on human behavior, three concepts can be very useful: youth and age dependency ratios, sex ratios, and age-sex population pyramids.

The *youth dependency ratio* is the number of children under age 15 divided by the number between 15 and 64. The number of those older than 64 divided by those

FIGURE 15.1   The Exponential World Population Growth From About 8000 BCE to 21st Century

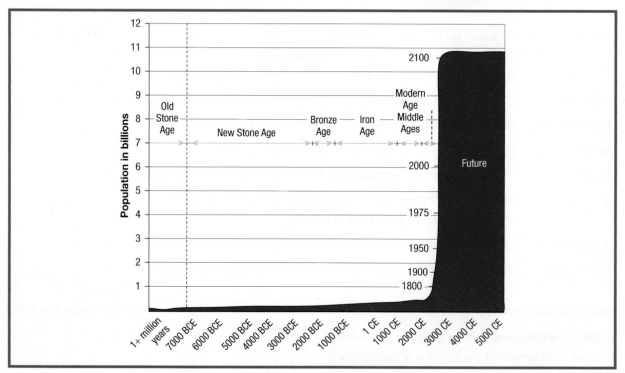

Source: Abu-Lughod (2001:50).

FIGURE 15.2   World Population Growth Rate, 1950–2050

Source: U.S. Census Bureau (2012f).

between 15 and 64 is called the *age dependency ratio.* Although many of the world's young people under 15 help support themselves and their families, and many older than 64 are likewise economically independent, these figures have been taken as the general ages when individuals are not contributing to the labor force. They represent the economic burden (especially in wealthy countries) of people in the population who must be supported by the working-age population. The **dependency ratio**, then, is *the ratio of those in both the young and aged groups compared with the number of people in the productive age groups between 15 and 64 years old.* Today, 90% of those in the world between the ages of 10 and 24, many of whom are dependent, live in the Global South (Sengupta 2014).

In several resource-poor countries, nearly half of the population is under 15 years of age. These include Kenya (42.1%, as mentioned above), Niger (49.8%), Uganda (48.7%), Congo (43.1%), and Afghanistan (42%). Working adults in less-developed countries have a tremendous burden in supporting the dependent population, especially if a high percentage of the population is urban and not able to support itself through farming.

Similarly, most Global North countries have high percentages of older dependent people over 64. In the European countries of Norway, Sweden, Denmark, Germany, and the United Kingdom, between 15% and 20% of the population is 65 or older. These countries have low death rates, resulting in the average life expectancy at birth being as high as 82.39 in Switzerland (World Factbook 2014h).

Consider the case of Japan, which faces the problem of its "graying" or aging population. In 2014, 24.8% of its population was 65 or older, and the average life expectancy had topped 84 years (World Factbook 2014h). The death rate is higher than the birth rate, and the population is shrinking in size. Only 13.2% of the population is under 15 years old. With a declining population and almost no influx of immigrants, there are not enough replacement workers to support the aging population. Japan may provide a glimpse into the future for other rapidly aging societies, including Germany, the United States, and China. These different societies, however, vary in their approach to immigration and population control policies, which will impact both the demographic challenges they face and how they handle them (see Figure 15.3 for a vivid depiction of the expected transformation in one century).

The *sex ratio* refers to the ratio of males to females in the population. For instance, the more females, especially females in their fertile years, the more potential there is for population growth. The sex ratio also determines the supply of eligible spouses. Other factors that influence marriage patterns include economic cycles, wars in which the proportion of males to females may decrease, and migrations that generally take males from one area and add them to another.

Population pyramids *are pyramid-shaped diagrams that illustrate sex ratios and dependency ratios* over time (see Figure 15.4). The graphic presentation of the age and sex distribution of a population tells us a great deal about that population. The structures are called pyramids

FIGURE 15.3   Japan Grows Old

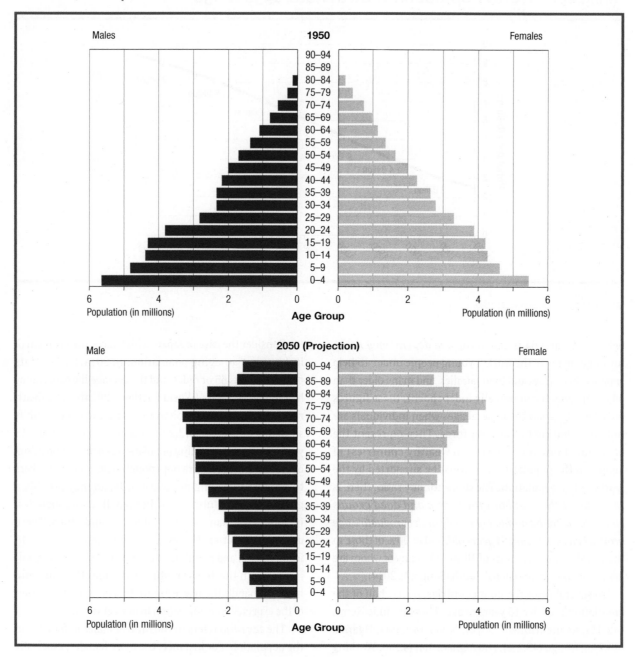

Source: Statistical Handbook of Japan (2010). 1950 pyramid is based on data from the results of the survey of the Statistics Bureau of Japan. 2050 pyramid is based on data of the National Institute of Population and Social Security Research, the Ministry of Health, Labour and Welfare.

because that is the shape they took until several decades ago. By looking up and down the pyramid, we can see the proportion of population at each age level. Looking to the right and left of the centerline tells us the balance of males to females at each age. The bottom line shows us the total population at each age.

The first pyramid shows the population of Germany with low birthrates and death rates. This is typical of Global North countries. The second pyramid—Uganda— is typical of Global South countries and illustrates populations with high birthrates and large dependent youth populations. As these images show, the world population has been getting both younger (the Global South) *and* older (the Global North), resulting in large numbers of people dependent on the working-age population between 15 and 65 years of age. As Global

South nations have more and more children, they create more potential parents in later years, adding momentum to the world's population growth. Fewer deaths of infants and children, due to immunizations and disease control, result in lower mortality rates, younger populations, and higher potential numbers of births in the future.

Thinking Sociologically

Consider your own country's population pyramid. You can find it at www.census.gov/population/international/. What can you tell about your country's level of development by studying the population pyramid? How might societies differ if they have a young versus old population?

FIGURE 15.4 Population Pyramids in Global North (Germany) and Global South (Uganda) Countries in 2014

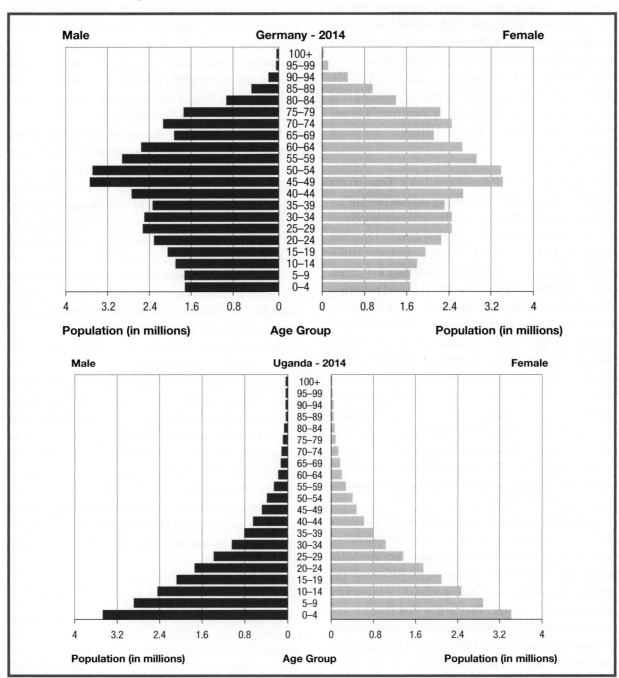

Source: SlideShare (2014).

Population Patterns: Theoretical Explanations

The earliest historical writings reveal that interest in population size is nothing new. Scriptures written many centuries ago, such as the Quran and the Bible, encourage population growth to increase the ranks of the faithful. Of course, population expansion made sense at the time these holy tracts were written, and populations grew slowly. Government leaders throughout the ages have adopted various philosophies about the best size of populations. The ancient Greek philosopher Plato argued that the ideal city-state should have 5,040 citizens and that measures should be taken to increase or decrease the population to bring it in line with this figure (Plato [ca. 350 BCE] 1960). However, the first significant scholarly analysis that addressed global population issues came from Thomas Malthus (1766–1834), an English clergyman and social philosopher.

Malthus's Theory of Population. In his "Essay on the Principle of Population," Malthus argued that humans are driven to reproduce and will multiply excessively without checks imposed to slow population growth (Malthus [1798] 1926). He noted that an unchecked population increases geometrically: 2 parents could have 4 children, 16 grandchildren, 64 great-grandchildren, and so forth—just with a continuous average family size of 4 children. Meanwhile, the means of subsistence (food) increases at best only arithmetically or lineally (5, 10, 15, 20, 25). Therefore, population growth must be controlled. Malthus described two types of checks that control population growth—positive checks that lead to higher death rates (wars, disease, epidemics, and food shortages leading to famine), and preventative checks that result in lower birthrates (delaying marriage and practicing abstinence). Hoping to avoid the positive checks, Malthus advocated for implementing the preventative checks. He did not approve of contraception, viewing it as immoral.

Contemporary neo-Malthusians like Paul and Anne Ehrlich favor contraception rather than simple reliance on the moral restraint that Malthus proposed. They also add to the formula of "too many people and too little food" the additional problem of a "dying planet"—caused by environmental damage. They argue that "the human predicament is driven by overpopulation, overconsumption of natural resources and the use of unnecessarily environmentally damaging technologies and socio-economic-political arrangements to service *Homo sapiens'* aggregate consumption." Successfully addressing these threats and avoiding the "collapse" of global society will require dramatic cultural and political shifts across the world (Ehrlich and Ehrlich 1990, 2013:1).

Looking at the world today, we see examples of the "positive" population checks described by Malthus. War decimated the populations of several countries during the world wars and has taken its toll on other countries in Central and Eastern Europe, Africa, and the Middle East since then. Waterborne diseases such as cholera and typhus strike after floods, and the floods themselves are often caused by large populations clearing and using almost all of the trees in their environment for fuel and building materials. In 2013 and 2014 alone, famines necessitated food aid in many countries including the Central African Republic, South Sudan, Syria, Somalia, and West Africa. Bosnia may require food aid after severe flooding (World Famine Timeline 2014).

Disease has also taken a toll on the world's population. In some villages in sub-Saharan and East African countries, AIDS has wiped out large percentages of the population, and many children must fend for themselves. Orphaned children take care of their younger siblings. PEPFAR (President's Emergency Plan for AIDS Relief), begun under President George W. Bush and continued under President Barack Obama, distributes generic forms of antiviral drugs to those with AIDS, and has helped bring the death toll down by 1.2 million. Without this relief effort, the loss of life would be even more staggering in this region of the world (Aguirre 2012).

While Malthus's work raised many issues still discussed today, his pessimistic vision of the future has not come to pass. He overemphasized *environmental determinism*, the idea that we can do little about the environment because it controls our lives. Malthus and neo-Malthusians were not able to anticipate the advances in agriculture that have increased the food supply tremendously. Nor did they foresee the importance of vaccines in controlling diseases. However, they have raised important issues that have helped government leaders in many parts of the world become aware of the need to plan for and take steps to control population growth (Bell 2012).

Thinking Sociologically

What are contemporary examples of what Malthus described as "positive" checks on population growth—war, disease, famine? Are family planning and contraception (a) suitable and (b) sufficient means to solve the problem of global overpopulation by humans? Can you think of other alternatives?

Demographic Transition: Explaining Population Growth and Expansion. Why should a change in the economic structure such as industrialization and movement from rural agricultural areas to cities have an impact on population size? The **demographic transition theory**, which *links trends in birthrates and death rates with patterns of economic and technological development*, offers one explanation.

This theory identifies four clear stages of development and posits that a fifth one is in process:

Stage 1: Populations have *high birthrates and death rates that tend to balance each other* over time. Births may outpace deaths until some disaster diminishes the increase. This has been the pattern for most of human history.

Stage 2: Populations still have high birthrates, but death rates decline (i.e., more people live longer) because of improvements in health care and sanitation, establishment of public health programs, disease control and immunizations, and food availability and distribution. This imbalance between continuing high births and declining deaths means that the *population growth rate is very high.*

Stage 3: Populations *begin to level off* due to access to contraception, wage increases, urbanization, increases in education levels and the status of women, and other changes. Most industrial societies are in this stage.

Stage 4: Birthrates and death rates are both low. Birthrates in some Global North countries drop below replacement level, resulting in declining population. Death rates remain fairly constant and low, though lifestyle diseases caused by smoking, obesity, and lack of exercise may increase death rates in some areas.

Stage 5: This stage has not yet come into full existence, but many demographers predict it will. As death rates remain stable and birthrates decline, the total population will begin to decrease for the first time. Japan and Germany are in the beginning of Stage 5. These stages are illustrated in Figure 15.5.

Demographic transition theory helps explain the developmental stages and population trends in countries around the world, but it does not consider some important factors that affect the size of populations:

1. People's age at marriage determines how many childbearing years they have (late marriage means fewer years until menopause).
2. Contraceptive availability determines whether families can control their number of children.
3. A country's resources and land may determine how much population a country can support.
4. The economic structure of a country, religious beliefs, and political philosophies affect attitudes toward birth control and family size.
5. Economic expansion rates influence a country's need for labor and its ability to create jobs.

FIGURE 15.5 **Stages of Demographic Transition**

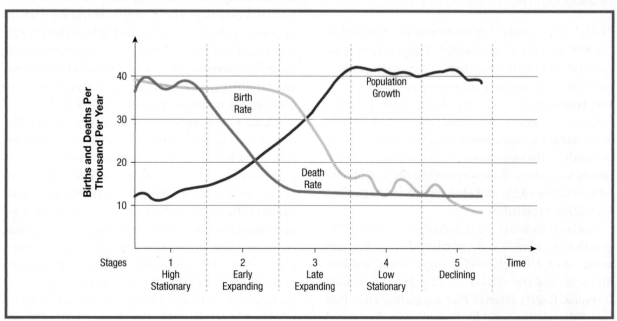

The *wealth flow theory* suggests that two possible strategies operate in couples' personal decisions about family size. When wealth flows from children to parents—that is, when children are an asset working on the family farm or laboring—parents have larger families. When wealth flows from parents to children, families tend to have fewer children (Caldwell 1982). To raise a child born in 2012 to 18 years in the United States, for instance, costs an average of more than $301,970 (adjusted for inflation), not including college expenses (Willis Report 2014).

Elements of both the demographic transition and wealth flow theories describe why families in poor nations tend to have more children than those in wealthier nations. Consider the following:

1. Many poor societies are agricultural societies where more children equal more people to work the farm.
2. Poor societies have higher rates of child mortality (leading parents to have more children, because they know some are likely to die at a young age).
3. Girls in poor societies tend to leave school early (if they attend at all), and to marry at a young age, leading to early childbearing.
4. Artificial contraception tends to be less available in poor nations.

With these facts in mind, Jeffry Sachs, an economist and leading expert on world poverty, advocates (along with many other social scientists) for efforts to keep girls in school longer and to improve health care and access to contraceptives in poor nations (Sachs 2011).

Conflict Theorists' Explanations of Population Growth. Karl Marx and Friedrich Engels did not agree with Malthus's idea that high fertility rates and population growth that outstrips food and resources produce poverty. They believed that social and structural factors built into the economic system—inequitable distribution and control of resources—cause poverty. Capitalist structures lead to wealth for the owners and create overpopulation and poverty for workers. Workers are expendable, kept in competition for low wages, used when needed, and let go when unprofitable to capitalists.

Socialist societies, Marx argued, could absorb the growth in population so the problem of overpopulation would not exist. In a classless society, all would be able to find jobs, and the system would expand to include everyone. Engels asserted that population growth in socialist societies could be controlled by the central government, as was done by the Chinese government when it imposed a "one child per family" policy in 1979. (The policy has gone through several revisions since that time.)

Conflict theorists also point out the impact that capitalism has on the health of people living in poor areas, as exemplified by the dumping of toxic waste from industries into predominantly poor areas with high percentages of people of color. This *environmental racism* relates directly to the social status differences of groups in society. For example, a well where the African American Holt-Orsted family got their drinking water was being polluted in 2007 with toxic chemicals that leaked from a nearby landfill. They continued to use this well, unaware of any problems, for nine years in their community of Dickson, Tennessee. Although some of the neighbors—those who were white—were notified within 48 hours after local waste treatment agencies learned of the danger (in 1993), the Holt-Orsted family was not informed and in fact was told by county officials that things were fine (Holt 2007; Huang 2011). By the time the Sheila Holt-Orsted was finally informed (in 2002) that the water the family had been using for showers, cooking, and beverages was contaminated with cancer-causing agents, Sheila had breast cancer and her father had terminal prostate cancer.

Four additional Holt-Orsted family members suffered from various other illnesses believed to be caused by the spills into the water supply. The family finally won their court case in 2011, but by then several family members had died from cancer (Holt 2007; Huang 2011). People of color are two to three times more likely to live in communities with hazardous waste problems. It has become a pressing issue in poor minority areas where housing was built on contaminated land (Bell 2012). A race- and class-based distribution of environmentally hazardous materials, as seen in the location of toxic dumps and landfills in predominantly poor and minority communities, occurs in countries across the world.

Of the many examples of environmental racism in the United States, consider the following: In Los Angeles, some minority schools are located in areas with high levels of airborne toxins; in Missouri, industrial-scale hog farms can be found in low-income counties; in Massachusetts, communities with high proportions of low-income minorities are 10 times more likely to experience chemical releases from industries than are high-income communities. Other low-quality-of-life indicators like poor-quality drinking water and noise pollution from highways are common in low-income and minority neighborhoods (Bell 2012). One classic study in Chicago focused on the impact of efforts to make Chicago a more eco-friendly or "green" city by encouraging more recycling. However, there were substantial problems of pollution, disease risk, and other costs to the neighborhoods where the recycling plants were located (Pellow 2002). Those involved in the *environmental justice movement* work to address such problems.

In a similar vein, if you sent your old computer to a recycling center, there is a good chance it ended up in a West African dump. To save money, many electronic recycling centers in Global North nations illegally send what they take in to Global South nations like Ghana, where governments are unable or unwilling to stop dumps from taking in e-waste. In a dump in Accra, the capital of Ghana, teenage boys can be seen smashing old computers and other electronic devices, so that they can sell the metals inside to local businesses. Exposed to the chemicals that leach out of the abandoned computers, they are being poisoned and injuring their health. It is sobering to realize that environmentally friendly policies (recycling, donating—rather than throwing away—electronic devices) aimed at prolonging the health of the Earth and the human population—have often been implemented in ways that hurt those who have the fewest resources— people living in poverty and minorities (Hugo 2010; Korgen and Gallagher 2013).

MESO-LEVEL INSTITUTIONAL INFLUENCES ON POPULATION CHANGE

Meso-level analysis focuses on institutions and ethnic subcultures within a country. In this section we examine how institutions influence birthrates and other population patterns. Populations change in three main ways: (1) *size* (overall number of people), (2) *composition* (the makeup of the population, including sex ratio, age distribution, and religious or ethnic representation in the population), and (3) *distribution* (density or concentration in various portions of the land).

The key *demographic processes* that cause population changes are **fertility** (*the birthrate*), **mortality** (*the death rate*), and **migration** (*movement of people from one place to another*). Populations change when births and deaths are not evenly balanced or when significant numbers of people move from one area to another. Migration does not change the size or composition of the world as a whole, but can

Overpopulation presents a challenge to food and water resources, and large populations damage the environment and provide little ecological recovery time. The top photo shows the smog from fires, factories, and automobiles—called "brown haze"—that routinely hovers over Cape Town, South Africa, in the morning. The bottom photo pictures a billboard in Shanghai advertising China's "One Child Only" policy.

affect size or makeup in a micro (family), meso (institution or ethnic subculture), or macro-level (national) population. Fertility is the most easily controllable factor impacting population change.

Institutions and Population Patterns

Jeanne, one of the coauthors of this book, was riding in the back of a "mammy wagon," a common means of transport in West Africa. Crowded in with the chickens and pigs and people, she did not expect the conversation that ensued. The man in his late 20s asked if she was married and for how long. Jeanne responded, "Yes, for three years." The man continued, "How many children do you have?" Jeanne answered, "None." The man commented, "Oh, I'm

 Fertility   Later-Life Migration in the United States

In an urban area in Cambodia (Kampuchea), residents crowd onto this truck, a common form of transportation. With a high fertility rate and migration from rural to urban areas, crowded transportation is common.

sorry!" Jeanne replied, "No, don't be sorry. We planned it that way!" This man had been married for 10 years to a woman 3 years younger than him and had eight children. The ninth was on the way. In answer to his pointed questions, Jeanne explained that she was not being cruel to her husband and that birth control was what prevented children, and no, it did not make sex less enjoyable. He expressed surprise that limiting the number of children was possible and rather liked the idea. He jumped at the suggestion that he visit the family planning clinic in the city. With his meager income, he and his wife were finding it hard to feed all their children. This story helps to illustrate the fact that knowledge of and access to family planning options are not uniformly available. Institutions affect access to those services.

Demographers consider micro-, meso-, and macro-level factors in attempting to understand fertility rates around the world. We know that personal knowledge and access are key factors. Couples' decisions to use or not use contraception, their ideas about the acceptability of abortion, and whether they want to have children (and how many) can also have an impact on national and global rates of population change. So choices at the micro level make a difference at the macro level. Consider the following meso-level institutional factors affecting the size of the population.

Economic Factors and Population Patterns.

Fertility fluctuates with actions in meso-level institutions such as the economy and the government. During economic depressions, for example, the rate of fertility tends to drop due to lack of family resources. Thus, meso-level structural factors—including level of economic prosperity within the nation, government policies to encourage or discourage births, changes in norms and values about sexuality within a society, and access to health care—all influence decisions within families about fertility.

Political Systems and Population Patterns. Some governments provide incentives to parents to have more children through *pronatalist policies* (those that encourage fertility), while others discourage high fertility with *antinatalist policies* (those that discourage fertility). Thus, meso-level social policies established by the political system can shape decisions of families at the micro level. Government policies can take several forms: (1) manipulating contraceptive availability; (2) promoting change in factors that affect fertility such as the status of women, education, availability of abortion, and degree of economic development; (3) using propaganda for or against having children; (4) creating incentives (maternity leaves, benefits, and tax breaks) or penalties (such as fines) for having children; and (5) passing laws governing age of marriage, size of family, contraception, and abortion.

Antinatalist policies arise out of concern over available resources and differences in birthrates among population subgroups. Singapore, a small island country in Asia, consists of one main island and many smaller islands. It is one of the most crowded places on Earth, with 7,405 people per square kilometer (compared to 34 in the United States, 4 in Canada, and 351 in Japan) (World Bank 2013b). The entire population of Singapore is urban, and 90% live in the capital city. The country has little unemployment and one of the highest per capita incomes in Asia. However, it depends on imports from other countries for most of its raw materials and food.

Some years ago, the central government in Singapore started an aggressive antinatalist plan. It made birth control widely available, and residents of Singapore who had more than two children were penalized with less health care, smaller housing, and higher costs for services such as education. As a result of these policies, Singapore now claims one of the lowest natural increase rates (the birthrate minus the death rate) in Southeast Asia, at 0.6% a year (Population Reference Bureau 2013b).

As noted earlier, China instituted its current antinatalist policy, which includes the "one child" rule, in 1979. The government discourages traditional preferences for early marriage, large families, and many sons by using fines, group pressure, privileges for small families, and easy availability of birth control and abortion. The government has reduced the fertility rate to 1.55 children per family. Unfortunately, there are side effects to such a stringent policy among a people who value male more than female children. There has been an increase in selective abortions by couples hoping to have sons, and instances of female infanticide in rural areas—killing of female infants when they are born—so that families can try for a male child. Recent challenges to the one-child policy come from two levels: (1) the micro level where individual women have been forced to have abortions, sometimes late in pregnancy, and (2) the macro level as Chinese society ages and birthrates are low, resulting in a shortage of young people to support the increasingly aging society (Zakaria 2012).

Examples of pronatalist government policies can be seen in Eastern Europe where governments are worried about the drop in birthrates. There are fewer young people to pay taxes and to do jobs needed in the society. Pronatalist policies established to raise birthrates include giving workers a day off to "have sex"; free summer camps for young couples—without condoms; cars and monetary gifts for new parents; and additional benefits for parents and their children. Abortions and even birth control have been restricted in some Eastern European countries to curb dropping population numbers (Stracansky 2013).

In the United States, it is sometimes hard to pin a simple label of antinatalist or pronatalist on the administration in power. Presidents Ronald Reagan, George H. W. Bush, and George W. Bush each implemented a "gag rule" (requiring parental notification) that limited the availability of birth control for teens in the United States. Presidents Bill Clinton and Barack Obama each eliminated the gag policy. On the other hand, President Clinton signed the Family and Medical Leave Act, which allows employees to take up to 12 weeks' (unpaid) leave to take care of a family member, without risk of losing their job.

While family planning programs and contraceptive use have increased in much of the world, availability and use in sub-Saharan Africa remains low. Global use of modern contraception was 57% in 2012, but 222 million Global South women who would like to control family size are not using contraception because of limited access and knowledge, fear of side effects, cultural or religious opposition, and gender-based barriers (World Health Organization [WHO] 2012a). The vast majority of the 16 million girls between 15 and 19 who give birth each year live in Global South countries (WHO 2014a).

 Thinking Sociologically

Do you think it is appropriate for governments to use enticements or penalties to encourage or discourage fertility decisions by couples? Why or why not? Identify several positive and several negative repercussions of either pronatalist or antinatalist policies discussed earlier.

Religion and Population Patterns. Religion is a primary shaper of norms and values in most societies, including those related to fertility. In some societies, children born out of wedlock are accepted into the mother's family. In other societies, a woman can be stoned to death for having a child or even sex out of wedlock.

Some religious groups oppose any intervention, such as birth control or abortion, in the natural processes of conception and birth. Roman Catholicism, for example, teaches that large families are a blessing from God and that artificial birth control is a sin. The Roman Catholic Church officially advocates natural family planning (NFP) to regulate conception, a less reliable method than artificial birth control, using medication, or physical barriers. Many Catholics, however, do use artificial birth control methods. In the United States, only 2% of Catholics rely on NFP while almost 70% rely on the birth control pill, an IUD (intrauterine device), or sterilization to control their fertility (Guttmacher Institute 2013).

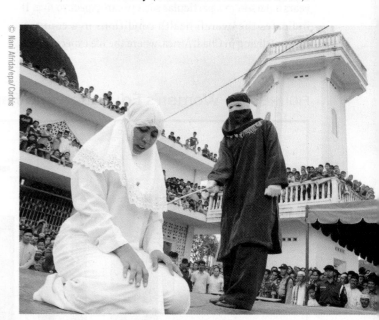

Nur Azizah binti Hanafiah, 22, receives a punishment of caning for having premarital sex with her boyfriend. Her community in the Aceh region of Indonesia follows a form of Islamic Sharia law. In some societies, she would have been stoned to death for having premarital sex.

Almost all (99%) of the sexually active women in the United States have used some form of contraception.

Education and Population. If a country wants to control population growth, providing better access to schools and raising the education level of women is a key to success. The higher women's status in society—as measured by education level and job opportunities—the lower their fertility (Population Reference Bureau 2013). Figure 15.6 shows the relationship between education and family size in five Global South countries (Population Reference Bureau 2012d). Note that the higher the education level, the lower the fertility rate and population growth.

Lower population growth means less pressure on governments to provide emergency services, such as food and water rations, for booming populations, and more attention to services such as schools, health care, and jobs. Most population experts encourage governments and other meso-level institutions in fast-growing countries to act aggressively to control population size. Consequences of population fluctuations affect affluent parts of the world as well as poor parts. The impact of the baby boom in the United States illustrates this, as discussed in the next "Sociology in Our Social World."

Factors Affecting Mortality Rates

Recall that life expectancy refers to the average number of years a person in a particular society can expect to live. It indicates the overall health conditions in a country. Imagine living in Chad, Africa, where the life expectancy at birth is 49.44 years. In this low-income, largely agricultural society, families tend to have many children (4.68, on average, or 37.3 per 1,000 population). Of every 1,000 babies born alive, 90.3 will die within the first year (IndexMundi 2014). Over 72% of men and women live in rural areas, where most are subsistence farmers, working small plots that may not provide enough food to keep their families from starving (World Factbook 2014a). When one plot is overfarmed and the soil depleted so that plants will no longer grow, the family moves to another and clears the land, depleting more arable land. This scenario repeats itself, leading to little arable land, shortages of food, malnutrition, and a population susceptible to illnesses and disease. The limited medical care that exists is mostly available in urban areas.

Some other African countries face similar situations, with life expectancy in South Africa at 49.56, Somalia at 51.58, and Zimbabwe at 55.68. Average life expectancy for sub-Saharan Africa as a whole is about 56 years (World Bank 2014a).

Why are these societies so dramatically different from Global North countries, many of which have average life expectancies into the '80s? The low life expectancy stems from lack of medical care, epidemics such as AIDS, wars and civil strife, corrupt governments, droughts and famine, malnutrition, resulting susceptibility to diseases, and high infant mortality. Table 15.2 shows the infant mortality rate around the world, meaning the number of infant deaths (children under 5 years) per 1,000 births. This is another key indicator of a country's overall well-being.

FIGURE 15.6   Women's Education and Family Size—Selected Countries

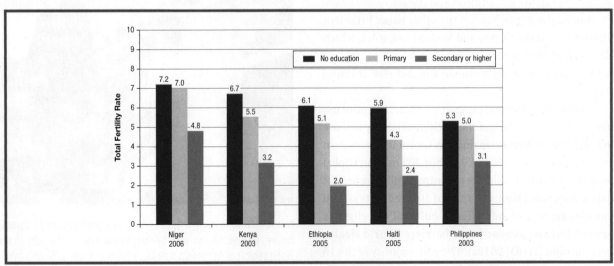

Source: Population Reference Bureau (2012d).

sociology in our social world

The Significance of the Baby Boom

At the end of World War II, the birthrate shot up temporarily in most countries involved in the war, as many young people who had been forced to delay marriage made up for lost time. The postwar economy was growing, people were employed in relatively well-paying positions, and the norms supported large families. In the United States, this baby boom lasted for 17 years, from 1946 to 1963.

The baby boom phenomenon has had many impacts. During the late 1960s, school boards and contractors were busy building schools to educate the growing number of children. By the 1980s, student numbers declined, and towns were consolidating schools and closing buildings. When the baby boomers entered the job market starting in the mid-1960s, there were great numbers of applicants for jobs, and employers could pay less. The supply was so great they were assured that someone would take the job.

Two decades later, it was much easier for young people to find jobs because there were fewer of them in that age range looking for starting-level positions. However, that generation is finding it hard to get promotions because the baby boomers have dominated so many of the high-level positions. In addition, trends in marketing and advertising have, for years, been dictated by the baby boomer generation because they are such a large segment of the consumer public.

By the 1960s, people's views of the ideal family size and the proper age for marriage changed. Zero-population-growth movements and environmental concerns slowed the rate of growth. The period from the late 1960s to early 1970s has been referred to as a "baby bust" or the "birth dearth." This fluctuation resulted in a population structure that did not look very much like a pyramid, as shown in Figure 15.7 on page 517.

In the mid-1970s and into the 1980s, when the baby boom generation started having babies, there was another baby boom—or a "boomer echo"—but it was much smaller because the baby boomers had smaller families. Currently, growth in the overall size of the U.S. population is due largely to immigration. White non-Hispanic deaths now outpace white non-Hispanic births. If not for immigration, the population in the United States might have actually begun to decline.

 Thinking Sociologically

After reading "Sociology in Our Social World," discuss what impact the baby boom and boomer echo have had on your opportunities for education and a career. How will retirement of baby boomers affect your opportunities?

Migration and Mobility: Where People Move and Why

Most of us have moved one or more times in our lives, a process called *migration*. Perhaps, we have moved to a larger house down the block, maybe to another area for

A sick and displaced Chadian woman watches as her malnourished infant sleeps at a health clinic run by Doctors without Borders. This mother knows that life expectancy for her child is less than 50 years.

a job opportunity or school, or even to another country altogether. The process of changing one's place of residence is called *geographic mobility*. Over the history of the human race, people have migrated to the far reaches of the globe. Because of adaptability to climatic and

Table 15.2 Infant Mortality Rates Around the World

Region	Infant Mortality Rate[a]
World	41
More affluent (Global North) countries	5
Less affluent (Global South) countries	49
Least affluent (the very poor Global South)	72
Africa	67
North America	6
Latin America	20
Asia	37
Europe	5

Source: Population Reference Bureau (2012e).

a. Deaths of children under 1 year per 1,000 births.

geographic barriers, humans have dispersed to more areas of the world than any other species. Even inhospitable locations such as the Arctic North and the South Pole have human settlements.

As noted in previous chapters, the *push–pull* model points out that some people are pushed from their original locations by wars, plagues, famine, political or religious conflicts, economic crises, or other factors and pulled to new locations by economic opportunities or political and religious tolerance. Most people do not leave a location unless they have been forced out or they have a viable alternative in the new location. They weigh the benefits of moving versus the costs (Weeks 2012).

Migration is often initiated at the micro level: a lucrative job offer in another location requires a move, the family dwelling becomes too small, a relative needs help, or a family member's health requires a different climate. If an opportunity arises, the individual or family may move. However, if the risks are high, if the information about migration is scarce, or if the move involves negative factors such as leaving family, individuals may decide to stay put. For rational choice theorists, assessment of costs and benefits by individuals impacts migration patterns.

Although the decision to move is often a personal or family one, the sociocultural environment also influences it. Examples of large groups of people leaving an area because of aspirations to improve their life chances, hopes of retaining a way of life, or expulsion by political, economic, or religious forces have existed throughout history. Chinese railroad workers came to the United States for economic reasons. Amish and Mennonite settlers from Europe sought religious freedom and preservation of their way of life. The Amish, a group originating in Germany, left Germany *en masse*, and members of this group now live entirely in North America. Italian immigration to the United States took place in a collective manner. When a family left Italy, it would usually move to a U.S. city where a relative or a previous acquaintance lived. Thus, residents of entire apartment buildings in the North End of Boston were from the same extended family, and entire city blocks of people came from the same town or region of southern Italy (Gans 1962). Many European countries are multicultural environments today because of immigrants from former colonies.

Those living at the receiving end have not always been welcoming, and in fact have often tried to isolate the newcomers in ghettos, preventing them from moving into other neighborhoods. Especially in difficult economic times, when competition for jobs is greatest, newcomers may find few employment opportunities (Foner 2005).

Immigration laws in the United States reflect the nation's attitudes toward immigrants at different periods. The United States tended to welcome immigrants during boom economic times and tried to repel them during recessions and depressions. Exclusionary acts include the Chinese Exclusion Act of 1882, which ended Chinese immigration; the Gentlemen's Agreement of 1907, which halted Japanese immigration; and the National Origins Act of 1924, which heavily restricted immigration from Southern and Eastern Europe and excluded nonwhites.

The Immigration and Nationality Act of 1965 abolished the policies that excluded Asians, Africans, and Latin Americans and based immigration policy on family relationships and skills. Current debates in the U.S. Congress over immigration reform, however, reveal the persistent contentious nature of policies related to immigration, including undocumented migration from Latin America.

After the Great Recession began in 2008, immigration to the United States slowed. In Mexico, an economic rebound and successful efforts to lower the birthrate have led to fewer people looking for jobs in the United States. Those factors, in combination with the economic recession, anti-immigrant environment, and tighter U.S. border controls, have led to fewer Mexicans making the trip to the United States and more returning to Mexico. In 2014, most new immigrants were from Asia rather than Latin America (Barrera 2013).

Immigrants seeking a better life often struggle in their new locations. Consider Mohammed from Senegal who traverses the streets of Verona, Italy, trying to make a living selling children's books and hoping he might have some money left to send back to his family. Mohammed speaks five languages and has a high school education, but opportunities in his homeland are limited, and he is an undocumented immigrant in Italy. European countries, especially those with former colonies, have large populations of immigrants from North Africa and the Middle East. These immigrants often face great peril in their attempts to gain entry into more prosperous nations; and once they arrive, many find themselves in crowded, unsanitary housing with little economic opportunity.

Social scientists study the impact of immigration, pointing out that immigration tends to yield significant economic gains for receiving countries. Scholars who study migration—especially long-distance migration that involves crossing into another society—point out that migrants are usually among the most hardworking, ambitious, optimistic, healthy, and well-adjusted people, for it takes considerable courage and motivation

🎙 Immigration

A giant dust storm (left) blacked out the sky of Goodwell, Oklahoma, during the Dust Bowl of the late 1800s, *pushing* many people off their farms and out of the plains states. By contrast, the California Gold Rush of the middle 1800s *pulled* thousands of migrants to the west coast in search of wealth.

to undertake migration to a new land. Wilkerson summarizes:

> *Any migration takes some measure of energy, planning, and forethought. It requires not only the desire for something better but the willingness to act on that desire to achieve it. Thus, the people who undertake such a journey are more likely to be either among the more educated in their homes of origin or those most motivated. (Wilkerson 2010:261)*

International Migration. More than 3.1% of the world's population is "on the go" each year. That is 214 million international migrants, or 1 out of every 33 persons in the world. Half are women. These migrants change the size and characteristics of populations around the world, expanding some and emptying out others (International Organization for Migration 2012).

Many people have taken great risks to enter Global North nations illegally in search of work. Luis is one such undocumented immigrant. His story, in the next "Sociology Around the World," illustrates the hardships that many migrants must endure as they seek a better life for themselves and their families. To these migrants, a better life awaits *if* they can reach it.

International migration is especially common where political turmoil, wars, famines, or natural disasters ravage a country. *Refugees*, those "who flee in search of refuge in times of war, political oppression, or religious persecution," numbered 43.7 million in 2011, half of them children. This is a 15-year high (UNHCR 2012). Roughly 27.5 million citizens are *internally displaced*, forcibly relocated within their own countries by violent conflict or environmental disaster. In China, pollution in large cities such as Beijing is creating an environmental disaster, causing some people to move out of the cities to small towns (Wong 2013b).

The ongoing crisis in Syria has added significantly to the numbers of refugees. By 2013, over 1.5 million Syrians had fled the nation. Over 500,000 sought refuge in the tiny neighboring nation of Jordan, which already harbored many Palestinian refugees. Ten percent of the Jordanian population now consists of refugees, and that number increases daily (PBS Newshour 2013).

A recent study of immigrants to the United States shows people born elsewhere who later acquire U.S. citizenship are more likely than their native-born neighbors to marry, less likely to divorce, and more likely to avoid poverty. In the 10 poorest U.S. states, native-born citizens earn $0.84 to every $1 earned by naturalized citizens. In the richest states, the ratio is $0.97 to $1. One reason for this difference in earnings comes from the fact that foreign-born naturalized citizens tend to bring with them the tools and attitudes they need to be successful. They had to have the wherewithal to leave their home country, find sponsors in the United States, navigate visa and green card requirements, and fulfill the requirements for U.S. citizenship. Those who can do all that tend to be self-reliant and willing to take risks, and have an entrepreneurial spirit (Giridharadas 2014).

Internal Migration in the United States. The rate of internal migration in the United States is high compared with that in most places in the world. Patterns of migration have primarily involved individual "pull" to economic opportunities and better housing. According to the U.S. Census, about 40% of people who move cite a housing reason, including a new or better home or apartment, a better neighborhood, cheaper housing, owning rather than renting, or establishing their own household (Demographics Livability 2014). During different historical periods, movement directions have varied. During the 20th century, up until the 1960s, people moved out of the southern states and into northern states. This included the Great Migration of 6 million black Americans who left the rural south for northern cities. Then the pattern reversed, and the flow started going south and west. Movement starting in the 1960s and increasing in the 1970s has been toward the Sunbelt, especially to California, Arizona, Texas, and Florida. Movement to the Pacific Coast and even Alaska has also increased, due to economic opportunities in these locations.

One major form of internal migration is *urbanization* (U.S. Census Bureau 2013d). The second half of this chapter focuses on the urbanization of the population across the globe. Although decisions about family size and migration are individual choices, what happens at the meso and macro levels influences these decisions, as we see in the next section.

Thinking Sociologically

Think about your own grandparents or great-grandparents. How long have your ancestors occupied the same house or lived in the same community? Do they go back more than one generation on the same property? If they have been mobile, what factors were critical in their decision to move? How has their mobility or stability influenced your family's experiences? How were they received in their new home(s)?

MICRO-LEVEL POPULATION PATTERNS

Understanding demography can be extremely important for comprehending social processes in your everyday life. While most Global North countries do not have massive famines or population explosions, population fluctuations influence them in many ways. Consider the life choice decisions you will make regarding education, employment, and retirement.

Keith, one of the coauthors of this book, lived in Boston, and his wife taught in a suburban school system there at a time when the fertility rate was falling. The

Sociology Around the World

From South to North of the U.S. Border

By Nancy Diggs

When Luis and the group of 60 undocumented immigrants made the journey across the Arizona desert, it was March; temperatures ranged as high as the nineties during the day to freezing at night. The group was told that they would be walking in the desert for about six hours, and to be sure to bring food and water for that time. To make sure they could travel quickly, they were told to carry nothing else. As often happens, not long after their start, their guide claimed that in order to avoid the Immigration and Naturalization Service [now U.S. Citizenship and Immigration Services] they would take a longer way—a march through the desert that would end up lasting a hellish two-and-a-half days, almost all the way without food or water. It was so hot during the day that when they chanced upon water tanks for animals, most of them rushed to gulp down the green and slimy water. Along the path, the travelers skirted the remains of one man who hadn't made it. Having been instructed to bring nothing but the clothes on their backs, they were not able to bury him.

At night in the desert cold, without extra clothing or blankets, Luis and his companions huddled together for warmth. In order not to be spotted, they were told to wear dark clothes and no white hats. Smoking and whistling were also forbidden. At last they came to a highway to be crossed, where they would wait until late at night when there was no traffic at all. When a car stopped on the road, the guide warned everyone not to move and to keep their eyes closed so the light wouldn't reflect off the whites of their eyes.

When all was dark and quiet, the guide called another coyote (a person who helps undocumented

In 2014, this group of immigrants from Honduras and El Salvador, most of them children, crossed the U.S.–Mexico border into Texas and were caught. The border fences cost millions of dollars but have not stopped the flow of undocumented migrants, who endure great peril to get to the United States.

immigrants into the United States in exchange for money), who came in about a half-hour with two vans. The sound of a helicopter caused everyone to push and shove in a vain attempt to squeeze 60 people into the two vehicles. Some had to remain behind, including Luis, who waited anxiously for the coyotes to return. Fortunately, there was a big incentive: Luis and his companions had not yet paid them.

At the next step of the journey, the immigrants were loaded into a truck trailer that was "incredibly hot," with no water, let alone air conditioning. After traveling some 400 miles, they eventually arrived in the Los Angeles area where they were able to buy plenty of food and drinks. After spending the night in a safe house, Luis and his group met their new American coyote who sent them off in different directions. Luis took a bus to Las Vegas where his uncle lived.

Source: Diggs (2011).

elementary school where she taught had four first-grade classrooms, with 28 children per room—112 first graders in the school. By the next year, the school felt the decline in the fertility rate six years earlier, and the number of first graders declined. Within four years, there were only 40 first graders in her school, with two classrooms and only 20 students per class. Some school systems lost half of their student population in a few years. One year, first-grade teachers were losing their jobs or having to move to another grade, and the next year, it was second-grade teachers who were scrambling. The third year, third-grade teachers were in oversupply, and so forth. With low demand, these were not times for college students to be pursuing teaching careers. A personal decision was being influenced by population trends—and this pattern continues.

We have already mentioned the impact of the baby boom (the high fertility rates from 1946 to about 1963) and the following baby bust (the drop in fertility for more than a decade following the baby boom). The population pyramid of the United States reveals the impact on the population (see Figures 15.7 and 15.8). As we can see, the U.S. population no longer looks anything like a pyramid. From these figures, we can tell a great deal about job prospects, retirement security, career decisions, and other outcomes of demographic changes. As that bulge for the

baby boomer group moves into the senior citizens' category, society will have new challenges.

 Thinking Sociologically

Why do population experts predict the population pyramid will look like Figure 15.8 by 2050? What factors in society might lead to this? What kinds of problems do you think this sort of configuration might cause?

Retirement is another topic for which population patterns are critical. When Social Security was established in the United States in the 1930s, life expectancy from birth was 58 for men and 62 for women (Social Security Administration 2013b). The number of people in the age-dependent categories of under 15 and over 65 was low. For each person who received Social Security in 1945, 42 workers paid Social Security taxes. Forty people, each paying $255 a year, could easily support a retired person, receiving $10,000 per year. However, the average life expectancy has shifted, and the age-dependent population has increased. Currently in the United States, nearly 14% of the population is over the age of 65, as opposed to 4% in the 1930s (World Factbook 2014k). Moreover, predictions are that by 2035, 20% of the population will be over 65. In 2013, there were just 2.8 workers contributing Social Security

FIGURE 15.7   **United States, 2010**

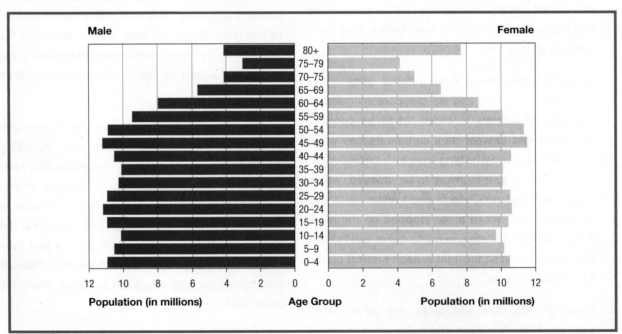

Source: NationMaster (2011).

FIGURE 15.8   United States, 2050

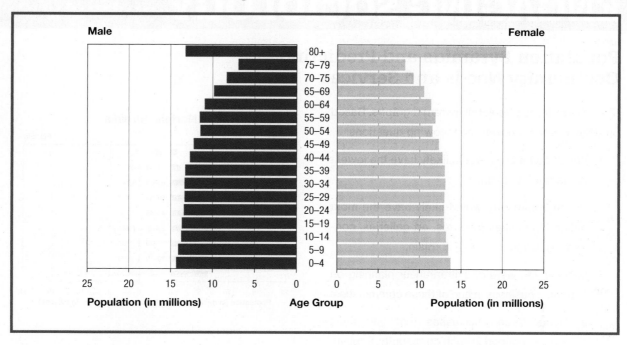

Source: NationMaster (2011).

taxes for each person covered by Social Security (Social Security Administration 2013a). When commentators and politicians say Social Security is in trouble, they refer to problems created by changes in the composition of the U.S. population.

In the 1980s, the U.S. administration and Congress saw the problem coming and for the first time began to save funds in a Social Security account for the baby boomers. They also passed laws requiring baby boomers to work longer before they qualify for Social Security. The fact that there are so many baby boomers—and that an extremely high percentage of citizens over the age of 65 vote—makes it unlikely that the government will cut back on benefits to this group. Still, members of the younger generation may not receive as much Social Security income as do current retirees. Meanwhile, Medicare, the insurance program for retired adults, has less money on hand than does the Social Security system. It appears that the aging population and need for funds may have a profound influence on your own family budget and retirement.

As noted in Chapter 6, population patterns also influence rates of deviance and juvenile delinquency. Most deviant acts are committed by young people in their mid-teens to early 20s. Thus, when the baby boom generation was in their teens and early 20s, in the 1960s and 1970s, the overall rates of deviance climbed higher. When the

birth dearth group was in their teens, overall rates of crime dropped because there were fewer teenagers. Thus, private and personal decisions by thousands of couples (micro level) may result in the crime rates for the entire country rising or falling 15 years later.

Because population trends shape your life, understanding those trends can help you use that knowledge to your advantage. To illustrate the power of demographic trends on individual decisions, the next "Engaging Sociology" on page 514 provides an exercise in problem solving using information from population pyramids of U.S. cities.

URBANIZATION: MOVEMENT FROM RURAL TO URBAN AREAS

Mumbai (Bombay), India; Caracas, Venezuela; Lagos, Nigeria; Shanghai, China; and New York City, United States—all are bustling *megacities* (cities and their surrounding metropolitan areas with more than 10 million people) with traffic congestion and people rushing to their destinations. Carts, bicycles, and taxis weave in and out of traffic jams. The local spices and other aromas scent the

Urban Nature

ENGAGING SOCIOLOGY

Population Pyramids and Predicting Community Needs and Services

Study these three population pyramid graphs. Based on what you see, answer the following questions:

1. Which community would likely have the lowest crime rate? Explain.

2. Which community would likely have the most cultural amenities (theatres, art galleries, concert halls, and so forth)? Explain.

3. Imagine you were an entrepreneur planning on starting a business in one of these communities.

   a. Name three businesses that you think would succeed in each community. Explain.

   b. Name one business that you think would not succeed in each community. Explain.

Source: U.S. Census Bureau.

Source: U.S. Census Bureau.

Source: U.S. Census Bureau.

air. Sidewalk merchants display vegetables and fruits unique to the country. Beggars and the homeless, often migrants from rural areas, dot the sidewalks, while merchants sell colorful wares. Cities provide a kaleidoscope of humanity as more of the world's population becomes urban.

Today, more than half of all people live in urban areas, and projections indicate that 7 out of 10 people will do so by 2050 (WHO 2013b). The U.S. Census breaks down the geographic regions of the nation into urbanized areas (of 50,000 or more), urban clusters (2,500–50,000), and rural

areas (all nonurban areas). In 1900, 60.4% of Americans lived in nonurban, or rural, areas, and in 1960, 36% did so. By 2010, just 19.3% of the population lived in rural parts of the country.

The move from rural to urban areas has always stemmed from the increased opportunities for employment and investment that come with living around more people. Globalization has made this more important than ever, as markets and job opportunities have become transnational. Population growth often spurs job growth. For example, in the United States, all but one of the ten urban areas with the most population growth between 2000 and 2010 also increased their number of jobs. The exception was Atlanta, which had a slight decline. While the growth in these urban areas in the United States focuses primarily in the low-density, suburban areas surrounding the cities, in other parts of the world, poor migrants to urban areas live in crowded slums. In many parts of the Global South, the rural poor, who come to cities to find opportunities, often live with no running water, electricity, or sewage disposal and lack basic services, including health care and education (Kotkin 2013; Kotkin and Cox 2011; World Bank 2013a).

Megacities around the world are part of a global trend that has gained momentum over several centuries—urbanization. The next "Engaging Sociology" feature on page 516 invites you to explore some consequences of major urbanization trends in the world (Brunn, Hays-Mitchell, and Zeigler 2011).

Urbanization accompanies *modernization*—transformation from traditional, mostly agrarian societies to contemporary bureaucratized states—and *industrialization*—transformation from an agricultural base and handmade goods to manufacturing industries. We explore urbanization in this section as a demographic trend that has major social implications for how people live and interact.

Most people live their lives in *communities*: locations that provide dwellings, a sense of identity and belonging, neighbors and friends, social involvements, and access to basic necessities. Our most intimate micro-level interactions take place in these communities. Yet our communities also connect us to larger meso- and macro-level social structures, such as political and religious organizations, world health organizations, and international relief agencies (e.g., UNICEF). In this section, we consider the development of communities—from rural areas and small towns to urban areas such as megacities.

CITIES AS MICRO-LEVEL LIVING ENVIRONMENTS

In the 17th and 18th centuries, when Europe was undergoing dramatic changes, small villages contrasted sharply with the rapidly growing urban centers. Ferdinand Tönnies (1855–1936) described living environments on a continuum from **Gemeinschaft**, a German word indicating *a small traditional community*, to **Gesellschaft**, meaning *a large, impersonal urban area*. He saw social life

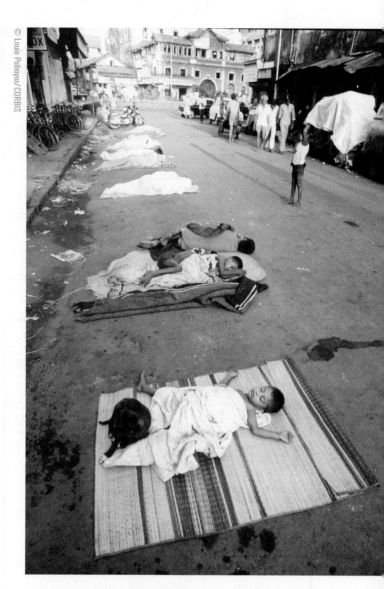

In Mumbai (Bombay), India, many children have no choice but to sleep on the streets each night.

as an evolution from family units to rural villages, towns, cities, nations, and finally cosmopolitan urban life (Tönnies [1887] 1963). Key elements of Gemeinschaft include family, friendship, relations to the land, common values, and traditions. On the other hand, formal relations, contracts, laws, and economies built on money characterize Gesellschaft. People in urban areas do not necessarily know one another or share common values. They tend to be employees of bureaucratic organizations, and act as individuals rather than members of a collectivity.

A number of other theorists living in the Europe of the 19th century suggested similar contrasts between rural and urban life. Émile Durkheim (1858–1917) described the social bonds that held society together and the changes that arose from industrialization and urbanization.

Small Towns   Urbanization

ENGAGING SOCIOLOGY

World Urbanization Trends

World Urbanization Prospects are reports published by the United Nations Population Division. They provide valuable data on past, present, and future urbanization trends in regions and subregions of the world. They also provide data on individual cities and urban areas. Consider the impact of major migration trends on the environment, friends and relatives left behind, dual-career families, maintaining one's culture, the impact of new cultural ideas spreading, and many more impacts. The major findings of the most recent edition follow in Figures 15.9–15.11.

FIGURE 15.9   Percentage of Population Residing in Urban Areas, 2014

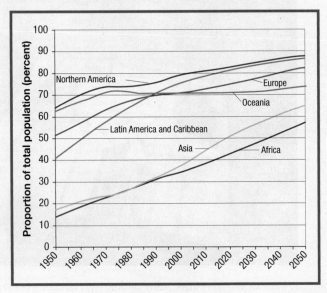

Source: United Nations Population Division (2014).

FIGURE 15.10   Urban and Rural Population of the World, 1950–2050

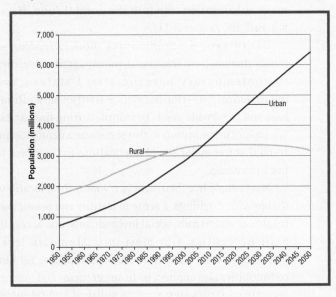

Source: United Nations Population Division (2014).

Sociological Data Analysis of Figure 15.9

- What do you learn from this figure about world urbanization trends? Which continents seem to be most urbanized?

- What might be some effects of urbanization on global climate change, the possibilities of globally transmitted diseases, political stability or instability, or the global economy?

- How might the global trend toward urbanization affect your own life?

Sociological Data Analysis of Figure 15.10

- When the size of the rural population declines, how might it affect the culture of a nation?

- Identify two positive and two negative consequences of this urbanization trend for a nation.

FIGURE 15.11   **Percentage of World's Urban Population by Region, 2014**

Source: United Nations Population Division (2014).

Sociological Data Analysis of Figure 15.11

- In 1950, North America had 15% of the world's population. That number has dropped to 8% and will drop again to 6% by 2050. Is that something that is cause for concern? Why or why not?

As discussed in Chapter 3, mechanical solidarity was Durkheim's term *for the glue that holds a society together through shared beliefs, values, and traditions typical of rural areas and simple societies.* In societies with mechanical solidarity, homogeneity of thought forms social bonds.

The social glue that holds modern industrial and postindustrial societies and people together is organic solidarity, *the social coherence (glue) based on a division of labor with each member playing a highly specialized role in the society and each person being dependent on others due to interrelated, interdependent tasks.* This interdependence of specialized tasks is the key to unity in more complex societies.

As noted earlier, for most of human history, humans lived in rural areas. *Rural sociology* considers patterns and behaviors among people at a distance from population centers. Over the past three centuries, and increasing rapidly over the past few decades, a rural exodus has been under way, with movement from rural to urban areas with more economic opportunities and better health care and education. Major population shifts from rural to urban areas were triggered by industrialization first in Europe and North America, and then in other areas of the world.

The early interpretations of urbanization, especially by European sociologists, were made through a rather pessimistic lens. The trend was seen largely as a decline of civil society. However, there are pluses as well as minuses in quality of life as people inhabit more densely populated areas. Many city planners have worked to make cities more habitable and "green," to encourage more people to live closer together in cities. We consume less energy if we live in densely populated areas because there are fewer people using individual transportation (cars) to get to destinations as shared public transit is more possible.

Thinking Sociologically

Consider a small town and a large city with which you are familiar. Do they seem to have unity and coherence based on organic or mechanical solidarity? Do the notions of Gemeinshaft and Gesellshaft seem to apply to them?

Life in the City

On warm evenings, the residents come out of their oppressive apartments to sit on the front steps. Children play ball in the street or splash in front of open fire hydrants. Neighbors chat about work and politics and other things neighbors share. In another neighborhood in the city, a professional couple has cocktails with friends from work in their renovated, air-conditioned Victorian home. In a nearby suburb, families return from sports practices, mow their lawns, and prepare dinner. Political, economic, and cultural factors help shape these different scenarios in the inner city and its surrounding area, as described by urban residential patterns and suburbanization.

Urban Residential Patterns. Some neighborhoods in cities, especially in ethnic immigrant concentrations, are close-knit. This is especially true when members of extended families live in the same area and provide support for one another. In major cities around the world, ethnic enclaves offer security, familiarity, and protection. For new migrants to cities, neighborhoods provide a place to gradually adapt to a strange new society and the dominant group. Immigrant groups often attempt to re-create their former, more intimate village-type settings within their urban neighborhood (Gans 1962). Ethnic communities can provide job opportunities and gradual acculturation into language and customs.

Supportive ethnic enclaves also exist in some U.S. African American inner-city neighborhoods of predominantly single mothers and children. In some neighborhoods, women create support networks—sustaining each other through sharing child care and resources (Stack 1998). However, in some low-income tenement areas, high turnover of residents and fear lead to little interaction (Renzetti 2003, Woldoff 2011). Let us look at some of the variables that affect how people experience city life.

Human Relationships in Cities. Does urban life affect people's thoughts and behavior? Sociologist Georg Simmel argued that two factors—the intensity and stimulation of city life and the economic effects on urban relations—cause people to have different attitudes, beliefs, and values from those in rural areas (Simmel [1902–1917]

1950). He thought that city dwellers have no choice but to be somewhat insensitive, to avoid intense relationships, and to keep most social relationships superficial to protect their privacy. However, he did not feel this was necessarily negative. Cities free people from the social constraints of close relationships in small towns. To visitors or strangers to city life, these behaviors seem callous and cold. However, they offer anonymity and freedom in a crowded environment (Goffman [1959] 2001).

Because urban residents live in heterogeneous, high-density areas, they seem to develop coping mechanisms for dealing with the people around them (Wirth 1964). They become removed from others to insulate themselves from too many personal claims and expectations of others. The depersonalization that results from lower commitment to a common community "goal" also leads to a higher tolerance for nonconformity in cities, resulting in more individual freedom—and, as a result, a higher level of deviance (Wirth 1964).

Urbanism also promotes diverse subcultures, and as people seek community this may encourage intimate social circles with an in-group of people with common

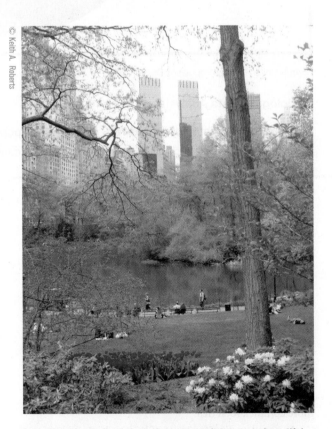
© Keith A. Roberts

In many cities today, urban planners work to create beautiful and environmentally and recreationally friendly environments. This scene in Central Park, New York City exists because urban planners had the foresight to put in several sizable parks.

interests rather than many superficial relationships. The larger numbers of people in cities make it possible for individuals with similar interests—from ethnic subcultures to gay communities to artist groups—to draw together as clubs, organizations, or neighborhoods. These little social worlds "touch but do not interpenetrate" according to Claude Fischer (1984:37). As long as there are enough members of a group, each can maintain its own identity. So rather than creating isolated individuals who interact defensively with others, urban life may create choices about lifestyle and enhance a different kind of community base, intensifying the interactions.

Despite these benefits of urban life in countries where cities have substantial resources to provide services, urbanization can have very different consequences in poor regions of the world. As noted earlier, rapidly growing cities in impoverished countries often face challenges to provide basic services—shelter, water, electricity, sanitation, schools, health care—for the increasing numbers of residents. Approximately one billion people live in urban slums in Global South cities (World Bank 2013a).

Thinking Sociologically

What do you see as the most important impact(s) on individuals or groups living in urban areas?

HOW DID CITIES EVOLVE? MESO-LEVEL ORGANIZATIONAL STRUCTURES

Human settlements have gone through massive transitions over the past 100,000 years, from small agricultural settlements to bustling crowded metropolises with millions of people. The first step toward the development of urban life came when those living nomadic lives became more settled. Archaeological evidence indicates that the earliest settlements were in the Middle East and North Africa, most probably in Oman about 125,000 years ago, as human nomads followed rivers into Arabia to Wadi Aybut in Dhofar (Southern Oman) (Global Arab Network 2010). Other early settlements have been excavated in Ethiopia, Morocco, United Arab Emirates, South Africa, Pakistan, and Israel. Starting about 10,000 years ago, with the advent of agriculture, domestication of animals, and the shift from food gathering to food production, small groups established permanent settlements. Among the first was Eridu in Iraq, a settlement of some 25 permanent compounds with a population of up to 200 in each compound and a grain storage facility in the center (see Figure 15.12).

FIGURE 15.12   Cities in Antiquity

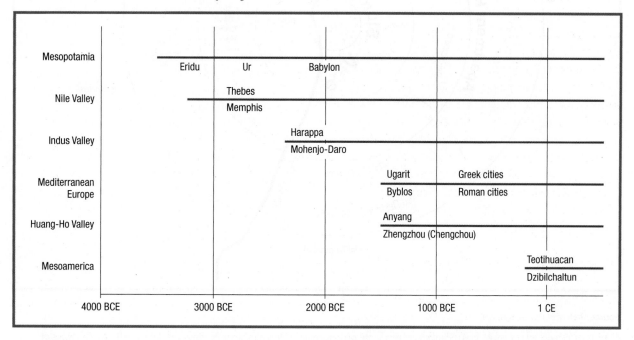

Source: Sjoberg (1965:56–57).

The people grew wheat and barley and domesticated dogs, goats, and sheep.

These settlements were not cities as we think of them today, however, because they had different cultural and economic structures, and there was little division of labor. Everyone shared roles, worked the land to support the population, and banded together for protection. Cities, in contrast, are large permanent settlements with nonagricultural specialists, a literate elite, and surplus food to support the social classes not involved in food production. They have been the source of intense fascination for many social science theorists. The next "Sociology Around the World" explores a very ancient and highly sophisticated city in the Middle East.

Theories of Urban Development

Urban scholars who studied problems in the city of Chicago were among the first sociologists in the United States. Referred to as the Chicago School, their studies of urban ecology focused on the patterns of land use and residential distribution of people in urban areas. These theorists pictured the city's growth pattern as a series of circles. Moving out from the center, each circle was dominated by a particular type of activity and residential pattern, from central city ghettoes and rooming houses to working-class apartments and bungalows, to middle-class housing, to upper-class suburbs (Park, Burgess, and McKenzie [1925] 1967). See Figure 15.13 for an illustration of this pattern.

FIGURE 15.13 Burgess's Theory of City Growth

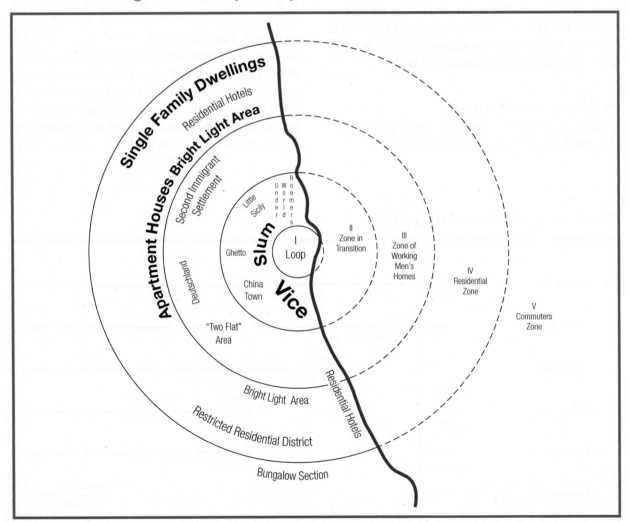

Source: Park et al. ([1925] 1967:55).

Note: The Chicago School envisioned urban growth as a series of concentric circles, with ethnicity, class, residential patterns, and types of activity evolving with each ring removed from the central city.

Sociology Around the World

Evolution of Early Cities: The Nabateans and Petra

By Ossama Zyoud

The Nabatean culture provides an example of the early development of urban areas. Once a nomadic Bedouin tribe, they migrated from the southern parts of Arabia (Middle East) around the year 600 BC to what became Petra, meaning "the cleft in the rock" (now located in the south of Jordan). When they began to settle down, the Nabateans started as cave and tent dwellers, living in primitive conditions; however, within 200 years they had developed a large city and were able to control all the trade routes across the Arabian peninsula.

Before settling in Petra, Nabateans attacked Egyptian caravans to get food and money. Gradually they started to offer (for a fee) basic services like food, water, and safe passage along the caravan trade routes that went through their territories. As more caravans passed, transporting precious items like frankincense, Chinese silk, and Indian spices to distant lands in Europe and Africa, the Nabateans gained power and gradually controlled more territory across Arabia. During the peak of the Nabatean civilization, their kingdom covered modern Jordan and parts of modern Saudi Arabia, Syria, and Lebanon. The king of the Nabateans sent ambassadors to the largest cities on the trading route to promote the main caravan stop that became the city of Petra.

Three factors determined the location for Petra, the large settlement that became the capital city of the Nabateans: location, protection, and water. The location was on the main caravan route near the Mediterranean Sea to the west, Bosra and Damascus in Syria to the north, Aqaba and Leuce Come on the Red Sea to the south, and the Arab Gulf across the desert. Protection was provided by the location of the city of Petra. It was easy to defend because it was surrounded by steep hills and the entrance was a narrow passage between high rocks. The hilly area of sandstone formations and natural caves, and a natural gorge that rises for almost 100 meters into the sky, offered safety and security for the caravans and encouraged them to pass by Petra. Rainwater was collected from a sophisticated system of channels carved by the Nabateans to take water to dams and other storage facilities.

The city was designed in two main parts: the residential area and the cemetery. Archaeologists are still excavating residential areas of the city, many of which were damaged in the 2nd century CE

Creative Commons Attribution-Share Alike 3.0.

The heyday of Petra under the rule of the Nabateans ended in 106 CE when Roman Empire Governor Cornelius Palma of Syria took over. Although the Nabatean dynasty came to an end, the city of Petra continued to flourish under the new Roman inhabitants. Today this early city is a UNESCO World Heritage site open to visitors and researchers alike.

(Continued)

(Continued)

when the Romans invaded. The upper part of the city with most of their tombs shows the greatness of Nabatean architecture and art. Because the Nabateans were nomadic Bedouins, they did not have architectural heritage, but borrowed ideas from neighboring civilizations to carve their stunning facades. Their ambassadors to the other urban centers and their caravan guests inspired them to carve some of the most unique facades in the area, mixing Greek, Roman, Mesopotamian, and Egyptian architectural styles together as is seen in most of the facades still standing in Petra today.

• •

Ossama Zyoud is an archaeologist from Jordan who worked on the excavations of the city of Petra as a member of Queen Rania Institute of Tourism and Heritage and Brown University at Petra.

Urban ecologists further refined the Chicago School's original ideas by exploring social, economic, political, and technological systems of cities' spatial patterns (Abu-Lughod 1991). Several processes constantly take place in urban areas: residential segregation; invasion by a new ethnic, religious, or socioeconomic group; and successive movement by that group. These processes are part of dynamic city life (Berry and Kasarda 1977).

Racial and ethnic segregation is a continuing and troubling issue in many urban areas of the United States. Despite some reductions in racism in the nation, U.S. cities—especially northern cities—have high levels of residential segregation. This segregation affects individual networking, school composition, and access to community resources. The next "Engaging Sociology" examines the likelihood that someone of a given race will have contacts in his or her neighborhood that cross racial lines. This figure is based on one city—Chicago, Illinois—but you can easily check the residential patterns in your city by going to www.censusscope.org/segregation.html.

Any effective solution to urban problems must address inequalities between groups and allocations of resources in urban areas. Some conflict theorists maintain that urban inequality results from the domination of cities by elites, who exploit and displace the poor (Gottdiener and Hutchison 2006). Cities produce profits for those who buy and sell property and for investors and politicians who redevelop urban areas. Sometimes, redevelopment pushes poor urban residents out of their neighborhoods, so there are winners and losers in the process.

Types of Cities

Although organizational structures of cities have changed and evolved over time, in the following section we focus on industrial and postindustrial cities.

Industrial Cities. The onset of industrialization in 17th- and 18th-century Europe started the trend toward urbanized nations, countries in which more than half of the population lives in urban areas. Rural peasants migrated to the cities in search of opportunities and to escape the tedium and poverty of agricultural existence and shortage of available farmland. The rapid influx of migrants often resulted in an unplanned urbanization process. Crowded conditions, poor sanitation, polluted water supplies, and poor working conditions all contributed to the misery of poor urban residents and to their short life expectancy compared with those living in the countryside.

Industrial cities became primarily commercial centers motivated by competition, a characteristic that differentiated them from preindustrial cities. The advent of power-driven machinery and the new capitalist factory system transformed and replaced the former craft and cottage industries and guild structures (Abu-Lughod 1991). Roads, waterways, and railroads made travel and communication between towns and cities easier and faster.

Around 1870, Great Britain became the first truly urban nation with more than 50% of the population living in urban areas. Economically changing conditions in the British Isles were conducive to urbanization and industrialization. Parliament had passed "enclosure acts" that enclosed common land people used for growing crops, fishing, and other means to make a living, pushing many rural citizens from the countryside to cities. In addition, raw materials from colonies; new technology for manufacturing; and financing for industry were all falling into place (Benevolo 1995; Mumford 1961).

ENGAGING SOCIOLOGY

Residential Segregation and Cross-Race Contact

The bar graph in Figure 15.14 illustrates typical contact of most residents with members of their own and other races in a metropolitan area. The Census Bureau creates *exposure indices* by calculating the average racial and ethnic composition of neighborhoods. In this graph, the first five columns represent the average neighborhood racial composition of a person of a given race. The far right column shows the racial composition of the metropolitan area as a whole. Study the line graphs and answer the following questions.

Interpreting Sociological Data

1. How likely are whites to experience diversity in their neighborhoods? How do the diversity levels

where most whites live compare with diversity of the city as a whole?

2. Which group experiences the most diversity and is likely to have more opportunities to encounter people from other racial groups?

3. Which groups experience the most segregation?

4. What might be some consequences of living in racially homogeneous neighborhoods? Which group might experience more negative consequences because of the homogeneity? Why?

5. Go to www.censusscope.org/segregation.html and enter a city near you to see the exposure indices for various racial groups in that city. What do you conclude?

FIGURE 15.14   **Exposure Indices for Race and Ethnic Groups: Chicago**

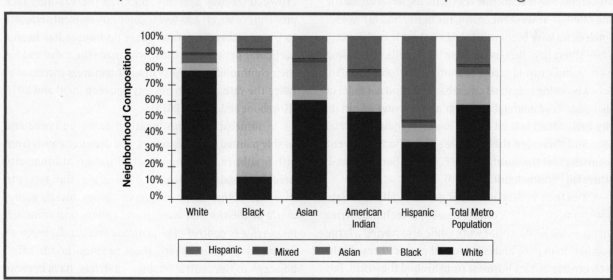

Source: Residential Segregation and Cross-Race, Chicago, Illinois. www.censusscope.org/segregation.html.

In the late 19th century in the United States, an increase in agricultural productivity aided urban growth. Fewer

farms began to produce much more food than ever before and the development of roads, trains, and other efficient means of transportation allowed farmers to efficiently move their produce to a growing urban population.

Suburbs also began to develop during this time period. With the advent of public transportation in the late 1800s and early 1900s, some city dwellers began to move to the outskirts of cities and beyond, to escape crowded city conditions. Private automobiles and telephones aided movement to the suburbs. Road systems were developed to accommodate the growing numbers of autos, and more businesses and services relocated to suburban areas.

Postindustrial Cities. Postindustrial cities have a high percentage of employees in the service sector—business headquarters, government and intergovernmental organizations, research and development, tourism, finance, health, education, and telecommunications (Bell [1976] 1999). They are primarily found in the most technologically advanced, wealthy nations. Washington, D.C., fits most of these characteristics, as does La Défense, an urban center on the outskirts of Paris, built as a commercial, service, and information exchange center to serve France.

Postindustrial cities are closely tied to the economic structures of capitalism, with global production systems and instant exchanges of information (Abu-Lughod 2001; Friedman 2005). In the transformation from industrial to postindustrial economies, from manufacturing to service economies, some people get left behind, and some cities get left behind. Major economic restructuring has changed the fate of cities around the world, for better and for worse. Some cities have become international centers of finance, while others have become hollowed-out shells, after losing their manufacturing base. For example, Detroit, Michigan, once a booming industrial city, is bankrupt and has miles of abandoned commercial buildings and housing within its city limits. Rust belt cities that have lost their industrial base and therefore their tax base struggle to reinvent themselves for the postindustrial economy. Some succeed; others fail ("Rustbelt Britain" 2013).

Cities such as Bengaluru (Bangalore), India, illustrate how some cities can contain new high-tech industries that provide white-collar work while also having a large population of poor and uneducated people. These high-tech centers attract business from around the world. For example, this book would have been typeset in the United States a few years ago, but with the competitive publication market, publishers find it economically prudent to outsource to India and save on costs.

Some urban areas are carefully planned. *New towns*, cities built in previously undeveloped areas as economically self-sufficient entities, provide all the needed urban amenities. Urban planners believe that these cities can relieve the congestion of urban areas, provide new economic bases and residences near jobs, and solve many problems faced by older cities. Some new towns have been success stories: Columbia, Maryland; Brasília, Brazil (the relatively new capital); and Canberra, Australia. *Transition towns* are a recent movement featuring locally grown food, community-owned power and water sources, and even local currencies (Flintoff 2013). However, these experiments require certain conditions and are difficult in many places. Consider cities around the world that experience influxes of poor migrants who squat (set up shelter) in any location available—abandoned buildings, cemetery mausoleums, hillsides surrounding cities. The next "Sociology Around the World" discusses archeological research indicating that large planned cities existed in North America before white Europeans even knew the continent existed.

As cities became overcrowded, people moved to the suburbs. Manufacturing firms, services, commerce, and retail trade followed (Clapson 2003; Gans 1982). The movement of economic activities formerly located in cities removes an economic base of cities. These internal migrations lock cities and suburbs into competition over jobs and tax revenues. When this happens, farmland and open lands disappear; energy and water demands increase, often straining public utilities; and sprawl leads to vast, crowded freeway systems. Suburbs increasingly face problems of poverty, as low-income city residents relocate to them. Recently, foreclosures on houses has been a particular problem for those who made the move and for their communities. Poverty in suburban areas increased at twice the rate of urban poverty between 2000 and 2011 (Kneebone and Berube 2013).

In some urban areas, neatly manicured lawns and freshly painted exteriors reflect new directions away from either suburbanization or deterioration of inner-city neighborhoods. The process of **gentrification** refers to *members of the middle and upper classes, mostly young white professionals, buying and renovating rundown properties in central-city locations and displacing poor residents*. In recent years, these neighborhoods, often adjacent to the central business districts, have become fashionable residential areas. For example, many neighborhoods in Washington, D.C., and Brooklyn have become gentrified—some to the point that relatively few people can now afford to live in certain neighborhoods (like Capitol Hill in Washington, D.C., and Williamsburg in Brooklyn). Walkability—the ability to walk to most "hot spots" in the city and dispense with owning a car—has

Sociology Around the World

City Planning in Prehistoric Central America: Teotihuacan

Teotihuacan, ancient city of pyramids, was a Mesoamerican city (located about 30 miles northeast of modern-day Mexico City) created by a society that had no metal tools, had not invented the wheel, and had no pack animals. At its height, between the 3rd and 6th century BCE about 2,100 years ago, Teotihuacan covered 8 square miles (20 square kilometers), which made it larger than imperial Rome (Jarus 2012). Its central religious monument, the Temple of the Sun, was as broad at its base as the great pyramid of Cheops in Egypt. Its population may have reached 100,000.

Strategically located astride a valley that was the gateway to the lowlands of Mexico, Teotihuacan flourished for over 500 years as a great urban commercial center. Yet it was more than a large city. It was the mecca of the New World, a religious and cultural capital that probably housed pilgrims from as far away as Guatemala. Perhaps most startling, Teotihuacan was a totally planned city. Those who designed the city laid out its two great pyramids, citadel, hundreds of lesser religious structures, and 4,000 other dwellings according to an exact design. They organized streets (and many of its buildings) on a perfect grid aligned with the city center. They even changed the shape of the river that divided the city to fit the grid pattern.

Planning for the construction of Teotihuacan's major temples must have been an incredible undertaking.

The Temple of the Sun, for instance, rises to a height of 215 feet and has a base of 725 square feet. These dimensions mean that it took about 1 million tons of sunbaked mud bricks to build the temple. When the Spaniards conquered Mexico in the 16th century, they were amazed to find Teotihuacan's ruined temples. Local inhabitants claimed that the temples had been built by giants. They showed the Spaniards the bones of giant elephants (which had lived there in prehistoric times) to prove their point.

Small buildings as well as large ones were cleverly conceived in Teotihuacan. Houses were apparently planned for maximum space and privacy. Apartments were constructed around central patios, with each patio designed to give dwellers light and air, as well as an efficient drainage system. In a Teotihuacan housing complex, a person could indeed live in relative comfort (Jarus 2012; Jordan-Bychkov and Domoch 1998).

become a primary standard for many young urbanites (Palmer 2012). This gentrification brings consumers and a tax base to the city.

For those low-income people who move because of rising costs, many are pushed into less attractive parts of town with fewer services and recreational areas, and often pay higher rents for less adequate housing. Alternative housing for displaced residents may be difficult to find, contributing to problems of homelessness. Conflict theorists view gentrification and other urban developments that favor the wealthy and displace or exclude the poor as exploitation by real estate capitalists.

In contrast, others argue that wealthy residents who choose the lifestyle of the city over suburbia help support viable, livable cities, bringing in an additional tax base.

Thinking Sociologically

What are some positive and negative aspects of gentrification for individuals and cities? Explain.

Megacities. As we look at Earth from space, some areas glow as depicted in the recent Oscar-winning film, *Gravity*. These glowing cities and their surrounding metropolitan areas of 10 million or more residents, called megacities, dot the globe. In the 1950s, the New York City metropolitan area (which comprises 30 counties, including cities and towns in the states of New York, New Jersey, Connecticut, and Pennsylvania) was the only place in the world that had 10 million people. At that time, there were 75 cities in the world with 1 to 5 million residents, mostly in the Global North. Table 15.3 shows the rapid change in this pattern with the 10 largest population centers in 2014. New York City now ranks eighth, as cities in the Global South move up in population; just three years ago, New York was ranked third largest city in the world.

As the world becomes more congested and cities continue to attract residents, cities start to merge or to become continuous urban areas without rural areas between them. Those who have driven from Boston to Washington, D.C., an area sometimes called BosWash, know the meaning of *megalopolis*, a spatial merging of two or more cities along major transportation corridors (Brunn et al. 2011).

THE URBAN ENVIRONMENT AND SOCIAL POLICY: MACRO-LEVEL PERSPECTIVES

The mountains rise from the sea, dotted with pastel-colored shanties. On the drive from the port city of La Guaira up into the mountains to the capital city of Caracas, Venezuela, one sees settlements nestled into the hillsides. The poor, who have come from the country to find opportunities in the capital, make shelters in the hills surrounding Caracas, often living with no running water, electricity, or sewage disposal. The laundry list of urban problems facing governments is overwhelming: excessive size and overcrowding; shortages of services, education, and health care; slums and squatters; traffic congestion; unemployment; and effects of global restructuring, including loss of agricultural land, environmental degradation, and resettlement of immigrants and refugees (Brunn, Williams, and Zeigler 2003). This section considers several of the many

Table 15.3   The 10 Largest Population Centers (population in millions)

2014 Rank	Urban Center	Population
1	Tokyo, Japan	37,126
2	Jakarta, Indonesia	26,063
3	Seoul, South Korea	22,547
4	Delhi, India	22,242
5	Shanghai, China	20,860
6	Manila, Philippines	20,767
7	Karachi, Pakistan	20,711
8	New York City, USA	20,464
9	São Paulo, Brazil	20,186
1	Mexico City	19,463

Source: Worldatlas (2014).

problems mentioned earlier in the chapter and now facing urban areas such as Caracas.

Rural Migrants and Overcrowding

In Cairo, Egypt, a huge, sprawling graveyard full of large mausoleums, the City of the Dead, has become home to thousands of families transplanted from rural areas. Cities in India such as Chennai (the former colonial name was Madras), Mumbai (Bombay), and Kolkata (Calcutta) have thousands of homeless migrants living on the sidewalks, on highway medians, and in river channels that flood during the rainy season.

Overcrowding exists in cities throughout the world but causes special problems in the Global South, when rural residents seek opportunities in urban areas. Poor migrants set up shacks of any material available—tin, cardboard, leaves, mud, and sticks—in settlements known as *barriadas* in Spanish, *shantytowns* in English, *bidonvilles* in French, *favelas* in Portuguese-speaking Brazil, and *bustees* in India. The majority of migrants to the city are young. They are pulled to the city in hopes of finding jobs and often have been pushed from the rural areas because of limited land on which to farm and too many mouths to feed.

As we have seen over the past three decades, the urban populations in Africa, Asia, and Latin America have grown rapidly, and many of the largest cities in the world are now in the Global South. Rural-to-urban migration and development of megacities dominate the economic and political discussions in many countries. The newcomers spill out into the countryside, engulfing towns along the way. Refer to Figure 15.10 for trends from 1950 to 2012 and projections through 2050, and Figure 15.11 for the population living in urban areas by more and less developed regions of the world (United Nations Population Division 2014).

Most Global South countries have little time or money to prepare infrastructures and provide services for the rapidly increasing numbers of urban residents. Technological development, job opportunities, and basic services have not kept up with the large migrations of would-be laborers. Lack of basic services has become a major problem, resulting in contagious diseases that can cause deadly epidemics due to lack of services and poor sanitary conditions. The next "Sociology in Our Social World" on page 528 describes one plague that ravaged much of Europe.

Crime and Delinquency in the City

In many cities across the globe, crime is a serious issue, particularly among those experiencing large influxes of

With few places to live, rural migrants to Egypt's largest city, Cairo, find shelter in the large ancient mausoleums in the burial grounds of the "City of the Dead."

rural residents and immigrants. When people are transient, when they move frequently, they tend to experience *anomie*. They have less commitment to community norms and the well-being of the local community. Add to that the desperate situation of the very poor, and you have a recipe for crime.

In rural communities and tribal cultures, strict norms govern behavior, but in urban areas, cohesiveness of families and ties with tribal groups are lessened. Thus crime is more likely to occur in urban settings with fewer social ties that foster conformity to norms. Policy makers need to address ways to build community and connections among urban dwellers, particularly for recent migrants from rural areas. When education, economic security, and social services increase, conformity again becomes a norm for these newcomers, replacing the sense of anomie experienced during the transition.

The study of urbanization teaches us that the social environment influences people's lives. Public sociologists can play a role in improving the conditions of urban areas, as described in the next "Sociologists in Action" on page 529.

Urban Planning for Structures That Meet Human Needs

Ideal city planning is quite a task. City planners must meet citizens' needs for housing, sanitation, education, food distribution, jobs, family life, and recreation. The problem is that most urban planners do not have the luxury of starting from scratch. They must work with decaying

sociology in our social world

"Ring Around the Rosey" and the Plague

Ring around the Rosey, Pockets full of posies, Ashes, Ashes, We all fall down!

Remember this nursery school rhyme? You probably did not understand the meaning of the rhyme as a child. It refers to the bubonic plague, which ravaged England and Europe in the early to mid-1600s, leaving dead and dying people in its wake. People infected with the plague developed red circular sores that released an unpleasant odor. People placed flowers (posies) in their pockets or on their bodies to cover up the smell. Because people were dying so rapidly, it was difficult to keep up with burials, and families or officials burned the dead to reduce the spread of the disease (ashes, ashes). So many people were sick and dying that "we all fall down." Although there are variations on this story, it is probably true that the rhyme was related to a major plague in London (Snopes.com 2007).

From 1603 to 1849, the clergy had the task of recording the deaths, the burials, and the cause of deaths that occurred. These records were circulated weekly, with a summary put out before Christmas. This process is one of the earliest records of vital statistics. In 1662, John Graunt from London published mortality records beginning from 1603 for the first known statistical analysis of demographic data. Among his findings was that "for every 100 people born in London, only 16 were still alive at age 36 and only 3 at age 66" (Stephan n.d.; Weeks 2012:73). The plague had an impact on social relationships, too. Many citizens avoided anyone who was a stranger, and some who contracted the disease died miserable lonely deaths because of others' fears of the disease.

As the Industrial Revolution advanced, so did income, housing, sanitation, and nutrition in London. All these improvements in people's lives reduced the incidence of plague and increased life expectancy. Modern plagues, such as avian influenza (bird flu) and severe acute respiratory syndrome (SARS), have claimed hundreds of lives this decade, but both have had a significantly smaller impact than the bubonic plague. The World Health Organization is monitoring bird flu and SARS throughout the world to ensure the effects never reach the tragic levels of the bubonic plague.

areas, being cognizant of meaningful landmarks and treasured sites. Planners may also have to undo mistaken or inadequate planning by previous administrations.

Leaders in some U.S. cities have begun to take more active roles on issues related to demographic and economic changes. For example, New York City has invested in diversifying the city's economy by recruiting a top-level university (Cornell) to develop a new high-tech graduate school. It is also creating an applied science district that will bring in new companies, new jobs, and tax revenues for the city. Building on its expertise in high tech and sustainability, Portland, Oregon, has created a "We Build Green Cities" marketing campaign to promote its clean tech companies, and created partnerships in other nations to expand the market for these companies (Katz and Bradley 2013).

Pandemics

SOCIOLOGISTS IN ACTION:
JAY WEINSTEIN

Improving Quality of Life by Transforming Community Structure

As is true of many urban centers, Detroit, Michigan, has its share of distressed neighborhoods. Dr. Jay Weinstein has been director of an interdisciplinary team attempting to bring about economic, social, and physical restructuring of some of these areas. By developing long-term relationships in several urban neighborhoods, the team has had success working with residents and others to improve conditions. Weinstein calls this approach *relationship brokering*—bringing people together to share perspectives and to clear up misperceptions between residents, local officials, service providers, and police. These efforts have helped empower residents to take action and improve their neighborhoods.

A major project along these lines, which began in 1990, is in the Detroit suburb of Taylor. For decades, residents of Taylor and the surrounding Down River area were painfully aware of the problems of their neighborhood, known by uncomplimentary names such as "Crack Ridge," "Hooker Heaven," and "Sin City." With about 7,500 people packed into one-half square mile, most residents lived in rental units controlled by the U.S. Department of Housing and Urban Development Section 8 program (subsidized private housing). An influential local newspaper published a series of articles showing that the neighborhood had earned the labels applied to it. The articles inspired local and federal political leaders to demand action. Weinstein and his colleagues were awarded a research grant by the City of Taylor Department of Community Development to assess the problems and make recommendations to improve the

community. The fact-finding stage revealed that the residents of the neighborhood were not the main perpetrators. Instead, the area had been under siege by nonresidents who came and went, drifting from apartment to apartment, or illegally occupying residences after threatening to harm the rightful owners.

The research team recommended a plan for a thorough physical, economic, social, and political reconstruction of the neighborhood. City and federal officials accepted the recommendations of the sociological team and set out on a 10-year program of implementation. Working with residents of the neighborhood and other citizens of the city, Taylor's mayor, city council, Department of Human Resources, police department, and many others tackled the problem, with Weinstein and his colleagues' help.

Today, the neighborhood has a new name (The Villages of Taylor), a new human services center, a new residential owner (a private nonprofit corporation established by the city), and many new or redesigned buildings. The population density has been reduced by more than 20%, without one person, other than drug dealers, displaced against his or her will. The average median income of Taylor now exceeds the national average. Former Secretary of Housing and Urban Development Shaun Donovan called Taylor "a model for the nation."

During his work in the Taylor neighborhood, Weinstein used triangulation (multiple methods of data collection), utilizing surveys, participant observation, census data, and other large data sets. He also used a symbolic interactionist approach to learn how residents view the community and how it operates. With this understanding of how their

(Continued)

(Continued)

neighborhood functions, residents and community leaders were able to transform their neighborhood.

• •

Dr. Jay Weinstein, professor emeritus at Eastern Michigan University, specializes in urban sociology, *demography, and social change. He has been a private consultant for more than 20 years, with contracts from international and local governments and nonprofit organizations. His studies have included analysis of demographic trends and changes in India, Albania, Bulgaria, and Jamaica.*

A number of global trends affect urban planning today (Brunn et al. 2011):

1. The process of urbanization—people migrating to cities—will continue, exacerbating the already difficult situation of providing services for people in the world's crowded urban areas.

2. Information and transportation technologies allow people in any part of the globe to be in contact. However, this may also reduce the feelings of belonging to a specific place, thus reducing commitment to work on city problems.

3. International boundaries diminish in importance as the flow of information, goods, services, labor, and capital increasingly ignores national boundaries. For example, migration of Asians to cities around the world will continue and will have an impact on these cities.

4. Economies will increasingly rely on brain work, including invention of new technologies, and high-tech manufacturing. Thus, the gap between haves and have-nots is likely to continue.

5. Conflicts between cultural and political groups, including religious and political extremists (as described in previous chapters) will impact urban life.

6. McDonaldization—the creation of a consumer world dominated by American food, music, fashion, and entertainment—will continue, even as we see an increasing diversity of people within the United States (Ritzer 2013b).

Awareness of these trends can help urban planners in their efforts to design cities to meet the needs of the future. Some analysts also believe that women have unique needs in the city that must be addressed by urban planners. For example, urban spaces designed with women in mind emphasize public spaces designed for safety, opportunities for participation, involvement in community development, and leisure activities such as informal places for meeting (Hayden and Baron 2007; UNESCO 2009; UN Habitat 2012).

Whether demographers, political leaders, and urban planners can keep up with the demands for even basic services in the Global South remains to be seen. This is especially true in areas of the world where poor rural people flock to cities for survival. This basic population pattern—urbanization—has consequences at the most global levels and at the most micro levels of human life. Our social world model—which looks at the connections of micro, meso, and macro levels of the social system—makes us cognizant of the consequences of decisions made by millions of individuals and families. It also makes us mindful of the consequences of global trends and forces for individuals and for cities.

Thinking Sociologically

Try planning an ideal city. First, list everything you need to consider, such as how big the city should be. Now think of organization: Who will handle what? Keep in mind services, maintenance, financing, and leadership.

Intersection of Demographic and Environmental Policy

Ecosystems—streams, rivers, inland and coastal wetlands, grasslands, and forests—provide critical resources and services that sustain human health and well-being (EcoSummit 2012). Yet our ecosystems are under stress, much of it caused by human activity. Extinction of species, lack of water and water pollution, resource exploitation, collapse of some global fisheries, and new diseases are the results of this breakdown. Major storms such as Typhoon Haiyan in the Philippines and infestations such as the southern pine beetle in the New Jersey Pine Barrens have been determined by scientists to be a result of global warming (Bradsher 2013; Gillis 2013). As scientists in the Royal Society make clear:

The combination of increasing global population and increasing overall material consumption has implications for a finite planet. As both continue to rise,

Urban Planning ▶   Pollution 🖥

signs of unwanted impacts and feedback (climate change reducing crop yields and irreversible changes such as species extinction) are growing alarmingly . . . Demographic change is driven by economic development, social and cultural factors as well as environmental change. (Royal Society 2012)

Additional infrastructure problems threaten to immobilize cities in the Global South. Traffic congestion and pollution are so intense in some cities that the slow movement of people and goods reduces productivity, jobs, health, and vital services. Pollution of the streets and air are chronic problems, especially with expansion of automobile use around the world. One scientific report in 2013 made the urgency of the issue very clear:

Warming of the climate system is unequivocal, and since the 1950s, many of the observed changes are unprecedented over decades to millennia. The atmosphere and ocean have warmed, the amounts of snow and ice have diminished, sea level has risen, and the concentrations of greenhouse gases have increased . . . Continued emissions of greenhouse gases will cause further warming and changes in all components of the climate system. Limiting climate change will require substantial and sustained reductions of greenhouse gas emissions. (Intergovernmental Panel on Climate Change 2013a:3, 14)

Older cities face deteriorating infrastructures, with water, gas, and sewage lines in need of replacement. In regions of China, parents confine their children to their homes, in order to keep them from breathing the outside air. In Beijing and other Chinese cities, the air has 40 times the

In 2013, air pollution was so thick in Beijing that people wore masks and entrepreneurs sold cans of fresh air for people to breathe.

pollutants deemed safe to breathe (Wong 2013a). In Global South countries, concern for these problems has brought some action and relief, but in impoverished countries where survival issues are pressing, environmental contamination is a low priority. Thus, the worst air pollution is now found in major cities in the Global South, such as Mexico City, São Paulo, and several Chinese cities, including Beijing.

In order to improve the Earth's ecosystems, we must rebalance consumption between the Global North and Global South; stabilize population growth, especially in Global South countries; bring those in extreme poverty (those who live on $1.25 or less per day) out of this condition; develop plans for urban growth; provide access to reproductive health and family planning; and adopt plans to reduce overall human consumption (Royal Society 2012). In order to increase the health of cities, we must also address urban crime. Rapidly growing cities can become hotbeds of deviance and crime.

Many factors, including population dynamics and urbanization, create change in a society. Some factors contributing to social dynamics push for innovation and change in a particular direction, and other factors retard change. The next chapter examines the larger picture of social transformation and change in our complex and multileveled social world.

WHAT HAVE WE LEARNED?

Population trends, including migration resulting in urbanization, provide a dynamic force for change in societies. Whether one is interested in understanding social problems, social policy, or factors that may affect one's own career, it is helpful to understand demographic processes. We ignore them at our peril—as individuals and as a society. If we overlook demographic patterns, family businesses can be destroyed, retirement plans obliterated, and the health of our communities sabotaged. Awareness of such patterns can enhance planning that leads to prosperity and enjoyment of our communities. Urban living creates problems, but it can have enormous benefits as well.

KEY POINTS

- Population analysis (called demography) looks at the composition, distribution, and size of a population and how variables of fertility, mortality, and migration impact society. (See pp. 492–494.)

- The population of the world has increased dramatically since industrialization. Its implications for society can be viewed in population pyramids. (See pp. 494–499.)

- Various theories explain the causes and repercussions of rapid population growth. (See pp. 500–503.)

- Many institutions affect and are affected by fertility and mortality rates at the meso level—government, religion, the economy, education, and health care. (See pp. 503–507.)

- Migration is also an important issue for society— whether the migration is international or internal—for it can change the size, distribution, and composition of a nation's citizenry. (See pp. 507–510.)

- Population patterns can also affect individual decisions at the micro level, from career choices to business decisions to retirement plans. (See pp. 510–513.)

- A major element of population migration has been urbanization. As populations become more densely concentrated, this creates a series of opportunities and problems for meeting human needs. (See pp. 513–515.)

- At the micro level, widespread or dense population concentration impacts relationships among people. In urban areas, social relations may be less closely knit, factors that can create anomie. On the positive side, it provides more choices for people as to their social relationships and lifestyles. (See pp. 515–519.)

- At the macro level, urban environments must be understood as ecosystems that have dense poverty and homelessness, major pollution issues, and higher crime rates. These are the focus of urban planners, who try to use sociological knowledge to plan for a better future. (See pp. 526–531.)

DISCUSSION QUESTIONS

1. Why is it important for policy makers to understand demographic trends in their communities and nation? Why should *you* be interested in such knowledge? How might it impact your understanding of and positions on issues related to (a) immigration, (b) education, (c) health care, and (d) Social Security legislation?

2. How many children (if any) do you think you would (ideally) like to have? Why? What might make this (ideal) number change?

3. What are some examples of (a) pronatalist and (b) antinatalist policies? Do you approve of such policies? Why or why not? How might your perspective differ depending on the demographics of your particular nation?

4. How is the social status of girls and women related to a society's ability to control population growth? If you were a male leader in the government of an overcrowded nation, why and how might you use this information to promote gender equality in your country? How might your ideas be perceived differently, depending on your sex?

5. What are some of the major reasons people leave their country of origin and move to another? Have you ever done so? Why? If not, under what circumstances would you be willing to leave the country in which you were born and move to another?

6. How do your attitudes toward those around you and your behavior differ in rural, suburban, and urban settings? Why?

CONTRIBUTING TO OUR SOCIAL WORLD: *WHAT CAN WE DO?*

At the Local Level

- The *U.S. Census Bureau* is always at work collecting, analyzing, and disseminating demographic information. It is a great source of data, ranging from information on your block to the whole nation. Invite a representative to your campus to discuss the Bureau's activities. You can check internship and job opportunities with the Census at www.census.gov/hrd/www/jobs/student.html.

- Check out your *local department of urban planning, urban and regional development, or community development* by Googling those terms and the name of your town, county, or province. Invite a representative to your campus or visit the department's offices. Discuss how population information is used in planning and service delivery contexts. Consider an internship with one of the organizations you find in your area.

At the Organizational or Institutional Level

- *The Population Association of America (PAA)* "is a non-profit, scientific, professional organization that promotes research on population issues," according to its website. At www.populationassociation.org, you can find information on demographic issues and ways to get involved in efforts to address them.

At the National and Global Levels

- The Population Reference Bureau (www.prb.org/About.aspx) "informs people around the world about population, health, and the environment, and empowers them to use that information to advance the well-being of current and future generations."

- *Planned Parenthood* (www.plannedparenthood.org) promotes family planning education and outreach programs throughout the United States. The International Planned Parenthood Federation (www.ippf.org) works in 180 nations. The organizations use volunteers and interns, as well as providing long-term employment opportunities.

- *World Vision* (www.worldvision.org/?open&lpos=facebook-sponsor_bot_Home) is "a Christian humanitarian organization, dedicated to working with children, families, and their communities worldwide to reach their full potential by tackling the causes of injustice and poverty." The organization provides many ways you can get involved in efforts to alleviate poverty and promote justice around the world.

- *The Population Council* (www.popcouncil.org) promotes family planning in order to reduce poverty, create healthier populations and communities, empower women, and improve lives across the globe. You can find fact sheets and other information at the group's website. You can also look for possible job and internship opportunities at www.popcouncil.org/employment/index.asp.

16 The Process of Change

We Can Make a Difference!

Individuals are profoundly influenced by the macro structures around them, but people are also capable of creating change, especially if they band together with others and approach change in an organized way.

MICRO

● ME (AND MY FAMILY)

● LOCAL ORGANIZATIONS AND COMMUNITY
Unemployment and business scandals cause personal losses.

MESO

● NATIONAL ORGANIZATIONS, INSTITUTIONS, AND ETHNIC SUBCULTURES
Family instability contributes to wobble and flux—that is, change—in other institutions and increases in delinquency rates.

MACRO

● SOCIETY
National government policies about trade, war, or immigration may cause change in families, the economy, or international relationships.

● GLOBAL COMMUNITY
World Bank loans or United Nations poverty programs may result in change for poor nations and stimulate international trade.

IN THIS CHAPTER

THINK ABOUT IT

Micro: Local Community	What do you think needs to change in your community?
Meso: National Institutions, Complex Organizations, and Ethnic Groups	How do complex organizations or ethnic groups enhance, hamper, or shape social change?
Macro: National and Global Community	How does training and support from national governments for technological innovation affect the process of change in your country and in the world?

Our planet is in peril, according to evidence from the Asian subcontinent to the Arctic and from Africa to the Americas (Tollefson 2012). Seven hundred and seventy-two scientists from around the world have signed on to the statement that "the world is not ready for the impacts of climate change, including more extreme weather and the likelihood that populated parts of the planet could be rendered uninhabitable" (Intergovernmental Panel on Climate Change [IPCC] 2014). The evidence presented by the IPCC depicts a dire future with extreme weather events.

A major factor in climate change is the waste humans create. Wet, dry, smelly, and sometimes recyclable—garbage is a problem, and we are running out of space to dispose of our refuse. We dump it in the ocean and see garbage surfacing on beaches and killing fish and birds (Heyes 2012). We bury it in landfills, and the surrounding land becomes toxic. Recycling and waste reduction efforts are relatively new movements in response to the urgent pleas from environmentalists about our polluted air, land, and water sources; dying oceans; and warming planet.

Recycling, salvaging items that can be reused, is part of a social reform movement—the environmental movement. However, few issues have simple solutions. The dumping and recycling have to take place somewhere. As noted in Chapter 15, many of the recycling plants and trash dumps are located in areas where poor people and racial and ethnic minorities live—part of a practice of *environmental racism*, in which members of lower socioeconomic classes and racial and ethnic minority groups face the brunt of environmental dangers, including pollutants and disease (Bell 2012).

At the micro level, individuals can help save the planet through responsible personal actions. At the meso level, the environmental movement can encourage local and regional governments to enact policies and plans to reduce waste and pollution and address environmental racism. At the macro level, world leaders need to hold all nations accountable for, and find ways to adapt to and mitigate, global warming. Our social world is, indeed, complex and interdependent.

Turn on the morning or evening news, and there are lessons about other aspects of our changing social world. We see headlines about medical advances and cures for disease; biological breakthroughs in cloning and the DNA code; terrorist bombings in Afghanistan, Israel, Iraq, Pakistan, Ukraine, and other parts of the world; famine in drought-afflicted sub-Saharan Africa; disasters such as earthquakes, hurricanes, tsunamis, and floods; and social activists calling for boycotts of chocolate, coffee, oil companies, Walmart, or other multinational corporations. Some events seem far away and hard to imagine: thousands killed by a tidal wave in India, hundreds swept away by mud from an erupting volcano in Colombia, a massive oil spill in the Gulf of Mexico, or a rise in

© REUTERS/Sean Gardner

Smoke billows from a controlled burn of spilled oil off the Louisiana coast in the Gulf of Mexico in 2010. Millions of gallons of oil have poured into the Gulf since an April 20, 2011, offshore rig explosion that killed 11 workers and ruptured British Petroleum's deep-sea well. Environmental issues do stimulate change.

Is Wal-Mart Good for America? ▶

terrorism reflecting divisions in world economic, political, and religious ideologies. Others may impact you directly—having affordable access to health insurance, living in an area suffering from the results of a drought or severe storm, or accessing financial aid for increasing college costs. Some of these are natural events, but most are the result of human actions.

Social change refers to *variations or alterations over time in the structure, culture (including norms and values), and behavior patterns of a society*. Some change is controllable, and some is out of our hands, but change is inevitable and ubiquitous. Change can be rapid, caused by some disruption to the existing system, or it can be gradual and evolutionary. Very often, change at one level in the social world occurs because of change at another level. Micro, meso, and macro levels of society often work together in the change process but are sometimes out of sync.

In this chapter, we explore the process of change, the causes of change, and some strategies for bringing about desired change. We consider the complexity of change in our social world, explanations and theories of social change, the role of collective behavior in bringing about change, planned change in organizations, macro-level social movements, technology, and environmental actions as they affect and are affected by change.

Our social world model is based on the assumption that change, whether evolutionary or revolutionary, is inevitable and ever present in the social world. The impetus for change may begin at the micro, meso, or macro level of analysis. Studies of the change process are not complete, however, until the level under study is understood in relation to other levels in the model, for each level affects the others in multiple ways.

 Thinking Sociologically

How do your activities impact the environment? Have you taken steps to address climate change? If so, what socializing agents prompted you to do so? If not, why do you think you have not?

THE COMPLEXITY OF CHANGE IN OUR SOCIAL WORLD

The Yir Yoront, a group of Australian aborigines, long believed that if their own ancestors did not do something, then they must not do it. It would be wrong and might cause evil to befall the group (Sharp 1990). However, contact with European cultures and missionaries brought new tools such as the steel axe, changing the role of men whose job it was to make stone axes. Gradually other European ways were introduced, changing the culture dramatically so that old ways were obsolete. The group's original culture disintegrated as it adopted others' ways, but a major contributor was the introduction of new technological ideas, especially the steel axe.

In the 1940s, missionaries gave steel axes to the Yir Yoront women, and the hunting and gathering economy changed due to changing roles of women and men. Men, who used to control the stone axes, lost their high status in the community when they had to borrow axes and other tools from women, and thus, the power structure of the community changed (BushTV 2010).

Obviously, the Yir Yoront were not a people who favored change or innovation. In contrast, *progress* is a positive word in much of Australia and in many other countries where change is seen as normal, even desirable. The traditions, cultural beliefs of a society, and internal and external pressures all affect the degree and rate of change in society (Berman 2011).

Change at the Individual Level: Micro-Level Analysis

One of the top U.S. entrepreneurs, Microsoft's Bill Gates, combines intelligence, business acumen, and philanthropy, qualities that appeal to American individualism. Gates has the power to influence others because of his fame, wealth, and personal organizational skills. He is able to bring about change in organizations through his ability to motivate people and set wheels in motion. Some people have persuasive power to influence decision making, based on expertise, wealth, privileged position, access to information, or the ability to use coercive force. Any of us, if we feel strongly about an issue, can rally others and bring about change in society. Each individual in society has the potential to be a change agent.

Individuals are active agents, and they can either stimulate or resist change. Sometimes they prod organizations to change, insisting on more family-supportive policies (like an on-site day-care center), better safety precautions for employees, or more environmentally friendly buildings and programs. For example, at the urging of students and others, colleges may develop more recycling programs, more energy-efficient buildings or transportation systems, and more degree programs that involve study of the environment.

Angelina Jolie (top) has used her fame as an Academy Award–winning actress to bring attention to problems of refugees, serving as a Special Envoy and Goodwill Ambassador for the United Nations High Commissioner for Refugees. Bill Gates (bottom) holds a child who is receiving a trial malaria vaccine at a medical research center in Mozambique. Gates announced a grant of $168 million to fight malaria, a disease that kills more than 1 million people a year, 90% of them children. Sometimes, social change occurs because of individual initiatives.

Sometimes individuals are not eager to change. They must be enticed or manipulated into change by organizations. When this does occur, most organizations—schools, businesses, volunteer associations—use one or more of the following strategies to persuade individuals to accept change: They appeal to individuals' values, use persuasion by presenting hard data and logic, convince individuals that the existing benefits of change outweigh the costs, remove uncooperative individuals from the organization ("addition by subtraction"), provide rewards or sanctions for acceptance of change to alter the cost–benefit ratio, or compel individuals to change by an order from authority figures. In any case, individuals are critically important parts of any understanding of social change.

Change at the Institutional Level: Meso-Level Analysis

Global climate change, an issue connected to pollution and use of the Earth's natural resources, affects people at all levels in the social system. Many meso-level organizations have developed policies and practices to reduce emission of pollutants and change the way they use resources. For example, many religious denominations have developed programs to be more "green" or "earth-friendly." The United Church of Christ is one such group, passing a resolution in July 2009 encouraging local churches to become "Earthwise Congregations." An example of one congregation within this meso-level denomination follows.

Mayflower United Church of Christ in Minneapolis was one of the first in the nation to seek the designation of an "Earthwise Congregation." The church has an action team that works on ways to help members have more energy-efficient homes, but it also brought a resolution to the congregation that by 2030, the church would be entirely carbon neutral. The resolution was approved, and fundraising began to change the heating system to solar energy. The roof of the church is now covered with 240 solar panels. Within 18 months, the church reported a reduction of carbon emissions of almost 50% (Mayflower Church 2013). Members of the congregation have also begun lobbying the state legislature to have more public transit, and especially more transportation that runs on electricity rather than oil-based fuels. Other United Church of Christ congregations are also taking actions, as are other communities of faith—inspired by denominational resolutions at the meso level.

Another example of meso-level change takes place at universities. Under pressure from college students, many have changed their policies about production of campus clothing. Multinational corporations like Gap and Nike, seeking higher profits, fostered the growth of sweatshops in the Global South. Many professors, students, and concerned citizens in the United States and other Global North nations began to insist that these companies establish acceptable labor and human rights conditions in their factories in the Global South. Their efforts gradually grew into an anti-sweatshop movement with strong labor and religious support and tens of thousands of active participants. College students on hundreds of campuses in the United States have taken up the anti-sweatshop cause, holding sit-ins on many campuses to force their college bookstores to ban the use of college logos on products not produced under acceptable labor conditions (Brecher, Costello, and Smith 2012). In doing so, they have helped shape the conditions for production of clothing on other continents.

Change at the National and Global Levels: Macro-Level Analysis

Change may also begin at the national level in response to some concern, or it may be stimulated by a global organization (like the United Nations or the World Bank) or by a global concern, like climate change. In this section, we discuss national and then global forces that can bring about change.

Societal-Level Change. Take a look at the impact of national policies and trends on the global environment and the constant change we bring to our planet. To illustrate the increasingly complex and biologically interdependent social world, consider that pollution of the environment by any one country now threatens other countries. Carcinogens, acid rain, and other airborne chemicals carry across national boundaries (Brecher et al. 2012). Heat-trapping gases have risen dramatically in the past several years causing pessimism about reversing the environmental effects (Borenstein 2013). In terms of population size, the United States is the third-largest country in the world after China and India. People in the United States comprise about 4.5% of the world's population but emit almost a fourth of the heat-trapping gases ("Global Warming and Climate Change" 2013). According to scientists, the Earth's surface has warmed by 1 degree in the past century. That does not sound like much until one considers that during the last ice age, the Earth's surface was only 7 degrees cooler than it is today. Small variations can make a huge difference, and those consequences are likely to be dire if the Earth's surface temperature increases by another 2 or 3 degrees. Currently, massive blocks of sea ice are melting each year at a rate that equals

A part of its "Earthwise" mission to protect the environment, this church in Minneapolis installed 240 solar panels as part of a commitment by the church to be carbon neutral by 2030.

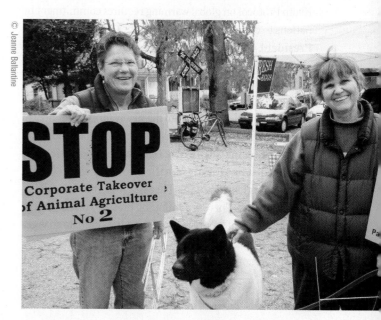

People at the local level often try to influence policies at the meso level. At this local community event, people lobby their neighbors on a state referendum in an upcoming election.

the size of Maryland and Delaware combined ("Global Warming and Climate Change" 2013). In the Northern Hemisphere, Greenland is home to many glaciers such as the huge Petermann Glacier. Warming recently caused the Petermann Glacier to calve (break off) an iceberg twice the size of Manhattan ("Iceberg Breaks Off" 2012).

Human Rights

In a warmer world, there is less snowfall, resulting in smaller mountain icecaps and, thus, a smaller spring runoff of crucial freshwater. In fact, 80% of the world's population today lives in areas with shortages of water for human use (Environment 911 2012).

While some of the environmental change may be rooted in natural causes, the preponderance of evidence suggests that human activity—the way we live our lives—is the primary cause (Gore 2012; IPCC 2013). So national policies and cultural attitudes within a country can have consequences at many levels of our social world.

 Thinking Sociologically

What do you think happens when people do not have enough water in their current location to survive? What happens when they try to move into someone else's territory to gain access to needed resources such as land and water?

Global climate change requires nations to work together for change, yet some nations resist change because they feel climate control efforts will impede economic progress. The Kyoto Protocol on global warming requires commitment by nations to curb carbon dioxide and other emissions, but U.S. President Bush rejected it because it "does not make economic sense" (Lindsay 2006:310–11). As of February 2014, 192 countries and the European Commission had approved the treaty. The exceptions are the United States, Afghanistan, the Vatican, and the newly formed country of South Sudan (United Nations Framework Convention on Climate Change 2014). The Obama administration has indicated support for dramatic efforts to curb climate change and global warming, but passage of a bill in Congress is still pending. There is continuing pressure on the United States to sign onto a global treaty to address climate change.

The two big quandaries are (1) the costs and benefits to various nations of participating in a solution and (2) the

Due to global climate change, ice on which polar bears depend is disappearing, as is the habitat of many other species that are becoming endangered.

question of time—will nations respond before it is too late to make a difference? Currently, impoverished countries bear most of the costs and consequences of pollution, while rich nations benefit from the status quo. It is becoming increasingly clear, though, that the rich will also pay a price. Not only will they have to face pollution, increasingly severe weather and intense storms, and contaminated food supplies from around the world, but if Global South countries cannot support their populations, affluent nations will also face increasing pressure from immigration (legal or not).

Yet fixing the environmental issues will be expensive for nations and may add to economic woes by temporarily hindering economic growth. Because slow-growth economies and recessions can lead to an unhappy public and political unrest, making changes to address climate change is not easy. However, such action is crucial because nations are still the most powerful units for allocating resources and for setting policy.

Global Systems and Change. As the world becomes more interconnected and interdependent, impetus for change increasingly comes from global organizations, international and transnational government agencies, and multinational corporations. As discussed in other chapters, nongovernmental organizations (NGOs) work on such efforts as eradicating polio or controlling AIDS and malaria. Some promote human rights, and others support local social movements for clean water, environmental protection, and access to health. One NGO, *Sociologists Without Borders*, works transnationally to develop globally inclusive sociology curricula, advance human rights, and support the needs of vulnerable groups.

New and shifting alliances between international organizations and countries link together nations, form international liaisons, and create changing economic and political systems. The following international alliances between countries, for example, are based primarily on economic ties:

- SADC: Southern African Development Community
- NAFTA: North American Free Trade Agreement
- CAFTA-DR: Dominican Republic–Central America Free Trade Agreement
- WIPO: World Intellectual Property Organization
- G7: Group of Seven—the most affluent and most powerful countries in the world
- OPEC: Organization of the Petroleum Exporting Countries

- APEC: Asia-Pacific Economic Cooperation
- EU: European Union
- AU: African Union

Consider NAFTA, which recently had its 20th anniversary. It was initiated in 1993 to establish a free trade area between Canada, the United States, and Mexico in order to facilitate trade in the region. Promoters, including many global corporations, promised that the agreement would create thousands of new high-wage jobs, raise living standards in each of the countries, improve environmental conditions, and transform Mexico from a poor developing country into a booming new market. Opponents (including labor unions, environmental organizations, consumer groups, and religious communities) argued the opposite—that NATFA would reduce wages; destroy jobs, especially in the United States; undermine democratic policy making in North America by giving corporations a free rein; and threaten health, the environment, and food safety (U.S. Trade Representative 2012).

Analyses of NAFTA show mixed results. It has helped boost intraregional trade between Canada, Mexico, and the United States, but has fallen short of generating the jobs and deeper regional economic integration its advocates promised decades ago (Council on Foreign Relations 2014). Trade has increased significantly, from $290 billion in 1993 to more than $1.1 trillion in 2012. There is some indication that tariffs are down and U.S. exports have increased (U.S. Trade Representative 2012). NAFTA has been more effective in increasing trade in agricultural commodities than nonagricultural products. Some analysts argue that there is improvement in the areas of environmental protection and labor rights, but many others argue that these areas have declined. The truth is hard to determine, but there are probably both gains and losses.

In the preceding discussion of changes at different levels of analysis, one principle carries through all: Change at one level leads to change in other levels, as it has done in the global cases of climate change and NAFTA. Changes at the macro level affect individuals, just as change at the micro level has repercussions at the meso and macro levels.

SOCIAL CHANGE: PROCESS AND THEORIES

The Process of Social Change

Something always triggers a social change. The impetus may come from within an organization or society, a source of change known as *strain*. Sometimes, it comes from outside an organization, what sociologists call *stress*. Let us consider two examples of *strain*: (1) conflicting goals and (2) contrasting belief systems within an organization.

Conflicting goals are seen in the case of the platinum mining industry and its union workers. In the Lonmin South African platinum mines (providing materials for catalytic converters and jewelry), 44 workers died in August 2012 and 2 more died in May 2014 during strikes against the company. Two feuding unions both demanded pay hikes, and violence broke out. As we write, the company is trying to settle the dispute by going directly to the miners with a pay offer. Individual miners work in difficult, dangerous conditions to try to meet their basic needs for food and shelter for their families. Sometimes they must live at the mines away from their families for many months, but when jobs are scarce, one does what one must. Company goals focus on the bottom line, being profitable in a competitive environment. The company argues that it cannot afford to raise wages and still be competitive, yet their profit margin has dropped as a result of the strikes (Herskovitz 2012; "Lonmin Profit Plunges" 2014). This conflict and others like it demonstrate how the needs of the workers can be at odds with those of the company, creating internal strain.

Contrasting belief systems (political, religious, economic, and social) within a society can also have a major effect on the type and rate of change. For example, some religious groups oppose stem cell research, which often uses the cells of fetuses created in test tubes. Yet other members of those same religious groups may believe this research will alleviate the suffering of loved ones and save lives. Although both sides in the organization believe they are pro-life, the internal conflicts can be disruptive and cause internal strain (Religious Tolerance 2014).

Stresses, those pressures for change that come from the organization's external environment, can be traced to several sources: the natural environment and natural disasters, population dynamics, actions of leaders, new technologies, changes in other institutions, and major historical events. For example, the natural environment can bring about either slow or dramatic change in a society. *Natural disasters* such as floods, hurricanes, tsunamis, heavy snows, earthquakes, volcanic eruptions, mudslides, tornadoes, and other sudden events are not planned occurrences, but they can have dramatic consequences. Disease epidemics are often unpredictable, such as the 2010 to 2013 cholera epidemic in Haiti (UNICEF 2014). Natural disasters and diseases are so important as a dramatic change agent that the sociology of disasters has become a specialty field within the discipline. The next "Sociology in Our Social World" describes one of the classic sociological studies of a disaster.

sociology in our social world

Disasters and Their Aftermath

A series of small villages were settled along a mountain creek in West Virginia known as Buffalo Creek. This was mining country, and at the top of the creek, a coal company had poured more than 1 million tons of wastewater and coal waste into a company-created basin. The restraining embankment of shale, clay, slag, and low-quality coal that created the reservoir was referred to by the coal company as an "impoundment," but the people themselves referred to it as a "dam."

Heavy rains in the winter of 1972 weakened this restraining wall, and on February 26, it broke, setting forth a massive flood of black sludge and oily, slag-filled wastewater down the valley toward the homes of 5,000 residents in the mountain villages. The first village hit was not just crushed; it disappeared entirely. This meant that the villages farther down the creek bed had not just filthy water coming at them but the remains of homes, churches, stores, vehicles, and bodies. By the time the water subsided, the flood had taken with it almost everything in its path.

Newspapers reported the economic loss and the staggering death toll, but lawyers, psychologists, and sociologists were interested in the human cost to survivors—costs to their sense of self, their mental and emotional well-being, and their family and friendship ties. Here was a community that had had an extraordinarily close-knit social network, where crime was virtually nonexistent, divorces were extraordinary, chemical abuse and mental problems were far below the national norms, and neighborhoods were like extended families. Yet the community had been ripped apart by the flood. Even three years after the flood, time had not healed the social and emotional wounds: Few marriages remained intact, problems of deviance and delinquency were rife, and more than 90% of the people interviewed were judged to be in need of psychological counseling.

The federal government's response to the flood in Buffalo Creek dealt mostly with the immediate needs for survival. Thus, mobile homes were brought in, and emergency food was provided, but people were placed in these shelters without taking into account their existing ties with family members, friends, and neighbors. Thus, people found themselves surrounded by strangers at a time when they desperately needed support and when they also had few interpersonal resources to forge new relationships.

The mental health symptoms tied to individual trauma include psychic numbness (feeling mentally blank and emotionally limp), constant anxiety about death, guilt at having survived when so many members of one's family had not, guilt for not having saved people who were seen being swept down the river, loss of the "furniture of self" (the symbols of one's life that might include one's home, family heirlooms, photographs of loved ones, and other artifacts that connect one to others and to a personal history), and loss of trust in the order of the universe or a loving God, who people believed was in control of life's events.

The "collective trauma," however, was even more important to understand than the individual trauma: "People find it difficult to recover from the effects of individual trauma so long as the community around them remains in shreds" (Erikson 1976:155). The collective trauma included five dimensions:

1. *Disorientation:* Many persons were so socially displaced that they could hardly orient themselves in time and space, even two or three years after the flood.

2. *Loss of morale and morality:* Following the flood, people were more likely to commit deviant acts and to think they were surrounded by immoral people.

3. *Loss of connection:* Marriages began to disintegrate, and people lost their sense of connection to others.

4. *Illness and identity:* People seemed to feel that the land was polluted and untrustworthy, with some people afraid to till the soil lest they find a body part of a family member or a neighbor buried there. Because the land was polluted, many people felt their own bodies were polluted, too.

5. *Loss of a sense of safety:* People slept in their clothes and boots, and whenever it rained,

many residents would run to the creek every hour to check on the water levels.

This disaster at Buffalo Creek indicates how much of our personal mental health rests in the health of the larger community. It helps us understand how anomie (normlessness) can create anxiety and disorientation. Most of all, it helps us understand that natural disasters and human catastrophes, such as the September 11 terrorist attacks, devastating storms such as Hurricane Katrina, and the daily killings in Syria, can have pervasive effects on individuals and communities.

Work on collective trauma forces us to be aware of the extent to which we depend on a larger community to regain our footing when a disaster disrupts our lives. We humans are, indeed, profoundly social beings. Changes that disrupt our social ties can have severe and wide-ranging consequences.

• •

Source: Kai Erikson, Everything in Its Path *(Simon & Schuster, 1976).*

Thinking Sociologically

Think of a recent natural disaster with which you are familiar. If you were in charge of the disaster relief effort, how might the findings from the Buffalo Creek study help you to determine what steps you would take to help the community or communities impacted by the disaster?

Population dynamics—birthrates and death rates, size of populations, age distribution, and migration patterns—can be important contributors to external stress on organizations. Where populations are growing at extremely rapid rates, government systems may be unable to meet the basic needs of the people.

Immigration due to political upheavals or motivated by anticipated economic opportunities can also create stress on the societies that receive the newcomers as they

© REUTERS/Edgar Su

Natural disasters—floods, hurricanes, tornadoes, earthquakes, volcanic eruptions—can be the cause of major social changes in a community, as shown in this photo after a tsunami hit the Philippines in 2013.

The Domiz Refugee Camp in the Kurdistan Region of Iraq is home to thousands of Syrian refugees. Immigration to avoid persecution can stimulate massive change for people and for countries.

attempt to meet the immigrants' needs. For example, many refugees from the conflict in Syria have fled to camps in the nearby countries of Turkey and Jordan, greatly taxing the capacities of those nations. Figure 16.1 shows the global hot spots for refugees entering other countries.

Leaders influence change through their policy decisions or the social movements they help generate. India's Mohandas K. (Mahatma) Gandhi taught the modern world nonviolent methods of bringing about change in political systems. The policies of Charles Taylor, former military dictator of Liberia, created long-term war that resulted in thousands of deaths. President Robert Mugabe of Zimbabwe locked his country in a downward spiral of economic turmoil and disease, killing thousands. These leaders' actions created internal strains in their own countries and external stressors resulting in discussions and sometimes change in the international community.

Technology also influences societal change. William F. Ogburn compiled a list of 150 social changes in the United States that resulted from the invention of the radio, such as instant access to information (Ogburn 1933). Other lists could be compiled for cell phones, automobiles, television, computers, and new technologies such as smartphones. Some of these changes give rise to secondary changes. For example, automobile use led to paved highways, complex systems of traffic patterns and rules, and gasoline stations. The next "Sociology in Our Social World" explores several issues involving the automobile and change.

FIGURE 16.1   Countries Receiving Refugees, Asylum Seekers, and Internally Displaced People: 2012

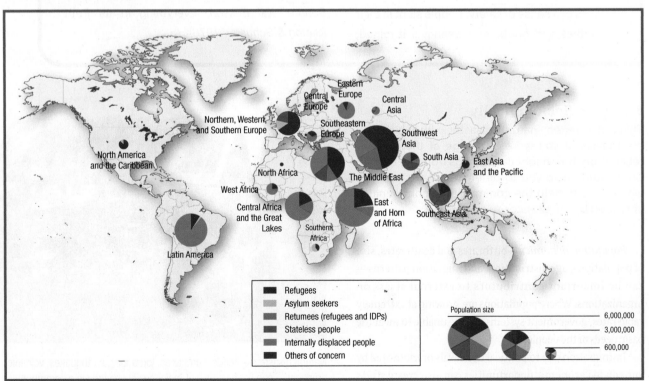

Source: United Nations Human Rights Council (2014).
Note: IDP = internally displaced person.

sociology in our social world

Technology and Change: The Automobile

Only a century ago, a newfangled novelty was spreading quickly from urban areas to the countryside: the automobile. At the turn of the 20th century, this strange horseless carriage was often referred to in rural areas as the "devil wagon." The introduction of this self-propelled vehicle was controversial; in the 1890s and early 1900s, some cities and counties had rules forbidding motorized vehicles. In Vermont, a walking escort had to precede the car by an eighth of a mile with a red warning flag, and in Iowa, motorists were required to telephone ahead to a town they planned to drive through to warn the community lest their horses be alarmed (Berger 1979; Clymer 1953; Glasscock 1937; Morris 1949). In most rural areas, motorists were expected to pull their cars to a stop or even to shut down the motor when a horse-drawn buggy came near. "Pig and chicken legal clauses" meant the automobile driver was liable for any injury that occurred when passing an animal near the road, even if the injury was due to the animal running away (Scott-Montagu 1904).

Automobiles were restricted to cities for nearly a decade after their invention because roads were inadequate outside of the urban areas and they often slid off muddy roads into ditches. Paving of roads became a necessity for automobile travel and, of course, made automobile travel much faster and more common. The expansion was stunning. Roughly 85,000 motored vehicles were in use in the United States in 1911. By 1930, the number was nearly 10 million, and in 2011 the estimated number of registered passenger vehicles was 253 million (Berger 1979; Statistica 2014).

Forms of entertainment began to change when people were able to be more mobile.

As the Model T made cars affordable, families no longer had only each other for socializing, and entertainment became available virtually any night of the week (Berger 1979; McKelvie 1926). Thus, dependence on family was lessened, possibly weakening familial bonds and oversight (Berger 1979). Even courting was substantially changed, as individuals could go farther afield to find a possible life partner, couples could go more places on dates, and two people could find more privacy.

Transportation that made traversing distances more possible changed how people related to a number of other institutions as well. Motorized buses made transportation to schools possible, and attendance rates of rural children increased substantially (U.S. Department of Interior Office of Education 1930). Because people could drive farther to churches, they often chose to go to city churches, where the preachers were more skilled public speakers and the music was of higher quality (Berger 1979). Many country churches consolidated or closed (Wilson 1924). The automobile was also a boon to the mental health of isolated farm women, allowing them to visit with neighbors (Berger 1979; McNall and McNall 1983).

As people could live in less congested areas but still get to work in a reasonable amount of time via an automobile, the suburbs began to develop around major cities. No longer did people locate homes close to shopping, schools, and places of worship. Still, a dispersed population needs to use more gasoline, thereby creating pollution. As the wealthy moved to expensive suburbs and paid higher taxes to support outstanding schools, socioeconomic and ethnic stratification between communities increased. These are some of the *unintended consequences* of the spread of the automobile. It sometimes takes decades before we can identify the consequences of the technologies we adopt.

Thinking Sociologically

What might be some long-term social consequences for our individual lives and societies of the widespread use of smartphones, microwave ovens, computer games, and cars that can navigate themselves and warn us of hazards around us?

The diffusion or spread of technology throughout the world is likely to be uneven, especially in the early stages of the new technology. For example, computer technology has advanced rapidly, but those advances began in corporate boardrooms, military bases, and university laboratories. Policies of governing bodies—such as funding for school computers—determine the rate of public access. Thus, only gradually are computers reaching the world's citizenry through schools, libraries, and eventually private homes. Clearly, internal strains and external stressors give impetus to the processes of change. The question is, "How do these processes take place?"

Theories of Social Change

Social scientists seek to explain the causes and consequences of social change, sometimes in the hope that change can be controlled or guided. Theories of change often reflect the events and belief systems of particular historical periods. For example, conflict theory developed during periods of change in Europe. It gained adherents in the United States during the 1960s, when intense conflict over issues of race and ethnic relations, the morality of the Vietnam War, and changes in social values peaked. Theories such as structural functionalism that focused on social harmony were of little help.

The major social change theories can be categorized as micro-level (symbolic interaction and rational choice theories) or meso- and macro-level (evolutionary, functional, conflict, and world systems theories). As we review these theories, many of them will be familiar to you from previous chapters. Here, we relate them to the process of change.

Micro-Level Theories of Change.

Symbolic Interactionism. According to symbolic interaction theory, human beings are always trying to make sense of the things they experience, figure out what an event or interaction means, and determine what action is required of them. Humans construct meanings that agree with or diverge from what others around them think. This capacity to define one's situation, such as concluding that one is oppressed, even though others have accepted the

circumstances as normal, can be a powerful impetus to change. It can be the starting point of social movements, cultural changes, and revolutions.

Some sociologists believe that individuals are always at the core of any social trends or movements, even if those movements are national or global (Blumer 1986; Giddens 1986; Simmel [1902–1917] 1950). After all, it is individuals who act, make decisions, and take action. There are a number of leaders, for example, who have changed the world—for better (Mahatma Gandhi) or worse (Adolf Hitler). Neither corporations nor nations nor bureaucracies make decisions—people do. The way in which an individual defines the reality he or she is experiencing makes a huge difference in how she or he will respond to it.

Social institutions and structures are always subject to maverick individuals "thinking outside the box" and changing how others see things. Individual actions can cause riots, social movements, planned change in organizations, and a host of other outcomes that have the potential to transform society. That people may construct reality in new ways can be a serious threat to the status quo, and those who want to protect the status quo try to ensure that people will see the world the same way they do. If change feels threatening to some members who have a vested interest in the current arrangements, those individuals who advocate change may face resistance. Consider the current state of the world, in which some nations are making rapid technological advances and others are resisting modernization as a threat to their traditional political and religious way of life.

Leaders may provide opportunities for group members to participate in suggesting, planning, and implementing change in order to help create acceptance and positive attitudes toward change. Several recent street demonstrations in Egypt and Ukraine against governments in power turned violent; at different points during the demonstrations, leaders attempted to engage the opposition in talks to calm the tensions. Symbolic interactionists might see this as either an effort to build a consensus about what social change is necessary or a method to appease those wanting change in order to remain in control and maintain much of the status quo.

Rational Choice. To rational choice theorists, behaviors are largely driven by individuals seeking rewards and reducing costs. They maintain that most individuals engage in activities that bring positive rewards and try to avoid actions that can have negative outcomes. A group seeking change can attempt to set up a situation in which the desired behavior is rewarded. The typology presented in Figure 16.2 shows the relationship between behaviors and sanctions.

Bringing about change may not, however, require a change in costs or rewards. It may be sufficient simply to change people's perception of the advantages and disadvantages of certain actions. Sometimes, people are not aware of all the rewards, or they have failed to accurately assess the costs of an action. For example, few citizens in the United States realize all the financial, health, and legal benefits of marriage. To change the marriage rates, we may not need more benefits to encourage marriage. We may do just as well to change the population's appraisal of the benefits already available.

Meso- and Macro-Level Theories of Change.

Social Evolutionary Theories. Social evolutionary theories at the macro level assume that societies change slowly from simple to more complex forms. Early unilinear theories maintained that all societies moved through the same steps and that advancement or progress was desirable and would lead to a better society. These theories came to prominence during the Industrial Revolution, when European social scientists sought to interpret the differences between their own societies and the "primitive societies" of other continents. Europe was being stimulated by travel, exposure to new cultures, and a spawning of new philosophies, a period called the Enlightenment. Europeans witnessed the development of mines, railroads, ships, weaponry, cities, educational systems, and industries, which they defined as "progress" or "civilization." World travelers reported that other peoples and societies did not seem to have these developments. These reports provided the empirical evidence that early sociologist Auguste Comte used in proposing his theory of unilinear development from simple to complex societies. Unilinear theories came to legitimate colonial expansion and exploitation of other people and lands seen as less developed and "inferior."

In a more recent version of evolutionary theory, Patrick Nolan and Gerhard Lenski discuss five stages through which most societies progress: hunter-gatherer, horticultural, agrarian, industrial, and postindustrial (Nolan and Lenski 2010; see also Chapter 3). This does not mean that some stages are "better" than others. It simply means that this is the typical pattern of change resulting from new technologies and more efficient harnessing of energy.

Contemporary evolutionary theories acknowledge that change takes place in multiple ways and not just in a straight line. The rapid spread of ideas and technologies means that societies today may move quickly from simple to complex, creating modern states. They skip steps or are selective about what aspects of technology they wish to adopt. For example, countries such as India and China are largely agricultural but are importing and developing the latest technology that allows them to skip over developmental steps. As noted in previous chapters, most African countries will not see landlines for phones but instead will have cell phones even in the more remote areas.

Some scholars disapprove of the phrase *developing countries* because it might imply that all societies are moving toward the type of social system characterized by the affluent or "developed" societies. As we have noted in earlier chapters, many now use the term *Global South* because poor countries are disproportionately located south of the 20th parallel north, whereas affluent nations are typically situated north of that latitude. Note that the term is a metaphor for all poor countries, meant to avoid an assumption of inevitable evolution toward Western cultures.

Functionalist Theories. Functional theorists assume that societies are basically stable systems held together by the shared norms and values of their members. The interdependent parts work together to make the society

FIGURE 16.2   Relationship Between Behaviors and Sanctions

		Sanction	
		Formal	Informal
Behavior	Positive	Bonuses, advances, fringe benefits, recognition	Praise, smile, pat on the back
	Negative	Demotion, loss of salary	Ridicule, exclusion, talk behind back

function smoothly. A change in one part of the society affects all the other parts, each changing in turn until the system resumes a state of equilibrium. Change can come from external or internal sources, from stresses in contact with other societies or from strains within.

Slow, nondisruptive change occurs as societies become more complex, and this may be a very functional adaptation. Rapid change, however, is often seen as dysfunctional or disruptive to stability by functional theorists. Because functionalists often view major change with suspicion, many sociologists have turned to conflict theories to help explain change, especially rapid or violent change.

Conflict Theories. Conflict theorists assume that societies are dynamic and that change and conflict are inevitable. According to Karl Marx, socioeconomic class conflict is the major source of tension leading to change in any society. Marx and Friedrich Engels predicted that the antagonistic relationship they saw developing between the workers (proletariat) and the owners of the production systems (bourgeoisie) in 19th-century England would lead to social revolution. From this, they believed a new world order would emerge in which the workers themselves would own the means of production. Thus, conflict between the owners and the workers would be the central factor driving social change (Marx and Engels [1848] 1969).

Other conflict theorists study variables such as gender, religion, politics, and ethnic or interest group problems in their analyses, feeling that these factors can also be the grounds for oppression and "us" versus "them" differences (Dahrendorf 1959). Some see conflict as useful for society because it forces societies to adapt to new conditions and leads to healthy change (Coser 1956). Conflicts over slavery and over gender inequality are examples of problems that cause stresses and strains, often resulting in an improved society.

World Systems Theory of Global Change. World systems theorists focus on how world history has influenced the status of individual countries today. Capitalist economies first appeared about 1500. Since then, except for a few isolated tribal groupings, almost all societies have been at least indirectly influenced by dominant capitalist world economic and political systems (Wallerstein 1974).

This theory divides the world system into three main parts: the core, semiperipheral areas, and peripheral areas (see Figure 16.3). Core countries

include most Western European states, Australia and New Zealand, Japan, Canada, the United States, and a few others (Wallerstein 1974). Historically, they have controlled global decision making, received the largest share of the profits from the world economic system, and dominated the peripheral areas politically, economically, and culturally by controlling the flow of technology and capital into and out of those countries. Peripheral countries, most of which are in Africa, Asia, and South America, provide cheap labor and raw materials for the core countries' needs.

The semiperipheral countries hold an intermediate position, trading with both the core and the peripheral countries. The Baltic regions of Eastern Europe, Brazil, Argentina, South Africa, India, the Philippines, Iran, and Mexico are among the semiperipheral areas. Because most semiperipheral countries are industrializing, they serve as areas to which core-country businesses and multinational corporations can move for continued growth, often in partnerships, as semiperipheral states aspire to join the core countries. The core and semiperipheral countries process raw materials, often taken from peripheral countries for little in return, and may sell the final products back to the peripheral countries. The semiperipheral countries and the peripheral countries need the trade and the resources of the core countries, but they are also at a severe disadvantage in competition and exploited by those at the core, resulting in an uneasy relationship.

Core countries have been a major force in the development of global institutions, such as the International Monetary Fund (IMF), that facilitate and attempt to control international capital flow. By increasing the frameworks for debt restructuring for peripheral countries, the IMF attempts to restore sustainability and growth to countries that default on their loans. At least 95 countries have restructured their

FIGURE 16.3   World Systems Theory

Core countries (wealthy countries of Europe, Japan, United States, Canada)

Semiperipheral countries (India)

Peripheral countries (many poor African, Asian, and Latin American nations)

Mob Mentality

debt under IMF guidelines since the 1950s (Das, Papaioannou, and Trebesch 2012). However, the IMF leaves countries little economic autonomy. The restructuring plans control what countries do even within their own national boundaries, creating debt dependencies on core countries that most poorer countries can never overcome (Dollars and Sense Collective 2012; Gibler 2012; Rothkopf 2012; Stiglitz 2012).

World systems theory is a global conflict theory, with core countries exploiting the poor countries. As we might expect from conflict theory, some groups of noncore countries have increased their collective power by forming alliances such as OPEC (Organization of the Petroleum Exporting Countries), OAS (Organization of African States), and SEATO (Southeast Asia Treaty Organization). These alliances present challenges to the historically core countries of the world system because of their combined economic and political power. For example, the price we pay at the gas pump reflects, in part, the power of OPEC to set prices.

When we understand international treaties and alliances as part of larger issues of conflict over resources and economic self-interests, the animosity of noncore countries toward core countries such as the United States begins to make sense. Likewise, the threat felt by the United States from countries that seem to be getting jobs once found in the United States is not entirely unfounded. The problem is an extraordinarily complex system that tends to leave the most vulnerable more at risk and the wealthiest even richer (Gibler 2012; Rothkopf 2012; Stiglitz 2012).

The climate crisis illustrates the world systems theory and rift between rich and poor nations. For example, the tiny Pacific islands such as Nauru soon will be under water due to global warming and water rising. Human activity, mostly from development in Global North countries, is causing what some groups of countries call "climate injustice," and Global South nations harmed by climate change now demand compensation for damages. After decades of climate talks with little change taking place, the divide between peripheral nations and core nations is becoming more stark. This world system outlook assumes that developed Global North countries are most to blame for climate change problems and therefore should be held accountable. However, nations like India and China, in the midst of phenomenal economic growth, now contribute to increasing global carbon emissions. The causes of climate change are complex and not solely due to the actions of Global North countries (Myers and Kulish 2013).

We have discussed examples of planned change, but sometimes behavior that results in change is unplanned, even spontaneous, as described in the following section.

 Thinking Sociologically

Where is your clothing made? Did a multinational corporation have it assembled in the Global South? What steps can you take to ensure that the workers who made your clothes receive tolerable working conditions and a fair wage?

COLLECTIVE BEHAVIOR: MICRO- TO MESO-LEVEL CHANGE

Individuals in local communities often come together over some issue that irritates or even enrages them, and these gatherings can evolve into mobs, riots, panics, or other forms of collective reaction to events. It is often at the micro or local level that change movements get started. These can evolve into large statewide, national, or even global movements with implications for the larger society, but since they begin with individuals in local communities deciding to take some sort of common action, we discuss it as a micro- to meso-level event. Political demonstrations and stock market sell-offs are forms of collective behavior that can stimulate change. In this section, we introduce a form of change that typically has uncertain outcomes.

Collective behavior refers to *spontaneous, unstructured, and disorganized actions that may violate norms; this behavior arises when people are trying to cope with stressful situations and unclear or uncertain conditions* (Goode 1992; Smelser 1963, 1988). Collective behavior falls into two main types: crowd behavior and mass behavior. It often starts as a response to an event or a stimulus. It could begin with a shooting or beating, a speech, a sports event, or a rumor. The key is that as individuals try to make sense of the situations they are in and respond based on their perceptions, collective social actions emerge.

Crowd behaviors—mobs, panics, riots, and demonstrations—are forms of collective behavior in which a crowd acts, at least temporarily, as a unified group (LeBon [1895] 1960). Crowds are often made up of individuals who see themselves as supporting a just cause. Because the protesters are in such a large group, they may not feel bound by normal social controls—either internal (normal moral standards) or external (fear of police sanctions).

Crowds can stimulate change in a society, but they can also become unruly and unpredictable, so governments spend a good deal of money and time equipping and training officers to control crowds. Here a Ukrainian woman participating in a protest places carnations into the shields of anti-riot policemen standing outside the presidential office in Kiev.

Mass behavior occurs when individual people communicate or respond in a similar manner to ambiguous or uncertain situations, often based on common information from word of mouth rumors, websites, social networking, and television. Examples include fashions and fads, such as the ALS (Lou Gehrig's disease) "ice bucket challenge." Unlike social movements, these forms of collective behavior generally lack a hierarchy of authority and clear leadership, a division of labor, and a sense of group action.

Theories of Collective Behavior

Social scientists studying group and crowd dynamics find that most members of crowds are respectable, law-abiding citizens, but faced with specific situations, they act out (Berk 1974; Turner and Killian 1993). Several explanations of individual involvement dominate the modern collective behavior literature.

Based on principles of rational choice theory, the *minimax strategy* suggests that individuals try to minimize their losses or costs and maximize their benefits (Berk 1974). People are more likely to engage in behavior if they feel the rewards outweigh the costs. Individuals may become involved in a riot if they feel the outcome—drawing attention to their plight, the possibility of improving conditions, solidarity with neighbors and friends, looting goods—will be more rewarding than the status quo or the possible negative sanctions.

Emergent norm theory points out that individuals have different emotions and attitudes guiding their behaviors in crowds than when they act alone (Turner and Killian 1993). The theory addresses the unusual situations, involving the breakdown of norms, in which most collective behavior takes place. Unusual situations may call for the development of new norms and even new definitions of acceptable behavior. The implication of this theory is that in ambiguous situations, people look to others for clues about what is happening or what is acceptable, and norms emerge in ambiguous contexts that may be considered inappropriate in other contexts. This is the most widely used approach to understanding collective behavior (Turner and Killian 1993).

Imagine you are at an athletic event. Someone in the crowd with a very loud voice begins to taunt a player from the visiting team. Initially some people around you laugh, but as the initiator begins to chant an insult, your friends and others around you begin to join in. Chances are good that in the camaraderie of the moment, you follow suit and start chanting the insult, too—even if it is very disrespectful. Normally you would not make such an insulting remark to someone's face, but in this situation where you are anonymous, the pattern of behavior emerged and you felt compelled to follow the crowd. This would be an example of an emergent norm affecting an entire crowd.

Value-added theory (sometimes called structural-strain theory) describes the conditions for crowd behavior and social movements. Key elements are necessary for collective behavior, with each new variable adding to the total situation until conditions are sufficient for individuals to begin to act in common. At this point, collective behavior emerges (Smelser 1963). These are the six factors identified that can result in collective behavior:

1. *Structural conduciveness:* Existing problems create a climate ripe for change. Consider the example of the independent country of Ukraine, caught between Russia and Western Europe. The (now deposed) president of Ukraine stated that he planned to align Ukraine with the West, but under pressure and promises from Russia changed his mind. This change angered many Ukrainians.

2. *Structural strain*: The social structure is not meeting the needs and expectations of the citizens, which creates widespread dissatisfaction with the status quo—the current arrangements. Ukrainians who felt the country would fare better if aligned with Western Europe demonstrated in the capital of Kiev.

3. *Spread of a generalized belief:* Common beliefs about the cause, effect, and solution of the problem evolve, develop, and spread. Charges spread that the pro-Russian president was corrupt, lived opulently, and had stolen money belonging to the Ukrainian people to support his lifestyle.

4. *Precipitating factor:* A dramatic event or incident occurs to incite people to action. The Ukrainian president left the capital Kiev in fear after the guards defending him left their posts. President Putin of Russia amassed Russian troops on the Ukrainian border, charging that the president of Ukraine had been rightfully elected and that Crimea should be part of Russia. Russian troops then entered Crimea, and Russia officially annexed it (declared it part of Russia).

5. *Mobilization for action:* Leaders emerge and set out a path of action, or an emergent norm develops that stimulates common action. Ukrainian leaders emerged to defend Ukraine against what they saw as Russian aggression. A newly elected Ukrainian president has sent troops to eastern Ukraine to defend it against Russians who want to align it with Russia.

6. *Social controls are weak:* If the police, the military, or political or religious leaders are unable to counter the mobilization, a social movement or other crowd behavior may form. Ukraine's new president, parliament, and army resisted the efforts of the pro-Russian groups (assisted by Russian troops) in eastern Ukraine to establish a separate (pro-Russian) state, but Ukrainian forces and resources are much less than Russia's. As we write these words, the outcome remains unclear.

When all six of the preceding factors are present, some sort of collective behavior will emerge. Those interested in controlling volatile crowds must intervene and take control when one or more of these conditions exists (Flynn 2014; Smelser 1963).

Thinking Sociologically

Think of an example of a crowd behavior or social movement. Which of the preceding theories best explains this act? Why?

Types of Collective Behavior

Collective behavior ranges from spontaneous violent mobs to temporary fads and fashions. Figure 16.4 shows the range of actions.

All six social factors that contribute to collective behavior were present in 2014 in Kiev, Ukraine, and the results were riots in the streets, the overthrow of the Ukrainian president, and the annexation of Crimea by Russia.

Mobs are emotional crowds that engage in violence against a specific target. Examples include lynchings, killings, and hate crimes. Near the end of the U.S. Civil War, self-appointed vigilante groups roamed the countryside in the South looking for army deserters, torturing and killing both those who harbored deserters and the deserters themselves. There were no courts and no laws, just "justice" in the eyes of the vigilantes. The members of these groups constituted mobs. The film *Cold Mountain* depicts these scenes vividly. Unless deterred, mobs often damage or destroy their target.

Riots—an outbreak of illegal violence against random or shifting targets committed by crowds expressing frustration or anger against people, property, or groups in power—begin when certain conditions occur. Often, a sense of frustration or deprivation sets the stage for a riot—hunger, poverty, poor housing, lack of jobs, discrimination, poor education, or an unresponsive or unfair judicial system. If the conditions for collective behavior are present, many types of incidents can be the precipitating factor setting off a riot. For example, in the summer of 2014, residents of Ferguson, Missouri, became outraged when a police officer shot and killed Michael Brown, an unarmed black 18-year-old. While some residents peacefully protested, others looted stores and threw rocks at police officers. The distinction between riots and mobs is illustrated in Figure 16.5.

Panic occurs when a large number of individuals become fearful or try to flee threatening situations beyond

FIGURE 16.4   Types of Collective Behavior

Spontaneous and often violent						Less spontaneous and seldom violent
Crowd behavior				Mass behavior		
Mob	Riot	Panic		Rumor	Fad	Fashion

their control, sometimes putting their lives in danger. Panic can occur in a crowd situation, such as a restaurant or theater in which someone yells "Fire," or it can occur following rumors or information spread by the media. Panic started by rumors set off the run on the stock market in October 1929. A large number of actions by individuals caused the stock market crash in the United States, with repercussions around the world. In 2008, the collapse of the global investment banking and securities trader Bear, Stearns & Co. resulted in turmoil in the financial markets. Only radical intervention by the federal government abated the immediate panic. Panics can result in collapse of an organization, destruction, or even death.

Rumors are forms of mass behavior in which unsupported or unproven reports about a problem, issue, or concern circulate widely throughout the public. Rumors

FIGURE 16.5   The Difference Between Riots and Mobs

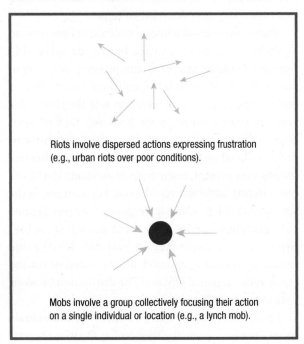

Riots involve dispersed actions expressing frustration (e.g., urban riots over poor conditions).

Mobs involve a group collectively focusing their action on a single individual or location (e.g., a lynch mob).

may spread only in a local area, but with electronic means available, rumors spread more widely and rapidly. Without authoritative information, ambiguous situations can produce faulty information on which decisions are made and actions are based. *Urban legends*, one example of widely spread but unverified messages, are unsubstantiated stories that sound plausible and become widely circulated. The people telling these stories usually believe them (Mikkelson and Mikkelson 2012). The next "Sociology in Our Social World" provides an example. (Go to www .snopes.com/college/college.asp for some additional entertaining urban legends about professors, exam scams, embarrassments, and other college pranks.)

Fads are temporary behaviors, activities, or material objects that spread rapidly and are copied enthusiastically by large numbers of people. Body modification, especially tattooing, appeals mostly to young people of all social classes. Tattoo artists emblazon IDs, secret society and organization emblems, fraternity symbols, and decorations to order on all parts of customers' bodies. Body modification has taken place for centuries, but it goes through fads (University of Pennsylvania 2010). Sometimes, fads become institutionalized—that is, they gain a permanent place in the culture. Other fads die out, replaced by the next hot item.

Fashions refer to a style of appearance and behavior temporarily favored by a large number of people. Examples include clothing styles, music genres, color schemes in home decor, types of automobiles, and architectural designs. Fashions typically last longer than fads but sometimes survive only a season, as can be seen in the clothing industry. Music styles such as "hardcore techno," "acid," "alternative hip hop," and "UK 2-step garage" were popular among some groups as the previous edition of this book was being written, but a couple of years later as we finished the fifth edition, the fads were "dub step," "indie," "electropop," "screamo," "Latin-pop," and "chiptune." These styles will probably be passé by the time you read this, replaced by new fads emerging in mass behavior.

Social Change and the Media ▶

sociology in our social world

Exam Stories: Testing the Truth

College exams are quickly approaching, so it is a good time to take a look at the latest chapter in the tome of teacher-student legend and rumors.

The first one was reported from Calgary, Alberta, by a civil engineering student at the University of Manitoba. This tale says a professor announced an open-book final examination in which the students could "use anything they are able to carry into the exam room." One innovative undergraduate, it is reported, carried in a graduate student who wrote his exam for him.

Another legend came from North Carolina. Supposedly, on the day before the final exam, the professor left his office unattended, with the door open and the examinations left sitting on his desk. A student who came by to ask a question found the room empty and quickly left with one of the exams. However, the professor had printed the exact number of exams that he needed, and the next morning, he counted them again before going to the classroom. Discovering that he was one short, he suspected that it had been stolen, so he trimmed a half inch from the bottom of the remaining exams. When the exam papers were turned in, the student whose paper was longer than the others' received a failing grade.

A student procrastinated on writing a paper. Twenty-four hours before the paper was due, he went to the university library and found an old paper on the topic. He copied it and turned it in. A few weeks later, the professor returned the papers, and he stopped by the student's desk. He supposedly said to the student, "Twenty-five years ago, when I wrote this paper, it got a B. I always thought it deserved an A." There was an A on the cover, but the professor added, "Try anything like this again, and I'll have you thrown out of school."

Another college legend goes like this: Jack, a less than industrious student, was taking an examination with two blue books, a pen, and a question that had him baffled. Being naturally bright, even if lazy, he solved the problem in the following way. In one of the blue books, he wrote a letter to his mother, telling her that he had finished his exam early but was waiting for a friend to finish and was taking the opportunity to write her a note. He said he had been studying very hard for this instructor, who was a nice guy but had pretty high standards. When the time was up, he handed in one blue book and quickly left with the unused one. When he got to his room, he opened his text, wrote the answer to the exam question, and mailed the blue book to his mother. When the instructor found the letter, he called Jack, who explained that he had written in two blue books and must have gotten them mixed up. The examination essay must be in the mail on the way to Boston where his mother lived, he explained. He offered to call his mother and have her send the envelope back as soon as she got it. He did, she did, and the blue book was returned, with the inner envelope postmarked the day of the test and the outer envelope postmarked Boston.

Finally, in an introductory chemistry class, two guys were taking chemistry, and they had

(Continued)

(Continued)

done so well on all the quizzes that by the last week of class they each had a solid A. These friends were so confident going into the final that for the weekend just before the exam they decided to drive some distance to party at another college. However, after a very good time and hangovers on Monday, they overslept and did not make it back to campus until late on Monday—the day of the exam. They found the professor and told him they missed the final because they had been away, had had a flat tire on the way back to campus, and were without a spare. The professor thought this over and agreed that they could make up the final on the following day. So the two studied intensely that night and went in the next day for the exam. The professor placed them in separate rooms

and handed each of them a test booklet and told them to begin. The first problem was simple and was worth 5 points. It looked like it was going to be an easy exam, and they were both relieved. They did the first problem and then turned the page. The next question was "Which tire? (95 points)."

Campus legends such as these help reduce the strain of college life and spread the reputations of legendary professors. Furthermore, they keep alive hopes of someday outfoxing the professors—or the students, depending on which side you are on.

• •

Source: www.snopes.com.

Each of these forms of collective behavior involves micro-level individual actions that cumulatively become collective responses to certain circumstances. Insofar as these various types of collective activity upset the standard routines of society and the accepted norms, they can unsettle the entire social system and cause lasting change. When we move to meso- and macro-level analyses, the established structures and processes of society become increasingly important. Much of the change at these levels is planned change.

PLANNED CHANGE IN ORGANIZATIONS: MESO-LEVEL CHANGE

The board of trustees of a small liberal arts college has witnessed recent drops in student enrollments that could cause the college to go out of business, but the college has a long tradition of fine education and devoted alumni. How does the college continue to serve future students and current alumni? The problem is how to plan change to keep the college solvent.

A company manufactures silicon chips for computers. Recently, the market has been flooded with inexpensive chips, primarily from Asia, where they are made more cheaply than this North American firm can possibly make them. Does the company succumb to the competition, figure out ways to meet it, or diversify its products? What steps should be taken to facilitate the change? Many companies in Silicon Valley, California, face exactly this challenge.

A Native American nation within the United States faces unemployment among its people due in large measure to discrimination by Anglos in the local community. Should the elders focus their energies and resources on electing sympathetic politicians, boycotting racist businesses, filing lawsuits, becoming entrepreneurs as a nation so they can hire their own people, or beginning a local radio station so they will have a communication network for a social movement? What is the best strategy to help this proud nation recover from centuries of disadvantage?

All these are real problems faced by real organizations. Anywhere we turn, organizations face questions involving change, questions that arise because of internal strains and external stresses. How organizational leaders deal with change will determine the survival and well-being of the organizations.

How Organizations Plan for Change

When working for an organization, we engage in the process of planning for change. Some organizations spend time and money writing long-range strategic plans and doing self-studies to determine areas for ongoing change. Sometimes, change is desired, and sometimes it is forced on the organization by *stresses* from society and more powerful organizations, or *strains* from individuals and groups within organizations pushing for new ideas. Moreover, a problem solved in one area can create unanticipated problems someplace else.

Organizational leaders must be prepared to guide their organization through planned and unplanned changes. Planned change involves strategic planning: deliberate, structured attempts, guided by stated goals, to alter the status quo of the social unit (Bennis, Benne, and Chin 1985; Ferhansyed 2008). Several important questions should be considered before undertaking planned change: How can we identify what needs to be changed? How can we plan or manage the change process successfully? What kind of systems adapt well to change? Here, we outline three of the many approaches to planned change. Keep in mind the levels of analysis as you read about change models.

Models for Planning Organizational Change. Change models fall into two main categories: (1) closed-system models, which deal with the internal dynamics of the organization, and (2) open-system models (such as our social world model), which consider the organization and its environment. *Closed-system models*, often called classical or mechanistic models, focus on the internal dynamics of the organization. The goal of change using closed models is to move the organization closer to the ideal of bureaucratic efficiency and effectiveness. An example is "time and motion studies," which analyze how much time it takes a worker to do a certain task and how it can be accomplished more efficiently. Each step in McDonald's process of getting a hamburger to the customer has been planned and timed for the greatest efficiency (Ritzer 2013b).

In some closed-system models, top executives legislate change, and it filters down to the workers. Other organizations follow a closed-system change model with an "organizational development approach." They involve participants in the organization in decision making

FIGURE 16.6   Open Systems Model

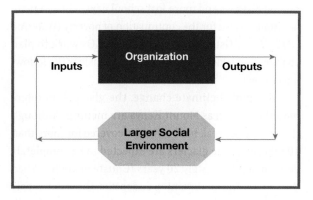

Thinking Sociologically

Using the model in Figure 16.6, fill in the parts as they relate to your college or university. For example, inputs might include students, federal student aid grants, new knowledge, and technology.

leading to change. The leadership is more democratic and supportive of workers, and the atmosphere is transparent—open, honest, and accountable to workers and investors. This model emphasizes that change comes about through adjusting workers' values, beliefs, and attitudes regarding new demands on the organization. Many variations on this theme have evolved, with current efforts including team building and change of the organizational culture to improve worker morale. Closed-system models tend to focus on group change that occurs from within the organization.

Open-system models combine both internal processes and the external environment. The latter provides the organization with inputs (workers and raw materials) and feedback (acceptability of the product or result). In turn, the organization has outputs (products) that affect the larger society. There are several implications of this model: (1) Change is an ever-present and ongoing process, (2) all parts of the organization and its immediate environment are linked, and (3) change in one part has an effect on the other parts. The model in Figure 16.6 illustrates the open system.

The Process of Planned Change. A huge issue in the Global South is the availability of clean drinking water. For example, in parts of Africa, women must spend as much as six hours a day carrying water to their homes. Because older daughters care for the younger siblings while the mother is away, many girls cannot attend school.

Sometimes the water found is not clean, leading to water-related diseases and more lost school days. This, in turn, has implications for the continuation of poverty (WaterAid 2012). Scientists and public policy NGOs work to plan changes and address such problems. Consider the following example.

With global climate change, the glaciers on top of mountains such as Mount Kenya are melting. Although that mountain peak has been snow covered for more than 10,000 years, the glaciers are expected to be completely gone in approximately 20 years (Cousteau 2008). When the snow at the mountaintop disappears, the water supply for hundreds of thousands of people and animals will

Petermann Glacier, 5 August 2009

Petermann Glacier 24 July 2011

These before and after shots of the Petermann Glacier in Greenland show a massive loss of glacier in just one calving (breaking off of chunks of ice at the edge of a glacier). For many parts of the world, glaciers are a major source of freshwater, but they are melting because of global climate change.

disappear (Maoncha 2013). One British NGO bringing about change in this area is WaterAid, launched in 1981. It has grown to become an international NGO that focuses entirely on water and sanitation issues, including hygiene. WaterAid now assists communities throughout the world to develop the most appropriate technologies for clean water, given the geographical features and changes in resources in their areas. This is an issue that requires careful planning and strategic use of resources if change is to be effective and have positive outcomes.

Using planned change, WaterAid reached 1.9 million people with safe water, 2.9 million people with sanitation, and an estimated 4.1 million people with hygiene promotion in 2013–2014 (WaterAid 2014). Some sociologists use their understanding of social processes to improve access to safe water and water management. This is illustrated by the work of Ruth Meinzen-Dick, described in the next "Sociologists in Action."

The process of planned change is like a puzzle with a number of pieces that differ for each organization but must fit together for the smooth operation of the organization. The goal of most organizations is to remain balanced and avoid threats or conflict. Most organizations and countries prefer to bring about change in a slow, carefully planned way. Unplanned change can be disruptive to the system.

At the societal and global macro levels, individuals and events outside the chambers of power often stimulate change, and there is much less control over how the change evolves. We turn next to an exploration of change at the macro level.

SOCIAL MOVEMENTS: MACRO-LEVEL CHANGE

Sochi, Russia, hosted the prestigious 2014 Winter Olympics. The Olympics purport to promote peace and goodwill around the globe. The Olympic torch, a symbol of peace and goodwill, traveled from Moscow to Sochi through 2,900 towns and villages to prepare for and celebrate the event. However, its journey and the opening of the games were far from peaceful and full of goodwill. Protests about Russia's policies toward gay rights dogged the torch and pregame political commentary, and major political leaders refused to attend the opening ceremonies. Russian legislation denigrating LGBTQ individuals and those spreading "propaganda" that "promotes" same-sex relationships sparked off protests and demonstrations around the world ("Sochi" 2014). Was this a

Same-Sex Marriage

SOCIOLOGISTS IN ACTION:
RUTH MEINZEN-DICK

Natural Resource Management in Developing Countries

What does a sociologist have to say about natural resource management? This is a question Ruth Meinzen-Dick has often been asked during her career. For 22 years, she has studied how farmers organize and relate to government and other organizations through her work at the International Food Policy Research Institute (IFPRI), part of a larger network of international agricultural research organizations.

Meinzen-Dick's interest in water management came from growing up in a dry part of India, where water was critical. She returned to India to study how small-scale irrigation systems were operated and found that farmers' organizations played an important role, even though the systems were formally under government management. Other students and faculty from different fields at Cornell University were finding similar patterns of farmer-managed irrigation systems in other parts of the world, so Meinzen-Dick was able to be part of a larger effort to understand the human side of water management. This was not just an academic exercise. Even while still in graduate school, Meinzen-Dick had a consultancy with the World Bank to review the extent of farmer participation in irrigation programs.

During her work at IFPRI, Meinzen-Dick has been able to continue studying what brings people together to manage water systems in developing countries and to compare this with the factors that encourage collective action for managing forests, rangelands, and other natural resources. This has involved field research in countries such as India, Pakistan, Zimbabwe, Kenya, and Uganda. She brought all this research together by coordinating an international network on Collective Action and Property Rights (CAPRi). This network helps people working on different aspects of agricultural research and natural resource management in developing countries to understand that the social institutions of property rights and collective action play a major role in shaping how people use and share resources. The CAPRi program provides training in quantitative and qualitative research methods to researchers and practitioners interested in collective action, property rights, and research strategies.

Much of Meinzen-Dick's professional life has involved working across disciplines. It has been especially important for her to communicate the findings of sociological research clearly to nonsociologists. Institutional economics and a strong background in quantitative analysis have been especially helpful for her in communicating with her colleagues—mostly economists. She says, "It is exhilarating when the research team achieves changes in government policies or development programs such as allowing farmers to have more voice in water management."

. . . .

Ruth Meinzen-Dick received her MA and PhD degrees in development sociology at Cornell University, with minors in agricultural economics and international agriculture. she is a senior research fellow at the International Food Policy Research Institute (IFPRI), with research in water resource management.

© AP Photo/Mary Gash

This photo shows Russian police attacking members of the Russian punk band Pussy Riot as they mock Russian antigay policies. This was one of hundreds of protests against the Russian policy prior to and during the Winter Olympic Games in Sochi.

social movement? We now turn to the definition of a social movement and discuss how social movements form and the results of such movements.

What Is a Social Movement?

From human rights and women's rights to animal rights and environmental protection, individuals seek ways to express their concerns and frustrations. Social movements are *consciously organized attempts outside of established institutions to enhance or resist change through group action*. Movements focus on a common interest of members, such as abortion policy. They have an organization, a leader, and one or more goals that aim to correct some perceived wrongs existing in society or even around the globe. Social movements are most often found in industrial or postindustrial societies although they can occur any place groups of people have a concern or frustration.

Social movements entail large groups of people who hold little power individually but do have power as united groups that promote or resist social change. The problems leading to social movements often result from the way resources—human rights, jobs, income, housing, money for education and health care, and power—are distributed. In turn, countermovements—social movements against the goals of the original movement—may develop, representing other opinions (McCarthy and Zald 1977).

Many individuals join social movements to change the world or their part of the world and affect the direction of history. In fact, some social movements have been successful in doing just that. Consider the movements

around the world that have protected lands, forests, rivers, and oceans, seeking environmental protection for the people whose survival depends on these natural resources. For example, the Chipko movement (meaning "embrace") has been fighting the logging of forests by commercial industries in a number of areas in India. Villagers, mostly women, who depend on the forests, use Gandhi-style nonviolent methods to oppose the deforestation. These women have set an example for environmentalists in many parts of the world who wish to save trees (Scribd 2011).

Stages of Social Movements

Why do people become involved in social movements such as PETA (People for the Ethical Treatment of Animals), pro-choice or pro-life movements, or political demonstrations against governments and their policies? Social movements begin because of cultural conflicts in society and because people who want to create—or resist—social change come together. Movements take the time and energy of individual volunteers, and these human resources must be focused as the movement evolves.

The *first stage* of a social movement involves setting the purpose of the movement. Long-standing problems or very recent events may create dissatisfaction and discontent in the general public or a part of the public. This discontent can galvanize people through a single event.

Sociologists have identified several conditions that give rise to the *preliminary stage*:

a. Individuals must *share some basic values and ideals*. They often occupy similar social statuses or positions and share concerns.

b. Social movements need to have a "*preexisting communication network*" that allows alienated or dissatisfied people to share their discontent (Farley 2011). Several recent political movements, such as MoveOn.org and Crossroads GPS, were carried out primarily on the Internet.

c. A *strain and a precipitating event* galvanize people around the issue. Effective leadership emerges—leaders who can mobilize people, organize the movement, and garner resources to fund the movement.

d. The people in the movement develop a *sense of efficacy*, a sense of confidence that they actually can be successful and change the system. Sometimes, as in the case of the civil rights movement, a sense of efficacy comes from a religious conviction that God will not let the movement fail (Farley 2011).

Women's Gain ▤   Pussy Riot ▤

The *second stage* in the development of a movement is popularization, in which individuals coalesce their efforts, define their goals and strategies, develop recruitment tactics, and identify leaders. The social movement enters the public arena. The leaders present the social problems and solutions as seen by the members of the social movement. Now the social movement enters the *third stage*, becoming institutionalized and a formal organization. This organized effort generates the resources and members for the social change efforts.

In some movements, the final *fourth stage* is fragmentation and demise. The group may or may not have achieved its goals, but fragmentation breaks apart the organization because the resources may be exhausted, the leadership may be inept or have lost legitimacy, or the leaders may be co-opted to join powerful mainline organizations. In the latter case, radical renewal movements may arise among those still strongly committed to the original cause (Mauss 1975).

Social movements sometimes focus on regional or even organizational modification, but typically, their focus is on national or global issues. For example, Amnesty International's primary interest is challenging countries with human rights violations. It publishes information on violations around the world and encourages supporters to advocate for those who face government persecution. One way to classify social movements is by their purpose or goals, as seen in the following section.

Types of Social Movements

Stonewall is a gay, lesbian, and bisexual rights movement that began when patrons of a gay bar fought back against a police raid in New York in 1969. After that incident, the concern about gay rights erupted from a small number of activists into a widespread movement for rights and acceptance. Stonewall now has gone global, with chapters in many other countries and continents.

Proactive social movements advocate moving forward with a new initiative—proposing something that did not exist before. One example is the effort by The Nonhuman Rights Project to give mammals such as chimpanzees legal rights of personhood. The Supreme Court ruled in the *Citizens United* case that corporations can be considered "persons." Now the Nonhuman Rights Project and Harvard Professor Steven Wise argue that dogs, cats, elephants, and other animals should be protected with rights of persons (such as right to body integrity) since

Flash mobs consist of groups of people who assemble suddenly in a public place, perform an unusual act for a brief time, and then quickly disperse, often for the purposes of entertainment, satire, or artistic expression. They are often fun and sometimes have a message critiquing the society or calling for change. This church-based flash mob in Minnehaha Park (Minneapolis) sang and danced to encourage voters to support same sex-marriage legislation in the 2012 election.

 Youth and Social Movements

they are aware, thinking, feeling, compassionate, communicating beings (Nonhuman Rights Project 2014). Regardless of whether you think this is an idea whose time has come or a harebrained notion, it would clearly change many aspects of society and move us in an entirely new direction.

Reactive social movements resist change, reacting against something that exists or against new trends or new social policies. The Climate Change Countermovement provides an example of a reactive social movement. It comprises 91 groups that have spent more than $1 billion from 141 nonprofit organizations and think tanks trying to debunk the conservation movement and climate change claims (Brulle 2014). They aim to counter the environmental movement and the change in policies that would result if that movement were successful in passing legislation and action.

Note that both liberals and conservatives can be involved in a reactive movement. When businesses want to build a corporation or plant in an area that will wipe out a native forest or destroy a historic area, liberals can be at the forefront of fighting "progress." Whether proactive or reactive, there are five main types of social movements: expressive, social reform, revolutionary, resistance or regressive, and globalized.

Expressive movements take place in groups, but they *focus on changing individuals and saving people from lifestyles the movement considers corrupt.* Many expressive movements are religious, such as the born-again Christian movements, Zen Buddhism, Scientology, and the Christian Science Church. Expressive movements also include secular psychotherapy movements and self-help or self-actualization groups.

Social reform movements *seek to change some specific dimension of society, usually involving legislative policy modification or appeals to the courts.* Movement members generally support the society as a whole but think things could be better if attention were given to issues such as environmental protection, women's rights, same-sex marriage, "just and fair" globalization, reducing the national debt, or abortion policy.

Social reform movements are not interested in disrupting the functioning of the entire society: They have one issue they think needs reform. For example, many individuals with disabilities are given little attention, hope, or opportunity to get ahead and are institution-alized or left to languish. However, social reform movements have advocated for legislation to promote the rights of the differently abled. One such movement is

Special Olympics International, begun by Eunice Kennedy Shriver in 1968 to give those with intellectual or physical disabilities an opportunity to excel in sports. Over 3 million athletes from 150 countries now participate in these games (www.specialolympics.org). The 2014 winter Paralympic Games were held in Sochi, Russia, featuring athletes with physical, mental, and sensorial disabilities. These events bring attention to the movement and issues faced by those with disabilities. Of particular interest were the advances the movement has helped to stimulate in physical adaptations for amputees, such as ice hockey using two sticks.

Revolutionary movements *attempt to transform society to bring about total change in society by overthrowing existing power structures and replacing them with new ones; these movements often resort to violent means to achieve their goals.* This has been the case with many revolutions throughout history. When we read in the paper that there has been a coup, we are learning about the ousting of an existing government such as when the military in Thailand declared martial law and seized power from the interim prime minister in May 2014.

Resistance or regressive movements *try to protect an existing system, protect part of that system, or return to what a system had been by overthrowing current laws and practices. They see societal change as a threat to values or practices and wish to maintain the status quo or return to a former status by reversing the change process* (Eitzen and Zinn 2012; Inglehart and Baker 2001). The Taliban religious movement in Afghanistan is a regressive movement against modernization, especially against the Western pattern of giving freedom and autonomy to women. The movement was successful in gaining power in the 1990s, imposing a harsh brand of Islamic law in the sections of Afghanistan under its control. The Taliban insists that its version of Islam is pure in that it follows a literal understanding of the Muslim holy book. Members of the movement maintain that someone who commits adultery should be stoned to death; the hands or arms of thieves should be amputated; and women who deviate from the Taliban interpretation of Muslim law should be mutilated, publically beaten, and sometimes executed (Valentine 2009).

Global transnational movements are *mobilized groups that take place across societies as international organizations.* Such groups focus on issues that affect the global community, such as the status of women, child labor, the rights of indigenous peoples, environmental

Occupy Wall Street ▶

degradation, global warming, and disease pandemics. Free the Slaves, an antislavery movement started by sociologist Kevin Bales, provides one example of a global transnational movement. Members of this movement have researched and written about the plight of the 27 million slaves in the world, "forced to work without pay, under threat of violence and unable to walk away" (Bales 2007; Bales, Trodd, and Williamson 2009; Bales and Soodalter 2010; Free the Slaves 2013).

The autoworkers' conflict with General Motors in Colombia is another example of a transnational or global social movement. A group of 68 autoworkers at a GM assembly plant outside of Bogotá formed a protest movement in May 2011. The issue was that a number of workers were fired when they could no longer perform their jobs due to disabling workplace injuries, including severe impairments to backs and rotator cuffs. Some of the workers will never be able to work again. Some health care companies hired by GM had changed medical records to read "injuries unrelated to occupation." After 15 months of protests, 13 protesters began a hunger strike, 8 of them sewing their mouths shut. International supporters began solidarity actions to put pressure on GM to enter into negotiations, and supporters in the United States sent money, wrote letters, and even engaged in fasting or hunger strikes themselves (Witness for Peace 2012). Intervention in 2013 by the United Auto Workers temporarily ended the hunger strike, but they were not able to resolve the issue. As of April 2014, the protest was continuing with some of the men starting a hunger strike again, swearing to fast until death if GM did not remedy the situation. As you can see, this is a local issue in Colombia that has mobilized people in other parts of the world.

Figure 16.7 summarizes the types of movements and the focus of each, from the micro to the macro level.

Globalization and Social Movements

Social movements provide compelling evidence that humans make choices and are capable of countering macro- and meso-level forces. As Stanley Eitzen and Maxine Baca Zinn put it,

Powerful social structures constrain what we do, but they can never control (us) entirely. Human

FIGURE 16.7   Types of Movements

This photo shows a statue of Nelson Mandela, who voted for the first time in South Africa in 1994. He had been a political prisoner for 26 years before becoming president of South Africa and winning the Nobel Peace Prize. Mandela provides a model for those committed to nonviolent revolutionary change.

beings are not passive actors. . . . Individuals acting alone, or with others, can shape, resist, challenge, and sometimes change the social structures that impinge on them. These actions constitute human agency. (Eitzen and Zinn 2012:269)

Since World War II, power in the global system has been dominated by a group of industrial giants calling themselves the Group of 8 (or the "G8"). As noted in earlier chapters, in March 2014, Russia was voted out by the other members because of its actions in Ukraine, so the group is now the G7. These nations control world markets and regulate economic and trading policies. Included among these elites are the dominant three—Japan from the East; Germany from central Europe; and the United States from the American continents. The other four, important but somewhat less powerful, members are Canada, France, Great Britain, and Italy.

The G7 nations, as we have mentioned in previous chapters, have the most power in the World Trade Organization, the World Bank, the IMF, and other regulatory agencies that preside over the global economy. These agencies have required poor countries to adhere to their demands or lose the right to loans and other support. The policies they have imposed, however, have sometimes been disastrous for poor countries, leading to debt burdens impossible to pay off.

The IMF points out that the loans are the only way poor countries can meet the UN Millennium Development Goals, but critics argue that the loans make poor countries dependent on wealthy countries and that the loans should be forgiven (International Monetary Fund 2013). They argue that if these were individuals rather than countries, we would call the poorer nations indentured servants or slaves (Brecher et al. 2012). One might think that hopelessness would reign supreme in these nations, yet social movements are arising in precisely these places and often joining forces across national boundaries (Eitzen and Zinn 2012; Ferree 2012; Muchhala 2012). Even some groups within the G7 nations—labor unions, college student groups, and religious bodies concerned about social justice—are joining the movements.

Global South nations, calling themselves the G77, have now united, rather like a labor union seeking collective unity among workers, in an attempt to gain some power and determine their own destinies (Brecher et al. 2012). Figure 13.4 displays the location of G7 and G77 countries.

Although workers risk losing jobs by participating in protests for higher wages and better working conditions, one result of globalization has been a rise in counter-movements. "Globalization from below" refers to the efforts by common people in small groups and protest movements to fight back (della Porta, Andretta, Mosca, and Reiter 2006; Eitzen and Zinn 2012). These countermovements seek to protect workers, defend the environment, and combat the bone-crunching poverty that plagues so much of the Global South. The argument goes like this:

It is the activity of people—going to work, paying taxes, buying products, obeying government officials, staying off private property—that continually re-creates the power of the powerful. . . . [The system, for all its power and resources, is dependent on common people to do the basic jobs that keep the society running.] This dependency gives people a potential power over the society—but one that can be realized only if they are prepared to reverse their acquiescence. . . . Social movements can be understood as the collective withdrawal of consent to established institutions. (Brecher et al. 2012:279)

The movement against globalization can be understood as withdrawing consent for globalization dominated by the most powerful nations and global corporations (Brecher et al. 2012). There are thousands of small resistance actions against what are sometimes perceived to be the oppressive policies of G7 transnational corporations (Hearn 2012). They involve micro-level actions to bring change at the macro level. Consider the following example:

Under heavy pressure from the World Bank, the Bolivian government sold off the public water system of its third-largest city, Cochabamba, to a subsidiary of the San Francisco–based Bechtel Corporation, which promptly doubled the price of water for people's homes. Early in 2000, the people of Cochabamba rebelled, shutting down the city with general strikes and blockades. The government declared a state of siege, and a young protester was shot and killed. Word spread all over the world from the remote Bolivian highlands via the Internet. Hundreds of e-mail messages poured into Bechtel from all over the world, demanding that it leave Cochabamba. In the midst of local and global protests, the Bolivian government, which had said that Bechtel must not leave, suddenly reversed itself and signed an accord accepting every demand of the protesters. (Brecher et al. 2012:284)

Many concerned citizens in the Global North now buy Fair Trade Certified goods such as coffee, cocoa, and fruits. This is an effort by individuals to support *globalization from below*—a different model of how to change the world. Activists believe that actions by individuals and small groups—globalization from below—can have a real impact on global problems. Consider how effective you think the actions taken by individuals and local groups can be by thinking about the issues in the next "Engaging Sociology."

ENGAGING SOCIOLOGY

Micro to Macro: Change From the Bottom Up

The idea of globalization "from the bottom up" suggests that the actions of a lot of people at the micro or local level can have a significant impact on how things develop at the macro level. Think about that process and what forces can enhance or retard that kind of change:

1. Are you familiar with cases in which "globalization from below" has made a difference in local, national, or international events? If so, what are those? If not, do a Google search and find two examples of globalization from below. Describe them.

2. Identify three structural challenges that might make it hard for people at the micro level to change the national and global forces that interfere with the quality of their lives.

3. Identify three reasons to be optimistic about why change from the bottom up can be successful.

4. To examine a specific example of a group that approaches globalization from below, do an Internet search of the Zapatistas or of their leader, Subcomandante Marcos. What are the pros and the cons of this movement? Do you think the Zapatistas have any chance of bringing change to the poor, disfranchised people of southern Mexico? Why or why not?

In summary, some social change is planned by organizations (planned change), some is initiated by groups outside the organizational structure (social movements), and some is unplanned and spontaneous (collective behavior). The most important point, however, is that actions taken by individuals affect the larger social world, sometimes even having global ramifications. Likewise, national and international changes and social movements influence the lives of individuals.

In the opening to this book, we asked whether you as an individual can make a difference. We present on page 564 an example of a "Sociologist in Action" who helps others bring about social change.

TECHNOLOGY, ENVIRONMENT, AND CHANGE

A lot is at stake for businesses, workers, environmentalists, policy makers, and others when considering the need for more energy sources. From renewable energy such as solar and wind power to gas and oil from fracking, strong opinions abound. One current example is the proposed Keystone XL Pipeline that would go from the Canadian tar sands source of oil to Texas refineries, crossing many states in the process. Proponents argue that it will be the safest, most advanced oil pipeline in North America, bringing jobs, long-term energy independence and an economic boost to both Canada and the United States. In addition, it will enhance the relationship between the two countries (TransCanada 2014).

Opponents argue that a technology failure along the pipeline could create havoc. The popularity of the movement to stop the construction of the pipeline illustrates that controversy can sometimes inspire or revitalize a group supporting social change, as happened with the environmentalists opposing the Keystone XL Pipeline project. Increasingly, U.S. oil is coming from deposits of tar sands in Alberta, Canada. This is not conventional crude oil. It is thick, sticky sand that companies extract by shooting steam deep underground to liquefy it, or they scrape it out of sprawling surface mines. These techniques of extraction are expensive, and they produce a lot more greenhouse gases than conventional oil wells. Still, high oil prices are now making tar sands oil profitable. If the network, known as the Keystone XL Pipeline, is approved, some 800,000 barrels of oil would be transported to refineries in Texas via large 36-inch pipes.

SOCIOLOGISTS IN ACTION:
ELLIS JONES

Empowering Everyday People: Democratizing Access to Social Change

On April 22, 1990, something changed for me. It was a Sunday. I was a student at the University of Southern California, and a friend invited me to walk down to a fair that was going on nearby. I didn't have any plans, so I decided to join him. Apparently, it was something called "Earth Day." There were tables and booths everywhere, and people were excitedly milling about from one to the next. Every booth I visited offered me a different way to make a positive environmental impact: recycling, composting, conserving water, reusing old clothes, and the list went on and on.

At the end of that day, I felt absolutely inspired to make the world a better place. In my mind, the environmental movement had experienced a stroke of true genius. They weren't asking people to join groups, attend meetings, or organize rallies. Instead, they had opened up a completely new realm of action for people—their own everyday lives. By engaging people in micro-activism rather than asking them to commit to the much more intensive work undertaken by full-time activists, they were essentially democratizing access to social change. It was a way to expand the environmental movement to almost anyone despite their limits of time, money, skills, or circumstances.

As soon as I realized this, I imagined that thousands of others were having the same revelation at that same moment of history. The environmental movement was laying the foundation for all other social movements to do exactly the same thing! The human rights movement, the social justice movement, the animal rights movement, the feminist movement, the LGBTQ movement, and all the rest would begin to adapt this new technique to engage people everywhere in actions they could take in their own lives to contribute to some much needed social change.

Granted, no particular action would add up to much in terms of impact, but if enough people were inspired to act, the collective impact of thousands, or tens of thousands, or perhaps even millions of people would redefine what kind of changes were possible around these issues. At the same time, all of these people would now feel more invested in the outcomes that they themselves had been working toward in their own way. Rather than relying solely on a relatively small group of activists to bear the weight of these daunting social and environmental problems, now everyone could take on a piece of that responsibility.

The more I thought about this potential, the more I became convinced that what people really needed (or at least what I really needed) was a book that would collect as many of these actions as possible into a single place. I was absolutely sure that someone would write it and I, in turn, would be first in line to buy it. Ten years later, I was a sociology graduate student at the University of Colorado at Boulder. I had waited, patiently, for the imaginary author of this hypothetical book to appear and s/he had yet to step forward. In the meantime, I was teaching *Social Problems* along with a number of other mainstay sociology courses and found that my own students were constantly asking what they could actually do about all of these problems we were spending so much time reading about, discussing, and analyzing.

I had waited 10 years and decided that was long enough. So I roped in two of my closest friends (also fellow sociology grad students), and we spent the next year writing a book that collected all the actions we could find, from every source we could get our hands on, and distilled the results into a single book. We added a section summarizing the latest data on some of the most significant social and environmental problems we seemed to be facing at the beginning of the 21st century, and the result was *The Better World Handbook: Small Changes That Make a Big Difference*. It has since sold 25,000 copies, been added to more than 300 college and university libraries worldwide, and been adopted in sociology classrooms across the country. The website (betterworldhandbook.com) has had over 550,000 unique visitors since it was created. In a very practical sense, sociology provided the three of us with the tools we needed to uncover, understand, and translate our world's social and environmental problems into a form that allows each of us to personally contribute to their resolution.

• •

Ellis Jones received his doctorate from the University of Colorado at Boulder, and is now an assistant professor of sociology at College of the Holy Cross in Worcester, Massachusetts.

A break in a tar sands pipeline in Michigan in 2010 resulted in 40 miles of the Kalamazoo River being basically closed to any public use (Wheaton 2014). TransCanada, the company that owns the pipeline, has admitted that it expects about two breaks per year over the 1,700 miles of pipe (Shogren 2012).

James Hansen, a former NASA climate scientist, published an open letter to the public calling the pipeline "game over for the climate" and urged people to take action. This jump-started the environmental movement, bringing in unexpected allies—including Texas landholders—and large numbers of young people (Wheaton 2014).

Environmentalists opposed to the Keystone XL Pipeline have built a human chain around the White House, clogged the State Department's public comment system with more than a million e-mails and letters, and had themselves arrested at protests across the country. The e-mail list of an organization called 350.org, which focuses on climate change, more than doubled to 530,000 people in less than a year. In addition, about 76,000 people have signed a "pledge of resistance," and an environmental group—the Sierra Club—raised more than $1 million in one week when it announced an anti-pipeline initiative (Wheaton 2014). The revitalized environmental movement is changing the landscape regarding the energy versus environment conflict (Wheaton 2014).

Technology refers to *the practical application of tools, skills, and knowledge to meet human needs and extend human abilities*. Technology and the environment cannot be separated, as we see from the debate over the Keystone pipeline. The raw products that fuel technology come from the environment, the wastes return to the environment, and technological mistakes affect the environment. This section discusses briefly the development and process of technology, the relationship between technology and the environment, and the implications for change at each level of analysis.

Throughout human history, there have been major transition periods when changes in the material culture brought about revolutions in human social structures and cultures (Toffler and Toffler 1980). For example, the

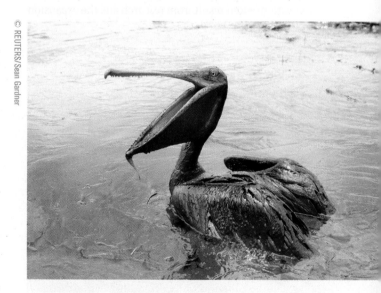

© REUTERS/Sean Gardiner

An exhausted oil-covered brown pelican struggled in a pool of oil on an island off the coast of Louisiana, part of the cost of a massive oil spill in 2010. Environmental disasters from oil spills have created new impetus for environmental movements.

agricultural revolution, which resulted from the use of the plow to till the soil, established new social arrangements and created food surpluses that allowed cities to flourish. With the Industrial Revolution came machines powered by steam and petrol, resulting in mass production, population increases, urbanization, the division of labor in manufacturing, social stratification, and the socialist and capitalist political-economic systems. Today, postindustrial technology, based on the microchip, fuels the spread of information, communication, transportation on a global level, and even exploration of outer space. It also allows us to store and retrieve masses of information in seconds. However, each wave of innovation initially affects only a portion of the world, leaving other people and countries behind and creating divisions between the Global North and the Global South.

Sociologist William Ogburn has argued that change is brought about through three processes: *discovery, invention, and diffusion.* Discovery is a new way of seeing reality. The material objects or ideas have been present, but they are seen in a new light when the need arises or conditions are conducive to the discovery. It is usually accomplished by an individual or a small group, a micro-level activity (Ogburn [1922] 1938, 1961, 1964).

Invention refers to combining existing parts, materials, or ideas to form new ones. There was no light bulb or combustion engine lying in the forest waiting to be discovered. Human ingenuity was required to put together something that had not previously existed. Technological innovations often result from research and the expansion of science, increasingly generated in meso-level institutions and organizations in society.

Diffusion is the spread of an invention or discovery from one place to another. The spread of ideas such as capitalism, democracy, and religious beliefs has brought about changes in human relationships around the world. Likewise, the spread of various types of music, film technology, telephone systems, and computer hardware and software across the globe has had important ramifications for global interconnectedness. Diffusion often involves expansion of ideas across the globe, but it also requires individuals to adopt ideas at the micro level.

Technology and Science

Science is *the systematic process of producing human knowledge; it uses empirical research methods to discover facts and test theories.* The question "How do we know what we know?" is often answered: "It's science." Whether social, biological, or physical, science provides a systematic way to approach the world and its mysteries. It uses empirical research methods to discover facts and test theories. Today, technology applies scientific knowledge to solve problems. Early human technology was largely the result of trial and error, not based on scientific knowledge or principles. Humans did not understand why boats floated or fires burned. Since the Industrial Revolution, many inventors and capitalists have seen science and technology as routes to human betterment and happiness. Science has become a major social institution in industrial and postindustrial societies, providing the bases of information and knowledge for sophisticated technology.

Indeed, one of the major transformations in modern society is the result of science becoming an institution. Prior to the 18th century, science was an avocation. People like Benjamin Franklin experimented in their backyards with whatever spare cash they had to satisfy their own curiosity.

Science in the contemporary world is both a structure and a social process. *Institutionalization* means creation of the organized, patterned, and enduring sets of social structures that provide guidelines for behavior and help the society meet its needs. Within these structures, actions are taken—the processes within the structure—that accomplish a goal such as conducting research. Innovation resulting in change will be very slow until a society has institutionalized science—providing extensive training and paying some people simply to do research. Modern science involves mobilizing financial

Technological innovation is now providing us with electricity through wind farms. The one depicted here is the first complete high-sea wind farm on the North Sea coast of Germany.

© REUTERS/Fabian Bimmer

resources and employing the most highly trained people (which, in turn, requires the development of educational institutions).

Specialization in science speeds up the rates of discovery. A researcher focuses on one area and gets much more in-depth understanding. Also, effective methods of communication across the globe mean that we do not need to wait several years for a research manuscript to cross the ocean and be translated into another language. Competition in science (now global) means that researchers move quickly on their findings. The first to create new drugs, devices, and other inventions tend to reap the most recognition and compensation.

We would not have automobiles, planes, missiles, space stations, computers, the Internet, and many of our modern conveniences without the institutionalization of science and without scientific application (technology). Science is big business, funded by industry and government. Most university researchers and some government-funded science institutes engage in *basic research* designed to discover new knowledge. Industry and some governmental agencies such as the military and the Department of Agriculture employ scientists to do *applied research* and discover practical uses for existing knowledge.

Scientific knowledge is usually cumulative, with each study adding to the existing body of research. However, radical new ideas can result in scientific revolutions (Kuhn 1970). Galileo's finding that the Earth revolves around the Sun and Darwin's theory of evolution are two examples of radical new ideas that changed history. More recently, cumulative scientific knowledge has resulted in energy-efficient engines that power cars and computer technology that has revolutionized communication.

Thinking Sociologically

Imagine what your life would have been like before home computers, e-mail, and the Internet. What would be different? (Note that you are imagining the world from only 30 years ago.) Ask your parents or grandparents what this recent past was like.

Technology and Change

The G7 has yearly meetings to regulate global economic policy and markets. The group's power enables those seven countries to dominate technology by controlling raw products—from natural gas and essential ores to sugarcane. In the process, powerful leaders of Global North countries profoundly influence which countries

Thomas Edison had more than 1,000 patented inventions, including the lightbulb, recorded sound, and movies, but perhaps his most influential invention was the research lab—in which people were paid to invent and to conduct research—at Menlo Park in New Jersey. This was the seminal step in the institutionalization of science.

will be rich or poor. Although some politicians say they believe in a free market economy, uninhibited by governmental interference, government officials intervene regularly in the global market, influencing nations' access to technology.

A nation's research and development (R&D) is an important measure of its investment in the future. For many years the biggest investors have been the European Union, the United States, and Japan, accounting in 2014 for $1.6 trillion or 78% of global R&D expenditures. However, as of 2022, China is expected to surpass the United States in R&D spending. While U.S. industry continues to support R&D, the government is under pressure to pare down federal spending and thus contributing less to it than in previous budgets.

This lack of U.S. investment in research is especially troubling, given what we know about the relationship between economic growth and R& D (Battelle 2013). For example, technological revolution in communications has resulted in fiber-optic cable and wireless microwave cell phones and satellite technologies that make it easier to communicate with people around the world. A cable starting in Europe is now circling Africa; the capabilities for high-speed Internet will enhance opportunities for businesses, health care to remote areas, and educational advances in countries that have few textbooks. We now live

📖 Research and Development   💻 The Elderly and the Internet in a global village, a great boon for those fortunate enough to have the education and means to take advantage of it (Drori 2006).

However, changes in technology do not always have a positive effect on less affluent countries. Consider, for example, the effects of the invention of artificial sweeteners on the demand for sugar. Sugar is the major source of income for the 50 million people who work in the beet and cane sugar industries around the globe. As new technologies bring substantial benefits to many in the world, these results can also harm people in other parts of the interconnected world. Changes in technology and the economy have forced many individuals to leave their native villages in search of paid labor positions in urban factories and the tourism industry, disrupting family lives.

Rapid technological change has affected generational relationships as well. It is not uncommon for younger generations to have more technological competence than their elders, and this sometimes creates a generational digital divide in competencies regarding use of computers, cell phones, and other electronic devices. In some settings, younger people are looked to for their expertise, whereas in the past, the elders were the source of knowledge and wisdom. Often the older members of a business or group feel devalued and demoralized late in their careers because those with technical competence view the older members as "outdated has-beens."

Popular video games such as *Grand Theft Auto V* and *BioShock Infinite* plus *BioShock 2* top the sales charts (Kotaku 2013), and forms of entertainment such as the Wii-U and Nintendo 3DS further the social distance between generations. With the changes brought about by technology come changes in the nonmaterial culture—values, political ideologies, and human relationships. Clearly, technology can have a variety of social impacts—both positive and negative.

In the opening to this book, we asked whether you as an individual can make a difference. In closing, we present an example of a sociologist in action who helps others bring about social change. We also provide, in the final "Engaging Sociology," a plan you can follow to make a difference.

Thinking Sociologically

First, read "Engaging Sociology: Making a Difference." Then use the steps to plan how you would bring about a change that would make a difference in your community, in your country, or in the world. Go to "Contributing to Our Social World: What Can We Do?" at the end of this and other chapters to find ways in which you could be actively involved in bettering society.

VISUAL SOCIOLOGY: *TRANSPORTATION SYSTEMS AND SOCIAL CHANGE*

© Keith Roberts

The modes of transportation for goods and people vary around the world, often reflecting the level of development of the region or country. Sometimes, technological progress has high costs, including pollution. Visit **edge.sagepub.com/ballantine5e** for an interactive photo essay about transportation systems and modernization.

········· ENGAGING SOCIOLOGY ·········

Making a Difference

If you want to bring about social change, consider the following steps used by public/applied sociologists: Because bringing about change requires cooperation, working in a group context is often essential. Flexibility, openness to new ideas, and willingness to entertain alternative suggestions are also key factors in successful change making. The following steps provide a useful strategy for planning change:

1. *Identify the issue:* Be specific and focus on what is to be changed. Without a clear focus, your target for change can get muddied or lost.

2. *Research the issue and use those findings:* Learn as much as you can about the situation or problem to be changed. Use informants, interviews, written materials, observation, existing data (such as U.S. Census Bureau statistics), or anything that helps you understand the issues. That will enable you to find the information you need to thoroughly understand the issue you wish to address.

3. *Find out what has already been done and by whom:* Other individuals or groups may be working on the same issue. Be sure you know what findings and intervention have already taken place. This can also help determine whether attempts at change have been tried, what has been successful, and whether further change is needed.

4. *Change must take into account each level of analysis:* When planning a strategy, you may focus on one level of analysis, but be sure to consider what interventions are needed at other levels to make the change effective or to anticipate the effects of change on other levels.

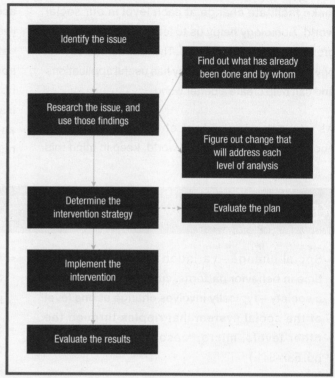

5. *Determine the intervention strategy:* Map out the intervention and the steps to carry it out. Identify resources needed, and plan each step in detail.

6. *Evaluate the plan:* Get feedback on the plan from those involved in the issue and from unbiased colleagues. If possible, involve those who will be affected by the intervention in the planning and evaluation of the change. When feasible, test the intervention plan before implementing it.

7. *Implement the intervention:* Put the plan into effect, watching for any unintended consequences. Ask for regular feedback from those affected by the change.

8. *Evaluate the results:* Assess what is working, what is not, and how the constituents that experience the change are reacting. Sociological knowledge and skills should help guide this process.

WHAT HAVE WE LEARNED?

Can you change the world? The underlying message of this chapter and the text is that the choices we make facilitate change at each level in our social world. Sociology helps us to learn how to work with groups to make a difference. The founders of sociology recognized that sociology has useful applications and can help create a better world.

As you face individual challenges to bring about change in your social world, keep in mind this

message: Change at one level affects all other levels. Sociology as a discipline is focused on gathering accurate information about the society in which we live. Sociologists often use their knowledge to advocate for changes that they think will make a better society. We hope that through his book and your course you have gained important sociological insights that will help you contribute to the dialogue about how to make our social world a better, more humane place.

KEY POINTS

- Social change—variation or alteration over time in behavior patterns, culture, or structure in a society—typically involves change at one level of the social system that ripples through the other levels, micro, meso, and macro. (See pp. 537–541.)

- *Strains* within an organization or group can induce change, as can *stresses* imposed from the outside environment. (See pp. 541–544.)

- Sociological theories—whether micro or macro—offer explanations for the causes of change. (See pp. 546–549.)

- At the micro level, change is often initiated through collective behavior, which can take several forms: crowds, mobs, riots, rumors, fads, and fashions. (See pp. 549–554.)

- At the meso level, change in organizations is often managed through a planned process. (See pp. 554–556.)

- Social movements often provide impetus for change at the macro level. Social changes can be induced at the micro level, but they can have impacts even at the global level. (See pp. 558–563.)

- Science and technology can also stimulate change, but science has its greatest impact for change when it is institutionalized. (See pp. 563–569.)

- Social structures constrain what we do, but individuals, especially when acting in concert with others, can challenge, resist, and change the social systems that constrain them. We can change our society through *human agency*. (See pp. 568–569.)

DISCUSSION QUESTIONS

1. What is the latest technological device you or your family has acquired? How has it changed your life? What are the (a) intended and (b) unintended consequences of your having it?

2. Every organization must adapt to change. Describe how an organization to which you belong coped with change. Was the adaptation successful? Why or why not? What was your role? Did you

feel as though you had some influence over the adaptation strategy? Why or why not?

3. Were you aware that the United States gives far less than the 0.7% of gross national product the United Nations has requested of nations, in order to achieve the UN Millennium Development Goals to decrease poverty, illiteracy, famine, and disease? Would be in the self-interest of the United States to contribute more or less? Why?

4. What type of social movement has helped bring about the dramatic increase in support for same-sex marriage over the past few years? Why? How do the results of this movement indicate the power of social movements to influence society at the micro, meso, and macro levels?

5. If you were to join a social movement today, which would you join? Why? What would you hope to achieve?

CONTRIBUTING TO OUR SOCIAL WORLD: WHAT CAN WE DO?

At the Local Level

- *Campus-wide Movements:* A wide range of social issues, including international peace, environmental issues, human rights, and specific student concerns such as campus safety and the rising cost of higher education, may have movements represented on your campus. Consider participating in such activities. If you feel strongly about an issue for which no movement exists, consider organizing one with a few like-minded students. You can find tools to create a campus movement at www.campusactivism.org/index.php, www.campusactivism.org/displayresource-471.htm, and www.thetaskforce.org/reports_and_research/campus_manual.

- Many *community movements* bring about change at the local level, sometimes with national and even international effects. Check with your professors, service learning and campus activities offices, and Chambers of Commerce to find community movements in your area.

At the Organizational or Institutional Level

- *Invite a movement leader to campus.* Consider inviting movement leaders to your campus for a lecture, or organize a conference that features several experts in a particular field. Environment, civil rights, and modern slavery are topics that have wide appeal. Professors who teach classes that cover these issues may be able to help you find a good speaker. Work with your sociology club or student government to provide funding for the speaker.

- *Volunteer Match* seeks to connect individuals with movements of interest to them. Its website (www.volunteermatch.org) has suggestions for getting involved in your local area.

At the National and Global Levels

- *The Jubilee Movement* promotes international debt forgiveness for the world's poorest countries — a solution that the U.S. government has embraced in principle. Named for the principle offered in the Hebrew scriptures that creditors are to cancel all debt owed to them every jubilee year (once every 49 years), the organization sponsors legislative programs, research work, and educational outreach activities throughout the world. The website of Jubilee USA (www.jubileeusa.org/about-us) provides information on ways in which you can get involved, and includes information about international debt, activities, and the history of the movement.

Glossary

Absolute poverty. Not having resources to meet basic needs, 221

Achieved status. Social status that is chosen or earned by decisions one makes and sometimes by personal ability, 132

Achieved stratification systems. Societal systems that allow individuals to earn positions through their ability, efforts, and choices, 216

Agents of socialization. The transmitters of culture—the people, organizations, and institutions that help us define our identity and teach us how to thrive in our social world, 107

Agricultural society. Relies primarily on raising crops for food, but makes use of technological advances such as the plow, irrigation, animals, and fertilization to continuously cultivate the same land, 64

Alienation. Feeling uninvolved, uncommitted, unappreciated, and unconnected to the group or the society, 141

Anomie. The state of normlessness that occurs when rules for behavior in society break down under extreme stress from rapid social change or conflict, 135

Arranged marriages. A pattern of mate selection in which someone other than the couple—elder males, parents, a match-maker—selects the marital partners, 320

Ascribed statuses. Social statuses that are often assigned at birth and that do not change during an individual's lifetime; gender, race, and ethnic status group are examples, 131

Ascribed stratification systems. Societal systems in which characteristics beyond the control of the individual—such as family background, age, sex, and race—determine one's position in society, 216

Assimilation. The structural and cultural merging of minority and majority groups in society, 249

Authoritarian governments. Governments in which one absolute monarch or dictator, or a small group of unelected people, holds all of the political power, 433

Authority. Power that people consider legitimate and that is recognized as rightful by those subject to it, 420

Beliefs. Ideas about life, the way society works, and where one fits in, 74

Bureaucracies. Specific types of large formal organizations that have the purpose of maximizing efficiency; they are characterized by formal relations between participants, clearly laid-out procedures and rules, and pursuit of shared goals, 138

Caste systems. The most rigid ascribed stratification systems. Individuals are born into a status, which they retain throughout life. That status is deeply embedded in religious, political, and economic norms and institutions, 216

Cause-and-effect relationships. Occur when there is a relationship between variables so that one variable stimulates a change in another, 44

Civil religion. The set of beliefs, rites, and symbols that sacralize the values of the society and place the nation in the context of transcendent meaning, often giving it divine significance, 393

Collective behavior. Actions that are unstructured and spontaneous and that may violate norms; this behavior arises when people are trying to cope with stressful situations and unclear or uncertain conditions, 549

Conflict theory. Theory that focuses on social groups competing for scarce resources, 37

Consensus crimes. Crimes for which members of society are in general agreement about the seriousness, 155

Content analysis. Entails the systematic categorizing and recording of information from written or recorded sources—printed materials, videos, radio broadcasts, or artworks, 46

Control group. A group in which the subjects are not exposed to the variable the researcher wants to test, 46

Controls. Steps used by researchers to eliminate all variables except those related to the hypothesis—especially those variables that might be spurious, 44

Correlation. A relationship between variables such as poverty and low levels of education, with change in one variable associated with change in another, 44

Counterculture. A group with expectations and values that contrast sharply with the dominant values of a particular society, 81

Crime. Deviant actions for which there are formal penalties imposed by the government, such as fines, jail, or prison sentences, 152

Cultural capital. The knowledge, skills, language mastery, style of dress, and values that provide a person with access to a particular status in society, 197

Cultural relativism. Requires setting aside cultural and personal beliefs and prejudices to understand another group or society through the eyes of its members and using its own community standards, 72

Culture. The way of life shared by a group of people—the knowledge, beliefs, values, rules or laws, language, customs, symbols, and material products within a society that help meet human needs, 58

Democratic governments. Governments characterized by accountability to citizens and a large degree of control by individuals over their own lives, 434

Democratic socialism. Collective or group planning of the development of society, but within a democratic political system; the good of the whole is paramount, 439

Demographic transition theory. Links trends in birthrates and death rates with patterns of economic and technological development, 501

Demography. The study of human populations, 494

Denominations. Centralized coordinating bodies or associations that link local congregations with a similar history and theology, 388

Dependency ratio. The ratio of those in both the young and aged groups compared with the number of people in the productive age groups between 15 and 64 years old, 497

Dependent variable. The variable in a cause-and-effect relationship that is affected by and comes after the independent variable in time sequence, 44

Deprofessionalization. The process through which a professional occupation loses autonomy, respect, and service orientation because the professionals come to be controlled by nonprofessionals and outside forces such as financial concerns, government regulations, technological changes, and administrators or management, 476

Deviance. The violation of social norms, 152

Discrimination. Differential treatment and harmful actions against minorities, 240

Dysfunctions. Actions that undermine the stability or equilibrium of society, 37

Empirical knowledge. Founded on information gained from evidence (facts), rather than intuition, 42

Endogamy. Norms that require individuals to marry inside certain human boundaries, whatever the societal members see as protecting the homogeneity of the group, 320

Environment. The setting in which the social unit operates, including everything that influences the social unit, such as its physical and organizational surroundings and technological innovations, 16

Estate systems. Characterized by the concentration of economic and political power in the hands of a small minority of political-military elite, with the peasantry tied to the land, 216

Ethnic group. A group within the human species that is based on cultural factors: language, religion, dress, foods, customs, beliefs, values, norms, a shared group identity or feeling, and sometimes loyalty to a homeland, monarch, or religious leader, 237

Ethnocentrism. The tendency to view one's own group and its cultural expectations as right, proper, and superior to others, 71

Evidence. Facts and information that are confirmed through systematic processes of testing, using the five senses, 42

Exogamy. Norms governing the choice of a mate that require individuals to marry outside of their own immediate group, 320

Experimental group. In a controlled experiment, the group in which people are exposed to the variable being studied to test its effect, 46

Experiment. All variables except the one being studied are controlled so researchers can study the effects of the variable under study, 46

Expressive movements. Focus on changing individuals and saving people from lifestyles the movement considers corrupt, 560

Extended family. Two or more adult generations that share tasks and living quarters. This may include brothers, sisters, aunts, uncles, cousins, and grandparents, 325

Family of orientation. The family into which we are born, 314

Family of procreation. The family we create ourselves, 314

Feminist theory. Critiques the hierarchical power structures that disadvantage women and other minorities, 40

Fertility. Demographic processes referring to the birthrate, 503

Formal agents of socialization. Official or legal agents (e.g., families, schools, teachers, religious organizations) whose purpose it is to socialize the individual into the values, beliefs, and behaviors of the culture, 107

Formal education. Schooling that takes place in a formal setting with the goal of teaching a predetermined curriculum, 344

Formal organizations. Modern rational organizations composed of complex secondary groups deliberately formed to pursue and achieve certain goals, 138

Formal sanctions. Rewards or punishments conferred by recognized officials to enforce the most important norms, 77

Free-choice marriage. A pattern of mate selection in which the partners select each other based primarily on romance and love, 321

Functional theory. Assumes that all parts of the social structure (including groups, organizations, and institutions), the culture (values and beliefs), and social processes (social change or child rearing) work together to make the whole society run smoothly and harmoniously, 36

Game stage. Stage in the process of developing a social self when a child develops the ability to take the role of multiple others concurrently (norms, values, and expectations of the generalized other) and conform to societal expectations, 103

Gemeinschaft. German term meaning "small traditional community," 515

Gender. A society's notions of masculinity and femininity—socially constructed meanings associated with being male or female—and how individuals construct their identity in terms of gender within these constraints, 271

Gender roles. Those commonly assigned tasks or expected behaviors linked to an individual's sex-determined statuses, 271

Generalized other. A composite of societal expectations that a child learns from family, peers, and other organizations, 103

Genocide. The systematic effort of one group, usually the dominant group, to destroy a minority group, 248

Gentrification. Refers to members of the middle and upper class, mostly young white professionals, buying and renovating run-down properties in central-city locations, and displacing poor residents, 524

Gesellschaft. German term meaning "a modern society with impersonal relationships," 515

Global culture. Behavioral standards, symbols, values, and material objects that have become common across the globe, 84

Global transnational movements. Mobilized groups that take place across societies as international organizations seek change in the status of women, child labor, rights of indigenous peoples, environmental degradation, global warming, disease pandemics, and other issues that affect the global community, 560

Globalization. The process by which the entire world is becoming a single interdependent sociocultural entity, more uniform, more integrated, and more interdependent, 84

Goal displacement. Occurs when the original motives or goals of the organization are displaced by new secondary goals, 142

Groups. Units involving two or more people who interact with each other because of shared common interests, goals, experiences, and needs, 134

Hate crimes. Criminal offenses committed against a person, property, or group that are motivated by the offender's bias against a religious, ethnic, or racial group; national origin; gender; or sexual orientation, 170

Health. A state of physical, mental, and social well-being or the absence of disease, 458

Herding societies. Societies in which the food-producing strategy is based on the society's domestication of animals, whose care is the central focus of their activities, 62

Horticultural societies. Societies in which the food-producing strategy is based on domestication of plants, using digging sticks and wooden hoes to cultivate small gardens, 63

Hunter-gatherer society. A society in which people rely on the vegetation and animals occurring naturally in their habitat to sustain life, 62

Hypothesis. An educated guess or prediction, 42

I. The spontaneous, unpredictable, impulsive, and largely unorganized aspect of the self, 100

Ideal culture. Consists of practices, beliefs, and values that are regarded as most desirable in society and are consciously taught to children, 74

Illness. Lack of health, 458

Imitation stage. A period when children under 3 years old are preparing for role-taking by observing others and imitating their behaviors, sounds, and gestures, 102

Independent variable. The variable in a cause-and-effect relationship that comes first in a time sequence and causes a change in another variable, 44

Industrial societies. Rely primarily on mechanized production, resulting in greater division of labor based on expertise, 64

Inequality. A social condition in which privileges, opportunities, and substantial rewards are given to people in some positions in society but denied to others, 187

Informal agents of socialization. Unofficial forces that shape values, beliefs, and behaviors in which socialization is not the express purpose; examples are the media, books, advertising, and the Internet, 109

Informal sanctions. Unofficial rewards or punishments such as smiles, frowns, or ignoring unacceptable behaviors, 77

In-group. A group to which an individual feels a sense of loyalty and belonging; it also may serve as a reference group, 137

Institutional racial discrimination. Any meso-level institutional arrangement that favors one racial group over another; this favoritism may result in intentional or unintentional consequences for minority groups, 245

Institutions. Organized, patterned, and enduring sets of social structures that provide guidelines for behavior and help each society meet its basic survival needs. While institutions operate mostly at the meso level, they also act to integrate micro and macro levels of society, 306

Interaction. The exchange of verbal and nonverbal messages, 94

Labeling theory. Explains how people can be labeled deviant after committing a deviant act, which can then lead them to carry out further acts that reflect that label, 159

Language. Conveys verbal and nonverbal messages among members of society; the foundation of every culture, 77

Latent functions. Unplanned or unintended consequences of actions or of social structures, 37

Laws. Norms formally encoded by those holding political power in society with formal punishment attached, 76

Levels of analysis. Social groups from the smallest to the largest, 13

Life expectancy. The average number of years a person in a particular society can expect to live, 493

Lifestyle. Includes attitudes, values, beliefs, behavior patterns, and other aspects of one's place in the world, shaped by socialization, 206

Looking-glass self. A reflective process that develops our *self* based on our interpretations and internalization of the reactions of others to us, 99

Macro-level analysis. Analysis of the largest social units in the social world, including entire nations, global forces, and international social trends, 18

Manifest functions. The planned outcomes of interactions, social organizations, or institutions, 36

Market or capitalist economic system. An economic system driven by the balance of supply and demand, allowing free competition to reward the efficient and innovators with profits; stresses individual planning and private ownership of property, 438

Master status. An individual's social status that becomes most important and takes precedence over other statuses, 132

Material culture. Includes all the objects we can see or touch; all the artifacts of a group of people, 73

Me. The part of the self that has learned the rules of society through interaction and role-taking, and it controls the *I* and its desires, 100

Means of production. Karl Marx's concept of property, machinery, and cash owned by capitalists, 38

Mechanical solidarity. Social cohesion and integration based on the similarity of individuals in the group, including shared beliefs, values, and emotional ties between members of the group, 61

Medicalization. Handling of some forms of deviance as well as some normal human functions (such as pregnancy and childbirth) in the health care system rather than the family, legal, or religious arenas, 460

Meritocracy. A social group or organization in which people are allocated to positions according to their abilities and credentials, as in level of education attained, 212

Meso-level analysis. Analysis of intermediate-size social units, smaller than the nation but large enough to encompass more than the local community or region, 18

Microculture. A group that affects only a small segment of one's life or influences a limited period of one's life, 79

Micro-level analysis. Analysis with a focus on individual or small group interaction in specific situations, 18

Migration. In terms of demographic processes, refers to the movement of people from one place to another, 503

Minority groups. Groups in a population that differ from others in some characteristics and are therefore subject to less power, fewer privileges, and discrimination, 233

Monogamy. The most familiar form of marriage in industrial and postindustrial societies; refers to marriage of two individuals, 323

Mortality. In terms of demographic processes, refers to the death rate, 503

Myths. Stories that transmit values and embody ideas about life and the world, 384

National culture. Common values and beliefs that tie citizens of a nation together, 84

National society. A population of people, usually living within a specified geographic area, who are connected by common ideas, cooperate for the attainment of common goals, and are subject to a particular political authority, 15

New religious movements (NRMs). Innovative religious groups that arise to meet specific needs not met through traditional religious organizations, and that can become established religions after several generations, 390

Nonmaterial culture. The thoughts, language, feelings, beliefs, values, and attitudes that make up much of our culture, 73

Nonverbal communication. Interactions without words using facial expressions, the head, eye contact, body posture, gestures, touch, walk, status symbols, and personal space, 128

Norms. Rules of behavior shared by members of a society and rooted in the value system, 76

Nuclear family. Consists of two parents and their children—or any two of the three, 325

Objectivity. Entails steps taken to ensure that one's personal opinions or values do not bias or contaminate data collection and analysis, 42

Observational studies (also called field research). Involve systematic, planned observation and recording of interactions or human behavior in their natural settings (where the activity normally takes place rather than in a laboratory), 45

Oligarchy. The concentration of power in the hands of a small group, 142

Organic solidarity. Refers to social cohesion (glue) based on division of labor, with each member playing a highly specialized role in the society and each person being dependent on others due to interdependent, interrelated tasks, 517

Organized crime. Ongoing criminal enterprises by an organized group whose ultimate purpose is economic gain through illegitimate means, 172

Out-group. A group to which an individual does not belong and a group that competes with or acts in opposition to an in-group, 137

Past-in-present discrimination. Practices from the past that may no longer be allowed but that continue to have consequences for people in the present, 246

Peer group. A group of people who are roughly equal in some status within the society, such as the same age or the same occupation, 107

Planned (or centralized) economic systems. Economic systems in which the government or another centralized group oversees production and distribution, 438

Play stage. Involves a child, usually between 3 and 5, having the ability to see things (role-take) from the perspective of one person at a time; simple role-taking or play-acting, 102

Pluralism. Occurs when each ethnic or racial group in a country maintains its own culture and separate set of institutions but has recognized equality in the society, 250

Pluralist power theorists. Argue that power is not held exclusively by an elite group but is shared among many power centers, each of which has its own self-interests to protect, 219

Polygamy. Marriage of one person to more than one partner at the same time, 323

Population pyramids. Pyramid-shaped diagrams that illustrate sex ratios and dependency ratios over time, 497

Population transfer. The removal, often forced, of a minority group from a region or country, 248

Populations. Permanent societies, states, communities, adherents of a common religious faith, racial or ethnic groups, kinship or clan groups, professions, and other identifiable categories of people, 494

Postindustrial society. A society that has moved from human labor and manufacturing to automated production and service jobs, largely processing information, 65

Power. Ability of a person or group to realize its own will in groups, even against the resistance of others, 417

Power elite. Power held by top leaders in corporations, politics and military; this interlocking elite makes major decisions guiding the nation, 219

Predatory crimes. Those crimes committed against individuals or property and are considered by the public to be the most serious crimes, 155

Prejudice. Attitudes of prejudgment about a group, usually negative and not based on facts, 240

Prestige. Refers to the esteem, recognition, and respect one receives, based on wealth, position, or accomplishments, 37

Primary deviance. A violation of a norm that may be an isolated act or an initial act of rule breaking, 159

Primary groups. Groups characterized by close, intimate, long-term contacts, cooperation, and relationships, 135

Public order crimes. See *victimless crimes*, 169

Public sociologists. Strive to better understand how society operates and to make practical use of their sociological findings, 49

Questionnaires. Contain questions and other types of items designed to solicit information from individual respondents appropriate to analysis of research questions, 45

Race. A socially created concept that identifies a group of individuals as "different" based on certain biologically inherited physical characteristics. This allows them to be singled out for dissimilar treatment, 233

Racism. Any meso-level institutional arrangement that favors one racial group over another; this favoritism may result in intentional or unintentional consequences for minority groups, 243

Rational choice (exchange) theory. A theory that focuses on humans as fundamentally concerned with self-interests, making rational decisions based on weighing costs and rewards of the projected outcome, 35

Rationality. The attempt to reach maximum efficiency with rules that are rationally designed to accomplish goals, 40

Rationalization (of social life). The attempt to maximize efficiency by creating rules and procedures focused solely on accomplishing goals, 138

Real culture. The way things in society are actually done, 74

Recidivism rates. The likelihood that someone who is arrested, convicted, and imprisoned will later be a repeat offender, 182

Reference groups. Groups composed of members who act as role models and establish standards against which members evaluate their conduct, 136

Relative poverty. Occurs when one's income falls below the poverty line, resulting in an inadequate standard of living relative to others in the individual's country, 221

Reproduction of class. The socioeconomic positions of one generation passing on to the next, 364

Resistance or regressive movements. Try to protect an existing system, protect part of that system, or return to what a system had been by overthrowing current laws and practices. They see societal change as a threat to values or practices and wish to maintain the status quo or return to a former status by reversing the change process, 560

Resocialization. The process of shedding one or more positions and taking on others; it involves learning new norms, behaviors, and values suitable to the newly acquired status, 106

Revolution. Social and political transformations of a nation that result when states fail to fulfill their expected responsibilities, 441

Revolutionary movements. Attempt to transform society to bring about a total change in society by overthrowing existing power structures and replacing them with new ones; these movements often resort to violent means to achieve goals, 560

Rituals. Ceremonies or repetitive practices, often to invoke a sense of awe of the sacred and to make certain ideas sacred, 385

Role conflict. Conflict between the roles of two or more social statuses, 133

Role strain. Tension among roles within a social status, 133

Role-taking. The process by which individuals take others into account by imagining themselves in the position of the other, 100

Roles. The expected behaviors, rights, obligations, responsibilities, and privileges assigned to a social status, 132

Sample. A group of systematically chosen people who represent a much larger group, 43

Sanctions. Rewards and penalties that reinforce norms, 77

Science. The systematic process of producing human knowledge; it uses empirical research methods to discover facts and test theories, 566

Secondary analysis. Uses existing data, information that has already been collected in other studies—including data banks such as the national census, 46

Secondary deviance. Occurs when an individual continues to violate a norm and begins to take on a deviant identity *because* of being labeled as deviant, 159

Secondary groups. Groups characterized by formal, impersonal, and businesslike relationships; often temporary, based on a specific limited purpose or goal, 136

Secularization. The diminishing influence and role of religion in everyday life; involves a movement away from supernatural and sacred interpretations of the world and toward decisions based on empirical evidence and logic, 405

Self. Refers to the perceptions we have of who we are, 98

Self-fulfilling prophecy. Occurs when a belief or a prediction becomes a reality, in part because of the prediction, 159

Sex. A biological term referring to ascribed genetic, anatomical, and hormonal differences between males and females, 270

Sexuality. Culturally shaped meanings both of sexual acts and of how we experience our own bodies—especially in relation to the bodies of others, 270

Sick role. A special position in society in which one is temporarily relieved of responsibilities and accepts a position of dependence, 469

Side-effect discrimination. Practices in one institutional area that have a negative impact because they are linked to practices in another institutional area; because institutions are interdependent, discrimination in one results in unintentional discrimination in others, 245

Significant others. Parents, guardians, relatives, siblings, or important individuals whose primary and sustained interactions with the individual are especially influential, 103

Slavery. When an individual or a family is bound in servitude as the property of a person or household, bought and sold, and forced to work, 191

Social capital. One's networks with others who have influence, 197

Social change. Variations or alterations over time in the behavior patterns, culture (including norms and values), and structure of society, 537

Social class. The wealth, power, and prestige rankings that individuals hold in society; a large group with similar rankings, 113

Social construction of reality. The process by which individuals and groups shape reality through social interaction, 30

Social institutions. Organized, patterned, and enduring sets of social structures that provide guidelines for behavior and help each society meet its basic survival needs, 15

Social interaction. Consists of two or more individuals purposefully relating to each other, 127

Social mobility. The extent of individual movement up or down in the class system, changing one's social position in society—especially relative to one's parents, 209

Social movements. Consciously organized attempts outside of established institutional mechanisms to enhance or resist change through group action, 558

Social networks. Refer to individuals linked together by one or more social relationships, connecting us to the larger society, 125

Social processes. Take place through actions of people in institutions and other social units or structures, 16

Social reform movements. Seek to change some specific dimension of society, usually involving legislative policy modification or appeals to the courts, 560

Social status. A social position in society, 131

Social stratification. How individuals and groups are layered or ranked in society according to their access to and possession of valued resources, 196

Social structure. The stable patterns of interactions, statuses, roles, and institutions that provide stability for the society and bring order to individuals' lives, 15

Social units. Interconnected parts of the social world ranging from small groups to societies, 15

Social world model. The levels of analysis in our social surroundings as an interconnected series of small groups, organizations, institutions, and societies, 13

Socialization. The lifelong process of learning to become a member of the social world, beginning at birth and continuing until death, 94

Socialized medicine. Provides a government-supported consumer service that ensures equal access to health care for all citizens of a country, 472

Society. An organized and interdependent group of individuals who live together in a specific geographical area and who interact more with each other than they do with outsiders; they cooperate for the attainment of common goals and share a common culture over time, 58

Sociological imagination. The recognition of the complex and interactive relationship between micro-level individual experiences and macro-level public issues, 8

Sociology. The scientific study of social life, social change, and the social causes and consequences of human behavior, 5

Spurious relationships. Occur when there is no causal relationship between the independent and dependent variables, but they vary together, often due to a third variable affecting both of them, 44

Status. A social position in society, 104

Stigma. Social disapproval that discredits a person's claim to a "normal" identity, 160

Stratification. See *social stratification*, 196

Structural-functional theory. See *functional theory*, 36

Subculture. The culture of a meso-level subcommunity that distinguishes itself from the dominant culture of the larger society, 80

Subjugation. The subordination of one group to another that holds power and authority, 248

Symbolic interaction theory (also called social constructionism or interpretative theory). Sees humans as active agents who create shared meanings of symbols and events, and then interact on the basis of those meanings, 33

Symbols. Actions or objects that represent something else and therefore have meaning beyond their own existence. Flags and wedding rings are examples, 33

Technology. The practical application of tools, skills, and knowledge to meet human needs and extend human abilities, 565

Terrorism. The planned use of random, unlawful (or illegal) violence or threat of violence against civilians to create (or raise) fear and intimidate citizens in order to advance the terrorist group's political or ideological goals, 449

Theocracy. Religion in which religious leaders rule society in accordance with God's presumed wishes, 393

Theoretical perspective. The broadest theories in sociology, presenting basic views of society, the social world, and social problems and that guide sociological research and analysis, 32

Theories. Statements or explanations regarding how and why two or more facts are related to each other and the connections between these facts, 32

Total institution. A place that cuts people off from the rest of society and totally controls their lives in the process of resocialization; examples are prisons and boot camps, 106

Totalitarian government. Any form of government that almost totally controls people's lives, 434

Transnationalism. The process by which immigrants create multinational social relations that link together their original societies with their new locations; this usually entails national loyalty to more than one country, 116

Triangulation. The utilization of two or more methods of data collection to enhance the amount and type of data for analysis and the accuracy of the findings, 46

Urbanization. The pattern of movement from rural areas to cities, 494

Values. Nonmaterial shared judgments about what is desirable or undesirable, right or wrong, good or bad; they express the basic ideals of any culture, 74

Variables. Concepts (ideas) that can vary in frequency of occurrence from one time, place, or person to another, 43

Victimless crimes. Acts (also called *public order crimes*) committed by or between consenting adults, 169

War. Armed conflict occurring within, between, or among societies or groups, 446

Wealth. One's income, property, and total assets, or how much one is worth, 204

White-collar (or occupational) crime. The violation of law committed by an individual or group in the course of a legitimate, respected occupation or financial activity, 173

References

AAANativeArts. 2011. "Facts About Alaskan Natives." Retrieved April 19, 2011 (www.aaanativearts.com/alaskan-natives/index.html).

Abadi, Ponta. 2013. "Kids' Toys: More Gendered Than Ever." *Ms. Magazine,* June 5. Retrieved January 16, 2014 (http://mismagazine.com/blog/2013/06/05/kids-toys-more-gendered-than-ever).

Abrahamson, K., J. G. Anderson, M. Anderson, J. Suitor, and K. Pillemer. 2009. "The Cumulative Influence of Conflict on Nursing Home Staff: A Computer Simulation Approach." *Research in Gerontological Nursing.* Retrieved January 15, 2010 (www.geronurseresearch.com/advanced.asp).

Abu-Lughod, Janet L. 1991. *Changing Cities: Urban Sociology.* New York: HarperCollins.

Abu-Lughod, Janet L. 2001. *New York, Chicago, Los Angeles: America's Global Cities.* Minneapolis: University of Minnesota Press.

Ackerman, Spencer. 2014. "Global Terrorism Rose 43% in 2013 Despite Al-Qaida Splintering, US Reports." *The Guardian.* Retrieved May 22, 2014 (www.theguardian.com/world/2014/apr/30/global-terrorism-rose-despite-al-qaida-splintering).

ACT. 2012. "The Condition of College & Career Readiness 2012." Retrieved July 10, 2014 (http://media.act.org/documents/CCCR12-NationalReadinessRpt.pdf).

ACT. 2013. "National and State Scores." Retrieved September 12, 2014 (http://www.act.org/newsroom/data/2013).

Addictionblog.org. 2011. "Why Do People Have Different Pain Tolerances?" July 2. Retrieved July 17, 2012 (http://drug.addictionblog.org/why-do-people-have-different-pain-tolerances/).

Adler, Patricia A. and Peter Adler. 1991. *Backboards and Blackboards: College Athletes and Role Engulfment.* New York: Columbia University Press.

Adler, Patricia A. and Peter Adler. 1998. *Peer Power: Preadolescent Culture and Identity.* New Brunswick, NJ: Rutgers University Press.

Adler, Patricia A. and Peter Adler. 2004. "The Gloried Self." Pp. 117–26 in *Inside Social Life,* 4th ed., edited by Spencer E. Cahill. Los Angeles: Roxbury.

A&E. 2012. *Intervention.* Retrieved July 16, 2012 (www.aetv.com).

Afghanistan Opium Survey. 2011. Retrieved April 13, 2012 (www.unodc.org/documents/crop-monitoring/Afghanistan/Executive_Summary_2011_web.pdf).

AFP. 2013. "China Blogger Sentenced for Bo Joke Denied Payout." *Bangkok Post,* January 1. Retrieved June 1, 2013 (www.bangkokpost.com/lite/news/333594/china-blogger-sentenced-for-bo-joke-denied-payout).

African Undersea Cables. 2013. *Many Possibilities.* Retrieved February 13, 2014 (http://manypossibilities.net/african-undersea-cables/).

Agius, Silvan. 2013. "Third Gender: A Step Toward Ending Intersex Discrimination." Retrieved January 16, 2014 (Spiegel.de/international/Europe/third-gender-option-in-germany-a-small-step-for-intersex-recognition-a-917650.html).

Aguirre, Adalberto and David V. Baker. 2007. *Structured Inequality in the United States,* 2nd ed. Englewood Cliffs, NJ: Prentice Hall.

Aguirre, Adalberto, Jr., and Jonathan H. Turner. 2011. *American Ethnicity: The Dynamics and Consequences of Discrimination,* 7th ed. Boston: McGraw-Hill.

Aguirre, Jessica Camille. 2012. "Generic Drugs Make Dent in Global AIDS Pandemic." NPR, July 13. Retrieved July 3, 2013 (www.npr.org/blogs/health/2012/07/11/156612196/generic-drugs-make-dent-in-global-aids-pandemic).

Ahmad, Nehaluddin. 2009. "Sati Tradition—Widow Burning in India: A Socio-legal Examination." *Web Journal of Current Legal Issues,* 2 WEB JCLI. Retrieved April 7, 2011 (http://webjcli.ncl.ac.uk-/2009/issue2/almad2/html).

Ahuja, Masuma. 2013. "Teens Are Spending More Time Consuming Media, on Mobile Devices." *The Washington Post*, March 13. Retrieved December 6, 2013 (http://articles.washingtonpost.com/2013-03-13/news/37675597_1_teens-cellphones-video-games).

Akers, Ronald. 1992. *Deviant Behavior: A Social Learning Approach,* 3rd ed. Belmont, CA: Wadsworth.

Akers, Ronald. 1998. *Social Learning and Social Structure: A General Theory of Crime and Deviance.* Boston: Northeastern University Press.

Akers, Ronald L., Marvin D. Krohn, Lonn Lanza-Kaduce, and Marcia Radosevich. 1979. "Social Learning and Deviant Behavior." *American Sociological Review* 44(August):635–54.

Alarcon, Arthur L. and Paula M. Mitchell. 2011. "Executing the Will of the Voters? A Roadmap to Mend or End the California Legislature's Multi-Billion Dollar Death Penalty Debacle." *Loyola of Los Angeles Law Review* 44(June):S41.

Alatas, Syed Farid. 2006. "Ibn Khaldun and Contemporary Sociology." *International Sociology* 21(6):782–95.

AlertNet. 2012. "World Refugee Day 2012—Refugee Camps in Eastern Africa Are Overflowing and Underfunded." June 20. Retrieved September 14, 2012 (www.trust.org/alertnet/news/world-refugee-day-2012-refugee-camps-in-eastern-africa-are-overflowing-and-underfunded-lwf-dadaab-camp-manager/).

Alexander, Michelle. 2010. *The New Jim Crow: Mass Incarceration in the Age of Color Blindness*. New York: The New Press.

Alexander, Michelle. 2011. "More Black Men Are in Prison Today Than Were Enslaved in 1850." October 10. Retrieved April 15, 2012 (www.huffingtonpost.com/2011/10/12/michelle-alexander-more-Black-men-are-in-prison-today-than-were-enslaved-in-1850_n_1007368.html).

Alexander, Victoria D. 2003. *Sociology of the Arts: Exploring Fine and Popular Forms*. Malden, MA: Blackwell.

Allegretto, Sylvia, Ary Amerikaner, and Steven Pitts. 2011. "Black Employment and Unemployment: Teen Employment Population Ratios by Race." Chart 14, p. 14. *Work in the Black Community*, February 4. University of California at Berkeley Labor Center. (Retrieved April 17, 2011 (http://laborcenter.berkeley.edu/blackworkers/monthly/bwreport_2011-02-04_27.pdf).

Alliance for Excellent Education. 2010. "High School Dropouts in America: Fact Sheet." Retrieved July 8, 2013 (www. all4ed.org).

Alpert, Emily. 2013, June 13. "More Americans Consider Themselves Multiracial." *Los Angeles Times*. Retrieved June 17, 2013 (www.latimes.com/news/local/la-me-multiracial-growth-20130613,0,6580186.story).

Altheide, David, Patricia A. Adler, Peter Adler, and Duane Altheide. 1978. "The Social Meanings of Employee Theft." P. 90 in *Crime at the Top,* edited by John M. Johnson and Jack D. Douglas. Philadelphia: Lippincott.

Alvarez, Lizette. 2013. "Girl's Suicide Points to Rise in Apps Used by Cyberbullies." *New York Times*, September 13. Retrieved January 16, 2014 (www.nytimes.com/2013/09/14/us/suicide-of-girl-after-bullying-raises-worries-on-web-sites.html?ref=cyberbullying&_r=0).

Amadeo, Kimberley. 2009. "NAFTA Pros and Cons." Retrieved December 20, 2009 (http://useconomy.about.com/b/2008/04/24/nafta-pros-and-cons.htm).

Amato, Paul R. 2000. "The Consequences of Divorce for Adults and Children." *Journal of Marriage and the Family* 62(November):1269–87.

Amato, Paul R. and Juliana M. Sobolewski. 2001. "The Effects of Divorce and Marital Discord on Adult Children's Psychological Well-Being." *American Sociological Review* 63(December):697–713.

American Academy of Pediatrics. 2008. "Fact Sheet: Children's Health Insurance." Retrieved January 9, 2010 (www.aap.org/research/factsheet.pdf).

American Academy of Pediatrics. 2013. "Different Types of Families: A Portrait Gallery." Retrieved February 24, 2014 (www.healthychildren.org/English/family-life/family-dynamics/types-of-families/pages/Different-Types-of-Familes-A-Portrait-Gallery.aspx).

American Association of Medical Colleges. 2013. "2013 State Physician Workforce Data Book." Retrieved April 2, 2014 (www.aamc.org/download/362168/data/2013statephysicianworkforcedatabook.pdf).

American Civil Liberties Union. 2013. *The War on Marijuana in Black and White*. Retrieved June 5, 2013 (www.aclu.org/files/assets/aclu-thewaronmarijuana-rel2.pdf).

American Hospital Association. 2012. "Health Forum." Retrieved July 17, 2012 (www.ahadataviewer.com/).

American Hospital Association. 2014. "Fast Facts on US Hospitals." Retrieved March 10, 2014 (www.aha.org/research/rc/stat-studies/fast-facts.shtml).

American Library Association. 2014. "Frequently Challenged Books of the 21st Century: 2013." Retrieved September 9, 2014 (http://www.ala.org/bbooks/frequentlychallengedbooks/top10).

American Medical Association. 2012. *Physician Characteristics and Distribution in the U.S.,* 2012 ed. Washington, DC: Author.

American Panel Survey. 2012. "Notes on Public Attitudes Toward Health Care Reform and the Supreme Court." Weidenbaum Center on the Economy, Government, and Public Policy, June 25. Retrieved August 1, 2012 (http://wc.wustl.edu).

American Psychological Association. 2008. "Report From: Working Group on Assisted Suicide and End-of-Life Decisions." Retrieved August 16, 2008 (www.apa.org/pi/aseol/introduction.html).

American Sociological Association. 2006. "'What Can I Do with a Bachelor's Degree in Sociology?' A National Survey of Seniors Majoring in Sociology." Washington DC: American Sociological Association Research and Development Department.

American Sociological Association. 2009. *21st Century Careers With an Undergraduate Degree in Sociology*. Washington, DC: Author.

American Sociological Association Task Force on Institutionalizing Public Sociologies. 2005. *Public Sociology and the Roots of American Sociology: Re-Establishing our Connection to the Public*. Washington, DC: Author.

Ammerman, Nancy. 1990. *Baptist Battles: Social Change and Religious Conflict in the Southern Baptist Convention*. New Brunswick, NJ: Rutgers University Press.

Ammerman, Nancy. 2006. "Denominationalism/Congregationalism." Pp. 353–72 in *Handbook of Religion and Social Institutions*, edited by Helen Rose Ebaugh. New York: Springer.

Ammerman, Nancy. 2009. "Congregations: Local, Social, and Religious." Pp. 562–80 in *Oxford Handbook of the Sociology of Religion*, edited by Peter Clarke. New York, Oxford: Oxford University Press.

Amnesty International. 2006. "Facts and Figures on the Death Penalty." Retrieved August 8, 2006 (http://web.amnesty.org/pages/deathpenalty-facts-eng, http://web.amnesty.org/pages/deathpenaltycountries-eng).

Amnesty International. 2011. "Death Penalty in 2010." Retrieved July 7, 2011 (www.amnesty.org/en/news-and-updates/report/death-penalty-2010-executing-countries-left-isolated-after-decade-progress).

Amnesty International. 2012. "Death Penalty 2011: Alarming Levels of Executions in the Few Countries That Kill." March 27. Retrieved April 16, 2012 (www.amnesty.org/en/news/deasth-penalty-2011-alarming-level-executions-few-countries—kill-2012-03-27).

Amnesty International. 2014. "Death Penalty 2013: Small Number of Countries Trigger Global Spike in Executions." Retrieved April 25, 2014 (www.amnesty.org/en/news/death-penalty-2013-small-number-trigger-global-spike-executions-2014-03-27).

Ananova. 2001. "Death Workers Sell Body Parts for Extra Christmas Cash." Retrieved December 4, 2005 (www.ananova.com/news/sm_465113.html).

Ananova. 2002. "Students Willing to Sell Body Parts to Fund Education." April 8. Retrieved August 26, 2006 (www.ananova.com).

Anderson, Benedict. 2006. *Imagined Communities: Reflections on the Origin and Spread of Nationalism,* rev. ed. London: Verso.

Anderson, David A. and Mykol Hamilton. 2005. "Gender Role Stereotyping of Parents in Children's Picture Books: The Invisible Father." *Sex Roles: A Journal of Research* 52(3/4):145.

Anderson, D. Mark and Daniel I. Rees. 2013. " The Legalization of Recreational Marijuana How Likely is the Worst-Case Scenario?" *The Journal of Policy Analysis and Management.* Retrieved October 17, 2013 (http://dmarkanderson.com/Point_Counterpoint_07_31_13_v5.pdf).

Anderson, Elijah. 2000. *Code of the Street: Decency, Violence, and the Moral Life of the Inner City.* New York: Norton.

Anderson, James G. and Carolyn E. Aydin. 2005. *Evaluating the Organizational Impact of Health Care Information Systems.* New York: Springer.

Anderson, Margaret and Patricia Hill Collins. 2010. *Race Class and Gender: An Anthology,* 7th ed. Belmont: Wadsworth.

Angier, Natalie 2013. "The Changing American Family." *The New York Times.* Nov. 25. Retrieved January 17, 2014 (www.nytimes.com/2013/11/26/health/families.html?_r=0).

Anglican Church in North America. 2013. "About." Retrieved July 13, 2013 (http://anglicanchurch.net/?/main/page/about-acna).

ANRED (Anorexia Nervosa and Related Eating Disorders, Inc.). 2007. "Statistics: How Many People Have Eating Disorders?" Retrieved April 17, 2010 (www.anred.com).

Answers.com. 2011. "Flag." Retrieved December 21, 2001 (http://www.answers.com/flag&r=67).

Answers.com. 2012. "How Many English Native Speakers Are There in the World?" Retrieved March 7, 2012 (http://wiki.answers.com/Q/How_many_English_native_speakers_are_there_in_the_world).

Anti-Defamation League. 2010. "ADL Audit: 1,211 Anti-Semitic Incidents Across the Country in 2009." Retrieved April 7, 2011 (www.adl.org/PresRele/ASUS_12/5814_12.htm).

Anti-Violence Resource Guide. 2012. "Facts About Violence." *Feminist.com.* Retrieved May 26, 2012 (www.feminist.com/antiviolence/facts.html).

Antonowicz, Anton. 2002. "Zarmina's Story." *Daily Mirror,* June 19. Retrieved February 7, 2013 (www.freerepublic.com/focus/news/702415/posts).

Antoun, Richard T. 2008. *Understanding Fundamentalism: Christian, Islamic, and Jewish Movements*, 2nd ed. Walnut Creek, CA: AltaMira.

Appleby, Julie. 2006. "Debate Surrounds End-of-Life Health Care Costs." *USA Today,* October 18. Retrieved April 4, 2008 (www.usatoday.com/money/industries/heaslth/2006-10-18-end-of-life-costs_x.htm).

Archer, Dale. 2013. "Could America's Wealth Gap Lead to a Revolt?" *Forbes,* September 4. Retrieved January 4, 2014 (www.forbes.com/sites/dalearcher/2013/09/04/could-americas-wealth-gap-lead-to-a-revolt/).

Armstrong, Karen. 2000. *The Battle for God.* New York: Knopf.

Arnold, David O., ed. 1970. *The Sociology of Subcultures.* Berkeley, CA: Glendessary.

Arrighi, Barbara A. 2000. *Understanding Inequality: The Intersection of Race, Ethnicity, Class, and Gender.* Lanham, MD: Rowman & Littlefield.

Arulampalam, Wiji, Alison L. Booth, and Mark L. Bryan. 2007. "Is There a Glass Ceiling Over Europe? Exploring the Gender Pay Gap Across the Wages Distribution." *Industrial and Labor Relations Review* 60(1):163–86.

ASCD. 2013. "The Whole Child Initiative." Retrieved February 8, 2013 (www.ascd.org/whole-child.aspx).

Aseltine, Robert H., Jr. 1995. "A Reconsideration of Parental and Peer Influences on Adolescent Deviance." *Journal of Health and Social Behavior* 36(2):103–21.

Ashley, David and David Michael Orenstein. 2009. *Sociological Theory,* 7th ed. Boston: Allyn & Bacon.

Aslan, Reza. 2011. *No god but God: The Origins, Evolution, and Future of Islam,* updated ed. New York: Random House.

"Assisted Suicide: Over My Dead Body." 2012. *The Economist,* October 20. Retrieved July 13, 2013 (www.economist.com/news/international/21564830-helping-terminally-ill-die-once-taboo-gaining-acceptance).

Association of American Colleges and Universities and Hart Research Associates. 2013. *It Takes More Than a Major: Employer Priorities for College Learning and Student Success.* Washington, DC. Retrieved May 22, 2013 (www.aacu.org/leap/documents/2013_EmployerSurvey.pdf).

"At Least 80 Electoral Votes Depended on Youth." 2012. Center for Information & Research on Civic Learning and Engagement. Retrieved November 1, 2012 (www.civicyouth.org/at-least-80-electoral-votes-depended-on-youth/).

Attewell, Paul. 2001. "The First and Second Digital Divides." *Sociology of Education* 74(3):252–59.

Audette, Nicole. 2014. "Congo: Rape as a Weapon of War and Wealth." *The Christian Science Monitor.* Retrieved May 11, 2014 (www.csmonitor.com/World/Africa/Africa-Monitor/2014/0321/Congo-Rape-as a weapon-of-war-and wealth).

Aulette, Judy Root. 2010. *Changing American Families.* Boston: Allyn & Bacon.

Avert. 2009. "Worldwide HIV and AIDS Statistics: Regional Statistics for HIV and AIDS, End of 2008." Retrieved April 13, 2010 (www.avert.org/worldstats.htm).

Avert. 2010. "Global HIV and AIDS Estimates, End of 2009." Retrieved May 14, 2011 (www.avert.org/worldstats.htm).

Ayers, Dennis. 2010. "Top 50 Favorite Gay Films!" *Afterelton,* September 20. Retrieved May 27, 2012 (www.afterelton.com/movies/2010/9/favorite-gay-films?page=0%20).

Ayers, William and Michael Klonsky. 2006. "Chicago's Renaissance 2010: The Small Schools Movement Meets the Ownership Society." *Phi Delta Kappan* (February):453–56.

Azize, Pary M., Ruth Endacott, Allegra Cattani, and Ann Humphreys. 2013. "Cultural Responses to Pain in UK Children of Primary School Age: A Mixed-Methods Study." *Nursing & Health Sciences,* August 29. Retrieved March 4, 2014 (http://onlinelibrary.wiley.com/doi/10.1111/nhs.12084/abstract).

Babbie, Earl. 2014. *The Basics of Social Research*, 6th ed. Belmont, CA: Thomsen/Wadsworth.

Babiarz, Kimberly Singer, Hongmei Yi, and Renfu Luo. 2013. "Meeting the Health-Care Needs of the Rural Elderly: The Unique Role of Village Doctors." *China & World Economy* 21(3):44–60.

BabyCenter. 2013. "100 Most Popular Baby Names of 2013." *Choosing a Name,* December. Retrieved January 16, 2014 (www.babycenter.com/top-baby-names-2013).

Bagby, Ihsan. 2003. "Imams and Mosque Organization in the United States: A Study of Mosque Leadership and Organizational Structure in American Mosques." Pp. 113–34 in *Muslims in the United States,* edited by Philippa Strum and Danielle Tarantolo. Washington, DC: Woodrow Wilson International Center for Scholars.

Bainbridge, William S. and Rodney Stark. 1981. "Suicide, Homicide, and Religion: Durkheim Reassessed." *Annual Review of the Social Sciences of Religion* 5:33–56.

Bakalian, Anny and Medhi Bozorgmehr. 2009. *Backlash 9/11: Middle Eastern and Muslim Americans Respond.* Berkeley: University of California Press.

Baker, Bruce D., David G. Sciarra, and Danielle Farrie. 2010. *Is School Funding Fair? A National Report Card.* Retrieved July 8, 2013 (www.schoolfundingfairness.org/National_Report_Card.pdf).

Baker, Peter and Dan Bilefsky. 2010. "Russia and U.S. Sign Nuclear Arms Reduction Pact." *The New York Times*, April 8. Retrieved July 14, 2012 (www.nytimes.com/2010/04/09/world/europe/09prexy.html).

Bales, Kevin. 1999. *Disposable People: New Slavery in the Global Economy,* updated ed. Berkeley: University of California Press.

Bales, Kevin. 2000. *New Slavery: A Reference Handbook,* 2nd ed. Santa Barbara, CA: ABC-CLIO.

Bales, Kevin. 2004. *Disposable People: New Slavery in the Global Economy,* 2nd ed. Berkeley: University of California Press.

Bales, Kevin. 2007. *Ending Slavery: How We Free Today's Slaves.* Berkeley: University of California Press.

Bales, Kevin. 2012. *Disposable People: New Slavery in the Global Economy,* 3rd ed. Berkeley: University of California Press.

Bales, Kevin. 2013. "Confronting Slavery With the Tools of Sociology." In *Sociologists in Action: Race, Class, Gender, and Intersections,* edited by Shelley White, Jonathan White, and Kathleen Odell Korgen. Thousand Oaks, CA: Sage.

Bales, Kevin and Ron Soodalter. 2010. *The Slave Next Door: Human Trafficking and Slavery in America Today.* Berkeley: University of California Press.

Bales, Kevin and Zoe Trodd. 2008. *To Plead Our Own Cause: Personal Stories by Today's Slaves.* Ithaca, NY: Cornell University Press.

Bales, Kevin, Zoe Trodd, and Alex Kent Williamson. 2009. *Modern Slavery: The Secret World of 27 Million People.* Oxford, UK: Oneworld Press.

Balfanz, Robert and John Gomperts. 2013. "What You Won't Hear at High School Graduation." CNN.com, June 6. Retrieved July 8, 2013 (www.cnn.com/2013/06/06/opinion/balfanz-high-school-graduation).

Ballantine, Jeanne H. and Floyd M. Hammack. 2012. *The Sociology of Education: A Systematic Analysis,* 7th ed. Upper Saddle River, NJ: Prentice Hall.

Barajas, Mark S. 2011. "Academic Achievement of Children in Single Parent Homes: A Critical Review." *The Hilltop Review* 5(1): Article 4. Retrieved September 13, 2012 (http://scholarworks.wmich.edu/hilltopreview/vol5/iss1/4).

Barash, David. 2002. "Evolution, Males, and Violence." *The Chronicle Review* (May 24):B7.

Barber, Benjamin R. 2006. "The Uncertainty of Digital Politics: Democracy's Relationship with Information Technology." Pp. 61–69 in *Globalization: The Transformation of Social Worlds,* edited by D. Stanley Eitzen and Maxine Baca Zinn. Belmont, CA: Wadsworth.

Barber, Bonnie L., Jacquelynne S. Eccles, and Margaret R. Stone. 2001. "Whatever Happened to the Jock, the Brain, and the Princes? Young Adult Pathways Linked to Adolescent Activity Involvement and Social Identity." *Journal of Adolescent Research* 16(5):429–55.

Barnes, P. M., B. Bloom, and R. Nahin. 2008. "Complimentary and Alternative Medicine Use Among Adults and Children: US 2007." *CDC National Health Statistics Report* 12(December).

Barnett, T. P., J. C. Adam, and D. P. Lettenmaier. 2005. "Potential Impacts of a Warming Climate on Water Availability in Snow-Dominated Regions." *Nature* 438(November 17):303–309.

Barrera, Juliana. 2013. "Asian Immigrants Surpass Hispanics as Biggest Immigrant Wave to U.S." *Huffington Post Latino Voices,* June 15. Retrieved March 17, 2014 (www.huffingtonpost.com/2013/06/15/asian-immigrants-surpass-hispanics_n_3446441html).

Barrett, David B., Todd M. Johnson, and Peter F. Crossing. 2011. "2010 Annual Megacensus of Religion." *Time Almanac.* Chicago: Encyclopedia Britannica, Inc.

Barrett, David, George Kurian, and Todd Johnson, eds. 2001. *World Christian Encyclopedia,* 2 vols. New York: Oxford University Press.

Barnett, W. Steven. 2013. "Does Head Start Work for Kids? The Bottom Line." In Valerie Strauss' column The Answer Sheet. *The Washington Post.* March 5. Retrieved July 10, 2013 (www.washingtonpost.com/blogs/answer-sheet/wp/2013/03/05/does-head-start-work-for-kids-the-bottom-line/).

Barry, Ellen. 2009. "Protests in Moldova Explode, With Help of Twitter." *New York Times*, April 8: A1. Retrieved October 6, 2012 (www.nytimes.com).

Barry, Ellen and Mansi Choksi 2013. "Gang Rape in India, Routine and Invisible." *New York Times*, October 26. Retrieved January 17, 2014 (www.nytimes.com/2013/10/27/world/asia/gang-rape-in-india-routine-and-invisible.html?_r=0).

Basch, Linda, Nina Glick Schiller, and Cristina Szanton Blanc. 1994. *Nations Unbounded: Transnational Projects, Postcolonial Predicaments, and Deterritorialized Nation-State.* Amsterdam: Gordon and Breach.

Basso, Keith H. 1979. *Portraits of the Whiteman: Linguistic Play and Cultural Symbols Among the Western Apache.* Cambridge, UK: Cambridge University Press.

Battelle. 2013. "2014 Global R&D Funding Forecast." December. Retrieved February 24, 2014 (www.battelle.org/docs/tpp/2014_global_rd_funding_forecast.pdf).

Beaubien, Jason. 2011. "In Haiti, Cell Phones Serve as Debit Cards." NPR, January 30. Retrieved June 8, 2013 (www.npr.org/2011/01/30/133305663/in-haiti-cell-phones-serve-as-debit-cards).

Beaver, David. 2012. "Sally Ride: Beauty of the Earth Is Only Half of It." The Overview Institute. Retrieved June 29, 2013 (www.overviewinstitute.org/featured-articles/45-sally-ride-beauty-of-the-earth-is-only-half-of-it).

Beckwith, Carol. 1983. "Niger's Wodaabe: People of the Taboo." *National Geographic* 164(4):483–509.

Beckwith, Carol. 1993. *Nomads of Niger.* New York: Harry N. Abrams.

Bedi, Rahul. 2012. "Indian Dowry Deaths on the Rise." *The Telegraph*, February 27. Retrieved May 26, 2012 (www.telegraph.co.uk/news/worldnews/asia/india/9108642/Indian-dowry-deaths-on-the-rise.html).

Belding, Theodore C. 2004. "Nobility and Stupidity: Modeling the Evolution of Class Endogamy." Retrieved August 7, 2008 (http://arxiv.org/abs/nlin.AO/0405048).

Bell, Daniel. 1973. *The Coming of Post-Industrial Society: A Venture in Social Forecasting.* New York: Basic Books.

Bell, Daniel. [1976] 1999. *The Coming of Post-Industrial Society: A Venture in Social Forecasting,* Special anniversary edition. New York: Basic Books.

Bell, Michael Mayerfeld. 2012. *An Invitation to Environmental Sociology,* 4th ed. Thousand Oaks, CA: Sage/Pine Forge.

Bellah, Robert N. 1970. "Civil Religion in America." Pp. 168–215 in *Beyond Belief: Essays on Religion in a Post-Traditionalist World.* New York: Harper & Row.

Bellah, Robert N. 1992. *The Broken Covenant: American Civil Religion in Time of Trial.* Chicago: University of Chicago Press.

Bellah, Robert N., Richard Madsen, William M. Sullivan, Ann Swidler, and Steven M. Tipton. 1996. *Habits of the Heart: Individualism and Commitment in American Life,* updated ed. Berkeley: University of California Press.

Benavot, Aaron, John Meyer, and David Kamens. 1991. "Knowledge for the Masses: World Models and National Curricula: 1920–1986." *American Sociological Review* 56(1):85–100.

Benevolo, Leonardo. 1995. *The European City.* Cambridge, MA: Blackwell.

Benguigui, Yamina. 2000. *The Perfumed Garden.* Brooklyn, NY: First Run Icarus Films.

Bennis, Warren G., Kenneth D. Benne, and Robert Chin. 1985. *The Planning of Change,* 4th ed. New York: Holt, Rinehart and Winston.

Benokraitis, Nijole V. 2012. *Marriages and Families: Changes, Choices, and Constraints—2010 Census Update,* 7th ed. Englewood Cliffs, NJ: Prentice Hall.

Beran, Tanya. 2012. "Bullying: What Are the Differences Between Boys and Girls?" *Education.com,* January 24. Retrieved January 17, 2014 (www.education.com/reference/article/Ref_Bullying_Differences).

Berger, Helen. 1999. *A Community of Witches: Contemporary Neo-Paganism and Witchcraft in the United States.* Columbia: University of South Carolina Press.

Berger, Helen A. and Douglas Ezzy. 2007. *Teenage Witches: Magical Youth and the Search for the Self.* New Brunswick, NJ: Rutgers University Press.

Berger, Michael L. 1979. *The Devil Wagon in God's Country: The Automobile and Social Change in Rural America, 1893–1929.* Hamden, CT: Archon.

Berger, Peter L. and Thomas Luckmann. 1966. *The Social Construction of Reality.* Garden City, NY: Doubleday.

Berk, Richard A. 1974. *Collective Behavior.* Dubuque, IA: Brown.

Berliner, David. 2001. *Our Schools vs. Theirs: Averages That Hide the True Extremes.* Center for Education Research, Analysis, and Innovation, January 28. Retrieved September 14, 2012 (http://nepc.colorado.edu/files/cerai-o1-02.htm).

Berman, Bruce J. 2011. "Of Magic, Invisible Hands and Elfs: How Not to Study Ethnicity in Africa." Presented at the ECAS4, Uppsala, Sweden, June 14–18.

Berman, Carol. 2010. "Glass Ceiling Is Still Solid." March 15. Retrieved May 25, 2012 (http://jobs.aol.com/articles/2010/03/15/glass-ceiling-is-still-solid-especially-if-you-have-an-mba/).

Bernhardt, Annette, Ruth Milkman, Nik Theodore, Douglas Heckathorn, Mirabai Auer, James DeFilippis, Ana Luz González, Victor Narro, Jason Perelshteyn, Diana Polson, and Michael Spiller. 2009. *Broken Laws, Unprotected Workers.* Retrieved June 3, 2013 (http://labor.ucla.edu/publications/reports/brokenlaws.pdf).

Berrey, Ellen. 2013. "Breaking Glass Ceilings, Ignoring Dirty Floors: The Culture and Class Bias of Diversity Management." *American Behavioral Scientist,* October 11. Retrieved January 17, 2014 (http://abs.sagepub.com/content/easrly/2013/10/11/0002764213503333.abstract).

Berry, Brian J. L. and John Kasarda. 1977. *Contemporary Urban Ecology.* New York: Macmillan.

Bertman, Stephen. 1998. *Hyperculture: The Human Cost of Speed.* Westport, CT: Praeger.

Better Factories. 2012. *Better Factories Cambodia Newsletter* 9(March). Retrieved May 28, 2012 (www.betterfactories.org/content/documents/1/Newsletter%20No.%2019_Eng.pdf).

Bettie, Julie. 2003. *Women Without Class: Girls, Race, and Identity.* Berkeley: University of California Press.

Beyer, Peter. 2000. "Secularization From the Perspective of Globalization." Pp. 81–93 in *The Secularization Debate,* edited by William H. Swatos, Jr. and Daniel V. A. Olson. Lanham, MD: Rowman & Littlefield.

Bibby, Reginald W. 2002. *Restless Gods: The Renaissance of Religion in Canada.* Toronto, Canada: Stoddard.

Billig, Michael. 1995. *Banal Nationalism.* Thousand Oaks, CA: Sage.

Birdwhistell, Raymond L. 1970. *Kinesics and Context: Essays on Body Motion Communication.* Philadelphia: University of Pennsylvania Press.

Bjelopera, Jerome P. and Kristin M. Finklea. 2012. "Organized Crime: An Evolving Challenge for U.S. Law Enforcement." Congressional Research Service. Retrieved April 13, 2012 (www.fas.org/sgp/crs/misc/R41547.pdf).

Blank, Rebecca M. 2002. "Evaluating Welfare Reform in the United States." *Journal of Economic Literature* 40(4):1105–166.

Blasi, Joseph, Douglas Kruse, and Aaron Bernstein. 2003. *In the Company of Owners.* New York: Basic Books.

Blau, Peter M. 1956. *Bureaucracy in Modern Society.* New York: Random House.

Blau, Peter M. 1964. *Exchange and Power in Social Life.* New York: John Wiley.

Blau, Peter and Otis Dudley Duncan. 1967. *The American Occupational Structure.* New York: John Wiley.

Blauner, Robert. 1972. *Racial Oppression in America.* New York: Harper & Row.

Blee, Kathleen M. 2008. "White Supremacy as Extreme Deviance." Pp. 108–17 in *Extreme Deviance,* edited by Erich Goode and D. Angus Vail. Thousand Oaks, CA: Pine Forge.

Blumer, Herbert. 1969. *Symbolic Interactionism: Perspective and Method.* Englewood Cliffs, NJ: Prentice Hall.

Blumer, Herbert. 1986. *Symbolic Interactionism: Perspective and Method.* Berkeley: University of California Press.

"Body Parts for Sale." 2008. *Science and Society,* May 6. ABC News. Retrieved January 11, 2010 (blogs.abcnews.com/scienceandsociety/2008/05/body-parts-for.html).

Boger, John Charles and Gary Orfield. 2009. *School Resegregation: Must the South Turn Back?* University of North Carolina Press.

Bokova, Irina and Laura Bush. 2012. "Literacy Is Key to Unlocking the Cycle of Poverty." *Houston Chronicle,* September 7. Retrieved January 28, 2013 (www.chron.com/opinion/outlook/article/Literacy-is-key-to-unlocking-the-cycle-of-poverty-3848564.php).

Bolduan, Kate 2009. "The Plight of Young Uninsured Americans." CNN Politics.com, March 7. Retrieved January 10, 2010 (www.cnn.com/2009/POLITICS/03/07/young.uninsured/index.html).

Boli, John. 2002. "Globalization." Pp. 307–13 in *Education and Sociology: An Encyclopedia,* edited by David L. Levinson, Peter W. Cookson, Jr., and Alan R. Sadovnik. New York: RoutledgeFalmer.

Bonacich, Edna. 1972. "A Theory of Ethnic Antagonism: The Split Labor Market." *American Sociological Review* 37(October): 547–59.

Bonacich, Edna. 1976. "Advanced Capitalism and Black-White Race Relations in the United States: A Split Labor Market Interpretation." *American Sociological Review* 41(February): 34–51.

Bond, Jeff. 2010. "The Anthropology of Garbage." *Columns,* March. Retrieved August 15, 2013 (www.washington.edu/alumni/columns/march10/garbage.html).

Bonilla-Silva, Eduardo. 2003. *Racism Without Racists: Color-Blind Racism and the Persistence of Racial Inequality in the United States.* Berkeley: University of California Press.

Bonilla-Silva, Eduardo. 2009. *Racism Without Racists: Color-Blind Racism and the Persistence of Racial Inequality in America,* 3rd ed. Lanham, MD: Rowman & Littlefield.

Bonilla-Silva, Eduardo and David G. Embrick. 2005. "Black, Honorary White, White: The Future of Race in the United States?" In *Negotiating the Color Line: Doing Race in the Color-Blind Era and Implications for Racial Justice,* edited by David Brunsma and Lynne Rienner. Boulder, CO: Lynne Rienner Publishers.

Booth, Alan and Paul R. Amato. 2001. "Parental Predivorce Relations and Offspring Postdivorce Well-Being." *Journal of Marriage and the Family* 63(February):197–212.

Borenstein, Seth 2013. "U.S. Scientists Report Big Jump in Heat-Trapping CO2." March 5. Retrieved June 20, 2013 (phys.org/news/2013-03-scientists-big-heat-trapping-co2.html).

Borg, Marcus J. 1994. *Meeting Jesus Again for the First Time.* San Francisco: Harper San Francisco.

Borg, Marcus. 2001. *Reading the Bible Again for the First Time.* New York: HarperCollins.

Boston Women's Health Book Collective. 2006. *Our Bodies, Ourselves: Menopause.* New York: Touchstone.

Bottomore, Tom. 1979. *Political Sociology.* New York: Harper & Row.

Boulding, Elise with Jennifer Dye. 2002. "Women and Development." In *Introducing Global Issues,* 2nd ed., edited by Michael T. Snarr and D. Neil Snarr. Boulder, CO: Lynne Rienner.

Bourdieu, P. and J. C. Passeron. 1977. *Reproduction in Education, Society and Culture.* London: Sage.

Bowen, Debra. 2008. "History Behind California's Primary Election System." Retrieved March 21, 2008 (www.sos.ca.gov/elections/elections_decline.htm).

Bowles, Samuel and Herbert Gintis. 1976. *Schooling in Capitalist America.* New York: Basic Books.

Bowles, Samuel and Herbert Gintis. 2002. "Schooling in Capitalist America Revisited." *Sociology of Education* 75(1):1–18.

Bowman, Bobbi. 2010. "A Portrait to Black America on the Eve of the 2010 Census." *The Root,* February 10. Retrieved June 5, 2012 (www.theroot.com/views/portrait-black-america-eve-2010-census).

Boy, Angie and Andrzej Kulczycki. 2008. "What We Know About Intimate Partner Violence in the Middle East and North Africa." *Violence Against Women* 14(1):53–70.

Bracey, Gerald W. 2005. "The 15th Bracey Report on the Condition of Public Education." *Phi Delta Kappan* (October): 138–53.

Bradley, Tamsin, Emma Tomalin, and Mangala Subramaniam. 2009. *Dowry: Bridging the Gap Between Theory and Practice.* London: Zed Books.

Bradsher, Keith. 2013. "Kerry Calls Typhoon a Warning of Climate Change." *New York Times,* December 18. Retrieved March 18, 2014 (www.nytimes.com/2013/12/19/world/asia/typhoon-haiyan-philippines-aid.html).

Brandon, Emily. 2012. "65-and-Older Population Soars." *US News Money,* January 9. Retrieved March 31, 2012 (http://money.usnews.com/money/retirement/articles/2012/01/09/65-and-older-population-soars).

Brandon, Mark E. 2005. "War and American Constitutional Order." In *The Constitution in Wartime: Beyond Alarmism and Complacency,* edited by Mark Tushner. Durham, NC: Duke University Press.

Brasher, Brenda E. 2004. *Give Me That On-Line Religion.* New Brunswick, NJ: Rutgers University Press.

Brecher, Jeremy, Tim Costello, and Brendan Smith. 2012. "Globalization and Social Movements." Pp. 272–90 in *Globalization: The Transformation of Social Worlds,* 3rd ed., edited by D. Stanley Eitzen and Maxine Baca Zinn. Belmont, CA: Wadsworth.

Bremner, Jason, Carl Haub, Marlene Lee, Mark Mather, and Eric Zuehlke. 2009. "World Population Highlights." *Population Bulletin* 64(3):3. Population Reference Bureau. Retrieved January 10, 2010 (www.prb.org/pdf09/64.3highlights.pdf).

Brenchley, Cameron. 2013. "High School Graduation Rate at Highest Level in Three Decades." U.S. Department of Education, January 23. Retrieved July 8, 2013 (www.ed.gov/blog/2013/01/high-school-graduation-rate-at-highest-level-in-three-decades/).

Brettell, Caroline B. and Carolyn F. Sargent. 2012. *Gender in Cross-Cultural Perspective,* 6th ed. Englewood Cliffs, NJ: Prentice Hall.

Brier, Noah Rubin. 2004. "Coming of Age." *American Demographics* 26(9):16.

Brill, Steven. 2013. "Bitter Pill: Why Medical Bills Are Killing Us." *Time,* March 4. Retrieved July 15, 2013 (www.time.com/time/covers/0,16641,20130304,00.html).

Brint, Steven, Mary F. Contreras, and Michael T. Matthews. 2001. "Socialization Messages in Primary Schools: An Organizational Analysis." *Sociology of Education* 74(July): 157–80.

British Columbia Ministry of Labour & Citizens' Services. 2006. *B.C. Stats Infoline* 6(40). October 6. Retrieved April 17, 2010 (www.bcstats.gov.bc.ca/releases/info2006/in0647.pdf).

Britton, Dana M. 2000. "The Epistemology of the Gendered Organization." *Gender and Society* 14(3):418–34.

Bromley, David G. and Anson D. Shupe, Jr. 1981. *Strange Gods: The Great American Cult Scare.* Boston: Beacon.

Brookover, Wilbur B. and Edsel L. Erickson. 1975. *Sociology of Education.* Homewood, IL: Dorsey.

Brookover, Wilbur B., Edsel L. Erickson, and Alan McEvoy. 1996. *Creating Effective Schools: An In-Service Program.* Holmes Beach, FL: Learning Publications.

Brooks, David. 2012. "Thurston Howell Romney." *New York Times,* September 17. Retrieved September 18, 2012 (www .nytimes.com/2012/09/18/opinion/brooks-thurston-howell-romney.html?_r=0).

Brooks, Rachel and Johanna Waters. 2010. "Student Mobility as a Response to Labour Market Congestion." Presented at International Sociological Association meetings in Sweden, July.

Broom, Leonard and Philip Selznick. 1963. *Sociology: A Text With Adapted Readings,* 3rd ed. New York: Harper & Row.

Brown, Dee. 2001. *Bury My Heart at Wounded Knee: An Indian History of the American West,* 30th anniversary ed. New York: Holt.

Brown, Donald E. 1991. *Human Universals.* Philadelphia: Temple University Press.

Brulle, Robert J. 2014. "Institutionalizing Delay: Foundation Funding and The Creation of U.S. Climate Change Counter-Movement Organizations." *Climactic Change* 122(4):681–94.

Bruner, Jerome. 1996. *The Culture of Education.* Cambridge, MA: Harvard University Press.

Brunn, Stanley D., Maureen Hays-Mitchell, and Donald J. Zeigler. 2011. *Cities of the World: World Regional Urban Development,* 4th ed. Lanham, MD: Rowman and Littlefield.

Brunn, Stanley D., Jack F. Williams, and Donald J. Zeigler. 2003. *Cities of the World: World Regional Urban Development,* 3rd ed. Lanham, MD: Rowman & Littlefield.

Brunsma, David. 2006. *Mixed Messages: Doing Race in the Color-Blind Era.* Boulder, CO; Lynne Rienner.

Brym, Robert J. and John Lie. 2007. *Sociology: Your Compass for a New World,* 3rd ed. Belmont, CA: Wadsworth.

Buchmann, Claudia, Dennis J. Condron, and Vincent J. Roscigno 2010. "Shadow Education, American Style: Test Preparation, the SAT and College Enrollment." *Social Forces* 89(2) 435–61.

Buechler, Steven. 2008. "What Is Critical About Sociology?" *Teaching Sociology* 36(4):318–30.

Bukhari, Zahid H. 2003. "Demography, Identity, Space: Defining American Muslims." Pp. 7–18 in *Muslims in the United States,* edited by Philippa Strum and Danielle Tarantolo. Washington DC: Woodrow Wilson International Center for Scholars.

Bullas, Jeff. 2012. "20 Interesting Facts, Figures and Statistics Revealed by Facebook." Jeffbullas.com. Retrieved September 25, 2012 (www.jeffbullas.com/2012/04/30/20-interesting-facts-figures-and-statistics-revealed-by-facebook/).

Burawoy, Michael. 2005. "For Public Sociology." *American Sociological Review* 56(2):4–28.

Bureau of Labor Statistics. 2012a. "Licensed Practical and Licensed Vocational Nurses." *Occupational Outlook Handbook,* March 29. Retrieved February 6, 2013 (http:// www.bls.gov/ooh/healthcare/licensed-practical-and-licensed-vocational-nurses.htm).

Bureau of Labor Statistics. 2012b. "Registered Nurses." *Occupational Outlook Handbook,* March 29. Retrieved February 6, 2013 (http://www.bls.gov/ooh/healthcare/regis tered-nurses.htm).

Burgess, Robert and Ronald L. Akers. 1966. "A Differential Association-Reinforcement Theory of Criminal Behavior." *Social Problems* 14:363–83.

Burn, Shawn Meghan. 2011. *Women Across Cultures: A Global Perspective,* 3rd ed. New York: McGraw-Hill.

BushTV. 2010. "Kowanyama Keeping Culture Alive." Retrieved September 12, 2014 (http://www.youtube.com/watch? v=QCcBaVEUFlo).

Business Insider. 2012. "Hundreds of Suicides in India Linked to Microfinance Organizations." Retrieved January16, 2014 (www.businessinsider.com/hundreds-of-suicides-in-India-linked-to -microfinance-organizations-2012-2).

Byrne, Jane. 2011. "Mars Goes Fair Trade With Maltesers." FoodNavigator.com, September 27. Retrieved June 25, 2013 (www.foodnavigator.com/Financial-Industry/Mars-goes-Fairtrade-with-Maltesers).

Cainkar, Louise A. 2009. Homeland Insecurity: The Arab American and Muslim American Experience After 9/11. New York: Russell Sage Foundation.

CAIR. 2014. "Vision and Mission." Retrieved September 16, 2014 (http://www.cair.com/about-us/vision-mission-core-principles.html).

Caldwell, John C. 1982. *Theory of Fertility Decline.* New York: Academic Press.

Calhoun, Craig, ed. 2007. *Sociology in America: A History.* Chicago: University of Chicago Press.

Cambodian Genocide Program. 2013. "The CGP, 1994–2013." Yale University. Retrieved June 28, 2013 (www.yale.edu/cgp/).

Camilli, Gregory, Sadako Vargas, Sharon Ryan, and W. Steven Barnett. 2010. "Meta-Analysis of the Effects of Early Education Interventions on Cognitive and Social Development." *Teachers College Record* 112(3):579–620.

Campbell, Denis. 2010. "The New Anorexics: Big Increase in Eating Disorders Among Women over 30." *The Guardian,* October 8. Retrieved May 27, 2012 (www.guardian.co.uk/soci ety/2010/oct/08/new-anorexics-women-over-30).

Campbell, Ernest Q. and Thomas F. Pettigrew. 1959. *Christians in Racial Crisis.* Washington, DC: Public Affairs Press.

Canada, Geoffrey. 1998. Reaching Up for Manhood: Transforming the Lives of Boys in America. Boston: Beacon Press.

Canadian Health Care. 2007. "Introduction." Retrieved May 14, 2011 (www.canadian-healthcare.org/).

Cancian, Francesca M. 1992. "Feminist Science: Methodologies That Challenge Inequality." *Gender and Society* 6(4): 623–42.

Caramanica, Jon. 2013. "Homphobia and Hip-Hop: A Confession Breaks a Barrier." *New York Times,* September 13. Retrieved September 15, 2013 (www.nytimes.com/2013/09/14/arts/ music/homophobia-and-hip-hop-a-confession-breaks-a-bar rier.html?emc=eta1).

Carlson, Allan C. and Paul T. Mero. 2005. *The Natural Family: A Manifesto.* The Howard Center for Family, Religion and Society and the Sutherland Institute. Retrieved July 11, 2013 (http://familymanifesto.net/fmDocs/FamilyManifesto.pdf).

Carnevale, Anthony P. 2012. "Postsecondary Education and Training As We Know It Is Not Enough." Urban Institute. Retrieved May 17, 2012 (www.urban.org/issues/reducing-poverty-economic-distress.cfm).

Carroll, Lizz. 2010. "Interracial Marriage: Which Groups Are More Likely to Wed?" *DiversityInc,* May 27. Retrieved April 10, 2011 (www.diversityinc.com/article/7719/Interracial-Marriage-Which-Groups-Are-More-Likely-to-Wed/).

Carroll, Rory. 2010. "Ecuador Declares State of Emergency as Country Thrown Into Chaos." September 30. Retrieved December 2, 2010 (www.guardian.co.uk/world/2010/sep/30/ equador-chaos-police-rafael-correa).

Carrothers, Robert M. and Denzel E. Benson. 2003. "Symbolic Interactionism in Introductory Textbooks: Coverage and Pedagogical Implications." *Teaching Sociology* 31(2):162–81.

Carson, E. Ann and William J. Sabol. 2012. December. "Prisoners in 2011." Bureau of Justice Statistics. Retrieved June 2, 2013 (www.bjs.gov/content/pub/pdf/p11.pdf).

Carter, Prudence. 2007. *Keep'n It Real: School Success Beyond Black and White*. Oxford: Oxford University Press.

Casasanto, Daniel. 2008. "Who's Afraid of the Big Bad Whorf? Crosslinguistic Differences in Temporal Language and Thought." *Language Learning* 58(1):63–79.

CASE. 2012. "Community College and Business Partnerships Take Root." February 14. *Community College Advancement News* 1(8).

Casella, Alexander. 2009. "Rural China Misses 'Barefoot Doctors.'" *Asia Times,* January 16. Retrieved January 10, 2010 (www.atimes.com/atimes/China/KA16Ad04.html).

Cashmore, Ellis and Barry Troyna. 1990. *Introduction to Race Relations*. London: Routledge.

Castiello, Umberto, Cristina Becchio, Stefania Zoia, Cristian Nelini, Luisa Sartori, Laura Blason, Giuseppina D'Ottavio, Maria Bulgheroni, and Vittorio Gallese. 2010. "Wired to Be Social: The Ontogeny of Human Interaction." *PLoS ONE* 5(10). Retrieved October 19, 2010 (www.plosone.org/article/info%3Adoi%2F10.1371%2Fjournal.pone.0013199).

Catalyst. 2013. "Women CEOs of the Fortune 500." January 3. Retrieved June 7, 2013 (www.catalyst.org/knowledge/women-ceos-fortune-500).

Catalyst. 2014a. "Statistical Overview of Women in the Workplace." Equity in Business Leadership, March 3. Retrieved September 2, 2014 (http://www.catalyst.org/knowledge/statistical-overview-women-workplace).

Catalyst. 2014b. "Women CEOs of the Fortune 1000." Equity in Business Leadership, August 27. Retrieved September 2, 2014 (http://www.catalyst.org/knowledge/women-ceos-fortune-1000).

Catalyst 2014c. "Women's Earnings and Income." Equity in Business Leadership, March 24. Retrieved May 11, 2014 (http://www.catalyst.org/knowledge/womens-earnings-and-income).

Cauchon, Dennis and Barbara Hansen. 2011. "Typical U.S. Family Got Poorer During the Past 10 Years." *USA Today*, September 13. Retrieved June 5, 2012 (www.usatoday.com/news/nation/story/. . ./census. . ./1).

CBS News. 2010. "The Cost of Dying." *60 Minutes,* December 3. Retrieved July 16, 2012 (www.cbsnews.com/2100-18560_162-5711689.html?tag=contentMain;contentBody).

CBC News. 2010. "Four in 10 First Marriages End in Divorce." October 4. Retrieved June 27, 2012 (www.cbc.ca/news/canada/story/2010/10/04/vanier-study004.html).

Center for American Progress. 2013. "The High Cost of Youth Unemployment." Retrieved September 11, 2014 (www.americanprogress.org/issues/labor/report/2013/04/05/59428/the-high-cost-of-youth-unemployment/).

Center for American Progress Immigration Team. 2012. "The Facts on Immigration Today." July 6. Retrieved July 30, 2012 (www.americanprogress.org/issues/2012/07/immigration_facts.html).

Center for American Women and Politics. 2014. "Historical Information About Women in Congress." Retrieved September 4, 2014 (http://www.cawp.rutgers.edu/fast_facts/levels_of_office/Congress-HistoricalInfo.php).

Center for Constitutional Rights. 2013. "Report: Torture and Cruel, Inhuman, and Degrading Treatment of Prisoners at Guantanamo Bay." March 19. Retrieved April 25, 2014 (http://ccrjustice.org/learn-more/reports:-torture-and-cruel,-inhuman,-and-degrading-treatment-prisoners-quantanamo).

Center for Education Policy. 2006. *Survey on Hours Spent on Subjects.* Menlo Park, CA: SRI International.

Center for Voting and Democracy. 2008. "Understanding Super Tuesday: State Rules on February 5 and Lessons for Reform." Retrieved March 21, 2008 (www.fairvote.org/?page=27&pressmode=showspecific&showarticle=185).

Center for Workforce Studies. 2011. *2011 State Physician Workforce Data Release*, March. "Figure 1. Active Physicians per 100,000 Population by Degree Type, 2009" (p. 2). Association of American Medical Colleges. Retrieved February 4, 2013 (https://www.aamc.org/download/181238/data/state_databook_update.pdf).

Center on Philanthropy. 2012. "Has America's Charitable Giving Climbed Out of Its Great Recession-Fueled Trough?" June 19. Retrieved September 19, 2012 (www.philanthropy.iupui.edu/news/article/has-americas-charitable-giving=climbed-out-of-its-great=recession-fueled-trough).

Centers for Disease Control and Prevention. 2009c. "Overweight and Obesity." July 27–29. Retrieved November 4, 2009 (www.cdc.gov/obesity/index.html).

Centers for Disease Control and Prevention. 2011a. "Births, Marriages, Divorces, and Deaths: Provisional Data for 2009." *National Vital Statistics Report 2009* 58(25).

Centers for Disease Control and Prevention. 2011b. "National Marriage and Divorce Rate Trends." Retrieved June 5, 2012 (www.cdc.gov/nchs/nvss/marriage_divorce_tables.htm).

Centers for Disease Control and Prevention. 2011c. "U.S. Divorce Rate .68% for 2009." *National Vital Statistics Report,* February 7. Retrieved April 12, 2011 (http://familylaw.typepad.com/stats/2011/02/us-divorce-rate-068-for-2009-table-of-state-totals.html).

Centers for Disease Control and Prevention. 2012. "Economic Facts About U.S. Tobacco Production and Use." Retrieved August 3, 2012 (www.cdc.gov/tobacco/data_statistics/fact_sheets/economics/econ_facts/).

Centers for Disease Control and Prevention. 2012. "National Ambulatory Medical Care Survey: 2009." Retrieved October 15, 2012 (http://www.cdc.gov/nchs/fastats/docvisit.htm).

Centers for Disease Control and Prevention. 2013. "National Marriage and Divorce Rate Trends." Retrieved February 26, 2014 (www.cdc.gov/nchs/nvss/marriage_divorce_tables.htm).

Centers for Disease Control and Prevention. 2013a. "NCHS Data Brief; Trends in Inpatient Hospital Deaths: National Hospital Discharge Survey, 2000–2010." Retrieved July 16, 2013 (www.cdc.gov/nchs/data/databriefs/db118.htm).

Centers for Disease Control and Prevention. 2013b. "Multistate Fungal Meningitis Outbreak Investigation." Retrieved July 13, 2013 (www.cdc.gov/hai/outbreaks/meningitis.html).

Centers for Disease Control and Prevention. 2013c. "Alcohol and Public Health." Retrieved March 3, 2014 (www.cdc.gov/alcohol/faqs.htm#alcoholismAbuse).

Centers for Disease Control and Prevention. 2013d. "Infant Mortality Statistics from the 2010 Period." Retrieved May 28, 2014 (www.cdc.gov/nchs/data/nvsr/nvsr62/nvsr62_08.pdf).

Centers for Disease Control and Prevention. 2014a. "Measles Cases and Outbreaks, January 1 to August 29, 2014." Retrieval September 7, 2014 (www.cdc.gov/measles/cases-outbreaks.html).

Centers for Disease Control and Prevention. 2014b. "Unmarried Childbearing." Retrieved May 12, 2014 (www.cdc.gov/nchs/fastats/unmarry.htm).

Centers for Disease Control and Prevention/National Center for Health Statistics. 2012a. "National Vital Statistics System: Marriages and Divorces." Retrieved January 24, 2013 (http://www.cdc.gov/nchs/mardiv.htm).

Centers for Disease Control and Prevention/National Center for Health Statistics. 2012b. "National Vital Statistics System: National Marriage and Divorce Rate Trends: Provisional Number of Divorces and Annulments and Rate: United States, 2000–2010." Retrieved January 24, 2013 (www.cdc.gov/nchs/nvss/marriage_divorce_tables.htm).

Centers for Disease Control and Prevention/National Center for Health Statistics/Office of Analysis and Epidemiology. 2012. "Health, United States, 2011." Retrieved February 2, 2013 (http://www.cdc.gov/nchs/hus.htm).

Centers for Medicare and Medicaid Services. 2012. *Health Care Indicators.* Baltimore, MD: Office of the Actuary, Office of National Health Statistics.

Centers for Medicare and Medicaid Services. 2013. "The Affordable Care Act: Helping Providers Help Patients: A Menu of Options for Improving Care." Retrieved July 15, 2013 (www.cms.gov/Medicare/Medicare-Fee-for-Service-Payment/ACO/downloads/ACO-Menu-Of-Options.pdf).

Centers for Medicare and Medicaid Services. 2014a. "Historical." Retrieved May 3, 2014 (www.cms.gov/Research-Statistics-Data-and-Systems/Statistics-Trends-and-Reports/NationalHealthExpendData/NationalHealthAccounts Historical.html).

Centers for Medicare and Medicaid Services. 2014b. "National Health Expenditure Projections 2012–2022." Retrieved March 10, 2014 (www.cms.gov/Research-Statistics-Data-and-Systems/Statistics-Trends-and-Reports/NationalHealth ExpendData/downloads/proj2012.pdf).

Chalfant, H. Paul and Charles W. Peck. 1983. "Religious Affiliation, Religiosity, and Racial Prejudice: A New Look at Old Relationships." *Review of Religious Research* 25(December):155–61.

Chamberlain, Houston Stewart. [1899] 1911. *The Foundations of the Nineteenth Century,* translated by John Lees. London, New York: John Lane.

Chambliss, William J. 1973. "The Saints and the Roughnecks." *Society* 11(December):24–31.

Chapman, Paige. 2010. "Report Calles for Distance Learning to Improve Higher Education Access and Efficiency in California." *The Chronicle of Higher Education,* October 29. Retrieved April 17, 2011 (http://chronicle.com/blogs/wired campus/distance-learning-can-improve-higher-education-access-and-efficiency-in-california/27978).

Charities Aid Foundation. 2012. "World Giving Index 2012," December. Retrieved June 15, 2013 (www.cafonline.org/PDF/WorldGivingIndex2012WEB.pdf).

Charles, Camille Z., Vincent J. Roscigno, and Kimberly C. Torres. 2007. "Racial Inequality and College Attendance: The Mediating Role of Parental Investments." *Social Science Research* 36(1):329–52.

Charon, Joel. 2010. *Symbolic Interactionism: An Introduction, and Interpretation, an Integration,* 10th ed. Englewood Cliffs, NJ: Prentice Hall.

Chase, Cheryl. 2000. "Genital Surgery on Children Below the Age of Consent: Intersex Genital Mutilation." In *Psychological Perspectives on Human Sexuality,* edited by L. Szuchman and F. Muscarella. New York: Wiley.

Chase-Dunn, Christopher and E. N. Anderson. 2006. *The Historical Evolution of World-Systems.* New York: Palgrave Macmillan.

Chaves, Mark. 1993. "Denominations as Dual Structures: An Organizational Analysis." *Sociology of Religion* 54(20):147–69.

Chaves, Mark. 1999. *Ordaining Women: Culture and Conflict in Religious Organizations.* Cambridge, MA: Harvard University Press.

Chaves, Mark. 2004. *Congregations in America.* Cambridge, MA: Harvard University Press.

Chaves, Mark and Philip S. Gorski. 2001. "Religious Pluralism and Religious Participation." *Annual Review of Sociology* 27:261–81.

Chen, Zeng-Yin and Howard B. Kaplan. 2003. "School Failure in Early Adolescence and Status Attainment in Middle Adulthood: A Longitudinal Study." *Sociology of Education* 76(2):110–27.

Cheng, Cecilia. 2005. "Processes Underlying Gender-Role Flexibility: Do Androgynous Individuals Know More or Know How to Cope?" *Journal of Personality* 73(3):645–73.

Cheng, Siwei and Yu Xie. 2013. "Structural Effect of Size on Interracial Friendship." *Proceedings of the National Academy of Sciences,* April 15.

Cherlin, Andrew. 1978. "Remarriage as an Incomplete Institution." *American Journal of Sociology* 84(3):634–50.

Cherlin, Andrew J. 2010. *The Marriage-Go-Round: The State of Marriage and the Family in America Today.* New York: Random House.

Cherlin, Andrew J. 2012. *Public and Private Families: An Introduction,* 7th ed. New York: McGraw-Hill.

Cherry, Donald, Christine Lucas, and Sandra L. Decker. 2010. "Population Aging and the Use of Office-Based Physician Services." National Center for Health Statistics. *NCHS Data Brief* 41(August). Retrieved July 17, 2012 (www.cdc.nchs.gov/data/databriefs/db41.pdf).

Cherry, Kendra. 2012. "Understanding Body Language." *About.com Psychology*. Retrieved September 25, 2012 (http://psychology.about.com/od/nonverbalcommunication/ss/understanding-body-language.htm).

Cheung, Cecilia Sin-Sze and Eva M. Pomerantz. 2012. "Why Does Parents' Involvement Enhance Children's Achievement? The Role of Parent-Oriented Motivation." *Journal of Educational Psychology* 14(3):820–32.

Chicago Public Schools. 2011. "Renaissance 2010." Retrieved September 13, 2012 (www.cps.edu/PROGRAMS/DISTRI CINITIATIVES/Pages/Renaissance 2010.aspx).

Child Trends. 2012. "Living Arrangements of Children, by Race and Hispanic Origin, 2012." U.S. Census Bureau, Current Population Survey. Retrieved February 19, 2014 (www.census.gov/hhes/families/data/cps2012.html).

Child Trends. 2013a. "Child Support Receipt." Retrieved February 19, 2014 (www.childtrends.org/wp-content/uploads/212/07/84_Child_Support_Receipt.pdf).

Child Trends. 2013b. "Family Structure: Indicators on Children and Youth." Retrieved February 19, 2014 (www.childtrends databank.org).

Child Trends. 2013c. "High School Dropout Rates." Retrieved April 3, 2014 (www.childtrends.org/?indicators=high-school-dropout-rates).

Child Trends Data Bank. 2012. "Sexually Active Teens." Retrieved September 13, 2012 (www.childtrendsdatabank.org/?q=node/315).

"Children and Watching TV." 2011. *American Academy of Child and Adolescent Psychiatry* 54(December). Retrieved May 24, 2012 (www.aacap.org/cs/root/facts_for_families/children_and_watching_tv).

Children's Defense Fund. 2011. "Number and Percentage of Uninsured Children in Each State." Retrieved April 7, 2011 (www.childrensdefense.org/policy-priorities/childrens-health/uninsured-children/uninsured-children-state.html).

Children's Defense Fund. 2013. "Cradle to Prison Pipeline Campaign." Retrieved January 15, 2014 (www.childrensde fense.org/programs-campaigns/cradle-to-prison-pipeline/).

ChildStats.gov. 2013. "America's Children: Key National Indicators of Well-Being, 2013." Retrieved February 25, 2014 (www.childstats.gov/americaschildren/famsoc2.asp).

ChinaDaily.com. 2012. "Tobacco Consumption Rises Amid Economic Slowdown." July 19. Retrieved August 2, 2012 (www.chinadaily.com.cn/business/2012-07-19/content_15598994.htm).

China.org. 2009. "Acupuncture, Herbal Medicine Become More Popular in U.S." Retrieved January 10, 2010 (www.china.org.cn/health/2009-06/25/content_18009726.htm).

Chiotakis, Steve. 2011. "U.S. Census: Only 16% Live in Rural America." *American Public Media*, July 28. Retrieved September 26, 2012 (www.marketplace.org/topics/business/us-census-only-16-live-rural-america).

Chivers, M. L., M. C. Seto, and R. R. Blanchard. 2007. "Gender and Sexual Orientation Differences in Sexual Response to Sexual Activities Versus Gender of Actors in Sexual Films." *Journal of Personality and Social Psychology* 93(6):1108–1121.

Christiano, Kevin J., William H. Swatos, Jr., and Peter Kivisto. 2008. *Sociology of Religion: Contemporary Developments*, Rev. ed. Walnut Creek, CA: AltaMira.

Chubb, John E. and Terry M. Moe. 1990. *Politics, Markets, and America's Schools*. Washington, DC: Brookings Institution.

Churchill, Winston. 2009. *Churchill by Himself: The Definitive Collection of Quotations,* edited by Richard Langworth. Jackson, TN: Public Affairs.

Cillizza, Chris. 2011. "Facebook, President Obama, and the Youth Vote in 2012." *The Washington Post*, April 20. Retrieved November 1, 2012 (www.washingtonpost.com/blogs/the-fix/post/facebook-president-obama-and-the-youth-vote-in-2012/2011/04/20/AF9zCwCE_blog.html).

Cisco. 2014. "Cisco Visual Networking Index: Global Mobile Data Traffic Forecast Update, 2013." Retrieved May 10, 2014 (www.cisco.com/c/en/us/solutions/collateral/service-provider/visual-networking-index-vni/white_paper_c11-520862.html).

Clapson, Mark. 2003. *Suburban Century: Social Change and Urban Growth in England and the USA*. Oxford and New York: Berg Publishers.

Clark, Warren and Grant Schellenberg. 2008. "Who's Religious?" *Statistics Canada*. Retrieved January 30, 2013 (http://www.statcan.gc.ca/pub/11-008-x/2006001/9181-eng.htm#half).

Clarke, Anne. 2007. "Amish Traditions—Shunning." *EzineArticles.com,* June 12. Retrieved December 13, 2009 (http://enzinearticles.com/?Amish-Traditions-Shunning&id=603322).

Clarke, Ronald R., ed. 1997. *Situational Crime Prevention: Successful Case Studies*, 2nd ed. New York: Harrow and Heston.

Clarkson, Lamar. 2011. "Divorce Rates Falling, Report Finds." *CNN Living,* May 19. Retrieved June 6, 2012 (http://articles.cnn.com/2011-05-19/living/divorce.rates.drop_1_divorce-rate-divorce-laws-marriage?_s=PM:LIVING).

Clausen, John A. 1986. *The Life Course: A Sociological Perspective*. Englewood Cliffs, NJ: Prentice Hall.

Cline, Michael E. 2008. "Comparison of Potential Demographic Influences on Church Membership of Two United Methodist Congregations in San Antonio, Texas." Pp. 237–49 in *Applied Demography in the 21st Century,* edited by Steve H. Murdock and David A. Swanson. Netherlands: Springer.

Clymer, Floyd. 1953. *Those Wonderful Old Automobiles*. New York: Bonanza.

CNBC. 2010. "Mob Money: An American Greed." July 7. Retrieved February 8, 2013 (www.cnbc.com/id/37593299/mob_money).

CNN. 2012. "Facts on Immigration in the United States." June 15. Retrieved July 30, 2012 (http://news.blogs.cnn.com/2012/06/15/facts-on-immigration-in-the-united-states/).

CNNMoney.com. 2010. "Fortune 500: Women CEOs." Retrieved January 20, 2013 (http://money.cnn.com/magazines/fortune/fortune500/2010/womenceos/).

CNN Politics. 2009. "Obama Reverses Abortion-Funding Policy." Retrieved July 25, 2011 (http://articles.cnn.com/2009-01-23/politics/obama.abortion_1_abortion-counseling-family-planning-family-planning?_s=PM:POLITICS).

Cockerham, William C. 2012. *Medical Sociology,* 12th ed. Englewood Cliffs, NJ: Prentice Hall.

Coghlan, Andy and Debora MacKenzie. 2011. "Revealed—The Capitalist Network That Runs the World." *NewScientist*. Retrieved June 23, 2013 (www.newscientist.com/article/mg21228354.500-revealed—the-capitalist-network-that-runs-the-world.html).

Cohen, Jessica and Wendy D. Manning. 2010 "The Relationship Context of Premarital Serial Cohabitation." *Social Science Research* 39(September):766–76.

Cohn, D'Vera, Paul Taylor, Mark Hugo Lopez, Catherine A. Gallagher, Kim Parker and Kevin T. Maass. 2013. "Gun Homicide Rate Down 49% Since 1993 Peak; Public Unaware." Pew Research Social & Demographic Trends, May 7. Retrieved June 1, 2013 (www.pewsocialtrends.org/2013/05/07/gun-homicide-rate-down-49-since-1993-peak-public-unaware/).

Cole, Stephen and Robert Lejeune. 1972. "Illness and the Legitimation of Failure." *American Sociological Review* 37(3):347–56.

Coleman, James S. 1968. "The Concept of Equality of Educational Opportunity." *Harvard Education Review* 38(Winter):7–22.

Coleman, James S. 1975. "What Is Meant By 'An Equal Educational Opportunity'?" *Oxford Review of Education* 1(1):27–29.

Coleman, James. 1990. *Equality and Achievement in Education*. Boulder, CO: Westview.

Coleman, James William. 2006. *The Criminal Elite: Understanding White Collar Crime,* 6th ed. New York: Worth.

Coleman-Jensen, Alisha, Mark Nord, Margaret Andrews, and Steven Carlson. 2011. "Household Food Security in the United States in 2010." ERR-125, U.S. Department of Agriculture, Economic Research Service, September. Retrieved May 17, 2012 (www.cbpp.org/cms/index.cfm?fa=view&id=2226).

Coleman-Jensen, Alisha, Mark Nord, Margaret Andrews, and Steven Carlson. 2012. *Household Food Security in the United States in 2011*. U.S. Department of Agriculture. Retrieved June 7, 2013 (www.ers.usda.gov/media/884525/err141.pdf).

College Board. 2013. "SAT Total Group Profile Report." Retrieved May 16, 2014 (http://media.collegeboard.com/digitalServices/pdf/research/2013/TotalGroup-2013.pdf).

"Colleges' Gender Gap." 2010. *Los Angeles Times*, January 25. Retrieved September 12, 2012 (http://articles.latimes.com/2010/jan/25/opinion/la-ed-gender25-2010jan25).

Collins, Patricia Hill. 2005. *Black Sexual Politics: African Americans, Gender and the New Racism*. New York: Routledge.

Collins, Patricia Hill. 2008. *Black Feminist Thought: Knowledge, Consciousness, and the Politics of Empowerment*. New York: Routledge.

Collins, Randall. 1971. "A Conflict Theory of Sexual Stratification." *Social Problems* 19(Summer):2–21.

Collins, Randall. 2004. "Conflict Theory of Educational Stratification." *American Sociological Review* 36:47–54.

Commonwealth Fund. 2013. *International Profiles of Health Care Systems, 2013*. Retrieved September 16, 2014 (http://www.commonwealthfund.org/publications/fund-reports/2013/nov/international-profiles-of-health-care-systems).

ComScore. 2010. "Social Networking Sites Reach a Higher Percentage of Women Than Men Worldwide." July 28. Retrieved May 25, 2012 (www.comscore.com/Press_Events/Press_Releases/2010/7/Social_Networking_Sites_REach_a-Higher_Percentage_of_Women_than_Men_).

Comte, Auguste. [1855] 2003. *The Positive Philosophy of Auguste Comte,* freely translated and condensed by Harriet Martineau. Whitefish, MO: Kessinger.

Condron, Dennis J. and Vincent J. Roscigno. 2003. "Disparities Within: Unequal Spending and Achievement in an Urban School District." *Sociology of Education* 76(January):18–36.

Conrad, Peter. 2007. *The Medicalization of Society: On the Transformation of Human Conditions Into Treatable Disorders*. Baltimore, MD: Johns Hopkins University Press.

Conrad, Peter, Thomas Mackie, Attev Mehrotra. 2010. "Estimating the Costs of Medicalization." *Social Science and Medicine* 70(12):1943–47.

Conrad, Peter and Joseph Schneider. 1992. *Deviance and Medicalization: From Badness to Sickness*. Philadelphia: Temple University Press.

Cook, Karen S., Jodi O'Brien, and Peter Kollock. 1990. "Exchange Theory: A Blueprint for Structure and Process." Pp. 158–81 in *Frontiers of Social Theory: The New Syntheses*, edited by George Ritzer. New York: Columbia University Press.

Cooke, Jennifer G. 2012. "Polio in Nigeria: The Race to Eradication." Center for Strategic and International Studies, February 10. Retrieved July 16, 2012 (http://csis.org/publication/polio-nigeria).

Cooley, Charles Horton. 1902. *Human Nature and the Social Order*. New York: Scribner.

Cooley, Charles Horton. [1909] 1983. *Social Organization: A Study of the Larger Mind*. New York: Schocken Books.

Coontz, Stephanie. 1997. *The Way We Really Are: Coming to Terms With America's Changing Families*. New York: Basic Books.

Coontz, Stephanie. 2005. Marriage, a History: From Obedience to Intimacy, or How Love Conquered Marriage. New York: Viking.

Coontz, Stephanie. 2011a. "On Marriage." January 4. Retrieved February 25, 2012 (www.youtube.com/watch?v=gwtb7jz8G4k).

Coontz, Stephanie. 2011b. "What Is the 'Traditional American Family'? Interview with Stephanie Coontz." *The Mother Company*, November 22. Retrieved May 25, 2012 (www.themotherco.com/2011/1/what-is-the-traditional-family/).

Copp, Jennifer E., Peggy C. Giordano, Monica A. Longmore, and Wendy D. Manning. 2013. "Stay/Leave Decision-Making in Non-Violent and Violent Dating Relationships." 2013 Working Paper Series. *Center for Family and Demographic Research*. Retrieved January 17, 2014 (www.bgsu.edu/organizations.cfdr).

Corbett, Christianne, Catherine Hill, Andresse St. Rose. 2008. "Where the Girls Are: The Facts About Gender Equity in Education." AAUW, May. Retrieved July 8, 2013 (www.aauw.org/research/where-the-girls-are/).

Cordain, L., S. B. Eaton, A. Sabastian, N. Mann, S. Lindeberg, B. A. Watkins, J. H. O'Keefe, and J. Brand-Miller. 2005. "Origins and Evolution of the Western Diet: Health Implications for the 21st Century." *American Journal of Clinical Nutrition* 82(August): 483–84.

Coser, Lewis A. 1956. *The Functions of Social Conflict*. New York: Free Press.

Council on the American Family. N.d. "Marriage and Families." Retrieved June 6, 2012 (http://caf-usa.org/).

Council on Foreign Relations. 2014. "NAFTA's Economic Impact." Retrieved February 23, 2014 (www.cfr.org/trade/naftas-economic-impact/p15790).

Council of Graduate Schools. 2014. "Doctoral Degrees by Field and Gender, 2012." Retrieved May 11, 2014 (www.aei-ideas.org/2013/09/women-earned-majority-of-doctoral-degrees-in-2012-for-4th-straight-year-and-outnumber-men-in-grad-school-141).

Cousteau, Jacques-Yves. 2008. "The Great Ocean Adventure." Lecture at Hanover College, January 15.

Cowen, Nick and Nigel Williams. 2012. "Comparisons of Crime in OECD Countries." *Civitas Crime*. Retrieved May 2, 2013 (www.civitas.org.uk/crime/crime_stats_oecdjan2012.pdf).

Crary, David and Denise Lavoie. 2013. "As Boston Buries Its Dead, More Evidence Gathered." AP, April 23. Retrieved August 23, 2014 (http://bigstory.ap.org/article/more-details-sought-mute-boston-bomb-suspect).

Crenshaw, Kimberlé. 1991. "Mapping the Margins: Intersectionality, Identity Politics, and Violence against Women of Color." *Stanford Law Review* 43(6):1241–99.

Creswell, John W. 2009. *Research Design: Qualitative, Quantitative, and Mixed Methods Approaches,* 3rd ed. Thousand Oaks, CA: Sage.

Crime Library. 2012. "Worst Cases of Bullying." Retrieved October 5, 2012 (www.gtrutv.com/library/crime/photogallery/worst-cases-of-bullying.html?curPhoto=3).

Croft, Michelle and Grover J. "Russ" Whitehurst. 2010. "The Harlem Children's Zone Revisited." The Brookings Institute. July 28. Retrieved January 10, 2014 (www.brookings.edu/blogs/up-front/posts/2010/07/28-hcz-whitehurst).

Cronkite, Walt. 2012. "Romney Says He's 'Fine' With Gay Couples Adopting Children." *CBS News,* May 10. Retrieved June 3, 2012 (www.cbsnews.com/8301-503544_162-57432292-503544/romney-says-hes-fine-with-gay-couples-adopting-children/).

Crosby, Faye J. 2004. *Affirmative Action Is Dead; Long Live Affirmative Action.* New Haven, CT: Yale University Press.

Crossette, Barbara. 1996. "Angkor Emerges From the Jungle." *New York Times*, January 28. Retrieved September 9, 2008 (http://query.nytimes.com/gst/fullpage.html?res=9500e0d91139f93ba15752c0a960958260&sec=travel&spon=&pagewanted=1).

"Cruellest Cut—Pakistan's Kidney Mafia." 2009. Retrieved January 11, 2010 (www.youtube.com/watch?v=vi7A_jK64qc).

Crummey, Robert O. 1970. *The Old Believers and the World of Antichrist: The Vyg Community and the Russian State, 1694–1855.* Madison: University of Wisconsin Press.

Cultural Survival. 2010. "Wodaabe." Retrieved July 7, 2013 (www.culturalsurvival.org/publications/cultural-survival-quarterly/cameroon/wodaabe).

Current.com. 2012. "The War Room With Jennifer Granholm: The Pros and Cons of Private Prisons." February 21. Retrieved October 7, 2012 (http://current.com/shows/the-pros-and-cons-of-private-prisons).

Current Population Survey. 2013. "The Diversifying Electorate—Voting Rates by Race and Hispanic Origin in 2012 (and Other Recent Elections)." Pp. 20–568. Retrieved January 4, 2014 (www.census.gov/prod/2013pubs/p20-568.pdf).

Curtiss, S. 1977. *Genie: A Psycholinguistic Study of a Modern-Day "Wild Child."* New York: Academic Press.

Cushing, Bill and Robert G. Bishop. 2008. *The Big Sort: Why the Clustering of Like-Minded America Is Tearing Us Apart.* Boston: Houghton Mifflin Harcourt.

Cushman, Thomas and Stjepan G. Mestrovic. 1996. *This Time We Knew: Western Responses to Genocide in Bosnia.* New York: New York University Press.

Cuzzort, R. P. and Edith W. King. 2002. *Social Thought Into the Twenty-First Century*, 6th ed. Belmont, CA: Wadsworth.

"Cybercrime: Smoking Gun." 2013. *The Economist,* February 23. Retrieved June 2, 2013 (www.economist.com/news/china/21572228-evidence-mounting-chinas-government-sponsoring-cybertheft-western-corporate).

DaCosta, Kimberly McClain. 2007. *Making Multiracials: State, Family, and Market in the Redrawing of the Color Line.* Stanford, CA: Stanford University Press.

Dahl, Robert A. 1961. *Who Governs?* New Haven, CT: Yale University Press.

Dahlberg, Frances. 1981. *Woman the Gatherer.* New Haven, CT: Yale University Press.

Dahrendorf, Ralf. 1959. *Class and Class Conflict in Industrial Societies.* Palo Alto, CA: Stanford University Press.

Daley, Suzanne, and Nicholas Kulish 2013. "Germany Fights Population Drop." *New York Times,* August 13. Retrieved March 17, 2014 (www.nytimes.com/2013/08/14/world/europe/germany-fights-population-drop.html).

Dalit Liberation Education Trust. 1995. *10th Anniversary Newsletter* (May). Madras: Human Rights Education Movement of India.

Dalton, Harlon. 2012. "Failing to See." Pp. 15–18 in *White Privilege,* edited by Paula S. Rothenberg. New York: Worth.

Danesi, Marcel. 2008. *Popular Culture.* Lanham, MD: Rowman & Littlefield.

D'Arcy, Yvonne. 2009. "The Effect of Culture on Pain." *Nursing Made Incredibly Easy!* 7(3):5–7.

Darr, Kurt. 2007. "Assistance in Dying: Part II. Assisted Suicide in the U.S." *Hospital Topics* 85(2):31–36.

Darwin, Charles. [1859] 1909. *On the Origin of Species.* New York: P. F. Collier.

Das, Udaibir S., Michael G. Papaioannou, and Christoph Trebesch. 2012. "Sovereign Debt Restructurings 1950-2010: Literature Survey, Data, and Stylized Facts." International Moetary Fund, August. Retrieved September 8, 2014 (www.un.org/esa/ffd/ecosoc/debt/2013/IMF_wp12_203.pdf).

Davidson, James D. 2008. "Religious Stratification: Its Origins, Persistence, and Consequences" *Sociology of Religionsocrel.oxfordjournals.org Sociology of Religion* 69(4):371–95.

Davis, Kingsley. 1940. "Extreme Social Isolation of a Child." *American Journal of Sociology* 45:554–65.

Davis, Kingsley. 1947. "A Final Note on a Case of Extreme Isolation." *American Journal of Sociology* 52:432–37.

Davis, Kingsley and Wilbert Moore. 1945. "Some Principles of Stratification." *American Sociological Review* 10(April): 242–45.

Day, Jennifer Cheeseman. 2011. U.S. "Population Profile of the U.S.: Percentage of the Population, by Race and Hispanic Origin." Census Bureau, Population Division Retrieved April 19, 2011 (http://www.census.gov/population/www/pop-profile/natproj.html).

Dealbook. 2009. "Pay Czar Said to Plan to Disclose Top Salaries." Retrieved January 20, 2013 (www.dealbook.nytimes.com/2009/09/17/pay-czar-seen-disclosing-top-executive-salaries/).

Death Penalty Information Center. 2013. "FBI Releases Report Including State Murder Rates for 2012: DPIC Analysis Posted October 28, 2013." Retrieved April 25, 2014 (www.deathpenaltyinfo.org/studies-fbi-releases-report-including-state-murder-rates-2012).

Death Penalty Information Center. 2014. "States With and Without the Death Penalty." Retrieved April 25, 2014 (www.deathpenaltyinfoorg/states-and-without-death-penalty).

Death With Dignity National Center. 2012. "Death with Dignity: The Laws & How to Access Them: Overview." Retrieved July 15, 2013 (www.deathwithdignity.org/access-acts).

Debenham, Lucy. 2014. "Communication—What Percent Is Body Language?" August 18. Retrieved August 29, 2014 (www.bodylanguageexpert.co.uk/communication-what-percentage-body-language.html).

DeBoskey, Bruce. 2012. "Women Changing the Face of Philanthropy." *The Denver Post,* July 22. Retrieved April 25, 2013 (www.denverpost.com/business/ci_21124380/women-changing-face-philanthropy).

Deerwester, Karen. 2013. "Boy Toys or Girl Toys: Children Are What They Play." *Examiner,* November 8. Retrieved January 16, 2014 (www.examiner.com/article/boy-toys-or-girl-toys-children-are-what-they-play).

DeGenova, Mary Kay, Nick Stinnett, and Nancy Stinnett. 2011. *Intimate Relationships, Marriages, and Families,* 8th ed. New York: McGraw-Hill.

Delfattore, Joan. 2004. "Romeo and Juliet Were Just Good Friends." Pp. 177–83 in *Schools and Society,* 2nd ed., edited by Jeanne H. Ballantine and Joan Z. Spade. Belmont, CA: Wadsworth.

Della Porta, Donatella, Massimillano Andretta, Lorenzo Mosca, and Herbert Reiter. 2006. *Globalization From Below: Transnational Activists and Protest Networks*. Minneapolis: University of Minnesota Press.

DeMartini, Joseph R. 1982. "Basic and Applied Sociological Work: Divergence, Convergence, or Peaceful Coexistence?" *Journal of Applied Behavioral Science* 18(2):205–206.

Deming, W. E. 2000. *Out of the Crisis*. Cambridge, MA: MIT Press.

DeMitchell, Todd A. and John J. Carney. 2005. "Harry Potter and the Public School Library." *Phi Delta Kappan* (October):159–65.

Demographics Livability 2014. "Why Do People Move? Here Are the Top Reasons for Relocation." June 12. Retrieved September 8,2014 (http://livability.com/blog/demographics/why-do-people-move-here-are-top-reasons-relocation).

Denali Commission. 2001. "Telecommunications Inventory Survey." Retrieved June 29, 2006 (www.commonwealth.north.org/transcripts/denalicom.html).

DeNavas-Walt, Carmen, Bernadette D. Proctor, and Jessica C. Smith. 2010. "Income, Poverty, and Health Insurance Coverage in the United States: 2009." U.S. Census Bureau, Report P60-238, Table B-2, pp. 62–67. Retrieved January 23, 2013 (http://www.census.gov/prod/2010pubs/p60-238.pdf).

DeNavas-Walt, Carmen, Bernadette D. Proctor, and Jessica C. Smith. 2011. "Income, Poverty, and Health Insurance Coverage in the United States: 2010." Retrieved January 28, 2013 (http://www.census.gov/prod/2011pubs/p60-239.pdf).

DeNavas-Walt, Carmen, Bernadette D. Proctor, and Jessica C. Smith. 2012. "Income, Poverty, and Health Insurance Coverage in the United States: 2011." U.S. Census Bureau Current Population Reports, September. Retrieved February 6, 2013 (http://www.census.gov/prod/2012pubs/p60-243.pdf).

DeNavas-Walt, Carmen, Bernadette D. Proctor, and Jessica C. Smith. 2013. "Income, Poverty, and Health Insurance Coverage in the United States." *Current Population Reports,* September. Retrieved September 5, 2014 (http://www.census.gov/prod/2013pubs/p60-245.pdf).

DePalma, Anthony. 1995. "Racism? Mexico's in Denial." *The New York Times*, June 11, p. E4.

DeParle, Jason and Sabrina Tavernise. 2012. " For Women Under 30, Most Births Occur Outside Marriage." *The New York Times*, February 17. Retrieved June 5, 2012 (www.nytimes.com/2012/02/18/us/for-women-under-30-most-births-occur-outside-marriage.html?pagewanted=all).

Department of Defense. 2012. *Sustaining U.S. Global Leadership: Priorities for 21st Century Defense*. Retrieved December 2, 2013 (www.defense.gov/news/defense_strategic_guidance.pdf).

DeSantis, Carol. 213. "Cancer Statistics About African Americans Released." American Cancer Society, February 4. Retrieved July 15, 2013 (http://www.cancer.org/cancer/news/expert voices/post/2013/02/04/cancer-statistics-about-african-amer icans-released.aspx).

Deutsch, Albert. 1944. "The First U.S. Census of the Insane (1840) and Its Use as Pro-Slavery Propaganda." P. 472 in *Bulletin of the History of Medicine* 15.

Deutsch, Morton and Ronald M. Krauss. 1960. "The Effect of Threat on Interpersonal Bargaining." *Journal of Abnormal and Social Psychology* 61:181–89.

Deutsch, Morton and Roy J. Lewicki. 1970. "'Locking-In' Effects During a Game of Chicken." *Journal of Conflict Resolution* 14(3):367–78.

Dews, C. L. Barney and Carolyn Leste Law, eds. 1995. *This Fine Place So Far From Home: Voices of Academics From the Working Class*. Philadelphia: Temple University Press.

Diamond, Jared M. 1999. *Guns, Germs, and Steel: The Fates of Human Societies*. New York: Norton.

Diamond, Jared. 2005. Collapse: How Societies Choose to Fail or Succeed. New York: Viking.

Diamond, Larry. 1992. "Introduction: Civil Society and the Struggle for Democracy." Pp. 1–28 in *The Democratic Revolution: Struggles for Freedom and Pluralism in the Developing World,* edited by Larry Diamond. New York: Freedom House.

Diamond, Larry. 2003. "Universal Democracy?" *Policy Review* (June/July). Retrieved August 28, 2008 (www.hoover.org/publications/poicyreview/3448571.html).

Diamond, Larry. 2009. The Spirit of Democracy: The Struggle to Build Free Societies Throughout the World. New York: Times Books/Henry Holt & Co.

Diekman, Amanda B. and Sarah K. Murmen. 2004. "Learning to Be Little Women and Little Men: The Inequitable Gender Equality of Nonsexist Children's Literature." *Sex Roles: A Journal of Research* 50(5/6):373.

Diep, Francie. 2011. "Fast Facts About the Japan Earthquake and Tsunami." *Scientific American,* March 14. Retrieved May 13, 2012 (www.scientificamerican.com/article.cfm?if=fast-facts-japan).

Diggs, Nancy Brown. 2011. *Hidden in the Heartland*. East Lansing: Michigan State University Press.

Diggs, Nancy Brown. 2014. *Breaking the Cycle: How Schools Can Overcome Urban Challenges*. New York: Rowman and Littlefield.

Dilon, Michele. 2009. *Introduction to Sociological Theory: Theorists, Concepts, and Their Applicability to the Twenty-First Century*. Malden, MA: Wiley-Blackwell.

DiMaggio, Paul and Walter Powell. 1983. "The Iron Cage Revisited: Institutional Isomorphism and Collective Rationality in Organizational Fields." *American Sociological Review* 48:147–60.

DiPrete, Thomas A., and Claudia Buchmann. 2013. *The Rise of Women: The Growing Gender Gap in Education and What It Means for American Schools*. New York: Russell Sage Foundation.

Disabled World. 2012. "2012 London Summer Paralympic Games." Retrieved September 9, 2012 (www.disabled-world.com/sports/paralympics/2012/).

DiversityInc. 2008. "Belonging Nowhere: The Biracial Children of Vietnam Veterans." October 13. Retrieved October 16, 2009 (diversityinc.com/content/1757/article/4574).

Divorce Rate. 2011. "Divorce Updates and Divorce Rate in 2011." Retrieved June 6, 2012 (http://divorcerate2011.com/divorce-updates).

Dixon, Patrick. 2011. "Steroid Use." *Global Change*. Retrieved May 23, 2012 (www.globalchange.com/steroids.htm).

Dobbelaere, Karel. 1981. *Secularization: A Multidimensional Concept.* Beverly Hills, CA: Sage.

Dobbelaere, Karel. 2000. "Toward an Integrated Perspective of the Processes Related to the Descriptive Concept of Secularization." Pp. 21–39 in *The Secularization Debate,* edited by William H. Swatos, Jr. and Daniel V. A. Olson. Lanham, MD: Rowman & Littlefield.

Dobbs, David. 2013. "The Social Life of Genes" *Pacific Standard,* September 3. Retrieved December 17, 2013 (www.psmag .com/health/the-social-life-of-genes-64616/).

Dockterman, Eliana. 2014. "Chore Wars: How the Division of Domestic Duties Really Affects a Couple's Sex Life" *Time,* February 18. Retrieved February 28, 2014 (http://healthland .time.com/2014/02/18/chore-wars-how-the-division-of-domestic-duties-really-affects-a-couples-sex-life/#ix zz2udTcoUJ0).

Doctors without Borders. 2012. "Swaziland: Community Takes Part in HIV Treatment." February 13. Retrieved July 16, 2012 (http://doctorswithout borers.org/news/article.cfm?id=5763 &cat=video&ref-tag-index).

"Doing Gender." 2011. *Creative Sociology.* August 10. Retrieved May (http://creativesociology.blogspot.com/2011/08/doing-gender.html).

Dollars and Sense Collective. 2012. Pp. 81–91 in *Globalization: The Transformation of Social Wor*lds, 3rd ed., edited by D. Stanley Eitzen and Maxine Baca Zinn. Belmont, CA: Wadsworth.

Domestic Violence Resource Center. 2012. "Domestic Violence Statistics." Retrieved June 21, 2012 (www.dvrc-or.org/domes tic/violence/resources/C61).

Domhoff, G. William. 2005. "The Class-Domination Theory of Power." *Who Rules America,* 6th ed. Retrieved May 16, 2012 (www2.ucsc .edu/whorulesamerica/power/class_domination.html).

Domhoff, G. William. 2008. "Who Rules America.net: Power, Politics, and Social Change." Retrieved March 24, 2008 (http://sociology.ucsc.edu/whoruleeesamerica).

Domhoff, G. William. 2009. *Who Rules America: Challenges to Corporate and Class Dominance.* Upper Saddle River, NJ: Prentice Hall.

Domhoff, G. William. 2014. *Who Rules America: The Triumph of the Corporate Rich,* 7th ed. New York: McGraw-Hill.

Domina, Thurston. 2005. "Leveling the Home Advantage: Assessing the Effectiveness of Parental Involvement in Elementary School." *Sociology of Education* 78(3):233–49.

Donadio, Rachel. 2010. "Vatican Revises Abuse Processes But Causes Stir. *New York Times,* July 15. Retrieved July 12, 2013 (www.nytimes.com/2010/07/16/world/europe/16vatican .html).

Dotinga, Randy. 2011. "Fewer Med Students Training as Primary Care Doctors-Study." U.S. News.com, April 26. Retrieved July 15, 2013 (http://health.usnews.com/health-news/managing-your-healthcare/healthcare/articles/2011/04/26/fewer-med-students-training-as-primary-care-doctors-study).

Dotzler, Robert J. and Ross Koppel. 1999. "What Sociologists Do and Where They Do It—The NSF Survey on Sociologists' Work Activities and Work Places." *Sociological Practice: A Journal of Clinical and Applied Sociology* 1(1):71–83.

Downey, Douglas B. and Shana Pribesh. 2004. "When Race Matters: Teachers' Evaluations of Students' Classroom Behavior." *Sociology of Education* 77(4):267–82.

"Dowry Deaths: One Woman Dies Every Hour." 2013. *The Times of India,* September 1. Retrieved January 18, 2014 (http:// articles.timesofindia.indiatimes.com/2013-09-01/ india/41662390_1_delhi-police-conviction-ncrb).

Drafke, Michael. 2008. *The Human Side of Organizations.* Englewood Cliffs, NJ: Prentice Hall.

"Drop in Hospital Death Rates May Mean More Americans Dying at Home." *CBS News,* 2013. March 27. Retrieved July 16, 2013 (www.cbsnews.com/8301-204_162-57576526/drop-in-hospital-death-rates-may-mean-more-americans-dying-at-home/).

Drori, Gili S. 2006. *Global E-Litism: Digital Technology, Social Inequality, and Transnationality.* New York: Worth.

Du Bois, W. E. B. [1899] 1967. *The Philadelphia Negro: A Social Study.* New York: Schocken.

Dufur, Mikaela J. and Seth L. Feinberg. 2007. "Artificially Restricted Labor Markets and Worker Dignity in Professional Football." *Journal of Contemporary Ethnography* 36(5):505–36.

Duhigg, Charles and David Kocieniewski. 2013. "How Apple Sidesteps Billions in Taxes." *New York Times,* April 28. Retrieved May 31, 2013 (www.nytimes.com/2012/04/29/busi ness/apples-tax-strategy-aims-at-low-tax-states-and-nations .html?pagewanted=all&_r=0).

Duncan, Arne. 2006. "Chicago's Renaissance 2010: Building on School Reform in the Age of Accountability." *Phi Delta Kappan* (February):457–58.

Durkheim, Émile. [1893] 1947. *The Division of Labor in Society,* translated by George Simpson. New York: Free Press.

Durkheim, Émile. [1895] 1982. *The Rules of the Sociological Method,* edited by Steven Lukes and translated by W. D. Halls. New York: Free Press.

Durkheim, Émile. [1897] 1964. *Suicide.* Glencoe, IL: Free Press.

Durkheim, Émile. [1915] 2002. In *Classical Sociological Theory,* edited by Craig Calhoun. Malden, MA: Blackwell.

Durkheim, Émile. 1947. *Elementary Forms of Religious Life.* Glencoe, IL: Free Press.

Durkheim, Émile. 1956. *Education and Society.* Translated by Sherwood D. Fox. Glencoe, IL: Free Press.

Dusenbery, Maya and Jaeah Lee. 2012. "Charts: The State of Women's Athletics, 40 Years After Title IX." *Mother Jones,* June 22. Retrieved May 2, 2013 (www.motherjones.com/ politics/2012/06/chasrts-womens-athletics-title-nine-ncaa).

Dworkin, Anthony Gary and Rosalind J. Dworkin. 1999. *The Minority Report: An Introduction to Racial, Ethnic, and Gender Relations,* 3rd ed. Fort Worth, TX: Harcourt Brace.

Dworkin, Anthony Gary and Pamela F. Tobe. 2012. "Teacher Burnout in Light of School Safety, Student Misbehavior, and Changing Accountability Standards." Pp. 199–211 in *Schools and Society: A Sociological Approach to Education,* edited by Jeanne H. Ballantine and Joan Z. Spade. Thousand Oaks, CA: Sage Pine Forge.

Dye, Thomas, R. 2002. *Who's Running America? The Clinton Years.* Upper Saddle River, NJ: Prentice Hall.

Dye, Thomas and Harmon Zeigler. 1983. *The Irony of Democracy.* North Scituate, MA: Duxbury Press.

Dyer, Richard. 2012. "The Matter of Whiteness." Pp. 9–14 in *White Privilege,* edited by Paula S. Rothenberg. New York: Worth.

Earls, Felton M. and Albert J. Reiss. 1994. *Breaking the Cycle: Predicting and Preventing Crime.* Washington, DC: National Institute of Justice.

"Eating Disorder Statistics." 2008. South Carolina Department of Mental Health. Retrieved May 27, 2012 (www.state.sc.us/dmh/anorexia/statistics/htm).

Eaton, S. B., M. J. Konner, and L. Cordain. 2010. "Diet-Dependent Acid Load, Paleolithic (Corrected) Nutrition, and Evolutionary Health Promotion." *American Journal of Clinical Nutrition* 91(February):295–97.

Ebaugh, Helen Rose Fuchs. 2005. *Handbook of Religion and Social Institutions.* New York: Springer.

Eckert, Penelope. 1989. *Jocks and Burnouts: Social Categories and Identity in High School.* New York: Teacher's College Press.

EcoSummit 2012. "Ecological Sustainability: Restoring the Planet's Ecosystem Services." *Fourth International Ecosummit.* Retrieved July 31, 2012 (www.ecosummit2012.org/).

"Ecosystems Report Links Human Well-Being With Health of Planet." 2006. *Popline* 28(January/February):1.

Eidelson, Josh. 2014. "Most Americans Think It's Illegal to Fire Someone for Being Gay. They're Wrong." *Bloomberg-Businesweek,* June 26. Retrieved September 9, 2014 (http://www.businessweek.com/articles/2014-06-23/discrimination-at-work-is-it-legal-to-fire-someone-for-being-gay).

Eder, Donna, Catherine Colleen Evans, and Stephen Parker. 1995. *School Talk: Gender and Adolescent Culture.* New Brunswick, NJ: Rutgers University Press.

Edney, Anna. 2012. "Meningitis Risk Spreads to 14,000 People Given Back-Pain Shot." Bloomberg News, October 12. Retrieved October 12, 2012 (www.sfgae.com/business/bloomberg/article/Meningitis-Risk-Spreads-to-14,000-People-Given-3941544.php).

Edwards, Harry. 2000. "Crisis of the Black Athlete on the Eve of the 21st Century." *Society* 37(3):9–13.

eHarmony. 2014. "Dating Advice and Relationship Advice." Retrieved September 10, 2014 (http://www.eharmony.com/dating-advice/#.VA4tsmRdXCw).

Ehrenreich, Barbara. 2001. *Nickel and Dimed: On (Not) Getting By in America.* New York: Henry Holt.

Ehrenreich, Barbara. 2005. *Bait and Switch: The (Futile) Pursuit of the American Dream.* New York: Henry Holt.

Ehrlich, Paul R. and Anne H. Ehrlich. 2013. "Can a Collapse of Global Civilization Be Avoided?" *Proceedings of the Royal Society B* 280. Retrieved July 3, 2013 (http://rspb.royalsocietypublishing.org/content/280/1754/20122845.full.pdf).

Ehrlich, Paul and Ann Ehrlich. 1990. *The Population Explosion.* New York: Simon and Schuster.

Eitzen, D. Stanley and George H. Sage. 2003. *Sociology of North American Sport.* Boston: McGraw-Hill.

Eitzen, D. Stanley and Maxine Baca Zinn, eds. 2006. *Globalization: The Transformation of Social Worlds.* Belmont, CA: Wadsworth.

Eitzen, D. Stanley and Maxine Baca Zinn. 2012. "Changing Global Structures: Resistance and Social Movements." Pp. 269–71 in *Globalization: The Transformation of Social Worlds,* 3rd ed., edited by D. Stanley Eitzen and Maxine Baca Zinn. Belmont, CA: Wadsworth.

Eitzen, D. Stanley and Maxine Baca Zinn. N.d. "Commonsense Sayings." *Sociological Conceptual Tools Room.* Retrieved February 9, 2013 (www.angelfire.com/or/sociologyshop/CONCEPTTOOLS.html#css).

Elam, Jerome. 2011. "Pedophiles and Pimps Score at Large Sporting Events Like Super Bowl XLVI." *The Washington Times,* January 17. Retrieved January 21, 2013 (http://communities.washingtontimes.com/neighborhood/heart-without-compromise-children-and-children-wit/2012/jan/17/pedophiles-and-pimps-score-large-sporting-events-s/).

Ellens, G. F. S. 1971. "The Ranting Ranters: Reflections on a Ranting Counter-Culture." *Church History* 40(March):91–107.

Ellison, Christopher G., J. A. Burr, and P. L. McCall. 1997. "Religious Homogeneity and Metropolitan Suicide Rates." *Social Forces* 76(1):273–99.

Ellison, Christopher G. and Daniel A. Powers. 1994. "The Contact Hypothesis and Racial Attitudes Among Black Americans." *Social Science Quarterly* 75(2):385–400.

Emerson, Michael O., with Rodney Woo. 2006. *People of the Dream: Multiracial Congregations in the United States.* Princeton, NJ: Princeton University Press.

Emery, Robert E. 2013. *Cultural Sociology of Divorce: An Encyclopedia.* Thousand Oaks, CA: Sage Knowledge.

Employment and Social Development Canada. 2014. "Family Life—Marriage." Retrieved February 26, 2014 (www4.hrsdc.gc.ca/.3ndic.1t.4r@-eng.jsp?iid=78).

Engels, Friedrich. [1884] 1942. *The Origin of the Family, Private Property, and the State.* New York: International Publishing.

England Church Records. 2014. "Introduction." Retrieved September 10, 2014 (https://familysearch.org/learn/wiki/en/England_Church_Records#Introduction).

Enloe, Cynthia. 2006. "Daughters and Generals in the Politics of the Globalized Sneaker." In *Beyond Borders: Thinking Critically About Global Issues,* edited by Paula S. Rothenberg. New York: Worth.

Environment 911. 2012. "Causes of Water Shortages." Retrieved February 8, 2013 (www.environment911.org/221.Causes_of_Water_Shortages).

Environmental Defense Fund. 2012. "Climate: Facts, Dangers and What You Can Do." Retrieved September 8, 2012 (www.edf.org/climate-facts-dangers-and-what-climate-change&gclid).

Environmental Protection Agency. 2004. "Terms of Environment." Retrieved (www.epa.gov/OCEPAterms/gterms.html).

Environmental Protection Agency. 2011. "Air Quality Trends." Retrieved September 7, 2012 (www.epa.gov/airtrends/aqtrends.html).

Environmental Protection Agency. 2012. "Greenhouse Gas Emissions." Retrieved February 8, 2013 (www.epa.gov/climatechange/ghgemissions/).

Erickson, Fritz and John A. Vonk. 2012. "100 People: A World Portrait." Retrieved January 4, 2014 (www.100people.org/statistics_100stats.php).

Erikson, Erik H. 1950. *Childhood and Society.* New York: Norton.

Erikson, Kai T. 1976. *Everything in Its Path: Destruction of Community in the Buffalo Creek Flood.* New York: Simon & Schuster.

Erikson, Kai T. 1987. "Notes on the Sociology of Deviance." Pp. 9–21 in *Deviance: The Interactionist Perspective*, 5th ed., edited by Earl Rubington and Martin S. Weinberg. New York: Macmillan.

Erikson, Kai T. [1966] 2005. *Wayward Puritans: A Study in the Sociology of Deviance*. Boston: Pearson Education.

Eshleman, J. Ross and Richard A. Bulcroft. 2006. *The Family*, 11th ed. Boston: Allyn & Bacon.

Eshleman, J. Ross and Richard A. Bulcroft. 2010. *The Family*, 12th ed. Boston: Allyn & Bacon.

Esim, Simel. 2014. "Cooperatives Considerable Clout in the Fight Against Child Labor." International Labour Organization, July 14. Retrieved September 5, 2014 (http://www.ilo.org/global/about-the-ilo/newsroom/comment-analysis/WCMS_249483/lang—en/index.htm).

Esperitu, Yen Le. 1992. Asian American Panethnicity: Bridging Institutions and Identities. Philadelphia: Temple University Press.

Espo, David. 2009. "$797 Billion Stimulus Plan Ok'd in Victory for Obama." *Los Angeles Daily News,* February 14. Retrieved February 24, 2009 (www.dailynews.com/search/ci_11703066).

Esquivel, Laura. 2001. *Like Water for Chocolate*. New York: Anchor.

Estrellado, Alicia F. and Jennifer (M. I.) Loh. 2013. "Factors Associated With Battered Filipino Women's Decision to Stay in or Leave an Abusive Relationship." *Journal of Interpersonal Violence*, November 7. Retrieved January 17, 2014 (http://jiv.sagepub.com/content/early/2013/11/07/0886260513505709.abstract).

Ethnic Majority. 2012. "African, Hispanic (Latino), and Asian American Members of Congress." Retrieved September 1, 2014 (www.ethnicmajority.com/congress.htm).

Etounga-Manguelle, Daniel. 2000. "Does Africa Need a Cultural Adjustment Program?" Pp. 65–77 in *Culture Matters: How Values Shape Human Progress,* edited by Lawrence E. Harrison and Samuel P. Huntington. New York: Basic Books.

Etzioni, Amitai. 1975. A Comparative Analysis of Complex Organizations. New York: Free Press.

Europa World Year Book. 2005. London: Europa.

European Commission. 2012 "Marriage and Divorce Statistics." Retrieved February 26, 2014 (http://epp.eurostat.ec.europa.eu/statistics_explained/index.php/Marriage_and_divorce_statistics).

European Commission. 2014. "EU Anti-Corruption Report." February 3. Retrieved April 25, 2014 (http://ec.europa.eu/dgs/home-affairs/e-library/documents/policies/organized-crime-and-human-trafficking/corruption/docs/acr_2014_en.pdf).

European Higher Education Area. 2014. "Bologna Process." Retrieved May 13, 2014 (www.ehea.info/).

Evans, Martin. 2012. "First Case of People Trafficking for Organs Uncovered in UK." *The Telegraph,* April 25. Retrieved January 19, 2013 (http://www.telegraph.co.uk/news/uknews/crime/9227137/First-case-of-people-trafficking-for-organs-uncovered-in-UK.html).

Evans, Tom. 2010. "Bosnian Leader: 'Ethnic Cleansing' Continues 15 Years After War." *CNN World,* March 1. Retrieved May 6, 2012 (http://articles.cnn.com/2010-03-01/world/bosnia.herzegovina_1_ethnic-cleansing-serb-bosnian-leader?_s=PM:WORLD).

Evon, Dan. 2012. "Laura Dekker Completes Round-the-World Journey." Retrieved February 23, 2012 (www.inquisitr.com/184540/laura-dekker-completes-round-the-world-journey-video/).

Ewert, Stephanie. 2013. "The Decline in Private School Enrollment." *SEHSD Working Paper Number FY12-117.* U.S. Census Bureau, January. Retrieved July 10, 2013 (www.census.gov/hhes/school/files/ewert_private_school_enrollment.pdf).

"Experts Weigh In on Texas Law Keeping Brain-Dead Pregnant Woman Alive." 2014. *CBS News,* January 3. Retrieved March 3, 2014 (www.cbsnews.com/news/experts-weight-inon-texas-law-keeping-brain-dead-woman-alive/).

Facebook.com. 2011. "Facebook Facts." Retrieved March 6, 2011 (www.facebook.com/press/info/php?statistics).

Fackler, Martin. 2007a. "Career Women in Japan Find a Blocked Path." *New York Times,* August 6. Retrieved November 8, 2009 (www.nytimes.com/2007/08/06/world/asia/06equal.html).

Fackler, Martin, 2007b. "Low-Crime Japan Seeks Answers to Killing of Mayor of Nagasaki." *New York Times,* April 19. Retrieved June 1, 2013 (http://www.nytimes.com/2007/04/19/world/asia/19japan.html?_r=0).

Fadiman, Anne. 1997. *The Spirit Catches You and You Fall Down.* New York: Noonday.

Fainaru-Wada, Mark and Justine Gubar. 2012. "The Unseen Faces of Sports Apparel." ESPN, January 9. Retrieved July 12, 2012 (http://espn.go.com/espn/otl/story/id/7435424/dallas=cowboys-dip=sports-apparel-business-comes-allegations-sweatshop-labor).

Family Research Council. 2014. "Marriage and Family." Retrieved September 16, 2014 (http://www.frc.org/Marriage-and-Family).

Farley, John E. 2011. *Majority-Minority Relations,* 6th ed. Englewood Cliffs, NJ: Prentice Hall.

Farmer, Paul. 1999. *Infections and Inequalities: The Modern Plagues.* Berkeley: University of California Press.

Farrer, Claire R. 2011. *Thunder Rides a Black Horse: Mescalero Apaches and the Mythic Present,* 3rd ed. Long Grove, IL: Waveland.

Fathi, David C. 2009. "Prison Nation." Human Rights Watch, April 9. Retrieved April 15, 2009 (www.hrw.org/en/news/2009/04/09/prison-nation).

Fausto-Sterling, Anne. 1992. *Myths of Gender: Biological Theories About Women and Men,* 2nd ed. New York: Basic Books.

Fausto-Sterling, Anne. 2000. "The Five Sexes, Revisited." *Sciences* 40(July/August):118.

Feagin, Joe R., 1983. *The Urban Real Estate Game: Playing Monopoly with Real Money.* Englewood Cliffs, NJ: Prentice Hall.

Feagin, Joe R. 2012. *The White Frame: Centuries of Racial Framing and Counter-Framing,* 2nd ed. New York: Routledge.

Feagin, Joe R. and Clairece Booher Feagin. 1986. *Discrimination American Style: Institutional Racism and Sexism.* Malabar, FL: Krieger.

Feagin, Joe R. and Clairece Booher Feagin. 2010. *Racial and Ethnic Relations,* 9th ed. Englewood Cliffs, NJ: Prentice Hall.

Featherman, David L. and Robert Hauser. 1978. *Opportunity and Change.* New York: Academic Press.

Federal Bureau of Investigation. 2006. "2006 Financial Crime Report." Retrieved February 8, 2008 (www.fbi.gov/publications/financial/fcs_report2006/financial_crime_2006.htm).

Federal Bureau of Investigation. 2009. "Crime in the United States: Expanded Homicide Data." Retrieved June 3, 2012 (www2.fbi.gov/ucr/cius2009/offenses/expanded_information/homicide.html).

Federal Bureau of Investigation. 2011a. "Child Pornography Prosecutions Soaring." February 5. Retrieved April 14, 2012 (http://rapecrisiscenter.org/sanfrancisco02053011.html).

Federal Bureau of Investigation. 2011b. "FBI 2010 Cybercrime Statistics." February 27. Retrieved April 14, 2012 (http://scamfraudalert.net/2011/02/27/fbi-2010-cybercrime-statistics/).

Federal Bureau of Investigation. 2012a. "Crime Rates Are Down." *Uniform Crime Report,* June 11. Retrieved October 6, 2012 (www.fbi.gov/news/stories/2012/june/crimes_061112/crimes_061112).

Federal Bureau of Investigation. 2012b. "Former New York State Senate Majority Leader Pedro Espada, Jr. Pleads Guilty to Tax Fraud and Will Not Challenge Jury Conviction for Stealing From Bronx Health Clinics." New York Field Office, October 12. Retrieved June 2, 2013 (www.fbi.gov/newyork/press-releases/2012/former-new-york-state-senate-majority-leader-pedro-espada-jr.-pleads-guilty-to-tax-fraud-and-will-not-challenge-jury-conviction-for-stealing-from-bronx-health-clinics).

Federal Bureau of Investigation. 2012c. "Hate Crime Statistics 2011." Retrieved June 1, 2013 (www.fbi.gov/news/stories/2012/december/annual-hate-crimes-report-released/annual-hate-crimes-report-released).

Federal Bureau of Investigation. 2014a. "FBI Releases Preliminary Semiannual Crime Statistics for 2013." Retrieved April 25, 2014 (www.fbi.gov/news/press-releases-fbi-releases-preliminary-semiannual-crime-statistics-for-2013).

Federal Bureau of Investigation. 2014b. "Uniform Crime Report: Crime in the United States 2012." Retrieved April 26, 2014 (www.fbi.gov/about-us/cjis/ucr/crime-in-the-u.s/2012/crime-in-the-u.s.-2012/crir).

Federal Bureau of Investigation. 2014c. "Hate Crime—Overview." Retrieved September 4, 2014 (http://www.fbi.gov/about-us/investigate/civilrights/hate_crimes/overview).

Federal Register. 2002. Office of the Federal Register, National Archives and Records 67.

Fedotov, Yury. 2012. "Briefing: Fight Against Transnational Organized Crime and Drug Trafficking." Retrieved April 18, 2013 (www.unodc.org/unodc/en/speeches/briefing-to-member-states-toc-7-february-2012.html).

Feeding America. 2013. "Hunger in America." Retrieved January 5, 2014 (http://feedingamerica.org/hunger-in-america.aspx).

Felix, Samantha. 2012. "Side by Side: How Obama and Romney's Social Media Battle Stacks Up." *Business Insider*, September 23. Retrieved November 1, 2012 (www.businessinsider.com/winner-of-the-obamaromney-social-media-campaign-2012-9?op=1).

Ferhansyed. 2008. "Fundamental Terminology of Planned Change." Retrieved December 21, 2009 (http://organizationdevelopment.wordpress.com/2008/08/10/fundamental-terminology-of-organization-development).

Fernandez, Eleazar S. 2011. *Burning Center, Porous Borders: The Church in a Globalized World.* Eugene, OR: Wipf and Stock.

Fernando, Suman. 2002. *Mental Health, Race and Culture,* 2nd ed. New York: Palgrave.

Ferree, Myra Marx. 2012. "Globalization and Feminism: Opportunities and Obstacles for Activism in a Global Arena." Pp. 291–320 in *Globalization: The Transformation of Social Worlds*, 3rd ed., edited by D. Stanley Eitzen and Maxine Baca Zinn. Belmont, CA: Wadsworth.

Ferree, Myra Marx and David A. Merrill. 2000. "Hot Movements, Cold Cognition: Thinking About Social Movements in Gendered Frames." *Contemporary Sociology: A Journal of Reviews* 12:626–48.

Fine, Gary Alan. 1990. "Symbolic Interactionism in the Post-Blumerian Age." Pp. 117–57 in *Frontiers of Social Theory: The New Synthesis,* edited by George Ritzer. New York: Columbia University Press.

"Finery for Infants." 1893. *New York Times,* July 23. Retrieved May 8, 2012 (http://query.nytimes.com/mem/archive-free/pdf?res=F20E17FB3B5F1A738DDDAA0A94DF405B8385F0D3).

Finke, Roger and Rodney Stark. 2005. *The Churching of America, 1776–1990: Winners and Losers in Our Religious Economy*, 2nd ed. New Brunswick, NJ: Rutgers University Press.

"First Born Children." 2008. Retrieved June 29, 2008 (http://social.jrank.org/pages/261/Firstborn-children.html).

Fischer, Claude S. 1984. *The Urban Experience,* 2nd ed. San Diego, CA: Harcourt Brace Jovanovich.

Fish, Virginia Kemp. 1986. "The Hull House Circle: Women's Friendships and Achievements." Pp. 185–227 in *Gender, Ideology, and Action: Historical Perspectives on Women's Public Lives*, edited by Janet Sharistanian. Westport, CT: Greenwood.

Fisher, Max. 2012. "Here's a Map of the Countries That Provide Universal Health Care (America's Still Not on It)." *The Atlantic,* June 28. Retrieved February 6, 2013 (http://www.theatlantic.com/international/archive/2012/06/heres-a-map-of-the-countries-that-provide-universal-health-care-americas-still-not-on-it/259153/).

Fisher, Max. 2013a. "How 35 Countries Compare on Child Poverty." *The Washington Post*. April 15. Retrieved Feb. 12, 2014 (www.washingtonpost.com/blogs/worldviews/wp/2013/04/15/map-how-3-countries-compare-on-child-poverty-the-u-s-is ranked-34th/).

Fisher, Max. 2013b. "This Map Shows Where the World's 30 Million Slaves Live." *Washington Post,* October 17. Retrieved February 17, 2014 (www.washingtonpost.com/blogs/worldviews/wp/2013/10/17/this-map-shows-where-the-worlds-30-million-slaves-live-there-are-60000-in-the-u-s/).

Fitch, Brian. 2010. "Attitudes and Performance." The Impact of Self-Fulfilling Prophecies." *FBI Law Enforcement Bulletin* 79(12):12–19.

Fitch, Catherine, Ron Goeken, and Steven Ruggles. 2005. "The Rise of Cohabitation in the United States: New Historical Estimates." Retrieved July 14, 2011 (http://www.hist.umn.edu/~ruggles/cohab-revised2.pdf).

"Five Rules for Online Networking." 2005. CNN.com, April 1. Retrieved July 25, 2006 (www.cnn.com/2005/US/Careers/03/31/online.networking).

"Flag-Burning Amendment Fails by a Vote." 2006. CNN.com, June 28. Retrieved August 16, 2008 (www.cnn.com/2006/POLITICS/06/27/flag.burning).

Flavin, Jeanne. 2004. "Employment, Counseling, Housing Assistance . . . and Aunt Yolanda? How Strengthening Families' Social Capital Can Reduce Recidivism." *Fordham Urban Law Journal* 3(2):209–16.

Flintoff, John-Paul. 2013. "Local, Self-Sufficient, Optimistic: Are Transition Towns the Way Forward?" *The Guardian,* June 14. Retrieved March 17, 2014 (www.theguardian.com/environment/2013/jun/15/transition-towns-way-forward).

Florida, Richard. 2004. *Cities and the Creative Class.* New York: Routledge.

Florida, Richard. 2012a. "Creative Class Group." March 2. Retrieved March 5, 2012 (www.creativeclass.com/richard_florida).

Florida, Richard. 2012b. "The Joys of Urban Tech." *The Wall Street Journal,* August 31. Retrieved September 25, 2012 (www.creativeclass.com/rfcgdb/articles/WSJ%20The%20Joys%20of%20Urban%20Tech.pdf).

Flynn, Simone I. 2014. "Social Movement Theory: Value-Added Theory." *Research Starters.* Retrieved February 24, 2014 (http://connection.ebscohost.com/c/essays/36268048/social-movement-theory-value-added-theory).

Foner, Nancy. 2005. *In a New Land: A Comparative View of Immigration.* New York: New York University Press.

Food and Agriculture Organization of the United Nations, Jacques Diouf. 2010–2011. *Women—Key to Food Security.* Retrieved October 1, 2012 (www.fao.org/docrep/014/am719e/am719e00.pdf).

Food Empowerment Project. 2014. "Slavery in the Chocolate Industry." Retrieved February 15, 2014 (www.foodispower.org/slavery-chocolate/).

Ford, Clennan S. 1970. *Human Relations Area Files: 1949–1969—A Twenty Year Report.* New Haven, CT: Human Relations Area Files.

Foundation Source Access. 2013. "Children and WaterAid." Retrieved February 9, 2013 (http://access.foundationsource.com/project/children-and-wateraid).

Foundation for Women. 2012. "Eliminating Global Poverty through Microcredit." Retrieved May 21, 2012 (www.foundationforwomen.org/).

Frank, Mark G. and Thomas Gilovich. 1988. "The Dark Side of Self- and Social Perception: Black Uniforms and Aggression in Professional Sports." *Journal of Personality and Social Psychology* 54(1):74–85.

Frankal, Elliot. 2011. "Compulsory Voting around the World." *The Guardian,* October 4. Retrieved May 21, 2014 (guardian.co.uk/politics.guardian.co.uk).

Freedom House. 2002. *Freedom in the World 2001–2002.* New York: Author.

Freedom to Marry. 2014a. "The Freedom to Marry Internationally." Retrieved September 10, 2014 (http://www.freedomtomarry.org/landscape/entry/c/international).

Freedom to Marry. 2014b. "Where State Laws Stand." Retrieved September 9, 2014 (http://www.freedomtomarry.org/states/).

Freeman, Jo. 1975. The Politics of Women's Liberation: A Case Study of an Emerging Social Movement and Its Relation to the Policy Process. New York: McKay.

Freese, J., B. Powell, and L. C. Steelman. 1999. *Rebel Without a Cause or Effect: Birth Order and Social Attitudes.* Washington, DC: American Sociological Association.

Free the Slaves. 2013. "Our Mission." Retrieved January 19, 2013 (www.freetheslaves.net).

Free the Slaves. 2013. "About Slavery: Slavery Map." Retrieved January 4, 2014 (www.freetheslaves.net/sslpage.aspx?pid=375).

Freston, Paul. 2007. "Evangelicalism and Fundamentalism: The Politics of Global Popular Protestantism." Pp. 205–26 in *Sage Handbook of the Sociology of Religion,* edited by James Beckford and N. J. Demerath III. Thousand Oaks, CA: Sage.

Freud, Sigmund. [1923] 1960. *The Ego and the Id.* New York: Norton.

Frey, Bruno S. 2004. *Dealing With Terrorism: Stick or Carrot?* Cheltenham, UK: Edward Elgar.

Friedman, Judith J. 2007. "Suburbs: Urban, Rural and Community Sociology." *Blackwell Encyclopedia of Sociology Online.* Retrieved July 30, 2012 (www.sociologyencyclopedia.com/public/tocnode?id=g978140512433125_ss1_298).

Friedman, Thomas L. 2005. *The World Is Flat: A Brief History of the Twenty-First Century.* New York: Farrar, Straus, & Giroux.

Friedman, Thomas L. 2006. "Opening Scene: The World Is Ten Years Old." pp. 21–29 in *Globalization: The Transformation of Social Worlds,* edited by D. Stanley Eitzen and Maxine Baca Zinn. Belmont, CA: Wadsworth.

Friedman, Thomas L. 2008. Hot, Flat and Crowded: Why We Need a Green Revolution—and How It Can Renew America. New York: Farrar, Straus & Giroux.

"Full Transcript of the Second Presidential Debate." 2012. *New York Times,* October 16. Retrieved November 1, 2012 (www.nytimes.com/2012/10/16/us/politics/transcript-of-the-second-presidential-debate-in-hempstead-ny.html?pagewanted=all&_r=0).

Furstenberg, F. F. 2003. "Growing Up in American Society: Income, Opportunities, and Outcomes." Pp. 211–33 in *Social Dynamics of the Life Course: Transitions, Institutions, and Interrelations,* edited by W. R. Heinz and V. W. Marshall. New York: A. deGruyter.

Future for All. 2008. "Future Technology and Society." Retrieved January 14, 2008 (www.futureforall.org).

Gaijinpot 2010. "Japanese Women Stand Low on the Corporate Ladder." August 30. Retrieved May 27, 2012 (http://injapan.gaijinpot.com/work-tips/2010/08/30/japanese-women-stand-low-on-the-corporate-ladder/).

Galanti, Geri-Ann. 2008. *Caring for Patients From Different Cultures,* 4th ed. Philadelphia: University Pennsylvania Press.

Galbraith, Kate. 2012. "Taking the Ick Factor Out of Recycled Water." *The New York Times,* July 25. Retrieved July 31, 2012 (www.nytimes.com/2012/07/26/business/global/26iht-green26.html).

Gallagher, Charles. 2004. "Transforming Racial Identity Through Affirmative Action." Pp. 153–70 in *Race and Ethnicity: Across Time, Space and Discipline,* edited by Rodney D. Coates. Leiden, Holland: Brill.

Gallup 2004. "Women in the Clergy: Perception and Reality." March 30. Retrieved September 20, 2012 (www.gallup.com/poll/11146/women-cleregy-perception-reality.aspx).

Gallup. 2009. "Muslim Americans: A National Portrait." The Muslim West Facts Project. Retrieved September 24, 2012 (www.gallup.com/strategicconsulting/153572/REPORT-Muslim-Americans-National-Portrait.aspx).

Gallup. 2011. "More Than 9 in 10 Americans Continue to Believe in God." June 3. Retrieved July 14, 2011 (www.gallup.com/poll/147887/americans-continue-believe-god.aspx).

Gallup. 2013. "Religion." Retrieved January 30, 2013 (http://www.gallup.com/poll/1690/religion.aspx).

Gallup, George, Jr., and D. Michael Lindsay. 1999. *Surveying the Religious Landscape: Trends in U.S. Beliefs.* Harrisburg, PA: Morehouse.

"Gang-Rape Victim Faces Lashes." 2007. Retrieved November 4, 2009 (www.news.com.au/story/0,23599,21332543-2,00.html).

Gannon, Shane Patrick. 2009. *Translating the Hijra: The Symbolic Reconstruction of the British Empire in India.* PhD thesis, University of Alberta.

Gans, Herbert J. 1962. The Urban Villagers: Group and Class in the Life of Italian-Americans. New York: Free Press.

Gans, Herbert J. 1971. "The Uses of Poverty: The Poor Pay All." *Social Policy* 2(2):20–24.

Gans, Herbert. 1982. *The Levittowners: Ways of Life and Politics in a New Suburban Community.* New York: Columbia University Press.

Gans, Herbert J. 1994. "Positive Functions of the Undeserving Poor: Uses of the Underclass in America." *Politics and Society* 22(3):269–83.

Gans, Herbert J. 1995. *The War Against the Poor.* New York: Basic Books.

Gans, Herbert J. 2007. "No, Poverty Has Not Disappeared." Reprinted in *Sociological Footprints,* edited by Leonard Cargan and Jeanne Ballantine. Belmont, CA: Wadsworth.

Gardner, Howard. 1987. "The Theory of Multiple Intelligences." *Annual Dyslexia* 37:19–35.

Gardner, Howard. 1999. *Intelligence Reframed: Multiple Intelligences for the 21st Century.* New York: Basic Books.

Gardom, James. 2011. "The End of Secularisation." *Cambridge GodThink,* March 30. Retrieved July 12, 2013 (http://godthink.org.uk/2011/03/30/the-end-of-secularisation/).

Gates, Bill. 2013. "Annual Letter." Retrieved February 5, 2013 (www.gatesfoundation.org/annualletter).

Gatta, Mary L. and Kevin McCabe. 2005. *Not Just Getting By: The New Era of Flexible Workforce Development.* Lanham, MD: Lexington Books.

Gatto, John Taylow. 2003. *The Prussian Connection.* New York: The Odysseus Group.

"Gay Adoption Nationwide." 2011. *AZ Living,* May 2. Retrieved June 3, 2012 (www.azcentral.com/news/azliving/articles/2011/05/02/20110502gay-dads-adoption-facts-resources.html).

The Gay Law Report. 2011. "Gay Facts and Statistics in 2011." January 3. Retrieved April 12, 2011 (http://www.gaylawreport.com/gay-facts-statistics-2011/).

Gender Equity Resource Center. 2013. "Definition of Terms: Heterosexism." Retrieved February 10, 2014 (http://geneq.berkeley.edu/lgbt_resources_definiton_of_terms#heterosexism).

"Gender Stereotypes Easing More for Girls than Boys." 2011. *USA Today.* Retrieved May 21, 2012 (www.usatoday.com/news/health/wellness/teen-ya/story/2011/05/Gender-stereotypes-easing-more-for-girls-than-boys/46886846/1).

"Gendercide: The War on Baby Girls." 2010. *The Economist,* March 4. Retrieved May 2, 2010 (www.economist.com/node/15606229).

Geocommons. 2009. "Infant Mortality Rates, World by Country, 2009." Retrieved February 9, 2013 (http://finder.geocommons.com/overlays/11932).

George, Blythe. 2011. "Native American Academic Performance: Does School Type Matter?" Academy for Public Policy and Analyses. Class of 2011, Research Paper No. 2, November. Retrieved July 10, 2013 (www.dartmouth.edu/~socy/pdfs/blythe_george_paper_urban_institute_2011.pdf).

"Getting Married in Japan." 2014. Retrieved September 8, 2014 (http://japanese.about.com/library/weekly/aa080999.htm).

Gettleman, Jeffery. 2008. "Mob Sets Kenya Church on Fire, Killing Dozens." *The New York Times,* January 2. Retrieved June 3, 2008 (www.nytimes.com/2008/01/02/world/africa/02kenya.html?pagewanted=1&ref=africa).

Gellner, Ernest. 1983. *Culture, Identity, and Politics.* Cambridge, UK: Cambridge University Press.

Gellner, Ernest. 1993. "Nationalism." Pp. 409–11 in *Blackwell Dictionary of Twentieth Century Thought,* edited by William Outhwaite and Tom Bottomore. Oxford, UK: Basil Blackwell.

Gellner, Ernest and John Breuilly. 2009. *Nations and Nationalism,* 2nd ed. Ithaca, NY: Cornell University Press.

Geobase. 2014. "The World: Life Expectancy (2014)." Retrieved March 10, 2014 (www.geoba.se/population/php?pc=world&type=15).

Ghosh, Palash. 2014. "Swara: The Horrors of Marrying Off Young Girls in Pakistan to Older Men to Settle Debts and Disputes." February 20. Retrieved September 5, 2014 (www.ibtimes.com/swara-horrors-marrying-young-girls-pakistan-older-men-settle-debts-disputes-1556721).

"The Ghost in Your Genes." 2009. BBC's Science and Nature. Retrieved November 12, 2009 (www.bbc.co.uk/sn/tvradio/programmes/horizon/ghostgenes.shtml).

Gibler, John. 2012. "Mexico's Ghost Towns." Pp. 68–72 in *Globalization: The Transformation of Social Worlds,* 3rd ed., edited by D. Stanley Eitzen and Maxine Baca Zinn. Belmont, CA: Wadsworth.

Giddens, Anthony. 1986. *The Constitution of Society.* Berkeley: University of California Press.

Gilbert, Dennis. 2011. *The American Class Structure in an Age of Growing Inequality,* 8th ed. Thousand Oaks, CA: Sage.

Gilchrist, John. 2003. *Anderson's Ohio Family Law.* Cincinnati, OH: Anderson.

Gilligan, Carol. 1982. *In a Different Voice: Psychological Theory and Women's Development.* Cambridge, MA: Harvard University Press.

Gillis, Justin 2013. "In New Jersey Pines, Trouble Arrives on Six Legs." *New York Times,* December 1. Retrieved March 18, 2014 (www.nytimes.com/2013/12/02/science/earth/in-new-jersey-pines-trouble-arrives-on-six-legs.html?_r=0).

Gillis, Chester. 1999. *Roman Catholicism in America.* New York: Columbia University Press.

Ginicola, Misty M. and Christina Saccoccio. 2008. "Good Intentions, Unintended Consequences: The Impact of NCLB on Children's Mental Health." *Emotional and Behavioral Disorders in Youth* (Spring):27–35.

Giridharadas, Anand. 2014. "The Immigrant Advantage." *New York Times,* May 25. Sunday Review, pp. 1, 5.

Girls Health. 2009. "Bullying." *Girlshealth.gov*. Retrieved May 21, 2012 (www.girlshealth.gov/bullying/).

Givens, David B. 2012. "Nonverbal Communication." *Center for Nonverbal Studies*. Retrieved September 25, 2012 (http://center-for-nonverba-studies.org/nvcom.htm).

Gladwell, Malcolm. 2010. "Small Change: Why the Revolution Will Not Be Tweeted." *The New Yorker*, October 4. Retrieved October 9, 2012 (http://www.newyorker.com).

Glasberg, Davita Silfen and Deric Shannon. 2011. *Political Sociology: Oppression, Resistance, and the State*. Thousand Oaks, CA: Sage.

"The Glass Ceiling Index." 2013. *The Economist*, March 13. Retrieved February 10, 2014 (www.economist.com/blogs/graphicdetail/2013/03/daily-chart-3)

Glasscock, C. B. 1937. *The Gasoline Age: The Story of the Men Who Made It*. Indianapolis, IN: Bobbs-Merrill.

Glaze, Lauren E. 2011. "Correctional Populations in the U.S. 2010." December 15. Retrieved April 15, 2012 (http://bjs.ojp.usdoj.gov/index.cfm?ty=tp&tid=13).

Global Arab Network. 2010. "British Archaeologist: 125,000 Years Ago First Human Settlement Began in Oman." April 9. Retrieved July 30, 2012 (www.english.globalarabnetwork.com/201004095443/Cu5000-years-ago-first-human-settlement-began-in-oman.html).

Global Campaign for Education. 2011. "100th Anniversary of International Women's Day." Retrieved April 17, 2011 (www.campaignforeducation.org/en/news/gces-news).

Global Citizen Corps. 2010. "Women's Rights." December 6. Retrieved April 8, 2011 (www.globalcitizencorps.org/groups/issue-human-rights/14178).

Global Fund for Women. 2012. "Status of Women Fact Sheet." Retrieved October 1, 2012 (www.globalfundforwomen.org/impact/media-center/fact-sheets/status-of-women-fact-sheet).

Global Issues. 2012. "World Military Spending." Retrieved July 27, 2012 (www.globalissues.org/print/article/75#WorldMilitarySpending).

Global Journal. 2013. *Top 100 NGOs*. Retrieved June 28, 2013 (http://theglobaljournal.net/top100NGOs/).

"Global Opium Production." 2011. *The Economist*, June 24. Retrieved April 13, 2012 (www.economist.com/node/16432922).

Global Post. 2014. "Cuba Ends 2013 With Lowest Infant Mortality Rate in Its History." January 2. Retrieved March 4, 2013 (www.globalpost.com/dispatch/news/agencia-efe/140102/cuba-ends-2013-lowest-infant-mortality-rate-its-history).

Global Security. 2009. "Guantanamo Bay Detainees." Retrieved April 14, 2012 (www.globalsecurity.org/military/facility/guantanamo-bay_detainees.htm).

Global Sports Development. 2013. "Steroid Use Among High School Athletes: Research Articles." November 12. Retrieved January 17, 2014 (http://globalsportsdevelopment.org/steroid-use-among-high-school-athletes/).

"Global Warming and Climate Change." 2013. *The New York Times*, January 8. Retrieved February 5, 2013 (http://topics.nytimes.com/top/news/science/topics/globalwarming/index.html).

Globe Women. 2013. "WEXPO: Women's Online Marketplace." Retrieved January 23, 2013 (http://www.wexpo.biz/).

Goffman, Erving. 1961. Asylums: Essays on the Social Situation of Mental Patients and Other Inmates. New York: Anchor.

Goffman, Erving. 1967. *Interaction Ritual*. New York: Anchor.

Goffman, Erving. [1959] 2001. *Presentation of Self in Everyday Life*. New York: Harmondsworth, UK: Penguin.

Goldberg, David Theo, ed. 1990. *Anatomy of Racism*. Minneapolis: University of Minnesota Press.

Goldman, Henry and Duane D. Stanford. 2012. "MYC Mayor Bloomberg Seeks Ban on Super-Size Soft Drinks." *Bloomberg News*, May 31. Retrieved July 17, 2012 (www.bloomberg.com/news/2012-05-31/nyc-mayor-bloomberg-seeks-ban-on-super-size-soft-drinks.html).

Gonzalez-Perez, Margaret. 2011. "The False Islamization of Female Suicide Bombers." *Gender Issues* 28(1/2):50–65.

Goode, William J. 1970. *World Revolution and Family Patterns*. New York: Free Press.

Goode, Erich. 1992. *Collective Behavior*. New York: Harcourt Brace Jovanovich.

Goode, Erich. 2012. *Drugs in American Society*, 8th ed. Boston: McGraw-Hill.

Goodman, Marc D. and Susan W. Brenner. 2002. "The Emerging Consensus on Criminal Conduct in Cyberspace." *International Journal of Law and Information Technology* 10(2):139–223.

Goodman, Amy and Juan Gonzalez. 2012. "Debating Tucson School District's Book Ban after Suspension of Mexican American Studies Program." *Democracy Now*, January 18. Retrieved January 28, 2013 (www.democracynow.org/2012/1/18/debating_tucson_school_district_book_ban).

Goodstein, Laurie. 2012. "Ugandan Gay Rights Group Sues U.S. Evangelist." *The New York Times*, March 14. Retrieved May 27, 2012 (www.nytimes.com/2012/03/15/us/ugandan-gay-rights-group-sues-scott-lively-an-american-evangelist.html).

GoodTherapy.org. 2012. "Complementary and Alternative Medicine (CAM)." Retrieved August 3, 2012 (www.goodtherapy.org/complementary-alternative-medicine.html).

Gordon, Milton. 1970. "The Subsociety and the Subculture." Pp. 150–63 in *The Sociology of Subcultures*, edited by David O. Arnold. Berkeley, CA: Glendessary.

Gore, Al. 2012. "Global Warming Is Real." *EarthSky*, April 30. Retrieved September 7, 2012 (http://earthsky.org/human-world/al-gore-at-hampshire-college-global-warming-is-real).

Gorski, Phillip S. 2000. "Historicizing the Secularization Debate: Church, State, and Society in Late Medieval and Early Modern Europe, ca 1300 to 1700." *Social Forces* (February): 138–67.

Gorski, Philip and Ates Altinordu. 2008. "After Secularization." *Annual Review of Sociology* 34:55–85.

Gottdiener, Mark and Ray Hutchison. 2006. *The New Urban Sociology*, 3rd ed. Boston: McGraw-Hill.

Gottfredson, Michael R. and Travis Hirschi. 1990. *A General Theory of Crime*. Palo Alto, CA: Stanford University Press.

Gottlieb, Lori. 2006. "How Do I Love Thee?" *The Atlantic*, March. Retrieved February 9, 2013 (http://www.theatlantic.com/magazine/archive/2006/03/how-do-i-love-thee/304602/).

Gould, Elise. 2012. "U.S. Lags Behind Peer Countries in Mobility." Economic Policy Institute, October 10. Retrieved June 12, 2013 (www.epi.org/publication/usa-lags-peer-countries-mobility/).

Gould, Stephen J. 1997. *The Mismeasure of Man*. New York: Norton.

Gouldner, Alvin W. 1960. "The Norm of Reciprocity: A Preliminary Statement." *American Sociological Review* 25(2): 161–78.

Gracey, Harry L. 1967. "Learning the Student Role: Kindergarten as Academic Boot Camp." Pp. 215–26 in *Readings in Introductory Sociology,* 3rd ed., edited by Dennis Wrong and Harry L. Gracey. New York: Macmillan.

Grandpa Junior. 2006. "If You Were Born Before 1945." Retrieved July 20, 2006 (www.grandpajunior.com/1945.shtml).

Granovetter, Mark. 2007. "Introduction for the French Reader." *Sociologica* 1(Suppl.):1–10.

Grant, Linda. 2004. "Everyday Schooling and the Elaboration of Race-Gender Stratification." Pp. 296–308 in *Schools and Society: A Sociological Approach to Education,* 2nd ed., edited by Jeanne H. Ballantine and Joan Z. Spade. Belmont, CA: Wadsworth.

Grant, Madison. [1916] 2011. *The Passing of the Great Race.* Burlington, IA: Ostara.

Gray, Emma. 2012. "Women and Poverty in the United States: 18 Essential Facts and Statistics." *The Huffington Post,* August 29. Retrieved May 5, 2013 (www.huffingtonpost.com/2012/08/29/women-and-poverty-united-states-facts-statistics_n_1838384.html#slide=more247419).

Gray, Robin Hattersley. 2012. "Sexual Assault Statistics." *Campus Safety Magazine,* March 6. Retrieved January 17, 2014 (www.campussafetymagazine.com/Channel/Public-Safety/articles/2012/03/Sexual-Assault-Statistics-and-Myths.aspx).

Greeley, Andrew M. 1972. *The Denominational Society.* Glenview, IL: Scott, Foresman.

Greeley, Andrew M. 1989. *Religious Change in America.* Cambridge, MA: Harvard University Press.

The Green Papers. 2008a. "Presidential Primaries, Caucuses, and Conventions." Retrieved March 21, 2008 (www.thegreenpapers.com/P08/CO-R.phtml).

The Green Papers. 2008b. "Presidential Primaries 2008: Republican Delegate Selection and Voter Eligibility." Retrieved March 21, 2008 (www.thegreenpapers.com/P08/R-DSVE.phtml?sort=a).

Greenan, Matthew. 2013. "New Indian Documentary on the Practice of Sati." Retrieved January 16, 2014 (http://greenanreport.wordpress.com/2013/05/12/new-indian-documentary-on-the-practice-of-sati/).

Greensboro Justice Fund. 2005. "Courage From the Past." *GJF Newsletter* (17, Summer):1.

Greenwald, Glenn and Ewen MacAskill. 2013. "NSA Prism Program Taps in to User Data of Apple, Google and Others." *The Guardian,* June 6 Retrieved June 30, 2013 (www.guardian.co.uk/world/2013/jun/06/us-tech-giants-nsa-data).

Grieco, Elizabeth M., Yesenia D. Acosta, G. Patricia de la Cruz, Christine Gambino, Thomas Gryn, Luke J. Larsen, Edward N. Trevelyan, and Nathan P. Walters. 2012. "The Foreign-Born Population in the United States: 2010." American Community Survey Reports. Retrieved June 17, 2013 (www.census.gov/prod/2012pubs/acs-19.pdf).

Grille, Robin. 2005. "Religious Extremism: A Parenting Style." In *Parenting for a Peaceful World.* Longueville Media.

Grossman, Cathy Lynn. 2012a. "Number of U.S. Mosques Up 74% Since 2000." *USA Today,* February 29. Retrieved June 7, 2012 (www.usatoday.com/news/religion/story/2012-02-29/islamic-worship-growth-us/53298792/1).

Grossman, Cathy Lynn. 2012b. "Survey Finds 19% Without Religious Affiliation." *USA Today,* February 29. Retrieved September 20, 2012 (www.usatoday.com/news/religion/story/2012-07-19/no-religion-affiliation/56344976/1).

Guardian. 2011. "Guantanamo Bay Detainees Full List." January 11. Retrieved April 14, 2012 (www.guardian.co.uk/world/. . ./guantanamo-bay-detainees-full-list).

Guarino-Ghezzi, Susan. 2013. *The Engaged Sociologist: Connecting the Classroom to the Community.* Thousand Oaks, CA: Sage.

Guarino-Ghezzi, S. and Carr, B. 1996. "Juvenile Offenders Versus the Police: A Community Dilemma." *Caribbean Journal of Criminology and Social Psychology* 1(2):24–43.

Guarino-Ghezzi, S. and Kimball, L. 1996, April. *Transitioning Youth From Secure Treatment to the Community.* Boston, MA: Department of Youth Services.

Guerino, Paul, Paige M. Harrison, and William J. Sabol. 2011. "Prisoners in 2010 (Revised)." December 15. Retrieved April 15, 2012 (http://bjs.ojp.usdoj.gov/index.cfm?ty=tp&tid=13).

Gumperz, John J. and Stephen C. Levinson, eds. 1996. *Rethinking Linguistic Relativity.* Cambridge, UK: Cambridge University Press.

Gusten, Susanne. 2012. "New Twists and Turns in Turkey's Head-Scarf Debate." *The New York Times,* February 1. Retrieved May 25, 2012 (www.nytimes.com/2012/02/02/world/middleeast/new-twists-and-turns-in-turkeys-head-scarf-debate.html?pagewanted=all).

Guttmacher Institute. 2012a. "Contraceptive Use in the United States." July. Retrieved September 13, 2012 (www.guttmacher.org/pubs/fb_contr_use.html).

Guttmacher Institute. 2012b. "Just the Numbers: The Impact of U.S. International Family Planning Assistance." April 27. Retrieved July 28, 2012 (www.guttmacher.org/media/inthenews/2012/04/27/index.html).

Guttmacher Institute. 2013. "Contraceptive Use in the United States." August. Retrieved March 17, 2014 (www.guttmacher.org/pubs/fb_contr_use.html).

Guttmacher Institute. 2014. "American Teens' Sexual and Reproductive Health." May. Retrieved May 13, 2014 (www.guttmacher.org/pubs/FB-ATSRH.html).

Haberkorn, Leonardo. 2014. "From Guantánamo to Uruguay, an Unlikely Journey." *The Miami Herald,* August 14. Retrieved September 15, 2014 (http://www.miamiherald.com/2014/08/14/4289381/from-guantanamo-to-uruguay-an.html).

Hadden, Jeffrey K. 2006. "New Religious Movements." Retrieved August 14, 2008 (www.hirr.hartsem.edu/denom/new_religious_movements.html).

Hagan, Frank E. 2011. *Introduction to Criminology,* 7th ed. Thousand Oaks, CA: Sage.

Hall, Edward T. 1959. *The Silent Language.* New York: Doubleday.

Hall, Edward T. 1983. *The Dance of Life.* Garden City, NY: Anchor Books/Doubleday.

Hall, Edward T. and Mildred Reed Hall. 1992. *An Anthropology of Everyday Life.* New York: Doubleday.

Hall, Richard H. 2002. *Organizations: Structures, Processes, and Outcomes,* 7th ed. Englewood Cliffs, NJ: Prentice Hall.

Hallett, Tim and Emily Meanwell. 2012. "Sociologists Explore the Changing Meaning of 'No Child Left Behind.'" Presented at American Sociological Association meetings, Denver, CO, August 18.

Hamilton, Rebecca. 2012. "Factbox: Which States Allow Same-Sex Marriage?" *Reuters*, February 13. Retrieved May 27, 2012 (www.reuters.com/article/2012/02/13/us-usa-gaymarriage-states-idUSTRE81C1YH2020213).

Hammersley, Martyn and Glenn Turner. 1980. "Conformist Pupils." In *Pupil Strategies: Explorations in the Sociology of the School,* edited by Peter Woods. London: Croom Helm.

Hampton, Keith, Lauren Sessions Goulet, Cameron Marlow, and Lee Rainie. 2012. "Why Most Facebook Users Get More Than They Give." Pew Internet and American Life Project, February 3. Retrieved January 10, 2013 (www.pewinternet.org/Reports/2012/Facebook-users.aspx).

Handel, Gerald, Spencer Cahill, and Frederick Elkin. 2007. *Children and Society: The Sociology of Children and Childhood Socialization.* New York: Oxford University Press.

Handwerk, Brian. 2004. "Female Suicide Bombers: Dying to Kill." *National Geographic News*, December 13. Retrieved July 5, 2008 (http://news.nationalgeographic.com/news/2004/12/1213_041213_tv_suicide_bombers.html).

Haniffa, Aziz. 2009. "Financial Crisis Bigger Than Al Qaeda, Says U.S. Intelligence Czar." *Rediff India Abroad*. February 13. Retrieved March 17, 2009 (www.rediff.com/money/2009/feb/15bcrisis-financial-crisis-bigger-threat-than-al-qaeda-says-us-intel-chief.htm).

Hansen, Randall and Katharine Hansen. 2003. "What Do Employers Really Want? Top Skills and Values Employers Seek From Job-Seekers" (Quintessential Careers). Retrieved June 23, 2008 (www.quintcareers.com/job_skills_values.html).

Hardin, Garrett. 1968. "The Tragedy of the Commons." *Science* 162(3859):1243–48.

Harding, David J. 2011. "Rethinking the Cultural Context of Schooling Decisions in Disadvantaged Neighborhoods: From Deviant Subculture to Cultural Heterogeneity." *Sociology of Education* 84 (October):322–39.

Hare, Jan and Lizbeth A. Gray. 2008. "All Kinds of Families: A Guide for Families." CYFERnet. Retrieved February 24, 2014 (www1.cyfernet.org/prog/fam/nontradfam.html).

Harlem Children's Zone. 2009. "The HCZ Project." Retrieved January 28, 2013 (www.hcz.org/about-us/the-hcz-project).

Harris, Judith Rich. 2009. *The Nurture Assumption: Why Children Turn Out the Way They Do,* rev. and updated edition. New York: Free Press.

Harris, Marvin. 1989. Cows, Pigs, War, and Witches: The Riddles of Culture. New York: Random House.

Hart, Betty and Todd R. Risley. 2003. "The Early Catastrophe: The 30 Million Word Gap by Age 3." *American Educator* 27(1):4–9.

Haskins, Ron, Julia B. Isaacs, and Isabel V. Sawhill. 2008. *Getting Ahead or Losing Ground: Economic Mobility in America*. The Brookings Institute. Retrieved June 7, 2013 (www.brookings.edu/research/reports/2008/02/economic-mobility-sawhill).

Hassard, Jack. 2012. "In Math and Science, Have American Students Fallen Behind?" *The Art of Teaching Science*. Retrieved September 14, 2012 (www.artofteachingscience.org/2012/07/29/obamas-personal-view-teaching-conflict-u-s-department-education/).

Haycock, Kati and Eric A. Hanushek. 2010. "An Effective Teacher in Every Classroom: A Lofty Goal, but How to Do It." *Education Next* 10(3):46–52.

Haub, Carl and Toshiko Kaneda. 2013. *World Population Data Sheet*. Washington, DC: Population Reference Bureau. Retrieved May 25, 2014 (www.prb.org/pdf13/2013-population-data-sheet_eng.pdf).

Hayden, Dolores and Patricia Baron. 2007. "Urban Planning and Women's Needs." *Journal of Planning Education and Research* 26(3):370.

Hayden, Tom. 2006. "Seeking a New Capitalism in Chiapas." Pp. 348–54 in *Globalization: The Transformation of Social Worlds,* edited by D. Stanley Eitzen and Maxine Baca Zinn. Belmont, CA: Wadsworth.

Hays, Jeffrey. 2011. "China's Barefoot Doctors: What Happened?" CR Studies, August 5. Retrieved August 2, 2012 (www.wengewang.org/read.php?tid=30852).

HealthReform.gov. 2010. "Coverage Denied: How the Current Health Insurance System Leaves Millions Behind." Retrieved January 10, 2010 (www.healthreform.gov/reports/denied_coverage/index.html).

Hearn, Kelly. 2012. "Big Oil Wreaks Havoc in the Amazon, but Communities Are Fighting Back." Pp. 313–16 in *Globalization: The Transformation of Social Worlds*, 3rd ed., edited by D. Stanley Eitzen and Maxine Baca Zinn. Belmont, CA: Wadsworth.

Hegewisch, Ariane, Claudia Williams, Heidi Hartmann, and Stephanie Keller Hudiburg. 2014. "The Gender Wage Gap: 2013." *Institute for Women's Policy Research,* March. Retrieved May 12, 2014 (www.iwpr.org/publications/pubs/the-gender-wage-gap-2013-differences-by-race-and-ethnicity-no-growth-in-real-wages-for-women).

Heilbroner, Robert L. and William Milberg. 2007. *The Making of Economic Society,* 12th ed. Englewood Cliffs, NJ: Prentice Hall.

Heilbroner, Robert L. and William Milberg. 2012. *The Making of Economic Society*. Upper Saddle River, NJ: Pearson.

Helfand, Duke. 2008. "Presbyterian Leaders OK Gay Clergy." *Los Angeles Times,* June 28. Retrieved August 18, 2008 (www.latimes.com/news/local/la-me-ordain28-2008jun28,0,7679148.story).

Hendry, Joy. 1987. *Becoming Japanese: The World of the Preschool Child.* Honolulu: University of Hawaii Press.

Henley, Nancy, Mykol Hamilton, and Barrie Thorne. 2000. "Womanspeak and Manspeak: Sex Differences in Communication, Verbal and Nonverbal." Pp. 111–15 in *Sociological Footprints,* edited by Leonard Cargan and Jeanne Ballantine. Belmont, CA: Wadsworth.

Hennigan, Ashley. 2012. "Missing Men: Addressing the College Gender Gap." *Higher Ed Live*. Retrieved September 12, 2012 (http://higheredlive.com/missing-men/).

Hensley, Christopher, M. Koscheski, and Richard Tewksbury. 2005. "Examining the Characteristics of Male Sexual Assault Targets in a Southern Maximum-Security Prison." *Journal of Interpersonal Violence* 20(6):667–79.

Hepworth, Kimberly. 2010. "Eating Disorders Today—Not Just a Girl Thing." *Journal of Christian Nursing,* July/September. Retrieved January 17, 2014 (http://nursing.ceconnection.com/nu/public/modules/2224).

Herskovitz, Jon. 2012. "Militant South African Union Tells Lonmin to Pay Up." Reuters, September 7. Retrieved September 8, 2012 (www.reuters.com/article/2012/09/07/us-safrica-mines-idUSBRE8860U820120907).

Hesse-Biber, Sharlene Nagy. 2007. *The Cult of Thinness,* 2nd ed. New York: Oxford University Press.

Hesse-Biber, Sharlene Nagy, and Patricia Lina Leavy. 2007. *Feminist Research Practice: A Primer.* Thousand Oaks, CA: Sage.

Hewitt, John P. 2007. Self and Society: A Symbolic Interactionism Social Psychology, 10th ed. Boston: Allyn & Bacon.

Hewitt, John P and David Shulman. 2011. *Self and Society: A Symbolic Interactionist Approach to Social Psychology*, 11th ed. Englewood Cliffs, NJ: Prentice Hall.

Hewlett, Sylvia Ann. 2013. "What's Holding Japanese Women Back." *Time Ideas*, September 27. Retrieved January 18, 2014 (http://ideas.time.com/2013/09/27/whats-holding-japanese-women-back/).

Heyes, J. D. 2012. "Plastic Waste Garbage Floating in Pacific Ocean Has Increased 100-Fold." *NaturalNews.com,* May 15. Retrieved September 7, 2012 (www.naturalnews.com/035866_garbage_floating_Pacific_Ocean.html).

HG.org Legal Resources. 2014. "Covenant Marriage Laws in the U.S." Retrieved February 19, 2014 (www.hg.org/divorce-law-covenant-marriage.html).

Hill, Catherine and Holly Kearl. 2011. "Crossing the Line: Sexual Harassment at School." Washington, DC: AAUW. November. Retrieved September 20, 2012 (www.aauw.org/learn/research/upload/CrossingTheLine.pdf).

Hill, Christopher. 1991. *The World Turned Upside Down: Radical Ideas During the English Revolution.* New York: Penguin.

Hinton, Christopher. 2010."Global Military Spending to Outpace GDP Growth in 2010." *Market Watch*, June 18. Retrieved May 10, 2011 (www.marketwatch.com/story/worlds-militaries-see-another-budget-busting-year-2010-06-18).

Hirschi, T. 1969. *Causes of Delinquency.* Berkeley: University of California Press.

Hitler, Adolf. [1939] 2014. *Mein Kampf: My Struggle.* White Wolf Publishers.

Hochschild, Arlie. 1989. *The Second Shift: Working Parents and the Revolution at Home.* New York: Viking.

Hochschild, Arlie. 1997. *The Time Bind: When Work Becomes Home and Home Becomes Work.* New York: Metropolitan Books.

Holland, Megan M. 2012. "Only Here for the Day: The Social Integration of Minority Students at a Majority White High School." *Sociology of Education* 85(April):101–20.

Holloway, Susan. 2001. "Mothers of Japanese Preschoolers." *GSE Term Paper* 8(1). University of California, Berkeley. Retrieved April 17, 2010 (http://gse.berkeley.edu/admin/publications/termpaper/fall01/fall01/html).

Holt, Sheila. 2007. *Talk of the Nation.* National Public Radio Interview by Cheryl Covley, March 26.

Homans, George C. 1974. *Social Behavior: Its Elementary Forms.* New York: Harcourt, Brace Jovanovich.

Hood, Roger. 2002. *The Death Penalty: A World-Wide Perspective,* 3rd ed. Oxford, UK: Clarendon Press.

Horn, Jordana. 2011. "US Sees Slight Increase in Anti-Semitic Incidents." *The Jerusalem Post,* October 4. Retrieved February 9, 2013 (www.jpost.com/JewishWorld/Jewish Features/Article.aspx?id=240522).

Hostetler, John A. 1993. *Amish Society,* 4th ed. Baltimore: John Hopkins University Press.

Houlihan, G. Thomas. 2005. "The Importance of International Benchmarking for U.S. Educational Leaders." *Phi Delta Kappan* (November):217–18.

Houlis, Anna Marie. 2011. "Gender Stereotypes in Picture Books Are Blamed for Affecting Children." June 13. Retrieved May 23, 2012 (http://annamariehoulis.wordpress.com/2011/06/13/gender-stereotypes-in-picture-books-are-blamed-for-affecting-children/).

Housing and Urban Development. 2008. "HUD Reports Drop in the Number of Chronically Homeless Persons" (News Release No. 08–113). Retrieved August 23, 2008 (www.hud.gov/news).

Howard, Adam. 2007. Learning Privilege: Lessons of Power and Identity in Affluent Schooling. New York: Taylor & Francis.

"How Finnish Schools Shine." 2012. *The Guardian*, May 21. Retrieved July 8, 2013 (www.guardian.co.uk/teacher-network/teacher-blog/2012/apr/09/finish-school-system).

Howard, Adam and Ruben Gaztambide-Fernandez, eds. 2010. *Educating Elites: Class Privilege and Educational Advantage.* Lanham, MD: Rowman and Littlefield.

Howard, Philip. 2011. "The Upside Downside of Social Media." *Reuters*, August 23. Retrieved October 3, 2012 (http://blogs.reuters.com).

Hozien, Muhammad. N.d. "Ibn Khaldun: His Life and Work." Retrieved May 7, 2009 (www.muslimphilosophy.com/ik/klf.htm).

Hu, Elise 2014. "Niche Online Dating Promises a Different Site for Every Preference." *National Public Radio,* February 12. Retrieved February 18, 2014 (www.gpb.org/news/2014/02/12/niche-online-dating-promises-a-different-site-for-every-preference).

Hu, Winnie. 2007. "Equal Cheers for Boys and Girls Draw Some Boos." *New York Times*. January 14. Retrieved February 11, 2014 (www.nytimes.com/2007/01/14/nyregion/14title.html).

Huang, Al. 2011. "'Poster Child' for Environmental Racism Finds Justice in Dickson, TN." *NRDC Switchboard,* December 8. Retrieved March 14, 2014 (http://archive.is/AsHA).

Huddy, Leonie and Stanley Feldman. 2006. "Worlds Apart: Blacks and Whites React to Hurricane Katrina." *Du Bois Review* 3(1):97–113. Retrieved July 7, 2011 (http://journals.cambridge.org/action/displayAbstract?fromPage=online&aid=462978).

Hudson, Heather E. 2011. "Digital Diversity: Broadband and Indigenous Populations in Alaska." Journal of Information Policy 1:378–93. Retrieved September 25, 2012 (jip.vmhost.psu.edu/ojs/index.php/jip/article/download/42/37).

Hudson, Heather E. 2012. "Toward Universal Broadband in Rural Alaska." Institute of Social and Economic Research, University of Alaska, Anchorage. Retrieved September 25, 2012 (www.iser.uaa.alaska.edu/Publications/2012_11-TERRA.pdf).

Huebler, Friedrich. 2008. "International Education Statistics." Retrieved December 6, 2009 (http://huebler.blogspot.com/2008/11/ptr.html).

Huebler, Friedrich. 2012. "Adult and Youth Literacy in 2010." *International Education Statistics,* May 31. Retrieved January 27, 2013 (http://huebler.blogspot.com/2012/05/literacy.html)

Heuer, Ruth and Stephanie Stullich. 2011. Comparability of State and Local Expenditures Among Schools Within Districts: A Report From the Study of School-Level Expenditures. Retrieved July 8, 2013 (www2.ed.gov/rschstat/eval/title-i/school-level-expenditures/school-level-expenditures.pdf).

Huffington Post. 2012b. "Shaken By USC Shooting, Chinese Students Still Seek US Colleges." June 4. Retrieved June 4, 2012 (www.huffingtonpost.com/2012/04/12/shaken-by-usc-shooting-ch_n_1420171.html).

Hughes, Melanie M. 2004. "Armed Conflict, International Linkages, and Women's Parliamentary Representation in Developing Nations." Master's thesis, Department of Sociology, Ohio State University.

Hugo, Peter. 2010. "A Global Graveyard for Dead Computers in Ghana." *New York Times Magazine.* Retrieved July 10, 2013 (www.cnn.com/2011/10/17/opinion/sachs-global-population).

Huizinga, David, Rolf Loeber, and Terence P. Thornberry. 1994. "Urban Delinquency and Substance Abuse: Initial Findings." OJJDP Research Summary. Washington, DC: Government Printing Office.

Human Planet 2012. "Wodaabe Flirtation Festival." Retrieved January 16, 2014 (http://dsc.discovery.com/tv-shows/human-planet/videos/wodaabe-flirtation-festival.htm).

"Human Trafficking: Trafficking by the Numbers." 2012. WGBH, October 8. Retrieved October 8, 2012 (www.wgbh.org/articles/Human-Trafficking-Trafficking-by-the-numbers-285).

Humes, Karen R., Nicholas A. Jones, and Roberto R. Ramirez. 2011. "2010 Census Briefs: Overview of Race and Hispanic Origins: 2010." March, p. 1. Retrieved April 7, 2011 (http://www.census.gov/prod/cen2010/briefs/c2010br-02.pdf).

Hunter College Women's Studies Collective. 2005. *Women's Realities, Women's Choices: An Introduction to Women's Studies,* 3rd ed. New York: Oxford University Press.

Hurst, Charles E. 2006. *Social Inequality: Forms, Causes and Consequences,* 6th ed. Boston: Allyn & Bacon.

Hurst, Charles E. 2013. *Social Inequality: Forms, Causes, and Consequences,* 8th ed. Pearson.

Hyde, Christopher. n.d. "Why Should California Pass a Law That Protects Aid in Dying for Terminally-Ill Patients Who Are Suffering at the End of Their Lives?" Retrieved July 16, 2012 (www.compassinandchoicesnca.org/pdf/88530_Hyde, Christopher.pdf).

Iannaccone, Laurence and William S. Bainbridge. 2010. "Economics of Religion." Pp. 461–75 in *The Routledge Companion to the Study of Religion,* 2nd ed., edited by John Hinnells. New York: Routledge.

Iannelli, Vincent. 2014. "Measles Outbreaks 2014." *Pediatrics. about.com* Retrieved March 10,2014. (http://pediatrics.about.com/od/measles-outbreaks.htm).

"Iceberg Breaks Off From Greenland's Petermann Glacier." 2012. *BBC News,* July 19. Retrieved February 8, 2013 (www.bbc.co.uk/news/world-europe-18896770).

Immigration Policy Center. 2010. "Immigrant Women in the United States: A Portrait of Demographic Diversity." Retrieved May 15, 2011 (www.immigrationpolicy.org/just-facts/immigrant-women-in-the-united-states-portrait-demographic-diversity).

Independence Hall Association. 2010. "Betsy Ross and the American Flag." Retrieved December 21, 2011 (http://www.ushistory.org/betsy/flagtale.html).

Index Mundi 2012a. "Angola Demographics Profile 2012." Retrieved October 12, 2012 (www.indexmundi.com/angola/demographics_profile.html).

Index Mundi. 2012b. "Countries." Retrieved February 7, 2013 (http://www.indexmundi.com/factbook/countries).

Index Mundi. 2012c. "Country Comparison: Health Expenditures." January 1. Retrieved February 4, 2013 (www.indexmundi.com/g/raspx?v=2225).

Index Mundi. 2012d. "Country Comparison: Population Growth Rate." Retrieved July 27, 2012 (www.indexmundi.com/g/r.aspx?v=24).

Index Mundi 2012e. "Haiti Demographics Profile 2012." Retrieved October 12, 2012 (www.indexmundi.com/haiti/demographics_profile.html).

Index Mundi. 2012f. "HIV/AIDS Adult Prevalence Rate—World." Retrieved August 26, 2012 (www.indexmundi.com/map/?v=32).

Index Mundi 2012g. "World Demographic Profile 2012." Retrieved July 29, 2012 (www.indexmundi.com/world/demographics_profile.html).

Index Mundi. 2012h. "World Literacy." Retrieved January 28, 2013 (www.indexmundi.com/world/literacy.html).

Index Mundi. 2013. "Sweden Life Expectancy at Birth" (2012 est.). Retrieved February 7, 2013 (http://www.indexmundi.com/sweden/life_expectancy_at_birth.html).

IndexMundi. 2013a. "Cuba Demographics Profile 2013." Retrieved March 4, 2014 (www.indexmundi.com/cuba/demographics_profile.html).

IndexMundi. 2013b. "Japan Demographics Profile 2013." Retrieved June 9, 2013 (www.indexmundi.com/japan/demographics_profile.html).

IndexMundi. 2013c. Japan Life Expectancy at Birth." Retrieved June 9, 2013 (www.indexmundi.com/japan/life_expectancy_at_birth.html).

IndexMundi. 2013d. "Population Growth Rate." Retrieved March 17, 2014 (www.indexmundi.com/united_kingdom/demo-graphic_profile.html).

IndexMundi. 2014. "Chad Demographic Profile 2014." Retrieved September 16, 2014 (www.indexmundi.com/chad/demographics_profile.html).

Infographics. 2012. "What's Happening? Twitter Facts and Figures." Retrieved September 25, 2012 (www.infographicsarchive.com/social-media/twitter-facts-and-figures/).

Infoplease. 2011. "Lowest Literacy Rates." Retrieved January 28, 2013 (www.infoplease.com/world/countries/lowest-literacy-rates.html).

Infoplease. 2012. "Most Widely Spoken Languages in the World." Retrieved August 19, 2014 (www.infoplease.com/ipa/A0775272.html).

Infoplease. 2013. "Lowest Life Expectancy, 2012." Retrieved February 4, 2013 (www.infoplease.com/world/countries/lowest-life-expectancy.html).

Ingersoll, Richard M. and Elizabeth Merrill. 2012. "The Status of Teaching as a Profession." In *Schools and Society: A Sociological Approach to Education,* edited by Jeanne H. Ballantine and Joan Z. Spade. Thousand Oaks, CA: Sage Pine Forge.

Inglehart, Ronald. 1997. *Modernization and Postmodernization: Cultural, Economic, and Political Change in 43 Societies.* Princeton, NJ: Princeton University Press.

Inglehart, Ronald and Wayne E. Baker. 2001. "Modernization's Challenge to Traditional Values: Who's Afraid of Ronald McDonald?" *The Futurist* 35(2):16–22.

Inniss, Janis Prince. 2010. "A Closer Look at Interracial Marriage Statistics." *Everyday Sociology*, August 2. Retrieved April 10, 2011 (nortonbooks.typepad.com/everydaysociology/2010/08/a-closer-look-at-interracial-marriage-statistics.html).

Innocence Project. 2012. "289 Exonerated." April 16. Retrieved April 16, 2012 (www.innocenceproject.org/).

In Sickness and In Wealth: Health in America. 2008. Unnatural Causes, July 3. Retrieved May 13, 2014 (www.youtube.com/watch?v=w98GSXBEyQw).

Intergovernmental Panel on Climate Change. 2013a. *Fifth Assessment Report.* Retrieved March 18, 2014 (www.ipcc.ch/report/).

Intergovernmental Panel on Climate Change. 2013b. "Working Group I Contribution to the IPCC Fifth Assessment Report." *Climate Change 2013: The Physical Science Basis.* Summary for Policymakers, September 27. Retrieved September 27, 2013 (http://graphics8.nytimes.com/packages/pdf/science/27climate-ipcc-report-summary.pdf).

Intergovernmental Panel on Climate Change. 2014. "Climate Change 2014: Mitigation of Climate Change." Retrieved May 27, 2014 (http://www.ipcc.ch/).

International Beliefs and Values Institute. 2012. "Mission." Staunton, VA: Mary Baldwin College. Retrieved March 23, 2012 (www.ibavi.org).

International Center for Prison Studies. 2014. "World Prison Brief." Retrieved May 13, 2014 (www.prisonstudies.org/).

"The International Digital Divide." 2011. *Science Daily*, February 8. Retrieved May 18, 2012 (www.sciencedaily.com/releases/2011/02/110208121345.htm).

International Food Policy Research Institute. 2013. "Global Hunger Index." September 20. Retrieved February 19, 2014 (http://outcomestories.ifpri.info/2013/09/20/the-global-hunger-index/).

International Humanist and Ethical Union. 2009. "Untouchability in Japan: Discrimination Against Burakumin." August 21. Retrieved December 4, 2009 (www.iheu.org/untouchability-japan-discrimination-against-burakumin).

International Institute for Democracy and Electoral Assistance. 2012. *Voter Turnout Since 1945: A Global Report.* Retrieved June 2, 2013 (www.idea.int/vt/).

International Institute for Democracy and Electoral Assistance. 2008. "Turnout in the World—Country by Country Performance." Retrieved April 17, 2010 (www.idea.int/vt/survey/voter_turnout_pop2.cfm).

International Labor Rights Forum. 2012. "Why Target Hershey for Labor Rights Abuses?" Retrieved February 15, 2014 (www.laborrights.org/stop-child-forced-labor/cocoa-campaign/why-target-hershey-for-labor-rights-abuses).

International Labour Organization. 2013. "Ten Million Child Labourers in Domestic Work." June 12. Retrieved February 15, 2014 (www.ilo/global/about-the-ilo/newsroom/news/WCMs_215170/lang—en/index.htm).

International Labour Organisation. 2014. "Cambodia." Retrieved January 18, 2014 (www.ilo.org/asia/countries/cambodia/lang—en/index.htm).

International Monetary Fund. 2003. "Proposal for a Sovereign Debt Restructuring Mechanism: A Factsheet." Retrieved September 29, 2006 (www.imf.org/external/np/exr/facts/sdrm.htm).

International Monetary Fund. 2013. "Debt Relief Under the Heavily Indebted Poor Countries (HIPC) Initiative." January 10. Retrieved February 7, 2013 (http://www.imf.org/external/np/exr/facts/hipc.htm).

International Organization for Migration. 2012. "Global Estimates and Trends." Retrieved July 30, 2012 (www.iom.int/jahia/Jahia/about-migration/facts-and-figures/lang/en).

Internet World Stats. 2014. "Internet Users in the World." Retrieved September 16, 2014 (http://www.internetworldstats.com/stats.htm).

Inter-Parliamentary Union. 2014. "Women in National Parliaments." Retrieved September 2, 2014 (www.ipu.org/wmn-e/classif.htm).

Interpol. 2007. "Interpol News." Retrieved July 27, 2009 (http://www.interpol.int/Public/News/news2009.asp).

Interuniversity Consortium for Political and Social Research. 2011. "Voting Behavior: The 2008 Election." Retrieved May 16, 2012 (http://www.icpsr.umich.edu/icpsrweb/SETUPS2008/voting.jsp).

In the Face of Pain. 2013. "Race and Pain: Fact Sheet." Retrieved March 4, 2014 (www.inthefaceofpain.com/content/uploads/2011/12/factsheet_Race.pdf).

Irvine, Leslie. 2004. *If You Tame Me: Understanding Our Connection With Animals.* Philadelphia: Temple University Press.

Irwin, John. 1985. *The Jail: Managing the Underclass in American Society.* Berkeley: University of California Press.

Irwin, John. 2005. *The Warehouse Prison: Disposal of the New Dangerous Class.* Los Angeles: Roxbury.

Irwin, John and Barbara Owen. 2007. *The Warehouse Prison: Disposal of the New Dangerous Class.* New York: Oxford University Press.

Isaacs, John. 2011. "Current U.S. and Russian Nuclear Weapons Stockpiles." Retrieved December 21, 2011 (http://armscontrolcenter.org/policy/nuclearweapons/articles/031009_current_nuclear_weapons_stockpiles/).

"Is Overpopulation a World Threat?" 2011. Helium. Retrieved July 28, 2011 (www.helium.com/debates/166036-is-overpopulation-a-world-threat/side_by_side).

"It Begins With Us." 2011. YouTube. Retrieved November 1, 2012 (www.youtube.com/watch?v=f-VZLvVF1FQ).

Jackman, Robert W. 1993. *Power Without Force: The Political Capacity of Nation-States.* Ann Arbor: University of Michigan Press.

Jackson, Philip W. 1968. *Life in Classrooms.* New York: Holt, Rinehart & Winston.

Jacoby, Jeff. 2009. "A Bad Sign Illegal Immigrants Are Leaving." Center for Immigration Studies. September 6. Retrieved April 17, 2010 (www.boston.com/. . ./2009/. . ./a_bad_sign_illegal_immigrants_are_leaving).

Jaeger, Mads Meier. 2011. "Does Cultural Capital Really Affect Academic Achievement? New Evidence from Combined Sibling and Panel Data." *Sociology of Education* 84 (October):281–98.

James, Deanna. 2013. "The Psychology of Eating Disorders." *PsychCentral*, August 8. Retrieved January 18, 2014 (http://psychcentral.com/blog/archives/2013/08/08/the-psychology-of-eating-disorders/).

James, Susan Donaldson. 2011. "Census 2010: One-quarter of Gay Couples Raising Children." *ABC News,* June 23. Retrieved June 5, 2012 (http://abcnews.go.com/Health/sex-couples-census-data-trickles-quarter-raising-children/story?id=13850332).

James, William. [1890] 1934. *The Principles of Psychology*. Mineola, NY: Dover.

Jao, Jui-Chang and Matthew McKeever. 2006. "Ethnic Inequalities and Educational Attainment in Taiwan." *Sociology of Education* 79(2):131–52.

Jarrett, R. L., P. J. Sullivan, and N. D. Watkins. 2005. "Developing Social Capital Through Participation in Organized Youth Programs: Qualitative Insights From Three Programs." *Journal of Community Psychology* 33(1):41–55.

Jarus, Owen. 2012. "Teotihuacan: Ancient City of Pyramids." *Live Science,* August 20. Retrieved March 18, 2014 (www.livescience.com/22545-teotihuacan.html).

Jaschik, Scott. 2010. "Women Lead in Doctorates." September 14. *Inside Higher Ed.* Retrieved January 28, 2013 (www.insidehighered.com/news/2010/09/14/doctorates).

Jaschik, Scott. 2013. "Prestige vs. Major." *Inside Higher Education*, December 10. Retrieved January 4, 2014 (www.insidehighered.com/news/2013/12/10/study-examines-impact-major-vs-impact-college-prestige-womens-earnings).

Jaslow, Ryan. 2013. "End of Life Care for Elderly Often Too Aggressive, Study Says." CBS News, February 6. Retrieved July 16, 2013 (www.cbsnews.com/8301-204_162-57567998/end-of-life-care-for-elderly-often-too-aggressive-study-says/).

Jay, Meg. 2012. "The Downside of Cohabiting before Marriage." *The New York Times Sunday Review,* April 14. Retrieved June 5, 2012 (www.nytimes.com/2012/04/15/opinion/sunday/the-downside-of-cohabiting-before-marriage.html?pagewanted=all).

Jayson, Sharon. 2011. "Cohabitation Numbers Jump 13%, Linked to Job Losses." *USA Today.* Retrieved June 5, 2012 (www.usatoday.com/news/nation/census/2010-09-24-cohabitation24ONLINE_ST_N.htm).

Jelen, Ted, ed. 2002. *Sacred Markets, Sacred Canopies: Essays on Religious Markets and Religious Pluralism.* New York: Rowman & Littlefield.

Jellinek, E. M. 1960. *The Disease Concept of Alcoholism.* New Haven, CT: Hillhouse.

Jencks, Christopher. 1972. *Inequality: A Reassessment of the Effects of Family and Schooling in America.* New York: Basic Books.

Jencks, Christopher, ed. 1979. *Who Gets Ahead? The Determinants of Economic Success in America.* New York: Harper & Row.

Jencks, Christopher. 1992. *Rethinking Social Policy: Race, Poverty, and the Underclass.* Cambridge, MA: Harvard University Press.

Johnson, Ben. 2012. "Chinese Officials: One-Child Policy Has Helped Prevent 400 Million Births." July 27. Retrieved July 28, 2012 (www.lifesitenews.com/news/chinese-officials-one-child-policy-has-prevented-400-million-births).

Johnson, Clifford M., Amy Rynell, and Melissa Young. 2012. "Publicly Funded Jobs: An Essential Strategy for Reducing Poverty and Economic Distress Throughout the Business Cycle." Urban Institute. Retrieved May 17, 2012 (www.urban.org/issues/reducing-poverty-economic-distress.cfm).

Johnson, David W. and Frank P. Johnson. 2006. *Joining Together: Group Theory and Group Skills,* 9th ed. Boston: Allyn & Bacon.

Johnson, Kenneth M. and Glenn V. Fuguitt. 2000. "Continuity and Change in Rural Migration Patterns, 1950–1995." *Rural Sociology* 65(1):27–49.

Johnson, Kevin. 2014. "Thousands of Prisoners Could Qualify for Clemency." *USA Today,* April 21. Retrieved April 25, 2014 (www.usatoday.com/story/news/nation/2014/04/21/prisoners-clemency-holder/7962929/).

Johnson, Nicholas. 2012. "Laboratories of Underfunding? State Financing for Antipoverty Programs." Urban Institute. Retrieved May 17, 2012 (www.urban.org/issues/reducing-poverty-economic-distress.cfm).

Johnson, Paul. 2005. "Majority of Americans Believe Homosexuality Should Not Be Illegal, Support Partner Rights: Gallup Poll." Retrieved August 22, 2006 (www.sodomylaws.org/usa/usnews141.htm).

Johnson, Robert. 2002. *Hard Time: Understanding and Reforming the Prison.* Belmont, CA: Wadsworth/Thompson Learning.

Johnson, Steven. 2009. "How Twitter Will Change the Way We Live (in 140 Characters or Less)." *Time,* June 15, pp. 32–37.

Joint Center for Political and Economic Studies. 2013. "Nickelodeon: Kids Watch 35 Hours of TV/Week—MTI Stats and Studies, 12/2/2013." Retrieved January 17, 2014 (http://jcpes.wordpress.com/2013/12/02/nickelodeon-kids-watch-35-hours-of-tvweek-mti-stats-and-studies-1222013/).

Jones, Sydney and Susannah Fox. 2009. "Generations Online in 2009." Pew Internet and American Life Project, January 28. Retrieved June 25, 2011 (www.pewinternet.org/Reports/2009/Generations-Online-in-2009.aspx).

Jordan, Amy B., James C. Hersey, Judith A. MdDivitt, and Carrie D. Heitzler. 2006. "Reducing Children's Television-Viewing Time: A Qualitative Study of Parents and Their Children." *Pediatrics* 118(5):1303–10.

Jordan, Winthrop D. 2012. *White Over Black: American Attitudes Toward the Negro 1550–1812,* 2nd ed. (Published for the Omohundro Institute of Early American History). Chapel Hill: University of North Carolina.

Jordan-Bychkov, Terry G., and Mono Domoch. 1998. *The Human Mosaic,* 8th ed. New York: Freeman.

Jory, Brian and Carry L. Yodanis. 2014. "Family Relationships, Marital Relationships." *Marriage and Family Encyclopedia*. Retrieved February 18, 2014 (http://family.jrank.org/pages/1316/Power.html).

Jourdan, Adam. 2013. "Divided Church of England Renews Pledge to Ordain Women Bishops." Reuters, July 8. Retrieved July 12, 2013 (http://uk.reuters.com/article/2013/07/08/uk-britain-church-women-idUKBRE9670SC20130708).

Julian, Tiffany and Robert Kominski. 2011. "Table 1: Annual Earnings by Level of Education and Work Status." *American Community Survey Reports,* September. Retrieved September 9, 2014 (http://www.census.gov/prod/2011pubs/acs-14.pdf).

Kaiser, Ashley and Freddie Cross. 2011. Beginning Teacher Attrition and Mobility: Results From the First Through Third Waves of the 2007–08 Beginning Teacher Longitudinal Study. National Center for Education Statistics. Retrieved July 8, 2013 (http://nces.ed.gov/pubs2011/2011318.pdf).

Kaiser Commission on Medicaid and the Uninsured. 2011. "The Uninsured: A Primer." Retrieved February 2, 2013 (http://www.kff.org/UNINSURED/UPLOAD/7451-07.PDF).

Kaiser Family Foundation. 2005. "Generation M: Media in the Lives of 8 to 18 Year-Olds—Report." Retrieved July 20, 2006 (www.kff.org/entmedia/7251.cfm).

Kaiser Family Foundation. 2010. "G8 leaders to Discuss Economic Policy, Developing World, Maternal and Child Health, Haitian Rebuilding." June 25. Retrieved July 13, 2012 (http://globalhealth.Kff.org/Daily-Reports/2010/June/25/GH-062510-G8-G20-Summits.aspx).

Kaiser Family Foundation. 2013. "The Global HIV/AIDS Epidemic." *Global Health Policy,* October 10. Retrieved April 2, 2014 (http://kff.org/global-health-policy/fact-sheet/the-global-hivaids-epidemic/).

Kan, Man Yee, Oriel Sullivan, and Jonathan Gershuny. 2011. "Gender Convergence in Domestic Work: Discerning the Effects of Interactional and Institutional Barriers from Large-Scale Data" *Sociology* 45(2):234–51.

Kane, Maggie. 2012. "Minnesota Clergy Unite Against Marriage Amendment." *Southwest Journal,* June 7. Retrieved September 26, 2012 (www.swjournal.com/index.php?&story=18542&page=152&category=63).

Kanter, Rosabeth Moss. 1977. *Men and Women of the Corporation.* New York: Basic Books.

Kanter, Rosabeth Moss. 2005. *Commitment and Community.* Cambridge, MA: Harvard University Press.

Kao, Grace. 2004. "Social Capital and Its Relevance to Minority and Immigrant Populations." *Sociology of Education* 77:172–76.

Kaplan, Howard B. and Robert J. Johnson. 1991. "Negative Social Sanctions and Juvenile Delinquency: Effects of Labeling in a Model of Deviant Behavior." *Social Science Quarterly* 72(1):117.

Karen, David. 2005. "No Child Left Behind? Sociology Ignored!" *Sociology of Education* 78(2):165–82.

Karraker, Katherine Hildebrant. 1995. "Parent's Gender-Stereotyped Perceptions of Newborns: The Eye of the Beholder Revisited." *Sex Roles* 33(9/10):687–701.

Karthikeyan, D. 2011. "Dalits Pay the Price for Their Political Assertion." *The Hindu: Tamil Nadu,* February 18, p. 1.

Kasperkevic, Jana. 2014. "How Much Can You Get for Selling Your Body (Parts)?" *The Guardian.* Retrieved May 27, 2014 (www.theguardian.com/money/us-money-blog/2014/jan/31/flu-government-sell-egg-sperm-body).

Katz, Jackson. 2006. *The Macho Paradox: Why Some Men Hurt Women and How All Men Can Help.* Naperville, IL: Sourcebooks.

Katz, Jonathan and Jennifer Bradley. 2013. *The Metropolitan Revolution.* Washington, DC: The Brookings Institution.

Kavilanz, Parija. 2010. "Doctor-Starved: America's Heartland in Crisis." CNN Money, March 28. Retrieved July 17, 2012 (http://money.cnn.com/2010/03/26/news/economy/health_care_rural_care_country_doctors/index.htm).

Kean, Sam. 2007. "What's in a Name?" *The New York Times,* October 28. Retrieved May 21, 2012 (www.nytimes.com/2007/10/28/magazine/28wwln-idealab-t.html).

Keck, Zachary. 2014. "US Drives Down Global Defense Spending." *The Diplomat,* April 15. Retrieved May 22, 2014 (http://thediplomat.com/2014/04/us-drives-down-global-defense-spending/).

Keigher, Ashley and Freddie Cross. 2010. "Teacher Attrition and Mobility." School and Staffing Survey. IES. NCES. Retrieved April 17, 2011 (http://nces.ed.gov/pubs2010/2010353.pdf).

Kelber, Harry. 2012. "Manufacturers Are Hiring Workers in America, But Offer a Sharp Drop in Wages and Benefits." *The Labor Educator,* January 2. Retrieved May 28, 2012 (www.laboreducator.org/It120102.htm).

Kennedy, Kelly. 2011. "Health Care Fraud Prosecutions on Pace to Rise 85%." *USA Today,* August 29. Retrieved April 13, 2012 (www.usatoday.com/news/washington/story/2011-08-29/Health-care-fraud-prosecutions-on-pace-to-rise-85/50180282/1).

Kerbo, Harold R. 2008. *Social Stratification and Inequality,* 7th ed. Boston: McGraw-Hill.

Kerckhoff, Alan C. 2001. "Education and Social Stratification Processes in Comparative Perspective." *Sociology of Education* (Extra Issue: Currents of Thought: Sociology of Education at the Dawn of the 21st Century):3–18.

Kessler, Sarah. 2011. "Study: 80% of Children Under 5 Use Internet Weekly." *Technology Live,* March 15. Retrieved April 9, 2013 (http://content.usatoday.com/communities/technologylive/post/2011/03/study-80-percent-of-children-under-5-use-internet-weekly/).

Kettl, Donald F. 1993. *Sharing Power: Public Governance and Private Markets.* Washington, DC: Brookings.

Khazaleh Lorenz. 2009. "Internet Fatwas Cautiously Support Divorce Among Women" *CULCOM,* October 29. Retrieved January 4, 2010 (www.culcom.uio.no/english/news/2009/bogstad.html).

Khazan, Olga. 2013. "The Countries Where Women Have the Best Lives." *The Atlantic,* March 8. Retrieved January 17, 2014 (www.theatlantic.com/international/archive/2013/03/the-countries-where-women-have-the-best-lives-in-charts/273848).

Khan, Shamus Rahman. 2011. *Privilege: The Making of an Adolescent Elite at St. Paul's School.* Princeton, NJ: Princeton University Press.

Kidder, Tracy. 2004. *Mountains Beyond Mountains.* New York: Random House.

Kilbourne, Jean. 1999. *Deadly Persuasion: Why Women and Girls Must Fight the Additive Power of Advertising.* New York: Free Press.

Kilbourne, Jean. 2000. *Killing Us Softly, III* (Video). Northampton, MA: Media Education Foundation.

Killian, Caitlin. 2006. *North African Women in France: Gender, Culture, and Identity.* Palo Alto, CA: Stanford University Press.

Kim, Min-Sun, Katsuya Tasaki, In-Duk Kim, and Hye-ryeon Lee. 2007. "The Influence of Social Status on Communication Predispositions Focusing on Independent and Inter-dependent Self-Construals." *Journal of Asian Pacific Communication* 17(2):303–329.

Kimmel, Michael S. and Michael A. Messner. 2009. *Men's Lives,* 8th ed. Boston: Allyn & Bacon.

Kindlon, Dan and Michael Thompson. 2000. *Raising Cain: Protecting the Emotional Life of Boys.* New York: Ballantine Books.

King, Edith W. 2006. *Meeting the Challenges of Teaching in an Era of Terrorism.* Belmont, CA: Thomson.

King, Neil, Jr. 2012. "Vote Data Show Changing Nation." *The Wall Street Journal*, November 8. Retrieved June 7, 2013 (http://online.wsj.com/article/SB1000142412788732407350457810 5360833569352.html#project%3DEXITPOLLS2012%26artic leTabs%3Darticle).

Kingkade, Tyler. 2012. "Youth Vote 2012 Turnout: Exit Polls Show Greater Share of Electorate Than in 2008." *Huffington Post*, November 7. Retrieved November 8, 2012 (www.huff ingtonpost.com/2012/11/07/youth-vote-2012-turnout-exit-polls_n_2086092.html).

Kinsey Institute for Research in Sex, Gender, and Reproduction. 2012. Retrieved May 20, 2012 (www.kinseyinstitute.org).

Kirchhoff, Suzanne M. 2010. "Economic Impacts of Prison Growth." Congressional Research Service, April 13. Retrieved June 2, 2013 (www.bjs.gov/content/pub/pdf/p11.pdf).

Kirkham, C. 2012. "Private Prison Corporation Offers Cash In Exchange For State Prisons." *The Huffington Post,* February 14. Retrieved September 16, 2014 (http://www.huffington post.com/2012/02/14/private-prisons-buying-state-prisons_n_1272143.html).

Kitano, Harry H., Pauline Aqbayani, and Diane de Anda. 2005. *Race Relations,* 6th ed. Englewood Cliffs, NJ: Prentice Hall.

Kitano, Harry H. L. and Roger Daniels. 2001. *Asian Americans: Emerging Minorities,* 3rd ed. New York: Pearson.

Kliff, Sarah. 2014. "Think America Has the World's Best Health Care System? You Won't After Seeing This Chart." *The Washington Post,* January 7. Retrieved March 12, 2014 (www .washingtonpost.com/blogs/wonkblog/wp/2014/01/07/think-america-has-the-worlds-best-health -care-system-you-wont-after-seeing-this-chart/).

Klinenberg, Eric. 2012. *Going Solo: The Extraordinary Rise and Surprising Appeal of Living Alone.* New York: Penguin.

Knapp, Mark L. and Judith A. Hall. 1997. *Nonverbal Communication in Human Interaction,* 4th ed. Fort Worth: Harcourt Brace.

Kneebone Elizabeth and Alan Berube. 2013. *Confronting Suburban Poverty in America.* Washington, DC: The Brookings Institute.

Knickmeyer, Ellen. 2008. "Turkey's Gul Signs Head Scarf Measure." February 23. Retrieved April 17, 2010 (www.wash ingtonpost.com/>world).

Koch, Jerome R. and Evans W. Curry. 2000. "Social Context and the Presbyterian Gay/Lesbian Debate: Testing Open Systems Theory." *Review of Religious Research* 42(2):206–214.

Kochhar, Rakesh. 2012. "Labor Force Growth Slows, Hispanic Share Grows." Pew Research Social and Demographic Trends, February 13. Retrieved February 6, 2013 (www.pews ocialtrends.org/2012/02/13/labor-force-growth-slows-his panic-growth-grows-2/).

Kodish, Bruce I. 2003. "What We Do With Language—What It Does With Us." *ETC: A Review of General Semantics* 60:383–95.

Kohlberg, Lawrence. 1971. "From Is to Ought." Pp. 151–284 in *Cognitive Development and Epistemology,* edited by T. Mischel. New York: Academic Press.

Kohn, Melvin. 1989. *Class and Conformity: A Study of Values,* 2nd ed. Chicago: University of Chicago Press.

Koleth, Elsa. 2012. "Asylum Seekers: An Update: Briefing Paper No. 1/2012." NSW Parliamentary Library. Retrieved July 30, 2012 (www.parliament.nsw.gov.au/prod/parment/publica tions.OD189A/SFile/Asylum%20seekers%20Final%20 March%20202012.pdf).

Konrad, Walicia. 2012. "As Medicare Fraud Evolves, Vigilance Is Required." *New York Times,* September 11. Retrieved April 18, 2013 (www.nytimes.com/2012/09/12/business/retire mentspecial/medicare-fraud-victimizes-patients-and-taxpay ers.html?_r=0).

Koos, Earl. 1954. *The Health of Regionville.* New York: Columbia University Press.

Korgen, Jeffry and Charles Gallagher. 2013. *The True Cost of Low Prices.* New York: Orbis Books.

Korgen, Kathleen Odell and David Brunsma. 2012. "Avoiding Race or Following the Racial Scripts? Obama and Race in the Recessionary Part of the Colorblind Era." In *Obama and the Biracial Factor: The Battle for a New American Majority,* edited by Andrew Jolivette. Bristol, UK: Policy Press.

Korgen, Kathleen Odell and Jonathan M. White. 2013. *The Engaged Sociologist: Connecting the Classroom to the Community,* 3rd ed. Thousand Oaks, CA: Sage.

Korgen, Kathleen Odell, Jonathan M. White, and Shelley K. White. 2013. *Sociologists in Action: Sociology, Social Change, and Social Justice,* 2nd ed. Thousand Oaks, CA: Sage.

Korte, Charles and Stanley Milgram. 1970. "Acquaintance Networks Between Racial Groups." *Journal of Personality and Social Psychology* 15:101–108.

Koschate-Reis, Miriam. 2009. "The Social Psychology of Embarrassment." Research project at the School of Psychology, University of St. Andrews. Retrieved March 31, 2012 (http:// sites.google.com/site/embarrassmentproject/home).

Kosmin, Barry and Ariela Keysar. 2009. *American Religious Identification Survey (ARIS 2008) Summary Report.* March. Hartford, CT: Trinity College.

Kotaku. 2013. "The 13 Most Popular Video Games of 2013, as Purchased by You." Retrieved February 14, 2014 (http:// kotaku.com/the-13-most-popular-video-games-of-2013-as-purchased-b-1487785780).

Kotkin, Joe and Wendell Cox. 2011. "Cities and the Census." *City Journal,* April 6. Retrieved July 1, 2013 (www.city-journal .org/2011/eon0406jkwc.html).

Kotkin, Joel. 2013. "America's Fastest—And Slowest—Growing Cities." *Forbes,* March 18. Retrieved July 1, 2013 (www .forbes.com/sites/joelkotkin/2013/03/18/americas-fastest-and-slowest-growing-cities/).

Kottak, Conrad Phillip. 2010. *Prime-Time Society: An Anthropological Analysis of Television and Culture*, updated ed. Walnut Creek, CA: Left Coast Press.

Kozol, Jonathan. 1991. *Savage Inequalities: Children in America's Schools.* New York: Crown.

Kozol, Jonathan. 2005. "Confections of Apartheid: A Stick-and-Carrot Pedagogy for the Children of Our Inner-City Poor." *Phi Delta Kappan* (December):265–75.

Kozol, Jonathan. 2006. The Shame of the Nation: The Restoration of Apartheid Schooling in America. New York: Crown.

Kozol, Jonathan. 2012. *Fire in the Ashes: Twenty-five Years Among the Poorest Children in America.* New York: Random House Crown Publishing Group.

Kramer, Laura. 2010. *The Sociology of Gender: A Brief Introduction,* 3rd ed. New York: Oxford University Press.

Kramer, Laura and Ann Beutel. 2014. *The Sociology of Gender: A Brief Introduction,* 4th ed. New York: Oxford University Press.

Kreider, Rose M. 2010a. "Estimates of Cohabiting Couples ASEC 2009 and 2010" (Table 1). U.S. Census Bureau, Current Population Survey, September 15. Retrieved October 14, 2012 (www.census.gov/population/www/socdemo/Inc-Opp-sex-2009-to-2010.pdf).

Kreider, Rose M. 2010b. "Increase in Opposite-Sex Cohabiting Couples From 2009 to 2010 in the Annual Social and Economic Supplement to the Current Population Survey." U.S. Census Bureau, September 15. Retrieved April 11, 2011 (www.census.gov/population/www/socdemo/Inc-Opp-sex-2009-to-2010.pdf).

Kreider, Rose. 2010c. "Working Paper on the Change in Cohabiting Couples from 2009 to 2010." Retrieved July 14, 2011 (http://www.census.gov/population/www/socdemo/Inc-Opp-sex-2009-to-2010.pdf).

Kreider, Rose M. and Diana B. Elliott. 2009. "America's Families and Living Arrangements: 2007." U.S. Census Bureau *Current Population Reports,* P20-561. Retrieved January 24, 2013 (http://www.census.gov/prod/2009pubs/p20-561.pdf).

Kreider, Rose M., and Renee Ellis. 2011. "Living Arrangements of Children: 2009." *U.S. Census Bureau,* June. Retrieved May 4, 2013 (www.census.gov/prod/2011pubs/p70-126.pdf).

Krieger, Lisa M. 2012. "The Cost of Dying: It's Hard to Reject Care Even as Costs Soar." *San Jose Mercury Sun.* Retrieved July 16, 2012 (www.mercurynews.com/health/ci_19898736).

Kristof, Nicholas D. 2009. "Where Sweatshops Are a Dream." *The New York Times,* January 14. Retrieved May 9, 2011 (www.nytimes.com/2009/01/15/opinion/15kristof.html).

Kristof, Nicholas and Sheryl WuDunn. 2009. *Half the Sky: Turning Oppression Into Opportunity for Women Worldwide.* New York: Alfred A. Knopf.

Kroenig, Matthew and Barry Pavel. 2012. "How to Deter Terrorism." *The Washington Quarterly* 35(2):21–36.

Kübler-Ross, Elizabeth. 1997. *Death, the Final Stage of Growth,* Rev. ed. New York: Scribner.

Kuhn, Manford. 1964. "Major Trends in Symbolic Interaction Theory in the Past Twenty-Five Years." *Sociological Quarterly* 5:61–84.

Kuhn, Thomas. 1970. *The Structure of Scientific Revolutions,* 2nd ed. Chicago: University of Chicago Press.

Kulkarni, Shefali. S. 2012 "Teen Pregnancies Hit New Low, But Disparities Remain." *NPR,* February 8. Retrieved July 12, 2013 (www.npr.org/blogs/health/2012/02/08/146573537/teen-pregnancies-decline-but-disparities-remain).

Kumlin, Johanna. 2006. "The Sex Wage Gap in Japan and Sweden: The Role of Human Capital, Workplace Sex Composition, and Family Responsibility." *European Sociological Review* (advance access published online on December 18). Retrieved April 17, 2010 (http://esr.oxford journals.org/cgi/content/abstract/23/2/203).

Kurtz, Lester R. 2007. *Gods in the Global Village,* 2nd ed. Thousand Oaks, CA: Pine Forge Press.

Lacayo, Richard. 1993. "Cult of Death." *Time* (March 15):36.

Lake, Nell. 2012. "Labor, Interrupted." *Harvard Magazine,* November-December. Retrieved July 15, 2013 (http://harvardmagazine.com/2012/11/labor-interrupted).

Lake, Robert. 1990. "An Indian Father's Plea." *Teacher Magazine* 2 (September):48–53.

Lamanna, Mary Ann and Agnes Riedmann. 2010. *Marriages and Families: Making Choices Throughout the Life Cycle,* 10th ed. Belmont, CA: Wadsworth.

Lambert, Yves. 2000. "Religion in Modernity as a New Axial Age: Secularization or New Religious Forms?" Pp. 95–125 in *The Secularization Debate,* edited by William H. Swatos, Jr. and Daniel V. A. Olson. Lanham, MD: Rowman & Littlefield.

Landler, Mark and Brian Stelter. 2009. "Washington Taps Into a Potent New Force in Diplomacy." *New York Times,* June 17, p. A12. Retrieved December 22, 2009 (www.nytimes.com).

Langfitt, Frank. 2011. "Mobile Money Revolution Aids Kenya's Poor, Economy." *NPR,* January 5. Retrieved June 8, 2013 (http://www.npr.org/2011/01/05/132679772/mobile-money-revolution-aids-kenyas-poor-economy).

Langton, Lynn, Michael Planty, and Nathan Sandholtz. 2013. "Hate Crime Victimization, 2003–2011." Bureau of Justice Statistics, March 21. Retrieved June 1, 2013 (www.bjs.gov/index.cfm?ty=pbdetail&iid=4614).

Lareau, Annette. 2003. *Unequal Childhoods: Class, Race, and Family Life.* Berkeley: University of California Press.

Larsen, Jensine. 2013. "The Day Women of the Congo Seized Control of the Internet." *The Huffington Post,* March 5. Retrieved May 3, 2013 (www.huffingtonpost.com/news/congo-rape-weapon-of-war).

Lasch, Kathryn E. 2002 "Culture and Pain." Pain: Clinical Updates, December. *International Association for the Study of Pain* X(5):1–9.

Lashbrook, Jeffrey. 2009. "Social Class Differences in Family Life." P. 224 in *Our Social World,* 2nd ed., edited by Jeanne H. Ballantine and Keith A. Roberts. Thousand Oaks, CA: Sage.

Lavoie, Denise 2013. "Victims in Meningitis Outbreak Hope for Criminal Charges against Compounding Pharmacy." *NBC News,* November 25. Retrieved March 3, 2014 (wwwnbcnews.com/health/health-news/victims-meningitis-outbreak-hope-criminal-charges- against-compounding-pharmacy-f2D11653410).

Lawrence, Alison. 2009. "Cutting Correction Costs: Earned Time Policies for State Prisoners." National Conference of State Legislatures. Retrieved June 2, 2013 (www.ncsl.org/documents/cj/earned_time_report.pdf).

Layton, Lyndsey. 2012. "High School Graduation Rate Rises in U.S." *The Washington Post,* March 18. Retrieved September 19, 2012 (www.washingtonpost.com/local/education/high-school-graduation-rate-rises-in-us/2012/03/16/gIQAxZ9rLS_story.html).

Lazare, Aaron. 2004. *On Apology.* New York: Oxford University Press.

Lazaridis, Gabriella. 2011. *Security, Insecurity and Migration in Europe.* Farnham, UK: Ashgate Publishing, Ltd.

Lazerwitz, Bernard, J. Alan Winter, Arnold Dashefsky, and Ephraim Tabory. 1998. *Jewish Choices: American Jewish Denominationalism.* Albany, NY: SUNY Press.

Leach, Edmund R. 1979. "Ritualization in Man in Relation to Conceptual and Social Development." Pp. 333–37 in *Reader in Comparative Religion,* 3rd ed., edited by William A. Lessa and Evon Z. Vogt. New York: Harper & Row.

Leavitt, Jacqueline and Susan Saegert. 1990. *From Abandonment to Hope: Community-Households in Harlem* (Columbia History of Urban Life). New York: Columbia University Press.

LeBon, Gustave. [1895] 1960. *The Crowd: A Study of the Popular Mind.* New York: Viking.

LeBow, Bob. 2004. *Health Care Meltdown: Confronting the Myths and Fixing Our Failing System.* Chambersburg, PA: Alan C. Hood.

Lebow, R.N. 1981. *Between Peace and War: The Nature of International Crisis.* Baltimore, MD: Johns Hopkins University Press.

Lechner, Frank J. and John Boli. 2005. *World Culture: Origins and Consequences.* Malden, MA: Blackwell.

Lederer, Edith M. 2012. "Human Trafficking Victims: 2.4 Million People Across the Globe Are Trafficked for Labor, Sex." *Huff Post World,* April 3. Retrieved January 21, 2013 (www.huffingtonpost.com/2012/04/03/human-trafficking-victims_n_1401673.html).

Lederman, Josh. 2012. "Voter Turnout Shaping Up to Be Lower Than 2008." *Huffington Post,* November 7. Retrieved November 11, 2012 (http://www.huffingtonpost.com/2012/11/07/voter-turnout_n_2088810.html).

Lee, B. C. and J. L. Werth. 2000. *Observations on the First Year of Oregon's Death With Dignity Act.* Washington, DC: American Psychological Association.

Lee, Gang, Ronald L. Akers, and Marian J. Borg. 2004. "Social Learning and Structural Factors in Adolescent Substance Use." *Western Criminology Review* 5(1):17.

Lee, Jennifer and Frank D. Bean. 2004. "America's Changing Color Lines: Immigration, Race/Ethnicity, and Multiracial Identification." *Annual Review of Sociology* 30(August):222–42.

Lee, Jennifer and Frank D. Bean. 2007. "Redrawing the Color Line?" *City and Community* 6(1):49–62.

Lee, Richard B. 1984. *The Dobe !Kung.* New York: Holt, Rinehart & Winston.

Lee, Suevon. 2012. "By the Numbers: The U.S.'s Growing For-Profit Detention Industry." *ProPublica,* June 20. Retrieved June 3, 2013 (www.propublica.org/article/by-the-numbers-the-u.s.s-growing-for-profit-detention-industry).

Leeder, Elaine J. 2004. *The Family in Global Perspective: A Gendered Journey.* Thousand Oaks, CA: Sage.

Legters, Nettie E. 2001. "Teachers as Workers in the World System." Pp. 417–26 in *Schools and Society: A Sociological Approach to Education,* edited by Jeanne H. Ballantine and Joan Z. Spade. Belmont, CA: Wadsworth.

Lehman, Edward C., Jr. 1985. *Women Clergy: Breaking Through Gender Barriers.* New Brunswick, NJ: Transaction.

Leit, R. A., J. J. Gray, and H. G. Pope. 2002. "The Media's Representation of the Ideal Male Body." *International Journal of Eating Disorders* (doi.wiley.com).

Lemert, Edwin M. 1951. *Social Pathology.* New York: McGraw-Hill.

Lemert, Edwin M. 1972. *Human Deviance, Social Problems, and Social Control,* 2nd ed. Englewood Cliffs, NJ: Prentice Hall.

Lemkau, Jeanne Parr. 2006. "Fences, Volcanoes, and Embargoes." Unpublished manuscript.

Lengermann, Patricia M., and Jill Niebrugge-Brantley. 1990. "Feminist Sociological Theory: The Near-Future Prospects." Pp. 316–44 in *Frontiers of Social Theory: The New Synthesis,* edited by George Ritzer. New York: Columbia University Press.

Lenski, Gerhard E. 1966. *Human Societies.* New York: McGraw-Hill.

Lentze, Georg. 2013. "Islamic Headscarf Debate Rekindled in France." *BBC News Europe,* April 2. Retrieved May 2, 2013 (http://www.bbc.com/news/world-europe-21997089).

Leon, Kim. 2009. "Covenant Marriage: What Is It and Does It Work?" *MissouriFamilies.org.* Retrieved June 6, 2012 (http://missourifamilies.org/features/divorcearticles/divorcefeature23.htm).

Lerner, Richard M. 1992. "Sociobiology and Human Development: Arguments and Evidence." *Human Development* 35(1):12–51.

Leslie, Gerald R. and Sheila K. Korman. 1989. *The Family in Social Context,* 7th ed. New York: Oxford University Press.

Leung, K., S. Lau, and W. L. Lam. 1998. *Parenting Styles and Academic Achievement: A Cross-Cultural Study.* Detroit, MI: Wayne State University Press.

Levin, Jack and Jack McDevitt. 2003. Hate Crimes Revisited: America's War on Those Who Are Different. Boulder, CO: Westview.

Levinson, David L. 2010. "Grand Solution or Grab Bag?" *The American Prospect* (November):14–17. Retrieved February 9, 2013 (www.prospect.org).

Levinson, Stephen C. 2000. "Yeli Dnye and the Theory of Basic Color Terms." *Journal of Linguistic Anthropology* 1:3–55.

Levitt, Judith. 2012. "Women as Priests." *New York Times,* September 29. Retrieved June 20, 2013 (www.nytimes.com/2012/09/30/opinion/sunday/women-as-priests.html).

Levitt, Peggy. 2001. *The Transnational Villagers.* Berkeley: University of California Press.

Levitt, Peggy. 2007. *God Needs No Passport: Immigrants and the Changing American Religious Landscape.* New York: New Press.

Levitt, Peggy, and Mary Waters, eds. 2006. *The Changing Face of Home: The Transnational Lives of the Second Generation.* Russell Sage Foundation. Retrieved June 27, 2011 (www.russellsage.org/publications/changing-face-home).

Levy, Audrey. 2008. "No to Forced Marriages!" *France Diplomatie.* Retrieved April 17, 2010 (www.diplomatie.gouv.fr/. . .no. . ./seen-from-france_4737.html).

Levy, Jenna. 2014. "U.S. Uninsured Rate Drops So Far in First Quarter of 2014." *Gallup Well-Being.* Retrieved March 10, 2014 (www.gallup.com/poll/167393/uninsured-rate-drops-far-first-quarter-2014.aspx).

Lewin, Tamar. 2006. "At Colleges, Women Are Leaving Men in the Dust." *The New York Times,* July 9, pp. A1, 18.

Lewis, Oscar. 1961. *The Children of Sánchez: Autobiography of a Mexican Family.* New York: Random House.

Lewis, Oscar. 1986. *La Vida: A Puerto Rican Family in the Culture of Poverty.* New York: Irvington.

Library of Congress. 2010. "Margaret Mead: Human Nature and the Power of Culture." July 27. Retrieved March 7, 2012 (www.loc.gov/exhibits/mead/field-sepik.html).

Lichter, Daniel T., Richard N. Turner, and Sharon Sassler. 2010. "Marriage and Family in the New Millenium: Papers in Honor of Steven L. Nock." *Social Science Research* 39(5):754–65. Retrieved April 11, 2011 (doi:10.1016/j.ssresearch.2009.11.002).

Lieberson, Stanley. 1980. *A Piece of the Pie: Blacks and White Immigrants Since 1880.* Berkeley: University of California Press.

Lieberson, Stanley, Susan Dumais, and Shyon Bauman. 2000. "The Instability of Androgynous Names: The Symbolic Maintenance of Gender Boundaries." *American Journal of Sociology* 105(5):1249–87.

Lin, June. 2010. "What Are the Main Criticisms of Whorf"s Theory of Linguistic Determinism and Relativity?" August 3. Retrieved March 21, 2012 (www.quora.com/What-are-the-main-criticisms-of-Whorfs-theory-of-linguistic-determinism-and-relativity).

Lincoln, Erik and Laurence Mamiya. 1990. *The Black Church in the African American Experience*. Durham, NC: Duke University Press.

Lindberg, Richard and Vesna Markovic. N.d. "Organized Crime Outlook in the New Russia: Russia Is Paying the Price of a Market Economy in Blood." Retrieved January 4, 2001 (www.search-international.com/Articles/crime/russiacrime.htm).

Lindow, Megan. June 20, 2009. "South Africa's Rape Crisis: 1 in 4 Men Say They've Done It." *Time/World*. Retrieved February 27, 2012 (www.time.com/time/world/article/0,8599,1906000,00.html).

Lindsay, James M. 2006. "Global Warming Heats Up." Pp. 307–13 in *Globalization: The Transformation of Social Worlds*, edited by D. Stanley Eitzen and Maxine Baca Zinn. Belmont, CA: Wadsworth.

Lindsey, Linda L. 2011. *Gender Roles: A Sociological Perspective*, 5th ed. Englewood Cliffs, NJ: Prentice Hall.

Linton, Ralph. 1937. *The Study of Man*. New York: D. Appleton-Century.

Lips, Hilary M. 2010. *Sex and Gender: An Introduction,* 9th ed. Boston: McGraw-Hill.

Lips, Hilary. 2013. *Gender: The Basics*. Taylor and Francis.

Liptak, Adam. 2008. "U.S. Prison Population Dwarfs that of Other Nations." April 23. *The New York Times*. Retrieved April 15, 2012 (www.nytimes.com/2008/04/23/world/americas/23iht-23prisons.12253738.html).

Liptak, Adam. 2012. "Justices Take Up Race as a Factor in College Entry." *The New York Times,* February 21. Retrieved May 12, 2012 (www.nytimes.com/2012/02/22/us/justices-to-hear-case-on-affirmative-action-in-higher-education.html?pagewanted=all).

Liptak, Adam. 2013. "Justices Step Up Scrutiny of Race in College Entry." *New York Times,* June 24. Retrieved June 25, 2013 (www.nytimes.com/2013/06/25/us/affirmative-action-decision.html?pagewanted=1&_r=0&hp).

Liptak, Adam and Maria Newman. 2005. *"New York Times* Reporter Jailed for Keeping Source Secret." *New York Times,* July 6. Retrieved March 3, 2012 (www.nytimes.com/2005/07/06/po9litics/06cnd-leak.html?pagewanted=all).

Lofgren, Orvar. 1999. *On Holiday: A History of Vacationing*. Berkeley: University of California Press.

Lofgren, Orvar. 2010. "The Global Beach." Pp. 37–55 in *Tourists and Tourism,* 2nd ed., edited by Sharon Bohn Gmelch. Long Grove, IL: Waveland Press.

Loftsdottir, Kristin. 2004. "When Nomads Lose Cattle: Wodaabe Negotiations of Ethnicity." *African Sociological Review* 8(2):55–76.

Longman, Timothy. 2005. "Rwanda: Achieving Equality or Serving an Authoritarian State?" Pp. 133–150 in *Women in African Parliaments,* edited by Gretchen Bauer and Hannah Britton. Boulder, CO: Lynne Reinner.

"Lonmin Profit Plunges on South Africa Platinum Strike." 2014. *BBC News*, May 12. Retrieved September 7, 2014 (www.bbc.com/news/business-27369966).

Lopatto, Elizabeth. 2013. "Unmarried Couples Living Together Is New U.S. Norm." *Bloomberg*. Retrieved February 19, 2014 (www.bloomberg.com/news/2013-04-04/unmarried-couples-living-together-is-new-u-s-norm.html).

Lopez, Mark Hugo and Anna Gonzalez-Barrera. 2014. "Women Outpace Men in College Enrollment." Pew Research Fact Tank, March 6. Retrieved May 16, 2014 (www.pewresearch.org/fact-tank/2014/03/06/womens-college-enrollment-gains-leave-men-behind/).

Lopez, Ian F. Haney. 1996. *White by Law*. New York: New York University Press.

Lopez-Garza, Marta. 2002. "Convergence of the Public and Private Spheres: Women in the Informal Economy." *Race, Gender, and Class* 9(3):175–92.

Lopreato, Joseph. 2001. "Sociobiological Theorizing: Evolutionary Sociology." Pp. 405–33 in *Handbook of Sociological Theory*. Secaucus, NJ: Springer.

Lorber, Judith. 1998. "Reinventing the Sexes: The Biomedical Construction of Femininity and Masculinity." *Contemporary Society* 27(5):498–99.

Lorber, Judith. 2009. *Gender Inequality: Feminist Theories and Politics*. New York: Oxford University Press.

Lorber, Judith and Lisa Jean Moore. 2007. *Gendered Bodies*. Los Angeles, CA: Roxbury.

Lorber, Judith and Lisa Jean Moore. 2011. *Gendered Bodies: Feminist Perspectives*, 2nd ed. New York: Oxford University Press.

Lorillard, Didi. 2011. "What's Going on With the Venerable State of Marriage?" *GoLocal Lifestyle*. Retrieved June 4, 2012 (www.golocalprov.com/lifestyle/modern-manners-etiquette-sharing-household-chores/).

Los Angeles Times. 2008. "Kenyans Recall the Screams of the Dying in Burning Church." January 3. Retrieved June 3, 2008 (http://articles.latimes.com/2008/jan/03/world/fg-church3).

Lotfi Yaser, Ali Ayar, and Simin Shams. 2012. "The Relation Between Religious Practice and Committing Suicide: Common and Suicidal People in Darehshahr, Iran." *Procedia—Social and Behavioral Sciences* July 16–18(50):1051–60.

Louk, Malysa Stratton. 2012. "Canadian Blogger Sentenced to Death in Iran; Journalists Detained." *Digital Journal*, January 30. Retrieved June 1, 2013 (http://digitaljournal.com/article/318744).

Loveless, Tom. 2009. "Tracking and Detracking: High Achievers in Massachusetts Middle Schools." Thomas B. Fordham Institute. Retrieved April 17, 2010 (http://edexcellence.net/. . ./news_tracking-and-detracking-high-achievers-in-massachusetts-middle-schools).

Loveless, Tom. 2013. "The Resurgence of Ability Grouping and Persistence of Tracking." The Brookings Institute, March 19. Retrieved July 8, 2013 (www.brookings.edu/research/reports/2013/03/18-tracking-ability-grouping-loveless?cid=em_brown032013).

Lowrey, Annie. 2013. "Slowdown in Health Costs' Rise May Last as Economy Revives." *New York Times,* May 6. Retrieved July 15, 2013 (www.nytimes.com/2013/05/07/business/slowdown-in-rise-of-health-care-costs-may-persist.html?pagewanted=all&_r=0).

Loy, Irwin. 2012. "Observers: Cambodian Vote Improved but Problems Remain." *Voice of America.* Retrieved July 25, 2012 (www.voanews.com/content/observers-cambodian-elections-improved-but-problems-remain/1146999.html).

Lucal, Betsy. 1999. "Building Boxes and Policing Boundaries: (De)constructing Intersexuality, Transgender and Bisexuality." *Sociology Compass.* Retrieved April 8, 2011 (www.blackwell-compass.com/subject/sociology/article_view?article_id=soco_tr_bpl100).

Lucas, Samuel R. and Mark Berends. 2002. "Sociodemographic Diversity, Correlated Achievement, and De Facto Tracking." *Sociology of Education* 75(4):328–48.

Luhby, Tami. 2012. "Worsening Wealth Inequality by Race." *CNN Money,* June 21. Retrieved April 28, 2013 (http://money.cnn.com/2012/06/21/news/economy/wealth-gap-race/index.htm).

Luhman, Reid and Stuart Gilman. 1980. *Race and Ethnic Relations: The Social and Political Experience of Minority Groups.* Belmont, CA: Wadsworth.

Lumsden, Charles J. and Edward O. Wilson. 1981. *Genes, Mind, and Culture: The Coevolutionary Process.* Cambridge, MA: Harvard University Press.

Luscombe, Belinda. 2010. "Marriage: What's It Good For?" *Time* 176(November 29):48–56.

Lutz, Ashley. 2012. "These 6 Corporations Control 90% of the Media in America. *Business Insider*, June 14. Retrieved June 30, (www.businessinsider.com/these-6-corporations-control-90-of-the-media-in-america-2012-6).

Ma, Yngyi and Gokhan Savas. 2014. "Which Is More Consequential: Fields of Study or Institutional Selectivity?" *The Review of Higher Education* 37(2):221–47.

Machiavelli, Niccolò. [1532] 2010. *The Prince.* Hollywood, FL: Simon & Brown.

MacDorman, Marian F. and T. J. Mathews. 2011. "Understanding Racial and Ethnic Disparities in U.S. Infant Mortality Rates." Centers for Disease Control and Prevention, National Center for Health Statistics: Data Brief #74. Retrieved August 28, 2012 (www.cdc.gov/nchs/data/databriefs/db74.pdf).

Machalek, Richard, and Michael W. Martin. 2010. "Evolution, Biology, and Society: A Conversation for the 21st Century Classroom." *Teaching Sociology* 38(1):35–45.

Macionis, John. 2012. *Sociology,* 14th ed. Upper Saddle River, NJ: Prentice Hall.

Mackey, Robert. 2011, April 23. "Social Media Accounts of the Protests in Syria." The Lede Weblog, *New York Times.* Retrieved October 3, 2012 (thelede.blogs.nytimes.com).

Mackey, Robert. 2012. "Update on Rage Over Anti-Islam Film." The Lede Weblog, *New York Times*, September 12. Retrieved October 2, 2012 (thelede.blogs.nytimes.com).

Mackey, Robert and Liam Stack. 2012. "Obscure Film Mocking Muslim Prophet Sparks Anti-U.S. Protests in Egypt and Libya." The Lede Weblog, *New York Times*, September 11. Retrieved October 2, 2012 (thelede.blogs.nytimes.com).

MacLeod, Jay. 2008. *Ain't No Makin' It: Aspirations and Attainment in a Low-Income Neighborhood,* 3rd ed. Boulder, CO: Westview.

Madden, Mary, Amanda Lenhart, Maeve Duggan, Sandra Cortesi, and Urs Glasser. 2013. "Teens and Technology." Pew Internet and American Life Project, March 13. Retrieved December 6, 2013 (www.pewinternet.org/Reports/2013/Teens-and-Tech/Main-Findings/Teens-and-Technology.aspx).

Madden, Mary and Kathryn Zickuhr. 2011. "65% of Online Adults Use Social Networking Sites." *Pew Internet.* Retrieved May 25, 2012 (http://pewinternet.org/Reports/2011/Social-Networking-Sites.aspx).

"The Madoff Case: A Timeline." 2009. *The Wall Street Journal,* March 12. Retrieved November 5, 2009 (http://online.wsj.com/article/SB112966954231272304.html?mod=googlenews.wsj).

Madyun, Na'im and Moo Sung Lee. 2010. "The Influence of Female-Headed Households on Black Achievement." *Urban Education* 45(4):424–47.

Maglaty, Jeanne. 2011. "When Did Girls Start Wearing Pink?" Retrieved May 9, 2013 (www.smithsonianmag.com/arts-culture/When-Did-Girls-Start-Wearing-Pink.html).

Mahoney, Brian. 2012. "NBA 'Set The Tone' with Black Coaches." *Athletic Business Daily* E-News, April 27. Retrieved May 10, 2012 (http://athleticbusiness.com/articles/lexisnexis.aspx?Inarticleid=1654581846&Intopicid=136030023).

Makhmalbaf, Mohsen, producer. 2003. *Kandahar: The Sun Behind the Moon* (Film).

"Male Dominance Causes Rape." 2008. *Journal of Feminist Insight*, December 8. Retrieved April 8, 2011 (http://journaloffeministinsight.blogspot.com/2008/12/male-dominance-causes-rape.html).

"Mali 'at War' With Tuareg Rebels." 2009. *Aljazeera*, May 19. Retrieved August 29, 2014 (http://www.aljazeera.com/news/africa/2014/05/mali-at-war-with-tuareg-rebels-201451815152681548.html).

Malthus, Thomas R. [1798] 1926. *First Essay on Population 1798.* London: Macmillan.

Mann, Charles C. 2005. 1491: New Revelations of the Americas Before Columbus. New York: Alfred A. Knopf.

Mann, Thomas E. and Norman J. Ornstein. 2012. *It's Even Worse Than It Looks: How the American Constitutional System Collided With the New Politics of Extremism.* New York: Basic Books.

Manning, Jennifer E. 2011. "Membership of the 112th Congress: A Profile." Congressional Research Service Report to Congress. Retrieved April 22, 2011 (www.senate.gov/reference/resources/pdf/R41647.pdf).

Maoncha, Merculine. 2013. "Sustainability: Lake Nakuru in the Great Rift Valley." *Thomson Reuters*, April 22. Retrieved February 24, 2014 (http://sustainability.thomsonreuters.com/2013/04/19/youth-perspective-lake-nakuru-in-the-great-rift-valley/).

Maquila Solidarity Network. 2014. "Support Grows for Cambodian Garment Workers After Violent Government Crackdown." January 17. Retrieved January 18, 2014 (http://en.maquilasolidarity.org/).

Marcus, Richard R. 2008. "Kenya's Conflict Isn't 'Tribal.'" *Los Angeles Times*, January 24. Retrieved June 3, 2008 (www.latimes.com/news/opinion/la-oew-marcus24jan24,0,4231203.story).

Marger, Martin N. 2012. *Race and Ethnic Relations: American and Global Perspectives*, 9th ed. Belmont, CA: Wadsworth.

Markoff, John and Somini Sengupta. 2011. "Separating You and Me? 4.74 Degrees." *The New York Times,* November 21. Retrieved September 25, 2012 (www.nytimes.com/2011/11/22/technolgoy/between-you-and-me-4-74-degrees.html).

Marmor, Theodore R. 1999. *The Politics of Medicare,* 2nd ed. Hawthorne, NY: Aldine de Gruyter.

Marti, Geraldo. 2009. "Affinity, Identity, and Transcendence: The Experience of Religious Racial Integration in Diverse Congregations" *Journal for the Scientific Study of Religion* 48(March):54–96.

Martin, Jenny Beth and Mark Meckler. 2012. *Tea Party Patriots: The Second American Revolution.* New York: Henry Holt and Company.

Martin, Patricia Yancey and Robert A. Hummer. 1989. "Fraternities and Rape on Campus." *Gender and Society* 3(4):457–73.

Martin, Scott C. 2006. *From Temperance to Alcoholism in America.* Baltimore: Johns Hopkins University Press.

Martineau, Harriet. [1837] 1962. *Society in America.* Garden City, NY: Doubleday.

Martineau, Harriet. 1838. *How to Observe Manners and Morals.* London: Charles Knight & Co.

Martins, Nichole, Dmitri C. Williams, Kristen Harrison, and Rabindra A. Ratan. 2009. "A Content Analysis of Female Body Imagery in Video Games." *Sex Roles* 61:824–36.

Marty, Martin E., and R. Scott Appleby, eds. 1991. *Fundamentalism Observed.* Chicago: University of Chicago Press.

Marty, Martin E. and R. Scott Appleby, eds. 2004. *Accounting for Fundamentalism: The Dynamic Character of Movements.* Chicago: University of Chicago Press.

Marx, Karl. [1844] 1963. "Contribution to the Critique of Hegel's Philosophy of Right." Pp. 43–59 in *Karl Marx: Early Writings,* translated and edited by T. B. Bottomore. New York: McGraw-Hill.

Marx, Karl. [1844] 1964. *The Economic and Philosophical Manuscripts of 1844.* New York: International Publishers.

Marx, Karl and Friedrich Engels. [1848] 1969. *The Communist Manifesto.* Baltimore: Penguin.

Marx, Karl and Friedrich Engels. 1955. *Selected Work in Two Volumes.* Moscow: Foreign Language Publishing House.

Mashberg, Tom. 2002. "Med Examiner's Office Has Secret Body-Parts Deal." *Boston Herald* (May 20):1.

Mason-Schrock, Douglas. 1996. "Transsexual's Narrative Construction of the 'True Self.'" *Social Psychology Quarterly* 59(3):176–92.

Massey, Douglas S. 2007. Categorically Unequal: The American Stratification System. New York: Russell Sage.

Massey, Douglas S. and Nancy A. Denton. 1998. *American Apartheid: Segregation and the Making of the Underclass.* Cambridge, MA: Harvard University Press.

Masters, William H. and Virginia Johnson. 1966. *Human Sexual Response.* Boston: Little, Brown.

Masters, William H. and Virginia Johnson. 1970. *Human Sexual Inadequacy.* Boston: Little, Brown.

Mathews, T. J. and Marian F. MacDorman. 2008. "Infant Mortality Statistics From the 2005 Period Linked Birth/Infant Death Data Set." *National Vital Statistics Reports* 27(2). Retrieved January 23, 2010 (www.cdc.gov/nchs/data/nvsr/nvsr57/nvsr57_02.pdf).

Matson, John. 2013. "Women Are Earning Greater Share of STEM Degrees, But Doctorates Remain Gender-Skewed." *Scientific American Magazine*, April 23. Retrieved January 18, 2014 (www.scientificamerican.com/article.cfm?id=women-earnings-greater-share-stem-degrees-doctorates-remain-skewed).

Mattingly, Marybeth and Liana C. Sayer. 2006. "Under Pressure: Trends and Gender Differences in the Relationship Between Free Time and Feeling Rushed." *Journal of Marriage and Family* 68(1):205–21.

Mauksch, Hans. 1993. "Teaching of Applied Sociology: Opportunities and Obstacles." Pp. 1–7 in *Teaching Applied Sociology: A Resource Book,* edited by C. Howery. Washington, DC: American Sociological Association Teaching Resources Center.

Mauss, Armand. 1975. *Social Problems as Social Movements.* Philadelphia: Lippincott.

Mavalankar, Dileep V., Kranti S. Vora, K. V. Ramani, Parvathy Raman, Bharati Sharma, and Mudita Upadhyaya. 2009. "Maternal Health in Gujarat, India: A Case Study." *Journal of Health, Population, and Nutrition* 27(April):235–48.

Mawani, Vrushti. 2011. "Marriage Majestic. William-Kate Wedding to Cost $70 Million." *Industry Leaders Magazine*, April 29. Retrieved June 5, 2013 (www.industryleadersmagazine.com/marriage-majestic-william-kate-wedding-to-cost-70-million/).

Mayflower Church. 2013. "Social Justice: Earthwise Congregation." Retrieved June 24, 2013 (www.ucc.org/environmental-ministries/about-us.html).

Mayo Clinic. 2011. "Domestic Violence Toward Women: Recognize the Patterns and Seek Help." Retrieved January 21, 2013 (www.mayoclinic.com/health/domestic-violence/WO00044).

Mayoux, Linda. 2002. "Women's Empowerment or Feminisation of Debt? Towards a New Agenda in African Microfinance." Report at the One World Action Conference in London, March 21–22.

Mayoux, Linda, ed. 2008. *Sustainable Learning for Women's Empowerment: Ways Forward in Micro-Finance.* Warwickshire, UK: ITDG Publishing.

McAdam, Doug. 1999. *Political Process and the Development of Black Insurgency, 1930–1970,* 2nd ed. Chicago: University of Chicago Press.

McAdam, Doug. 2003. "Beyond Structural Analysis: Toward a More Dynamic Understanding of Social Movements." Pp. 281–98 in *Social Movements and Networks: Relational Approaches to Collective Action*, edited by Mario Diani and Doug McAdam. New York: Oxford University Press.

McArdle, Megan 2012. "The College Bubble: Is College a Lousy Investment?" *Newsweek*, September 17, pp. 22–26.

McCabe, Janice, Emily Fairchild, Liz Grauerholz, Bernice A. Pescosolido, and Daniel Tope. 2011. "Gender in Twentieth-Century Children's Books: Patterns of Disparity in Titles and Central Characters." *Gender and Society* 25(2):197–226.

McCaghy, Charles H., Timothy A. Capron, J. D. Jamieson, and Sandra Harley Carey. 2006. *Deviant Behavior: Crime, Conflict, and Interest Groups,* 7th ed. Boston: Allyn & Bacon.

McCarthy, John D. and Mayer N. Zald. 1977. "Resource Mobilization and Social Movements: A Partial Theory." *American Journal of Sociology* 82(6):1212–41.

McCormick, John. 1992. "A Housing Program That Actually Works." *Newsweek*, June 22, p. 61.

McCrone, David. 1998. *The Sociology of Nationalism.* London: Routledge.

McCrummen, Stephanie. 2008. "Women Run the Show in a Recovering Rwanda." *The Washington Post*, October 27. Retrieved May 6, 2011 (www.washingtonpost.com/wp-dyn/content/article/2008/10/26/AR2008102602197.html).

McEvoy, Alan W. and Jeff B. Brookings. 2008. *If She Is Raped: A Guidebook for the Men in Her Life,* 4th ed., abridged. Tampa, FL: Teal Ribbon Books.

McGuire, Meredith. 2002. *Religion: The Social Context,* 5th ed. Belmont, CA: Wadsworth.

McIntosh, Peggy. 1992. "White Privilege and Male Privilege: A Personal Account of Coming to See Correspondences through Work in Women's Studies." Pp. 70–81 in *Race, Class, and Gender: An Anthology,* edited by Margaret A. Anderson and Patricia Hill Collins. Belmont, CA: Wadsworth.

McIntosh, Peggy. 2002. "White Privilege: Unpacking the Invisible Knapsack." Pp. 97–101 in *White Privilege: Essential Readings on the Other Side of Racism,* edited by Paula S. Rothenberg. New York: Worth.

McKelvie, Samuel R. 1926. "What the Movies Meant to the Farmer." *Annals of the American Academy of Political and Social Science* 128(November):131.

McKernan, Signe-Mary, Caroline Ratcliffe, Eugene Steuerle, and Sisi Zhang. 2013. "Less Than Equal: Racial Disparities in Wealth Accumulation." *Urban Institute.* Retrieved May 11, 2014 (www.urban.org/UploadedPDF/412802-Less-Than-Equal-Racial-Disparities-in-Wealth-Accumulation.pdf).

McKie, Linda and Samantha Callan. 2012. *Understanding Families: A Global Introduction.* Thousand Oaks: Sage.

McKinley, James C. 2012. "Hip-Hope World Gives Gay Singer Support." *New York Times.* July 6. Retrieved September 15, 2013 (www.nytimes.com/2012/07/07/arts/music/frank-ocean-draws-praise-for-declaring-his-homosexuality.html?pagewanted=all&_r=0).

McKinnish, Terra, Randall Walsh, and Kirk White. 2008. "Who Gentrifies Low Income Neighborhoods?" Retrieved April 17, 2010 (papers.ssrn.com/so13/papers.cfm?abstract_id=1139352).

McMichael, Philip. 2012. *Development and Social Change: A Global Perspective.* Los Angeles: Sage.

McNall, Scott G. and Sally Allen McNall. 1983. *Plains Families: Exploring Sociology Through Social History.* New York: St. Martin's Press.

McPhail, Deborah, Brenda Beagan, and Gwen E. Chapman. 2012. "'I Don't Want to Be Sexist But . . .' Denying and Re-Inscribing Gender Through Food." *Food, Culture & Society* 15(3):473–89.

McVey, G., S. Tweed, and E. Blackmore. 2004. "Dieting Among Preadolescent and Young Adolescent Females." *CMAJ* (May 11): 1559–61. Retrieved May 23, 2012 (www.ncbi.nlm.nih.gov/pubmed/15136549).

Mead, Frank, Samuel Hill, and Craig Atwood, eds. 2005. *Handbook of Denominations in the United States,* 12th ed. Nashville, TN: Abingdon Press.

Mead, George Herbert. [1934] 1962. *Mind, Self, and Society.* Chicago: University of Chicago Press.

Mead, Margaret. [1935] 1963. *Sex and Temperament in Three Primitive Societies.* New York: William Morrow.

Mears, Bill. 2014. "Michigan's Ban on Affirmative Action Upheld by Supreme Court." *CNN Justice,* April 23. Retrieved May 11, 2014 (www.cnn.com/2014/04/22/justice/scotus-michigan-affirmative-action/).

Mehan, Hugh. 1992. "Understanding Inequality in Schools: The Contribution of Interpretive Studies." *Sociology of Education* 65(1):1–20.

Mehra, Bharat, Cecelia Merkel, and Ann P. Bishop. 2004. "The Internet for Empowerment of Minority and Marginalized Users." *New Media and Society* 6:781–802.

Mehsud, Saud. 2012. "Pakistani Girl Shot by Taliban Defied Threats for Years." *Reuters,* October 10. Retrieved October 11, 2012 (www.reuters.com/article/2012/10/10/us-pakistan-girl-family-idUSBRE8990T720121010).

Melton, J. Gordon. 1993. "Another Look at New Religions." *Annals of the American Academy of Political and Social Science* (May): 97–112.

Melton, J. Gordon, James Bevereley, Constance Jones, and Pamela S. Nadell. 2009 *Melton's Encyclopedia of American Religions,* 8th ed. Detroit, MI: Gale/Cengage.

Meltzer, B. 1978. "Mead's Social Psychology." Pp. 15–27 in *Symbolic Interactionism: A Reader in Social Psychology,* 3rd ed., edited by J. Manis and B. Meltzer. Boston: Allyn & Bacon.

Meltzer, Bernard N., John W. Petras, and Larry T. Reynolds. 1975. *Symbolic Interactionism: Genesis, Varieties and Criticism.* London: Routledge & Kegan Paul.

Memmott, Mark. 2013. "Teen Pregnancies Continue to Decline, New Report Shows." *NPR,* May 23. Retrieved July 12, 2013 (www.npr.org/blogs/thetwo-way/2013/05/23/186277188/teen-pregnancies-continue-to-decline-new-report-shows).

Mental Health America. 2011. "Bullying in Schools: Harassment Puts Gay Youth at Risk." Retrieved April 17, 2011 (www.nmha.org/index.cfm?objectid=CA866DCF-1372-4D20-C8EB26EEB30B9982).

Mercola, Dr. 2013. "Want More Tolerant Kids? Keep Them Away from the TV." December 12. Retrieved Jan. 17, 2014 (http://articles.mercola.com/sites/articles/archive/2013/12/12/children-watching-tv.aspx).

Merriam-Webster. 2014. "Black." Retrieved April 9, 2014 (www.merriam-webster.com/dictionary/black).

Merton, Robert K. 1938. "Social Structure and Anomie." *American Sociological Review* 3(October):672–82.

Merton, Robert K. [1942] 1973. *The Sociology of Science: Theoretical and Empirical Investigations.* Chicago: University of Chicago Press.

Merton, Robert K. 1948. "The Self Fulfilling Prophecy." *The Antioch Review* 8(2):193–210.

Merton, Robert K. 1949. "Discrimination and the American Creed." Pp. 99–126 in *Discrimination and American Welfare,* edited by Robert M. MacIver. New York: Harper.

Merton, Robert K. 1968. *Social Theory and Social Structure,* 2nd ed. New York: Free Press.

MetLife. 2013. *The MetLife Survey of the American Teacher: Challenges for School Leadership.* February. Retrieved July 8, 2013 (www.metlife.com/assets/cao/foundation/MetLife-Teacher-Survey-2012.pdf).

Metropolitan Community Churches. 2008. "Churches." Retrieved March 1, 2008 (www.mcchurch.org/AM/Template.cfm?Section=Find_an_MCC).

Metropolitan Community Churches. 2011. "Beliefs." Retrieved April 8, 2011 (http://www.blackwell-compass.com/subject/sociology/article_view?article_id=soco_tr_bpl100).

Metropolitan Community Churches. 2012. "Our Churches." Retrieved January 30, 2013 (http://mccchurch.org/our churches).

Meyer, Elaine. 2012. "Is the Wealth Gap Creating a Health Gap?" 2x2 Project, December 5. Retrieved May 13, 2014 (http://the2x2project.org/health-gap-wealth-gap/).

Michael, John. N.d. "Pros and Cons of Private Prisons." Retrieved February 9, 2012 (www.ehow.com/info_8110862_pros-cons-private-prisons.html).

Michels, Robert. [1911] 1967. *Political Parties.* New York: Free Press.

Migration Information Source. 2011. Retrieved May 15, 2011 (www.migrationinformation.org/Resources/unitedstates.cfm).

Mike, Valerie. 2003. "Evidence and the Future of Medicine." *Evaluation and the Health Professions* 26(2):127–52.

Mikkelson, Barbara and David P. Mikkelson. 2012. "Urban Legends." Retrieved January 1, 2012 (www.snopes.com/college/college.asp).

Milgram, Stanley. 1967. "The Small World Problem." *Psychology Today* 1:61–67.

Milkie, Melissa. 1999. "Social Comparisons, Reflected Appraisals, and Mass Media. The Impact of Pervasive Beauty Images on Black and White Girl's Self Concept." *Social Psychology Quarterly* 62(2):190–210.

Mills, C. Wright. 1956. *The Power Elite.* New York: Oxford University Press.

Mills, C. Wright. 1959. *The Sociological Imagination.* New York: Oxford University Press.

Mills, Theodore M. 1984. *The Sociology of Small Groups,* 2nd ed. Englewood Cliffs, NJ: Prentice Hall.

Milner, Murray. 2006. *Freaks, Geeks, and Cool Kids: American Teenagers, Schools, and the Culture of Consumption.* London: Routledge.

Mincy, Ronald B. 2006. *Black Males Left Behind.* Washington, DC: Urban Institute Press.

Minkoff, Debra C. 1995. *Organizing for Equality.* New Brunswick, NJ: Rutgers University Press.

"Misery of the Maquiladoras." 2011. *Socialist Worker,* November 18. Retrieved May 27, 2012 (http://socialistworker.org/2011/11/18/misery-of-the-maquiladoras).

Mishel, Lawrence and Natalie Sabadish. 2012. *CEO Pay and the Top 1%: How Executive Compensation and Financial-Sector Pay Have Fueled Income Inequality.* Economic Policy Institute, May 2. Retrieved June 5, 2013 (www.epi.org/publication/ib331-ceo-pay-top-1-percent/).

Misztal, Bronislaw and Anson D. Shupe. 1998. *Fundamentalism and Globalization: Fundamentalist Movements at the Twilight of the Twentieth Century.* Westport, CT: Praeger.

Moen, Bob. 2014. "Wyoming Becomes Latest to Legalize Gay Marriage." *ABC News.* October 21. Retrieved October 22, 2014 (http://abcnews.gocom/US/wireStory/wyoming-prepares-legalize-sex-marriage-26336559)

Molotch, Harvey. 2003. Where Stuff Comes From: How Toasters, Toilets, Cars, Computers, and Many Other Things Come to Be as They Are. London: Routledge.

Moore, Valerie Ann. 2001. "Doing Racialized and Gendered Age to Organize Peer Relations: Observing Kids in Summer Camp." *Gender and Society* 15(6):835–58.

Morello, Carol, and Dan Keating. 2009. "Number of Foreign-Born U.S. Residents Drops." September 22. Retrieved January 5, 2010 (www.washingtonpost.com/wp-dyn/content/article/2009/09/21/AR2009092103251.html).

Morey, Peter and Amina Yaqin. 2011. *Framing Muslims: Stereotyping and Representation After 9/11.* Cambridge, MA: Harvard University Press.

Morgan, David. 2012. "One in Four Americans Without Health Coverage." Reuters, April 19. Retrieved August 1, 2012 (www.reuters.com/article/2012/04/19/us-usa-healthcare-insurance-idUSBRE83117420120419).

Morris, Edward W. 2005. "From 'Middle Class' to 'Trailer Trash': Teachers' Perceptions of White Students in a Predominately Minority School." *Sociology of Education* 78(2):99–121.

Morris, Joan M. and Michael D. Grimes. 1997. *Caught in the Middle: Contradictions in the Lives of Sociologists From Working Class Backgrounds.* Westport, CT: Praeger.

Morris, Lloyd R. 1949. *Not So Long Ago.* New York: Random House.

Morris, Martina, Mark Stephen Handcock, Marc A. Scott, and Annette D. Bernhardt. 2001. *Divergent Paths: Economic Mobility in the New American Labor Market.* New York: Russell Sage.

Morrison, Maureen. 2010. "New Data Shed Light on Women's Internet Usage." *Ad Age*, August 3. Retrieved May 25, 2012 (http://adage.com/article/adagestat/data-research-women-s-internet-usage/145224/).

Morozov, Evgeny. 2009. "How Dictators Watch Us on the Web." *Prospect.* Retrieved October 9, 2012 (http://www.prospectmagazine.co.uk/magazine/how-dictators-watch-us-on-the-web/).

Mou, Yi and Wei Peng. 2009. "Gender and Racial Stereotypes in Popular Video Games." IGI Global OnDemand.

Muchhala, Bhumika. 2012. "Students Against Sweat Shops." Pp. 303–12 in *Globalization: The Transformation of Social Worlds,* 3rd ed., edited by D. Stanley Eitzen and Maxine Baca Zinn. Belmont, CA: Wadsworth.

"Mukhtar Mai—History of a Rape Case." 2005. BBC News. Retrieved July 13, 2008 (http://news.bbc.co.uk/2/hi/south_asia/4620065.stm).

Mumford, Lewis. 1961. *The City in History: Its Origins, Transformations, and Prospects.* New York: Harcourt, Brace, & World.

Munsey, Christopher. 2012. "Hostile Hallways." *American Psychological Association: Monitor on Psychology* 43(February):58.

Murdock, George Peter. 1967. *Ethnographic Atlas.* Pittsburgh: University of Pittsburgh Press.

Murray, Rheana. 2012. "PICTURED: Agony of the Child Brides Forced to Marry as Young as Six to Men up to Eight Times Their Age." October 12. Retrieved September 5, 2014 (www.dailynews.com/news/world/photos-life-child-bride-article-1.1182062).

Murstein, Bernard I. 1987. "A Clarification and Extension of the SVR Theory of Dyadic Pairing." *Journal of Marriage and the Family* 49(November):929–33.

"Muslims and Multicultural Backlash." 2011, July. Retrieved March 23, 2012 (http://harvardpress.typepad.com/hup_publicity/2011/07/framing-muslims-morey-yaqin.html).

Mutamba, John. 2005. "Strategies for Increasing Women's Participation in Government." Expert Group Meeting on Democratic Governance in Africa, Nairobi, Kenya, December 6–8.

Mydans, Seth. 2002. "In Pakistan, Rape Victims Are the 'Criminals." *New York Times*, May 17, p. A3.

Mydans, Seth. 2009. "For Khmer Rouge Guard, It Was Kill or Be Killed." March 1. Retrieved July 11, 2009 (www.nytimes .com/2009/03/01/world/asia/01iht-guard.1.20501994.html).

Myers, John P. 2003. *Dominant-Minority Relations in America: Linking Personal History With the Convergence in the New World.* Boston: Allyn & Bacon.

Myers, Steven Lee and Nicholas Kulish 2013. "Growing Clamor about Inequities of Climate Crisis." New York Times, November 16. Retrieved February 24, 2014 (www.nytimes .com/2013/11/17/world/growing-clamor-about-inequities-of-climate-crisis.html?_r=0).

Myrdal, Gunnar. 1964. *An American Dilemma.* New York: McGraw-Hill.

Nagai, Tyrone. 2010. "Multiracial Identity and the U.S. Census." *ProQuest Discovery Guides,* January (pp. 10–13). Retrieved January 21, 2013 (www.csa.com/discoveryguides/census/review.pdf).

Nagel, Joane. 1994. "Constructing Ethnicity: Creating and Recreating Ethnic Identity and Culture." *Social Problems* 41(1):152–76.

Nagourney, Adam and Rick Lyman. 2013. "Few Problems With Cannabis for California." *New York Times,* October 26. Retrieved October 27, 2013 (www.nytimes.com/2013/10/27/us/few-problems-with-cannabis-for-california.html?_r=0).

Nakamura, Lisa. 2004. "Interrogating the Digital Divide: The Political Economy of Race and Commerce in the New Media." Pp. 71–83 in *Society On-Line: The Internet in Context,* edited by Philip N. Howard and Steve Jones. Thousand Oaks, CA: Sage.

Nall, Jeff. 2012. "Combating Slavery in Coffee and Chocolate Production." *Toward Freedom,* January 5. Retrieved May 1, 2012 (http://www.towardfreedom.com/labor/2673-combating-slavery-in-coffee-and-chocolate-production).

Nancy Brown Diggs. 2011. *Hidden in the Heartland.* East Lansing, MI: Michigan State University Press.

National Alliance to End Homelessness. 2012. "The State of Homelessness in America 2012." Retrieved July 31, 2012 (www.endhomelessness.org/content/asrticle/detail/4361/).

National Alliance to End Homelessness. 2014. "Snapshot of Homelessness." Retrieval May 9, 2014 (http://www.endhomelessness.org/pages/snapshot_of_homelessness).

National Archives and Records Administration. 2008. "What Is the Electoral College?" Retrieved March 21, 2008 (www .archives.gov/federal-register/electoral-college/about.html).

National Center for Complementary and Alternative Medicine. 2013. "Complementary, Alternative or Integrative Health: What's in a Name?" *National Institutes of Health,* May. Retrieved March 10, 2014 (http://nccam.nih.gov/health/whatiscam).

National Center for Education Statistics. 2006. "Revenues and Expenditures for Public Elementary and Secondary Education" (Table 1). National Center for Education Statistics. Retrieved April 17, 2011 (http://nces.ed.gov/ccd/pubs/npefs03/tables.asp).

National Center for Education Statistics. 2011. "ACT Score Averages and Standard Deviations, by Sex and Race/Ethnicity, and Percentage of ACT Test Takers, by Selected Composite Score Ranges and Planned Fields of Study: Selected Years, 1995 through 2010" (Table 155). *Digest of Education Statistics.* Retrieved September 14, 2012 (http://nces.ed.gov/programs/digest/d10/tables/dt10_155.asp).

National Center for Education Statistics. 2012a. "Higher Education: Gaps in Assess and Persistence Study." Indicator 24: College Entrance Exams. Retrieved September 14, 2012 (http://nces.ed.gov/pubs2012/2012046/chapter 4_8.asp).

National Center for Education Statistics. 2012b. "Postsecondary Graduation Rates." Retrieved September 12, 2012 (http://nces.ed.gov/programs/coe/indicator_pgr.asp).

National Center for Education Statistics. 2012c. "Fact Facts: Do You Have Information on Postsecondary Enrollment Rates?" Institute of Education Sciences. Retrieved June 16, 2013 (Nces.ed.gov/fastfacts/display.asp?id=98).

National Center for Education Statistics. 2014. "Public High School Graduation Rates." *The Condition of Education.* Retrieved August 13, 2014 (http://nces.ed.gov/programs/coe/indicator_coi.asp).

National Center for Injury Prevention and Control. 2011. "The National Intimate Partner and Sexual Violence Survey: 2010." Atlanta, GA: Centers for Disease Control and Prevention, November. Retrieved May 29, 2012 (www.cdc.gov/ViolencePrevention/pdf/NISVS_Executive_Summary-a.pdf).

National Coalition on Health Care. 2008. "Health Insurance Cost." Retrieved April 17, 2010 (www.nchc.org OR www .whitehouse2.org/. . ./305-facts-from-the-national-coalition-on-health-care).

National Conference of State Legislatures. 2011. "The Affordable Care Act: A Brief Summary." Retrieved July 13, 2013 (www .ncsl.org/portals/1/documents/health/hraca.pdf).

National Conference of State Legislatures. 2013. "State Laws Regarding Marriages Between First Cousins." Retrieved April 21, 2013 (www.ncsl.org/issues-research/human-services/state-laws-regarding-marriages-between-first-cousi.aspx).

National Consumers League. 2013. "Parents: Take Control Over Your Child's Viewing, Surfing, and Texting Habits." Retrieved December 6, 2013 (www.ncinet.org/technology/149-parental-controls/537-parental-controls).

National Council of La Raza. 2011. "Who Makes Up the U.S. Hispanic Population?" Retrieved January 21, 2013 (www.nclr .org/index.php/about_us/faqs/most_frequently_asked_questions_about_hispanics_in_the_us/).

National Eating Disorders Association. 2009. "National Eating Disorders Association Unveils Powerful & Provocative Ad Campaign." Retrieved June 1, 2013 (http://mediasmarts.ca/body-image/body-image-advertising-and-magazines).

National Education Association. 2012. "Raising Compulsory School Age Requirements: A Dropout Fix?" NEA Education Policy and Practice Department, Center for Great Public Schools. Retrieved August 13, 2014 (www.nea.org/assets/docs/PB40raisingcompulsoryschoolage2012.pdf).

National Geographic Society. December 8, 2011. "7 Billion." Retrieved February 25, 2012 (http://itunes.apple.com/us/aoo/7-billion/id473524096?mt=8).

National Health Service Corps. 2011. "Mission and History." U.S. Department of Health and Human Services." Retrieved July 17, 2012 (http://nhsc.hrsa.gov/corpsexperience/aboutus/missionhistory/index.html).

National Institutes of Health. 2007. "The Use of Complementary and Alternative Medicine in the United States." Retrieved April 4, 2008 (http://nccam.nih.gov/news/camsurvey_fs1.htm).

National Institutes of Health. 2008. "10 Most Common CAM Therapies Among Adults." Retrieved February 9, 2013 (http://nccam.nih.gov/sites/nccam.nih.gov/files/news/cam stats/2007/72_dpi_CHARTS/chart4.htm).

National Institutes of Health. 2012. "Stem Cell Information: Stem Cell Basics." February 13. Retrieved March 7, 2012 (http://stemcells.nih.gov/info/basics/basics4.asp).

National Marriage Project. 2012. "About the National Marriage Project: Mission." Retrieved October 9, 2012 (http://nationalmarriageproject.org/about/).

National Opinion Research Center. 2010. "More Than 60% of Marriages Break Up Because of Adultery." Retrieved February 28, 2011 (www.norc.uchicago.edu/).

National Postsecondary Education Cooperative. 2004. "How Does Technology Affect Access in Postsecondary Education? What Do We Really Know?" (NPEC 2004–831), prepared by Ronald A. Phipps for NPEC Working Group on Access-Technology. Washington, DC.

National Public Radio. 2008. "Poppy Growing in Afghanistan." *Morning Edition,* February 9.

National Public Radio. 2010. "Affirmative Action: How Far Have We Come?" *All Things Considered,* August 15. Retrieved May 12, 2012 (www.npr.org/templates/story/story.php?storyId=129216337).

National Public Radio. 2013. "Closing the 'Word Gap' Between Rich and Poor." Retrieved January 5, 2014 (www.wbur.org/npr/257922222/closing-the-word-gap-between-rich-and-poor).

National Science Foundation. 2005. *Children, TV, Computers and More Media: New Research Shows Pluses, Minuses.* Retrieved July 20, 2006 (www.eurekalert.org/pub_releases/2005-02/nsf-ctc021005.php).

National Vital Statistics System, Centers for Disease Control and Prevention. 2011. "National Marriage and Divorce Rate Trends." Retrieved April 12, 2011 (www.cdc.gov/nchs/nvss/marriage_divorce_tables.htm).

National Women's Law Center. 2012. "Health Care and Reproductive Rights." July 5. Retrieved July 9, 2012 (www.nwlc.org/repro).

Nationmaster. 2010. "Crime Stats: China vs. Cuba." Retrieved July 5, 2011 (www.nationmaster.com/compare/China/Cuba/Crime).

Nationmaster. 2011. "United States Population Pyramids." Retrieved May 19, 2011 (www.nationmaster.com/country/us/Age_distribution).

NationMaster. 2014a. "Education: School Enrollment, Primary." Retrieved September 11, 2014 (http://www.nationmaster.com/country-info/stats/Education/School-enrollment,-primary/%25-net).

NationMaster. 2014b. "Physicians per 1,000 People." Retrieved September 15, 2014 (http://www.nationmaster.com/country-info/stats/Health/Physicians/Per-1%2C000-people).

Neuman, Michelle J. 2005. "Global Early Care and Education: Challenges, Responses, and Lessons." *Phi Delta Kappan* (November):188–92.

Neurological Correlates. 2008. "The 30% on Medicare Spent of Last-Year-of-Life Care: Let's Not Forget We're Humans." Retrieved January 8, 2010 (neurologicalcorrelates.com/wordpress/2008/03/12/about-30-of-medicare-is-spent-on-end-of-life-care-what-should-we-do-about-it).

New America Foundation. 2013. "Federal Education Budget Process: School Finance Federal, State, and Local K–12 School Finance Overview." June 30. Retrieved July 10, 2013 (http://febp.newamerica.net/background-analysis/school-finance).

New America Foundation, 2014a. "No Child Left Behind-Overview." April 24. Retrieved May 13, 2014 (http://febp.newamerica.net/background-analysis/no-child-left-behind-overview).

New America Foundation 2014b. "School Finance: Federal, State, and Local K–12 School Finance Overview." April 21. Retrieved May 13, 2014 (http://febp.newamerica.net/background-analysis/school-finance).

Newcombe, Tod. 2012. "Urban Areas Defy Crime Trends." *Governing the State and Localities,* August. Retrieved July 31, 2012 (www.governing.com/columns/urban-notebook/urban-areas-defy-crime-trends.html).

"New Federal Report: Sexual Abuse Plagues U.S. Prisons and Jails." 2010. *Just Detention,* August 26. Retrieved March 8, 2011 (www.businesswire.com/).

Newman, Andy. 2008. "What Women Want (Maybe)." *The New York Times,* June 12):E6.

Newman, David. 2009. *Families: A Sociological Perspective.* New York: McGraw-Hill.

Newman, Matthew L., Carla J. Groom, Lori D. Handelman, and James W. Pennebaker. 2008. "Gender Differences in Language Use: An Analysis of 14,000 Text Samples." *Discourse Process* 45:211–36.

New Media Trend Watch. 2013. "Demographics: Percentage of Population Online." Retrieved December 6, 2013 (www.newmediatrendwatch.com/markets-by-country/17-usa/123-demographics).

Newport, Frank. 2006. "Mormons, Evangelical Protestants, Baptists Top Church Attendance List." Gallup. Retrieved April 17, 2010 (www.gallup.com/. . ./mormons-evangelical-protestants-baptists-top-church-attendance-list.aspx).

Newport, Frank. 2009. "This Christmas, 78% of Americans Identify as Christian." Gallup, December 24. Retrieved September 26, 2012 (www.gallup.com/poll/124793/This-Christmas-78-Americans-Identify-Christian.aspx).

Newport, Frank. 2010. "American's Church Attendance Inches Up in 2010." Gallup, June 25. Retrieved September 20, 2012 (www.gallup.com/poll/141044/americans-church-attendance-inches-2010.aspx).

Newport, Frank. 2012a. "Nearly One in Five Americans Would Not Vote for a Mormon Presidential Candidate." Gallup, June 21. Retrieved September 24, 2012 (www.gallup.com/video/155270/Nearly-One-Five-Americans-Not-Vote-Mormon-Candidate.aspx).

Newport, Frank. 2012b. "The Highly Religious Choose Romney, the Less Religious, Obama." Gallup. Retrieved September 24, 2012 (www.gallup.com/video/154112/Highly-Religious-Choose-Romney-Less-Religious-Obama.aspx).

Newport, Frank. 2012c. "In U.S., 46% Hold Creationist View of Human Origins." Gallup, June 1. Retrieved September 24, 2012 (www.gallup.com/poll/155003/Hold-Creationist-View-Human-Origins.aspx).

Newport, Frank. 2012d. "Hispanic Catholics Pro-Obama; Non-Hispanic Catholics Pro Romney." Gallup, May 1. Retrieved September 24, 2012 (www.gallup.com/poll/154424/Hispanic-Catholics-Pro-Obama-Non-Hispanic-Catholics-Pro Romney.aspx).

Newport, Frank. 2012e. "More Than Nine in Ten Americans Continue to Believe in God." Gallup. Retrieved September 26, 2012 (www.gallup.com/poll/147887/americans-continue-believe-god.aspx).

Newport, Frank. 2012f. *God Is Alive and Well*. New York: Gallup Books.

Newport, Frank. 2013. "In U.S., Four in 10 Report Attending Church in Last Week." Retrieved January 28, 2014 (www.gallup.com/poll/166613/four-report-attending-church-last-week.aspx).

Newport, Frank and Igor Himelfarb. 2013. "In U.S., Record-High Say Gay, Lesbian Relations Morally OK." *Gallup Politics*, May 20. Retrieved January 18, 2014 (www.gallup.com/poll/162689/record-high-say-gay-lesbian-relations-morally.aspx).

Newport, Frank and Elizabeth Mendes. 2009. "About One in Six U.S. Adults Are Without Health Insurance." Gallup, July 22. Retrieved April 7, 2011 (http://www.gallup.com/poll/121820/one-six-adults-without-health-insurance.aspx).

The New York Times. 2013. "Syria—Uprising and Civil War." Retrieved January 20, 2013 (http://topics.nytimes.com/top/news/international/countriesandterritories/syria/index.html?8qa).

New York Times Almanac. 2011. "Major Languages of the World." New York: Penguin Reference, p. 505.

News of Future. 2012. "1 Million Hydrogen-Fueled Cars in U.S." Retrieved March 7, 2012 (www.newsoffuture.com/million_hydrogen_fueled_cars_in_us_future_energy.html).

Nichols, Larry A., George A. Mather, and Alvin J. Schmidt. 2006. *Encyclopedic Dictionary of Cults, Sects, and World Religions*, Revised and updated ed. Grand Rapids, MI: Zondervan.

Nightingale Alliance. 2007. "Fast Facts." Retrieved January 20, 2008 (www.nightingalealliance.org/cgi-bin/home.pl?section=3).

Niolon, Richard. 2010. "Children of Divorce and Adjustment." *PsychPage*, September 19. Retrieved June 26, 2012 (www.psychpage.com/family/childrenadjust.html).

Nock, Steven L., Laura Ann Sanchez, and James D. Wright. 2008. *Covenant Marriage: The Movement to Reclaim Tradition in America*. New Brunswick, NJ: Rutgers University Press.

Noel, Donald. 1968. "A Theory of the Origin of Ethnic Stratification." *Social Problems* 16(Fall):157–72.

Noguera, Pedro A. 2011. "A Broader and Bolder Approach Uses Education to Break Cycle of Poverty." *Phi Delta Kappan Magazine* 93(3):9–14.

Noguera, Pedro, and Robby Cohen. 2006. "Patriotism and Accountability: The Role of Educators in the War on Terrorism." *Phi Delta Kappan* 87(8):573–78.

Nolan, Cathal J. 2002. "Terrorism." Pp. 1648–49 and "War" in *The Greenwood Encyclopedia of International Relations*. London: Greenwood.

Nolan, Patrick and Gerhard Lenski. 2008. *Human Societies*. Boulder, CO: Paradigm.

Nolan, Patrick and Gerhard Lenski. 2010. *Human Societies: An Introduction to Macrosociology*, 11th ed. Boulder, CO: Paradigm.

Nolan, Patrick D., Jennifer Triplett, and Shannon McDonough. 2010. "Sociology's Suicide: A Forensic Autopsy." *The American Sociologist* 41:292–305.

No More Deaths. 2012. "Deaths on AZ Border Since October 1, 2011." Retrieved July 30, 2012 (www.nomoredeaths.org/Information/deaths.html).

The Non-Human Rights Project. 2014. Retrieved March 20, 2014 (www.nonhumanrightsproject.org/).

Nonprofit Vote. 2012. "America Goes to the Polls 2012." Retrieved June 2, 2013 (www.nonprofitvote.org).

North American Free Trade Agreement. 2011. "Mexico Is Taking Back Manufacturing Work." *Bloomberg News*. Retrieved May 27, 2012 (www.teamnafta.com/index.php/Latest/2011-Labor-and-Wage-Report-for-Mexico.html).

Norton, M. and Ariely D. 2011. "Building a Better America—One Wealth Quintile at a Time." *Perspectives in Psychological Science* 6(1):9–12.

Noss, David S. and John B. Noss. 1990. *A History of the World's Religions*. New York: Macmillan.

Nossiter, Adam. 2014. "Wielding Whip and a Hard New Law, Nigeria Tries to 'Sanitize' Itself of Gays." *New York Times*, February 8. Retrieved February 8, 2014 (www.nytimes.com/2014/02/09/world/africa/nigeria-uses-law-and-whip-to-sanitize-gays.html?hp&_r=0).

Nuclear Threat Initiative. 2010. "Obama's Nuclear Nonproliferation and Disarmament Agenda: Building Steam or Losing Traction." January 15. Retrieved April 10, 2010 (www.nti.org/e_research/e3_obama_administration_agenda.html).

Oakes, Jeannie. 2005. *Keeping Track: How Schools Structure Inequality*, 2nd ed. New Haven, CT: Yale University Press.

Oakes, Jeannie, Amy Stuart Wells, Makeba Jones, and Amanda Datnow. 1997. "Detracking: The Social Construction of Ability, Cultural Politics, and Resistance to Reform." *Teacher's College Record* 98(3):482–510.

Oberlander, Jonathan. 2002. "The U.S. Health Care System: On a Road to Nowhere?" *Canadian Medical Association Journal* 167(2):163–69.

O'Brien, Denise. 1977. "Female Husbands in Southern Bantu Societies." In *Sexual Stratification: A Cross-Cultural View*, edited by Alice Schlegel. New York: Columbia University Press

O'Brien, Jody. 2011. *The Production of Reality*, 5th ed. Thousand Oaks, CA: Sage

O'Connel, Sanjida. 1993. "Meet My Two Husbands." *Guardian*, March 4, Sec. 2, p. 12.

O'Connor, Liz, Gus Lubin and Dina Spector. 2013. "The Largest Ancestry Groups in the United States." Business Insider, August 13. Retrieved September 5, 2014 (www.businessinsider.com/largest-ethnic-groups-in-america-2013-8).

Occupational Outlook Handbook. 2012. "Agricultural Workers." *Bureau of Labor Statistics*. Retrieved July 30, 2012 (www.bls.gov/ooh/farming-fishing-and forestry/agricultural-workers.html).

OECD Family Database. 2010. "Cohabitation Rate and Prevalence of Other Forms of Partnership." Retrieved June 5, 2012 (www.oecd.org/dataoecd/52/27/41920080/pdf).

Office of Management and Budget. 2010. "Table of United States Metropolitan Statistical Areas." U.S. Census Bureau, March 29. Retrieved July 30, 2012 ().

Ogburn, William F. [1922] 1938. Social Change, With Respect to Culture and Original Nature. New York: Viking.

Ogburn, William F. 1933. *Recent Social Trends*. New York: McGraw-Hill.

Ogburn, William F. 1961. "The Hypothesis of Cultural Lag." Pp. 1270–73 in *Theories of Society: Foundations of Modern Sociological Theory*, Vol. 2, edited by Talcott Parsons, Edward Shils, Kaspar D. Naegele, and Jesse R. Pitts. New York: Free Press.

Ogburn, William F. 1964. In *On Culture and Social Change: Selected Papers,* edited by Otis Dudley Duncan. Chicago: University of Chicago Press.

Ogunwole, Stella U., Malcolm P. Drewery, Jr., and Merarys Rios-Vargas. 2012. "The Population with a Bachelor's Degree or Higher by Race and Hispanic Origin: 2006–2010." American Community Survey Briefs, U.S. Census, May. Retrieved February 10, 2013 (http://www.census.gov/prod/2012pubs/acsbr10-19.pdf).

Oi, Mariko. 2013. "Japan Crime: Why Do Innocent People Confess?" *BBC News Magazine,* January 2. Retrieved April 26, 2014 (www.bbc.com/magazine-20810572).

O'Keefe, J. H., and L. Cordain. 2004. "Cardiovascular Disease Resulting From a Diet and Lifestyle at Odds With Our Paleolithic Genome: How to Become a 21st-Century Hunter-Gatherer." *Mayo Clinic Proc.* 79(May):703–704, 707.

Oller, Kimbrough. 2006. "Development and Evolution in Human Vocal Communication." *Biological Theory* 1(4):349–51.

Olsen, Marvin E. 1970. "Power as a Social Process." Pp. 2–10 in *Power in Societies,* edited by Marvin Olsen. New York: Macmillan.

Olson, C. L., H. D. Schumaker, and B. P. Yawn. 1994. "Overweight Women Delay Medical Care." *Archives of Family Medicine* 3(10).

One in Four, Inc. N.d. Retrieved November 6, 2009 (www.oneinfourusa.org).

Ong, Michael, Elisa K. Tong, Quan Gan, Teh-wei Hu, Yuan Jiang, Yan Yang, and Yi Nan. 2007. "360 Million Smokers in China and High Prevalence of Smoking Among Physicians." *American Journal of Preventative Medicine,* August 8. Retrieved April 17, 2010 (www.news-medical.net/news/2007/08/08/28574.aspx).

OpenSecrets.org. 2012a. "Overview: Stats at a Glance." Retrieved June 7, 2013 (www.opensecrets.org/overview/index.php?cycle=2012&type=A&display=A).

OpenSecrets.org. 2012b. "2012 Presidential Race." Retrieved June 7, 2013 (www.opensecrets.org/pres12/#out).

Oregon Public Health Division. 2012. "Table 1: Characteristics of End-of-Life Care of 596 DWDA Patients Who Have Died From Ingesting a Lethal Dose of Medication as of February 29, 2012, by Year, Oregon, 1998–2011." Retrieved July 16, 2012 (http://www.compassionoforegon.org/wp-content/uploads/2010/08/year14-tbl-11.pdf).

Oregon's Euthanasia Law. 2010. "Law Library." Retrieved January 11, 2010 (http://law.jrank.org/pages/6602/Euthanasia-Oregon-s-Euthanasia-law.html).

Organisation for Economic Co-operation and Development. 2012. "Balance of Economic Power Will Shift Dramatically Over the Next 50 Years, Says OECD." Retrieved September 12, 2014 (http://www.oecd.org/newsroom/balanceofeconomicpowerwillshiftdramaticallyoverthenext50yearssaysoecd.htm).

Organisation for Economic Co-operation and Development. 2013. "Health at a Glance 2013: OECD Indicators." Retrieved May 28, 2014 (http://dx.doi.org/10.1787/health_glance-2013-en).

Organisation for Economic Co-operation and Development. 2014. "OECD Family Database—Trends in Parental Leave Policies Since 1970." Retrieved February 27, 2014 (www.oecd.org/els/family/PF2.5%20Trends%20in%20leave%20entitlements%20around%20childbirth%20since%201970%20-%2010%20oct%202012%20-%20FINAL.pdf).

"Organized Crime." 2011. Retrieved August 6, 2011 (http://law.jrank.org/pages/11951/Organized-Crime.html).

Ostroff, Stephen M. 2013 "Perspectives: The Role of the Traveler in Translocation of Disease." Chapter 1 in *Travelers' Health.* Retrieved March 10, 2014 (www.cdc.gov/travel/yellowbook/2014/chapter-1-introduction/perspective-the-role-of-the-traveler-in-translocation-of-disease).

Oswald, Ramona Faith. 2000. "A Member of the Wedding? Heterosexism and Family Ritual." *Journal of Social and Personal Relationships* 17(June):349–68.

Oswald, Ramona Faith. 2001. "Religion, Family, and Ritual: The Production of Gay, Lesbian, and Transgendered Outsiders-Within." *Review of Religious Research* 43(December):39–50.

Otieno, Christine. 2013. "Nigeria Polio." Immunising the Vaccine Fears." BBC News, April 26. Retrieved July 13, 2013 (www.bbc.co.uk/news/world-africa-22307412).

O'Toole, Tara and Donald A. Henderson. 2006. "A Clear and Present Danger: Confronting the Threat of Bioterrorism." Pp. 239–45 in *Globalization: The Transformation of Social Worlds,* edited by D. Stanley Eitzen and Maxine Baca Zinn. Belmont, CA: Wadsworth.

Otterman, Sharon. 2010. "Lauded Harlem Schools Have Their Own Problems." *New York Times.* October 12. Retrieved July 10, 2013 (www.nytimes.com/2010/10/13/education/13harlem.html?pagewanted=all&_r=0).

"Overseas Population Spending Threatened." 2006. *Popline* 29 (March/April):1.

Pager, Devah, Bruce Western, and Bart Bonikowski. 2009. "Discrimination in a Low Wage Labor Market: A Field Experiment." *American Sociological Review* 74(October): 777–99.

Palmer, Craig. 1989. "Is Rape a Cultural Universal? A Re-examination of the Ethnographic Data." *Ethnology* 28(Jan):1–16.

Palmer, Kim. 2012. "Young Home Buyers Seek 'Walkability.'" *Minneapolis Star Tribune,* August 6. Retrieved Aug. 10, 2012 (www.startribune.com/lifestyle/homegarden/164822116.html?refer=y).

Papalia, Diane E., and Ruth Duskin Feldman. 2011. *A Child's World: Infancy Through Adolescence,* 12th ed. Boston: McGraw-Hill.

Pareto, Vilfredo. [1911] 1955. "Mathematical Economics." In *Encyclopedie des Sciences Mathematique.* New York: Macmillan.

Park, Robert Ezra, Ernest W. Burgess, and Roderick D. McKenzie. [1925] 1967. *The City.* Chicago: University of Chicago Press.

Parker, Kim, and Wendy Wang. 2013. "Time in Work and Leisure, Patterns by Gender and Family Structure." *Pew Research Social and Demographic Trends.* Retrieved February 28, 2014 (www.pewsocialtrends.org/2013/03/14/modern-parenthood-roles-of-moms-and-dads-converge-as-they-balance-work-and-family/7/).

Parker-Pope, Tara. 2013. "Are Doctors Nicer to Thinner Patients?" *New York Times.* April 29. Retrieved October 29, 2013 (http://well.blogs.nytimes.com/2013/04/29/overweight-patients-face-bias/).

Parkinson, C. Northcote. 1957. *Parkinson's Law.* Boston: Houghton Mifflin.

Parsons, Talcott. 1951a. *The Social System*. New York: Free Press.

Parsons, Talcott. 1951b. *Toward a General Theory of Action*. New York: Harper & Row.

Parsons, Talcott. 1971. *The System of Modern Societies*. Englewood Cliffs, NJ: Prentice-Hall.

Parsons, Talcott. 1975. "The Sick Role and Role of the Physician Reconsidered." *Milbank Memorial Fund Quarterly* 53(3):257–78.

Parsons, Talcott, and Robert F. Bales. 1953. *Family, Socialization, and Interaction Process*. Glencoe, IL: Free Press.

Partners in Prepaid. 2012. "Haiti Leads in Mobile Payments." April 23. Retrieved June 8, 2013 (www.partnersinprepaid.com/topics/articles/haiti-leads-in-mobile-payments.html).

Passel, Jeffrey and D'Vera Cohn. 2012. "U.S. Foreign-Born Population: How Much Change From 2009 to 2010?" Pew Research Center, January 9. Retrieved July 30, 2012 (www.pewhispanic.org/2012/01/09/u-s-foreign-born-population-how-much-change-from-2009-to-2010/).

Pasternak, Susan. 2013. "Of That $554 Billion, Medicare Spent 28 Percent, or About $170 Billion, on Patients' Last Six Months Of Life." *The Medicare Newsgroup*, June 3. Retrieved July 13, 2013 (www.medicarenewsgroup.com/context/understanding-medicare-blog/understanding-medicare-blog/2013/06/03/end-of-life-care-constitutes-third-rail-of-u.s.-health-care-policy-debate).

Patriana, Zarah. 2013. "Hershey's and Fair Trade: Is it a Victory?" *Global Exchange,* May 7. Retrieved June 25, 2013 (www.globalexchange.org/blogs/fairtrade/2013/05/07/hersheys-and-fair-trade-is-it-a-victory/).

Paulson, Amanda. 2013. "Record Number of International Students: Where They're From, Where They Study." The Christian Science Monitor, November 11. Retrieved January 4, 2014 (www.csmonitor.com/USA/2013/1111/Record-number-of-international-students-where-they-re-from-where-they-study).

Paxton, Pamela and Tess Pearce. 2009. "How Does Social Class Affect Socialization Within The Family?" Exploring Social Science Research, April 24. Retrieved March 1, 2011 (http://ibssblog.wordpress.com/2009/04/24/how-dues-social-class-affect-socialisation-within-the-family/).

Paxton, Pamela and Melanie M. Hughes. 2007. *Women, Politics, and Power: A Global Perspective*. Thousand Oaks, CA: Pine Forge.

Payne, Ed. 2014. "Doctors Keep Brain-Dead Pregnant Woman on Life Support Until Baby's Birth." *CNN,* February 4. Retrieved February 3, 2014 (www.cnn.com/2014/02/04/world/americas/canada-brain-dead-woman/).

Pazzanese, Christina. 2013. "Understanding India's Rape Crisis" Retrieved January 17, 2013 (http://news.harvard.edu/gazette/story/2013/09/udnerstanding-indias-rape-crisis/).

PBS. 2012. "World's Biggest Congregation" *Religion and Ethics Newsweekly,* August 10. Retrieved October 3, 2012 (www.pbs.org/wnet/religionandethics/episodes/january-27-2012/worlds-biggest-congregation/10162/).

PBS Newshour. 2009. "Comparing International Health Care Systems." October 6. Retrieved January 25, 2010 (www.pbs.org/newshour/globalhealth/july-dec09/insurance_1006.html).

PBS Newshour. 2013. "Jordan Struggles with Next Door's Chaos and Influx of Syrian Refugees." Retrieved July 3, 2013 (www.pbs.org/newshour/bb/middle_east/jan-june13/jordan_05-31.html).

PBS NOW. 2009. "Africa: House Calls and Health Care." December 18.

Pearce, Fred. 2010. "As Longevity Grows, The World Might Become a Better Place." *Washington Post*, May 25. Retrieved July 28, 2011 (www.washingtonpost.com/wp-dyn/content/article/2010/05/24/AR2010052402607.html).

Peek, Lori. 2011. *Behind the Backlash: Muslim Americans After 9/11*. Philadelphia: Temple University Press.

Pelaez, Vicky. 2013. "The Prison Industry in the United States: Big Business or a New Form of Slavery?" *Global Research*, January 31. Retrieved June 3, 2013 (www.globalresearch.ca/the-prison-industry-in-the-united-states-big-business-or-a-new-form-of-slavery/8289).

Pellow, David Naguib. 2002. *Garbage Wars: The Struggle for Environmental Justice in Chicago*. Cambridge, MA: MIT Press.

People's Daily Online. 2011. March 11. Retrieved May 15, 2012 (http://english.peopledaily.com.cn/90001/98649/7315789.html).

PEPFAR. 2013. "Secretary of State John Kerry Marks Tenth Anniversary of PEPFAR." Retrieved July 15, 2013 (www.pepfar.gov/press/releases/2013/210773.htm).

Perez, Marvin G. 2013. "Coffee Consumption Increases in U.S., Association Survey Shows." *Bloomberg News,* March 22. Retrieved February 14, 2014 (www.bloomberg.com/news/2013-03-22/coffee-consumption-increases-in-u-s-association-survey-shows.html).

Perez, Miguel. 2011. "The Latino Backlash Is Coming Sooner Than Republicans Expected." April 6. Retrieved April 7, 2011 (http://www.paragoulddailypress.com/articles/2011/04/06/opinion/doc4d9ba4c6c2ef4312670875.txt).

Perlroth and Sanger. 2013. "Cyberattacks Seem Meant to Destroy, Not Just Disrupt." *New York Times,* March 28. Retrieved June 3, 2013 (www.nytimes.com/2013/03/29/technology/corporate-cyberattackers-possibly-state-backed-now-seek-to-destroy-data.html?pagewanted=all)/.

Persell, Caroline Hodges. 2005. "Race, Education, and Inequality." pp. 286–24 in *Blackwell Companion to Social Inequalities,* edited by M. Romero and E. Margolis. Oxford, UK: Blackwell.

Persell, Caroline Hodges and Peter W. Cookson, Jr. 1985. "Chartering and Bartering: Elite Education and Social Reproduction." *Social Problems* 33(2):114–29.

Pescosolido, Bernice A., 1992. "Beyond Rational Choice: The Social Dynamics of How People Seek Help." *American Journal of Sociology* 97(4):1113.

Pescosolido, Bernice A. and Carol A. Boyer. 2010. "The American Health Care System: Beginning the 21st Century With High Risk, Major Challenges, And Great Opportunities." Pp. 391–411 in *The New Blackwell Companion to Medical Sociology,* edited by William C. Cockerham. Malden, MA: Wiley-Blackwell.

Pescosolido, Bernice A. and Sharon Georgianna. 1989. "Durkheim, Suicide, and Religion: Toward a Network Theory of Suicide." *American Sociological Review* 54(February):33–48.

Pettigrew, Thomas F. and Linda R. Tropp. 2000. "Does Intergroup Contact Reduce Prejudice? Recent Meta-Analytic Findings." Pp. 93–114 in *Reducing Prejudice and Discrimination,* edited by Stuart Oskamp. London: Psychology Press, Taylor and Francis Group.

Pew Center on the States. 2011. "State of Recidivism: The Revolving Door of American Prisons." The Per Charitable Trusts, April 3, p. 2. Retrieved April 16, 2012 (www.percent eronthestates.org/initiatives_detail.aspx?initiativeID).

Pew Charitable Trusts. 2012. *Pursuing the American Dream: Economic Mobility Across Generations*. Retrieved June 7, 2013 (www.pewstates.org/uploadedFiles/PCS_Assets/2012/Pursuing_American_Dream.pdf).

Pew Forum on Religion and Public Life. 2008. "U.S. Religious Landscape Survey, 2008." Retrieved March 2, 2008 (http://religions.pewforum.org/pdf/report-religious-landscape-study-full.pdf).

Pew Forum on Religion and Public Life. 2009. "Most Latino Evangelicals Pray Every Day." June 11. Retrieved September 26, 2012 (www.pewforum.org/Frequency-of-Prayer/Most-Latino-Evangelicals-Pray-Every-Day.aspx).

Pew Forum on Religion and Public Life. 2012a. "'Nones' on the Rise: One-in-Five Adults Have No Religious Affiliation." Retrieved October 10, 2012 (www.pewforum.org/uploaded Files/Topics/Religious_Affiliation/Unaffiliated/NonesOn TheRise-full.pdf October 9).

Pew Forum on Religion and Public Life. 2012b. "U.S. Religious Landscape Survey." September 18. Retrieved September 18, 2012 (http://religions.pewforum.org/reports).

Pew Forum on Religion and Public Life. 2008. "Chapter 1: Religious Beliefs and Practices." *U.S. Religious Landscape Survey*, June. Retrieved September 12, 2014 (http://reli gions.pewforum.org/pdf/report2-religious-landscape-study-full.pdf).

Pew Forum on Religion and Public Life. 2013. "Changing Attitudes on Gay Marriage." Retrieved July 12, 2013 (http://features.pewforum.org/same-sex-marriage-attitudes/slide3.php).

Pew Hispanic Center. 2011. "Hispanics Account for 56% of Nation's Growth in Past Decade." Retrieved April 7, 2011 (http://pewhispanic.org/).

Pew Internet and American Life Project. 2010. "Change in Internet Access by Age Group, 2000–2009." February 3. Retrieved February 27, 2011 (www.pewinternet.org/Infographics/2010/Internet-access-by-age-group-over-time.aspx).

Pew Internet and American Life Project. 2012. "Demographics of Internet Users." Retrieved March 5, 2012 (http://www.pewin ternet.org/Static-Pages/trend-Data/Whos-Online.aspx).

Pew Research Center. 2010a. "The Decline of Marriage and Rise of New Families." *Pew Social & Demographic Trends*, November 18. Retrieved March 8, 2012 (www.pewsocialtrends .org/2010/11/18/the-decline-of-marriage-and-rise-of-new-families/).

Pew Research Center. 2010b. *Gender Equality Universally Embraced, but Inequalities Acknowledged*. July 1. Retrieved July 9, 20113 (www.pewglobal.org/files/pdf/Pew-Global-Attitudes-2010-Gender-Report.pdf).

Pew Research Center. 2011. "The Generation Gap and the 2012 Election." November 3. Retrieved July 29, 2012 (www.peo ple-press.org/2011/11/03/section-1-how-generations-have-changed/).

Pew Research Center Internet and American Life Project. 2012. "Teens Fact Sheet." Retrieved August 29, 2014 (http://www .pewinternet.org/fact-sheets/teens-fact-sheet/).

Pew Research Center Internet and American Life Project. 2014. "Social Networking Fact Sheet." Retrieved May 11, 2014 (www.pewinternet.org/fact-sheets/social-networking-fact-sheet/).

Pew Research Center for the People and the Press. 2012. "More Support for Gun Rights, Gay Marriage Than in 2008, 2004." Retrieved July 12, 2013 (www.people-press.org/files/legacy-pdf/4-25-12%20Social%20Issues.pdf).

Pew Research Center Religion and Public Life Project. 2014. "Gay Marriage Around the World." *Religion and Public Life Report*, February 5. Retrieved Feb 19, 2014 (www.pewforum.org/2013/12/19/gay-marriage-around-the-world-2013/).

Phillips, Richard. 2013. "Animal Communication" Lecture at *Tuesdays with a Liberal Arts Scholar*, University of Minnesota, May 6.

Phipher, Mary. 1994. Reviving Ophelia: Saving the Selves of Adolescent Girls. New York: Ballantine Books.

Phoenix Declaration. 2012. "A New Declaration for a New Decade." Retrieved September 20, 2012 (www.nolongersilent .org/Phoenix-Declaration-2012.html).

Phys.Org. 2009. "Humans Spread Out of Africa Later." Retrieved October 9, 2012 (http://phys.org/news171286860.html).

Piaget, Jean. 1989. *The Child's Conception of the World*. Savage, MD: Littlefield, Adams Quality Paperbacks.

Piaget, Jean, and Barbel Inhelder. [1955] 1999. *Growth of Logical Thinking*. London: Routledge & Kegan Paul.

Pickard, Ruth, and Daryl Poole. 2007. "The Study of Society and the Practice of Sociology." Previously unpublished essay.

Pieterse, Jan Nederveen. 2004. *Globalization and Culture*. Lanham, MD: Rowman & Littlefield.

"Plan for Lifetime Success Through Education." 2008. Retrieved April 17, 2010 (www.barackobama.com/pdf/issues/Prek-12EducationFactSheet.pdf; www.americanthinker.com/2008/. . ./obamas_national_public_educati.html).

Plass, Jan L, with Melissa Biles, Jonathan Frye, and Tsu-Ting Huang. 2012. "Video Games & the Future of Learning." New York University, April 30. Retrieved July 8, 2013 (www.nyu .edu/about/news-publications/publications/connect-infor mation-technology/2012/04/30/video-games-and-the-future-of-learning.html).

Plato. [ca. 350 BCE] 1960. *The Laws*. New York: Dutton.

Ploughshares. 2011. "Armed Conflicts Report." Retrieved July 13, 2012 (www.ploughshares.ca/content/armed-conflicts-report-0).

Plumer, Brad. 2013. "Ten Charts Show How the U.S. Has Changed for The Better since MLK's Speech." *The Washington Post Wonkblog*, August 28. Retrieved September 29, 2013 (www .washingtonpost.com/blogs/wonkblog/wp/2013/08/28/ten-charts-show-how-the-u-s-has-changed-for-the-better-since-mlks-march/).

Political Geography Now. 2014. "How Many Countries Are There in the world?" February. Retrieved May 22, 2014 (www.pol geonow.com/2011/04/how-many-countries-are-there-in-the-world.html).

Pollack, William. 1999. Real Boys: Rescuing Our Sons From the Myths of Boyhood. New York: Owl Books.

Pollard, Kelvin. 2011. "The Gender Gap in College Enrollment and Graduation." *Population Reference Bureau*. Retrieved September 12, 2012 (www.prb.org/Articles/2011/gender-gap-in-education.aspx).

"Pope Condones Condom Use in Exceptional Cases – Book." 2010. *BBC News*, November 20. Retrieved July 11, 2013 (www.bbc.co.uk/news/world-europe-11804398).

Popenoe, David. 2002. "Debunking Divorce Myths." *National Marriage Project.* New Brunswick, NJ: Rutgers. Retrieved November 30, 2009 (health.discovery.com/centers/loverelationships/articles/divorce.html).

Population Reference Bureau. 2010a. "World Population Clock." Retrieved May 13, 2011 (www.prb.org/Articles/2010/worldpopulationclock2010.aspx).

Population Reference Bureau. 2010b. "World Population Data Sheet." Retrieved July 27, 2011 (www.prb.org/pdf10/10wpds_eng.pdf).

Population Reference Bureau. 2012a. "Fact Sheet: World Population Trends 2012." Retrieved August 25, 2012 (www.prb.org/Publications/Datasheets/2012/world-population-data-sheet/fact-sheet-world-population.aspx).

Population Reference Bureau. 2012b. "Human Population: Women." Retrieved August 25, 2012 (www.prb.org/educators/teachersguides/humanpopulation/women.aspx).

Population Reference Bureau. 2012c. "PRB's 2012 World Population Clock." Retrieved June 9, 2013 (www.prb.org/Publications/Datasheets/2012/2012populationclock.aspx).

Population Reference Bureau. 2012d. "World Population Data Sheet." Retrieved August 25, 2012 (www.prb.org/pdf12/2012-population-data-sheet_eng.pdf).

Population Reference Bureau. 2013a. "Rate of Natural Increase." Retrieved March 17, 2014(www.prb.org/DataFinder/Topic/Rankings.aspx?ind=16).

Population Reference Bureau. 2013b. "Total Fertility Rate, 2012." Retrieved February 7, 2013 (http://www.prb.org/DataFinder/Topic/Rankings.aspx?ind=17).

Population Reference Bureau. 2013c. "Traditional Families Account for Only 7 Percent of U.S. Households." Retrieved February 24, 2014 (www.prb.org/Publications/Articles/2003/TraditionalFamiliesAccountforOnly7PercentofUSHouseholds.aspx).

Population Reference Bureau. 2013d. "World Population Growth, 1950–2050: Exponential Growth." Retrieved February 5, 2013 (www.prb.org/Educators/TeachersGuides/HumanPopulation/PopulationGrowth.aspx).

Population Reference Bureau. 2013e. "The World's Youth 2013 Data Sheet." Retrieved May 12, 2014 (www.prb.org/Publications/Datasheets/2013/youth-datasheet-2013.aspx/).

Potok, Mark. 2013a. "DOJ Study: More Than 250,000 Hate Crimes a Year, Most Unreported." Southern Poverty Law Center, March 26. Retrieved June 1, 2013 (www.splcenter.org/blog/2013/03/26/doj-study-more-than-250000-hate-crimes-a-year-a-third-never-reported/).

Potok, Mark. 2013b. "The Year in Hate and Extremism." *Intelligence Report* 149. Retrieved November 9, 2013 (http://www.splcenter.org/home/2013/spring/the-year-in-hate-and-extremism).

Potok, Mark. 2013c. "Editorial: Boston and Beyond." *Intelligence Report* 150. Retrieved June 17, 2013 (www.splcenter.org/get-informed/intelligence-report/browse-all-issues/2013/summer/boston-and-beyond).

Powell, Andrea D. and Arnold S. Kahn. 1995. "Racial Differences in Women's Desires to Be Thin." *International Journal of Eating Disorders* 17(2):191–95.

Powell, Brian, Catherine Bolzendahl, Claudia Geist, and Lala Carr Steelman. 2010. *Counted Out: Same-Sex Relations and Americans' Definitions of Family.* New York: Russell Sage Foundation.

Powley, Elizabeth. 2003. "Strengthening Governance: The Role of Women in Rwanda's Transition." In *Women Waging Peace,* edited by S. N. Anderlini. Washington, DC: Hunt Alternatives Fund.

Pramis, Joshua. 2013. "Number of Mobile Phones to Exceed World Population by 2014." February 28. Retrieved January 6, 2014 (www.digitaltrends.com/mobile/mobile-phone-world-population-2014/).

Preston, David L. 1988. *The Social Organization of Zen Practice: Constructing Transcultural Reality.* Cambridge, UK: Cambridge University Press.

Preston, Jennifer. 2011. "The Year in Media: Social Media and Egypt's Revolution." Media Decoder Weblog, *New York Times,* December 21. Retrieved October 6, 2012 (http://mediadecoder.blogs.nytimes.com).

"Primary Calendar: Democratic Nominating Contests." *New York Times.* 2008. Retrieved March 30, 2008 (http://politics.nytimes.com/election-guide/2008/primaries/democraticprimaries/index.html).

Project Ploughshares. 2013. "Armed Conflicts Report." Retrieved May 23, 2014 (http://batchgeo.com/map/01f8889add78ece0a88eccffc6d000cb).

Project Vote Smart. 2008. "State Presidential Primary and Caucus Dates." Retrieved April 17, 2010 (www.votesmart.org/election_president_state_primary_dates.php).

Proudman, Charlotte Rachael. 2012. "Sex and Sharia: Muslim Women Punished for Failed Marriages." *The Independent,* April 2. Retrieved May 24, 2012 (http://blogs.independent.co.uk/2012/04/02/sex-and-sharia-muslim-women-punished-for-failed-marriages/).

Putnam, Robert. 2001. *Bowling Alone: The Collapse and Revival of American Community.* New York: Simon & Schuster.

Pyle, Ralph E. 2006. "Trends in Religious Stratification: Have Religious Group Socioeconomic Distinctions Declined in Recent Decades?" *Sociology of Religion* 67(Spring):61–79.

Quesnal-Vallee and Jenkins. 2010. "Social Policies and Health Inequalities." Pp. 455–83 in *The New Blackwell Companion to Medical Sociology,* edited by William C. Cockerham. Malden, MA: Wiley/Blackwell.

Quinney, Richard. 2002. *Critique of Legal Order: Crime Control in Capitalist Society.* New Brunswick, NJ: Transaction.

Radcliffe-Brown, A. R. 1935. "On the Concept of Functional in Social Science." *American Anthropologist* 37(3):394–402.

Radelet, Michael L. and Traci L. Lacock. 2009. "Do Executions Lower Homicide Rates? The Views of Leading Criminologists." *The Journal of Criminal Laws and Criminology* 99(2).

Raina, Shruti. 2012. "Gender Bias in Education." *International Journal of Research Pedagogy and Technicalogy in Education* 1(2):37–45. Retrieved July 10, 2013 (http://ijems.net/issue02Dec.IJEMSp05.pdf).

Rani, M., S. Bonu, and N. Diop-Sidibe. 2004. "An Empirical Investigation of Attitudes Towards Wife-beating Among Men and Women in Seven Sub-Saharan African Countries." *African Journal of Reproductive Health* 8(3):116–36.

Rankin, Bruce H. and Işik A. Aytaç. 2006. "Gender Inequality in Schooling: The Case of Turkey." *Sociology of Education* 79(1):25–43.

Ranu, Manju, Sekhur Bonu, and Nafissalon Diop-Sidibe. 2004. "An Empirical Investigation of Attitudes Towards Wife-Beating Among Men and Women in Seven Sub-Saharan African Countries." *African Journal of Reproductive Health*. Women's Health and Action Research Centre. Retrieved June 3, 2012 (www.jstor.org/discover/10.2307/3583398?uid=3739840&uid=2129&uid=2&uid=70&uid=4&uid=3739256&sid=56228966303).

Rappoport, Leon. 2003. *How We Eat: Appetite, Culture and the Psychology of Food*. Toronto, Ontario, Canada: ECW Press.

Read, Kristen. 2011. "Number of Internet Users Worldwide Climbs to 2 Billion." UN International Telecommunications Union, January 28. Retrieved March 18, 2011 (http://graphicartsmag.com/news/2011/01/number-of=internet-users-worldwide).

Reason. 2011. "In-Depth Study: After Divorce, 44% of Women Fell Into Poverty." *Family Research Council,* May 31. Retrieved June 6, 2012 (http://primacyofreason.blogspot.com/2011/05/in-depth-study-after-divorce-44-of_31.html).

Regnerus, Mark D. 2007. *Forbidden Fruit: Sex and Religion in the Lives of American Teenagers*. New York: Oxford University Press.

Regnerus, Mark. 2012. "How Different Are the Adult Children of Parents Who Have Same-Sex Relationships? Findings From the New Family Structures Survey." *Social Science Research* 41(4):752–70.

Reich, Ashley. 2013. "This Map Of U.S. Divorce Rates Shows Where Marriages Go to Die." *Huffington Post,* November 4. Retrieved February 26, 2014 (www.huffingtonpost.com/2013/11/04/us-divorce-rate_n_4184261.html).

Reid, T. R. 2009. *The Healing of America: A Global Quest for Better, Cheaper and Fairer Health Care*. New York: Penguin Press.

Reid, Scott A. and Sik Hung Ng. 2006. "The Dynamics of Intragroup Differentiation in an Intergroup Social Context." *Human Communication Research* 32:504–525.

Reiman, Jeffrey and Paul Leighton. 2010a. The Rich Get Richer and the Poor Get Prison: Ideology, Class, and Criminal Justice, 9th ed. Boston: Pearson.

Reiman, Jeffrey and Paul Leighton. 2010b. *The Rich Get Richer and the Poor Get Prison: A Reader*. Boston: Allyn & Bacon.

Reinhardt, Uwe E. 2008. "Why Does U.S. Health Care Cost So Much? (Part II: Indefensible Administrative Costs)." *New York Times,* November 21. Retrieved August 28, 2012 (http://economix.blogs.nytimes.com/2008/11/21/why-does-us-health-care-cost-so-much-part-ii-indefensible-administrative-costs/).

Religious Congregations and Membership Study. 2010. "2010 U.S. Religion Census." Retrieved September 25, 2012 (www.rcms2010.org/compare.php).

Religious Tolerance. 2006. "Trends Among Christians in the U.S." Retrieved December 13, 2009 (www.religioustolerance.org/chr_tren.htm).

Religious Tolerance. 2009. "U.S. Divorce Rates for Various Faith Groups, Age Groups, and Geographic Areas." Retrieved April 17, 2010 (www.religious tolerance.org/chr_dira.htm).

Religious Tolerance. 2010. "Stem Cell Research: All Viewpoints." Retrieved September 8, 2012 (www.religioustolerance.org/res_stem.htm).

Religious Tolerance. 2012. "The Status of Women, Currently and Throughout History." Retrieved November 30, 2012 (http://www.religioustolerance.org/women.htm).

ReligiousTolerance.org. 2013. "Inclusive Religious Websites." Retrieved July 12, 2013 (www.religioustolerance.org/var_rel.htm).

Religious Tolerance. 2014. "Stem Cell Research: All Viewpoints." Retrieved March 4, 2014 (www.religioustolerance.org/res_stem.htm).

Religious Worlds. 2007. "New Religious Movements." Retrieved August 14, 2008 (www.religiousworlds.com/newreligions.html).

Renick, Oliver. 2011. "Disconnected: 70 Percent of World Doesn't Have Internet, Despite Rising Phone Usage." *Laptop,* October 31. Retrieved May 18, 2012 (http://blog.laptopmag.com/disconnected-70-percent-of-world-doesn%E2%80%99t-have-internet-despite-rising-phone-usage).

Renzetti, Claire. 2003. "Urban Violence Against Women." *Speech,* September 30, Dayton, OH: Wright State University.

Residents of Hull House. [ca. 1895] 1970. *Hull House Maps and Papers*. New York: Arno.

Reuters. 2011. "France Starts Ban on Full-Face Veil, Factbox on Veils In Europe." Reuters, April 11. Retrieved May 25, 2012 (http://blogs.reuters.com/faithworld/2011/04/11/france-starts-ban-on-full-face-veil-factbox-on-veils-in-europe/).

Reuters. 2012. "91 Are Charged With Fraud, Billing Millions to Medicare." *The New York Times,* October 4. Retrieved October 6, 2012 (www.nytimes.com/2012/10/05/business/medicare-fraud-charged-against-91.html).

Reuters. 2013. "Richest 1 Percent Owns 46 Pct of Global Wealth—Credit Suisse." October 9. Retrieved January 4, 2014 (http://in.reuters.com/article/2013/10/09/creditsuisse-wealth-idINL6N0HZ0MD20131009).

Richardson, John. 2010. "Workfare Program Makes Welfare Work." October 18. Retrieved May 17, 2012 (www.onlinesentinel.com/news/workfare-programmakes-welfare-work_2010-10-17.html).

Rice, William. 2013. "Types of Terrorism." Prezi, March 8. Retrieved May 13, 2014 (http://prezi.com/zyhuxjslaame/copy-of-types-of-terrorism/).

Rideout, Victoria. 2013. "Zero to Eight: Children's Media Use in America." Common Sense Media Retrieved December 30, 2013 (www.commonsensemedia.org/sites/default/files/research/zero-to-eight-2013.pdf).

Rideout, Victoria J., Ulla G. Foehr, and Donald F. Roberts. 2010. "Generation M2: Media in the Lives of 8- To 18-Year-Olds." A Kaiser Family Foundation Study, January. Retrieved March 2, 2011 (www.kff.org/entmedia/upload/8010.pdf).

Riegle-Crumb, Catherine, and Chelsea Moore. 2013. "The Gender Gap in High School Physics: Considering the Context of Local Communities." *Social Science Quarterly,* April 1. Retrieved Jan. 17, 2014 (http://onlinelibrary.wiley.com/doi/10.1111/ssqu.12022/abstract).

Riehl, Carolyn. 2001. "Bridges to the Future: Contributions of Qualitative Research to the Sociology of Education." *Sociology of Education* (Extra Issue):115–34.

Riley, Charles. 2011. "One California Budget Fix: Abolish Death Row." CNN Money, June 20. Retrieved April 16, 2012 (http://money.cnn.com/2011/06/20/news/economy/california_death-penalty/index.htm).

Riordan, Cornelius. 2004. *Equality and Achievement: An Introduction to the Sociology of Education*. Upper Saddle River, NJ: Prentice Hall.

Risman, Barbara J. and Pallavi Benerjee. 2013. "Kids Talking About Race: Tween-agers in a Post-Civil Rights Era." *Sociological Forum* 28(2):213–35.

Ritzer, George. 2007. *The Globalization of Nothing,* 2nd ed. Thousand Oaks, CA: Pine Forge.

Ritzer, George. 2011. *Globalization: The Essentials*. Malden, MA: Wiley.

Ritzer, George. 2013a. *Introduction to Sociology*. Thousand Oaks, CA: Sage.

Ritzer, George. 2013b. *The McDonaldization of Society,* 20th anniversary edition. Thousand Oaks, CA: Sage.

Ritzer, George and Douglas J. Goodman. 2004. *Sociological Theory,* 6th ed. New York: McGraw-Hill.

Roach, Ronald. 2004. "Survey Reveals 10 Biggest Trends in Internet Use." *Black Issues in Higher Education*, October 21.

Robbins, Mandy. 1998. "A Different Voice: A Different View." *Review of Religious Research* 40(1):75–80.

Robbins, Richard H. 2011. *Global Problems and the Culture of Capitalism,* 5th ed. Upper Saddle River NJ: Prentice Hall.

Roberts, Christine. 2012. "Most 10 Year-Olds Have Been on a Diet." Daily News. Retrieved January 17, 2014 (www.nydailynews.com/news/national/diets-obsess-tweens-study-article-1.1106653).

Roberts, Dorothy. 1997. *Killing the Black Body: Race, Reproduction, and the Meaning of Liberty*. New York: Pantheon.

Roberts, Dorothy. 2002. *Shattered Bonds: The Color of Child Welfare*. New York: Basic Books.

Roberts, Judith C. and Keith A. Roberts. 2008. "Deep Reading, Cost/Benefit, and the Construction of Meaning: Enhancing Reading Comprehension and Deep Learning in Sociology Courses." *Teaching Sociology* 36(April):125–40.

Roberts, Keith A. 2003. *Interviews With Ohio Residents in Communities Considering Tax Levies*. Unpublished manuscript.

Roberts, Keith A. and Karen A. Donahue. 2000. "Professing Professionalism: Bureaucratization and Deprofessionalization in the Academy," *Sociological Focus* 33(4):365–83.

Roberts, Keith A. and David Yamane. 2012. *Religion in Sociological Perspective*, 5th ed. Thousand Oaks, CA: SAGE/Pine Forge Press.

Robertson, Roland. 1992. *Globalization: Social Theory and Global Culture*. London: Sage.

Robertson, Roland. 1997. "Social Theory, Cultural Relativity and the Problem of Globality." Pp. 69–90 in *Culture, Globalization and the World System,* edited by Anthony King. Minneapolis: University of Minnesota Press.

Robertson, Roland and Jan Aart Scholte, eds. 2007. *Encyclopedia of Globalization*. London: Routledge.

Robillard, Kevin. 2012. "Study: Youth Vote Was Decisive." *Politico,* November 7. Retrieved November 1, 2012 (www.politico.com/news/stories/1112/83510.html).

The Robinhood Tax. 2010. Retrieved February 10, 2013 (http://robinhoodtax.org/).

Robinson, Bruce. 2007. "Physician Assisted Suicide." *Religious Tolerance,* June 2. Retrieved October 20, 2009 (www.religioustolerance.org/euth_us2htm).

Rodricks, Dan. 2012. "Catholics, Contraception and the Heretic Faithful." *The Baltimore Sun,* February 8. Retrieved Feb. 5, 2013 (http://articles.baltimoresun.com/2012-02-08/news/bs-ed-rodricks-catholics-20120208_1_cafeteria-catholics-church-leaders-protest-catholic-identity).

Rodriguez, Eric M. and S. C. Ouellette. 2000. "Gay and Lesbian Christians: Homosexual and Religious Identity Integration in the Members of a Gay-Positive Church." *Journal for the Scientific Study of Religion* 39(3):333–47.

Roethlisberger, Fritz J. and William J. Dickson. 1939. *Management and the Worker*. Cambridge, MA: Harvard University Press.

Roisen, Ron. 2012. "Mrs. Marty Mann and the Early Medicalization of Alcoholism." *The Atlantic,* February 22. Retrieved July 16, 2012 (www.theatlantic.com/health/archive/2012/02/mrs-marty-mann-and-the-early-medicalization-of-alcoholism/252286/).

Roksa, Josipa and Daniel Potter. 2011. "Parenting and Academic Achievement: Intergenerational Transmission of Educational Advantage." *Sociology of Education* 84(October):299–321.

Roof, Wade Clark. 1999. *Spiritual Marketplace: Baby Boomers and the Remaking of American Religion*. Princeton, NJ: Princeton University Press.

Rorem, Annie and Hamilton Lombard. 2014. "Ancestry: Who Do You Think You Are?" Stat Chat from the Demographics Research Group at UVA. Retrieved Sept. 5,2014 (http://statchatva.org/2014/03/13/ancestry-who-do-you-think-you-are/).

Rosen, Karen. 2007. "Women Still Lag in College Sports." June 6. Retrieved March 7, 2008 (www.oxfordpress.com/sports/content/shared/sports/stories/2007/WOMEN_SPORTS_0606_COX.html).

Rosenbaum, James E. 1999. "If Tracking Is Bad, Is Detracking Better? A Study of a Detracked High School." *American Schools* (Winter):24–47.

Rosenberg, Matt. 2012. "Maquiladoras in Mexico: Export Assembly Plants for the United States." *About.com Geography*. Retrieved May 28, 2012 (http://geography.about.com/od/urbaneconomicgeography/a/maquiladoras.htm).

Rosenthal, Elisabeth. 2013. "As Drug Costs Rise, Bending The Law Is One Remedy." *New York Times*, October 22. Retrieved March 12, 2014 (http://nyti.ms/17HuF6G).

Rosenthal, Robert and Lenore Jacobson. 1968. *Pygmalion in the Classroom*. New York: Holt, Rinehart & Winston.

Rossi, Alice S. 1984. "Gender and Parenthood." *American Sociological Review* 49(February):1–19.

Rossides, Daniel W. 1997. *Social Stratification: The Interplay of Class, Race, and Gender*. Englewood Cliffs, NJ: Prentice Hall.

Rothbard, Nancy P. and Jeanne M. Brett. 2000. "Promote Equal Opportunity by Recognizing Gender Differences in the Experience of Work and Family." In *The Blackwell Handbook of Principles of Organizational Behavior,* edited by Edwin A. Locke. Malden, MA: Blackwell.

Rothenberg, Paula S. 2006. *Beyond Borders: Thinking Critically About Global Issues*. New York: Worth.

Rothenberg, Paula S. 2010. *Race, Class, and Gender in the United States: An Integrated Study,* 8th ed. New York: Worth.

Rothenberg, Paula S. 2011. *White Privilege: Essential Readings on the Other Side of Racism,* 3rd ed. New York: Worth Publishers.

Rothkopf, David. 2012. "Two Septembers." Pp. 100–103 in *Globalization: The Transformation of Social Worlds*, 3rd ed., edited by D. Stanley Eitzen and Maxine Baca Zinn. Belmont, CA: Wadsworth.

Rothman, Robert A. 2005. *Inequality and Stratification: Race, Class, and Gender*, 5th ed. Englewood Cliffs, NJ: Prentice Hall.

Royal Society. 2012. *People and the Planet*. April. Retrieved July 31, 2012 (royalsociety.org/uploadedFiles/Royal_Society_Content/policy/projects/people-planet/2012-04-25-People Planet.pdf).

Rubin, Beth C. 2008. "Detracking in Context: How Local Constructions of Ability Complicate Equity-Geared Reform." *Teachers College Record* 110(3):646–99.

Rubin, Jeffrey Z. 1974. "The Eye of the Beholder: Parents' Views on Sex of Newborns." *American Journal of Orthopsychiatry* 44(4):512–19.

Rubin, Richard. 2012. "Romney's 47% Comments Distance Him from Bush-Era Republicans." *San Francisco Chronicle*, September 18. Retrieved September 24, 2012 (www.sfgate.com/business/bloomberg/article/Romney-s-47-Comments-Distance-Him-From-3875115.php).

Rumbaut, Ruben G. and Alejandro Portes. 2001. *Ethnicities: Children of Immigrants in America*. Los Angeles: University of California Press.

Rumberger, Russell W. 2011. *Dropping Out: Why Students Drop Out of High School and What Can Be Done About It*. Cambridge, MA: Harvard University Press.

"Rustbelt Britain: The Urban Ghosts." 2013. *The Economist*, October 12. Retrieved March 17, 2014 (www.economist.com/news/britain/21587799-these-days-worst-urban-decay-found-not-big-cities-small-ones-urban-ghosts).

Ryan, Paul, Eric Cantor, and Kevin McCarthy. 2010. *Young Guns: A New Generation of Conservative Leaders*. New York: Simon and Schuster.

Rydgren, Jens. 2004. "Mechanisms of Exclusion: Ethnic Discrimination in the Swedish Labour Market." *Journal of Ethnic and Migration Studies* 30(4):687–716.

Saad, Lydia. 2010. "Americans' Acceptance of Gay Relations Crosses 50% Threshold." Gallup Politics, May 25. Retrieved May 27, 2012 (www.gallup.com/poll/135764/americans-acceptance-gay-relations-crosses-threshold.aspx).

Saad, Lydia. 2012. "U.S. Confidence in Organized Religion at Low Point." *Gallup Politics*, July 12. Retrieved September 20, 2012 (www.gallup.com/poll/155690/confidence-organized-religion-low-point.aspx).

Saad, Lydia. 2013. "In U.S., 52% Back Law to Legalize Gay Marriage in 50 States." Gallup, July 29, 2013. Retrieved February 8, 2014 (www.gallup.com/poll/163730/back-law-legalize-gay-marriage-states.aspx).

Sabol, William J., Heather C. West, and Matthew Cooper. 2009. "Prisoners in 2008." *Bureau of Justice Statistics Bulletin*. U.S. Department of Justice, December. Retrieved December 20, 2009 (bjs.ojp.usdoj.gov/content/pub/pdf/p08.pdf).

Sachoff, Mike. 2008. "18% of U.S. Households Have No Internet Access." WebProNews.com, May. Retrieved February 27, 2011 (http://www.webpronews.com/18-of-us-households-have-no-internet-access-2008-05).

Sachs, Jeffrey. 2011. "With 7 Billion on Earth, a Huge Task Before Us." Retrieved July 10, 2013 (www.cnn.com/2011/10/17/opinion/sachs-global-population)

Sadker, Myra and David Sadker. 2005. *Teachers, Schools, and Society*, 7th ed. New York: McGraw-Hill.

Sadovnik, Alan R. 2007. *Sociology of Education: A Critical Reader*. New York: Routledge.

Saez, E. 2012. *Striking It Richer: The Evolution of Top Incomes in the United States* (Updated with 2009 and 2010 estimates). March 2. Retrieved June 18, 2012 (http://elsa.berkeley.edu/~saez/saez-UStopincomes-2010.pdf).

Safdar, Khadeeja. 2012. "Median Income Falling, Even as More Find Jobs." *The Huffington Post*, March 7. Retrieved May 16, 2012 (www.huffingtonpost.com/2012/03/07/media-income-2011_n_1324859.html).

Safe Horizon. 2014. "Domestic Violence: Statistics & Facts." Retrieved February 18, 2014 (www.safehorizon.org/index/what-we-do-2/domestic-violence—abuse-53/domestic-violence-statistics—facts-195.html).

Sager, Ira, Ben Elgin, Peter Elstrom, Faith Keenan, and Pallavi Gogoi. 2006. "The Underground Web." Pp. 261–70 in *Globalization: The Transformation of Social Worlds*, edited by D. Stanley Eitzen and Maxine Baca Zinn. Belmont, CA: Wadsworth.

Saha, Lawrence and A. Gary Dworkin. 2006. "Educational Attainment and Job Status: The Role of Status Inconsistency on Occupational Burnout." Paper presented at the International Sociological Association, July 23–29, Durban, South Africa.

Saharan Vibe. 2007. "Wodaabe Beauty Ceremony." February 19. Retrieved November 6, 2009 (saharanvibe.blogspot.com/2007/02/wodaabe-beauty-ceremony.html).

Salzman, Michael B. 2008. "Globalization, Religious Fundamentalism and the Need for Meaning." *International Journal of Intercultural Relations* 32(July):318–27.

"Same Sex Couples Get Wal-Mart Benefits." 2013. *Minneapolis Star Tribune*, August 28, p. D1.

Substance Abuse and Mental Health Services Administration. N.d. "Epidemiological Data: What Can It Tell You?" Retrieved March 4, 2014 (http://captus.samhsa.gov/prevention-practice/epidemiology-and-prevention/epidemiological-data).

Samovar, Larry A. and Richard E. Porter. 2003. *Intercultural Communication*. Belmont, CA: Wadsworth.

Sanday, Peggy Reeves. 1996. *A Woman Scorned: Acquaintance Rape on Trial*. Berkeley: University of California Press.

Sanday, Peggy Reeves. 2007. *Fraternity Gang Rape: Sex, Brotherhood, and Privilege on Campus*. New York: New York University Press.

Sanday, Peggy and Ruth Gallagher Goodenough, eds. 1990. *Beyond the Second Sex*. Philadelphia: University of Pennsylvania Press.

Sandberg, Sheryl. 2013. *Lean In: Women, Work, and the Will to Lead*. New York: Alfred A. Knopf.

Sapir, Edward. 1929. "The Status of Linguistics as a Science." *Language* 5:207–214.

Sapir, Edward. 1949. In *Selected Writings of Edward Sapir in Language, Culture, and Personality*, edited by David G. Mandelbaum. Berkeley: University of California Press.

Sapiro, Virginia. 2003. *Women in American Society: An Introduction to Women's Studies*, 5th ed. Mountain View, CA: Mayfield.

Sapolsky, Robert. 2011. "The Trouble With Testosterone." In *The Kaleidoscope of Gender*, 3rd ed., edited by Joan Z. Spade and Catherine G. Valentine. Thousand Oaks: Pine Forge.

Sargeant, Kimon Howland. 2000. *Seeker Churches: Promoting Traditional Religion in a Nontraditional Way*. New Brunswick, NJ: Rutgers University Press.

Sassen, Saskia. 2012. *Cities in a World Economy*, 4th ed. Thousand Oaks, CA: Sage.

Sassler, Sharon and Amanda J. Miller. 2011. "Waiting to Be Asked: Gender, Power, and Relationship Progression Among Cohabiting Couples." *Journal of Family Issues* 32(April): 482–506.

Sauter, Michael B. and Alexander E. M. Hess. 2013. "The States Where the Most People Go Hungry: 24/7 Wall St." September 9. Retrieved January 5, 20142013 (www.huffingtonpost .com/2013/09/08/states-food-insecurity_n_3890209 .html=slide=2885737).

Sauter, Michael B., Samuel Weigley, and Alexander E.M. Hess. 2013. "Ten Countries That Hate America Most." March 13. Retrieved October 3, 2013 (http://247wallst.com/special-report/2013/03/13/ten-countries-that-hate-america-most/ 2/).

Saxbe, Darby E., Rena L Repetti, and Anthony P. Graesch. 2011. "Time Spent in Housework and Leisure: Links With Parents' Physiological Recovery From Work." *Journal of Family Psychology* 25(April):271–81.

Scarce, Rik. 1999. "Good Faith, Bad Ethics: When Scholars Go the Distance and Scholarly Associations Do Not." *Law and Social Inquiry* 24(4):977–86.

Schabloski, Alyssa Kim. 2008. *Health Care Systems Around the World*. Insure the Uninsured Project, p. 3. Retrieved February 3, 2013 (www.itup.org/Reports/Fresh%20Thinking/Health_ Care_Systems_Around_World.pdf).

Schadenberg, Alex. 2013. "Oregon Assisted Suicide Deaths Hit Record High in 2012." *LifeNews*, January 30. Retrieved March 3, 2014 (www.lifenews.com/2013/01/30/oregon-assisted-suicide-deaths-hit-record-high-in-2012/).

Schaefer, Richard T. 2007. *Racial and Ethnic Groups*, 11th ed. Upper Saddle River, NJ: Prentice Hall.

Schaefer, Richard T. 2012. *Racial and Ethnic Groups*, 13th ed. Upper Saddle River, NJ: Prentice Hall.

Schaefer, Richard T. and Jenifer Kunz. 2007. *Racial and Ethnic Groups*. Upper Saddle River, NJ: Pearson/Prentice Hall.

Schiller J. S., J. W. Lucas, B. W. Ward, and J. A. Peregoy. 2010. "Summary Health Statistics for U.S. Adults: National Health Interview Survey, 2010." *National Center for Health Statistics—Vital Health Statistics* 10(252). Retrieved August 28, 2012 (www.cdc.gov/nchs/data/series/sr_10/ sr10_252.pdf).

Schmalleger, Frank. 2006. *Criminology Today: An Integrative Introduction*, 4th ed. Upper Saddle River, NJ: Prentice Hall.

Schmalleger, Frank. 2012. *Criminology Today: An Integrative Introduction*, 6th ed. Upper Saddle River, NJ: Prentice Hall.

Schoeman, Ferdinand. 1991. "Book Review: Heavy Drinking: The Myth of Alcoholism as a Disease." *The Philosophical Review* 100(3):493–98.

Schneider, Barbara and James S. Coleman. 1993. *Parents, Their Children, and Schools*. Boulder, CO: Westview.

Schneider, Linda and Arnold Silverman. 2006. *Global Sociology*, 4th ed. Boston: McGraw-Hill.

Schneider, Barbara and Linda J. Waite. 2005. *Being Together, Working Apart: Dual-Career Families and the Work-Life Balance*. Cambridge University Press.

Schoepflin, Todd. 2011. "Doing Gender." *Creative Sociology*, August 10. Retrieved May 25, 2012 (http://creativesociology .blogspot.com/2011/08/doing-gender.html).

"School Finance." 2011. *Education Week*. June 20. Retrieved September 14, 2012 (www.edweek.org/ew/issues/school-finance/).

Schwartz, Nelson D. 2013. "Where Factory Apprenticeship Is Latest Model From Germany." *New York Times,* November 30. Retrieved May 13, 2014 (www.nytimes.com/2013/12/01/ business/where-factory-apprenticeship-is-latest-model-from-germany.html?_r=0).

Science Daily. 2011b. "Prison Education Programs Reduce Inmate Prison Return Rate, Study Shows." October 4. Retrieved April 16, 2012 (www.sciencedaily.com/releases/ 2011/10/111004180121.htm).

Scott, Ellen K., Andrew S. London, and Nancy A. Myers. 2002. "Dangerous Dependencies: The Intersection of Welfare Reform and Domestic Violence." *Gender and Society* 16(6):878–97.

Scott-Montagu, John. 1904. "Automobile Legislation: A Criticism and Review." *North American Review* 179(573):168–77.

Scribd. 2011. "Chipko Movement." Retrieved January 1, 2012 (www.scribd.com/doc/27513230/Chipko-Movement).

Scribd. 2012. "Afghanistan in Transition: Illicit Drugs and Afghanistan." May. Retrieved July 30, 2012 (www.scribd.com/ doc/93907735/Illicit-Drugs-Afghanistan-Key-Trends).

Sedghi, Ami. 2013. "How Did Venezuela Change Under Hugo Chávez?" *The Guardian,* March 6. Retrieved July 15, 2013 (www.guardian.co.uk/news/datablog/2012/oct/04/venezu ela-hugo-chavez-election-data#data).

Sengupta, Somini. 2014. "U.N. Report Says Progress for Women Is Unequal." *New York Times*. February 12. Retrieved February 20, 2014 (www.nytimes.com/2014/02/13/world/un-report-says-progress-for-women-is-unequal.html?_r=0).

Sentencing Project. 2012a. "Facts About Prisons and Prisoners." Retrieved May 30, 2012 (www.sentencingproject.org/doc/publi cations/publications/inc_factsAboutPrisons_jan2012.pdf).

Sentencing Project. 2012b. "Rate of Incarceration per 100,000, by Gender and Race, 2010." Retrieved September 12, 2012 (www.sentencingproject.org/template/page.cfm?id=122).

Sentencing Project. 2014. "Facts About Prisons and People in Prison." Retrieved September 4, 2014 (http://www.sentenc ingproject.org/doc/publications/inc_Facts%20About%20 Prisons.pdf).

Sernau, Scott. 2010. *Social Inequality in a Global Age*. Thousand Oaks, CA: SAGE/Pine Forge Press.

Sessions, David. 2012. "Evangelicals Struggle to Address Premarital Sex and Abortion." *The Daily Beast,* July 13. Retrieved September 20, 2012 (www.thedailybeast.com/ articles/2012/07/13/evangelicals-struggle-to-address-pre marital-sex-and-abortion.html).

Shackle, Samira. 2012. "Mukhtar Mai—the Gang Rape Victim Who Defied Her Attackers." *New Statesman,* October 19. Retrieved April 24, 2014 (www.newstatesman.com/world-affairs/2012/10/mukhtar-mai-gang-rape-victim-who-defided-her-attackers).

Shade, Leslie Regan. 2004. "Bending Gender Into the Net: Feminizing Content, Corporate Interests, and Research Strategy." Pp. 57–70 in *Society On-Line: The Internet in Context,* edited by Philip N. Howard and Steve Jones. Thousand Oaks, CA: Sage.

Shah, Anup. 2009b. "World Military Spending." Retrieved December 17, 2009 (www.globalissues.org/article/75/world-military-spending).

Shaffer, David Williamson, Kurt R. Squire, Richard Haverson, and James P. Gee. 2005. "Video Games and the Future of Learning." *Phi Delta Kappan* (October):95–112.

Shah, Anup. 2011. "World Military Spending." Retrieved December 21, 2011 (www.globalissues.org/article/75/world-military-spending).

Shah, Anup. 2012. "World Military Spending: Expenditures in 2011." Retrieved February 10, 2013 (www.globalissues.org/print/article/75=WorldMilitarySpending).

Shah, Taimoor and Alissa J. Rubin. 2012. "In Poppy War, Taliban Aim to Protect a Cash Crop." *The New York Times,* April 12. Retrieved April 14, 2012 (www.nytimes.com/2012/04/12/world/asia/taliban-poppy-war-targets-tractors-and -police.html).

Shapiro, Jordan. 2013. "Are Your Kids Average? National Study on Kids and Digital Media." *Forbes,* October 28. Retrieved December 30, 2013. (www.forbes.com/sites/jordanshapiro/2013/10/28/are-your-kids-average-national-study-on-kids-and-digital-media/).

Sharp, Henry S. 1991. "Memory, Meaning, and Imaginary Time: The Construction of Knowledge in White and Chipewayan Cultures." *Ethnohistory* 38(2):149–73.

Sharp, Lauriston. 1990. "Steel Axes for Stone-Age Australians." Pp. 410–24 in *Conformity and Conflict,* 7th ed., edited by James P. Spradley and David W. McCurdy. Glenview, IL: Scott Foresman.

Shaw, Clifford R. and Henry D. McKay. 1929. *Delinquency Areas.* Chicago: University of Chicago Press.

Shaw, Susan M. and Janet Lee. 2005. *Women's Voices, Feminist Visions: Classic and Contemporary Readings,* 3rd ed. Boston: McGraw-Hill.

Sheridan, Mary Beth and William Branigin. 2010. "Senate Ratifies New U.S.-Russia Nuclear Weapons Treaty." *The Washington Post*, December 22. Retrieved June 28, 2013 (www.washingtonpost.com/wp-dyn/content/article/2010/12/21/AR2010122104371.html?sid=ST2010122205900).

Sherif, Muzafer and Carolyn Sherif. 1953. *Groups in Harmony and Tension.* New York: Harper & Row.

Sherkat, Darren E. 2012. "The Editorial Process and Politicized Scholarship: Monday Morning Editorial Quarterbacking and a Call for Scientific Vigilance." *Social Science Research* 41(6):1346–49.

Sherkat, Darren E. and Christopher G. Ellison. 1999. "Recent Developments and Current Controversies in the Sociology of Religion." *Annual Review of Sociology* 25:363–94.

Sherwood, I-Hsien. 2012. "Latest Presidential Election 2012 Map." *Latinos Post.* Retrieved November 12, 2012 (www.latinospost.com/articles/6570/20121107/latest-presidential-election-2012-map-obama-beats.htm).

Shihri, Abdullah. 2007. "Saudi King Pardons Woman Who Was Gang Raped." *The Guardian,* December 17. Retrieved April 24, 2014. (www.theguardian.com/world/2007/dec/18/saudiarabia.southafrica).

Shin, Jean H. and Karina J. Havrilla. 2008. "Proposition 187." In *Encyclopedia of Race, Ethnicity, and Society,* edited by Richard T. Shaefer. Retrieved February 6, 2013 (http://knowledge.sagepub.com/view/ethnicity/n439.xml).

Shirley, Craig. 2012. "Better Off Circa 2012." *Politico,* September 5. Retrieved October 11, 2012 (www.politico.com/news/stories/0912/80719.html).

Shogren, Elizabeth. 2012. "When This Oil Spills, It's 'A Whole New Monster.'" National Public Radio, August 16. Retrieved March 16, 2014 (www.npr.org/2012/08/16/158025375/when-this-oil-spills-its-a-whole-new-monster).

Short, Katherine. 2009. "Voter Participation Rate, 2008." Retrieved April 17, 2010 (www.askquestions.org/details.php?id=21094).

Shriver, Eunice Kennedy. 2007. *Add Health Study.* Washington, DC: National Institute of Child Health and Human Development. Retrieved December 24, 2009 (www.nichd.nih.gov/health/topics/add_health_study.cfm).

Shu, Xiaoling. 2004. "Education and Gender Egalitarianism: The Case of China." *Sociology of Education* 77(4):311–36.

Siegel, Larry J. 2009. *Criminology: Theories, Patterns, and Typologies,* 10th ed. Belmont, CA: Thomson/Wadsworth.

Siegel, Larry J. 2011. *Criminology: Theories, Patterns, and Typologies,* 11th ed. Belmont, CA: Thomson/Wadsworth.

Simmel, Georg. [1902–1917] 1950. *The Sociology of Georg Simmel,* translated by Kurt Wolff. Glencoe, IL: Free Press.

Simmel, Georg. 1955. *Conflict and the Web of Group Affiliation,* translated by Kurt H. Wolff. New York: Free Press.

Simmons, Rachel. 2002. *Odd Girl Out: The Hidden Culture of Aggression in Girls.* Orlando, FL: Harcourt.

Simon, David R. 2006. *Elite Deviance,* 8th ed. Boston: Allyn & Bacon.

Sine, Richard. 2002. "Garment Workers Say Gap Aided in Cambodian Strife." Retrieved September 2, 2008 (http://laborcenter.berkeley.edu/press/sfchronicle_dec02.shtml).

Sink, Todd and Brian Ceh 2011. "Relocation of the Urban Poor in Chicago: HOPE VI Policy Outcomes." *GeoForum* 42(January):71–82.

SIPRI Military Expenditure Database. 2012. Retrieved July 13, 2012 (http:milexdata.sipri.org).

"6.7% of World Has a College Degree." 2010. Retrieved March 11, 2011 (www.huffingtonpost.com/2010/05/19/percent-of-world-with-col_n_581807.html).

Sizer, Theodore R. 1984. *Horace's Compromise: The Dilemma of the American High School.* Boston: Houghton Mifflin.

Sjoberg, Gideon. 1965. "The Origin and Evolution of Cities." *Scientific American* 213(September):56–57.

Skocpol, Theda. 1979. *States and Social Revolutions: A Comparative Analysis of France, Russia, and China.* Cambridge, UK: Cambridge University Press.

Skocpol, Theda and Vanessa Williamson. 2012. *The Tea Party and the Remaking of Republican Conservatism.* New York: Oxford University Press.

Slaughter, Anne-Marie. 2012. "Why Women Still Can't Have it All." *The Atlantic*, July/August. Retrieved January 17, 2014 (www.theatlantic.com/magazine/archive/2012/07/why-women-still-cant-have-it-all/309020/).

SlideShare. 2014. "Population Pyramids 2014." Retrieved September 16, 2014 (http://www.slideshare.net/sbsgeog/population-pyramids-2014).

Smelser, Neil J. 1963. *Theory of Collective Behavior.* New York: Free Press.

Smelser, Neil J. 1988. "Social Structure." Pp. 103–29 in *Handbook of Sociology,* edited by Neil J. Smelser. Newbury Park, CA: Sage.

Smelser, Neil J. 1992. "The Rational Choice Perspective: A Theoretical Assessment." *Rationality and Society* 4: 381–410.

Smith, Adrian. 2012. "Private vs. Public Facilities, Is It Cost Effective and Safe?" Corrections.com, June 11. Retrieved September 1, 2014 (www.corrections.com/news/article/30903-private-vs-public-facilities-is-it-cost-effective-and-safe).

Smith, Alex Duval. 2011. "South Africa's Maternal Mortality Rate Increases Fourfold." *The Guardian*, August 12. Retrieved July 17, 2012 (www.guardian.co.uk/global-development/2011/aug/12/south-africa-maternal-mortality-health).

Smith, Christian and Robert Faris. 2005. "Socioeconomic Inequality in the American Religious System: An Update and Assessment." *Journal for the Scientific Study of Religion* 44(1):95–104.

Smith, Christian and Melinda Lundquist Denton. 2005. *Soul Searching: The Religious and Spiritual Lives of American Teenagers.* New York: Oxford University Press.

Smith, Christian, with P. Snell. 2009. *Souls in Transition: The Religious and Spiritual Lives of Emerging Adults.* New York: Oxford University Press.

Smith, Daniel R. and David F. Ayers. 2006. "Culturally Responsive Pedagogy and Online Learning: Implications for the Globalized Community College." *Community College Journal of Research and Practice* 30.

Smith, Jacquelyn. 2013. "Billionaire CEOs with the Biggest Paychecks." Retrieved January 4, 2014 (www.forbes.com/sites/briansolomon/2014/the-worlds-youngest-billionaires-23-under -40/).

Smith, Mark K. 2008. "Howard Gardner and Multiple Intelligences." *The Encyclopedia of Informal Education.* Retrieved April 17, 2011 (http://www.infed.org/thinkers/gardner.htm).

Smith Drug War Chronicle. 2009. "Prohibition: UN Drug Chief Says Black Market Drug Profits Propped Up Global Banking System Last Year." Retrieved November 4, 2009 (http://stopthedrugwar.org/chronicle/570/costa_UNODC_drug_trade_banks).

Snarr, Michael T. and D. Neil Snarr. 2008. *Introducing Global Issues*, 4th ed. Boulder, CO: Lynne Rienner Publishers

Snopes.com. 2007. "Ring Around the Rosie." Retrieved July 31, 2012 (www.snopes.com/language/literary/rosie.asp).

Snow, David A. and L. Anderson. 1993. *Down on Their Luck: A Study of Homeless Street People.* Berkeley: University of California Press.

Snyder, Denson R. 1971. *The Hidden Curriculum.* New York: Alfred A. Knopf.

Snyderman, Nancy and Chiara Sottile. 2013. "'It's Getting a Lot Harder to Do This': Doctor Shortage Strains Practices." NBC News, May 25. Retrieved July 15, 2013 (http://dailynightly.nbcnews.com/_news/2013/05/25/18042694-it-is-getting-a-lot-harder-to-do-this-doctor-shortage-strains-practices?lite).

Sobolewski, Juliana M. and Paul R. Amato. 2007. "Parents' Discord and Divorce, Parent-Child Relationships, and Subjective Well-Being in Early Adulthood: Is Feeling Close to Two Parents Always Better Than Feeling Close to One?" *Social Forces* 85(March):1105–124.

"Sochi 2014: Gay Rights Protests Target Russia's Games." 2014. BBC News, February 5. Retrieved Feb. 24, 2014 (www.bbc.co.uk/news/world-europe-26043872).

Social Security Administration. 2013a. "Social Security Basic Facts." Retrieved July 1, 2013 (www.ssa.gov/pressoffice/basicfact.htm).

Social Security Administration. 2013b. "Social Security History." Retrieved February 6, 2013 (www.ssa.gov/history/lifeexpect.html).

Social Security and Medicare Boards of Trustees. 2013. "A Summary of the 2013 Annual Reports." Retrieved July 13, 2013 (www.ssa.gov/oact/trsum/).

Social Security Online. 2010. "Isabella Reigns as New Queen of Baby Names: Takes Top Spot on Social Security's Most Popular Baby Names List." May 7. Retrieved April 7, 2011 (http://www.ssa.gov/pressoffice/pr/baby-names2009-pr.htm).

Social Security Online. 2012. "History." Retrieved February 6, 2013 (www.prb.org/DataFinder/Topic/Rankings.aspx?ind=17).

Sommerville, C. John. 2002. "Stark's Age of Faith Argument and the Secularization of Things: A Commentary." *Review of Religious Research* (Fall):361–72.

Sons of Union Veterans of the Civil War. 2010. "The United States' Flag Code." Retrieved December 212, 2011 (http://suvcw.org/flag.htm).

Souers, Joanna Mae. 2012. "Cuba Leads the World In Lowest Patient Per Doctor Ratio; How Do They Do It?" *The Social Medicine Portal,* July 30. Retrieved March 4, 2014 (www.socialmedicine.org/2012/07/30/about/cuba-leads-the-world-in-lowest-patient-per-doctor-ratio-how-do-they-do-it/).

Southern Poverty Law Center. 2014. "Active U.S. Hate Groups." Retrieved September 1, 2014 (www.splcenter.org/get-informed/hate-map).

Sowell, Thomas. 1994. *Race and Culture: A World View.* New York: Basic Books.

Spacey, John. 2012. "Japan's Crime Rate." *Japan Talk,* June 30. Retrieved April 18, 2013 (www.japan-talk.com/jt/new/japans-crime-rate).

Spade, Joan Z. 2004. "Gender in Education in the United States." Pp. 287–95 in *Schools and Society: A Sociological Approach to Education,* 2nd ed., edited by Jeanne H. Ballantine and Joan Z. Spade. Belmont, CA: Wadsworth.

Spar, Debora. 2013. Wonder Women: Sex, Power, and the Quest for Perfection. New York: Macmillan.

Sperling, Gene B. 2006. "What Works in Girls' Education." PBS Wide Angle. Retrieved July 11, 2009 (www.pbs.org/wnet/wideangle/episodes/time-for-school-series/essay-what-works-in-girls-education/274).

Srinivasan, Padma and Gary R. Lee. 2004. "The Dowry System in Northern India: Women's Attitudes and Social Change." *Journal of Marriage and Family* 66:1108–17.

Stack, Carol B. 1998. *All Our Kin: Strategies for Survival in a Black Community* (Reissued). New York: Harper & Row.

Standler, Ronald B. 2012. "Annotated Legal Cases on Physician-Assisted Suicide in the USA." *Carbon Mitigation Initiative,* July 12. Retrieved July 16, 2013 (cmi.princeton.edu/).

Stanley, Angela. 2011. "Black, Female and Single." *The New York Times Sunday Review,* December 10. Retrieved June 5, 2012 (www.nytimes.com/2011/12/11/opinion/sunday/black-and-female-the-marriage-question.html?pagewanted=all).

Staples, Brent. 2001. "Black Men and Public Space." Pp. 244–46 in *The Production of Reality*, edited by Jodi O'Brien and Peter Kollock. Thousand Oaks, CA: Pine Forge Press.

Stark, Rodney. 2000. "Secularization, R.P.I." Pp. 41–66 in *The Secularization Debate*, edited by William H. Swatos, Jr., and Daniel V. A. Olson. Lanham, MD: Rowman & Littlefield.

Stark, Rodney and Roger Finke. 2000. *Acts of Faith: Explaining the Human Side of Religion*. Berkeley: University of California Press.

Starr, Paul D. 1982. The Social Transformation of American Medicine. New York: Basic Books.

State of Alaska. 2006. "Workplace Alaska: How to Apply." Retrieved July 5, 2006 (http://notes3.state.ak.us/WA/MainEntry.nsf/WebData/HTMLHow+to+Apply/?open).

State of Delaware. 2008. "Presidential Primary Election." Retrieved March 21, 2008 (http://elections.delaware.gov/information/elections/presidential_2008.shtml).

StateMaster. 2013. "Education Statistics." Retrieved September 12, 2014 (http://www.statemaster.com/).

Statistic Brain. 2014. "High School Dropout Statistics." *Education Week*, Children Trends Database. Retrieved August 13, 2014 (http://www.statisticbrain.com/high-school-dropout-statistics/).

Statistica. 2014. "Number of Vehicles Registered in the United States from 1990 to 2011." Retrieved February 23, 2014 (www.statistica.com/statistics/183505/number-of-vehicles-in-the-united-stastes-since-1990/).

Statistical Handbook of Japan. 2010. "Population." Retrieved May 13, 2011 (www.stat.go.jp/english/data/handbook/c02cont.htm#cha2_2).

Statistics Canada. 2013. "Crude Marriage Rate and Crude Divorce Rate, Canada." Retrieved February 26, 2014 (www.statcan.gc.ca/pub/89-503-x/2010001/article/11546/c-g/c-g006-eng.htm).

Steele, Tracey L. 2005. *Sex, Self, and Society: The Social Context of Sexuality*. Belmont, CA: Thomson Wadsworth.

Steele, Tracey and Norma Wilcox. 2003. "A View From the Inside: The Role of Redemption, Deterrence, and Masculinity on Inmate Support for the Death Penalty." *Crime and Delinquency* 49(2):285–313.

Stelter, Brian. 2009. "In Coverage of Iran, Amateurs Take the Lead." Mediadecoder Weblog, *New York Times*, June 17. Retrieved December 22, 2009 (http://mediadecoder.blogs.nytimes.com).

Stephan, Ed. N.d. "John Graunt's Billsof Mortality." Retrieved March 18, 2014 (www.edstephan.org/Graunt/bills.html).

Stephen, Eric M., Jennifer Rose, Lindsay Kenney, Francine Rosselli-Navarra, and Ruth S. Weissman. 2014. "Adolescent Risk Factors for Purging in Young Women: Findings From the National Longitudinal Study of Adolescent Health." *Journal of Eating Disorders* 2(1). Retrieved January 16, 2014 (www.jeatdisord.com/).

Stern, Jessica. 2003. *Terror in the Name of God: Why Religious Militants Kill*. New York: HarperCollins.

Stevenson, Mark 2013. "At 20 Years, Nafta Didn't Close Mexico Wage Gap." Retrieved January 18, 2014 (http://news.yahoo.com/20-years-nafta-didn-39-t-close-mexico-064658474—financial.html).

Stewart, Susan D. 2007. *Brave New Stepfamilies: Diverse Paths Toward Stepfamily Living*. Thousand Oaks, CA: Sage.

Stiglitz, Joseph E. 2012. "A Real Cure for the Global Economic Crackup." Pp. 104–109 in *Globalization: The Transformation of Social Worlds*, 3rd ed., edited by D. Stanley Eitzen and Maxine Baca Zinn. Belmont, CA: Wadsworth.

Stillwell, Robert. 2010. "Public School Graduates and Dropouts From the Common Core of Data: School Year 2007–08." Retrieved July 14, 2011 (nces.ed.gov/pubs2010/2010341.pdf).

Stillwell, Robert, Jennifer Sable, and Chris Plotts. 2011. "Public School Graduates and Dropouts From the Common Core of Data." Retrieved September 11, 2014 (http://nces.ed.gov/pubs2011/2011312.pdf).

Stockholm International Peace Research Institute. 2010. "World Military Expenditures Increase Despite Financial Crisis." June 2. Retrieved May 10, 2011 (www.sipri.org/media/pressreleases/2010/100602yearbooklaunch).

Stoessinger, John. 1993. *Why Nations Go to War*. New York: St. Martin's Press.

Stone, Brad and Noam Cohen. 2009. "Social Networks Spread Defiance Online." *The New York Times*, June 16. Retrieved June 30, 2009 (www.nytimes.com/2009/06/16/world/middleeast/16media.html?_r=1&ref=world).

Stop Child Trafficking Now. 2012. "Child Trafficking Statistics." Retrieved May 1, 2012 (http://sctnow.org/contentpages.aspx?parentnavigationid=5827-4e7a-bde1-f61690fa44a8).

Stout, David. 2009. "Violent Crime Fell in 2008, F.B.I. Report Says." *The New York Times*, September 14. Retrieved November 4, 2009 (www.nytimes.com/2009/09/15/us/15crime.html).

Stracansky, Pavol 2013. "Curbs on Abortion Spread Across East Europe." *Inter Press Service*, July 12. Retrieved March 17, 2014 (www.ipsnews/net/2013/07/curbs-on-abortion-spread-across-east-europe/).

Straus, Murray and Richard J. Gelles. 1990. *Physical Violence in American Families*. New Brunswick, NJ: Transaction.

Straus, Murray A., Richard J. Gelles, and Suzanne K. Steinmetz. 2006. *Behind Closed Doors: Violence in the American Family*. New Brunswick, NJ: Transaction.

Strauss, Valerie. 2011. "ACT Scores Show Problems With College Readiness." *The Washington Post*, August 17. Retrieved July 8, 2013 (www.washingtonpost.com/blogs/answer-sheet/post/2011-act-scores-show-problems-with-college-readiness/2011/08/16/gIQABKu4JJ_blog.html).

Stringer, Donna M. 2006. "Let Me Count the Ways: African American/European American Marriages." Pp. 170–76 in *Intercultural Communication: A Reader*, edited by Larry A. Samovar, Richard E. Porter, and Edwin R. McDaniel. Belmont, CA: Wadsworth.

Stryker, Sheldon. 1980. *Symbolic Interactionism: A Social Structural Version*. Menlo Park, CA: Benjamin Cummings.

Stryker, Sheldon. 2000. "Identity Competition: Key to Differential Social Involvement." Pp. 21–40 in *Identity, Self, and Social Movements*, edited by Sheldon Styker, Timothy Owens, and Robert White. Minneapolis: University of Minnesota Press.

Stryker, Sheldon and Anne Stratham. 1985. "Symbolic Interaction and Role Theory." Pp. 311–78 in *Handbook of Social Psychology*, edited by Gardiner Lindsey and Eliot Aronson. New York: Random House.

Stutz, Fredrick P. and Barney Warf. 2005. *The World Economy.* Upper Saddle River, NJ: Prentice Hall.

Sullivan, Brian. 2013. "HUD Repots Continued Decline in U.S. Homelessness Since 2010." HUD.gov, November 21. Retrieved February 17, 2014 (http://portal.hud.gov/hudpor tal/HUD?src=/press/press_releases_media_advisories/2013/HUDNo.13-173).

"Supreme Court DOMA Decision Rules Federal Same-Sex Marriage Ban Unconstitutional." 2013. *Huffington Post,* June 26. Retrieved June 26, 2013 (www.huffingtonpost.com/2013/06/26/supreme-court-doma-decision_n_3454811.html?ref=topbar).

Sutherland, Anne. 1986. *Gypsies: The Hidden Americans.* Prospect Heights, IL: Waveland.

Sutherland, Anne. 2001 "Complexities of U.S. Law and Gypsy Identity." Pp. 231–42 in *Gypsy Law: Romani Legal Traditions and Culture,* edited by Walter O. Weyrauch. Berkeley: University of California Press.

Sutherland, Edwin H., Donald R. Cressey, and David Luckenbil. 1992. *Criminology.* Dix Hills, NY: General Hall.

Sutton, Joe. 2013. "Maryland Governor Signs Death Penalty Repeal." CNN.com, May 2. Retrieved June 2, 2013 (www.cnn.com/2013/05/02/us/maryland-death-penalty).

Swank, Eric, Breanne Fahs, and David M. Frost. 2013. "Region, Social Identities and Disclosure Practices as Predictors of Heterosexist Discrimination against Sexual Minorities in the United States." *Sociological Inquiry* 83(2):238–58.

Sway, Marlene. 1988. *Familiar Strangers: Gypsy Life in America.* Urbana: University of Illinois Press.

Sweet, Stephen. 2001. *College and Society: An Introduction to the Sociological Imagination.* Boston: Allyn & Bacon.

Szymanski, Linda A., Ann Sloan Devlin, Joan C. Chrisler, and Stuart A. Vyse. 1993. "Gender Role and Attitude Toward Rape in Male and Female College Students." *Sex Roles* 29:37–55.

Talbot, Margaret. 2008. "Red Sex, Blue Sex." *The New Yorker,* November 3. Retrieved December 24, 2009 (www.newyorker.com/reporting/2008/11/03/081103fa_fact_talbot).

Tamney, Joseph B. 1992. *The Resilience of Christianity in the Modern World.* Albany: State University of New York Press.

Tanenhaus, Sam. 2012. "History vs. the Tea Party." *New York Times,* January 14. Retrieved July 15, 2012 (www.nytimes.com/2012/01/15/sunday-review/gop-history-vs-the-tea-party.html?pagewanted=all).

Tareen, Sophia and Jason Keyser. 2012. "Chicago Teachers Strike: No Deal Reached Yet, Talks Continue on Day 5." *Huffington Post*, September 14. Retrieved September 14, 2012 (www.huffingtonpost.com/2012/09/14/chicago-teachers-strike-n_0_n_1883626.html).

Taseer, Shehrbano. 2011. "True Survivor." *The Daily Beast,* May 1. Retrieved April 12, 2012 (www.thedailybeast.com/newsweek/2011/05/01/true-survivor.html).

Taub, Diane E. and Penelope A. McLorg. 2010. "Influences of Gender Socialization and Athletic Involvement on the Occurrence of Eating Disorders." Pp. 73–82 in *Sociological Footprints: Introductory Readings in Sociology*, 11th ed., edited by Leonard Cargan and Jeanne H. Ballantine. Belmont, CA: Wadsworth Cengage Learning.

Tavris, Carol and Carol Wade. 1984. *The Longest War,* 2nd ed. San Diego, CA: Harcourt Brace Jovanovich.

Tea Party Patriots. 2012. "About Tea Party Patriots." Retrieved June 13, 2012 (http://www.teapartypatriots.org/about/?gclid=CLyk15G6y7ACFcIUKgod00KPXw).

TechWench. 2010. "Physical Books to Be Overshadowed by E-Books Within 5 Years." October 19. Retrieved April 17, 2011 (www.techwench.com/physical-books-to-be-overshad owed-by-e-books-within-5-years/).

"Teen Ends Globe-Circling Voyage in St Maarten." 2012. *USA Today,* January 21. Retrieved February 23, 2012 (www.usato day.com/news/world/story/2012-01-21/teen-sails-globe/52723684/1).

Terra Networks. 2013. *Kony 2012 Viral Campaign Sheds Light on Ugandan Violence.* Retrieved March 30, 2012 (http://en.terra .com/latin-in-america/news/kony_2012_viral_campaign_sheds_light_on_ugandan_violence/hof18171/ECID=US_ENGLISH_terrausa_SEMSearch_Kony).

Teixeira, Ruy. 2008. "The Decline of the White Working Class and the Rise of a Mass Upper Middle Class." Brookings Institution. Retrieved June 27, 2008 (www.brookings.edu/experts.aspx).

Teixeira, Ruy. 2012a. *America's New Swing Region: Changing Politics and Demographics in the Mountain West.* Washington DC: The Brookings Institution.

Teixeira, Ruy. 2012b. "The Emerging Democratic Majority Turns 10." *The Atlantic,* November. Retrieved November 10, 2012 (www.theatlantic.com/politics/archive/2012/11/the-emerg ing-democratic-majority-turns-10).

Teixeira, Ruy and John Halpin. 2012. "The Obama Coalition in the 2012 Election and Beyond." *Center for American Progress,* December. Retrieved November 19, 2013 (www.american progress.org/wp-content/uploads/2012/12/ObamaCoalition-5 .pdf).

"10 Countries Spending the Most on Health Care: 24/7 Wall St." 2012a. *Huffington Post,* March 29. Retrieved August 1, 2012 (www.huffingtonpost.com/2012/03/29/healthcare-spending-countries_n_1388306.html#s825346&title=1_United_States).

Therborn, Goran. 1976. "What Does the Ruling Class Do When It Rules?" *Insurgent Sociologist* 6:3–16.

Theroux, David J. 2012. "Secular Theocracy: The Foundations and Folly of Modern Tyranny." *The Independent Institute,* January 11. Retrieved July 13, 2012 (www.independent.org/newsroom/article.asp?id=3206).

Thiagaraj, Henry. 2006. *Human Rights From the Dalit Perspective.* Chennai, India: Oneworld Educational Trust.

ThisNation.com. 2014. "The United States Congress Quick Facts." Retrieved September 4, 2014 (http://www.thisnation .com/congress-facts.html).

Thomas, V. J. and F. D. Rose. 1991. "Ethnic Differences in the Experience of Pain." *Social Science and Medicine* 32(9):1063–1066.

Thompson, A. C. 2009. "Katrina's Hidden Race War." *The Nation,* January 5. Retrieved July 7, 2011 (www.thenation.com/arti cle/katrinas-hidden-race-war).

Thompson, Derek. 2011. "How Women in the Workforce Are Changing America." *The Atlantic,* March 9. Retrieved June 9, 2012 (www.theatlantic.com/business/archive/2011/03/how-women-in-the-workforce-are-chang ing-america/72235/).

Thorne, Barrie. 1993. *Gender Play: Girls and Boys in School.* New Brunswick, NJ: Rutgers University Press.

Thumma, Scott and Dave Travis. 2007. *Beyond Megachurch Myths: What We Can Learn From America's Largest Churches.* Hoboken, NJ: Jossey-Bass.

Tippett, Rebecce, Avis Jones-Deweever, Maya Rockeymoore, Darrick Hamilton, and William Darity, Jr. 2014. "Beyond Broke Why Closing the Racial Wealth Gap is a Priority for National Economic Security." Retrieved September 16, 2014 (http://globalpolicysolutions.org/resources/beyond-broke-report/).

Tipton, Steven M. 1990. "The Social Organization of Zen Practice: Constructing Transcultural Reality." *American Journal of Sociology* 96(2):488–90.

Toffler, Alvin and Heidi Toffler. 1980. *The Third Wave.* New York: Morrow.

Tofugu. 2011. "The Burakumin: Japan's Invisible Race." November 18. Retrieved May 6, 2012 (www.tofugu.com/2011/11/18/the-burakumin-japans-invisible-race/).

Tolbert, Pamela S. and Richard H. Hall. 2008. *Organizations: Structures, Processes, and Outcomes,* 10th ed. Upper Saddle River, NJ: Prentice Hall.

Tollefson, Jeff. 2012. "Heatwaves Blamed on Global Warming." *Nature.* Retrieved September 7, 2012 (www.nature.com/news/heatwaves-blamed-on-global-warming-1.11130).

Tönnies, Ferdinand. [1887] 1963. *Community and Society.* New York: Harper & Row.

Topix.com. 2010. "Fired for Being Gay? It's Legal in 29 States." Retrieved July 10, 2011 (www.topix.com/forum/state/de/TP9N5JVK30FRS3NLO).

Tough, Paul. 2008. *Whatever It Takes: Geoffrey Canada's Quest to Change Harlem and America.* Boston: Houghton Mifflin Harcourt.

TransCanada 2014. "Keystone XL Pipeline Project." Retrieved May 28, 2014 (http://keystone-xl.com/).

"Transnational Crime in the Developing World." 2011. Cited in "The 12 Most Profitable International Crimes." Retrieved April 13, 2012 (http://247wallst.com/2011/02/10/the-12-most-profitable-international-crimes/).

Transparency International. 2012. "Global Corruption Barometer 2010/11." Retrieved October 6, 2012 (http://gcb.transparency.org/gcb201011/infographic/).

Travers, Jeffrey and Stanley Milgram. 1969. "An Experimental Study of the Small World Problem." *Sociometry* 32:425–43.

Truman, Jennifer L. 2011a. "Criminal Victimization, 2010." National Crime Victimization Survey, U.S. Department of Justice, September. Retrieved May 26, 2012 (www.bjs.gov/content/pub/pdf/cv10.pdf).

Truman, Jennifer L. 2011b. "Rate of Total Violent Crime Victimization Declined by 13% in 2010." U.S. Bureau of Justice Statistics, September 15. Retrieved April 13, 2012 (www.bjs.ojp.usdoj.gov/index.cfm?ty=pbdetail&iid=2224).

Trust in Education. 2013. "Life as an Afghan Woman." Retrieved January 16, 2014 (www.trustineducation.org/why-afghanistan/life-as-an-afghan-woman/).

Tull, Matthew. 2012. "The Consequences of Male Gender Role Stress." About.com. Retrieved February 6, 2014 (http://ptsd.about.com/od/relatedconditions/a/MaleGenderRoleStres.htm).

Tumin, Melvin M. 1953. "Some Principles of Social Stratification: A Critical Analysis." *American Sociological Review* 18(August):387–94.

Turnbull, Colin M. 1962. *The Forest People.* New York: Simon & Schuster.

Turner, Bryan S. 1991a. "Politics and Culture in Islamic Globalism." Pp. 161–81 in *Religion and Global Order,* edited by Roland Robertson and William R. Garrett. New York: Paragon.

Turner, Bryan S. 1991b. *Religion and Social Theory.* London: Sage.

Turner, Jonathan H. 2003. *The Structure of Sociological Theory,* 7th ed. Belmont, CA: Wadsworth.

Turner, Ralph H. and Lewis M. Killian. 1993. "The Field of Collective Behavior." Pp. 5–20 in *Collective Behavior and Social Movements,* edited by Russell L. Curtis, Jr. and Benigno E. Aguirre. Boston: Allyn & Bacon.

20-first. 2010. "It's Official at Last: Women Outnumber Men in US Workforce." Retrieved May 25, 2012 (www.20-first.com/1317-0-its-official-at-last-women-outnumber-men-in-us-workforce.html).

UNAIDS. 2009. "AIDS Epidemic Update." November. Retrieved January 11, 2010 (www.avert.org/worldstats.htm).

UNAIDS. 2012a. "AIDS Dependency Crisis: Sourcing African Solutions." Retrieved August 3, 2012 (www.unaids.org/en/media/contentassets/documents/unaidspublication/2012/JC2286_Sourcing-African-Solutions_en.pdf).

UNAIDS. 2012b. "Swaziland Country Report on Monitoring the Political Declaration on HIV and AIDS." March. Retrieved July 16, 2012 (www.unaids.org/en/dataanalysis/monitoringcountry progress/progressreports/2012countries/ce_SZ_Narrative_Report[1].pdf).

UNESCAP. 2007. "Gender Inequality Continues—at Great Cost." The Economic and Social Survey for Asia and the Pacific 2007. Retrieved April 9, 2010 (www.unescap.org/survey2007/backgrounder/gender_inequality.asp).

UNESCO. 1969. "Four Statements on the Race Question." Retrieved September 5, 2014 (http://unesdoc.unesco.org/images/0012/001229/122962eo.pdf).

UNESCO. 1978. "Declaration on Race and Racial Prejudice." Retrieved September 5, 2014 (http://www.unrol.org/files/Declaration%20on%20Race%20and%20Racial%20Prejudice.pdf).

UNESCO. 2005. Education for All Global Monitoring Report 2005: The Quality Imperative. Paris: Author.

UNESCO. 2009. "Women and Accessibility in Town Centers: Open Sesame Project, UK." Retrieved January 6, 2010 (www.unesco.org/most/westeu23.htm).

UNESCO. 2010. "Education (All Levels) Profile—India." Institute of Statistics. Retrieved September 13, 2012 (http://stats.uis.unesco.org/unesco/TableViewer/document.aspx).

UNESCO. 2012. "World Atlas of Gender Equality in Education." Retrieved September 11, 2014 (www.uis.unesco.org/Education/Documents/unesco-world-atlas-gender-education-2012.pdf).

UNESCO Institute for Statistics. 2012. "Primary School Curricula on Reading and Mathematics in Developing Countries." *Technical Paper* 8. Retrieved January 28, 2013 (www.uis.unesco.org/Education/. . .tp8-education-curriculum-reading-math-2012-en3.pdf).

UNESCO Institute for Statistics. 2013. "UIS Fact Sheet: U.S. and Adult Literacy." Retrieved May 1, 2014 (www.uis.unesco.org/literacy/Documents/fs26-2013-literacy-en.pdf).

UNESCO Institute for Statistics. 2014. "India." Retrieved September 11, 2014 (http://www.uis.unesco.org/DataCentre/Pages/country-profile.aspx?code=IND&regioncode=40535).

UN.GIFT. 2014. "Trafficking for Organ Trade." *Global Initiative to Fight Human Trafficking*. Retrieved March 10, 2014 (www.ungift.org/knowledgehub/en/about/trafficking-for-organ-trade.html).

UN Habitat. 2012. "Issues and Trends." United Nations Human Settlements Programme. Retrieved July 31, 2012 (www.scribd.com/doc/99074172/Gender-and-Urban-Planning).

UNHCR. 2012. "UNHCR Report Shows Highest Number of Refugees in 15 Years." June 19. Retrieved July 30, 2012 (www.euronews.com/2012/06/19/unhrc-report-shows-highest-number-of-refugees-in-15-yeasrs/).

UN Human Development Report. 2011. "Sustainability and Equity: A Better Future for All." Retrieved September 9, 2012 (http://hdr.undp.org/en/reports/global/hdr2011/).

UNICEF. 2005. "Convention on the Rights of the Child." Retrieved July 23, 2012 (www.unicef.org/crc/index_30229.html).

UNICEF. 2011. "Basic Education and Gender Equality: Equal Access to Education." Retrieved July 29, 2012 (www.unicef.org/education/index_access.html).

UNICEF. 2013. "Estimates of Under-Five, Infant, and Neonatal Mortality by Millennium Development Goal Region." Retrieved September 16, 2014 (www.childinfo.org/files/Child_Mortality_Report_2013.pdf).

UNICEF. 2014. "Update on Haiti's Children." Retrieved February 23, 2014 (www.unicefusa.org/work/emergencies/Haiti/?gclid=CJ6zxOK847wCFdE-Mgodt1IANg).

UNIFEM. 2002. "Report of the Learning Oriented Assessment of Gender Mainstreaming and Women's Empowerment Strategies in Rwanda." Retrieved April 7, 2008 (www.unifem.org/attachments/products/rwanda_assessment_report_eng.pdf).

United Church of Christ. 2007. "Toxic Waste and Race at Twenty: 1987–2007." Environmental Justice/Environmental Racism. Retrieved April 22, 2009 (www.ejnet.org/ej).

United Nations. 2009. "World Food Program: Swaziland." November. Retrieved April 13, 2010 (www.wfp.org/countries/swaziland).

United Nations. 2010. "Violence Against Women." Ch. 6 in *The World's Women: Trends and Statistics*. Retrieved April 11, 2012 (http://unstats.un.org/unsd/demographic/products/Worldswomen/WW2010%20Report_by%20chapter(pdf)/Vnce%20against%20women.pdf).

United Nations. 2011. *The Millennium Development Goals Report 2011*. Retrieved January 23, 2013 (www.un.org/millenniumgoals/11_MDG%20Report_EN.pdf).

United Nations. 2012. "Status of Ratification of the Kyoto Protocol." United Nations Framework Convention on Climate Change. Retrieved September 7, 2012 (http://unfccc.int/kyoto_protocol/status_of_ratification/items/).

United Nations. 2013. "A Promise Is a Promise." United Nation's Secretary General's Campaign UNiTE to End Violence Against Women. Retrieved June 10, 2013 (www.un.org/en/women/endviolence/pdf/apromiseisapromise.pdf).

United Nations, Department of Economic and Social Affairs, Population Division. 2011. *World Population Prospects: The 2010 Revision. Vol. 1: Comprehensive Tables*. "Table A30. Life Expectancy at Birth by Major Area, Region and Country: Estimates and Projections, 1950–2050." Retrieved February 4, 2013 (http://books.google.com/books?idf=ghTtZ89QOt4C&pg=PA6=life%20expectancy%20in%20China%20in%201955%2040.8%20years&f=false).

United Nations, Department of Economic and Social Affairs, Population Division. 2012a. "Data on Cities and Urban Agglomerations." *World Urbanization Prospects: The 2011 Revision*. Retrieved December 22, 2012 (http://esa.un.org/unpd/wup/CD-ROM/Urban-Agglomerations.htm).

United Nations, Department of Economic and Social Affairs, Population Division. 2012b. "Total, Urban and Rural Populations by Major Area" (Table 7). *World Urbanization Prospects: The 2011 Revision*. Retrieved October 13, 2012 (http://esa.un.org/unup/pdf/WUP2011_Highlights.pdf).

United Nations, Department of Economic and Social Affairs, Population Division. 2012c. "Urban and Rural Populations by Development Group, 1959–2050" (Figure 1). P. 3 in *World Urbanization Prospects: The 2011 Revision*. Retrieved February 7, 2013 (http://esa.un.org/unup/pdf/WUP2011_Highlights.pdf).

United Nations Educational, Scientific and Cultural Organization. 1951. *Statement on Race*. Retrieved January 22, 2013 (http://unesdoc.unesco.org/images/0017/001789/178908eb.pdf).

United Nations Human Rights Council. 2014. *Displacement: The New 21st Century Challenge. Global Trends 2012*. Retrieved March 21, 2014 (www.refworld.org/docid/51c169d84.html).

United Nations Framework Convention on Climate Change. 2014. "Status of Ratification of the Kyoto Protocol." *United Nations Framework Convention on Climate Change*. Retrieved February 23, 2014 (http://unfccc.int/kyoto_protocol/status_of_ratification/items/2613.php).

United Nations Office on Drugs and Crime. 2014a. "Transnational Organized Crime: The Globalized Illegal Economy." Retrieved April 25, 2014 (www.unodc.org/toc/en/crimes/organized-crime.html).

United Nations Office on Drugs and Crime. 2014b. "Human Trafficking FAQs." Retrieved September 5, 2014 (http://www.unodc.org/unodc/en/human-trafficking/faqs.html#How_widespread_is_human_trafficking).

United Nations Population Division. 2014. "World Urbanization Prospects 2-14." Retrieved September 16, 2014 (http://esa.un.org/unpd/wup/Highlights/WUP2014-Highlights.pdf).

United Nations Population Fund. 2007. "Maternal Mortality Figures." *State of the World*. Retrieved April 17, 2010 (unic.un.org/imucms/LegacyDish.aspx?loc=11&pg=795).

United Nations Population Fund. 2009. "Because Everyone Counts: Giving Birth Should Not Be a Matter of Life and Death." Retrieved February 7, 2013 (www.unfpa.org/webdav/site/global/shared/safemotherhood/docs/maternalhealth_factsheet_en.pdf).

United Nations Population Fund. 2014. "Big Gains Made on Women's Health, But Access Still Unequal." Retrieved Feb. 20, 2014 (info@populationandsustainability.org).

University of Michigan Documents Center. 2003. "Documents in the News—1997/2003: Affirmative Action in College Admissions." Retrieved April 17, 2010 (www.lib.umich.edu/files/libraries/govdocs/pdf/affirm/pdf).

University of Pennsylvania. 2010. "Body Modification." Retrieved November 18, 2010 (penn.museum/sites/body_modification/bodmodpierce.shtml).

UN News Center. 2010. "Senior UN Official Cites Evidence of Growing Support for Abolishing Death Penalty." February 24. Retrieved March 8, 2011 (www.un.org/apps/news/story.asp?NewsID=33877&Cr=death+penalty&Cr1=).

UN News Center. 2012. "Millions of Children in Cities Face Poverty and Exclusion." *The State of the World's Children 2012*, February 28. Retrieved May 14, 2012 (www/im/prg/apps/news/story.asp?NewsID=41395&Cr=children&Cr1).

Upbin, Bruce. 2011. "The 147 Companies That Control Everything." *Forbes*, October 22. Retrieved July 13, 2012 (www.forbes.com/sites/bruceupbin/2011/10/22/the-147-companies-that-control-everything/).

UPI. 2008. "Annan Says Kenyan Conflict 'Evolving.'" January 27. Retrieved September 16, 2014 (http://www.upi.com/Top_News/2008/01/27/Annan-says-Kenyan-conflict-evolving/UPI-19121201438711/).

UPI.com. 2010. "12 Percent in U.S. Foreign Born." October 19. Retrieved May 5, 2012 (www.upi.com/Top_News/US/2010/10/19/12-percent-in-US-foreign-born/UPI-87261287522622/).

UPI. 2014. "OECD: Switzerland Tops 34 Nations for Life Expectancy at 82.8." *Health News UPI*. Retrieved January 2014 (www.upi.com/Health_News/2014/01/07/OECD/Switzerland-tops-34-nations-for-life-expectancy-at-828/UPI-32701389078243/).

Urban Institute. 2004. "Family Support, Substance Abuse Help, and Work Release Programs Are Essential as Ex-Prisoners Restart Lives in Baltimore." Retrieved April 17, 2010 (www.urban.org/url.cfm?ID=900688).

USAID. 2014. "USAID Announces New Award to Prevent and Repair Obstetric Fistula." January 6. Retrieved March 4, 2014 (www.usaid.gov/news-information/press-usaid-announce-new-award-prevent-and-repair-obstetric-fistula).

U.S. Bureau of Labor Statistics. 2012a. "American Time Use Survey Summary" (2011 Results). Retrieved January 24, 2013 (http://www.bls.gov/news.release/atus.nr0.htm).

U.S. Bureau of Labor Statistics. 2012b. "Women's Earnings as a Percent of Men's in 2010." January 10. Retrieved May 25, 2012 (www.bls.gov/opub/ted/2012/ted_20120110.htm).

U.S. Bureau of Labor Statistics. 2013a. "America's Young Adults at 25: School Enrollment, Training, and Employment Transitions Between Ages 23 and 25 Summary." March 1. Retrieved June 12, 2014 (www.bls.gov/news.release/nlsyth.nr0.htm).

U.S. Bureau of Labor Statistics. 2013b. "Earnings and Unemployment Rates By Educational Attainment." *Current Population Survey*, May 22. Retrieved June 16, 2013 (www.bls.gov/emp/ep_chart_001.htm).

U.S. Bureau of Labor Statistics. 2013c. "Overview of BLS Statistics on Unemployment." Retrieved September 11, 2014 (http://www.bls.gov/bls/unemployment.htm).

U.S. Bureau of Labor Statistics. 2014a. "Economic News Release: American Time Use Survey—2013 Results." Retrieved September 8, 2014 (www.bls.gov/news.release/atus.nr0.htm).

U.S. Bureau of Labor Statistics. 2014b. "Injuries, Illnesses, and Fatalities." Retrieved September 4, 2014 (www.bls.gov/iif/).

U.S. Bureau of Labor Statistics 2014c. "Occupational Outlook Handbook." Registered Nurses" and "Licensed Practical and Vocational Nurses." Retrieved March 10, 2014 (www.bls.gov/ooh/healthcare/registered-nurses.htm) and (www.bls.gov/ooh/healthcare/licensed-practical-andlicensed-vocational-nurses.htm).

U.S. Bureau of Labor Statistics. 2014d. "Table 2. Median Usual Weekly Earnings of Full-Time Wage and Salary Workers by Selected Characteristics, Quarterly Averages, Not Seasonally Adjusted." Retrieved September 9, 2014 (http://www.bls.gov/news.release/pdf/wkyeng.pdf).

U.S. Census Bureau. 2010. "Income, Poverty and Health Insurance Coverage in the United States: 2009." Retrieved September 15, 2014 (http://www.census.gov/newsroom/releases/archives/income_wealth/cb10-144.html).

U.S. Census Bureau. 2011. "Income (in Dollars) by Educational Level and Race/Ethnicity" (Table 228). Retrieved April 19, 2011 (http://www.census.gov/compendia/statab/2011/tables/11s0228.pdf).

U.S. Census Bureau. 2012a. "Educational Attainment in the United States: 2010 (Table 2)." Retrieved August 16, 2014 (www.census.gov/hhes/socdemo/education/data/cps/2010/tables.html).

U.S. Census Bureau. 2012b. "Growth in Urban Population Outpaces Rest of Nation, Census Bureau Reports." Retrieved July 1, 2013 (www.census.gov/newsroom/releases/archives/2010_census/cb12-50.html).

U.S. Bureau of the Census. 2012c. *Statistical Abstract of the United States: 2012*. "Table 229. Educational Attainment By Race and Hispanic Origin 1970–2010." Retrieved June 17, 2013 (www.census.gov/compendia/statab/2012/tables/12s0229.pdf).

U.S. Census Bureau. 2012d. "Table 232. Mean Earnings by Highest Degree Earned: 2009." Retrieved September 5, 2014 (http://www.census.gov/compendia/statab/2012/tables/12s0232.pdf).

U.S. Census Bureau. 2012e. "Table 696. Money Income of Families—Percent Distribution by Income Level in Constant (2009) Dollars: 1980 to 2009." Retrieved September 5, 2014 (http://www.census.gov/compendia/statab/2012/tables/12s0695.pdf).

U.S. Census Bureau. 2012f. "World Population: 1950–2050." Retrieved October 13, 2012 (www.census.gov/population/international/data/idb/worldpopgraph.php).

U.S. Census Bureau. 2012g. *Statistical Abstract of the United States*. Retrieved September 16, 2014 (http://www.census.gov/compendia/statab/).

U.S. Census Bureau. 2013a. "Current Population Survey (CPS)—Definitions." Retrieved September 8, 2014 (http://www.census.gov/cps/about/cpsdef.html).

U.S. Census Bureau 2013b. "Families in Poverty by Type of Family: 2011 and 2012." *Current Population Survey, 2012 and 2013*. Retrieved February 19, 2014 (www.census.gov/prod/2013pubs/p60-245.pdf).

U.S. Census Bureau. 2013b c. "Same-Sex Couple Households." Retrieved February 19, 2014 (www.census.gov/hhes/samesex/files/SScplfactsheet_final.pdf).

U.S. Census Bureau. 2013d. "U.S. and World Population Clock." June 9. Retrieved June 9, 2013 (www.census.gov/popclock/).

U.S. Census Bureau. 2014. "State & County Quick Facts." Retrieved August 22, 2014 (http://quickfacts.census.gov/qfd/states/00000.html).

U.S. Debt Clock. 2013. Retrieved November 12, 2013 (http://www.usdebtclock.org/).

U.S Department of Commerce. 2011. "Commerce Department's U.S. Census Bureau Reports 55 Percent of Americans Have Married Once in their Lifetimes." Retrieved February 19, 2014 (www.commerce.gov/blog/2011/05/18/commerce-department%E2%80%99s-us-census-bureau-reports-55-percent-americans-have-married-onc).

U.S. Department of Defense. 2011. *Dictionary of Military and Associated Terms,* January 31. Retrieved January 19, 2013 (http://ra.defense.gov/documents/rtm/jp1_02.pdf).

U.S. Department of Defense. 2012. "Department of Defense Antiterrorism Program Memo: Instruction No. 2000.12." March 1. Retrieved July 28, 2012 (www.dtic.mil/whs/direc tives/corres/pdf/200012p.pdf).

U.S. Department of Education. 2004–05. "Integrated Postsecondary Education Data System: Glossary." Retrieved July 10, 2009 (http://nces.ed.gov/ipeds/glossary/?charindex=D).

U.S. Department of Education for Civil Rights. 2012. *Title VI Enforcement Highlights*. Retrieved July 8, 2013 (www2.ed.gov/documents/press-releases/title-vi-enforcement.pdf).

U.S. Department of Energy. 2006. "Energy Consumption: Energy Kids Page." Retrieved November 8, 2006 (www.eia.doe.gov/kids/energyfacts/saving/efficiency/savingenergysecondary.html).

U.S. Department of Health and Human Services. 2011. "NHE Fact Sheet." Retrieved April 7, 2011 (www.cms.gov/NationalHealthExpendData/25_NHE_Fact_Sheet.asp).

U.S. Department of Health and Human Services. 2012. "A Profile of Older Americans: 2012." Administration on Aging. Retrieved March 10, 2014 (www.aoa.gov/Aging_Statistics/Profile/2012/docs/2012profile.pdf).

U.S. Department of Health and Human Services. 2014a. *Health Insurance Marketplace: Summary Enrollment Report for the Initial Annual Open Enrollment Period. ASPE Issue Brief.* Retrieved May 3, 2014 (http://aspe.hhs.gov/health/reports/2014/MarketPlaceEnrollment/Apr2014/ib_2014Apr_enrollment.pdf).

U.S. Department of Health and Human Services. 2014. "2014 Poverty Guidelines." Retrieved February 19, 2014 (http://aspe.hhs.gov/poverty/14poverty.cfm).

U.S. Department of Housing and Urban Development. 2013. *The 2013 Annual Homeless Assessment Report (AHAR) to Congress*. Retrieved February 17, 2014 (www.onecpd.info/resources/documents/AHAR-2013-Part1.pdf).

U.S. Department of Interior Office of Education. 1930. *Availability of Public School Education in Rural Communities* (Bulletin No. 34, edited by Walter H. Gaummitz). Washington, DC: Government Printing Office.

U.S. Department of Justice. 2009. "Crime in the U.S.: Violent Crime." Federal Bureau of Investigation. Retrieved April 12, 2012 (www2.fbi.gov/ucr/cius2009/offenses/violent_crime/index.html).

U.S. Department of Justice. 2010. "Crime Clock Statistics." *Crime in the United States, 2009*. Retrieved July 7, 2011 (http://www2.fbi.gov/ucr/cius2009/about/crime_clock.html).

U.S. Department of Justice. 2014. "2011 Crime Clock Statistics." Retrieved August 30, 2014 (http://www.fbi.gov/about-us/cjis/ucr/crime-in-the-u.s/2011/crime-in-the-u.s.-2011/offenses-known-to-law-enforcement/crime-clock).

U.S. Department of Labor. 2011a. "Highlights of Women's Earnings in 2010." *Report 1031*. Retrieved June 5, 2012 (www.bls.gov/cps/cpswom2010.pdf).

U.S. Department of Labor. 2011b. "List of Goods Produced by Child Labor or Forced Labor." Retrieved February 14, 2014 (www.dol.gov/ilab/programs/ocft/PDF/2011TVPRA.pdf).

U.S. Department of Labor. 2012. "Usual Weekly Earnings of Wage and Salary Workers." Bureau of Labor Statistics News Release, April 17. Retrieved June 10, 2012 (www.bls.gov/news.release/pdf/wkyeng.pdf).

U.S. Department of Labor. 2013a. "Employee Rights and Responsibilities under the Family and Medical Leave Act." Retrieved February 19, 2014 (www.dol.gov/whd/regs/compliance/posters/fmlean.pdf).

U.S. Department of Labor (2013b). Should it be Bureau of Labor Statistics. 2013. "Median Weekly Earnings by Age, Sex, Race, and Hispanic or Latino Ethnicity, First Quarter 2013." Retrieved February 19, 2014 (www.bls.gov/opub/ted/2013/ted_20130419.htm).

U.S. Department of State. 2011. *Country Reports on Terrorism 2010*. Retrieved July 14, 2012 (www.state.gov/documents/organization/170479.pdf).

"U.S. Elections Map: State by State Guide." 2008. BBC News. Retrieved February 8, 2013 (http://news.bbc.co.uk/2/hi/in_depth/629/629/7223461.stm).

U.S. Elections Project. 2012. "Turnout 1980–2012." Retrieved November 12, 2012 (http://elections.gmu.edu/voter_turnout.htm).

U.S. Environmental Protection Agency. 2009. "Ag101: Demographics." Retrieved March 30, 2010 (www.epa.gov/oecaagct/ag101/demographics/html).

U.S. Flag Code. 2008. "U.S. Flag Code (4 US Code 1)." Retrieved August 28, 2008 (http://suvcw.org/flag.htm).

U.S. General Accounting Office. 2004. "Defense of Marriage Act: Update to Prior Report." GAO-04-353R, January 23. Retrieved June 30, 2012 (http://www.gao.gov/products/GAO-04-353R).

U.S. Government Accountability Office. 2012. "Budget and Federal Debt." Retrieved September 27, 2012 (www.gao.gov/special.pubs/longterm/debt/budgetdebt.html#affect budget).

U.S. Government Accountability Office, 2014. "Long-Term Federal Budget Simulations." Spring 2014 Update. Retrieved September 16, 2014 (http://www.gao.gov/assets/670/662489.pdf).

"The U.S. Illiteracy Rate Hasn't Changed In 10 Years." 2013. *Huffington Post,* September 6. Retrieved May 1, 2014 (www.huffingtonpost.com/2013/09/06/illiteracy-rate_n_3880355.html).

"U.S. Life Expectancy Ranks 26th in the World, OECD Report Shows." 2013. *Huffington Post,* November 21. Retrieved December 5, 2013 (www.huffingtonpost.com/2013/11/21/us-life-expectancy-oecd_n_4317367.html).

U.S. Senate. 2011. "Ethnic Diversity in the Senate." Retrieved April 22, 2011 (www.senate.gov/artandhistory/history/common/briefing/minority_senators.htm).

U.S. Trade Representative. 2012. "Joint Stats From 2012 NAFTA Commission Meeting." Retrieved September 8, 2012 (www.ustr.gov/).

Valentine, Simon Ross. 2009. "The Tehrik-i-Taliban Pakistan: Ideology and Beliefs." *Pakistan Security Research Unit*. Retrieved February 24, 2014 (www.eisf.eu/resources/item/?d=1623).

Van Conoley, R. 2012. "The Illegal Sale of Human Body Parts for Profit—Part 1." *Sanity and Sense,* April 1. Retrieved August 2, 2012 (Sanityandsense.com/2012/04/01/the-illegal-sale-of-human-body-parts-for-profit-part-1/).

Vanderminden, Jennifer and Sharyn J. Potter. 2010. "Challenges to the Doctor-Patient Relationship in the 21st Century." In *The New Blackwell Companion to Medical Sociology,* edited by William C. Cockerham. Malden, MA: Wiley/Blackwell.

Van Houtte, Mieke and Peter A. Stevens. 2009. "School Ethnic Composition and Students Integration Outside and Inside Schools in Belgium." *Sociology of Education* 82(July): 217–39.

Varul, Matthias Zick. 2010. "Talcott Parsons, the Sick Role and Chronic Illness." *Body Society* 16(2):72–94.

Veblen, Thorstein. 1902. *The Theory of the Leisure Class: An Economic Study of Institutions.* New York: Macmillan.

Verbeek, Stjin and Rinus Penninx. 2009. "Employment Equity Policies in Work Organisations." Pp. 69–94 in *Equal Opportunity and Ethnic Inequality in European Labour Markets: Discrimination, Gender, and Policies of Diversity*, edited by Karen Kraal, Judith Roosblad, and John Wrench. Amsterdam: University of Amsterdam Press.

Vervaeck, Armand and James Daniell. 2011. "Japan Tohoku Tsunami and Earthquake: The Death Toll Is Climbing Again." Earthquake Report, August 15. Retrieved May 13, 2012 (Httlp://earthquake-report.com/2011/08/04/japan-tsunami-following-up-the-aftermath-part-16-june/).

Vespa, Jonathan, Jamie M. Lewis, and Rose M. Kreider. 2013. "America's Families and Living Arrangements: 2012." U.S. Census Bureau, August. Retrieved May 15, 2014 (www.census.gov/prod/2013pubs/p20-570.pdf).

Victor, Barbara. 2003. Army of Roses: Inside the World of Palestinian Women Suicide Bombers. Emmaus, PA: Rodale Books.

Vijayakumar, Gowri. 2012. "Girls and Education: A Global Approach." May 20. Retrieved January 28, 2013 (www.socwomen.org/web/images/stories/resources/fact_sheets/fact_2_2012-girlseducation.pdf).

Vinograd, Cassandra. 2013. "Teen Pregnancy: 7.3 Million Teenage Births in Developing World, UN Says." Retrieved March 12, 2014 (www.huffingtonpost.com/2013/10/30/teen-pregnancy-developing-world_n_4176898.html).

Vivat International. 2012. "Poverty." Retrieved January 23, 2013 (vivatinternational.org/our-work/poverty-eradication/).

Voting and Democracy Research Center. 2008. "Primaries: Open and Closed." Retrieved March 21, 2008 (www.fairvote.org/?page=1801).

Wade, Lisa. 2012. "The New Elite: Attributing Privilege and Class vs. Merit." *Sociological Images: Inspiring Sociological Imaginations Everywhere,* June 21. Retrieved September 14, 2012 (http://thesocietypages.org/socimages/2012/06/21/the-new-elite-attributing-privilege-to-class-vs-merit/).

Wade, Lisa. 2013a. "The Number of People in Private Prisons Has Grown by 1,664% in the Last 19 Years." *PolicyMic,* January 25. Retrieved April 26, 2014 (www.policymic.com/articles/24142/the-number-of-people-in-private-prisons-has-grown-by-1-664-in-the-last-19-years).

Wade, Lisa. 2013b. "The Truth About Gender and Math." *Sociological Images,* March 7. Retrieved Jan. 17, 2014 (http://thesocietypages.org/socimages/2013/03/07/the-truth-about-gender-and-math/).

Waite, Linda J. and Maggie Gallagher. 2000. *The Case for Marriage: Why Married People Are Happier, Healthier, and Better Off Financially.* New York: Doubleday.

Walk Free Foundation. 2013. "The Global Slavery Index 2013." Retrieved January 2, 2014 (www.globalslaveryindex.org/).

Wallenstein, Peter. 2002. *Tell the Court I Love My Wife: Race, Marriage, and Law—An American History.* New York: Macmillan

Wallerstein, Immanuel. 1974. *The Modern World System.* New York: Academic Press.

Wallerstein, Immanuel. 1979. *The Capitalist World Economy.* London: Cambridge University Press.

Wallerstein, Immanuel. 1991. *Geopolitics and Geoculture: Essays on the Changing World-System.* Cambridge, MA: Cambridge University Press.

Wallerstein, Immanuel. 2005. "Render Unto Caesar? The Dilemmas of a Multicultural World." *Sociology of Religion* 66(2):121–33.

Wallerstein, Judith. 1996. *Surviving the Breakup: How Children and Parents Cope With Divorce.* New York: Basic Books.

Wallerstein, Judith S. and Sarah Blakeslee. 1996. *The Good Marriage: How and Why Love Lasts.* New York: Warner Books.

Wallerstein, Judith S. and Sarah Blakeslee. 2004. *Second Chances: Men, Women and Children a Decade After Divorce,* 15th ed. Boston: Houghton Mifflin.

Wallis, Jim. 2005. God's Politics: *Why the Right Gets It Wrong and the Left Doesn't Get It.* New York: HarperCollins.

Wallis, Jim. 2013. *On God's Side: What Religion Forgets and Politics Hasn't Learned About Serving the Common Good.* Grand Rapids, MI: Brazos Press.

Walmsey, Roy. 2011. *World Prison Population List,* 9th ed. International Centre for Prison Studies. Retrieved January 20, 2013 (http://www.idcr.org.uk/wp-content/uploads/2010/09/WPPL-9-22.pdf).

Walum, Laurel Richardson. 1974. "The Changing Door Ceremony: Some Notes on the Operation of Sex Roles in Everyday Life." *Urban Life and Culture* 2(4):506–515.

Wang, Tina. 2009. "China Health Care Markets." *Forbes,* January 22. Retrieved January 10, 2010 (www.forbes.com/2009/01/22/china-health-care-markets-econ-cx_twdd_0122markets04.html).

War Child. 2014. "Child Soldier: Some Words Don't Belong Together." Retrieved August 21, 2014 (www.warchild.org.uk/issues/child-soldiers?gclid=CJ_78cL7bYCFSdgMgod11wAmQ).

Ward, Martha C. and Monica Edelstein. 2014. *A World Full of Women,* 6th ed. Boston: Allyn & Bacon.

Warner, R. Stephen. 1993. "Work in Progress Toward a New Paradigm for the Sociological Study of Religion in the United States." *American Journal of Sociology* 98(5):1044–1093.

Warner, R. Stephen. 2005. *A Church of Our Own: Disestablishment and Diversity in American Religion.* New Brunswick, NJ: Rutgers University Press.

Washington, Jesse. 2011. "The Disappearing Black Middle Class." *Chicago Sun Times,* July 10. Retrieved May 4, 2012 (www.suntimes.com/news/nation/6397110-418/the-disappearing-black-middle-class.html).

WaterAid. 2012. "Annual Review 2010/11." Retrieved September 9, 2012 (www.wateraid.org/uk/about_us/annual_report/default.asp).

WaterAid. 2013. "Precipitation for Education." Retrieved February 10, 2013 (www.wateraid.org/other/Print.asp).

WaterAid. 2014. "Statistics." Retrieved September 8, 2014 (www.wateraid.org/us/the-water-story/the-crisis/statistics?pageEEF299BDEFB04B4A89206672AC6D5578=2#filterContent).

Waters, Tony. 2012. *Schooling, Childhood, and Bureaucracy: Bureaucratizing the Child.* Basingstoke, UK: Palgrave Macmillan.

Watkins, Tom. 2013. "U.S. Woman Killed in Syria Identified by Relatives Via Online Images." CNN.com, May 31. Retrieved May 31, 2013 (www.cnn.com/2013/05/31/world/meast/syria-civil-war/index.html).

Watson, Ivan and Gul Tuysuz. 2013.."Turkish-Armenian Blogger Sentenced to Turkish Prison for Blasphemy." CNN.com, May 23. Retrieved June 1, 2013 (www.cnn.com/2013/05/23/world/meast/turkey-blasphemy-sentence).

Watts, Jonathan. 2012. "Air Pollution Could Become China's Biggest Health Threat, Expert Warns." *The Guardian,* March 16. Retrieved August 2, 2012 (www.guardian.co.uk/environment/2012/mar/16/air-pollution-biggest-threat-china).

Way, Niobe. 2011. *Deep Secrets: Boys' Friendships and the Crisis of Connection.* Cambridge, MA: Harvard University Press.

Weaver, Janelle. 2010. "Social Life Starts in the Womb." *Science*Shot, October 12. Retrieved October 19, 2010 (http://news.sciencemag.org/sciencenow/2010/10/scienceshot-social-life-starts-in.html?rss=1&utm_source=twitterfeed&utm_medium=twitter).

Weber, Max. [1904–1905] 1958. *The Protestant Ethic and the Spirit of Capitalism,* translated by Talcott Parsons. New York: Scribner.

Weber, Max. 1946. *From Max Weber: Essays in Sociology*, translated and edited by Hans H. Gerth and C. Wright Mills. New York: Oxford University Press.

Weber, Max. 1947. *The Theory of Social and Economic Organization*, translated and edited by A. M. Henderson and Talcott Parsons. New York: Oxford University Press.

WebSiteOptimization.com. 2010. "U.S. Broadband Penetration Jumps to 45.2%—U.S. Internet Access Nearly 75%." April 13. Retrieved March 1, 2011 (www.websiteoptimization.com/bw/0403/).

Webster's Unabridged English Dictionary. 1989. New York: Gramercy Books.

Weeks, John R. 1999. *Population: An Introduction to Concepts and Issues,* 7th ed. Belmont, CA: Wadsworth.

Weeks, John R. 2012. *Population: An Introduction to Concepts and Issues,* 11th ed. Belmont, CA: Wadsworth.

Weil, Elizabeth. 2008. "Teaching to the Testosterone." *New York Times Magazine*, March 2, p. 38.

Weinberg, George. 1972. *Society and the Healthy Homosexual.* New York: St. Martin's Press.

Weisenberg, Faye and Elizabeth Stacey. 2005. "Reflections on Teaching and Learning Online: Quality Program Design, Delivery, and Support Issues From a Cross-Global Perspective." *Distance Education,* 26(3).

Weiss, Gregory L. and Lynne E. Lonnquist. 2012. *The Sociology of Health, Healing, and Illness,* 7th ed. Englewood Cliffs, NJ: Prentice Hall.

Weiss, Robin Elise. 2010. "Pregnancy and Childbirth." Retrieved January 9, 2010 (pregnancy.about.com/od/cesareansections/ss/cesarian.htm).

Weitzman, Lenore J., Deborah Eifler, Elizabeth Hokada, and Catherine Ross. 1972. "Sex-Role Socialization in Picture Books for Preschool Children." *American Journal of Sociology* 77(May):1125–50.

Wells, Amy Stuart and Jeannie Oakes. 1996. "Potential Pitfalls of Systemic Reform: Early Lessons From Research on Detracking." *Sociology of Education* 69(Extra Issue):135–43.

Wessinger, Catherine. 2000. *How the Millennium Comes Violently: From Jonestown to Heaven's Gate.* New York: Seven Bridges.

West, Candace and Don H. Zimmerman. 1987. "Doing Gender." *Gender and Society* 1(2):125–51.

West, Heather C. and William J. Sabol. 2008 "Prisoners in 2007." Bureau of Justice Statistics Bulletin. U.S. Department of Justice. Retrieved December 23, 2008 (www.ojp.usdoj.gov/bjs/pub/pdf/p07.pdf).

Westermann, Ted D. and James W. Burfeind. 1991. *Crime and Justice in Two Societies: Japan and the United States.* Pacific Grove, CA: Brooks/Cole.

Western Jurisdictional Conference. 2012. "Passed: A Statement of Gospel Obedience." Western Jurisdictional Conference of the United Methodist Church, July 20. Retrieved September 26, 2012 (www.pnwumc.org/gc2012/passed-a-statement-of-gospel-obedience/).

Whaley, Floyd. 2012. "New Internet Law in Philippines Takes Effect, Raising Fears." *New York Times*, October 3. Retrieved October 6, 2012 (http://www.nytimes.com).

Wheaton, Sarah. 2014. "Pipeline Fight Lifts Environmental Movement." New York Times. January 24. Retrieved March 21, 2014 (www.nytimes.com/2014/01/25/us/keystone-xl-pipeline-fight-lifts-environmental-movement.html?action=click&module=Search&region=searchResults%230&version=&url=http%3A%2F%2Fquery.nytimes.com%2Fsearch%2Fsitesearch%2F%3Faction%3Dclick%26region%3DMasthead%26pgtype%3DHomepage%26module%3DSearchSubmit%26contentCollection%3DHomepage%26t%3Dqry659%23%2Fenvironmental+movement&_r=1).

White House. 2011. "Fact Sheet: New Actions on Guantanamo and Detainee Policy." March 7. Retrieved April 14, 2012 (www.whitehouse.gov/sites/default/files/Fact_Sheet_—_Guantanamo_and_Detainee_Policies.pdf).

White House. 2013. "Health Reform in Action." Retrieved February 2, 2013 (www.whitehouse.gov/issues/health-care).

White, Kevin. 2002. An Introduction to the Sociology of Health and Illness. London: Sage.

White, Shelley, Jonathan White, and Kathleen Odell Korgen. 2013. *Sociologists in Action: Race, Class, and Gender.* Thousand Oaks, CA: Sage.

Whitney, Lance. 2012. "2011 Ends with Almost 6 Billion Mobile Phone Subscriptions." CNET News. Retrieved May 18, 2012 (http://news.cnet.com/8301-1023_3-57352095-93/2011-ends-with-almost-6-billion-mobile-phone-subscriptions/).

WHO, UNICEF, UNFPA, and World Bank. 2012. "Trends in Maternal Mortality: 1990–2010." Work Health Organization. Retrieved July 17, 2012 (http://africa.unfpa.org/public/pid/10773).

The Whole Child. 2012. "Award-Winning Programs Demonstrate Excellence in Summer Learning." August 30. Retrieved September 14, 2012 (www.wholechildeducation.org/blog/award-winning-programs-demonstrate-excellence-in-summer-learning).

Whorf, Benjamin Lee. 1956. *Language, Thought, and Reality.* New York: John Wiley.

Whyte, William H. 1956. *The Organization Man.* New York: Simon and Schuster.

Wilcox, Norma and Tracey Steele. 2003. "Just the Facts: A Descriptive Analysis of Inmate Attitudes Toward Capital Punishment." *The Prison Journal* 83(4):464–82.

Wilcox. W. Bradford and Elizabeth Marquardt. 2011. *2011 State of Our Unions.* Retrieved October 9, 2012 (http://stateofourunions.org/2011/SOOU2011.pdf).

Wilhoit, Sarah 2014. "Demand That U.S. Coffee Companies Stop Using Child and Slave Labor Overseas." Retrieved February 14, 2014 (http://forcechange.com/62236/demand-that-u-s-coffee-companies -stop-using-child-and-slave-labor-overseas/).

Wilkerson, Isabel. 2010. *The Warmth of Other Suns: The Epic Story of America's Great Migration.* New York: Vintage/Random House.

Williams, Brian K., Stacey C. Sawyer, and Carl M. Wahlstrom. 2013. *Marriages, Families, and Intimate Relationships,* 3rd ed. Boston: Allyn & Bacon.

Williams, Christine L. 2006. *Inside Toyland: Working, Shopping, and Social Inequality.* Berkeley: University of California Press.

Williams, Christine L. 2013. "The Glass Escalator, Revisited: Gender Inequality in Neoliberal Times." *Gender and Society* 27(5):609–29.

Williams, Dmitri, Mia Consalvo, Scott Caplan, and Nick Yee. 2009. "Looking for Gender: Gender Roles and Behaviors Among Online Gamers." *Journal of Communication* 59):700–25.

Williams, Robin Murphy, Jr. 1970. *American Society: A Sociological Interpretation,* 3rd ed. New York: Alfred Knopf.

Willis, Paul. 1979. *Learning to Labor: How Working Class Kids Get Working Class Jobs.* Aldershot, Hampshire, England: Saxon House.

Willis Report. 2014. "The Costs of Raising a Child in 2014." Retrieved May 24, 2014 (www.myfoxla.com/story/24695222/the-costs-of-raising-a-child-in-2014).

Wilson, Edward O. 1980. *Sociobiology.* Cambridge, MA: Belknap.

Wilson, Edward O. 1987. *The Coevolution of Biology and Culture.* Cambridge, MA: Harvard University Press.

Wilson, Edward O., Michael S. Gregory, Anita Silvers, and Diane Sutch. 1978. "What Is Sociobiology?" *Society* 15(6):1–12.

Wilson, K. 1993. *Dialectics of Consciousness: Problems of Development, the Indian Reality.* Madras: Oneworld Educational Trust.

Wilson, Kate, Vlad Lavrov, Martina Keller, Thomas Jajer, and Gerard Ryle. 2012. "Skin, Bones and Tissue for Sale: How the Dead Are Being Used for Grisly Trade in Human Body Parts." *Daily Mail,* July 17. Retrieved August 2, 2012 (www.dailymail.co.uk/news/article-2175006/Skin-bones-tissue-sale-How-dead-used-grisly-trade-human-body-parts.html).

Wilson, Megan. 2012. "Big Business Sides with Obama on Affirmative Action Case Before High Court." *The Hill,* October 28. Retrieved May 31, 2013 (http://thehill.com/homenews/administration/264329-big-business-sides-with-obama-on-affirmative-action-case-before-supreme-court).

Wilson, Warren H. 1924. "What the Automobile Has Done to and for the Country Church." *Annals of the American Academy of Political and Social Science* 116(November):85–86.

Wilson, William Julius. 1978. *The Declining Significance of Race: Blacks and Changing American Institutions.* Chicago: University of Chicago Press.

Wilson, William Julius. 1984. "The Black Underclass." *The Wilson Quarterly* (Spring):88–89.

Wilson, William Julius. 1993a. *The Ghetto Underclass: Social Science Perspectives.* Newbury Park, CA: Sage.

Wilson, William Julius. 1993b. "The New Urban Poverty and the Problem of Race." *The Tanner Lecture on Human Values,* October 22 (printed in *Michigan Quarterly Review,* 247–73).

Wilson, William Julius. 1996. *When Work Disappears.* New York: Alfred A. Knopf.

Wimberly, Ronald C. and William H Swatos, Jr. 1998. "Civil Religion." Pp. 94–96 in *Encyclopedia of Religion and Society,* edited by William H. Swatos, Jr. Altamira Press.

Winders, Bill. 2004. "Changing Racial Inequality: The Rise and Fall of Systems of Racial Inequality in the U.S." Paper presented at the Annual Meeting of the American Sociological Association, San Francisco.

Wing, Nick. 2013. "Countries *With the Largest Number of Prisoners per 100,000 of the National Population, as of 2013.*" *Huffington Post,* August 13. Retrieved April 25, 2014 (www.huffingtonpostcom/2013/08/13/incarceration-rate-per-capita_n_3745291.html).

Wingfield, Adia Harvey. 2009. "Racializing the Glass Escalator: Reconsidering Men's Experiences With Women's Work." *Gender and Society* 23(5):5–26.

Winkler, Celia. 2002. Single Mothers and the State: The Politics of Care in Sweden and the United States. London: Rowman and Littlefield.

Winkler, Karen J. 1991. "Revisiting the Nature vs. Nurture Debate: Historian Looks Anew at Influence of Biology on Behavior." *Chronicle of Higher Education,* May 22, pp. A5, A8.

Winnick, Terri A. 2006. "Medical Doctors and Complementary and Alternative Medicine: The Context of Holistic Practice." *Health: An Interdisciplinary Journal for the Social Study of Health, Illness and Medicine* 10(2):149–73.

Winslow, Robert W. and Sheldon X. Zhang. 2008. *Criminology: A Global Perspective.* Upper Saddle River, NJ: Pearson Prentice Hall.

Wire Side Chat. 2014. "How Can Teachers Develop Students' Motivation—and Success?" Retrieved September 11, 2014 (http://www.educationworld.com/a_issues/chat/chat010.shtml).

Wirth, Louis. 1964. "Urbanism as a Way of Life." *American Journal of Sociology* 44(1):1–24.

Witness for Peace. 2008. *Venezuelan Delegation on Health Care,* March (Personal communication; interviews with members of the delegation).

Witness for Peace. 2012. "Mediation With GM Fails, Workers Re-Start Hunger Strike." September 3. Retrieved October 14, 2012 (http://witnessforpeace.org/).

Witt, Susan D. 2000. "The Influence of Television on Children's Gender Role Socialization." *Childhood Education* 76. Retrieved May 24, 2012 (www.eric.ed.gov/ERICWebPortal/recordDetail?accno=EJ610307).

Witters, Dan. 2014. "Highest Uninsured States Less Likely to Embrace Health Law." Gallup Well-Being, February 7. Retrieved March 10, 2014 (www.galup.com/poll/167321/highest-uninsured-states-less-likely-embrace-health-law.aspx).

Witzig, Ritchie. 1996. "The Medicalization of Race: Scientific Legitimation of a Flawed Social Construct." *Annals of Internal Medicine: American College of Physicians* 125(8): 675–76.

Woldoff, Rachel A. 2011. *White Flight/Black Flight: The Dynamics of Racial Change in an American Neighborhood.* Ithaca, NY: Cornell University Press.

Wolf, Richard. 2010. "Number of Uninsured Americans Rises to 50.7 Million." *USA Today,* September 17. Retrieved April 7, 2011 (www.usatoday.com/news/nation/2010-09-17-uninsured17_ST_N.htm).

Wolf, Richard. 2014. "Legal Fight for Gay Marriage Reaches Virginia Court." February 5. Retrieved February 6, 2014 (www.usatoday.com/story/news/nation/2014/02/04/gay-lesbian-marriage-court-virginia/5193233/).

Women's Sports Foundation. 2005. "Women's Sports: Title IX Q and A" (May). Retrieved April 17, 2010 (www.womenssportsfoundation.org/. . ./Title-IX/. . ./Briefing-Paper-Five).

Wong, Edward. 2013a. "In China, Breathing Becomes a Childhood Risk." *New York Times*. April 22. Retrieved July 1, 2013 (www.nytimes.com/2013/04/23/world/asia/pollution-is-radically-changing-childhood-in-chinas-cities.html?pagewanted=all).

Wong, Edward. 2013b. "Urbanites Flee China's Smog for Blue Skies." *New York Times,* November 22. Retrieved March 17, 2014 (www.nytimes.com/2013/11/23/world/asia/urbanites-flee-chinas-smog-for-blue-skies.html?_r=0).

Wood, Julia T. 2008. *Gendered Lives: Communication, Gender, and Culture,* 8th ed. Belmont, CA: Wadsworth.

Wood, Julia T. and Nina M. Reich. 2006. "Gendered Communication Styles." Pp. 177–86 in *Intercultural Communication,* 11th ed., edited by Larry A. Samovar, Richard E. Porter, and Edwin R. McDaniel. Belmont, CA: Wadsworth.

Woodberry, Robert D. and Christian S. Smith. 1998. "Fundamentalism et al: Conservative Protestants in America." *Annual Review of Sociology* 24:25–26.

Woods, Andrew K. 2011. "These Revolutions Are Not All Twitter (Op-Ed)." *New York Times*, February 1. Retrieved October 6, 2012 (http://www.nytimes.com).

Worldatlas. 2014. "Largest Cities in the World." March 16. Retrieved April 15, 2014 (www.worldatlas.com/citypops.htm).

World Almanac. 2014. "World Adherents of Religions by Continental Area 2012." New York: World Almanac Books: 701.

World Bank. 2012a. "Girls' Education: Learning for All." Retrieved September 14, 2012 (http://web.worldbank.org/WBSITE/EXTERNAL/TOPICS/EXTEDUCATION/o,,contentMDK:20298916~menuPK:617572~pagePK:148956~piPK:216618~theSitePK:282386,00.html).

World Bank. 2012b. "Physicians (per 1,000 People)." Retrieved August 2, 2012 (Data.worldbank.org/indicator/SH.MED.PHYS.ZS).

World Bank. 2013. *Internet Users (Per 100 People).* Retrieved December 17, 2013 (http://data.worldbank.org/indicator/IT.NET.USER.P2).

World Bank. 2013a. "Featured Conversation: Slums and Service Delivery for the Urban Poor." Striking Poverty. Retrieved July 1, 2013 (www.forbes.com/sites/joelkotkin/2013/03/18/americas-fastest-and-slowest-growing-cities/).

World Bank 2013b. "Population Density (People Per Square KM of Land Area)." Retrieved June 9, 2013 (http://data.worldbank.org/indicator/EN.POP.DNST).

World Bank. 2013c. "Ratio of Female to Male Secondary Enrollment (%)." Retrieved June 15, 2013 (http://data.worldbank.org/).

World Bank. 2014a. "Sub-Saharan Africa (Developing Only)." Retrieved September 16, 2014 (http://data.worldbank.org/region/sub-saharan-africa).

World Bank. 2014b. "Voices and Agency: Empowering Women and Girls for Shared Prosperity." Retrieval September 10, 2014 (www.worldbank.org/en/topic/gender/publication/voice-and-agency-empowering-women-and-girls-for-shared-prosperity).

World Coalition. 2012. "World Database." World Coalition Against the Death Penalty. Retrieved May 29, 2012 (http://www.worldcoalition.org/worldwide-database.html).

World Development Report. 2012. *World Development Report: Gender Equality and Development.* World Bank. Retrieved October 1, 2012 (http://go.worldbank.org/6R2KGVEXPO).

World Economic Forum. 2012. "Seven Billion and Growing: A 21st-Century Perspective on Population." Retrieved July 28, 2012 (http://reports.weforum.org/global-agenda-council-2012/councils/population-growth/).

World Factbook. 2011. "Field Listing: Suffrage." Retrieved May 6, 2011 (https://www.cia.gov/library/publications/the-world-factbook/fields/2123.html#210).

World Factbook. 2014a. "Chad." Retrieved September 15, 2014 (https://www.cia.gov/library/publications/the-world-factbook/geos/cd.html).

World Factbook. 2014b. "China." Retrieved September 15, 2014 (https://www.cia.gov/library/publications/the-world-factbook/geos/ch.html).

World Factbook. 2014c. "Congo." Retrieved September 15, 2014 (https://www.cia.gov/library/publications/the-world-factbook/geos/cg.html).

World Factbook. 2014a d. "GDP—Per Capita." Retrieved April 18, 2014 (https://www.cia.gov/library/publications/the-world-factbook/rankorder/2004rank.html).

World Factbook. 2014e. "India." Retrieved September 15, 2014 (https://www.cia.gov/library/publications/the-world-factbook/geos/in.html).

World Factbook. 2014f. "Infant Mortality Rate." Retrieved April 18, 2014 (https://www.cia.gov/library/publications/the-world-factbook/rankorder/2091rank.html).

World Factbook. 2014g. "Kenya." Retrieved September 15, 2014 (https://www.cia.gov/library/publications/the-world-factbook/geos/ke.html).

World Factbook. 2014c h. "Life Expectancy at Birth." Retrieved April 18, 2014 (https://www.cia.gov/library/publications/the-world-factbook/rankorder/2102rank.html).

World Factbook. 2014i. "Niger." Retrieved September 15, 2014 (https://www.cia.gov/library/publications/the-world-factbook/geos/ng.html).

World Factbook. 2014j. "Uganda." Retrieved September 15, 2014 (https://www.cia.gov/library/publications/the-world-factbook/geos/ug.html).

World Factbook. 2014k. "United States." Retrieved September 15, 2014 (https://www.cia.gov/library/publications/the-world-factbook/geos/us.html).

World Famine Timeline 2014. "Famine." Retrieved May 24, 2014 (www.mapreport.com/subtopics/d/0.html#2013)

World Food Programme. 2013. "10 Things You Need to Know about Hunger in 2013." January 2. Retrieved Jan. 5, 2014 (www.wfp.org/stories/10-things-you-need-to-know-about-hunger-2013).

World Health Organization. 2009. Retrieved April 17, 2010 (apps.who.int/whosis/database/core/WHO2009–12–27–151422.csv).

World Health Organization. 2011. "The Top 10 Causes of Death." Retrieved August 29, 2012 (www.who.int/mediacentre/factsheets/fs310/en/index.html).

World Health Organization. 2012a. "Family Planning: Fact Sheet No. 351." July. Retrieved July 29, 2012 (www.who.int/mediacentre/factsheets/fs351/en/index.html).

World Hunger Education Service. 2012b. "Hunger in America: 2012 United States Hunger and Poverty Facts." Retrieved May 17, 2012 (www.worldhunger.org/articles/Learn/us_hunger_facts.htm).

World Hunger Education Service. 2013. "2013 World Hunger and Poverty Facts and Statistics." Retrieved September 16, 2014 (http://www.worldhunger.org/articles/Learn/world%20hunger%20facts%202002.htm).

World Health Organization. 2013a. "Antimicrobial Resistance." Fact Sheet 194, May. Retrieved March 10, 2014 (www.who.int/mediacentre/factsheets/fs194/en/).

World Health Organization. 2013b. "Urban Population Growth." Retrieved July 1, 2013 (www.forbes.com/sites/joelkotkin/2013/03/18/americas-fastest-and-slowest-growing-cities/).

World Health Organization. 2014a. "Adolescent Pregnancy." *Maternal, Newborn, Child, and Adolescent Health*. Retrieved March 17, 2014 (www.who.int/maternal_child_adolescent/topics/maternal/adolescent_pregnancy/en/).

World Health Organization. 2014b. "The Top 10 Causes of Death." Retrieved May 28, 2014 (www.who.int/mediacentre/factsheets/fs310/en/index1.html).

World Resources Institute. 2007. "Ask Earth Trends: How Much of the World's Resource Consumption Occurs in Rich Countries?" *EarthTrends*. Retrieved April 14, 2008 (http://earthtrends.wri.org/updates/node/236).

Worldometers. 2014. "Current World Population." Retrieved March 18, 2014 (www.worldometers.info/world-population/).

WorldWideLearn. 2007. "Guide to College Majors in Sociology." Retrieved June 23, 2008 (www.worldwidelearn.com/online-education-guide/social-science/sociology-major.htm).

World Wildlife Fund. 2012. "The Living Planet Report." Retrieved September 7, 2012 (www.panda.org/lpr).

Wöss, Josef. 2012. "Tackling the Ageing Challenge: The Labour Market as a Key Determinant." Retrieved August 25, 2012 (www.esip.org/files/RT2_Josef%20W%C3%B6ss.pdf).

Wright, John W., ed. 2007. *The New York Times Almanac 2008*. New York: Penguin Reference.

Wright, Stuart A. 1995. *Armageddon in Waco: Critical Perspectives on the Branch Davidian Conflict*. Chicago: University of Chicago Press.

Wuthnow, Robert. 1988. *The Restructuring of American Religion: Society and Faith Since World War II*. Princeton, NJ: Princeton University Press

Yablonski, Lewis. 1959. "The Gang as a Near-Group." *Social Problems* 7(Fall):108–117.

Yamane, David. 1997. "Secularization on Trial: In Defense of a Neosecularization Paradigm." *Journal for the Scientific Study of Religion* 36(1):109–122.

Yamane, David. 2007. "Civil Religion." Pp. 506–507 in *The Blackwell Encyclopedia of Sociology*, Vol. II, edited by George Ritzer. Oxford: Blackwell.

Yamane, David and Sarah MacMillen. 2006. *Real Stories of Christian Initiation: Lessons for and from the RCIA*. Collegeville, MN: Liturgical Press.

Yardley, Jim. 2013. "Bangladesh Pollution, Told in Colors and Smells." *New York Times,* July 14. Retrieved July 15, 2013 (www.nytimes.com/2013/07/15/world/asia/bangladesh-pollution-told-in-colors-and-smells.html?pagewanted=1&_r=0&ref=global-home).

Yen, Hope. 2009. "Multiracial Americans Become Fastest-Growing U.S. Group." *The Huffington Post,* May 28. Retrieved May 5, 2012 (www.huffingtonpost.com/2009/05/29/multiraction-americans-bec_n_208989.htlm).

Yinger, J. Milton. 1960. "Contraculture and Subculture." *American Sociological Review* 25(October):625–35.

Yoon, Mi Yung. 2001. "Democratization and Women's Legislative Representation in Sub-Saharan Africa." *Democratization* 8(2):169–90.

Yoon, Mi Yung. 2004. "Explaining Women's Legislative Representation in Sub-Saharan Africa." *Legislative Studies Quarterly* 29(3):447–68.

Yoon, Mi Yung. 2005. "Sub-Saharan Africa." Chapter 7 in *Sharing Power: Women, Parliament, Democracy,* edited by Manon Tremblay and Yvonne Galligan. Aldershot, UK: Ashgate.

Yoon, Mi Yung. 2008. "Special Seats for Women in the National Legislature: The Case of Tanzania." *Africa Today* 55(Fall):61–85.

Yoon, Mi Yung. 2011a. "More Women in the Tanzanian Legislature: Do Numbers Matter?" *Journal of Contemporary African Studies* 29(January):83–98.

Yoon, Mi Yung. 2011b. "Factors Hindering 'Larger' Representation of Women in Parliament: The Case of Seychelles." *Commonwealth and Comparative Politics* 49(February):98–114.

Young, Jeffrey. 2012. "Health Insurance Costs More, Covers Less, Survey Says." *The Huffington Post*, March 3. Retrieved August 1, 2012 (www.huffingtonpost.com/2012/03/08/health-insurance-costs-n-1327861.html).

youthxchange. 2007. "Women's Literacy." (youthxchange.net/utils/download.asp?filename . . . pdf).

YubaNet.com. 2011. "World's Fastest Growing Populations . . ." October 26. Retrieved July 27, 2012 (http://yubanet.com/world/World-39-s-fastest-growing-populations-increasingly-vulnerable-to-impacts-of-climate-change.php).

Yunus, Muhammad and Alan Jolis. 1999. *Banker to the Poor: Micro-Lending and the Battle Against World Poverty*. New York: Public Affairs.

Zaimov, Stoyan. 2013. "African Anglicans Say Gay Bishops Affirmation Shatters Hopes of Reconciliation." *The Christian World,* January 10. Retrieved July 12, 2013 (www.christianpost.com/news/african-anglicans-say-gay-bishops-affirmation-shatters-hopes-of-reconciliation-88038/).

Zakaria, Fareed. 2012. "Could China's One-Child Policy Change?" Retrieved July 28, 2012 (www.cnn.com/WORLD/fareed .zakaria.qa/archive/index.html).

Zborowski, Mark. 1952. "Cultural Components in Response to Pain." Journal of Social Issues 8(4):16–30.

Zeleny, Jeff. 2009. "Obama Vows, 'We Will Rebuild' and 'Recover'." New York Times. February 25. Retrieved February 25, 2009 (www.nytimes.com/2009/02/25/us/politics/25 obama.html?scp=1&sq=obama%20vows%20we%20will%20 rebuild&st=cse).

Zernike, Kate. 2012. "Former Rutgers Student Found Guilty of Hate Crimes." March 17. Retrieved April 16, 2012 (www.bos tonglobe.com/news/nation/2012/03/16/defendent-rutgers-spying-case-guilty-hate-crimes/7KF8AAexk3gih01WS4W09/ story/html)

Zhang, Baohui, Alexi A. Wright, Haiden A. Huskamp, Matthew E. Nilsson, Matthew L. Maciejewski, Craig C. Earle, Susan D. Block, Paul K. Maciejewski, and Holly Prigerson. 2009. "Health Care Costs in the Last Week of Life." Archives of Internal Medicine. 16(5):480–488.

Zhao, Yong. 2005. "Increasing Math and Science Achievement: The Best and Worst of the East and West." Phi Delta Kappan (November):219–22.

Ziel, Magda. 2013 "Sati Widow Burning Still Going On." HubPages. Retrieved January 16, 2014 (http://whitemuse .hubpages.com/hub/Sati-Still-Being-Done-in-India).

Zimbardo, Philip C. 2004. "Power Turns Good Soldiers Into 'Bad Apples.'" Boston Globe (May 9). Retrieved July 5, 2008 (www .boston.com/news/globe/editorial_opinion/oped/arti cles/2004/05/09/power_turns_good_soldiers_into_bad_apples).

Zimbardo, Philip C., Craig Haney, Curtis Banks, and David Jaffe. 1973. "The Mind Is a Formidable Jailer: A Pirandellian Prison." The New York Times (April 8):38–60.

Zull, James E. 2002. The Art of Changing the Brain: Enriching the Practice of Teaching by Exploring the Biology of Learning. Sterling, VA: Stylus.

Index

About the Authors

Jeanne H. Ballantine is University Professor of Sociology at Wright State University in Dayton, Ohio. She received an M.A. from Columbia University and a Ph.D. from Indiana University, with a specialty in sociology of education. She has been teaching and writing for more than 30 years and has written or coauthored several texts, including *Our Social World: Introduction to Sociology, Sociological Footprints, Sociology of Education: A Systematic Analysis, Schools* and *Society: A Sociological Approach, and Teaching Sociology of Education*. She has also published in other areas, including gender and teaching of sociology, and has held leadership positions in ASA Section on Teaching and Learning, the ASA Section on Sociology of Education, the ASA Departmental Resources Group, the American Educational Research Association (AERA), and the International Sociological Association (ISA) Research Committee on Sociology of Education. She has won numerous awards, including the ASA Distinguished Contributions to Teaching Award.

Keith A. Roberts, Professor Emeritus of Sociology at Hanover College, has not only won teaching awards, but has been honored by several sociological associations for "Distinguished Contributions to Teaching"—including the ASA's 2010 Award. He has published on teaching and conducted workshops around the country. He is a member of the Departmental Resources Group of the ASA, which among other activities involves consulting work with departments of sociology on curriculum and on teaching issues. He is the co-author of *Religion in Sociological Perspective, Fifth Edition* (SAGE, 2012), *Our Social World* (SAGE, 2011) and *Our Social World, Condensed* (SAGE, 2010), and a monograph on Writing in the Undergraduate Sociology Curriculum. He is active in the ASA Section on Teaching and Learning, and for 21 years organized and led workshops for high school sociology teachers. Keith has taught a wide range of sociology courses at a two-year college, at a Research 1 University, and at a selective liberal arts college.

Kathleen Odell Korgen is Professor of Sociology at William Paterson University in Wayne, New Jersey. Kathleen has co-authored or co-edited numerous books that teach students to use the sociological tools they gain in their classes and to find inspiration from public sociologists and fellow sociology students. These books include *The Engaged Sociologist: Connecting the Classroom to the Community, Sociologists in Action: Sociology, Social Change, and Social Justice* and *Sociologists in Action on Inequalities: Race, Class, Gender, and Sexuality*. She has also written or edited the following books on race relations and racial identity: *Race Policy and Multiracial Americans* (forthcoming), *Multiracial Americans and Social Class, Crossing the Racial Divide: Close Friendships Between Black and White Americans*, and *From Black to Biracial*. Kathleen works as a consultant for other sociology departments as a member of the Departmental Resources Group of the American Sociological Association. She has received William Paterson University's Award for Excellence in Scholarship/Creative Expression and the University's Award for Excellence in Teaching.

◉ SAGE researchmethods

The essential online tool for researchers from the world's leading methods publisher

Find exactly what you are looking for, from basic explanations to advanced discussion

More content and new features added this year!

Discover **Methods Lists**— methods readings suggested by other users

"I have never really seen anything like this product before, and I think it is really valuable."

John Creswell, University of Nebraska–Lincoln

Watch video interviews with leading methodologists

Explore the **Methods Map** to discover links between methods

Search a custom-designed taxonomy with more than 1,400 qualitative, quantitative, and mixed methods terms

Uncover more than 120,000 pages of book, journal, and reference content to support your learning

Find out more at
www.sageresearchmethods.com